**PROBLEMS
IN
SOCIAL
PSYCHOLOGY**

PROBLEMS IN SOCIAL PSYCHOLOGY

SELECTED READINGS

Edited by

CARL W. BACKMAN

PROGRAM DIRECTOR FOR SOCIOLOGY AND SOCIAL PSYCHOLOGY
NATIONAL SCIENCE FOUNDATION

and

PAUL F. SECORD

PROFESSOR OF PSYCHOLOGY
UNIVERSITY OF NEVADA

**McGRAW-HILL
BOOK COMPANY**
NEW YORK
ST. LOUIS
SAN FRANCISCO
TORONTO
LONDON
SYDNEY

**PROBLEMS IN
SOCIAL PSYCHOLOGY**

Copyright © 1966 by McGraw-Hill, Inc.
All Rights Reserved.
Printed in the United States of America.
This book, or parts thereof, may not
be reproduced in any form without
permission of the publishers.
*Library of Congress Catalog
Card Number 66-14802*

1234567890BN7321069876

PREFACE

The use of a collection of research reports can accomplish two objectives. First, it can serve to highlight significant and substantive contributions to an area of knowledge. Second, it can convey to the student a sense of the nature and process of scientific inquiry. While we have been mindful of both of these objectives in selecting the studies included in this volume, we have, whenever possible, emphasized the second in the belief that it is here that a book of readings can make its most distinctive pedagogical contribution. The student can master the substantive aspects of a science from a textbook but short of engaging in the research process himself, the best means of learning about the process of scientific inquiry is to encounter examples of problems which scientists face in a variety of research contexts. This emphasis has necessitated a somewhat greater volume of editorial comment than is found in most books of readings. Unless made explicit, methodological lessons are frequently missed. In part, this omission reflects most students' concern for knowing about the results of research rather than about the details of the method. In part, however, it simply reflects the fact that the student normally does not have the background knowledge necessary to appreciate the significance of a particular problem, especially when it is embedded in a research report originally prepared for a professional audience.

With this in mind we have attempted in the introductions to each part and each selection to provide sufficient context for an understanding of the material, underscoring the substantive or methodological lesson that can be learned from it. Occasionally a postscript has been added to a selection when new data or ideas have emerged that have altered or underscored some point.

This book has been primarily prepared for college students taking social psychology for the first time (usually sophomores and juniors), as a supplement to other modern texts in social psychology. The liberal use of orienting and integrative statements throughout the book also makes it suitable for those instructors who prefer to use a book of readings without a textbook. Because of the attention given to methodology, the book may also be useful for a course in experimental social psychology, following the first course in that subject. Since equal attention has been given to social psychological problems as formulated by sociologists and psychologists, these readings should be suitable for use in either discipline.

In producing this book, we have become indebted to many persons. Most of all we are grateful to those investigators who graciously permitted us to include their works in this collection. In a very real sense, the book is theirs and not ours. For typing, obtaining permissions, and sundry secretarial tasks we thank Alma Smith.

For assistance in proofreading and compiling the indexes we are indebted to Edmund Doherty.

CARL W. BACKMAN
PAUL F. SECORD

CONTENTS

CONTENTS

viii

The purpose of this volume is to describe the ongoing processes of social psychological research in a manner that conveys the spirit and method of scholarly inquiry. To do this we have chosen the problem as a central theme. All scholarly activity begins with a problem. It may be a precisely formulated statement of a hypothesized relation between two or more variables or it may be simply a desire to know more about some aspect of human experience. Such problems may be classified in a number of ways. Some are methodological in character, others substantive; some have strategic value, others do not.

The solution to a methodological problem increases the **certainty** of knowledge. For example, developing ways to control actions of the experimenter by which he inadvertently affects the behavior of his subjects increases our confidence that the results are due to variations in the experimental variable rather than to some characteristic of the interaction between the experimenter and his subjects.

Substantive problems are those whose solution increases the **sum** of knowledge in a field, the number of predictable relations between variables. Problems of this kind vary in their strategic quality. A problem is strategic to the degree that its solution leads to the solution of other problems. New theories that make sense out of findings from different lines of inquiry, suggest new empirical relations, lead to the discovery of a new process, or identify a powerful but hitherto unknown variable are examples of problem solutions of high strategic value.

That problems differ in strategic quality is implicit in the distinction that has long been drawn between pure and applied research. So-called **pure research** problems, since they are embedded in a network of theory, are more apt to be strategic. Their solution is related by bonds of theory to the solution of other problems. An investigation concerning the determinants of conformity to norms or rules of conduct is more strategic than one concerning the determinants of juvenile delinquency, because solutions arrived at in the former might well lead to an understanding of a wide variety of forms of deviant and conforming behavior including delinquency itself.

The strategic character of a problem is not always immediately clear; sometimes it may be recognized only after the research is completed or after subsequent research developments have taken place. Solutions to applied problems have occasionally resulted in theoretical ramifications that in retrospect lead them to be classified as highly strategic. Just as the distinction between pure and applied research is not hard and fast, similarly the strategic character of a problem is not always certain. The selections that follow attempt to identify, where possible, the strategic character of a particular investigation by placing it in proper context in the research of the field.

There are three broad ways in which an investigator tackles and solves a problem. One is through the development of a new theoretical insight. Such an effort ranges from the development of a new concept that directs attention to a crucial dimension of a phenomenon to the elaboration of a theoretical rationale that relates and makes sense

INTRODUCTION

out of a number of hitherto unconnected observations. Such concepts as **need disposition** or **role expectation** illustrate the development of new concepts. Both of these concepts serve to focus attention on certain regularities of individual behavior and their source, the former on certain learned tendencies to orient and behave toward aspects of the biosocial environment in a characteristic way, the latter on a system of shared behavioral expectations that provide structure to human interaction. The development in recent years of theories of cognitive balance illustrates how new theoretical rationales contribute to problem solution. A wide variety of findings, ranging from those concerned with the effects of mass communication on public opinion to studies of the determinants of a person's self conceptions, can be organized and made understandable in terms of a series of propositions drawn from these balance theories.

A second way in which a scientific problem is solved is through the careful piecing together of diverse findings of a series of investigations. In this process, certain principles emerge that bring order to the findings. The recent survey of the literature by Heslin and Dunphy (1964), reproduced in this volume, offers a convenient illustration. These investigators, reviewing the findings from a large number of studies, concluded that the diverse findings on the determinants of member satisfaction could be explained in terms of three variables. The first was status consensus: the degree to which members agreed on their relative ranking on various dimensions. The second was the degree to which members perceived progress toward the group goal; the third, their perceived freedom to participate.

The third manner in which solutions to a scientific problem are arrived at is through crucial observations that delineate a previously unknown relation between variables. Ideally such observations are made in a manner that excludes as far as possible interpretations other than the one proposed by the investigator. The various experimental designs discussed in the first selection of this volume are structured so as to obtain such observations. Other selections amply illustrate all three approaches to problem solution.

This volume is organized into seven parts. At the beginning of each part is a brief introduction intended to place the studies in that part in their appropriate context. Each article, in turn, is preceded by a somewhat more detailed introduction, intended to accomplish three things. First, the selection is placed in the context of research on the particular topic being dealt with. From this the student can gauge the strategic character of the work. Second, the substantive and methodological ideas that should be gained from a reading of the article are made explicit. Finally, where necessary, explanatory notes concerning elements within the selection that might be difficult to grasp are included.

Part One is concerned primarily with two methodological problems that are especially crucial for social science. The first is the problem of causal inference; the second, that of generalization beyond the conditions of the original investigation; or, as they are labeled in the first selection, the problems of internal and external validity. These problems are interrelated. Conditions that minimize one often maximize the other.

Social psychologists, like other scientists, are interested in establishing at a specified degree of certainty that one factor or variable does, in fact, influence another. Three conditions must be met to make such an inference. First, there must be evidence of covariation. Changes in one variable should be accompanied by changes in the other. A second condition concerns the temporal order of the variables. There must be some basis for inferring that the variable considered the effect did not precede in time the variable labeled as the antecedent or cause. Finally, an investigator must provide some basis for excluding alternative explanations—explanations that offer some other factor as the cause. In experiments the bases for these several inferences are inherent in the experimental design and operations. In nonexperimental designs inferences are made on other grounds.

The demonstration of a causal relation in a given research situation is rarely an end in itself. Generally the social scientist, like any other scientist, would like to state with some degree of confidence that this relation obtains in other contexts as well. The social psychologist is especially interested in making this generalization, since his province is the behavior of individuals in interaction with other individuals—the stuff of everyday life. For this reason, he conducts not only laboratory experiments but also field investigations in natural settings. This combination of laboratory and field data enables him to develop principles that apply to human interaction outside the laboratory. The sociologist especially has made substantial contributions here, for his major concern is with the group and larger organizations, with structures and processes that make up the fabric of everyday interaction between people.

The problem of causal inference, along with that of generalization, is common to all scientific disciplines, but is especially acute in the behavioral sciences where the human element plays a large role. The human factor is always present in any scientific study, in that the scientist is human and subject to human error. But in the natural sciences elaborate instrumentation reduces decision processes to a simple level where error is minimized. In contrast, the behavioral scientist often relies on extremely complex judgments made by him or his assistants, thus creating openings for error to creep in.

More unique to the situation faced by the behavioral scientist is the fact that the object of their investigations, human behavior, changes its character when it is subjected to scrutiny. The study of human beings involves interaction between the person being studied and the investigator, a situation which introduces factors other than the hypothesized causes.

The first selection focuses on both causal inference and generalization, or as they are referred to there, the problems of internal

PART ONE

METHODS IN SOCIAL PSYCHOLOGY

and external validity. Their close interrelation is demonstrated; often attempts to solve problems regarding the first raise barriers to a solution of the second. Frequently, controlling or excluding factors other than those whose causal significance is being evaluated curtails the external validity of the findings. The causal relation holds only in the highly unique situation created by the investigator; outside this situation, where accompanying influences are allowed to operate, the relation is seriously modified or negated.

Much of the first selection is concerned with ways of eliminating the effects of extraneous variables in an attempt to isolate a causal relation. The next selection, on the social psychology of the experiment, focuses on just one class of extraneous variables: those influences stemming from the subjects' perception of the **demand characteristics** of the experimental situation. Demand characteristics refer to those cues in the experimental situation which convey to the subjects the experimenter's hypothesis.

In retrospect it is surprising that for so many years psychologists viewed experimental subjects as responding only to whatever the experimenter consciously and purposely introduced into the situation, but it is indeed true that until relatively recently the influence on experimental results of the subjects' attempt to structure and make sense of what is frequently a rather novel situation for him has been virtually ignored. This is all the more surprising in view of the fact that, as the subsequent selection on opinion research documents, social psychologists for many years have been aware that interview responses are influenced by far more than the content of the questions asked. The characteristics of the interviewer, his sex, race, ethnic and religious background, as well as other aspects of the interview situation as perceived by the respondent, influence his replies.

The first two selections focus largely on situations where causal inferences can be made on the basis of active experimental manipulation and control of the observational situation. In contrast, the fourth selection is concerned with methods of causal inference in situations where an investigator could not, or for a variety of reasons did not, structure his observations so as to provide the necessary evidence for causal inference. Here the investigator, through an internal analysis of his data, arrives at the basis for causal inference.

In the last selection, a similar problem of causal inference is faced in the discussion of problems of proof when using the method of participant observation. While this method is used less today than in the past, it is still employed in the study of organizations and other types of ongoing social units. Using this method, the investigator immerses himself in the stream of activity of the units under study, and, like a clinician exploring the personality of an individual in therapy, constructs an explanatory model. In contrast to the standardized procedures of an experiment or the structure of a questionnaire or formal interview in survey research, the lack of structure in participant observation poses special problems of observer bias. In addition, the rather lengthy process of analysis of essentially qualitative material creates special problems of communicating to other scientists the conviction of a scientific proof.

VALIDITY OF EXPERIMENTS IN SOCIAL SETTINGS *

In the following selection Campbell distinguishes between the two problems which are the focus of the readings in Part One, and which are often reiterated throughout the book. The problem of *internal validity* is essentially one of establishing a causal relation between the variables within a given research context—a particular laboratory experiment, a particular sample survey, or some other study. The problem of *external validity* is that of showing that the relation does hold in contexts other than the initial one. These two problems are interrelated in that attempts to reduce the one often magnify the other.

In the research process an investigator establishes the internal validity of a causal relation essentially by a process of elimination. His study is designed so as to provide the basis for excluding interpretations of the results other than the causal relation proposed. Fundamental to this process of excluding alternatives is the principle that elements *common* to two or more situations cannot account for observed *differences* between these situations. This is apparent in the classical experiment in which two situations are equated in all respects save the experimental variable whose introduction is thought to produce the differences in the observed outcome. For example, in a learning experiment the superior performance of the experimental group cannot be due to superior intelligence if the experimental and control groups have been equated in that respect.

To control or eliminate the effects of an extraneous variable both the effects of a variable by itself (main effects) and its effects in combination with other variables (interaction effects) must be kept in mind. The latter is a particularly vexing problem in research on human behavior because of the sensitivity of the human being and the difficulties inherent in isolating him from influences both within and outside the experimental situation that might interact with the effect of the variable under study. As we have become increasingly aware in social psychological research, the measuring process itself may interact with and cause the experimental variable to have effects different from those which it would have in the absence of these influences. For example, assessing an individual's attitudes before subjecting him to a communication may alert him to aspects of the communication that differ from his attitudes, producing a reaction to it different from what he might experience if he were not pretested.

More complex designs that allow an investigator to control and assess both main and interaction effects are needed. The interaction problem is also related to external validity. To what degree are the effects observed in the experimental setting generalizable to other settings, other samples of subjects, and other values of the particular experimental variable? To the extent that features of the new context modify interactions, generalization becomes hazardous.

The first selection is admittedly difficult, particularly for persons unfamiliar with experimental design. For them it would be best to focus on the main line of argument, ignoring some of the smaller details which they find difficult to understand.

1.

Factors Relevant to the Validity of Experiments in Social Settings[1]

DONALD T. CAMPBELL
NORTHWESTERN UNIVERSITY

What do we seek to control in experimental designs? What extraneous variables which would otherwise confound our interpretation of the experiment do we wish to rule out? The present paper attempts a specification of the major categories of such extraneous variables and employs these categories in evaluating the validity of standard designs for experimentation in the social sciences.

Validity will be evaluated in terms of two major criteria. First, and as a basic minimum, is what can be called *internal validity:* did in fact the experimental stimulus make some significant difference in this specific instance? The second criterion is that of *external validity, representativeness,* or

* The selection following the editorial introduction is reprinted from "Factors relevant to the validity of experiments in social settings," *Psychological Bulletin,* 1957, **54,** 297–312, by permission of the author and the American Psychological Association.

[1] A dittoed version of this paper was privately distributed in 1953 under the title "Designs for Social Science Experiments." The author has had the opportunity to benefit from the careful reading and suggestions of L. S. Burwen, J. W. Cotton, C. P. Duncan, D. W. Fiske, C. I. Hovland, L. V. Jones, E. S. Marks, D. C. Pelz and B. J. Underwood, among others, and wishes to express his appreciation. They have not had the opportunity of seeing the paper in its present form, and bear no responsibility for it. The author also wishes to thank S. A. Stouffer (33) and B. J. Underwood (36) for their public encouragement.

generalizability: to what populations, settings, and variables can this effect be generalized? Both criteria are obviously important although it turns out that they are to some extent incompatible, in that the controls required for internal validity often tend to jeopardize representativeness.

The extraneous variables affecting internal validity will be introduced in the process of analyzing three pre-experimental designs. In the subsequent evaluation of the applicability of three true experimental designs, factors leading to external invalidity will be introduced. The effects of these extraneous variables will be considered at two levels: as simple or main effects, they occur independently of or in addition to the effects of the experimental variable; as interactions, the effects appear in conjunction with the experimental variable. The main effects typically turn out to be relevant to internal validity, the interaction effects to external validity or representativeness.

The following designation for experimental designs will be used: X will represent the exposure of a group to the experimental variable or event, the effects of which are to be measured; O will refer to the process of observation or measurement, which can include watching what people do, listening, recording, interviewing, administering tests, counting lever depressions, etc. The Xs and Os in a given row are applied to the same specific persons. The left to right dimension indicates temporal order. Parallel rows represent equivalent samples of persons unless otherwise specified. The designs will be numbered and named for cross-reference purposes.

THREE PRE-EXPERIMENTAL DESIGNS AND THEIR CONFOUNDED EXTRANEOUS VARIABLES

The one-shot case study. As Stouffer (32) has pointed out, much social science research still uses Design 1, in which a single individual or group is studied in detail only once, and in which the observations are attributed to exposure to some prior situation.

X O 1. One-Shot Case Study

This design does not merit the title of experiment, and is introduced only to provide a reference point. The very minimum of useful scientific information involves at least one formal comparison and therefore at least two careful observations (2).

The one-group pretest-posttest design. This design does provide for one formal comparison of two observations, and is still widely used.

O_1 X O_2 2. One-Group Pretest-Posttest Design

However, in it there are four or five categories of extraneous variables left uncontrolled which thus become rival explanations of any difference between O_1 and O_2, confounded with the possible effect of X.

The first of these is the main effect of *history.* During the time span between O_1 and O_2 many events have occurred in addition to X, and the results might be attributed to these. Thus in Collier's (8) experiment, while his respondents[2] were reading Nazi propaganda materials, France fell, and the obtained attitude changes seemed more likely a result of this event than of the propaganda.[3] By history is meant the specific event series other than X, i.e., the extra-experimental uncontrolled stimuli. Relevant to this variable is the concept of experimental isolation, the employment of experimental settings in which all extraneous stimuli are eliminated. The approximation of such control in much physical and biological research has permitted the satisfactory employment of Design 2. But in social psychology and the other social sciences, if history is confounded with X the results are generally uninterpretable.

The second class of variables confounded with X in Design 2 is here designated as *maturation.* This covers those effects which are systematic with the passage of time, and not, like history, a function of the specific events involved. Thus between O_1 and O_2 the respondents may have grown older, hungrier, tireder, etc., and these may have produced the difference between O_1 and O_2, independently of X. While in the typical brief experiment in the psychology laboratory, maturation is unlikely to be a source of change, it has been a problem in research in child development and can be so in extended experiments in social psychology and education. In the form of "spontaneous remission" and the general processes of healing it becomes an important variable to control in medical research, psychotherapy, and social remediation.

There is a third source of variance that could explain the difference between O_1 and O_2 without a recourse to the effect of X. This is the effect of *testing* itself. It is often true that persons taking a test for the second time make scores systematically different from those taking the test for the first time. This is indeed the case for intelligence tests, where a second mean may be expected to run as much as five IQ points higher than the first one. This possibility makes important a distinction between *reactive* measures and *nonreactive* measures. A reactive measure is one which modifies the phenomenon under study, which changes the very thing that one is trying to measure. In general, any measurement procedure which makes the subject self-conscious or aware

---

[2] In line with the central focus on social psychology and the social sciences, the term *respondent* is employed in place of the terms *subject*, *patient*, or *client*.

[3] Collier actually used a more adequate design than this, an approximation to Design 4.

of the fact of the experiment can be suspected of being a reactive measurement. Whenever the measurement process is *not* a part of the normal environment it is probably reactive. Whenever measurement exercises the process under study, it is almost certainly reactive. Measurement of a person's height is relatively nonreactive. However, measurement of weight, introduced into an experimental design involving adult American women, would turn out to be reactive in that the process of measuring would stimulate weight reduction. A photograph of a crowd taken in secret from a second story window would be nonreactive, but a news photograph of the same scene might very well be reactive, in that the presence of the photographer would modify the behavior of people seeing themselves being photographed. In a factory, production records introduced for the purpose of an experiment would be reactive, but if such records were a regular part of the operating environment they would be nonreactive. An English anthropologist may be nonreactive as a participant-observer at an English wedding, but might be a highly reactive measuring instrument at a Dobu nuptials. Some measures are so extremely reactive that their use in a pretest-posttest design is not usually considered. In this class would be tests involving surprise, deception, rapid adaptation, or stress. Evidence is amply present that tests of learning and memory are highly reactive (**35, 36**). In the field of opinion and attitude research our well-developed interview and attitude test techniques must be rated as reactive, as shown, for example, by Crespi's (**9**) evidence.

Even within the personality and attitude test domain, it may be found that tests differ in the degree to which they are reactive. For some purposes, tests involving voluntary self-description may turn out to be more reactive (especially at the interaction level to be discussed below) than are devices which focus the respondent upon describing the external world, or give him less latitude in describing himself (e.g., **5**). It seems likely that, apart from considerations of validity, the Rorschach test is less reactive than the TAT or MMPI. Where the reactive nature of the testing process results from the focusing of attention on the experimental variable, it may be reduced by imbedding the relevant content in a comprehensive array of topics, as has regularly been done in Hovland's attitude change studies (**14**). It seems likely that with attention to the problem, observational and measurement techniques can be developed which are much less reactive than those now in use.

Instrument decay provides a fourth uncontrolled source of variance which could produce an O_1-O_2 difference that might be mistaken for the effect of X. This variable can be exemplified by the fatiguing of a spring scales, or the condensation of water vapor in a cloud chamber. For psychology and the social sciences it becomes a particularly acute problem when human beings are used as a part of the measuring apparatus, as judges, observers, raters, coders, etc. Thus O_1 and O_2 may differ because the raters have become more experienced, more fatigued, have acquired a different adaptation level, or have learned about the purpose of the experiment, etc. However infelicitously, this term will be used to typify those problems introduced when shifts in measurement conditions are confounded with the effect of X, including such crudities as having a different observer at O_1 and O_2, or using a different interviewer or coder. Where the use of different interviewers, observers, or experimenters is unavoidable, but where they are used in large numbers, a sampling equivalence of interviewers is required, with the relevant N being the N of interviewers, not interviewees, except as refined through cluster sampling consideration (**18**).

A possible fifth extraneous factor deserves mention. This is statistical *regression*. When, in Design 2, the group under investigation has been selected for its extremity on O_1, O_1-O_2 shifts toward the mean will occur which are due to random imperfections of the measuring instrument or random instability within the population, as reflected in the test-retest reliability. In general, regression operates like maturation in that the effects increase systematically with the O_1-O_2 time interval. McNemar (**22**) has demonstrated the profound mistakes in interpretation which failure to control this factor can introduce in remedial research.

The static group comparison. The third pre-experimental design is the Static Group Comparison.

$$X \quad O_1$$
$$- - - - -$$
$$ O_2$$

3. The Static Group Comparison

In this design, there is a comparison of a group which has experienced X with a group which has not, for the purpose of establishing the effect of X. In contrast with Design 6, there is in this design no means of certifying that the groups were equivalent at some prior time. (The absence of sampling equivalence of groups is symbolized by the row of dashes.) This design has its most typical occurrence in the social sciences, and both its prevalence and its weakness have been well indicated by Stouffer (**32**). It will be recognized as one form of the correlational study. It is introduced here to complete the list of confounding factors. If the Os differ, this difference could have come about through biased *selection* or recruitment of the persons making up the groups; i.e., they might have differed anyway without the effect of X. Frequently, exposure to X (e.g., some mass communication) has been voluntary and the two groups have an inevitable systematic difference on the factors determining the choice involved, a difference which no amount of matching can remove.

A second variable confounded with the effect of X in this design can be called experimental *mortality*. Even if the groups were equivalent at some prior time, O_1 and O_2 may differ now not because individual members have changed, but because a biased subset of members have dropped out. This is a typical problem in making inferences from comparisons of the attitudes of college freshmen and college seniors, for example.

TRUE EXPERIMENTAL DESIGNS

The pretest-posttest control group design. One or another of the above considerations led psychologists between 1900 and 1925 (**2, 30**) to expand Design 2 by the addition of a control group, resulting in Design 4.

$O_1 \ X \ O_2$ 4. Pretest-Posttest Control Group
$O_3 \ \ \ \ O_4$ Design

Because this design so neatly controls for the main effects of history, maturation, testing, instrument decay, regression, selection, and mortality, these separate sources of variance are not usually made explicit. It seems well to state briefly the relationship of the design to each of these confounding factors, with particular attention to the application of the design in social settings.

If the differences between O_1 and O_2 were due to intervening historical events, then they should also show up in the O_3-O_4 comparison. Note, however, several complications in achieving this control. If respondents are run in groups, and if there is only one experimental session and one control session, then there is no control over the unique internal histories of the groups. The O_1-O_2 difference, even if not appearing in O_3-O_4, may be due to a chance distracting factor appearing in one or the other group. Such a design, while controlling for the shared history or event series, still confounds X with the unique session history. Second, the design implies a simultaneity of O_1 with O_3 and O_2 with O_4 which is usually impossible. If one were to try to achieve simultaneity by using two experimenters, one working with the experimental respondents, the other with the controls, this would confound experimenter differences with X (introducing one type of instrument decay). These considerations make it usually imperative that, for a true experiment, the experimental and control groups be tested and exposed individually or in small subgroups, and that sessions of both types be temporally and spatially intermixed.

As to the other factors: if maturation or testing contributed an O_1-O_2 difference, this should

appear equally in the O_3-O_4 comparison, and these variables are thus controlled for their main effects. To make sure the design controls for instrument decay, the same individual or small-session approximation to simultaneity needed for history is required. The occasional practice of running the experimental group and control group at different times is thus ruled out on this ground as well as that of history. Otherwise the observers may have become more experienced, more hurried, more careless, the maze more redolent with irrelevant cues, the lever-tension and friction diminished, etc. Only when groups are effectively simultaneous do these factors affect experimental and control groups alike. Where more than one experimenter or observer is used, counter-balancing experimenter, time, and group is recommended. The balanced Latin square is frequently useful for this purpose (**4**).

While regression is controlled in the design as a whole, frequently secondary analyses of effects are made for extreme pretest scorers in the experimental group. To provide a control for effects of regression, a parallel analysis of extremes should also be made for the control group.

Selection is of course handled by the sampling equivalence ensured through the randomization employed in assigning persons to groups, perhaps supplemented by, but not supplanted by, matching procedures. Where the experimental and control groups do not have this sort of equivalence, one has a compromise design rather than a true experiment. Furthermore, the O_1-O_3 comparison provides a check on possible sampling differences.

The design also makes possible the examination of experimental mortality, which becomes a real problem for experiments extended over weeks or months. If the experimental and control groups do not differ in the number of lost cases nor in their pretest scores, the experiment can be judged internally valid on this point, although mortality reduces the generalizability of effects to the original population from which the groups were selected.

For these reasons, the Pretest-Posttest Control Group Design has been the ideal in the social sciences for some thirty years. Recently, however, a serious and avoidable imperfection in it has been noted, perhaps first by Schanck and Goodman (**29**). Solomon (**30**) has expressed the point as an *interaction* effect of testing. In the terminology of analysis of variance, the effects of history, maturation, and testing, as described so far, are all *main* effects, manifesting themselves in mean differences independently of the presence of other variables. They are effects that could be added on to other effects, including the effect of the experimental variable. In contrast, interaction effects represent a joint effect, specific to the concomitance of two or more conditions, and may occur even when no main effects are present. Applied to the testing variable, the interaction effect might involve not a shift due solely or directly to the measurement process, but rather a sensitization of respondents to the experimental variable so that when X was preceded by O there would be a change, whereas both X and O would be without effect if occurring alone. In terms of the two types of validity, Design 4 is internally valid, offering an adequate basis for generalization to other sampling-equivalent *pretested* groups. But it has a serious and systematic weakness in representativeness in that it offers, strictly speaking, no basis for generalization to the *unpretested* population. And it is usually the *unpretested* larger universe from which these samples were taken to which one wants to generalize.

A concrete example will help make this clearer. In the NORC study of a United Nations information campaign (**31**), two equivalent samples, of a thousand each, were drawn from the city's population. One of these samples was interviewed, following which the city of Cincinnati was subjected to an intensive publicity campaign using all the mass media of communication. This included special features in the newspapers and on the radio, bus cards, public lectures, etc. At the end of two months, the second sample of 1,000 was interviewed and the results compared with the first 1,000. There were no differences between the two groups except that the second group was somewhat more pessimistic about the likelihood of Russia's cooperating for world peace, a result which was attributed to history rather than to the publicity campaign. The second sample was no better informed about the United Nations nor had it noticed in particular the publicity campaign which had been going on. In connection with a program of research on panels and the reinterview problem, Paul Lazarsfeld and the Bureau of Applied Social Research arranged to have the initial sample reinterviewed at the same time as the second sample was interviewed, after the publicity campaign. This reinterviewed group showed significant attitude changes, a high degree of awareness of the campaign and important increases in information. The inference in this case is unmistakably that the initial interview had sensitized the persons interviewed to the topic of the United Nations, had raised in them a focus of awareness which made the subsequent publicity campaign effective for them but for them only. This study and other studies clearly document the possibility of interaction effects which seriously limit our capacity to generalize from the pretested experimental group to the unpretested general population. Hovland (**15**) reports a general finding which is of the opposite nature but is, nonetheless, an indication of an interactive effect. In his Army studies the initial pretest served to reduce the effects of the experimental variable, presumably by creating a commitment to a given position. Crespi's (**9**) findings support this expectation. Solomon (**30**) reports two studies with

school children in which a spelling pretest reduced the effects of a training period. But whatever the direction of the effect, this flaw in the Pretest-Posttest Control Group Design is serious for the purposes of the social scientist.

The Solomon four-group design. It is Solomon's (**30**) suggestion to control this problem by adding to the traditional two-group experiment two unpretested groups as indicated in Design 5.

$$O_1 \ X \ O_2$$
$$O_3 \quad\ \ O_4 \qquad \text{5. Solomon Four-Group Design}$$
$$X \ O_5$$
$$O_6$$

This Solomon Four-Group Design enables someone to control and measure both the main and interaction effects of testing and the main effects of a composite of maturation and history. It has become the new ideal design for social scientists. A word needs to be said about the appropriate statistical analysis. In Design 4, an efficient single test embodying the four measurements is achieved through computing for each individual a pretest-posttest difference score which is then used for comparing by t test the experimental and control groups. Extension of this mode of analysis to the Solomon Four-Group Design introduces an inelegant awkwardness to the otherwise elegant procedure. It involves assuming as a pretest score for the unpretested groups the mean value of the pretest from the first two groups. This restricts the effective degrees of freedom, violates assumptions of independence, and leaves one without a legitimate base for testing the significance of main effects and interaction. An alternative analysis is available which avoids the assumed pretest scores. Note that the four posttests form a simple two-by-two analysis of variance design:

	NO X	X
Pretested	O_4	O_2
Unpretested	O_6	O_5

The column means represent the main effect of X, the row means the main effect of pretesting, and the interaction term the interaction of pretesting and X. (By use of a t test the combined main effects of maturation and history can be tested through comparing O_6 with O_1 and O_3.)

The posttest-only control group design. While the statistical procedures of analysis of variance introduced by Fisher (**10**) are dominant in psychology and the other social sciences today, it is little noted in our discussions of experimental arrangements that Fisher's typical agricultural experiment involves no pretest: equivalent plots of ground receive different experimental treatments and the subsequent yields are measured.[4] Applied to a social experiment as in testing the influence of a motion picture upon attitudes, two randomly assigned audiences would be selected, one exposed to the movie, and the attitudes of each measured subsequently for the first time.

$A \; X \; O^1$ 6. Posttest-Only Control Group
$A \quad \; O_2$ Design

In this design the symbol A had been added, to indicate that at a specific time prior to X the groups were made equivalent by a random sampling *assignment*. A is the point of selection, the point of allocation of individuals to groups. It is the existence of this process that distinguishes Design 6 from Design 3, the Static Group Comparison. Design 6 is not a static cross-sectional comparison, but instead truly involves control and observation extended in time. The sampling procedures employed assure us that at time A the groups were equal, even if not measured. A provides a point of prior equality just as does the pretest. A point A is, of course, involved in all true experiments, and should perhaps be indicated in Designs 4 and 5. It is essential that A be regarded as a specific point in time, for groups change as a function of time since A, through experimental mortality. Thus in a public opinion survey situation employing probability sampling from lists of residents, the longer the time since A, the more the sample underrepresents the transient segments of society, the newer dwelling units, etc. When experimental groups are being drawn from a self-selected extreme population, such as applicants for psychotherapy, time since A introduces maturation (spontaneous remission) and regression factors. In Design 6 these effects would be confounded with the effect of X if the As as well as the Os were not contemporaneous for experimental and control groups.

Like Design 4, this design controls for the effects of maturation and history through the practical simultaneity of both the As and the Os. In superiority over Design 4, no main or interaction effects of pretesting are involved. It is this feature that recommends it in particular. While it controls for the main and interaction effects of pretesting as well as does Design 5, the Solomon Four-Group Design, it does not measure these effects, nor the main effect of history-maturation.

[4] This is not to imply that the pretest is totally absent from Fisher's designs. He suggests the use of previous year's yields, etc., in covariance analysis. He notes, however, "with annual agricultural crops, knowledge of yields of the experimental area in a previous year under uniform treatment has not been found sufficiently to increase the precision to warrant the adoption of such uniformity trials as a preliminary to projected experiments" (**10**, p. 176).

It can be noted that Design 6 can be considered as the two unpretested "control" groups from the Solomon Design, and that Solomon's two traditional pretested groups have in this sense the sole purpose of measuring the effects of pretesting and history-maturation, a purpose irrelevant to the main aim of studying the effect of X (**25**). However, under normal conditions of not quite perfect sampling control, the four-group design provides in addition greater assurance against mistakenly attributing to X effects which are not due it, inasmuch as the effect of X is documented in three different fashions (O_1 vs. O_2, O_2 vs. O_4, and O_5 vs. O_6). But, short of the four-group design, Design 6 is often to be preferred to Design 4, and is a fully valid experimental design.

Design 6 has indeed been used in the social sciences, perhaps first of all in the classic experiment by Gosnell, *Getting Out the Vote* (**11**). Schanck and Goodman (**29**), Hovland (**15**) and others (**1, 12, 23, 24, 27**) have also employed it. But, in spite of its manifest advantages of simplicity and control, it is far from being a popular design in social research and indeed is usually relegated to an inferior position in discussions of experimental designs if mentioned at all (e.g., **15, 16, 32**). Why is this the case?

In the first place, it is often confused with Design 3. Even where Ss have been carefully assigned to experimental and control groups, one is apt to have an uneasiness about the design because one "doesn't know what the subjects were like before." This objection must be rejected, as our standard tests of significance are designed precisely to evaluate the likelihood of differences occurring by chance in such sample selection. It is true, however, that this design is particularly vulnerable to selection bias and where random assignment is not possible it remains suspect. Where naturally aggregated units, such as classes, are employed intact, these should be used in large numbers and assigned at random to the experimental and control conditions; cluster sampling statistics (**18**) should be used to determine the error term. If but one or two intact classrooms are available for each experimental treatment, Design 4 should certainly be used in preference.

A second objection to Design 6, in comparison with Design 4, is that it often has less precision. The difference scores of Design 4 are less variable than the posttest scores of Design 6 if there is a pretest-posttest correlation above .50 (**15**, p. 323), and hence for test-retest correlations above that level a smaller mean difference would be statistically significant for Design 4 than for Design 6, for a constant number of cases. This advantage to Design 4 may often be more than dissipated by the costs and loss in experimental efficiency resulting from the requirement of two testing sessions, over and above the considerations of representativeness.

Design 4 has a particular advantage over Design 6 if experimental mortality is high. In Design

4, one can examine the pretest scores of lost cases in both experimental and control groups and check on their comparability. In the absence of this in Design 6, the possibility is opened for a mean difference resulting from differential mortality rather than from individual change, if there is a substantial loss of cases.

A final objection comes from those who wish to study the relationship of pretest attitudes to kind and amount of change. This is a valid objection, and where this is the interest, Design 4 or 5 should be used, with parallel analysis of experimental and control groups. Another common type of individual difference study involves classifying persons in terms of amount of change and finding associated characteristics such as sex, age, education, etc. While unavailable in this form in Design 6, essentially the same correlational information can be obtained by subdividing both experimental and control groups in terms of the associated characteristics, and examining the experimental-control difference for such subtypes.

For Design 6, the Posttest-Only Control Group Design, there is a class of social settings in which it is optimally feasible, settings which should be more used than they now are. Whenever the social contact represented by X is made to single individuals or to small groups, and where the response to that stimulus can be identified in terms of individuals or type of X, Design 6 can be applied. Direct mail and door-to-door contacts represent such settings. The alternation of several appeals from door-to-door in a fund-raising campaign can be organized as a true experiment without increasing the cost of the solicitation. Experimental variation of persuasive materials in a direct-mail sales campaign can provide a better experimental laboratory for the study of mass communication and persuasion than is available in any university. The well-established, if little-used, split-run technique in comparing alternative magazine ads is a true experiment of this type, usually limited to coupon returns rather than sales because of the problem of identifying response with stimulus type (**20**). The split-ballot technique (**7**) long used in public opinion polls to compare different question wordings or question sequences provides an excellent example which can obviously be extended to other topics (e.g., **12**). By and large these laboratories have not yet been used to study social science theories, but they are directly relevant to hypotheses about social persuasion.

Multiple X designs. In presenting the above designs, X has been opposed to No-X, as is traditional in discussions of experimental design in psychology. But while this may be a legitimate description of the stimulus-isolated physical science laboratory, it can only be a convenient shorthand in the social sciences, for any No-X period will not be empty of potentially change-inducing stimuli. The experience of the control group might better be categorized as another type of X, a con-

trol experience, an X_C instead of No-X. It is also typical of advance in science that we are soon no longer interested in the qualitative fact of effect or no-effect, but want to specify degree of effect for varying degrees of X. These considerations lead into designs in which multiple groups are used, each with a different X_1, X_2, X_3, X_n, or in multiple factorial design, as X_{1a}, X_{1b}, X_{2a}, X_{2b}, etc. Applied to Designs 4 and 6, this introduces one additional group for each additional X. Applied to 5, The Solomon Four-Group Design, two additional groups (one pretested, one not, both receiving X_n) would be added for each variant on X.

In many experiments, X_1, X_2, X_3, and X_n are all given to the same group, differing groups receiving the Xs in different orders. Where the problem under study centers around the effects of order or combination, such counterbalanced multiple X arrangements are, of course, essential. Studies of transfer in learning are a case in point (**34**). But where one wishes to generalize to the effect of each X as occurring in isolation, such designs are not recommended because of the sizable interactions among Xs, as repeatedly demonstrated in learning studies under such labels as proactive inhibition and learning sets. The use of counterbalanced sets of multiple Xs to achieve experimental equation, where natural groups not randomly assembled have to be used, will be discussed in a subsequent paper on compromise designs.

Testing for effects extended in time. The researches of Hovland and his associates (**14, 15**) have indicated repeatedly that the longer range effects of persuasive Xs may be qualitatively as well as quantitatively different from immediate effects. These results emphasize the importance of designing experiments to measure the effect of X at extended periods of time. As the misleading early research on reminiscence and on the consolidation of the memory trace indicate (**36**), repeated measurement of the same persons cannot be trusted to do this if a reactive measurement process is involved. Thus, for Designs 4 and 6, two separate groups must be added for each posttest period. The additional control group cannot be omitted, or the effects of intervening history, maturation, instrument decay, regression, and mortality are confounded with the delayed effects of X. To follow fully the logic of Design 5, four additional groups are required for each posttest period.

True experiments in which O is not under E's control. It seems well to call the attention of the social scientist to one class of true experiments which are possible without the full experimental control over both the "when" and "to whom" of both X and O. As far as this analysis has been able to go, no such true experiments are possible without the ability to control X, to withhold it from carefully randomly selected respondents while presenting it to others. But control over O does not seem so indispensable. Consider the following design.

A X O_1
A $\quad$ O_2
$\quad (O)$
$\quad (O)$
$\quad (O)$

6. Posttest Only Design, where O cannot be withheld from any respondent

The parenthetical Os are inserted to indicate that the studied groups, experimental and control, have been selected from a larger universe all of which will get O anyway. An election provides such an O, and using "whether voted" rather than "how voted," this was Gosnell's design (**11**). Equated groups were selected at time A, and the experimental group subjected to persuasive materials designed to get out the vote. Using precincts rather than persons as the basic sampling unit, similar studies can be made on the content of the voting (**6**). Essential to this design is the ability to create specified randomly equated groups, the ability to expose one of these groups to X while withholding it (or providing X_2) from the other group, and the ability to identify the performance of each individual or unit in the subsequent O. Since such measures are natural parts of the environment to which one wishes to generalize, they are not reactive, and Design 4, the Pretest-Posttest Control Group Design, is feasible if O has a predictable periodicity to it. With the precinct as a unit, this was the design of Hartmann's classic study of emotional vs. rational appeals in a public election (**13**). Note that 5, the Solomon Four-Group Design, is not available, as it requires the ability to withhold O experimentally, as well as X.

FURTHER PROBLEMS OF REPRESENTATIVENESS

The interaction effect of testing, affecting the external validity or representativeness of the experiment, was treated extensively in the previous section, inasmuch as it was involved in the comparison of alternative designs. The present section deals with the effects upon representativeness of other variables which, while equally serious, can apply to any of the experimental designs.

The interaction effects of selection. Even though the true experiments control selection and mortality for internal validity purposes, these factors have, in addition, an important bearing on representativeness. There is always the possibility that the obtained effects are specific to the experimental population and do not hold true for the populations to which one wants to generalize.

Defining the universe of reference in advance and selecting the experimental and control groups from this at random would guarantee representativeness if it were ever achieved in practice. But inevitably not all those so designated are actually eligible for selection by any contact procedure. Our best survey sampling techniques, for example, can designate for potential contact only those available through residences. And, even of those so designated, up to 19 per cent are not contactable for an interview in their own homes even with five callbacks (**37**). It seems legitimate to assume that the more effort and time required of the respondent, the larger the loss through nonavailability and noncooperation. If one were to try to assemble experimental groups away from their own homes it seems reasonable to estimate a 50 per cent selection loss. If, still trying to extrapolate to the general public, one further limits oneself to docile preassembled groups, as in schools, military units, studio audiences, etc., the proportion of the universe systematically excluded through the sampling process must approach 90 per cent or more. Many of the selection factors involved are indubitably highly systematic. Under these extreme selection losses, it seems reasonable to suspect that the experimental groups might show reactions not characteristic of the general population. This point seems worth stressing lest we unwarrantedly assume that the selection loss for experiments is comparable to that found for survey interviews in the home at the respondent's convenience. Furthermore, it seems plausible that the greater the cooperation required, the more the respondent has to deviate from the normal course of daily events, the greater will be the possibility of nonrepresentative reactions. By and large, Design 6 might be expected to require less cooperation than Design 4 or 5, especially in the natural individual contact setting. The interactive effects of experimental mortality are of similar nature. Note that, on these grounds, the longer the experiment is extended in time the more respondents are lost and the less representative are the groups of the original universe.

Reactive arrangements. In any of the experimental designs, the respondents can become aware that they are participating in an experiment, and this awareness can have an interactive effect, in creating reactions to X which would not occur had X been encountered without this "I'm a guinea pig" attitude. Lazarsfeld (**19**), Kerr (**17**), and Rosenthal and Frank (**28**), all have provided valuable discussions of this problem. Such effects limit generalizations to respondents having this awareness, and preclude generalization to the population encountering X with non-experimental attitudes. The direction of the effect may be one of negativism, such as an unwillingness to admit to any persuasion or change. This would be comparable to the absence of any immediate effect from discredited communicators, as found by Hovland (**14**). The result is probably more often a cooperative responsiveness, in which the respondent accepts the experimenter's expectations and provides pseudo-confirmation. Particularly is this positive response likely when the respondents are self-selected seekers after the cure that X may offer. The Hawthorne studies (21), illustrate such sympathetic changes due to awareness of experimentation rather than to the specific nature of X. In some settings it is possible to disguise the experimental purpose by providing plausible façades in which X appears as an incidental part of the background (e.g., **26, 27, 29**). We can also make more extensive use of experiments taking place in the intact social situation, in which the respondent is not aware of the experimentation at all.

The discussion of the effects of selection on representativeness has argued against employing intact natural preassembled groups, but the issue of conspicuousness of arrangements argues for such use. The machinery of breaking up natural groups such as departments, squads, and classrooms into randomly assigned experimental and control groups is a source of reaction which can often be avoided by the use of preassembled groups, particularly in educational settings. Of course, as has been indicated, this requires the use of large numbers of such groups under both experimental and control conditions.

The problem of reactive arrangements is distributed over all features of the experiment which can draw the attention of the respondent to the fact of experimentation and its purposes. The conspicuous or reactive pretest is particularly vulnerable, inasmuch as it signals the topics and purposes of the experimenter. For communications of obviously persuasive aim, the experimenter's topical intent is signaled by the X itself, if the communication does not seem a part of the natural environment. Even for the posttest-only groups, the occurrence of the posttest may create a reactive effect. The respondent may say to himself, "Aha, now I see why we got that movie." This consideration justifies the practice of disguising the connection between O and X even for Designs 6, as through having different experimental personnel involved, using different façades, separating the settings and times, and embedding the X-relevant content of O among a disguising variety of other topics.[5]

Generalizing to other Xs. After the internal validity of an experiment has been established, after a dependable effect of X upon O has been found, the next step is to establish the limits and relevant dimensions of generalization not only in terms of populations and settings but also in terms of categories and aspects of X. The actual X in any one experiment is a specific combination of stimuli, all confounded for interpretative purposes, and only some relevant to the experimenter's intent and theory. Subsequent experimentation should be designed to purify X, to discover that aspect of the original conglomerate X which is responsible for the effect. As Brunswik (3) has emphasized, the representative sampling of Xs is as relevant a problem in linking experiment to theory as is the sampling of respondents. To define a category of Xs along some dimension, and then to sample Xs for experimental purposes from the full range of stimuli meeting the specification while other aspects of each specific stimulus complex are varied, serves to untie or unconfound the defined dimension from specific others, lending assurance of theoretical relevance.

In a sense, the placebo problem can be understood in these terms. The experiment without the placebo has clearly demonstrated that some aspect of the total X stimulus complex has had an effect; the placebo experiment serves to break up the complex X into the suggestive connotation of pill-taking and the specific pharmacological properties of the drug—separating two aspects of the X previously confounded. Subsequent studies may discover with similar logic which chemical fragment of the complex natural herb is most essential. Still more clearly, the sham operation illustrates the process of X purification, ruling out general effects of surgical shock so that the specific effects of loss of glandular or neural tissue may be isolated. As these parallels suggest, once recurrent unwanted aspects of complex Xs have been discovered for a given field, control groups especially designed to eliminate these effects can be regularly employed.

Generalizing to other Os. In parallel form, the scientist in practice uses a complex measurement procedure which needs to be refined in subsequent experimentation. Again, this is best done by employing multiple Os all having in common the theoretically relevant attribute but varying widely in their irrelevant specificities. For Os this process can be introduced into the initial experiment by employing multiple measures. A major practical reason for not doing so is that it is so frequently a frustrating experience, lending hesitancy, indecision, and a feeling of failure to studies that would have been interpreted with confidence had but a single response measure been employed.

Transition experiments. The two previous paragraphs have argued against the *exact* replication of experimental apparatus and measurement procedures on the grounds that this continues the confounding of theory-relevant aspects of X and O with specific artifacts of unknown influence.

---

[5] For purposes of completeness, the interaction of X with history and maturation should be mentioned. Both affect the generalizability of results. The interaction effect of history represents the possible specificity of results to a given historical moment, a possibility which increases as problems are more societal, less biological. The interaction of maturation and X would be represented in the specificity of effects to certain maturational levels, fatigue states, etc.

On the other hand, the confusion in our literature generated by the heterogeneity of results from studies all on what is nominally the "same" problem but varying in implementation, is leading some to call for exact replication of initial procedures in subsequent research on a topic. Certainly no science can emerge without dependably repeatable experiments. A suggested resolution is the *transition experiment*, in which the need for varying the theory-independent aspects of X and O is met in the form of a multiple X, multiple O design, one segment of which is an "exact" replication of the original experiment, exact at least in those major features which are normally reported in experimental writings.

Internal vs. external validity. If one is in a situation where either internal validity or representativeness must be sacrificed, which should it be? The answer is clear. Internal validity is the prior and indispensable consideration. The optimal design is, of course, one having both internal and external validity. Insofar as such settings are available, they should be exploited, without embarrassment from the apparent opportunistic warping of the content of studies by the availability of laboratory techniques. In this sense, a science is as opportunistic as a bacteria culture and grows only where growth is possible. One basic necessity for such growth is the machinery for selecting among alternative hypotheses, no matter how limited those hypotheses may have to be.

SUMMARY

In analyzing the extraneous variables which experimental designs for social settings seek to control, seven categories have been distinguished: history, maturation, testing, instrument decay, regression, selection, and mortality. In general, the simple or main effects of these variables jeopardize the internal validity of the experiment and are adequately controlled in standard experimental designs. The interactive effects of these variables and of experimental arrangements affect the external validity or generalizability of experimental results. Standard experimental designs vary in their susceptibility to these interactive effects. Stress is also placed upon the differences among measuring instruments and arrangements in the extent to which they create unwanted interactions. The value for social science purposes of the Posttest-Only Control Group Design is emphasized.

REFERENCES

1. ANNIS, A. D., & MEIER, N. C. The induction of opinion through suggestion by means of planted content. *J. soc. Psychol.,* 1934, **5**, 65–81.

2. BORING, E. G. The nature and history of experimental control. *Amer. J. Psychol.,* 1954, **67**, 573–589.

3. BRUNSWIK, E. *Perception and the representative designs of psychological experiments.* Berkeley: Univer. California Press, 1956.

4. BUGELSKI, B. R. A note on Grant's discussion of the Latin square principle in the design and analysis of psychological experiments. *Psychol. Bull.,* 1949, **46**, 49–50.

5. CAMPBELL, D. T. The indirect assessment of social attitudes. *Psychol. Bull.,* 1950, **47**, 15–38.

6. CAMPBELL, D. T. On the possibility of experimenting with the "Bandwagon" effect. *Int. J. Opin. Attitude Res.,* 1951, **5**, 251–260.

7. CANTRIL, H. *Gauging public opinion.* Princeton: Princeton Univer. Press, 1944.

8. COLLIER, R. M. The effect of propaganda upon attitude following a critical examination of the propaganda itself. *J. soc. Psychol.,* 1944, **20**, 3–17.

9. CRESPI, L. P. The interview effect in polling. *Publ. Opin. Quart.,* 1948, 12, 99–111.

10. FISHER, R. A. *The design of experiments.* Edinburgh: Oliver & Boyd, 1935.

11. GOSNELL, H. F. *Getting out the vote: an experiment in the stimulation of voting.* Chicago: Univer. of Chicago Press, 1927.

12. GREENBERG, A. Matched samples. *J. Marketing,* 1953–54, **18**, 241–245.

13. HARTMANN, G. W. A field experiment on the comparative effectiveness of "emotional" and "rational" political leaflets in determining election results. *J. abnorm. soc. Psychol.,* 1936, **31**, 99–114.

14. HOVLAND, C. E., JANIS, I. L., & KELLEY, H. H. *Communication and persuasion.* New Haven: Yale Univer. Press, 1953.

15. HOVLAND, C. I., LUMSDAINE, A. A., & SHEFFIELD, F. D. *Experiments on mass communication.* Princeton: Princeton Univer. Press, 1949.

16. JAHODA, M., DEUTSCH, M., & COOK, S. W. *Research methods in social relations.* New York: Dryden Press, 1951.

17. KERR, W. A. Experiments on the effect of music on factory production. *Appl. Psychol. Monogr.,* 1945, No. 5.

18. KISH, L. Selection of the sample. In L. Festinger and D. Katz (Eds.), *Research methods in the behavioral sciences.* New York: Dryden Press, 1953, 175–239.

19. LAZARSFELD, P. F. Training guide on the controlled experiment in social research. Dittoed. Columbia Univer., Bureau of Applied Social Research, 1948.

20. LUCAS, D. B., & BRITT, S. H. *Advertising psychology and research.* New York: McGraw-Hill, 1950.

21. MAYO, E. *The human problems of an industrial civilization.* New York: Macmillan, 1933.

22. McNEMAR, Q. A critical examination of the University of Iowa studies of environmental influences upon the IQ. *Psychol. Bull.,* 1940, **37**, 63–92.

23. MENEFEE, S. C. An experimental study of strike propaganda. *Soc. Forces,* 1938, **16**, 574–582.
24. PARRISH, J. A., & CAMPBELL, D. T. Measuring propaganda effects with direct and indirect attitude tests. *J. abnorm. soc. Psychol.,* 1953, **48**, 3–9.
25. PAYNE, S. L. The ideal model for controlled experiments. *Publ. Opin. Quart.,* 1951, **15**, 557–562.
26. POSTMAN, L., & BRUNER, J. S. Perception under stress. *Psychol. Rev.,* 1948, **55**, 314–322.
27. RANKIN, R. E., & CAMPBELL, D. T. Galvanic skin response to Negro and white experimenters. *J. abnorm. soc. Psychol.,* 1955, **51**, 30–33.
28. ROSENTHAL, D., & FRANK, J. O. Psychotherapy and the placebo effect. *Psychol. Bull.,* 1956, **53**, 294–302.
29. SCHANCK, R. L., & GOODMAN, C. Reactions to propaganda on both sides of a controversial issue. *Publ. Opin. Quart.,* 1939, **3**, 107–112.

30. SOLOMON, R. W. An extension of control group design. *Psychol. Bull.,* 1949, **46**, 137–150.
31. STAR, S. A., & HUGHES, H. M. Report on an educational campaign: the Cincinnati plan for the United Nations. *Amer. J. Sociol.,* 1949–50, **55**, 389.
32. STOUFFER, S. A. Some observations on study design. *Amer. J. Sociol,* 1949–50, **55**, 355–361.
33. STOUFFER, S. A. Measurement in sociology. *Amer. sociol. Rev.,* 1953, **18**, 591–597.
34. UNDERWOOD, B. J. *Experimental psychology.* Appleton-Century-Crofts, 1949.
35. UNDERWOOD, B. J. Interference and forgetting. *Psychol. Rev.,* 1957, **64**, 49–60.
36. UNDERWOOD, B. J. *Psychological research.* New York: Appleton-Century-Crofts, 1957.
37. WILLIAMS, R. Probability sampling in the field: a case history. *Publ. Opin. Quart.,* 1950, **14**, 316–330.

DEMAND CHARACTERISTICS OF THE EXPERIMENT *

A recent methodological contribution having profound implications is systematic research programs on sources of bias in psychological experiments. Although investigators reported on such biases as early as 1904, they have all too often been ignored.[a]

Quite possibly many experimental findings in social psychology and in other areas of sociological and psychological research are products of biasing factors rather than the supposed independent or causal variables of the experiments. This possibility has produced an intensive social psychological analysis of the experiment, focusing on the interaction between the experimenter and his subjects, which generates these sources of bias.

One series of studies has shown that experimental assistants familiar with the purpose of the experiment they are conducting are more apt to obtain the desired findings from their subjects than assistants who do not know the purpose of the experiment.[b] This is due not to conscious dishonesty, but to subtle, not fully identified cues in the experimenter's behavior that convey to the subject the experimenter's hypothesis. Considering the subject's contribution to these biases, Orne notes the extreme suggestibility of the individual when he is playing the role of subject—he acts almost as though he were hypnotized. This appears to make him particularly sensitive to cues stemming from the experimenter's behavior.

Various other sources have been suggested by Mills.[c] For example, in a reanalysis of a classic study by Schachter,[d] Mills suggests that the subjects' rejection of a group member who had taken an extreme position in the group discussion was a form of scapegoating or displaced aggression against the experimenter. Schachter had varied the cohesiveness or attractiveness of his groups by assembling into groups some subjects who had previously indicated a preference for their group activity and others who had indicated a preference for an activity other than that of the group in which they were placed. He also varied the relevance of the group activity: some groups were allowed to engage in activities that they had been formed to carry out, and others, to engage only in activities irrelevant to their purpose. In a subsequent group discussion the paid participant, who took a deviant position on the issue under discussion, was rejected most by groups of low cohesive-

*The selection following the editorial introduction is reprinted from "On the social psychology of the psychological experiment with particular reference to the demand characteristics and their implications," *American Psychologist,* 1962, **17**, 776–783, by permission of the author and the American Psychological Association.

[a] B. L. Kintz, D. J. Delprato, D. R. Mettee, C. E. Persons, & R. H. Shappe. The experimenter effect. *Psychol. Bull.,* 1965, **63**, 223–232.

[b] R. Rosenthal. On the social psychology of the psychological experiment: The experimenter's hypotheses as an unintended determinant of experimental results. *Amer. Scientist,* 1963, **51**, 268–282.

[c] T. M. Mills. A sleeper variable in small groups research: The experimenter. *Pacific Sociol. Rev.,* 1962, **5**, 21–28.

[d] S. Schachter. Deviation, rejection, and communication. In L. Festinger et al. (eds.), *Theory and experiment in social communication.* Ann Arbor, Mich.: Research Center for Group Dynamics, 1950.

ness engaging in irrelevant activities. This result, Mills asserts, cannot be explained in terms of Schachter's theoretical framework. It can, however, be explained in terms of the subjects' reaction to the experimenter. He suggested that the subjects in these groups were frustrated by the caprice of the experimenter in assigning them to less desirable groups and requiring them to engage in irrelevant activities and that they directed their consequent feelings of aggression concerning him toward the deviant group member, who was a more suitable target.

Not only the relation between the experimenter and the subject but also the subject's motivation for volunteering, his conception of the role of subject in a psychological experiment, and even the manner in which he has been recruited[e] affect his responses to the experimental situation.

These findings greatly complicate the problems of causal inference and generalization. To what degree are the findings of any experiment a function of the independent variable and to what degree are they a product of other aspects of the total experience of the experimental subjects? To the extent that the latter influences prevail, both causal inferences and generalization beyond the particular research context are risky. In the following selection, Orne provides a way of conceptualizing the problem of bias in experimental settings and suggests means by which the effects of bias can be assessed and separated from the variables under study.

2.

On the Social Psychology of the Psychological Experiment: with particular reference to demand characteristics and their implications[1]

MARTIN T. ORNE[2]
UNIVERSITY OF PENNSYLVANIA

It is to the highest degree probable that the subject['s] *. . . general attitude of*

[e] K. W. Bach, T. C. Hood, & Mary L. Brehm. The subject role in small group experiments. *Soc. Forces*, 1964, **43**, 181–187.
[1] This paper was presented at the Symposium, "On the Social Psychology of the Psychological Experiment," American Psychological Association Convention, New York, 1961.

The work reported here was supported in part by a Public Health Service Research Grant, M-3369, National Institute of Mental Health.

[2] I wish to thank my associates Ronald E. Shor, Donald N. O'Connell, Ulric Neisser, Karl E. Scheibe, and Emily F. Carota for their comments and criticisms in the preparation of this paper.

mind is that of ready complacency and cheerful willingness to assist the investigator in every possible way by reporting to him those very things which he is most eager to find, and that the very questions of the experimenter . . . suggest the shade of reply expected. . . . Indeed . . . it seems too often as if the subject were now regarded as a stupid automaton. . . . A. H. PIERCE, 1908[3]

Since the time of Galileo, scientists have employed the laboratory experiment as a method of understanding natural phenomena. Generically, the experimental method consists of abstracting relevant variables from complex situations in nature and reproducing in the laboratory segments of these situations, varying the parameters involved so as to determine the effect of the experimental variables. This procedure allows generalization from the information obtained in the laboratory situation back to the original situation as it occurs in nature. The physical sciences have made striking advances through the use of this method, but in the behavioral sciences it has often been difficult to meet two necessary requirements for meaningful experimentation: reproducibility and ecological validity.[4] It has long been recognized that certain differences will exist between the types of experiments conducted in the physical sciences and those in the behavioral sciences because the former investigates a universe of inanimate objects and forces, whereas the latter deals with animate organisms, often thinking, conscious subjects. However, recognition of this distinction has not always led to appropriate changes in the traditional experimental model of physics as employed in the behavioral sciences. Rather the experimental model has been so successful as employed in physics that there has been a tendency in the behavioral sciences to follow precisely a paradigm originated for the study of inanimate objects, i.e., one which proceeds by exposing the subject to various conditions and observing the differences in reaction of the subject under different conditions. However, the use of such a model with animal or human subjects leads to the problem that the subject of the experiment is assumed, at least implicitly, to be a *passive responder* to stimuli—an assumption difficult to justify. Further, in this type of model the experimental stimuli themselves are usually rigorously defined in terms of what *is done* to the subject. In contrast, the purpose of this paper will be to focus on what the human subject *does* in the laboratory: what motivation the subject is likely to have in the experimental situation, how he usually perceives behavioral research, what the

[3] See reference list (Pierce, 1908).
[4] Ecological validity, in the sense that Brunswik (1947) has used the term: appropriate generalization from the laboratory to nonexperimental situations.

nature of the cues is that the subject is likely to pick up, etc. Stated in other terms, what factors are apt to affect the subject's reaction to the well-defined stimuli in the situation? These factors comprise what will be referred to here as the "experimental setting."

Since any experimental manipulation of human subjects takes place within this larger framework or setting, we should propose that the above-mentioned factors must be further elaborated and the parameters of the experimental setting more carefully defined so that adequate controls can be designed to isolate the effects of the experimental setting from the effects of the experimental variables. Later in this paper we shall propose certain possible techniques of control which have been devised in the process of our research on the nature of hypnosis.

Our initial focus here will be on some of the qualities peculiar to psychological experiments. The experimental situation is one which takes place within the context of an explicit agreement of the subject to participate in a special form of social interaction known as "taking part in an experiment." Within the context of our culture the roles of subject and experimenter are well understood and carry with them well-defined mutual role expectations. A particularly striking aspect of the typical experimenter-subject relationship is the extent to which the subject will play his role and place himself under the control of the experimenter. Once a subject has agreed to participate in a psychological experiment, he implicitly agrees to perform a very wide range of actions on request without inquiring as to their purpose, and frequently without inquiring as to their duration.

Furthermore, the subject agrees to tolerate a considerable degree of discomfort, boredom, or actual pain, if required to do so by the experimenter. Just about any request which could conceivably be asked of the subject by a reputable investigator is legitimized by the quasi-magical phrase, "This is an experiment," and the shared assumption that a legitimate purpose will be served by the subject's behavior. A somewhat trivial example of this legitimization of requests is as follows:

A number of casual acquaintances were asked whether they would do the experimenter a favor; on their acquiescence, they were asked to perform five push-ups. Their response tended to be amazement, incredulity and the question "Why?" Another similar group of individuals were asked whether they would take part in an experiment of brief duration. When they agreed to do so, they too were asked to perform five push-ups. Their typical response was "Where?"

The striking degree of control inherent in the experimental situation can also be illustrated by a set of pilot experiments which were performed in the course of designing an experiment to test whether the degree of control inherent in the

hypnotic relationship is greater than that in a waking relationship.[5] In order to test this question, we tried to develop a set of tasks which waking subjects would refuse to do, or would do only for a short period of time. The tasks were intended to be psychologically noxious, meaningless, or boring, rather than painful or fatiguing.

For example, one task was to perform serial additions of each adjacent two numbers on sheets filled with rows of random digits. In order to complete just one sheet, the subject would be required to perform 224 additions! A stack of some 2,000 sheets was presented to each subject —clearly an impossible task to complete. After the instructions were given, the subject was deprived of his watch and told, "Continue to work; I will return eventually." Five and one-half hours later, the *experimenter* gave up! In general, subjects tended to continue this type of task for several hours, usually with little decrement in performance. Since we were trying to find a task which would be discontinued spontaneously within a brief period, we tried to create a more frustrating situation as follows:

Subjects were asked to perform the same task described above but were also told that when finished with the additions on each sheet, they should pick up a card from a large pile, which would instruct them on what to do next. However, every card in the pile read:

> You are to tear up the sheet of paper which you have just completed into a minimum of thirty-two pieces and go on to the next sheet of paper and continue working as you did before; when you have completed this piece of paper, pick up the next card which will instruct you further. Work as accurately and as rapidly as you can.

Our expectation was that subjects would discontinue the task as soon as they realized that the cards were worded identically, that each finished piece of work had to be destroyed, and that, in short, the task was completely meaningless.

Somewhat to our amazement, subjects tended to persist in the task for several hours with relatively little sign of overt hostility. Removal of the one-way screen did not tend to make much difference. The postexperimental inquiry helped to explain the subjects' behavior. When asked about the tasks, subjects would invariably attribute considerable meaning to their performance, viewing it as an endurance test or the like.

Thus far, we have been singularly unsuccessful in finding an experimental task which would be discontinued, or, indeed, refused by subjects in

[5] These pilot studies were performed by Thomas Menaker.

an experimental setting.[6,7] Not only do subjects continue to perform boring, unrewarding tasks, but they do so with few errors and little decrement in speed. It became apparent that it was extremely difficult to design an experiment to test the degree of social control in hypnosis, in view of the already *very high degree of control in the experimental situation itself.*

The quasi-experimental work reported here is highly informal and based on samples of three or four subjects in each group. It does, however, illustrate the remarkable compliance of the experimental subject. The only other situations where such a wide range of requests are carried out with little or no question are those of complete authority, such as some parent-child relationships or some doctor-patient relationships. This aspect of the experiment as a social situation will not become apparent unless one tests for it; it is, however, present in varying degrees in all experimental contexts. Not only are tasks carried out, but they are performed with care over a considerable period of time.

Our observation that subjects tend to carry out a remarkably wide range of instructions with a surprising degree of diligence reflects only one aspect of the motivation manifested by most subjects in an experimental situation. It is relevant to consider another aspect of motivation that is common to the subjects of most psychological experiments: high regard for the aims of science and experimentation.

A volunteer who participates in a psychological experiment may do so for a wide variety of reasons ranging from the need to fulfill a course requirement, to the need for money, to the invoiced hope of altering his personal adjustment for the better, etc. Over and above these motives, however, college students tend to share (with the experimenter) the hope and expectation that the study in which they are participating will in some material way contribute to science and perhaps ultimately to human welfare in general. We should expect that many of the characteristics of the experimental situation derive from the peculiar role relationship which exists between subject and experimenter. Both subject and experimenter share the belief that whatever the experimental task is, it is important, and that as such no matter how much effort must be exerted or how much discom-

fort must be endured, it is justified by the ultimate purpose.

If we assume that much of the motivation of the subject to comply with any and all experimental instructions derives from an identification with the goals of science in general and the success of the experiment in particular,[8] it follows that the subject has a stake in the outcome of the study in which he is participating. For the volunteer subject to feel that he has made a useful contribution, it is necessary for him to assume that the experimenter is competent and that he himself is a "good subject."

The significance to the subject of successfully being a "good subject" is attested to by the frequent questions at the conclusion of an experiment, to the effect of, "Did I ruin the experiment?" What is most commonly meant by this is, "Did I perform well in my role as experimental subject?" or "Did my behavior demonstrate that which the experiment is designed to show?" Admittedly, subjects are concerned about their performance in terms of reinforcing their self-image; nonetheless, they seem even more concerned with the utility of their performances. We might well expect then that as far as the subject is able, he will behave in an experimental context in a manner designed to play the role of a "good subject" or, in other words, *to validate the experimental hypothesis.* Viewed in this way, the student volunteer is *not* merely a passive responder in an experimental situation but rather he has a very real stake in the successful outcome of the experiment. This problem is implicitly recognized in the large number of psychological studies which attempt to conceal the true purpose of the experiment from the subject in the hope of thereby obtaining more reliable data. This maneuver on the part of psychologists is so widely known in the college population that even if a psychologist is honest with the subject, more often than not he will be distrusted. As one subject pithily put it, "Psychologists always lie!" This bit of paranoia has some support in reality.

The subject's performance in an experiment might almost be conceptualized as problem-solving behavior; that is, at some level he sees it as his task to ascertain the true purpose of the experiment and respond in a manner which will support the hypotheses being tested. Viewed in this light, the totality of cues which convey an experimental hypothesis to the subject becomes significant determinants of subjects' behavior. We have labeled the sum total of such cues as the *"demand characteristics of the experimental situation"* (Orne, 1959a). These cues include the rumors or campus scuttlebutt about the research, the information

---

[6] Tasks which would involve the use of actual severe physical pain or exhaustion were not considered.

[7] This observation is consistent with Frank's (1944) failure to obtain resistance to disagreeable or nonsensical tasks. He accounts for this "primarily by *S*'s unwillingness to break the tacit agreement he had made when he volunteered to take part in the experiment, namely, to do whatever the experiment required of him" (p. 24).

[8] This hypothesis is subject to empirical test. We should predict that there would be measurable differences in motivation between subjects who perceive a particular experiment as "significant" and those who perceive the experiment as "unimportant."

conveyed during the original solicitation, the person of the experimenter, and the setting of the laboratory, as well as all explicit and implicit communications during the experiment proper. A frequently overlooked, but nonetheless very significant source of cues for the subject lies in the experimental procedure itself, viewed in the light of the subject's previous knowledge and experience. For example, if a test is given twice with some intervening treatment, even the dullest college student is aware that some change is expected, particularly if the test is in some obvious way related to the treatment.

The demand characteristics perceived in any particular experiment will vary with the sophistication, intelligence, and previous experience of each experimental subject. To the extent that the demand characteristics of the experiment are clear-cut, they will be perceived uniformly by most experimental subjects. It is entirely possible to have an experimental situation with clear-cut demand characteristics for psychology undergraduates which, however, does not have the same clear-cut demand characteristics for enlisted army personnel. It is, of course, those demand characteristics which are perceived by the subject that will influence his behavior.

We should like to propose the heuristic assumption that a subject's behavior in any experimental situation will be determined by two sets of variables: (*a*) those which are traditionally defined as experimental variables and (*b*) the perceived demand characteristics of the experimental situation. The extent to which the subject's behavior is related to the demand characteristics, rather than to the experimental variable, will in large measure determine both the extent to which the experiment can be replicated with minor modification (i.e., modified demand characteristics) and the extent to which generalizations can be drawn about the effect of the experimental variables in nonexperimental contexts [the problem of ecological validity (Brunswik, 1947)].

It becomes an empirical issue to study under what circumstances, in what kind of experimental contexts, and with what kind of subject populations, demand characteristics become significant in determining the behavior of subjects in experimental situations. It should be clear that demand characteristics cannot be eliminated from experiments; all experiments will have demand characteristics, and these will always have some effect. It does become possible, however, to study the effect of demand characteristics as opposed to the effect of experimental variables. However, techniques designed to study the effect of demand characteristics need to take into account that these effects result from the subject's *active* attempt to respond appropriately to the *totality* of the experimental situation.

It is perhaps best to think of the perceived demand characteristics as a contextual variable in the experimental situation. We should like to

emphasize that, at this stage, little is known about this variable. In our first study which utilized the demand characteristics concept (Orne, 1959b), we found that a particular experimental effect was present only in records of those subjects who were able to verbalize the experimenter's hypothesis. Those subjects who were unable to do so did not show the predicted phenomenon. Indeed we found that whether or not a given subject perceived the experimenter's hypothesis was a more accurate predictor of the subject's actual performance than his statement about what he thought he had done on the experimental task. It became clear from extensive interviews with subjects that response to the demand characteristics is not merely conscious compliance. When we speak of "playing the role of a good experimental subject," we use the concept analogously to the way in which Sarbin (1950) describes role playing in hypnosis: namely, largely on a nonconscious level. The demand characteristics of the situation help define the role of "good experimental subject," and the responses of the subject are a function of the role that is created.

We have a suspicion that the demand characteristics most potent in determining subjects' behavior are those which convey the purpose of the experiment effectively but not obviously. If the purpose of the experiment is not clear, or is highly ambiguous, many different hypotheses may be formed by different subjects, and the demand characteristics will not lead to clear-cut results. If, on the other hand, the demand characteristics are so obvious that the subject becomes fully conscious of the expectations of the experimenter, there is a tendency to lean over backwards to be honest. We are encountering here the effect of another facet of the college student's attitude toward science. While the student wants studies to "work," he feels he must be honest in his report; otherwise, erroneous conclusions will be drawn. Therefore, if the subject becomes acutely aware of the experimenter's expectations, there may be a tendency for biasing in the opposite direction. (This is analogous to the often observed tendency to favor individuals whom we dislike in an effort to be fair.) [9]

Delineation of the situations where demand characteristics may produce an effect ascribed to experimental variables, or where they may obscure such an effect and actually lead to systematic data

---

[9] Rosenthal (1961) in his recent work on experimenter bias has reported a similar type of phenomenon. Biasing was maximized by ego involvement of the experimenters, but when an attempt was made to increase biasing by paying for "good results," there was a marked reduction of effect. This reversal may be ascribed to the experimenters' becoming too aware of their own wishes in the situation.

in the opposite direction, as well as those experimental contexts where they do not play a major role, is an issue for further work. Recognizing the contribution to experimental results which may be made by the demand characteristics of the situation, what are some experimental techniques for the study of demand characteristics?

As we have pointed out, it is futile to imagine an experiment that could be created without demand characteristics. One of the basic characteristics of the human being is that he will ascribe purpose and meaning even in the absence of purpose and meaning. In an experiment where he knows some purpose exists, it is inconceivable for him not to form some hypothesis as to the purpose, based on some cues, no matter how meager; this will then determine the demand characteristics which will be perceived by and operate for a particular subject. Rather than eliminating this variable then, it becomes necessary to take demand characteristics into account, study their effect, and manipulate them if necessary.

One procedure to determine the demand characteristics is the systematic study of each individual subject's perception of the experimental hypothesis. If one can determine what demand characteristics are perceived by each subject, it becomes possible to determine to what extent these, rather than the experimental variables, correlate with the observed behavior. If the subject's behavior correlates better with the demand characteristics than with the experimental variables, it is probable that the demand characteristics are the major determinants of the behavior.

The most obvious technique for determining what demand characteristics are perceived is the use of postexperimental inquiry. In this regard, it is well to point out that considerable self-discipline is necessary for the experimenter to obtain a valid inquiry. A great many experimenters at least implicitly make the demand that the subject not perceive what is really going on. The temptation for the experimenter, in, say, a replication of an Asch-group pressure experiment, is to ask the subject afterwards, "You didn't realize that the other fellows were confederates, did you?" Having obtained the required, "No," the experimenter breathes a sigh of relief and neither subject nor experimenter pursues the issue further.[10] However, even if the experimenter makes an effort to elicit the subject's perception of the hypothesis of the experiment, he may have difficulty in obtaining a valid report because the subject as well as he himself has considerable interest in appearing naive.

Most subjects are cognizant that they are not

[10] Asch (1952) himself took great pains to avoid this pitfall.

supposed to know any more about an experiment than they have been told and that excessive knowledge will disqualify them from participating, or, in the case of a postexperimental inquiry, such knowledge will invalidate their performance. As we pointed out earlier, subjects have a real stake in viewing their performance as meaningful. For this reason, it is commonplace to find a pact of ignorance resulting from the intertwining motives of both experimenter and subject, neither wishing to create a situation where the particular subject's performance needs to be excluded from the study.

For these reasons, inquiry procedures are required to push the subject for information without, however, providing in themselves cues as to what is expected. The general question which needs to be explored is the subject's perception of the experimental purpose and the specific hypotheses of the experimenter. This can best be done by an open-ended procedure starting with the very general question of, "What do you think that the experiment is about?" and only much later asking specific questions. Responses of "I don't know" should be dealt with by encouraging the subject to guess, use his imagination, and in general, by refusing to accept this response. Under these circumstances, the overwhelming majority of students will turn out to have evolved very definite hypotheses. These hypotheses can then be judged, and a correlation between them and experimental performance can be drawn.

Two objections may be made against this type of inquiry: (*a*) that the subject's perception of the experimenter's hypotheses is based on his own experimental behavior, and therefore a correlation between these two variables may have little to do with the determinants of behavior, and (*b*) that the inquiry procedure itself is subject to demand characteristics.

A procedure which has been independently advocated by Riecken (1958) and Orne (1959a) is designed to deal with the first of these objections. This consists of an inquiry procedure which is conducted much as though the subject had actually been run in the experiment, without, however, permitting him to be given any experimental data. Instead, the precise procedure of the experiment is explained, the experimental material is shown to the subject, and he is told what he would be required to do; however, he is not permitted to make any responses. He is then given a postexperimental inquiry as though he had been a subject. Thus, one would say, "If I had asked you to do all these things, what do you think that the experiment would be about, what do you think I would be trying to prove, what would my hypotheses be?" etc. This technique, which we have termed the pre-experimental inquiry, can be extended very readily to the giving of pre-experimental tests, followed by the explanation of experimental conditions and tasks, and the administration of postexperimental tests. The subject is requested to behave on these tests as though he had been exposed to the experimental treatment that was described to him. This type of procedure is not open to the objection that the subject's own behavior has provided cues for him as to the purpose of the task. It presents him with a straight problem-solving situation and makes explicit what, for the true experimental subject, is implicit. It goes without saying that these subjects who are run on the pre-experimental inquiry conditions must be drawn from the same population as the experimental groups and may, of course, not be run subsequently in the experimental condition. This technique is one of approximation rather than of proof. However, if subjects describe behavior on the preinquiry conditions as similar to, or identical with, that actually given by subjects exposed to the experimental conditions, the hypothesis becomes plausible that demand characteristics may be responsible for the behavior.

It is clear that pre- and postexperimental inquiry techniques have their own demand characteristics. For these reasons, it is usually best to have the inquiry conducted by an experimenter who is not acquainted with the actual experimental behavior of the subjects. This will tend to minimize the effect of experimenter bias.

Another technique which we have utilized for approximating the effect of the demand characteristics is to attempt to hold the demand characteristics constant and eliminate the experimental variable. One way of accomplishing this purpose is through the use of simulating subjects. This is a group of subjects who are not exposed to the experimental variable to which the effect has been attributed, but who are instructed to act *as if* this were the case. In order to control for experimenter bias under these circumstances, it is advisable to utilize more than one experimenter and to have the experimenter who actually runs the subjects "blind" as to which group (simulating or real) any given individual belongs.

Our work in hypnosis (Damaser, Shor, & Orne, 1963; Orne, 1959b; Shor, 1959) is a good example of the use of simulating controls. Subjects unable to enter hypnosis are instructed to simulate entering hypnosis for another experimenter. The experimenter who runs the study sees both highly trained hypnotic subjects and simulators in random order and does not know to which group each subject belongs. Because the subjects are run "blind," the experimenter is more likely to treat the two groups of subjects identically. We have found that simulating subjects are able to perform with great effectiveness, deceiving even well-trained hypnotists. However, the simulating group is not exposed to the experimental condition (in this case, hypnosis) to which the given effect under investigation is often ascribed. Rather, it is a group faced with a problem-solving task: namely, to utilize whatever cues are made available by the experimental context and the experimenter's con-

crete behavior in order to behave as they think that hypnotized subjects might. Therefore, to the extent that simulating subjects are able to behave identically, it is possible that demand characteristics, rather than the altered state of consciousness, could account for the behavior of the experimental group.

The same type of technique can be utilized in other types of studies. For example, in contrast to the placebo control in a drug study, it is equally possible to instruct some subjects not to take the medication at all, but to act as if they had. It must be emphasized that this type of control is different from the placebo control. It represents an approximation. It maximally confronts the simulating subject with a problem-solving task and suggests how much of the total effect could be accounted for by the demand characteristics—assuming that the experimental group had taken full advantage of them, an assumption not necessarily correct.

All of the techniques proposed thus far share the quality that they depend upon the active cooperation of the control subjects, and in some way utilize his thinking process as an intrinsic factor. The subject does *not* just respond in these control situations but, rather, he is required *actively* to solve the problem.

The use of placebo experimental conditions is a way in which this problem can be dealt with in a more classic fashion. Psychopharmacology has used such techniques extensively, but here too they present problems. In the case of placebos and drugs, it is often the case that the physician is "blind" as to whether a drug is placebo or active, but the patient is not, despite precautions to the contrary; i.e., the patient is cognizant that he does not have the side effects which some of his fellow patients on the ward experience. By the same token, in psychological placebo treatments, it is equally important to ascertain whether the subject actually perceived the treatment to be experimental or control. Certainly the subject's perception of himself as a control subject may materially alter the situation.

A recent experiment[11] in our laboratory illustrates this type of investigation. We were interested in studying the demand characteristics of sensory deprivation experiments, independent of any actual sensory deprivation. We hypothesized that the overly cautious treatment of subjects, careful screening for mental or physical disorders, awesome release forms, and, above all, the pres-

---

[11] This experiment is described in: Orne, M. T., & Scheibe, K. E., The contribution of non-deprivation factors in the production of sensory deprivation effects: the psychology of the "panic button." *J. abnorm. soc. Psychol.*, 1964, **68**, 3–12.

ence of a "panic (release) button" might be more significant in producing the effects reported from sensory deprivation than the actual diminution of sensory input. A pilot study (Stare, Brown, & Orne, 1959), employing preinquiry techniques, supported this view. Recently, we designed an experiment to test more rigorously this hypothesis.

This experiment, which we called Meaning Deprivation, had all the *accoutrements* of sensory deprivation, including release forms and a red panic button. However, we carefully refrained from creating any sensory deprivation whatsoever. The experimental task consisted of sitting in a small experimental room which was well lighted, with two comfortable chairs, as well as ice water and a sandwich, and an optional task of adding numbers. The subject did not have a watch during this time, the room was reasonably quiet, but not soundproof, and the duration of the experiment (of which the subject was ignorant) was four hours. Before the subject was placed in the experimental room, 10 tests previously used in sensory deprivation research were administered. At the completion of the experiment, the same tasks were again administered. A microphone and a one-way screen were present in the room, and the subject was encouraged to verbalize freely.

The control group of 10 subjects was subjected to the identical treatment, except that they were told that they were control subjects for a sensory deprivation experiment. The panic button was eliminated for this group. The formal experimental treatment of these two groups of subjects was the same in terms of the objective stress—four hours of isolation. However, the demand characteristics had been purposively varied for the two groups to study the effect of demand characteristics as opposed to objective stress. Of the 14 measures which could be quantified, 13 were in the predicted direction, and 6 were significant at the selected 10% alpha level or better. A Mann-Whitney U test has been performed on the summation ranks of all measures as a convenient method for summarizing the overall differences. The one-tailed probability which emerges is $p = .001$, a clear demonstration of expected effects.

This study suggests that demand characteristics may in part account for some of the findings commonly attributed to sensory deprivation. We have found similar significant effects of demand characteristics in accounting for a great deal of the findings reported in hypnosis. It is highly probable that careful attention to this variable, or group of variables, may resolve some of the current controversies regarding a number of psychological phenomena in motivation, learning, and perception.

In summary, we have suggested that the subject must be recognized as an active participant in any experiment, and that it may be fruitful to view the psychological experiment as a very special form of social interaction. We have proposed that the subject's behavior in an experiment is a function of the totality of the situation, which includes the experimental variables being investigated and at least one other set of variables which we have subsumed under the heading, demand characteristics of the experimental situation. The study and control of demand characteristics are not simply matters of good experimental technique; rather, it is an empirical issue to determine under what circumstances demand characteristics significantly affect subjects' experimental behavior. Several empirical techniques have been proposed for this purpose. It has been suggested that control of these variables in particular may lead to greater reproducibility and ecological validity of psychological experiments. With an increasing understanding of these factors intrinsic to the experimental context, the experimental method in psychology may become a more effective tool in predicting behavior in nonexperimental contexts.

REFERENCES

ASCH, S. E. *Social psychology.* New York: Prentice-Hall, 1952.

BRUNSWIK, E. *Systematic and representative design of psychological experiments with results in physical and social perception.* (Syllabus Series, No. 304) Berkeley: Univer. California Press, 1947.

DAMASER, ESTHER C., SHOR, R. E., & ORNE, M. T. Physiological effects during hypnotically-requested emotions. *Psychosom. Med.,* 1963, **25**, 334–343.

FRANK, J. D. Experimental studies of personal pressure and resistance: I. Experimental production of resistance. *J. gen. Psychol.,* 1944, **30**, 23–41.

ORNE, M. T. The demand characteristics of an experimental design and their implications. Paper read at American Psychological Association, Cincinnati, 1959. (a)

ORNE, M. T. The nature of hypnosis: Artifact and essence. *J. abnorm. soc. Psychol.,* 1959, **58**, 277–299. (b)

PIERCE, A. H. The subconscious again. *J. Phil., Psychol., scient. Meth.,* 1908, **5**, 264–271.

RIECKEN, H. W. A program for research on experiments in social psychology. Paper read at Behavioral Sciences Conference, University of New Mexico, 1958.

ROSENTHAL, R. On the social psychology of the psychological experiment: With particular reference to experimenter bias. Paper read at American Psychological Association, New York, 1961.

SARBIN, T. R. Contributions to role-taking theory: I. Hypnotic behavior. *Psychol. Rev.,* 1950, **57**, 255–270.

SHOR, R. E. Explorations in hypnosis: A theoretical

and experimental study. Unpublished doctoral dissertation, Brandeis University, 1959.

STARE, F., BROWN, J., & ORNE, M. T. Demand characteristics in sensory deprivation studies. Unpublished seminar paper, Massachu-

setts Mental Health Center and Harvard University, 1959.

METHODOLOGICAL PROBLEMS IN OPINION RESEARCH DATA*

While systematic research has only recently been carried out on the demand characteristics of an experiment, it has long been known that the behavior of respondents in an interview is more than a simple function of the content of the questions posed. In the selection below, based on research in the 1940s Hyman demonstrates that a wide variety of influences are at work. Some of these are attributed to characteristics of the interviewer, others to characteristics of the respondent, and still others to the effect of these characteristics and the demands of the interview situation on the interaction between the two parties.

Sources of interview bias are rather similar to the more recent findings on experimenter bias. Like subjects in experiments, respondents in interviews are apt to give the investigator what they perceive he wants, or perhaps what they perceive will least offend him. That interviewer expectancies formed from the early phases of the interview regarding the attitude of the respondent bias the later phases of the interview is reminiscent of findings reported by Rosenthal and his colleagues.[a] They used a number of experimenters who in reality were subjects themselves. For some "experimenters" the first two subjects (accomplices) behaved in accordance with the experimenter's supposed hypothesis, and, for others, contrary to his hypothesis. They found that the experimenters obtained from their later subjects behavior similar to that of the initial subjects, regardless of the direction of the initial behavior. In survey research as well as in experimental designs, then, the human factor is apt to complicate the problems of internal and external validity.

3.

Problems in the Collection of Opinion-Research Data[1]

HERBERT HYMAN
COLUMBIA UNIVERSITY

ABSTRACT
A central problem in the collection of data is the effect of the interviewer on the quality of the results. This paper describes research findings of the National Opinion Research Center's project on the isolation, measurement, and control of interviewer effect. Variations in results derive from interviewer fallibility, unreliability of respondents, and, finally, interactional processes. Disparities in the group memberships of interviewer and respondent affect the results; beliefs the interviewer has about the respondent produce expectations which in turn affect results. Experiments on the role of situational factors in mediating interviewer effects and on the validity of interviewer data are described.

Opinion research has availed itself of many methods for the collection of data. The methods are as varied as the kinds of data which research workers have regarded as relevant, and there is almost no limit to what has been regarded as relevant. I did not invent the following examples of genius in devising circuitous methods of getting at sociopsychological phenomena; they can be documented:[2] (1) the collection of historical records of behavior used as inferential measures of opinion, e.g., the use of statistics on the sub-

* The selection following the editorial introduction is reprinted from "Problems in the collection of opinion-research data," *American Journal of Sociology*, 1950, **55**, 362–370, by permission of the author and the University of Chicago Press.

[a] R. Rosenthal, G. W. Persinger, Linda L. Vikan-Kline, & K. L. Fode. The effect of early data returns on data subsequently obtained by outcome-biased experimenters. Unpublished manuscript, Harvard University, 1961.

[1] A paper read before the University of Chicago Seminar on Communications and Public Opinion, September 30, 1949. The data presented are from the findings of the National Opinion Research Center's project on the "Isolation, Measurement, and Control of Interviewer Effect," which is supported by the Rockefeller Foundation and sponsored by the Committee on Measurement of Opinion, Attitudes and Consumer Wants of the National Research Council and the Social Science Research Council.

[2] R. R. Willoughby, "Liberalism, Prosperity, and Urbanization," *Journal of Genetics and Psychology*, XXXV (1928), 134–36; S. M. Stoke and E. D. West, "Sex Differences in Conversational Interests," *Journal of Social Psychology*, II (1931), 120–26; a study by Deegan cited in G. Seward, "Sex Roles in Post War Planning," *Journal of Social Psychology* (SPSSI Bulletin), XIX (1944), 163–85; H. T. Moore, "Innate Factors in Radicalism and Conservatism," *Journal of Abnormal and Social Psychology*, XXXV (1929), 220–38; and G. Eckstrand and A. R. Gilliland, "The Psychogalvanometric Method for Measuring the Effectiveness of Advertising," *Journal of Applied Psychology*, XXXII (1948), 415–25.

scriptions to the *Nation* as a basis for conclusions about radicalism and its correlates; (*2*) the collection of behavioral data based on observation used as inferential measures of opinion, e.g., the use of statistics derived from listening to conversations as a basis for drawing conclusions about sex differences in values; (*3*) the collection of data derived from the content analysis of mediums, e.g., the characterization of unmarried women in recent novels used as a clue to attitudes toward the status of women; (*4*) even the collection of data based on measurements of psychophysical indices, e.g., reaction time, muscular steadiness, as correlates of a man's ideology or the measurement of the secretion of sweat as a clue to the reaction to advertisements. These examples—and many others that can be found in the literature—suggest that there apparently is no limit to the imagination of the social scientist in devising indirect approaches. Apart from the creative tendencies of the scientist, these indirect approaches reflect a distrust of the most obvious method in opinion research, the interview, since they all show a common aversion to asking a question in order to find out a man's opinions.

On the other hand, during the last two or three decades, the social psychologist, like the experimentalist and the clinician, has made increasing use of the direct approach wherein reliance is placed in substantial degree at least upon the subject's own verbal reports. The procedures have ranged from the application of quasi-clinical devices, such as thematic apperception tests or interpretations of slips of the tongue, and those involving routine self-administered questionnaires to those involving the ordinary techniques of asking questions in the course of an interview. And the routine interviews vary from the single polling or intensive interview through such elaborate methods as a series of repeated interviews with the same individual to the genetic study of attitudes based on the reported entire life-history of the individual. Interviewing has also varied in technical respects from that of a group situation to a private interview and in terms of such details as method of recording, type of sponsorship, degree of anonymity, and the like:

This experience in the use of the direct approach has certainly revealed weaknesses, some of which are inherent in the method and some in the lack of discipline and insight in its application. There are always tough questions as to the reliability and validity of the data elicited by it. But before the method is discarded in favor of such indirect and inferential methods as those exemplified above, its demonstrated weaknesses should themselves be subjected to careful research to see whether they cannot be remedied. We have been engaged in this very type of methodological research at the National Opinion Research Center.

Therefore, I shall limit this discussion to some of the problems of collection of data by the methods of interviewing that prevail in most public opinion research. Against the vista of all possible methods for collecting data about opinions, this may seem narrow, but certainly the interview is the essential method in the field of opinion research. The interview is also central in the methods of clinical psychology, psychiatry, and ethnology, so that whatever *basic* knowledge we can gain about interviewing methods is applicable to many of the social sciences and is of general value. To the best of my knowledge, no evaluations have been made in ethnology of the effect that different interviewers have on the results they report as fact about a culture. And I know of only one isolated wartime study of the differences in diagnoses obtained by different psychiatrists.[3] In the report of one of the most ambitious undertakings in the history of clinical psychology, the assessment of men for OSS duties, I can find only one tiny datum on the effect of different interviewers on the assessment ratings given to OSS candidates.[4] In the light of these gaps in our knowledge, it would certainly seem that any evidence bearing on the quality of data collected by interviewing methods would be a notable contribution. Perhaps, merely by example, fields other than opinion research will be stimulated to inquire into the quality of their interview data.

The two-year study now in progress at the National Opinion Research Center is concerned with the isolation, measurement, and control of interviewer effects in *opinion* research, and we are indebted for financial support to the Rockefeller Foundation and for sponsorship to the Committee on Measurement of Opinion, Attitudes and Consumer Wants of the National Research Council and the Social Science Research Council. The findings represent the work of many colleagues in my own organization as well as the co-operation of individuals in many other research centers. There are many different ways to conceptualize our work. It is difficult to describe all the findings of these two years of work in a concise presentation, but I shall try to summarize some of our thinking and some of the findings.

Every day, throughout the United States, hundreds of people are asked questions by a public opinion interviewer, and thousands of these answers are put through an elaborate process of tabulation and analysis, and then elegant conclusions are drawn about the state of American

[3] Great Britain Air Ministry, *Psychological Disorders in Flying Personnel of the Royal Air Force, Investigated during the War*, 1939–1945 (London: H.M. Stationery Office, 1947).
[4] OSS Assessment Staff, *Assessment of Men: Selection of Men for the Office of Strategic Services* (New York: Rinehart, 1948).

public opinion. Would we have obtained a different set of results and a different picture of American public opinion if we had sent another corps of interviewers out to ask the same questions of the same people? And if the results would be different, how different? Obviously, in so far as different interviewers get different results, we know that our conclusions may be in error. We do know from past studies in this field, by Rice and by Shapiro and Eberhart, to cite only a few, that there are interviewer effects operating on our data.[5] The magnitude of these effects is presumed to be small in most instances, but on occasion the tabulations based on the work of different interviewers assigned to equivalent samples have differed by as much as 50 percentage points. In our own work at NORC we have extended this body of data by a few studies in which we have been able to measure the magnitude of the differences in results obtained by interviewers assigned to equivalent respondents.

Presumably such studies should yield some empirical or historical basis for stating the margins of uncertainty that apply to future survey findings as a consequence of factors within the interview situation. Conceivably we can qualify our findings in future surveys in the light of such past knowledge about interviewer effects. However, in order to do this, we would need an archive of past estimates of interviewer effects under a wide variety of representative conditions. Only then might one know what appropriate allowance to make for error in any particular type of survey. This seems like an almost hopeless task when one considers the number of ways in which surveys can vary. The magnitude of these effects might be dependent on the types of respondents who are being sampled, the types of information being measured, the kinds of interviewers used, the mode of questioning, and the like. And for any given survey the combination of factors and conditions may be so peculiar that none of our past estimates of interviewer effects would apply. Or a given survey may be similar to past ones in certain respects and different in other respects. And if one does not know which particular factors are the *determinants* of interviewer effects, one has no basis for judging what the magnitude of interviewer effects might be in the new situation. It would only be by research that inquires not only into the magnitude but also into the determinants that one would know what are the essential factors to consider in deciding the susceptibility of a given survey to interviewer effects and in applying a past estimate.

Consequently, we have done only a limited

number of such studies in which the mere magnitude of interviewer effects has been measured and have concentrated much more on understanding the sources of such effects.

What contributes to these effects? Classically, interviewer effects have been interpreted in terms of the interaction between interviewer and respondent. It was thought that the respondent is affected by the personality or characteristics of the interviewer and alters what he says in the light of the particular interviewer who speaks to him. In part, interviewer effects have nothing to do with the interaction that occurs between interviewer and respondent. These effects derive simply from the fact that interviewers are human beings, not machines, and they therefore do not all work identically nor are they infallible in performing difficult tasks. This is certainly suggested by what we might call "interviewer effects" in surveys involving sampling of physical materials.[6] When field staffs are assigned the task of rating the quality of a sample of telephone poles, one cannot argue that the telephone pole reacts to the personality of the investigator. And the fact that different field workers may obtain different results in evaluating physical materials shows that some of the sources of error reside purely in the field worker and are not dependent on interaction in the immediate situation. And this is in line with a whole body of psychological theory ranging from classical research on testimony to the modern dynamic theory in the psychology of perception that individuals perceive the world in a way that is not dependent purely on their sensory acuity but on their wishes and personality structure and that there are large individual differences in judging, perceiving, and other functions.

In our own work specifically on interviewer effects, we have some experiments which show that the differences in results can be accounted for without any references to the interaction between interviewer and respondent. For example, in one experiment the mere changing of the method of recording that the interviewer is required to use in a regular survey changed the results. In another experiment in which the interviewer was required to listen to a dummy interview on a phonograph record and take down the answers, we found errors. The recording operation is purely in the hands of the interviewer, and consequently any effects operating cannot be attributed to the respondent's altering his behavior.

In part some of the interviewer effects observ-

[5] S. A. Rice, "Contagious Bias in the Interview," *American Journal of Sociology*, XXXV (1929), 420–23; and S. Shapiro and J. Eberhart, "Interviewer Differences in an Intensive Interview Survey," *International Journal of Opinion and Attitude Research*, I, No. 2 (1947), 1–17.

[6] See, for example, W. E. Deming, "On the Sampling of Physical Materials," a paper read at a meeting of the International Statistical Institute, Bern, Switzerland, in September, 1949.

able in a survey derive purely from the respondents and really have nothing to do with the interviewer. They simply represent the unreliability of reports that respondents as human beings make. This is certainly suggested by classical studies of the unreliability of results from self-administered questionnaires, in which variations occur in the absence of any interviewer. It is also suggested by panel studies in which respondents are reinterviewed by the same interviewer after a lapse of time in which we find considerable change in the reporting of unchanged facts. In one minor experiment by the NORC, in which a small group of respondents in Mississippi was interviewed twice with the same questionnaire within a time interval of less than one hour by two competent interviewers, the results of the two interviews bear almost no resemblance to each other and seem to be nothing but answers at random, one thrown out at one moment in time and a different answer at another moment in time. This was, luckily, an extreme and unusual finding, but it certainly supports the notion that interviewer effects are to some extent merely unreliability of report.

Consequently, we may go too far at times in interpreting the variations in survey results as due to the sensitive reactions of respondents to the interviewer's characteristics, and we may err in thinking that the type of social situation common in public opinion research is one in which the respondent hangs on every word, gesture, and nuance of the interviewer's behavior and orients his own behavior accordingly. In one study we reinterviewed a small group of respondents within a few days after the regular survey interview and inquired about their feelings when they were interviewed originally. We found a few individuals who could not even recall what the interviewer looked like. I particularly remember the answer of the respondent who, upon being asked what he remembered most about the previous interviewer, was stumped for a while and then remarked after a few minutes of serious thought, "She was tall," and the answer of another respondent who, after being asked what he was most impressed by in the previous interview, said, "it was in one ear and out the other—it was the goddamnedest lot of bull." For such respondents whatever interaction there is with the interviewer must be at best minimal.

There are certain types of interviewer effects, however, that would best be accounted for by hypothesizing some interaction between interviewer and respondent. For example, a whole series of studies shows that survey results for specialized attitudes are affected by the disparities or similarities in the group membership of interviewer and respondent. For example, in two

NORC surveys samples of Christian respondents in New York City were asked whether Jews in America had too much influence in the business world. Among those who were interviewed by Christian interviewers, 50 per cent said the Jews had too much influence, but among those interviewed by Jewish interviewers, only 22 per cent said so. In another survey in which respondents were asked whether they agreed with the statement "Prison is too good for sex criminals; they should be publicly whipped or worse," among women respondents who were interviewed by men interviewers 61 per cent agreed with this statement; whereas when women were interviewed by women interviewers, only 49 per cent agreed. It would seem either that women are less bloodthirsty when they are in the company of their own species or, put more precisely, that they feel more compelled to give the conventional and sanctioned attitude to a male interviewer. In another survey, in which one group of Negroes was interviewed by white interviewers and an equivalent group by Negro interviewers, similar effects were observed. For example, when asked whether the Army is unfair to Negroes, 35 per cent of those interviewed by Negroes said "Yes," but only 11 per cent of those interviewed by whites were willing to express this critical attitude. It is well documented that responses vary with the disparity between interviewer's and respondent's sex, class, color, religion, and other group-membership factors.[7] And the systematic direction of these effects is such that one would not attribute them to mere unreliability but to the way in which the respondent alters his behavior in accordance with the kind of person who speaks to him.

A number of additional experiments suggest the mechanism by which such interactions or effects are mediated. A study by Robinson and Rohde showed that there was an orderly change in the anti-Semitic opinions expressed depending on the degree to which the interviewer looked Jewish and emphasized this fact by using a Jewish name.[8] There is also evidence from secret-ballot surveys, in which the interviewer asks no questions, does no recording of answers, but merely hands the respondent a printed ballot on which the respondent registers his opinion, that the results vary with the type of interviewer who merely proffers the ballot to the respondent.[9] This kind of evidence suggests not that the interviewer communicates his bias by a specific mechanism of intonation or probing or specific reactions to what

---

[7] See, for example, Daniel Katz, "Do Interviewers Bias Poll Results?" *Public Opinion Quarterly*, VI (1944), 248–68; and Hadley Cantril and Associates, *Gauging Opinion* (Princeton: Princeton University Press, 1944), chap. viii.

[8] D. Robinson and S. Rohde, "Two Experiments with an Anti-Semitism Poll," *Journal of Abnormal and Social Psychology*, XLI (1946), 136–44.

[9] Frederick Mosteller *et al.*, *The Pre-election Polls of 1948* (Social Science Research Council Bull. 60, 1949), chap. vii.

is said but simply that respondents perceive something about the interviewer immediately from his mere appearance or behavior, interpret this for some reason in a certain way, and in turn alter their behavior. And the meaning they give to whatever they perceive may depend on a complex of cultural factors. For example, the study on the effect of the color of the interviewer on the opinions reported by Negroes was conducted in Memphis, and the change in results cited was 24 percentage points. When the identical question was asked in Harlem by Negro versus white interviewers, the change was only 7 percentage points—24 percentage points in Memphis, 7 in New York City. Clearly the respondents must have perceived the color of the interviewer in both cities, but the impact of color and the meaning given to this physical phenomenon was a product of the cultural patterns in the North as compared with those in the South, and the interviewer effects mirror these cultural forces.

One can use the findings of such experiments in building a better theoretical foundation in social psychology. We are now leaning away from our old notion that an attitude is a fixed thing that influences behavior and toward the idea that attitudes have situational components and may or may not come into play depending on a variety of environmental factors. We can fill in some of the concrete material for such a theory by interpreting the interview situation as a miniature of the larger social setting and seeing some of the interviewer effects as analogies to the influence of social factors on the expression of attitudes.

The way the *respondent* perceives the interviewer is only one side of the coin. Interviewer effects also derive from the way the *interviewer* perceives the respondent and subsequently alters his method of questioning, probing, recording, and the like. In the course of intensive interviews with interviewers designed to reveal their existential world, we noted that they had certain expectations about how their respondents would answer given questions. These expectations guide the interviewer at various choice-points throughout the interview and affect his decisions about probing it and recording. As one interviewer put it, "Once they start talking, I can predict what they'll say." These expectations seem to be built on the basis of certain beliefs about the respondent. And these beliefs are of two main types. On the one hand, interviewers may entertain oversimplified stereotypes about the attitudes or behavior or roles that correspond to given status characteristics or group memberships. Merely on the basis of perceiving that the respondent is a man or woman, rich rather than poor, or Negro rather than white, they expect his answers to be of a certain nature, and this spuriously inflates the relation between group membership and certain attitudes. Such reactions by the interviewer to the group membership of the respondent and the corresponding reactions of respondents to the group membership of the inter-

viewer, as mentioned earlier, provide incidental evidence of the pervasive influence of group membership on human behavior.

J. J. Feldman of the NORC's Chicago staff found differences in the results obtained by interviewers given equivalent samples on certain questions dealing with the extent to which the respondent and the spouse made purchases of given types of commodities. These differences seem to be explained best by the beliefs that different interviewers had as to the normal buying roles of men and women, e.g., whether a woman would normally have an automobile repaired or a man would normally buy house furnishings. A second type of belief that operates in the interviewer to produce expectations and therefore interviewer effects might be called "attitude structure expectations." Interviewers, like most human beings, seem to believe that other human beings have a logically consistent and integrated structure of attitudes. Consequently, on the basis of the early answers of respondents, they build up some belief as to what his further attitudes will be and anticipate that the later answers will fall in line. Such expectations presumably operate to produce spurious intercorrelations between attitudes. Harry Smith of the NORC's New York staff had interviewers listen to prepared phonograph records which simulated two normal interviews and record the answers they heard on a questionnaire. In both these records, lukewarm, equivocal answers were inserted which were identical in substance for both respondents. On one record the answers were imbedded in a context of previous answers that built up a picture of an isolationist respondent, and on the other the context of previous answers was that of an internationalist. One result will be vivid enough to demonstrate that attitude-structure expectations really influence the perception and recording of the answer. On a question whether the United States was spending too much on foreign aid, both respondents gave an answer which impartial judges, viewing the answer out of context, coded as "we're spending about the right amount." But among the 117 interviewers tabulated, only 20 percent classified the isolationst's answer as the "right amount" whereas 75 per cent classified the internationalist's answer as the "right amount." This difference is accounted for essentially by the fact that 53 per cent classified the isolationist as saying "we're spending too much."

The process by which such expectations are built up and can be maintained despite contradictory material can be illustrated by phenomenological data collected in the course of Smith's experiment. One of the interviewers was asked to report aloud his thinking as he participated in the experiment. No suggestion whatsoever was given to him that he describe the respondent or report on his expectations. Nevertheless, the following portions of his running account show the immediate formation of a picture of the respondent and the dynamics by which such expectations are maintained: After hearing the answer to Question 1: "I do have some impressions. The respondent seems very doubtful about giving his opinion—a little suspicious. I don't have too much respect for this particular respondent. My immediate impression is that he's one of those types of individuals who thinks in very personal terms." Following the answer to Question 2: "I was right. Immediately he's going off on tangents. He's not really interested in the survey. He's interested in getting rid of any personal feelings he has. I feel he's an old geezer." At Question 7 the first experimental answer was inserted which was a mild contradiction of the previous answers. However, instead of changing his beliefs, the interviewer rationalized the contradiction in such a way as to maintain his former impression. He remarked: "He's still wary about giving his *real* opinion. He started to backtrack."

Traditionally, it has been argued in discussions of interviewer bias that the interviewer is motivated to influence the results in the direction of his own attitude or ideology, and little attention has been given to the role of such cognitive factors as expectations. The relative importance of these two sources of bias can be illustrated, in a somewhat oversimplified fashion, by another finding from Smith's experiment.

In the finding already cited on the question of whether the United States was spending too much on foreign aid, it is seen that the influence of expectations built up by the context of previous answers was to cause 75 per cent of the subjects to code the internationalist's answer as "the right amount" whereas only 20 per cent coded the same answer in the isolationist context as "the right amount." Here we have the effect of expectations, in the aggregate, for interviewers holding *all* kinds of attitudes. Now, if we compare the results that interviewers who themselves are internationalist produced on the internationalist recording with the results that interviewers who themselves are isolationist produced on the isolationist recording, we should presumably enhance the difference between the two results, since we are compounding the two sources of bias—expectation *plus* interviewer's own attitude. We actually find for this comparison that 78 per cent of the internationalist interviewers score the internationalist respondent as saying "the right amount" whereas only 19 per cent of the isolationist interviewers classify the isolationist respondent as saying "the right amount." Adding the factor of interviewer attitude hardly increases the bias.

Such expectations must certainly operate in other fields of interviewing as sources of bias. In clinical work we tacitly recognize the existence of such expectations by talking of the "insightfulness" of the clinician. The difference is simply that we bar them as "biases" in public opinion research whereas we sanction them in clinical work.

As suggested earlier, interviewer effects may simply represent the fallibility of the human beings who are our interviewers and do not derive from any interaction between respondent and interviewer. Not all interviewers are identical in their structures, and their human failings appear when they are confronted with the difficult tasks we assign them. We have undertaken a few projects which start from the assumption that the situational features of the interview, the specific processes we require the interviewer to engage in, the pressures we put upon him in the interview, may either facilitate or reduce interviewer variations and interviewer errors. We must accept the inherent limitations of our human materials, and perhaps the next best thing is to examine our procedures and manipulate the interview process in such a way as to inhibit the *operation* of the human factors that would potentially create errors. Such an approach is eminently practical in that the survey process is flexible and within our control, and it would also seem to be more sophisticated theoretically. Instead of seeing bias as a fixed entity residing purely within the individual, we now see it as a product of the individual working within a certain type of environment, the interview.

In one such experiment Paul Sheatsley of the NORC's New York Staff hypothesized that interviewers wish to avoid asking tedious, embarrassing, difficult questions.[10] If we design our surveys so that such questions are supposed to be asked only if the respondent has given a certain answer previously, the interviewer might be prone to elicit or record the answer that permits him to avoid the difficult subquestions. Note that this point of view is not that the interviewer has some long-term desire to bias the answers and does it but that the bias is created by the temporary situational pressures upon the interviewer. This hypothesis was tested by having interviewers work with two equivalent ballots on two equivalent samples. In the one instance the ballot was so designed that a certain answer to an initial question called for the asking of four additional annoying subquestions; in the other instance, the opposing answer to the same question called for the four subquestions to be asked. If the pressure of the subquestions causes interviewers to distort results so as to avoid the additional work, the results on the initial question should be different

---

[10] Paul B. Sheatsley, "The Influence of Subquestions on Interviewer Performance," *Public Opinion Quarterly*, XIII (1949), 310–13.

in the two matched samples. In this instance, we found that there was no effect.

In another experiment of this same type we required interviewers, on the one hand, to classify the answers they received into pre-coded categories and in a matched control survey merely to record the answers verbatim. If the classification process releases the biasing tendencies of the interviewers, we should find differences in the results.[11] In brief we found that in the *aggregate* the classification process does not affect the data. However, among inexperienced members of the field staff the classification process does affect the results they obtain.

In line with our interest in the situational features of the interview, in the specific processes that mediate or create interviewer effects, we have naturally turned toward the idea of hidden observation of the total interview. In the two experiments just cited we have been able to *infer* the effects of given aspects of the process by special experimental designs. However, if we can bring the total interview situation into view, we can see what contribution each and every aspect of the total process makes to the final effects. We will be able to collect such information from a study being done by the American Jewish Committee to which we have contributed financial support and advice. In the study, stooge respondents are being interviewed by a crew of interviewers and a hidden wire recording of the entire interview is being made. From this study, which is still in progress, we will ultimately have information on errors in interviewer behavior in such separate aspects of the interview as the question-asking, the probing, and the recording. We will be able to state whether such errors change in magnitude progressively in time, whether the respondent's behavior in turn alters the interviewer's performance, whether errors are distributed among all questions or concentrated in certain types of question, whether there is a given type of interviewer who is prone to all kinds of error, or whether interviewing skills are discrete.

In many of the experiments cited thus far, we can demonstrate interviewed differences in the results and allocate these effects to certain characteristics of the interviewer or of the respondent or of the situation itself or of the interaction between interviewer and respondent. However, from a practical point of view, these experiments are not very helpful unless they establish what kinds of interviewers or procedures give us better or more valid results. Merely to reduce the variability in results might not improve their quality. Conceivably we might even screen our staff so as to get a homogeneous group of interviewers who would get identical results, all bad. Such thinking led us to undertake an experiment in Denver in which groups of interviewers are given equivalent assignments on a survey which includes questions on age, ownership of telephone, automobile ownership, charitable contributions, voting behavior in a series of elections, and a number of other characteristics. For each of these characteristics we have reliable information from official records about the actual status of *each individual* in the sample. Consequently, we will not only be able to state whether different interviewers obtain different results but, knowing which interviewers of given types obtain more valid results, we will be guided in the selection of personnel. These data are now being analyzed and will be published in the future by J. D. Cahalan, Helen Crossley, Hugh Parry, and others and, apart from their import for the problem of interviewer effects, will be a notable contribution to the almost untouched problem of validity.

In the nature of the case the emphasis in this paper has been upon defective work. But there are many surveys where one finds little variation in the results for different interviews, and no one should contend that opinion research does not belong in the company of other sciences because of the unreliability of the interviewing methods. I am convinced that these types of error occur elsewhere and that opinion research is merely leading the way in subjecting its interviewing methods to critical examination. The problem of interviewer effects has now come into its own.

ANALYSIS OF SURVEY DATA *

Survey research questions are framed in the context of everyday social situations; consequently, the

problem of generalization or external validity is less formidable than in experimental research. But in survey research the problem of internal validity is more difficult to deal with; an investigator must accept a lower level of certainty in his causal inferences. As noted earlier, three conditions must be met in order to infer that one variable stands in a causal relation to another. First, there must be evidence of covariation, evidence that a change in one variable is accompanied by systematic changes in the other. Second, there must be some

[11] An elaborate analysis of this study will be reported shortly by C. H. Stember and Herbert Hyman.

* The selection following the editorial introduction is reprinted from "Problems of survey analysis," in R. K. Merton, and P. F. Lazarsfeld (eds.), *Continuities in Social Research: Studies in the Scope and Method of "The American Soldier,"* New York: Free Press, 1950, pp. 136–147, by permission of the authors and the publisher.

basis for deciding that the supposed consequence or effect did not precede in time the variable labeled the antecedent or cause. Finally, there must be some basis for excluding the possibility that the covariation results from the influence of some third variable.

In an experiment these three conditions are inherent in the experimental design and analysis. In survey research this is usually not the case. While covariation is easily demonstrated, it is more difficult to ascertain the temporal order of variables and to prove that covariation is not due to some third variable. For the latter problem in particular the solutions available require adoption of a lower level of certainty of causal inferences. This is so because in survey research the subgroups used in the survey analysis often differ in other characteristics besides the independent variable focused upon. Thus, any difference in their responses might well be due to these other variables instead of the one of dominant concern. This problem seldom arises in experiments, where subjects can be assigned to the experimental and control conditions by random methods, which maximize the probability that the two groups differ only to a random extent on all characteristics. Statistical procedures may then be used to determine whether the relation discovered exceeds what might be expected from random variation.

In survey analysis, groups may be equated after collection of the data by forming subgroups similar in the characteristics to be controlled. But here the statistical analyst can only equate his groups on the attributes identified by the interview or questionnaire. Thus, only those attributes that he suspects might be related to the respondent's behavior and that were consequently incorporated in the survey design can be controlled. Obviously there are practical limits on the number of attributes that he can simultaneously control, and there are other attributes of which he may be unaware even if he could control them. Inevitably, his conclusions must be tempered by the possibility that some uncontrolled third variable has created a spurious relation.

In the selection which follows, Kendall and Lazarsfeld draw illustrative materials from a number of investigations carried on during the Second World War by behavioral scientists with the Research Branch of the Information and Education Division of the War Department. Many of these studies, originally designed for the practical purposes of the Armed Forces, became the subject of secondary analyses, and added considerably to social psychological theory and method in the postwar years. One such gain was a codification and clarification of some of the methods of survey analysis discussed below.

4.

Problems of Survey Analysis

PATRICIA KENDALL
PAUL F. LAZARSFELD
COLUMBIA UNIVERSITY

Section 1—APPROXIMATIONS OF SURVEY RESULTS TO CONTROLLED EXPERIMENTATION

Even when not explicitly stated, the presentation of a relationship between two variables suggests a causal connection between them. We do not report that combat veterans are more dissatisfied than non-veterans with certain Army policies without implying that somehow the experience of combat changes the perspectives and attitudes of soldiers.

The scientific model designed to study cause-and-effect relationships of this sort is the *controlled experiment*, in which the responses of an experimental group, exposed to the crucial stimulus, are compared with those of an exactly equivalent control group, from which the stimulus has been withheld. The difficulties of carrying out such experiments in the social sciences are well known.[1] It is important, therefore, to consider the kinds of approximations provided by survey materials.

Sub-group comparisons

The type of approximation most often used in survey analysis involves a comparison of the frequency with which groups *characterized in different ways* express a certain attitude or indicate a particular behavior. Thus in *The American Soldier* we find that:

> There was a marked relationship between job satisfaction and chance to choose one's Army job. Those who asked for and got their Army jobs were much more satisfied than those who did not get the jobs they asked for, or who did not get a chance to ask. (I, Chap. VII, Chart II and Table 1.)

> There was a relationship between the theater in which the soldier served and his personal adjustment. For example, men stationed overseas reported themselves in less good spirits than did men stationed in the United States. (I, 155-189. See especially Table 1.)

In the first example it is the experience of having asked for and obtained the job they wanted which distinguished soldiers in the "experimental" group

---

[1] Stouffer and his associates indicate at a number of points where experimentation would have been necessary to provide final answers to the questions which they raise, and why such experimentation was impossible. See, for example, II, 205, fn. 14.

from those in the "control" group. In the second case the distinction is in terms of the soldier's location. To what extent can we attribute differences in job satisfaction, on the one hand, and different levels of personal adjustment, on the other hand, to these "stimuli"?

There are two main difficulties in equating the simple cross-tabulations of survey materials to real experimentation. One of these is the danger that spurious factors are present in the relationship. The second is the difficulty of establishing clearly the time sequence of the variables involved.

Spurious factors. To illustrate the problem of spurious factors, let us consider the relationship between theater of service and answers to the question, "In general, how would you say that you feel most of the time, in good spirits or in low spirits?" We recall that men stationed overseas reported themselves in less good spirits than did men stationed in the United States who had not yet been overseas. One possibility which occurs to us is that length of service might operate as a spurious factor in this relationship. It might be that men stationed overseas had, on the average, served for longer periods of time, and that men with records of long service had lower morale. If this were the case, we would not be justified in saying that personal esprit was determined by theater of service. Experimentally, this would express itself in the following way: two groups of soldiers, equated according to length of service, would show no differences in morale even when one group was shipped to an overseas theater.

In order to minimize the danger that spurious factors of this kind remain undetected, we employ analytical procedures which enable us to examine the relationship between the assumed cause and the assumed effect *when the influence of the possible spurious factor is eliminated.*[2] We divide the sample into different groups according to length of service in the Army. Within each of the groups we examine the relationship between theater of service and personal esprit. In this way we are able to observe the original relationship when the possible spurious factor is "controlled" or "held constant."

Often it is not enough to introduce only one control. There are a number of other possible spurious factors in the relationship which we have considered. For example, the men overseas probably held higher rank and served in different branches of the Army. There might also have been educational differences between the two groups. All of these are factors which could have produced differences in the proportions saying that they were in "good spirits"; consequently, all of them must be controlled. For these reasons, it is necessary to carry out the comparison between

ing way. Half of a group of soldiers, selected at random, would be shipped overseas, while the other half remained in the United States. After a lapse of time the morale of both groups would be compared. If it turned out that the group randomly selected for shipment overseas showed significantly lower spirits, we would have the necessary evidence that it was overseas service which brought about a decline in morale.

As long as we can only control factors after the fact, however, our findings are always open to doubts. If we study the relationship through a statistical analysis of survey materials, rather than by experimentation, we can, at best, control four or five factors. Let us assume that we consider length of service in the Army, rank, branch of service and education to be important factors. It might be that none of these is important, and that we overlook the really relevant spurious factor. Perhaps certain soldiers were less popular than others; their lack of popularity might be reflected in low spirits, and it might also mean that their officers were more likely to put them on lists for shipment overseas. In this case, both overseas service and low spirits are the result of personality differences, and there is no causal connection between them. The Research Branch analysts are clearly aware of this danger and they constantly caution the reader against it. (See, for example, I, 48; II, 35, 127, 163, 226, 403, and 507.)

In actual survey analysis, the control of spurious factors requires a constant weaving back and forth between speculations as to the possible factors and examination of the data when the influence of each factor has been eliminated. There is one particularly important result in *The American Soldier* which illustrates this process very well.

> The closer the contact of white with Negro soldiers, the greater the willingness of the whites to serve in mixed Negro-white companies. (I, 594, Chart XVII)[4]

This relationship is one in which typically we might suspect that spurious factors are operating.

---

[4] One of the frustrations in any analysis, but perhaps a particular problem in secondary analyses, is the fact that one is frequently forced to base important cross-tabulations on very few cases. Thus in the chart just cited, there were only 80 men who had served in a company which had a Negro platoon, only 68 who had served in an unmixed company in a regiment with mixed companies, and 112 who served in all white companies within a division containing mixed companies. The more elaborate the cross-tabulations, the more serious this limitation of vanishing cases. Thus in a table showing the incidence of anxiety symptoms at different time periods, holding constant age and education, we find

Whenever we deal with a variable like "amount of contact" or "closeness of contact" we have a feeling that the persons who are found at various points along these continua made their way there voluntarily. That is, we suspect the presence of "self-selection" factors; those who have close contact with Negroes may do so because of initially favorable or "tolerant" attitudes. If this were the case, it would not surprise us to find that their attitudes following contacts with Negroes were also favorable.

The way in which the Army's "racial experiment" came about reduced the likelihood that these self-selective processes were at work. The Negro platoons were placed *at random* within Infantry companies needing replacements. While the Negro men had volunteered for combat service, men in the white companies were not consulted about their willingness to serve in mixed companies.

While the real-life situation seemed to meet those conditions required for controlled experimentation, the Research Branch sought additional checks. For example, the companies which had suffered the greatest casualties, and were therefore most likely to receive replacements, might have become more tolerant toward other men as a result of their combat experience. If this were the case, the men in mixed companies could be expected to have initially more favorable attitudes toward service with Negroes. In order to check this possibility, the Research Branch made use of a retrospective question: The soldiers in mixed companies were asked to recall how they had felt about serving with Negroes prior to the actual experience of doing so. The results indicated an even more *un*favorable attitude initially than was observed among men not serving in mixed companies.[5]

Another possibility is that the persons in charge of assigning replacements put the Negro platoons in companies which they felt would receive them more favorably. There was undoubtedly some leeway in deciding which companies got which replacements, and the officers responsible for those decisions may not have distributed the troops at random. Again, if this were the case, we would conclude that the original relationship was a spurious one. Partial evidence that it was *not* the case is seen in the fact that there were as many Southerners serving in the mixed as in the unmixed companies.[6]

The interweaving of speculations about possible spurious factors and actual analysis of the data

---

percentages based on 9, 21, 22, and 32 cases, clearly too few to yield significant or reliable figures. (See II, 431, Table 8)

[5] This result is not reported in the text of *The American Soldier*. Stouffer refers to it in a recent article, "Some observations on study design," *American Journal of Sociology*, LV (1949–50), 355–361.

[6] *Ibid.*

emerges very clearly from this example. The original relationship was one which is typically suspect as being spurious. But the results were obtained in a situation which seemed to reproduce, in real life, the conditions required in controlled experimentation. There was more reason to believe, therefore, that the original relationship was a reasonable approximation of what might have been found through actual experimentation. But the analysts did not lose sight of the possibility that spurious factors were in operation. They introduced suitable controls and checks. Even though these did not destroy the original relationship, we cannot say that the causal connection between contact with Negroes and favorable attitudes toward them has been demonstrated. The connection is more *probable* after the checks have been introduced than it was beforehand, but it is never quite certain.

The time order of variables. Clearly to be distinguished from the problem of spurious factors is the second difficulty in approximation procedures. In order even to consider whether the statistical relationship between two variables is a causal one, the variables must stand in a determinate time relation, with the assumed cause *preceding* the assumed effect. (When we say that Variable *A* precedes Variable *B* in time, we mean that A was *acquired* or *developed* first.)

Often the time order between two variables is quite clear. If we relate formal educational level to rank in the Army, we can be quite sure that education precedes rank. Or, if we study the relation between civilian occupation and type of Army job, there is little doubt that Army job follows after civilian occupation in time.

There are some instances in which the same attribute is used as an index of different phenomena, so that its time order, rather than being fixed, is determined by the particular problem being considered. Suppose, for example, that we related each man's rank to the length of time which he had been in the Army. Now "length of time in the Army" can stand for a variety of different phenomena. We might consider it an index of the time when the soldier entered the Army; given this meaning, it would *antecede* promotion. We would then look at the relationship to see whether those who had entered the Army during early stages of the war were more likely to be promoted. But "length of time in the Army" can also indicate the amount of experience which the soldier has at the time that he is interviewed. Looked at in this way, length of service is a characteristic which follows *after* the soldier has acquired his rank. We then ask whether those with particular ranks are more experienced than others.

Finally, there are some instances in which the time sequence of two or more variables is indeterminate. One such case is the relationship between attitudes toward one's officers and willingness for combat. (II, 126, Table 7)[7] Which of these attitudes developed or was acquired first? Does a soldier reluctant to go into combat "rationalize" his feelings by saying that his officers are not good? Or does a soldier with favorable attitudes toward his officers develop a feeling of confidence which makes him willing for combat? Because of our inability to answer these questions, because we do not know and cannot know which of the attitudes developed first, we cannot discuss whether there is a causal connection between them. (As we shall see in the next section, panel techniques often enable one to circumvent these difficulties.)

It is very difficult to answer these questions of time sequence with the materials of only one survey. But it is possible that in some cases clues to the time order will be found. In *The American Soldier*, for example, the authors are interested in the relationship between marital status and rank. They found (I, 118-120, see especially Chart V) that married men were more likely to have higher rank, even when age and length of service in the Army were controlled. But which came first, marriage or promotion? Is it that married men are more likely to be promoted, or that promotion encourages the soldier to marry? With knowledge only of marital status and rank, very little can be said. But fortunately Research Branch analysts obtained one other bit of information which provided some clue to the time sequence: they knew whether the soldier had been married prior to his entrance into the Army or whether he had married after becoming a soldier. These data enabled them to make the following observations. They noted that there was very little relationship between rank and having been married prior to entering the Army. On the other hand, there was some relationship between rank and marriage taking place after induction. This leads them to suggest that "marriage was even more likely to be a·*resultant* of promotion or of expected promotion than to be a factor *predisposing promotion*." (I, 120, authors' italics.) The clue to the sequence of the variables was the fact that where the time order was known one kind of relationship existed; where it was unknown, another relationship, suggesting another time sequence, prevailed.[8]

---

[7] In all but one or two instances, Stouffer and his associates successfully resisted the temptation to discuss the relationship between two untimed attitudes as if one might be a cause of the other. That a correlation between untimed attitudes cannot ever reveal a causal connection does not mean, however, that such correlations are not of interest. Often they help in clarifying the meaning of one of the attitudes.

[8] But note that even where clues to the *direction* of the relationship can be found, we cannot be sure that the relationship is not a spurious one. Thus it may be that there is a particular personality type, let us call it "stable"

Panel techniques

While the data of one survey may sometimes suggest the time order of variables whose sequence is apparently indeterminate, they give us nothing more than clues to be checked by other means. So-called panel techniques provide the relatively best device for establishing a time sequence of two variables. In a panel study, the same respondents are interviewed at different time periods. In those cases where the respondent changes between successive interviews, it is possible to determine when a particular attitude or behavior pattern developed.

These techniques contribute many new analytical devices.[9] While it is not possible to discuss all of these here, reference to one finding in *The American Soldier*, of substantive interest as well as methodological value, may give a general idea. It was found that non-commissioned officers had more conformist attitudes toward Army discipline than did privates. This relationship could be explained in a variety of ways. The non-com might have a better understanding of the importance of discipline or he might endorse disciplinary measures in order to bolster his own position. It could also be, however, that a private with what one might call an authoritarian personality has a better chance of being promoted. One of the panel studies carried out by the Research Branch shows that this latter relationship is involved in the original result. On the first interview the analysts divided the respondents according to their answers to a number of questions on discipline. Then a

TABLE 1   Distribution of Conformity Scores Among Privates in November, 1943

	NUMBER OF CASES	PERCENTAGE OF THESE CASES PROMOTED BY MARCH, 1944
Relatively high score	68	31
Medium score	138	28
Relatively low score	112	17

or "dependable," which predisposes an individual both to marriage and to being promoted. Indeed the two problems exist independently of each other: knowledge of the time sequence indicates nothing about the persistence of the relationship when control factors are introduced; conversely, confidence that the relationship is not a spurious one tells nothing of the time sequence of the variables.

[9] See Paul F. Lazarsfeld, "The Use of Panels in Social Research," *Proceedings of the American Philosophical Society*, **92** (1948), 405–410. The Bureau of Applied Social Research of Columbia University is currently working on a project to codify and evaluate these analytical devices.

few months later they ascertained what proportion of the original respondents had become non-coms. Some of the findings are as follows: (See I, 265, Chart XI)

Through their analysis of these panel materials, the investigators were able to establish that privates who held conformist attitudes were more likely to be promoted during a subsequent six months period than were their relatively more rebellious barracks mates. As Table 1 shows, among those who had indicated a relatively high degree of conformity in the Fall of 1943, nearly one-third had been promoted by the following Spring, as compared with only one-sixth of the men who had originally received a low score on the conformity index.

The Research Branch of the Army was aware of the desirability of panel studies in investigations of changing attitudes or behavior.[10] Because of the peculiar conditions under which the Research Branch operated, however, it was possible for them to set up only two full-scale panel studies. One of these, from which the preceding result was taken, was a study of Infantry recruits. It is called on at various points in the two volumes: it is used to show that the better adjusted soldiers, those who reported themselves in good spirits, accepted their Army role, were satisfied with their Army jobs, and so on, consistently had better chances to be promoted at a later date (I, 147-154); data from the same study reveal the stability of response to the type of question used in gauging levels of adjustment (I, 163 and I, 208, Table 6); it also is called on to show that, compared with "normal" soldiers, a sample of recruits subsequently diagnosed as psychoneurotic were significantly less well adjusted during the early stages of their Army careers. (II, 414, Table 1)

In other instances, the analysts could only state that panel studies would have been appropriate had they been available. In discussing the relation of job choice to job satisfaction, for example, the authors indicate that a panel study would be required to eliminate all doubts about the relationship. (I, 289) Similarly, in their discussion of the deterioration in the effective force of formal sanctions as related to time in combat, they point out the need for a panel study. (II, 114) In all, there are a dozen points where the authors indicate that their results would have been better founded had they been based on panel materials.[11]

[10] See especially I, 198. This and the following few pages contain a very lucid and thoughtful discussion of the methodological problems involved in studying trends in attitudes, or in other words, using time as a variable. (I, 197–206)

[11] For other examples, see I, 344–346; II, 149, 207–208, 240, 436 and 625. In other sections the need for panel studies, while not explicitly stated, is implicit. See, for example, the discussion of personal adjustment as related to

Retrospective questions

One of the main difficulties in a panel study is keeping the original sample intact. This is a problem even in studies of civilian populations: respondents move; some become ill and unable to participate further in the study; others become bored and refuse to participate. The enormity of these difficulties in studies of soldiers during a global war is obvious.

Because of these handicaps we sometimes use *retrospective questions* as a substitute for panel techniques. By asking the respondents to recall what their attitudes were at some earlier period (generally prior to a crucial experience whose effect we are trying to study), we attempt to reconstruct what would have been observed had there been a previous interview. We ask, "How did you feel about *y* before *x* took place?" We remember that the Research Branch used a question of this kind in checking the relationship between service in bi-racial companies and the willingness of whites to serve with Negroes. In addition to stating their present willingness to serve in mixed companies, the respondents were asked to recall what their attitudes had been before Negro platoons were put in their companies.

There are a number of grounds on which one might object to the use of retrospective questions as a substitute for panel techniques. First of all, it is difficult to know how accurate respondents are in their retrospection. Do they tend to remember selectively? Do they discount the extent to which they have actually changed their attitudes or habits? Secondly, there is the problem of specifying the exact time period to which the subjects should retrospect. "Before *x* took place" covers a wide time range.

Wherever possible, then, the accuracy of the retrospections should be checked. This was done in an interesting way at one point in *The American Soldier*. In investigating the effects of combat on the incidence of psychosomatic symptoms, the researchers used a number of different procedures. First of all, they cross-tabulated such variables as nearness to combat and length of time in combat with questions about psychosomatic symptoms. In one study of combat veterans, however, they included a retrospective question. In addition to asking, "Since you have been on active combat duty, are you ever bothered by (hand tremors, stomach disturbances, fainting spells, nightmares, shortness of breath, and pressure in the head)?" they also asked, "During your civilian and military life, but before you went on active combat duty, were you ever bothered by . . . ?" Comparison of the retrospective form of the question with the post-combat form reveals a marked increase in the proportion of men experiencing many anxiety symptoms. (II, 449, Table 17)

But how accurate were these retrospections? As a check, the analysts compared the pre-combat answers of the veterans with those given by Infantrymen in training in the United States. The close correspondence of the answers provided some assurance that the combat veterans did not distort their answers, either consciously or unconsciously, to any extent. (II, 448, Table 16)[12]

These, then, are perhaps the major procedures through which the data obtained through surveys and utilized in secondary analyses can be made more nearly equivalent to experimental results.[13]

---

combat experience (I, 195–229) and the analysis of changes in attitudes at the conclusion of the war. (II, 562 ff.) It is also interesting that in his recent review of the second volume, three of the four specific findings which George Murdock points to as having special importance were obtained from these two panel studies. (The fourth was obtained in a controlled experiment.) *See The American Sociological Review*, **14** (1949), p. 815.

[12] There is one caution to be noted in connection with this kind of check on the accuracy of retrospections. At Time II we ask respondents to recall their attitudes of Time I. If these retrospections are checked, it should be with data collected at Time I. In a highly dynamic situation, checks based on data obtained at Time II may introduce a distortion. Let us consider what this distortion might have been in the Research Branch study. The authors note that the Army adopted a permissive attitude toward fear and anxiety symptoms among the troops. (II, 196 ff.) But this attitude might have been more apparent at later stages of the war, so that soldiers were more willing to express their anxiety at Time II, let us say, than they had been at Time I. If this were the case, and if the checks had been based on data obtained only at Time II, then the actual extent of increase in anxiety symptoms would have been underestimated. (Actually the checks were based on material collected both at "Time I" and "Time II".)

[13] In a recent article ("Some Observations on Study Design," *American Journal of Sociology*, LV, 1949–50, 355–361), Stouffer himself suggests a general scheme through which the interrelationships of controlled experiments, panel studies, surveys, and so on, can be shown. His paper is an elaboration of pp. 47–48 in the first volume of *The American Soldier*.

PARTICIPANT OBSERVATION:
THE ANALYSIS OF QUALITATIVE FIELD DATA*

The problems of causal inference when using the method of participant observation are so great that most social psychologists avoid its use. And yet there are certain research situations where it is the only feasible method. Where experimental intervention or the systematic asking of questions would radically alter the social phenomenon under study, it appears to be the only alternative. Also, where the phenomenon displays its true character only at the moment of occurrence and is subsequently distorted by recall, participant observation is superior to interviewing after the event. Similarly, where the researcher with limited resources is faced with the task of grasping in some total manner the structure and functioning of an ongoing social unit, such as a treatment facility, work unit, school, or prison, it is often the only practical alternative.

Although for certain situations the method of participant observation is the only suitable method, its proper use is in many ways more difficult than survey or experimental procedures. In part this is because the specific techniques of analysis long codified in experimental and survey research need yet to be clarified and systematized for this approach. In part, however, the difficulties are inherent in the fact that safeguards against errors, such as the rules of observation and analysis that govern experimental and survey procedures, must be built into the cognitive and perceptual organization of the researcher who employs the methods of participant observation. To illustrate, the progressive sequence of collecting observations, analyzing or interpreting them, and making new observations can in participant observation easily lead to progressive bias, because of the perceptual tendency to perceive in a manner which supports one's cognitive organization. The problem here is that observations are more subjective in nature, and estimates of relations or associations between variables quantitative in only a crude sense. This subjectivity of observation and grossness of estimates of magnitude leave the door wide open for perceptual bias to enter. To compensate for this susceptibility to bias, the participant observer must constantly search out negative cases that dispute his formulation. This requires considerable mental discipline.

An additional problem concerns the presentation of the empirical materials in support of one's model of explanation. Unlike the experimenter or the survey researcher who can summarize his quantitative findings in a table or two, the participant observer normally deals with a voluminous mass of qualitative materials, in the form of field notes, that defy succinct presentation. Since any presentation of results must necessarily be highly selective, a report of research based on participant observation is difficult to present without raising the suspicion that the report favors supporting evidence and slights negative instances. In the following selection Becker discusses some of these issues and suggests the directions in which solutions may be sought.

5.

Problems of Inference and Proof in Participant Observation[1]

HOWARD S. BECKER
STANFORD UNIVERSITY

The participant observer gathers data by participating in the daily life of the group or organization he studies.[2] He watches the people he is studying to see what situations they ordinarily meet and how they behave in them. He enters

[1] This paper developed out of problems of analysis arising in a study of a state medical school. The study is sponsored by Community Studies, Inc., of Kansas City, Missouri. It is directed by Everett C. Hughes; Anselm Strauss is also a member of the research team. Most of the material presented here has been worked out with the help of Blanche Geer, who has been my partner in field work and analysis in this study. I am grateful to Alvin W. Gouldner for a thorough critique of an earlier draft.

Substantive papers on the study, whose findings are made use of throughout, include: Howard S. Becker and Blanche Geer, "The Fate of Idealism in Medical School," *American Sociological Review*, **23** (February, 1958), pp. 50–56, and "Student Culture in Medical School," *Harvard Educational Review*, **28** (Winter, 1958), pp. 70–80. Another paper on participant observation by the same authors is "Participant Observation and Interviewing: A Comparison," *Human Organization*, **16** (Fall, 1957), pp. 28–32.

[2] There is little agreement on the specific referent of the term *participant observation*. See Raymond L. Gold, "Roles in Sociological Field Observations," *Social Forces*, **36** (March, 1958), pp. 217–223, for a useful classification of the various procedures that go by this name. Our own research, from which we have drawn our illustrations, falls under Gold's type, "participant-as-observer." The basic methods discussed here, however, would appear to be similar in other kinds of field situations.

---

* The selection following the editorial introduction is reprinted from "Inference and proof in participant observation," *American Sociological Review*, 1958, **23**, 652–660, by permission of the author and the American Sociological Association.

into conversation with some or all of the participants in these situations and discovers their interpretations of the events he has observed.

Let me describe, as one specific instance of observational technique, what my colleagues and I have done in studying a medical school. We went to lectures with students taking their first two years of basic science and frequented the laboratories in which they spend most of their time, watching them and engaging in casual conversation as they dissected cadavers or examined pathology specimens. We followed these students to their fraternity houses and sat around while they discussed their school experiences. We accompanied students in the clinical years on rounds with attending physicians, watched them examine patients on the wards and in the clinics, sat in on discussion groups and oral exams. We ate with the students and took night call with them. We pursued internes and residents through their crowded schedules of teaching and medical work. We stayed with one small group of students on each service for periods ranging from a week to two months, spending many full days with them. The observational situations allowed time for conversation and we took advantage of this to interview students about things that had happened and were about to happen, and about their own backgrounds and aspirations.

Sociologists usually use this method when they are especially interested in understanding a particular organization or substantive problem rather than demonstrating relations between abstractly defined variables. They attempt to make their research theoretically meaningful, but they assume that they do not know enough about the organization *a priori* to identify relevant problems and hypotheses and that they must discover these in the course of the research. Though participant observation can be used to test *a priori* hypotheses, and therefore need not be as unstructured as the example I have given above, this is typically not the case. My discussion refers to the kind of participant observation study which seeks to discover hypotheses as well as to test them.

Observational research produces an immense amount of detailed description; our files contain approximately five thousand single-spaced pages of such material. Faced with such a quantity of "rich" but varied data, the researcher faces the problem of how to analyze it systematically and then to present his conclusions so as to convince other scientists of their validity. Participant observation (indeed, qualitative analysis generally) has not done well with this problem, and the full weight of evidence for conclusions and the processes by which they were reached are usually not presented, so that the reader finds it difficult to make his own assessment of them and must rely on his faith in the researcher.

In what follows I try to pull out and describe *the basic analytic operations carried on in participant observation*, for three reasons: to make these operations clear to those unfamiliar with the method; by attempting a more explicit and systematic description, to aid those working with the method in organizing their own research; and, most importantly, in order to propose some changes in analytic procedures and particularly in reporting results which will make the processes by which conclusions are reached and substantiated more accessible to the reader.

The first thing we note about participant observation research is that analysis is carried on *sequentially*,[3] important parts of the analysis being made while the researcher is still gathering his data. This has two obvious consequences: further data gathering takes its direction from provisional analyses; and the amount and kind of provisional analysis carried on is limited by the exigencies of the field work situation, so that final comprehensive analyses may not be possible until the field work is completed.

We can distinguish three distinct stages of analysis conducted in the field itself, and a fourth stage, carried on after completion of the field work. These stages are differentiated, first, by their logical sequence: each succeeding stage depends on some analysis in the preceding stage. They are further differentiated by the fact that different kinds of conclusions are arrived at in each stage and that these conclusions are put to different uses in the continuing research. Finally, they are differentiated by the different criteria that are used to assess evidence and to reach conclusions in each stage. The three stages of field analysis are: the selection and definition of problems, concepts, and indices; the check on the frequency and distribution of phenomena; and the incorporation of individual findings into a model of the organization under study.[4] The fourth stage of final analysis involves problems of presentation of evidence and proof.

SELECTION AND DEFINITION OF PROBLEMS, CONCEPTS, AND INDICES

In this stage, the observer looks for problems and concepts that give promise of yielding the greatest understanding of the organization he is studying,

[3] In this respect, the analytic methods I discuss bear a family resemblance to the technique of *analytic induction*. Cf. Alfred Lindesmith, *Opiate Addiction* (Bloomington: Principia Press, 1947), especially pp. 5–20, and the subsequent literature cited in Ralph H. Turner, "The Quest for Universals in Sociological Research," *American Sociological Review*, **18** (December, 1953), pp. 604–611.

[4] My discussion of these stages is abstract and simplified and does not attempt to deal with practical and technical problems of participant observation study. The reader should keep in mind that in practice the research will involve all these operations simultaneously with reference to different particular problems.

and for items which may serve as useful indicators of facts which are harder to observe. The typical conclusion that his data yield is the simple one that a given phenomenon exists, that a certain event occurred once, or that two phenomena were observed to be related in one instance; the conclusion says nothing about the frequency or distribution of the observed phenomenon.

By placing such an observation in the context of a sociological theory, the observer selects concepts and defines problems for further investigation. He constructs a theoretical model to account for that one case, intending to refine it in the light of subsequent findings. For instance, he might find the following: "Medical student X referred to one of his patients as a 'crock' today."[5] He may then connect this finding with a sociological theory suggesting that occupants of one social category in an institution classify members of other categories by criteria derived from the kinds of problems these other persons raise in the relationship. This combination of observed fact and theory directs him to look for the problems in student-patient interaction indicated by the term "crock." By discovering specifically what students have in mind in using the term, through questioning and continued observation, he may develop specific hypotheses about the nature of these interactional problems.

Conclusions about a single event also lead the observer to decide on specific items which might be used as indicators[6] of less easily observed phenomena. Noting that in at least one instance a given item is closely related to something less easily observable, the researcher discovers possible shortcuts easily enabling him to observe abstractly defined variables. For example, he may decide to investigate the hypothesis that medical freshmen feel they have more work to do than can possibly be managed in the time allowed them. One student, in discussing this problem, says he faces so much work that, in contrast to his undergraduate days, he is forced to study many hours over the weekend and finds that even this

is insufficient. The observer decides, on the basis of this one instance, that he may be able to use complaints about weekend work as an indicator of student perspectives on the amount of work they have to do. The selection of indicators for more abstract variables occurs in two ways: the observer may become aware of some very specific phenomenon first and later see that it may be used as an indicator of some larger class of phenomena; or he may have the larger problem in mind and search for specific indicators to use in studying it.

Whether he is defining problems or selecting concepts and indicators, the researcher at this stage is using his data only to speculate about possibilities. Further operations at later stages may force him to discard most of the provisional hypotheses. Nevertheless, problems of evidence arise even at this point, for the researcher must assess the individual items on which his speculations are based in order not to waste time tracking down false leads. We shall eventually need a systematic statement of canons to be applied to individual items of evidence. Lacking such a statement, let us consider some commonly used tests. (The observer typically applies these tests as seems reasonable to him during this and the succeeding stage in the field. In the final stage, they are used more systematically in an overall assessment of the total evidence for a given conclusion.)

The credibility of informants. Many items of evidence consist of statements by members of the group under study about some event which has occurred or is in process. Thus, medical students make statements about faculty behavior which form part of the basis for conclusions about faculty-student relations. These cannot be taken at face value; nor can they be dismissed as valueless. In the first place, the observer can use the statement as evidence *about the event*, if he takes care to evaluate it by the criteria an historian uses in examining a personal document.[7] Does the informant have reason to lie or conceal some of what he sees as the truth? Does vanity or expediency lead him to mis-state his own role in an event or his attitude toward it? Did he actually have an opportunity to witness the occurrence he describes or is hearsay the source of his knowledge? Do his feelings about the issues or persons under discussion lead him to alter his story in some way?

Secondly, even when a statement examined in this way proves to be seriously defective as an accurate report of an event, it may still provide useful evidence for a different kind of conclusion. Accepting the sociological proposition that an individual's statements and descriptions of events

---

[5] The examples of which our hypothetical observer makes use are drawn from our own current work with medical students.

[6] The problem of indicators is discussed by Paul F. Lazarsfeld and Allen Barton, "Qualitative Measurement in the Social Sciences: Classification, Typologies, and Indices," in Daniel Lerner and Harold D. Lasswell, editors, *The Policy Sciences: Recent Developments in Scope and Method*, Stanford: Stanford University Press, 1951, pp. 155–192; "Some Functions of Qualitative Analysis in Sociological Research," *Sociologica*, **1** (1955), pp. 324–361 (this important paper parallels the present discussion in many places); and Patricia L. Kendall and Paul F. Lazarsfeld, "Problems of Survey Analysis," in R. K. Merton and P. F. Lazarsfeld, editors, *Continuities in Social Research*, Glencoe: Free Press, 1950, pp. 183–186.

[7] Cf. Louis Gottschalk, Clyde Kluckhohn, and Robert Angell, *The Use of Personal Documents in History, Anthropology, and Sociology*, New York: Social Science Research Council, 1945, pp. 15–27, 38–47.

are made from a perspective which is a function of his position in the group, the observer can interpret such statements and descriptions as indications of the individual's perspective on the point involved.

Volunteered or directed statements. Many items of evidence consist of informants' remarks to the observer about themselves or others or about something which has happened to them; these statements range from those which are a part of the running casual conversation of the group to those arising in a long intimate tete-a-tete between observer and informant. The researcher assesses the evidential value of such statements quite differently, depending on whether they have been made independently of the observer (volunteered) or have been directed by a question from the observer. A freshman medical student might remark to the observer or to another student that he has more material to study than he has time to master; or the observer might ask, "Do you think you are being given more work than you can handle?", and receive an affirmative answer.

This raises an important question: to what degree is the informant's statement the same one he might give, either spontaneously or in answer to a question, in the absence of the observer? The volunteered statement seems likely to reflect the observer's preoccupations and possible biases less than one which is made in response to some action of the observer, for the observer's very question may direct the informant into giving an answer which might never occur to him otherwise. Thus, in the example above, we are more sure that the students are concerned about the amount of work given them when they mention this of their own accord than we are when the idea may have been stimulated by the observer asking the question.

The observer-informant-group equation. Let us take two extremes to set the problem. A person may say or do something when alone with the observer or when other members of the group are also present. The evidential value of an observation of this behavior depends on the observer's judgment as to whether the behavior is equally likely to occur in both situations. On the one hand, an informant may say and do things when alone with the observer that accurately reflect his perspective but which would be inhibited by the presence of the group. On the other hand, the presence of others may call forth behavior which reveals more accurately the person's perspective but would not be enacted in the presence of the observer alone. Thus, students in their clinical years may express deeply "idealistic" sentiments about medicine when alone with the observer, but behave and talk in a very "cynical" way when surrounded by fellow students. An alternative to judging one or the other of these situations as more reliable is to view each datum

as valuable in itself, but with respect to different conclusions. In the example above, we might conclude that students have "idealistic" sentiments but that group norms may not sanction their expression.[8]

In assessing the value of items of evidence, we must also take into account the observer's role in the group. For the way the subjects of his study define that role affects what they will tell him or let him see. If the observer carries on his research incognito, participating as a full-fledged member of the group, he will be privy to knowledge that would normally be shared by such a member and might be hidden from an outsider. He could properly interpret his own experience as that of a hypothetical "typical" group member. On the other hand, if he is known to be a researcher, he must learn how group members define him and in particular whether or not they believe that certain kinds of information and events should be kept hidden from him. He can interpret evidence more accurately when the answers to these questions are known.

CHECKING THE FREQUENCY AND DISTRIBUTION OF PHENOMENA

The observer, possessing many provisional problems, concepts, and indicators, now wishes to know which of these are worth pursuing as major foci of his study. He does this, in part, by discovering if the events that prompted their development are typical and widespread, and by seeing how these events are distributed among categories of people and organizational sub-units. He reaches conclusions that are essentially quantitative, using them to describe the organization he is studying.

Participant observations have occasionally been gathered in standardized form capable of being transformed into legitimate statistical data.[9] But the exigencies of the field usually prevent the collection of data in such a form as to meet the assumptions of statistical tests, so that the observer deals in what have been called "quasi-statistics."[10] His conclusions, while implicitly numerical, do not require precise quantification. For instance, he may conclude that members of freshmen medical fraternities typically sit together

[8] See further, Howard S. Becker, "Interviewing Medical Students," *American Journal of Sociology*, **62** (September, 1956), pp. 199–201.

[9] See Peter M. Blau, "Co-operation and Competition in a Bureaucracy," *American Journal of Sociology*, **59** (May, 1954), pp. 530–535.

[10] See the discussion of quasi-statistics in Lazarsfeld and Barton, "Some Functions of Qualitative Analysis . . .," *op. cit.*, pp. 346–348.

during lectures while other students sit in less stable smaller groupings. His observations may indicate such a wide disparity between the two groups in this respect that the inference is warranted without a standardized counting operation. Occasionally, the field situation may permit him to make similar observations or ask similar questions of many people, systematically searching for quasi-statistical support for a conclusion about frequency or distribution.

In assessing the evidence for such a conclusion the observer takes a cue from his statistical colleagues. Instead of arguing that a conclusion is either totally true or false, he decides, if possible, how *likely* it is that his conclusion about the frequency or distribution of some phenomenon is an accurate quasi-statistic, just as the statistician decides, on the basis of the varying values of a correlation coefficient or a significance figure, that his conclusion is more or less likely to be accurate. The kind of evidence may vary considerably and the degree of the observer's confidence in the conclusion will vary accordingly. In arriving at this assessment, he makes use of some of the criteria described above, as well as those adopted from quantitative techniques.

Suppose, for example, that the observer concludes that medical students share the perspective that their school should provide them with the clinical experience and the practice in techniques necessary for a general practitioner. His confidence in the conclusion would vary according to the nature of the evidence, which might take any of the following forms: (*1*) *Every* member of the group said, *in response to a direct question,* that this was the way he looked at the matter. (*2*) *Every* member of the group *volunteered* to an observer that this was how he viewed the matter. (*3*) *Some given proportion* of the group's members either *answered* a direct question or *volunteered* the information that he shared this perspective, but none of the others was asked or volunteered information on the subject. (*4*) Every member of the group was asked or volunteered information, but *some given proportion said* they viewed the matter from the differing perspective of a prospective specialist. (*5*) No one was asked questions or volunteered information on the subject, but *all members were observed to engage in behavior* or to make other statements from which the analyst *inferred* that the general practitioner perspective was being used by them as a basic, though unstated, premise. For example, all students might have been observed to complain that the University Hospital received too many cases of rare diseases that general practitioners rarely see. (*6*) *Some given proportion* of the group *was observed* using the general practitioner perspective as a basic premise in their activities, but *the rest*

of the group was not observed engaging in such activities. (*7*) *Some proportion* of the group *was observed* engaged in activities implying the general practitioner perspective while *the remainder* of the group was observed engaged in activities implying the perspective of the prospective specialist.

The researcher also takes account of the possibility that his observations may give him evidence of different kinds on the point under consideration. Just as he is more convinced if he has many items of evidence than if he has a few, so he is more convinced of a conclusion's validity if he has *many kinds* of evidence.[11] For instance, he may be especially persuaded that a particular norm exists and affects group behavior if the norm is not only described by group members but also if he observes events in which the norm can be "seen" to operate—if, for example, students tell him that they are thinking of becoming general practitioners and he also observes their complaints about the lack of cases of common diseases in University Hospital.

The conclusiveness which comes from the convergence of several kinds of evidence reflects the fact that separate varieties of evidence can be reconceptualized as deductions from a basic proposition which have now been verified in the field. In the above case, the observer might have deduced the desire to have experience with cases like those the general practitioner treats from the desire to practice that style of medicine. Even though the deduction is made after the fact, confirmation of it buttresses the argument that the general practitioner perspective is a group norm.

It should be remembered that these operations, when carried out in the field, may be so interrupted because of imperatives of the field situation that they are not carried on as systematically as they might be. Where this is the case, the overall assessment can be postponed until the final stage of postfield work analysis.

CONSTRUCTION OF SOCIAL SYSTEM MODELS

The final stage of analysis in the field consists of incorporating individual findings into a generalized model of the social system or organization under study or some part of that organization.[12] The concept of social system is a basic intellectual tool of modern sociology. The kind of participant observation discussed here is related directly to this

[11] See Alvin W. Gouldner, *Patterns of Industrial Bureaucracy,* Glencoe, Ill.: Free Press, 1954, pp. 247–269.

[12] The relation between theories based on the concept of social system and participant observation was pointed out to me by Alvin W. Gouldner. See his "Some Observations on Systematic Theory, 1945–55," in Hans L. Zetterberg, editor, *Sociology in the United States of America,* Paris: UNESCO, 1956, pp. 34–42; and "Theoretical Requirements of the Applied Social Sciences," *American Sociological Review,* **22** (February, 1957), pp. 92–102.

concept, explaining particular social facts by explicit reference to their involvement in a complex of interconnected variables that the observer constructs as a theoretical model of the organization. In this final stage, the observer designs a descriptive model which best explains the data he has assembled.

The typical conclusion of this stage of the research is a statement about a set of complicated interrelations among many variables. Although some progress is being made in formalizing this operation through use of factor analysis and the relational analysis of survey data,[13] observers usually view currently available statistical techniques as inadequate to express their conceptions and find it necessary to use words. The most common kinds of conclusions at this level include:

(1) Complex statements of the necessary and sufficient conditions for the existence of some phenomenon. The observer may conclude, for example, that medical students develop consensus about limiting the amount of work they will do because (a) they are faced with a large amount of work, (b) they engage in activities which create communication channels between all members of the class, and (c) they face immediate dangers in the form of examinations set by the faculty.

(2) Statements that some phenomenon is an "important" or "basic" element in the organization. Such conclusions, when elaborated, usually point to the fact that this phenomenon exercises a persistent and continuing influence on diverse events. The observer might conclude that the ambition to become a general practitioner is "important" in the medical school under study, meaning that many particular judgments and choices are made by students in terms of this ambition and many features of the school's organization are arranged to take account of it.

(3) Statements identifying a situation as an instance of some process or phenomenon described more abstractly in sociological theory. Theories posit relations between many abstractly defined phenomena, and conclusions of this kind imply that relationships posited in generalized form hold in this particular instance. The observer, for example, may state that a cultural norm of the medical students is to express a desire to become a general practitioner; in so doing, he in effect asserts that the sociological theory about the functions of norms and the processes by

which they are maintained which he holds to be true in general is true in this case.

In reaching such types of conclusions, the observer characteristically begins by constructing models of parts of the organization as he comes in contact with them, discovers concepts and problems, and the frequency and distribution of the phenomena these call to his attention. After constructing a model specifying the relationships among various elements of this part of the organization, the observer seeks greater accuracy by successively refining the model to take account of evidence which does not fit his previous formulation;[14] by searching for negative cases (items of evidence which run counter to the relationships hypothesized in the model) which might force such revision; and by searching intensively for the interconnections *in vivo* of the various elements he has conceptualized from his data. While a provisional model may be shown to be defective by a negative instance which crops up unexpectedly in the course of the field work, the observer may infer what kinds of evidence would be likely to support or to refute his model and may make an intensive search for such evidence.[15]

After the observer has accumulated several partial-models of this kind, he seeks connections between them and thus begins to construct an overall model of the entire organization. An example from our study shows how this operation is carried on during the period of field work. (The reader will note, in this example, how use is made of findings typical of earlier stages of analysis.)

When we first heard medical students apply the term "crock" to patients we made an effort to learn precisely what they meant by it. We found, through interviewing students about cases both they and the observer had seen, that the term referred in a derogatory way to patients with many subjective symptoms but no discernible physical pathology. Subsequent observations indicated that this usage was a regular feature of student behavior and thus that we should attempt to incorporate this fact into our model of student-patient behavior. The derogatory character of the term suggested in particular that we investigate the reasons students disliked these patients. We found that this dislike was related to what we discovered to be the students' perspective on medical school: the view that they were in school to get experience in recognizing and treating those

[13] See Alvin W. Gouldner, "Cosmopolitans and Locals: Toward an Analysis of Latent Social Roles," *Administrative Science Quarterly*, **2** (December, 1957), pp. 281–306, and **3** (March, 1958), pp. 444–480; and James Coleman, "Relational Analysis: The Study of Social Structure with Survey Methods," mimeographed.

[14] Note again the resemblance to analytic induction.
[15] See Alfred Lindesmith's discussion of this principle in "Comment on W. S. Robinson's 'The Logical Structure of Analytic Induction,'" *American Sociological Review*, **17** (August, 1952), pp. 492–493.

common diseases most likely to be encountered in general practice. "Crocks," presumably having no disease, could furnish no such experience. We were thus led to specify connections between the student-patient relationship and the student's view of the purpose of his professional education. Questions concerning the genesis of this perspective led to discoveries about the organization of the student body and communication among students, phenomena which we had been assigning to another part-model. Since "crocks" were also disliked because they gave the student no opportunity to assume medical responsibility, we were able to connect this aspect of the student-patient relationship with still another tentative model of the value system and hierarchical organization of the school, in which medical responsibility plays an important role.

Again, it should be noted that analysis of this kind is carried on in the field as time permits. Since the construction of a model is the analytic operation most closely related to the observer's techniques and interests he usually spends a great deal of time thinking about these problems. But he is usually unable to be as systematic as he would like until he reaches the final stage of analysis.

FINAL ANALYSIS AND THE PRESENTATION OF RESULTS

The final systematic analysis, carried on after the field work is completed, consists of rechecking and rebuilding models as carefully and with as many safeguards as the data will allow. For instance, in checking the accuracy of statements about the frequency and distribution of events, the researcher can index and arrange his material so that every item of information is accessible and taken account of in assessing the accuracy of any given conclusion. He can profit from the observation of Lazarsfeld and Barton that the "analysis of 'quasi-statistical data' can probably be made more systematic than it has been in the past, if the logical structure of quantitative research at least is kept in mind to give general warnings and directions to the qualitative observer."[16]

An additional criterion for the assessment of this kind of evidence is the state of the observer's conceptualization of the problem at the time the item of evidence was gathered. The observer may have his problem well worked out and be actively looking for evidence to test an hypothesis, or he may not be as yet aware of the problem. The evidential value of items in his field notes will

[16] "Some Functions of Qualitative Analysis . . .," *op. cit.*, p. 348.

vary accordingly, the basis of consideration being the likelihood of discovering negative cases of the proposition he eventually uses the material to establish. The best evidence may be that gathered in the most unthinking fashion, when the observer has simply recorded the item although it has no place in the system of concepts and hypotheses he is working with at the time, for there might be less bias produced by the wish to substantiate or repudiate a particular idea. On the other hand, a well-formulated hypothesis makes possible a deliberate search for negative cases, particularly when other knowledge suggests likely areas in which to look for such evidence. This kind of search requires advanced conceptualization of the problem, and evidence gathered in this way might carry greater weight for certain kinds of conclusions. Both procedures are relevant at different stages of the research.

In the post field work stage of analysis, the observer carries on the model building operation more systematically. He considers the character of his conclusions and decides on the kind of evidence that might cause their rejection, deriving further tests by deducing logical consequences and ascertaining whether or not the data support the deductions. He considers reasonable alternative hypotheses and whether or not the evidence refutes them.[17] Finally, he completes the job of establishing interconnections between partial models so as to achieve an overall synthesis incorporating all conclusions.

After completing the analysis, the observer faces the knotty problem of how to present his conclusions and the evidence for them. Readers of qualitative research reports commonly and justifiably complain that they are told little or nothing about the evidence for conclusions or the operations by which the evidence has been assessed. A more adequate presentation of the data, of the research operations, and of the researcher's inferences may help to meet this problem.

But qualitative data and analytic procedures, in contrast to quantitative ones, are difficult to present adequately. Statistical data can be summarized in tables, and descriptive measures of various kinds and the methods by which they are handled can often be accurately reported in the space required to print a formula. This is so in part because the methods have been systematized so that they can be referred to in this shorthand fashion and in part because the data have been collected for a fixed, usually small, number of

[17] One method of doing this, particularly adapted to testing discrete hypotheses about change in individuals or small social units (though not in principle limited to this application), is "The Technique of Discerning," described by Mirra Komarovsky in Paul F. Lazarsfeld and Morris Rosenberg, editors, *The Language of Social Research*, Glencoe, Ill.: Free Press, 1955, pp. 449–457. See also the careful discussion of alternative hypotheses and the use of deduced consequences as further proof in Lindesmith, *Opiate Addiction, passim.*

categories—the presentation of data need be nothing more than a report of the number of cases to be found in each category.

The data of participant observation do not lend themselves to such ready summary. They frequently consist of many different kinds of observations which cannot be simply categorized and counted without losing some of their value as evidence—for, as we have seen, many points need to be taken into account in putting each datum to use. Yet it is clearly out of the question to publish all the evidence. Nor is it any solution, as Kluckhohn has suggested for the similar problem of presenting life history materials,[18] to publish a short version and to make available the entire set of materials on microfilm or in some other inexpensive way; this ignores the problem of how to present *proof*.

In working over the material on the medical school study a possible solution to this problem, with which we are experimenting, is a description of the natural history of our conclusions, presenting the evidence as it came to the attention of the observer during the successive stages of his conceptualization of the problem. The term "natural history" implies not the presentation of every datum, but only the characteristic forms data took at each stage of the research. This involves description of the form that data took and any significant exceptions, taking account of the canons discussed above, in presenting the various

---

[18] Gottschalk, Kluckhohn, and Angell, *op. cit.*, pp. 150–156.

statements of findings and the inferences and conclusions drawn from them. In this way, evidence is assessed as the substantive analysis is presented. The reader would be able, if this method were used, to follow the details of the analysis and to see how and on what basis any conclusion was reached. This would give the reader, as do present modes of statistical presentation, opportunity to make his own judgment as to the adequacy of the proof and the degree of confidence to be assigned the conclusion.

CONCLUSION

I have tried to describe the analytic field work characteristic of participant observation, first, in order to bring out the fact that the technique consists of something more than merely immersing oneself in data and "having insights." The discussion may also serve to stimulate those who work with this and similar techniques to attempt greater formalization and systematization of the various operations they use, in order that qualitative research may become more a "scientific" and less an "artistic" kind of endeavor. Finally, I have proposed that new modes of reporting results be introduced, so that the reader is given greater access to the data and procedures on which conclusions are based.

A **distinctive possession** of the human being is his rich and varied inner experience. This experience is not only a legitimate object of study in its own right, but is also both a product of and a stimulus to interaction among persons. Certain actions by an individual produce feelings of like or dislike for him as well as more definite impressions of his personality and character. Similarly, feelings of like or dislike for another person can motivate an individual to behave in particular ways toward him. Thus, understanding of human interaction requires knowledge of the part played in it by human experience.

In the course of his interactions with other persons, the individual learns certain modes of perceiving and knowing his world, and from time to time experiences various feelings that color his perceptions and judgments. The study of these perceptions and cognitions and their determinants is known as **social perception**, and is the subject matter of this section of the book. One movement in social perception is concerned primarily with the influence of personal and social factors on the perception of relatively simple physical objects or stimuli. The other deals with the more complex problem of how impressions of other persons are formed and how our feelings toward them are determined.

During the 1950s social psychologists became excited and enthusiastic about the effects of social factors on the perception of the physical world. Their initial research suggested that our perceptions were distorted by such social factors as our emotional state immediately prior to the perception, by the tendency of the stimulus object to make us anxious or guilty, or by the positive or negative value of the object. Thus, it seemed that, instead of perceiving the world accurately, an individual was apt to perceive it according to his own experience and his drives, wishes, and values. Such processes could not be discovered without precisely controlled laboratory studies. If this new position could be demonstrated to be correct, it would have great significance in explaining how an individual's behavior persisted in the face of environmental pressures to the contrary stemming from the real nature of the world. Not only could abnormal and bizarre behavior be more readily explained, but omnipresent individual differences in personality would no longer be so mysterious.

As research continued, however, the internal validity of the initial investigations was questioned. More adequate experimental designs indicated that failures to accurately perceive stimulus objects were not quite so readily produced as had been thought and that the influence on perception apparently stemming from such social factors as motives or values might, instead, be due to other associated variables. Many of the conclusions from initial research efforts were shown to result primarily from the particular method of investigation used. Thus, their external validity was low; often they could not be generalized to nonexperimental situations or even to more adequately designed experiments.

The first three articles in Part Two deal with variations in the recognition of a stimulus object resulting from such variables as the value of the stimulus object or the frequency of experience with it and the effects of the positive or negative value of an object on judg-

PART TWO

SOCIAL FACTORS IN PERCEPTUAL- COGNITIVE PROCESSES

ment of its size. The introduction to each article briefly describes the problem initially formulated by investigators and explains those technical aspects of the experimentation that require some background knowledge.

The last three articles in Part Two deal with the perception of persons under widely different conditions. In everyday situations, opinions and evaluations of other persons are formed under widely varying circumstances. Conditions vary in three major respects: (1) the amount of information available to the perceiver that can be used to form an impression of the other person, (2) the quantity of interaction between the perceiver and the other person, and (3) the extent to which the relation between the perceiver and the other person is well established. For example, when one meets a stranger, the amount of information and of interaction is very limited and no relation is yet established. At the opposite extreme, an individual has considerable information about a friend and much interaction with him, as well as a definite relation to him. The factors that determine the perception of the other person are apt to be quite different under these two conditions.

The first of the three selections deals with impressions of personality formed from limited information and in the absence of interaction with or an established relation to the stimulus person. The concept of stereotyping, which applies to judgments made in similar circumstances, is treated in the subsequent article. The final article demonstrates that the relation between the perceiver and other persons, as well as his relation to the stimulus person, affects his perception of the stimulus person.

WORD VALUES AND WORD FREQUENCY*

A favorite research approach to social perception has been the use of "impoverished" stimulus situations. The perceiver is presented with ambiguous or blurred stimulus patterns or with stimulus objects presented for only a fraction of a second under conditions of low illumination. Such conditions were thought to maximize the influence of social factors on what is perceived, so that their operation could be observed in the laboratory. One device for presenting stimulus material under restricted conditions is the tachistoscope, which exposes the material for a precisely determined brief fraction of a second. The perceiver is successively presented with a variety of exposure times. The unit of time at which the stimulus material is correctly recognized by the perceiver is known as the *recognition threshold* or the *visual duration threshold*.

Behavioral scientists expressed considerable interest in the effects on recognition threshold of the

perceiver's previous experience with the stimulus material and its emotional value to him. Early experiments yielded somewhat contradictory results concerning the relative influence of these two factors. In the selection below, Johnson, Thomson, and Frincke describe a series of experiments which help to resolve some of the questions raised by previous research.

For those who are unfamiliar with the technique, it is necessary to describe the method employed to measure the value of the stimulus words used in the experiments. The value of each word was measured by a special technique called the "good-bad" scale of the Semantic Differential[a]. This consists of a series of bipolar scales that have been demonstrated through intensive analysis to represent the evaluative connotations of a concept. In making ratings, subjects place toward the favorable end of the scale concepts toward which they have positive feelings, such as mother, democracy, education, money. Concepts carrying negative con-

* The selection following the editorial introduction is reprinted from "Word values, word frequency, and visual duration thresholds," *Psychological Review*, 1960, **67**, 332–342, by permission of the authors and the American Psychological Association.

[a] C. E. Osgood, G. J. Suci, & P. H. Tannenbaum. *The measurement of meaning.* Urbana, Ill.: The University of Illinois Press, 1957.

notations, such as Communism, poverty, and ignorance, would be rated toward the unfavorable ends of the scales. Examples of several such scales are the following:

generous:____:____:____:____:____:____: stingy
warm:____:____:____:____:____:____: cold
large:____:____:____:____:____:____: small

For each stimulus word, the subject checks the space on each of the bipolar scales that best describes his feeling about the stimulus word. On these scales, positively valued concepts tend to be rated as generous, warm, and large; negatively valued concepts as stingy, small, and cold.

6.

Word Values, Word Frequency, and Visual Duration Thresholds

RONALD C. JOHNSON
UNIVERSITY OF HAWAII

CALVIN W. THOMSON
SAN JOSE STATE COLLEGE

GERALD FRINCKE
SACRAMENTO STATE COLLEGE

A number of studies have shown a relation to exist between word frequency, word value, and visual duration thresholds. Certain issues have developed concerning the interpretation of the observed relations. Two types of interpretation of results can be distinguished:

1. Those interpretations that claim word frequency to be the major determinant of visual duration threshold. This point of view contends that the responses made to the tachistoscopic presentation of words are learned in the same manner that other responses are learned. Differences in the visual duration thresholds of words can then be accounted for in terms of word frequency so that the introduction of such tenuous and "unanchored" variables as perceptual selectivity and perceptual defense is a violation of the law of parsimony. Thus, the problems that exist with regard to the differential visual duration thresholds of words are problems in learning, not problems in perception.
2. Those interpretations that attempt to show that differences in the visual duration thresholds of words are due, all or in part, to differences in the affective qualities (values, goodness–badness, affective tone, emotional valence) attached to words. These affective qualities affect visual duration thresholds directly, through perceptual selectivity and/or perceptual defense. Visual duration thresholds of words are determined by variables that can be called perceptual variables instead of or along with those variables that usually bear upon learning.

We wish to center our introductory discussion around those few studies which, for us, best exemplify the two positions described above. Solomon and Howes (1951) take the position that differences between words can be accounted for on the basis of word frequency. The perceptual process does not differ in any fundamental way from the learning process. They say:

> Emotional factors undoubtedly operate to an important extent in the building of word frequencies in a given life history. In this way they would be related to word frequency and, indirectly, to the duration thresholds. . . . But to date we can find no evidence to suggest that emotional factors operate in the tachistoscopic situation independently of their effect on word frequency (p. 267).

According to Solomon and Howes (1951, p. 258) visual duration threshold can be accurately predicted from a knowledge of population-wide word frequency as given in the Thorndike-Lorge tables (1944). There is no need to bring in concepts such as perceptual selectivity or perceptual defense in order to explain differences in visual duration thresholds of words. To Solomon and Howes emotional factors operate only in producing idiosyncratic variation in word frequency. These differences in frequency account for differences in the visual duration thresholds of words such as those found between the visual duration threshold of a value-oriented word for subjects (Ss) who score high as opposed to low on specific scales of the Allport-Vernon Study of Values. They do not have any other influence on visual duration threshold.

The second position concerning the relation between word frequency, word value and visual duration threshold is clearly expressed by Postman and Schneider (1951). Faced with the problem of salvaging value as a variable influencing visual duration threshold, they say that

> It may . . . be more profitable theoretically to regard both frequency of word usage and duration thresholds as dependent variables, both manifestations of more fundamental psychological properties attributed to the organism, such as "habits," hypotheses, or even, perhaps, "personal values" (p. 277).

While not denying that word frequency can account for a considerable proportion of the variance in visual duration thresholds of words, they claim that values (called directive factors in this paper) directly influence the visual duration thresholds of infrequent words.

Postman, in a later article (1953), suggests that

the frequency of usage of a specific word is determined by its reinforcing qualities. He suggests that frequent as opposed to infrequent words differ systematically in affective tone. He presents evidence to show that the sheer number of pleasant words is much greater than that of unpleasant words. Postman says, "Social control over environmental stimuli will, then, tend to create a correlation between frequency and positive value" (p. 68). Whether called values, directive states, or affective qualities, certain emotive or affective aspects of words influence their general (e.g., Thorndike-Lorge) frequency. Affective quality determines frequency, not merely in an idiosyncratic way as Solomon and Howes (1951) suggest, but also in a very general sense for all words used by all individuals.

It has been hypothesized from this second position that values can influence visual duration threshold in two ways. The affective qualities of words influence visual duration threshold *directly* as in the case of an *S*'s Allport-Vernon score influencing his thresholds for infrequent value oriented words (Postman & Schneider, 1951). (It has been shown that the *S* who values an area such as aesthetics highly reports infrequent "aesthetic" words at lower thresholds than an individual who does not value aesthetics highly. However, as Solomon and Howes point out, this may be due to "idiosyncratic" differences in frequency of exposure.) The affective qualities of words influence visual duration threshold *indirectly*, since the frequency of general usage of any word is determined to a considerable extent by the affective tone of that word, with this frequency then acting as a determiner of visual duration threshold (Postman, 1953).

A third position might also be taken concerning the relations between word frequency, word value, and visual duration threshold. Postman (1953) touches upon this last possible interpretation. He says, "Finally, we cannot entirely discount the possibility that familiarity resulting from frequency may be in itself a source of positive value" (p. 68).

It appears, historically, as if the first point of view—that emphasizing word frequency, playing down the influence of value except as it produces idiosyncratic differences in word frequency—has won out. None of the three positions described above have been proven to be untenable, however. Indeed, we have all of the original questions left, plus a few new ones as well. The questions that we see as being testable and requiring further investigation are these:

1. Is word value related, in a general sense, to word frequency? All of the three positions described above would admit the existence of a relation between value and frequency—they would diverge in opinion with regard to the generality of the relationship. It is true that a knowledge of word frequency allows us to predict visual duration threshold. But why is the frequent word frequent? Perhaps we should go one step beyond frequency to determine whether other attributes of words vary systematically with frequency.

2. If a general relation between value and frequency exists, does it exist because more positively valued words are used more frequently or because one increases positive affect merely by increasing frequently? Or does the dependent-independent relationship depend on the experimental procedure used?

3. If value and frequency are rated in a general, not merely an idiosyncratic sense, then one would have to separate out the influences of each on visual duration threshold. Are there significant differences in visual duration threshold between "good" and "bad" words of equal population-wide frequency? Are there significant differences between frequent and infrequent words equal in affective tone?

These are the three problems that we have attempted to deal with in the series of experiments reported below.

Our first concern was to determine whether a general relation exists between word value and word frequency. As we noted above, there is reason to suspect that emotional factors do operate in the building of word frequency. In a large sample of words for which we have actual measures of goodness, the words in the semantic atlas prepared by Jenkins, Russell, and Suci (1958), one finds better than a two to one preponderance of good over bad words. While the words in this atlas are not a random selection of words in the English language, the sources from which the words were selected seem unlikely to be systematically biased in frequency of pleasant as opposed to unpleasant words. One is led to believe that this ratio is characteristic of the entire English language when examining proportions of pleasant to unpleasant words in a sample of 150 words selected at random from the Thorndike-Lorge tables for use in the experiments in Series I, discussed below. Of these 150 words, 95 were on the good end (4.00 or less) of the semantic differential, a ratio of approximately 2:1. It seems highly probable that the sheer number of pleasant words in the English language is far greater than the number of unpleasant words.

It seems equally likely that the frequency with which any specific word is used also depends to a considerable extent on its goodness or badness: hence on its reinforcing qualities. This question is amenable to determination. As Solomon and Howes (1951) state, "In the absence of further data it seems best merely to define word frequency for English words as the frequency of words in the Thorndike-Lorge tables" (pp. 264–265). If affective factors operate in the building of word frequency, then pleasantly toned words should have higher frequencies in the Thorndike-Lorge word count than unpleasantly toned words. Experiment I was designed to determine whether this was the case.

EXPERIMENT *I*

In the first of this series of experiments we attempted to determine whether the pleasantness of words—in this case measured by the good–bad scale of the semantic differential—was related to word frequency as measured by the Thorndike-Lorge tables.

We selected a sample of words from the Thorndike-Lorge tables. This sample of words consisted of two words selected at random from within every alphabetic category (except X) in the tables. These words were rated on the good–bad dimension of the semantic differential by 24 Ss, all freshmen taking an introductory psychology course. The rank order correlation between the goodness and the L count frequency of these words was $+.63$. Another random sample of 50 words was taken from the Thorndike-Lorge word list in the manner described above. These words were rated by 28 Ss, a different group than those who made the first set of ratings. The rank order correlation between goodness and L count frequency in this list was $+.40$, again significant to the .01 level of confidence. A third random sample of 50 words was drawn from the Thorndike-Lorge tables. These words were rated by 24 Ss, none of whom had taken part in previous experiments. The correlation between L count frequency and goodness for this set of words was $+.38$. All of these three correlations are significant to the .01 level. The results of these experiments, regardless of differences in the magnitude of the correlations, indicate that there is a positive and significant correlation between word frequency and goodness. Value attributes of words are related to word frequency—and not merely in an idiosyncratic way, but in a far more general sense as well.

EXPERIMENT *II*

Solomon and Howes (1951) list 30 frequent and 30 infrequent words that they used in a study of the relation of word frequency to visual duration threshold. Five frequent and 5 infrequent words had to do with each of the six value areas of the Allport-Vernon Study of Values. Frequent and infrequent words were sometimes, but not always, synonymous. We paired these words, matching the first frequent with the first infrequent word, and so on, through the two lists. Position of presentation within pairs was determined by coin flip. These 30 pairs of words were presented to 34 freshman introductory psychology students, none

of whom had taken part in any previous psychological experiments. Ss were told to "encircle the most pleasantly toned word of each pair." In 26 of the word pairs, the more frequent word was chosen by the majority of the Ss as the most pleasantly toned. (The 4 exceptions, in which the least frequent word was chosen as the more pleasantly toned, were the word pairs limousine-automobile, economics-assets, orchestra-ensemble, and celestial-heavenly.) A sign test (Guilford, 1956, p. 248) indicates that this preference for the more frequent word in each pair could occur by chance less than one time in a hundred. Again, the more frequent word is rated as the better word.

In the experiment discussed below we attempted to determine whether frequency and goodness were related when nonsense syllables were used as stimulus materials.

EXPERIMENT *III*

Twenty-two Ss rated two separate visually represented lists of nonsense syllables for goodness, as measured by the semantic differential. An interval of one week separated the ratings of the two lists. Each list consisted of eight 100%, eight 47–53%, and eight 0% association value (Glaze, 1928) nonsense syllables in random order. Syllables were selected at random from within each block of ten Glaze syllables as listed in the *Handbook of Experimental Psychology* (Stevens, 1951, pp. 540–546) at each of the association values used. Then the eight syllables used in each list at each association level were drawn from this pool of randomly selected syllables. We believed that if frequency of exposure was related to goodness, then the higher the association value of the syllable, the better the syllable should be rated. This seemed likely, since the association value of nonsense syllables appears to be determined largely by the frequency of occurrence of the letter combinations in meaningful words (Underwood, 1959). Table 1, showing two sets of syllables and their mean ratings of goodness, indicates this to be the case.

A Mann-Whitney (1947) test of the significance of differences between syllables of 100% and 47–53% association values in List 1 indicates that the 100% list is rated as somewhat better ($P < .10$). The difference in goodness between 47–53% and 0% syllables is significant ($P < .01$); Mann-Whitney tests of List 2 show the 100% and the 47–53% list to differ in goodness ($P < .01$); and the 47–53% list and the 0% list to differ significantly ($P < .05$) as well.

Just as the goodness and the frequency of meaningful words in the English language are related to one another, so also is goodness related to the association value of nonsense syllables; the higher the association value, the better the syllable.

Our data indicate that value and frequency are related. We have moved at least somewhat beyond the empirical fact that word frequency is related to visual duration threshold. We know something else about the stimulus qualities of frequent as opposed to infrequent words; frequent words are not only more frequent but are better as well. Our second question then becomes relevant. Does a manipulation of frequency cause systematic variation in value or do differences in value produce differences in word frequency, or does the independent–dependent status of each of these variables vary depending on the experimental procedures used? Experiment IV bears upon this question.

EXPERIMENT *IV*

Fourteen Ss rated the goodness of twenty nonsense words. These words were from the list of words used by Solomon and Postman (1952) in their study of the effect of "built in" frequency on visual duration threshold. The words used were: JANDARA, AFWORBU, BIWOJNI, NANSOMA, ENANWAL, IKTITAK, SARICIK, ZABULON, CIVADRA, LOKANTA, KADIRGA, ADAFNAW, BORULCE, NIJARON,

TABLE 1 Ratings of Nonsense Syllables of Differing Association Values on the Good–Bad Dimension of the Semantic Differential

100% SYLLA-BLES	RATING	47–53% SYLLA-BLES	RATING	0% SYLLA-BLES	RATING
List 1					
BUL	4.72	WOB	4.59	ZEQ	4.91
FES	3.41	KAW	4.33	WUH	4.48
HON	2.11	DUX	4.33	XIW	5.36
JIN	2.98	BOZ	4.00	WUQ	5.26
RAC	3.98	VOK	3.46	QIH	4.87
ROV	3.74	GEY	2.93	GUV	4.39
SUR	2.72	TIZ	3.52	VEC	3.91
WIL	2.46	VOZ	4.30	XUR	5.28
List 2					
DUL	4.27	BEK	3.46	YUF	4.46
BAL	2.35	PIJ	5.17	QIF	4.44
LOV	1.44	WEP	4.71	ZUK	5.04
SAR	3.23	RIQ	4.46	ZIF	4.06
LIK	2.50	YAF	3.96	XAD	4.85
HAV	2.35	LUB	4.15	XUC	5.35
WAT	3.46	GOW	3.75	QUJ	5.00
ROV	3.54	RUV	3.83	GUQ	5.98

ENSHIMI, INDULAM, TAVHANE, UDIBNON, DILIKLI, and MECBURI. Mean goodness scores were obtained. One week later each S was tested individually. When the S entered the experimental room he was given the following instructions (from Solomon & Postman, 1952):

> This is an experiment concerning the effectiveness of repetition in learning to pronounce strange words correctly. It has a direct bearing on the problem of reading words in a foreign language, as compared to hearing the words spoken. In addition, we are interested in knowing whether the relative effectiveness of the two kinds of learning methods depends on general reading ability.
>
> We are going to give you a deck of cards. On each card is printed a strange word. We would like you to look at each card carefully and then pronounce the word in the way it would be pronounced if it were a word in the English language. Proceed steadily from card to card, turning over each one after you have finished with it. Go right through the deck and then stop unless you have serious doubts about your pronunciations.

The experimenter (E) handed the S a pack of 90 3″ × 5″ cards. In this pack were the words listed above. The first five words above were presented 10 times apiece, the next five, 5 times apiece, the next five, 2 times apiece, and the last five, once each. The cards were shuffled thoroughly after each S completed this task, so that they were in a relatively random order.

All responses were taped in order to lend realism to the expressed purpose of this new situation. Since Ss had participated in another experiment on the pronounceability of words, it seems likely that (although the Ss had seen the words before while rating them on the semantic differential) they were misled as to the purpose of this experiment. Each S rated the nonsense words a second time following this pronounceability test.

Figure 1 indicates the mean preexposure and postexposure ratings for words of each frequency of exposure. While the differences between ratings prior to exposure were not significant, a Kruskal and Wallis H test (1952) shows that words of differing frequencies of exposure do differ significantly in the postexposure test ($P < .01$, $H = 7.83$).

In this experimental situation a manipulation of word frequency alters Ss' evaluations of word goodness. One can, however, think of instances where the reverse might well occur. The most obvious example of this is in verbal conditioning, where the differential reinforcement of a class of words produces systematic variation in the frequency with which this class of words is emitted.

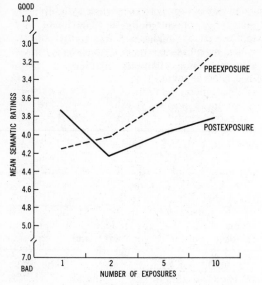

FIGURE 1. Ratings of nonsense words before and after word frequency was manipulated.

evident—there is a relation between word frequency and Ss' ratings of word goodness. Since this is so, our third question also becomes relevant. Since value and frequency are generally related, it became necessary to experiment with samples of words matched in frequency, varying in goodness, plus samples of words varying in frequency, matched in goodness, in order to separate out the influence of value and of frequency on visual duration threshold. This was attempted in Experiment V.

EXPERIMENT V

We had various groups of Ss rate the goodness of a large number of words on the semantic differential. These groups rated 60 words of a Thorndike-Lorge G count of 12, 13, or 14, three random samples of 50 words each (described in Experiment I), and 39 words, one sample 30 words plus 9 words which happened to appear on the other lists, from Jenkins' semantic atlas. From these words, and from Jenkins' atlas, we selected 17 pairs of words matched in frequency, varying in goodness, and 17 pairs of words matched in goodness, varying in frequency. (Some words among those matched in goodness were rated by Jenkins' Ss and by our own. Although the rank

We would suspect that in this case frequency of emission (and hence of reinforcement) alters the affective quality of the words. Reinforcement might then produce further variation of frequency.

No matter whether frequency of exposure alters value or vice versa, or both, one thing is

TABLE 2   Words Used in the Tachistoscopic Experiment

	WORDS OF MATCHED GOODNESS						WORDS OF MATCHED FREQUENCY					
	Frequent			Infrequent			Good			Bad		
Word	SD Rating	Threshold	Word	SD Rating	Threshold	Word	G Count	Threshold	Word	G Count	Threshold
Sample 1											
Think	2.34	.0373	Income	2.52	.0500	Rally	12	.1092	Stammer	12	.1538
Butter	1.97	.0692	Caress	1.97	.1085	Glisten	13	.0777	Corrupt	12	.0985
Doctor	1.60	.0369	Ivory	1.68	.0262	Prosper	13	.1046	Defect	14	.0815
Health	1.97	.0492	Piano	1.97	.0546	Ivory	13	.0262	Hinder	13	.0969
Sleep	2.22	.0362	Radiant	2.08	.0662	Ginger	13	.0446	Wretch	12	.1285
Sweet	1.93	.0631	Patriot	1.90	.0992	Alert	14	.0392	Sneer	12	.0785
Mother	1.73	.0315	Vision	1.57	.0546	Deputy	13	.0446	Scandal	13	.1123
House	2.46	.0323	Agile	2.74	.0623	Vehicle	13	.0492	Dismal	13	.1162
Flower	1.87	.0369	Bible	1.87	.0462	Caress	12	.1085	Penalty	13	.0469
Sample 2											
Mountain	2.73	.0687	Bodice	2.74	.0965	Bodice	2	.0965	Slime	4	.0713
Water	2.43	.0217	Dough	2.47	.0757	Candy	32	.0409	Beggar	29	.1087
Window	2.68	.0400	Gradual	2.63	.0965	Engine	A	.0565	Bitter	A	.1704
Green	2.93	.0296	Elegant	3.00	.0852	Brave	A	.0739	Anger	A	.0417
Smooth	2.57	.0522	Zenith	2.62	.0330	Statue	32	.0748	Divorce	29	.0948
Father	2.36	.0800	Jelly	2.49	.0800	Cushion	21	.0900	Inferior	19	.1948
Pretty	2.13	.0661	Refresh	2.09	.0661	Garment	40	.1043	Grief	45	.0687
Street	2.77	.0496	Lenient	2.77	.1522	Church	AA	.0530	Danger	AA	.0583

order correlation of goodness ratings between our own and Jenkins' sample of Ss was +.98, for a group of 30 of these words, there was some variation in ratings between the two samples. Whenever this occurred, we used the mean goodness rating assigned by our Ss.) The first 9 words from each list were presented to the first group of 26 Ss; the last 8 to a second group of 23 Ss. The four lists of words, divided as they were presented to two sample populations, are presented in Table 2.

The words were put on slides in the form of bold faced capital letters. The words were presented to Ss by means of a Revere 888 tachistoscope. Each S sat 18 feet from the screen on which the words were projected. The testing room was fully illuminated while the tachistoscope was used at the smallest possible lens opening. The ratio of room illumination to screen illumination was 1:1.08. The words were presented in random order with the order remaining constant in all presentations to any specific S but with the order varying between Ss. A modified method of limits was used in which each of the 36 words was presented once at each of the following speeds: 1/100, 1/50, 1/25, 1/5, 1/2, and 1 second. Under the conditions of presentation used in this experiment, only one word was recognized at 1/100 of a second while all words were recognized at 1 second.

Each S's mean visual duration threshold for frequent as opposed to infrequent and good as opposed to bad words was obtained. The Ss in the first sample ($N = 26$), exposed to the first group of words, differed significantly in mean thresholds for good vs. bad words ($t = 3.56$, $P < .01$, using the formula for correlated data), with good words reported at lower thresholds. These Ss also differed in mean thresholds for frequent vs. infrequent words ($t = 2.33$, $P < .05$), with frequent words reported at lower thresholds. The Ss in the second sample ($N = 23$), exposed to the second group of words, differed significantly in mean thresholds for good vs. bad words ($t = 3.25$, $P < .01$), with good words reported at lower thresholds, and in threshold for frequent vs. infrequent words ($t = 3.82$, $P < .01$), with frequent words reported at lower thresholds.

DISCUSSION

We attempted to obtain data relevant to three specific questions. Let us look at these questions, along with the relevant data.

1. Is value related, in a general sense, to word frequency? Our data is unequivocally affirmative. Whether dealing with samples of words in the English language, with frequent vs. infrequent words in various Allport-Vernon value areas, or with nonsense syllables, frequency, as measured by the Thorndike-Lorge tables and by association value, and positive value, as measured by the good–bad scale of semantic differential, are significantly related in a general sense.

2. If this general relation exists, does it exist because more positively valued words are used more frequently or because one increases positive value merely by increasing frequency? We found that a manipulation of frequency produces systematic variation in Ss' ratings of the goodness of words. It seems highly probable, however, that the reverse may also be true—that by increasing the goodness of words, one also increases frequency. At this point it seems likely that the independent-dependent relation between goodness and frequency would depend on the experimental situation. We would not hazard a guess as to the effect of each on the other in general speech, although a relation between frequency and goodness has been shown to exist.

The data gathered in the first three experiments suggest that other attributes of the stimulus vary systematically as one varies frequency. Perhaps this is true for other forms of learning also. The fourth experiment would suggest the possibility that a manipulation of the frequency of occurrence of a stimulus and a contiguous response, in itself and without any regard to drive reduction, changes the reinforcing qualities of the stimulus. Perhaps we should look beyond the influence of frequency on response probability and ask *why* frequency changes response probability. Is it the difference in association value (and hence, in frequency of occurrence) that causes 100% association value syllables to be learned more rapidly than 0% syllables? Or is it the variation in affective quality accompanying differing frequencies of occurrence? Since the relation beween goodness and frequency is not perfect, one can obtain syllables that vary from 0 to 100% in association value, yet are equal in semantic rating—this should provide a test for our question.

These results seem to have considerable social consequence. If word frequency and word goodness are related, and if a manipulation of the frequency of occurrence of a word produces systematic variation in word value, then one wonders whether ideas and personal values are manipulable in the same fashion. If so, then perhaps those elements of society that believe in censorship would find support in these experiments for one of their major assumptions, viz., that frequent exposure to an idea or a set of behaviors —violence, drinking alcoholic beverages, or what have you—lessens the "evil" associated with the idea of behavior. The validity of their second major assumption—that if we make a thing evil enough, people won't do this thing—is, of course, a very different problem.

If the more frequent becomes demonstrably better merely because it is more frequent, one can well understand the values of advertising. If it is generally true that the most frequent words in the English language are also the most good, the logical conclusion that this would lead to is that ads would be more effective if written at an even lower vocabulary level than is currently used. "Oh, brave new world. . . ."

3. If value and frequency are related, what are the influences of each on visual duration threshold when the other variable is held constant? Words equal in frequency, varying in value, are correctly reported by *S*s at different mean thresholds, with good words being correctly identified at significantly lower thresholds than are bad words. Words equal in goodness, varying in frequency, are reported by *S*s at different mean thresholds, with frequent words being correctly identified at significantly lower thresholds.

While it has been generally accepted that values have some secondary effect on visual duration thresholds, it is also generally accepted that the influence of values on threshold is small, producing idiosyncratic variations in frequency and hence influencing thresholds in this way. Our results indicate that values influence threshold even when frequency of exposure is held constant, and that this influence is approximately equal to that of frequency with value held constant, using these lists of words.

Since word goodness, independent from frequency, does significantly influence visual duration threshold, we are left with the problem of "Why?" The terms "perceptual selectivity" and "perceptual defense" are descriptive, not explanatory. We have no answers here, although we would like to discuss several possible explanations.

One interpretation of the fact that good words are perceived at lower threshold than bad words of the same frequency might be called the "simple" guess theory. Good words appear to be about twice as common as bad words in the English language. Specific good words are likely to be more frequently used than specific bad words. It seems, then, that good words occur between three and four times as frequently as bad words in terms of usage. Even though the frequency of occurrence of the stimuli are equaled, by matching good and bad words for Thorndike-Lorge frequency, response probabilities probably are still not equal. If an *S* sees a word in a tachistoscope but identifies only a "g—— d——" he is probably three or four times more likely, on the basis of responses made in the past, to fill in the gaps with a good word, such as "gradual," rather than a bad word, such as "goudge." This simple guess explanation may be partially correct but is not too satisfying to us, since an examination of our *S*s' responses to words on the good–bad lists indicates that there seems to be a rather

strong likelihood that when *S*s guess at but miss a bad word, they respond with another bad word —incorrect but still bad, while when they respond incorrectly to the tachistoscope presentation of a good word, the incorrect response is usually another good word. This finding runs contrary to the idea that perceptual defense is a significant variable but also suggests that something more systematic than mere guessing is involved in errors and in correct responses to tachistoscopically presented words.

A second explanation for the differences in *S*s' mean visual duration thresholds might be called the "complex" guess theory. This explanation is derived from Bruner and Postman's (1949) hypotheses theory of perception and cognition. According to Postman (1951) hypotheses are, "in the most general sense, expectancies or predispositions of the organism which serve to select, organize, and transform the stimulus information that comes from the environment" (p. 249). The strength or availability of certain hypotheses is stronger than that of others. This strength is a function of the following factors: frequency of past confirmation of the hypothesis, number of alternative hypotheses, motivational relevance, and cognitive support. The first two factors—frequency of past confirmation and number of alternative hypotheses—fit well into the simple guess theory, while the last factor, that of cognitive support, may not be relevant to this discussion. The factor of motivational relevance might possibly, however, produce differential predictions between the two explanatory devices that we have labeled simple and complex guessing. As Postman (1951) puts it: "The stronger the motivational support for a given hypothesis, the less of appropriate information is required to confirm it" (p. 255). We would limit this statement somewhat by tying it only to the effect of reward or reinforcement on the number of cues required for the confirmation of a hypothesis. It may be that the differential reinforcement of various stimuli causes those stimuli (as well as those responses) that have most frequently led to reinforcement in the past to be more readily observable or available in the present. The availability of a specific response may well depend on the frequency that this response has been rewarded in the past—but perhaps because that aspect of the stimulus situation that has called forth the rewarded response in the past has become more salient—has become more of a "figure" as opposed to the other stimuli becoming more like the "ground." To paraphrase our quotation from Postman given above: The more reinforcing or rewarding a word is, the less cues are needed for the recognition of this word. We are advancing the proposition that reinforcement not only influences the probability that a given response will be emitted, but also that reinforcement causes that aspect of the stimulus situation that is salient at the time that the rewarded response is made to become more likely to be salient at the next presentation of the stimulus. If this is true, then even if word frequencies of good and bad words are equal and even if habitual modes of response (such as guessing good words) are controlled, the stimulus qualities of rewarding or reinforcing words would be such that less information is needed before the word is correctly recognized than would be the case for words which were presented with equal frequency but were not equally reinforcing. Something that might be called perceptual sensitivity might then be said to exist. This sensitivity would not, however, be a unique perceptual process, but would instead depend on those old standbys in all forms of learning: frequency and reinforcement, a little intermingled to be sure, but still observably present.

We have no way of testing out the "why" question with these data, although the types of wrong guesses made in our study incline us away from the simple guess theory. We believe that the data presented in this study are valuable chiefly in reviving the concept of perceptual selectivity, not in solving the problem of why what is called perceptual selectivity exists. By systematically varying frequency of exposure and frequency of reinforcement and nonreinforcement of nonsense syllables in future experiments, we hope to eventually be able to deal with the question of why good words are perceived at lower mean thresholds than are bad words.

SUMMARY

Three positions may be taken concerning the relation between word value and word frequency, and the relation of each of these to visual duration threshold. Two of these points of view would suggest a general relation to exist between word frequency and word value. Three experiments demonstrate the existence of this relationship. The more frequent a word or a nonsense syllable occurs in the English language, the better it is likely to be rated on the good–bad scale of the semantic differential. Since this relation does exist, we attempted to test out, in Experiment 4, one possible explanation of *why* the relation exists. A manipulation of the frequency of nonsense words produces systematic variation in the rated goodness of these nonsense words. Words that are frequent are also very likely to be rated as good. Hence, to separate out the influence of word value and of word frequency on visual duration threshold, we tachistoscopically presented lists of words matched in frequency, varying in goodness; matched in goodness, varying in frequency. Subjects reported the good

words at significantly lower thresholds than the matched bad words; the frequent words at significantly lower thresholds than matched infrequent words. Both frequency and value appear to operate in producing differential visual duration thresholds for words. Possible explanations and certain implications of these findings were discussed.

REFERENCES

BRUNER, J. S., & POSTMAN, L. Perception, cognition, and behavior. *J. Pers.,* 1949, **18,** 12–31.

GLAZE, J. A. The association value of nonsense syllables. *J. genet. Psychol.,* 1928, **35,** 255–267.

GUILFORD, J. P. *Fundamental statistics in psychology and education.* (3rd ed.) New York: McGraw-Hill, 1956.

JENKINS, J. J., RUSSELL, W. A., & SUCI, G. J. An atlas of semantic profiles of 360 words. *Amer. J. Psychol.,* 1958, **71,** 688–699.

KRUSKAL, W. H., & WALLIS, W. A. Use of ranks in one criterion variance analysis. *J. Amer. Statist. Ass.,* 1952, **47,** 583–621.

MANN, H. B., & WHITNEY, D. R. On a test of whether one of two random variables is stochastically larger than the other. *Ann. math. Statist.,* 1947, **18,** 50–60.

POSTMAN, L. Towards a general theory of cognition. In J. H. Rohrer & M. Sherif (Eds.), *Social psychology at the crossroads.* New York: Harper, 1951. Pp. 242–272.

POSTMAN, L. The experimental analyses of motivational factors in perception. In J. S. Brown (Ed.), *Current theory and research in motivation.* Lincoln: Univer. Nebraska Press, 1953. Pp. 59–108.

POSTMAN, L., & SCHNEIDER, B. H. Personal values, visual recognition, and recall. *Psychol. Rev.,* 1951, **58,** 271–284.

SOLOMON, R. L., & HOWES, D. H. Word frequency, word value, and visual duration thresholds. *Psychol. Rev.,* 1951, **58,** 256–270.

SOLOMON, R. L., & POSTMAN, L. Usage as a determinant of visual duration thresholds of words. *J. exp. Psychol.,* 1952, **43,** 195–201.

STEVENS, S. S. (Ed.) *Handbook of experimental psychology.* New York: Wiley, 1951.

THORNDIKE, E. L., & LORGE, I. *The teacher's word book of 30,000 words.* New York: Bureau of Publications, Teachers College, 1944.

UNDERWOOD, B. J. Verbal learning and the educative process. *Harvard educ. Rev.,* 1959, **29,** 107–117.

POSTSCRIPT

Stricker[a] has noted that the experiments reported above use the semantic differential, which measures

---

[a] G. Stricker. Word values, word frequency, and visual duration thresholds. *Psychol. Rev.,* 1961, **68,** 420–422.

value by a method different from earlier studies. Generally these earlier investigations used a multiple-choice procedure: the perceiver chose the word he most preferred in each set of words presented to him. While it is quite true that this earlier procedure differs from the semantic differential method described in our introduction, the experimenters point out that the value of a word as measured in the earlier investigations is inextricably associated with the frequency of experience with that word. Their use of the semantic differential enabled them to control the effects of "value," so that effects on the visual duration threshold due solely to frequency could be assessed.[b]

The experiments described have demonstrated that (*1*) the more frequently a word occurs in the English language, the more positively it is valued, (*2*) when words are of equal frequency but differ in value, the more highly valued ones are perceived at a lower threshold, and (*3*) when words are of equal value but different in frequency, the frequent words are perceived at a lower threshold.

The tentative nature of scientific conclusions is illustrated by an experiment carried out subsequently to those which have just been described. Another characteristic of words that is frequently stressed in experimentation is their meaningfulness or "association" value. The association value of a word is determined by presenting it to a subject and asking him to report, in a fixed time period, other words that are suggested by the stimulus word. In an experiment using this variable, the meaningfulness of a word was found to be correlated with its frequency, and when meaningfulness was controlled, frequency did *not* affect visual thresholds.[c] Good–bad distinctions, however, continued to affect recognition thresholds even when meaningfulness was controlled. The investigators concluded that value, as measured by the semantic differential, and meaningfulness, as measured by word association, significantly affect recognition thresholds, but that frequency has little effect on thresholds when these other variables are controlled.

SUBLIMINAL STIMULATION: AN OVERVIEW*

The idea that something that cannot be perceived can yet be known and responded to has always fascinated man. Ancient beliefs in the occult illustrate this. Twentieth-century examples include the persistent belief in extrasensory perception by a few psychologists and many laymen and the surge of interest in *subliminal perception* in the past ten or fifteen years. The term *subliminal* comes from *limen*, meaning threshold. Any stimulus can be varied in intensity or duration to the point where it is so weak or so brief that it cannot be perceived. When this occurs, it is said to be subliminal. If a person gives an emotional or other indirect response to a subliminal stimulus, that phenomenon is referred to as subliminal perception. The phrase subliminal perception is really a contradiction in terms, since subliminal refers to stimuli that cannot be perceived, and perception implies response to a stimulus. But subliminal perception has come into common use to refer to a situation where a person gives an emotional or other indirect response to a subliminal stimulus. As with the previous selection, in the present article McConnell, Cutler, and McNeil clear up some of the confusion resulting from the use of inadequate experimental methods and from misunderstandings concerning the nature of perception and the threshold concept.

7.

Subliminal Stimulation: An Overview

JAMES V. McCONNELL
RICHARD L. CUTLER
ELTON B. McNEIL
UNIVERSITY OF MICHIGAN

Seldom has anything in psychology caused such an immediate and widespread stir as the recent claim that the presentation of certain stimuli below the level of conscious awareness can influence people's behavior in a significant way. The controversy was precipitated primarily by a commercial firm which claimed that the subliminal presentation of the words "Eat Popcorn" and "Drink Coca-Cola" fantastically stimulated the respective sales of these products among the motion picture audiences who received the stimulation. Despite the fact that detailed reports of the experiment have not been made directly available in any published form, this technique was seized upon as the newest of the "new look" promises of the application of psychology to advertising. While such claims and demonstrations will be considered in greater detail below, it is important to note here that they have given rise to a series

[b] R. C. Johnson, G. Frincke, & Lea Martin. Meaningfulness, frequency, and affective character of words as related to visual duration thresholds. *Canadian J. Psychol.*, 1961, **15**, 199–204.
* The selection following the editorial introduction is reprinted from "Subliminal stimulation: An overview," *American Psychologist*, 1958, **13**, 229–242, by permission of the authors and the American Psychological Association.

[c] Ibid.

of charges and countercharges, the effects of which have reached the United States Congress and the Federal Communications Commission (**7, 117**).

Rarely does a day pass without a statement in the public press relating to the Utopian promise or the 1984 threat of the technique (**8, 17, 29, 37, 42, 45, 118, 132**). Since the process of choosing up sides promises to continue unabated, it appears wise to provide the potential combatants with a more factual basis for arriving at their positions than presently seems available. Meanwhile, the present writers have cautiously sought to avoid aligning themselves behind either of the barricades.

Obviously, the notion that one may influence the behavior of another individual without the individual's knowing about it is a fascinating one. It is of extreme interest, not only to psychologists and advertisers, but also to politicians, psychiatrists, passionate young men, and others, whose motives would be considered more or less sacred by the larger society. Equally obvious is the need for a clarification of the issues surrounding the application of subliminal perception. This clarification must involve the assessment of available scientific evidence, the answering of a series of technical questions, and the examination of what, if any, levels of behavior may indeed be influenced. Finally, a series of extremely complex ethical issues needs to be explored. It is the purpose of the present paper to undertake this task, in the hope of providing information upon which possible decisions involving its application may be based.

RECENT HISTORY OF THE TECHNIQUE

The custom of providing a chronological review of the literature will be violated in this paper, inasmuch as three separate threads of investigation seem worth tracing: (*a*) the recent demonstrations by advertisers which first aroused large-scale public interest in subliminal perception, (*b*) systematic research by psychologists relating directly to the influencing of behavior without the individual's awareness that he is being influenced, and (*c*) psychological research concerned primarily with the influence of inner states of the organism upon the threshold for conscious recognition of certain stimuli.

Recent advertising demonstrations

While the advertising possibilities of subliminal stimulation were recognized by Hollingworth (**59**) as early as 1913, the intensive work in its application to this area has been carried out within the past two years. In 1956, BBC-TV, in conjunction with one of its regular broadcasts, trans-

mitted the message "Pirie Breaks World Record" at a speed assumed to be subliminal (**85**). At the conclusion of the regular program, viewers were asked to report whether they had noticed "anything unusual" about the program. While no reliable statistical data are available, it seems possible that those few viewers responding to the message possessed sufficiently low thresholds so that for them the message was supraliminal.

A demonstration by the commercial enterprise which has been most vocal in its claims for the advertising promise of the technique consisted of projecting, during alternate periods, the words "Eat Popcorn" and "Drink Coca-Cola" during the regular presentation of a motion picture program. As a result of this stimulation, reports contend,[1] popcorn sales rose more than 50% and Coca-Cola sales 18%, as compared to a "previous period." Despite the likelihood of serious methodological and technical defects (exposure time was reported as 1/3,000 sec., far faster than any previously reported stimulation), this demonstration has been the one which has caused the most stir in both the fields of advertising and psychology. There were no reports, however, of even the most rudimentary scientific precautions, such as adequate controls, provision for replication, etc., which leaves the skeptical scientist in a poor position to make any judgment about the validity of the study.

In a later demonstration for the press, technical difficulties permitted the viewers to become consciously aware of the fact that they were being stimulated. Although described as a purposeful and prearranged part of the demonstration, it left many of the reporters present unconvinced that the technical difficulties inherent in the technique have been surmounted.

The FCC, turning its attention to the problem, has reported that one TV station (WTWO, Bangor, Maine) has experimented with the transmission of public service announcements at subliminal levels, with "negative results" (**117**).

The uncontrolled and unsystematic nature of the demonstrations reported above makes very difficult the task of reaching a trustworthy conclusion about the effectiveness of subliminal stimulation in advertising. Whether the technique represents a promising means of communicating with the individual at a level of his unconsciousness or whether it reflects only the hyperenthusiasm of an entrepreneurial group remain unanswered questions.

Research on behavior without awareness

In the hope of providing a more substantial foundation upon which to base judgments of the

---

[1] The essential facts of this study have not been reported in any journal. The discussion of this experiment and the findings reported by the commercial enterprise responsible for the study is based on reports in several general news accounts appearing in the popular press (**7, 8, 16, 17,** etc.)

validity of advertising claims for subliminal stimulation, a systematic review of relevant scientific work was undertaken. While we believe that our review was comprehensive, we have decided not to provide an extensive critical discussion of the various studies, choosing instead to present summative statements and conclusions based upon what seems to be sufficient evidence and consensus in the literature.[2]

The work of experimental psychologists in subliminal stimulation dates from Suslowa (119) in 1863, as reported by Baker (5). Suslowa's experiments concerned the effect of electrical stimulation upon subjects' ability to make two-point threshold discriminations. He found that, even when the intensity of the electrical stimulation was so low that the subjects were not aware of its presence, their ability to discriminate one- from two-point stimulation was somewhat reduced.

In 1884, Peirce and Jastrow (94) were able to show that subjects could discriminate differences between weights significantly better than chance would allow, even though the differences were so small they had no confidence whatsoever in their judgments.

Numerous experimenters have relied upon this criterion of "zero confidence" to establish that discrimination of stimuli presented below the level of conscious awareness is possible. For example, Sidis (107) showed that subjects could reliably distinguish letters from numbers, even when the stimuli were presented at such a distance from them that the subjects thought they were relying on pure guesswork for their judgments.

In what was essentially a replication of Sidis' research, Stroh, Shaw, and Washburn (116) found evidence to support his conclusions. They found similar results when auditory stimuli (whispers) were presented at a distance such that the subjects were not consciously aware that they were hearing anything.

Several experiments have provided further support for Peirce and Jastrow's initial conclusions (44, 127). Baker (5) found subjects able to discriminate diagonal from vertical crossed lines, and a dot-dash from a dash-dot auditory pattern. Miller (88) presented five geometric figures at four different levels of intensity below the threshold and found that, while subjects could discriminate which was being presented a significant proportion of the time, their ability to discriminate was reduced as the intensity of stimulation was further reduced. More recently, a series of studies by Blackwell (11) has shown that subjects can reliably identify during which of four time periods a subliminal spot of light is presented upon a homogeneous field. Blackwell, however, stresses that reliability of discrimination decreases

as the intensity of the stimulus is further lowered. Several other supporting studies are available (28, 97, 130) which show essentially the same results, namely, that even when subjects have zero confidence in their judgments, they can discriminate reliably (though not perfectly) between stimuli.

In his review, Adams (1) points out certain general weaknesses inherent in studies of this type, but agrees with the present authors that discrimination can occur under certain circumstances. However, it is interesting to note that, in nearly all studies reporting relevant data, the reliability of the subjects' judgments increases directly with the intensity of the stimuli. If a valid extrapolation can be drawn from this finding, it would be that accuracy of perception increases as the stimulation approaches a supraliminal level.

A second series of studies has involved presenting subjects with variations of the Mueller-Lyer illusion, in which the angular lines have differed, subliminally, in hue or brightness from the background. The first of these studies, reported by Dunlap in 1909 (36), gave clear evidence that the subjects were influenced in their judgments of line length, even though they could not "see" the angular lines. Several replications of this study have been carried out, and while at least three have found partial support for Dunlap's conclusions (14, 59, 86), others have failed to find the phenomenon (123). In another experiment conducted by Sidis in 1898 (107) subjects asked to fixate on a number series in the center of a card, and then asked to pick a number from this series, systematically chose that number which was written in the periphery of the card, even though they were not consciously aware of its presence. Coover (28) in 1917 showed essentially the same results by asking subjects to pick a number at random while they were fixating on a letter in the upper right portion of a card. He found that subjects tended to pick the number printed in the lower left of the card, even though they did not *usually* know it was there. In similar experiments, Collier (27) and Perky (95) showed that subjects could be made to produce drawings, even though they were not aware that they were being influenced in their actions. While these studies are not unequivocal in their findings, nor generally rigorous in their methodology, they too seem to support the contention that behavior of a sort can be influenced by subliminal means. However, they require cautious interpretation, since the degree of the subject's attention to the stimuli seems clearly to be a factor. Further, as contrasted to those studies where the subject is actually aware in advance of at least the general nature of the stimulation, these studies reveal a somewhat less pronounced effect of subliminal stimulation upon the subject's behavior.

---

[2] The reader who wishes a more complete technical critique of studies in the field is referred to reviews by Adams (1), Collier (27), Coover (28), Lazarus and McCleary (76), and Miller (90).

While the studies reported above seem to indicate that discrimination without awareness may occur, it may reasonably be asked whether stimulation below the level of conscious awareness can produce any but the most simple modifications in behavior. A series of studies (**24, 26, 73, 109**), beginning with Newhall and Sears in 1933 (**92**), have attempted to show that it is possible to condition subjects to subliminal stimuli. Newhall and Sears found it possible to establish a weak and unstable conditioned response to light presented subliminally, when the light had been previously paired with shock. Baker (**6**) in 1938 reported the successful conditioning of the pupillary reflex to a subliminal auditory stimulus, but later experimenters have failed to replicate his results (**57, 128**). In a now classic experiment, McCleary and Lazarus (**79**) found that nonsense syllables which had previously been associated with shock produced a greater psychogalvanic reflex when presented tachistoscopically at subliminal speeds than did nonshock syllables. Deiter (**34**) confirmed the McCleary and Lazarus findings and showed further that, when verbal instructions were substituted for the shock, no such differences were produced. Bach and Klein (**4**) have recently reported that they were able to influence subjects' judgments of whether the line drawing of a face (essentially neutral in its emotional expression) was "angry" or "happy" by projecting the appropriate words at subliminal speeds upon the drawing.

A series of related studies (**58, 65, 89, 99, 105, 121, 122**) have shown that, even when the subject is not aware that any cue is being given, certain responses can be learned or strengthened during the experimental process. For example, Cohen, Kalish, Thurston, and Cohen (**25**) showed that, when the experimenter said "right" to any sentence which the subject started with "I" or "We," the number of such sentences increased significantly. Klein (**69**) was able to produce both conditioning and extinction without awareness, using the Cohen et al. technique.

Several experimenters have used subliminal or "unnoticed" reward-punishment techniques to modify subjects' responses in a variety of situations, including free or chained association tasks, performance on personality tests, and interview elicited conversation (**35, 41, 50, 56, 72, 78, 93, 120, 125, 126**). Typical is the work of Greenspoon (**48**), who reinforced the use of plural nouns by saying "mm-humm" after each plural mentioned by the subject. He found that, even though none of his subjects could verbalize the relationship between their response and his reinforcement, their use of plural nouns doubled. Sidowski (**108**) demonstrated essentially the same

thing using a light, of which the subject was only peripherally aware, as a reinforcer for the use of plural words. Weiss (**129**), however, failed to find any increase in the frequency of "living things" responses, using a right-wrong reinforcement to free associations by the subjects.

This evidence suggests that subjects may either (*a*) "learn" certain subliminally presented stimuli or (*b*) make use of subliminal reinforcers either to learn or strengthen a previously learned response. Again, the critical observations of Adams (**1**) and the introduction of other possible explanations by Bricker and Chapanis (**15**) make necessary a cautious interpretation of these results.

Effects of inner states upon thresholds

Whatever the possibility that subliminal stimulation may significantly alter behavior, there is excellent evidence that certain inner states of the organism, as well as externally induced conditions, may significantly alter the recognition threshold of the individual. This, of course, has important implications for the susceptibility of the individual to the effects of subliminal stimulation. It is well known that physiological factors, such as fatigue, visual acuity, or satiation, may change the threshold of an individual for various kinds of stimuli.

Recent evidence has accumulated to show that, in addition to these physiological factors, certain "psychological states," such as psychological need, value, conflict, and defense, may also significantly influence thresholds, as well as other aspects of the perceptual process. Early work in this area is reported by Sanford (**102, 103**) who showed that subjects who had been deprived of food were more prone to produce "food-relevant" responses to a series of ambiguous stimuli. McClelland and Atkinson (**80**) showed that levels of the hunger drive were systematically related to the ease with which food responses were made when no words were presented on the screen.

While a complete review of the experimental work on "perceptual defense" and "selective vigilance" would take us too far afield, it seems wise to indicate, by example, some of the inner state factors which allegedly produce variations in recognition threshold. Bruner and Postman (**19, 20, 21**) and Bruner and Goodman (**18**) were able to show that such factors as symbolic value, need, tension and tension release, and emotional selectivity were important in the perceptual process. Ansbacher (**3**) had earlier demonstrated that the perception of numerosity was significantly affected by the monetary value of the stimuli. Rees and Israel (**101**) called attention to the fact that the mental set of the organism was an important factor in the perceptual process. Beams and Thompson (**9**) showed that emotional factors were important determiners of the perception of the magnitude of need-relevant objects. Other studies bearing upon the issue of inner state determiners of perception are reported by Carter and Schooler (**23**), Cowen and Beier (**31, 32**), and Levine, Chein, and Murphy (**77**).

More specifically related to the issue of altered recognition thresholds is a study by McGinnies (**82**) in which he demonstrated that emotionally toned words had generally higher thresholds than neutral words. Blum (**13**) has shown that subjects tend to be less likely to choose conflict-relevant stimuli from a group presented at subliminal speeds than to choose neutral stimuli. Lazarus, Ericksen, and Fonda (**75**) have shown that personality factors are at least in part determiners of the recognition threshold for classes of auditory stimuli. Reece (**100**) showed that the association of shock with certain stimuli had the effect of raising the recognition threshold for those stimuli.

While many writers have contended that the variations in threshold can be accounted for more parsimoniously than by introducing "motivational" factors such as need and value (**60, 61, 111**), and while the issue of the degree to which need states influence perception is still unresolved (**22, 39, 40, 62, 74, 83**), it is apparent that the recognition threshold is not a simple matter of intensity nor speed of presentation. Recent work by Postman and others (**47, 96, 98**), which has sought to illuminate the prerecognition processes operating to produce the apparent changes in threshold, does not alter the fact that individual differences in the perceptual process must be taken into account in any further work on the effects of subliminal stimulation.

UNANSWERED METHODOLOGICAL QUESTIONS

Having now concluded that, under certain conditions, the phenomenon of subliminal perception does occur, we turn our attention next to the many unanswered questions which this conclusion raises. For example, what kinds of behavior can be influenced by subliminal stimulation? What types of stimuli operate best at subthreshold intensities? Do all subliminal stimuli operate at the same "level of unconsciousness," or do different stimuli (or modes of stimulation) affect different levels of unconsciousness? What characteristics of the perceiver help determine the effectiveness of subliminal stimulation? All of these questions, as well as many others of a technological nature, will be discussed in the ensuing paragraphs.

A few words of caution concerning the word "subliminal" seem in order, however. It must be remembered that the psychological limen is a statistical concept, a fact overlooked by far too many current textbook writers. The common definition of the limen is "that stimulus value which gives a response exactly half the time" (**44**, p. 111). One of the difficulties involved in analyzing the many studies on subliminal perception is the fact that many experimenters have assumed that, because the stimuli which they employed were below the

statistical limen for a given subject, the stimuli were therefore never consciously perceivable by the subject. This is, of course, not true. Stimuli slightly below the statistical limen might well be consciously perceivable as much as 49% of the time. Not only this, but thresholds vary from moment to moment, as well as from day to day. All this is not to deny that stimuli which are so weak that they are never consciously reportable under any circumstances may not indeed influence behavior. We simply wish to make the point that the range of stimulus intensities which are in fact "subliminal" may be smaller than many experimenters in the past have assumed. It has been commonly assumed that the several methods of producing subliminal stimuli, i.e., reducing intensity, duration, size, or clarity, are logically and methodologically equivalent. While this may be true, it remains to be demonstrated conclusively.

Types of behavior influenced by subliminal stimulation

One of the first questions that springs to mind concerns the types of response which can be elicited with subliminal stimulation. Let us assume for the moment that the below-threshold advertisements used in commercial demonstrations were the sole cause of increased popcorn buying among the movie audiences subjected to the ads. How did this come about? Did the stimulus "Eat Popcorn" elicit an already established response in some members of the audience? Or did the frequent repetitions of the stimulus message cause a shift in attitude towards popcorn eating which eventually resulted in the purchase of popcorn at the first opportunity the audience had? Did the ads merely raise an already existing, presumably learned, but weak need for popcorn to an above the action-threshold level, or did the ads actually create a need for popcorn where no need had existed beforehand? Did members of the audience rise like automatons during the course of the movie and thus miss part of the feature in order to satisfy a sudden craving for popcorn or in order to respond to a suddenly evoked stimulus-response connection? Or did they wait until a "rest period" to do their purchasing? How many patrons bought popcorn only after they had seen the film and were heading home? How many people purchased popcorn on their way *in* to see the next movie they attended? How many of those who purchased popcorn did so for the first time in their lives, or for the first time in recent memory? What if the message presented had been "Buy Christmas Seals," which are available only in one season? How many people failed to buy popcorn at the theater, but purchased it subsequently at the local supermarket?

Unfortunately, these pertinent questions have yet to be answered. Let us tentatively accept this demonstration that impulse buying of inexpensive items such as popcorn and Coca-Cola can be influenced by subliminal advertising, without yet knowing what the mechanism involved is. It remains to be demonstrated, however, that such ads could make a person of limited means wreck himself financially by purchasing a Cadillac merely because the ads told him to do so. Nor do we know if deep-seated, strongly emotional attitudes or long established behavior patterns can be shifted one way or another as a result of subliminal stimulation. The answers to these questions must come from further experimentation.

As we have already seen, people can make use of subthreshold stimuli in making difficult perceptual judgments in situations where they are required to call up images of various objects (95) and in situations where they are asked to "read the experimenter's mind" (88). Kennedy (68) believes that some extrasensory-perception (ESP) experimenters may have obtained positive results because the "senders" unconsciously transmitted slight auditory and visual cues to their "receivers," and offers many experimental findings to back up his belief. Kennedy's studies also point up the difficult dilemma faced by people who object to subliminal stimulation as being an immoral or illegal attempt to influence other people. All of us, apparently, are constantly attempting to influence the people around us by means of sounds and movements we are unconscious of making. Correspondingly, all of us make some unconscious use of the cues presented to us by the people around us.

It also seems fairly clear that learning can take place when the stimuli to which the organism must respond are presented subliminally. Hankin (51) learned to predict changes in the flight of birds by utilizing wing-tip adjustments which were too slight to be consciously (reportably) noticeable. As we stated previously, Baker (6) obtained a conditioned pupillary response to subliminal auditory stimuli, although other investigators failed to replicate his findings. Miller (89) had subjects look at a mirror while trying to guess geometrical forms in an ESP-type experiment. Stimuli far below the statistical limen were projected on a mirror from behind. When the subjects were rewarded by praise for correct guesses and punished by electric shock for wrong guesses, learning took place. It is interesting to note that neither punishment alone nor reward alone was sufficient to produce learning.

Whether different types of learning than those reported above can take place using subliminal stimulation, and indeed how broad a range of human behavior can be influenced in any way whatsoever by subliminal stimulation, are questions which remain unanswered.

Levels of unconsciousness affected by subliminal stimulation[3]

We must now differentiate between stimuli which a subject cannot bring to awareness under any conditions (completely subliminal stimuli) and those stimuli of which he is merely not aware at the moment but could be made aware of should his set be changed. At any given moment, a vast conflux of stimuli impinges upon a subject's receptors. Few of the sensations arising from this stimulation ever enter the focus of attention. As Dallenbach was fond of reminding his Freshman classes: "Until I mentioned it, you were quite unaware that your shoes are full of feet." A great many experimenters have demonstrated that subjects could make use of stimuli well above the threshold of awareness but which could not be consciously reported on. Thus in one phase of her experiment, Perky (95) raised the intensity of the visual stimuli she was using to such a level that other psychologists who had not participated in the study apparently refused to believe that the subjects had not been aware of the stimuli. Perky's subjects, however, operating under a set to call up "images" of the stimuli presented, did not notice even relatively intense stimuli. Correspondingly, Newhall and Dodge (91) presented visual stimuli first at below-threshold intensities, then increased the intensities so slowly that the subjects were not aware of them even when the stimuli were well above threshold. When the stimuli were turned off suddenly, however, the subjects experienced afterimages. Thus certain stimuli may be well above threshold and yet be "subliminal" in the sense that they cannot be reported on under certain experimental conditions.

There are other levels of "unconsciousness" which are deserving of our attention, however. Much work has been done at the animal level in which conditioning has been attempted upon animals with various parts of the brain removed (33, 43). The same is true of animals under various types of anesthesia (106, 115). Miller, in summarizing the experimental data dealing with conditioning and consciousness, concludes:

> (*a*) That conditioning can take place in other parts of the nervous system than the cortex—even in the spinal cord;
>
> (*b*) That, if conditioned responses are evidences of consciousness, then consciousness is not mediated solely by the cortex;
>
> (*c*) That it may be possible to de-

---

[3] For an excellent review of the many meanings of the word "unconsciousness," readers are referred to Miller's book of the same name (**90**).

velop conditioning . . . at more than one level of the nervous system at the same time;

    (*d*) And that . . . animals are conditionable even when anesthetized (**90**, p. 100).

The nervous system has many levels of anatomical integration. Should we be surprised to discover that incoming stimuli may have an effect on a lower level and not on a higher and that under certain conditions this effect can later be demonstrated in terms of behavioral changes? We shall not be able to speak clearly of the effects of subliminal stimulation upon the various "levels of unconsciousness" until we have some better method of specifying exactly what these levels are and by what parts of the nervous system they are mediated. Experimentation is badly needed in this area.

Technological problems involved in stimulating subjects subliminally

The paucity of data presented by those dealing with subliminal perception on a commercial basis, as well as the equivocal nature of their results, suggests that there are many technological problems yet to be solved by these and other investigators. For example, during a two-hour movie (or a one-hour television show), how many times should the stimulus be repeated to make sure that the "message" gets across to the largest possible percentage of the audience? Should the stimulus be repeated every second, every five seconds, only once a minute? Is the effect cumulative, or is one presentation really enough? Is there a satiation effect, such that the audience becomes "unconsciously tired" of the stimulation, and "unconsciously blocks" the incoming subliminal sensations? Should the stimuli be presented "between frames" of the movie (that is, when the shutter of the film projector is closed and the screen momentarily blank as it is 24 times each second), or should the message be presented only when the screen already has a picture on it? How close to the threshold (statistical or otherwise) should the stimuli be? How many words long can the message be? If the message must be short, could successive stimulations present sequential parts of a longer advertisement? How much of the screen should the stimuli fill? Should the stimuli be presented only during "happier" moments in the film, in order to gain positive affect? Does any affect transfer at all from the film to the ad? Should one use pictures, or are words best? Must the words be familiar ones? And what about subliminal auditory, cutaneous, and olfactory stimulation?

As we have stated before, there has been so much talk and so little experimentation, and much of what experimentation has been done is so inadequately reported, that we can merely hazard guesses based on related but perhaps not always applicable studies.

To begin with, we can state with some assurance that, the closer to the threshold of awareness the stimuli are, the more effect they are likely to have. Study after study has reported increased effectiveness with increased intensity of stimulation (**5, 14, 88, 97, 104**). The main difficulty seems to be that thresholds vary so much from subject to subject (**112**), and from day to day (**114**), that what is subliminal but effective for one person is likely to be subliminal but ineffective for a second, and supraliminal for a third. As is generally the case, anyone who wishes to use the technique of subliminal stimulation must first experiment upon the specific group of people whom he wishes to influence before he can decide what intensity levels will be most efficacious.

Somewhat the same conclusion holds for the question of how many times the stimuli should be presented. While under some conditions subliminal stimuli which did not influence behavior when presented only once seemed to "summate" when presented many times (**10, 66**), Bricker and Chapanis (**15**) found that one presentation of a stimulus slightly below the (statistical) limen was enough to increase the likelihood of its being recognized on subsequent trials. We interpret this to mean that too many presentations may well raise the "subliminal" stimuli above the limen of awareness if the stimuli themselves are not carefully chosen.

As for the physical properties of the message itself, we can but guess what the relevant issues are. Both verbal and pictorial presentations apparently are effective in the visual modality, but no one has tested the relative effectiveness of these two types of stimulation. Quite possibly subsequent experimentation will show that words are best for some situations (such as direct commands), while pictures are best for others.[4] It can be stated unequivocally, however, that advertisers should look to their basic English when writing their subliminal commercials. Several studies have shown that, the more familiar a subject is with the stimulus he is to perceive, the more readily he perceives it (**22, 54, 63, 110**). We interpret these studies to mean that unfamiliar stimuli may be ineffective when presented subliminally, even though familiar messages may "get through."

The exact length the message should be, its composition, and the background in which it should be presented are variables upon which no work has been done and about which no conclu-

---

[4] Perhaps much of the work on sensory preconditioning is applicable here. When Ellson (**38**) presented his subjects with both a light and a buzzer for many trials, then presented the light alone, subjects "heard" the buzzer too.

sions can presently be drawn. Suffice it to say, however, that a message which would be short enough to be perceived by one person might be too long for another person to perceive under any conditions.

Which modalities are most useful for subliminal stimulation? While most of the work has been done on the visual modality, Vanderplas and Blake (124) and Kurland (71) have found subthreshold auditory stimuli to be effective, and earlier in this paper we have reported similar studies with cutaneous stimulation. Advertisers who wish to "sneak up on" their patrons by presenting subliminal stimuli in one modality while the patrons are attending to supraliminal stimuli from another modality are probably doomed to failure, however. Collier (27) presented subliminal geometric forms simultaneously to both the visual and the cutaneous modalities and found little, if any, lowering of thresholds. Correspondingly, it should be remembered that Hernandez-Peon et al. (55) found that some part of the nervous system acts as a kind of gating mechanism, and when an organism is attending strongly to one modality, the other modalities are probably "shut off" to most incoming stimuli.

Even if experimenters succeed in finding answers to many of the questions raised above concerning the physical characteristics of the stimuli to be employed, it is quite probable that they will have succeeded in discovering the source of only a small part of the variance operant in subliminal perception. For, as always, the major source of variance will come from the perceiver himself.

Characteristics of the perceiver which affect subliminal perception

The following section of this paper might well be considered a plea for the recognition that individual differences exist and that they must be taken into account by anyone who wishes to deal with individuals. We know next to nothing about the relationships between such factors as age, sex, social class, etc. and subliminal perception. Perhaps only one study is relevant: Perky (95) found that children were as much influenced by subthreshold visual stimulation as were naive adults. It is quite likely that many differences in the perception of subliminal stimuli do exist between individuals of differing classes, ages, and sexes. As always, only experimentation can determine what these differences are.

We do have some idea, however, of how what might be called "personality factors" influence subliminal perception. First and foremost, there seems little doubt but that a high need state affects perception. Gilchrist and Nesberg (46) found that, the greater the need state, the more

their subjects tended to overestimate the brightness of objects relevant to that need. It should be noted that they were dealing with difference limens, not absolute limens, but other studies to be quoted later show the same effect for absolute limens. It should be noted also that Gilchrist and Nesberg apparently overlooked evidence in their own data that a strong need affects judgments of non-need-related objects in the same direction (but not as much) as it does need-related objects. Wispe and Drambarean, dealing with visual duration thresholds, concluded that "need-related words were recognized more rapidly as need increased" (131, p. 31). McClelland and Lieberman (81) found that subjects with high need achievement scores had lower visual thresholds for "success" words than did subjects not scoring as high on need achievement. Do all of these findings mean that subliminal ads will work only when some fairly strong need (of any kind) is present in the viewers? Only experimentation can answer this question.

What about abnormalities of personality? What effect do they have? Kurland (71) tested auditory recognition thresholds using emotional and neutral words. He found that hospitalized neurotics perceived the emotional words at significantly lower thresholds than did a group of normal subjects. Does this mean that neurotics are more likely to respond to low-intensity subliminal commands than normals? Should advertisers take a "neurotic inventory" of their audiences?

A more pertinent problem is posed by the findings of Krech and Calvin (70). Using a Wechsler Vocabulary Score of 30.5 as their cutting point, they found that almost all college students above this score showed better visual discriminations of patterns presented at close to liminal values than did almost all students scoring below the cutting point. Does this mean that the higher the IQ, the better the subliminal perception? What is the relationship between the value of the absolute limen and intelligence? Will advertisers have to present their messages at such high intensities (in order that the "average man" might perceive the message) that the more intelligent members of the audience will be consciously aware of the advertising?

One further fascinating problem is posed by Huntley's work (64). He surreptitiously obtained photographs of the hands and profiles of his subjects, as well as handwriting samples and recordings of their voices. Six months later each subject was presented with the whole series of samples, among which were his own. Each subject was asked to make preference ratings of the samples. Huntley reports evidence of a significant tendency for subjects to prefer their own forms of expression above all others, even though in most cases they were totally unaware that the samples were their own and even though many subjects were unable to identify their own samples when told they were included in the series. If an advertiser is making a direct appeal to one specific individual, it would seem then that he should make use of the photographs and recordings of that individual's behavior as the subliminal stimuli. If an advertiser is making an appeal to a more general audience, however, it might be that he would find the use of pictures and recordings of Hollywood stars, etc., more efficacious than mere line drawings, printed messages, and unknown voices.

Nor can the advertiser afford to overlook the effects of set and attention. Miller (**88**), Perky (**95**), and Blake and Vanderplas (**12**), among others, discovered that giving the subject the proper set lowered the recognition threshold greatly. In fact, in many cases the stimulus intensity which was subliminal but effective for sophisticated subjects was far too subliminal to have much, if any, effect upon naive subjects. Thus advertisers might do well to tell their audiences that subliminal messages were being presented to them, in order to bring all members of that audience closer to a uniform threshold. Does this not, however, vitiate some of the effect of subliminal advertising?

As for attentional effects, we have presented evidence earlier (**46**) that strong needs seem to have an "alerting" effect upon the organism, lowering recognition thresholds for *all* stimuli, not just need-related stimuli. In addition to this, two studies by Hartmann (**52, 53**), as well as two by Spencer (**113, 114**) lead us to the belief that subliminal stimuli might best be presented when either the television or movie screen was blank of other pictures. Perhaps, then, subliminal commercials in movie houses should be shown between features; while on television the commercials should consist of an appropriate period of apparent "visual silence," during which the audience would not be aware of the subliminal stimulation presented, but might react to it later.

One fact emerges from all of the above. Anyone who wishes to utilize subliminal stimulation for commercial or other purposes can be likened to a stranger entering into a misty, confused countryside where there are but few landmarks. Before this technique is used in the market place, if it is to be used at all, a tremendous amount of research should be done, and by competent experimenters.

THE ETHICS OF SUBLIMINAL INFLUENCE

From its beginnings as a purely academic offshoot of philosophy, psychology has, with ever increasing momentum, grown in the public perception as a practical and applied discipline. As psychologists were called upon to communicate and interpret their insights and research findings to lay persons, it was necessary to make decisions about what constituted proper professional behavior,

since it was evident that the misuse of such information would reflect directly on the community of psychologists. As a growing number of our research efforts are viewed as useful to society, the problem of effective and honest communication becomes magnified, although its essential nature does not change. Recently, to our dismay, the announcement of a commercial application of long established psychological principles has assumed nightmarish qualities, and we find ourselves unwillingly cast in the role of invaders of personal privacy and enemies of society. A kind of guilt by association seems to be occurring, and, as future incidents of this kind will, it threatens to undermine the public relations we have built with years of caution and concern for the public welfare. The highly emotional public reaction to the "discovery" of subliminal perception should serve as an object lesson to our profession, for in the bright glare of publicity we can see urgent ethical issues as well as an omen of things to come. When the theoretical notion $E = MC^2$ became the applied reality of an atom bomb, the community of physicists became deeply concerned with social as well as scientific responsibility. Judging from the intensity of the public alarm when confronted with a bare minimum of fact about this subliminal social atom, there exists a clear need for psychologists to examine the ethical problems that are a part of this era of the application of their findings.

The vehemence of the reaction to the proposed use of a device to project subliminal, or from the public's point of view "hidden," messages to viewers indicates that the proposal touches a sensitive area. One of the basic contributors to this reaction seems to be the feeling that a technique which avowedly tampers with the psychological status of the individual ought to be under the regulation or control of a trusted scientific group. As a professional group, psychologists would fit this description, for in the *Ethical Standards of Psychologists* (**2**) there is a clear statement of their motives and relationship to society:

> Principle *1.12-1* The psychologist's ultimate allegiance is to society, and his professional behavior should demonstrate an awareness of his social responsibilities. The welfare of the profession and of the individual psychologist are clearly subordinate to the welfare of the public. . . .

Both this statement and the long record of responsible behavior of the members of the profession would certainly seem to be sufficient to reduce any anxiety the public might have over the possible unscrupulous use of this or any other device.

It is precisely the fact that the public *is* aware that decisions about the use of subliminal perception devices rest not with psychologists but with commercial agencies that may be distressing to the public. The aura of open-for-business flamboyance and the sketchily presented percentages in the first public announcement tended to reinforce existing apprehensions rather than allay them.

Although subliminal perception happens now to be the focus of a great deal of reaction, it is merely the most recent in a succession of perturbing events to which the public has been exposed. It has become the focus of, and is likely to become the whipping boy for, a host of techniques which now occupy the twilight zone of infringement of personal psychological freedom. It must be remembered that to the lay person the notion of an unconscious part of the "mind" is eerie, vague, and more than a little mysterious. Unable fully to comprehend the systematic and theoretical aspects of such a concept, he must be content with overly popularized and dramatic versions of it. In every form of mass media the American public has been exposed to convincing images of the bearded hypnotist (with piercing eye) who achieves his nefarious ends by controlling the unconscious of his victim. It has been treated to the spectacle of the seeming reincarnation of Bridey Murphy out of the unconscious of an American housewife and, in *Three Faces of Eve,* to complex multiple personalities hidden in the psychic recesses of a single individual. With such uncanny and disturbing images as an emotional backdrop, the appearance of *The Hidden Persuaders* on the best seller lists formed the indelible impression of the exploitation of the unconscious for purposes of profit and personal gain. In combination, this growth of emotionally charged attitudes toward the unconscious and the suspicions about commercial morality came to be a potentially explosive set of tensions which was triggered off by the first commercial use of subliminal techniques.

What is to be the psychologist's position in regard to future developments with subliminal perception? The apparent discrepancy between the claims being made for the technique and the available research evidence suggests a need for considerable scientific caution as well as extensive investigation. The responsibility of psychologists in this instance is clearly indicated in the code of ethics:

> Principle *2.12-1* The psychologist should refuse to suggest, support, or condone unwarranted assumptions, invalid applications, or unjustified conclusions in the use of psychological instruments or techniques.

The flurry of claim and opinion about the effectiveness of subliminal methods seems to be based more on enthusiasm than controlled scientific experimentation, and it is here that psychology can be of service. Until acceptable scientific answers are forthcoming, we believe psychologists should guard against a premature commitment which might jeopardize public respect for them. The course of scientific history is strewn with the desiccated remains of projects pursued with more vigor than wisdom.

Scientific caution is essential, but it falls short of meeting the ethical issue raised by the nature of subliminal perception itself. The most strident public objections have been directed toward the possibility that suggestions or attempts to influence or persuade may be administered without the knowledge or consent of the audience. Assurances that widespread adoption of this technique would provide increased enjoyment through the elimination of commercial instrusions, or that the users will establish an ethical control over the content of the messages presented, can only fail to be convincing in light of past experience. The suggestion that the public can be taught means of detecting when it is being exposed to a planned subliminal stimulation is far from reassuring since such a suggestion implies that the ability to defend oneself warrants being attacked. A captive audience is not a happy audience, and even the plan to inform the viewers in advance concerning the details of what is to be presented subliminally may not prevent the public from reacting to this technique as a demand that it surrender an additional degree of personal freedom. Fresh from similar encounters, the public may not allow this freedom to be wrested from it.

Finally, the argument that a great deal of our normal perception occurs on the fringe of conscious awareness and that subliminal events are no more effective than weak conscious stimuli rests on opinion and not fact. This seems particularly dangerous clinical ground on which to tread since the effect, on behavior, of stimuli which may possibly be inserted directly into the unconscious has yet to be explored. Assurances that this technique can only "remind" a person of something he already knows or "support" a set of urges already in existence but cannot establish a completely new set of urges or needs are reckless assertions having no evidence to support them. So it seems that the aspect of subliminal projection which is marked by the greatest potential risk to the individual's emotional equilibrium is the aspect about which the least is scientifically known.

The psychologist's ethical quandary, then, stems directly from the inescapable implication of deviousness in the use of such a technique. The appropriate guidelines for conduct are provided in this ethical statement:

> Principle *2.62-2* It is unethical to employ psychological techniques for devi-

ous purposes, for entertainment, or for other reasons not consonant with the best interests of a client or with the development of psychology as a science.

It is obvious that "devious purposes" and "the best interests . . . of psychology as a science" are not self-defining terms and must be interpreted by the individual psychologist in light of the circumstances of each situation. It is a trying and complex decision to make. If in his mature judgment the intended uses of the principles of subliminal perception do not meet acceptable ethical standards, the psychologist is obligated to dissociate himself from the endeavor and to labor in behalf of the public welfare to which he owes his first allegiance. In this respect, the responsibility of the social scientist must always be that of watchdog over his own actions as well as the actions of those to whom he lends his professional support.

The furor which promises to accompany the further application of a variety of devices involving subliminal perception is certain to embroil psychology in a dispute not of its own choosing. The indiscriminate and uncontrolled application of psychological principles is increasing at a fearsome rate in the form of motivation research, propaganda, public relations, and a host of other "useful" practices based on the work of psychologists. In a very real sense this era of applied psychology will be a test of the workability of the psychologist's code of ethics and promises to stimulate the profession to give further consideration to its responsibility for assisting society to use its findings wisely.

REFERENCES

1. ADAMS, J. K. Laboratory studies of behavior without awareness. *Psychol. Bull.*, 1957, **54**, 383–405.
2. AMERICAN PSYCHOLOGICAL ASSOCIATION, Committee on Ethical Standards for Psychology. *Ethical standards of psychologists.* Washington: APA, 1953.
3. ANSBACHER, H. Perception of number as affected by the monetary value of the objects. *Arch. Psychol.*, 1937, **30**, No. 215.
4. BACH, S., & KLEIN, G. S. Conscious effects of prolonged subliminal exposures of words. *Amer. Psychologist*, 1957, **12**, 397. (Abstract)
5. BAKER, L. E. The influence of subliminal stimuli upon verbal behavior. *J. exp. Psychol.*, 1937, **20**, 84–100.
6. BAKER, L. E. The pupillary response conditioned to subliminal auditory stimuli. *Psychol. Monogr.*, 1938, **50**, No. 3 (Whole No. 223).
7. Ban on subliminal ads, pending FCC probe, is urged. *Adv. Age*, 1957, **28**, No. 45.

8. BATTELLE, PHYLLIS. The lady objects to id tampering. *Publishers Auxiliary*, 1957, **92**, No. 40.
9. BEAMS, H. L., & THOMPSON, G. G. Affectivity as a factor in the perception of the magnitude of food objects. *Amer. Psychologist*, 1952, **7**, 323. (Abstract)
10. BEITEL, R. J., JR. Spatial summation of subliminal stimuli in the retina of the human eye. *J. gen. Psychol.*, 1934, **10**, 311–327.
11. BLACKWELL, H. R. Personal communication, 1958.
12. BLAKE, R. R., & VANDERPLAS, J. M. The effects of prerecognition hypotheses on veridical recognition thresholds in auditory perception. *J. Pers.*, 1950–1951, **19**, 95–115.
13. BLUM, G. S. Perceptual defense revisited. *J. abnorm. soc. Psychol.*, 1955, **56**, 24–29.
14. BRESSLER, J. Illusion in the case of subliminal visual stimulation. *J. gen. Psychol.*, 1931, **5**, 244–250.
15. BRICKER, P. D., & CHAPANIS, A. Do incorrectly perceived tachistoscopic stimuli convey some information? *Psychol. Rev.*, 1953, **60**, 181–188.
16. BRITT, S. H. Subliminal advertising—fact or fantasy? *Adv. Age*, 1957, **28**, 103.
17. BROOKS, J. The little ad that isn't there. *Consumer Rep.*, 1957, **23**, No. 1.
18. BRUNER, J. S., & GOODMAN, C. C. Value and need as organizing factors in perception. *J. abnorm. soc. Psychol.*, 1947, **42**, 33–44.
19. BRUNER, J. S., & POSTMAN, L. Emotional selectivity in perception and action. *J. Pers.*, 1947, **16**, 69–77.
20. BRUNER, J. S., & POSTMAN, L. Tension and tension-release as organizing factors in perception. *J. Pers.*, 1947, **16**, 300–308.
21. BRUNER, J. S., & POSTMAN, L. Symbolic value as an organizing factor in perception. *J. soc. Psychol.*, 1948, **27**, 203–208.
22. BRUNER, J. S., & POSTMAN, L. Perception, cognition, and behavior. *J. Pers.*, 1949, **18**, 14–31.
23. CARTER, L. F., & SCHOOLER, K. Value, need, and other factors in perception. *Psychol. Rev.*, 1949, **56**, 200–207.
24. CASON, H., & KATCHER, NAOMI. An attempt to condition breathing and eyelid responses to a subliminal electric stimulus. *J. exp. Psychol.*, 1934, **16**, 831–842.
25. COHEN, B. D., KALISH, H. I., THURSTON, J. R., & COHEN, E. Experimental manipulation of verbal behavior. *J. exp. Psychol.*, 1954, **47**, 106–110.
26. COHEN, L. H., HILGARD, E. R., & WENDT, G. R. Sensitivity to light in a case of hysterical blindness studied by reinforcement-inhi-

bition and conditioning methods. *Yale J. Biol. Med.,* 1933, **6,** 61–67.

27. COLLIER, R. M. An experimental study of the effects of subliminal stimuli. *Psychol. Monogr.,* 1940, **52,** No. 5 (Whole No. 236).

28. COOVER, J. E. Experiments in psychical research. *Psychical Res. Monogr.,* 1917, No. 1.

29. COUSINS, N. Smudging the subconscious. *Saturday Rev.,* 1957, **40,** No. 40.

30. COWEN, E. L., & BEIER, E. G. The influence of "threat-expectancy" on perception. *J. Pers.,* 1950–1951, **19,** 85–94.

31. COWEN, E. L., & BEIER, E. G. A further study of the "threat-expectancy" variable in perception. *Amer. Psychologist,* 1952, **7,** 320–321. (Abstract)

32. COWEN, E. L., & BEIER, E. G. Threat-expectancy, word frequencies, and perceptual prerecognition hypotheses. *J. abnorm. soc. Psychol.,* 1954, **49,** 178–182.

33. CULLER, E., & METTLER, F. A. Conditioned behavior in a decorticate dog. *J. comp. Psychol.,* 1934, **18,** 291–303.

34. DEITER, J. The nature of subception. Unpublished doctoral dissertation, Univer. of Kansas, 1953.

35. DIVEN, K. Certain determinants in the conditioning of anxiety reactions. *J. Psychol.,* 1937, **3,** 291–308.

36. DUNLAP, K. Effect of imperceptible shadows on the judgments of distance. *Psychol. Rev.,* 1900, **7,** 435–453.

37. DuSHANE, G. The invisible word, or no thresholds barred. *Science,* 1957, **126,** 681.

38. ELLSON, D. G. Hallucinations produced by sensory conditioning. *J. exp. Psychol.,* 1941, **28,** 1–20.

39. ERIKSEN, C. W. The case for perceptual defense. *Psychol. Rev.,* 1954, **61,** 175–182.

40. ERIKSEN, C. W. Subception: Fact or artifact? *Psychol. Rev.,* 1956, **63,** 74–80.

41. ERIKSEN, C. W., & KUETHE, J. L. Avoidance conditioning of verbal behavior without awareness: A paradigm of repression. *J. abnorm. soc. Psychol.,* 1956, **53,** 203–209.

42. FINK, A. A. Questions about subliminal advertising. New York: Author, 1957.

43. FOLEY, J. P., JR. The cortical interpretation of conditioning. *J. gen. Psychol.,* 1933, **9,** 228–234.

44. FULLERTON, G. S., & CATTELL, J. McK. On the perception of small differences. *Univer. Penn. Publ., Philos. Ser.,* 1892, No. 2.

45. "Ghost" ads overrated. *Sci. Newsltr.,* 1957, **72,** No. 17.

46. GILCHRIST, J. C., & NESBERG, L. S. Need and perceptual change in need-related objects. *J. exp. Psychol.,* 1952, **44,** 369–376.

47. GOODNOW, JACQUELINE J., & POSTMAN, L. Probability learning in a problem-solving situation. *J. exp. Psychol.,* 1955, **49,** 16–22.

48. GREENSPOON, J. The reinforcing effect of two spoken sounds on the frequency of two responses. *Amer. J. Psychol.,* 1955, **68,** 409–416.

49. GUILFORD, J. P. *Psychometric methods.* New York: McGraw-Hill, 1936.

50. HAGGARD, E. A. Experimental studies in affective processes: I. Some effects of cognitive structure and active participation on certain autonomic reactions during and following experimentally induced stress. *J. exp. Psychol.,* 1943, **33,** 257–284.

51. HANKIN, H. *Common sense.* New York: Dutton, 1926.

52. HARTMANN, G. W. I. The increase of visual acuity in one eye through the illumination of the other. *J. exp. Psychol.,* 1933, **16,** 383–392.

53. HARTMANN, G. W. II. Changes in visual acuity through simultaneous stimulation of other sense organs. *J. exp. Psychol.,* 1933, **16,** 393–407.

54. HENLE, MARY. An experimental investigation of past experience as a determinant of visual form perception. *J. exp. Psychol.,* 1942, **30,** 1–21.

55. HERNANDEZ-PEON, R., SCHERRER, H., & MICHEL, J. Modification of electrical activity of cochlear nucleus during "attention" in unanesthetized cats. *Science,* 1955, **123,** 331–332.

56. HILDUM, D. C., & BROWN, R. W. Verbal reinforcement and interviewer bias. *J. abnorm. soc. Psychol.,* 1956, **53,** 108–111.

57. HILGARD, E. R., MILLER, J., & OHLSON, J. A. Three attempts to secure pupillary conditioning to auditory stimuli near the absolute threshold. *J. exp. Psychol.,* 1941, **29,** 89–103.

58. HILGARD, E. R., & WENDT, G. R. The problem of reflex sensitivity to light studied in a case of hemianopsia. *Yale J. Biol. Med.,* 1933, **5,** 373–385.

59. HOLLINGWORTH, H. L. *Advertising and selling.* New York: Appleton, 1913.

60. HOWES, D. A statistical theory of the phenomenon of subception. *Psychol. Rev.,* 1954, **61,** 98–110.

61. HOWES, D. On the interpretation of word frequency as a variable affecting speed of recognition. *J. exp. Psychol.,* 1954, **48,** 106–112.

62. HOWES, D., & SOLOMON, R. L. A note on McGinnies' "Emotionality and perceptual defense." *Psychol. Rev.,* 1950, **57,** 235–240.

63. HOWES, D., & SOLOMON, R. L. Visual duration

threshold as a function of word probability. *J. exp. Psychol.*, 1951, **41**, 401–410.

64. HUNTLEY, C. W. Judgments of self based upon records of expressive behavior. *J. abnorm. soc. Psychol.*, 1953, **48**, 398–427.

65. IRWIN, F. W., KAUFMAN, K., PRIOR, G., & WEAVER, H. B. On "Learning without awareness of what is being learned." *J. exp. Psychol.*, 1934, **17**, 823–827.

66. KARN, H. W. The function of intensity in the spatial summation of subliminal stimuli in the retina. *J. gen. Psychol.*, 1935, **12**, 95–107.

67. KENNEDY, J. L. Experiments on "unconscious whispering." *Psychol. Bull.*, 1938, **35**, 526. (Abstract)

68. KENNEDY, J. L. A methodological review of extra-sensory perception. *Psychol. Bull.*, 1939, **36**, 59–103.

69. KLEIN, G. S., MEISTER, D., & SCHLESINGER, H. J. The effect of personal values on perception: An experimental critique. *Amer. Psychologist*, 1949, **4**, 252–253. (Abstract)

70. KRECH, D., & CALVIN, A. Levels of perceptual organization and cognition. *J. abnorm. soc. Psychol.*, 1953, **48**, 394–400.

71. KURLAND, S. H. The lack of generality in defense mechanisms as indicated in auditory perception. *J. abnorm. soc. Psychol.*, 1954, **49**, 173–177.

72. LACEY, J. I., & SMITH, R. L. Conditioning and generalization of unconscious anxiety. *Science*, 1954, **120**, 1045–1052.

73. LACEY, J. I., SMITH, R. L., & GREEN, A. Use of conditioned autonomic responses in the study of anxiety. *Psychosom. Med.*, 1955, **17**, 208–217.

74. LAZARUS, R. S. Subception: Fact or artifact? A reply to Eriksen. *Psychol. Rev.*, 1956, **63**, 343–347.

75. LAZARUS, R. S., ERIKSEN, C. W., & FONDA, C. P. Personality dynamics and auditory perceptual recognition. *J. Pers.*, 1950–1951, **19**, 471–482.

76. LAZARUS, R. S., & MCCLEARY, R. A. Autonomic discrimination without awareness: A study of subception. *Psychol. Rev.*, 1951, **58**, 113–122.

77. LEVINE, R., CHEIN, I., & MURPHY, G. The relation of the intensity of a need to the amount of perceptual distortion. *J. Psychol.*, 1942, **13**, 283–293.

78. LYSAK, W. The effects of punishment upon syllable recognition thresholds. *J. exp. Psychol.*, 1954, **47**, 343–350.

79. MCCLEARY, R. A., & LAZARUS, R. S. Autonomic discrimination without awareness: An interim report. *J. Pers.*, 1949, **18**, 171–179.

80. MCCLELLAND, D. C., & ATKINSON, J. W. The projective expression of needs: I. The effect of different intensities of the hunger drive on perception. *J. Psychol.*, 1948, **25**, 205–222.

81. MCCLELLAND, D. C., & LIEBERMAN, A. M. The effect of need for achievement on recognition of need-related words. *J. Pers.*, 1949, **18**, 236–251.

82. MCGINNIES, E. Emotionality and perceptual defense. *Psychol. Rev.*, 1949, **56**, 244–251.

83. MCGINNIES, E. Discussion of Howes' and Solomon's note on "Emotionality and perceptual defense." *Psychol. Rev.*, 1950, **57**, 229–234.

84. MANDLER, G., & KAPLAN, W. K. Subjective evaluation and reinforcing effect of a verbal stimulus. *Science*, 1956, **124**, 582–583.

85. MANNES, MARYA. Ain't nobody here but us commercials. *Reporter*, 1957, **17**, No. 6.

86. MANRO, H. M., & WASHBURN, M. F. Effect of imperceptible lines on judgment of distance. *Amer. J. Psychol.*, 1908, **19**, 242–243.

87. Michigan State prof. tells weaknesses of invisible commercials. *Publishers Auxiliary*, 1957, **92**, No. 40.

88. MILLER, J. G. Discrimination without awareness. *Amer. J. Psychol.*, 1939, **52**, 562–578.

89. MILLER, J. G. The role of motivation in learning without awareness. *Amer. J. Psychol.*, 1940, **53**, 229–239.

90. MILLER, J. G. *Unconsciousness*. New York: Wiley, 1942.

91. NEWHALL, S. M., & DODGE, R. Colored after images from unperceived weak chromatic stimulation. *J. exp. Psychol.*, 1927, **10**, 1–17.

92. NEWHALL, S. M., & SEARS, R. R. Conditioning finger retraction to visual stimuli near the absolute threshold. *Comp. psychol. Monogr.*, 1933, **9**, No. 43.

93. NUTHMANN, ANNE M. Conditioning of a response class on a personality test. *J. abnorm. soc. Psychol.*, 1957, **54**, 19–23.

94. PEIRCE, C. S., & JASTROW, J. On small differences of sensation. *Mem. Nat. Acad. Sci.*, 1884, **3**, 73–83.

95. PERKY, C. W. An experimental study of imagination. *Amer. J. Psychol.*, 1910, **21**, 422–452.

96. PHILBRICK, E. B., & POSTMAN, L. A further analysis of "learning without awareness." *Amer. J. Psychol.*, 1955, **68**, 417–424.

97. PILLAI, R. P. B. K. A study of the threshold in relation to the investigations on subliminal impressions and allied phenomena. *Brit. J. educ. Psychol.*, 1939, **9**, 97–98.

98. POSTMAN, L., & JARRETT, R. F. An experimental

analysis of "learning without awareness."
Amer. J. Psychol., 1952, **65,** 244–255.

99. RAZRAN, G. Stimulus generalization of conditioned responses. *Psychol. Bull.,* 1949, **46,** 337–365.

100. REECE, M. M. The effect of shock on recognition thresholds. *J. abnorm. soc. Psychol.,* 1954, **49,** 165–172.

101. REES, H. J., & ISRAEL, H. E. An investigation of the establishment and operation of mental sets. *Psychol. Monogr.,* 1935, **46,** No. 6 (Whole No. 210).

102. SANFORD, R. N. The effects of abstinence from food upon imaginal processes: A preliminary experiment. *J. Psychol.,* 1936, **2,** 129–136.

103. SANFORD, R. N. The effects of abstinence from food upon imaginal processes: A further experiment. *J. Psychol.,* 1937, **3,** 145–159.

104. SCHAFER, T. H. Influence of the preceding item on units of the noise masked threshold by a modified constant method. *J. exp. Psychol.,* 1950, **40,** 365–371.

105. SEARS, R. R., & COHEN, L. H. Hysterical anesthesia, analgesia, and astereognosis. *Arch. Neurol. Psychiat.,* 1933, **29,** 260–271.

106. SETTLAGE, T. The effect of sodium amytal on the formation and elicitation of conditioned reflexes. *J. comp. Psychol.,* 1936, **22,** 339–343.

107. SIDIS, B. *The psychology of suggestion.* New York: Appleton, 1898.

108. SIDOWSKI, J. B. Influence of awareness of reinforcement on verbal conditioning. *J. exp. Psychol.,* 1954, **48,** 355–360.

109. SILVERMAN, A., & BAKER, L. E. An attempt to condition various responses to subliminal electrical stimulation. *J. exp. Psychol.,* 1935, **18,** 246–254.

110. SMOKE, K. L. An objective study of concept formation. *Psychol. Monogr.,* 1932, **42,** No. 4 (Whole No. 191).

111. SOLOMON, R. L., & HOWES, D. H. Word frequency, personal values, and visual duration thresholds. *Psychol. Rev.,* 1951, **58,** 256–270.

112. SOLOMON, R. L., & POSTMAN, L. Frequency of usage as a determinant of recognition thresholds for words. *J. exp. Psychol.,* 1952, **43,** 195–201.

113. SPENCER, L. T. The concept of the threshold and Heymans' law of inhibition: I. Correlation between the visual threshold and Heymans' coefficient of inhibition of binocular vision. *J. exp. Psychol.,* 1928, **11,** 88–97.

114. SPENCER, L. T., & COHEN, L. H. The concept of the threshold and Heymans' law of inhibition. II. *J. exp. Psychol.,* 1928, **11,** 194–201.

115. STERLING, K., & MILLER, J. G. Conditioning under anesthesia. *Amer. J. Psychol.,* 1941, **54,** 92–101.

116. STROH, M., SHAW, A. M., & WASHBURN, M. F. A study in guessing. *Amer. J. Psychol.,* 1908, **19,** 243–245.

117. Subliminal ad okay if it sells: Lessler; FCC peers into subliminal picture on TV. *Adv. Age,* 1957, **28,** No. 48.

118. Subliminal ads wash no brains, declare Moore, Becker, developers of precon device. *Adv. Age,* 1957, **28,** No. 48.

119. SUSLOWA, M. Veranderungen der Hautgefule unter dem Einflusse electrischer Reizung. *Z. Rationelle Med.,* 1863, **18,** 155–160.

120. TAFFEL, C. Anxiety and the conditioning of verbal behavior. *J. abnorm. soc. Psychol.,* 1955, **51,** 496–501.

121. THORNDIKE, E. L. *The fundamentals of learning.* New York: Teachers College, Columbia Univer., 1932.

122. THORNDIKE, E. L., & ROCK, R. T. Learning without awareness of what is being learned or intent to learn it. *J. exp. Psychol.,* 1934, **17,** 1–19.

123. TITCHNER, E. B., & PYLE, W. H. Effect of imperceptible shadows on the judgment of distance. *Proc. Amer. phil. Soc.,* 1907, **46,** 94–109.

124. VANDERPLAS, J. M., & BLAKE, R. R. Selective sensitization in auditory perception. *J. Pers.,* 1949, **18,** 252–266.

125. VERPLANCK, W. S. The control of the content of conversation: Reinforcement of statements of opinion. *J. abnorm. soc. Psychol.,* 1955, **51,** 668–676.

126. VERPLANCK, W. S. The operant conditioning of human motor behavior. *Psychol. Bull.,* 1956, **53,** 70–83.

127. VINACKE, W. E. The discrimination of color and form at levels of illumination below conscious awareness. *Arch. Psychol.,* 1942, **38,** No. 267.

128. WEDELL, C. H., TAYLOR, F. V., & SKOLNICK, A. An attempt to condition the pupillary response. *J. exp. Psychol.,* 1940, **27,** 517–531.

129. WEISS, R. L. The influence of "set for speed" on "learning without awareness." *Amer. J. Psychol.,* 1955, **68,** 425–431.

130. WILLIAMS, A. C. Perception of subliminal visual stimuli. *J. Psychol.,* 1938, **6,** 187–199.

131. WISPE, L. G., & DRAMBAREAN, N. C. Physiological need, word frequency, and visual duration thresholds. *J. exp. Psychol.,* 1953, **46,** 25–31.

132. WOOLF, J. D. Subliminal perception is nothing new. *Adv. Age,* 1957, **28,** No. 43.

VALUE AND PERCEPTUAL JUDGMENT OF MAGNITUDE*

The previous two selections investigated perception under impoverished stimulus conditions; the stimulus material was presented for only a brief fraction of a second under dim illumination. Such circumstances magnify the possible influence of social factors. So that laboratory findings might have more external validity, other investigators have attempted to demonstrate that value could also influence perceptions or judgments made under conditions where they would normally be quite accurate. Judgments of the *size* of objects were chosen for study, since errors in this kind of judgment are usually minimal. Experimenters undertook to prove that such judgments could also be influenced by the positive or negative value that the perceiver attached to the objects.

Early experimentation led to the concept of *perceptual accentuation*, the idea that valued objects are perceived as larger than objects of the same physical size but of no value. As experimentation continued, misinterpretations resulting from inadequacy of method were identified, and some experiments, for no apparent reason, failed to demonstrate perceptual accentuation. In the present selection, Tajfel brings order to this research topic by classifying the conditions under which perceptual accentuation occurs and does not occur and by calling attention to two perceptual processes that underlie the phenomenon—the *intraserial* effect and the *interserial* effect.

8.

Value and the Perceptual Judgment of Magnitude[1]

H. TAJFEL
UNIVERSITY OF OXFORD, ENGLAND

Problems connected with the influences exercised by motivational factors on perception have been subject to much debate in recent years. It seems that the dust of controversy is beginning to settle. A reaction is setting in (e.g., 17) against premature attempts to construct theories which would cope with the enormous variety of facts in this field, even before many of the facts have been

* The selection following the editorial introduction is reprinted from "Value and perceptual judgment of magnitude," *Psychological Review*, 1957, **64**, 192–204, by permission of the author and the American Psychological Association.
[1] I wish to express my gratitude to Professor J. S. Bruner for encouragement and advice; and to Dr. W. Sluckin and Mr. D. Graham from the University of Durham for many useful suggestions.

properly established. These general theories were based in part on an a priori assumption that all the phenomena concerned can be reduced to, and formulated in terms of, a few very wide and non-specific principles. No one can tell at present whether such an assumption is justified; but its hasty acceptance seems to have led to a confusion of experimental issues which has not been avoided either by those who stressed the importance of motivational variables in perception or by those who persistently denied it. The primary concern of this paper is with only one of these issues: the phenomena of perceptual overestimation, presumably due to value or some related variables. One of the reasons for this concern is that there exists a body of positive experimental findings in this field which cannot be ignored, and for which a consistent explanation has not yet been offered.

In the last fifteen years or so about twenty experiments on various aspects of overestimation have been conducted. Of those, only two have yielded unambiguously negative results (3, 21). Partly negative results have been reported by Carter and Schooler (8), and by Klein, Schlesinger, and Meister (19). All other workers were able to conclude that, in the situations which they were using, "motivational" or "value" variables had an effect on their subjects' perceptual judgments of magnitude. Shifts in judgments of size (e.g., 1, 2, 5, 6, 7, 10, 20, 26), weight (e.g., 9), number (e.g., 25), and brightness (e.g., 13) have been reported.

All this evidence cannot be dismissed as an accumulation of experimental artifacts. Furthermore, perceptual accentuation need not be considered as a "maladaptive" phenomenon. The fact that it may represent a departure from the "objective reality" leads to a general criticism which consists in pointing out that in order to survive we must perceive the world as it is, that we usually do, and that therefore the fleeting phenomena of overestimation are more typical of the specific laboratory situations in which they have been demonstrated than of perception under normal conditions. There is, however, a possibility that the shifts in the judgments of magnitude which concern us here do not interfere with an adequate handling of the environment. They may even be of help.

A CLASSIFICATION

The experiments on overestimation fall naturally into two classes. In one group, changes in the magnitude of the stimuli under investigation are relevant to the changes in value. The experiments on coins provide an example here: in general, the larger the coin, the greater its value. The experiment of Dukes and Bevan (9), in which judgments of weight of jars filled with sand were compared with judgments of weight of jars filled with candy, would also be "relevant" in this sense: heavier jars would presumably contain more candy, and thus have greater "value." On the other hand, several experiments have been reported in which changes in value have in no apparent way been related to changes in the physical dimension which the subjects were requested to judge. Thus, in the experiment by Lambert, Solomon, and Watson (20), the color of the disc was the determinant of its value, as red discs only were associated with reward; but judgments of size were requested of the subjects. In the experiments by Bruner and Postman (6) and by Klein, Schlesinger, and Meister (19), discs containing a swastika were among the stimuli used. Judgments of their size were compared with judgments of size of discs containing neutral symbols. Here again, the size of the swastika has no easily conceivable relationship to its degree of relevance. Further examples from both classes of experiments could be given.

"RELEVANT" DIMENSIONS AND THE ACCENTUATION OF DIFFERENCES

Let us first deal with the "relevant" group of experiments. The stimuli whose magnitudes were judged in these investigations form, by definition, a series varying concurrently in at least two dimensions: the physical dimension (size or weight), and the "dimension" of value. The concern of most experimenters has been to show (or to deny) that the stimuli of the series in which a variation in magnitude was paired in the environment with a variation in value were judged larger

TABLE 1

STIMULI	PERCENTAGE INCREASE FROM ACTUAL TO PERCEIVED EXTENSION
Cardboard discs	16.81
Aluminum discs	16.20
Coins judged when present	33.91
Coins judged from memory	38.69

Converted from Carter and Schooler, p. 202. Judgments of the "dime" and of the corresponding discs in other series have not been taken into account in this table, as the "dime" represents an exception in the concomitant variations of size and value in coins.

than stimuli of objectively equivalent magnitudes belonging to a different, "neutral," series. Thus, judgments of size of coins were compared with judgments of size of cardboard or metal discs, and judgment of weight of jars filled with candy with similar judgments of jars filled with sand. Little attention has been paid to the perceived differences *between* the magnitudes of the stimuli in the "valued" series, as compared with the corresponding relationships in the "neutral" series.

It seems that some, at least, of the apparent contradictions between the various experimental results can be resolved if this intraserial aspect of the situation is considered. On the basis of an argument to be developed later, a prediction can be made that in a "relevant" series, where value changes concurrently with the dimension subjected to investigation, the differences between the stimuli of the series will be perceived as larger than the objectively equivalent differences between the stimuli of a neutral series, where no such association exists between value and magnitude. This comparison of the perceived differences within the two series would acquire its fullest meaning when intraindividual data are considered. Large individual variations are to be expected in the fineness of discrimination for both relevant and neutral series, but the tendency for a larger accentuation of differences in the former is likely to appear in most subjects, independently of the absolute values of the differences.

All the results to date in the "relevant" group of experiments support this contention. The quantitative difference, as expressed by subjects' judgments, between the two extremes of a series has been adopted as a rough measure of the accentuation of differences. This limitation was found necessary for two reasons. In the first place, coins, for example, differ not only in size and value. Secondly, it is possible that other determinants of quantitative judgment, such as the interaction of various generalization gradients (cf., e.g., 18), might counteract in some segments of the series the expected accentuation of differences.

A glance at Fig. 1 in the early study of Bruner and Goodman (5) shows that the perceived difference between the smallest and the largest coins (extension of the scale of judgments) is much larger than the corresponding extensions for discs. A conversion of the data in the experiment by Carter and Schooler (8, Table I, p. 202) to similar extensions, for all subjects combined, shows that:

a. In all series of stimuli (coins, aluminum and cardboard discs) the perceived extensions are larger than the actual ones;
b. The relative differences between the actual and the perceived extensions are about twice as large for the series of coins as for both series of discs (see Table 1).

Carter and Schooler imply this when they ". . . suggest that there is a constant error involved in making these size judgments such that small coins are underestimated and large coins are overestimated in size" (8, p. 205); but they do not seem to draw further conclusions.

Bruner and Rodrigues (7) have introduced in their well-controlled experiment the notion of "relative increase in overestimation" in which some of the suggestions made here are already implicit. Half of their subjects emphasized the purchasing power of money. The other half were assigned to an "accuracy set" in which the experimenters' concern with accurate judgments of size was stressed. A conversion of their data similar to the above conversion of Carter and Schooler's data gives similar results (see Table 2).

This table is suggestive in several ways:

a. The same general tendency as in Carter and Schooler's data emerges: the relative extensions for the value series are considerably larger than for both neutral series.

b. All extensions in the "accuracy set" are larger than the corresponding extensions in the "value set." This is not inconsistent with the general proposition put forward here that the relevance of a series of stimuli is related to an emphasis of the differences between them. It is reasonable to assume that an appeal for accuracy of judgment would lead to similar results in its stress on clear discrimination between the stimuli of the series.

c. The differences between the extensions of the value and the neutral series are less marked in the "accuracy" than in the "value" set. This is also consistent with the position adopted in this paper. An appeal for accuracy would have little effect in a series associated with value, where the accentuation of differences between the stimuli exists already as a long-standing product of past experience (cf. McCurdy's discussion of the role of schemata in the perception of coins, 22). This same appeal would have comparatively more effect in the case of a neutral series.

One further example: Dukes and Bevan (9) found that for their "positive" series (jars filled with candy) the variability of responses was less marked than for the "neutral" series (jars filled with sand). This is related to smaller j.n.d.'s in the positive than in the neutral series. In other words, the differences between the stimuli of the positive series were more clearly and consistently perceived than the objectively equivalent differences in the neutral series, and the scale of judgments was more extended for the positive than for the neutral series.

This summary of evidence suggests that the results of the "relevant" experiments on overestimation cannot be solely the product of some simple and rather mysterious process of overestimation. As has already been pointed out, the interest of the experimenters was confined mainly to the comparisons of the perceptual judgments

of stimuli in a value series with the judgments of physically equivalent stimuli in a neutral series. The subjects were invited to make comparisons between the valued stimuli and either a neutral standard or elements of a parallel neutral series (with the exception of the experiment by Dukes and Bevan, in which comparisons *between* the stimuli of the value series were also included). However, the implications of the fact that the stimuli associated with value do form a series cannot be ignored; during the experiments the subjects were repeatedly exposed to the various elements of this series, and the "belongingness," in the case of coins, would be further enhanced by familiarity.

In view of the evidence concerning the effects that all elements of a series, past and present, have on the quantitative judgments of its individual members (e.g., 14, 18), it may reasonably be assumed that the judgments of magnitude given by the subjects in the "relevant" overestimation experiments were not only determined by the perceived relationship, at the time of judgment, between a stimulus of the value series and a standard. They must have been affected as well by the background of perceived relationships between this particular stimulus and all other stimuli of the same series. This assumption is further supported by the evidence that the effects exercised by a particular stimulus on judgments pertaining to a series of stimuli increase as a function of the extent to which this stimulus is perceived as forming part of the series which is being judged (4).

In other words, in the "relevant" experiments on overestimation two aspects of the situation must be taken into account: The *inter*serial and the *intra*serial. The first consists of the perceived relationships of magnitude between any stimulus of the value series and the neutral stimuli; the second is concerned with the perception of relationships between the stimuli of a value series as compared with the corresponding relationships in an objectively identical neutral series.

TABLE 2

STIMULI	PERCENTAGE INCREASE FROM ACTUAL TO PERCEIVED EXTENSION	
	Value Set	Accuracy Set
Coins (on table)	68.2	73.7
Metal discs	34.9	55.7
Paper discs	20.9	39.8

Converted from Bruner and Rodrigues, table 6, p. 21.

The phenomenon of accentuation of differences between the stimuli in a value series can be isolated in its "pure" form when the following two requirements are satisfied: the subjects' judgments must be based on comparisons between the various stimuli of this series, and not between these stimuli and some extraneous ones; and the value and neutral series must be objectively identical, value being the only experimental variable in which they differ. These requirements were satisfied in some experiments recently completed by the writer (27).[2]

An ordered series of ten weights was used, and the subjects were requested to judge their heaviness in terms of seven category numbers. Each subject underwent an equal number of sessions under the "value" and under the "neutral" conditions. An experimental session consisted of two parts: in the first part, the entire series was presented several times in random order, but no judgments were reported by the subject. In the second part, following the first after an interval of about three minutes, all the stimuli were presented again several times, and judgments of weight were requested at each presentation. In the value condition, a small paper bonus (gift certificate, exchangeable for a book) accompanied each presentation of one of the two heaviest (or two lightest) stimuli of the series during the first part of the session. No rewards were given in the first part of the neutral sessions. In this way, the effects of the two experimental conditions, introduced in the first part of the sessions, on judgments of weight in the second part could be assessed. A total of 60 adult subjects were used in the four experiments. They were told, as part of the instructions, that the purpose of the experiment was to investigate the effects of monotony on the speed of performing a simple task which consisted of discriminating between weights. The "small paper tokens," which they were to receive from time to time, were being introduced in order "to vary the degree of monotony." A questionnaire, which was presented to the subjects after completion of all the experiments, revealed that none of them doubted the truth of these statements. The subsequent disclosure of the experimenter's bad faith caused considerable surprise.

Data consisted of differences in the extensions of the scales of judgment between the two conditions for each of the subjects. Results can be briefly summarized as follows: in the first two experiments, in which rewards were associated with the two heaviest and the two lightest stimuli of the series, respectively, extensions of the scales

of judgments were significantly larger for the value than for the neutral condition. In a third experiment, in which rewards were associated indiscriminately with all the stimuli of the series, no such effect occurred. In a fourth experiment, the procedure was the same as in the first and second experiments, apart from the fact that the paper "bonuses," passed by the experimenter to the subjects at each presentation of either one of the two heaviest or one of the two lightest stimuli, were devoid of all value. Once again, no significant effect on the extension of the scale of judgments was observed.

All this evidence is, to say the least, strongly suggestive. The advantages of using accentuation of differences as an explanatory device for overestimation are threefold:

a. It accounts for some seemingly contradictory results, such as the underestimation of the small end of the value series reported in some studies (7, 8); it also accounts for Bruner and Rodrigues' (7) "relative overestimation."

b. It does not require an introduction of *deus ex machina* principles to account for the phenomenon of overestimation in the "relevant" class.

c. With some extensions, it can be applied to the "interserial" differences in the "relevant" experiments, and to most experiments on overestimation which fall outside the "relevant" class.

The first point above does not require further elaboration. The second can be supported by some lines of argument, independent of each other.

McCurdy (22) has recently pointed out that by exaggerating the differences between the various coins, memory commits a "good error." In his ingenious attempt to relate the results of the studies on coins to the concept of schemata, he limited his discussion to series of coins where strong schemata could have developed through long familiarity with the stimuli. However, this would not account for the results of those experiments in which accentuation of differences in the value series, as compared with the neutral series, was found to exist (9, 27), in spite of the fact that the conditions for the development of the schemata were, as far as one can judge, not notably different for the two series.

What is the nature of the experience with coins, or with any series of stimuli, where it is important to discriminate sharply between the elements of the series? Discriminative responses to stimuli in such series are not usually made in terms of precise quantitative labels attached to individual stimuli. They are made in terms of "larger than," or "smaller than," the neighboring elements of the series. Minimizing the differences entails a risk of confusion; accentuating them is an additional guarantee of a successful response. However, the normal routine of responding in terms of "larger" or "smaller" is upset in most experi-

[2] This investigation was supported by a grant from the Durham Colleges Research Fund.

ments on overestimation. The usual technique for correct handling of coins, for example, which is based primarily on an awareness of the relevant differences between a particular coin and other coins of the series, present or absent, is not quite adequate, as unusually precise individual quantitative labels are requested in the experiments. These absolute labels, whether obtained through matching or through some kind of verbal categorizing, may be expected to reveal an accentuation of differences between the stimuli, since they would reflect, and possibly exaggerate, what is otherwise implicit in the relative judgments of comparison pertaining to the series.

It is in this sense only that the results yielded by the studies on overestimation can be treated as experimental artifacts. In this context, it is not particularly important to find out whether the stimuli are really "seen" as larger or smaller. They are *reproduced* as such; to ask the subject to match a variable standard to a stimulus, or to assign to the stimulus a quantitative verbal label, is essentially asking him to reproduce its size. This reproduction, which involves an activity very different from stating vaguely that an object is sizably larger or smaller than something else, lends itself easily to a sharpening of the relevant distinctive feature of it, which is, in this instance, its difference in size from the next object in the series. The phenomenon is not unfamiliar: Gibson reported some time ago (12) that a sharpening of differences occurred in the early stages of aircraft recognition training, when his subjects were asked to draw the silhouettes of the various aircraft.

A prediction is possible here to the effect that shifts in the estimates of magnitudes would either not occur or promptly disappear if the training to discriminate between the elements of a series, along which discrimination is important for the subject, was directed towards the accuracy of individual quantitative labels rather than towards a clear distinction in relative terms between the stimuli. This is exactly what happened in an experiment by Smith, Parker, and Robinson (25) in which accuracy of report was a condition of obtaining the reward. Prizes were offered to the subjects who would report correctly the greatest number of *dots* forming clusters which were flashed successively on a screen. In a control group, prizes went to those subjects who reported correctly on the number of dots in the greatest number of *clusters*. No information about the accuracy of their estimates was available to the subjects during the experiment. The first group showed overestimation in the early stages of the experiment, but after a certain number of trials the performance of both groups converged.

An experiment is being designed at present to test a further implication of the present argument: that in any ordered series, training to discriminate in comparative terms between the stimuli will result in larger estimated differences between the elements of the series than training to label the stimuli quantitatively in familiar units of measurement.

These assumptions of a "functional" mechanism underlying the accentuation of differences may be supplemented by some evidence coming from a different quarter. It consists of the findings about the effects of multidimensionality on the acuity of discrimination along a series. Eriksen and Hake (11) have reported recently that when the method of absolute judgments is used, the number of discriminable steps for a series of stimuli is greater when the stimuli vary concurrently in two or more dimensions than when they vary in one dimension only. More specifically, they found that discriminability was considerably greater when the "stimuli varied in size and hue, size and brightness, hue and brightness, and size, hue, and brightness" (p. 159) than when they varied in only one of these dimensions. Eriksen and Hake suggest that their results were due to a kind of summation, to "the ability of Ss to make fairly independent judgments of stimulus values along each of the component dimensions" (p. 158). They add, however:

> We cannot assume that this is always the case for compound stimuli. For some stimuli, judgments made of values in the separate dimensions may be interrelated. That is, the evocation of a particular response tendency by a component of a compound stimulus may change the likelihood of evocation of other response tendencies by other components of the stimulus. We could expect this to occur when Ss have learned by long experience to associate the occurrence of certain values in one dimension with the occurrence of particular values in another.

This interrelation may account in part for such perceptual "errors" as the size-weight illusion. Ryan (23, quoted by Hochberg, 15) writes: ". . . O is not really reporting *weight* at all, but *specific gravity*, and the illusion is really not an illusion at all. O is simply unable to report on weight being influenced by the striking differences in density involved." In the field of size estimation, Holzman and Klein (16) have recently reported that heavy discs were judged larger by their subjects than light discs of identical size, and that black discs were judged smaller than grey discs of identical size and weight. They add wistfully that these results ". . . do not exclude the possibility that value and need may indeed be important variables in size judgments" (p. 40).

Two conclusions can be drawn from the above: the first, supported by Eriksen and Hake's results, is that under some conditions of judgment, and in a situation new to the subject, compounding of concurrently varying dimensions will result in a clearer perception of differences between the stimuli along a series. The second is related to the first, and already outlined in the above quotation from Eriksen and Hake: when the association between dimensions has been a long-standing one, new training may not be capable of inducing changes in discriminability. In such cases, judgments along one of the dimensions have already been influenced, previous to the experiment, by concomitant changes in other dimensions. In other words, it is likely that the Eriksen and Hake situation represents the incipient stages of a process which, if given an opportunity to develop further, might lead to interrelations such as those that Ryan suspects to be responsible for the size-weight illusion, or that Holzman and Klein (16) found between the estimated size and the actual weight of their discs. Interrelations of this kind exist, of course, when there is a consistent pairing, in the environment, of changes in more than one dimension.

Such pairing exists by definition in series where magnitude and value vary concurrently. The difficulty is that value is not a "dimension" in the physical sense. It is, however, an important attribute of the stimuli in such series, if only because efficient discrimination between the stimuli in terms of differences in value is, in most cases, more important than discrimination in terms of the physical dimension. It is not reasonable to expect that subjects who, in an experiment, judge a series of coins in terms of size, judge it in terms of size alone. This would be a feat of abstract behavior difficult for adults, and even more so for children. As Vernon (28) points out in her discussion of the experiment by Bruner and Goodman (5): "It seems fairly certain that . . . there was an inability to isolate a single aspect from a global percept" (p. 187). Or, as Hochberg writes in another context (15): ". . . the subjects are responding in terms of a dimension which specifies the most about the stimulus series with the least number of categories, rather than in terms of the dimension expected by the experimenter."

In the experiment on weights described earlier (27), value is the only "dimension of difference" between the two series. It would also be a supplementary and important difference between two series which differ not only with regard to value, but also with regard to some other dimensions. In the first case, the difference in value is the only contributing factor to a more pronounced accentuation of differences in the value in the neutral series; in the second, it is one of the contributing factors. Once again, this does not necessarily

mean that the subjects "see" the stimuli in the value series as being more different from each other, or larger, or smaller. They respond *as if* they perceived them as such, as this is as far as the phenomenology of it can go for the time being.

"RELEVANT" DIMENSIONS AND THE ACCENTUATION OF DIFFERENCES

The accentuation of differences *between* the stimuli of a value series may partly account for the results obtained in the "relevant" experiments on overestimation. However, it has no direct bearing on the problems raised by the results of the "irrelevant" group of experiments; nor does it help to understand why in the "relevant" group a rather consistent trend towards overestimation of the value series should be superimposed, as it were, on the sharpening of differences within it.

The preceding discussion is not, however, entirely irrelevant to these problems. As was pointed out earlier, in a "relevant" series the subjects' judgments are simultaneously determined by the perceived differences between the stimuli of the series, and between a particular stimulus of the series and an extraneous stimulus. In the "irrelevant" experiments, where the magnitude under investigation seems in no way related to the presence or absence of value, the fact that one stimulus is "valued" and another "neutral" would form an additional distinctive feature between them, superimposed on the physical differences. Examples of such experiments have been given above (6, 19, 20). Beams' study (2) on overestimation of size of favorite food objects by children provides another example. The common feature of these experiments is that the subjects are requested to judge along a dimension which, in usual circumstances, does not help to discriminate between the objects in terms of their value. Children, who in the experiment by Lambert *et al.*, (20) were asked to report on the size of the chips, had just experienced a situation in which the value of the chips was determined by their color. The refugees, who in the study by Klein *et al.* (19) were judging the size of discs containing the swastika, would be unlikely, in any other circumstances, to pay special attention to the *size* of the emblem.

In these experiments the valued and the neutral objects belong to sharply distinctive categories of experience, and size is certainly not the basis of classification. In such cases, to judge size exclusively on the basis of size would, once again, be possible only if the subjects were able to abstract one element, and not an important one, out of a complex compound of experience. A more likely assumption is that the qualitative "motivational" differences between the two kinds of stimuli function in the direction of accentuating the perceived differences between their "irrelevant" magnitudes.

This would lead to the prediction that, all else constant, the perceived differences of magnitude between valued (or otherwise relevant) and neutral stimuli would be larger than the corresponding differences between two sets of neutral stimuli. It does not, however, allow for the prediction that the valued stimuli would be perceived as *larger* than the neutral ones.

Some interesting indications which may suggest a way out of this difficulty can be found in the experimental literature. In the group of studies on "irrelevant" magnitudes, three experiments seem typical of those which yielded negative (or partially negative) results. Klein *et al.* (19) reported that their subjects did not reliably overestimate the discs containing the swastika. Bevan and Bevan (3), who used a "quasi-representative design" and a heterogeneous assortment of objects with their two children, found that the ratio of estimated to real size was not higher for the liked than for the disliked or neutral objects. Finally, Lysak and Gilchrist (21) found that increasing complexity of design was a significant determinant of increasing overestimation; but dollar bills were not judged larger than the corresponding rectangles, nor was there any correlation between overestimation and value of various dollar bills. Experiments by Lambert *et al.* (20) and by Beams (2), already referred to, are representative of those in which positive results were reported.

The experiments of Klein *et al.* (or at least the parts of them involving the swastika) and of Bevan and Bevan (3) have one feature in common: the value of the objects used has nothing to do with their size. The data, as they are presented, do not allow one to draw conclusions about an accentuation of differences beween the size of valued and neutral stimuli; but if there was such an accentuation, there are no grounds to assume on the basis of the present argument that it should work, with any degree of consistency, in the direction of overestimating the valued objects.

On the other hand, it seems reasonable to say that the dictum "the bigger the better" expresses a profound truth to Beams' 10- to 12-year-old *S*s when they are confronted with a piece of fruitcake, a sugar cookie, or a "marshmallow-covered chocolate cupcake" (2, p. 197). Lambert *et al.* worked with much younger children (3 to 5 years old); the number of chips of a particular color which they received was related to the amount of candy which was the final compensation for their efforts. It would not be surprising if this, in view of the age of the subjects, had a great deal to do with their judgments of size.

The negative results of Lysak and Gilchrist (21) lend further support to the thesis that the accentuation of differences will tend consistently towards an overestimation of valued objects *only* when there exists a valued series in which there is some discernible relationship between magnitude and value. Their adult subjects knew from long experience that the value of dollar bills does not vary as a function of their size. They may have accentuated the differences in size between the bills and the corresponding rectangles, but not necessarily or consistently by overestimating the bills more than the control stimuli.

A comparison of this study with other experiments performed on adult subjects helps to bring out more clearly its particular features which may account for the lack of positive results. In the experiment by Klein *et al.*, there is no tendency to overestimate the disc bearing the swastika; but in one of their two experimental situations, all results pertaining to the disc bearing the dollar sign are significant (19, Table 3, p. 103). This is further substantiated by Solley and Lee (26) who attempted ". . . to determine whether the differences in perceived size of discs with symbols drawn upon them, as reported by Bruner and Postman, could be better explained by their hypothesis of symbolic value than by the more general Gestalt principle of closure" (p. 142). They report an overestimation of the discs containing a dollar sign (as compared with discs containing a figure of presumably equal degree of closure), but no such effect with the discs containing a swastika. The fact that a symbol of money drawn on a disc is strongly suggestive of the familiar series of coins, whose value increases with their size, may well be responsible for these results.

The negative outcome of the experiment by Lysak and Gilchrist must also be taken in conjunction with an almost identical experiment by Dukes and Bevan (10), who reported positive results. They used a number of rectangular cards, identical in size but differing in value, and engaged in "gambling" with their subjects. A number representing its value was stamped on each of the cards. The cards were drawn at random from a bag, and at each draw the subject won or lost an amount of money proportional to the positive or negative number printed on the card. As soon as each drawn card was returned to the bag, the subject was asked to match its size with one of a series of blank reference cards spread out in front of him. Dukes and Bevan's hypothesis was that "as the monetary value printed on the test card increases from zero, the subject, regardless of winning or losing, will tend to select larger reference cards as his estimates" (10, p. 47). This was confirmed: a significant correlation emerged between the ratios of estimated to actual sizes and the monetary value, positive or negative, of the test cards.

The situation was almost identical with one of the arrangements of Lysak and Gilchrist's experiment (21). If the fact of conflicting results were to be ascribed, here or in other cases, to relatively unimportant differences in procedure, attempts to generalize results from a great number of psychological experiments would have to suffer a serious setback. There is, however, one essential difference between the two experiments: Lysak and Gilchrist's subjects *knew* that all the dollar bills, with which they were presented, were of equal size. This bit of information about the cards used was not available to Dukes and Bevan's subjects. What is more, Dukes and Bevan included in their instructions the following sentence: "Here is a bag containing small white cards, *varying slightly in size*" (10, p. 44, italics mine). It would be only natural for the subjects to assume that this variation followed some regular pattern, and that this pattern consisted of an increase in size corresponding to the increase in value. Here again, a continuous variation along the dimension of value has carried over to the judgments of the physical dimension, and this has been further helped by a hint from the experimenter.

But there is some evidence that the same could have happened even without the hint. In an experiment by Ashley, Harper, and Runyon (1), a "grayish metal slug" was presented several times to the subjects. At different presentations of the slug they were told that "it was made of either lead, silver, white gold, or platinum" (p. 568). Judgments of the size of the slug reflected its imaginary value; the size of the variable standard "that was called equal to the slug increased as the cost of the metal increased" (p. 572). As in the preceding example, a progressive increase in value is related to an imaginary increase in size, while the actual size is kept constant.

The evidence summarized so far lends strong support to the view that both the positive and the negative results of the studies on overestimation can be best understood in terms of a hypothesis of accentuation of differences. This accentuation would work along two axes: between the stimuli of a series in which there is a concomitant variation of value and magnitude; and between the valued stimuli and the neutral ones. In the latter case, the accentuation would tend towards a relative overestimation of the valued stimuli only under certain conditions, which have been discussed above.

SOCIAL PERCEPTION

Some implications of the present discussion go beyond the problems raised by the phenomenon of overestimation. It may be said that, in a sense, "overestimation" as discussed in this paper is a special case and a convincing experimental paradigm of a more general aspect of social perception. Many social objects and events are sharply classified in terms of their value or relevance.

When judgments concerning some quantifiable or ratable aspects of stimuli which fall into distinct categories are called for, differences in value or relevance cannot fail to influence the quantitative judgments in the direction of sharpening the objectively existing differences between the stimuli. A very similar conception has recently been formulated by Hochberg (15), and applied by him to the perception of in- and out-group individuals:

> If a group of individuals is perceived as different from the non-group individuals, the perceived differences between those within the group and those outside the group will automatically be sharpened, and the differences perceived between the members of the group (i.e., intragroup differences), and between those outside the group will be lessened.

These judgmental effects of categorization are probably fairly general; it is likely, however, that they are particularly pronounced when judgments are made in dimensions in which scaling in magnitude is simultaneously a scaling in value. Thus, it may well be that an accentuation of differences in size will hardly occur between two paintings, one liked and one indifferent or disliked. But when skin color, or height, or some facial traits of social "value" are concerned, there will be a marked sharpening of differences in the degree of these characteristics perceived as belonging to individuals who are assigned to different categories. Some evidence of this is provided by a recent study on "perceptual accentuation and the Negro stereotype" conducted by Secord, Bevan, and Katz (24). Their results suggest that a group of prejudiced Ss sharpened the differences in the degree of Negroid physiognomic traits possessed respectively by Negroes and whites, more than did a group of nonprejudiced Ss. It is likely that the same is happening in the case of more abstract social judgments which are implicitly quantitative, such as, for example, those concerning the relative frequency of crimes in various social groups, as perceived by people who have an axe to grind.

SUMMARY

The thesis put forward in this paper is that the apparently conflicting results of studies concerned with perceptual overestimation can be best understood if this phenomenon is considered as a special case of accentuation of perceived differences. This would work in two directions. First, in a series of stimuli in which there exists a concomitant variation of value and of some physical dimension, the perceived differences between the elements of the series would be larger than in a corresponding neutral series. Secondly, the perceived differences in magnitude between the stimuli which possess the attribute of value and those which do not would tend to be more accentuated than the corresponding differences between neutral stimuli. This would not, however, always result in overestimation. The sharpening of differences resulting in overestimation of valued stimuli would occur only when, in the class of stimuli with the attribute of value, an increase in some physical magnitude is correlated with the increase in value. In other cases, there are no grounds for assuming that an accentuation of perceived differences between the two classes of stimuli would tend consistently towards an overestimation of the valued stimuli.

In this way, overestimation is seen as one instance of a more general phenomenon. The accentuation of differences between classes of stimuli occurs when these stimuli differ in some respects other than the dimension along which the subjects are reporting their judgments of quantity. The presence or absence of "value" or "relevance" is one such contrast. It is probable that this contrast is responsible not only for the results obtained in the field of overestimation. It may also lead to the sharpening of differences between the quantifiable or ratable aspects of social objects and events. This occurs when the dimension along which judgments are made is not the primary basis for assigning the various stimuli into their sharply distinctive categories.

REFERENCES

1. ASHLEY, W. R., HARPER, R. S., & RUNYON, D. L. The perceived size of coins in normal and hypnotically induced economic states. *Amer. J. Psychol.,* 1951, **64,** 564–572.
2. BEAMS, H. L. Affectivity as a factor in the apparent size of pictured food objects. *J. exp. Psychol.,* 1954, **47,** 197–200.
3. BEVAN, W., & BEVAN, D. C. Judged size and personal relevance: an exercise in quasi-representative design. *J. gen. Psychol.,* 1956, **54,** 203–207.
4. BROWN, D. R. Stimulus-similarity and the anchoring of subjective scales. *Amer. J. Psychol.,* 1953, **66,** 199–214.
5. BRUNER, J. S., & GOODMAN, C. C. Value and need as organizing factors in perception. *J. abnorm. soc. Psychol.,* 1947, **42,** 33–44.
6. BRUNER, J. S., & POSTMAN, L. Symbolic value as an organizing factor in perception. *J. soc. Psychol.,* 1948, **27,** 203–208.
7. BRUNER, J. S., & RODRIGUES, J. S. Some determinants of apparent size. *J. abnorm. soc. Psychol.,* 1953, **48,** 17–24.
8. CARTER, L. F., & SCHOOLER, K. Value, need, and other factors in perception. *Psychol. Rev.,* 1949, **56,** 200–207.
9. DUKES, W. F., & BEVAN, W. Accentuation and response variability in the perception of personally relevant objects. *J. Pers.,* 1952, **20,** 457–465.
10. DUKES, W. F., & BEVAN, W. Size estimation and monetary value: a correlation. *J. Psychol.,* 1952, **34,** 43–53.
11. ERIKSEN, C. W., & HAKE, H. W. Multidimensional stimulus differences and accuracy of discrimination. *J. exp. Psychol.,* 1955, **50,** 153–160.
12. GIBSON, J. J. Social perception and the psychology of perceptual learning. In M. Sherif & M. O. Wilson (Eds.), *Group relations at the crossroads.* New York: Harper, 1953. Pp. 120–138.
13. GILCHRIST, J. C., & NESBERG, L. S. Need and perceptual change in need-related objects. *J. exp. Psychol.,* 1952, **44,** 369–376.
14. HELSON, H. Adaptation-level as a basis for a quantitative theory of frames of reference. *Psychol. Rev.,* 1948, **55,** 297–313.
15. HOCHBERG, J. E. Psychophysics and stereotypy in social perception. In *Emerging problems in social psychology,* in press.
16. HOLZMAN, P. S., & KLEIN, G. S. Intersensory and visual field forces in size estimation. *Percept. Mot. Skills,* 1956, 1, 37–42.
17. JENKIN, N. Affective processes in perception. *Psychol. Bull.,* 1957, **54,** 100–127.
18. JOHNSON, D. M. *The psychology of thought and judgment.* New York: Harper, 1955.
19. KLEIN, G. S., SCHLESINGER, H. J., & MEISTER, D. E. The effect of values on perception: an experimental critique. *Psychol. Rev.,* 1951, **58,** 96–112.
20. LAMBERT, W. W., SOLOMON, R. L., & WATSON, P. D. Reinforcement and extinction as factors in size estimation. *J. exp. Psychol.,* 1949, **39,** 637–641.
21. LYSAK, W., & GILCHRIST, J. C Value, equivocality and goal availability. *J. Pers.,* 1955, **23,** 500–501. (Abstract)
22. McCURDY, H. G. Coin perception studies and the concept of schemata. *Psychol. Rev.,* 1956, **63,** 160–168.
23. RYAN, T. A. Interrelations of the sensory systems in perception. *Psychol. Bull.,* 1940, **37,** 659–698.
24. SECORD, P. F., BEVAN, W., & KATZ, B. The Negro stereotype and perceptual accentuation. *J. abnorm. soc. Psychol.,* 1956, **53,** 78–83.
25. SMITH, K. R., PARKER, G. B., & ROBINSON, G. A. An exploratory investigation of autistic perception. *J. abnorm. soc. Psychol.,* 1951, **46,** 324–326.
26. SOLLEY, C. M., & LEE, R. Perceived size: closure versus symbolic value. *Amer. J. Psychol.,* 1955, **68,** 142–144.
27. TAJFEL, H. The role of value in the formation of a scale of judgments. *Bull. Brit. psychol. Soc.,* 1956, **29,** 14. (Abstract)
28. VERNON, M. D. The functions of schemata in perceiving. *Psychol. Rev.,* 1955, **62,** 180–192.

FORMING IMPRESSIONS OF PERSONALITY*

Studies of impression formation generally use experimental situations that are most similar to those everyday situations where the main information we have about another person consists of statements by a mutual acquaintance or written material about the persons. Veness and Brierley continue an earlier series of experiments which start with the pioneer work of Asch[a] (1946). In Asch's study, groups of college students were told that a list of traits belonging to a particular person would be read to them and that they should try to form an impression of the kind of person described. After hearing the list read twice, they were asked to write a brief characterization of the person in just a few sentences. Asch found that his subjects readily accomplished the task, in spite of the meagre information provided concerning the hypothetical person.

A basic concept in such work is that of centrality. Trait lists describing a person appear to contain certain terms that have a strong effect on the impression formed, and other terms that make only a minor contribution to an evaluation of the stimulus person. For example, the term *warm* appearing in a list generates a strong impression of friendliness, generosity, kindness, sociability, and has many additional connotations. The term *cold* also has a strong effect, of an opposite nature. Such terms have been called *central* traits. In contrast, such traits as *polite* or *blunt* do not have as much influence on the impression formed. Such traits are termed *peripheral*.

Veness and Brierley vary earlier forms of experimentation by having the stimulus person, a speech expert, describe herself on a tape recording. Instead of conveying the impression of warmth or coldness in verbal terms, the impression of warmth was conveyed by varying voice quality. One group received the impression of warmth, and another, of coldness. Other traits were conveyed in direct verbal terms, by her self-description. Another experimental treatment reported in this article presents traits descriptive of a person in written form, instead of orally, as is usually done. The results of these experimental procedures are reported and analyzed, with particular emphasis on the concept of central traits.

The first of these two experiments increases external validity in that the stimulus person is presented much as she would be in a life situation. The second augments internal validity by demonstrating that impression formation takes place in a similar manner when traits are presented in written form—effects are not simply an artifact of oral presentation of trait cues.

9.

Forming Impressions of Personality: Two Experiments

THELMA VENESS
DOROTHY W. BRIERLEY
BIRKBECK COLLEGE, UNIVERSITY OF LONDON

Asch's experiment on forming impressions of personality on the basis of lists of traits, one trait being different for the two experimental groups, is reduplicated with certain variations. In the first experiment, the traits are embodied in a descriptive passage reproduced on tape, the variable trait being represented by changes in tone of voice. The second experiment makes only a slight modification on Asch's original experiment, and confirms his main findings: however, the data are, in part, differently analysed. The results of the two experiments are discussed in relation to theoretical points raised by Asch, some of which have been recently disputed by Wishner.

INTRODUCTION

Asch's experiments on forming impressions of personality from lists of trait names, using the technique of varying one trait only (Asch, 1946), have been followed by a number of studies using the same technique (Mensch & Wishner, 1947; Kelley, 1950) and others using different experimental situations but also investigating the way in which personality impressions are formed on the basis of similar stimulus material (Cofer & Dunne, 1952; Shapiro & Tagiuri, 1958). Subjects seem to have little difficulty in forming intelligible impressions of a hypothetical person described by a few characteristics only, suggesting that the 'implicit personality theory' (Bruner & Tagiuri, 1954) we apply when we form initial impressions of real people may owe much to systematized expectations based on relatively few cues. Even when apparently incompatible information is provided (Asch, 1946; Haire & Grunes, 1950; Gollin,

* The selection following the editorial introduction is reprinted from "Forming impressions of personality: Two experiments," *British Journal of Social and Clinical Psychology*, 1963, **2**, 11–19, by permission of the authors and publisher.

[a] S. E. Asch. Forming impressions of personality. *J. abnorm. soc. Psychol.*, 1946, **41**, 258–290.

1958), many people are able to find means of reconciliation that permit them to form coherent personality impressions.

While Asch's experimental technique has largely been accepted without criticism, with one exception, certain of his theoretical points (Asch, 1946, 1952) have aroused controversy. Asch, with his preference for field rather than association explanations, spoke of the traits themselves 'seeking organization', rather than of past experience leading to expectations of certain relationships between traits (Bruner, Shapiro & Taguiri, 1958) or of the logical relatedness of traits (Hays, 1958). Further, the principles of organization were adumbrated: the given traits organize themselves in a hierarchical way, certain traits occupying a central position. The warm–cold variable was the one which best illustrated this situation, and several later studies, with one exception (Kjeldergaard & Jenkins, 1958), have also claimed that this variable takes up a central position. Until challenged by Wishner (1960), the evidence for the centrality of this variable seemed overwhelming. Hays (1958), in a study in which 'centrality' is defined, in part, in terms of implication, demonstrated that the terms 'warm' and 'cold' were ones which implied many other traits while not being implied by them. (Indeed, Shapiro & Taguiri (1958), using a technique in which variations were made in the response list instead of the stimulus list, found that 'warm' was seldom inferred from the given characteristics 'intelligent' and 'independent.') Asch himself extended his analysis of the effects of 'warm' and 'cold' by studying their metaphorical uses in various languages, concluding that common functional relations are involved in metaphor, 'warm' always denoting physically and psychologically a property that brings us closer, 'cold' one that excludes and isolates (Asch, 1958). On this basis, one would expect the warm–cold variable to have a certain prepotency when we are forming first impressions, so that Wishner's refutation of its centrality in experimental impression-formation is unexpected and worthy, therefore, of close scrutiny.

The experiments to be reported were conducted before they could benefit from Wishner's work. The findings will be evaluated, however, in the light of his discussion.

EXPERIMENT *I*

The one criticism made of Asch's procedure, by Luchins (1948), was that it was divorced from reality in dealing only with trait names and hypothetical persons. Kelley (1950) used the Asch technique but introduced real persons. The present experiment attempts to meet Luchins' criticism by presenting stimulus material in the form of tape-recordings of a human voice, whereas the warm-cold variation is represented in the manner of speaking.

Subjects

Sixty women students, in the second year of a course of training to be non-graduate teachers, were divided randomly into two groups of 30. They were told only that the experiment was concerned with the way in which first impressions of people are formed.

Stimulus material

Two tape-recordings were made by the same speaker, a woman unknown to the subjects, speaking the same passage but adapting her voice to give an impression of either warmth or coldness.[1] In the talk, the speaker was describing her job and Asch's six non-central traits were implied as closely as possible, without direct mention. The passage was as follows, with the relevant traits inserted in brackets:

> Good afternoon. I have been asked to speak to you today about my work as a veterinary surgeon and to give you some idea of the variety and interest which I derive from my large and far-flung country practice in North Wales. I qualified as a vet. after training at Liverpool University and I was fortunate to complete my very long training in the minimum time. (INTELLIGENT.) I then obtained a post as assistant to a vet. who was already in established practice and who gave me every opportunity for making use of my newly-acquired professional skills. (SKILFUL.) My work is virtually of two kinds; firstly with small animals, mostly pets, who are brought to morning and evening surgery by their owners for treatment of major or minor ailments or accidents; secondly it is with larger animals of the scattered farms in the valleys and hills around the town itself. In addition to tending sick animals in this way, I am responsible to the Ministry of Health for the testing of herds of cattle for tuberculosis. This has to be done at regular intervals and has become a part of almost every day's work, after morning surgery, and is something with which my assistant is, as yet, unqualified to help me.
>
> My day begins with the arrival of the postman at half-past six and, very often, with the ringing of the telephone, as farmers are early risers and crises

---

[1] Thanks are due to Miss Muriel Judd, Senior Lecturer in Speech and Drama at the college, for invaluable training and assistance in making the recordings.

so often happen during the night, (IN-DUSTRIOUS.) Surgery over by ten o'clock, I set out in my car for the neighbouring and distant farms. The problems of weather, transport, distances, bad roads and difficult hills are very great in a country practice, but my assistant and I have managed not to let such difficulties deter us from our purpose of reaching a sick animal at all costs. (DE-TERMINED.) And because of these hazards of mountain roads and unforeseen weather changes, I have found it essential to learn how to service my own car and keep it in running repair. All too often in the early days of my work here, I found myself having to change a wheel or dismantle the carburettor. (PRACTICAL.) Some parts of the countryside are very lonely, so I always carry a crowbar in my car. I wondered at first whether a gun would be a better weapon of defence, if put to the test, but the crowbar is easy to wield and it gives one a feeling of security. (CAUTIOUS.)

Long distance visits are usually completed by mid-afternoon, and then I return home to deal with telephone calls, messages and emergency visits to surgery. Sometimes I have to make further local visits. Evening surgery is rarely over by seven o'clock and even then I have my records to complete after supper. But I recommend this work as being interesting, varied and worth while, and ideal for those who enjoy life in the open air and the country, and who are not afraid of hard work.

Procedure

The experimental groups each heard one of these recordings and they were then asked to write free character sketches of the person. Finally, they

TABLE 1   Discrepancies between the Cold Groups of Experiments 1 and 2

TRAITS	NOS. SELECTING THEM (N = 30)	
	EXPERIMENT 1	EXPERIMENT 2
Generous	7	24
Ruthless	16	0
Self-centred	21	7
Humorous	4	17
Sociable	5	22
Popular	5	23
Important	20	29
Restrained	28	14

were given a checklist like that used by Asch (see Table 3), except that the words 'warm' and 'cold' were added, and they were asked to underline the word of each pair that best fitted the person described.

RESULTS AND DISCUSSION

All six non-central traits were mentioned in a number of the free character sketches in each group, at least by a very close synonym, suggesting that the passage was adequate in conveying the characteristics intended. All 30 subjects who heard the 'warm' recording underlined 'warm' on the checklist, whereas only 18 of the 'cold' group underlined 'cold.'

Considering only these 48 subjects, who did receive the impression intended, their selections among the remaining pairs of traits in the checklist agreed to a significant degree with those marked in Experiment 2 below (in which no actual person was used, reproducing, for the most part, Asch's original experiment). Comparing the warm groups of the two experiments, by ranking the eighteen characteristics according to number of selections, rho is 0.92; for the two cold groups, it is 0.63.

There are discrepancies, however, between the two experiments, the most marked of which are shown in Table 1. These suggest a greater attribution of 'warm' qualities (e.g., generous, humorous, sociable) and a lesser attribution of 'cold' qualities (ruthless, self-centred, restrained) on the part of the cold group in the first experiment compared with the cold group of the second. These results should be considered together with the fact that 12 of the cold group did not identify the speaker as cold. There are at least two possible reasons for this. The acting may have been inadequate, and a naturally warm voice not sufficiently concealed: however, 60 per cent of those who were intended to hear a cold voice did, in fact, do so. The more likely explanation is that the occupation described, that of veterinary surgeon, was even more potent in conjuring up expectations than the coldness of the voice: Asch himself (1946) had different results on his checklist according to whether the original traits were attributed to a man, a woman or a child. Certain social and occupational roles are readily associated with warmth from the nature of the relationships or work involved, and an occupation devoted to the nurturance of animals is likely to be among these. The cold group in this experiment was, therefore, confronted with incompatible information, as in the experiments of Pepitone & Hayden (1955) and Haire & Grunes (1950). Some dealt with the situation by ignoring the less definite information.

Centrality

In the case of the 80 per cent of subjects who did not receive the intended impression, the subsequent selection of traits was very similar to that of Experiment 2, where the descriptions 'warm' and 'cold' were made explicitly. This is substantial justification of the attempt to represent these characteristics by manner only. While the efficacy of other traits has not been tested in the same fashion, it is difficult to imagine the use of this experimental method for the presentation of other pairs of qualities demonstrated by Wishner as being central in his sense—'humane' and 'ruthless', for example. The warm–cold dimension is a pervasive one—i.e. it can be expressed by voice, gesture and posture as well as in the content of speech—and this makes it likely to be an important dimension in impression-formation. And, with its connotations of acceptance and rejection, it will be for many people a highly relevant dimension on which to classify people being met for the first time. For some, however, an occupational or similar social classification gives information even more relevant to their expectation systems.

Asch's claim that the warm–cold variable occupied a central position in impression-formation rested on two findings. One of these will be discussed later: that when the subjects were asked to mark the given traits according to their importance in impression-formation, warm and cold were ranked high. More important was the effectiveness of these two traits, as distinct from others Asch tried, in giving differential results on the checklist. This is where Wishner has produced contrary evidence. Claiming that Asch's differential results would be entirely predictable from independent measures of the relationship between the so-called central and other traits, he was able to substantiate this, with a high degree of success, by first asking student subjects to assess their University instructors on relevant semantic differential scales, which afforded the independent measures of relationship required. This alone, of course, does not weaken Asch's claim that warm–cold is a central variable. But Wishner then applied the procedure to make another pair of traits equally 'central,' in the sense of differentiating on a checklist, when this new checklist consisted of traits found independently to be related to the new central variable.

While there is no need to dispute Wishner's main contention that traits interact in predictable ways, which Asch appears to have denied, there are points that should be made about Wishner's experiments. First, his demonstrations are not complete. He has failed to test also whether the warm–cold variable would be effective with the checklist specially composed for the 'humane–ruthless' variable. But, more important, the independent measures of the relation between traits were obtained from the assessments of one occupational group only—University teachers—and by subjects by whom they were already known. Asch's experiments invited the subjects to 'create' persons not already known, and the experiment described above demanded impressions of someone being met for the first time. In first encounters the warm–cold variable may be very important,

as argued above, while it may become far less important in someone familiar and with whom one has a formalized relationship, as student with teacher. Moreover, in the assessment of certain occupational groups (such as University lecturer compared, say, with veterinary surgeon) this particular variable may be less salient, and the interaction of traits may be different. In fact, Wishner's findings support his theoretical position to a greater extent than might be expected from so biased a sample of persons to be assessed. Some of the negative findings, however, may be explicable by reference to the particular expectations aroused by the social role studied (for example, 'inflexible' having a negligible correlation with 'unintelligent' and 'popular' with the blunt-polite dimension when University teachers are rated; but high degrees of association when a person has to be 'created'), although to pursue the argument thoroughly it would be necessary to know the distributions of assessments on each trait. That there will be systematic differences in the interrelation of traits associated with different occupations has yet to be shown, however.

Although Wishner is probably right when he says 'a trait is central for those traits correlated with it and peripheral for those traits uncorrelated with it' (p. 108), it could still be the case that certain traits will have more traits in all correlated with them, which increases their chances of being 'central' in Wishner's sense.

EXPERIMENT 2

It seems to have escaped notice that in the original experiment the stimulus lists of traits were *read* to the subjects, despite the possibility of unequal emphasis being given, unintentionally, to the seven words. The transition to visual presentation occurred in 1950 (Haire & Grunes; Kelley), but without explicit mention and in association with other procedural modifications. The experiment now to be reported is a repetition of Asch's original experiment but with visual presentation, performed partly to check this point and partly to gather material that could be analysed more closely than is possible from the published accounts of Asch's data.

Subjects

Sixty women students from the same training college were used, these being in the third year.

Procedure

The traits used by Asch were typed on sheets of paper, thirty containing the word 'warm' in the middle of the list, thirty 'cold'. These were interleaved randomly for distribution. The subjects were asked, in both written instructions and verbally, to read them several times, trying to form an impression of the person described, since afterwards they would be asked to write brief character sketches. These were written after one minute of reading time. Meanwhile, checklists of pairs of traits, those used by Asch (see Table 3) were distributed and the subjects were asked to mark those appropriate to the person conceptualized. Finally, they were asked to turn back to the original seven traits and indicate their rank order of importance in forming their impressions.

RESULTS AND DISCUSSION

Influence of the warm–cold variable

The closeness of the results on the checklist to those of Asch can be seen from Table 2, in which Asch's results have been converted into percentages, and only one of each pair of traits is shown. Discrepancies exist, but they are small, and in no case is the warm–cold influence in the opposite direction.

Table 3 summarizes the findings for the present experiment. To what extent can it be said that the giving of warm or cold has modified the personality traits selected? One way of answering this question statistically is by taking out, from each pair, the trait with the higher score for the warm group and comparing these scores with those received from the cold group. On the Wilcoxon Signed-Rank Test, the difference is significant at the 1 per cent level.

Examining the pairs of traits singly, compari-

TABLE 2   Comparison of Asch's and Present Results on the Checklist: Experiment 2

TRAITS	WARM GROUP		COLD GROUP	
	Asch per cent	Present per cent	Asch per cent	Present per cent
Generous	91	93	8	23
Wise	65	77	25	23
Happy	90	97	34	53
Good-natured	94	90	17	23
Humorous	77	80	13	13
Sociable	91	90	38	16
Popular	84	93	28	16
Reliable	94	100	99	100
Important	88	50	99	66
Humane	86	83	31	33
Good-looking	77	70	69	46
Persistent	100	100	97	100
Serious	100	77	99	96
Restrained	77	50	89	93
Altruistic	69	70	18	10
Imaginative	51	63	19	10
Strong	98	90	95	83
Honest	98	100	94	93

sons can be made by the Chi-Square Test, bearing in mind the strictures of Kjeldergaard & Jenkins (1958) against differences at the 5 per cent level with traits which are probably not independent. For ten of the 18 pairs the proportions of selections from the warm and cold groups differ to a degree significant at the 1 per cent level.

It would seem that the reading of 'warm' or 'cold' in the original list has again quite substan-

TABLE 3   Selection of Traits on Checklist: Experiment 2

TRAIT	WARM PER CENT	COLD PER CENT	TRAIT	WARM PER CENT	COLD PER CENT
*Generous	93	23	Ungenerous	0	56
*Shrewd	16	70	Wise	77	23
*Unhappy	0	26	Happy	97	53
*Irritable	7	37	Good-natured	90	23
*Humorous	80	13	Humourless	0	73
*Sociable	90	16	Unsociable	0	70
*Popular	93	16	Unpopular	0	53
Unreliable	0	0	Reliable	100	100
Important	50	66	Insignificant	7	13
*Ruthless	7	53	Humane	83	33
Good-looking	70	46	Unattractive	13	36
Persistent	100	100	Unstable	0	0
Frivolous	7	0	Serious	77	96
Restrained	50	93	Talkative	40	3
*Self-centred	17	70	Altruistic	70	10
*Imaginative	63	10	Hard-headed	30	70
Strong	90	83	Weak	3	16
Dishonest	0	0	Honest	100	93

* Significantly different at the 1 per cent level (χ^2).

TABLE 4 *Mean Ranks of Peripheral Traits: Experiment 2*

TRAITS	WARM GROUP	COLD GROUP
Intelligent	5½	6
Skilful	2	2
Industrious	7	4
Determined	5½	7
Practical	4	3
Cautious	3	5

tially modified the impression formed. Moreover, as Bruner, Shapiro & Tagiuri (1958) pointed out, the traits selected are not necessarily denoted by the given one: thus, 'wise' and 'imaginative' are markedly associated with warmth, but are certainly not logically implied by it.

Centrality of the warm–cold variable
The ranking of traits for their importance in impression-formation again demonstrated the dominance of warm and cold: 50 per cent of the warm group and 60 per cent of the cold group placed warm or cold in the first or second rank. In speaking of the centrality of these traits, Asch meant, in part, that the peripheral traits would fall into different hierarchical constellations according to the nature of the central trait. This is shown numerically in two ways with the present data. First, while an equal number in each group (14) put warm or cold in the first place, in the warm group the trait receiving the next highest number of 'firsts' is 'intelligent,' and in the cold group, it is 'determined.' Second, and more important, it can be seen from Table 4 that the mean rankings of the peripheral traits differ in the two groups: these are calculated from the rankings of the 28 subjects who put warm or cold first. The trait 'industrious,' which carries a low mean rank in association with 'warm,' illustrates most clearly the point that relative importance can be transformed by the central traits.

Totality of the impression
Luchins (1948) has criticized Asch's claim that in the character sketches an entire person is represented. Unfortunately Asch makes little detailed reference to this material. Luchins himself, on repeating the experiment, found that a high proportion of the character sketches consisted of the trait names, or synonyms for them, strung out as sentences.

The subjects of the present experiment showed little tendency to be restricted to the given traits. One index of this is the occurrence of sentences bearing no direct relationship, apparently, to any of the given traits: sentences such as 'Someone interested in weird, unorthodox forms of art and music and with highbrow taste for the theatre.' As many as 59 per cent of all the sentences written (from the assessments of two judges working

separately) are independent in this sense. Comparing only the subjects who ranked warm and cold in first place, in their assessment of relative importance in impression-formation, the influence of the warm–cold variable is not apparent in the attribution of gender, there being an equal number of males and females described in each group. There is a difference in mention of occupation (and, by implication, of age): occupations are ascribed more often by the cold group, always with the assumption that the person is an older man or woman, holding a position of responsibility usually, such as a business man or a manageress. Finally, an analysis of the descriptions of physical appearance, given by about half the subjects, yields this difference, that whereas the cold people are always tall and thin, the warm ones are as likely to be small and plump.

REFERENCES

ASCH, S. E. (1946). Forming impressions of personality. *J. abnorm. soc. Psychol.* **41**, 258–290.

ASCH, S. E. (1952). *Social Psychology.* New York: Prentice-Hall.

ASCH, S. E. (1958). The metaphor: a psychological enquiry. In *Person Perception and Interpersonal Behaviour.* (Tagiuri, R. & Petrullo, L., eds.). Stanford: Stanford U.P. Pp. 86–94.

BRUNER, J. & TAGIURI, R. (1954). The perception of people. In *Handbook of Social Psychology.* (Lindzey, G., ed.). Cambridge, Mass.: Addison-Wesley. Pp. 634–654.

BRUNER, J., SHAPIRO, D. & TAGIURI, R. (1958). The meaning of traits in isolation and in combination. In *Person Perception and Interpersonal Behaviour.* (Tagiuri, R. & Petrullo, L., eds.). Stanford: Stanford U.P. Pp. 277–288.

COFER, C. N. & DUNN, J. T. (1952). Personality ratings as influenced by verbal stimuli. *J. Pers.* **21**, 223–227.

GOLLIN, E. S. (1958). Organizational characteristics of social judgment: a developmental investigation. *J. Pers.* **26**, 139–154.

HAIRE, M. & GRUNES, W. F. (1950). Perceptual defenses: processes protecting an organised perception of another personality. *Hum. Relat.* **3**, 403–412.

HAYS, W. L. (1958). An approach to the study of trait implication and trait similarity. In *Person Perception and Interpersonal Behaviour.* (Tagiuri, R. & Petrullo, L. eds.). Stanford: Stanford U.P. Pp. 289–299.

KELLEY, H. H. (1950). The warm–cold variable in first impressions of persons. *J. Pers.* **18**, 431–439.

KJELDERGAARD, P. M. & JENKINS, J. J. (1958). Personality ratings as influenced by verbal stimuli—some negative findings. *J. Pers.* **26**, 51–60.

LUCHINS, A. S. (1948). Forming impressions of personality: a critique. *J. abnorm. soc. Psychol.* **43**, 318–325.

MENSH, I. N. & WISHNER, J. (1947). Asch on 'Forming impressions of personality', further evidence. *J. Pers.,* **16**, 188–191.

PEPITONE, A. & HAYDEN, R. (1955). Some evidence for conflict resolution in impression formation. *J. abnorm. soc. Psychol.* **51**, 302–307.

SHAPIRO, D. & TAGIURI, R. (1958). Some effects of response control on trait impression. *J. Pers.* **26**, 42–50.

WISHNER, J. (1950). Re-analysis of 'Impressions of Personality'. *Psychol. Rev.* **67**, 96–112.

SOCIAL CLASS AND THE NEGRO STEREOTYPE *

Often in everyday situations, we have only categorical information concerning a person. We know only that he is a Negro, a lawyer, or an elderly retired person. As might be expected, if we evaluate or form an opinion of that person, our impression will be strongly colored by this categorical information. This act of assigning attributes to a person solely according to the category to which he belongs is known as *stereotyping*.

Generally speaking, the concept of stereotyping implies three characteristics: (*1*) persons are categorized according to certain identifying attributes (skin color, religion, age, etc.), (*2*) perceivers agree on the traits that the persons in the category possess, and (*3*) a discrepancy exists between traits that they are believed to have and those they actually possess. Although studies of stereotyping support these observations, they are sometimes a source of misunderstanding. They illustrate how the use of a single method of investigation of a problem can easily lead to a faulty interpretation. When a perceiver is provided only with an ethnic identification of a group of persons and no other information, he is virtually forced to ignore individual differences and to respond to the group as a class of persons. This does *not* mean that he will respond in exactly the same way when confronted with individual members of the ethnic group.

The present selection is relevant to this point. Bayton, McAlister, and Hamer demonstrate that when members of an ethnic group are identified in terms of different social classes, the traits belonging to the stereotyped impression of them vary markedly. Thus, it supports the view that additional information concerning stimulus persons may profoundly change the impression formed. This does not mean that the concept of stereotyping is useless. When research comparing the traits assigned to different categories of persons is considered, the concept is seen to have some validity. Much research has repeatedly demonstrated that perceivers agree in assigning distinctively different traits to various categories of persons. Such consensus reveals that social forces are shaping the perceptions of each class of persons in a given direction. Moreover, there are many situations in everyday life where we respond to others mainly in terms of their group identification instead of reacting to them as individuals. But caution must be exercised in assuming that a perceiver might always react similarly in a face-to-face confrontation with a person belonging to a particular category.

10.

Race-Class Stereotypes

JAMES A. BAYTON
LOIS B. McALISTER
JESTON HAMER
HOWARD UNIVERSITY

INTRODUCTION

Research on racial stereotypes usually involves the following procedure. The subjects are asked to select from a list of characteristics those they think apply to given racial groups—"White Americans," "the Negro," "the Jew," etc. It has often been demonstrated that this procedure yields definite, race-linked stereotypes.[1,2,3,4] It would appear, however, that there is at least one possible fallacy in this approach. The results of such research carry the implication that the possessors of a given stereotype do not make sub-group distinctions within the larger group being stereotyped. For example, are white American's aware of class differences among Negroes; do those who stereotype "the Negro" as being "lazy," "superstitious,"

---

* The selection following the editorial introduction is reprinted from "Race-class stereotypes," *Journal of Negro Education,* 1956 (Winter), 75–78, by permission of the senior author and the publisher.

---

[1] J. A. Bayton, "Racial Stereotypes of Negro College Students." *Journal of Abnormal and Social Psychology,* 36: 97–102 (1941).

[2] R. Blake and W. Dennis, "Development of Stereotypes Concerning the Negro." *Ibid.,* 38: 525–531 (1943).

[3] G. M. Gilbert, "Stereotype Persistence and Change among College Students." *Ibid.,* 46: 245–254 (1951).

[4] D. Katz and K. Braly, "Racial Stereotypes of 100 College Students." *Ibid.,* 28: 280–290 (1933).

"happy-go-lucky," and "physically-dirty" regard these characteristics as being equally typical for upper- and lower-class Negroes? If the subjects in research on stereotypes were given an opportunity to make such sub-group distinctions, patterns might emerge which are different from those attached to the group-at-large.

The present research investigates racial stereotypes in terms of class within race. It is our hypothesis that racial stereotypes vary according to class-designations within the races being stereotyped. In addition, the design is such that the prepotency of race and class, as independent dimensions for sterotyping, can be investigated.

PROCEDURE

The subjects were 92 white and 180 Negro college students. The white subjects attended a border-state university which had, at the time, very few Negroes enrolled in the undergraduate college. The Negro subjects attended a university which is essentially all-Negro in its student population.

The Katz and Braly[4] technique was used to obtain the stereotypes. The subjects were asked to select from a list of 85 adjectives any which they thought described each of the following groups: Upper-class white Americans, upper-class Negroes, lower-class white Americans, and lower-class Negroes. After selecting as many adjectives per group as were thought to be descriptive, the subjects starred the five adjectives which they considered most typical of the group in question. The latter items formed the basis for the stereotypes.

RESULTS

The stereotypes for upper-class white Americans and upper-class Negroes by white and Negro subjects are given in Table 1. White and Negro subjects described both upper-class white Americans and upper-class Negroes as *intelligent, ambitious, industrious, neat,* and *progressive.* The two groups of subjects assigned *pleasure-loving* and *sophisticated* to upper-class white Americans but not to upper-class Negroes. They both assigned *ostentatious* to upper-class Negroes but not to upper-class white Americans. Traits assigned to upper-class white Americans by white subjects but not by Negro subjects were *aggressive, alert,* and *materialistic.* Similarly, Negro subjects said upper-class Negroes are *efficient, conceited* and *materialistic.* The white subjects, rather than the Negro subjects, saw upper-class Negroes as *courteous, musical, honest,* and *reserved.* In contrast, the Negro subjects, but not the white subjects, assigned *tradition-loving, conservative,* and *scientifically-minded* to upper-class white Americans.

Table 2 contains the stereotypes of lower-class white Americans and lower-class Negroes. Both groups of subjects assigned *ignorant, lazy, loud,*

and *physically dirty* to the two lower-class racial groups. The white subjects characterized both lower-class groups as being *happy-go-lucky, unreliable,* and *pleasure-loving.* Negro subjects assigned *happy-go-lucky* only to lower-class Negroes. Lower-class white Americans were called *rude* by the two groups of subjects, but only the Negro subjects attributed this characteristic to lower-class Negroes. Both groups of subjects described lower-class Negroes as being *superstitious;* only the Negro subjects assigned this item to lower-class white Americans. Lower-class white Americans were assigned *deceitful, sly, stubborn* and *tradition loving* by Negro subjects but not by white subjects. White subjects, but not Negro subjects, said lower-class Negroes are *musical* and *ostentatious. Materialistic* and *practical* were assigned to lower-class white Americans by white subjects only. *Very religious, sensitive, talkative,* and *pugnacious* were items used only by the Negro subjects in reference to lower-class Negroes.

The items assigned to white Americans of both classes by white subjects were *materialistic* and *pleasure-loving.* Negro subjects attributed *tradi-*

TABLE 1 Stereotypes of Upper-class Whites and Upper-class Negroes by 92 White and 180 Negro Subjects

Reactions of White Subjects

UPPER-CLASS WHITES		UPPER-CLASS NEGROES	
Trait	Per Cent	Trait	Per Cent
Intelligent	59	Intelligent	53
Ambitious	49	Ambitious	51
Materialistic	45	Ostentatious	29
Pleasure-loving	33	Industrious	28
Industrious	25	Courteous	27
Neat	23	Neat	25
Sophisticated	22	Musical	24
Aggressive	18	Progressive	22
Alert	18	Honest	18
Progressive	18	Reserved	15

Reactions of Negro Subjects

UPPER-CLASS WHITES		UPPER-CLASS NEGROES	
Trait	Per Cent	Trait	Per Cent
Intelligent	48	Intelligent	61
Ambitious	28	Ambitious	35
Progressive	27	Progressive	25
Sophisticated	26	Neat	24
Tradition-loving	21	Ostentatious	23
Industrious	19	Sophisticated	23
Pleasure-loving	19	Industrious	21
Conservative	18	Materialistic	17
Scientifically-minded	18	Pleasure-loving	15
Neat	17	Efficient	13
		Conceited	13

tion-loving to both classes of white Americans. White subjects gave *musical* and *ostentatious* to the two classes of Negroes. There was no item that was assigned to the two classes of Negroes by the Negro subjects.

DISCUSSION

The above results indicate that when subjects are given an opportunity to stereotype races in terms of classes within the races, the resulting stereotypes vary more as a function of class than of race. This is true for subjects representing the different racial groups. The sharpest distinctions were between the two classes—upper and lower rather than between the two races, white and

TABLE 2 Stereotypes of Lower-class Whites and Lower-class Negroes by 92 White and 180 Negro Subjects

Reactions of White Subjects

LOWER-CLASS WHITES		LOWER-CLASS NEGROES	
Trait	Per Cent	Trait	Per Cent
Happy-go-lucky	20	Superstitious	66
Materialistic	20	Lazy	39
Ignorant	19	Physically dirty	34
Lazy	19	Unreliable	34
Loud	19	Musical	30
Rude	19	Loud	26
Unreliable	17	Ignorant	26
Pleasure-loving	16	Happy-go-lucky	24
Physically dirty	15	Ostentatious	19
Practical	14	Pleasure-loving	17

Reactions of Negro Subjects

Physically dirty	36	Loud	55
Ignorant	34	Superstitious	44
Rude	33	Very religious	35
Lazy	19	Lazy	28
Loud	18	Ignorant	26
Deceitful	18	Physically dirty	21
Sly	14	Sensitive	19
Stubborn	14	Happy-go-lucky	17
Superstitious	14	Talkative	15
Tradition-loving	14	Pugnacious	14
		Rude	14

Negro. This finding does not negate previous research on stereotypes which has revealed race differences. It is altogether possible that when subjects are asked to stereotype "white Americans" and "the Negro" they assume that *most* white Americans tend toward the upper-class position while *most* Negroes tend toward lower-class status. In the present investigation no question was raised as to the relative proportions of each race that fall within the two class positions.

In the race-class stereotype situation the prepotency of class over race is seen in the common core of items assigned to a respective class regardless of race. The upper-class, white or Negro, is seen as being intelligent, ambitious, industrious, neat, and progressive. In contrast, the lower-class, white and Negro, is characterized as being ignorant, lazy, loud and physically dirty. There is little evidence of purely race-linked stereotyping when the class factor is in the situation. This is observed, however, in the case of the white subjects who assigned musical and ostentatious to Negroes of both classes.

The prepotency of class over race as revealed in the stereotypes does not necessarily mean that this relationship would exist in actual interrace contacts. It is possible that some white people while granting that upper-class Negroes are intelligent, industrious, neat, etc., would still respond to them as Negroes with respect to maintaining segregation. They might deny to such Negroes privileges which they would grant white persons who actually possess rude, lazy, and ignorant characteristics. Even so, one would anticipate some differentiation of response to Negroes which would depend upon the class with which they are identified by whites. A similar situation seems to exist in the relations of Negroes to whites which vary in terms of the perceived class-positions they associate with whites.

SUMMARY

1. Stereotypes were obtained for upper-class whites, upper-class Negroes, lower-class whites, and lower-class Negroes. The subjects were 92 white and 180 Negro college students.
2. For both groups of subjects the stereotypes were more class-linked than race-linked. Regardless of race, upper-class persons were stereotyped as being intelligent, ambitious, industrious, neat, and progressive. Lower class persons were assigned ignorant, loud, lazy, and physically dirty, regardless of race. With this procedure there was little evidence of purely race-linked stereotyping.

EFFECTS OF GROUP SUPPORT ON THE EVALUATION OF AN ANTAGONIST✳

Situations where a perceiver interacts with a stimulus person toward whom he has some particular relation are vastly more complicated with respect to person perception. Impressions in such situations are not formed only on the basis of information concerning the other person; they are in part determined by the nature of the interaction and the relation between perceiver and perceived. The selection below, by Strickland, Jones, and Smith, illustrates some of these complexities. It reveals that under certain circumstances the judgment of the stimulus person is related to the justifiability of the *perceiver's* actions toward the stimulus person.

The experimental situation is arranged to give the perceiver the illusion that he is interacting with the stimulus person. The actual "exchange" of information is mediated by the experimenter. Such techniques permit the study of isolated variables that are likely to be relevant in face-to-face interaction, while introducing a degree of experimental control that could not be achieved in free interaction.

11.

Effects of Group Support on the Evaluation of an Antagonist[1]

LLOYD H. STRICKLAND
DARTMOUTH COLLEGE

EDWARD E. JONES
WILLIAM P. SMITH
SAN DIEGO STATE COLLEGE

Our impressions of others are determined not alone by information which these others directly provide; the verbal and gestural responses of a "stimulus person" (*SP*) are typically assessed by a perceiver in relation to the situation in which they occur (Jones & Thibaut, 1958). In many cases, the perceiver himself is a component of this situation. He must therefore consider his own behavior as a condition affecting the other's responses and the meaning he assigns to them. If *A*, for example, is aware of his own role in the instigation of hostile behavior in *B*, he is less likely to think of *B* as hostile or unpleasant, than he would if he were unaware of the provocation he himself provided.

It seems to follow that, in the typical social interaction, evaluations of others on the basis of their responses are contingent on the perceiver's evaluation of his own behavior. If the perceiver behaves in a "good" fashion and this elicits a "bad" response (e.g., a negative evaluation, a frown, a critical comment) from the *SP*, the latter will be judged as personally bad by the perceiver. If the perceiver is unconvinced that his own behavior is good, worthy, or appropriate, he will be less likely to form a negative evaluation of *SP*. This line of reasoning suggests an experimental situation in which one person (the *SP*) responds with hostility to the behavior of another (the perceiver) which is or is not highly valued by the perceiver himself.

A potential determinant of this valuation is the extent to which the perceiver's initiating response has normative support in some relevant group. A hostile reaction to behavior that has such normative support would seem to invite retaliation in the form of a negative impression. Hostile reaction to the same initiating response unsupported by social sanction would result in a less derogatory impression of the hostile respondent.

In simplified form, this is the reasoning behind the main prediction of the experiment described below. Consider an experimental procedure involving three primary steps or stages. In Step I, one group member (*S*) chooses influence messages to transmit to the target person or *SP* (not a group member); in Step II *S* learns that others in the group do (Group Support) or do not (No Support) endorse the particular messages selected; in Step III, *S* hears the *SP* severely criticize his messages and derogate their source. In such a situation, the main experimental hypothesis is that *perceivers in the group support condition will be more negative in their final impressions of the SP than will perceivers in the no support condition.*

Although it is theoretically quite possible that *S*s could respond to such a situation by rejecting their group in the No Support condition or succumbing to various forms of withdrawal and

✳ The selection following the editorial introduction is reprinted from "Effects of group support on the evaluation of an antagonist," *Journal of Abnormal and Social Psychology,* 1960, **61**, 73–81, by permission of the authors and the American Psychological Association.

[1] This study was initiated in the program of the Organization Research Group of the Institute for Research in Social Science at the University of North Carolina. The ORG is supported by the Office of Naval Research Nonr-855(04). Analysis and writing time was made available to Jones on National Science Foundation contract G8857 administered by Duke University.

perceptual distortion, the experiment was designed to minimize such alternative reactions and thus to promote differential perceptions of the *SP*. Several postexperimental measures failed to reveal any tendency for *S*s in either group to adopt these different ways of managing the problem created by the *SP*'s hostility. Therefore, these alternative reactions will not be considered further.

METHOD

Procedure

Ninety males *S*s, recruited from introductory psychology courses, were observed in groups of three. Each group was told that the experiment was part of a broader research project concerned with opinion change and reactions to propaganda. The experimental rationale emphasized that any propagandist must be aware of the "characteristics of his audience," which could be inferred by the audience's response to an influence attempt. *S*s were told that one of their group would eventually present a number of persuasive arguments about "big time athletics" to a fourth student (who would be in an adjacent, soundproof room) while the two remaining *S*s would be "innocent bystanders." Their job was two-fold: (*a*) evaluate the persuasive arguments to be used; (*b*) observe the reactions of the fourth student and make some inferences about "just what kind of a person you think he is." It was explained to the group that the issue of "big time athletics" on the college campus had been chosen as the influence topic because of the differences in opinion on this subject, and that the *S*s had been selected to participate in the experiment because they had all had about the same scores on an Attitude-Toward-Big-Time-Athletics questionnaire, which they had filled out in class early in the semester. An attempt actually was made to compose groups of persons whose scores were relatively homogeneous and extreme in the *pro* or *con* direction, although it was not always possible to compose the groups of extremes. The fourth student was presented as one whose questionnaire responses reflected that he was "more or less undecided on the issue".

E stated that he would first interview the fourth student (henceforth referred to as the *SP*) in the next room. This interview would be carried through a microphone to a loudspeaker in the laboratory, so that the three *S*s might obtain an initial impression of him which would aid in their selection of good arguments supporting their own position. *E* left the room and turned on a previously recorded taped interview.

In this initial interview, an attempt was made to create a rather neutral but mildly likeable *SP*. He was presented as a sophomore, undecided on his major, who enjoyed intramural sports but was concentrating on his studies. He stated that he didn't care one way or the other about "big time" sports—he enjoyed going to ball games but didn't think sports "should push everything out of the picture."

After hearing this brief interview, the *S*s filled out a 10-item rating scale designed to reveal their "first impressions" of *SP*. They then were asked to bring up in a brief discussion those points (favoring their own position) which might be successful in influencing the interviewee. This was done in order to involve the *S*s more strongly in the issue and to increase the saliency of group membership by stressing attitudinal similarity and the cooperative nature of the task of finding arguments. Each *S* was then seated in his own private cubicle and assigned a letter (supposedly, *A*, *B* or *C*) for identification. The ostensible purpose of this procedure was to preserve the anonymity of the responsible *S*, whose arguments were to be transmitted to *SP*, vis-à-vis the innocent bystanders, who would be evaluating *S*'s arguments. Actually all three *S*s received *B* identification cards.

Each *S* then selected from a list of 13 typical, one-paragraph arguments, the five which he thought most likely to influence *SP*, after having rated each of the 13 on a six-point scale from Poor to Excellent. He made these choices by placing a checkmark in a column headed B, in the left-hand margin of the pages, beside those preferred arguments. *E* collected these sheets, supposedly to record *S*'s choices and to check in the adjoining A and C columns the choices of *B*'s partners. They were then returned to *S*.

In this way, the major independent variable was manipulated: in the Group Support condition, each *S* (*B*) perceived that *A* and *C* had agreed with his choices in four of five cases. In the No Support condition, *S* found his partners in close agreement with each other but in slight agreement with him.

Following the return of these argument selection sheets to the *S*s, *B* was formally selected (presumably by lot) as the letter designation of the Communicator, leaving the nonexistent *A* and *C* to function as Innocent Bystanders. All *S*s were instructed to select, from a pile of hand-written copies of the arguments, the five that *B* chose. *B* was told to rank order them in terms of their probable increasing effectiveness—*A* and *C* were to write brief evaluative comments about them. The rank-ordered arguments were collected from each *S*, and *E* announced that he would bring them to *SP*, let him read them, and then interview him about his reactions to them.

In the next interview, also prerecorded on tape, *SP* appeared initially vague and evasive. As he reviewed each argument (in *S*'s designated order), he became increasingly derogatory, not debating the point made by the argument, but disparaging the attempt to change anyone's mind with such poor material. After completing his review of the arguments, *SP* made a few additional unkind remarks about *S* and then asked *E* if he could leave, preferring not to meet his fellow *S*s. After granting this permission, *E* returned to the adjoining laboratory and required the *S*s to complete the following:

1. A brief, free-response personality sketch of *SP*, and a statement of arguments *S* might use were he to attempt to influence *SP* again.
2. A second, private rating of SP on the same scale form used in the initial impression rating.

3. A re-rating of all 13 arguments on the original six-point poor-excellent scale.
4. A "cohesiveness" measure, in which S designated (a) how much he would like to work with his fellow group members again, and (b) how much he felt they would prefer him as Communicator again.
5. A "public" rating of SP, on a parallel form of the scale used in the first and second ratings, purportedly to serve as the basis for a group discussion about SP and final composite group rating of him. It was expected that the predicted differential change in the private ratings would be augmented in making the public ratings.
6. A recognition-recall measure, in which S attempted to designate those five arguments initially preferred by himself and his two partners.

After these procedures were completed E informed the Ss about the method and purposes of the experiment and determined the extent to which their suspicions had been aroused.

Rating scale
As indicated above, each S rated the SP on three different occasions, before the derogation, after the derogation (private), and once again (public). Since the final two ratings were made consecutively, it was necessary to use two equivalent forms of the scale. In order to insure that the actual positive or negative results obtained were not solely a function of the particular items comprising the scale, approximately half of the Ss were given Form I to use on the first and second rating and Form II to use on the third (i.e., public) rating. The order of form administration was reversed for the remaining Ss. Each form of the scale consisted of 5 trait pairs (or 10 items) which measured the perceived characteristics: likeability, adjustment, warmth, intelligence, and conceit. The ratings were made on a six-point scale reflecting the degree of agreement with simple declarative statements about the person being rated. The scale was constructed in such a way that a positive statement like: "He seems to be a very warm and affectionate person" was in all cases matched by its negative counterpart in a different item such as: "He strikes me as a hostile and unsympathetic person." Many of

the items on both forms of the scale were taken from a very similar scale described by Jones, Hester, Farina and Davis (1959). Data on reliability are included in the earlier study, but in view of the way in which the scales were used in the present study, separate reliability analyses were run on each scale. The split-half correlations of the change scores on Forms I and II were .57 and .61 respectively (corrected by the Spearman-Brown prophecy formula). Obviously, the scales each measure other variables in addition to overall favorability or "halo," but the reliability coefficients seem adequate to provide a meaningful test of changes in general evaluation of the SP.

Design and distribution of subjects
Although primary interest lies in the effects of the manipulation of group support, the two additional control variables make the design somewhat more complex. As Table 1 indicates, the design involved three dichotomous variables resulting in eight separate cells of Ss. Table 1 also indicates the number of Ss actually observed in each condition. It will be apparent that a large number of Ss were suspicious before, or became suspicious during the course of, the experiment. Ss were classified as suspicious if they acknowledged any doubts about the status of the SP during the postexperimental group discussion led by E. This is a very stringent criterion of suspicion, since some Ss were probably influenced by statements of suspicion made by others in their group, or their suspicions may have reached a threshold of awareness during the tedium of filling out the final questionnaires. Nevertheless, for most of the analyses to be presented below, all suspicious Ss by this criterion were excluded. The fact that 29% of the Ss expressed some degree of suspicion clearly raises some questions about the representativeness of the remaining sample. More will be said about this later, but the main reason for suspicion is easy to locate: the SP was forced by the conditions of the experiment to respond with very vague generalities, and to avoid any reference to the content of the arguments he had presumably received. This unavoidable circumstance combined with

TABLE 1   Experimental Design and Distribution of Ss

	GROUP SUPPORT					NO SUPPORT				
	Pro BTA		Anti BTA		Total		Pro BTA		Anti BTA	Total
Rating form sequence:	*I–II*	*II–I*	*I–II*	*II–I*		*I–II*	*II–I*	*I–II*	*II–I*	
Good Ss	9	6	6	8	29	6	6	8	7	27
Suspicious*	7	5	0	2	14†	3	0	4	5	12‡
Total	16	11	6	10	43	9	6	12	12	39

* Although suspicious Ss appear to be unevenly distributed between conditions, a chi square test reveals that this distribution does not, in fact, depart from chance.   † None of these Ss spontaneously expressed suspicion in the free-response impression sketch.   ‡ Five of these Ss did spontaneously express suspicion.

the surprise and incredibility of the actual derogation of *S,* made it difficult for some *S*s to accept the *SP* as a naive fourth *S.* It should be noted that eight *S*s were discarded because of failure to comply with the instructions (e.g., they sent unpreferred arguments to *SP*), or because they felt their stand on Big-Time Athletics had been misidentified.

RESULTS

Success of experimental manipulations

Response to the SP. The script for the tape recorded response to the *S*'s arguments was constructed with the purpose of instigating the *S*s to hostility. Almost without exception, *S*s did in fact change their ratings in a negative direction. Pooling the change scores of all *S*s and comparing the mean against the null expectation of zero change results in a *t* value of 16.4, $p < .001$, leaving little doubt that the *SP*'s recorded comments had their intended effect.

Perception of social support. A crucial condition for an adequate test of the major hypothesis is that the degree of support for the *S*'s arguments, conveyed to him through an exchange of bogus ballots, should be actually perceived as high or low in line with the degree of agreement indicated. Suffice it to say that *S*s in the two conditions are strikingly different from each other ($p < .001$) in amount of agreement perceived (on the recognition–recall measure).

It is possible, of course, that agreement perceived has no implications beyond the purely cognitive ability to recall the bogus ballots distributed. To what extent does each *S* actually infer that the group is behind him, and accepts him as spokesman? Does this inference vary with support treatment? On the postexperimental questionnaire the *S*s were asked to predict whether the other two members of the group would like to have them as "communicator" again. By classifying the responses as yes or no, a chi square test was

computed indicating a clear association between support condition and perceived acceptance ($\chi^2 = 5.22$, $df = 1$, $p < .025$). Thus, *S*s in the No Support condition felt that the group was unhappy with their performance and would not be likely to support them in the same role again.

The effects of variation in group support

Summary rating evaluation. The main hypothesis of the present study was that *S*s in the Group Support condition would show a greater increase in negative evaluation of the *SP* than would *S*s in the No Support condition. This prediction was expected to hold regardless of variation in such control variables as attitude toward athletics and rating form used. Before examining the evidence concerning this main hypothesis, it may be pointed out that neither of these control variables was seen to have any effects of significance in analyzing the main rating data. For presentational simplicity, therefore, no further reference will be made to these variables unless they are specifically relevant to a particular point of difference.

The data most clearly relevant to the main hypothesis are presented in Table 2 and analyzed in Table 3. Here it may be seen that the difference between Group Support and No Support conditions is consistently in the predicted direction for Before, After, and Change scores. The difference between After scores of the two treatment groups is highly significant, the difference between Before scores is significant at the 5% level, and the crucial difference between Change scores does not approach significance.

Interpretation of this pattern of findings is complicated by the quite unexpected difference in Before scores. This result requires explanation in and of itself, because *S*s were randomly assigned to the two treatment groups and at the time the Before measure was taken, *S*s had not been exposed to any differential treatment. The apparent explanation is a curious and unusual one: *S*s in the Group Support condition who initially liked the *SP* tended to become suspicious that he was not responding spontaneously and were later discarded as *S*s; *S*s in the no support condition who initially disliked the *SP* also tended to become

TABLE 2   Mean Before, After and Change Scores, Summary Rating Evaluations

	GROUP SUPPORT					NO SUPPORT				
	Pro BTA		Anti BTA		Total	Pro BTA		Anti BTA		Total
Form	*I*	*II*	*I*	*II*		*I*	*II*	*I*	*II*	
N	9	6	6	8	29	6	6	8	7	27
Before*	3.67	3.92	4.22	4.09	*3.95*	4.63	4.00	4.41	4.26	*4.34*
After*	2.81	3.03	3.30	3.35	*3.11*	3.78	3.40	3.79	3.96	*3.75*
Change†	.86	.89	.92	.74	*.84*	.85	.60	.62	.30	*.59*

* The higher the score, the more favorable the overall evaluation.   † The higher the score, the greater the change in the negative direction.

suspicious. The net result of this interaction between support treatment and initial impression, as it affects arousing suspicion, is that usable, nonsuspicious Ss have significantly different Before scores. The causes of this differential suspicion will be discussed below, but the consequence of the systematic variation in Before scores is the major concern in the present context. It is difficult to interpret the Change scores at face value when the group which is predicted to show the greater decline in rating starts out significantly lower. Both the "floor" effect and the tendency for regression toward the mean would tend to suppress the Change scores in the group support treatment, where the greatest change is predicted. Such a regression effect would be especially likely, given the moderate reliability of the Change scores.

There turns out to be no simple or single way of handling this problem. Two bits of evidence do tend to clarify the picture, however, in the direction of partial support for the major hypothesis of difference between Group Support and No Support conditions. First of all, if the Before scores for the two main treatment conditions are matched by discarding 11 Ss, a t test for matched groups shows the Group Support and No Support conditions to be significantly different ($p < .05$, one-tailed test). This is, of course, a rather wasteful procedure and one which limits the ease of generalization to a broader population of college students.

Secondly, looking at the regression of After scores on Before scores, the coefficient for the No Support Ss ($b = 1.09$) is significantly greater than the coefficient for the Group Support Ss ($b = .42$), the probability value of the difference being less than .01. Examination of the scatter plots for the two conditions indicates that this difference is mainly a function of the initially favorable Ss, who show much more marked decline in the Group Support than in the No Support condition.

Support for this last notion appears when the Before scores for the two treatments are split at the overall median. The difference between Before score means for the two high subgroups is not significant, and these Ss, who are initially favorable to the SP, show significantly greater negative change ($p < .01$) in the Group Support condition than in the No Support condition.

With the low subgroups, Ss in the Group Support condition had significantly lower Before scores than those in the Support condition ($p < .01$) but not significantly greater Change scores. Thus, the problem of interpretation concerns only those Ss who were initially unfavorable; the results for the initially favorable Ss are straightforward.

To summarize, then, the hypothesis that evaluative ratings will become more negative in the Group Support than in the No Support condition receives only qualified support. A more accurate statement of the general hypothesis would be:

those Ss who show an initially favorable impression of a person who later derogates them for their action will show a greater decline in evaluation when their actions have received normative support than when they have not.

Free response descriptions. In addition to the summary evaluation provided by averaging the item scores on the rating scale, it is important to consider any support for the main hypothesis derived from analysis of the impression sketches contributed by each S immediately after the derogation of his arguments. Although the sketches were rich in variety, most of the Ss seemed concerned with "explaining" the SP's behavior, either by referring to his rigidity, stupidity, and inflexibility, or to his honesty and sense of independence.

Before discussing the effects of the group support variable on these free response descriptions, it is necessary to consider once again the related problems of sampling and suspicion. Since the impression sketches were only written once, after the Ss had heard both parts of the tape recording, it is obviously impossible to obtain a measure of change from a "before score" baseline. But the significant difference in Before score on the ratings of nonsuspicious Ss has already been noted, thus tending to confound any differences in the same direction which might be observed on the "after" impression sketches. As a way of handling this problem, the sample was reconstituted for the purpose of this particular analysis. From the total pool of Ss, only those were discarded who showed any signs of suspicion in the impression sketch itself, although some of them later reported varying degrees of suspicion under questioning. The remaining sample contained 43 Ss in the

TABLE 3 *Summary of Analysis of Variance* Results* (Summary rating evaluations: before, after, and change scores)

SOURCE	df	BEFORE		AFTER		CHANGE	
		MS	F	MS	F	MS	F
Support (A)	1	.25	4.17†	.75	9.38‡	.12	2.4
Attitude (B)	1	.06		.24		.05	
Form (C)	1	.05		.00		.05	
A × B	1	.07		.00		.02	
A × C	1	.10		.03		.01	
B × C	1	.00		.02		.01	
A × B × C	1	.09		.06		.01	
Error	48	.06		.08		.05	

* Because of the unequal cell frequencies, the approximation technique presented by Snedecor (1946) was used. † $P < .05$. ‡ $P < .005$.

Group Support condition and 34 *S*s in the No Support condition. The primary reason for extending the sample in this way was to assure greater comparability between the Before scores (rating scale summaries) of the Group Support and No Support *S*s. This purpose was accomplished since the difference in Before scores between the extended subsamples did not approach significance. We are presumably free, then, to interpret any difference between support conditions on the impression sketches as largely the result of experimental manipulations rather than sampling variation.

Each of the impression sketches was placed by two coders in one of five carefully described rating categories arrayed on the dimension of overall favorability. As evidence of the reliability of coding, 58% of the placements were identical, and 98% of the placements fell in identical or adjacent categories. In cases of disagreement, the final score assigned was the average of the two ratings.

The final distribution of ratings was quite bimodal and skewed, with more of the impression sketches being clearly negative in tone. For this reason, the scores were split as near to the median as possible and the resulting two by two table (More Favorable–Less Favorable, Group Support–No Support) was submitted to a chi square test. The obtained value of 11.97 (corrected for continuity, $df = 1$) is significant at the .001 level indicating a strong association between support condition and the expression of hostility—those in the Group Support condition express more hostility in their impression sketches than those in the No Support condition.

In general, the Group Support *S*s were more likely than the No Support *S*s to refer to the *SP* as prejudiced, ignorant, egotistical, indifferent, or confused. The No Support *S*s, on the other hand, were more likely to refer to the *SP* as likeable, rational, and honest.

Publicity of ratings and group support

As indicated above, a comparison of the change in summary rating evaluations for Group Support and No Support *S*s provides qualified support for the main hypothesis. That is, the Group Support *S*s show greater negative change than do the No Support *S*s. To what extent does this reflect a private change in judgment, and to what extent are we dealing with differences in the inhibition versus facilitation of the *expression* of hostility? It might be argued that at least some of the *S*s held the vague expectation that they would have to justify their ratings to their fellow group members. If this were the case, then these *S*s would feel more safety in expressing their hostility on the rating scale in the Group Support than in the No Support condition.

No one has yet discovered a simple way of measuring the difference between private feelings and public expression of these feelings. Some form of expression is inevitably bound up with the measurement of attitudes or impressions. However, some partial evidence relevant to this point is provided in the design of the present experiment. It will be recalled that the *S*s filled out two forms of the rating scale after the derogation. First they rated the *SP* on one 10-item form under instructions which stressed the anonymity of the ratings and the fact that they would only be seen by *E*. This "private" After scale was always the same form as the Before scale. Then they were asked to fill out a different 10-item scale under the explicit instructions that each member's ratings would serve as the basis for a three-person group discussion, a discussion which would lead eventually to a common rating of the *SP*. If the observed changes in rating reported above were entirely a function of inhibition or facilitation of reporting one's hostility, there should be no difference between private and public ratings. If social inhibition and facilitation exercise independent effects, we should expect the difference between Group Support and no support conditions to be even greater on the public ratings.

There are several kinds of analysis that would be appropriate in answering this question, but perhaps the most straightforward involves tabulating the number of *S*s who become more negative and the number of *S*s who become less negative going from the private to public rating form in the Support and No Support conditions. By omitting the few *S*s who did not change in either direction, the resulting two by two table shows that 14 out of 25 Group Support *S*s were more negative in their public ratings, whereas only 6 out of 25 No Support *S*s became more negative and 19 more positive. This difference is significant by chi square test at the .05 level. In other words, when faced with the prospect of publicizing and defending their ratings to the other two group members, the Group Support *S*s became somewhat more hostile on the average. When faced with the same prospect, the No Support *S*s became considerably less hostile on the average.

The interpretation of this finding is complicated by the fact that almost all of this difference is attributable to the group of *S*s rating the *SP* privately on Form II and publicly on Form I. Those *S*s going from Form I to Form II show a slight and nonsignificant change in the same direction. Since there are no differences between Form I and Form II means for any other comparison (Before ratings, Change ratings, private After ratings) it is difficult to know what to make of this variation. However, since the overall effect is significant when both forms are pooled (both by chi square and t test) it seems reasonable to state the guarded conclusion that there are independent inhibitory effects stemming from the anticipation of group confrontation in the No Support condition and (to a lesser extent) facilitating effects in the Group Support condition. This does not mean that the private ratings were entirely unaffected by such factors, but it does suggest that they largely reflect the S's internalized impression of the SP.

Suspicion as an alternative to changes in evaluation

As noted above, there was no reliable tendency for any of the Ss to reject the group, devaluate the arguments, or misperceive the degree of support in order to maintain their initial impression of the SP. It is possible, however, to consider suspicion as one form of alternative reaction to the experimental situation. As already reported, Ss in the Group Support condition who initially liked the SP tended to become suspicious, whereas, those in the No Support condition who initially *disliked* the SP tended to become suspicious. What is the psychological significance of becoming suspicious in the present context? Presumably, Ss in a psychological experiment become suspicious because (a) the situation is poorly rationalized by the E, there are incongruous features which destroy credibility, etc., or (b) S desperately wants to believe that the situation is not as described. In most cases of suspicion these two factors probably reinforce each other—especially when something unpleasant or stressful is done to the S. In the present experiment two kinds of Ss became suspicious. Let us examine each of these in turn.

Considering first those Ss in the Group Support condition who initially liked the SP, it may simply be hard for them to believe that a person for whom they have esteem and respect is responding with such antagonism to so little provocation. The incredulousness of these Ss may be heightened by their awareness that two other Ss have checked almost the identical five arguments which were sent. We may speculate, then, that these Ss became suspicious primarily because of the cognitive-affective incongruity of the experimental situation.

As for those Ss in the No Support condition who dislike the SP initially, the unpleasantness of their position should be noted. They dislike the SP and the SP appears to dislike them. And yet, the other two group members have indicated that they would have sent different arguments had either of them been communicators. In this situation of unrelieved antagonism and lack of support, it may be that the S is highly motivated to perceive any cues of artificiality or incongruity.

The fact that different kinds of people may have become suspicious in the two conditions

raises the issue of confounding in the rating results. However, including most of the suspicious Ss (as in the free response data) results in even greater differences in the predicted direction. Furthermore, there is no a priori reason for assuming that suspicion would consistently bias the results to favor confirmation of the hypothesis.

DISCUSSION

The present research grew out of a general concern with the conditions of interaction which affect the perception and evaluation of a stimulus person. It is to be noted that the behavior of the person being judged was constant and identical from S to S. The meaning of this behavior, however, was shown to vary with the interaction context from which it stemmed. In the experiment, a stimulus person responded in an abusive, antagonistic fashion to a series of arguments chosen by an experimental S. We would naturally expect the S to modify his impression of the SP in a negative direction, and we have seen that this is indeed the case. But the intensity or degree of negative feelings expressed depends on the implied value S attaches to his own eliciting behavior. The more S is convinced that his arguments are reasonable, just, and valid, the more righteous and therefore intense we would expect his hostility to become. In the realm of communication about controversial issues, the degree of consensual support for an argument is an important source of its perceived validity (see, for example, Festinger, 1954). The presence or absence of such social support was the main experimental variation in the present study. The results show that Ss who perceive support for their behavior respond with greater hostility than those who perceive no such support. As predicted, this differential hostility was reflected in the Ss' verbal impressions of the derogating SP and in their attempts to characterize the SP on a rating scale (though with the latter measure those who initially disliked the SP showed no such differential change).

The present results fit nicely into the discussion by Jones and Thibaut (1958) of the importance of interaction context in person perception, and the method for demonstrating these contextual effects is basically similar to that employed by Jones and Daugherty (1959) and Jones, Hester, Farina and Davis (1959). However, the obtained findings can be accommodated by a number of theoretical positions and seem not to embarrass any others. It is possible, for example, to interpret the results by a simple extension of Heider's (1958) notions of cognitive balance in the P-O-X unit. The individual S (P) is led to dislike or devalue SP (O) because they disagree about *S*'s verbal product (*X*). Following Cartwright and Harary (1956), this particular *P-O-X* unit can be represented as an *s*-digraph in which *P* dislikes *O*, *O* dislikes *P*, *P* likes *X*, and *O* dislikes *X*. Given the fact that *P* likes *X* (*S* values his own chosen arguments) and that *O* dislikes *P* and *X* (as revealed by *SP*'s derogation of both the arguments and the person who thought them up), *P* must dislike *O* for the structure to be balanced. In order to handle the present experimental results, however, it is necessary to introduce a further quantitative assumption: the magnitude of *P*'s liking for *X* will determine the magnitude of his *dis*like for *O*.

In the context of frustration-aggression theory, the present results might be viewed in terms of the degree to which *S*'s hostility toward *SP* is inhibited or facilitated by the Group Support manipulation. *S*s in the Group Support condition may be compared with the members of a cohesive in-group who are secure in the conviction that their beliefs and behavior are not only meaningful but morally right. A considerable amount of anecdotal evidence on witch hunts, lynchings, etc., could be cited to make the point that hostility toward out-group members can be vastly intensified when justified as serving a righteous moral passion. This could be true both because the threat to a highly moral position is viewed as more "frustrating" than the threat to a position more neutral in morality, and because the in-group provides direct positive sanctions for the expression of aggression in the service of a moral cause. The present results provide circumstantial evidence for both of these effects in the laboratory context. There is a difference between the private and the public ratings, the latter seeming to facilitate hostility in the Group Support and inhibit it in the No Support condition. However, the fact that the private ratings show the same difference to a significant if lesser degree, indicates that the present results are not entirely the effect of the group's power to release or suppress aggression in its members. At least we may speculate that this power becomes internalized as the individual responds to others in terms of the normative support inherent in his position.

SUMMARY

The present experiment was concerned with variations in person perception as a function of the perceiver's role in instigating a stimulus person to hostility. While the stimulus person's hostile remarks were always constant across *S*s, the perceiver was led to believe that his instigating behavior either was or was not sanctioned by a group of fellow *S*s. This variation in group support was accomplished by manipulating the extent to which the other group members agreed with a set of arguments transmitted by the perceiver to the stimulus person.

The major findings were generally in line with the hypotheses in that:

1. There was a tendency for the *S*s' evaluative ratings of the stimulus person to become more negative when they perceived that they had group support for their communication (which prompted the derogation by the stimulus person) than when they perceived no such support. This difference was significant when consideration was restricted to those *S*s in each condition who were initially favorably disposed toward the stimulus person.
2. In postderogation free-response "personality sketches," Group Support *S*s evidenced significantly greater hostility toward the stimulus person than did the No Support *S*s.
3. When anticipating the publication of their judgments to the other members of their group, the Group Support *S*s became somewhat more hostile, while the No Support *S*s became considerably less hostile.

In discussing these findings, the importance of considering the interaction context in studying person perception was stressed. The results were also discussed in terms of cognitive balance and frustration-aggression theories.

REFERENCES

CARTWRIGHT, D., & HARARY, F. Structural balance: A generalization of Heider's theory. *Psychol. Rev.*, **63**, 1956, 277–293.

FESTINGER, L. A theory of social comparison processes. *Hum. Relat.*, **7**, 1954, 117–140.

HEIDER, F. *The psychology of interpersonal relations.* New York: Wiley, 1958.

JONES, E. E., & THIBAUT, J. W. Interaction goals as bases of inference in interpersonal perception. In R. Tagiuri & L. Petrullo (Eds.), *Person perception and interpersonal behavior.* Stanford: Stanford Univer. Press, 1958, 151–178.

JONES, E. E., & DAUGHERTY, B. N. Political orientation and the perceptual effects of an anticipated interaction. *J. abnorm. soc. Psychol.*, **59**, 1959, 340–349.

JONES, E. E., HESTER, S. L., FARINA, A., & DAVIS, K. E. Reactions to unfavorable personal evaluation as a function of the evaluator's perceived adjustment. *J. abnorm. soc. Psychol.*, **59**, 1959, 363–370.

The process of social influence is fundamental to social psychology. The means by which individuals or organizations influence other persons or groups underlies most processes of development and change, such as socialization, mass communication, group formation, leadership, politics, psychotherapy, and education. Part Three conceptualizes social influence processes in terms of change in attitudes and behavior. The principles delineated in this part are sufficiently general to be applied to virtually any of the more specific topics of influence, such as socialization or psychotherapy. Early scientific conceptions of persuasion, propaganda, and other forms of social influence were similar to those of the layman in emphasizing the content and style of communications and the prestige of the communicator. The first selection follows this older tradition in examining the qualities of the communicator that make him believable, but it differs from earlier research in using high-powered statistical techniques made possible only through modern digital computers.

The second selection examines the consequences of discrepancies of varying amounts between the communicator's attitude position and that of the respondent. Using the respondent's involvement in the issue as an additional variable, the point at which maximum attitude change will occur is specified in terms of this involvement and the discrepancy between the positions of communicator and respondent, and this prediction is tested empirically. In recent years, research has greatly emphasized the structural relation between cognitions, feelings, and behavior as a source of attitude change or as source of resistance to persuasive communications. Most of the remaining selections are devoted to various facets of this current research development.

The final two selections are of a different character. They take into account the fact that social influence is a complex process having many facets that must be considered in their relation to one another. To implement this view, a more adequate and comprehensive theory of social influence needs to be developed. The next to the last selection takes a modest step in this direction by thoroughly analyzing changes that take place in the psychological situation when an action contrary to one's attitude is induced. The final selection takes communication out of the restricted conditions of the laboratory and examines the process as it is influenced by features of the social situation, with particular emphasis on the diffusion of innovations throughout a society or subgroup.

PART THREE

SOCIAL INFLUENCE PROCESSES

PERCEIVED CHARACTERISTICS OF THE COMMUNICATOR *

Although the focus of communication research today is on dynamic processes rather than such older problems as the influence of the characteristics of the communicator, these older questions have by no means been fully answered. While it is true that the communicator may be perceived in

* The selection following the editorial was written especially for this volume and is being printed with permission of the authors.

varied ways by different respondents, that the content of his communication influences how he is perceived, and even that the relation of the recipient to other persons determines the communicator's image, it is still likely that regularities will be discovered relating the perception of the communicator to the effectiveness of his communications.

One respect in which communicators vary is their credibility—the extent to which they are believed. Several studies have shown that the credibility of a communicator is related to the extent to which his communications are accepted. But what makes a communicator credible is not entirely clear. Speculative analysis has suggested that two major components of credibility are expertness and trustworthiness. Schweitzer and Ginsburg report some empirical data pertaining to these and other attributes of credibility.

12.

Factors of Communicator Credibility[1]

DON SCHWEITZER
GERALD P. GINSBURG
UNIVERSITY OF NEVADA

Individual differences among communicators in the effectiveness of their persuasive messages has been amply demonstrated. Asch (1948), for example, found that agreement with a statement and even the meaning of a statement can be altered by attributing it to different communicators. Similar findings have been reported by Haiman (1949), Paulson (1954), and Horowitz and Pastore (1955). Some communicators quite clearly are more effective in getting their messages across and are more likely to be believed than are others. However, these studies did not undertake to identify the characteristics which determine such inter-communicator differences in effectiveness and believability. Instead, identification of the characteristics of persuasive communicators was attacked by the Yale group (Hovland, Janis, and Kelley, 1953) in their studies on communication and persuasion under the rubric of *communicator credibility*. The present study constitutes an investigation of the components of that construct. In particular, the authors have attempted to assess empirically the presumed determinants of communicator credibility.

Hovland, Janis, and Kelley (1953) used credibility to refer to the recipient's judgment of the "believableness" of a communicator. They argued that as the credibility of a communicator increases, the probability also increases that his influence attempts will be successful. According to those authors, communicator credibility is composed of two factors—expertness and trustworthiness. Expertness is concerned with the extent to which the communicator is considered to be a

[1] The authors gratefully acknowledge the services of Diana Poehlman, who coded the data in Phase I, and of the Data Processing Center of the University of Nevada and the Western Data Processing Center at University of California, Los Angeles.

source of valid information. It is assumed to depend on qualities of a communicator which cause him to be perceived as "knowing what he is talking about." This would include such qualities as experience, training, holding a position of leadership, age, and background. For example, when students enter a classroom for the first time the credibility of the teacher for the class members would be due largely to their attribution to him of these qualities; that is, his credibility would be based upon the level of experience attributed to him by the class.

Trustworthiness is more difficult to define. Hovland et al. (1953) suggest that appearance, attitude, manner, and perceived intent of the communicator are important in assessing a communicator's trustworthiness. Trustworthiness can be viewed as the recipient's judgment of the extent to which a communicator is a reliable source of information.

A number of studies of credibility have been based on this model. (See, for example, Hovland and Weiss, 1951; Kelman and Hovland, 1953; and Hovland and Mandell, 1953.) These studies follow the general form of varying credibility as a whole, or one of its factors, and noting the effect of this variation on stated opinion concerning the topic of the communication. However, this model of credibility was developed *a priori* and has not been tested empirically. The studies just cited take the model as a given. Such research is helpful in determining the effect of credibility in altering attitudes toward a communication but it cannot be taken as a test of the model itself. It is unlikely to identify those characteristics of communicators which determine their credibility.

The purpose of the present study, then, was to determine the characteristics of communicators that affect recipients' judgments of the communicator's credibility. A list of characteristics was empirically derived and subjected to a factor analysis in order to assess the adequacy of the *a priori* model of communicator credibility offered by Hovland and his associates.

METHOD

The present study involved two phases. In the first phase subjects were asked to list the relevant characteristics of several highly credible people with whom they had had personal contact. A set of bipolar rating scales was constructed from the lists generated in Phase I. In Phase II these rating scales were used in a judgmental task and the results were factor analyzed to yield information about the number and composition of the dimensions involved in judgments of credibility. The factor analysis was done by the principal axis method with normalized varimax rotation.

Phase I
Twenty-four students from an upper division summer school class in Educational Psychology were instructed

to think of one person who fit into each of four situations specified on separate pages of an experimental booklet. The four specified situations were receiving communications from an expert, from someone whom the subject trusted, from someone who had sold him something, and from someone who had changed the subject's mind about something. The Ss were further instructed to list the characteristics of these four people that made them believe their communications. As an example, the situation concerning the trusted person read as follows:

> Think of one person that you would consider worthy of your trust. That person's initials are ———. Now consider the instances when that person has talked to you, either formally or informally. Please list the characteristics of that person which made you believe what he said.

The Ss were instructed to think of some specific acquaintance for each of the four situations so as to minimize the likelihood of their listing the characteristics contained in social stereotypes of credible persons. The four situations to which the Ss responded were selected so as to elicit characteristics related to each of the two major components of credibility (expertness and trustworthiness) plus two other situations in which credibility obviously plays a part (in addition, one of these situations—the salesman—has not received any attention in credibility studies). This procedure ensured an adequate representation of characteristics for the formation of trustworthiness and expertness factors in Phase II, if such dimensions actually are used to judge the credibility of a speaker.

After completing the lists of characteristics, the subjects were asked to answer a series of questions aimed at determining what they thought the experiment was about. In addition to a direct question about the purpose of the study the subjects were asked upon what they based their opinion, whether they had any hunches about what the experimenter expected and if so, what it was they thought he expected and what led them to believe this. These questions were included in order to determine whether the subjects had responded in terms of the instructions given them in the booklet or in terms of some other structuring of the situation which they arrived at independently of the instruction.

The lists of characteristics generated by the subjects were collated into four lists, one for each situation. The frequency with which each characteristic appeared was noted. The four lists were then combined into one list and finally were coded into general categories.[2] Each of the general categories was given a label and a definition which reflected the meanings of the responses in that category. The coding process

yielded twenty-four categories plus three individual responses which could not be coded into any of the categories. The categories were used to form rating scales as described below in Phase II.

Phase II

The purpose of this phase was to investigate the factor structure of judgments of the credibility of both highly credible speakers and speakers of low credibility. This was implemented by forming bipolar rating scales based on the categories obtained in Phase I and having an independent group of subjects rate two hypothetical speakers on the scales. The judgmental responses were factor analyzed in order to assess the dimensions involved in judgments of communicator credibility.

The rating scales were derived in the following manner. From each of the twenty-four categories derived in Phase I, the most representative and most frequently mentioned characteristics were selected and paired with their opposites. From this list, two pairs from twenty-three of the twenty-four categories were selected to be included in the final set of scales.[3] Two criteria were used to select the pairs to be included in the final set of scales. First, the pair had to adequately represent the category from which it was selected; second, neither member could have a strongly negative connotation. Negatively connoted terms were avoided in an attempt to reduce the effects of any bias that the subjects might have had against characterizing others in strongly negative terms.

The forty-six pairs finally selected were ordered at random except for the restriction that the two pairs from any given category had to be separated by at least two pairs from other categories. To reduce response bias the negative member was presented first for half of the pairs. Each pair of words was used as the polar terms of a seven place rating scale. The set of rating scales served as the measuring instrument in this phase of the study.

Data for Phase II were collected from 181 students enrolled in General Psychology. Each subject was given an experimental booklet which contained complete instructions and the introductions for two hypothetical speakers, each of which was followed by the list of rating scales. The instructions informed the Ss that they would be asked to rate two individuals on a number of scales, and gave detailed instructions on how to use the rating scale.

The topic of the would-be speeches was "The Home Disaster Shelter." The first introduction concerned a Professor Hugo Meier. He was made to appear highly credible in terms of the characteristics mentioned by Hovland, Janis, and Kelley (1953). The

---

[2] The coding was done independently by two persons, both very familiar with the study. There were few inconsistencies, and these were resolved through discussion only after each coder had completely finished his task.

[3] The category labeled "Appearance" was eliminated because subjects were not going to see any communicators and, therefore, could not be expected to judge them on this variable.

TABLE 1   Rotated Factor Matrix—Lo C Intro

VARIABLE NUMBER	VARIABLE NAME	LOADING	ORDER OF COM-PONENTS	OTHER FACTORS LOADED	PROPORTION OF COMMON VARIANCE
FACTOR I					.260
1	Closed minded	.429	2	XVIII	
2	Unstable	.495	3	II	
5	Intuitive	.507	1		
13	Gives poor advice	.594	2	XVII	
15	Uninspiring	.561	3	IV	
18	Not helpful	.634	2	(not in table)	
21	Unfair	.721	1		
24	Braggard	.495	1		
25	Unaware of needs of others	.684	1		
26	Not dedicated to his field	.742	1		
29	Dishonest	.808	1		
32	Untrustworthy	.708	1		
33	Crude	.494	1		
38	Displays common sense	.488	2	II; V	
39	Unconcerned	.747	1		
40	Disloyal to listeners	.678	1		
42	Insincere	.840	1		
45	Devious	.682	1		
FACTOR II					.157
2	Unstable	.601	2	I	
3	Amateur	.980	1		
6	Inconsistent	.526	2	VII; XV	
10	Inexperienced	.871	1		
11	Lacks professional manner	.542	3	XI	
16	Lacks foresight	.444	2	XXI	
23	Lacks expert knowledge	.416	1		
27	Informed	.462	1		
30	Infrequently tackles problems	.483	3	XIII	
38	Displays common sense	.454	3	I; V	
43	Unintelligent	.529	2	XVI	
44	Plans for future	.318	4		
FACTOR III					.118
9	Lacks command of English	.830	1		
12	Partial	.641	1		
19	Not well mannered	.533	1		
22	Poor speaker	.637	1		
28	Does not use correct English	.769	1		
FACTOR IV					.093
15	Uninspiring	.634	2	I	
17	Unbelievable	.725	1		
18	Not helpful	.522	3	I	
31	Boring	.430	1		
36	Persuasive	.668	1		
38	Displays common sense	.410	3	I; II	
46	Bright	.498	1		
FACTOR V					.051
6	Inconsistent	.443	3	II; XV	
7	Dissimilar to me	.714	1		
20	Does not share my likes and dislikes	.664	1		

introduction stated that he had received a Ph.D. degree, served on the "President's Special Committee on Civil Preparedness," published two books and innumerable articles on the topic of civil preparedness and organized civil preparedness programs on the city, state, and national levels. In addition, hypothetical quotations lauding Dr. Meier were included. These quotations were attributed to Edward R. Murrow and *The New York Times.*

The second introduction concerned a Mr. Otto Schmidt, who was made to appear low in credibility. The description stated that he had never finished high school, accused him of shrewd business maneuvering, and said that his businesses had been investigated by the Better Business Bureau on three occasions. Included also was a hypothetical quotation from the local press that was far from complimentary to Mr. Schmidt.

RESULTS AND DISCUSSION

The subjects in Phase I made a total of 430 responses, with a mean of eighteen responses per subject. The mean numbers of responses per subject for the four situations were 5.08, 4.67,

4.00, and 4.17 respectively. All but three of the responses were coded into the twenty-four categories mentioned earlier. The answers to the questions concerning the subjects' hunches about the study indicated that the subjects had responded in terms of the instructions given to them. Thus, the purpose of the first phase was adequately met: the four situations elicited approximately equal numbers of responses, almost all of the responses were coded into a set of general descriptive categories, and subjects responded in terms of the instructions.

The analysis of the rating scale data of Phase II was carried on in several stages. First, the means and variances of the responses to the forty-six rating scales were computed separately for the introduction of the highly credible speaker (Hi C Intro) and for the introduction of the speaker with low credibility (Lo C Intro). Then the rating data were factor analyzed, again sep-

TABLE 1   *(continued)*

VARIABLE NUMBER	VARIABLE NAME	LOADING	ORDER OF COMPONENTS	OTHER FACTORS LOADED	PROPORTION OF COMMON VARIANCE
FACTOR VI					.035
35	Halting presentation	.570	1		
41	Easily flustered	.562	1		
FACTOR VII					.032
34	Sure of himself	.662	1		
FACTOR VIII					.029
4	Indiscrete	.597	1		
FACTOR IX					.029
8	Immodest	.739	1		
FACTOR X					.028
37	Cold	.605	1		
FACTOR XI					.022
14	Involved in his field	.591	1		
FACTOR XII					.016
11	Lacks professional manner	.544	2	II	
FACTOR XIII					.016
6	Inconsistent	.521	3	II; VII	
FACTOR XIV					.016
43	Intelligent	.471	3	II	
FACTOR XV					.016
1	Closed minded	.428	3	I	
FACTOR XVI					.015
30	Infrequently tackles problems	.536	2	II	
FACTOR XVII					.011
13	Gives poor advice	.441	3	I	

arately for each of the two introductions. An examination of the means and variances is useful for interpretation of the two factor structures.

As expected, the Hi C Intro speaker was judged in generally favorable terms, while the Lo C Intro speaker was rated in generally unfavorable terms. Furthermore, the mean responses (summed over subjects) for the forty-six scales were more extreme (closer to 1 or 7) under the Hi C Intro than under the Lo C Intro. This was reflected in the much greater variance of the Hi C Intro means than of the Lo C Intro means ($t = 23.94$, $p < .001$), although the means of the two distributions of mean responses did not differ significantly ($t = .07$). In addition, there was more agreement among Ss under the Hi C Intro than under the Lo C Intro (the mean of the forty-six Hi C Intro variances was significantly smaller than that of the Lo C Intro variances, tested by t-test for correlated variances, $p < .01$). A plausible implication of these comparisons is that categories for the description of people with negative characteristics are less well defined and more poorly learned in our culture than are categories for the description of people with favorable characteristics. This would lead to lower consensus under the Lo C Intro than under the Hi C Intro. We will return to this point, as well as consider an alternative explanation, after an examination of the factor structures.[4]

In order to interpret the factor structures the following scheme was adopted. First, those scales which loaded .400 or greater on one, and only one, factor were considered to be the "primary components" of that factor. These are the most salient scales and the terms which define them constitute the major portion of the definition of the factor. Second, those scales which loaded .400 or greater on one factor but had a smaller loading that was also .400 or greater on another factor constitute "second order components" of factors. Third, those scales which loaded .400 or greater on a factor but also had a higher loading on another factor constitute "third order components" of factors. Fourth, those scales that had no loading of .400 or greater constitute "fourth order components" of the factor upon which they had the highest loading. Those factors on which no scales loaded .400 or greater were not considered. Table 1 contains the rotated factors and components of factors, as defined above, which were found in the responses to the Lo C Intro and Table 2 presents comparable data for the

[4] An alternative basis for the lower Lo C Intro consensus is the possible inappropriateness of the rating scales for judging speakers of low credibility, since the scales were originally developed in terms of highly credible people (Phase I). This point will be discussed later.

Hi C Intro. The scale name is given together with the loading, the order of each component, and, where appropriate, the other factors upon which the scales loaded. The proportion of common variance explained by each factor is also included. The rotated factor structures generated by each of the two sets of data first will be considered separately and then will be compared.

A total of twenty-eight factors emerged in the rotated factor matrix for the Lo C Intro. This matrix, shown in Table 1, accounts for 74.2 percent of the total variability of this set of responses. The first factor is a very global one that can best be interpreted as indicating a lack of trustworthiness. It is not, however, as precise as one would expect from the Hovland, Janis, and Kelley conceptualization. In addition to the components one would expect to find in terms of their model, the obtained factor contains such first order components as "intuitive," "braggard," "crude," and "unconcerned." The second factor in the matrix is also very global in nature. It clearly indicates a lack of expertise. Thus far the data seem to support the Hovland, Janis, and Kelley model, except for the inclusion of several characteristics not mentioned by them. The emergence of additional factors, however, casts doubts as to the total adequacy of their model.

Factors III and IV of this matrix refer to expectations concerning the communicator's mode of presentation. The third factor indicates that the communicator was expected to lack the techniques of public speaking and to be inept in the use of English. The fourth factor reveals that this communicator was expected to be persuasive but boring and unbelievable. The fifth factor indicates that the subjects perceive this communicator as unlike themselves. Factor VI, like Factors III and IV, is concerned with mode of presentation. Here again, the speaker was expected to lack the techniques of public speaking. Factors VII through XI are all unitary factors, the meanings of which are clear from the table.[5]

The factor matrix generated by the responses to the other introduction (Hi C Intro) is shown in Table 2. It contains twenty-seven factors and accounts for 59.79 percent of the variance. The first factor in the matrix indicates that the subjects expected the speaker to be trustworthy. However, the inclusion of such components as "humble," "refined," and "warm" indicates that this communicator also was expected to be gracious. Factors II through IV are related to expectations concerning the mode of presentation of this communicator. Factor II indicates that the highly credible communicator was expected to be inspiring and stimulating, while Factor III reveals that he was expected to be professional, and Factor IV shows that he was expected to

[5] Due to a clerical error, "discreet" was misspelled as "discrete" in the instrument. It is possible that the term emerged as a unitary factor because of the misspelling.

possess the techniques of public speaking. Factors V, VI, and VII reflect expectations that the speaker will be straightforward, open minded, and adept in the use of English, respectively. The remaining factors in the matrix reveal that the communicator having high credibility was perceived as logical, sincere, professional, aware of the needs of others, problem oriented, expert, discrete, informed, a good advisor, having foresight, and impartial.

A comparison can now be made between the two factor structures. First, it should be noted that more factors were generated in describing the communicator having high credibility. Second, the factors found in the Lo C Intro matrix are of a more global nature than are those found in the other matrix. It should also be noted that the substance of the factors differs between the two situations. All of these points are related to the issue raised earlier, namely, that the categories used to describe persons with negative characteristics are not as well defined in our culture as are those used to describe persons with positive characteristics. This assertion is supported by the moderate values of the means, the size of the variances, the number and global nature of the factors and the substantive makeup of the factors related to the communicator who is low in credibility.

There is, however, another possible interpretation of these results. It may be that the characteristics used to describe communicators of low credibility are not simply the opposite of those used to describe communicators of high credibility. It should be remembered that subjects in the first phase were asked to list characteristics of communicators which made them believe what these communicators said. The terms used to define the scales in the second phase were these positive characteristics and their opposites. It may be that the crucial characteristics necessary to define communicators of low credibility were not obtained by this procedure. Regardless of which of these interpretations is correct, the fact still remains that the two factor structures differed considerably, and such a fact is not consistent with the Hovland, Janis, and Kelley model of credibility.

The present results differ on many points from what would be predicted by the Hovland, Janis, and Kelley model. The factors that emerged for the highly credible communicator are much more specific than those for the communicator with low credibility. Many more factors are necessary to describe the communicator of high credibility. An "expert" factor does not emerge for the highly credible communicator. Many factors in addition to "expertness" and "trustworthiness" are required to describe either of the communicators. Although no claim is made for the stability of the particular factors that emerged in this analysis, it does seem clear that the Hovland, Janis, and Kelley model is incomplete.

There are, however, certain limitations of the present study that should be noted. First, the matrix may have been very different if a different population had been sampled. (The decision to use students was based on the fact that the previous research in this area was done using students as subjects.) For instance, it may be the case that an expertness factor would have emerged for the Hi C Intro if a different population had been used. Students are confronted every day by experts and the possession of this quality may not be crucial for their judgments of high credibility, whereas the absence of this characteristic may be all that is necessary for them to judge a communicator as low in credibility. Perhaps the Hovland, Janis, and Kelley factors form a baseline of high credibility, for students at least. College students who are motivated enough to take summer school classes may well be more impressed by the absence of a given characteristic ("intelligence," for example) than they are by its presence. This could account for the absence of an expert factor in Table 2. For college students, who are accustomed to hearing expert communicators, the presence of other variables as determiners of high credibility is understandable. The importance of this point is obvious. Very different factor structures may have been found if a different population had been sampled. If the interpretation that the characteristic mentioned by Hovland, Janis, and Kelley actually form a sort of baseline for high credibility, at least for students, is accepted, then the problem of listing the characteristics that will increase credibility above this baseline becomes a primary one. This study strongly suggests that the characteristic of being inspiring and stimulating is involved. It is also suggested that communicators having high credibility are perceived as warm and honest.

A second limitation of the present study is imposed by the procedures used. If the factors that emerged here are indeed crucial variables in judgments of credibility, that fact should be demonstrable in experimental situations similar to those used by Hovland, Janis, and Kelley. A factor analytic study can only be used to suggest hypotheses that should be tested in situations that permit actual manipulation of the variables.

The results of this study have several important implications for the concept of communicator credibility which are not precluded by the limitations discussed above. In the first place, it seems very likely that the recipient's judgment of the credibility of a communicator is based upon more than perceptions of what Hovland et al. (1953) call "trustworthiness" and "expertness." In the second place, the perceived characteristics which underlie low credibility are not necessarily the opposites of the characteristics which underlie

TABLE 2   Rotated Factor Matrix—Hi C Intro

VARIABLE NUMBER	VARIABLE NAME	LOADING	ORDER OF COM-PONENTS	OTHER FACTORS LOADED	PROPORTION OF COMMON VARIANCE
FACTOR I					.145
8	Modest	.373	4		
19	Well mannered	.545	2	VII	
21	Fair	.488	2	XXI	
24	Humble	.704	1		
29	Honest	.396	4		
32	Trustworthy	.662	1		
33	Refined	.551	1		
37	Warm	.616	1		
40	Loyal to listeners	.610	1		
FACTOR II					.077
15	Inspiring	.666	1		
31	Stimulating	.641	1		
46	Bright	.412	2	V	
FACTOR III					.066
6	Consistent	.603	1		
10	Experienced	.478	2	XIV	
11	Possesses professional manner	.512	1		
18	Helpful	.375	4		
FACTOR IV					.063
22	Polished speaker	.549	1		
35	Smooth presentation	.631	1		
36	Persuasive	.373	4		
FACTOR V					.058
38	Displays common sense	.556	1		
45	Straightforward	.670	1		
46	Bright	.403	3	II	
FACTOR VI					.052
1	Open minded	.589	1		
17	Convincing	.362	4		
FACTOR VII					.050
9	Has command of English	.629	1		
19	Well mannered	.432	3	I	
28	Uses correct English	.586	1		
FACTOR VIII					.047
2	Stable	.478	1		
5	Logical	.555	1		
43	Intelligent	.351	4		
FACTOR IX					.046
39	Concerned	.334	4		
42	Sincere	.573	1		
44	Plans for future	.540	1		
FACTOR X					.042
3	Professional	.579	1		
14	Involved in his field	.483	1		

high credibility. For example, the absence of trustworthiness and expertness cues may be condition enough for a judgment of low credibility, but the presence of those cues may not be enough for a judgment of high credibility. Thirdly, the perceived trustworthiness and perceived expertness of a communicator appear to be determined by a wider set of characteristics than those suggested by Hovland, et al. (1953). Finally, the results of the present study strongly suggest that the particular cues, or perceived characteristics, which influence the recipient's judgment of credibility will vary across communication contexts and across populations of recipients. For example, cues which imply expertness of a speaker may not be influential in effecting judgments of high credibility in a college context, where expertness of the speaker is part of the everyday environment. In summary, it is important to recognize that

the present data do not refute the Hovland, et al. concept of communicator credibility with its underlying determinants of trustworthiness and expertness. Instead, they lend further support to the model but very strongly argue that it is incomplete and is sorely in need of extension. Furthermore, the data suggest several directions which extensions might follow.

REFERENCES

ASCH, S. E. The doctrine of suggestion, prestige and imitation in social psychology. *Psychol. Rev.,* 1948, **55,** 250–276.

HAIMAN, F. S. An experimental study of the effects

TABLE 2 (continued)

VARIABLE NUMBER	VARIABLE NAME	LOADING	ORDER OF COMPONENTS	OTHER FACTORS LOADED	PROPORTION OF COMMON VARIANCE
FACTOR XI					.040
25	Aware of the needs of others	.495	1		
26	Dedicated to his field	.557	1		
FACTOR XII					.037
30	Frequently tackles problems	.640	1		
FACTOR XIII					.037
7	Dissimilar to me	.671	1		
20	Shares my likes and dislikes	.444	1		
FACTOR XIV					.034
10	Experienced	.415	3	III	
23	Possesses expert knowledge	.573	1		
FACTOR XV					.029
4	Discrete	.553	1		
FACTOR XVI					.026
27	Informed	.511	1		
FACTOR XVII					.025
13	Gives good advice	.539	1		
FACTOR XVIII					.024
16	Shows foresight	.505	1		
FACTOR XIX					.023
12	Impartial	.474	1		
FACTOR XX					.019
34	Sure of himself	.430	1		
FACTOR XXI					.016
21	Fair	.438	3	I	

of ethos in public speaking. *Speech Monogr.*, 1949, **16**, 190–202.
HOROWITZ, M. W., & PASTORE, N. Relationship of
motive to author and statement. *Science,*
1955, **121,** 110–111.
HOVLAND, C. I., JANIS, I. L., & KELLEY, H. H. *Communication and persuasion.* New Haven,
Conn.: Yale Univer. Press, 1953.
HOVLAND, C. I., & MANDELL, W. An experimental
comparison of conclusion-drawing by the
communicator and by the audience. *J.*

abnorm. soc. Psychol., 1952, **47,** 581–
588.
HOVLAND, C. I., & WEISS, W. The influence of source
credibility on communication effectiveness. *Publ. Opin. Quart.*, 1951, **15,** 635–
650.
KELMAN, H. C., & HOVLAND, C. I. Reinstatement of
the communicator in delayed measurement of opinion change. *J. abnorm. soc.
Psychol.*, 1953, **48,** 327–335.
PAULSON, S. F. The effects of the prestige of the
speaker and acknowledgment of opposing
arguments on audience retention and
shift of opinion. *Speech Monogr.*, 1954,
21, 267–271.

INVOLVEMENT, DISCREPANCY, AND ATTITUDE CHANGE*

The degree to which an influence attempt is successful depends to some extent on the difference
between the attitude position of the communicator
and that of the respondent. Several earlier studies
indicate that the greater the discrepancy, the more
the attitude change. Also significant is the intensity
of feeling which the respondent has concerning his
attitude position. Hovland, Harvey, and Sherif[a]
noted that when the respondent has high involvement in his own attitude position, the communicator's position must be within a certain distance
of the respondent's position, a range termed the
latitude of acceptance. Beyond this point, communications are less influential or are rejected entirely.
Thus, under conditions of low involvement, attitude
change would appear to be directly related to the
discrepancy between communicator and respondent; but under conditions of high involvement, this
relation holds only up to a point, beyond which
attitude change is reduced, does not occur, or is
even opposite to the communicator's position.

In the selection below Freedman reports empirical data that confirm for the two conditions the
relation between attitude change and the discrepancy between the communicator and respondent.
Some conceptual improvements are also offered.
The suggestion is made that, if the discrepancy is
sufficiently extreme under low-involvement conditions, attitude change will also be reduced. Moreover, a parsimonious explanation of these differing
relations for high and low involvement is offered
in terms of difficulty of change as a function of
discrepancy and involvement, as follows.

Difficulty of *attitude change* would appear to be

a function of the discrepancy between the position
of the respondent and that of the communicator:
the greater the discrepancy, the greater the difficulty of change. But *rejection of the communication*
is no more difficult with a more discrepant position; in fact, if the communicator's position is extreme, rejection of his message may be easier
because he appears biased or irrational. Thus,
maximum change will occur when the discrepancy
is at a point where attitude change is just slightly
easier than rejection of the communication. This is
a point where any further discrepancy in positions
would make rejection of the message easier than
attitude change. The relation of involvement in
one's own position is now clear. Such investment
of affect makes attitude change more difficult, and
rejection of the message easier; consequently, maximum attitude change occurs with a smaller discrepancy between the positions of communicator
and respondent.

13.

Involvement, Discrepancy, and Change[1]

JONATHAN L. FREEDMAN
STANFORD UNIVERSITY

*S*s took a position under high or low
involvement; were subsequently exposed to information which was slightly,
moderately, or extremely discrepant
from the initial position; and the
amount of change in their positions

* The selection following the editorial introduction is reprinted
from "Involvement, discrepancy, and change," *Journal of
abnormal and Social Psychology*, 1964, **69**, 290–295, by permission of the author and the American Psychological Association.
ª C. I. Hovland, O. J. Harvey, & M. Sherif. Assimilation and
contrast effects in reactions to communication and attitude
change. *J. abnorm. soc. Psychol.*, 1957, **55**, 244–252.

1 This study is based on a dissertation presented to Yale Uni-
versity in candidacy for the degree of Doctor of Philosophy.
It was conducted while the author held a United States Public
Health Service research fellowship.

The author is extremely grateful for the guidance and encouragement he received from the late Carl I. Hovland who
served as chairman of the dissertation committee until his
death.

was measured. Under low involvement, there was more change with greater discrepancy; but under high involvement, the relationship was nonmonotonic, with maximum change occurring at moderate discrepancy. The situation is analyzed in terms of the relative difficulty of position change and rejection of the information as alternative modes of resolution.

When a person is exposed to information that is discrepant from his own opinion, there is a tendency for him to change his position in the direction of the information. What effect does the size of the discrepancy between his initial position and the information have on the amount of change? Despite the considerable amount of research that has dealt with this basic situation, the answer to this question is not clear. A number of studies have demonstrated that in general the greater the discrepancy, the more change occurs (Fisher & Lubin, 1958; Fisher, Rubinstein, & Freeman, 1956; Goldberg, 1954; Harvey, Kelley, & Shapiro, 1957; Hovland & Pritzker, 1957; Zimbardo, 1960). It has been suggested, however (Hovland, 1959; Hovland, Harvey, & Sherif, 1957) that under conditions of high involvement in the initial position this relationship breaks down; and that extreme discrepancy may produce little or even negative change. The present paper presents an experiment designed to provide evidence bearing directly on this suggestion.

To begin with it is essential to have a clear understanding of what is meant by "involvement." Unfortunately it appears to have been used in at least two quite different ways by different authors. While probably the most common usage is to refer to interest in, concern about, or commitment to a particular position on an issue, it has also sometimes referred to general level of interest in or concern about an issue without reference to a specific position. Since a person can be greatly interested in an issue without having yet taken a stand on it, these two meanings of the terms are clearly different. In their discussion Hovland et al. (1957) appear to be using the term in the former, more specific sense and that is how it will be used in this paper. That is, involvement will refer to degree of concern about or commitment to a specific response or position.

How has the effect of involvement and discrepancy on change been explained? Hovland et al. (1957) compared the attitude-change situation to that in psychophysics in which near or remote anchors are given. When the anchor is near, assimilation occurs and all judgments move toward the anchor; when the anchor is very far away, contrast occurs and all judgments move away from the anchor. It is suggested that a similar phenomenon occurs in attitude-change situations. Slightly or moderately discrepant information produces movement away from the initial position; but information that is so discrepant that it falls within the latitude of rejection produces no change or even produces a "boomerang" effect, with subjects moving away from the new information.

What does this imply about the relationship between discrepancy and change? In the first place, although Hovland and Sherif do not state this explicitly, it seems reasonable to assume that if assimilation occurs, there will be greater change with larger discrepancies. An extremely close external anchor would be expected to produce very small displacements in judgments of the closest stimuli, because the displacement would be limited by the size of the discrepancy between the anchor and the stimuli. Although the relative change (that is, absolute change divided by size of the discrepancy) would be very high, the absolute change would be small. A somewhat more remote anchor, which was still close enough to cause assimilation, would be expected to produce greater absolute change, because the total amount of change possible would be greater. The various attitude-change studies cited above also lends support to this assumption. Thus, as long as the discrepant information falls within the latitude of acceptance, larger discrepancies should produce greater change. Once the information falls outside the latitude of acceptance, however, little or no change is expected to occur. Therefore, as discrepancy increases, amount of change increases up to a point and then decreases. Or, in other words, the relationship between discrepancy and change is nonmonotonic, with maximum change occurring at moderate levels of discrepancy.

This nonmonotonic relationship between discrepancy and change should hold regardless of the degree of involvement in the initial position, but involvement should be an important determinant of the level of discrepancy at which maximum change occurs. With low involvement the latitude of acceptance is relatively wide and it is consequently difficult to get beyond it into the latitude of rejection; with high involvement the latitude of acceptance is narrower and it is considerably easier to get into the latitude of rejection. Thus, with low involvement only extremely discrepant information will fall within the latitude of rejection, whereas with high involvement relatively moderate information may be rejected. Since the point at which the latitude of rejection is reached is the point of maximum change, and since this point should be more moderate for high- than for low-involvement conditions, maximum change should occur at a more moderate level of discrepancy for high than for low involvement.

The present experiment was designed to test

this hypothesis. The general design was to take an issue on which the subjects initially had no opinion; have them take a position under conditions of high or low involvement; present them with information that was slightly, moderately, or highly discrepant from their initial position; and measure the amount of change. On the basis of pretesting the three levels of discrepancy were selected so that all would be more moderate than the maximal change point for the low-involvement condition, but the high discrepancy information would fall beyond the point of maximum change for the high-involvement subjects. Therefore it was predicted that within the range of discrepancies used there would be more change with greater discrepancy under conditions of low involvement; but with high involvement, maximum change would occur at the moderate level of discrepancy.

METHOD

In order to minimize the possibility that the subjects had previous opinions on the issue and to maximize the objectivity of the information, a concept formation task was employed as the "issue." A number of concept instances were presented and the subjects were required to decide what the correct concept was. This first description of the concept was considered their initial position. The instances were constructed so that only one consistent concept could be formed and only subjects who gave this response were included in the experimental analysis. Additional concept instances were then presented which were discrepant from the subjects' first response, and subjects were told that these new instances were examples of the same concept. The new instances were thus essentially discrepant information. After seeing the new instances, subjects were asked to give a final description of the concept and the amount of change from the initial concept to this last one was measured, and is considered a measure of position change.

The subjects were 119 freshmen from an introductory psychology class at the University of Bridgeport and 96 students from North Haven high school. In both samples, participation in the experiment was required by the school. Ninety-one subjects were eliminated because of failure to give the appropriate response to the first series of concept instances. An additional 14 subjects did not give any response to the second part of the test and could therefore not be included in the results. The remaining 110 subjects were divided about equally among experimental conditions, with no difference between conditions even approaching significance. Although the number of subjects eliminated was very high, this was due primarily to the difficulty of the concept formation task which was the same for all groups. This means that the remaining subjects were probably a somewhat

select group (in that they were better able to cope with the concept formation task), but there is no reason to expect this selection to affect the various experimental groups differentially.

The experiment was described as a test being conducted as part of a survey of college and high school students. The subjects were run in groups ranging from four to eight. The test situation, the test booklet, and the instructions were designed to create an atmosphere which resembled a typical group intelligence test or scholastic aptitude test. When the subject entered the room he was asked to take a seat at which a booklet was placed. When all subjects had arrived, the signal to begin was given. Silence was strictly enforced.

All instructions and materials were in the test booklet which was entitled "Yale Personality Survey." It contained, in order, a personality questionnaire, the concept formation test, and a short questionnaire concerning the concept formation test.

All subjects first took a 25-item personality test. This questionnaire was administered in order to increase the subjects' interest and motivation by impressing them with the fact that the survey concerned important things about themselves. It was also expected that this would make it more credible that the concept formation test was a test of intelligence and perceptiveness, as it was described.

The concept formation test was presented next. The materials and procedure were similar to those employed in standard concept formation studies (cf. Hunt & Hovland, 1960). Concept instances consisted of a rectangle containing three figures in a row. The figures varied in shape (circle, triangle, or square) and size (large or small); and additional variation was produced by the number of a particular shape or size that was included (one, two, or three) and each figure's position (first, second, or third). There were thus four dimensions: shape, size, number, and position; three with three values, and one with two.

Three concept problems were shown, with the first being the critical one and the others serving merely as buffer items to minimize the possibility that the subjects would remember the exact instances that were used. The subjects were first presented with eight instances labeled either "alpha" or "not-alpha," and they were given detailed instructions which explained that their task was to discover what characteristics defined an alpha. Responses were recorded on a separate answer sheet and consisted of verbal descriptions of the identifying characteristic (e.g., alpha is a triangle in the second position). The eight instances were chosen so that only one answer was consistent with all of them, and all subjects who did not give the correct answer were discarded from the sample.

Discrepancy manipulation

After working on these problems, the subjects were told that they would be shown some additional instances of each of the concepts they had just seen, beginning with the first concept. It was stressed that these new instances were examples of exactly the same concept, and that in order for a solution to be correct it had to be consistent with all instances. To be certain that all subjects remembered their first answer and to increase its salience, subjects were required to copy their answers from the separate answer sheet on to the instruction page.

Sixteen instances were then presented one at a time, with each labeled either alpha or not-alpha as in Part I. Of these 16 new instances, 5 were discrepant from the first response given by the subjects, but all were consistent with a new response. That is, by responding with the new concept subjects would be consistent with all 16 instances. Also, since it was virtually impossible for the subject to remember the first 8 instances exactly, it would appear that he was responding consistently with all instances. Thus, this new concept is essentially the position advocated by the new instances. Discrepancy was defined as the number of common elements between the initial concept and the advocated concept. In the low-discrepancy condition the two concepts shared three elements; in moderate discrepancy they shared two; and in high discrepancy they shared no elements.

These 16 instances were presented for 15 seconds each, and immediately after each, the subject was given 20 seconds to record his current guess as to the correct solution on an answer page. After the last instance, the subject gave his final description of the concept. All timing was done by having the subjects turn pages on a signal from the experimenter.

Immediately before and after the presentation of the new instances, subjects were given an objective identification test on which they were to indicate whether each of 12 unlabeled instances was an alpha or a not-alpha. After the second identification test, subjects were asked a number of questions designed to measure the success of the involvement manipulation, degree of acceptance of the instructions, and to assess the possibility that involvement groups exerted differential effort on the two parts of the test.

Involvement manipulation

Before the concept formation test was presented, the high-involvement (*HI*) group was given instructions designed to emphasize the importance of their first response as an indicator of intelligence and perceptiveness; while the low-involvement (*LI*) subjects were led to believe that the first response was relatively unimportant as a personality indicator.

The key phrases from the high-involvement instructions were:

> It is extremely important to form an impression quickly and accurately. . . . Therefore, speed of solution is the most important aspect of this test. Your score depends mainly on how close your first answer is to the correct answer.

Low-involvement instructions included the following:

> The first part of the test will not be marked. . . . Your score cannot be based on these first impressions.

The rationale for this manipulation was that the subjects who thought that their score depended primarily on the first response would be more concerned about having that response be correct than those subjects who thought the second response counted more. Since involvement is defined as concern about a response, the manipulation should cause the former to be more involved in their first response than the latter.

Note that a special effort was made to equate the groups in level of interest in and concern about the test as a whole. All subjects were given the same instructions about the importance of the test and its relevance to intelligence and perceptiveness; and all were urged to work hard and concentrate on both parts of the test. The only difference between high- and low-involvement groups was in the instructions dealing with the relative significance of the initial and final responses.

The two sources of data concerning amount of change are the difference between initial and final description of the concept, and between first and last identification tests. Since the concept descriptions have more intuitive similarity to "opinions" as used in attitude-change studies, the results will be presented in terms of change from initial to final concept description. All results are virtually identical for both measures.

Scoring for amount of change in the concept descriptions was based on the assumption that perfect maintenance consists of retaining the original concept intact, with no elements subtracted or changed. In addition, it was felt that subtracting elements was a more serious change than adding new ones; and that forming a concept which included the original intact but provided for exceptions (e.g., a disjunctive concept of the form either *A* or *B*) was in essence no change at all. Rating was done on a 7-point scale, ranging from 0 (no change) to 6 (maximum change). All analyses are based on scoring done by the author, since an interrater reliability coefficient based on the scoring of 25 randomly selected protocols was .98.

RESULTS

Check on the manipulation

The instructions were designed to produce either high or low involvement in the first concept description. A direct check on this manipulation is provided by responses to the question: "Which part of the problem was more important?" Over 90% of the subjects responded consistently with the manipulation instructions (that is, *HI* subjects said the first part; *LI* subjects, the second part). The difference is highly significant. Thus, as far as this direct check indicates, the manipulation was successful in producing greater involvement in their first response for the *HI* group.

Another check on the manipulation is provided

by the amount of change by the two groups. Since high involvement is defined as greater concern with the first response being correct, there should be greater resistance to changing the first response with high than with low involvement. As may be seen in Table 1 and Figure 1, at each level of discrepancy *HI* subjects changed less than *LI* subjects, although at moderate discrepancy the difference was slight. The overall difference between *HI* and *LI* groups is highly significant ($F = 6.95$, $p < .02$). In addition, 54% of *HI* subjects showed no change at all, whereas the comparable figure for *LI* subjects is only 32%. This difference is significant ($\chi^2 = 5.59$, $p < .02$).

A possible alternative explanation of this difference might be that *LI* subjects worked harder than *HI* subjects on the second set of instances and the former therefore changed more (see Cohen, 1959). A check on this possibility is provided by responses to a posttest question which asked subjects to rate how hard they worked on all parts of the test, with possible responses ranging from "not hard at all" to "very hard." Since there were no appreciable differences between groups in amount of effort expended on either part of the test nor in total effort, it seems unlikely that difference between groups in amount of change was due to differential effort. Thus, it seems reasonable to assume that the manipulation was successful in producing differential involvement in the initial response.

Involvement and discrepancy

The major results are presented in Table 1 and Figure 1, which show the amount of change for each involvement and discrepancy condition. The main hypothesis was that there would be more change with greater discrepancy under low involvement, but with high involvement maximum change would occur at the moderate level of discrepancy. As may be seen in the figure, the results are in line with this prediction. With low involvement change increases monotonically with discrepancy; while under conditions of high involvement, the relationship is nonmonotonic.

A trend analysis (McNemar, 1962) of the three means in each condition demonstrates that the linear trend is significant in the low-involvement condition ($F = 3.71$, $p < .07$) and the quadratic trend is significant in the high-involvement condition ($F = 4.05$, $p < .05$). Neither the quadratic component under low involvement nor the linear component under high involvement approaches significance ($F < 1$ for each). Thus, the results are consistent with the hypothesis and indicate that within the range used the relationship between discrepancy and amount of change is monotonic for low involvement and nonmonotonic for high involvement with maximum change at moderate discrepancy.

DISCUSSION

Although the present results are consistent with the suggestion by Hovland et al. (1957), the analysis these authors offer in terms of latitudes of acceptance and rejection is more a description of the situation than an explanation. The main point of their analysis is that with high involvement extremely discrepant information is rejected and therefore does not cause position change. But the central question remains why rejection of the information occurs rather than position change. This may be answered by analyzing the effect of discrepancy and involvement on the relative difficulty of employing these two modes of resolution.

As discrepancy increases, the difficulty of changing the position also increases, because a greater change is necessary. Assuming that there is some resistance to change, it is harder to change a great deal than to change only a little. Thus, reducing the discrepancy by position change would be considerably harder when discrepancy is extreme than when it is slight. The difficulty of rejecting the information, however, does not increase with greater discrepancy. Extremely discrepant information sometimes tends to appear biased or fanatical and is consequently easier to reject. In any case, extremely discrepant information is no harder to reject than moderate information. Therefore, since position change becomes

FIGURE 1. Mean amount of change from initial to final response.

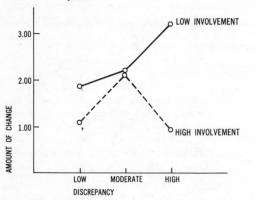

TABLE 1 Amount of Change from Initial to Final Position

CONDITION	DISCREPANCY		
	Low	Moderate	High
Low involvement	1.85	2.16	3.15
High involvement	1.14	2.12	0.94

harder with increasing discrepancy and rejection does not, the difficulty of employing position change must increase relative to the difficulty of rejection.

It follows from this that at some point along the discrepancy continuum position change should become more difficult than rejection of the information. At that point, the subject will reject the information and will not change his position. Since this point will be different for different subjects, a further increase in discrepancy will result in even less change because the point will have been reached by more subjects. Thus, maximum change will occur when the discrepancy is just below the level at which change becomes easier than rejection. Less discrepancy will produce less change because subjects have less far to change; while more discrepancy will produce less change because subjects will reject the information instead.

According to this analysis the relationship between discrepancy and change is nonmonotonic regardless of the degree of involvement in the initial position. Degree of involvement is important, however, because it affects the point along the discrepancy continuum at which the downturn in amount of change occurs. This point will be determined by any factors which affect the difficulty of employing either position change or rejection of the information. Increases in difficulty of changing the initial position will decrease the discrepancy level at which the downturn occurs; while increases in the difficulty of rejecting the information will increase the level. Since an increase in involvement in the initial position will make change more difficult, it should decrease the degree of discrepancy at which the downturn occurs. This is what was found in the present experiment. On the other hand, an increase in the prestige of the communicator will make rejection more difficult and should increase the level of discrepancy. This prediction was supported by the results of a recent experiment by Aronson, Turner, and Carlsmith (1963).

Note that in both of these experiments the downturn was actually found in only one condition. It was not found in the low-involvement condition of the present study nor in the high-prestige condition of the Aronson et al. study. This may be explained by the limited range of discrepancies employed. If the discrepancy level were made extreme enough presumably the downturn would occur eventually. Thus, although the present analysis asserts that the relationship between discrepancy and change is nonmonotonic under both high and low involvement, with low involvement it may appear to be monotonic for a broad range of discrepancies.

Additional support for this analysis is provided by inspection of the amount of change by those subjects in the various conditions who did change. According to the analysis, the decrease in amount of change under high involvement and high discrepancy is caused by a shift in the method of resolution employed from position change to rejection of the information. It follows from this that those subjects who did change (that is, did not reject the information) should change more under high than moderate discrepancy (although, of course, fewer should change). This is what the data show. The mean change under high involvement for those subjects who change is 4.25 for high discrepancy and 2.77 for moderate discrepancy ($t = 1.92$, $p < .06$). In other words, if they change, they change more the greater the discrepancy; but at some point fewer subjects change, thus causing a decrease in the mean amount of change. This implies (as Zimbardo, 1960, also discusses) that if all modes of resolution other than position change were eliminated, there would be a direct, positive relationship between discrepancy and change. Since it is virtually impossible to eliminate alternative modes entirely, however, the present results and analysis should generally hold.

REFERENCES

Aronson, E., Turner, Judy, & Carlsmith, J. M. Communicator credibility and communication discrepancy. *J. abnorm. soc. Psychol.*, 1963, **67**, 31–36.

Cohen, A. R. Communication discrepancy and attitude change: A dissonance theory approach. *J. Pers.*, 1959, **27**, 386–396.

Fisher, S., & Lubin, A. Distance as a determinant of influence in a two-person serial interaction situation. *J. abnorm. soc. Psychol.*, 1958, **56**, 230–238.

Fisher, S., Rubinstein, I., & Freeman, R. W. Intertrial effects of immediate self-committal in a continuous social influence situation. *J. abnorm. soc. Psychol.*, 1956, **52**, 200–207.

Goldberg, S. C. Three situational determinants of conformity to social norms. *J. abnorm. soc. Psychol.*, 1954, **49**, 325–329.

Harvey, O. J., Kelley, H. H., & Shapiro, M. M. Reactions to unfavorable evaluations of the self made by other persons. *J. Pers.*, 1957, **25**, 393–411.

Hovland, C. I. Reconciling conflicting results derived from experimental and survey studies of attitude change. *Amer. Psychologist*, 1959, **14**, 8–17.

Hovland, C. I., Harvey, O. J., & Sherif, M. Assimilation and contrast effects in reactions to communication and attitude change. *J. abnorm. soc. Psychol.*, 1957, **55**, 244–252.

Hovland, C. I., & Pritzker, H. A. Extent of opinion change as a function of amount of change advocated. *J. abnorm. soc. Psychol.*, 1957, **54**, 257–261.

Hunt, E. B., & Hovland, C. I. Order of consideration of different types of concepts. *J. exp.
Psychol.*, 1960, **59**, 220–225.

McNemar, Q. *Psychological statistics.* New York:
Wiley, 1962.

Zimbardo, P. G. Involvement and communication
discrepancy as determinants of opinion
conformity. *J. abnorm. soc. Psychol.*,
1960, **60**, 86–94.

RESPONSE REINFORCEMENT AND ATTITUDE CHANGE *

Most current research on attitude change is conducted within the theoretical context of dissonance
theory or other balance theories. Central to such
approaches is an emphasis on consistency among
the cognitive, affective, and behavioral components
of an attitude. Thus, if strong pressures impel an
individual to behave in a manner contrary to his
attitude, especially over an appreciable period of
time, he is apt to change his attitude to make it
consistent with his new behavior. But in their enthusiasm for this approach to social influence, investigators should not lose sight of the possible
contribution of some of the older research traditions to an understanding of attitude change.

One of the oldest lines of research in psychology pertains to learning processes. A tremendous
body of literature on learning has accumulated,
and very sophisticated theories have been developed. Because of the high internal validity of
learning theory, continued attempts are made to
apply it to an ever-increasing range of phenomena.
During the last decade, intensive efforts have been
made to apply learning theory to clinical phenomena. More recently, there have been signs that
a learning theory orientation is being increasingly
applied to social psychology. For an adequate application, however, extensive programs of research
on attitude change conducted within a context of
learning theory are necessary.

Scott's work, appearing below, does demonstrate, at least, that reinforcement of the expression of attitudes is apt to strengthen them. This
was found to be true even when the individual was
led to express attitudes that were initially contrary
to his own.

14.

Attitude Change by Response Reinforcement: Replication and Extension[1]

WILLIAM A. SCOTT
UNIVERSITY OF COLORADO

Within the framework of *S-R* learning theory an
attitude may be regarded, like a habit, as an im-

plicit anticipatory response which mediates overt
behaviors, and arises out of them through response reinforcement (6). Such a conception provided the basis for an earlier study (9) of the
effect on attitudes of rewarding relevant verbal
behaviors. The purposes of the present experiment were to substantiate the earlier results with
different operations, to investigate the effects of
response reinforcement on subjects with neutral,
as well as extreme, attitudes, and to determine
whether or not the induced attitude changes were
"permanent."

Briefly, the design of the earlier study (9)
was as follows: Pairs of students were selected
from a number of general psychology classes and
asked to debate any of three different issues on
which they had previously expressed their opinions. However, both members were required to
defend sides of the issue opposite to those which
they actually held. The excellence of their presentations was to be judged by class vote, but
this vote was falsified so that a predetermined
member of each pair won. Posttests of subjects'
attitudes showed that the "winners" had changed
in the direction of debate significantly more than
the "losers" and more than a group of control
S's, while the "losers" did not change significantly
more than the controls.

This study had used only *S*'s with initially extreme attitudes, and no provision had been made
for a second posttest to determine the extent to
which the attitude changes persisted. Therefore,
a new experiment was designed to fill these gaps.
Although the design was conceptually similar to
the previous one, the actual operations differed
in several respects: different issues were presented,
S's debated under different conditions, and the
nature of the reinforcing stimuli was different.
Given these innovations in operations (not in
conceptualization), it was felt that corroborative
results would better serve to substantiate the
theory on which the experiments were based than
would replication by identical operations.

METHOD

Attitudes of students toward three different controversial issues were assessed in several General Psychology classes, by the following open questions:

* The selection following the editorial introduction is reprinted
from "Attitude change by response reinforcement: Replication
and extension," *Sociometry*, 1959, **22**, 328–335, by permission
of the author and the American Sociological Association.

[1] The research reported in this article was supported by a

grant from the Foundation for Research on Human Behavior
(Ann Arbor, Michigan).

1. Curriculum. If you had the job of laying out a curriculum of required courses for all undergraduates at CU, what kinds of courses would you lay most emphasis on—those related to the study of scientific facts and research methods, or courses dealing with social problems and courses which help the student learn more about people?

2. Fraternities and sororities. Some people feel that fraternity and sorority life contributes a great deal to the development of the student during his college career. Others feel that fraternities and sororities work to the detriment of students by taking their attention away from more important academic matters. What do you think about this?

3. Ideal husband or wife. If you were thinking of getting married, which kind of a husband or wife would you rather have: One who is mainly interested in people and enjoys being with people, or one who has a wide variety of interests and creative talent in some area?

Immediately after this pretest, a general invitation was addressed to the classes to participate in an elimination debate contest, the winners of which would share a $100 cash prize. The investigator's interest was reported to be "to find out what kinds of people hold what kinds of attitudes." A couple of weeks later volunteers were contacted by phone and asked to take a particular side of one of the three issues for debate. The sides were assigned irrespective of Ss' initial positions, so that some debators defended their own opinions, some the opposite opinions, and some debated "off-neutral" (they expressed no clear opinion on the pretest, but were assigned a definite position in the debate). The only restrictions were to keep these three groups (same, opposite, and off-neutral) approximately equal and to give equal representation to each of the three issues. S's were told that debate positions were being assigned irrespective of actual attitudes, because "the purpose of the study is to see how well people can present opinions they don't actually hold, and how well their opponents can judge their own true attitudes."

The debates took place in a small research room, with the two S's seated at one end of a long table, and three judges at the opposite end. For every debate, two of the judges were professors of psychology, and the third was a mature graduate student; E was one of the judges at every debate, but the other judging professor and the graduate student were changed several times throughout the experiment. Introductions were formal, as was the decorum of the entire procedure. None of the S's had known his opponent prior to that time. It was explained that the winner of this first debate would be contacted for a second debate, and if he won that, as well as a third debate, he would receive a $20 prize. S's presented their initial arguments for five minutes each, followed by two-minute rebuttals in reverse order.

Each judge, in turn, rendered his decision on the relative merits of the two performances. The reasons

he offered for his decision were confined to the manner of presentation (style, clarity, convincingness, etc.), rather than to the content of the talk, in order to minimize the possible influences of prestige suggestion which might be entailed if the judgment referred to the substance of the argument (e.g., "that was a good point"). The winner in each case had been predetermined in systematic fashion, so that all the judges had to do during the debate was to jot down plausible reasons for their decisions.

Following the judgment, S's were led to small individual rooms near the debate room, where they filled out questionnaires on the three issues, identical with those from the pretest. E indicated that "we are interested in seeing how you feel about these matters at this time," without explicitly indicating that opinions were expected either to change or to remain constant. In addition there was the question, "How do you think your opponent *really* feels about this issue?" included simply to maintain the pretext previously offered for the study.

Winning S's were called back about ten days later to debate a different issue. Their positions were again assigned irrespective of their true attitudes, and the debating situation was as before, except that judgments of win or lose were based on merit (as the judges saw it).[2] There were no predetermined winners or losers, so occasionally there was a split vote among the three judges; but E always voted last, in order to make the decision as clear and definite as possible. A second posttest of attitudes toward the three issues was obtained. (S's wrote in separate rooms.)

Winners of the second debate were recalled for a third time, to debate the remaining issue of the three. The consequences of this contest were made clear, and S's were given the choice of "winner take all" ($20) or "split the prize" ($15 and $5). Three pairs chose the former division; two, the latter. Again the voting of judges was genuine; a third posttest of attitudes toward all three issues was obtained.

Attitudes expressed in the pretest and on the three posttests were typed on 3″ x 5″ cards, numbered in such a way as to disguise their sources (see 9). These were then coded by E on a seven-point attitude scale, representing a neutral position and three degrees of intensity toward each extreme of the issue—e.g.:

1. Greek organizations are very definitely a help.
2. Greek organizations are a help.
3. Greek organizations are mainly a help, but also some hindrance.
4. Don't know; not ascertained; equally a help and a hindrance; depends on the individual.

---

[2] This shift in the basis for determining winners was largely for ethical reasons. Though a random choice of winners was necessary for purposes of experimental control, once this had been achieved on the first round of debates, there appeared to be no reason why virtue should not be rewarded.

5. Greek organizations are mainly a hindrance, but also some help.
6. Greek organizations are a hindrance.
7. Greek organizations are very definitely a hindrance.

Check-coding, by an independent judge, of a sample of these attitudes showed their coding reliability to be .87.

RESULTS

Of principal interest is the comparison of winners and losers on the first round of debates, for in that series they were randomly determined. The results are presented in the top part of Table 1, which shows that winners tended to change toward the side debated more than did losers or controls. (The control group was composed of those volunteers who could not be scheduled during the first debate series. Their posttest attitudes were assessed just after the third debate series, approximately one month after the pretest.)

Attitude changes following the second and third debates were comparable to those in the first debate (see bottom of Table 1). It will be recalled that, here, the decisions were not predetermined, but depended on performance as estimated by the judges.

Also of interest are the findings concerning "permanence" of the effects of reinforcement. As previously noted, all 20 S's who participated in the second debate were tested concerning their attitudes toward the issue of the first debate. From their responses it is possible to estimate the

TABLE 2 *Mean Attitude Change as a Function of the Relationship between S's Pretest Attitude and Debate Position*

GROUP OF SUBJECTS	N	MEAN CHANGE*	S.D. OF CHANGE	DIFFERENCE IN MEAN-CHANGES
Debating opposite side				
(A) Winners	10	+2.77	1.97	A vs. B:
(B) Losers	10	+0.90	1.05	t = 2.53; p < .05
Debating off-neutral				
(A) Winners	11	+1.47	1.25	A vs. B:
(B) Losers	13	+0.54	1.44	t = 1.62; p < .10
Debating own side				
(A) Winners	7	+0.63	0.86	A vs. B:
(B) Losers	13	−0.77	1.89	t = 2.15; p < .05

* A positive sign indicates a mean change in the direction of debate. One-tail tests of significance are reported.

degree of "savings" from the first posttest to the second posttest—approximately ten days later. It is clear from the data in Table 1 ("first debate: Winners ten days later") that attitudes expressed on the second posttest are different, both from the pretest attitudes, and from the first posttest attitudes. Thus, there is a significant degree of savings from the first reward experience, even though the reinforcement is not explicitly repeated; but the amount of savings is less than the amount of initial change.

Since S's were assigned debate positions regardless of their own true attitudes, it is possible

TABLE 1 *Mean Attitude Changes of Winners, Losers, and Controls*

GROUP OF SUBJECTS	N	MEAN CHANGE*	S.D. OF CHANGE	DIFFERENCE IN MEAN-CHANGES
First debate				
(A) Winners	20	+1.67	1.55	A vs. B: t = 2.76; p < .01
(B) Losers	20	+0.15	1.83	A vs. C: t = 3.80; p < .001
(C) Controls	15	+0.24	0.47	B vs. C: t = −0.20; NS
(D) Winners ten days later	20	+1.20	1.66	D vs. C: t = 2.40; p < .05
Second debate				
(A) Winners	10	+1.40	1.80	A vs. B: t = 1.29; NS
(B) Losers	10	+0.36	1.62	
Third debate				
(A) Winners	5	+2.80	1.72	A vs. B: t = 2.88; p < .05
(B) Losers	5	−0.20	1.17	

* A positive sign indicates a mean change in the direction of debate; or, for control S's, a mean change opposite to their original position. For control S's with initially neutral attitudes the directions of changes were assigned alternately positive and negative signs. One-tail tests of significance were used throughout.

to see whether or not the response reinforcement was effective when it operated in the same direction as S's initial attitude, or when it aimed at moving him from a neutral position. Table 2 shows the results of the debates, grouped according to the relationship between S's initial attitude and his debate position. When S's debated "opposite sides," the absolute change of winners was largest (2.77 on a seven-point scale). When debating "off-neutral," the mean change was 1.47, and the mean change of winners debating their "own sides" was 0.63 toward a more extreme position in the same direction. A comparison of absolute changes in position is deceptive, however, since S's debating "opposite sides" had the greatest room for movement, and those debating "own sides" had the least. Relative to the amount of movement (in the direction of reinforcement) possible, the three groups showed changes of 55 per cent, 49 per cent, and 63 per cent, respectively. But since there is no way of comparing scale intervals at various points on the dimension, it would be mere sham to conclude anything about the relative effects of response reinforcement under the three circumstances. All one can say is that winners tended to change in the direction of debate more than losers did, regardless of whether they debated their own positions, opposite positions, or off-neutral.

DISCUSSION

The results of this study suggest, first of all, that the effects of response reinforcement on attitude change are not necessarily transitory, but may be preserved up to periods of at least ten days. On the one hand, this may seem surprising, since, during the interval between tests, S's were presumably living within the same social contexts that had supported their initial attitudes. Thus one might expect them to revert to their old positions as soon as they were removed from the reinforcing situation. On the other hand, the occasion for the second posttest was so nearly identical with that for the first posttest, that the cues present could well have served to reintegrate the former response, even though it did not conform to S's true attitude at that time. In a more imaginative study, one might attempt a follow-up assessment of S's attitudes in a completely different context, with someone other than E eliciting the relevant response.

A second result suggests that response reinforcement can be effective either in strengthening previously held attitudes, in changing them, or in creating new ones (if those S's who debated "off-neutral" can be said to have developed "new" attitudes). There was no evidence to indicate that S's with neutral attitudes were more amenable to change than those with more extreme views. Such an outcome might have been expected in the light of the frequently reported finding that people who hold intense attitudes, or who are quite certain

of their opinions, are relatively resistant to pressures to change (1, 2, 5, 7, 8). However, with less than interval-scale measures, it is difficult to compare relative movements at different positions on the attitude scale. Moreover, the status of the initially "neutral" attitudes is by no means clear, since that category included S's who expressed balanced opinions on both sides of the issue as well as those who replied "no opinion." It seems to this writer that neutrality of an attitude as such is probably not the critical feature for predicting susceptibility to change, but rather it is the degree to which the attitude, of whatever direction or strength, is embedded in a cognitive structure of other supporting attitudes and cognitive elements. (This quality of "embeddedness" has been referred to elsewhere as *cognitive consistency* [10, 11].)

The major significance of the study, however, would seem to lie in its confirmation of previously obtained results (9) not by exact replication, but by "methodological triangulation" (3). Whereas the earlier experiment required S's to debate in front of their fellow classmates and "rewarded" them by class vote, the present procedure involved debates in a private setting with reinforcement by judges' decisions and monetary reward. Moreover, the issues debated were different from those previously used. Thus one can safely maintain that the hypothesized relationship is not exclusively dependent on the particular methods chosen to assess it. When a number of different sets of empirical operations yield comparable results, it is reasonable to presume that they reflect a valid relationship (i.e., one that is independent of the measuring procedures), rather than just a reliable relationship (one that depends on a particular instrument or experimental design) (cf., 4).

SUMMARY

S's were invited to participate in a series of debates, in which they defended positions on three different issues irrespective of their own opinions. Comparison of their pretest attitudes with those expressed immediately following the debates indicated that S's who "won" (by judges' decision) tended to change their attitudes in the direction of the positions presented. This result confirmed that of a previous experiment in which S's debated under different conditions and were reinforced by vote of their classmates. The effect on "winners" in this study occurred regardless of whether they debated their own side of the argument, the opposite side, or from an initially neutral position. Some permanence of the change was evidenced on a second posttest about ten days after the initial winning. "Losers" in the debate did not change their attitudes significantly more than a control group of non-debaters.

REFERENCES

1. BIRCH, H. G., "The Effect of Socially Disapproved Labelling upon Well-structured Attitudes," *Journal of Abnormal and Social Psychology*, 1945, 40, 301–310.

2. BURDICK, H. A., "The Relationship of Attraction, Need Achievement, and Certainty to Conformity under Conditions of a Simulated Group Atmosphere," *Dissertation Abstracts*, 1956, 16, 1518–1519.

3. CAMPBELL, D. T., *A Study of Leadership among Submarine Officers*, Columbus: Ohio State University, Personnel Research Board, 1953.

4. CAMPBELL, D. T., and D. W. FISKE, "Convergent and Discriminant Validation by the Multitrait-multimethod Matrix," *Psychological Bulletin*, 1959, 56, 81–105.

5. CARLSON, E. R., "Attitude Change through Modi-

fication of Attitude Structure," *Journal of Abnormal and Social Psychology*, 1956, 52, 256–261.

6. DOOB, L. W., "The Behavior of Attitudes," *Psychological Review*, 1947, 54, 135–156.

7. HOCHBAUM, G. M., "The Relation between Group Members' Self-confidence and their Reactions to Group Pressures to Uniformity," *American Sociological Review*, 1954, 19, 678–687.

8. OSGOOD, C., and P. H. TANNENBAUM, "The Principle of Congruity in the Prediction of Attitude Change," *Psychological Review*, 1955, 62, 42–55.

9. SCOTT, W. A., "Attitude Change through Reward of Verbal Behavior," *Journal of Abnormal and Social Psychology*, 1957, 55, 72–75.

10. SCOTT, W. A., "Rationality and Non-rationality of International Attitudes," *Conflict Resolution*, 1958, 2, 8–16.

11. SCOTT, W. A., "Cognitive Consistency, Response Reinforcement, and Attitude Change," *Sociometry*, 1959, 22, 219–229.

DISSONANCE AND ATTITUDE CHANGE: A FUNCTION OF BALANCE OR VOLITION?*

Cognitive dissonance is a term representing an inconsistency between two or more cognitive elements. The term *cognitive element* refers to any knowledge, opinion, or belief about the environment, about oneself, or about one's behavior. Two cognitive elements are in a dissonant relation if, considering these two alone, the obverse of one element would follow from the other. Thus, the knowledge that smoking increases the probability of contracting lung cancer (an end to be avoided) is dissonant with the knowledge that one smokes two packs of cigarettes daily. Dissonance gives rise to pressures to change the elements so as to reduce the amount of dissonance.

In perhaps the most frequent application of dissonance theory, the individual is subjected to pressure from the experimenter that induces him to engage in behavior contrary to his attitudes. To reduce dissonance he is expected to change his attitude to make it consistent with his behavior. A series of studies suggests that dissonance is greatest and attitude change at a maximum when pressures on the individual are just barely sufficient to induce him to engage in behavior contrary to his attitudes. Pressures considerably in excess of this amount appear to arouse less dissonance and less attitude change: the individual readily engages in the discrepant behavior, but does not change his attitude. Thus, when cognitive elements associated with *not* engaging in the behavior are almost equal to those favoring engaging in the behavior, dissonance and attitude change are at a maximum. This optimum state is a situation approaching balance of the opposing elements.

As research of this type progressed, it became apparent that situations representing different degrees of dissonance are associated with not one but two variables. One is the balance of elements just referred to: balance is high with maximum dissonance and low with minimum dissonance. But another variable associated with dissonance situations is the extent to which the individual feels that he has *voluntarily* committed himself to engage in an action contrary to his attitudes. In virtually all dissonance situations that occur naturally and also in almost all experimental situations, the balance of elements and the feeling of freedom of choice are directly associated. That is, the more evenly the elements for and against engaging in the behavior are balanced, the more the individual believes he is free to commit or not commit himself to the discrepant behavior. Thus, these variables are referred to as *confounded*: they covary together so that it is impossible to tell whether one or both of them are responsible for the creation of dissonance and the consequent attitude change.

To determine the relative importance of these variables for dissonance arousal, differences in volition that vary *inversely* with the relative balance of the two sets of elements must be created. Below, Cohen† and Brehm describe an ingenious experiment in which freedom of choice is made to vary inversely with the relative balance of the elements. This reverse relation was created by making the elements associated with engaging in the be-

---

* The selection following the editorial introduction is reprinted from *Explorations in Cognitive Dissonance*, New York: John Wiley & Sons, 1962, by permission of the senior author and the publisher.

† A. R. Cohen is now deceased.

havior *illegitimate*. The condition involving strong pressure to participate in attitude-discrepant behavior was most imbalanced, but because the pressure was highly illegitimate, the individual felt that he was free to refuse if he wished. The condition involving low pressure was more balanced, but because the pressure was only slightly illegitimate, the individual did not feel as free to refuse participation.

To sum up, in one condition the elements associated with engaging or not engaging in the behavior are quite imbalanced and, in addition, subjects feel that they are free to engage voluntarily in the behavior requested by the experimenter or to refuse to do so. In the other condition, the elements associated with engaging in the behavior are evenly balanced, but the subjects feel less free to make their own decision about complying with the experimenter's request. Thus, if it turns out that the former of these conditions brings about more attitude change, volition will emerge as the crucial variable. On the other hand, if the second condition results in more attitude change, the relative balance of opposing elements would appear to be more important than free choice in creating changes in attitudes.

15.

An Experiment on Illegitimate Coercion, Volition, and Attitude Change

ARTHUR R. COHEN
NEW YORK UNIVERSITY

JACK W. BREHM
DUKE UNIVERSITY

Cohen and Brehm performed the following experiment in order to separate the hypothesized effects of the inducing force and those of volition. In line with the above reasoning, they used an illegitimate coercive force to make college students agree to participate in an unpleasant task. A questionnaire measured the participants' perceptions of the coercive force, volition, and task valuation. The effect of the illegitimate coercion was made clear by having conditions of low and high threat as well as a control condition that involved no threat. The procedure itself is in large part identical to that used by Brehm in the study on coercion and attitude change; it will only be summarized except where there were differences.

The subjects consisted of 30 Yale undergraduates—ten in each experimental condition—who were fraternity pledges recruited from four different campus fraternities. Arrangements had been made with the pledgemasters of the various fraternities to send pledges to the experimental room "to help out in some research for a short period of time."

The general condition of illegitimacy was established in the following way. First, the pledges were told by their pledgemasters that they were

DISSONANCE AND ATTITUDE CHANGE:
A FUNCTION OF BALANCE OR VOLITION?

113

to report for a *short* project of 15 to 20 minutes duration, whereas the experimenter then demanded that they sign up for a boring and profitless task that would take 3 to 4 hours. Above all, however, the experimenter was a professor who had no connection whatsoever with any of the fraternities involved. To make the coercion completely illegimate, then, the experimenter threatened to have the pledge's fraternity penalize him if he failed to participate in the unexpectedly long task. Since such an influence by a professor on a fraternity's business would be very unusual, it was expected that the attempted coercion would be seen by the pledge as illegitimate. The exact procedure follows.

When the subject arrived, he was told that he was expected to participate in 3 to 4 continuous hours of copying random numbers. It was emphasized that participation would be extremely dull and that there was nothing the subject would learn from it, but that his help was needed in order to "establish norms for other research." After being shown an example of the task, the subject was given one of the following coercion manipulations:

High coercion. "Now we need your cooperation, and if you don't cooperate, I'm afraid we'll have to report you as uncooperative to your pledgemaster and the other fellows and really push for some severe penalties. This can have very bad effects; we'll try to see that it has very strong consequences for extending your pledge period considerably and even for keeping you out of the house permanently."

Low coercion. "Now we need your cooperation, and if you don't cooperate, I'm afraid we'll have to report you as uncooperative to your pledgemaster and the other fellows and see that you get some hours of extra duty as a pledge."

In the *Control condition*, the subjects were told: "Now we need your cooperation." Nothing was said to them about any possible penalties for noncooperation.

After the manipulation, the subject was given a schedule sheet on which to indicate his free hours. All subjects with the exception of one in the Low Coercion condition agreed to participate and filled out a schedule sheet.

Perception of the coercive force, perceived choice about whether or not to participate (volition), and evaluation of the number-copying task were measured on a questionnaire given immediately after commitment to participation. The questionnaire was introduced as being purely for the use of the Interfraternity Council in evaluating the use of pledges in research, and its anonymity was stressed. *A priori* questions and multiple response scales were used to measure the variables of interest; these were also used in the Brehm experiment.

Here we may briefly note that measures of satisfaction, volition, and threat were all taken on *a priori* 81-point scales with nine identified points. The present experiment made use of one additional measure taken on the postquestionnaire. The subjects were asked, "How annoyed were you by the request that you participate in the proposed research?" This was answered on an 81-point *a priori* scale with nine identified points running from "Not annoyed at all" to "Extremely annoyed." Threat, volition, and annoyance were scored from zero to eight; the higher the number, the greater the respective response. The satisfaction measure was scored from −4 to +4; the more positive the figure, the greater the satisfaction.

Results

The test of whether dissonance depends on the coercive force itself or on volition arising from the coercion assumes that the experimental conditions have resulted in a direct relationship between coercion and violition: the greater the coercion, the greater the volition. The effect of the coercion manipulation was measured by a question on the severity of threat, and the mean responses to this question are presented in column 1 of Table 1. These data show that little or no threat was seen in the Control and Low Coercion conditions, and that considerable threat was seen in the High Coercion condition, which is significantly different from the Control condition at the 2% level.

Whether or not the threat was perceived as illegitimate can be inferred from the amount of annoyance reported by subjects. Although being given a choice may tend to minimize annoyance in experimental subjects compared to Control subjects, it should still be possible to compare the two experimental conditions. The relevant data, column 2 of Table 1, show that subjects in the High Coercion condition were more annoyed than were

subjects in the Low Coercion condition (p less than .05).

Since subjects in the High Coercion condition perceived more threat and were more annoyed than subjects in the Low Coercion condition, according to our theeoretical argument, they may reasonably be expected to have felt relatively more volition in regard to complying with the experimenter's request. Subjects' responses to the question on felt volition are shown in column 3 of Table 1. Although the only statistically reliable difference is that between the High Coercion and Control conditions (beyond the 1% level), there is a clear trend for High Coercion subjects to report feeling more volition than Low Coercion subjects. Thus our coercion manipulation *has produced a difference in volition that is directly related to the amount of coercive force applied.* Since this is the condition necessary for distinguishing between the effects on dissonance of the coercive force *per se* and of volition, we may now proceed to an inspection of the data relevant to the questions of central interest.

If coercion is the controlling determinant of the magnitude of dissonance, then revaluation of the task should vary inversely with coercion (and volition) as has been demonstrated in other research. But if volition is the controlling determinant of dissonance, then revaluation should vary *directly* with coercion (and volition). The measure of revaluation—subjects' satisfaction with being assigned to the experiment—is given in column 4 of Table 1. It shows very clearly that subjects in the High Coercion condition are more satisfied than subjects in either the Low Coercion condition (p less than .05) or the Control condition (p less than .01). These results therefore support the contention that volition is an important determinant of the magnitude of dissonance.

There is at least one equivocality about our interpretation of these data in that we cannot be sure that the severe threat was judged to be as likely to be carried out as was the mild threat. It is possible that the fraternity pledges would think it plausible for a professor to get them some hours of extra duty, but implausible that a professor could get them excluded from the fraternity altogether. If this were true, it could mean that subjects in the High Coercion condition perceived the effective force on them as being quite low rather than as very high. Hence they would be expected to experience high dissonance compared to the Low Coercion subjects for whom there was a realistic threat, and the results of the study would therefore be understandable as a straightforward effect of the amount of force resulting in compliance. But, on the other hand, it is not clear why the High Coercion subjects would have felt relatively more annoyed if they really perceived that the threatened punishment would not likely be carried out. It seems more plausible, therefore, to assume that the High Coercion subjects took the threat quite seriously and reacted to it with feelings of high volition. On the whole,

TABLE 1 *Mean Ratings of Postquestionnaire Items by Experimental Groups*

	1. SEVERITY OF THREAT	2. ANNOYANCE	3. VOLITION	4. SATISFACTION
High coercion ($N = 10$):	4.00*	2.88	3.14	+1.09
Low coercion ($N = 10$):	2.18	1.61	2.04	− .70
Control ($N = 10$):	1.46	2.64	.95	−1.58

* In all cases, the higher the mean figure, the greater the response in question.

then, the data support the proposition that volition can affect the magnitude of dissonance *independently of the ratio of dissonant to consonant cognitions.*

An interesting implication of our view of the role of volition in the arousal of dissonance is that even though a person may choose between nearly equally attractive alternatives, if he is forced to make that choice, then the amount of resulting dissonance will be relatively low. More generally, the magnitude of dissonance resulting from a choice is directly proportional to the degree of volition in making the choice. Thus we may hypothesize that *as the pressure to make a choice increases, the magnitude of postchoice dissonance and consequent revaluation of alternatives decreases.*

POSTSCRIPT

While one experiment can scarcely be regarded as conclusive, the outcome of the study just reported poses important questions concerning the nature of dissonance. Yet, a search of the very recent literature on dissonance theory has failed to uncover any further studies directly addressed to this important question of whether the crucial determinant of dissonance is imbalance of opposing forces or the amount of volition the individual experiences in committing himself to the discrepant behavior. In one sense, this is rather curious, for this question pertains to the very nature of dissonance; in another, however, the absence of such studies is not so strange when the difficulty of separating these confounded variables experimentally is considered. Several recent studies, however, do further stress the importance of choice or volition in dissonance arousal. Although in all of them this variable is probably confounded with degree of imbalance of opposing forces, they at least suggest the importance of voluntary commitment in dissonance arousal.

One study[a] reports that when a person has voluntarily complied with a request, a communicator having lower credibility will bring about more attitude change than one having higher credibility. No

such difference in communicator effectiveness occurred when compliance was forced. This result stems from the fact that it is more difficult to justify voluntary compliance to the demands of a communicator having low credibility than to one having high credibility. This greater dissonance is resolved by changing one's attitude in the direction advocated.

Another investigation[b] underscores the importance of voluntary compliance or noncompliance in a somewhat similar fashion. College students and military reservists were exposed to a persuasive communication advocating the eating of fried grasshoppers as part of an experiment. The communicator either had negative or positive personality qualities that were, however, irrelevant to the persuasive communication itself. Of those subjects who complied and ate grasshoppers (approximately 50 per cent in each condition), those exposed to the negative communicator increased their liking of grasshoppers to a greater extent than those exposed to the positive communicator. Those who did not comply increased their distaste for grasshoppers. As before, the reasoning is that voluntary commitment to eating grasshoppers is more dissonant when the communicator has negative qualities than when he has positive ones; hence, the greater the increase in liking of grasshoppers in order to resolve this dissonance.

One final study[c] with a similar theme yielded similar results. Subjects were either allowed to choose between two tasks, or were assigned to one of them arbitrarily. After performing the task, some subjects were given negative information, and others, positive information about their performance. The greater dissonance aroused by a negative performance in a chosen task was resolved by a larger increase in liking for that task—justifying one's choice. The reverse was true for those who were arbitrarily assigned to a task: they disliked more the assigned task.

ATTITUDINAL CONSISTENCY: COGNITION AND AFFECT ✳

The concepts of balance, consistency, and dissonance may be used not only to explain attitude change, but they can also be applied to explain various degrees of resistance to change. Consistency may exist between cognitive, affective, or behavioral elements. In general, the greater the

consistency among such elements, the greater the resistance to change. Specific research designs, however, may deal with only two types of elements, and investigations vary in the operations they use to measure consistency. Thus, several different studies are presented in this section to illustrate these various ways of representing consistency and to show how it creates resistance to change.

[a] F. A. Powell. Source credibility and behavioral compliance as determinants of attitude change. *J. Pers. Soc. Psychol.*, 1965, **2**, 669–676.

✳ The selection following the editorial introduction is reprinted from "Cognitive reorganization in response to the hypnotic reversal of attitudinal affect," *Journal of Personality*, 1960, 28, 39–63, by permission of the author and Duke University Press.

[b] P. G. Zimbardo, M. Weisenberg, I. Firestone, & B. Levy. Communicator effectiveness in producing public conformity and private attitude change. *J. Pers.*, 1965, 33, 233–255.
[c] C. W. Greenbaum, A. Cohn, & R. M. Krauss. Choice, negative information, and attractiveness of tasks. *J. Pers.*, 1965, 33, 46–59.

The selection below focuses on the *internal* consistency of an attitude in that it deals with consistency between the cognitive and affective components of an attitude toward a given object. The affective component refers to feelings; normally these are dealt with in research by using a measuring scale that places them along a continuum from very positive to very negative. The cognitive component consists of the individual's ideas about the attitude object.

Early attempts to change attitudes usually induced changes in the cognitive component, and predicted changes in the direction of positive affect on attitude items. For example, attempts to reduce prejudice toward a minority group through education presented the target individuals with factual information about the minority-group persons that contradicted some of the prejudiced beliefs about them. Although such studies did not specifically isolate cognitive and affective components, they tacitly assumed consistency between these constituents of an attitude. Attitudes were assessed before and after the delivery of information, and were expected to become more favorable. The selection below operates in a reverse direction from these earlier approaches; a change in the *affective* component is induced, and corresponding changes in cognitive components are expected to follow. Moreover, in the present study, cognitive and affective components are separately identifiable, and the linkage between them is precisely specified.

A major proposition of the study is that cognitive and affective components of attitudes are congruent with each other. The cognitive component is defined in a special way so that its consistency with the affective component may be readily assessed. By making the cognitive component a set of beliefs about the value-attaining or value-blocking powers of the attitude object, the experimenter to measure consistency need only assess an individual's values, his beliefs about how the attitude object attains or blocks these values, and his positive or negative affect toward the object. For example, suppose an individual has a positive attitude toward socialized medicine. If his attitude is consistent, he would also have beliefs that socialized medicine achieves some objectives that he positively values. He might place a positive value on the health and economic security of our older citizens. A belief that socialized medicine helps to achieve these aims by providing more medical attention and by avoiding the impoverishment of these citizens because of the high cost of medical treatment would be consistent with his values and his favorable position on socialized medicine.

The demonstration that attitude components tend toward consistency with each other implies that if one component is firmly anchored, the other will be difficult to change, especially for more than a temporary period. Various data from other studies suggest that the affective component of attitudes is often anchored in certain physiological functions and also in the concomitant values subscribed to by the individual. This may explain why even those cognitive components of attitudes that are contrary to objective evidence are sometimes stubbornly resistant to attempts to change them.

16.

Cognitive Reorganization in Response to the Hypnotic Reversal of Attitudinal Affect[1]

MILTON J. ROSENBERG
UNIVERSITY OF CHICAGO

Traditionally there have been two vantage points from which social psychologists have regarded "attitudes." When examined historically an attitude is seen as an end product of certain schedules of social learning (e.g., Doob, 1947; Hovland, Janis, & Kelley, 1953). When examined functionally an attitude is seen as a complex response set somehow serving the individual in adapting to his inner and outer worlds (e.g., Adorno, Frenkel-Brunswik, Levinson, & Sanford, 1950; Smith, Bruner, & White, 1956).

Confronted with the task of determining how attitudes undergo change the first approach directs attention toward variables delineated in laws of learning; the second directs attention toward variables delineated in laws of conflict resolution and personality dynamics. While these approaches have contributed toward construction of an adequate theory of attitude dynamics, they tend to neglect a set of variables that may be assumed to stand and mediate between attitude-change influences and attitude-change effects. This set of "intervening" variables may be classified as relating to the structure of attitudes.

In recent years there has been discernible an emerging structural focus whose prime concern is to define and model the attitude concept in terms of separate psychological processes organized into comparatively stable constellations by virtue of their common reference to some single object or class of objects (Abelson & Rosenberg, 1958; Krech & Crutchfield, 1948; Peak, 1955, 1958; Rosenberg, 1956; Smith, 1949; Tolman, 1951; Woodruff & DiVesta, 1948). Such an approach, when applied to attitude-change phenomena, directs attention not to historic or adaptive forces making for attitude change but rather to the question of "What happens *inside* attitudes as they change?"

[1] The author is indebted to Dr. Charles W. Gardner for his valuable guidance in the selection and training of the hypnotic *S*s and also to Dr. Phillip Zimbardo for his assistance in collecting some of the data. Part of the data analysis was carried out under contract 609(27) with the Office of Naval Research.

The present paper reports a recent experiment designed to test an hypothesis derived from a structural theory of attitude change. This theory is based upon the conceptual delineation of two major components of the structure of an attitude, namely: the affective and cognitive components.

The affective component is defined as the pattern of feeling regularly aroused by the psychological presence of the attitude object. An example would be the complex of hate, anger, loathing, and/or condescension felt by some person when he reads, hears, or thinks about Negroes moving into white neighborhoods.

The cognitive component is defined as the set of beliefs (held by the person) about the value-attaining and value-blocking powers of the attitude object viewed as an instrumental agency. For example, in justifying his negative affect toward Negroes moving into white neighborhoods the person would be likely to contend that this would lead to open discord and violence, would foster miscegenation, and would lower the worth of property.

A major theoretical proposition is, simply, that the affective and cognitive components of an attitude are, at any given point in the history of that attitude (except when it is in process of "changing"), congruent with each other. Such congruence was demonstrated in an earlier study (Rosenberg, 1956) where it was shown that strong and stable positive affect toward an attitude object is associated with beliefs relating that object to the attainment of positive values and the blocking of negative values. On the other hand, strong negative affect toward an attitude object was shown to be associated with beliefs relating that object to the attainment of negative values and the blocking of positive values. In contrast, it was confirmed that moderate positive or negative attitudinal affects are associated with beliefs that relate the attitude object to less important values or, if to important values, then with less confidence as to the existence of clear-cut instrumental relationships between the attitude object and the values in question.

An attempt was made to extrapolate from these findings on attitude structure to the area of attitude dynamics by way of the following general propositions: When the affective and cognitive components of an attitude are mutually consistent, the attitude is in a stable state; when the affective and cognitive components are mutually inconsistent, the attitude is in an unstable state and will undergo reorganizing activity until such reorganization eventuates in the attainment of affective-cognitive consistency. (A necessary extension of this proposition is that when certain special features of the competing components make the reestablishment of consistency either impossible or too costly, activity will continue until the person manages to put the irreconcilable inconsistency more or less permanently beyond the range of active awareness.)

This general proposition suggests two derivative propositions: (*a*) if a person somehow undergoes a change in his beliefs about an attitude object, his affect toward that object will show corresponding change or else the new beliefs will give way to a re-establishment of those that they originally replaced; and (*b*) if a person somehow undergoes a change in his affect toward an attitude object, his beliefs about that object will show corresponding change or else the new affect will give way to a re-establishment of the one that it originally replaced.

Data reported by Carlson (1956) are consistent with some hypotheses that can be derived from the first of these two propositions. With his demonstration that alteration of the cognitive component of an attitude generates an accommodating alteration in affect toward the attitude object, it seemed desirable to submit the converse proposition to experimentation. Therefore at the inception of the present experiment it was hypothesized that significant and irreversible alteration of an attitudinal affect will eventuate in spontaneous reorganization of the person's beliefs about the value-attaining and value-blocking powers of the attitude object.

It was recognized that while "real life" experience does provide reinforcement schedules which act directly to change previously stable affects, few analogous experimental operations are readily available. The one operation that seemed most promising in this regard was the use of hypnotic suggestion.

The remainder of this paper is given over to the description and discussion of an experiment in which attitudinal affects were changed by hypnosis with the affective and cognitive components of the attitudes being tested both before and after the delivery of the hypnotic suggestion.

METHOD

Subjects

From a larger group of volunteers drawn from the professional and graduate schools of Yale University, 22 *S*s were selected on the basis of their hypnotizability. Of these *S*s 11 were able, after receiving between two to five hours of individual hypnotic practice, to achieve the level of deep hypnosis at which it is possible to successfully implant posthypnotic suggestions to be carried out with amnesia for the fact that such suggestions have been received. These 11 *S*s were assigned to the experimental group. Membership in this group meant that the *S* was to be given posthypnotic suggestions of change in affect toward certain attitude objects. Membership in the control group, on the other hand, meant that the *S* was to go through just the same kind of measurement as the experimental group members but without receiving any posthypnotic suggestions of affect change.

From the point of view of ideal design it would have been fortunate if the control group could have been composed of persons as deeply hypnotizable as the Ss assigned to the experimental group, but the comparative scarcity of such persons made this impossible. The practical expedient followed was to assign to the control group eleven Ss who, while not capable of consistently achieving posthypnotic amnesia, were at least able to demonstrate various classic sensory-motor hypnotic phenomena. It was felt that with still further practice most, if not all, of these Ss could be trained to achieve the deeper hypnotic condition at which amnesic compliance with posthypnotic suggestions is regularly obtained.

In anticipation of some findings presented below it should be noted that a comparison of experimental and control-group Ss shows that they do not differ significantly in test-retest stability except in those attitude areas that were subjected to hypnotic manipulation for members of the experimental group.

Procedure

After the S had been assigned to either the experimental or the control group he was given an attitude questionnaire designed to measure his affective responses toward seven different social issues. These issues were: labor's right to strike, the city-manager plan, the U.S. being more conciliatory toward the U.S.S.R., the provision of comprehensive federal medical insurance, living in Los Angeles, Negroes moving into white neighborhoods, and the U.S. and Canada uniting to form a single nation. The questionnaire also required the S to rank each of these seven issues from most to least interesting. A modified Coombs (1952) scaling procedure was used through which 16 scale positions were generated. These scale positions covered a range running from extreme positive affect to extreme negative affect.

Either one week later (for six Ss in each group) or two weeks later (for five Ss in each group) each S was run through another session. In this session the S's cognitive structures for one of his two highest interest attitude areas and for one of his two lowest interest attitude areas were tested both before and after a half-hour interval. During this half-hour interval each experimental S was hypnotized and given suggestions of affect change for the two attitude areas on which he had been tested. During the comparable period the control Ss merely rested in a physical setting identical to that in which the experimental Ss received the hypnotic suggestion of affect change (i.e., on a couch in a darkened room). But instead of being put into hypnosis each control S was given the instruction that he try to "fall asleep."

The approach used in testing cognitive structure was similar to that employed in earlier studies by Rosenberg (1956) and Carlson (1956). In this procedure, called the "Cognitive Structure Test," the S works with 31 "value cards." Upon each of these cards is printed a different value term. Examples are "All human beings having equal rights," "People being well educated," "Making one's own decisions," "America having high prestige in foreign countries." The S first judges each of the 31 values in terms of its importance to him, using a scale with a range of 21 points. The scale runs from −10 (which stands for "Gives me maximum dissatisfaction") through 0 (which stands for "Gives me neither satisfaction nor dissatisfaction") to +10 (which stands for "Gives me maximum satisfaction"). He then judges each of these same values in terms of whether, and to what extent, he thinks it will be attained or blocked as a consequence of the instrumental effects of the attitude object. On this task he uses an 11-point scale running from −5 (which stands for "Extreme blocking") through 0 (which stands for "Neither blocked nor attained") to +5 (which stands for "Extreme attainment"). Thus at the end of the testing procedure there are available for each value term the S's judgments of its importance and of the attitude object's potential for attaining or blocking its realization These two judgments are algebraically multiplied for each value term respectively so that a positive product is obtained when a positive value is seen as attained or a negative value as blocked, while a negative product is obtained when a positive value is seen as blocked or a negative value as attained. In turn the 31 products are algebraically summed. The resulting quantity is taken as an index of the over-all extent to which values of varying intensity are seen as threatened or enhanced by the attitude object. This index of cognitive structure was computed for the high- and low-interest attitudes of each of the 22 S's respectively.

During the hypnotic session immediately following the first administration of the Cognitive Structure Test each experimental S was hypnotized to a deep and stable level. He was then given suggestions of affect reversal with regard to the two attitude objects on which he had been tested for associated cognitive structure. For example one of the Ss was given exactly the following hypnotic instructions:

> When you awake you will be very much in favor of Negroes moving into white neighborhoods. The mere idea of Negroes moving into white neighborhoods will give you a happy, exhilarated feeling. Although you will not remember this suggestion having been made, it will strongly influence your feelings after you have awakened.
>
> Also, when you awake you will be very opposed to the city-manager plan. The mere idea of the city-manager plan will give you a feeling of loathing and disgust. Although you will not remember this suggestion having been made, it will strongly influence your feelings after you have awakened.
>
> Only when the signal to remember

is given will you remember these suggestions and only then will your feelings revert to normal.

All hypnotic suggestions, whatever the specific attitude area, followed this form. It should be noted that this procedure for the hypnotic production of affect reversal does not make recourse to any cognitive-argumentative material. The intention is to exert direct manipulative influence only upon the affective component of the attitude. Thus the S is simply commanded to feel differently toward the attitude object; he is not given any communications about the relations of the attitude object to any value concepts.

After the delivery of the hypnotic suggestions the experimental S was awakened. He was then retested on the original attitude questionnaire. Following this the Cognitive Structure Test was readministered.

As has already been noted, the procedure used with the control Ss differed from that used with the experimental Ss only in that the former took a half-hour of rest (without any hypnotic induction or implantation of posthypnotic suggestions) between the two separate administrations of the Cognitive Structure Test.

In another part of the experiment the same 11 control Ss went through similar testing procedures with regard to two attitude objects other than the ones involved in the portion of the experiment that has just been described; i.e., again they were tested twice on affect toward, and beliefs about, a high-interest and low-interest attitude object, respectively. But in between these two test administrations they received instructions to "role-play" affective changes toward the two objects involved. The explanation of this portion of the study is deferred to a later section of this report.

The testing procedures were represented to all Ss as part of one experiment and the hypnotic experience (for the experimental Ss) as part of a totally different experiment. For the experimental Ss all testing was administered by a person other than the S's hypnotist.

RESULTS

Evidence on the comparability of the experimental and control groups

The major hypothesis in this study predicted that Ss receiving a posthypnotic suggestion of change in affect toward an attitude object would show

not only more of such change but also more change in their beliefs about the attitude object than would a group of control Ss not subjected to the hypnotic suggestion. As a necessary condition to the testing of this hypothesis it had to be demonstrated that, except when subjected to hypnotic manipulation, the attitudinal affects of experimental Ss show as much test-retest reliability as do those of control Ss.

The findings reported in Table 1 indicate that when the groups are compared on attitude items not subjected to hypnotic manipulation the hypothesis of no difference between the groups cannot be rejected. Thus when the experimental and control Ss are compared on their mean affect-change scores (i.e., the mean number of steps S shifted on an attitude scale with a range of sixteen steps) for the attitude items that were not hypnotically manipulated (i.e., five attitude items for each hypnotic S and seven for each control S) the application of the Mann-Whitney Rank Sum Test (Mosteller & Bush, 1954) reveals that the chance probability of the difference between the two groups is greater than .90.[2] Inspection of the actual change scores of individual Ss indicates that in both experimental and control groups the sizes of the individual mean affect-change scores are small enough to suggest that they are essentially chance fluctuations. In the experimental-hypnotic group the median of the distribution of the affect-change means for all nonmanipulated attitude items is 1.4 scale steps. In the control group the comparable median is 1.3.

The experimental and control Ss were also compared on the amounts of affect change they manifested on each of the separate attitude items from first to seventh in interest respectively, but eliminating from these analyses any hypnotic Ss who had received a suggestion of affect reversal on the topic in question. In addition the two groups were compared in terms of the specific attitude content areas (e.g., mean affect change

[2] All probability values given in this report are two-tailed and, unless indicated, are obtained through application of the Rank Sum Test.

TABLE 1 *Experimental Group and Control Group (under Test-Retest Condition) Compared for Amount of Affect Change*

INDEX	DIFFERENCE BETWEEN GROUPS (MANN-WHITNEY z)	p	DIRECTION OF DIFFERENCE
Mean affect-change score for nonmanipulated attitude objects	.07	$> .90$	
Affect-change score for high-interest attitude object	3.30	$< .001$	Exp > Cont
Affect-change score for low-interest attitude object	3.80	$< .0002$	Exp > Cont

on the topic "City-Manager Plan" etc.), disregarding the interest rank that the subject had assigned to the topic and eliminating from these analyses any hypnotic S who had received a suggestion of affect reversal on the topic in question. In all of these comparisons the differences between the two groups are not great enough to permit rejection of the null hypothesis.

On the basis of these findings it seems clear that while differing in level of hypnotizability the two groups do not differ in the characteristic (i.e., test-retest stability of attitudinal affect) of greatest relevance to the testing of the present hypothesis.

Evidence on the effectiveness of the hypnotic manipulations

All of the findings so far reviewed refer to group comparisons on attitude items that were not hypnotically manipulated for members of the experimental group. To determine whether the hypnotic manipulation of attitudinal affect is an effective one, tests similar to those already described were carried out.

Table 1 reports the results of a comparison of the affect-change scores of the experimental Ss on their respective hypnotically manipulated high-interest and low-interest attitudes with the equivalent affect change scores of the control Ss. The chance probability of the obtained difference is less than .001 for the high-interest attitude area and less than .0002 for the low-interest attitude area.

In both cases inspection shows the differences to be due to the experimental Ss having greater affect-change scores than the control Ss. In fact the affect-change scores of the control Ss are small enough and enough dispersed in both directions to suggest that they merely reflect the reliability limits of the kind of attitude scale employed in this experiment.

Another way of checking the effectiveness of the hypnotic manipulation is to compare the hypnotic Ss' mean affect-change scores on the manipulated-attitude items to their mean affect-change scores on the nonmanipulated items. In all 11 cases the former exceeds the latter. By the sign test procedure a two-tailed probability of less than .001 is obtained. It should be added that in their verbal responses after hypnosis, and both before and during the posthypnotic testing, most of the experimental Ss gave evidence that their expressions of affect alteration were not isolated to the questionnaire but rather reflected actual "internalized" changes.

The results reported up to this point seem clearly to confirm the following conclusion: through the use of posthypnotic suggestion it was possible to produce sizeable alterations in the

experimental Ss' expressed and felt affects toward attitude concepts of both high and low interest respectively; these affective alterations significantly exceeded the reliability limits of the affect-measuring instrument, whether those limits are ascertained through the performance of a control group or of the experimental group itself.

The cognitive consequences of hypnotically induced affect change

While the findings given above are relevant to establishing both the effectiveness of the affect manipulation and the validity of the affect measure, the main concern of this report is with the prediction that when a strong affect change has been induced it will be consolidated through a further process of cognitive reorganization in which the subject abandons old, and adopts new, ways of perceiving and thinking about the attitude object.

The basic test of this prediction employs the data gathered through the two administrations of the Cognitive Structure Test. It has been explained above that this test elicits from the S his perceptions about the kind (positive or negative) and degree of instrumental effectiveness possessed by the attitude object with separate regard to each of 31 "values." It was explained too that each of these values is also judged in terms of its sign (positive or negative) and the intensity of that sign. The cognitive-structure index computed by algebraic summation of all 31 (instrumentality $\times$ value-intensity) products is taken as the representation, in a single positive or negative number, of the S's pattern of beliefs about the attitude object's value-serving and value-blocking characteristics.

For each of the 22 Ss four such cognitive-structure indices were computed: one index referred to the S's beliefs about the value-attaining and value-blocking powers of the high-interest attitude object as those beliefs were elicited during the first administration of the Cognitive Structure Test; another index, otherwise identical, was based upon the beliefs elicited during the second administration of the Cognitive Structure Test; and similarly the two other indices were based upon the beliefs about the low-interest attitude object as those beliefs were elicited during the first and second test administrations respectively. From these indices there were computed for each S two difference scores: one representing change in the cognitive structure of the high-interest attitude object, the other representing change in the cognitive structure of the low-interest attitude object.

As Table 2 indicates, when the experimental and control groups are compared it is found that the two groups differ significantly in extent of cognitive change from the first to the second test of cognitive structure. The finding that in their beliefs about the high-interest attitude object the experimental Ss show more cognitive change than the control Ss has a chance probability of less than .01. The comparable finding involving the low-interest attitude object has a chance probability of less than .0002.

Examination of the rank distributions of the difference scores obtained from the two groups reveals that the median cognition-change scores with reference to the high-interest attitude object are 21 for the control group and 167 for the experimental group respectively. The highest cognition-change score obtained from the control group is 57; the highest from the experimental group is 642. Comparably the median cognition-change scores with reference to the low-interest attitude object are 1 for the control group and 130 for the experimental group respectively. The highest cognition-change score obtained from the control group is 21; the highest from the experimental group is 434.

On the basis of these data it is concluded that verification has been obtained for the original hypothesis: i.e., that the production (at least through a hypnotic procedure) of a reversal in affect felt toward an attitude object is followed by significant and consistent changes in the person's beliefs about that object. One possible objection to this conclusion is that in the present study the experimental Ss' cognitive structures were tested only for the two objects that were involved in the hypnotic suggestions. This made it impossible, with the data of the present experiment, to rule out the possibility that even when affect toward an object is not manipulated, hypnotizable persons such as those in our experimental group would show considerable instability in their beliefs about that object. Two answers to this objection are available. The first is that if our experimental population were characterized by such instability their cognitive changes should as frequently go in one direction as in the other. In fact the case is clearly otherwise: in 21 out of 22 instances the cognitition-change scores of the experimental Ss are due to patterns of belief change which are consistent in direction with the hypnotically implanted affects. A second answer to the objection noted above is simply that in a subsequent experiment, to be reported separately, members of another group of hypnotic Ss were tested on the belief patterns associated with three different attitude objects; one of these attitude objects was subjected to hypnotic manipulation and two were not subjected to such manipulation. The

data indicate, at highly acceptable levels of statistical verification, that with these hypnotic Ss the cognitive structures associated with nonmanipulated attitudinal affects hold constant over a large number of different testing sessions while those associated with the manipulated object undergo the kind of reorganization found in the present experiment.

Instrumentality change and value change in the cognitive reorganization process

Beyond the verification of the original hypothesis it is possible from the present data to inquire further into certain details of the general process assumed in that hypothesis. Thus it may be asked: do the experimental Ss alter their cognitive structures by changing their beliefs about the attitude object's instrumental bearing upon the group of values; do they change their evaluation of the values themselves; or do they show both types of change? Simply stated the last mentioned of these possibilities is the one which seems best to describe the performances of all the experimental Ss.

Supporting this generalization are some findings made possible by the computation of four additional indices. One of these indices was designated as the mean change in intensity of values associated with the high-interest attitude object. A second was designated as the mean change in intensity of values associated with the low-interest attitude object. To compute the first of these indices the following steps were executed. It was determined which of the 31 values were seen by the S as instrumentally affected by the high-interest attitude object (simply by excluding any value terms in reference to which the attitude object had been judged, on both administrations of the Cognitive Structure Test, as having zero instrumentality). For each of these values there was computed the difference between its value-intensity ratings on the first and second test administrations respectively. These differences were summed and divided by their number, thus yielding the mean change in intensity of values associated with the high-interest attitude object. An identical procedure was employed with reference to all values seen by the S as instrumentally af-

TABLE 2 *Experimental Group and Control Group* (*under Test-Retest Condition*) *Compared for Amount of Cognition Change*

INDEX	DIFFERENCE BETWEEN GROUPS (MANN-WHITNEY z)	p	DIRECTION OF DIFFERENCE
Cognition-change score for high-interest attitude object	2.62	$< .01$	Exp > Cont
Cognition-change score for low-interest attitude object	3.87	$< .0002$	Exp > Cont

fected by the low-interest attitude object. This yielded the mean change in intensity of values associated with the low-interest attitude object.

When the hypnotic and control groups are compared on these indices it is found (see Table 3) that both with regard to the groups of values seen as related to the high-interest attitude object and the low-interest attitude object respectively, the hypnotic Ss show greater change than the control Ss. Inspection of the Cognitive Structure Test records indicates that the experimental Ss' changes in ratings of value intensity are in the directions consistent with the altered attitudinal affects.

That the cognitive reorganizing achieved by the hypnotic Ss is not based upon value-intensity changes alone is made clear by the use of two additional indices. One of these indices is designated as the mean change in instrumentality of the high-interest attitude object and the second is the mean change in instrumentality of the low-interest attitude object. To compute the former the following steps were executed: it was determined which of the 31 values were seen by the S as instrumentally affected by the high-interest attitude object (by simply excluding any value terms in reference to which the attitude object had been judged, on both Cognitive Structure Test administrations, as having zero instrumentality); for each of these values there was computed the difference between its instrumentality ratings (the extent to which the attitude object is seen as tending to prevent or enhance its realization) on the first and second test administrations respectively; these differences were summed and divided by their number, thus yielding the mean change in instrumentality of the high-interest attitude object. An identical procedure was employed with reference to all values seen by the Ss as instrumentally affected by the low-interest attitude object. This yielded the mean change in instrumentality of the low-interest attitude object.

When the two groups are compared on these indices it is found (Table 3) that both with regard to the group of values seen as related to the high-interest and low-interest attitude objects respectively, the hypnotic Ss show significantly greater change than the control Ss in their perceptions of how these values are influenced by the attitude objects. Inspection of the Cognitive Structure Test records reveals that for the hypnotic Ss the direction of change is generally consistent with the altered affects.

Combining the two groups of findings just presented it is clear that the hypnotic Ss achieve cognitive reorganization both through changing their perceptions about the attitude object's instrumental bearing upon values and also through changing their evaluation of those values.

To further clarify the meaning of these findings it will be useful to regard some items from the test records of a typical experimental S. Before hypnotic manipulation the S, a medical student, was strongly opposed to "the federal government undertaking to provide comprehensive medical insurance for all persons." The hypnotic suggestion was merely that he would be strongly in favor of this policy. After hypnosis the subject placed himself at the extreme positive end of the affective scale referring to federal medical insurance.

On the Cognitive Structure Test various types of change are observed. The most frequent of these is the simple reversal of instrumentality from positive to negative or negative to positive. Thus before hypnosis the S sees "federal medical insurance" as violating the positive value "serving the interests of the group to which one belongs"; after hypnosis he perceives it as fostering the realization of this same value. He accomplishes many other changes of this sort and, either spontaneously or when queried, argues for the correctness of these new beliefs.

Another type of instrumentality change involves the reduction of an object-value relationship to the absence of any relationship. An example is that before hypnosis the S asserts that federal medical insurance violates the positive value "people having the right to participate in making decisions which will affect them"; after hypnosis

TABLE 3 *Experimental Group and Control Group (under Test-Retest Condition) Compared for Amount of Instrumentality Change and Value-intensity Change*

INDEX	DIFFERENCE BETWEEN GROUPS (MANN-WHITNEY z)	p	DIRECTION OF DIFFERENCE
Mean change in intensity of values associated with high-interest attitude object	3.15	$< .002$	Exp > Cont
Mean change in intensity of values associated with low-interest attitude object	3.40	$< .001$	Exp > Cont
Mean change in instrumentality of high-interest attitude object	3.80	$< .0002$	Exp > Cont
Mean change in instrumentality of low-interest attitude object	3.74	$< .0002$	Exp > Cont

he no longer sees any connection between federal medical insurance and the attainment or blocking of this value.

A third type of change is one in which a value formerly seen as unaffected by the attitude object is later discovered by the S to be affected in a manner consistent with the implanted attitudinal affect. Thus the present S, before hypnosis, asserts a zero instrumentality relationship between federal medical insurance and the value "change and variety; having new types of experience." After hypnosis he asserts that federal medical insurance will facilitate the attainment of this value and explains that as he sees it, physicians cooperating with such a program "will encounter a wider range of patients and types of disease and thus their work experience will be more interesting."

In addition to the three types of instrumentality change just illustrated the present S also makes some changes in his ratings of the values. For example before hypnosis he classifies "everyone being assured of a good standard of living" as a negative value (-3 in its intensity) and sees federal medical insurance as serving the attainment of this negative value; after hypnosis he still believes that federal medical insurance will facilitate "everyone being assured of a good standard of living" but this value phrase is now judged as representing a positive and desirable goal and receives a value-intensity rating of $+5$.

Weaker forms of value change are also found in which the S modifies a former belief by reducing the intensity of its involved value without actually changing its sign.[3]

Comparative effects of hypnotic and role-playing manipulations[4]

In all of the foregoing discussion it has been tacitly assumed that in their posthypnotic responses on both the affective and cognitive measures, the experimental Ss are giving valid reports of how, at the time of testing, they really feel and think about the attitude objects. Interview evidence in support of this assumption is briefly described below.

However it could be argued that on the basis of the data so far presented the original hypothesis is not unequivocally established; that the

hypnotic Ss only *seem* to undergo affective and related cognitive change, but that in reality they are "role playing" and thus merely responding "as if" they felt the suggested affects.

In anticipation of this possible line of interpretation the original experimental design included a plan for a special role-playing control procedure by which its validity could be gauged. On the assumption that the hypnotic Ss experience real affect change when given the posthypnotic suggestion, it was predicted that in their responses on both the affective and cognitive measures they would show less extreme change than a group of Ss who were instructed to role-play the occurrence of affect change. This prediction was based upon the expectation that if, after hypnosis, the experimental Ss were giving their presently true feelings and beliefs these would have been partially limited by their prehypnotic feelings and beliefs; their originally opposite responses would have exerted some restraining force upon the extent of change achieved after hypnosis. For Ss who were merely role-playing the occurrence of change, the original feelings and beliefs would not exert as much, if any, restraining force upon their test responses.

Brief mention has already been made of the procedure that was employed to test this prediction: in addition to his participation in the test-retest reliability procedure, each of the control Ss was also run through a role-playing control condition. For six of these Ss the reliability control procedure was administered first and the role-playing control condition a week later; for the other five control Ss this sequence was reversed.

Under the role-playing condition each S first took the Cognitive Structure Test. (He had already taken the affect-measuring instrument either one or two weeks earlier.) The object-instrumentality portion of the Cognitive Structure Test was administered twice; once for one of the S's two highest interest attitude objects and once for one of his two lowest interest attitude objects. For none of the Ss were these the same as the attitude objects used in the reliability control condition. A randomization procedure was applied so that the numbers of Ss working with the attitude objects of highest or next highest interest and lowest or next lowest interest under the reliability and role-playing control conditions respectively were roughly equal.

After completion of the first administration of the Cognitive Structure Test the S was asked to rest upon a couch in a darkened room for half an hour. Before arising he was told the following:

> In a moment I will ask you to get up.
> Before I do I have some instructions

---

[3] Research in progress is addressed to the question of whether in a subsequent experiment with a different group of hypnotic Ss, instrumentality and value-intensity changes were enabled by reorganization of the implicit meanings of the value terms. A provisional conclusion is that while some of these changes are based upon subjective redefinition of the values, others occur under conditions of value constancy.

[4] Some of the data reported in this section have bearing also upon some important issues in hypnotic theory. Since space and continuity requirements would not permit a discussion of these matters in the present paper, a portion of these data is examined for its relevance to the theory of hypnosis in a separate publication (Rosenberg, 1959).

for you. From the time you get up until the end of today's session everything you say and do should be consistent with a role that I am now going to assign to you. The role you are to play is defined in terms of the following feelings. . . .

The wording of the remainder of the role-playing instruction then continued with instructions of affect reversal exactly equivalent to those used with the hypnotic Ss. The S was then retested with both the affective and cognitive structure measures.

As indicated in Table 4, the role-playing Ss show significantly greater change in their stated affects toward the high-interest attitude object than do the hypnotic Ss ($p < .02$). When the two groups are compared for extent of affect change toward the low-interest attitude object the role-playing Ss again show more of such change but not significantly more ($p < .15$).

Similarly, when compared on the extent of related cognitive change it is found (see Table 5) that both with regard to the high-interest and the low-interest attitude objects the role-playing Ss show significantly more change than the hypnotic Ss. The former difference has a chance probability of less than .05; the latter has a chance probability of less than .01.

Thus, in support of the prediction given above, it is found that while the hypnotic Ss shows significantly more affective and cognitive change when compared to the performances of control Ss in a test-retest reliability procedure, they show significantly less affective and cognitive change when compared to the performances obtained from these same control Ss under a "role-playing" procedure.

These confirmations of the original prediction are taken as supporting the hypothesis from which it was derived: i.e., that the hypnotic Ss are, during the immediate posthypnotic phase, experiencing truly altered affects and beliefs.

Beyond its bearing upon this issue the comparison of the performance of the hypnotic and role-playing Ss suggests that, in general, the hypnotic Ss strive to limit their ways of changing so as to keep their images of themselves as intact as possible.

Supporting this impression is the finding (see Table 4) that the role-playing Ss show significant affective change not only in the two attitude areas mentioned in the role-playing instructions but also in the five nonmanipulated attitude areas. The hypnotic Ss on the other hand restrict their affect changes only to the two areas subjected to manipulation (see Table 1). When the mean affect change for the five nonmanipulated areas is computed the difference between the role-playing and hypnotic groups is found to have a chance probability of less than .001. The meaning of this finding is clarified by interview data which reveal that role-playing Ss typically take the sort of approach epitomized by the following comment: "Well, I figured that to be against Negroes that way I would have to be quite a reactionary type, so naturally in all the other questions (attitude items) I changed to the reactionary position. But of course this has nothing to do with what I really feel."

Similarly it is found that when the cognitive performances of the two groups are compared (see Table 6), the role-playing Ss show more change in their ratings of the values associated with both the high-interest attitude object ($p <$

TABLE 4 *Experimental Group and Control Group (under Role-playing Condition) Compared for Amount of Affect Change*

INDEX	DIFFERENCE BETWEEN GROUPS (MANN-WHITNEY z)	p	DIRECTION OF DIFFERENCE
Mean affect-change score for nonmanipulated attitude objects	3.45	$< .001$	Cont-RP $>$ Exp
Affect-change score for high-interest attitude object	2.45	$< .02$	Cont-RP $>$ Exp
Affect-change score for low-interest attitude object	1.51	$< .15$	Cont-RP $>$ Exp

TABLE 5 *Experimental Group and Control Group (under Role-playing Condition) Compared for Amount of Cognition Change*

INDEX	DIFFERENCE BETWEEN GROUPS (MANN-WHITNEY z)	p	DIRECTION OF DIFFERENCE
Cognition-change score for high-interest attitude object	2.10	$< .05$	Cont-RP $>$ Exp
Cognition-change score for low-interest attitude object	2.60	$< .01$	Cont-RP $>$ Exp

.004) and the low-interest attitude object ($p <$ .004) than do the hypnotic Ss. When compared on their mean changes in instrumentality judgments for both the high- and low-interest attitude objects respectively the two groups of Ss do not differ significantly from each other.[5]

These last findings and those having to do with affect change in the nonmanipulated attitude areas are offered as suggesting that the hypnotic Ss, unlike the role-playing Ss, are motivated to hold consistently to their usual ways of judging attitude objects and value concepts. If the presence of such motivation is acknowledged it would follow that the actual significant changes obtained from these Ss in their affective and cognitive responses toward the manipulated attitude objects are experienced by them as real; if these changes were not so experienced there would be no way to account for their occurrence in the face of the assumed motivation for response consistency.

Awareness of attitude change

To what extent is the hypnotic S aware that he has changed his ways of thinking and feeling about the attitude object? Four of the experimen-

---

[5] The fact that the hypnotic Ss, though they show change both in the mean intensity of attitude-related values and in the mean instrumentality of the attitude object (see Table 3), show significantly less of the former than do the role-playing Ss may be interpreted in terms of such "cognitive balance" theories as those of Abelson and Rosenberg (1958), Cartwright and Harary (1956), and Heider (1946, 1958). Abelson and Rosenberg conceive an attitudinal belief as a perceived positive or negative relationship between two "objects," each of which carries a positive or negative affective sign. An "imbalanced" belief is one containing either one or three negative signs. From this point of view the situation after hypnosis is one in which change in the affective sign of the attitude object has created an imbalance in a large number of previously balanced beliefs (relating that object to various separate value terms). Restoration of balance may be accomplished by changing either the sign of the relationship or of the value term. But the fact that many of the value terms figure in other beliefs (about other attitude objects) will limit the extent to which they can be changed without imbalancing those other beliefs. No such restriction limits the S when he undertakes to change relational signs.

tal Ss in the present study show no evidence whatsoever of such awareness. When queried before amnesia removal they insist that their present feelings and beliefs are identical with the ones they held at the beginning of the experiment. When confronted with the evidence of their having undergone change, they express great surprise and typically explain, "I guess I misunderstood the instructions the first time I took the test." When Ss are aware of having changed, such awareness is frequently limited by a rationalization to the effect that, during the premanipulation testing, the S misunderstood the instructions or the meaning of some of the test stimuli. Other Ss simply reject their previous approaches as wrong and judge their present ways of thinking and feeling as correct and justified. As one of these Ss said, "I wasn't thinking right before. Now I see the whole thing more clearly and more rationally."

Before amnesia removal none of the experimental Ss showed any suspicion that the changes in his feeling and thinking were due to hypnotic manipulation; to the contrary, all insisted that they had reported their true responses and all seemed to accept fully the fiction that the testing they underwent was part of one experiment and the hypnosis part of another. When, after the completion of all testing and interviewing, the hypnotic amnesia was removed and the experiment fully explained, most of the Ss seemed to be able to re-establish their original attitudes. However there was some incidental evidence in connection with the low-interest attitude object that at least one, and possibly two, of the Ss had not yet managed to re-establish fully the prehypnotic pattern of affect and cognition.

DISCUSSION

The main findings of this experiment confirm the original hypothesis that the production of a significant change in the affective component of a social attitude will eventuate in an accommodating

---

TABLE 6 *Experimental Group and Control Group (under Role-playing Condition) Compared for Amount of Instrumentality Change and Value-intensity Change*

INDEX	DIFFERENCE BETWEEN GROUPS (MANN-WHITNEY z)	p	DIRECTION OF DIFFERENCE
Mean change in intensity of values associated with high-interest attitude object	2.94	< .004	Cont-RP > Exp
Mean change in intensity of values associated with low-interest attitude object	3.05	< .004	Cont-RP > Exp
Mean change in instrumentality of high-interest attitude object	1.38	< .20	Cont-RP > Exp
Mean change in instrumentality of low-interest attitude object	1.56	< .15	Cont-RP > Exp

reorganization of the S's cognitions about the object of that attitude. Taken together with earlier findings reported by Rosenberg (1956) and Carlson (1956), these data suggest further the validity of a theoretical orientation in which attitude change generally is viewed as the result of a process that begins with the production of inconsistency between the affective and cognitive components of the attitude. The production of such inconsistency may be accomplished through communications designed to alter either component in a previously stable attitude. Once established, such inconsistency will be dealt with by attitude-reorganizing activity that continues until affective-cognitive consistency has been re-established. (An important special case is that if, by virtue of the comparative strengths and rigidities of the competing components, re-establishment of consistency is impossible then another type of outcome may occur: processes of selective inattention may be used to avoid any further encounter with the inconsistency.)

It should be clear that the final outcome of such a process of inconsistency reduction need not be the establishment of a stable altered attitude. Affective-cognitive inconsistency may be dealt with either by accommodating the unchanged component to the changed component or by reverting to the initial state of affairs. This latter type of outcome is the one obtained when, after initial rehearsal of change communications, these communications are rejected by the receiver. Whether the attitude-changing or attitude-restoring outcome is obtained would be due to a number of factors. One of these would be the sheer potency of the original communication in comparison to the original strength of the attitude component(s) against which it is directed. In the present experiment the use of a hypnotic command of affect reversal may be judged to have been a highly potent communication. But apart from communication potency other variables must be assumed to play a prominent role in the establishment of irreversible inconsistency. Among such variables are ones having to do with order of presentation (Hovland, 1957) and with the personality of the S (Hovland & Janis, 1959).

It seems likely too that certain aspects of the original affective-cognitive structure of an attitude may predict to the ease with which an inconsistency-establishing alteration of either of its major components may be created. Thus there is some evidence in unreported data from the present study that the fewer the number of beliefs contained within the cognitive component of the attitude, the more extreme will be the affect change produced through the hypnotic command of affect reversal.

Numerous other variables might be conceived

to influence the general process of inconsistency production and reduction which is here asserted to underlie attitude-change effects. Some of these variables would exert influence not during the initial stage of inconsistency establishment but rather during the phase of inconsistency reduction or the phase in which the outcome of such inconsistency reduction is consolidated. The present experiment is here interpreted not as delineating all such variables but rather as suggesting the validity and applicability of a general theoretical approach to attitude dynamics into which such variables may be fitted.

One clear value of this approach is that it permits a reduction of attitude-change effects into two types of sequences. The first of these is the one in which the alteration of one's beliefs about an attitude object generates an inconsistency between those beliefs and a previously established affect and this inconsistency is reduced by consequent affect change. Apart from experimental demonstrations of its operation a large part of the range of "persuasion through communication" effects can be understood and predicted in terms of this sequence.

The second conceivable type of change sequence, and the one represented by the present experiment, is the one in which alteration of one's affective orientation toward an object generates an inconsistency between that affective orientation and previously established beliefs; this inconsistency is reduced by consequent cognitive reorganization. It might be contended that though the present data demonstrate the reality of this sequence with regard to a special and unusual form of affect manipulation (i.e. hypnosis), it does not seem generally applicable to many nonexperimental phenomena. However it is the author's impression that a wide variety of attitude change phenomena do feature just this sequence, either in pure form or in joint operation with the first mentioned sequence. Whenever attitude change (or for that matter, original attitude learning) proceeds through the administration of reward or punishment for the imitation or rehearsal of affects expressed by other persons, the attitude-dynamic sequence demonstrated in this experiment is likely to be in operation.

While many issues of general psychological importance are involved in this approach to the problem of attitude dynamics, most of these will not be discussed here. One such issue does, however, require some comment: in the face of the present conception of attitude as featuring affective-cognitive consistency how can we explain the inconsistencies that are sometimes observed in experimental Ss or survey respondents? Many such inconsistencies would seem to be due to deficient methodology or to misuse of attitude measurement devices. It is a common observation that Ss who lack an attitude (in the sense of stable affective response) toward a specific object will nevertheless respond to an affective scale by choosing some nonneutral position. Whether accomplished through unreliable reference to related objects or by calculating the expectations of the tester, such responses will necessarily lack an associated body of clearly consistent cognitions.

Yet it is not unknown for an *S* who seems to hold a real and stable affect toward an object to report beliefs most of which are "inconsistent" with that affect. This is usually due to the use of a method in which the *S* is not allowed to deal with the goals and values that are for him relevant and salient to his evaluation of the attitude object.

Scott, in an interesting article (1959), contends that some attitudes are consistent and others are not; but the data offered to demonstrate inconsistency between attitudinal affect and cognition are based upon a version of the present author's Cognitive Structure Test so altered as to permit the very methodological errors mentioned above. (E.g., only eight value terms are used and these with no assurance of their salience for the attitude object.) However, the finding that, when they were exposed to a relatively weak change influence, "cognitively consistent *S*s were more likely to retain their initial attitudes than the inconsistent ones" suggests that some of Scott's "inconsistent" *S*s were in fact inconsistent in the unrecognized sense that they lacked any initial stable affective response toward the attitude object.

On the basis of the present author's observation any *S* who has given evidence of having a *stable* affective set toward a particular social object will, under interview conditions, report a number of supporting beliefs. If some test device is to be employed to get at these beliefs it must provide the *S* with a wide enough range of stimuli, a range that includes all or most of the goal states to which, as the *S* sees it, the object is really related. Nor do we have any right to expect that persons will be so consistent in relating their affects to their beliefs as to be incapable of entertaining some few beliefs that *are* inconsistent with the experienced affect: in postulating a strain toward affective-cognitive consistency, it is not forgotten or denied that individuals are capable, to demonstrably different degrees, of some tolerance of ambiguity. Neither is it contended that latent inconsistency is a sufficient condition for the production of attitude reorganization. Rather it is suggested that the motivation to achieve and maintain a pattern of consistency beween one's stable affects toward, and one's beliefs about, an attitude object is active only when the person's own needs, or expectations directed at him, lead him to "think about" and "express" his attitudes (Abelson & Rosenberg, 1958). That there are realms beyond articulate formulation and examination in which affective-cognitive inconsistency may persist under conditions of selective inattention and avoidance is a point that has already been acknowledged.

Beyond its relevance to the development of a structural theory of attitude dynamics the present study suggests certain conclusions about hypnosis. Of these the one most directly pertinent to the present discussion is that when it is employed as a technique of affect manipulation, hypnosis (or rather the *S*'s manner of adapting to it) may exert some indirect influence upon the ways in which he goes about reorganizing his affect-related cognitions. An investigation into this aspect of the phenomenon has been reported elsewhere (Rosenberg & Gardner, 1958).

A last conjecture is that in the light of the data that have been presented in this paper, it seems conceivable that hypnotic techniques have been used (in combination with other procedures) for the production of large scale affective-cognitive reorientation of the sort demonstrated in the confessions of the accused in certain totalitarian "show-trials."

SUMMARY

Attitudinal affective-cognitive inconsistency was produced in 11 hypnotic *S*s through the use of posthypnotic suggestions of affect reversal. The *S*s showed significantly more change in both their affects and beliefs about the attitude objects involved than did 11 control *S*s not subjected to posthypnotic suggestion. These and other findings were interpreted as confirming certain aspects, and as consistent with other aspects, of a structural theory of attitude dynamics.

REFERENCES

ABELSON, R. P., & ROSENBERG, M. J. Symbolic psycho-logic: a model of attitudinal cognition. *Behav. Sci.,* 1958, 3, 1–13

ADORNO, T. W., FRENKEL-BRUNSWIK, ELSE, LEVINSON, D. J., & SANFORD, R. N. *The authoritarian personality.* New York: Harper and Brothers, 1950.

CARLSON, E. R. Attitude change and attitude structure. *J. abnorm. soc. Psychol.,* 1956, 52, 256–261.

CARTWRIGHT, D., & HARARY, F. Structural balance: a generalization of Heider's theory. *Psychol. Rev.,* 1956, 63, 277–293.

COOMBS, C. H. A theory of psychological scaling. *Univer. of Mich. Engng. Res. Bull.* No. 34. Ann Arbor: Univer. Michigan Press, 1952.

DOOB, L. W. The behavior of attitudes. *Psychol. Rev.,* 1947, 54, 135–156.

HEIDER, F. Attitudes and cognitive organization. *J. Psychol.,* 1946, 21, 107–112.

HEIDER, F. *The psychology of inter-personal relations.* New York: John Wiley and Sons, 1958.

HOVLAND, C. I. (ED.) *The order of presentation in*

persuasion. New Haven: Yale Univer. Press, 1957.

HOVLAND, C. I., & JAMES, I. L. (Eds.) *Personality and persuasability.* New Haven: Yale Univer. Press, 1959.

HOVLAND, C. I., JANIS, I. L., & KELLEY, H. H. *Communication and persuasion.* New Haven: Yale Univer. Press, 1953.

KRECH, D., & CRUTCHFIELD, R. *Theory and problems of social psychology.* New York: McGraw-Hill, 1948.

MOSTELLER, F., & BUSH, R. R. Selected quantitative techniques. In G. Lindzey (Ed.) *Handbook of social psychology.* Cambridge: Addison-Wesley, 1954. Pp. 289–334.

PEAK, HELEN. Attitude and motivation. In M. R. Jones (Ed.), *Nebraska symposium on motivation.* Lincoln: Univer. Nebraska Press, 1955.

PEAK, HELEN. Psychological structure and psychological activity. *Psychol. Rev.,* 1958, 65, 325–347.

ROSENBERG, M. J. Cognitive structure and attitudinal affect. *J. abnorm. soc. Psychol.,* 1956, 53, 367–372.

ROSENBERG, M. J. A disconfirmation of the description of hypnosis as a dissociated state. *Int. J. clin. exp. Hypnos.,* 1959, 7, 187–204.

ROSENBERG, M. J., & GARDNER, C. W. Some dynamic aspects of posthypnotic compliance. *J. abnorm. soc. Psychol.,* 1958, 57, 351–366.

SCOTT, W. A. Cognitive consistency, response reinforcement, and attitude change. *Sociometry,* 1959, 22, 219–229.

SMITH, M. B. Personal values as determinants of a political attitude. *J. Psychol.,* 1949, 28, 477–486.

SMITH, M. B., BRUNER, J. S. & WHITE, R. W. *Opinions and personality.* New York: John Wiley and Sons, 1956.

TOLMAN, E. C. A psychological model. In T. Parsons and E. A. Shils (Eds.), *Toward a general theory of action.* Cambridge: Harvard Univer. Press, 1951.

WOODRUFF, A. D., & DiVESTA, F. J. The relationship between values, concepts, and attitudes. *Educ. psychol. Measmt.,* 1948, 8, 645–660.

RESISTANCE TO PERSUASION AND PRIOR BELIEF DEFENSES *

A belief might be expected to be more resistant to change if an individual anticipates that it might be challenged and if he has a fund of arguments with which to counter the attack. This leads to the rather surprising suggestion that the most widely held beliefs in a society are especially susceptible to attack. Such beliefs are apt to prevail only because there is little information dissonant with them. Because the beliefs are widespread, the individual rarely encounters any contrary information or any pressures to change them. Thus, he has little motivation to actively associate these beliefs with other ideas that he subscribes to. In particular, he does not need to develop rational arguments to defend them.

This reasoning has important social implications: censorship of information contrary to the central beliefs of a society is apt to make these beliefs vulnerable to attack. An attack upon a belief might be expected to produce ideas that refute the counterarguments, and these refutations would subsequently serve to ward off future attacks. A belief might also be bolstered by providing arguments in direct support of it without attacking it. McGuire's report, given below, briefly reviews the results of studies comparing these two forms of

defense and goes on to test several additional hypotheses pertaining to the relative persistence over time of beliefs supported in these two ways. His discussion illustrates how a clearly stated theoretical proposition lends itself to extension to new situations and is gradually elaborated to cover an increasingly wider range of phenomena.

17.

Persistence of the Resistance to Persuasion Induced by Various Types of Prior Belief Defenses[1]

WILLIAM J. McGUIRE
COLUMBIA UNIVERSITY

A number of previous studies have tested the relative efficacy of various types of prior defenses in making a person's belief resistant to change when he is later confronted with massive counterarguments against the belief. None of these previous studies were designed to measure the effect on resistance of varying the time interval between the defense and the attack. By systematically varying this interval, the present experiment investigates the relative persistence of the immunity of persuasion conferred by the different types of

* The selection following the editorial introduction is reprinted from "Persistence of the resistance to persuasion induced by various types of prior belief defenses," *Journal of Abnormal & Social Psychology,* 1962, **64**, 241–248, by permission of the author and the American Psychological Association.

[1] This study was supported, in part, by a grant from the National Science Foundation, Division of Social Sciences.

prior defenses. It is of some interest to know for each type of defense the rate at which its conferred immunity decays over time. Of even greater theoretical interest are comparisons among the decay rates for the different types of defense.

The predictions regarding these differential decay rates derive from the same postulates as gave rise to the earlier predictions, tested and confirmed in previous experiments, regarding the relative immunizing effectiveness of various defenses *without* regard to the time interval between defense and attack. Hence, it is useful to mention several of the relevant previous findings and their theoretical bases. The previous studies, and the present one as well, used cultural truisms as the beliefs being defended and attacked—for example, the belief that "We should brush our teeth after every meal if at all possible." It had been postulated that there is little belief-dissonant information available regarding such cultural truisms in the person's normal ideological environment. This unavailability, combined with the characteristic tendency to avoid even such belief-dissonant material as is available, would have left the person underestimating the vulnerability of his belief and, hence, unmotivated to acquire bolstering material and unprepared to deal with strong counterarguments when he is forced to expose himself to them.

From this theoretical analysis follow several of the previously confirmed hypotheses regarding immunization against persuasion which are relevant to the hypotheses being tested in the present experiment. One of these previous findings (McGuire & Papageorgis, 1961) is that prior refutational defenses are superior to prior supportive defenses in making cultural truisms resistant to subsequent persuasion. Refutational defenses involve mention and refutation of possible counterarguments against the belief, while ignoring arguments positively supporting the belief. Supportive defenses do mention and elaborate arguments positively supporting the belief, while ignoring possible counterarguments against it. This superiority of the refutational defense would follow from the above theoretical assumptions, since the refutational defense contains a threatening element—mention of the counterarguments to whose existence the subject has probably given little, if any thought—which stimulates him to bolster his belief. The supportive defense of the truism, on the other hand, seems to labor the obvious, so that the subject is little motivated to assimilate the positive arguments and is left, if anything, even less motivated to bolster further the belief he regards as obvious.

It was also demonstrated (Papageorgis & McGuire, 1961) that the refutational defense confers resistance to subsequent attacks even by novel counterarguments, different from those explicitly refuted in the defense. This conferral of generalized immunity by the refutational defense also follows from the theoretical assumptions. The immunizing efficacy derives not only from weakening the credibility of the specific counterarguments refuted, but also from the threat induced stimulation to bolster one's defense. Hence, the refutational defense increases resistance even to attacks by counterarguments other than those refuted.

The foregoing theoretical interpretation of the previous findings gives rise to three predictions regarding the temporal persistence of the resistance conferred by the different types of prior defense. First, it is hypothesized that the supportive defense will not only be initially inferior to the refutational in the amount of resistance it confers, but in addition that such resistance, as it does confer, will decay more rapidly than that conferred by the refutational defense. This prediction follows from the above interpretation that the immunizing efficacy of the supportive defense derives solely from the acquaintance with the positive arguments which it contains and which tend to be forgotten over time; the efficacy of the refutational defenses, on the other hand, derives in part from the threat induced motivation to bolster one's defenses. Since for some time the subject will continue to act on the motivation, the forgetting of the refutational material will be partly offset by this continued acquisition of bolstering material.

The second hypothesis is that the temporal decay of conferred immunity occurs more rapidly against attacks by the same counterarguments as had been explicitly refuted than against attacks by novel counterarguments. The theoretical basis for this prediction is quite similar to that yielding the first hypothesis. The immunity to attacks by the very counterarguments refuted derives from both recall of the specific refutations, which decays over time, and the amount of bolstering material the subject has acquired on the basis of his induced motivation, which increases over time. The immunity to attacks by novel counterarguments derives solely from the latter mechanism. Hence, conferred resistance to novel counterarguments should tend to catch up over time with resistance to the very counterarguments refuted.

The third hypothesis, which follows as a corollary of the second, is that the refutational defense has a delayed-action effect in conferring resistance to attacks by novel counterarguments. The refutations per se should not confer any resistance in this case, at least, not in so far as the counterarguments used in the attack are indeed novel. Hence, any resistance conferred derives from the second mechanism, the motivation to bolster one's belief induced by exposure to the threatening counterarguments during the defense. Acting on this motivation requires time, particularly in the monolithic ideological environment that tends to surround cultural truisms. Hence, the resistance to attack by novel arguments will continue to grow for sometime after the threatening pre-exposure. As time passes, the induced motivation will, of course, itself decay so that the total time function will be nonmonotonic. But for a time at least the conferred immunity will grow.

To test these temporal-trend predictions adequately it is important that we have some idea of the time parameters involved. It was in part to explore these parameters that the time interval between defense and attack was deliberately varied, from experiment to experiment, in the previous studies in this series. For example, in McGuire (1961a), the attack came immediately after the defense; in McGuire and Papageorgis (1961), 2 days intervened; and in Papageorgis and McGuire (1961), the interval was 1 week. Hence, it is possible to make a crude test of the three temporal-trend hypotheses by cross-experimental comparisons. The results based on such cross-experimental comparisons are depicted in Figure 1a and can be seen to be in accord with each of the three hypotheses. This confirmation of the predictions cannot be regarded as definitive since extraneous conditions varied somewhat from experiment to experiment. For example, the issues, defensive and attacking messages, and types of subjects all differed somewhat among the experiments. The confirmations are sufficiently clear, however, that we were encouraged to vary systematically the time intervals within the present experimental design over comparable magnitudes.

METHOD

Procedure. The study was represented to the subjects as an investigation of personality correlates of verbal skills, a deception that was bolstered by several tasks the subjects were called upon to perform during the experimental sessions. Each of the 160 subjects took part in two experimental sessions. During the first they received 600-word mimeographed messages defending their initial beliefs on medical truisms such as "Everyone should visit his doctor at least once a year for a routine physical check up." The subject was told that he would be scored on his ability to analyze such technical passages and he was given 4 minutes to read and, in each paragraph, underline the shortest clause that summarized the main point being made in the paragraph. This underlining task was introduced to encourage careful reading and to disguise the persuasive purpose of the messages. He was then given various personality tests, not relevant to the hypotheses under discussion, to disguise further the persuasive intent of the study.

The second session came either 2 days (for 80 subjects) or 7 days (for the other 80) later. In the second session, each subject received further defen-

sive messages on additional medical truisms and then, within the same booklet, additional messages attacking the previously defended truisms and, in control conditions described under Design, previously undefended truisms as well. As in the first session, the subject was given 4 minutes to read and underline the crucial clauses in each of these defensive and attacking messages. Another personality questionnaire was then administered and then the subject was asked to fill out an opinion questionnaire indicating his own beliefs on the medical issues dealt with in the messages, on the pretext that we wished to check on whether the subject's personal opinions on the topics discussed in the passages affected his ability to read these passages analytically. The subjects then filled out a questionnaire designed to ascertain the extent to which the desired experimental conditions obtained,[2] after which the true nature of the experiment and the nature of and reasons for the deceptions were explained to the subject.

Defensive and attacking messages. Two types of defensive messages were employed. The "supportive" defense had an introductory paragraph mentioning that the truism in question was obviously valid but that it was wise to consider some of the reasons why it was indeed valid. Two arguments in support of the belief were then mentioned. There followed two paragraphs each developing in a calm, factual way one of the two supportive arguments. These supportive messages avoided any mention of possible counterarguments against the truism.

The "refutational" defenses began with a similar introductory paragraph mentioning that the truism was obviously valid but that, since occasionally one heard misguided counterarguments attacking it, it was wise to consider some of these counterarguments and show wherein they erred. Two counterarguments against the truism were then mentioned. The following two paragraphs each refuted in a calm, factual way one of these counterarguments. These refutational messages avoided mention of arguments directly

---

[2] This Critique of the Experiment final questionnaire was designed to measure the adequacy of the time allowances, how much the subject had heard of the experiment in advance and whether he suspected its persuasive intent. About 20% of the subjects complained that some section of the test had been given either a too long or a too short time allowance; more than half the complaints were that the time allowed for the noncrucial personality test was too short. The subjects were indeed rushed through this section to keep the session down to 50 minutes. A surprising number admitted having heard something about the experiment in advance, despite our request to the subjects that they refrain from discussing it with anyone until the end of the experimental period. Hearing that the test involved a reading comprehension test or that it dealt with medical topics was admitted by 31 out of the 160 subjects. In addition, 4 heard that one's opinions were measured. When called upon to suggest what else—besides verbal skills—the experiment could have measured, only 5 suggested any purpose having to do with opinion change, persuasion, or propaganda.

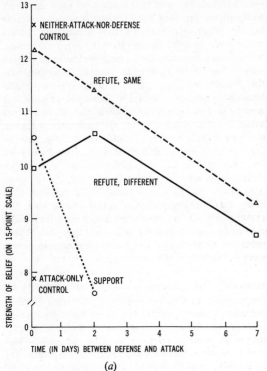

(a)

form using a different pair of supportive arguments. Hence, 24 messages in all were employed in the present study, 6 on each of four issues.[3]

Opinion questionnaire. Beliefs on the four issues were measured by a 17-item opinion questionnaire. Each item consisted of an assertion on one of the issues (e.g., "Everyone should brush his teeth after every

FIGURE 1. Persistence of the resistance to persuasion conferred by three types of prior defense: supportive, refutation of the same counterarguments as used in the attack, and refutation of counterarguments different from those used in the attack. (*a*) Based on data from previous experiments. (Zero interval points are based on data from McGuire, 1961a; 2-day interval points, on McGuire and Papageorgis, 1961, and McGuire, 1961b; and 7-day points, on Papageorgis and McGuire, 1961.) (*b*) Based on data from the present experiment as shown in Table 1.

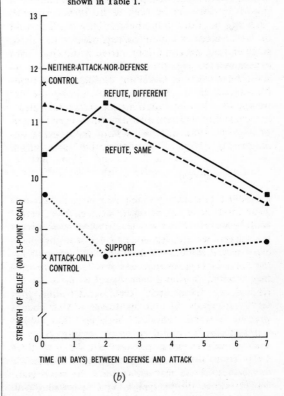

(b)

supporting the truism—they merely refuted counterarguments against it.

The attacking messages were similar in format to the defensive, each being about 600 words in length and divided into three paragraphs. The introductory paragraphs stated that most laymen would be surprised to learn that advanced medical and scientific work was beginning to cast some doubt on the validity of the truism in question and, hence, it would be wise to ponder some of these recently discovered counterarguments against the belief, two of which were then mentioned. Each of the following two paragraphs expounded in a calm, factual manner the validity of one of these counterarguments. When the attacking message followed a refutation defense, one of two alternatives was used. Half of the subjects received attacks employing the very counterarguments refuted; the other half of the subjects received attacks employing novel counterarguments, different from those previously refuted.

Since the experimental design called for each subject's serving in four different defensive conditions, it was necessary to prepare supportive defense, refutational defense, and attacking messages on four different truisms. Furthermore, since half the refutational defenses had to be followed by attacks employing the same counterarguments as refuted and half by novel counterarguments, it was necessary to prepare two alternative forms of the refutational defense message and of the attacking messages on each issue, each dealing with a different pair of counterarguments. For symmetry of design, we prepared alternative forms of the supportive defense on each issue, each

[3] All 24 of the defensive and attacking messages used in this study have been deposited with the American Documentation Institute. Order Document No. 7058 from ADI Auxiliary Publications Project, Photoduplication Service, Library of Congress; Washington 25, D. C., remitting in advance $2.25 for microfilm or $5.00 for photocopies. Make checks payable to: Chief, Photoduplication Service, Library of Congress.

meal if at all possible.") followed by a graphic scale containing 15 numbered categories with Definitely False at one end and Definitely True at the other. The subject was told to make an "X" in whichever of the categories best indicated his own agreement with the statement. There were four items on each issue.[4] The scores cited in the Results section and in Table 1 are based on the mean of the four items on each issue, with the possible range going from 1.00, for complete rejection of the truism, to 15.00 for complete agreement therewith. One of the 17 items was a repeat to serve as a reliability check. The two responses to this repeated item yielded an intrasubject correlation of .82.

Experimental design. The design included four blocks of subjects. The subjects in the first block received refutational defenses on all four issues. They received such defenses on two issues in a first session 2 days previous to the attack; and the defenses on the other two issues at the second session immediately before the attack. In each session the defense on one issue involved refutations of the same counterarguments as would be used in the attack, and on the other issue, the refutation of alternative counterarguments to those that would be used in the attack. The subjects in the second block received the same treatments as those in the first block, except that for them the first session preceded the attacks by 1 week rather than 2 days.

The subjects in the third block received defenses on only two issues. Both of these were supportive defenses, one coming in the first session 2 days before the attack and one in the second session just before the attack. As regards the other two undefended issues, one was attacked in the second session to ascertain the impact of the attacks in the absence of any prior defense and one was not attacked to obtain an estimate of the initial belief levels in the absence of both defense and attack. The subjects in the fourth block received the same treatments as those in the third, except that for them the first session preceded the attacks by 1 week rather than 2 days.

Since there were four issues and two alternative sets of materials on each issue, eight subconditions were necessary in each block to allow the materials to be systematically rotated around the four treatment conditions. Five subjects served in each of these eight "materials" subconditions, so that 40 subjects served in each of the four blocks.[5]

The purpose of this rather complex design was to allow more sensitive tests of the theoretically relevant

[4] This opinion questionnaire has been deposited with ADI and can be obtained by writing for the document mentioned in Footnote 3.
[5] The design of the present study is described in detail in Table A of the ADI document mentioned in Footnote 3.

and likely-to-be-small treatment effects. Thus, all comparisons between refutational defenses, for example, those predicted in the second and third hypotheses, involve intrasubject analyses. Likewise, comparisons between the supportive defense (which usually has the smallest effect—see for example, McGuire & Papageorgis, 1961) and no defense conditions also involve sensitive intrasubject analyses. It is true that comparisons between the refutation defenses on the one hand and the supportive defense, or the no defense control conditions involve across-subject comparisons, but such variations have been demonstrated in previous studies to produce sizable differentials.

The complexity of the design did necessitate the computation of several different error terms to evaluate the differential effects presented in the Results section below. In general, the error terms are based on the residual variance in the conditions being compared. The individual differences variance was removed when the comparison involved repeated measures on the same subject, for example, the effects of refutation of same vs. alternative counterarguments; or an interaction effect between type of defense and time of attack; or the effect of a supportive defense vs. no defense. When the comparison was between a refutational defense and a supportive or a no defense condition, the large between-subject residual variance, including individual differences among the subjects, was used as the error term.

Subjects. All 160 subjects were selected from a pool of students enrolled in the introductory psychology course at the University of Illinois. Among those who indicated at the beginning of the semester that they were regularly available on the days and hours chosen for running the experiment, the selection was random. About 75% of the 220 subjects requested to appear actually participated in the experiment and the data reported below are based on the first 160 of those who appeared for both sessions. The majority were sophomores and about 55% were females.

RESULTS AND DISCUSSION

General effects. The two control conditions set the probable limits within which the differential immunization effects can take place. The mean belief level in the neither-attack-nor-defense control condition is 11.74 on the 15-point scale, and can be taken as an estimate of the initial belief level on the four truisms. Actually the estimate is probably conservative, since it is based on the indicated belief on an issue unmentioned in the messages, but taken after the receipt of messages strongly attacking three other truisms and, hence, may reflect a general wariness on the part of the subject (see McGuire & Papageorgis, 1961, and Papageorgis & McGuire, 1961, for data on the accuracy with which such postcommunication beliefs on control, unmentioned issues estimate the initial level of the beliefs). The mean belief level in the other control condition (attack-only) is 8.49, indicating that in the absence of any defense, the attacks were effective in reducing the beliefs 3.25 points on the 15-point scale ($p < .001$). The overall belief level in all three defense-and-attack conditions at all three time intervals is 10.17, which is almost exactly midway between the neither-attack-nor-defense and the attack-only means and significantly ($p < .01$) different from either. Furthermore, the means in all nine defense-and-attack conditions (see Table 1) do lie between the two means of the neither-attack-nor-defense and attack-only conditions.

Relative persistence after supportive and refutational defenses. The supportive defenses conferred less resistance to the attack than did the refutational defenses regardless of whether the attack came immediately, 2 days, or 1 week after the attack. When the attack followed immediately, the superiority of the combined refutational defense conditions to the supportive was significant at the .01 level, but this superiority was primarily due to the conditions in which the very counter-arguments used in the attack were refuted: the superiority over the supportive reached only the .20 level of significance when counter-arguments alternative to those used in the immediate attack were refuted.

Where 2 days intervened between the attack and defense, this superiority of the combined refutational to the supportive defense became even more pronounced ($p < .001$). Whereas the immediate resistance conferred by the supportive defense had decayed ($p < .05$) almost completely after the 2-day interval, that conferred by the refutational defense actually showed a trivial gain from the immediate to the 2-day interval. As can be seen in Table 2, this gain yielded an F of only 1.05. This interaction effect between the supportive vs. refutation type-of-defense variable and the immediate vs. 2-day interval variable is significant at the .01 level and confirms the first

hypothesis. It will be noted that this interaction effect is in the opposite direction to that to be expected on the basis of a simple regression effect: the resistance conferred by the supportive defense is not only less to immediate attacks, but such as it is, it also decays more rapidly than the greater immediate resistance conferred by the refutation.

There is an alternative theoretical interpretation of this superior persistence of the immunity conferred by the refutational defense, an explanation related to the "sleeper effect" described by Hovland and his colleagues (Hovland, Lumsdaine, & Sheffield, 1949, Ch. 7; Hovland & Weiss, 1951; Kelman & Hovland, 1953). According to these theorists, if a persuasive message is initially accompanied by a discounting cue, its opinion change impact might actually increase with time passage, or at least decline relatively slowly (Weiss, 1953) as compared with a message not so accompanied. The recall of the persuasive content does, of course, decay over time but so does the recall of the discounting cue, thus, reducing or even reversing the net decay of induced opinion change. In the present situation the refutational defense could be interpreted as containing a discounting cue, namely, mention of the refuted counterarguments, the forgetting of which dampens the decay of the initially induced opinion change. The supportive defense contains no such incidental discounting cue, so that its greatest impact should be felt immediately and decay thereafter without any mitigating effect of a simultaneously decaying discounting factor. Some credence is given to this interpretation by the results of an earlier study (McGuire & Papageorgis, 1961) indicating that the direct strengthening effect prior to any attack was somewhat greater ($.05 < p < .10$) with the supportive than the

---

TABLE 1   *Persistence of the Resistance to Persuasion Conferred by Three Types of Prior Belief Defense*

INTERVAL BETWEEN DEFENSE AND ATTACK	TYPE OF DEFENSE WHICH PRECEDED THE ATTACK			ATTACK WITHOUT PRIOR DEFENSE	NEITHER ATTACK NOR DEFENSE
	Supportive Arguments	Refutation of Counterarguments Used in the Attacks	Refutation of Alternative Counterarguments		
Immediate	9.71 (80)*	11.36 (80)	10.41 (80)		
Two days	8.51 (40)	11.08 (40)	11.45 (40)	8.49 (80)	11.74 (80)
Seven days	8.82 (40)	9.49 (40)	9.68 (40)		

Note.—Scores in the cells are final belief levels on the Truisms as measured on a 15-point scale. * Numbers in parentheses indicate the number of individual scores on which the cell mean is based.

refutational defense, even though the latter conferred more resistance ($p < .01$) to an attack 2 days later.

Relative resistance after refutation of same and of alternate counterarguments. As can be seen in Figure 1b, the resistance conferred by the refutational-same defense, i.e., the defense involving prior refutation of the very counterarguments to be used in the attack, declines monotonically as the interval between defense and attack increases. The decline from the immediate to the 2-day interval is not significant but that from 2 days to 1 week is significant on the .01 level. A quite different, nonmonotonic time trend can be seen with the refutational-different defense, i.e., the defense involving prior refutation of counterarguments different from the ones that are actually to be used in the attack on the given belief. Although this type of defense was inferior ($p < .05$) to the refutation-same defense in conferring resistance to the immediate attack, it has become trivially superior when the attacks do not come until 2 days later (see Table 2). The interaction effect between this same vs. different refutational-defense variable and the immediate vs. 2-day interval variable appears on all four issues in-

dividually, and the effect combined over issues is significant above the .05 level. Hence, the second hypothesis—that the decay of the resistance conferred against attacks by different counterarguments will be slower than that to attacks by the same counterarguments as had been refuted—is confirmed. As can be seen in Figure 1b, there is actually greater resistance in the "different" refutation condition than in the "same" at both the 2- and 7-day intervals, which is embarrassingly more than the theory demands but this differential is trivial in magnitude.

The results also corroborate the third hypothesis, regarding a delayed-action effect in the resistance conferred by refutation of counterarguments different from those used in the attack. As can be seen in Table 2, the resistance conferred by this type of defense is greater against an attack 2 days later than against an immediate attack on all four issues individually, as well as in the combined results ($p < .05$).

In general, the results from this experiment agree closely with the cross-experimental comparisons from the previous studies in the introductory section. As can be seen from a comparison of Figures 1a and 1b, the two sets of curves are quite similar in shape and even as regards absolute parameters, except that in the present experiment, the refutational-different defense tends to be somewhat more effective than in the previous experiments. The general implication of the

TABLE 2 *Mean Belief Scores (on a 15-point Scale) and Analysis of Variance in the Conditions Involving Attacks by the Same or by Novel Counterarguments Immediately after and Two Days after the Refutation Defenses, with Issue-by-Issue Submeans*

ISSUES	REFUTATIONAL-SAME DEFENSE		REFUTATIONAL-DIFFERENT DEFENSE		ALL TREATMENTS
	Immediate Attack	Attack after 2 Days	Immediate Attack	Attack after 2 Days	
Chest X ray	10.10	8.50	8.96	9.92	9.42
Penicillin	12.59	12.95	11.92	12.48	12.41
Toothbrushing	10.35	9.92	9.84	10.78	10.18
Annual physical	12.41	12.92	10.92	12.62	12.04
All issues	11.36	11.08	10.41	11.45	11.01

SOURCE	SS	df	MS	F
Type defense (refutational-same vs. refutational-different)	248	1	248	2.19
Time (immediate attack vs. 2 days)	119	1	119	1.05
Type × time	552	1	552	4.88*
Issues	5,965	3	1,988	17.59†
Issues × treatments	517	9	57	0.50
Subject	17,755	79	225	1.99
Residual	16,425	145	113	
Total	41,581	239		

* $p < .05$. † $p < .001$.

study, particularly when considered in the context of the previous studies in this series, is to corroborate further the initial postulate: that the supportive defense confers resistance to persuasion only in so far as the material presented is assimilated and retained—an activity that the subject is little motivated to carry out in the case of a "truism." The resistance conferred by the refutational defense, on the other hand, derives not only from the assimilation and retention of the bolstering material actually presented but also from the motivational effect of the pre-exposure to threatening material, the mention of the counterarguments, contained in the refutational defense. If this interpretation is correct, then the temporal differentials found among the defenses in this study should be reduced as we move from the truisms used in this study, with respect to which the defense stimulating threat is particularly necessary and possible, to beliefs on more controversial issues. The results do seem fairly general as regards truisms, as can be seen in the trivial magnitude of the Issues × Treatments interaction effects (see Table 2).

SUMMARY

Theoretical considerations like those which led to the predictions tested in the previous studies of this series on immunizing beliefs against persuasion yielded several hypotheses regarding differential persistence of the immunity conferred by various types of prior belief-defenses. First, it was predicted that the immunity conferred by refutational defenses would decay less rapidly than that conferred by the supportive defenses. Secondly, within the refutational-defense conditions, it was predicted that the conferred resistance to attacks by counterarguments other than the explicitly refuted ones would decay less rapidly than resistance to attacks by the very counterarguments refuted. A related third prediction was that there would be a delayed action effect in the immunity to attacks by novel counterarguments conferred by the refutational defense.

Each of the 160 college students subjects served in two experimental sessions. The first involved reading defensive articles on medical truisms. The defenses involved either arguments supporting the truism, or refutations of counterarguments against

the truism, either the very counterarguments to be used in the later attack or alternative counterarguments. The second session came either 2 days (for 80 subjects) or 7 days (for the other 80) after the first, and involved a second defensive treatment on another truism and then attacks on the previously defended and undefended truisms. The subjects' beliefs on all the truisms were then measured. All three hypotheses received substantial confirmation.

REFERENCES

HOVLAND, C. I., LUMSDAINE, A. A., & SHEFFIELD, F. *Experiments on mass communication.* Princeton: Princeton Univer. Press, 1949.

HOVLAND, C. I., & WEISS, W. The influence of source credibility on communication effectiveness. *Publ. opin. Quart.,* 1951, 15, 635–650.

KELMAN, H., & HOVLAND, C. I. "Reinstatement" of the communicator in delayed measurement of opinion change. *J. abnorm. soc. Psychol.,* 1953, 48, 327–335.

MCGUIRE, W. J. The effectiveness of supportive and refutational defenses in immunizing and restoring beliefs against persuasion. *Sociometry,* 1961, 24, 184–197. (a)

MCGUIRE, W. J. Resistance to persuasion conferred by active and passive prior refutation of the same and alternative counterarguments. *J. abnorm. soc. Psychol.,* 1961, 63, 326–332. (b)

MCGUIRE, W. J., & PAPAGEORGIS, D. The relative efficacy of various types of prior belief-defense in producing immunity against persuasion. *J. abnorm. soc. Psychol.,* 1961, 62, 327–337.

PAPAGEORGIS, D., & MCGUIRE, W. J. The generality of immunity to persuasion produced by pre-exposure to weakened counterarguments. *J. abnorm. soc. Psychol.,* 1961, 62, 475–481.

WEISS, W. A "sleeper" effect in opinion change. *J. abnorm. soc. Psychol.,* 1953, 48, 173–180.

COGNITIVE BALANCING AS A DEFENSIVE PROCESS *

Several forms of attitudinal consistency have been illustrated in the previous selections. Abelson's analysis, offered here, conceives of balance among cognitive and affective elements in more formal

* The selection following the editorial introduction is reprinted from "Modes of resolution of belief dilemmas," *Journal of Conflict Resolution,* 1959, 3, 343–352, by permission of the author and publisher.

terms. The manner in which states of imbalance among the properties of the system may be changed in order to restore balance is analyzed. Formal theoretical statements of this kind have great value. They lead to more precise hypotheses, to a clearer specification of experimental operations, and to the identification of apparent inconsistencies in concepts or principles. The conceptual system described here can be used to represent the types of defensive processes used by the individual to resist persuasive communications. These communications create imbalance which may be resolved in several different ways without accepting the communication.

18.

Modes of Resolution of Belief Dilemmas[1]

ROBERT P. ABELSON
YALE UNIVERSITY

INTRODUCTION

This is a paper about intrapersonal conflict resolution. We first identify the kind of conflict to be considered. There are two levels of analysis of intrapersonal conflict: the action level and the belief level, the former dealing with external motor responses and the latter with internal affective and cognitive processes. Particular instances of conflict may, for theoretical convenience, be localized at one or another of these levels. For example, one may ask how a person acts when simultaneously motivated to approach and to avoid an external object (3, 9, 10). Or one may ask instead what happens to the cognitive representation of an external object when the object simultaneously incurs favorable and unfavorable cognitions (12). The present paper is addressed to the latter type of question. We shall not consider the problem of whether and how the action level is to be reduced to the belief level or vice versa. We only consider conflicts between one belief and another or, more generally, conflicts within a belief structure. The term "belief dilemma" is intended to enforce the distinction between the variety of conflict here considered and conflict in general.

BELIEF DILEMMAS

The model of cognitive structure to be described is similar at various points to other recent models (6, 8, 13).

First, we imagine a cognitive representation, a "cognitive element," corresponding to any attitude object. Associated with such a cognitive element is a numerical value, positive if the object is liked, negative if the object is disliked. Next, we suppose that between each pair of cognitive elements there may exist some kind of perceived relation. Assigned to each relation is another numerical value, positive if the relation

is "associative," negative if the relation is "dissociative" (11). Examples of associative relations are: is, has, includes, likes, helps, produces, implies. Examples of dissociative relations are: avoids, hates, hinders, defeats, destroys, is incompatible with. A zero value indicates a null, or irrelevant, relation.

Given an attitude issue or "conceptual arena" (1), a certain set of cognitive elements would be relevant for a given individual. The set of relevant elements and the particular relations among them define the *content* of the individual's belief system on the issue. The form, or *structure*, of belief may be expressed independently of the content according to the array of numerical affect values and relation values defined above.

A belief structure may or may not contain inconsistencies. By inconsistency is meant not logical inconsistency but psychological inconsistency, or, as it has been variously referred to, imbalance (7), incongruity (12, 13), or dissonance (5). We shall use the term "imbalance."

Heider (7), Festinger (5), and Osgood and Tannenbaum (12) have all postulated a motivation for the reduction of imbalance. There is said to be a tendency, a pressure, toward the attainment of cognitive balance. An essential qualification to this postulate has been pointed out by Abelson and Rosenberg (1). There are innumerable inconsistencies in anyone's belief system which may lie dormant and unthought about. Pressure toward cognitive balance, if always operative on all cognitive elements, would produce much more balance in belief systems than one finds empirically. It is much more plausible to assume that this pressure operates only when the issue is salient; that is, when the issue is being "thought about," or, if this is too rational a terminology, when "cognitive work" is applied on the issue. General methods for identifying the presence of imbalance in a structure of any size have been given elsewhere (1, 4). Here we confine our analysis to a simple case of imbalance: two elements and the relation between them.

There are six possible cases to be considered: two positively valued objects, related associatively or related dissociatively; one positively valued object and one negatively valued object, related dissociatively or related associatively; and two negatively valued objects, related associatively or related dissociatively. In each of these three pairs of cases, the first possibility is balanced, the second one is imbalanced. This may be clarified by reference to Figure 1.

An imbalanced dyad will be said to constitute a belief dilemma when the intensity of affect toward the objects is strong and when the dyad is often salient (i.e., often present in thought).

MODES OF RESOLUTION

Four possible modes of resolution are specified below. Each can manifest itself in several ways.

[1] This paper was written at the Center for Advanced Study in the Behavioral Sciences.

The modes are labeled: (*a*) denial, (*b*) bolstering, (*c*) differentiation, and (*d*) transcendence.

Denial refers to a direct attack upon one or both of the cognitive elements or the relation between them. The value felt toward the object, whether positive or negative, is denied, or the opposite is asserted; or the sign of the relation between the elements is explained away, or the opposite is asserted. Examples are: the man on a diet professing that he never liked rich foods anyway, the groom convincing himself of his avid belief in his bride's religion, John Calvin interpreting the scriptures to show that Christ never really condemned usury. If an attempt at denial is successful, it will convert an imbalanced structure into a balanced one. However, denial attempts may run into various difficulties, as, for example, when the denial is too great a distortion of reality or conflicts with other elements in the larger belief system. For example, the Boston colonists faced in 1773 with the odious taxation on tea went so far as to vote that "it is the sense of this Body that the use of tea is improper and pernicious." It is unlikely that this denial of the desirability of tea, albeit effective in encouraging group action, was effective in suppressing the taste for tea of the individuals concerned.

The mechanism called "bolstering" consists of relating one or the other of the two cognitive objects in a balanced way to other valued objects (Fig. 2), thereby minimizing the relative imbalance in the structure. This mechanism plays an important part in Festinger's theory of cognitive dissonance (5). He points out many situations in which the introduction of new cognitive elements is useful in reducing dissonance. This is a mechanism not for eliminating imbalance entirely but only for drowning it out, so to speak. Examples are: the smoker who is worried about lung cancer telling himself that smoking is extremely enjoyable, good for his nerves, and socially necessary; and the proponent of a large standing army, unwelcome in peacetime, claiming that it is good character training for the nation's youth. The mechanism of bolstering may be used in conjunction with the mechanism of denial. For example, in the example of the large standing army the advocate might also say that the large standing army was not contrary to peaceful purposes; in fact, it aided the cause of peace to have a large standing army.

The two mechanisms listed thus far have the property that they preserve the identity of the cognitive elements. The meaning of the attitude objects remains the same even though attitude toward the objects may be weakened by denial or strengthened by bolstering. Another mode of resolution arises if we consider the possibility of differentiation of the cognitive elements. An element may be split into two parts with a strong dissociative relation between the parts. To see how this mechanism might restore cognitive balance, consider the issue of hydrogen-bomb testing.

For many people, continued hydrogen-bomb testing is positively valued, but poisoning of the atmosphere is negatively valued. These two cognitive objects are associatively related—there is a causal connection of some degree. This dyad is therefore imbalanced. But there is bomb testing and there is bomb testing: one might differentiate this attitude object into two—testing "dirty bombs" and testing "clean bombs." It is only the testing of dirty bombs that contributes to poisoning of the atmosphere; the testing of clean bombs presumably does not. Thus the imbalance is resolved. To take another example, the facts of evolution, positively valued, are contradictory to the Bible which is also positively valued. But there are two Bibles: the Bible as literally interpreted and the Bible as figuratively interpreted. The Bible as figuratively interpreted is not contradictory to the facts of evolution but may be seen as concordant with them. In a third example, from an experiment by Asch (2), subjects who feel unfavorable toward "politicians" are confronted with a highly prestigeful source who glorifies the political profession. Many subjects get off the hook by differentiating statesmen (good

FIGURE 1. Cognitive structures with two elements and one relation. An unbroken line symbolizes an associative (positive) relation; a broken line a dissociative (negative) relation. The mechanism of denial aims toward the conversion of a structure on the right into one on the left, either through change of affect toward the element ("denial of the element") or change in the sign of the relation ("denial of the relation").

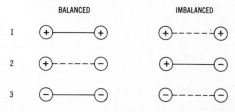

BALANCED   IMBALANCED

FIGURE 2. The mechanism of bolstering in reducing cognitive imbalance. In the bolstered structure (right) the units *AC, AD, . . .* are all balanced. The relative effect of the imbalanced unit *AB* is thus reduced.

ORIGINAL STRUCTURE   BOLSTERED STRUCTURE

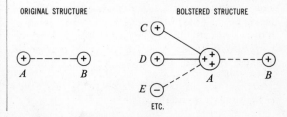

politicians) from wardheelers (bad politicians). In these examples one element is differentiated into two parts, a new part and an old part. The old part retains the relation with the other element in the structure, but the affect toward it is changed. The new part, on the other hand, retains the old affect toward the differentiated element, but the sign of the relation with the other element is changed. These changes are reviewed in Figure 3.

It is interesting to note the large number of dimensions along which objects can be differentiated. They may be differentiated according to the internal content of the object, the object as viewed in a social context versus a personal context, the object as it is versus as it should be, the object as it is versus the object as it will be, etc.

The mechanism of transcendence is in a sense obverse to the mechanism of differentiation. Elements, instead of being split down, are built up and combined into larger units organized on a

FIGURE 3. The mechanism of differentiation in restoring cognitive balance.

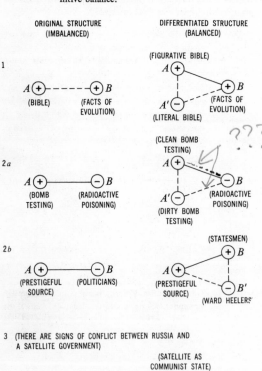

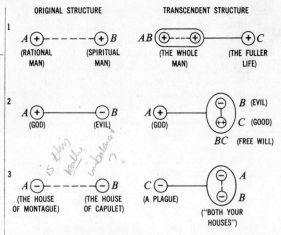

FIGURE 4. The mechanism of transcendence in restoring cognitive balance.

superordinate level, as indicated in Figure 4. For example, the dilemma pitting science against religion is transcended by the consideration that both the rational man and the spiritual man must be jointly cultivated to reach a fuller life or a better society or a deeper understanding of the universe. Thus the dilemma is transcended by imbedding the conflicting parts in a new concept instrumental to some higher purpose. The theosophical dilemma of God's presumed permissiveness toward evil is sometimes resolved by appeal to transcendent concepts. In the intriguing case study (6) of a group of individuals who prepared for a cataclysm that never occurred, it is reported that the group leader offered a transcendent resolution for the belief crisis: the cataclysm was said to have been stayed by God because of the group's devotion.

CHOICE AMONG THE MODES OF RESOLUTION

Presumably, the individual with an imbalanced cognition will strive to choose among the various modes of resolution. Imbalanced structure would then be under a variety of pressures to change. The theoretical specification of which particular changes are likely to take place is a complex problem. Several working propositions are sketched here. A more rigorous theory is in the process of development.

Proposition 1. There will be a hierarchy of resolution attempts in general proceeding in the following order: denial, bolstering, denial, differentiation, and transcendence.

The hierarchy of resolution attempts is based upon the relative ease of achieving success with each of the methods. The reason denial appears twice in the listing is that there are usually two points in the process at which denial may enter. If we consider the situation in which imbalance is introduced by forced or accidental exposure to propaganda or opinions seeking to establish new cognitive relations or to contradict previously held affect values, a first opportunity for denial may arise by a rejection of the relevance of the new material. If the initial denial fails, bolstering will be attempted and then another attempt at denial, this time buttressed by further thought about the issue. The presumption here is that denial and bolstering are simpler cognitive mechanisms than differentiation and transcendence, although they are not necessarily more effective in reducing cognitive imbalance. Differentiation is difficult because it requires intellectual ability, flexibility, and because, when there is strong affect toward a cognitive object, it is not easily split apart. Transcendence is presumably still more difficult, for it requires the existence of a compelling superordinate structure in which a given imbalance may be imbedded.

Proposition 2. When two cognitive elements stand in imbalanced relation to each other and the affect toward one is more intense than toward the other, the tendency will be to apply bolstering toward the more intensely affected element and/or denial toward (*a*) the less intensely affected element and/or (*b*) the relation between the elements.

Proposition 2a. The probability that an attempt will be made to bolster an element is high if other elements relevant to it are strong and stand in balanced relation to it (Fig. 2) and is low if other relevant elements are weak or stand in imbalanced relation to it.

Corollary. Elements for which the individual's affect is intensely socially supported are readily subject to bolstering attempts when caught in a strong dilemma.

Proposition 2b. The probability that an attempt will be made to deny an element is high if other relevant elements are strong and stand in imbalanced relation to it and is low if other relevant elements are weak or stand in balanced relation to it.

Corollary. Elements with which considerable shame or guilt is associated (e.g., elements connoting the overindulgence of appetites) are readily subject to denial attempts when caught in a strong dilemma (i.e., when firmly related in imbalanced fashion to a strongly affected element). See Example 1.

Proposition 2c. Relations between cognitive elements are readily denied when the external evidence for the relation is remote, ambiguous, under suspicion of bias, or dependent upon specific circumstances which can readily be perceived as inapplicable in general.

Proposition 2d. A relation between cognitive elements *A* and *B* is readily subject to denial attempts when there is available an element *A'*, formally similar to *A* and standing in associative relation with it, such that *the relation between A' and B is of opposite sign as between A and B, and is stronger.*

Proposition 2e. A relation between cognitive elements *A* and *B* is readily subject to denial attempts when there is available an element *A'*, formally similar to *A*, yet standing psychologically in dissociative relation to *A*, such that *the relation between A' and B is of the same sign as between A and B, but stronger* (the "mote-beam" technique).
   See Example 2 (from the point of view of a liberal but very proud southerner).

Proposition 3. If the affects toward two cognitive elements which stand in imbalanced relation to each other are nearly equal and the resolutions suggested in Proposition 2 fail, the converse resolutions will be attempted; that is, there will be attempts to bolster the less intense element and/or to deny the more intense element.

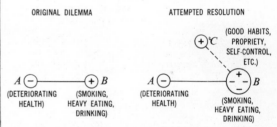

NOTE:—THE ELEMENT *C* MUST BE COMPELLING FOR THE RESOLUTION TO BE STABLE. IF ORIGINAL POSITIVE AFFECT TOWARD *B* IS STRONG, THE STABILITY OF THE ATTEMPTED RESOLUTION IS JEOPARDIZED.

EXAMPLE 1

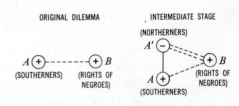

EXAMPLE 2

Proposition 4. The classical relationship between the intensity and extremity of attitude may be explained in terms of a succession of dilemma resolutions in individual histories with the attitude object.

Explanation. The mechanism of bolstering used in the service of dilemma resolution increases the intensity of affect toward the object. An object which has been repeatedly bolstered is therefore the object of an intense attitude. But repeated bolstering also increases the extremity of attitude. In bolstering, the attitude object is connected with other objects. New reasons and supports are given for it; it is seen to be instrumental to other values; it is seen to be supported by various people and groups. In short, it is imbedded in a cognitive system of ever widening circumference. If scope of cognitive support is equated with extremity of attitude, then the relationship between extremity and intensity follows.

Those individuals who do not invoke bolstering will in general be the ones with moderate attitudes of low intensity.

IMBALANCED STRUCTURE

BOLSTERING ATTEMPT

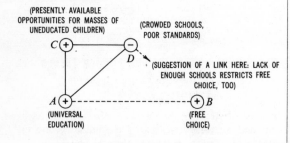

DIFFERENTIATED STRUCTURE

(ELEMENTS *A* AND *D* HAVE BECOME DIFFERENTIATED)

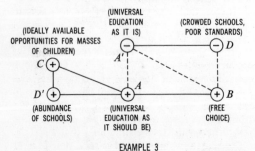

EXAMPLE 3

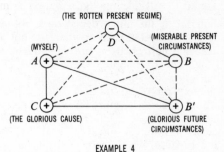

EXAMPLE 4

Proposition 5. If, in the search for new elements to bolster an original element in imbalance, further imbalance is created (usually because the new elements are imbalanced with each other), differentiation of the original element is encouraged.

See Example 3 (it is pointed out to an individual that universal public school education, by being compulsory, violates the democratic ideal of individual free choice—some parents might want to keep children out of school).

Proposition 6. When an element is differentiated it is crucial to the maintenance of the resolution that the old part and the new part of the element be strongly dissociated.

Proposition 7. Transcendent resolutions are likely to be invoked only in the case of chronically insoluble dilemmas. However, once a transcendent resolution is achieved, it may be found applicable to a variety of dilemmas.

Proposition 8. Mass propaganda efforts seek dilemma resolutions effective for a large number of people simultaneously.

See Example 4 (a nation in a period of hard times).

Revolutionary propaganda aims to bolster *A* and differentiate *B* along a time dimension. The dissociated parts of *B* are each doubly bolstered, as follows:

(*English translation:* "You are now part of the glorious Cause. Reject with us your miserable present circumstances. Look forward to the glorious future when all will be different. The rotten present regime despises you and is responsible for your misery. The Cause will attack the regime and lead you to the glorious future. The regime will try to prevent this but we shall triumph.")

Explicit in this analysis is the reason revolutionists should be so concerned over public apathy.

Those "Indifferents" who are not dissatisfied with their present circumstances have no dilemma to resolve, and consequently the propaganda does not "take" (unless the Indifferents can be convinced that their situation is indeed grim).

REFERENCES

1. ABELSON, R. P., & ROSENBERG, M. J. "Symbolic Psychologic: A Model of Attitudinal Cognition." *Behavioral Science*, III (1958), 1–13.
2. ASCH, S. E. "Studies in the Principles of Judgments and Attitudes: II. Determination of Judgments by Group and Ego Standards." *Journal of Social Psychology*, XII (1940), 433–65.
3. BROWN, J. S. "Principles of Intrapersonal Conflict. *Conflict Resolution*, I (1957), 135–54.
4. CARTWRIGHT, D., & HARARY, F. "Structural Balance: A Generalization of Heider's Theory," *Psychological Review*, LXIII (1956), 277–93.
5. FESTINGER, L. *Theory of Cognitive Dissonance*. Evanston, Ill.: Row, Peterson & Co., 1957.
6. FESTINGER, L., RIECKEN, H., & SCHACHTER, S. *When Prophecy Fails*. Minneapolis: University of Minnesota Press, 1956.

7. HEIDER, F. "Attitudes and Cognitive Organization." *Journal of Psychology*, XXI (1946), 107–12.
8. HEIDER, F. *The Psychology of Interpersonal Relations*. New York: John Wiley & Sons, 1958.
9. LEWIN, K. "Environmental Forces in Child Behavior and Development." In C. Murchison (ed.), *A Handbook of Child Psychology*. Worcester, Mass.: Clark University Press, 1931.
10. MILLER, N. "Experimental Studies of Conflict." In J. McV. Hunt, (ed.), *Personality and the Behavior Disorders*. New York: Ronald Press Co., 1944.
11. OSGOOD, C. E., SAPORTA, S., and NUNNALLY, J. C. "Evaluative Assertion Analysis." *Litera*, III (1956), 47–102.
12. OSGOOD, C. E., and TANNENBAUM, P. H. "The Principle of Congruity in the Prediction of Attitude Change." *Psychological Review*, LXII (1955), 42–55.
13. OSGOOD, C. E., SUCI, G. T., and TANNENBAUM, P. H. *The Measurement of Meaning*. Urbana: University of Illinois Press, 1957.

ATTITUDE CHANGE AND THE PSYCHOLOGICAL SITUATION *

Laboratory experiments on attitude change are usually restricted to relatively brief situations and ordinarily those changes that are induced are assessed only within a relatively short period of time. Such experiments are unlikely to identify all of the particular conditions that create permanent changes in attitudes or behavior.

The first step toward acquiring such information is a careful analysis of the psychological consequences of a change in behavior or attitude. In the selection to follow, Kelman analyzes what happens when an individual is induced to behave contrary to his attitude, and places particular emphasis upon resulting changes in the psychological situation, such as the emergence of new forces that may perpetuate the change or restore the **status quo.**

Although the ideas offered need to be tested through empirical study, conceptualizations of this kind are valuable in bringing together ideas that were previously unrelated and in enabling the de-

velopment of appropriate research designs for future experimental work.

19.

The Induction of Action and Attitude Change

HERBERT C. KELMAN
UNIVERSITY OF MICHIGAN

It has often been noted that when a person is induced, somehow, to take a particular action toward an object, he also changes his attitudes toward the object in such a way as to bring them in line with the action he has taken. By induction of action I refer to any manipulation of situational forces that causes the person to take an action step toward an object that he would not otherwise have taken, given the nature of his attitudes toward the object. Thus, if we conceive of a person's relationship to an object as varying along a dimension of "degree of positive association"—i.e., the degree to which he engages in actions that bring him into contact with the object and that involve active support for it—then we are concerned with those situations in which the person is somehow induced to take a step further

* The selection following the editorial introduction is reprinted from "The induction of action and attitude change," in S. Coopersmith (Ed.), *Personality Research*, Copenhagen: Munksgaard, 1962. Pp. 81–110, by permission of the author, editor, and publisher.

along the dimension of positive association with the object than he was prepared to go.

In the absence of induction, the degree of positive association (i.e., the nature of the action that the person will take) depends on the strength of the person's favorable attitude toward the object. More precisely, in the situations with which we shall be concerned, it depends on the strength of approach tendencies relative to the strength of avoidance tendencies. Now, by exerting pressure on the person, or by introducing some form of social facilitation, or by presenting him with a fait accompli and thus forcing his hand, one may induce him to take some overt action or make a public pronouncement indicating support of the object in question and associating himself with it favorably and concretely, in a way that is not warranted by his existing attitude toward the object. Note that we are dealing with a situation in which a specific action is directly induced through manipulation of situational forces that are extraneous to the object itself: the person has not taken the action because he has been presented with new information about the object and persuaded to change his underlying attitude, but because it was somehow demanded by momentary social considerations. In actuality, of course, it is very rare that an induction of action does not at the same time contain some new information that also bears on the underlying attitude, but I would like to consider that situation as the limiting case.

Given, then, a situation in which action is induced through momentary situational forces, what happens once these forces are removed? In line with the person's earlier attitudes, we would predict that he would now return to his previous level of association with the object; and this is, in fact, what frequently happens in situations of this sort. It is also possible, however, that, having taken the action, the person will change his attitudes in such a way as to bring him closer to the object. When this has happened, of course, we would expect the person to remain at the induced level of association even after the momentary forces have been removed, and to take similar and further action steps voluntarily, without further induction.

The question to which this paper addresses itself is: what are the conditions under which the induction of action does lead to attitude change, and what are some of the mechanisms and processes that account for this phenomenon when it does occur?

The answer to this question has important implications for our understanding of individual and social change. There are many instances in which specific and partial action steps vis-a-vis an object are induced by situational forces. When do such steps lead to changes that go beyond the immedi-

ate situation, changes in the underlying attitudes toward the object that would assure continued and repeated action in the induced direction? Thus, for example, when a public health communication induces people to take an X-ray, under what conditions will this action produce changes in general habits relating to preventive medical care? When a psychotherapist maneuvers a patient to sign up for a therapy session, under what conditions will the patient actually attend the session, remain in therapy, and seriously engage himself in the therapeutic process? When an advertising campaign, through the use of special inducements, gets people to buy a product, under what conditions will a stable change in their preferences result? When a legal decision requires association between Negroes and whites, under what conditions will prejudiced attitudes decline?

Some recent work in this general area has created the impression that if the person is somehow tricked into taking the action, by whatever means, forces toward attitude change will automatically arise. The position of the present paper is that such forces arise only under special circumstances, depending on the processes and experiences that the induced action makes possible, on the structure of initial attitudes, and on the nature of the action itself. It is to these various conditions that I would now like to turn my attention.

ACTION AS THE OCCASION FOR RE-EXAMINING ATTITUDES

One of the reasons why the induction of action may lead to attitude change is that this *action may provide the occasion for the person to re-examine his attitudes toward the object.* That is, the situational demands on the person to take or consider taking a particular action may be such as to bring into play an active process of re-evaluation of his position. In the context of the action he has been induced to take, he may reconsider his original attitude toward the object, either from the point of view of its value-implications (i.e., he may ask himself whether his existing attitude is conducive to the maximization of important values and congruent with his value system) or from the point of view of its role-implications (i.e., he may ask himself whether his existing attitude meets the expectations derived from important role relationships and reference groups). This process of re-examination may provide attitudinal support for the induced action and lead to attitude change. The resulting attitude change would, then, be occasioned by the induction of overt action, but it would actually be produced by the internal processes that precede and accompany the action.

The probability that the induction of action will lead to attitude change via this particular route depends on the nature of the induction—specifically on the kinds of internal processes that this induction makes possible and necessary. One variable that is likely to be particularly important in this connection is the degree of pressure exerted on the individual which, in turn, determines the freedom of choice left to him. In an experiment that I carried out some years ago (1953), for example, children were induced—through the offer of extraneous prizes—to write essays about comic books that went counter to their original position on the issue. All of the children were exposed to a persuasive communication, and all were induced to take the specific action—but the nature of the induction differed for different groups. In one group (the High Restriction condition) the situation was so structured (through manipulation of the prize and the expectation communicated by the experimenter) that subjects saw little choice about taking the induced action. In another group (the Low Restriction condition) the possibilities of taking the induced action or an alternative course were more evenly balanced. As one might expect, the amount of conformity was greatest in the High Restriction condition, but it was the subjects in the Low Restriction group that showed the greatest amount of attitude change. The indications are that these subjects, because of the possibility and hence the necessity of choosing, engaged in a more active process of re-examining their attitudes prior to and during the action itself, thus producing attitudinal support for the action they were taking. In the High Restriction group this process occurred more rarely and, moreover, an oppositional process was set into motion because of resentment of the experimenter's pressure.

There are two ways, incidentally, in which a high degree of choice with respect to the induced action may facilitate attitude change. Given a high degree of choice, the person may be undecided as to whether or not he should carry out the induced action. In the process of arriving at the necessary decision and firming it up, he would be likely to re-examine his attitudes and to marshal forces in support of the action that he finally selects. Of course, in this type of situation, he may decide not to take the induced action and this negative decision would now have considerable attitudinal support. But if he does take the action, it is likely to be accompanied by attitude change. A high degree of choice may facilitate attitude change even if the person is not undecided about taking the action. The situational forces may be so strong that the person is automatically inclined to accept the induction, but the fact that he is given the choice may in a sense force him to find attitudinal support for the action he has already decided to take. Here attitude change may result from a process of active self-persuasion.

Another feature of induced action that is likely to facilitate attitude change by bringing a re-examination of underlying attitudes into play is the requirement of improvisation and elaboration as the action is carried out. King and Janis (1956), for example, created an experimental role-playing situation in which subjects were asked to defend a position contrary to their own. This experience was more likely to lead to attitude change if the subjects were required to improvise their arguments than if they were merely asked to read a prepared script. Presumably, in the Improvisation condition they had to engage in an active process of re-examining their attitude toward the object in question.

In short, we have seen that induction of action may lead to attitude change if the nature of the induction is such as to bring supportive processes into play. The change in attitude occurs because the person re-examines his relationship to the object in the context of taking the induced action. The situational requirement to take or consider taking the action has served to force the issue, and has provided the occasion for the person to re-examine his attitudes. The process of re-examination, in turn, has produced the change. The probability that attitude change will occur via this mechanism depends primarily on the amount of choice the induction permits and requires of the individual. Needless to say, we are dealing here with an active process of attitude reorganization, occasioned by the induced action.

ACTION AS THE OCCASION FOR NEW EXPERIENCES

A second reason why the induction of action may lead to attitude change is that the *action may provide the occasion for the occurrence of new experiences in relation to the object*. Once the person has taken a particular action, he may have certain new experiences that were unanticipated, in the sense that the expectation of these experiences did not form the basis of his taking the action in the first instance. These new experiences and the information they provide may, in turn, be of such a nature as to produce a reorganization of attitudes.

One consequence of the induced action is that it gives the person some new experience with the attitude object itself and thus may provide him with new information about it. Given this new information, his attitude toward the object may change depending, of course, on the nature of the new information. If the attitude object is another person or group of people, for example, then the action may bring the person, at least temporarily, into closer contact and communication with the other which may not have been part of his prior experience. This new contact, in turn, may at least make it possible for new information about the other to emerge and a restructuring of attitudes to result. (Cf. Newcomb's [1947] autistic hostility hypothesis.) Whether attitudes toward the other in fact become more favorable depends, of course, on what happens in the course of the new contact—how the other behaves, how much opportunity there is for the characteristics of the other to manifest themselves, how easy it is to distort and reinterpret the other's behavior, and so on. Similar considerations arise if the attitude object is a social issue or organization of some sort. The person may be induced, for example, to support a certain community agency in some specific way. As a result of the closer contact with the agency into which this action has brought him, he may find that this agency is more effective, more useful, more conducive to the maximization of his own values than he had realized. Or, the person may find that the action itself—which had originally been induced by situational forces—is inherently satisfying to him. It may produce some desirable consequences, and help in the solution of a problem or the accomplishment of his ends. As a result, he may come to see the action in a new light and restructure his attitudes toward the object to which this action referred.

In short, action toward an object is likely to be followed by some new experiences with this object. If these experiences provide favorable information about the object—i.e., if they show that the object is worthy of the person's positive association, if they serve, in a sense, to validate the action—then attitude change in line with the action is likely to result. I have been referring to new experiences that provide favorable information about the object and thus increase the strength of approach tendencies toward it. There is also the possibility that the person's experiences following action will provide him with new information that helps to lower avoidance tendencies relating to the object. He may find, for example, that the other person or group is not as unpleasant as he had anticipated, that the procedure he adopted is not as difficult and costly, and so on. This new information, similarly, may lead to a restructuring of attitudes.

Another consequence of the induced action is that it may lead to certain new social experiences which indirectly provide new information about the attitude object. Given this new information, again, the person's attitude toward the object may change. Thus, the person may find that the action he has taken brings him into agreement with an important reference group—or perhaps, does not bring him into disagreement with the group, as he had feared. This is one of the features, for example, of the well-known group decision studies carried out by Lewin (1958) and his associates: in most of these studies, the group decision turned out to be unanimous or near-unanimous; thus, when subjects announced their decision to take the induced action, they found themselves in agreement with the other members of the group and found the group-based barriers to change removed. A later study by Edith Bennett Pelz (Bennett, 1955) has shown very nicely that the perception of group consensus is one of the two variables that seem to account for the effectiveness of the group decision procedure. The new information about group consensus, then, to which the person is exposed subsequent to action, may introduce forces toward attitude change via the process of identification.

Similarly, the person may receive certain direct social rewards as a result of adopting the induced action: others may praise him for what he has done, for example. Or, he may find that the disapproval from others that he had anticipated is in fact not forthcoming—that the action is, in fact, socially quite acceptable. Such information may also facilitate attitude change, perhaps by increasing the person's commitment to the action he has taken. Studies by Scott (1957; 1959) suggest that social reinforcement of this type may indeed lead to attitude change in an experimental role-playing situation.

In short, we have seen that induction of action may lead to attitude change if the action provides the person with new experiences in relation to the object—whether these be intrinsic experiences with the object itself, or social experiences that have reference to the object. The change is based on the new information derived from these experiences. The probability of its occurrence depends, first and foremost, on the nature of this new information. If the new information is favorable—if the experience is rewarding—then attitude change in the direction of the induced action may occur. If the new information is unfavorable, of course—if the experience is unpleasant—then it may even happen that attitude change in the opposite direction takes place. The probability of favorable change also depends on the person's openness to the new information, which is probably related, among other things, to the nature of the induction.

ACTION AS THE BASIS OF A NEW PSYCHOLOGICAL SITUATION

The two sets of factors that I have discussed so far refer to attitude changes that have been *occasioned* by the induced action, but are not dynamically related to the action itself. That is, the induction of action may provide the occasion for the person's re-examination of his attitudes before and while he takes the action. Similarly, the induction of action may provide the occasion for the occurrence of certain new experiences in relation to the object. It is these processes or these experiences occasioned by the action that provide the dynamics for attitude change. There is also the possibility, however, that the action itself may directly provide the dynamics for attitude change, by virtue of the new psychological situation that it creates for the actor. It is to this possibility that I would like to devote the remainder of the present paper.

As a direct consequence of having taken the action, the person finds himself in a new psychological situation. Or, to use Lewinian terminology —which seems particularly appropriate here— once he has taken the action, the person's life space has become altered. The new psychological situation is such that new forces have come into play, or that existing forces have moved to a higher or lower level. As a result, the strengths of approach and avoidance tendencies toward the attitude object may be different from what they were in the pre-action situation.

Action produces these changes in the person's psychological situation and in the resulting approach and avoidance tendencies for two reasons: (1) because action represents locomotion into a new region in which the balance of approach and avoidance tendencies is likely to be different; and (2) because the action itself introduces a new element into the person's life space which is likely to affect the balance of approach and avoidance tendencies. If the new psychological situation in which the person finds himself after having taken the action is such that—for one or both of these reasons—approach tendencies have become relatively stronger, then attitude change in line with the action is likely to result.

I shall discuss four variables—or, more correctly, four classes of variables—which are likely to have a bearing on the balance of approach and avoidance tendencies following action and which are, therefore, likely to affect the probability of attitude change. The first two of these variables refer to the *pre-existing structure of the person's relationship to the attitude object,* which determines the balance of forces in the new region into which the person has locomoted. The second two variables refer to the *nature of the action* that the person has taken, which determines the new forces that have been introduced into the person's life space by the action itself. Let me examine these four variables in turn.

The relative steepness of the approach and avoidance gradients

I have already indicated that the situations with which we are concerned usually involve an approach-avoidance (or a double approach-avoidance) conflict; and I have also introduced the concept of "degree of positive association" with the attitude object. The strength of both approach and avoidance tendencies can be presented as a function of the degree of positive association with the object. Let us assume, for the moment, that approach and avoidance tendencies are related to degree of association in the same way as they are related to distance from the goal object in Miller's (1944) model of conflict. According to this model, the avoidance gradient is steeper than the approach gradient (see Figure 1). The

person will, normally, move up to the point at which the two gradients cross. At this point he will experience conflict. Miller speaks of this point as a stable equilibrium: if, for any reason, the person moves beyond this point he will very soon return to it, because he would find himself in a region in which avoidance tendencies outweigh approach tendencies.

Now, in the situation with which we are concerned, the person has been induced, through temporary situational forces, to enter into a degree of association which he would not have chosen voluntarily: in other words, he has been induced to take an action which brings him beyond the point of conflict (see Figure 1). If, then, the structure of approach and avoidance gradients is of this classical variety (i.e., if the avoidance gradient is steeper than the approach gradient), then we would predict that, other things being equal, induction of action would be unlikely to lead to attitude change. As soon as the momentary forces are removed, the person would tend to revert to his earlier level of association with the object: the tendency to continue association— to approach the object behaviorally and affectively —would be outweighed by the tendency to avoid it. Let me give some hypothetical examples that would fit this model. A Catholic physician who intellectually accepts the necessity of birth control but would not go so far as to give out birth control information is pushed into doing so—perhaps while he is serving as a public health officer in an underdeveloped country; he is very disturbed by this, however, and as soon as he leaves the special situation he reverts to his earlier practice. A young man with a middle class background, who talks a good radical game, is induced by social pressure to go out on a picket line, but withdraws as soon as the pressure is re-

FIGURE 1. Degree of positive association.

moved. A white man who comes from a racially segregated society but holds certain liberal values is suddenly thrown into close contact with Negroes; this confrontation is threatening to him and he terminates the contact as soon as possible. In these examples, the induced action has taken the person beyond the point of conflict into a region of closer association with the object in which avoidance tendencies come more strongly to the fore. The person, thus, reverts to his earlier level and opportunities for attitude change are minimal.

There is no reason to assume, however, that approach and avoidance gradients would always be structured in this way. Miller's model refers largely to cases in which avoidance is based on an acquired drive—typically fear—and approach on a physiological drive, such as hunger. Because of the character of these underlying motivations, the avoidance gradient is likely to be steeper: the acquired drive is more affected by situational factors and hence its strength varies more sharply as a function of distance from the goal. In the type of situation with which we are concerned, however, there is no a priori reason to assume that the avoidance gradient will always be steeper than the approach gradient. Let us postulate a situation in which the opposite is true, and examine the implications of this possibility (see Figure 2).

If the approach gradient were steeper than the avoidance gradient, the person would normally not find himself in a situation of overt conflict: he would tend to stay away from any association with the object and would not voluntarily move to the equilibrium point. If, however, he is induced by situational forces to take an action that brings him beyond the point of intersection of the two gradients, then he will find himself in a region in which approach tendencies outweigh avoidance tendencies. To be sure, it would be

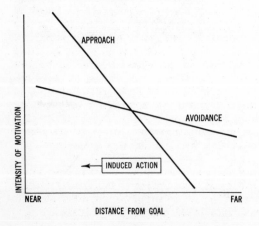

FIGURE 2.   Degree of positive association.

more difficult to induce action when the person's relationship to the object is structured in this way, because he would have to be pushed, as it were, a longer distance. If the induction is successful, however, then he is much more likely to continue to associate with the object—behaviorally and affectively—once the initial pressure is removed, and to display attitude change in the direction implied by the action.

Now, does this type of structure of approach and avoidance gradients with respect to an object represent a reasonable possibility? Let me present some hypothetical examples that would fit this model. A citizen who is relatively indifferent to a national cause is forced to support this cause by paying special taxes; this induced action arouses his latent patriotic sentiments and increases his involvement with and future voluntary support of the cause. (This consideration played a part in President Kennedy's plan—which he later abandoned—to raise taxes as a way of arousing the American public's concern with the Berlin crisis. Similar considerations, no doubt, play a part in the taxation imposed by the Algerian rebels. Of course, the success of such maneuvers depends on the existence of nationalist sentiments that are thus activated; in their absence, resentment would be the primary reaction.) To take other examples: A non-Zionist Jew is induced to visit Israel as part of a general tour; the association with the country that he thus experiences brings his relatively latent Jewish identifications to the fore and causes him to maintain a closer association even after he returns home. An ex-physician who has given up practice for one or another reason is forced to take on the physician's role in an emergency situation; this newly induced association may lead him to reestablish his practice. A member of a minority group who is relatively assimilated to the majority culture is pushed into closer association with his group—perhaps as a result of majority discrimination; he now continues this association voluntarily.

In the above examples, the induced action has taken the person into a region of closer association with the object in which approach tendencies come more strongly to the fore. The person is, thus, likely to remain at the new level of association and to change his attitude accordingly. The examples I have given refer, essentially, to cases in which latent approach tendencies exist but are outweighed by other considerations in the person's current life space. As long as the person's degree of association with the attitude object remains low, these tendencies continue to be latent. Once the degree of association is increased, however, through the manipulation of certain extraneous forces, the approach tendencies rise sharply. That is, at the higher levels of association, the latent nationalist sentiments and so on come to the fore. Contrast this with the case in which the avoidance gradient is steeper than the approach gradient. Here we have a situation in which relatively latent avoidance tendencies exist. As long as the person's association with the object remains at a low level, they are outweighed by the approach tendencies. When he is pushed into closer association, however, the avoidance rises sharply and the latent resistances come to the fore.

We have seen, then, that both types of relationship to the attitude object are possible: one in which the avoidance gradient is relatively steeper than the approach gradient, and one in which the opposite is true. The effects of induction of action on attitude change would depend, then, on the relative steepness of the two gradients. The crucial question is: What are the variables that determine the steepness of these gradients? In general it can be supposed (in line with Miller's assumption) that steepness is related to the extent to which the motivation aroused by the object depends on situational cues. There are probably a variety of variables that enter the picture, but I would like to dwell on one pair of hypotheses that I consider particularly germane here. In my earlier work (1958; 1961) I have distinguished between two different processes on which attitude change may be based. One of these, identification, refers to the acceptance of new attitudes because they permit the person to maintain or achieve a satisfying self-defining relationship to the influencing agent— e.g., because they are in line with the expectations of a reference group or because they meet the requirements of a role that the person wishes to enact. The other process, internalization, refers to the acceptance of new attitudes because of their congruence with the person's value system.

I would like to propose that, to the extent that a person's attitude toward an object is *internalized* the gradient of approach or avoidance along the dimension of degree of association would tend to be relatively flat. Thus, if the person favors a particular object because he sees it as conducive to the maximization of one or more of his values, the strength of his approach to the object would be relatively unaffected by such situational cues as his degree of association with the object at the moment. The approach tendency, in this case, is integrated with the person's value system and should therefore manifest itself at all levels of association (which does not mean that it would always be the dominant determinant of his behavior, for it may be outweighed by opposing tendencies). Similarly, if the person opposes a particular object because he sees it as detrimental to the maximization of his values, the strength of his avoidance would be relatively unaffected by his degree of association.

On the other hand, to the extent that a person's attitude toward an object is *based on identification*, the gradient of approach or avoidance along the dimension of degree of association would tend to be relatively steep. Thus, if a person favors an object because such an attitude is in line with

the expectations that circumscribe one of his roles, the strength of his approach to the object would vary considerably as a function of such situational cues as his degree of association with the object. The approach tendency, in this case, is tied to his *being in the role*—i.e., it is an aspect of role behavior—and should therefore manifest itself more strongly under conditions of active association with the object. Both the person's awareness of role expectations with regard to the object, and the strength of these expectations themselves, increase as the degree of association with the object increases. Similarly, if the person opposes an object because such an attitude is in line with role expectations, the strength of his avoidance would vary considerably as a function of degree of association. In short, the manifestation of identification-based attitudes is more dependent on situational cues, and hence varies more sharply with the degree to which the situation brings role requirements into salience— which, in turn, varies with the degree of association with the object.

If we look back at the examples I gave, in which the avoidance gradient was relatively steep, we see that they refer to situations in which avoidance (more than approach) is based on the person's relationship to important reference groups —the Catholic church for the physician induced to give out birth control information, his middle class ties for the young man induced to go on a picket line, and white society for the man induced to associate with Negroes. Under these circumstances, we would expect the avoidance gradient to be relatively steep. A further qualification that is probably necessary here is that we are dealing with cases in which avoidance is anchored in a relatively latent reference group, i.e., a reference group that does not constitute the person's key membership group at the moment.

If we look back at the examples I gave, in which the approach gradient was relatively steep, we see that they refer to situations in which approach (more than avoidance) is anchored in important reference groups—his nation for the man induced to pay taxes, his ethnic group for the visitor to Israel and for the minority group member, and the profession into which he was trained for the ex-physician. Again, we are dealing with cases in which approach is anchored in a reference group that is relatively latent in the person's current life space.

Let me summarize this part of the discussion by proposing the following two hypotheses:

Hypothesis 1a. Induction of action is more likely to lead to attitude change if the *approach* component of the person's relationship to the object is identification-based than if it is internalized.

Hypothesis 1b. Induction of action is more likely to lead to a reversion to the original level of association and less likely to lead to attitude change if the avoidance component of the person's relationship to the object is identification-based than if it is internalized.

In other words, induction of action is likely to be effective in producing attitude change to the extent that the approach tendencies are in the domain of role considerations rather than value considerations. It is likely to be ineffective to the extent that the avoidance tendencies are in the domain of role considerations rather than value considerations. These relationships should be particularly marked if the roles in question are relatively latent in the person's current life space.

The concentration of resistance in the region of induced action

So far I have been making the assumption that there is a direct positive relationship between strength of avoidance and degree of association. The avoidance curve may, however, have other shapes in the kind of situation with which we are concerned, and this may have various consequences for the effectiveness of inducing action.

One possibility that is of particular interest is the case in which the person's relationship to the object is characterized by the existence of a paramount barrier. That is, there is a point on the dimension of degree of association at which the strength of avoidance of the object reaches its peak. Beyond that point, avoidance tendencies drop sharply (see Figure 3). Thus, there is no strong resistance to a relatively high degree of association with the object, but the resistance is concentrated in a relatively narrow zone. Given this kind of structure of the person's relationship to the object, he is likely to continue his associa-

FIGURE 3. Degree of positive association.

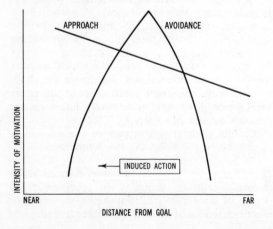

tion and to change his attitude accordingly if induction of action has taken him through and beyond the zone in which resistance is concentrated.

Let me give a trivial example which illustrates what I have in mind in a graphic way. A person wants to go swimming, runs up to the water and puts his toes in or even goes in up to his knees, but finds it too cold and immediately runs back. He knows that once in the water he would probably enjoy it, but it is the initial period of adjustment that causes the difficulty. He hovers at the edge, running back and forth, and overtly displaying typical conflict behavior. At this point, someone comes by and pushes him into the water and blocks his exit for a few moments, or someone shames him into going in, or a pretty girl walks by whom he is trying to impress. Assuming that the water is not in fact terribly cold, chances are that once he is inside the person will enjoy it and stay there voluntarily. Induction of action was effective in this case because it took the person through the zone of maximal resistance—past the paramount barrier—into a region in which approach tendencies clearly predominate.

This example suggests the nature of situations that are likely to be structured in this way. They are situations in which the person's avoidance of the object is *not* generated primarily by the characteristics of the object itself, but by *the price he would have to pay in order to enter into closer association with the object.* In other words, the resistance is generated by a particular action step with respect to the object and the demands that this step makes on the person. For some reason, this particular step is "difficult"—typically in that it represents a period of adjustment to a new situation during which the costs outweigh the rewards.

The sources of difficulty of the step in question—the nature of the price that the person is required to pay—may vary. The step may represent some new task with which the person is not familiar, and which thus requires an initial period of frustration and insecurity. It may consist in getting to know certain new people, or new kinds of people, to whom the person is not accustomed. It may require adjustment to a new type of interaction which presents special difficulties, anxieties, or embarrassments (e.g., the type of interaction involved in psychotherapy). Or, finally, it may simply be the act of admitting that there has been a change in the situation. This would be true, for example, in situations in which people have to change their relationship to others from one of superior status to one of equal status—such as in areas that are in the process of desegregation or decolonization. The ex-superior may be quite willing to relate to the others at this new level, but the initial step of recognizing and openly acknowledging that this change has taken place may represent humiliation, loss of face, and a threat to self-esteem, and may thus arouse resistance.

In all of these situations, the person may be

quite willing to accept a new role or a new relationship, or to engage in new activities or new types of interaction, but he avoids them because of the existence of a powerful barrier to the necessary intermediate step. His resistance is not to the attitude object, but to the particular step that is required if he is to associate with that object at a new level. Induction of action—by temporarily increasing approach tendencies (for example, through the application of pressure) or temporarily decreasing avoidance tendencies (for example, through social facilitation, support and reassurance, or the introduction of a fait accompli) —may succeed in taking the person through and beyond the difficult intermediate step. He will then find himself in a new situation, in which the existing forces favor continued association with the object and hence the development and strengthening of favorable attitudes toward it.

To summarize, let me propose the following hypothesis:

Hypothesis 2. Induction of action is more likely to lead to attitude change if the initial resistance to this action is generated by the demands of the action itself than if it is generated by the attitude object.

It is assumed here that induction is such as to take the person beyond the zone in which resistance is concentrated.

The degree of commitment to future action

So far I have dealt with the effects of the *pre-existing structure* of the person's relationship to the attitude object on the consequences of inducing action. Now I would like to turn to variables that relate to the *nature of the action* itself. The fact that the person has taken a particular action introduces new forces into his life space, which *may* produce attitude change in the direction of the induced action. Whether they do or not depends, of course, on the nature of these forces, which in turn depends on certain characteristics of the action itself.

When a person takes an action step, it often carries some implication for future action. Having taken one step, he may in some sense have committed himself to additional steps which will maintain or increase his degree of association with the object. The person now finds himself in a new situation in which he is tied to the object in a more or less irrevocable way—in Heider's (1958) terms, a relation of "unit formation" between the person and the object has been established. The tie is irrevocable in the sense that to break it—to fail to carry out further action and maintain further association—would entail great expense. In other words, having taken the action, the person now finds himself in a situation in which the price for reverting to his earlier level of association with the object would be higher than the price for remaining at the new level: it is easier to go on at this point than it is to go back.

There are a variety of action situations that are particularly marked by this characteristic. If the action consists of buying a particular product, the person is committing himself to further association with it. Once he has made the investment, he is motivated to use the product, for the alternative would involve a financial loss. (Lewin, in his discussion of food habits [1958], spoke of the crucial importance of the act of buying food products because this act represents a turning point at which many forces change their direction.) If the action consists of taking a public stand on an issue or making a public commitment to future action, the person is motivated to carry through. Failure to do so would lead to disapproval from others, loss of prestige, loss of face. If the action consists of a personal decision—a self-commitment—it creates a state of psychological irrevocability. Failure to carry out a decision would lead to a loss of self-esteem and of the sense of personal stability. If the action consists of joining an organization or signing up for something, the person is automatically committing himself to a series of steps, which form part of the larger package. Breaking the association may require initiative and lead to complications. If the action consists of taking an initial small step under pressure, the person may be undermining his own ability to resist further and larger steps. This would be true, for example, in a situation that involves interrogation or bribery: by taking a small step, the person becomes caught in the web, as it were.

In all of these situations, the action has been of such a nature as to tie the person to the object and imply continued association and further action. The action has created a situation in which the forces in the direction of association are stronger than those in the opposite direction: for one or another reason, it would be more difficult or more costly to cut the tie than to maintain it, to break the commitment than to carry it out. Sometimes, the very forces that originally pointed to resistance now point to further action.

If the psychological situation in which the person finds himself after taking the induced action is of this nature, new forces toward attitude change will be brought into play. Being committed to further association with the object, the person is likely to be open to and to search for new information that would help to make the anticipated association more effective, more comfortable, more rewarding. The nature of this information would typically be such as to lend attitudinal support to the association and to lead to the development or strengthening of favorable attitudes toward the object—in other words, to bring attitudes into line with the action taken and the future action that is anticipated. Thus, for example, the person will be open to information about ways of using the product he bought or the organization he joined, in line with his desire to make the anticipated association more effective. He will be open to information that will help him defend the object to which he has become linked, in preparation for such a necessity. He will be open to information that suggests the virtues of the object and the fact that others have viewed it favorably, or that points to the correctness of his decision, for such information would help him anticipate future association with less tension and anxiety. (Cf. Janis' [1959] discussion of post-decisional conflicts.)

In short, preparation for future association and action makes the person more ready to expose himself to information that supports the object and thus facilitates attitude change in the direction of the action. Note that I am not assuming here a general motivation to bring attitudes into line with an action that has been taken. The forces toward attitude change derive, rather, from the requirement for further association with the object and the commitment to future action. The anticipation of these brings certain preparatory processes into play, which create an openness for favorable information about the object and thus tend to bring attitudes into line with the induced action (assuming, of course, that sufficiently favorable information is in fact available).

Let me summarize by proposing the following hypothesis:

Hypothesis 3. Induction of action is likely to lead to attitude change to the extent that the induced action represents a commitment to continued association with the attitude object and future action in support of it.

Corollaries of this hypothesis can, of course, be formulated in terms of the variables that create commitment to future action by virtue of the fact that they make reversion difficult or costly. For example, the more public the commitment, the greater the likelihood that attitude change will result, since a public commitment makes continued association more imperative.

The degree of personal involvement in the induced action

New forces may enter into the person's life space not only because of his knowledge that he is committed to future action, but also because of the very knowledge that he has taken a particular action toward the object. In other words, having taken a particular action, the person finds himself in a new psychological situation in which the fact that he has taken this action is represented as an item of relevant information. This new information, to the extent that the person takes it into account, may introduce new forces in the direction of attitude change.

There are two interrelated mechanisms whereby the knowledge of having taken the action may lead to attitude change. One involves the direct effect of having acted in support of the object on the subsequent perception and evaluation of that object. One of the major elements in our definition of an object is the way in which we characteristically act toward it. The book of children's definitions, entitled "*A hole is to dig*," it seems to me, points to a basic psychological phenomenon that is not only restricted to children. Thus, if a person has been induced to act in a friendly way toward another, he will come to define that other—in part—as "someone to whom I have acted in a friendly way." His own action toward the other will tend to become a salient characteristic of the other. This definition, in turn, may lead to a new evaluation of the other as "someone who is worthy of friendly actions on my part." The same consideration would hold for other objects. That is not to say that the objective characteristics of the object are irrelevant, but simply that the person's own supportive action toward the object represents one new datum about the object which may then enter into its evaluation. At the very least, having acted in support of the object may make the person more open to favorable information about it. How important this datum is for the person's evaluation of the object depends on the nature of the action, to which I shall return in a moment. But first let us look at the second mechanism whereby the knowledge of having taken a particular action may lead to attitude change.

The second mechanism involves the effect of having acted in support of the object on the person's self-evaluation, which may in turn affect his perception and evaluation of the object. If the person associates himself with an object toward which he holds a negative attitude, his self-evaluation may decline. Depending on the strength of his negative attitude and its centrality for his self-concept, the action will be ego-alien and produce psychological tension in the form of guilt (e.g., for having betrayed a cause), shame (e.g., for having been too weak to resist pressure), embarrassment, disappointment in one's self, annoyance with one's self, or what have you. There are various ways in which the person can reduce these negative self-evaluations, one of which is attitude change. By changing his attitude toward the object, he can manage to avoid or reduce the negative implications of his actions. His guilt would be reduced, for example, if he could convince himself that the cause he betrayed was not worthy of his loyalty; his shame would be reduced if he could convince himself that he was not simply yielding to pressure but acting in line with his own preferences. In short, the motivation to reduce negative self-evaluation stemming from the knowledge that one has acted contrary to one's belief may set into motion forces toward attitude change that would bring the attitude into line with the action.

Whether or not knowledge that he has taken a particular action will in fact bring forces toward attitude change into play—by either of the two mechanisms I described—will depend on the individual's degree of personal involvement in the induced action. That is, the knowledge that he has acted in a certain way toward a particular object will become an important datum in the person's evaluation of the object and of himself only to the extent that he regards this action as really part of himself, as representing his own behavior. This, in turn, depends on the character of the action itself.

The action will have a high degree of personal involvement to the extent that the person *chose* to engage in it. If the induction situation allows the person some degree of choice about taking or not taking the action, and he chooses to take it, it will tend to represent a relatively high level of personal involvement. I have already discussed this variable as one which increases the likelihood that a process of re-examination of attitudes prior to and during the action will be set into motion. But it should also affect the psychological situation in which the person finds himself after taking the action and introduce forces toward attitude change. Recent studies by Cohen (1960) and Brehm (1960) present some evidence for this assumption.

The action will also have a high degree of personal involvement to the extent that its execution requires the person's active participation. For example, he will tend to be involved if he takes initiative in carrying out various action steps, puts effort into the task, and in other ways invests much of himself in it. Finally, the action will have a high degree of personal involvement to the extent that it represents a complex of interrelated role behaviors within some social system rather than a specific, isolated act. The person will be more involved in the action if it serves to identify him with the whole system.

The greater the personal involvement in the induced action, in terms of one or more of the manifestations of involvement that I have listed, —the more important does the knowledge of this action become in the person's definition and evaluation of the object. An action at a high level of involvement is more likely to force itself into the picture as a relevant datum to be considered in subsequent evaluation of the object and, hence, the contemplation of such past action is more likely to produce stronger forces toward attitude change. Similarly, the greater the personal involvement in the action, the more important does the knowledge of the action become in his self-evaluation. An action at a high level of involvement is, by definition, part of the self and representative of it and, hence, a relevant datum in self-evaluation for which the person

cannot easily escape responsibility. Thus, if this action has negative implications for the self, its contemplation should produce stronger forces toward reduction of negative self-evaluation. Moreover, the greater the personal involvement in the action, the greater the probability that reduction of negative self-evaluation will take the form of attitude change rather than certain other forms—such as minimizing or disavowing the action.

These considerations can be summarized in terms of the following hypothesis:

Hypothesis 4. Induction of action is likely to lead to attitude change to the extent that the induced action becomes personally involving for the actor.

Corollaries of this hypothesis can be formulated in terms of the variables that create personal involvement. For example, attitude change is likely to be greatest if the person has chosen to engage in the action, if it has required his active participation, or if it has identified him with a role complex.

The involvement variable in Hypothesis 4 may very well be positively related to the degree of commitment to future action of Hypothesis 3. An action that is involving is also likely to be one that represents a commitment to future action. Both variables imply a commitment to the object, though perhaps one might say that Hypothesis 3 refers to the *fact* of commitment and Hypothesis 4 to the *act* of commitment. In any event, these two variables do not necessarily go hand in hand and they do imply different operations on the part of the influencing agent.

SUMMARY

In summary, I have discussed the effects of induced action on attitude change. Three types of factors that may account for attitude change as a result of induced action were considered: *1*) the re-examination of the person's attitudes toward the object before and while he takes the action, occasioned by the induction; *2*) exposure to new experiences in relation to the object which yields new information about it, occasioned by the action; and *3*), changes in the psychological situation in which the person finds himself as a result of having taken the action and the new forces that are thus brought into play. The bulk of the discussion dealt with this third set of factors. Four hypotheses were presented regarding the conditions under which the new psychological situation in which the person finds himself are likely to favor attitude change. Two of these hypotheses refer to the pre-existing structure of the person's relationship to the attitude object. They concern two variables: the relative steepness of the approach and avoidance gradients, and the concentration of resistance in the region of induced action. The other two hypotheses refer to the nature of the action itself. The variables with which they are concerned are the degree of commitment to future action and the degree of personal involvement in the induced action.

The three sets of factors are by no means independent of one another. Some of the same variables that lead to a re-examination of attitudes prior to action also affect the psychological situation following upon action. Similarly, the psychological situation in which the person finds himself after action will determine his openness to any new experience to which he might be exposed. It is not my intention, then, to propose completely independent mechanisms whereby action may lead to attitude change. The only purpose of the distinctions I have made is to provide some degree of analytic clarification which can help in the formulation of empirical research.

This paper is part of a research program on social influence and behavior change, supported by grant M-2516 from the National Institute of Mental Health.

REFERENCES

BENNETT, EDITH B. Discussion, decision, commitment, and consensus in "group decision." *Human Relat.,* 1955, 8, 251–273.

BREHM, J. W. A. dissonance analysis of attitude-discrepant behavior. In C. I. Hovland & M. J. Rosenberg (Eds.), *Attitude organization and change.* New Haven: Yale Univer. Press, 1960. Pp. 164–197.

COHEN, A. R. Attitudinal consequences of induced discrepancies between cognitions and be-

havior. *Publ. Opinion Quart.,* 1960, 24, 297–318.

HEIDER, F. *The psychology of interpersonal relations.* New York: Wiley, 1958.

JANIS, I. L. Motivational factors in the resolution of decisional conflicts. In M. R. Jones (Ed.), *Nebraska symposium on motivation.* Lincoln: Nebr. Univer. Press, 1959. Pp. 198–231.

KELMAN, H. C. Attitude change as a function of response restriction. *Human Relat.,* 1953, 6, 185–214.

KELMAN, H. C. Compliance, identification, and internalization: Three processes of attitude change. *J. Confl. Resol.,* 1958, 2, 51–60.

KELMAN, H. C. Processes of opinion change. *Publ. Opinion Quart.,* 1961, 25, 57–78.

KING, B. T. & JANIS, I. L. Comparison of the effectiveness of improvised versus non-improvised role playing in producing opinion changes. *Human Relat.,* 1956, **9,** 177–186.

LEWIN, K. Group decision and social change. In Eleanor E. Maccoby, T. M. Newcomb & E. L. Hartley (Eds.), *Readings in social psychology* (3rd ed.). New York: Holt, 1958. Pp. 197–211.

MILLER, N. E. Experimental studies of conflict. In J. McV. Hunt (Ed.), *Personality and the behavior disorders* (Vol. 1). New York: Ronald, 1944. Pp. 431–465.

NEWCOMB, T. M. Autistic hostility and social reality. *Human Relat.,* 1947, 1, 69–86.

SCOTT, W. A. Attitude change through reward of verbal behavior. *J. abnorm. soc. Psychol.,* 1957, 55, 72–75.

SCOTT, W. A. Attitude change by response reinforcement: Replication and extension. *Sociometry,* 1959, 22, 328–335.

PERSUASIVE COMMUNICATION AND THE SOCIAL STRUCTURE *

Because of their very nature laboratory studies set up conditions that are apt to increase the effectiveness of an influence attempt: they sometimes introduce factors that do not exist outside the laboratory. The laboratory communicator benefits from the prestigious position he occupies in the institutional structure; he is generally much more credible than typical communicators in field situations. Outside the laboratory the respondent may avoid exposure to certain communications; he switches television to another channel, reads only those portions of the newspaper that interest him, and, by and large, voluntarily listens mainly to communicators whose opinions are not too dif-

ferent from his own. In the laboratory he is a captive target; he cannot avoid hearing the communication. In the field situation he may enlist group support for resisting communications; often, when he is exposed to a communication he is in the company of persons whose attitudes resemble his own and thus provide support for resisting the communication. In the laboratory he is often an isolated target, unable to communicate with other members of the group and sometimes not having any knowledge of their attitudes on the communication topic. Frequently the issues differ; in general, opinion polls ask questions about such ego-involving topics as civil rights, national defense, and medical care, issues on which the individual has definite positions resistant to change. Most, but not all, of the issues used in the laboratory are topics about which the subject has no strong feelings and on which he is susceptible to change.

* The selection following the editorial introduction is reprinted from "Traditions of research on the diffusion of innovation," *American Sociological Review*, 1963, **28**, 237–252, by permission of the authors and American Sociological Association.

These various differences between laboratory and field conditions limit the external validity or generalizability of laboratory studies.

Such differences make it necessary to supplement laboratory findings with studies of communication as it occurs in the larger social structure. Most of the research discussed to this point has dealt with the influence of communications at the individual level. The experimental situations often consist of one individual influencing another or one individual communicating to a group of other individuals. But communications outside the laboratory move through a much more complex structure. People are organized into groups. Specific channels of communication may be identified in small groups, organizations, communities, and whole societies. Communications move through these channels at a certain pace, sometimes slowly and sometimes quickly. Each individual or group link in the communication network may act as a relay or a filter for a particular influence attempt, stopping or facilitating its passage, transmitting it faithfully or in a distorted form.

In this selection, Katz and his colleagues examine the diffusion of innovations (new ideas or technologies) through the social structure. Lines of research from social anthropology, sociology, and mass communications are brought to bear on this central problem. Although no one selection can deal with all the facets of communication within the context of the social structure, the selection chosen helps to provide a broad perspective on this problem.

20.

Traditions of Research on the Diffusion of Innovation[1]

ELIHU KATZ
ISRAEL INSTITUTE OF
APPLIED SOCIAL RESEARCH
JERUSALEM, ISRAEL

HERBERT HAMILTON
UNIVERSITY OF ILLINOIS

MARTIN L. LEVIN
EMORY UNIVERSITY

The process of diffusion is defined as the (1) *acceptance,* (2) *over time,* (3) of some specific *item*—an idea or practice, (4) by individuals, groups or other *adopting units,* linked to (5) specific *channels* of communication, (6) *to a social structure,* and (7) to a given system of values, or *culture.* The elements of this definition are treated as an "accounting scheme" in terms of which diffusion studies in the fields of sociology, anthropology, rural sociology, mass communications, etc., are reviewed and problems of research design are explicated.

It is hardly news that the diffusion of innovation is one of the major mechanisms of social and technical change. Indeed, around the turn of the century anthropologists were greatly impressed with the significance of diffusion, even overly impressed. In sharp contrast to the European diffusionists,[2] however, the Americans avoided grand, all-embracing theories of cultural development. Instead they worked modestly, investigating rather specific items—elements of the maize-complex, the horse-complex, the sun dance—tracing their distribution in space and, insofar as possible, in time. The work remained primarily historical and descriptive, although some important generalizations about the generic aspects of diffusion were advanced.[3]

[1] Preliminary formulations of portions of this paper were presented at the meetings of the American Sociological Association, Chicago, 1959, and the American Anthropological Association, Mexico City, 1959. We wish to thank Robert L. Crain and Manning Nash for reading and commenting on the present version; readers of the earlier version are too numerous to mention. The overall project of which this paper is a part has received the support of the Foundation for Research on Human Behavior and the Social Science Research Committee of the University of Chicago.

[2] Robert H. Lowie, *History of Ethnological Theory* contains an excellent treatment of the early anthropological movements and schools, including evolutionism and diffusion. In this connection also see Alexander Goldenweiser's "Cultural Anthropology" in Harry Elmer Barnes (ed.), *History and Prospects of the Social Sciences,* New York: Alfred A. Knopf, 1925. A. L. Kroeber's article "Diffusionism" in the *Encyclopedia of the Social Sciences* is a brief, interesting description of the early diffusionist work in the context of the development of anthropology, and Melville Herskovits, *Man and His Works,* Chapters 30 and 31, New York: Alfred A. Knopf, 1938, can also be examined with profit as an informative survey of the various early movements in anthropology. For various sides of the argument concerning the early work on diffusion see G. Elliot Smith, *et al., Culture: The Diffusion Controversy,* New York: Norton, 1927.

[3] Among the more suggestive of these studies for our purposes are the following: Robert H. Lowie, "Plains Indians Age Societies," *Anthropological Papers,* American Museum of Natural History, 11 (1916), pp. 877–1031; Robert H. Lowie, "Ceremonialism in North America," *American Anthropologist,* 16 (October-December, 1914), pp. 602–631; Paul Radin, "A Sketch of the Peyote Cult of the Winnebago: A Study in Borrowing," *Journal of Religious Psychology,* 7 (January, 1914), pp. 1–22; Leslie Spier, "The Sun Dance of the Plains Indians: Its Development and Diffusion," *Anthropological Papers,* American Museum of Natural History, XVI (1921), pp. 451–527; Clark Wissler, "Material Culture of the North American Indians," *American Anthropologist,* 16 (Oc-

Influenced in part by these anthropoloists, several empirically minded sociologists of the 20's and 30's also demonstrated an interest in diffusion.[4] Studies were made of the spread of the city-manager plan, of a third-party movement, of amateur radio as a hobby, and the like. The guiding theoretical concerns had to do with the influence of the metropolis on its satellites, the effectiveness of natural anl legal boundaries as barriers to diffusion, the flow of innovation from region to region across the country, as well as the hypothesis of a "concentric circle" pattern of diffusion which was shared with the anthropologists. The underlying assumption was always that informal communication among adopters was the key to diffusion.

In both of these fields, diffusion studies came to a halt by about 1940.[5] In anthropology, atten-

tion shifted to the closely related problem of acculturation[6] in which emphasis is placed on ongoing (rather than historical) situations of intergroup contact, on patterns of culture traits rather than single items and, typically, on pairs of interacting societies rather than longer chains of connected groups.[7]

It is less clear why diffusion studies failed to hold the interest of sociologists, though they were never as prevalent as in anthropology. It seems a reasonable guess, however, that the revolution in communication which began with the rapid spread of radio in the late 20's and early 30's diverted their attention.

THE REVIVAL OF INTEREST IN DIFFUSION RESEARCH

But the mass media are incapable of influencing people (though they may inform them) as directly or as simultaneously as had been imagined.[8] Indeed, the study of mass media "effects," with its primarily psychological bias, is now broadening to take account of the *social* processes involved in the spread of influence and innovation.[9] This seems an altogether reasonable next step for former students of mass media "campaigns." For, if the mass media are not as all-powerful as was originally imagined, the problem of understanding the furious rate at which new ideas and behavior travel through society still remains. In

tober-December, 1914), pp. 477–505; Clark Wissler, "Costumes of the Plains Indians," *Anthropological Papers*, American Museum of Natural History, **17** (1915), pp. 39–91; Clark Wissler, "The Ceremonial Bundles of the Blackfoot Indians," *Anthropological Papers*, American Museum of Natural History, VII (1914), pp. 65–289.

[4] See, for example, Raymond V. Bowers, "The Direction of Intra-Societal Diffusion," *American Sociological Review*, **2** (December, 1937), pp. 826–836; F. S. Chapin, *Cultural Change*, New York: Century, 1928; Edgar C. McVoy, "Patterns of Diffusion in the United States," *American Sociological Review*, **5** (April, 1940), pp. 219–227; H. Earl Pemberton, "Culture Diffusion Gradients," *American Journal of Sociology*, **42** (September, 1936), pp. 226–233.

[5] In the 1920's and 1930's, a method of diffusion research commonly referred to as "age-area" analysis was developed. This method involved reconstructing the temporal movement and spread of cultural traits and complexes from geographic data on the spatial distribution of the cultural elements under investigation. Especially noteworthy in this regard was the work of Clark Wissler, who developed it to its most refined degree. See his *Man and Culture*, New York: Thomas Y. Crowell Co., 1923, and *The Relation of Nature to Man in Aboriginal America*, New York: Oxford University Press, 1926. While a very important contribution to the field in its day, this approach was subjected to a searching critique by Roland Dixon in *The Building of Culture*, New York: Scribners, 1928. This kind of criticism, no doubt, contributed appreciably to the subsequent decline of distributional diffusion studies generally. Still, there has been a continued production of such studies and, indeed, one occasionally encounters especially interesting investigations at least partly employing this approach, such as the recent work by David F. Aberle and Omer C. Stewart, "Navaho and Ute Peyotism: A Chronological and Distributional Study," *University of Colorado Studies*, Series in Anthropology No. 6, 1957. Furthermore, those interested in archaeology seem to have maintained an even more central concern for diffusion analysis along these distributional lines. See, for example, the spirited discussion

of the paper by Munro S. Edmondson, "Neolithic Diffusion Rates," *Current Anthropology*, **2** (1961), pp. 71–102.

[6] Acculturation or culture contact studies were heralded by Robert Redfield, Ralph Linton and Melville J. Herskovits, in their "Memorandum on the Study of Acculturation," *American Anthropologist*, **38** (January-March, 1936), pp. 149–152.

[7] Indeed, a large segment of diffusion studies has tended to concern itself with adjustive responses to contact rather than the transmission of items beween groups. This paper will explicitly avoid consideration of the now predominant concern with the social and cultural consequences of change. Our focus is on the processes of *communication* of change. Studies concerned with non-diffusion aspects of change are helpful, however, in drawing attention to the interrelationships among diffusion processes, socialization processes and adjustive processes in culture change. For an interesting empirical study illustrative of the link between socialization processes and (resistance to) acculturation, see Edward M. Bruner, "Primary Group Experience and the Processes of Acculturation," *American Anthropologist*, **58** (August, 1956), pp. 605–623.

[8] For a discussion of some of the social and psychological factors involved in the transmission of influence via the mass media, see Joseph T. Klapper, *The Effects of Mass Communication*, New York: Free Press, 1960, Part One.

[9] The design of research in mass communication has recently begun to take account of interpersonal relations as structures which relay and reinforce (or block) the flow of influence and innovation. See Elihu Katz, "The Two-Step Flow of Communication: An Up-to-Date Report on an Hypothesis," *Public Opinion Quarterly*, **21** (Spring, 1957), pp. 61–78.

short, there is a revival of interest in diffusion processes.[10]

The sociologists of communication who found themselves interested in diffusion discovered, somewhat to their surprise, that relevant studies were being carried on in a number of closely related fields. The most conspicuous case is that of rural sociology which has accumulated, over the last two decades, several hundred studies of the communication and acceptance of new farm practices.[11] Similarly, researchers in the field of education have tried to understand the rate of acceptance of innovations by school systems and have looked at such things as the spread of the kindergarten or supplementary reading.[12] Public health is interested in the acceptance of new health practices—the Salk vaccine, for example.[13] Marketing researchers, of course, are interested in the spread of acceptance of new products (although they have done far less work on this problem than one might imagine),[14] folklorists have documented the extent to which children's games, for example, have spread from region to region;[15] and so on. Like sociology, anthropology has also experienced something of a return to some of the interests of the more sober schools of diffusion, as a by-product of the current effort to evaluate the progress of the varied programs

for planned change in underdeveloped areas of the world.[16]

THE STATE OF DIFFUSION RESEARCH

Ironically, it almost seems as if diffusion research in the various research traditions can be said to have been "independently invented!" Indeed, diffusion researchers in the several traditions which we have examined scarcely know of each other's existence. The recent "discovery" of rural sociology by students of mass communications and vice versa is a good case in point.[17] As a result, each tradition has emphasized rather different variables and a characteristically different approach. This paper attempts to integrate these diverse points of view.

To accomplish this, we shall first propose a working conception of diffusion from a sociological point of view. This will be done in terms of a tentative set of component elements, each of which can be formulated as a key variable (sometimes as several variables) intrinsic to, or bearing upon, the diffusion process. Taken together, they constitute a kind of "accounting scheme" for the study of diffusion.

Following the enumeration of the component elements, each will be considered in some detail, paying particular attention to problems of conceptualization and operational definition. Then, we shall attempt to "locate" the characteristic emphases of each of the research traditions in terms of one or more of these elements of the diffusion process.

DEFINING DIFFUSION

Viewed sociologically, the process of diffusion may be characterized as the (*1*) *acceptance*, (*2*) over *time*, (*3*) of some specific *item*—an idea or practice, (*4*) by individuals, groups or other *adopting units*, linked (*5*) to specific *channels*

[10] In the few relevant studies so far, the tendency has been to follow a communication as it passes from one individual to the next, to establish the nature of the relationship between the interacting individuals and thus to infer the relevant social networks; in other words, structures of social relations are derived from the flow of interpersonal communication. The alternative method—that of mapping the potentially relevant structures of social relations *prior* to tracing the flow of influence—would seem to be somewhat more desirable, if more difficult.

[11] For an overview of work in this field together with selected bibliography, see Herbert F. Lionberger, *Adoption of New Ideas and Practices*, Ames, Iowa: Iowa State University Press, 1960.

[12] See Paul R. Mort and Frances G. Cornell, *American Schools in Transition*, New York: Teachers College, Columbia University, 1941; and Walter Cocking, "The Regional Introduction of Educational Practices," New York: Bureau of Publications, Teachers College, Columbia University, 1951.

[13] For numerous references, see Steven Polgar, "Health and Human Behavior: Areas of Interest Common to Social and Medical Sciences," *Current Anthropology*, 3 (April, 1962), pp. 159–179, particularly the section on Health Action Programs and, to a certain extent, the section on Dynamics of Health Status. Anthropologists have been particularly active in this area.

[14] The most interesting study, from our point of view, is *The Tastemakers* (Vol. I), a report of the Public Opinion Index for Industry, Princeton, New Jersey: Opinion Research Corporation, April, 1959.

[15] See, for example, Iona and Peter Opie, *The Lore and Language of Schoolchildren*, London: Oxford Univrsity Press, 1959.

[16] There is a burgeoning literature on this subject. See the studies reported in recent volumes of *Human Organization* and *Economic Development and Cultural Change*; the several collections of case studies, particularly Benjamin Paul (ed.), *Health, Culture and Community*, New York: Russell Sage Foundation, 1955; and recent volumes such as Charles Erasmus, *Man Takes Control*, Minneapolis: University of Minnesota Press, 1961; and George M. Foster, *Traditional Cultures and the Impact of Technological Change*, New York: Harper, 1962.

[17] For an account of the confrontation between students of mass communication and of rural sociology, see Elihu Katz, "Communication Research and the Image of Society: Convergence of Two Traditions," *American Journal of Sociology*, 65 (March, 1960), pp. 435–440.

of communication, (6) to a *social structure*, and (7) to a given system of values, or *culture*.

Altogether, there are very few studies in any of the traditions of diffusion research which have incorporated *all* of these elements. In fact, the traditions differ from each other precisely in their tendency to "favor" certain of the elements rather than others.

Now we shall consider each of the components in turn.

(1) *Acceptance*. Acceptance is the dependent variable in most studies of diffusion though, strictly speaking it is time-of-acceptance that is really of interest. Ideally, in other words, diffusion studies seek to classify acceptors in terms of the timing of their acceptance of an item or to compare the relative rate of acceptance in one community with another. More often than not, however, information about time is lacking and, instead, one learns—for a given point in time—which individuals have and have not accepted an innovation or what proportion of community members, in different communities have accepted.

Most diffusion studies define acceptance rather arbitrarily. Where information on time is available, date of "first use" is frequently employed as the measure of acceptance, the season of first-use of hybrid corn, for example.[18] But, obviously, first-use may or may not be followed by continued use and some recent studies, therefore, have insisted on the distinction between "trial" and "adoption." Thus, a measure of "sustained use" might be appropriate for some purposes, but, for other purposes, it may be of interest to consider only "ever use."[19]

For anthropologists, however, this is a much more serious matter. First of all, anthropologists tend to be skeptical about the extent to which a given item is perceived and used in the same manner in different societies. If the sewing machine is prominently displayed on the open porch, but never used for sewing, it may be argued that it is no longer the "same" item. For anthropologists, that is, acceptance tends to refer not to the form

of an item alone but to form-meaning-function.[20] Consider the acceptance of Christianity, for example, as discussed in the anthropological literature. With respect to its appearance in a given society, anthropologists would tend to ask: (1) Is it the "same" item? (2) Is it internalized in the personalities of the group? (3) Is it central to the social institutions of the group? Indeed, one of the factors underlying the distinction between "acculturation" (a prestigeful concept) and "diffusion" (a less prestigeful one) in anthropology, appears to be related to the "level" of acceptance (internalization and centrality) involved.[21]

This is a good example, perhaps, of the utility of confronting several traditions with each other within a manageable framework. Obviously, some kind of distinction must be made between mere external acceptance of a form and its internalization; and, obviously, attention must be given to the extent to which function travels together with form. But these ideas should not be treated merely as *cautionary*; they are also suggestive of hypotheses. Indeed, writing in a very similar vein, Gabriel Tarde—the social theorist of diffusion *par excellence*—suggested that "inner" changes precede "outer" changes in the sense that the diffusion of an idea precedes the diffusion of the tangible manifestation of that idea or, in other words, that there is a "material lag" rather than a "cultural lag" in the transfer of items across societal boundaries. Some theorists would agree; others, obviously, would not.[22] In any case, the implication is that diffusion research ought not to be misled by the argument over whether "mere diffusion" or penetration to deeper levels is more important but, rather, whether these correspond to separable episodes in the spread of any given item and, if so, how they are related.

(2) *Time*. If any one of the elements may be said to be more characteristic of the diffusion process than the others, it is time. It is the element of time that differentiates the study of diffusion both from the study of mass communication "campaigns" with their assumed immediacy of impact and from traditional distributional studies. Diffusion takes time; for example, it took ten years for hybrid corn—an unusually success-

---

[18] See Bryce Ryan and Neal Gross, "The Diffusion of Hybrid Seed Corn in Two Iowa Communities," *Rural Sociology*, **7** (March, 1943), pp. 15-24.

[19] Gaining acceptance for most contraceptive techniques, for example, is much more a problem of "sustained use" than of "first use." See Reuben Hill, J. Mayone Stycos and Kurt Back, *The Family and Population Control*, Chapel Hill: University of North Carolina Press, 1959. Obviously, the distinction is appropriate wherever first use does not lead directly to continued use. See A. Apodaca, "Corn and Custom," in E. H. Spicer (ed.), *Human Problems in Technological Change*, New York: Russell Sage Foundation, 1952, for a study of the acceptance of an innovation which was later discontinued.

[20] The form-meaning-function distinction is stressed particularly in Ralph Linton, *The Study of Man*, New York: Appleton-Century, 1936, pp. 402-404.

[21] For good examples of the applicability of the notion of levels of incorporation of an innovation into a receiving society, see Edward P. Dozier, "Forced and Permissive Acculturation," *American Indian*, **7** (Spring, 1955), pp. 38-44; and Edward H. Spicer, "Spanish-Indian Acculturation in the Southwest," *American Anthropologist*, **56** (August, 1954), pp. 663-678.

[22] In his analysis of the diffusion of the sun dance, Spier explicitly cites his data as evidence, at least in this case against Tarde. See Leslie Spier, *op. cit.*, p. 501.

ful innovation—to reach near-complete acceptance in Iowa communities. Nevertheless, there are very few studies, so far, that have taken systematic account of time in the study of diffusion.

In part, this neglect is a result of the difficulty of obtaining data. Studies which have taken account of time have relied on one of the following three methods: *recall* (where a respondent, or an informant, dates the acceptance of an innovation), *records* (where time-of-acceptance is a matter of record, for some reason), and *inferences* (such as in the archaeological dating methods of stratigraphy or Carbon-14).

Some of the early diffusion studies by sociologists had access to data on time because they studied innovations intended for adoption by municipalities—the city manager scheme, for example.[23] A current study of the diffusion of fluoridation has such data for the same reason.[24] The dates of acceptance of such innovations are a matter of public record.

Anthropologists who were studying diffusion in the 20's and 30's gave considerable thought to the development of a methodology for inferring time from spatial distributions. Clark Wissler, for example, was able to demonstrate that a particular distribution of pottery around a hypothesized point of origin did, indeed, correspond to a known succession of types of pottery as established stratigraphically.[25] Wissler further indicated that "students of culture generally assume that widely distributed trait complexes are the older," though he immediately cautions that such an assumption may result in serious error insofar as the rates of diffusion of different sorts of items may vary.

Early sociological students of diffusion faced a similar obstacle though they had more data on time. It is relatively easy to establish, for example, the date on which 10 per cent of the population of a city or state owned a refrigerator or a radio. Then, treating the city or the state as if they were "adopters" of refrigerators and radios makes it tempting to suggest that certain cities are influencing others to adopt or that there seems to be a certain kind of geographical movement from state to state. A genuinely pioneering (though perhaps unconvincing) effort to strengthen this sort of tenuous ecological analysis with data gathered from individuals was made by Bowers in the 30's.[26] Bowers studied the diffusion of amateur radio as a hobby and demonstrated, for example, that the proportion of amateurs to pop-

ulation was at its highest in 1914-15 in cities of 25,000-100,000; five years later the peak was in cities of 10,000-25,000; during the following five years, the heaviest concentrations were in still smaller cities. From this distribution, he infers that people in the larger cities had influenced those in smaller places. Then, by means of a mail questionnaire, an attempt was made to test this inference by asking licensed amateur radio operators to report on the sources which were influential in their decisions to become "hams."

If students of pre-history sorely felt the lack of data on time, it is a nice anomaly that students of "consumer" innovations in the mid-twentieth century are experiencing the same problem. It may be possible to ask a farmer to try to recall the season during which he first planted hybrid corn, but it is very difficult to be certain that such information is reliable. How much more is this the case for innovations which are less central to their adopters and inherently less datable than is the season of first use of a new kind of seed. One can perhaps ask about the date of purchase of major appliances, but it is almost impossible to rely on recall for most other things. A promising source for data of this kind is the type of consumer panel in which households are asked to keep a record of all their purchases, entering them in some sort of log on a daily or weekly basis; however, there are many difficulties with this procedure.[27] Occasionally, unusual opportunities present themselves for obtaining data on adoption dates. The study of the diffusion of new drugs among physicians, for example, had access to prescriptions on file in local pharmacies, making it possible to date each doctor's first use of a new drug.[28]

Time is a crucial ingredient in the diffusion process, however, not simply because it enables the researcher to identify the characteristics of early-adopting individuals or to establish the direction of the flow of influence. It is also important because it provides a basis for the charting of diffusion curves, thus making possible the development of mathematical descriptions of variations in the diffusion process. Time, and the

[23] See, for example, McVoy, *op. cit.*

[24] See Robert L. Crain, "Inter-City Influence in the Diffusion of Fluoridation," unpublished Ph.D. dissertation, Department of Sociology, University of Chicago, 1962.

[25] See *Man and Culture, op. cit.* Also see the work of Margaret T. Hodgen, "Geographical Diffusion as a Criterion of Age," *American Anthropologist,* **44** (1942), pp. 345-368. The article by Edmondson, *op. cit.*, is based on Carbon-14 datings.

[26] See Bowers, *op cit.*

[27] There is considerable difficulty in maintaining the representativeness of the consumer-panel sample, and constant programmed turnover is one of the strategies of doing so; for diffusion research, however, turnover represents a complication. Moreover, if one approaches the diffusion problem in a situation where individual adopters are widely dispersed—such as in a national study of some consumer innovation, for example—one must cope with the added complexity of differing beginning dates in different regions, etc.

[28] See James S. Coleman, Elihu Katz and Herbert Menzel, "The Diffusion of an Innovation among Physicians," *Sociometry,* **20** (December, 1957), pp. 253-270.

number of adopters at a given time, are continuous and easily quantified variables; hence, the study of diffusion is one of the areas of social science which lends itself immediately to the construction of mathematical models. For example, one can construct theoretical models of the diffusion process given certain assumptions and compare the results with those actually observed in the real world. On the basis of such a comparison, one can infer whether a given item is "contagious" or not, that is, whether the item spread as a function of the extent of previous adoptions or the character of contacts with previous adopters.[29] Hagerstrand, a geographer, was able to demonstrate that the most probable adopter of a new farm practice is the farmer living in the vicinity of someone who has just adopted it; and on the macro-level an innovation spreads from primary centers until the original source of influence is exhausted, whereupon some new center springs up.[30] Crain found essentially the same phenomenon at work in the case of fluoridation where the unit of adoption is a municipality

rather than an individual.[31] Similarly, attempts have been made to specify, *a priori*, the probable influence of different patterns of social relations on the spread of innovation. The work reported by Stuart Dodd is a good example.[32] The same kind of logic suggests that similar innovations may be described by similar curves of diffusion and, if this is so, part of the problem of classifying innovations (to be discussed below) will be open to solution.[33]

(3) A specific item. The discussion of acceptance has already made clear part of the problem of specifying the particular item under study. Obviously, one would like to ascertain whether the meaning of a given item for one individual, or for one society, is the same as it is for another. In a related sense, one would also like to know whether or not a given item is part of a larger "complex" of items to which it adheres. On the other hand, this does not preclude—as some people seem to think—the legitimacy of studying the diffusion of an isolated item, concentrating on form alone regardless of possible "adhesions" and regardless of possible variations in function. In any event, these problems are somewhat reduced when the items involved are practices more than ideas, items of lesser rather than greater pervasiveness, and when the study is concentrating on diffusion with a particular culture rather than across cultures. This, perhaps, makes somewhat clearer why anthropologists, more than others, have raised questions in this area.

The major problem of specifying the item in diffusion research derives from these considerations. It is the problem of how to classify items so that the results obtained are generalizable to other items. This problem is not unique to diffusion research, of course, but it is perhaps particularly obvious in this context. Suppose one studies the diffusion of hybrid corn, or of fluoridation, or of 2-4-D weed spray. Unless some scheme of classification exists which would make it possible to say that a given new item is rather more like a 2-4-D weed spray than it is like hybrid corn, each study simply becomes a discrete case which cannot be generalized.

Such a classification system is particularly difficult because, like all "content analysis," one must make guesses about the meaning of the item to its potential audience. Of course, to a certain extent this can be studied empirically. Suppose, for example, that the dimension of "radicalness"—that is, the extent to which an innovation is a major departure from some previous mode of acting—were an important one, as many observers seem to think. One might pre-test the

[29] An impressive amount of work is going on in this area, much of it beyond the competence of the present authors. The major contributions include the following: Stuart C. Dodd, "Diffusion Is Predictable: Testing Probability Models for Laws of Interaction," *American Sociological Review,* **20** (August, 1955), 392–401; and Stuart C. Dodd and Marilyn McCurtain, "The Logistic Law in Communication," in National Institute of Social and Behavioral Science, Symposia Studies Series No. 8, *Series Research in Social Psychology,* Washington, D.C., 1961; Melvin DeFleur and Otto Larsen, *The Flow of Information,* New York: Harper, 1958; Georg Karlsson, *Social Mechanisms,* Glencoe, Ill.: The Free Press, 1958; Torsten Hagerstrand, "Monte Carlo Simulation of Diffusion," University of Lund, Sweden, 1960 (unpublished); and James S. Coleman, "Diffusion in Incomplete Social Structures," Baltimore: Department of Social Relations, Johns Hopkins University, 1961 (unpublished). Two economists who have worked intensively with diffusion curves are Zvi Griliches, "Hybrid Corn: Explorations in the Economics of Technological Change," *Econometrica,* **25** (October, 1957), pp. 501–522; and Edwin Mansfield, "Technical Change and the Rate of Imitation," Pittsburgh: Graduate School of Industrial Administration, Carnegie Institute of Technology (unpublished). See also a noteworthy series of articles by bio-physicist Anatol Rapoport entitled, "Spread of Information through a Population with Socio-Structural Bias," *Bulletin of Mathematical Biophysics* 15 and 16 (1953–54). Related work in the epidemiology of contagious disease is that of N. T. J. Bailey, *The Mathematical Theory of Epidemics,* London: Charles Griffin, 1957. Steven Polgar has written a paper that is relevant here on "The Convergence of Epidemiology and Anthropology," School of Public Health, University of California at Berkeley (unpublished).

[30] Hagerstrand, *op cit.*

[31] Crain, *op cit.*

[32] Dodd and McCurtain, *op cit.*

[33] This is more difficult than it sounds, perhaps, but it is a lead worth following.

actual use of an innovation—a visual telephone, for example—to discover the kinds of behavioral and attitudinal changes which it implies in order to rank it, at least as perceived by its early users, on a radicalness scale.

But the trouble is that nobody is quite sure what dimensions of an item are relevant, and very little research has been done to try to find out. There are some exceptions, however. Wilkening in the United States and Emery and Oeser in Australia have traced the spread of several different agricultural innovations through the same communities, and on the basis of their differential rates and patterns of acceptance have speculated about some of the dimensions which affect diffusion.[34] A major study of the diffusion of educational practices also speculates about why different sorts of innovations seem to spread in different patterns.[35] Dimensions that have been suggested by these authors and others center on economic-sounding considerations such as (1) extent of capital outlay required; (2) extent of anticipated profitability; (3) certainty of profitability or efficacy, and extent of possible loss or danger (risk). Of course, these are not strictly financial matters at all.

The most promising works on this problem have been several attempts to explicate the most traditional of the dimensions in terms of which innovations have been classified: material vs. non-material items. Barnett and others have suggested that material items find more ready acceptance because (1) they are more easily communicated; (2) their utility is more readily demonstrable; and (3) typically, they are perceived as having fewer ramifications in other spheres of personal and social life.[36] Following Barnett, Menzel classified several different kinds of medical innovations in terms of his estimates of their (1) communicability, (2) risk, and (3) pervasiveness, hypothesizing that early adopters of each item would have certain characteristics.[37] He suggested, for example, that integration into the local medical community would be characteristic of early adopters of a new drug which "required" communication but neither risk nor pervasiveness, whereas acceptance of a psychotherapeutic technique would be likely to "require" a certain emancipation from the local community and thus

[34] Eugene A. Wilkening, *Acceptance of Improved Farm Practices in Three Coastal Plains Communities*, Raleigh: North Carolina Agricultural Experiment Station, Bulletin 98, 1952; and F. E. Emery, Oscar Oeser and Joan Tully, *Information Decision and Action: A Study of the Psychological Determinants of Changes in Farming Techniques*, Carleton: Melbourne University Press, 1958.

[35] Mort and Cornell, *op. cit.*

[36] Barnett, *op. cit.*, pp. 374–377.

[37] Herbert Menzel, "Innovation, Integration and Marginality," *American Sociological Review*, 25 (October, 1960), pp. 704–713.

lesser integration. The results obtained were promising and represent the opening up of an important direction for diffusion research.

(4) *Units of adoption.* Another way in which items can be usefully classified is in terms of the units of adoption for which they are intended. Most studies in sociology, rural sociology and marketing have considered only consumer-type items, those intended for adoption by an individual. But some innovations are intended for—indeed, they may "require"—groups, in the sense that it "takes two to tango" (or to telephone, or to perform the peyote ritual, etc.). And among such group-oriented innovations, a further distinction seems useful. There are items which require collective adoptions but permit any given individual to adopt or not (the telephone, for example); there are other items, however, where the group adopts as a single unit leaving no room for individual options (fluoridation, for example).

Just as the item may "require" one or another adopting unit, a given culture may "prescribe" one rather than another adopting unit as appropriate. The *kibbutz* prescribes a group decision even for consumer-type innovations intended for use by individuals; similarly, the simultaneous conversion of an entire village to Christianity reflects the acceptance of a corporate decision, made by the chief perhaps, as binding upon all. Anthropologists are much more likely than those in other traditions to focus on the group as an adopting unit. Sometimes, this is just another way of talking about individuals as, for example, when it is reported that Village *A* adopted a certain kind of plow but Village *B* did not. But, often, the group is indeed the unit of adoption in the sense that the group "decides," or the culture "prescribes," that there be a collective decision.

Thus, the unit of adoption may vary as a function of the "requirements" of the item or the "prescription" of the culture. And, just as in the case of the other elements in the diffusion process, the adopting unit functions as a variable to facilitate or block the flow of acceptance of innovation. For example, items which "require" collective adopting units may be resisted, therefore, by cultures which "prescribe," or favor, the individual as the unit of adoption and vice versa. Resistance to fluoridation, in the United States, in terms of minority rights is one such example; resistance to consumer innovations by Israeli *kibbutzim* is another. By the same token, an appeal for acceptance of an innovation is less likely of success when directed to the "wrong" adopting unit—as when family planning campaigns aim at, say, the wife, but the culture "prescribes," or the technique "requires," joint agreement by both spouses.[38]

(5) *Channels.* So far, almost nothing has been said about the channels which transmit information and influence concerning an innovation. Indeed, except for occasional studies which noted the role of highways or of caravan routes, channels—like time—are missing in most of the early studies of anthropologists and sociologists. Even when it seemed certain, from distributional evidence or other inferences, that an innovation traveled from Tribe *A* to Tribe *B*, it was often unclear *how* this took place. On the other hand, if there is any single thing that is most wrong with contemporary studies of diffusion in the fields of mass communication, rural sociology and marketing research, it is that there is too much emphasis on channels. The typical design for research in these fields has been based, almost exclusively, on the assumption that people can be asked to recall the channels of information and influence that went into the making of their decisions to adopt an innovation or to make some sort of behavioral change. This approach in mass media research is known as "reconstruction" or "reason analysis."[39] It is of some methodological interest, too, because it reverses the usual experimental design of "campaign" studies which begin with stimuli and try to track down their effects. Reason analysis, instead, begins with an effect and seeks to reconstruct how it came about. It is this approach which is, in a sense, responsible for the rediscovery of the importance of interpersonal relations in the flow of influence and innovation in modern society. It is only very recently that students of mass communications and marketing have begun to include interpersonal relations among the channels of diffusion. This contrasts sharply with the rural sociologists who have long been aware—though they have not formulated it systematically until rather recently—that there is a "two-step flow" from the county agent to an influential farmer and thence to other farmers.

While a concern with channels is the predominant emphasis in several fields, it is a conspicuous lack in several others. Early anthropological studies, particularly those dealing with historical instances of diffusion, have been criticized for their (necessary, in part) lack of attention to process. Still, there were occasional studies pointing to probable means of transportation and communication such as Wissler's research on the horse in relation to the diffusion of Plains Indian culture traits[40] or the analyses of the role of roads and highways by various authors,[41] and there was even a noteworthy study of the personalities and roles of key agents in the transmission of change.[42] More recent anthropological studies of acculturation of technical assistance campaigns have given close attention to the character of the contacts between donor and recipient societies, a subject to which we shall return in the section on social structure below.

An interesting new development in decision-making research has been the attempt, by several rural sociologists, to explore the psychological stages of the decision-making process and then to discover which media function most effectively within each stage.[43] For example, for the initial

---

[38] For further discussion of the points raised in this section, see Elihu Katz, "Notes on the Unit of Adoption in Diffusion Research," *Sociological Inquiry*, **32** (1962), pp. 3–9.

[39] For discussions of "reason analysis," see Paul F. Lazarsfeld and Morris Rosenberg (eds.), *The Language of Social Research*, Glencoe: The Free Press, 1955; and Hans Zeisel, *Say It with Figures*, New York: Harper, 1957.

[40] Clark Wissler's "The Influence of the Horse in the Development of Plains Culture," *American Anthropologist*, **16** (January-March, 1914), pp. 1–25, is the early classic paper on the role of "physical" means of transportation as a facilitator of diffusion. Also see the later study of Erna Gunther, "The Westward Movement of Some Plains Traits," *American Anthropologist*, **52** (April-June, 1950), pp. 174–180.

[41] See, for good examples, Stuart Rice, *Quantitative Methods in Politics,* New York: Knopf, 1928, pp. 154–155; A. T. and G. M. Culwick, "Culture Contact on the Fringe of Civilization," *Africa*, **8** (April, 1935), pp. 163–170; and, more recently, Charles J. Erasmus, "Agricultural Changes in Haiti: Patterns of Resistance and Acceptance," *Human Organization*, **2** (Winter, 1952), pp. 20–26. Some of these studies, it should be noted, are concerned rather more with channels of *distribution* than with channels of communication.

[42] Paul Radin, *op. cit.,* pp. 1–22. More recent examples include Richard N. Adams, "Personnel in Culture Change," *Social Forces,* **30** (December, 1951), pp. 185–189; Homer G. Barnett, "Personal Conflicts and Social Change," *Social Forces,* **20** (December, 1941), pp. 160–171; Wesley L. Bliss, "In the Wake of the Wheel," in Spicer (ed.), *Human Problems in Technological Change,* pp. 23–32; Henry F. Dobyns, "Experiment in Conservation," in Spicer, *ibid.,* pp. 209-223; Allan R. Holmberg, "The Wells That Failed," in Spicer, *ibid.,* pp. 113-123; Bertram Hutchinson, "Some Social Consequences of Nineteenth Century Missionary Activity Among the South African Bantis," *Africa,* **27** (April, 1957), pp. 160–175; I. Schapera, "Cultural Changes in Tribal Life," in Schapera (ed.), *The Banta-Speaking Tribes of South Africa,* London: Routledge and Sons, Ltd., 1937; Omer Stewart, *Washo-Northern Paiute Peyotism: A Study in Acculturation,* Berkeley: University of California Press, 1944; Fred Voget, "Individual Motivation in the Diffusion of the Wind River Shoshone Sundance to the Crow Indians," *American Anthropologist,* **50** (October-December, 1948), pp. 634–646; Fred Voget, "A Shoshone Innovator," *American Anthropologist,* **52** (January-March, 1950), pp. 52–63.

[43] See James H. Copp, Maurice L. Sill and Emory J. Brown, "The Function of Information Sources in the Farm Practice

"awareness" stage of receiving information, the mass media are obviously more efficient than interpersonal relations, but the reverse is true for the stage of "acceptance." The importance of this work is that it makes even more salient one of the central themes of this decision-making tradition, which is that the channels are better viewed as complementary rather than competitive. In other words, it has become clear to many of those who have studied the role of the media in the making of decision that different media are appropriate for different tasks and, consequently, that there is little worth to the gross question, which medium is more effective?

Where these studies begin to be more interesting is when they are carried out within a larger framework of structural and cultural factors. Ryan and Gross, for example, used the decision-making approach to confirm the hypothesis which they found implicit in the logistic growth curve obtained for the spread of hybrid corn: that early adopters influenced the acceptance of the new seed by later adopters.[44]

What should be clear by now, however, is that the place of many of these channel studies needs to be reconceptualized. To the extent that they focus on interpersonal channels—that is, on the "relay" functions of interpersonal networks—they are concerned with social structure. And, if the sequence of events is taken into account whereby some persons are influenced by the mass media and others influenced by other persons, we have the beginnings of a diffusion study.

Ideally, a diffusion study should classify individuals according to their place in a social structure—that is, according to their relationships with other people. What we need to know is when this kind of differential placement in the social structure is also related to differential access to, or acceptance of, influence stemming from outside the group regardless of whether the channel of influence is television or a troubadour or a traveling salesman. Then, we want to know whether differential placement in relationship to others has something to do with passing on, or reinforcing, information concerning the innovation. Thus studies of "who influences whom" fall into place both as structural studies and channel studies. Their content ranges from the role of a prestigeful person in introducing the sun dance to the Crow Indians[45] to the influential role of women with large families in the realm of marketing.[46]

In short, what is needed is a wedding of studies of the channels of decision-making and the social-

structural approach to the study of diffusion so that influence and innovation can be traced as to how they make their way into a social structure from "outside" and as they diffuse through the networks of communication "inside."

(6) Social structure. From the point of view of diffusion research, then, the social structure functions in several different ways. First of all, it constitutes a set of boundaries within which items diffuse. Secondly, as has already been demonstrated, the social structure describes the major channels of person-to-person communication through which diffusion flows. Additionally, social structure has to do with the distribution and differentiation of statuses and roles and the characteristic patterns of interaction among the occupants of varying positions. At least as far as diffusion is concerned, each of these functions may be seen to follow from the definition of social structure in terms of the frequency and the character of interpersonal contacts.

Consider boundaries, for example. Apart from making it possible to talk about the rate and extent of spread of an item within a system, boundaries are of interest to diffusion research because the frequency and character of social relations across a boundary differ from those within a boundary. Some studies have taken as problematic the determination of the effective boundaries within which diffusion takes place. For example, in his pioneering study of the diffusion of political influence, Stuart Rice discovered that state boundary lines acted as barriers to the diffusion of political influence except, interestingly, when residents of both sides of a state boundary shared a common marketing area.[47] A number of studies have dealt with the boundaries which arise in connection with systems of social and ethnic stratification. Acceptance of an innovation by a lower social stratum, for example, may block acceptance by higher strata and, by the same token, upper-status groups—as Gillin has shown —may actually try to block the diffusion of symbolically meaningful items to groups of lesser status.[48] The approach fits very well with classical sociological ideas about fashion changes in stratified societies.[49] The same kind of thinking is

Adoption Process," *Rural Sociology,* **23** (June, 1958), pp. 146–157; and Everett M. Rogers and George M. Beal, "The Importance of Personal Influence in the Adoption of Technical Changes," *Social Forces,* **36** (May, 1957), pp. 329–334.

[44] Ryan and Gross, *op cit.*

[45] See Fred Voget, "Individual Motivation . . . ," *op. cit.*

[46] See Katz and Lazarsfeld, *op. cit.,* Part III.

[47] Stuart Rice, *op. cit.*

[48] See John Gillin, "Parallel Cultures and the Inhibition to Acculturation in a Guatemalan Community," *Social Forces,* **24** (October, 1945), pp. 1–14; on this same theme, see the theoretical discussion by George Devereux and Edwin Loeb, "Antagonistic Acculturation," *American Sociological Review,* **8** (April, 1943), pp. 133–147.

[49] See Georg Simmel, "Fashion," reprinted in *American Journal of Sociology,* **62** (May, 1957), pp. 541–558.

characteristic of studies which have treated inter-group cleavages and rivalries within societies as boundaries to diffusion.[50] Several studies have inquired into the strategies of boundary-maintenance: Freed, for example, has analyzed the ways in which the traditional Amish and Eastern-European Jewish communities managed to constitute social structures limiting incursions of influence from the world outside.[51] Finally, a number of anthropologists have confronted the problem of classifying the character of the social relations that exist across boundaries. Spicer, for example, tries to classify the variable relations between the Spanish conquerors and certain Indian tribes in terms of dimensions such as directed vs. non-directed, forced vs. permissive, hostile vs. friendly, and the like. From an analysis of these social interrelations, and the communications channels which they imply, have come various ideas about the kinds of items and changes which are likely to be associated with them.[52]

Curiously, more work has been done on the implications for diffusion of the structure of social relations across boundaries than within boundaries. Certainly very few studies have been done on the basic problem of comparing the ways in which different kinds of structural arrangements within a group condition the diffusion of a given item. There are some notable exceptions, however. Larsen and Hill, for example, studied the differential patterns of spread of a message in a working class and in a college community, and also in summer-camp communities of varying degrees of stability.[53] Lionberger studied variations in

the flow of information as between residents in matched neighborhoods and "non-neighborhoods,"[54] and Stuart Dodd found that variations in social relations resulting from differences in city size and population density affect the rate and extent of diffusion of airborne leaflets.[55] Asking a different question about social-structural relations, Albert argues, on the basis of a comparison of the rate of acceptance of European influences in Ruanda and Urundi that, under certain conditions, innovation will diffuse more rapidly in more centrally organized societies.[56] Oscar Lewis has reported several cases of attempted assistance to underdeveloped communities where the social structure of these communities played a key role in the fate of the project. Based on his restudy of the Mexican village of Tepoztlán, Lewis describes an effort to introduce a modern medical service which encountered resistance from those sectors of the village that would now be called the power structure of the community.[57] In a second study Lewis describes the strategic significance of intro-community factions and cleavages for the eventual fate of innovations entering a village in India.[58] To the extent that a society is more complex, networks of social relations become increasingly specialized. Thus, in the study of the diffusion of new drugs among doctors, networks of professional relations and networks of social relations were both found to carry influence, though at rather different rates and at rather different phases of the diffusion process.[59] A related point is made by Edmondson to the

[50] For example, Homer Barnett, "Applied Anthropology in 1860," *Applied Anthropology*, 1 (April-June, 1942), pp. 19–32.

[51] Stanley A. Freed, "Suggested Type Societies in Acculturation Studies," *American Anthropologist*, 59 (February, 1957), pp. 55–68. Also see Joseph W. Eaton, "Controlled Acculturation: A Survival Technique of the Hutterites," *American Sociological Review*, 17 (June, 1952), pp. 333–340; and Eric Wolf, "Aspects of Group Relations in a Complex Society: Mexico," *American Anthropologist*, 58 (December, 1956), pp. 1065–1078.

[52] Thus, the combination of directed, permissive, friendly, intense and intimate contacts in the case of the Cahita led to the "fusion" of native and donor cultural elements while, in the case of the Athabascan, undirected, unforced, but hostile, intermittent and impersonal relations led to what Spicer calls "reorientation" or the adoption of a limited number of traits which, however, were extensively modified by the recipient culture. See Edward H. Spicer, "Spanish-Indian Acculturation in the Southwest," *op. cit.* For a related attempt to classify type of intergroup relations, see Edward P. Dozier, "Forced and Permissive Acculturation," *op. cit.*

[53] See Otto N. Larsen and Richard J. Hill, "Mass Media and

Interpersonal Communication," *American Sociological Review*, 19 (August, 1954), pp. 426–433; and "Social Structure and Interpersonal Communication," *American Journal of Sociology*, 63 (March, 1958), pp. 497–505.

[54] Herbert F. Lionberger and Edward Hassinger, "Neighborhoods as a Factor in the Diffusion of Farm Information in a Northeast Missouri Farming Community," *Rural Sociology*, 19 (December, 1954), pp. 377–384.

[55] See Stuart Dodd, "Formulas for Testing Opinions," *Public Opinion Quarterly*, 22 (Winter, 1958–59), pp. 537–554.

[56] Ethel M. Albert, "Socio-Political Organization and Receptivity to Change: Some Differences between Ruanda and Urundi," *Southwestern Journal of Anthropology*, 16 (Spring, 1960), pp. 46–74.

[57] Oscar Lewis, "Medicine and Politics in a Mexican Village," in Benjamin Paul (ed.), *Health, Culture and Community*, *op. cit.*, pp. 403–434.

[58] Oscar Lewis, *Group Dynamics in a North-Indian Village, A Study of Factions*, New Delhi, India: Programme Evaluation Organization, Planning Commission, 1954. The importance of social cleavages and factions in relation to the adoption and use of new items is suggested by other studies as well, including A. R. Holmberg, "The Wells That Failed," in Edward Spicer (ed.), *Human Problems in Technological Change*, New York: Russell Sage Foundation, 1952, pp. 113–123; and also J. D. N. Versalius, "Social Factors in Asian Rural Development," *Pacific Affairs*, 30 (June, 1957), pp. 160–172.

[59] Coleman, Katz and Menzel, *op. cit.*

effect that the uniform rate of spread which he finds in his study of rates of culture-trait diffusion in the Neolithic may be a product of the essential similarity in the roles of all potential adopters; he speculates that the rise of specialists might change the picture substantially.[60]

More typical of current diffusion research is the use of social-structural factors to classify *individuals* rather than groups, both in terms of relative status and in terms of differential roles. A large number of rural studies take account of such factors as size-of-farm, age, education, membership in formal organizations and the like.[61] While it is true that, in general, these variables are related to the acceptance of innovation in predictable ways, there are occasional surprises. A number of studies have shown that older people are more likely to accept certain innovations (those that contain a "revivalistic" element, for example)[62] and, similarly, another study found persons of lesser education to be earlier acceptors of the Salk Vaccine under certain circumstances.[63] It is true that these standard variables do account for a considerable part of the variance in many studies, but they leave very many questions unanswered. And there are, of course, other structural variables which have been examined. Thus, Wilkening has studied the effect on innovation in farming of authoritarian vs. non-authoritarian family heads.[64] Larsen and Hill, and Lionberger, are concerned with the ways in which social status within a primary group makes people differentially accessible to others both inside and outside the group.[65] The study of the diffusion of a new drug among physicians focuses on the consequences of differential integration in the medical community for time-of-adoption,[66] while a pioneering study in the field of marketing is concerned with the influence of a composite variable called "mobility" on time-of-adoption of new consumer goods.[67]

By the same token, group members have been studied in terms of the frequency and character of their contacts *outside* the group. Rural-sociological studies have taken accounts of such things as trips to the city, visiting outside the region, and personal contacts with agents of change such as salesmen, county agents and others who come into the community from the "outside world."[68] Certain anthropologically oriented studies of technological change in developing areas have taken similar account of contacts outside the community as a factor making for individual differences in the acceptance of innovation.[69] This kind of thinking, of course, leads directly to questions concerning the applicability of the hypothesis of the "two-step flow of communication" not only to mass communications but to interpersonal diffusion as well: Does influence tend to flow from individuals with relatively more contact with the "outside world" (not only the mass media) to those who stay "at home"?

(7) Value systems. Social structures function, too, as anchorages for shared attitudes and values or, in other words, for culture. By the same token, roles are anchorages for certain individual differences in outlook and personality, though roles are not the only factor associated with personality. Attitudes, values and personality represent one of the major sets of variables that have been related to the acceptance of innovation and, if we consider them both at the level of the individual and of the group, it becomes possible to point out some interesting parallels between ostensibly unrelated traditions of research.

The central idea is that of "compatability" or "fit" between the culture of a group or the personality of the individual and the elements of a proposed innovation. On the group level, there are a number of anthropological studies underlining this principle.[70] Among early studies,

[60] Edmondson, *op. cit.*

[61] For the influence of such variables on the acceptance of new farm practices see Lionberger, *Adoption of New Ideas and Practices, op. cit.*, Chaps. 8 and 9.

[62] See Fred Voget, "Individual Motivation . . . ," *op. cit.*, and the literature on nativistic movements generally.

[63] See John C. Belcher, "Acceptance of the Salk Polio Vaccine," *Rural Sociology*, 23 (June, 1958), pp. 158–170. Other studies of the diffusion of acceptance of the Salk Vaccine in other circumstances find the usual inverse relationship with education, social status, etc. Compare John A. Clausen, Morton A. Seidfeld and Leila C. Deasy, "Parent Attitudes toward Participation of Their Children in Polio Vaccine Trials," *American Journal of Public Health*, 44 (December, 1954), pp. 1526–1536.

[64] Eugene A. Wilkening, "Changes in Farm Technology as Related to Familism, Family Decision Making and Family Integration," *American Sociological Review*, 19 (February, 1954), pp. 29–37.

[65] Larsen and Hill, "Social Structure and Interpersonal Communication," *op. cit.*; Herbert F. Lionberger, "The Relation of Informal Social Groups to the Diffusion of Farm Information in a Northwest Missouri Farm Community," *Rural Sociology*, 19 (September, 1954), pp. 233–243.

[66] Coleman, Katz and Menzel, *op. cit.*

[67] See *The Tastemakers, op. cit.*

[68] For example, Ryan and Gross, *op. cit.*, F. E. Emery and O. A. Oeser, "*Information, Decision and Action*, Melbourne: Melbourne University Press, 1958.

[69] For example, Rose K. Goldsen and Max Ralis, *Factors Related to the Acceptance of Innovations in Bang Chan, Thailand*, Ithaca: Cornell Thailand Project, Interim Reports Series, No. 3, 1957.

[70] For a general discussion, and many specific examples, see Homer G. Barnett, *Innovation*, New York: McGraw-Hill, 1953. This general conception has long been a fundamental postulate of anthropological thinking about cultural change. See, for ex-

Lowie's, Wissler's, Radin's and Spier's studies on various aspects of diffusion among American Indians all emphasize the role of culture in making for selective borrowing.[71] Somewhat later, Elsie Clews Parsons also stressed that traits were taken over by Mexican Indian townspeople from the Spanish and from others when they could "be fitted into an old form of behavior and (were) compatible with existing emotional attitudes."[72] Since these early studies, anthropologically oriented research on diffusion has typically taken account of this principle. Furthermore, resistance to proposed innovations as well as acceptance has often been explained in terms of this conception; in such cases, of course, the emphasis is upon the incompatibility between the receiving culture and the innovation.[73]

But all too few of these studies are compara-

tive in the sense of setting out to demonstrate that a given item is acceptable to relatively comparable groups which, however, differ in values. One such example may be found in Oliver's study of the greater acceptability of new plant foods in a community many of whose rituals centered on the pig as compared with a community where *taro*, a plant, was a center of ritual and an important element in many institutional relations.[74] Hawley reports on a similar comparative situation where Catholicism found greater acceptance among the patrilineally oriented Eastern Pueblo but was incompatible with the matrilineally oriented Western Pueblo.[75] In much the same way, Saxon Graham seeks to explain the differential penetration of television and other leisure-time innovations in the middle and working classes in terms of the hospitality offered by the different sets of values of the two classes.[76]

On the individual level, the notion of compatibility, or fit, is equally applicable. Here can be located the whole tradition of motivation research in marketing. For motivation research is, in essence, the exploration of the symbolic meaning attributed by consumers to given items, seeking, ultimately, to tailor the item or its image to the consumer's personality.[77] Studying the introduction of television in England, Himmelweit established that even when class membership is held constant, different value orientations characterize early and late adopters.[78] The former seemed more present-oriented while the latter were more future-oriented and perhaps inner-directed. In addition, rural sociologists have occasionally dealt with the problem of the functional compatibility of a new practice in relation to the personality characteristics of the individual.[79]

In any case, this classification brings very different research traditions into touch. Neverthe-

---

ample, in addition to the references cited in footnote 2, Boas' thinking in an early paper (1911) later reprinted in *Race, Language and Culture*, New York: Macmillan, 1940, p. 299. Somewhat later Linton ably stated the important elements of earlier anthropological thinking on this problem in *The Study of Man*, New York: Appleton Century Co., 1936. It should be noted that virtually from the beginning this conception of cultural compatibility has been applied to two distinctly different aspects of change phenomena. On the one hand, the compatibility conception has been applied to the problem of what might be called "symbolic" or "meaningful" fit between an innovation and the "mentality" of human targets of change; or perhaps more accurately, the compatibility between the meanings and symbolic significance of the innovation as perceived by the actors in question and their own system of values, attitudes and moods. On the other, the notion of compatibility has been applied to what might be referred to as "functional fit," i.e., the problem of the compatibility between the innovation and the adopting system viewed from the standpoint of the *consequences* of accepting and using the innovation.

[71] Cf. footnote 3, above.

[72] See Elsie Clews Parsons, *Mitla, Town of the Souls*, Chicago: University of Chicago Press, 1936, p. 536.

[73] For example, Charles J. Erasmus, *op. cit.*, describes a situation among Haitian farmers, especially the backward ones, where the strong acceptance of a norm opposing "too much" material success acts to block and/or delay the diffusion of improved agricultural methods. Others who have emphasized this point include Charles P. Loomis and Glen Gresham, "The New Mexican Experiment in Village Rehabilitation," *Applied Anthropology*, 2 (June, 1943), pp. 13–37; F. L. Bailey, "Suggested Techniques for Inducing Navaho Women to Accept Hospitalization During Childbirth," *American Journal of Public Health*, 38 (October, 1948), pp. 1418–1423; Morris E. Opler and Rudra Dott Singh, "Economic, Political and Social Change in a Village of North Central India," *Human Organization*, 11 (Summer, 1952), pp. 5–12; Bertram Hutchinson, "Some Social Consequences of Nineteenth Century Missionary Activity among the South African Bantu," *Africa*, 27 (April, 1957), pp. 160–175.

[74] Douglas L. Oliver, "A Case of a Change in Food Habits in Bougainville, British Solomon Islands," *Applied Anthropology*, 1 (January-March, 1942), pp. 34–46.

[75] Florence Hawley, "The Role of Pueblo Social Organization in the Dissemination of Catholicism," *American Anthropologist*, 48 (1946), pp. 407–415.

[76] Saxon Graham, "Class and Conservatism in the Adoption of Innovations," *Human Relations*, 9, 1 (1956), pp. 91–100.

[77] See George H. Smith, *Motivation Research in Advertising and Marketing* (New York: McGraw-Hill, 1953). An excellent example of work in this tradition is the early study of Maison Haire, "Projective Techniques in Marketing Research," *Journal of Marketing*, 14 (April, 1950), pp. 649–656, demonstrating that the initial resistance to instant coffee was based on an image that the product symbolized housewifely laziness.

[78] Hilde Himmelweit, *et al.*, *Television and the Child*, London: Oxford University Press, 1958.

[79] For example, Irving A. Spaulding, "Farm Operator Time-Space Orientations and the Adoption of Recommended Farming Practices," Rhode Island Agricultural Experiment Station Bulletin, No. 330, 1955; Everett M. Rogers, "Personality Correlates of the Adoption of Technical Practices," *Rural Sociology*, 22 (September, 1957), pp. 267–268.

less, although the long-run aim may be the same, the dependent variables tend to be different. Hawley and Graham, for example, are concerned with the comparative extent of penetration of the item being studied in groups with different values. On the individual level, Himmelweit is concerned with the acceptance of TV by a given date. Motivation researchers, however, hardly ever study actual acceptance; their dependent variable is more likely to be "propensity to accept" and even that is often vaguely defined. Indeed, it may be said that this entire line of work requires that a distinction be made between the potential adopter's perception of the compatibility of an item and some objective evaluation of its compatibility, particularly over a longer period. This distinction parallels, to some extent, the earlier allusions to the difference between first use of an item and continued use. The item may be perceived as attractive to begin with, but experience with the item may involve unanticipated consequences which prove the longer-run incompatibility. Thus, the ease with which Puerto Rican women were willing to begin use of contraception does not jibe with the difficulties of inducing them to continue regular use.[80] In turn, this raises a more general question concerning the tendency to overlook the fact that most innovative items consist of complex elements some of which may "fit" while others may not.

Apart from the notion of functional fit, however, there are other subheadings within the cultural dimension which must be accounted for. Thus, there is a set of ideas, both on the group and on the individual level, which would seem to have more to do with a *general orientation toward innovation* than with the specific compatibility between certain innovations and certain values. Rural sociologists have conducted several studies of variations in ethnic attitudes toward innovation.[81] On the individual level, too, early vs. late adopters, or adopters vs. non-adopters, have been studied in terms of orientations such as sacred-secular, scientific-traditional, cosmopolitan-local and the like.[82]

CONCLUSIONS

We have tried (*1*) to present an overview of the basic elements of the process of diffusion, and (*2*) to indicate, with respect to this accounting

scheme, where each of a variety of research traditions has contributed as well as where it has fallen short, and (*3*) to specify problems which deserve further study.[83] We have drawn specifically on the early work on diffusion in anthropology, sociology and education, and on more contemporary work stemming from the sociology of mass communication, rural sociology, studies of acculturation and of technical change, public health and marketing. We have hardly begun to explore the work in folklore, geography, archeology, and other fields.

From the point of view of further development of the basic components, we have suggested (*1*) that the dependent variable, which we have been calling *acceptance,* must be more clearly defined; (*2*) that considerable ingenuity is needed to date the acceptance of innovations by their adopters, for *time* is the key to diffusion research; (*3*) that considerable effort must be invested in the development of a "content analytic" scheme for classifying *the item* which is diffusing; (*4*) that attention must be given to the *unit of adoption* "required" by an item in the light of the unit which is "prescribed" or the unit which is the "target" of a communication campaign; (*5*) that interpersonal *channels* of communication must be viewed as elements of social structure; (*6*) that work is urgently needed on the comparative study of the same item diffusing in different *social structures* and, finally, (*7*) that the notion of "compatibility" between a given *culture* or personality and an item must be formulated much more strictly.

From the point of view of the various traditions, we have tried to suggest how the work of each tradition contributes to a generic design for diffusion research. Thus, anthropology brings into clear focus the group as the unit of adoption, and intergroup, rather than intragroup, contacts; it

[80] See Hill, Stycos and Back, *op. cit.* Also see Apodaca, "Corn and Custom," in Spicer (ed.), *op. cit.*

[81] For example, Harold A. Pederson, "Cultural Differences in the Acceptance of Recommended Farm Practices," *Rural Sociology,* 16 (March, 1951), pp. 37–49; C. R. Hoffer, "Acceptance of Improved Farm Practices among Farmers of Dutch Descent," Michigan State College Agricultural Experiment Station, Special Bulletin No. 316, June 1942.

[82] For example, Emery and Oeser, *op. cit.*; Ryan and Gross, *op. cit.*

[83] It deserves to be noted that, in 1952, a subcommittee of the Rural Sociological Society proposed a classification system for diffusion studies which resembles this one in part. It divided studies into those emphasizing (1) differential acceptance of farm practices as a function of status, role and motivation; (2) differential acceptance as a function of socio-cultural systems; (3) diffusion as the study of cultural change; and (4) diffusion as a problem of the communication of information. The present paper differs, first of all, in that it advocates the integration of these several approaches in each study, though it also views the elements of the diffusion process as headings in terms of which to organize the various traditions of diffusion research. Secondly, as far as the specific classification schema is concerned, our inclination is to view categories one and two as parallel; accordingly we have grouped the individual (category one) and group (category two) factors together, dividing them only according to whether they are cultural or structural in emphasis.

devotes considerable attention to the structure of social relations between donor and recipient as central to an understanding of the fate of an item moving from one group to the other; it raises the question of "levels" of acceptance. Another contribution of the work in anthropology centers around the concept of compatibility—that is, the extent to which a given culture is receptive to a given new item. But almost no attention is given to channels, and little information is available about the progress of an item over time.

Early sociological work on diffusion also focused on corporate units of adoption (the municipality) as did educational research (the school system). In both these traditions, measures of time-of-adoption were explicitly formulated. Geographical proximity and urban-rural relations are the typical social structures in which channels of communication are thought, in some mysterious way, to inhere.

More recent work in mass communication, rural sociology, public health and marketing has focused explicitly on the individual as the unit of adoption and on his perception of the channels of communication which influence his decision to adopt. Rural sociology has continually taken account of interpersonal relations as a channel but this has not been true of mass communication or marketing research until recently. In each of these fields, there appears to be a growing interest in exploring the social structures in which adopting units are linked, and to introduce time as a variable. If it becomes possible to combine this approach satisfactorily and still take account of the ways in which other channels of communication, including the mass media, impinge on these structures the problem of designing diffusion research for modern society will be well on its way to solution. But there are no easy answers so far.

Part Four is concerned with the emergence, maintenance, and change of group structure and its consequences for group functioning and member satisfaction. Group structure is found in the regularities of feelings, thoughts, and behaviors of members in interaction with one another. Such regularities have been conceptualized in terms of two kinds of structures, the institutional and the subinstitutional. The former refers to regularities whose source lies in systems of shared expectations, norms, or rules of conduct that constrain the behavior of group members. The latter refers to regularities whose source is somewhat more primitive. Whereas institutional controls are maintained through the application of such secondary reinforcers as money or social approval, subinstitutional regularities are maintained by the direct exchange of rewards inherent in the behavior of the interacting participants.[a]

These two structures may be illustrated by considering parent-child interaction. In part, the parent's behavior stems from the normative or institutional expectation that the parent has a right to give guidance to the child and the child has an obligation to obey the parent. These rights and obligations are apt to be enforced by other persons or agents. Both the parent and his child agree on the expectations for their mutual behavior, and they are aware that conformity or nonconformity will result in the approval or disapproval of others. In part, however, their interaction also arises out of a past history which makes their current interaction directly rewarding. For example, the child has learned that when he is afraid he can depend on his parent to comfort him, and his parent experiences direct satisfaction when he engages in such nurturant behavior.

While a number of selections focusing on conformity are relevant to the institutional structure, the primary focus in this section is on subinstitutional regularities, or what Homans[b] has termed elementary social behavior. Such behavior has been studied in two settings. The first has been the small group laboratory; the second has been the study of informal groups in larger organizational settings. Five such structures have been the major conceptual focus for research. These include the sociometric or affect structure, and the power, communication, status, and leadership structures. Aspects of these structures have in turn been related to group productivity and member satisfaction, as well as to the emergence of norms and the extent and distribution of conformity to norms.

The organization of this section revolves around these topics. The first three selections are concerned with interpersonal attraction and the sociometric structure. The next two are concerned with social power. These are followed by three selections dealing with various aspects of status, and, in some instances, with communication. Conformity is the focus of the next two selections and leadership the subject of the four which follow. The determinants of productivity and member satisfaction are then dealt with in two selections and the section concludes with two articles on the determinants of intergroup attitudes.

---

[a] G. C. Homans. *Social behavior: Its elementary forms.* New York: Harcourt, Brace & World, Inc., 1961.
[b] *Ibid.*

PART FOUR

GROUP STRUCTURE AND PROCESS

THE PREDICTION OF INTERPERSONAL ATTRACTION✳

Two major strains of research in social psychology have revolved around the determinants of interpersonal attraction. One has been the sociometric movement. Beginning with the early work of Moreno,[a] hundreds of studies have been made of the patterns of attraction between members of groups, as reflected in choices on sociometric questionnaires. In a sociometric test, group members choose others in terms of some criterion, such as an associate in some activity or simply as a friend or liked object. The responses of group members can be described as a structure in terms of points connected by arrows of varying lengths indicating the degree and direction of affectional bonds between members. While this representation, called a *sociogram*, is probably the most popularly known method of illustrating the affect structure of the group, other methods of analysis are also used when relating features of the affect structure to individual and group variables. The second line of research has revolved around the choice of mates in the courtship process. Typically such research compares the characteristics of each member of the marital dyad. A perennial question has been whether opposites or similars are attracted to each other.[b]

Two trends have characterized these lines of research. Early research concentrated largely on characteristics of the overchosen or the underchosen. Later research took into consideration characteristics of the chooser as well as those of the object of his choice. The present trend suggests a further shift away from focusing on individual characteristics to one that emphasizes elements in the history of the relation, such as previous reciprocal reinforcements, and variables outside the relation, such as the availability of alternative relations. Paralleling this trend has been a progressively more theoretical orientation of much of the research. Today a number of theories attempt to organize, to make sense out of, and to suggest new relations among the voluminous research findings on attraction.

These two functions of theory, organizing existing knowledge and suggesting hypotheses leading to new knowledge, are well demonstrated in the selection that follows. Newcomb first reviews some of the major findings concerning the determinants of interpersonal attraction. He then formulates two theoretical propositions that appear consistent with these findings and proceeds to put these to an empirical test. His research design is also instructive. He attempted to test his hypothesis in situations as close to everyday life as possible, thus maximizing the external validity of his study. At the same time, he attempted to eliminate to some extent the effect of extraneous variables by starting with initial strangers. Finally, measuring variables at various points in time allowed him to determine their temporal order. These last two features add to the internal validity of the study.

21.

The Prediction of Interpersonal Attraction[1]

THEODORE M. NEWCOMB
UNIVERSITY OF MICHIGAN

During the past 30 years, according to my estimate, 9,426 articles and books, plus or minus 2,712, have been published in English on the topic of "attitudes." A large proportion of them deal with attitudes toward people—most commonly toward family members, toward categories like ethnic, religious, or occupational groups, or toward prominent individuals like Franklin D. Roosevelt or Adolf Hitler. At the level of psychological generalization, such studies have probably taught us more about the organization of individual personality, and about group influences upon individual motivation and cognition, than about the nature of person-to-person relationships. At any rate it seems appropriate to pose the question whether persons, as objects of attitudes, have properties that distinguish them from other classes of objects. If so, it is possible that the determinants of attitudes toward persons are in some respects different from those of other attitudes. Since it is convenient to have a distinctive label for something that one wishes to keep distinct, I shall use the term "attraction" to refer to attitudes toward persons as a class of objects.

Today I shall be primarily (though not exclusively) concerned with the motivational-affective aspects of attraction. Though I shall be referring mostly to its simpler manifestations—like choos-

* The selection following the editorial introduction is reprinted from "The prediction of interpersonal attraction," *American Psychologist*, 1956, 1, 575–586, by permission of the author and the American Psychological Association.

[a] J. L. Moreno. *Who shall survive?* (2d ed.) Beacon, N.Y.: Beacon House, Inc., 1953.

[b] R. G. Tharp. Psychological patterning in marriage. *Psychol. Bull.*, 1963, **60**, 97–117.

[1] Address of the President at the Sixty-Fourth Annual Convention of the American Psychological Association, Chicago, Illinois, September 2, 1956.

ing to spend time with a person, or expressing a generally favorable attitude toward him—I want to note, in passing, that there are several dimensions of attraction which are operationally distinctive and (to me, at any rate) conceptually necessary. Though I shall not stop to label these dimensions, what they all have in common is degree and direction on an approach-avoidance continuum, together with associated cognitive content.

I think it not much of an exaggeration to say that there exists no very adequate theory of interpersonal attraction. It has often seemed to me that even we psychologists, who like to pride ourselves in recognizing that nothing occurs apart from its necessary and sufficient conditions, have come very close to treating the phenomenon of personal attraction as an exception to the general rule. It is almost as if we, like our lay contemporaries, assumed that in this special area the psychological wind bloweth where it listeth, and that the matter is altogether too ineffable, and almost passeth even psychological understanding.

I hope you will regard this last comment as being in part, but not *in toto,* a rhetorical exaggeration. The fact is, of course, that both theoretical and empirical efforts have been devoted to the problem. To some of these I now turn.

Perhaps the simplest—and, in many ways, still the most convincing—of the notions concerning determinants of positive attraction is that of *propinquity*. In its baldest form, the proposition of propinquity reads as follows: other things equal, people are most likely to be attracted toward those in closest contact with them. Everyday illustrations readily leap to mind. Adults generally have strongest attraction toward those children, and children toward those adults, with whom they are in most immediate contact—which is to say, their own children and their own parents. And this commonly occurs, let me remind you, in spite of the fact that neither parents nor children choose each other. Or, if we are willing to accept the fact of selection of marriage partners as an index of positive attraction, then the available data are strongly in support of a theory of propinquity. If we use an adequate range of distance —miles, or city blocks rather than yards, or within-block distances—there is a neat, monotonic relationship between residential propinquity and probability of marriage, other criteria of eligibility being held constant (e.g., **1, 2, 3**).

It is, of course, a truism that distance per se will have no consequences for attraction; what we are concerned with is something that is made possible, or more likely, with decreasing distance. I think we may also consider it a truism that that something is behavior. Further, it is behavior on the part of one person that is observed and responded to by another: it is interaction. So widespread and so compelling is the evidence for the relationship between frequency of interaction and positive attraction that Homans (**9**) has ventured

to hypothesize that "If the frequency of interaction between two or more persons increases, the degree of their liking for one another will increase." Actuarially speaking, the evidence is altogether overwhelming that, *ignoring other variables*, the proposition is correct in a wide range of situations.

Why should this be so? Accepting the proposition only in an actuarial sense, and ignoring for the moment the other variables obviously involved, what theoretical considerations will enable us to make psychological sense out of it? The principle which comes first to mind is that of *reward and reinforcement*. Two simple assumptions will enable us to make direct use of this principle: first, that when persons interact, the reward-punishment ratio is more often such as to be reinforcing than extinguishing; and second, that the on-the-whole rewarding effects of interaction are most apt to be obtained from those with whom one interacts most frequently. These assumptions, together with the principles of reward and reinforcement and canalization, would account for the general association of frequency of interaction with positive attraction; they would not, of course, account for the many observed exceptions to the generalization.

To return to my earlier illustrations, this set of assumptions and principles would not apply in exactly the same way to the facts of attraction between parents and children and to the facts of marital selection. One difference, of course, is that selection is possible in the latter but not in the former case. As applied to the facts of parent-child attraction, the principle of propinquity asserts, in effect, that we are attracted to those whom "fate" has made rewarding. As applied to the facts of marital selection, the principle of propinquity says little more, in addition to this, than that the likelihood of being rewarded by interaction varies with opportunity for interaction. The problem of selection, among those with whom opportunity for interaction is the same, still remains.

The principle of *generalization* has often been called upon to account for selective attraction among those with whom opportunities for interaction are the same. Many Freudians, in particular, have assumed that in adolescence or adulthood attractions are largely determined by personal qualities resembling those of parents or siblings, initially determined by the Oedipus configuration —as illustrated by the old refrain, "I want a girl just like the girl that married dear old Dad." This principle, together with its variants, obviously cannot be omitted from a complete theory of interpersonal attraction, but neither can it be considered as a major contribution to it, since, in itself, it says nothing about the initial basis of attraction but only about extensions from one already attractive person to another, similar one. Perhaps the chief contribution of the principle of generalization lies in the enhanced probability that thresholds for interaction with persons resembling those toward whom one is already attracted are lower than for other persons; if so, then the likelihood of the rewards of interaction with such persons is greater than for other persons.

There is an interesting consequence of the proposition that attraction toward others varies with the frequency of being rewarded by them. Opportunities for being rewarded by others vary not only with propinquity, as determined by irrelevant considerations like birth and residence, but also with the motivations of the potentially rewarding persons. This suggests that the likelihood of being continually rewarded by a given person varies with the frequency with which that person is in turn rewarded, and thus we have a proposition of *reciprocal reward:* the likelihood of receiving rewards from a given person, over time, varies with the frequency of rewarding him. This proposition is significant for my problem in various ways, especially because it forces further consideration of the conditions under which continued interaction between the same persons is most likely, and under which, therefore, the possibilities of continued reciprocal reward are greatest.

The first of these may be most simply described as the possession by two or more persons of common interests, apart from themselves, that require interdependent behavior. If you like to play piano duets, or tennis, you are apt to be rewarded by those who make it possible for you to do so, and at the same time you are apt to reward your partner. Insofar as both partners are rewarded, another evening of duets or another set of tennis is likely to ensue, together with still further opportunities for reciprocal reward. Thus attraction breeds attraction.

The second condition favorable to continued reciprocal rewards has to do with complementary interests (rather than with similar ones) that require interdependent behavior. These are symbiotic relationships, like that in which cow and cowbird become attracted to each other: the cow provides sustenance for the bird in the form of parasitic insects, the removal of which is rewarding to both. Or, at the human level, consider the exchange of gratifications between a pair of lovers. Here, too, under conditions of complementary rather than of similar motivations, the general rule is that attraction breeds attraction.

There have also been interesting attempts, of late, to test the proposition that symbiotic personality needs tend to characterize marriage partners—who, it may be presumed, are reciprocally attracted to a greater than average degree. Pro-

fessor E. L. Kelly's work, some of which was reported on this occasion one year ago (**11**), has quite consistently revealed the existence of similar rather than complementary traits, both among spouses twenty-odd years married and among engaged couples. It is interesting, however, that his findings since last year suggest a curvilinear relationship between initial homogeneity and marriage durability; the best prognosis is provided by neither too much nor too little similarity. These findings, however, are not conclusive for my present problem—first, because there are many determinants of marriage durability other than personal attraction; and second, because comparatively few of the traits that he measured were such as could either confirm or disconfirm the hypothesis of personality symbiosis.

This problem has, however, been directly attacked by Professor Robert Winch, using measures derived from Murray's list of needs. My own perusal of his research reports (**17, 18**) suggests no conclusive findings for my problem, but if his personality ratings are free from contamination it seems clear that, within his sample of 25 middle-class couples, traits or needs can be found with regard to which spouses are more likely to be different than alike—in particular a dimension labeled "assertive-receptive." It is not possible, from Winch's data (nor from any other data known to me), to estimate how much of the variance in marital selection can be accounted for in terms of symbiotic personality needs. But it is surely a plausible notion that an individual with strong needs for assertiveness is more likely to find himself rewarded in this area of his life by interaction with a person who is receptive to his assertiveness than with one who is not.

The most detailed of the analyses of sociometric structures, especially those of Jennings (**10**), reveal analogous kinds of personality symbiosis; the over-chosen need the under-chosen, and vice versa. Many of the phenomena of choosing and accepting "leaders" (cf. **7**) are also understandable from this point of view.

There is another common notion about interpersonal attraction, to the effect that it varies with similarity, as such: birds of a feather flock together. It is not a very useful notion, however, because it is indiscriminate. We have neither good reason nor good evidence for believing that persons of similar blood types, for example, or persons whose surnames have the same numbers of letters, are especially attracted to one another. The answer to the question, Similarity with respect to what?, is enormously complex—because similarities of many kinds are associated with sheer contiguity, for one thing. I shall therefore content myself with the guess (for which fairly good evidence exists[2]) that the possession of similar characteristics predisposes individuals to be attracted

---

[2] Such evidence will be presented in my forthcoming monograph.

to each other to the degree that those characteristics are both observable and valued by those who observe them—in short, insofar as they provide a basis for similarity of attitudes.

Up to this point I have noted that we acquire favorable or unfavorable attitudes toward persons as we are rewarded or punished by them, and that the principles of contiguity, of reciprocal reward, and of complementarity have to do with the conditions under which rewards are most probable. From now on I shall be primarily concerned with a special subclass of reciprocal rewards—those associated with communicative behavior.

The interaction processes through which reciprocal reward occurs have to do not with the exchange of energy but with the exchange of information, and are therefore communicative. I prefer the term "communicative behavior" to "social interaction" because it calls attention to certain consequences that are characteristic of information exchange, but not of energy exchange, among symbol-using humans. The use of symbols, needless to say, involves the expenditure of energy, but—even in so obvious an example as that of receiving a slap in the face—it is the consequences of the information exchange rather than the energy exchange which interest us, as psychologists.

I shall note two of these consequences, in the form of very general propositions—though each of them is in fact subject to very specific limitations. The first is this: Communicators tend to become more similar to each other, at least momentarily, in one or more respects, than they were before the communication. At the very least (assuming more or less accurate receipt of a message that has been intentionally sent), both sender and receiver now have the information that the sender wishes to call the attention of the receiver to the object of communication—i.e., that which the symbols symbolize. If we stipulate still further conditions, the proposition will apply to a wider range of similarity. Suppose, for example, that a person has just expressed an opinion about something—say the United Nations; to the degree that he is sincere, and insofar as the receiver trusts his sincerity, the communication (if accurately received) will be followed by increased cognitive similarity, to the effect that the transmitter holds the stated opinion. Now suppose we add a further stipulation—that the receiver not only trusts the sender's sincerity but also respects his knowledgeability; under these conditions the opinions of sender and receiver are likely to be more similar than they were before.

It is this last kind of similarity—i.e., that of attitudes—that has a special importance for the problem of interpersonal attraction. In fact, the proposition, as applied to similarity of attitudes toward objects of communication, has already introduced, as independent variables, certain dimensions of attraction—namely, trust and respect. Change toward similarity in one kind of attitude

following communication, I have asserted, varies with another kind of attitude—i.e., attraction.

My second proposition reverses this relationship: Attraction toward a co-communicator (actual or potential) varies with perceived similarity of attitudes toward the object of communication. Before specifying the limited conditions under which this proposition applies, let me briefly present its rationale.

While there are, of course, many exceptions, it is a highly dependable generalization that the life history of every human has made accurate communication rewarding far more often than punishing. Such is our dependence upon one another, from the very beginnings of communicative experience, and such is our indebtedness to culture, which is transmitted via communication, that success in the enterprise of becoming socialized depends upon success in transmitting and receiving messages. Insofar as accurate communication is in fact rewarding, reward value will attach to the co-communicator—which is to say that positive attraction toward him will increase (other things equal) with frequency of accurate communication with him. Please note the qualification: "insofar as accurate communication is in fact rewarding"; there are many messages—e.g., "I hate you"—the accurate receipt of which is not in fact rewarding.

If, as I have maintained, increased similarity in some degree and manner is the regular accompaniment of accurate communication, it would be no surprise to discover that increased similarity becomes a goal of communication, and that its achievement is rewarding. And if, as I have also maintained, the reward value of successful communication attaches to the co-communicator, then it follows that the two kinds of reward effects—perception of increased similarity as rewarding, and perception of the co-communicator as rewarding—should vary together. This, in brief, is the rationale of my second proposition.

It is, however, a very general statement, and its usefulness can be enhanced by a further specification of conditions. I shall mention only two of them. First, the discovery of increased similarity is rewarding to the degree that the object with regard to which there is similarity of attitudes is valued (either negatively or positively). The discovery of agreement between oneself and a new acquaintance regarding some matter of only casual interest will probably be less rewarding than the discovery of agreement concerning one's own pet prejudices. The reward value of increased similarity increases, secondly, with the common relevance of the attitude object to the communicators. The success of a certain presidential candidate, for example, is likely to be seen as having consequences for both, whereas matters regarded as belonging in the area of personal taste—like taking cream in one's coffee—are viewed as devoid of common consequences. The discovery of similarity of the latter kind is not very likely to have much reward value.

The thesis that interpersonal attraction varies with perceived similarity in regard to objects of importance and of common relevance is, from one point of view, opposed to the thesis of complementarity. In my own view, however, they are not in opposition; indeed, I regard the thesis of complementarity as a special case of similarity. Let me illustrate. Suppose, as Winch's data may indicate, that an assertive person is more likely to be attracted toward a receptive than toward another assertive person, as a marriage partner. It is my guess that this would most probably occur if they have similar attitudes to the effect that one of them should be assertive and the other receptive. (Whether or not they use these words—and whether, indeed, they are able to verbalize the matter at all—does not matter.) In short, I am attempting to defend the thesis that interpersonal attraction always and necessarily varies with perceived similarity regarding important and relevant objects (including the persons themselves). While I regard similarity of attitudes as a necessary rather than a sufficient condition, I believe that it accounts for more of the variance in interpersonal attraction than does any other single variable.

As the foregoing implies, and as I have elsewhere suggested (13), attraction and perceived similarity of attitude tend to maintain a constant relationship because each of them is sensitive to changes in the other. If newly received information about another person leads to increased or decreased attraction toward him, appropriate changes in perceived similarity readily ensue—often at the cost of accuracy. And if new information—either about the object or about another person's attitudes toward it—leads to perceptions of increased or decreased similarity with him, then the direction or the degree of attraction toward him easily accommodates itself to the situation as newly perceived. Change in attraction is one, but only one, of the devices by which some sort of tension state, associated with perceived discrepancy about important and relevant objects, is kept at a minimum.

At the outset, I raised the question whether persons, as objects of attitudes, have properties that distinguish them from other objects. I ought now to acknowledge that I have already assumed that they do. I have been assuming that persons, as *objects* of attitudes, also *have* attitudes of their own—and, in particular, that they have (or can have) attitudes toward the *same* objects as do persons who are sources of attitudes toward the object-persons. Further, I have been assuming

that object-persons have the same capacities for being disturbed by perceived discrepancies as do those who are attracted toward them. In degree, if not *in toto*, these are distinctively human characteristics, as G. H. Mead long ago noted (12), and any theory of interpersonal attraction that is at all distinctive from a general theory of attitudes must, I believe, pay homage to this fact.

The remainder of this paper is devoted to some tests of specific predictions derived from the two propositions already presented, which may be telescoped as follows: Insofar as communication results in the perception of increased similarity of attitude toward important and relevant objects, it will also be followed by an increase in positive attraction. I shall therefore consider perceived similarity of attitude as a predictor of attraction. I shall also, for obvious reasons, be interested in actual, or objective, similarity.

Since the findings which I shall present were obtained in a single research setting, I shall stop briefly to note the nature of that setting. I started with the research objective of observing the changing interrelationships, over time, between attraction and similarity of attitudes. Since it seemed important to start with a base line of zero, as far as attraction was concerned, it was necessary to find a population of persons who were complete strangers to each other. It also seemed desirable to provide a setting in which it would be possible for a high degree of positive attraction to develop, and in which regular and repeated observations could be made. All of these requirements seemed to be met by the following arrangements. A student house was rented; male transfer students, all strangers to the University of Michigan, were offered the opportunity (several weeks before their planned arrival at the University) of receiving free room rent for a full semester; in return they were to spend four or five hours a week in responding to questionnaires and interviews, and in participating in experiments. Among those who submitted applications to live in the house under these conditions, 17 (the capacity of the house) were selected, no two of whom had ever lived in the same city, nor attended the same school. All 17 men arrived within a 24-hour period, and all responded to a questionnaire within a very few hours thereafter. The men were given no voice in the selection of roommates, but (within the limits of University regulations) they were given complete freedom to conduct the house, including the cooking and eating arrangements, as they chose. The entire procedure was repeated, with a different but strictly comparable group, one year later. So far, however, the data have not been very fully analyzed, and unless otherwise noted the findings that I shall report are from the second year only.

In this setting, data were obtained by questionnaire and interview, at semi-weekly intervals. A wide range of attitude responses was obtained, as well as rather complete data concerning interpersonal attraction. Measures of the latter were derived both from responses to direct questions about how favorably each house member felt toward each of the others, and from reports by each about informal, freely associating subgroups of two or more. It turned out that there were some important differences between these two measures of attraction. The "General Liking" responses (as we labeled the former) were the more amenable to parametric measurement, and unless otherwise specified those findings that I shall mention here depend upon this measure. But the "clique" measure (as we came to call it) was probably the more valid index of attraction for the purpose of testing many of our hypotheses, since it was based upon the reports of many observers having constant opportunity to notice who spent most time, and therefore had most opportunity for communication, with whom. The General Liking measure was probably the more sensitive toward the negative pole of attraction, since a full sixth of all pairs received zero scores on the other measure; but toward the positive pole it was often a more valid index of "admiration at a distance" than of direct contact and communication.

I turn now to some specific predictions. First, if the basic generalization is correct, it should follow that, regardless of the content of communication, positive attraction will increase with opportunity for communication, other things equal. The only additional assumption involved in this prediction is that the likelihood of being rewarded by a co-communicator increases with opportunity for communication. I might add that there is nothing new about this prediction; it is, in fact, a restatement of our old friend, the principle of propinquity. Previous studies—e.g., by Festinger, Schachter, and Back (5) and by Deutsch and Collins (4)—have provided convincing support for it.

Our own data give partial, but not complete, support for the prediction. Perhaps the best illustration of our findings that I can offer stems from an experimental "failure." During our first project year, roommate assignments had, literally, been drawn from a hat. In planning for the second year, however, we decided to assign roommates by experimental criteria. Half of the roommate combinations were therefore assigned in such manner as to insure (as we thought) that *minimal* attraction between roommates would result, and *maximal* attraction in the other half of the combinations. (Our assignments were based upon data provided by mail, some weeks before the men arrived.) Our predictions received no support whatever; from the very beginning, and during each of the succeeding 15 weeks, the mean level of attraction between roommates—including those for whom we had predicted low attraction—was higher than for all non-roommate pairs. It is also worth reporting that, at the beginning but not at the end of the semester, mean attrac-

tion among all pairs living on each of the two floors of the house was higher than for all inter-floor pairs. During the final week, 90 per cent of all inter-roommate choices were in the upper three-eighths of all choices.

These findings, as I have said, were obtained during our second year. Now I must report that, during the first year, the relationship between attraction and room propinquity was nothing like so close. I shall not stop to give you the actual figures, but at the end of the semester inter-roommate attraction was only slightly higher than that between non-roommates. This inconsistency would be frustrating, indeed, if there were no other variables to which the differences could be related; after describing these other variables, I shall show that they account for much of this inconsistency with regard to proximity. Meanwhile, the proposition under consideration is that proximity, alone, cannot account for attraction, but only to the degree that it facilitates the development of perceived similarity of attitude does it contribute to attraction.

The remainder of my predictions, unlike the first, take into account the content of communication. They are of the following general form: If and when increased attraction between pairs of persons does occur with opportunity for communication, it will be associated with increased similarity of attitude toward important and relevant objects.

The first of these predictions is based upon the additional assumption that one's self is a valued object to oneself. If so, then attraction should vary closely with self-other agreement about oneself. More specifically, insofar as a person's presumably ambivalent self-orientations are predominantly positive, his attraction toward others will vary directly with their attraction toward him. In testing this proposition, reciprocal attraction may be treated either as "objective" (i.e., as actually expressed by others toward the individual being considered) or as "perceived" (i.e., as that individual estimates that others will express attraction toward himself). The latter prediction, however—that one's attraction toward others varies with their perceived attraction toward oneself —seems almost untestable except in circular fashion; there are few ways in which it can be demonstrated in a "natural" situation, that attraction toward others is the dependent variable and that perceived attraction toward oneself the independent variable.

Whatever the causal direction, our data show that an individual's distribution of General Liking among his associates is related to their liking for him. The relationship is almost as close on the fourth day as at the end of the fourth month, and as a general tendency is highly significant,

Produce

though there are individual exceptions. One can predict an individual's liking for another individual with much better than chance accuracy if one knows the latter's liking for the former, at any time after the fourth day.

The prediction will be a good deal more accurate, however, if it is made from an individual's *estimate* of how well he is liked by the other. At any time from the second week on (when such estimates were first made), about three of every four estimates of another person's liking for oneself were in the same half of the distribution as own liking for that other person. Median rank-order correlations were .86 at the end, and .75 at the beginning, between each man's liking for each other man and his estimate of the reciprocals. As might be expected, this relationship was especially close at the extremes; 5 out of 6 predictions of liking for other persons would be in the correct quarter of the distribution, if based only upon subjects' estimates that they are in the highest or lowest quarter of reciprocated liking. Such findings correspond closely to those previously reported by Tagiuri (16).

Apparently the close relationship between General Liking and its estimated reciprocal is but slightly influenced by communication. At any rate, the relationship does not increase significantly from near-strangership to close acquaintance, nor is the relationship significantly closer for roommates, at the end of the four-month period, than for non-roommates. Neither, as a matter of fact, does accuracy in estimating reciprocal liking increase with further acquaintance, for most subjects. Estimates of others' liking for oneself are so closely correlated with own liking for those same persons (the relationship approaches the self-correlation of either measure, at any given time), that most of the variance of either can be accounted for by the other. Whatever influences either of them influences both in about the same way.

These facts—that perceived reciprocation remains closely tied to own liking without increasing in accuracy over time—do not mean that estimated reciprocation is purely autistic. On the contrary, it tends to be quite accurate, differing from chance distributions at beyond the .001 level. Two of every three estimates, at all times, are in the correct half. What these facts do mean, apparently, is that both attraction toward others and its estimated reciprocal are jointly determined by autistic and by "realistic" factors, in such manner as to remain closely bound together in a relationship that does not change over time. I believe that a clue to the manner of interaction between autistic and "realistic" influences is provided by the following additional fact. Without exception, the men whose liking status rose with

time either became more accurate in their estimates of reciprocation or maintained the earlier degree of accuracy, while those whose status declined tended to become less accurate. Our subjects had no difficulty in adapting, realistically, to the fact of rising sociometric status, but acceptance of declining status was only partial. All subjects distributed about the same range of liking scores, but each tended to receive a distinctive distribution. Estimated reciprocals represent a compromise between own liking for the individual in question and *amour propre*.

The proposition that perceived similarity in valuing the self contributes heavily to variance in attraction, together with the assumption that self-valuation tends to remain high at all times, is thus well supported. All persons, at all times, are liked according as they are judged to agree with oneself about oneself. These judgments become more accurate over time to the degree that one's actual changes in status make it possible to judge them accurately and at the same time continue to believe that one's own likings are reciprocated. For those who are discovering that their actual status is relatively low, the conflict—or, more specifically, the strain of perceived discrepancy—thus aroused is reduced at the cost of accuracy.

I have already implied that attraction is hypothetically predictable from cognitive as well as from cathectic similarity regarding objects of importance. I shall present findings concerning cognitive similarity regarding only one kind of object —persons. Each subject was asked to describe himself as well as the other house members by checking adjectives drawn from a list prepared by Professor Harrison Gough (8). Each was also asked to describe his "ideal self," by using the same list, and to describe himself as he thought other house members would describe him. By comparing these responses with self-descriptions, we obtained measures of perceived similarity regarding the self. (This work closely parallels that by Fiedler [6] concerning "assumed similarity."

Attraction turns out to be closely related to perceived agreement (at considerably less than the .001 level). When the same data are analyzed individually, only two of 17 subjects fail to show the relationship in the predicted direction, and only one of these reverses it. This finding is more impressive than it would be if it resulted from attributing only favorable judgments of oneself to high-liked others, and only unfavorable judgments to low-liked others. Actually, eight of the ten subjects who accepted unfavorable adjectives as describing themselves, and who indicated that one or more others agreed with them, showed more agreement in these unfavorable descriptions with high-liked than with low-liked others. The relationship between attraction and perceived agreement on favorable items is, not surprisingly, a good deal closer. At any rate, the finding that attraction varies with perceived cognitive agreement about the self is not merely an artifactual result of the common-sense assumption that one is attracted toward those who are believed to think well of one. Judging from our data, it is also true —and perhaps contrary to common sense—that we are attracted to those whom we perceive as seeing both our foibles and our virtues as we ourselves see them. Many psychotherapists, I am told,[3] can readily confirm this observation. I believe, by the way, that the patient's perception of converging attitudes toward himself, by himself and therapist, has much to do with the phenomena of positive attraction in "transference."[4]

My next prediction deals not with the self as object of attitudes but with other house members. Of all the objects about which we obtained responses, nothing compared in importance or in group relevance with the house members themselves. Very early they became differentiated in attraction status, so that it was easy to measure similarity, on the part of any pair of persons, in attraction toward the remaining members. Correlations were calculated between the attraction scores of each member and those of each other member (there were 136 such pairs, each year) toward all of the other 15 members; this was done for each of the 16 weeks that the group lived together. Thus the proposition could be tested that the greater the similarity between any two members in assigning General Liking scores to the other 15 members, the higher their attraction for each other. A related prediction is that this relationship will increase with communication—that is, with time.

Both propositions receive clear support, according to both criteria of attraction. On the fourth day the relationship between within-pair General Liking and within-pair correlation of General Liking for remaining members is barely significant, and only slightly higher a week later. It increases fairly steadily till, at the end of four months, two-thirds of all within-pair attractions would be correctly placed in the upper or lower half of the distribution, judging only from the fact of being in the upper or the lower half of the distribution of correlations. This finding emerges more clearly by comparing the mean within-pair correlations for various categories of within-pair attraction, as shown in Figure 1.

Individuals in high agreement with each other about the other 15 house members clearly tend to be attracted to each other. The opposite tendency is much less pronounced; none of the categories involving subjects in the lower eight ranks has a mean correlation much below the average of the total set of pairs. The lowest of all the mean cor-

relations (shown by the X in Figure 1) is that of all pairs of which one member—and only one—is in the lowest quarter of attraction (ranks 13–16). For these 44 pairs the mean correlation is .35— not significantly different from zero. Thus, the correlations predict not only to within-pair attraction but also (particularly at the extremes) to interpersonal mutuality, regardless of level of attraction; the relationship between them, as calculated by X^2, is in fact significant at the .001 level.

Though it has, in general, proven easier to predict to high than to low attraction, those lowest in our house totem pole deserve a paragraph. The lowest three in our second-year group were truly rejected (according to objective criteria which I cannot stop to specify); they were literally disliked as none others were. (The next lowest two, on the other hand, were near-isolates, who were withdrawn and more or less ignored but not generally disliked.) All six of the attraction responses given and received within this set of three rejects were among the lowest possible three ranks, their average being exactly 15, when 15.5 is the lowest possible average; they were liked by each other even less than others liked them. At the same time, the three intra-pair correlations among these three rejects are slightly above the average for the entire group of subjects, and .7 sigmas above the mean correlation for the same individuals with all others except the rejects themselves (.52 as compared with .39). In short, they disliked each other but tended to agree with each other about the remaining individuals more than they agreed with the remaining individuals. This, of course, is very perverse of them, and it is tempting to conclude that such wilful thwarting of my favorite hypotheses is all of a piece with their personalities, as rejected persons. I shall content myself, however, with suggesting that these three rejects developed a special set of standards: personal inoffensiveness

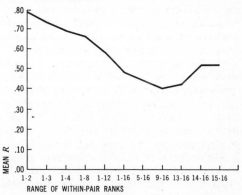

FIGURE 1. Mean within-pair correlations of attraction toward other members.

---

[3] Dr. Keith Sward, in particular, has called this to my attention.
[4] Cf. Rogers (**15**, pp. 66–96) for empirical evidence to the effect that, in at least one case of successful psychotherapy, the correlation between the patient's self-sort and the therapist's description of the patient, by a sorting of the same items, increased over time. I do not know of other data on this point.

in others was highly valued. If such standards did indeed exist, I believe they were developed by each of the three men in relative independence of the other two. They disliked each other too much to be very much influenced by each other. Such agreement as there was among them concerning the remaining men occurred, we know, without benefit of much communication, and it is well to be reminded that attitudinal similarity can occur on the part of individuals in the same predicament facing the same objective world, quite independently of one another's influence.

Since these two predictors (estimated reciprocation and within-pair agreement) are far from perfectly correlated (their relationship is indicated by a contingency coefficient of .60), one may ask about their comparative and their combined predictive power. The statistical breakdowns will eventually be published, and so I shall not present them here. The fact is that if one merely wishes to pin-point the individual instances of high attraction, the estimated reciprocal, alone, is the most successful of all predictors; 97 per cent of the highest quarter of attractions are selected by the criterion of the upper half of the estimated reciprocals. But if one wishes to account for maximum variance, and at both ends of the distribution, the combined criteria are better than either alone. As indicated by a coefficient of contingency of .53 between the combined predictors and actual attraction scores, almost one-third of the variance in attraction is thus accounted for. As shown in Figure 2, high attraction is particularly well predicted by the joint criteria; virtually none of those predicted as high are in fact in the lower half of attraction scores.

These findings, based upon small numbers, would be subject to much suspicion were they not perfectly consistent. Whether by very loose or by very restrictive criteria, the predicted relationships

emerge; the more restrictive the criteria, the greater the excess over chance expectations.

At a theoretical level, I consider it highly significant that these two predictors, the combined effects of which are more successful than either alone, include one subjective index (estimates of reciprocal attraction) and one that is objective, in the sense of describing a relationship between a pair of persons and not referring to either person alone. Theoretically speaking, this is as it should be. Doubtless most forms of social behavior, like attraction, are jointly determined by individual characteristics and by relationships to others—relationships which pertain to the recipient of behavior quite as much as to the behaver himself.

Now let me return, briefly, to our finding that, in one year but not in the other, the mere fact of being a roommate accounted for much of the variance in the development of attraction. I have already implied that propinquity is a facilitator but not a sufficient condition for the development of positive attraction. It should follow, therefore, that attraction between roommates will be relatively high only insofar as their propinquity contributes to the development of one or more of the conditions favorable to high attraction. This is exactly what our data show: roommates scored much higher on both predictor variables during the second year than did non-roommates, but not during the first year.

As shown in Figures 3 and 4, the year-to-year differences in the relationship between attraction and room proximity are paralleled by comparable differences in the relationship between proximity and one of the predictor variables, namely, within-pair correlation of attraction toward the other members. Roommates differ from all others by one full standard deviation at the end of the second year, but by only one-fifth of a standard deviation at the end of the first year. According to the other predictor variable, perceived reciprocality of liking, the differences are of exactly the same order, and the curves are correspondingly parallel.

It seems likely, therefore, that proximity contributes to attraction only by way of the predictor variables. As to why room proximity facilitated the development of the predictor variables in such a way as to lead to high roommate attraction in one year but not in the other, I can only say that I have some reason to believe that more detailed analysis will provide at least partial answers.

You are doubtless wondering about the generality of the proposition that attraction is predictable from similarity of attitude toward important and relevant objects, since the only objects that I have mentioned, so far, are persons. Although our analyses are far from complete, they indicate that the proposition also applies to objects other than persons, though at lower levels of confidence. But it is already clear that, in this research setting, there were no objects which compared in relevance, *for all members*, to house members

FIGURE 2. Per cent of 256 attraction scores selected, at each of four levels, by joint criteria (estimated reciprocals and within-pair correlations).

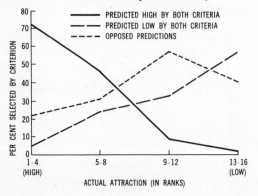

PREDICTED HIGH BY BOTH CRITERIA
PREDICTED LOW BY BOTH CRITERIA
OPPOSED PREDICTIONS

PER CENT SELECTED BY CRITERION

1-4 (HIGH)   5-8   9-12   13-16 (LOW)

ACTUAL ATTRACTION (IN RANKS)

themselves. We sampled a range of attitudes that extended virtually from cabbages to kings; there were several pairs of subjects for whom kings (or at least presidents) were highly relevant, and there may have been some whose within-pair attraction was influenced by attitudes toward cole slaw. There were, however, no *single* non-person objects of sufficient relevance for *all* members to account for very much variance in the attraction level among all pairs.

One way of describing this complication is to note that our subjects knew so much about so many of each others' attitudes that no single one was crucial for all pairs. This predicament is well illustrated by a series of experimental findings. On several occasions, outsiders were brought in to present a point of view on a controversial topic; our subjects' General Liking for these speakers, about whom they knew nothing apart from the one topic, was (as predicted) closely correlated with perceived agreement with them. Perhaps the moral to this story is that, if one wants uncomplicated findings, one should stick to brief, laboratory-like, rather than to long-term, "natural," situations.

There were two ways in which we were able, nevertheless, to show relationships between attraction and similarity in attitude toward non-person objects. The first of these was by regarding highly generalized values as objects. For example, agreement in Allport-Vernon scores was related to attraction, for the total population of 136 pairs; the significance levels ranged from .05 to .01, depending upon the exact measures of each variable. If Osgood's three-dimensional measure of meaning structure (14) may be regarded as a highly generalized attitude, of both cognitive and cathectic nature, toward things-in-general, then the results of using this measure are also relevant. "Semantic harmony," derived from responses to a wide range of stimulus words (e.g., father, politics, sex, money), was significantly related to at least one of our measures of attraction, for all 136 pairs.

Our second approach was to take as an index of attitude similarity the *number* of non-person objects about which there was a given degree of similarity, rather than the *degree* of similarity regarding a single object. This index was related to attraction, for at least one of our two sets of subjects, though not, apparently, at significance levels below .05. This was one of the few measures, by the way, of pre-acquaintance similarity which successfully predicted, among all pairs, to later attraction. If, as appears to be the case, its predictive value tended to increase with time, this finding would be consistent with the assumption that, over time, our subjects tended to sort each other out as they gradually discovered one another's attitudes on a wide range of issues.

I have two brief and final comments concerning the significance of findings such as I have been presenting. First, as to the very limited setting in which they were obtained, there is no reason to

believe that the particular students whom we happen to have studied differed very greatly from other groups of young-adult peers, in the kinds of relationships here reported, at comparable stages of acquaintance. Indeed, it is likely that the very fact of their homogeneity in regard to age and sex and student status tended to reduce the variance of many of their attitudes; if so, at least some of the predictors here reported would prove still more satisfactory with more varied groups. I feel, therefore, that I am not grossly over-extending the application of my own findings when I report, with considerable confidence, that the conditions under which attraction develops and changes or remains stable are orderly ones. It is

FIGURE 3. Deviation from means of general liking and of within-pair correlations of liking for other members, as related to room proximity.

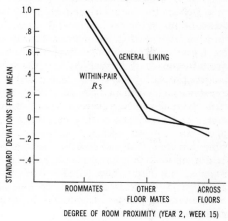

FIGURE 4. Deviation from means of general liking and of within-pair correlations of liking for other members, as related to room proximity.

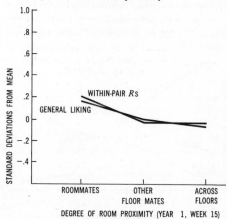

possible, moreover, to formulate statements of these conditions into a consistent body of propositions.

Secondly, as to the common-sense nature of much that I have reported, none of you has been overcome with astonishment on learning, for example, that our subjects tended to like those by whom they thought they were liked, or by those who, they thought, would describe them in most favorable terms. My concern is not so much to point out that some of our findings are *un*expected—e.g., that perceived agreement with others concerning one's own *un*favorable traits is a reasonably good predictor of positive attraction. Nor is it to repeat the ancient truism that no one knows whether what every one knows is true is really true until it has been properly tested. Rather, I want to note that several different propositions (some conforming to common sense and some not), which superficially have nothing to do with one another, are derivable from the same set of assumptions.

The fact seems to be that one can predict to interpersonal attraction, under specified conditions, from frequency of interaction, from the perception of reciprocated attraction, from certain combinations of personality characteristics, and from attitudinal agreement. There is no self-evident reason why such diverse variables, viewed commonsensewise, should belong together; one might almost suspect that they had been drawn out of a hatful of miscellaneous variables. But predictive propositions about those variables all flow, as I have tried to show, from a very few psychological assumptions. I believe the confluence to be both theoretically required and empirically supported. These considerations seem to me to lend confidence to the point of view that a limited theory about a limited class of objects—namely, persons—can profit by taking account of the significant properties of those objects and in particular those properties closely related to the fact of human dependence upon communication.

You may remember an old story whose punch line is "Vive la différence"—Thank God for the little difference. If we are inclined to take a favorable view of positive interpersonal attraction, perhaps we should also be grateful for similarities: Vive la similarité!

REFERENCES

1. BOSSARD, J. H. S. Residential propinquity as a factor in marriage selection. *Amer. J. Sociol.*, 1932, 38, 219–224.

2. CAMPBEL, W. D. The importance of occupation, as compared with age and residence, in marital selection. Unpublished master's thesis, Univer. of Michigan, 1939.

3. DAVIE, M. R., & REEVES, R. J. Propinquity of residence before marriage. *Amer. J. Sociol.*, 1939, 44, 510–517.

4. DEUTSCH, M., & COLLINS, M. E. *Interracial housing: A psychological evaluation of a social experiment.* Minneapolis: Univer. of Minnesota Press, 1951.

5. FESTINGER, L., SCHACHTER, S., & BACK, K. *Social pressures in informal groups.* New York: Harper, 1950.

6. FIEDLER, F. Assumed similarity measures as predictors of team effectiveness. *J. abnorm. soc. Psychol.*, 1954, 49, 381–388.

7. GIBB, C. A. Leadership. In G. Lindzey (Ed.), *Handbook of social psychology.* Cambridge, Mass.: Addison-Wesley, 1954. Vol. II, pp. 877–920.

8. GOUGH, H. *Reference handbook for the Gough Adjective Checklist.* Berkeley: Inst. Personality Assessment and Research, Univer. of California, 1955 (mimeographed).

9. HOMANS, G. C. *The human group.* New York: Harcourt Brace, 1950.

10. JENNINGS, HELEN H. *Leadership and isolation.* (2nd Ed.) New York: Longmans, Green, 1950.

11. KELLY, E. L. Consistency of the adult personality. *Amer. Psychologist*, 1955, 10, 659–681.

12. MEAD, G. H. *Mind, self, and society.* Chicago: Univer. of Chicago Press, 1934.

13. NEWCOMB, T. M. An approach to the study of communicative acts. *Psychol. Rev.*, 1953, 60, 393–404.

14. OSGOOD, C. E. The nature and measurement of meaning. *Psychol. Bull.*, 1952, 49, 197–237.

15. ROGERS, C. R. *Studies in client-centered psychotherapy.* III: The case of Mrs. Oak. Washington: Psychological Service Center Press, 1951.

16. TAGIURI, R. Relational analysis: An extension of sociometric method with emphasis upon social perception. *Sociometry*, 1952, 15, 91–104.

17. WINCH, R. F., KTSANES, T., & KTSANES, VIRGINIA. Empirical elaboration of the theory of complementary needs in mate-selection. *J. abnorm. soc. Psychol.*, 1955, 51, 508–513.

18. WINCH, R. F., & MORE, D. M. Quantitative analysis of qualitative data in the assessment of motivation: Reliability, congruence, and validity. *Amer. J. Sociol.*, 1956, 61, 445–452.

POSTSCRIPT

Since the above statement, Newcomb has placed his theoretical propositions in the broader framework of balance theory.[a] As such, the theory is stated in system terms. A system consisting of *A*'s

[a] T. M. Newcomb. *The acquaintance process.* New York: Holt, Rinehart and Winston, Inc., 1961.

attraction toward B, A's attitude toward X, and his perception of B's attitude toward X is balanced when A's attraction toward B is positive and he perceives B's attitude toward X as similar to his own. Where A is attracted to B and perceives B's attitude toward X as different from his own the system is imbalanced and tendencies arise to restore balance. These may take a number of forms. A in this instance may decide that he is mistaken about B's attitude toward X and misperceive it as similar to his own. He may attempt to change B's attitude in the direction of his own, or actual or perceived changes may be made in the importance

or in the common relevance of the attitude. Finally, the system may be restored to balance by A's reducing his attraction to B. These alternative ways of resolving balance suggest that this reformulation in system terms allows the theory to be used to explain perceptual and influence processes in the dyad as well as attraction. Thus, the power of the theory has been considerably enhanced.

EXCHANGE THEORY AND INTERPERSONAL ATTRACTION [*]

The most inclusive theory of interpersonal attraction is that proposed by Thibaut and Kelley. The major findings of thirty years of research on sociometric choice appear understandable in its terms. These findings we have summarized elsewhere[a] and are as follows:

To summarize the determinants of choice on a sociometric test, a person is likely to choose the following individuals: (*1*) those with whom he has a greater opportunity to interact, (*2*) those who have characteristics most desirable in terms of the norms and values of the group, (*3*) those who are most similar to him in attitudes, values, and social-background characteristics, (*4*) those whom he perceives as choosing him or assigning favorable characteristics to him, (*5*) those who see him as he sees himself, and (*6*) those whose company leads to gratification of his needs.

When each finding is examined from the standpoint of rewards and costs of persons in interaction, attraction is seen to arise toward those persons who maximize rewards and minimize costs. To illustrate, when two individuals are in close proximity to each other they can interact at low cost. Thus, the reward-cost outcome which they experience is apt to be high. That similarity of attitude, particularly toward the self, should lead to liking is consistent with exchange theory; satisfaction of the need for consensual validation of the self concept appears to be a powerful reward for most persons. Newcomb's propositions covering these relations may be viewed as a special case of the more general theory proposed by Thibaut and Kelley.

The idea that the exchange of rewards produces liking is not unique to this formulation, but what is unique is the notion that satisfactions derived from rewards and costs are always relative to the expectations of the participants. These expecta-

tions are known as the *comparison level*, a concept that has considerably augmented the explanatory power of the theory. At several points in the selection below, empirical findings in a variety of research contexts are understandable only in terms of this concept.

22.

Evaluation of the Dyad

JOHN W. THIBAUT
UNIVERSITY OF NORTH CAROLINA

HAROLD H. KELLEY
UNIVERSITY OF CALIFORNIA, LOS ANGELES

The outcomes a person receives in the course of interaction have a certain absolute significance to him. If they are offered to him, he will always prefer outcomes better than those he has, no matter how favorable the level of outcomes he has reached, for if they are offered they are instigated, and if they are better it is true by definition that he will prefer them. Further, he will attempt to repeat the activities he finds to yield good outcomes, and he will try to avoid activities that produce unsatisfactory ones. However, a good deal of what social psychology knows about how people evaluate themselves and their circumstances indicates that these evaluations also involve a good deal of *relativity of judgment*. Much of the work on the level of aspiration (e.g., Lewin, et al., 1944), reference group effects (Merton, 1957), and status behavior (Hollingshead, 1949) suggests that the person typically evaluates his circumstances in relation to those he believes other people achieve or in relation to those he has experienced in the past. He strives especially hard to reach certain levels, (e.g., those attained by his siblings), and he is particularly unhappy if he falls below a certain minimum (perhaps the standard of living he had achieved several years ago).

To take account of these phenomena, we introduced the notion of *comparison level* (*CL*) as a

[*] The selection following the editorial introduction is reprinted from *The Social Psychology of Groups*, New York: John Wiley & Sons, 1959, pp. 89–99, by permission of the authors and the publisher.

[a] P. F. Secord & C. W. Backman. *Social psychology*. New York: McGraw-Hill Book Company, 1964. Pp. 246–247.

standard or reference point against which, in some sense, the relationship of the moment is evaluated. We distinguish two special instances of CL that seem necessary for the analysis of interpersonal relations. The first, referred to merely as CL, provides a standard against which an evaluation is made of how satisfactory or unsatisfactory the relationship is. The second, referred to as CL_{alt}, provides a standard in terms of which decisions about remaining in or leaving the relationship are made. Here we focus upon the CL, its relation to satisfaction and attraction, and its determinants. The distinction between these two types of standards has not been made in the literature on attraction, power, and the like, and there is often some unclarity about the kind of reference point dealt with. Those studies which are concerned largely with subjective states reflecting satisfaction, personal morale, etc., are considered here. Those that delve into dependency and the exercise of power come in for discussion in relation to CL_{alt}.

The reader will also note the bearing of the present discussion upon nonvoluntary relationships. When, for various reasons, the person's existing outcomes are considerably below his CL, a number of consequences result, the interpretation of which relies upon the present general analysis of CL.

THE COMPARISON LEVEL

In defining the CL the primary intention is to locate a psychologically meaningful mid-point for the scale of outcomes—a neutral point on a scale of satisfaction-dissatisfaction. If the outcomes in a given relationship surpass the CL, that relationship is regarded as a satisfactory one. And, to the degree the outcomes are supra-CL, the person may be said to be attracted to the relationship. If the outcomes endured are infra-CL, the person is dissatisfied and unhappy with the relationship. If possible he would leave the group, so we may say his attraction to the group is negative. Locating the CL, then, enables us to analyze the subjective consequences of membership in a dyad. Although we can expect feeling tone to deteriorate as the person receives increasingly poor outcomes, the CL indicates a point (or at least a region) on the outcome continuum where the mood changes from positive to negative and where the orientation changes from *toward* the dyad to *away from* it.

How, then, should the CL be defined if it is to be a neutral point in this sense? We have chosen to define the CL as being some modal or average value of all the outcomes known to the person (by virtue of personal or vicarious experience), each outcome weighted by its salience (or the degree to which it is instigated for the person at the moment). A person's CL depends not only upon outcomes he has experienced or seen others experiencing but also upon which of these are actively stimulating to him—are obtruded on him, are vivid and perhaps implicitly rehearsed as he makes an evaluation of his circumstances. This salience depends in part upon momentary cues which serve as reminders of certain relationships and alternatives. To the degree this is true, CL is subject to situation-to-situation and moment-to-moment variations. Perhaps more important, because of their relative stability, are the outcomes the salience of which is independent of the immediate situation—outcomes for which the person provides dependable self-instigations or, so to speak, self-reminders.

In the following section we examine some of the evidence pertaining to the effect upon CL of experienced outcomes. On the assumption that instigations are supra-threshold for all experienced outcomes, we would expect to find a direct association between the quality of the known outcomes and the location of the CL, the latter being reflected in feelings of satisfaction with presently attained outcomes. In a subsequent section we consider those outcomes which are likely to be salient, both in specific circumstances and generally. Because there are important and pervasive individual differences in this regard, we then consider the personality predispositions that may be interpreted as affecting the particular set of experienced outcomes the person tends to maintain generally at a high level of salience.

For readers of Helson (1948), we might say that the CL represents the adaptation level to the instigated outcomes. This adaptation level is affected mainly by direct or indirect information available to the person about the goodness of outcomes in other relationships, but it is also conditioned partly by outcomes in the present relationship. Finally, there are what Helson calls "residual" considerations, idiosyncratic factors such as, in our case, individual differences in the weights assigned to the reward- versus cost-components particularly for favorable unattained outcomes—individual differences, that is, in "optimism" versus "pessimism."

EXPERIENCED OUTCOMES

If all of the outcomes a person has experienced or knows about are salient, then the CL reflects the quality of these outcomes. A person who has experienced superior outcomes, for example, in alternative relationships, will have a higher CL and, therefore, will be less satisfied with the level in the present relationship than will another person who has known only the mediocrity of the present situation.

This interpretation may be made of discrepancies between parents and children in evaluating the standard of living in the home. Koos (1946) provides observations of families with foreign-born parents and low-income families in which the children have opportunities outside the home to learn to expect a higher material standard of living. This leads the children to be dissatisfied with the level of living attained in the parental home.

Data from the studies of the American soldier (Stouffer, et al., 1949) may also be interpreted in these terms. For example, as compared with the less well educated soldiers, better educated ones were less satisfied with their status and opportunities for promotion. The authors interpret this greater dissatisfaction with the same circumstances in terms of the higher aspirations that the more educated men bring to the army. As compared to the outcomes they had enjoyed or anticipated enjoying as civilians, considering their relatively superior social and economic backgrounds, the better educated found their army status to be quite poor.

The results from level-of-aspiration studies are also relevant to this point. The level of aspiration consists of a person's statement about his expected level of performance on some task; for example, the number of arithmetic problems he will solve, the number of hits he will make on a target. Because the person's rewards (from recognition or experience of achievement) are presumably closely related to his performance level, the aspiration level is essentially an indication of the outcomes the person expects from interaction with the task. Because of this close relation with the CL, the evidence on determinants of aspiration levels probably reveals much about the factors underlying CL.

Two main results issue from the most pertinent of such studies (Chapman and Volkman, 1939, Festinger, 1942):

(1) Subjects tend to expect to do about as well as others similar to themselves, better than people they consider generally inferior to themselves, and poorer than people they consider generally superior to themselves.

(2) The effects of information about the performance of others is reduced by having direct experience with the task itself. If a person has enough experience with the task, information about how others perform on it will have relatively little effect on his future level of aspiration. Thus both one's personal experience and knowledge about others' experience play a role in these levels, but personal experience seems to be given priority.

SALIENT OUTCOMES

We suggested earlier that not all of the outcomes experienced are likely to be equally salient, hence not all equally weighty, in the determination of CL. Certain outcomes will be highly salient because of the particular circumstances in which the person is asked to make an evaluation of his situation. Others are likely to be salient under almost all circumstances because of some special significance they have to the individual.

Consider first the specific instigations and reminders which, by their immediate or recent presence, heighten the salience of some outcomes. Perhaps the best evidence on the effects of such instigations comes from studies in which people from similar backgrounds and presently receiving objectively similar outcomes are asked under different circumstances to evaluate their outcomes. For example, if a person is asked to say how well off he is considering the plight of the displaced peoples of Europe, he is almost certain to give a different response (a more "satisfied" one) than if the question suggests a more opulent set of outcomes for the comparison. Many such variations in "frame of reference" produced by different question wordings indicate fluctuations in CL as a function of the particular outcomes, persons, or relationships the question brings to mind. For example, Hyman (1942) found that an individual's judgment of his status changes as the reference group provided in the instructions was varied.

Variations in the other persons who are in one's immediate vicinity may have similar effects. For example, Stouffer and his associates (1949) found several instances in which outcomes were evaluated in a manner inconsistent with their objective quality. These findings are interpreted in terms of the effects of other persons near at hand. Among the many similar comparisons that appear in the data, let us take Negro troops stationed in northern versus southern installations and non-combat troops in the United States versus those in rear-areas overseas. In these cases a relatively high degree of satisfaction was found under what were objectively poorer conditions. Noncombat troops overseas showed higher satisfaction with army life than did noncombat troops in the United States, presumably because the salient alternatives for the overseas troops were the rigors and hardships of the combat soldier, whereas the troops at home compared their plight with that of a prosperous civilian population. Similarly for Negro soldiers:

Relative to most Negro civilians whom he saw in Southern towns, the Negro soldier had a position of comparative wealth and dignity. His income was high, at least by general Southern standards. Moreover, in spite of the Army carryover of many civilian practices of segregation, the Negro soldier received treatment more nearly on an equality with the white soldier than the treatment of the Negro civilian in the South as compared with the white civilian. Officially, the Army policies always insisted upon equality of treatment of the races, even when this meant separate treatment, and throughout the war repeated though often unsuccessful efforts were made by the War Department to translate these policies into practice and to enforce them even against the private wishes of some white commanding officers.

Consider, on the other hand, the Northern Negro stationed in the North. The differential in income and status between soldier and civilian was not the same as that in the South. The industrial earning power of one's Northern Negro civilian acquaintances was at an all-time high, very often far exceeding that of the Negro soldier. Moreover, the contrast between the racial practices of the Army and the racial practices of Northern civilian society was, frequently, the reverse of the contrast in the South. Although the Northern Negro was accustomed to countless irritations and instances of discrimination in Northern civilian life, he was not confronted to the same extent with official policies of racial segregation as existed in the Army [pp. 563-564].

Salience and control

Consider next the question of which outcomes are likely to be salient whether or not there exist momentary instigations to them. An hypothesis proposed here is that the generally and persistently salient outcomes are those perceived by the individual as instances of variations in rewards and costs for which he himself is primarily responsible —variations over which he has some degree of control. The following considerations are offered in support of this hypothesis.

As a person's outcomes fluctuate with changes in interaction and in his memberships, he adjusts his behavior in an effort to maintain better outcomes and avoid poorer ones. Of the total variability in his outcomes, only part is responsive to such attempts, namely, the portion that is in some manner under his control. The remaining variability is introduced by the exercise of external control over him by other persons or agencies. As his behavior has no effect on these variations, the adaptive solution would seem to involve a recognition of external control and an acceptance of its indocility to his efforts.

We might imagine that it would be highly adaptive if the human organism, in the course

of his evolution, had developed the capacity to respond with acceptance toward such arbitrary incursions into his life, being gratified by some events and hurt by others, but responding always in a consummatory rather than an instrumental way. This mode of responding has the adaptation value of avoiding costly attempts to adjust or rectify unalterable outcomes. On the other hand, it is highly useful for the organism to be able to give full attention to variations in outcomes that lie within his own range of control. A high sensitivity to such variations has the value of enabling him to attain more nearly the level of outcomes that is maximal in view of his ability to control his environment.

Our hypothesis suggests this to be true: that the person is indeed especially sensitive to variations subject to his own control and relatively insensitive to variations caused by others over and beyond his control. The outcomes under his control will tend to be highly salient under most circumstances; those under the control of others are salient only if they are currently being experienced or if obtrusive cues are present in the immediate situation. It is, then, the former variations that will predominate in determining the CL. The level forming the transition from satisfaction to dissatisfaction depends, according to this view, primarily upon the rewards and costs seen as instances of variations in outcomes for which one is himself responsible. By virtue of the tendency for selective salience or instigation of the different classes of outcomes, the CL depends in part upon the person's conception of his own power, his ability to cope with the contingent demands of others, and the realms over which he believes his own causal efficacy extends. The CL thus begins to approximate the modal value of the range of outcomes over which the person believes his control prevails. It is largely an indication of what the individual feels he "deserves" and only in small part an indication of what he expects or anticipates on the basis of all the outcomes he has experienced. The reason is, to repeat, that the outcomes are weighted (instigated) according to perceived responsibility for them.

What implications does this line of reasoning have for the kinds of outcomes that would be likely to be especially salient, hence heavily weighted in the CL? To begin with, outcomes the person receives by virtue of temporary ascribed status will have less effect on CL than those received by virtue of achieved status. (See Linton, 1945, for the distinction between "achieved" and "ascribed" status.) When the individual is indulged with magnificent rewards by a generous fate, his CL will be relatively little affected; or, when he is deprived of favorable outcomes by the action of external control, his CL will be relatively little affected. Of course, with repeated experiences of either sort, the instigations to them become so strong that CL ultimately will move in the direction of the good or bad fate. All we suggest is that in the short run these experiences change the person's outcomes without greatly affecting his *CL*. Consequently, with entrance into a high or a low ascribed status, there is initially a period of great satisfaction or dissatisfaction as the *CL* lags behind the experienced outcomes. As the *CL* finally catches up with the repeatedly experienced outcomes, the situation becomes more neutral in feeling tone.

Outcomes the person has commonly experienced are also more likely to be perceived as within the realm of self determination than those he has rarely experienced or only heard about. The latter would include most of the extremely high and extremely low outcomes, especially the high ones, which are outside or close to the limits of the individual's personal experience. These ordinarily appear to be outcomes a person would not attain (or be forced to endure) without the intervention of either a kind or cruel fate. Thus extreme outcomes, particularly the high ones (for anyone can assure himself of low outcomes) and those the individual person has never personally experienced, are not likely to be viewed as outcomes he reaches by employment of his own control. Subjectively these are the outcomes that have a low probability of attainment. It is on these grounds that we believe that outcomes of low perceived likelihood of attainment carry little weight in the determination of the *CL*. Outcomes of high probability of attainment, on the other hand, are perceived to be part of the range covered by one's control and are ordinarily heavily weighted in determining the location of *CL*.

If there exists a high subjective probability of attaining a very favorable outcome, the *CL* should rise. Failure to achieve such an outcome should then place the person below *CL*. By contrast, had the person's subjective probability of success been lower, his *CL* would not have risen, and failure to attain the outcome would be less likely to place him below *CL*. Spector (1956) has stated a variant of this hypothesis as follows:

> *On failing to achieve* an attractive goal, an individual's morale will be higher if the probability of achieving that goal had been perceived to be low than if it had been perceived to be high [p. 52, author's italics].

In an experiment designed to test this hypothesis and a set of closely related ones Spector varied the perceived probability of being promoted up a hierarchy of simulated military rank. His results confirmed the hypothesis stated above: among the subjects who were not promoted, those who had perceived the probability of their being promoted as high were more dissatisfied than those less sanguine about their chances.

An earlier report of the same relationship between expectation and morale comes from field research. In their study of the American soldier in World War II, Stouffer, et al. (1949), found a higher degree of satisfaction with the promotion system among enlisted men in the Military Police, in which promotions were relatively infrequent, than among Air Corps enlisted men, in which the rate of promotion was quite high. In line with the hypothesis stated above, the airman's discontent may come from the dashing of too high hopes.

Our analysis of the relation between control and *CL* further suggests that another person's outcomes will have an effect upon *CL* to the degree that the other's realm of power is seen to coincide with one's own. This is akin to Festinger's (1954) hypothesis that a person will tend to compare himself with others whose ability or competence is very similar to his own. Because similarity in ability is likely to induce a perception of similar power vis-à-vis the fates, we might expect the circumstances of persons similar in ability to the individual to contribute heavily to his *CL*. This would also be true of persons who occupy a social position similar to that of the individual, since similar social positions usually carry roughly equivalent power implications. Consistent with these expectations are Hyman's (1942) findings that friends and work associates are used more often in evaluating one's status than is the total society or the population at large.

The findings of Stern and Keller (1953) contain the further suggestion that there are societal differences in the range of persons with whose outcomes an individual compares his own. In a study conducted in France a count was made of the social groups spontaneously mentioned in interviews regarding living conditions and aspirations. Most frequently mentioned were social class and family, followed by references to occupational groups, age groups, and friends or colleagues. The authors suggest the generalization that, "In a society where there is little social mobility, one's horizon of possibility is relatively limited, thus confining comparison between oneself and others to members of one's family, occupation, and social circle. In a society of greater social mobility, the self-other comparison is allowed freer range and takes in more groups, as well as groups outside of one's membership or 'in-group' environment" [p. 216]. We would interpret this to mean that in a society in which the typical individual's realm of control over his outcomes is rather extensive there is considerable breadth to the class of persons whose outcomes contribute to his *CL*.

The effect of another person's outcomes will depend, of course, upon what causal interpretation is placed upon their occurrence. For example, a man who wins the Irish sweepstakes and thereby comes into a large sum of money would, by our reasoning, have little effect upon his brother's *CL*.

However, if the man acquires wealth by virtue of his own skill and efforts, his brother is likely to think of these rewards when evaluating his own outcomes.

INDIVIDUAL DIFFERENCES AND THE COMPARISON LEVEL

Consider two quite extreme cases lying on a continuum of power or control: at one end is located a person having very much power and at the other a person having very little. We can say that the person having much power is able dependably to insure himself of a wide range of outcomes, from very unfavorable ones (anyone can get these in abundance) to very favorable ones. The person having little power is able dependably to insure himself of a much more modest range of outcomes, from very unfavorable ones to mediocre ones.

If we assume that the person holding high power has a veridical perception of it, he will appear confident and sure of himself and will experience a high subjective probability of attaining favorable outcomes. Furthermore, he may be expected to respond differently to the reward and the cost components of very superior outcomes which lie above his present level of attainment. For he will have learned that thinking about and anticipating better outcomes creates only temporary tension which, by virtue of the effectiveness of his ensuing instrumental activities, is usually followed by actually attaining them. From the point of view of thorough mobilization of action, it is even advantageous for him to emphasize the positive aspects of new ventures and de-emphasize the negative ones. Thus, for a person with such high competence and confidence, instigations to behavior may be expected to come primarily from the reward components of superior outcomes. Instigations from the cost components should be very slight. This means that the reward components of such outcomes will carry relatively heavy weights, and the cost components relatively light ones, in determining this person's CL. The CL, then, is likely to be high.

For the person holding very little power, the prediction is quite different. Instigations to his behavior will very likely derive mainly from the cost components of superior outcomes and only negligibly from the reward components. Hence the cost components of such outcomes will be heavily weighted, and the reward components only lightly weighted, in locating this person's CL. The CL is likely to be low.

As intimated above, these two different orientations toward rewards and costs may be quite adaptive, each in its own way. The reward orientation of the powerful person motivates him to approach all of the favorable outcomes lying within the range of his power. The cost orientation of the powerless person helps him to avoid instigations to outcomes that he canot dependably attain.

Although the preceding argument has been developed in terms of the person's actual power and his veridical perception of it, the perception will not always coincide with the fact. It is well known that there are ideological contributions to the developing percept of one's own power relative to that of external sources. Thus the person's beliefs about this may depend upon how his parents indoctrinate him with respect to his responsibility for his own fate or upon the particular ideology about the individual's causal potency that pervades his culture (Kardiner, 1945). These factors may create notions about one's power that are quite discrepant with the facts. In this event the present theory is to be applied in terms of the perceived rather than the actual power. We merely note here that overestimations of one's power may often be corrected in the long run: the CL will be excessively high in the light of attained outcomes, with frustration chronic until the perception becomes more veridical. Underestimations of power may go uncorrected, however. The person will maintain modest levels of aspiration and comfortably surpass them without being presented with any impressive clues as to his unrealized potential.

Idealization

Suppose that each of these persons experiences a very satisfactory relationship, say in marriage. The powerful person, we may assume, will assign much of the causality for the success of his marriage (and the consequent favorable outcomes) to his own high range of control. By our hypothesis that one's own perceived realm of control contributes heavily to the determination of CL, this person's CL should be high from the outset of the relationship.

The powerless person will be more likely to assign causality for *his* happy marriage to external agencies, such as fate, good luck, unprovoked good will, and enigmatic forces. His CL will be expected to rise very gradually as instigations from favorable outcomes in the marriage take effect.

Now suppose that each of the marriages is revoked, say by the death of the spouse. The powerful person, instigated primarily by the reward components of the now unattainable outcomes, will be expected to recall the marriage in an idealized way, overemphasizing the rewards, underemphasizing the costs. Consequently his CL should rise even higher than its level during marriage.

The powerless person, instigated primarily by costs, is more likely to recall the marriage in a "debunking" way, overestimating its costs, depreciating its rewards (although social constraints would usually limit the public expression of out-right disparagement of the late spouse). His *CL* should fall.

Is there any evidence for such effects on the *CL* from past events? We may first note that there is considerable evidence for the existence of a phenomenon that looks very much like *idealization*. Consider a study based on interviews with widows. Dickinson and Beam (1931) report that to the widow the earlier marriage experiences now appear "sexually golden." "Sex life with the husband was interesting and desirable" [p. 276]. She remembers intercourse to have been very frequent and highly satisfactory—considerably more so than reported by women presently living with their husbands. "The dead sexual life takes on the value of all dead things, creates its own ideal and feeds the living desire" [p. 274]. Thus the widow may be ". . . sexually avid but unwilling to marry any man who compares unfavorably with the idealization of the husband's memory . . ." [p. 270].

This apotheosis of the past has received literary documentation, notably in Daphne Du Maurier's character "Rebecca," the first wife, whose reputation for perfection continued to grow long after she had been succeeded by a wife of merely remarkable talents. Following the motif of this novel, Gouldner (1954, pp. 79–83) has characterized as the "Rebecca Myth" this source of employee resistance to new industrial managers. Gouldner describes a situation in one of the plants of a large industrial corporation in which the old manager "Doug" had been succeeded by a new manager "Peele." "Doug" was remembered as a model manager: he set a comparison level that "Peele" had difficulty meeting. "Almost to a man, workers in the plant were in the spell of a back-ward-looking reverie. They overflowed with stories which highlighted the differences between the two managers, the leniency of Doug and the strictness of Peele" [p. 80].

An English study (Scott, et al., 1956) on the social consequences of transferring steelworkers from two obsolete plants to one large new plant revealed the same effect of idealization on the comparison level. Of the two managers of the older plants, one became manager of the new plant and the other was given a less important post outside the new plant hierarchy. The men whose old manager had been removed—". . . occasionally referred to the new . . . manager in a disparaging way; more often, indeed much more often, they spoke of their past manager . . . very favourably" [p. 235]. Summing up their observations, the authors conclude: "It is not unreasonable to assume that a tendency to idealize the virtues of a past plant manager and to magnify the failings of the present one was in operation here, . . ." [p. 235].

The comparison level may be elevated as much by idealizations of the future as of the past. It is generally thought that persons facing marriage tend to develop fantastic expectations of how their partner will behave in marriage and of the satisfactions to be achieved there. One of the main objections made by marriage counselors to pre-marital autoeroticism is that it is likely to involve fantasies of beautiful and talented partners whom an actual husband or wife will be unable to replace (Dickinson and Beam, 1931). Stories are also told of soldiers who, having been isolated from real women and limited to fantasy association with pin-up girls of movie magazines and fiction, find the women they return to rather disappointing.

Regarding this phenomenon, as it occurs with young people with limited social contacts, Sullivan (1953) has the following comment:

> Some of these isolated early adolescents suffer a particular handicap from this reverie substitution for the interpersonal experience, in that they develop quite strongly personified imaginary companions; and the singularly personal source of the idealized characteristics may be a severe barrier later on to finding anybody who strikes them as really suitable for durable interpersonal relations [p. 277].

A quite different type of research, which may not at first sight seem particularly relevant, is reported by Pepitone (1950). Adolescent boys appeared before an experimentally controlled board of adults who were to decide whether the subject-applicant would receive a prize (a ticket to an important college basketball game). Subjects who were highly motivated to win a prize, as contrasted with those not so highly motivated, showed marked "facilitative" distortions in their judgments of the adult board members. For example, in the first part of the experiment, highly motivated subjects judged the board member who played a friendly role toward the subject as having a disproportionate amount of power over the prize-awarding decision. And in the second part highly motivated subjects judged the board member who held the greatest power (i.e., the "head" member) as being more friendly toward themselves than did the less highly motivated subjects. This facilitative distortion resembles idealization in that the persons who most want the prize are optimistically judging the situation to be favorable to their attaining it. We would expect this to characterize the powerful person described earlier, who indirectly reveals his confidence by overestimating the power of the board member who is friendly to his interests or, alternatively, by emphasizing the friendliness of the most powerful board member. But what of low-power persons? Why are there not some pessimistic individuals who magnify the amount of unsympathetic external control present in the prize-attainment situation?

Both kinds of persons *do* appear in an experiment by Klein (1954), thereby calling into question the generality of Pepitone's findings. Klein administered the Stroop test (which measures the degree to which performance on a sorting task is impaired by interference from irrelevant information) to a large group of male college students. On the basis of these test scores, he then selected two extreme groups of subjects, one of which showed maximum and the other minimum impairment of performance, that is, a high-interference and a low-interference group. On the basis of more or less good evidence, the first group could be characterized as "compulsive" and "constricted," the second group as "outgoing," "confident," "exploratory." Just prior to the experiment itself, half of the subjects in each group were made thirsty by experimental means and the thirst of the other half was fully satiated. In the experiment the subjects made size estimations of pictures of objects, some of which were thirst-relevant (e.g., an ice-cream soda). Klein's results show that his low-interference subjects (exploratory) yield data that roughly parallel the Pepitone findings: with increasing need (thirst), there was an increasing tendency to overestimate the size of need-relevant objects. However, his high-interference (constricted) subjects showed the opposite relationship: as need increased, the size of need-relevant objects was increasingly *underestimated.*

To speculate further, the overestimations characteristic of Klein's low-interference subjects and the underestimations of his high-interference subjects are suggestive of recent interpretations of differences between those who score high and those who score low on the McClelland-type measure of need-achievement. For example, Atkinson (1953) summarizes experimental results by describing high need-achievement in terms of a confident orientation which ". . . is essentially positive motivation to experience feelings of accomplishment and success . . ." and low need-achievement as an avoidant orientation which implies ". . . relatively greater anxiety about failure" [p. 389]. If this interpretation is correct,[1]

---

[1] We hesitate to take any definite stand on the disagreement between interpretations like those of Atkinson and those of Alper (1948, 1952, 1957). Alper provides experimental and clinical evidence for the thesis that high need-achievement represents fear of failure and low need-achievement represents self-confidence, thus reversing the polarity that Atkinson describes. The issue awaits further research and standardization of measurement. Here we are interested only in raising the question as to the relationship, whatever its direction, between achievement motivation and a dimension the extremes

Atkinson's research on the relationship between achievement motivation and recall of tasks may reveal further facets of our powerful-confident and powerless-constricted types. One way of summarizing part of Atkinson's findings and interpretations is to say that when the achievement motive is aroused (by presenting tasks in a formal, serious way as having important consequences for the subjects' college careers) those subjects whose achievement motivation is high tend subsequently to recall a relatively high proportion of their failures, whereas subjects with low achievement motivation tend to recall relatively more of their successes. These findings are quite consistent with our view that the confident, powerful person can afford to entertain instigations from unattained outcomes (important but incompleted tasks), whereas the less powerful person learns to avoid such instigations and quickly puts such experiences out of mind. The latter might not have undertaken such tasks in the first place had not the experimental situation required it.

It is probable that the complexity of the Klein and Atkinson results, as contrasted with those of many of their predecessors, can be attributed at least in part to their recruiting procedures, as Atkinson [pp. 388–389] himself remarks. The subjects in many of the earlier studies, which relied heavily on volunteer recruits, would be expected to include large numbers of confident, outgoing persons who were unafraid of failure, whereas Klein and Atkinson both used preselection procedures that insured not a random or representative sample but at least one which contained the pertinent extremes.

An experiment reported by Horwitz (1958) provides a fitting capstone to this discussion because it deals simultaneously with a number of the variables considered separately in the studies just summarized. In this experiment all subjects performed a series of tasks on which success would presumably be highly rewarding to everyone. Each subject's goal was to learn how to do the tasks so that he could improve his performance on a later retest. Each subject was permitted to complete correctly half the tasks and the other half was not completed at all. This score of 50 per cent was interpreted to some subjects as indicating almost certain *success* on the retest and to others, almost certain *failure*. Persons in the success condition would be expected, then, to be little concerned about their wrong answers (the incompleted tasks), but in the failure condition these same items should be the occasion for considerable concern. However, a fair number of subjects in the success condition were found to express considerable concern over their wrong answers and a sizable number in the failure condition, to express little concern. These subjects, whom Horwitz describes as having nonveridical attitudes

---

of which may be labeled "hope for success" and "fear of failure."

toward their success or failure, might be viewed as being pessimistic about success, even though it is promised them, or, when failure is in the offing, as devaluating the loss sustained in doing poorly. Thus they resemble the personalities we have described as powerless and lacking in self-confidence. The remaining subjects, exhibiting "veridical" attitudes, might be considered as powerful, outgoing persons.

The resemblance is further manifested when "veridical" and "nonveridical" subjects are compared on their responses to a TAT picture: veridical subjects tend to give active themes (e.g., working on a problem) and nonveridical subjects, passive themes (e.g., worrying, daydreaming, activity unrelated to an achievement task). On the assumption that all subjects are originally instigated to do well in the experiment, Horwitz interprets the nonveridical subjects as inhibiting tendencies to engage in goal-striving behavior. When failing, they are said to block off attempts to improve and to inhibit awareness that they care about doing well. When successful, they feel "in luck" and are afraid that their own activities might destroy their lucky streak. It must be obvious to the reader that this pattern corresponds closely to our description of the person who perceives his own power to be inadequate relative to that of external agents.

Finally, Horwitz reports that the nonveridical subjects performed more poorly on the retest, and, in line with Atkinson's findings, their recall of the tasks consisted of a larger proportion of successes than did that of the veridical subjects.

The evidence cited in the disparate array of studies mentioned above leads us to reaffirm our view of the way in which individual differences affect *CL*. There will be wide individual differences in personal attributes: at one extreme, *positive motivation to experience success* or confidence and outgoingness, and, at the other, *constriction* and a *fear of failure*. The positive attributes might be expected to dispose the person to emphasize (to weight heavily) the rewards and/or to de-emphasize the costs that were associated with a past activity or that will be associated with a future one. This is idealization. Similarly, we would expect the person at the other end of the continuum (constricted, fearing failure) to de-emphasize (to weight lightly) the rewards and/or emphasize the costs of future or past situations. From such individuals we would expect pessimism about the future and "debunking" of the past.

GENERALITY OF COMPARISON LEVEL

We may propound the general hypothesis that the more satisfactory any given relationship has been found to be, the higher will be the comparison level for evaluating any new relationship.

Let us begin by considering the quite opposite claim that a kind of substitution tendency exists such that if the person achieves very satisfactory

AND INTERPERSONAL ATTRACTION
EXCHANGE THEORY
187

states in one relationship then he will be more willing to settle for somewhat less satisfactory states in others. Conversely, then, those who achieve quite unsatisfactory outcomes in one relationship might be expected to demand compensatory advantages in others. The only relevant evidence comes from studies of level of aspiration. Although these studies provide a very imperfect test of the hypothesis, they are germane insofar as the goal setting is affected by motivations to improve one's outcomes. Consistent with the substitution hypothesis are the scattered findings that at least some of the individuals who repeatedly perform badly on tasks tend to set high goals for themselves, as high as those set by more successful individuals. In general, the habitually unsuccessful people show great interindividual variability in their goal-setting behavior (Lewin, et al., 1944, pp. 343–344).

However, aside from this special effect of very little success, the original hypothesis appears to be somewhat better supported than the substitution one: highly successful persons tend to set higher goals than moderately successful persons.

Another kind of evidence can be approached through Benoit-Smullyan's (1944) status equilibration hypothesis, which is stated as follows:

> As a result of status conversion processes which are normally at work in every society, there exists a real tendency for the different types of status to reach a common level, i.e., for a man's position in the economic hierarchy to match his position in the political hierarchy and for the latter to accord with his position in the hierarchy of prestige, etc. [p. 160].

Benoit-Smullyan's hypothesis is slightly different from ours, since it emphasizes the tendency to equalize positions on different status dimensions within a given society or organization rather than a tendency to demand equally good outcomes, whatever their type or dimension, from different social organizations or relationships.

In a study designed to test this hypothesis Fenchel, Monderer, and Hartley (1951) asked subjects (sophomore men) to rate their present and desired standing in each of five specific groups: a school group, social club, friends, family, and the college student body. If we assume that the rating of present standing reflects the satisfactoriness of the reward-cost position the person is attaining in a given group, we would expect the statuses desired in the different groups to converge upon a common level. This follows from our hypothesis that the satisfaction a person achieves in each relationship will tend to set the standard (comparison level) of what he expects and wants in other relationships. Although the results are beset with methodological problems which can only partly be met within the units of the data in hand, they are consistent with such a convergence effect. The data were analyzed by determining the discrepancy between desired and present standing and comparing this for groups in which present standing is *low* versus those in which it is *high*. This discrepancy score was found to be greater for those of low, as compared with high, present standing—a finding taken to indicate that although present standings vary over most of the scale ratings of desired standings tend to be relatively concentrated at the upper end of the scale. If this effect is a real one, it appears to operate in the upward direction, that is, convergence toward the more satisfactory outcomes. This may be true of desired statuses but not true of realistically expected statuses.

The phenomenon we are pointing to here is a special case of the tendency for aspiration levels in different situations to be interdependent. How well a person does on one task affects not only his aspirations for further performances on it but also, to some degree, his aspirations with regard to other tasks, the degree of transfer effect depending upon the amount of similarity between the tasks (Lewin, et al., 1944, pp. 339, 343–344).

The general conception a person has about how well he can perform on tasks in general, which has been referred to in the literature as his "ego-level," is probably related to his general feelings of self-esteem. Our present suggestion is that a similar ego-level exists with regard to individual attainment in social relationships. As a result of many experiences in many relationships, the person develops a general and relatively constant expectation of the satisfaction he can achieve in association with others—a generalized conception of his worth in interpersonal relationships.

SUMMARY

Although a person is always assumed to prefer better outcomes to poorer ones, certain levels of outcome are of special significance in his evaluation of a relationship. This chapter defines and discusses the comparison level (*CL*) which constitutes a kind of zero or neutral point on the outcome scale. To the degree the outcomes an individual obtains in a given relationship surpass the *CL*, to that degree he is attracted to and satisfied with the relationship. To the degree obtained outcomes fall short of the *CL*, he is dissatisfied with the relationship.

The comparison level depends in general upon the outcomes which are salient (actively stimulating or vividly recalled) at any given time. If we assume that all the recently experienced outcomes are salient, then the better they have been, the higher the *CL*

and the less the satisfaction with any given level. Thus *CL* tends to move to the level of outcomes currently being attained. In other words, the person adapts to the presently experienced levels: after a shift upward to a new level, the once longed for outcomes gradually lose their attractiveness; after a downward shift to a new lower level, the disappointment gradually wears off and the once dreaded outcomes become accepted.

The foregoing generalizations do not always hold, however, because of the fact that not all the outcomes a person has recently experienced or learned about are equally salient. With variations in the particular instigations or reminders that are present (e.g., the particular persons brought to mind for comparison), there appear to be corresponding fluctuations in *CL*.

It is also proposed that salience of outcomes depends upon the person's conceptions of his power or control over his own fate. This is based on the assumption that it is highly adaptive for a person, on the one hand, to pay attention to and remember outcomes for which he has had major causal responsibility and, on the other hand, simply to accept and forget outcomes determined by external forces. A number of consequences follow from this proposition. For example, with an improved level of outcomes, the person's *CL* will rise more if he believes them to represent products of his own causal potency than if he views them as resulting from arbitrary actions of the external world. It is speculated that the latter category usually includes both infrequently received and extreme outcomes and those of low probability of attainment. This analysis is consistent with evidence that dissatisfaction with failing to attain a desired state is less if there was little optimism about attaining it in the first place.

There are, of course, individual differences in optimism and confidence about attaining good outcomes. These are viewed as tending to reflect the power the individual perceives himself to have and, in some degree, his actual effectiveness vis-à-vis his environment. It is also suggested that these individual differences are reflected in the manner in which the person permits himself to think about good, but presently unattainable, states. Arguing again from an adaptation and learning viewpoint, we may hypothesize that more powerful and confident persons will tend to emphasize the reward aspects of such states and de-emphasize the cost components. Conversely, less powerful and confident persons will emphasize costs and play down the rewards. A number of lines of evidence reveal the former tendency—to *idealize* unattainable states. Furthermore, recent work on personality variables points to an individual difference dimension at one extreme of which are found persons exhibiting an idealization tendency and at the other, persons who show the opposite, "debunking" tendency. It is to be expected that *CL* will tend to be higher for the first kind of person than for the second, with a consequent difference, on the average, in their evaluations of the relationships and situations they experience.

The question is raised as to whether an individual's CL is general over different relationships (with attained levels in one relationship affecting the CL operative in evaluating others) or specific to different types of relationships. Some indirect evidence suggests that there is at least some generality, a given CL representing the outcomes expected in a broad variety of relationships.

REFERENCES

ALPER, THELMA G. Memory for completed and incompleted tasks as a function of personality: Correlation between experimental and personality data. *J. Pers.*, 1948, 17, 104–137.

ALPER, THELMA G. The interrupted task method in studies of selective recall: A reevaluation of some recent experiments. *Psychol. Rev.*, 1952, 59, 71–88.

ALPER, THELMA G. Predicting the direction of selective recall: Its relation to ego strength and *n* achievement. *J. abnorm. soc. Psychol.*, 1957, 55, 149–165.

ATKINSON, J. W. The achievement motive and recall of interrupted and completed tasks. *J. exp. Psychol.*, 1953, 46, 381–390.

BENOIT-SMULLYAN, E. Status types and status interrelations. *Amer. sociol. Rev.*, 1944, 9, 151–161.

CHAPMAN, D. W., and J. A. VOLKMANN. A social determinant of the level of aspiration. *J. abnorm. soc. Psychol.*, 1939, 34, 225–238.

DICKINSON, R. L., and L. BEAM. *A thousand marriages.* Baltimore: Williams and Wilkins, 1931.

FENCHEL, G. H., J. H. MONDERER, and E. L. HARTLEY. Subjective status and the equilibration hypothesis. *J. abnorm. soc. Psychol.*, 1951, 46, 476–479.

FESTINGER, L. Wish, expectation and group performance as factors influencing level of aspiration. *J. abnorm. soc. Psychol.*, 1942, 37, 184–200.

FESTINGER, L. A theory of social comparison processes. *Hum. Relat.*, 1954, 7, 117–140.

GOULDNER, A. W. *Patterns of industrial bureaucracy.* Glencoe, Ill.: Free Press, 1954.

HELSON, H. Adaptation-level as a basis for a quantitative theory of frames of reference. *Psychol. Rev.*, 1948, 55, 297–313.

HOLLINGSHEAD, A. B. *Elmtown's youth.* New York: Wiley, 1949.

HORWITZ, M. The veridicality of liking and disliking. In R. Tagiuri and L. Petrullo (Eds.), *Person perception and interpersonal behavior.* Stanford: Stanford University Press, 1958, Pp. 191–209.

HYMAN, H. H. Psychology of status. *Arch. Psychol.*, 1942, No. 269.

KARDINER, A. *Psychological frontiers of society.* New York: Columbia University Press, 1945.

KLEIN, G. S. Need and regulation. In M. R. Jones (Ed.), *Nebraska symposium on motivation.* Lincoln: University of Nebraska Press, 1954, Vol. II. Pp. 224–274.

KOOS, E. L. *Families in trouble.* New York: King's Crown Press, 1946.

LEWIN, K., TAMARA DEMBO, L. FESTINGER, and PAULINE SEARS. Level of aspiration. In J. McV. Hunt (Ed.), *Personality and the behavior disorders.* New York: Ronald Press, 1944. Pp. 333–378.

LINTON, R. *The cultural background of personality.* New York: Appleton-Century, 1945.

MERTON, R. K. *Social theory and social structure.* Glencoe, Ill.: Free Press, 1957.

PEPITONE, A. Motivational effects in social perception. *Hum. Relat.*, 1950, 3, 57–76.

SCOTT, W. H., J. A. BANKS, A. H. HALSEY, and T. LUPTON. *Technical change and industrial relations.* Liverpool: Liverpool University Press, 1956.

SPECTOR, A. J. Expectations, fulfillment, and morale. *J. abnorm. soc. Psychol.*, 1956, 52, 51–56.

STERN, E., and SUZANNE KELLER. Spontaneous group reference in France. *Pub. Opin. Quart.*, 1953, 17, 208–217.

STOUFFER, S. A., E. A. SUCHMAN, L. C. DEVINNEY, SHIRLEY A. STAR, and R. M. WILLIAMS. *The American soldier.* Vol. I. *Adjustment during army life.* Princeton: Princeton University Press, 1949.

SULLIVAN, H. S. *The interpersonal theory of psychiatry.* New York: W. W. Norton, 1953.

THE COMPROMISE PROCESS AND THE AFFECT STRUCTURE OF GROUPS *

Choice patterns that develop in a group cannot be explained solely in terms of the reward-cost value of the characteristics of the chooser and chosen.

A consideration of the significance of these characteristics for possible outcomes in alternative relations is necessary. The final structure of choices in a group is shaped by a process of compromise in which each person's position reflects the overall value of his characteristics to others, with persons of approximately equal value choosing each other. The selection which follows explains this

* The selection following the editorial introduction is reprinted from "The compromise process and the affect structure of groups," *Human Relations*, 1964, **17**, 19–22, by permission of the authors and Tavistock Publications.

process in terms of the instability of relations between people whose characteristics are of markedly different value.

Where persons differ in the value of their characteristics, the one with the more valued attributes will not be satisfied with his less fortunate partner, who, in turn, may be subjected to excessive costs in the relation. Thus, each seeks a partner more suited to his own level. While this compromise process may be somewhat incompatible with a romantic conception of mate selection, it explains why most people find a mate despite the fact that relatively few persons have characteristics representing the cultural ideal. If we suppose that the comparison levels of the persons are appropriately adjusted in this process we also have the explanation of why people at both ends of the continuum of desirability are equally happy and "in love" with the person they marry.

Since some of the underlying reasoning in this selection is based on a theory of attraction proposed by Thibaut and Kelley, it would be well to review the previous selection before reading this one.

23.

The Compromise Process and the Affect Structure of Groups[1]

*CARL W. BACKMAN
PAUL F. SECORD*
UNIVERSITY OF NEVADA

Any group of persons observed over a period of time exhibits certain regularities in patterns of association. Where members have some choice as to whom to associate with in a given activity, some persons are chosen more frequently than others. Each individual, moreover, regularly chooses certain persons and ignores others. Such regularities have been conceptualized in terms of sociometric structure, or choice patterns. Most commonly, determinants of choice have been investigated by comparing persons frequently chosen with those infrequently chosen. No analysis based on the characteristics of the group's members, however, will provide a complete explanation of choice. One reason is that persons may not accurately assess the characteristics of others, and another is that the final structure that emerges is always a compromise. The group structure moves toward an equilibrium in which each person's position in the affect structure is the best that he can

[1] This investigation was supported by a grant (M-3620) from the National Institute of Mental Health, United States Public Health Service.

obtain in terms of his reward-cost outcomes. Two individual features of the sociometric structure may be thought of as resulting from this compromise process or trend toward equilibrium. These are the development of mutuality and the tendency to choose persons equal to oneself in choice status.

Over time, the attraction between persons becomes increasingly mutual. Newcomb (1961), in a living group study, has compared pairs composed of high, intermediate, and low attraction as to how each pair member ranked the other member on attractiveness relative to others in the house at the beginning and at the end of fifteen weeks. He found that at each attraction level mutuality increased with increasing acquaintance. Initially mutuality was very low, but at the end of fifteen weeks of acquaintance, mutuality was high at three of the four levels of attraction. He suggests that these findings are consistent with the principle that systems tend toward a balanced state. Assuming that the common focus of orientation in this case is the self and further that persons usually evaluate themselves positively, the perception that another who is liked does not return the feeling would be strain-inducing. One way of reducing such strain would be to decrease one's attraction toward this person.

A related proposition is that persons choose others who are equal in choice status. According to Homans (1961), the finding by Jennings (1950) that girls chose as leisure-time companions others who were equal to them in their work-living status is consistent with the proposition. Homans's interpretation of this is based on the relation between positions in two different sociometric structures, one representing personal liking or attraction, and the other evaluation with respect to contribution to the group. But the work of Newcomb as well as the data to be presented below suggest that on just the simple criterion of liking, those who are equal in attraction status choose each other.

As a part of a larger study (Backman & Secord, 1962), 31 members of a college sorority were instructed to rank each other from 1 to 30 from most-liked to least-liked. This operation was performed progressively, by first dividing the 30 other members into four quarters (the 7 most-liked, the 8 next most-liked, the 8 next most-liked, and the 7 who were least-liked). In the final step, each member placed the numbers from 1 to 30 before the names of the girls in the four groups, assigning the numbers 1 to 7 in the first group, 8 to 15 to the second, etc.

The hypothesized tendency toward choosing persons whose choice status was similar was tested in two ways, first, with mutuality ignored, and second, with mutuality taken into account. The first method was as follows. The sum of the ranks each member received from all other members was determined and considered an index of his "popularity." Then the popularity index obtained by each individual was paired with the index obtained by the person he had ranked as being best-liked. A correlation coefficient was computed for these 30 paired popularity rankings. A similar procedure was used for the second best-liked and the third best-liked person. The three coefficients obtained by this method were 0·29, 0·33, and 0·22. While all were in the predicted direction, none was significant at the five per cent level.

For the analysis based on mutuality, a mutual choice was defined as characterizing a pair if both members ranked each other 1, 2, or 3. Of the maximum number of 90 mutual pairs that might theoretically exist, 23 were actually found to occur. Considering only these 23 pairs, the popularity index of each member was paired with that of the other member. Since entries are made twice, once for A's choice of B, and again for B's choice of A, a total of 46 paired values is obtained. These are not, of course, independent of each other because of the double-entry, but the appropriate statistic for such data is the intraclass correlation coefficient (McNemar, 1962, p. 284). This statistic uses an analysis of variance technique to provide a measure of association, ranging from some indeterminant point below zero to 1·00. The smaller the within-pair variance relative to the between-pair variance, the higher the correlation. The obtained coefficient was 0·50, suggesting substantial agreement between the popularity rankings of members of the same mutual pair (between-pair variance, 21,025; within-pair variance, 7,058; $F=2.98$; $df=45/46$; $p<0.01$).

The relatively low correlations obtained when mutuality was not considered were reported because, at first thought, this analysis might seem to be an appropriate test of the hypothesis. A careful consideration of the nature of sociometric choice, however, suggests that an analysis that ignores mutuality is not appropriate. When popularity status levels of chooser and chosen are compared without regard to mutuality, a strong attenuating factor is introduced into the correlations. Given the fact that, in any group, there are certain highly popular individuals who, by definition, are chosen by many others, the correlation between the popularity status of members and the popularity of those they choose as best-liked would inevitably be attenuated. In other words, the many individuals who choose as best-liked the few popular persons in the group can scarcely have the same high popularity status as those they choose. But if our hypothesis is that those who choose *each other* tend to be equal in popularity status, an analysis of *mutual* pairs is required. This analysis yielded an appreciable and significant correlation. Perhaps the failure to consider mutuality has resulted in overlooking the tendency to choose others having equal status in spite of the many sociometric studies of groups appearing in the literature. Although mutual choice among high-status pairs has been frequently noted (Homans, 1961; Riecken &

Homans, 1954; Newcomb, 1961), implying that high-status persons choose others at their level, the fact that this is a general principle applying at all status levels has not been emphasized.

The question may yet be raised as to whether choice of others with equal status does in fact occur at all levels. The obtained correlation of 0·50 might possibly be due mainly to the contribution from the high-status pairs. Therefore, the group was divided into two halves, consisting of those pairs having the highest status and those having the lowest. A comparison of the within-person variance for each of these groups with the total between-pair variance yielded correlations of 0·66 and 0·42, respectively. Thus, although the high-status pairs have a slightly greater tendency to choose at their own level, a similar and appreciable tendency exists for the low-status pairs.

DISCUSSION

Recently Thibaut & Kelley (1959) and Homans (1961) have independently arrived at two general theoretical formulations which are remarkably similar and which are consistent with the findings presented here. Both theories attempt to explain social behavior in terms of the rewards exchanged and the costs incurred in interaction. As such, both include a theory of interpersonal attraction. While these authors differ in some details and in some of the terms used, both view liking as a function of the degree to which persons achieve in their interaction with others a reward-cost ratio in excess of some minimum level.

The term reward is, of course, a familiar one. Any activity on the part of one person that contributes to the gratification of the needs of another can be considered, from the standpoint of the latter, a reward. The term cost is similarly a very broad concept. The costs of engaging in any activity not only include 'punishment' incurred in carrying out that activity, such as fatigue or anxiety, but also, as Homans argues, include the value of rewards forgone by engaging in this activity rather than alternative activities. Mutuality and the choice of persons who are similar in choice status to the chooser may be thought of as an outcome of the stabilization of relations where each person is obtaining his best available cost-reward outcomes.

An examination of certain hypothetical departures from this state of equilibrium should identify the forces driving toward balance. First, two assumptions are made. One is that the order of persons by choice status represents the order of value attached to their behavior and to their other characteristics. A second assumption, true by definition, is that the order of choice status reflects the quantity of alternative relations available to each member. The greater the number of persons choosing a given person the greater the number who are willing to establish a relation with him. Consider first the case where person *A* of low choice status is attracted to person *B* of high choice status. The development of a mutually satisfactory relation in this instance is unlikely, because either one or the other is apt to experience outcomes that are lower than in some alternative relation. *B*'s profit in such a relation is apt to be relatively low because of the low value of *A*'s behavior. In this instance we would expect him not to continue the relation.

In certain circumstances, *B* might be able to exact from *A* behavior that is of high value to him, but, since by assumption it is not typical of *A*, this behavior would normally be produced only at high cost to *A*. Were this the case, the outcomes to *A* would be low and he would withdraw from the relation. Such a relation would be maintained only in those instances where the initial assumptions stated earlier do not hold. For example, they would not hold where some aspects of *A*'s behavior are of particular value to *B* but not to others, or where this behavior can be produced by *A* at low cost, or, finally, where *B* is discouraged either through inaccurate assessment of his alternatives or by force of circumstance from establishing more valuable alternative relations. That movements toward mutuality and equality of choice status between choosers are observable fairly early in a group, particularly in the high-ranking choices, suggests that persons become relatively adept at gauging their chances of satisfactory outcomes in a relation. This undoubtedly stems from previous experiences with relations that varied in this respect. Probably 'crushes' in early dating characterized by lack of mutuality and equality provide valuable training, leading persons in the courtship process to select and fall in love with those whose value in the marriage market is roughly the same.

The compromise process, then, consists of adjustments in relations among group members in the direction of a state of equilibrium characterized by an end result in which each person's reward-cost outcomes are maximized. This state of balance is characterized by many mutual choices, predominantly between persons equal in choice status.

REFERENCES

BACKMAN, C. W. & SECORD, P. F. (1962). Liking, selective interaction, and misperception in congruent interpersonal relations. *Sociometry,* December.
HOMANS, G. C. (1961). *Social behavior: its elementary forms.* New York: Harcourt, Brace & World.
JENNINGS, HELEN H. (1950). *Leadership and isolation.* New York: Longmans, Green.
MCNEMAR, Q. (1962). *Psychological statistics.* (Third edition.) New York: Wiley.
NEWCOMB, T. M. (1961). *The acquaintance process.* New York: Holt, Rinehart & Winston.
RIECKEN, H. W. & HOMANS, G. C. (1954). Psychological aspects of social structure. In G. Lindzey (Ed.), *Handbook of social psychology,* Vol. II. Cambridge, Mass.: Addison-Wesley. Pp. 786–832.
THIBAUT, J. W. & KELLEY, H. H. (1959). *The social psychology of groups.* New York: Wiley.

THE NATURE OF SOCIAL POWER*

Early investigations of social power attempted to identify the determinants of power by discovering what characteristics distinguished persons with high power. Today it is realized that this approach fails to uncover certain sources of power. The power of person *A* over person *B* is not solely a function of *A*'s characteristics; it is also a function of *B*'s. In fact, as in the case of attraction, for a complete understanding of their relative power, one must look beyond the *A-B* relation to the relations *A* and *B* have with other persons. This contemporary view is reflected in the theory of power presented by Emerson in the selection below.

Two important points about the nature of power are apparent in Emerson's representation of power

* The selection following the editorial introduction is reprinted from "Power-dependence relations," *American Sociological Review,* 1962, 27, 31–40, by permission of the author and the American Sociological Association.

in terms of the pair of equations $\begin{aligned}Pab &= Dba\\Pba &= Dab\end{aligned}$. The power of *A* over *B* is equal to the dependency of *B* on *A* and the power of *B* over *A* is equal to the dependency of *A* on *B*. First, the power of one individual must always be considered from the standpoint of the dependency of the other person on him. Second, this double equation underscores the idea that the power relation is usually transitive —a two-way relation, with each member of a pair having some power over the other.

An examination of the determinants of dependency provides an understanding of both the basis of power and the ways in which the power relation moves toward a balance of equality. Dependency is conceived as a function of the degree to which each individual is motivated to achieve goals mediated by the other, and the availability of these goals to each of the pair outside this relation. This suggests the nature of the balancing operations that come into play in response to tensions generated in a relation of unequal power. Withdrawal, in which the least powerful member reduces his motivational investment in the goals mediated by the more powerful, restores the relation to a balanced state. Cultivation of a new relation by the less powerful member—extending the power network—similarly reduces his dependency and restores balance. An increase in the more powerful member's motivational investment in goals mediated by the weaker, increasing the former's dependency, has the effect of restoring balance. The last balancing operation, blocking the alternative avenues to goal achievement of the more powerful member, increases his dependency and brings the power of the other into balance.

Emerson suggests that these four ways of correcting imbalance in power account for a number of social phenomena. The normative structure of social life arises out of the last-mentioned balancing operation, in which group members stand as a coalition, enforcing rules of conduct that ensure successful group functioning. This is illustrated by the ever-present threat of expulsion that faces the child who violates the rules of fairness in a group of children at play. Another basic social phenomenon is similarly derived from this formulation. The third balancing operation, increasing the dependency of the more powerful on the weaker, is thought to be the prototype of processes underlying the emergence of status. The power of those group members on whom the others are most dependent is reduced by giving them honor and esteem, thus increasing motivational investment on their part in their relations with other group members.

This selection is an excellent example of how a theory helps to relate and make meaningful in a parsimonious manner hitherto unconnected and little understood phenomena. While readers without sufficient background in sociology may find the selection difficult, they should be able to grasp the overall outline of the theoretical argument as well as a number of crucial ideas about power and power processes.

24.

Power-Dependence Relations

RICHARD M. EMERSON
UNIVERSITY OF WASHINGTON

A simple theory of power relations is developed in an effort to resolve some of the ambiguities surrounding "power," "authority," "legitimacy," and power "structures," through bringing them together in a coherent scheme. After defining a reciprocal *power-dependence relation*, attention is focused upon properties of balance and "balancing operations" in such relations. The

theory dictates exactly four generic types of balancing process, and discussion of these leads directly into processes of group formation, including the emergence of group norms, role structure and status hierarchy, all presented as the outcome of balancing tendencies in power relations. Within the framework of this theory, authority appears quite naturally to be legitimized power, vested in roles, and "legitimation" is seen as a special case of the coalition process through which norms and role-prescriptions are formed. Finally, through treating both persons and groups as actors in a *power-network* (two or more connected power-dependence relations) the door is opened for meaningful analysis of complex power structures. Brief reference is made to findings from two experiments pertaining to hypotheses advanced in this theory.

Judging from the frequent occurrence of such words as *power, influence, dominance* and *submission, status* and *authority*, the importance of power is widely recognized, yet considerable confusion exists concerning these concepts.[1] There is an extensive literature pertaining to power, on both theoretical and empirical levels, and in small group[2] as well as large community contexts.[3] Unfortunately, this already large and rapidly growing body of research has not achieved the cumulative character desired. Our *integrated* knowledge of power does not significantly surpass the conceptions left by Max Weber.[4]

This suggests that there is a place at this moment for a systematic treatment of social power. The underdeveloped state of this area is further suggested by what appears, to this author, to be

[1] See the Communications by Jay Butler and Paul Harrison on "On Power and Authority: An Exchange on Concepts," *American Sociological Review*, **25** (October, 1960), pp. 731–732. That both men can be essentially correct in the points they make yet fail to reconcile these points, strongly suggests the need for conceptual development in the domain of power relations.

[2] Among many studies, see Ronald Lippitt, Norman Polansky, Fritz Redl and Sidney Rosen, "The Dynamics of Power," *Human Relations*, **5** (February, 1952), pp. 37–64.

[3] Floyd Hunter, *Community Power Structure*, Chapel Hill: University of North Carolina Press, 1953.

[4] Max Weber, in *The Theory of Social and Economic Organization*, New York: Oxford University Press, 1947, presents what is still a classic formulation of power, authority and legitimacy. However, it is characteristic of Weber that he constructs a typology rather than an organized theory of power.

a recurrent flaw in common conceptions of social power; a flaw which helps to block adequate theoretical development as well as meaningful research. That flaw is the implicit treatment of power as though it were an attribute of a person or group ("*X* is an influential person." "*Y* is a powerful group," etc.). Given this conception, the natural research question becomes "Who in community *X* are the power *holders*?". The project then proceeds to rank-order persons by some criterion of power, and this ordering is called the *power-structure*. This is a highly questionable representation of a "structure," based upon a questionable assumption of *generalized power*.[5]

It is commonly observed that some person *X* dominates *Y*, while being subservient in relations with *Z*. Furthermore, these power relations are frequently intransitive! Hence, to say that "*X* has power" is vacant, unless we specify "over whom." In making these necessary qualifications we force ourselves to face up to the obvious: power is a property of the social relation; it is not an attribute of the actor.[6]

In this paper an attempt is made to construct a simple theory of the power aspects of social relations. Attention is focused upon characteristics of the relationship as such, with little or no regard for particular features of the persons or groups engaged in such relations. Personal traits, skills or possessions (such as wealth) which might be relevant to power in one relation are infinitely variable across the set of possible relations, and hence have no place in a general theory.

THE POWER-DEPENDENCE RELATION

While the theory presented here is anchored most intimately in small group research, it is meant to apply to more complex community relations as

[5] See Raymond E. Wolfinger, "Reputation and Reality in the Study of 'Community Power'," *American Sociological Review*, **25** (October, 1960), pp. 636–644, for a well taken critical review of Floyd Hunter's work on these very points. The notion of "generalized power" which is not restricted to specific social relations, if taken literally, is probably meaningless. Power may indeed be generalized across a finite set of relations in a power network, but this notion, too, requires very careful analysis. Are you dealing with some kind of halo effect (reputations if you wish), or are the range and boundary of generalized power anchored in the power structure itself? These are questions which must be asked and answered.

[6] Just as power is often treated as though it were a property of the person, so leadership, conformity, etc., are frequently referred to the personal traits of "leaders," "conformers" and so on, as if they were distinguishable types of people. In a sociological perspective such behavior should be explicitly treated as an attribute of a relation rather than a person.

well. In an effort to make these conceptions potentially as broadly applicable as possible, we shall speak of relations among *actors,* where an actor can be either a person or a group. Unless otherwise indicated, any relation discussed might be a person-person, group-person or group-group relation.

Social relations commonly entail *ties of mutual dependence* between the parties. *A depends* upon *B* if he aspires to goals or gratifications whose achievement is facilitated by appropriate actions on *B*'s part. By virtue of mutual dependency, it is more or less imperative to each party that he be able to control or influence the other's conduct. At the same time, these ties of mutual dependence imply that each party is in a position, to some degree, to grant or deny, facilitate or hinder, the other's gratification. Thus, it would appear that the power to control or influence the other resides in control over the things he values, which may range all the way from oil resources to ego-support, depending upon the relation in question. In short, *power resides implicitly in the other's dependency*. When this is recognized, the analysis will of necessity revolve largely around the concept of dependence.[7]

Two variables appear to function jointly in fixing the dependence of one actor upon another. Since the precise nature of this joint function is an empirical question, our proposition can do no more than specify the directional relationships involved:

Dependence (Dab). The dependence of actor *A* upon actor *B* is (*1*) directly proportional to *A*'s *motivational investment* in goals mediated by *B*, and (*2*) inversely proportional to the *availability* of those goals to *A* outside of the *A-B* relation.

In this proposition "goal" is used in the broadest possible sense to refer to gratifications consciously sought as well as rewards unconsciously obtained through the relationship. The "availability" of such goals outside of the relation refers to alternative avenues of goal-achievement, most notably other social relations. The costs associated with such alternatives must be included in any assessment of dependency.[8]

If the dependence of one party provides the basis for the power of the other, that power must be defined as a potential influence:

Power (Pab). The power of actor *A* over actor *B* is the amount of resistance on the part of *B* which can be potentially overcome by *A*.

[7] The relation between power and dependence is given similar emphasis in the systematic treatment by J. Thibaut and H. H. Kelley, *The Social Psychological of Groups*, New York: John Wiley and Sons, 1959.

[8] The notion of "opportunity costs" in economics is a similar idea. If an employee has alternative employment opportunities, and if these opportunities have low associated cost (travel, etc.), the employee's dependence upon his current employer is reduced.

Two points must be made clear about this definition. First, the power defined here will not be, of necessity, observable in every interactive episode between A and B, yet we suggest that it exists nonetheless as a potential, to be explored, tested, and occasionally employed by the participants. Pab will be empirically manifest only *if* A makes some demand, and only *if* this demand runs counter to B's desires (resistance to be overcome). Any operational definition must make reference to *change* in the conduct of B attributable to demands made by A.

Second, we define power as the "resistance" which can be overcome, without restricting it to any one domain of action. Thus, if A is dependent upon B for love and respect, B might then draw A into criminal activity which he would normally resist. The reader might object to this formulation, arguing that social power is in fact restricted to certain channels. If so, the reader is apparently concerned with "legitimized power" embedded in a social structure. Rather than begin at this more evolved level, we hope to derive legitimized power in the theory itself.

The premise we began with can now be stated as $Pab=Dba$; the power of A over B is equal to, and based upon, the dependence of B upon A.[9] Recognizing the reciprocity of social relations, we can represent a power-dependence relation as a pair of equations:

$$Pab=Dba$$
$$Pba=Dab.$$

Before proceeding further we should emphasize that these formulations have been so worded in the hope that they will apply across a wide range of social life. At a glance our conception of dependence contains two variables remarkably like supply and demand ("availability" and "motivational investment," respectively).[10] We prefer the term *dependency* over these economic terms because it facilitates broader application, for all we need to do to shift these ideas from one area of application to another is change the motivational basis of dependency. We can speak of the economic dependence of a home builder upon a loan

[9] In asserting that power is based upon the dependency of the other, it might appear that we are dealing with *one* of the bases of power ("reward power") listed by John R. P. French, Jr. and Bertram Raven, "The Bases of Social Power," *Studies in Social Power*, D. Cartwright, editor, Ann Arbor, Michigan: Institute for Social Research, 1959. However, careful attention to our highly generalized conception of dependence will show that it covers most if not all of the forms of power listed in that study.

[10] Professor Alfred Kuhn, Department of Economics, University of Cincinnati, has been working on a theory for power analysis soon to be published. The scheme he develops, though very similar to the one presented here, is put together in a different way. It is anchored more tightly to economic concepts, and hence its implications lead off in different directions from those presented below.

agency as varying directly with his desire for the home, and hence capital, and inversely with the "availability" of capital from other agencies. Similarly, a child may be dependent upon another child based upon motivation toward the pleasures of collective play, the availability of alternative playmates, etc. The same generic power-dependence relation is involved in each case. The dependency side of the equation may show itself in "friendship" among playmates, in "filial love" between parent and child, in "respect for treaties" among nations. On the other side of the equation, I am sure no one doubts that mothers, lovers, children, and nations enjoy the power to influence their respective partners, within the limit set by the partner's dependence upon them.

Finally, because these concepts are meant to apply across a wide variety of social situations, operational definitions cannot be appropriately presented here. Operational definitions provide the necessary bridge between generalizing concepts on the one hand, and the concrete features of a specific research situation on the other hand. Hence, there is no *one* proper operational definition for a theoretical concept.[11]

BALANCE AND IMBALANCE

The notion of reciprocity in power-dependency relations raises the question of equality or inequality of power in the relation. If the power of of A over B (Pab) is confronted by equal opposing power of B over A, is power then neutralized or cancelled out? We suggest that in such a balanced condition, power is in no way removed from the relationship. A pattern of "dominance" might not emerge in the interaction among these actors, but that does not imply that power is inoperative in either or both directions. A *balanced* relation and an *unbalanced* relation are represented respectively as follows:

$$\begin{array}{cc} Pab=Dba & \qquad Pab=Dba \\ \| \quad \| & \qquad \vee \quad \vee \\ Pba=Dab & \qquad Pba=Dab \end{array}$$

Consider two social relations, both of which are balanced, but at *different levels* of dependence (say Loeb and Leopold, as compared with two casual friends). A moment's thought will reveal the utility of the argument that balance does not neutralize power, for each party may continue to

[11] Many different operational definitions can serve one theoretical concept, and there is no reason to require that they produce intercorrelated results when applied in the same research situation. While the controversies surrounding "operationalism" have now been largely resolved, there remains some confusion on this point. See, for example, Bernice Eisman, "Some Operational Measures of Cohesiveness and Their Interrelations," *Human Relations*, 12 (May, 1959), pp. 183–189.

exert profound control over the other. It might even be meaningful to talk about the parties being controlled by the relation itself.

Rather than cancelling out considerations of power, reciprocal power provides the basis for studying three more features of power-relations: first, a power advantage can be defined as *Pab* minus *Pba,* which can be either positive or negative (a power disadvantage);[12] second, the *cohesion* of a relationship can be defined as the average of *Dab* and *Dba,* though this definition can be refined;[13] and finally, it opens the door to the study of *balancing operations* as structural changes in power-dependence relations which tend to reduce power advantage.

Discussion of balancing tendencies should begin with a concrete illustration. In the unbalanced relation represented symbolically above, *A* is the more powerful party because *B* is the more dependent of the two. Let actor *B* be a rather "unpopular" girl, with puritanical upbringing, who wants desperately to date; and let *A* be a young man who occasionally takes her out, while dating other girls as well. (The reader can satisfy himself about *A*'s power advantage in this illustration by referring to the formulations above.) Assume further that *A* "discovers" this power advantage, and, in exploring for the limits of his power, makes sexual advances. In this simplified illustration, these advances should encounter resistance in *B*'s puritanical values. Thus, when a power advantage is *used,* the weaker member will achieve one value at the expense of other values.

In this illustration the tensions involved in an unbalanced relation need not be long endured. They can be reduced in either of two ways: (*1*) the girl might reduce the psychic costs involved in continuing the relation by redefining her moral values, with appropriate rationalizations and shifts in reference group attachments; or (*2*) she might renounce the value of dating, develop career aspirations, etc., thus reducing *A*'s power. Notice that the first solution does *not* of necessity alter the unbalanced relation. The weaker member has sidestepped one painful demand but she is still vulnerable to new demands. By contrast, the second solution alters the power relation itself. In general, it appears that an unbalanced relation is unstable for it encourages the use of power which in turn sets in motion processes which we will

call (*a*) cost reduction and (*b*) balancing operations.[14]

COST REDUCTION

The "cost" referred to here amounts to the "resistance" to be overcome in our definition of power—the cost involved for one party in meeting the demands made by the other. The process of cost reduction in power-dependence relations shows itself in many varied forms. In the courting relation above it took the form of alteration in moral attitudes on the part of a girl who wanted to be popular; in industry it is commonly seen as the impetus for improved plant efficiency and technology in reducing the cost of production. What we call the "mark of oppression" in the character structure of members of low social castes (the submissive and "painless" loss of freedom) might well involve the same power processes, as does the "internalization of parental codes" in the socialization process. In fact, the oedipal conflict might be interpreted as a special case of the tensions of imbalance in a power-dependence relation, and cost reduction takes the form of identification and internalization as classically described. "Identification with the aggressor" in any context would appear to be explainable in terms of cost reduction.

In general, *cost reduction* is a process involving change in values (personal, social, economic) which reduces the pains incurred in meeting the demands of a powerful other. It must be emphasized, however, that these adjustments do not necessarily alter the balance or imbalance of the relation, and, as a result, they must be distinguished from the more fundamental *balancing operations* described below. It must be recognized that cost reducing tendencies will take place even under conditions of balance, and while this is obvious in economic transactions, it is equally true of other social relations, where the "costs" involved are anchored in modifiable attitudes and values. The intense cohesion of a lasting social relation like the Loeb-Leopold relation mentioned above can be attributed in part to the cost reduction processes involved in the progressive formation of their respective personalities, taking place in the interest of preserving the valued relation. We suggest that cost reducing tendencies generally will function to deepen and stabilize social relations over and above the condition of balance.

BALANCING OPERATIONS

The remainder of this paper will deal with balancing processes which operate through changes

[12] J. Thibaut and H. H. Kelley, *op. cit.,* pp. 107–108.

[13] This definition of cohesion, based upon dependency, seems to have one advantage over the definition offered by Leon Festinger, *et al., Theory and Experiment in Social Communication,* Ann Arbor: Research Center for Group Dynamics, University of Michigan Press, 1950. The Festinger definition takes into account only one of the two variables involved in dependency.

[14] The "tensions of imbalance," which are assumed to make an unbalanced relation unstable, are closely related to the idea of "distributive justice" discussed by George C. Homans, *Social Behavior: Its Elementary Forms,* New York: Harcourt, Brace and World, Inc., 1961. All of what Homans has to say around this idea could be fruitfully drawn into the present formulation.

in the variables which define the structure of the power-dependence relation as such. The formal notation adopted here suggests *exactly four generic types* of balancing operation. In the unbalanced relation

$$\begin{matrix} Pab = Dba \\ \vee \qquad \vee \\ Pba = Dab \end{matrix}$$

, balance can be restored either by an increase in *Dab* or by a decrease in *Dba*. If we recall that *dependence* is a joint function of two variables, the following alterations will move the relation toward a state of balance:

1. If *B* reduces motivational investment in goals mediated by *A*;
2. If *B* cultivates alternative sources for gratification of those goals;
3. If *A* increases motivational investment in goals mediated by *B*;
4. If *A* is denied alternative sources for achieving those goals.

While these four types of balancing operation are dictated by the logic of the scheme, we suggest that each corresponds to well known social processes. The first operation yields balance through motivational withdrawal by *B*, the weaker member. The second involves the cultivation of alternative social relations by *B*. The third is based upon "giving status" to *A*, and the fourth involves coalition and group formation.

In some of these processes the role of power is well known, while in others it seems to have escaped notice. In discussing any one of these balancing operations it must be remembered that a prediction of which one (or what combination) of the four will take place must rest upon analysis of conditions involved in the concrete case at hand.

In the interest of simplicity and clarity, we will illustrate each of the four generic types of balancing operation in relations among children in the context of play. Consider two children equally motivated toward the pleasures of collective play and equally capable of contributing to such play. These children, *A* and *B*, form a balanced relation if we assume further that each has the other as his only playmate, and the give-and-take of their interactions might well be imagined, involving the emergence of such equalitarian rules as "taking turns," etc. Suppose now that a third child, *C*, moves into the neighborhood and makes the acquaintance of *A*, but *not B*. The *A-B* relation will be thrown out of balance by virtue of *A*'s decreased dependence upon *B*. The reader should convince himself of this fact by referring back to the proposition on dependence. Without any of these parties necessarily "understanding" what is going on, we would predict that *A* would slowly come to dominate *B* in the pattern of their interactions. On more frequent occasions *B* will find himself deprived of the pleasures *A* can offer, thus slowly coming to sense his own dependency more acutely. By the same token *A* will more frequently find *B* saying "yes" instead of "no" to his proposals, and he will gain increased awareness of his power over *B*. The growing self-images of these children will surely reflect and perpetuate this pattern.

OPERATION NUMBER ONE: WITHDRAWAL

We now have the powerful *A* making demands of the dependent *B*. One of the processes through which the tensions in the unbalanced *A-B* relation can be reduced is *motivational withdrawal* on the part of *B*, for this will reduce *Dba* and *Pab*. In this illustration, child *B* might lose some of his interest in collective play under the impact of frustrations and demands imposed by *A*. Such a withdrawal from the play relation would presumably come about if the other three balancing operations were blocked by the circumstances peculiar to the situation. The same operation was illustrated above in the case of the girl who might renounce the value of dating. It would seem to be involved in the dampened level of aspiration associated with the "mark of oppression" referred to above.

In general, the denial of dependency involved in this balancing operation will have the effect of moving actors away from relations which are unbalanced to their disadvantage. The actor's motivational orientations and commitments toward different areas of activity will intimately reflect this process.

OPERATION NUMBER TWO: EXTENSION OF POWER NETWORK

Withdrawal as a balancing operation entails subjective alterations in the weaker actor. The second operation takes place through alterations in a structure we shall call a *power network*, defined as two or more *connected* power-dependence relations. As we have seen in our illustration, when the *C-A* relation is connected through *A* with the *A-B* relation, forming a simple linear network *C-A-B*, the properties of *A-B* are altered. In this example, a previously balanced *A-B* relation is thrown out of balance, giving *A* a power advantage. This points up the general fact that while each relation in a network will involve interactions which appear to be independent of other relations in the network (e.g., *A* and *B* are seen to play together in the absence of *C*; *C* and *A* in the absence of *B*), the internal features of one relation are nonetheless a function of the entire network. Any adequate conception of a "power structure" must be based upon this fact.

In this illustration the form of the network throws both relations within it out of balance, thus stimulating one or several of the balancing operations under discussion. If balancing operation number two takes place, *the network* will be extended by the formation of new relationships. The tensions of imbalance in the *A-B* and *A-C* relations will make *B* and *C* "ready" to form new friendships (*1*) with additional children *D* and *E*, thus lengthening a linear network, or (*2*) with each other, thus "closing" the network. It is important to notice that the lengthened network balances some relations, but not the network as a whole, while the closed network is completely balanced under the limiting assumptions of this illustration. Thus, we might offer as a corollary to operation number two: Power networks tend to achieve closure.[15]

If the reader is dissatisfied with this illustration in children's play relations, let *A* be the loan agent mentioned earlier, and *B*, *C*, . . . *N* be home builders or others dependent upon *A* for capital. This is the familiar monopoly situation with the imbalance commonly attributed to it. As a network, it is a set of relations connected only at *A*. Just as the children were "ready" to accept new friends, so the community of actors *B*, *C*, . . . *N* is ready to receive new loan agencies. Balancing operation number 2 involves in all cases the *diffusion* of dependency into new relations in a network. A final illustration of this principle can be found in institutionalized form in some kinship systems involving the extended family. In the case of the Hopi, for example, Dorothy Eggan has described at length the diffusion of child dependency among many "mothers," thus draining off much of the force of oedipal conflicts in that society.[16] We have already suggested that oedipal conflict may be taken as a special case of the tension of imbalance, which in this case appears to be institutionally handled in a manner resembling operation number two. This is not to be taken, however, as an assertion that the institution evolved as a balancing process, though this is clearly open for consideration.

[15] The notion of closed versus open networks as discussed here can be directly related to research dealing with communication networks, such as that reported by Harold J. Leavitt, "Some Effects of Communication Patterns on Group Performance," *Journal of Abnormal and Social Psychology*, **46** (January, 1951), pp. 38–50, in which the limiting assumptions involved in this discussion are fully met by experimental controls. In discussing those experiments in terms of the concepts in this theory we would consider each actor's dependence upon other actors for *information*. A formal treatment of such networks is suggested by A. Bavelas, "A Mathematical Model For Group Structure," *Applied Anthropology*, **7** (Summer, 1948), pp. 16–30.

[16] Dorothy Eggan, "The General Problem of Hopi Adjustment," *American Anthropologist*, **45** (July-September, 1943), pp. 357–373.

It is convenient at this juncture to take up balancing operation number 4, leaving number 3 to the last.

OPERATION NUMBER FOUR: COALITION FORMATION

Let us continue with the same illustration. When the *B-C* relation forms, closing the *C-A-B* network in the process of balancing, we have what appears to be a coalition of the two weaker against the one stronger. This, however, is not technically the case, for *A* is not involved in the *B-C* interactions; he simply exists as an alternative playmate for both *B* and *C*.

The proper representation of coalitions in a triad would be (*AB*)-*C*, (*AC*)-*B*, or (*BC*)-*A*. That is, a triadic network reduces to a coalition only if two members unite as a single actor in the process of dealing directly with the third. The difference involved here may be very small in behavioral terms, and the distinction may seem overly refined, but it goes to the heart of an important conceptual problem (the difference between a closed "network" and a "group"), and it rests upon the fact that two very different balancing operations are involved. The *C-A-B* network is balanced through the addition of a third relation (*C-B*) in operation number two, but it is still just a power network. In operation number 4 it achieves balance through collapsing the two-relational network into one group-person relation with the emergence of a "collective actor." Operation number two reduces the power of the stronger actor, while number 4 increases the power of weaker actors through collectivization. If the rewards mediated by *A* are such that they can be jointly enjoyed by *B* and *C*, then the tensions of imbalance in the *A-B* and *A-C* relations can be resolved in the (*BC*)-*A* coalition.

In a general way, Marx was asking for balancing operation number 4 in his call to "Workers of the world," and the collectivization of labor can be taken as an illustration of this balancing tendency as an historic process. Among the balancing operations described here, coalition formation is the one most commonly recognized as a power process. However, the more general significance of this balancing operation seems to have escaped notice, for the typical coalition is only one of the many forms this same operation takes. For this reason the next section will explore coalition processes further.

THE ORGANIZED GROUP

We wish to suggest that the coalition process is basically involved in all organized group functioning, whether the group be called a coalition or not. We believe this illuminates the role which power processes play in the emergence and maintenance of group structure in general.

In the typical coalition pattern, (*AB*)-*C*, *A* and

B constitute a collective actor in the sense that they act as one, presenting themselves to their common environment as a single unit. A coalition, as one *type* of group, is characterized by the fact that (*a*) the common environment is an actor to be controlled, and (*b*) its unity is historically based upon efforts to achieve that control. Now, all we need do to blend this type of group with groups in general is to *dehumanize* the environmental problem which the group collectively encounters. Thus, instead of having the control of actor *C* as its end, the group attempts to control *C* in the interest of achieving *X*, some "group goal." Now, if *C* also aspires toward *X*, and if *C* is dependent upon the group for achieving *X*, *C* might well be one of the group members—any member. Thus, in a three-member group we have three coalition structures as intragroup relations, each representable as ([*AB*]-*C*)-*X*, with *A*, *B* and *C* interchangeable.

The situation involved here is reminiscent of the rapidly forming and reforming coalitions in unconsolidated children's play groups. As the group consolidates, these coalitions do not drop out of the picture; they become stabilized features of group structure, and the stabilization process is identical with "norm formation." In fact, the demands made by (*AB*) of *C* in the power process within ([*AB*]-*C*) are exactly what we normally call *group norms* and *role-prescriptions*. Such norms are properly viewed as the "voice" of a collective actor, standing in coalition against the object of its demands. This reasoning suggests an idealized conception of group structure, based upon two types of collective demands:

(*1*) *Role-prescriptions.* Specifications of behavior which all group members expect (demand) of one or more but not all members.

(*2*) *Group norms.* Specifications of behavior which all group members expect of all group members.

Certain actions, when performed by some member or members, need not be performed by all other members to properly facilitate group functioning. These will tend to be incorporated in role-prescriptions, which, taken together, provide a division of labor in a role structure. Roles are defined and enforced through a consolidation of power in coalition formation. Likewise with group norms. Thus, the structure of a group (its norms and prescriptions) will specify the makeup of the coalition a member would face for any group-relevant act he might perform.

This conception of group structure is idealized in the sense that it describes complete consensus among members, even to the point of group identification and internalization of collective demands (members expect things of themselves in the above definitions). Balancing operations, along with cost reduction, should move group structure toward this ideal.

AUTHORITY

It should be clear that in introducing conceptions of group *structure* we have in no way digressed from our discussion of power *processes,* for the emergence of these structural forms is attributed directly to operation number four, closely resembling coalition formation. Even the most formalized role-prescription is properly viewed as the "voice" of all members standing as a coalition in making its demand of the occupant of the role. Whenever a specific member finds occasion to remind another member of his "proper" job in terms of such prescriptions, he speaks with the *authority* of the group behind him; he is "authorized" to speak for them. In this sense, every member has authority of a kind (as in civil arrest), but authority is usually used to refer to power vested in an office or role. The situation is basically the same, however, in either case. The occupant of such a role has simply been singled out and commissioned more explicitly to speak for the group in the group's dealings with its members. That authority is *limited* power follows from logical necessity when role-prescriptions are treated as they are here. A dean, for example, can force faculty member *A* to turn in his grades on time because the demand is "legitimate," that is, supported by a coalition of all other faculty members joining with the dean in making the demand. If that dean, however, were to employ sanctions in an effort to induce that member to polish the dean's private car, the "coalition" would immediately re-form around the faculty member, as expressed in role-prescriptions defining the boundary of "legitimate power" or authority. The dean's authority is power contained and restricted through balancing operation number four, coalition formation.

The notion of legitimacy is important, for authority is more than balanced power; it is *directed* power which can be employed (legitimately) only in channels defined by the norms of the group. A person holding such authority is commissioned; he does not simply have the right to rule or govern—he is obliged to. Thus, authority emerges as a transformation of power in a process called "legitimation," and that process is one special case of balancing operation number four.[17]

---

[17] The process of legitimation has sometimes been described as a tactic employed by a person aspiring to power or trying to hold his power, rather than a process through which persons are granted restricted power. For example, C. Wright Mills states: "Those in authority attempt to justify their rule over institutions by linking it, as if it were a necessary consequence, with widely believed in moral symbols, sacred emblems, legal formulae. These central conceptions may refer

Earlier in this section we referred to the common phenomenon of rapidly forming and reforming coalitions in children's play groups. Our reasoning suggests that it is precisely through these coalition processes that unifying norms emerge. These fluctuating coalitions can be taken as the prototype of organized group life wherein the tempo of coalition realignment is accelerated to the point of being a blur before our eyes. Stated more accurately, the norms and prescriptions define implicitly the membership of the coalition which would either support or oppose any member if he were to perform any action relevant to those norms.

OPERATION NUMBER THREE: EMERGENCE OF STATUS

One important feature of group structure remains to be discussed: status and status hierarchies. It is interesting that the one remaining balancing operation provided in this theory takes us naturally to the emergence of status ordering. Operation number three increases the weaker member's power to control the formerly more powerful member through increasing the latter's motivational investment in the relation. This is normally accomplished through giving him status recognition in one or more of its many forms, from ego-gratifications to monetary differentials. The ego-rewards, such as prestige, loom large in this process because they are highly valued by many recipients while given at low cost to the giver.

The discussion of status hierarchies forces us to consider *intra*-group relations, and how this can be done in a theory which treats the group in the singular as *an* actor. The answer is contained in the idealized conception of group structure outlined above. That conception implies that every intra-group relation involves at once every member of the group. Thus, in a group with members A, B, C, and D, the relations A-B, A-C, etc. do not exist. Any interactions between A and B, for example, lie outside of the social system

to god or gods, the 'vote of the majority,' 'the will of the people,' 'the aristocracy of talent or wealth,' to the 'divine right of kings,' or to the allegedly extraordinary endowments of the ruler himself. Social scientists, following Weber, call such conceptions 'legitimations,' or sometimes 'symbols of justification.' " (*The Sociological Imagination*, New York: Oxford University Press, 1959, p. 36). Whether we view the process of legitimation in the context of the *formation* of such collective conceptions, or in the context of calling upon them to justify action, the process is fundamentally that of mobilizing collective support to oppose those who challenge power. Power so supported is authority, and the process fits the general model of coalition formation.

in question unless one or both of these persons "represents" the group in his actions, as in the coalition pattern discussed at length above. The relations which do exist are $(ABCD)$-A, $(ABCD)$-B, $(ABCD)$-C and $(ABCD)$-D as a minimum, plus whatever relations of the $(ABCD)$-(AB) type may be involved in the peculiar structure of the group in question. Thus, in a group of N members we have theoretical reason for dealing with N *group-member* relations rather than considering all of the $\frac{N(N-1)}{2}$ possible member-member relations. Each of these group-member relations can now be expressed in the familiar equations for a power-dependence relation:

$$Pgm_i = Dm_i g$$
$$Pm_i g = Dgm_i.$$

To account for the emergence of a status hierarchy within a group of N members, we start with a set of N group-member relations of this type and consider balancing operations in these relations.

Let us imagine a five member group and proceed on three assumptions: (*1*) *status* involves differential valuation of members (or roles) by the group, and this valuation is equivalent to, or an expression of, Dgm_i; (*2*) a member who is highly valued by the group is highly valued in other *similar* groups he belongs to or might freely join; and (*3*) all five members have the same motivational investment in the group at the outset. Assumptions 2 and 3 are empirical, and when they are true they imply that Dgm and Dmg are inversely related across the N group-member relations. This in turn implies a state of imbalance of a very precarious nature so far as group stability is concerned. The least dependent member of a group will be the first to break from the group, and these members are precisely the most valued members. It is this situation which balancing operation number three alleviates through "giving status" to the highly valued members, thus gaining the power to keep and control those members.

These ideas are illustrated with hypothetical values in Table 1, with imbalance represented as power advantage (PA). Balancing operations will tend to move PA toward zero, as shown in column 6 after the highly valued members A and B have come to depend upon the group for the special rewards of status, and in column 9 after the least valued members D and E have withdrawn some of their original motivational investment in the group. The table presents three stages in status crystallization, and the process of crystallization is seen as a balancing process. The final stage (columns 7, 8, and 9) should be achieved only in groups with very low membership turnover. The middle stage might well be perpetual in groups with new members continually coming in at the lower levels. In such "open" groups, status striving should be a characteristic feature and can be taken as a direct manifestation of the tensions of imbalance. In the final stage, such strivers have either succeeded or withdrawn from the struggle.

Among the factors involved in status ordering, this theory focuses attention upon the extreme importance of the *availability* factor in dependency as a determinant of status position and the values employed in status ordering. In considering *Dgm* (the relative value or importance the group attaches to member roles), it is notably difficult to rely úpon a functional explanation. Is the pitcher more highly valued than the center fielder because he is functionally more important or because good pitchers are harder to find? Is the physicist valued over the plumber because of a "more important" functional contribution to the social system, or because physicists are more difficult to replace, more costly to obtain, etc.? The latter considerations involve the availability factor. We suggest here that the *values* people use in ordering roles or persons express the dependence of the system upon those roles, and that the *availability* factor in dependency plays the decisive part in historically shaping those values.[18]

CONCLUSION

The theory put forth in this paper is in large part contained implicitly in the ties of mutual dependence which bind actors together in social systems. Its principal value seems to be its ability to pull together a wide variety of social events, ranging

from the internalization of parental codes to society-wide movements, like the collectivization of labor, in terms of a few very simple principles. Most important, the concepts involved are subject to operational formulation. Two experiments testing certain propositions discussed above led to the following results:

1. Conformity (*Pgm*) varies directly with motivational investment in the group;
2. Conformity varies inversely with acceptance in alternative groups;
3. Conformity is high at both status extremes in groups with membership turnover (see column 5, Table 1);
4. Highly valued members of a group are strong conformers *only if* they are valued by other groups as well. (This supports the notion that special status rewards are used to hold the highly valued member who does not depend heavily upon the group, and that in granting him such rewards power is obtained over him.);
5. Coalitions form among the weak to control the strong (balancing operation number three);
6. The greatest rewards within a coalition are given to the less dependent member of the coalition (balancing operation number three, analogous to "status giving").

Once the basic ideas in this theory have been adequately validated and refined, both theoretical and empirical work must be extended in two main directions. First, the interaction process should be studied to locate carefully the factors leading to *perceived* power and dependency in self and others, and the conditions under which power, as a potential, will be employed in action. Secondly, and, in the long run, more important, will be study of *power networks* more complex than those referred to here, leading to more adequate under-

---

[18] "Motivational investment" and "availability," which jointly determine dependency at any point in time, are functionally related through time. This is implied in our balancing operations. While these two variables can be readily distinguished in the case of *Dmg*, they are too intimately fused in *Dgm* to be clearly separated. The values by which a group sees a given role as "important" at time 2, evolve from felt scarcity in that role and similar roles at time 1.

TABLE 1 *Hypothetical Values Showing the Relation between Dgm and Dmg in a Group with Five Members*

MEMBER	BEFORE BALANCING			AFTER OPERATION #3			AFTER OPERATION #1		
	1 *Dgm*	2 *Dmg**	3 *PAgm*†	4 *Dgm*	5 *Dmg*	6 *PAgm*†	7 *Dgm*	8 *Dmg*	9 *PAgm*†
A´	5	1	−4	5	5	0	5	5	0
B	4	2	−2	4	4	0	4	4	0
C	3	3	0	3	3	0	3	3	0
D	2	4	2	2	4	2	2	2	0
E	1	5	4	1	5	4	1	1	0

* Assuming that all members have the same motivational investment in the group at the outset, and that highly valued members (*A* and *B*) are valued in other groups as well. † Power Advantage *PAgm=Dmg−Dgm.*

standing of complex power structures. The theory presented here does no more than provide the basic underpinning to the study of complex networks. There is every reason to believe that modern mathematics, graph theory in particular,[19] can be fruitfully employed in the analysis of complex networks and predicting the outcome of power plays within such networks.

LEGITIMATE POWER, COERCIVE POWER, AND OBSERVABILITY [*]

French and Raven[a] have introduced fruitful dimensions of conceptualization in the study of power. They distinguish five types of power in terms of the bases upon which one person may exert influence on another. These include reward power, coercive power, legitimate power, referent power (based on identification), and expert power. In a series of studies these investigators have attempted to relate a number of features of the influence process to the basis of power employed. One of these earlier investigations is reproduced below. This selection is not only illustrative of how conceptual refinement aids in the process of learning more about a phenomenon, but also of how unanticipated reactions of subjects to features of the experimental situation make interpretation of results difficult. As to the former, this investigation suggests the value of the distinction between coercive power and legitimate power. Exercise of legitimate power increases private acceptance of an influence attempt, whereas exercise of coercive power does not.

As to unanticipated subject responses, this selection provides a number of interesting instances. First, as the investigators suggest, the power of the influencer, a supervisor, may well have been enhanced in this experimental setting by the subjects' perception of the legitimacy of the experiment. Second, while it might have been expected that a supervisor who did not have group support would be able to exert little legitimate power over the rate of work of the subjects, it appeared that some reacted to his attempt to slow them down by overconforming as a way of expressing resentment—as if they felt, "I'll show you how slowly I can really go!" Thus, the supervisor's influence under these conditions was greater than anticipated. Finally, the responses of the subjects to at least one of the questionnaire items appeared to be influenced by the subjects' unwillingness to respond in a manner that might have led the experimenter to view them unfavorably.

25.

Legitimate Power, Coercive Power, and Observability in Social Influence[1]

BERTRAM H. RAVEN
UNIVERSITY OF CALIFORNIA, LOS ANGELES

JOHN R. P. FRENCH, JR.
UNIVERSITY OF MICHIGAN

In an earlier theoretical paper (6), we defined five bases for social power in the small group: *Reward power*, based on the perception by the individual, P, that the agent, O, can mediate rewards for him; *coercive power*, based on P's perception that O has the ability to mediate punishments for him; *legitimate power*, based on the perception by P that O has a legitimate right to prescribe behavior for him; *referent power*, based on P's identification with O; and *expert power*, based on P's perception that O has some special knowledge or expertness. We then compared these types of power according to domain, degree of dependence of the given type of power upon O, the importance of publicity in contributing toward influence, and the effects of the use of a given type of power upon the continuing relationship between the individual and the agent. In a second article, legitimate power was successfully manipulated in an experimental situation (15). It is our purpose here to investigate further the effects of legitimate power as compared to the effects of coercion.

Legitimate power involves some value or standard, accepted by the individual, by virtue of which the agent can assert his power. The reader will note similarities to the concept of *legitimacy of authority* which has long been explored by

* The selection following the editorial introduction is reprinted from "Legitimate power, coercive power, and observability in social influence," *Sociometry*, 1958, **21**, 83–97, by permission of the authors and the American Sociological Association.

[a] J. R. P. French, Jr., & B. H. Raven. The bases of social power. In D. Cartwright (ed.), *Studies in social power*. Ann Arbor, Mich.: University of Michigan Press, 1959. Pp. 118–149.

[19] F. Harary and R. Norman, *Graph Theory as a Mathematical Model in the Social Sciences.* Ann Arbor: Institute for Social Research, 1953. An effort to apply such a model to power relations can be found in John R. P. French, Jr., "A Formal Theory of Social Power," *The Psychological Review,* **63** (May, 1956), pp. 181–194.

[1] This study was conducted at the Research Center for Group Dynamics under contract with the Office of Naval Research. For their assistance in this experiment, we are deeply indebted to Mr. Albert Meister, Mrs. Jacqueline Meister, Mrs. Elinor D. Grayer, and Miss Barbara Rackow.

sociologists, particularly by Weber (17) and more recently by Goldhammer and Shils (8). In varying social settings, the age, the sex, or the clan of O will determine the areas within which he may prescribe behavior for P. Acceptance of the social structure may also be a basis for legitimate power. Legitimate power in formal organizations is largely a relationship between offices rather than between persons. Assuming that the factory worker accepts the right of his supervisor to hold his position, that supervisor will, by virtue of this occupancy, have the legitimate right to prescribe behavior for his worker; the worker will, in turn, feel obligated to accept these orders. The manner in which the office is attained may be crucial, therefore, to the power of O over P. We have experimentally demonstrated that a member whose group has elected him to a position of authority will thereby achieve legitimate power over remaining members (15). Thus the election procedure is a formal means for designating the legitimate occupant of an office, and investing him with the legitimate power of that office. This has been recognized all too well by totalitarian rulers who go to great pains to go through the trappings of "elections" in order to reduce the necessity for use of coercive power. In this experiment, we will again manipulate legitimate power by mobilizing group support through an election procedure. This method of varying legitimate power is based ultimately on our subjects' democratic values regarding the election of leaders.

Legitimate and coercive power are similar in that each produces initial changes which are dependent upon O, the influencing agent. That is, even if P does not see the reason for the change, or accept the intrinsic value of the influence, he will nevertheless conform, in order to avoid punishment (*coercive power*), or because he accepts the right of O to influence him (*legitimate power*). The two types of power are different in that observability is important for coercive power, but not for legitimate power: P will conform to O's *coercive* induction to the extent that P feels that O will become aware of the degree of influence. In the case of legitimate power, the communication of the extent of change to O is unimportant. That coercion results in "public," rather than "private" influence has already been suggested by a number of investigators (2, 3, 5, 6, 9, 10, 11, 12, 13, 14, 15). The contrasting private influence resulting from legitimate power had, to our knowledge, not been explored prior to this experiment, though it is currently receiving additional investigation (5).

In addition, we expect that whereas the individual who exercises legitimate power will become more personally attractive to P, the coercive power figure will be less accepted as the result of such power. The use of coercive power should also reduce the legitimate power of O (6, 15).

EXPERIMENTAL PROCEDURE

All subjects were female volunteers from undergraduate courses at the University of Michigan. There were from eight to eleven members in each experimental group. Three paid participants took part as members of each group. Postexperimental interviews revealed that all subjects believed that the paid participants were ordinary volunteers like themselves.

As each subject entered the room, she was introduced to other group members and given a place card with her name on it. In addition, cohesiveness was also increased by giving subjects the impression that they had been assigned to compatible groups (1), by encouraging discussion, and by giving the group a success experience in solving a puzzle (putting two painted cardboard solids together so as to make a pyramid). This last procedure also served to introduce the subjects to their task—cutting out cardboard forms from which these puzzles could be built.

Speed and accuracy were stressed and, as an additional force toward increased speed, each subject was told that she would get a ten-cent base wage, plus one cent for each piece that she cut.

Election of the supervisor

In order to work properly, the experimenter said, the subjects would need a supervisor to assure that subjects were cutting with proper speed and accuracy. The supervisor would be selected through election, a method which had supposedly been accepted as efficient by all previous subjects.

The three paid participants—Ellie, Jackie, and Barbara—took an active part in the election procedure. By prior arrangement, Jackie would nominate either Ellie or Barbara, depending on the experimental condition. The motion would be rapidly seconded by the remaining paid participant. Both the nominator and seconder expressed strong feeling for their choice. Two other girls would also be nominated, though usually less wholeheartedly. The experimenter would present a fictitious tally of votes on the board, and announce that the paid participant had been elected, receiving nearly half again as many votes as her nearest competitor.

The manipulation of group support

Each subject was then seated at a separate booth, so as to reduce group effects on rate of cutting. Subjects were also asked not to communicate with one another. After two minutes, the elected supervisor went to each booth, picked up the completed cards, examined them, and returned to her desk. At this point, the manipulation of group support was introduced. A paid participant at one of the booths (either Ellie or Barbara, whichever one was *not* elected supervisor) would call the supervisor. There followed a heated, whispered discussion between supervisor and worker, unintelligible to subjects, but apparently involving an exchange of jobs. The elected supervisor turned to the experimenter for advice, but he said that he was "completely out of this situation."

In the *group support (Sup)* condition, Ellie, who had been nominated and elected supervisor, ended the discussion with Barbara and continued in her job as supervisor for the remainder of the experiment. For the remaining half of the groups, the *no group support (NoSup)* condition, Barbara had been elected supervisor. After their discussion, Barbara and Ellie would change jobs—Ellie supervising, Barbara cutting, though with some reluctance. The change was emphasized by a loud question from Jackie, "Did you change with her?", which was answered in the affirmative. Thus in every condition, Ellie would eventually become supervisor, thus controlling for personality differences. In the *Sup* condition, she assumed this position through election; in the *NoSup* condition, she became supervisor with no visible group support. This was the only difference in procedure between the two conditions.

The supervisor's inductions and measures of private acceptance

Approximately every four minutes, the supervisor would make her round of all the subjects, collect the cut cards, examine them carefully, and place them in an individually marked envelope. It was her job to examine the pieces cut by the subjects and to determine if they were working with proper speed and accuracy. Since there were to be no verbal communications, a form was provided the supervisor which included two nine-point rating scales—a scale of speed-evaluation ("1. *Very much too fast. Go much slower!*" to "9. *Very much too slow. Go much faster!*") and a scale of accuracy ("1. *Almost perfect*" to "9. *Definitely inferior. Cut much more accurately!*"). The supervisor could then check a point on either or both scales to indicate her evaluation. Since the guidelines over which subjects had to cut were very heavy, and subjects were told to cut in the center of the line, the subject could not be certain of her accuracy. In fact, the supervisor's evaluation followed a prearranged plan, such that regardless of the subject's production, she was consistently rated as "*too fast*" and "*inaccurate*" and asked to "*go slower.*"

Each time, after the supervisor had indicated her rating, the subjects were asked to indicate on the form their own rating of speed and accuracy, which might or might not be in agreement with the supervisor. These forms were collected by the experimenter as soon as they were marked by subjects. It was emphasized that these forms were not to be seen by the supervisor; they were, in this sense, an indication of degree of private acceptance of the supervisor's inductions. There were two periods during which the supervisor provided no rating, but the experimenter passed out forms on which the subjects could still indicate their self-ratings.

The manipulation of coercive power

In half the groups, the subjects were told that an earlier supervisor had asked permission to fine subjects for nonconformity. The experimenter expressed some doubts as to the legitimacy of such fines, but agreed that a supervisor should be allowed this option of fining subjects up to a maximum of 15 cents a visit, if she wished to do so, the money to be deducted from the subject's earnings at the end of the experimental session. The fine could be indicated at the bottom of the evaluation form. In fact, the supervisor in the *Fine* condition administered a fifteen-cent fine at the beginning of the second slow-down period (17 minutes) and a similar fine at the beginning of

EXPERIMENTAL TIME SINCE BEGINNING TO CUT	PERIOD	SUPERVISOR'S RATING ON FORM
2'	First round by elected supervisor	No form
3'	Discussion, followed by change of supervisors in *NoSup* condition	No form
5'	Begin first round by *de facto* supervisor. Begin B_1 base period.	No form
9'	Begin B_2 base period	Form passed out by *E*, no supervisor's rating
13'	First slow-down period	"2. *Too fast*" "7. *Somewhat poorly done*"
17'	Second slow-down period	"1. *Very much too fast*" "8. *Definitely inferior*"
21'	Third slow-down period	"2. *Too fast*" "7. *Somewhat poorly done*"
25'	Final visit	Form passed out by *E*. No supervisor rating.

the third slow-down period (21 minutes). No penalties were administered in the *NoFine* condition. Thus we had four experimental variations: *Sup-NoFine*, *NoSup-NoFine*, *SupFine*, and *NoSup-Fine*. (The number of subjects in each condition were, 32, 31, 28, and 23, respectively, for a total of 114 subjects in all.)

Final questionnaire

After the supervisor had made her last visit, the experimenter administered a questionnaire relating to the experiment. Finally, subjects were interviewed as a group, paid for their productivity (actually fines were not collected, and each subject received 40 cents as a token payment), and a complete explanation of the experiment was rendered.

The effectiveness of the manipulation of group support

In order to check on the effectiveness of this manipulation, the final questionnaire asked, *"Imagine that this group will continue working in this way for an extended period of time. To what extent do you feel that the other members of your group would stand behind your supervisor in his direction of the group?"* Responses ranged from 1. *"Considerable support"* to 9. *"Not much group support."* The mean for *Sup* subjects (3.9) was significantly different from that for *NoSup* subjects (5.4); $p < .001$ by Marshall's test[2] (16). Obviously the election was accepted and did affect perceived group support.[3]

Thus we had a situation in which groups of subjects were faced with a noninterdependent group task, wherein they cut cardboard forms under the direction of the supervisor. In some cases, the supervisor was given group support through a "rigged" election; in others the supervisor assumed this position without benefit of election. In some cases, the supervisor used coercive power, fining subjects for nonconformity; in others, no such fines were levied. Through an analysis of the number of cards cut following influence attempts, we could now measure differential public influence under the four condi-

[2] Since the hypotheses tested are directional, one-tail tests have been used, unless otherwise stated.

[3] It would seem appropriate here to compare this experiment with the one reported previously in which group support was manipulated in a similar manner, and the subjects worked on the same task (15). In the present experiment, the election procedure has been considerably strengthened. Also subjects worked in the same room rather than being separated. This allowed the change in supervisors to take place more dramatically, emphasizing the group support variable further. Interdependence was reduced in the present experiment, since subjects in the earlier study assumed that their fellow subjects were utilizing the pieces which were cut. The use of a form for evaluation, rather than giving it verbally, allowed for more control and also for a measurement of private influence.

tions. Through the subjects' private ratings of their work, given to the experimenter, we could compare private influence—not visible to the supervisor. Questionnaire data would allow for testing of our other hypotheses.

HYPOTHESES AND RESULTS

In the discussion that follows, we shall present our hypotheses and rationale, along with the data bearing on these hypotheses. The individual who is the subject of influence shall be referred to as *P*, and the other individual, attempting influence as *O*. A fuller discussion of the bases for these hypotheses is presented elsewhere (6).

Hypothesis 1. The more P perceives his group as supporting O in his position, the more will P perceive that O has a legitimate right to that position. After the work session, subjects were asked to rank their first three choices for supervisor, *"in terms of what you know now."* The data from this question are presented in Table 1. It is obvious that subjects in *Sup* condition were much more likely than those in the *NoSup* condition to feel that Ellie, the *de facto* supervisor, should have held that position ($p < .001$).

A direct question, "To what extent do you feel that someone else other than *Ellie* should have been supervisor?", yielded results at a comparable level of significance, further substantiating the hypothesis.

Hypothesis 2. The more P perceives that O has a legitimate right to his position, the more will P perceive that O is justified in prescribing behavior for him.

A correlation between questions showed that subjects who felt that they had the right supervisor were also more likely to feel that she was justified in prescribing behavior for them ($r =$

TABLE 1 *Final Rankings of* De Facto *Supervisor*

CONDITION	FIRST	SECOND	THIRD	NOT VOTED FOR	TOTAL
Sup-NoFine	16	6	5	5	32
NoSup-NoFine	8	3	5	15	31
Sup-Fine	11	5	3	9	28
NoSup-Fine	4	1	1	17	23

Tests of significance, by Marshall's test (16): *Sup* vs *NoSup*, $p = .001$; *Sup-NoFine* vs *NoSup-NoFine*, p = .002; *Sup-Fine* vs *NoSup-NoFine*, p = .003; *Fine* vs *NoFine*, p = .07; *Sup-NoFine* vs *Sup-Fine*, p = .11; *NoSup-Fine* vs *NoSup-NoFine*, p = .08.

.31, $p < .001$). A better test of this hypothesis should come through the test of a sub-hypothesis, derived from Hypotheses 1 and 2.

Hypothesis 2a. The more P perceives his group as supporting O in his position, the more will P perceive that O is justified in prescribing behavior for him.

Responses to a question, *"To what extent do you feel that the things which your supervisor asked you to do were justified?"*, with a scale ranging from 1. *"Completely justified"* to 9. *"Definitely not justified,"* showed clear differences resulting from group support in the noncoercive conditions. (Mean, *Sup-NoFine* = 2.6; Mean, *NoSup-NoFine* = 3.7; $p = .03$ by Marshall's test.) However, these differences were reduced when coercion was introduced, such that the overall difference between the *Sup* and *NoSup* conditions was not significant ($p = .10$). Analysis of questionnaire responses also indicated a significant positive correlation between (*a*) believing that the supervisor would continue to receive group support and (*b*) feeling that the supervisor was justified in prescribing behavior ($r = .46$, $p < .001$).

TABLE 2 Percentage Reduction Following Inductions*

PERIOD	NO FINE		FINE	
	Group Support	No Support	Group Support	No Support
I	26.7%	25.2%	23.7%	25.5%
II	32.3	29.0	33.5	33.2
III	41.3	36.5	43.6	43.5
Average	33.4	30.2	33.6	34.0
Base rate, cards per 4 minutes	6.9	6.7	6.6	7.1

* The formulae which took into account the number of cards reduced per four-minute period proportionate to the base rate were:

$$\frac{B-I}{B}, \quad \frac{B-II}{B}, \quad \frac{B-III}{B}, \quad \text{and} \quad \frac{B - \dfrac{I+II+III}{3}}{B},$$

where B = number of cards cut per period during the basal periods; I, II, and III are the number of cards cut, respectively, during the first, second, and third slow-down periods. Differences between percentages were not significant.

Hypothesis 3. The more P perceives his group as supporting O in his position, the more will O have legitimate power over P.

Hypothesis 3a. The more P perceives his group as supporting O in his position, the more will O be able to exert public influence over P.

Hypothesis 3b. The more P perceives his group as supporting O in his position, the more will O be able to exert private influence over P.

We have said that group support is one means of establishing the legitimate occupancy of a position. With such legitimate occupancy, P also attributes to O the right to prescribe behavior for P. The ability to influence P which results, we have called the *legitimate power* of O over P. In our theoretical discussion, we compared the types of influence that result from legitimate power with those which result from other types of power (6). Legitimate power leads to a behavior system on the part of P whose stability does not depend upon whether or not that behavior is observable to O. In our discussion here, we will refer to *public influence* as that influence on P which is observable to O. *Private influence* is that influence which is not observable to O. Both types of influence, we predicted, should occur as the result of legitimate power.

The test for Hypothesis 3a came from an examination of the reduction in rate of cutting in response to the slow-down inductions. A base rate, B, was calculated for each subject by averaging the number of cards cut by that subject during the two basal periods. The percentage reduction from that base rate for each of the subsequent periods is shown in Table 2.

As can be seen from the data in Table 2, this hypothesis was not supported. In the noncoercive conditions, the differences were all in the predicted direction, but in no case did they approach significance. In the coercive conditions, the rate of reduction for *Sup* and *NoSup* were practically identical.

One explanation of this failure to support the hypothesis comes from statements by some of the subjects in postsession interviews. These indicated that some subjects would express their resentment and resistance through overconformity, as if to say, "Well, if you insist I will go slower. I will show you how slow I can go and it really doesn't help any." This same reaction was observed in two earlier studies (7, 15). This explanation receives further support from the reduced differences within the coercive conditions, and also in the significantly greater variance in conformity in the *NoSup* conditions.

Data relating conformity with attraction towards the supervisor are also consistent with the overconformity interpretation (Table 3). Several previous experiments would lead us to predict that greater personal attraction towards the supervisor would result in a greater amount of influence. Instead, we see little difference in the *Sup* condition, and an opposite trend in the *No-Sup* condition. For subjects who liked their supervisor personally, the predicted difference between the *Sup* and *NoSup* conditions is significant ($p = .04$, t-test). There is no significant difference between conditions for those subjects who disliked their supervisor. Clearly this is a phenomenon which deserves further investigation.

In order to test the private influence of the supervisor upon her workers, we utilized the ratings given by the subjects of their own work, to see whether or not they would accept privately the suggestions by their supervisor that their work was inaccurate and too rapidly done. Most subjects initially rated their speed and accuracy as "5. *Just about right*" and "5. *Fairly well done*," so that it was not necessary to take the base rating into account in calculating private conformity. Also similar trends held for accuracy and speed for the various experimental conditions. We therefore calculated a total private conformity (*TPC*) score for each subject as follows: We reversed the speed ratings so as to make them comparable to the accuracy ratings (a rating of 1 became 9, 2 = 8, 3 = 7, etc.) and added the ratings for both accuracy and speed (a total of ten ratings) which the subjects gave themselves. The higher the *TPC* score, the greater the private conformity with the inductions of the supervisor. Table 4 shows the mean *TPC* ratings for the four experimental conditions.

Private influence, as measured by the *TPC* scores, was apparently greater in the *Sup* than in the *NoSup* conditions ($p = .05$, by analysis of variance; $p = .01$, t-test). The difference was especially sharp among those subjects in the *Fine* conditions ($p = .02$, t-test), but not significant in the *NoFine* conditions ($p = .12$, t-test). It seems that the nonlegitimate supervisor who administered fines was least likely to obtain private influence.

TCP scores were also significantly correlated with the responses to the question, "*To what extent did you feel that the things your supervisor asked you to do were justified?*" The more legitimate the prescriptions of the supervisor, the greater the degree of private influence ($r = .39$, $p = .001$).

Hypothesis 4. The more P perceives that O has a legitimate right to his position, the greater will be the attraction of P toward O.

This hypothesis already received support in a previous experiment (15) and we wished to see if the relationship would still obtain under the present conditions. When *O* operates in a manner which is not in keeping with his legitimate positions, personal rejection should take place (6). The evidence indicates that such was the case.

Attraction, as measured by responses to the question, "*How much did you like your supervisor?*", correlated significantly ($p = .001$) with 1. "*To what extent do you feel that the things your supervisor asked you to do were justified?*" ($r = .55$); with 2. "*To what extent do you feel that someone other than Ellie should have been supervisor?*" ($r = .82$); and with 3. "*To what extent do you feel that the other members of your group would support your supervisor in her direction of the group?*" ($r = .56$).

Again the direction of the causal relationship might be in question, so that a more adequate test is the comparison of experimental conditions. As we can see in Table 5, the subjects in the *Sup* conditions were indeed more attracted to their supervisor than those in the *NoSup* condition ($p = .003$ by Marshall's test). This is true both for *Fine* ($p = .007$) and *NoFine* subjects ($p = .01$). Hypothesis 4 can be considered as supported.

TABLE 3 Relationship between Personal Attraction and Percentage Reduction Following Induction

ATTRACTION TOWARD SUPERVISOR	GROUP SUPPORT	NO SUPPORT
"Liked very much" "Definitely liked" "Liked fairly well"	42.8% (47)*	35.2% (24)
"Neither liked nor disliked" "Felt some dislike"	41.2% (13)	42.7% (29)

* Number of subjects.

TABLE 4 Mean "Total Private Conformity" Scores*,†

	NO FINE	FINE	COMBINED
Group support	48.2	47.3	47.8
No group support	46.6	44.1	45.6
Combined	47.4	45.9	

* A higher score indicates greater private acceptance of supervisor's influence. † Analysis of variance:

SOURCE	Df	VARIANCE	F	p
Support	1	141.1	5.05	.05
Fine	1	68.1	2.44	ns
$S \times F$	1	26.2	.94	ns
Error	110	27.9		

Hypothesis 5. The more P perceives that O can punish him for nonconformity, the more will O have coercive power over P.

Coercive power depends upon the ability of O to punish P (6). As contrasted with legitimate power, coercive power will not occur if there are not other forces on P to remain in the situation (3, 13). The individual worker who is threatened with punishment will not obey if he can comfortably leave his position. Both legitimate and coercive power will result in public influence. However, legitimate power will lead also to private influence, whereas coercive power does not. To the extent that the power of O is *coercive*, it will not affect influence unless P considers it likely that the resulting influence will somehow be communicated to O. In fact, we have further suggested that under some conditions, the use of coercion may undermine the legitimate power of O (See Hypothesis 6) and reduce the attraction of P toward O (Hypothesis 7). The result may then be negative private influence—a change in a direction opposite to that desired by O.

Hypothesis 5a. The more P perceives that O can punish him for nonconformity, the more will O be able to exert public influence over P. In Table 2, we note that the first fine seemed to have no effect in increasing influence in any of the conditions. The second fine and third fine did increase conformity in the *NoSup* condition, the decreased production in response to slow-down inductions being significantly less in the *NoSup-Fine* variation than in the *NoSup-NoFine* variation ($p = .03$, *t*-test). The fine produced no significant effect in production where the supervisor had group support. Perhaps the failure to gain more adequate support for this hypothesis may be attributable to the subjects' acceptance of the legitimacy of the experiment itself, feeling that they must follow instructions no matter what. In any event, this hypothesis, in which we might

have been most confident prior to the experiment, received only fragmentary support.

Hypothesis 5b. The ability of O to punish P for nonconformity will not increase the private influence of O over P. We would therefore predict that private conformity, as measured by TPC scores, would not be greater in the *Fine* than in the *NoFine* conditions. This hypothesis was confirmed, as we can see in Table 4. In fact, we note that the TCP scores were uniformly *lower* in the *Fine* conditions, indicating lower private acceptance of inductions even though there was no difference in public influence. Analysis of variance revealed no significant difference however. The greatest difference between *Fine* and *NoFine* conditions occurred in the nonlegitimate groups ($p = .04$, *t*-test). When the effects of group support and fine were combined (comparing the *Sup-NoFine* and the *NoSup-Fine* conditions), the difference was significant at the .001 confidence point (*t*-test). Thus coercive power does not increase private acceptance of influence and may even have a boomerang effect.

Hypothesis 6. The attempt by O to use coercive power will reduce the legitimacy of O as perceived by P. In our theoretical discussion, we had pointed out that the use of coercion by O makes P less willing to accept the legitimate right of O to occupy that position of authority (6). The test of this hypothesis comes from the question mentioned earlier, *"To what extent did you feel that the things your supervisor asked you to do were justified?"*, with a nine-point scale from 1. *"Completely within her rights"* to 9. *"Definitely not justified."* The mean difference was in the opposite direction though not great (3.1 and 3.8 for the *Fine* and *NoFine* subjects, respectively, $p = .08$ by two-tailed Marshall's test), most of this difference was in the *Sup* conditions. It is possible that when the subjects accepted the legitimacy of the supervisor, a fine served to underline the supervisor's authority.

The question *"To what extent do you feel that someone other than Ellie should have been supervisor?"* showed no significant differences. In Table 1, we note that Ellie received more final votes for supervisor when she did not use fines, though this was a low level of significance ($p = .07$ by Marshall's test).

Yet, in response to the question, *"To what extent do you feel that other members of your group would stand behind your supervisor in his direction of the group?"*, fined subjects felt that she would get significantly less support than did nonfined subjects ($p = .006$ by Marshall's test). It may be that the subjects were unwilling to admit that they would let the fine reduce their own support of the supervisor, though they felt that others would be so influenced. In any case, Hypothesis 6 remains unsupported.

TABLE 5 Mean Attraction toward Supervisor*

	NO FINE	FINE	COMBINED
Group support	3.8	5.0	4.4
No group support	5.5	6.7	6.0
Combined	4.6	5.8	

* A low score means greater attraction. Significance of differences by Marshall's test: *Sup* vs *NoSup*, $p = .003$; *Sup-NoFine* vs *NoSup-NoFine*, $p = .01$; *Sup-Fine* vs *NoSup-Fine*, $p = .007$; *NoFine* vs *Fine*, $p = .02$; *Sup-NoFine* vs *Sup-Fine*, $p = .03$; *NoSup-Fine* vs *NoSup-NoFine*, $p = .03$.

Hypothesis 7. The attempt to use coercive power over P will reduce the attraction of P toward O. As measured by responses to *"How much did you like the supervisor in your group?"*, Table 5 shows that the subjects in the *Fine* conditions were less attracted toward their supervisor ($p = .02$ by Marshall's test). This was true within both the *Sup* ($p = .03$) and *NoSup* ($p = .03$) conditions. Personal attraction as measured by this item is also significantly related to private conformity on the *TPC* scores ($r = .22$, $p. = .02$). It is interesting to contrast this relationship with that involving public influence. Though subjects here show more private influence if they like their supervisor, we earlier indicated an opposite relationship with respect to public influence. (See Hypothesis 5*b*.) It seems that coercion decreases private influence and personal attraction, while increasing public influence.

SUMMARY AND DISCUSSION

It was our purpose in this experiment to explore further the bases and effects of legitimate power and to compare these with coercive power. Accordingly, we created two group work situations. In one, the supervisor was represented as having group support, through election; in the other the supervisor took over her job without group support. Within each of these conditions, half the subjects were fined for "nonconformity" and the remainder were not fined. As predicted, group support resulted in greater acceptance of the legitimacy of office—subjects were significantly more likely to feel that the elected supervisor had a right to hold that office, and to feel that the supervisor was justified in prescribing behavior for them. Legitimacy also increased the personal attraction of worker towards supervisor, while coercion reduced this attraction. The workers privately accepted the influence of the legitimate supervisor, whereas the use of coercion did not increase private acceptance. The predictions were all significantly supported. However, the predicted increase in public conformity as the result of legitimacy and coercion did not occur. Nor did coercion reduce perceived legitimacy.

This implies that the net effect of nonlegitimate and coercive influence may be an increased discrepancy between private and public opinion and behavior, with its resulting tensions. Eventually, we might predict that the worker would leave the situation, become hostile towards the supervisor, reject further influence completely, or otherwise express this tension.

It is interesting that in all four experimental conditions, the subjects publicly conformed considerably to the requests of the supervisor that they reduce their speed, even if they did not privately accept the inductions. We have offered several explanations for this. First, there is interdependence—the belief by subjects that their products might be used by others, and the resulting tendency to accept the judgment of the supervisor. Presumably, this interdependence may then add power to the supervisor. In this experiment, we did reduce interdependence from a prior study (15) and did find that the percentage conformity in this experiment was indeed decreased by over ten per cent in comparison with the previous investigation. Secondly, the legitimacy of the experiment itself may be an additional variable. The subjects, having volunteered for an experiment, may feel that they must do what they are asked within very broad limits (4). An attempt has been made to control for this factor in a later experiment (5). Finally, there is the possibility that subjects indicated their rejection of the supervisor through "overconformity." By "overconformity" we mean the compliance with the inductions of the influencer over and beyond the presumed desires of the influencer, while privately rejecting the influence. This recalls the behavior of the IWW workers who were reputed to systematically disrupt operations of factories by conforming in minute detail, going beyond orders. Interviews with subjects indicated that this might have occurred here in at least some cases. We have suggested that such behavior is especially likely to occur when communication through normal means has been reduced—overconformity may then become the means by which nonacceptance of influence is communicated. These are some of the factors which must be taken into account in further studies of social influence.

REFERENCES

1. BACK, K. W., "Influence through Social Communication," *Journal of Abnormal and Social Psychology*, 1951, 46, 9–23.

2. DITTES, J. E., and H. H. KELLEY, "Effects of Different Conditions of Acceptance upon Individual Judgment," *Journal of Abnormal and Social Psychology*, 1956, 53, 100–107.

3. FESTINGER, L., "An Analysis of Compliant Behavior," in M. Sherif and M. O. Wilson (eds.), *Group Relations at the Crossroads*, New York: Harper, 1953, 232–256.

4. FRANK, J. D., "Experimental Studies of Personal Pressure and Resistance: I. Experimental Production of Resistance," *Journal of General Psychology*, 1944, 30, 23–64.

5. FRENCH, J. R. P., Jr., G. Levinger, and H. W. Morrison, "The Legitimacy of Coercive Power" (unpublished).

6. FRENCH, J. R. P., Jr., and B. H. RAVEN, "The Bases of Social Power," in D. Cartwright, *et al., Studies in Social Power*, Ann Arbor, Institute for Social Research (in press).

7. FRENCH, J. R. P., Jr., and R. SNYDER, "Leadership and Interpersonal Power," in D. Cartwright, *et al., Studies in Social Power,* Ann Arbor, Institute for Social Research (in press).

8. GOLDHAMMER, H., and E. A. SHILS, "Types of Power and Status," *American Journal of Sociology,* 1939, 45, 171–178.

9. JAHODA, M., "Psychological Issues in Civil Liberties," *American Psychologist,* 1956, 11, 234–240.

10. KATZ, D., and R. L. SCHANCK, *Social Psychology,* New York: Wiley, 1938.

11. KELLEY, H. H., and E. H. VOLKHART, "The Resistance to Change of Group-anchored Attitudes," *American Sociological Review,* 1952, 17, 453–465.

12. KELMAN, H., "Three Processes of Acceptance of Social Influence: Compliance, Identification, and Internationalization," paper read at the meetings of the American Psychological Association, August, 1956.

13. LEWIN, K., *Field Theory in Social Science,* New York: Harper, 1951.

14. RAVEN, B. H., "Social Influence on Options and the Communication of Related Content," *Journal of Abnormal and Social Psychology* (in press).

15. RAVEN, B. H., and J. R. P. FRENCH, JR., "Group Support, Legitimate Power, and Social Influence—A Preliminary Experiment" (unpublished).

16. SMITH, K., "Distribution-free Statistical Methods and the Concept of Power Efficiency," in D. Katz and L. Festinger (eds.), *Research Methods in the Behavioral Sciences,* New York: Dryden, 1953.

17. WEBER, M., *The Theory of Social and Economic Organization,* Oxford: Oxford University Press, 1947.

UPWARD COMMUNICATION IN INDUSTRIAL HIERARCHIES *

The pragmatic payoff for scientific research is the application of its findings to the solution of problems in everyday settings. Whether this can be done will depend on the external validity of the research in question. A conclusion regarding the relation between two variables in a laboratory experiment can be generalized only to the extent that this relation is not modified by variables in the everyday setting that were controlled or not present in the laboratory. Where the effects of such influences in a particular setting are unknown, only a test in that situation will ensure validity. The selection below illustrates this application; it tests in large organizations the external validity of the relation between status and communication as derived largely from laboratory research.

This selection is an excellent illustration of research in another sense: it represents an ideal paradigm of the survey study. Following suggestions from previous research, Read first formulated a theory relating the mobility aspirations of subordinates to their communication behavior, as mediated by the variables of trust in and perceived influence of the superior. He then prepared a series of questionnaire items representing these variables. He next administered the questionnaire to a sample of subordinates and superiors in three business firms, selecting both individuals and firms so as to maximize external validity. Finally, he analyzed his results in a manner that allowed him

* The selection following the editorial introduction is reprinted from "Upward communication in industrial hierarchies," *Human Relations,* 1962, **15**, 3–15, by permission of the author and Tavistock Publications.

to assess the probability that his predicted relations could have occurred by chance alone.

26.

Upward Communication in Industrial Hierarchies

WILLIAM H. READ[1]
McGILL UNIVERSITY, MONTREAL

This study is concerned with communication in large organizations. The particular focus is upon motivational and attitudinal factors which affect the accuracy with which members at one administrative level communicate upward to a higher level.

The majority of studies of communication within hierarchies have dealt with inter-level communication in small groups. Festinger (1950) has pointed out that the structuring of groups into hierarchies automatically introduces restraints against free communication, particularly criticisms and aggressively-toned comments by low-status members towards those in higher-status positions.

[1] The study reported here was based upon a dissertation submitted in partial fulfillment of the requirements for the Ph.D. degree, University of Michigan, 1959. It was part of a larger project supported by the Foundation for Research on Human Behavior, Ann Arbor, Michigan, and directed by Professor Norman R. F. Maier. The writer wishes to express his appreciation for the guidance and inspiration provided by Professor Maier, and is also deeply indebted to Professor Stanley E. Seashore for his supervision of the dissertation during Professor Maier's absence in 1959.

Kelley (1951), Thibaut (1950), and Back *et al.* (1950) have shown that selective screening of information from low- to high-status members is a characteristic of communication in social groups, and serves as a 'psychological substitute' for actual movement upward on the part of aspiring low-status members.

More recently, Cohen (1958) has emphasized the 'instrumentality' of upward communication. The findings of Hurwitz, Zander, and Hymovitch (1953) support this instrumental view of communication. They reported that group members tend to perceive those with greater power as instrumental to the need satisfactions of these group members, hence 'lows' behave toward 'highs' in a manner designed to maximize good relations and minimize feelings of unease in their interactions with high-power persons.

The instrumental nature of communication upward through levels in larger hierarchical organizations such as industrial concerns is usually accepted as a fact of organizational life. Pleasant matters are more likely to be communicated upward than unpleasant ones, achievements are more likely to be passed upward than information about errors or difficulties encountered at lower levels. Yet the highly integrated effort required to achieve organizational purposes demands a relatively free upward and downward flow of information, both pleasant and unpleasant, problem-related as well as achievement-related. This screening of information passed upward is likely to be at a maximum when the information content is of a type which might reflect negatively upon the competence and thus, indirectly, upon the security or progress of members of the subordinate level: content such as the problems, current and unsolved, faced by members at this level.

The present study attempts to isolate variables accounting for the accuracy with which subordinate executives at one level of administration in industrial organizations communicate upward a specific type of information—the work-related problems experienced by these subordinates.

MOBILITY

One such variable is mobility—the mobility aspirations of lower-status members in industrial organizations. Henry (1949), in his analysis of the test profiles of executives, and Miner and Culver (1955), in a more recent study, attest that the most salient single characteristic of executives in industry is striving for advancement (and its accompanying fear of failure). One would expect that the more the executives are upwardly mobile, that is, the more they value vertical promotion in the hierarchy, the less accurately they will communicate upward 'negative' aspects of their work performance. The stronger the mobility aspirations of subordinates, the more will they com-

municate to their superiors in a way that will maximize positive, and minimize negative, aspects. Thus they would be likely to withhold, restrict, or distort information about the problems, current and unsolved, which they experience in their day-to-day work.

The major hypothesis in this study is that a negative relationship exists between upward mobility of members of industrial organizations and the accuracy with which these members communicate upward in the hierarchy. More specifically, it was predicted that the stronger the mobility aspirations of the subordinate, the less accurate would be his communication of problem-related information to his immediate superior.

MODIFYING CONDITIONS: TRUST AND PERCEIVED INFLUENCE

It was expected that the relationship between mobility and accuracy in communication would be modified by two conditions, both considered important dimensions of the superior-subordinate relationship. These were *interpersonal trust* of the subordinate for his superior, and the subordinate's perception of his superior's *influence* over that subordinate's career.

Mellinger (1956) reported that accurate information between two individuals is less likely to occur under conditions of mistrust than under conditions of trust. He demonstrated that individual A will restrict or distort information about an item X to the extent that he thinks individual B might misuse this item of information (to the possible detriment of A). This finding suggests that the highly mobile subordinate would feel a special threat to his progress in communicating anything 'negative', such as information about his unsolved problems, to a superior he does not trust, since this information might be used against him by that superior. It was expected that the predicted negative relationship between mobility and communication would be greater under conditions of low trust (of subordinate for superior) than under conditions of high trust.

The second modifying variable, perceived influence, was also expected to modify the mobility-communication relationship. The study of Pelz (1951) has indicated that supervisors, even at the same hierarchical level, vary considerably in the influence they are able to exert in their respective units. Pelz used influence, that is, the supervisor's potential control over the subordinate's work environment, as a modifying variable in the relationship between supervisory practices and employee attitudes. The present study focuses more specifically upon the superior's influence as it directly affects the subordinate's career, particularly his promotion and advancement in the organization.

It was predicted that the greater the influence the upwardly mobile subordinate perceived his superior to have (and thus the stronger that superior's position to satisfy or thwart the subordinate's aspirations), the greater would be the subordinate's tendency to withhold problem-related information from such a superior, or to restrict it. In short, it was predicted that influence would modify the negative relationship between mobility and communication—the greater the degree of perceived influence, the greater the negative relationship between mobility and communication upward.

In summary, the predicted negative relationship between mobility and communication would be conditioned or modified by (a) the subordinate's trust in his superior's motives and intentions, and (b) the subordinate's perception of his superior's degree of influence. These predictions suggest that an extreme condition for barriers to upward communication in industrial hierarchies would be present when a highly mobile subordinate has limited trust in a superior he believes to be powerful or influential.

METHOD

The study was conducted in three major industrial organizations in the U.S.A. One operating unit was selected in each company as a source of subjects. These units were selected on the basis of three main criteria, namely, that the chosen units should (a) provide access to executives in a variety of functions, (b) be typical of the company in its organizational structure, and (c) have a relatively stable history as to executive personnel changes.

A. Selection of subjects
In each unit of each of the three organizations, subjects were selected at random from the third level of supervision, that is, the supervisory level that was separated from non-supervisory employees by two intervening levels. For each of the chosen third-level supervisors, a corresponding subordinate was chosen from the second level of supervision. In this way, 52 superiors and their 52 respective subordinates were selected, or a total of 104 middle-management personnel from three companies.

B. Description of the measures
1. Accuracy of upward communication. The measure of accuracy of upward communication was derived from interview data provided by exploratory research conducted prior to the present study. These data consisted of descriptions of major problems experienced by 35 middle-level executives, as reported by these executives and, independently, by their immediate superiors. Contrasting descriptions of these major problems had been taken from five industries and utilities in the Michigan area, and the measure of accuracy of upward communication was derived for use in the present study in the following way:

All problems reported in this exploratory study were sorted according to type, then edited and combined to form a list representing five major problem types. These were (a) co-ordination and communication, (b) budget and cost, (c) technical, (d) pressures and deadlines, and (e) administration and supervision. The most frequently reported problems were listed within each type, making a total of 30 separate problems listed. For example, under budget and cost were listed such items as 'handling unforeseen costs' and 'deciding upon the feasibility of certain expenditures.' Under the technical category were listed items such as 'getting enough equipment and supplies.'

Because of the striking frequency with which the same problems were reported by the five companies in the exploratory study, together with the fact that these problems covered a very broad range of those encountered by executives, they were considered representative enough to apply to executives in the new settings selected for the present study.

Accuracy of upward communication was operationalized as the degree of agreement between superior and subordinate about the relative degree of difficulty these problems caused the subordinate, i.e. the degree to which they were problems to subordinates. Low agreement was taken to indicate relatively poor or inaccurate communication of this type of information; high agreement indicated the reverse.

This measure is based on the assumption that the superior's major source of knowledge of his subordinate's current work problems is the subordinate's communication of them in some way to that superior (hence agreement or disagreement between the two would reflect accuracy of upward communication). This was viewed as a reasonable assumption in view of the obviously limited opportunity an executive would have to observe directly the subordinate's experience with day-to-day problems. However, in order to provide a check on other possible sources of feedback the superior might have regarding the subordinate's problems (from peers or from other departments), each member of the subordinate-superior pairs in the sample was asked to state who was in the 'best position to know' about the subordinate's problems. All of the superiors and all but two of the subordinates in the sample designated the superior as in the 'best position'. This was a rough and rather subjective check, but provided at least some assurance that agreement or disagreement between the two about this type of information reflected accuracy of communication between the two, and not the adequacy or inadequacy of some other communication channel.

Both members of the 52 executive pairs were asked to rank-order the problems within each cateory or type according to the difficulty criterion. Using Kendall's *tau,* the two rank orders were correlated for each problem category. A mean *tau* over the five problem categories provided the overall statistical index of agreement for each executive pair.

2. *Mobility.* Three parallel but independent measures of degree or strength of mobility aspirations among subordinates were used. One measure consisted of a list of two-alternative, forced-choice items, ten in number, representing choices of hypothetical moves to other positions within the organization. One alternative in each pair of alternatives was the choice of a higher-level position, but with an unpleasant condition attached. The other alternative consisted of a hypothetical transfer to a position equivalent to the one presently held, but with a rewarding or pleasant condition attached. This questionnaire was scored simply by adding the total number of promotion alternatives chosen, yielding a possible score range of 0 to 10. This measure represented an attempt to determine strength of mobility aspirations from an indication of the price the individual would pay for promotion upward in the organization. For example, one item posed the alternatives:

> 'Promotion to a high position in which there is a great deal of pressure and stress
>
> or
>
> Transfer across to an intensely interesting position with little work pressure or stress.'

Nine other items such as this provided the measure of the expressed *mobility need* of subordinates.

Two other measures of mobility aspirations were used. These measures were sociological in nature, with the degree of mobility aspiration inferred from the amount of actual vertical occupational movement that the subordinate executives had experienced. These measures were of *work-life* and *inter-generational* mobility.

The study by Warner and Abegglen (1955) has shown that the mobility *experiences* of executives, particularly of those who have made the long climb up the occupational ladder, strongly affect their relationships with those above them in the industrial hierarchy. Their study suggested that both work-life and inter-generational experiences of progress and advancement are likely to be continuing forces in the executive's behavior even when conscious mobility aspirations may not be expressed.

Work-life mobility was operationalized as the degree to which the subordinate had moved upward through occupational levels from his first job to his present executive position. The second, inter-generational mobility, the degree the subordinate had moved upward from the position held by his father.

The Detroit Area Study revision of the 1950 U.S. Census Occupational Code provided the scale for measuring both work-life and inter-generational mo-

bility. This scale consisted of seven occupational levels, from 'low' to 'high' in skill and responsibility, and, except for minor revisions, was identical to the U.S. Census scale.

Scores of 1 to 7 were arbitrarily assigned to the seven levels of occupation on the scale ('laborers' to 'professional and kindred'), and these scores were used as measures of both the work-life and inter-generational dimensions of mobility. Thus, for work-life mobility, the subordinate who reported that his first full-time job had been 'drugstore clerk' would be assigned a score of 3—he had moved up 3 levels to his present executive position (the top level on the occupational scale, since all but one or two subordinates were engineers by profession). Likewise, a report of 'construction laborer' would be scored 7 on work-life mobility—he had moved from the bottom to the top of the occupational ladder. Scores for inter-generational mobility were derived in an identical way, except that the father's full-time occupation was taken as the base. Thus a subordinate who reported 'construction laborer' as his father's occupation would be given an inter-generational mobility score of 7—again, a move from bottom to top, inter-generationally.[2]

3. *Modifying variables: Trust and influence.* The measure of interpersonal trust was derived from four questions, each with five alternative answers, scaled in terms of degree, in the Likert fashion, from 'most' to 'least' interpersonal trust. By assigning weights of one to five to these alternatives and summing, the possible score range for the four items was 4 to 20. The questions were intended to reflect the subordinate's trust or confidence in the superior's motives and intentions with respect to matters relevant to the subordinate's career and status in the organization.

The interpersonal trust scale is shown below:

Interpersonal trust scale
1. Does your superior take advantage of opportunities that come up to further your interests by his actions and decisions?
2. How free do you feel to discuss with your superior the problems and difficulties you have in your job without jeopardizing your position or having it 'held against' you later on?
3. How confident do you feel that your superior keeps you fully and frankly informed about things that might concern you?
4. Superiors at times must make decisions which seem to be against the interests of their subordinates. When this happens to you as a subordinate,

---

[2] Intercorrelations among the three parallel measures of mobility were: Need and Work-life, .22, Work-life and Inter-generational, .37, and Inter-generational and Need, .08, indicating quite limited common variance among the measures.

how much trust do you have that your superior's decision is justified by other considerations?

The intercorrelations among the four trust items for the 52 subordinates were found to range between .39 and .68, indicating relatively high homogeneity of items.

The measure of perceived influence likewise consisted of a four-item scale. These items attempted to assess the subordinate's perception of the degree of *his superior's influence or potential control over four aspects of the subordinate's career,* namely, the subordinate's long-range progress in the company, his reputation as a manager, immediate rewards (wage increases, etc.), and his access to 'tools' (equipment, staff additions) needed to perform his job successfully. The perceived influence scale is shown below:

Perceived influence scale
1. In general, how much do you feel that your superior can do to further your career in this company?
2. To what degree does working for your present superior help your reputation in this company?
3. How much weight would your superior's recommendation have in any decision which would affect your standing in the company, such as promotions, transfers, wage increases, etc.?
4. How often is your superior successful in overcoming restrictions (such as policy or budget) in getting you the things you need in your job, such as equipment, personnel, etc.?

The intercorrelations among the four perceived influence items ranged from —.07 to .62, indicating less homogeneity than with the trust items. However, the existence of only one negative correlation was considered minimum but sufficient justification for summing the separate scores to yield a total perceived influence score.

C. General procedure
All the questionnaires outlined above were administered in face-to-face interviews with the 52 subjects, thus affording the researcher an opportunity to answer questions, assure anonymity, and clarify the

meaning of any item. This questionnaire session was part of a fairly long interview in which other job areas (in addition to problems) were explored as part of a larger study of management communication.

Since the present study focuses upon the subordinate—his attitudes and motives as they affect his upward communication—the only one of the questionnaires outlined above which the superior member of the management pair was asked to fill in was the problem list. He was required to rank-order the problems within each category in order of the difficulty they caused the subordinate. These, as stated, were matched against the subordinate's rank-ordering of the same problems and *taus* were then computed over the five categories for each pair.

D. Statistical method
Pearson product-moment correlations were used throughout to test the hypotheses in this study. The relationships between the independent variables (mobility scores) and the dependent variable (the mean *tau* measures of accuracy of upward communication) are expressed as correlations coefficients for an N of 52 cases. To test these same relationships modified by the separate as well as the joint effects of interpersonal trust and perceived influence, the distributions of scores on these conditioning variables were arbitrarily dichotomized into high and low. With the use of r to z transformations, correlations were computed between the independent and dependent variables for conditions of low and high trust, high and low influence, and for the joint low-trust, high-influence and high-trust, low-influence conditions. The correlations between these high and low conditions were in each case compared for the significance of the difference.

RESULTS
The hypothesis of a negative relationship between mobility and accuracy of upward communication was supported for two of the three measures of mobility, need and work-life, but was not supported for the third, inter-generational mobility. The correlations are shown in *Table 1.*[3]

The results in *Table 1* indicate that, for the group of 52 middle-management executives, the stronger the expressed need to achieve advancement within the organization, as well as the degree of mobility they had experienced from initial job to present one, the less accurate their communication to immediate superiors.

Effects of modifying conditions
Analysis of results indicates that the relationship between mobility need and accuracy of upward communication was strikingly modified by the

TABLE 1 Correlations between Three Parallel Measures of Mobility and Accuracy of Upward Communication

MOBILITY MEASURE	r	N
Need	—.38*	52
Work-life	—.41*	52
Inter-generational	.08	49

* Significant at the .01 level of confidence ($p < .01$).

[3] In reporting the significance of results, ps greater than .20 are shown as 'n.s.', not significant. In view of the small Ns, differences resulting in p values within the range of .10 to .20 are regarded as worth noting. P values of .10 and less are regarded as statistically significant.

TABLE 2 Correlations between Mobility Need and Accuracy of Upward Communication, Modified by the Separate and Joint Effects of Two Conditioning Variables

CONDITIONING VARIABLES	COMPARISON OF CORRELATIONS		p DIFF.
Trust	High trust	Low trust	
N high = 28	$*r_{ne} = -.16$	$r_{ne} = -.66$	<.01
N low = 24			
Influence	Low influence	High influence	
N low = 31	$r_{ne} = -.40$	$r_{ne} = -.55$	n.s.
N high = 21			
	High trust, low influence	Low trust, high influence	
Both			
N h−l = 17	$r_{ne} = -.07$	$r_{ne} = -.65$	<.05
N l−h = 10			

Note. Correlation between mobility need and upward communication for all cases is −.38. * Subscript n refers to strength of mobility need, subscript c refers to accuracy of upward communication.

interpersonal trust condition, but very little by the degree of the superior's influence or power (as perceived by the subordinate).

As the data in Table 2 show, the prediction of a greater negative mobility-communication relationship for the perceived influence condition holds only directionally, but is significantly greater in the negative direction when the condition of low trust prevails beween a subordinate executive and his immediate superior.

The results in Table 2 also indicate that communication is less accurate under the combined low-trust, high-influence condition, but this significant result is probably due to the very strong effects of interpersonal trust on the mobility-communication relationship.

The results thus far indicate that, in industrial hierarchies, the stronger the mobility needs among executives, the less accurately they communicate problem-related information; and the less trust they hold for their immediate superiors, the greater is this tendency toward inaccurate communication. There is also some indication that communication inaccuracy is increased when superiors are perceived as high-influence figures and are, at the same time, not fully trusted. However, unilateral subordinate-superior trust appears to have the greatest single effect upon accuracy of communication.

The analysis of results for work-life mobility is show in Table 3.

The modifying effect of trust is again evident, though the difference between correlations for high and low trust is only marginally significant. The tendency toward inaccurate communication by the subordinate who has experienced a rel-

atively high degree of vertical mobility during his work-life is greater when he has limited trust in his superior's motives and intentions.

A comparison of the remaining correlations in Table 3 suggests, but does not confirm, that both

TABLE 3 Correlations between Work-life Mobility and Accuracy of Upward Communication, Modified by the Separate and Joint Effects of Two Conditioning Variables

CONDITIONING VARIABLES	COMPARISON OF CORRELATIONS		p DIFF.
Trust	High trust	Low trust	
N high = 28	$*r_{we} = -.37$	$r_{we} = -.66$	.20
N low = 24			
Influence	Low influence	High influence	
N low = 31	$r_{we} = -.40$	$r_{we} = -.46$	n.s.
N high = 21			
	High trust, low influence	Low trust, high influence	
Both			
N h−l = 17	$r_{we} = -.41$	$r_{we} = -.49$	n.s.
N l−h = 10			

Note. Correlation between work-life mobility and upward communication for all 52 cases is −.41. * Subscript w refers to degree of work-life mobility, subscript c refers to accuracy of upward communication.

TABLE 4 Correlations between Inter-generational Mobility and Accuracy of Upward Communication, Modified by the Separate and Joint Effects of Two Conditioning Variables

CONDITIONING VARIABLES	COMPARISON OF CORRELATIONS		p DIFF.
Trust	High trust	Low trust	
N high = 28	$*r_{ie} = .11$	$r_{ie} = .02$	n.s.
N low = 21			
Influence	Low influence	High influence	
N low = 30	$r_{ie} = -.04$	$r_{ie} = .10$	n.s.
N high = 19			
	High trust, low influence	Low trust, high influence	
Both			
N h−l = 17	$r_{ie} = .13$	$r_{ie} = .07$	n.s.
N l−h = 10			

Note. Three of the 52 responses to the inter-generational scale were unclassifiable, hence the total N = 49. The correlation for all 49 cases is .08. * Subscript i refers to degree of inter-generational mobility, subscript c to accuracy of upward communication.

the influence and the combined trust-influence conditions have an effect on accuracy of upward communication.

The results in *Table 4* show little or no effect of trust or influence on the mobility-communication relationship.

The lack of any significant results in *Table 4* indicates that inter-generational mobility is not a significant determinant of communication accuracy.

These overall results for the total sample of 52 subordinate executives were found to hold fairly consistently for the three different companies sampled in the study. *Table 5* shows a company-by-company break-down of the mobility-communication relationship for the three parallel measures of mobility.[4]

The results in *Table 5* show consistency from company to company for mobility need and for inter-generational mobility. Inspection of the differences between mean scores of the variables in the three companies indicated that the total r of $-.41$ (*Table 1*) between work-life mobility and communication is somewhat inflated owing to clustered sampling. However, the negative direction of two of the three correlations in *Table 5* provides some assurance that this overall correlation is not entirely spurious.

TABLE 5 *Correlations between Three Measures of Mobility and Accuracy of Upward Communication for Executives in Each of Three Companies*

COMPANY	MOBILITY NEED N	r
A	16	−.41†
B	17	−.41†
C	19	−.22
	WORK-LIFE MOBILITY	
A	16	.04
B	17	.17
C	19	−.67‡
	INTER-GENERATIONAL MOBILITY	
A	15*	.20
B	17	.37
C	17*	−.06

* One response from Company *A* and two from Company *C* were unclassifiable, hence were not included. † Significant at .10–.20 level ($p < .20$). ‡ Significant at .01 level ($p < .01$).

[4] A further break-down according to the modifying conditions of trust and perceived influence for each company was not possible because of the relatively small size of the total N.

DISCUSSION

The results have generally supported the major prediction that, in industrial hierarchies, mobility aspiration among subordinate executives is negatively related to accuracy of upward communication. The findings have paralleled those of small-group studies which have rather consistently shown that individuals in power hierarchies tend to screen information passed upward, and to withhold or refrain from communicating information that is potentially threatening to the status of the communicator. The present study confirms that this tendency prevails in formal, large-scale organizations, is stronger among upwardly mobile members, and is strongly modified by the communicator's attitudes toward those above him in the hierarchy.

More specifically, the present study suggests that two aspects of mobility aspiration are related to inaccurate communication: (*a*) the expressed present needs of organizational members to advance upward in the hierarchy, and (*b*) the status-seeking tendencies of members who have experienced a long climb up the organizational ladder during their work-lives. One may only speculate on the lack of significant results for the inter-generational aspect of mobility. It may be that the psychological remoteness of one's familial relationship for those well along in their career lives would make it less strong as a motivating force than either one's conscious need or desire to advance, or one's career experiences.

Of particular note is the modifying effect of interpersonal trust on the communication-mobility relationship. This finding not only lends emphasis to the crucial importance of attitudinal factors in communication, but also suggests that free and accurate information exchange may depend significantly upon positive and harmonious relationships between organizational members, particularly those who differ in formal power. It must be pointed out, however, that high mobility aspirations strongly militate against accurate communication of potentially threatening information *even when high trust prevails*. It is only that low trust of the superior's motives and intentions intensifies or strengthens the tendency of highly ambitious subordinates to withhold or in some way prevent accurate upward communication.

The present research has implications for the effective co-ordination between middle-level executives in industrial hierarchies. The results of this study imply that upward mobility and the associated distortion of communication may introduce strains and imbalance into day-to-day co-ordination between the two. These strains can perhaps best be traced through in terms of decisions which require maximum information about the subordinate's work problems. First, periodic and important assessments must be made by the superior with respect to the general progress of the subordinate and the quality of his work performance. The findings of this study imply that these assessments are not likely to be made with any clear perspective on the problems and obstacles the upwardly mobile subordinate experiences in his work, unless the superior has other sources of information than the subordinate himself. Thus a judgement about the effectiveness the subordinate has shown in goal-achievement cannot be tempered by accurate knowledge of the problems he has encountered in his attempts to achieve the goals.

Second, decisions which the superior must make with regard to the general functioning of his subordinate's work unit or section may well be limited by a lack of awareness by the superior of problems affecting that unit. For example, one would expect that decisions regarding the allocation of manpower within the subordinate's unit would be based on the present problems the subordinate is experiencing with regard to allocation. Third, to the extent that the subordinate insulates his superior from clear knowledge of work-related problems, he has in effect insulated himself from whatever expert knowledge and judgement the superior might apply in solving these problems.

To the extent that the results of the present study hold for all levels of an organizational hierarchy, then the organization, to the degree that it fosters upward aspirations, introduces a system by which problem-related information is filtered through successive levels, and problems that might call for concerted action and decision at the top are effectively blocked at levels below. Perhaps this explains, at least to some extent, the 'fog of uncertainty' (Dalton, 1959, p. 234) that characterizes executives' work. One can be certain, however, that this potential dysfunction in organizations is not an all-or-nothing affair. Channels other than upward communication exist which can take over when problem information is blocked, and a certain amount of distortion of information can be expected in any organization. Furthermore, some insulation of one level of an organization from another undoubtedly has adaptive value. Inaccurate communication of problems may indicate, at least to some extent, that these problems are being handled at the appropriate level and may reflect effective delegation of duties.

SUMMARY

The purpose of this study was to test hypotheses about the relationship between upward mobility among executives and the accuracy with which they communicate problem-related information upward in industrial hierarchies. This relationship was found in general to be a significant negative one. The relationship was found to be conditioned or modified by the degree of interpersonal trust held by these executives for their superiors, and there is some evidence to suggest that the relationship is also conditioned by the degree of the superiors' influence as perceived by their subordinates.

These results indicate that the motives and attitudes of organizational members strongly affect the manner in which and degree to which they exchange work-related information with each other.

REFERENCES

BACK, K., FESTINGER, L., HYMOVITCH, B., KELLEY, H. H., SCHACHTER, S. & THIBAUT, J. (1950). The methodology of studying rumor transmission. *Hum. Relat.* **3**, 307–12.

COHEN, A. R. (1958). Upward communication in experimentally created hierarchies. *Hum. Relat.* **11**, 41–53.

DALTON, M. (1959). *Men who manage*. New York: Wiley.

FESTINGER, L. (1950). Informal social communication. *Psychol. Rev.* **57**, 217–82.

HENRY, W. E. (1949). The business executive: psychodynamics of a social role. *Amer. J. Sociol.* **54**, 286–91.

HURWITZ, J. I., ZANDER, A. F. & HYMOVITCH, B. (1953). Some effects of power on the relations among group members. In D. Cartwright and A. Zander (Eds.), *Group dynamics*. Evanston, Ill.: Row Peterson; London: Tavistock Publications.

KELLEY, H. H. (1951). Communication in experimentally created hierarchies. *Hum. Relat.* **4**, 39–56.

MELLINGER, G. D. (1956). Interpersonal trust as a factor in communication. *J. abnorm. soc. Psychol.* **53**, 304–09.

MINER, J. B. & CULVER, J. E. (1955). Some aspects of the executive personality. *J. appl. Psychol.* **39**, 348–53.

PELZ, D. (1951). Leadership within a hierarchical organization. *J. soc. Issues,* **7**, 49–55.

THIBAUT, J. (1950). An experimental study of the cohesiveness of underprivileged groups. *Hum. Relat.* **3**, 251–78.

WARNER, W. L. & ABEGGLEN, J. C. (1955). *Big business leaders in America*. New York: Harper.

STATUS CONGRUENCE AND COGNITIVE CONSISTENCY*

In an earlier selection by Emerson a general theory provided an underlying explanation of hitherto unrelated phenomena. The following selection also illustrates this function of theory. Findings in three areas of social psychological interest are brought together under a theory of expectancy congruence. Basic to this theory is a postulated tendency to achieve and maintain an internally consistent and externally valid set of expectations concerning the environment. This tendency is thought to arise out of the organism's experience with the functional necessities of individual and group life. Instances of cognitive dissonance, status incongruence, and role conflict, Sampson suggests, are explainable as special cases of this broader theory. He also proposed that certain findings, which hitherto have defied explanation in terms of the theories in each of these areas, can be handled by the broader theory of expectancy congruence. Should systematic research on this theory bear out these claims, we will have an instance of a considerable theoretical advance in social psychology.

27.

Status Congruence and Cognitive Consistency[1]

EDWARD E. SAMPSON
UNIVERSITY OF CALIFORNIA, BERKELEY

By employing the concept of expectancy and developing a theory of expectancy congruence, an attempt is made to understand the basic similarity between societal tendencies towards status congruence or equilibration and psychological tendencies towards cognitive consistency. The functional importance of the tendency towards expectancy congruence is examined, with particular emphasis being given to its consequences for interpersonal behavior. The implications of this expectancy model for reinterpreting the status congruence literature and for reexamining some aspects of the cognitive consistency literature are discussed.

In the following paper, we present a theoretical framework, referred to as a theory of expectancy congruence, which attempts to integrate the sociological literature on status crystallization[2] and the psychological literature on cognitive consistency. The paper will be organized into several major sections. The first section discusses the theory and research dealing with status crystallization. The second briefly outlines psychological developments in the area of cognitive consistency. The next section presents our theory of expectancy congruence, integrating the material of the first two sections. We conclude by examining further aspects of the theory and by re-examining the status crystallization literature in light of the theory of expectancy congruence.

APPROACHES TO STATUS CONGRUENCE

For many years, sociologists and social psychologists have been interested in social class or social status, as an independent and as a dependent variable in their theory and research.[3] The approaches of Max Weber[4] and more recently of Parsons[5] and of Lenski[6] has emphasized that a

* The selection following the editorial introduction is reprinted from "Status congruence and cognitive consistency," *Sociometry*, 1963, **26**, 146–162, by permission of the author and the American Sociological Association.

[1] The theoretical development reported in this paper provides the framework for a series of experiments on status congruence presently being conducted under Grant No. MH–06506–01 of the Public Health Service.

[2] In this paper, we shall use the terms status crystallization, status equilibration, and status congruence to refer to the same phenomena: the degree of correspondence across various dimensions of status ranking.

[3] See for example, Urie Bronfenbrenner, "Socialization and Social Class Through Time and Space," in Eleanor E. Maccoby, Theodore M. Newcomb, and Eugene L. Hartley, editors, *Readings in Social Psychology*, New York: Henry Holt, 1958, pp. 400–425; Richard Centers, *The Psychology of Social Classes*, Princeton University Press, 1949; August B. Hollingshead and Frederick C. Redlich, *Social Class and Mental Illness*, New York: John Wiley & Sons, 1958; Daniel R. Miller and Guy E. Swanson, "The Study of Conflict," in Marshall R. Jones, editor, *Nebraska Symposium on Motivation*, Lincoln, Neb.: University of Nebraska Press, 1956; Robert R. Sears, Eleanor E. Maccoby, and Harry Levin, *Patterns of Child Rearing*, Evanston, Ill.: Row, Peterson & Co., 1957; and W. Lloyd Warner and Paul S. Lunt, *The Social Life of a Modern Community*, New Haven: Yale University Press, 1941; and *idem.*, *The Status System of a Modern Community*, New Haven: Yale University Press, 1942.

[4] Max Weber, "Class, Status, Party," in Hans H. Gerth and C. Wright Mills, translators and editors, *From Max Weber: Essays in Sociology*, New York: Oxford University Press, 1946.

[5] Talcott Parsons, "An Analytical Approach to the Theory of Social Stratification," Ch. 7, *Essays in Sociological Theory, Pure and Applied*, Glencoe, Ill.: Free Press, 1949.

[6] Gerhard Lenski, "Status Crystallization: A Nonvertical Dimension of Social Status," *American Sociological Review*, **19** (August, 1954), pp. 405–413.

given individual may be ranked in many different systems of stratification. This observation has suggested the importance of examining the relationships that exist between these systems or dimensions as well as the second-order relationships with other social and psychological variables. It is to be noted that this approach differs from that discussed by Warner and Lunt[7] and Centers,[8] who were mainly concerned with discovering which dimensions provided the best indicator of an individual's "real" social class or which combination or weighting of dimensions was most predictive of behavior. By contrast, this newer emphasis attempts to discover the consequences of differential placement along the various ranking dimensions, by utilizing an index of differential ranking as a major independent variable.

Research using this latter approach has been reported by Lenski,[9] Adams,[10] and Exline and Ziller.[11] Lenski's work relates an index of status crystallization to the individual's political attitudes, whereas the research reported by Adams and by Exline and Ziller relates this index to small group morale and productivity.[12] In order to provide a concrete basis on which to build our theoretical framework, we shall briefly summarize some of the most relevant theory and research involving the status variable.

Lenski examined four status systems—income, occupation, education, and race or ethnic position—computing an index of crystallization across these dimensions for a sample of individuals. A person who ranked in similar positions across the dimensions was referred to as "high crystallized," while a person who ranked differently across the dimensions (regardless of the pattern) was referred to as "low crystallized." Lenski related this index of crystallization to expressed political attitudes and behavior, finding that liberal attitudes were positively related to low crystallization. He interpreted his findings as suggesting that the low crystallized person was dissatisfied with the present state of affairs, felt frustrated, and sought social change. This was in contrast to the satisfaction and relative lack of frustration of the

highly crystallized person. This finding and interpretation seem to imply what Benoit-Smullyan[13] referred to as a status equilibration tendency; that is, a tendency for a person's position in one hierarchy to match his position in another. It is also akin to the point made by Homans[14] in his discussion of the costs incurred from a condition of status incongruence. It suggests that differential ranking—at least on the four dimensions which Lenski selected—is an undesirable, costly state, giving rise to pressures to move towards a state of congruence or equilibrium. We shall have reason to deal in more detail with this point when we relate this material to the literature in psychology dealing with a principle of cognitive consistency, especially, Festinger's theory of cognitive dissonance.[15]

Adams computed an index of status congruence for a group of air crews on dimensions such as age, rank, amount of flight time, education, length of service, etc. His findings indicated that air crews with high congruence were characterized by their increasing friendship, greater mutual trust, and greater intimacy as compared to low congruent crews. In interpreting his results, Adams, like Lenski, turned to the dissatisfaction and frustration of the individuals in incongruent positions, who thereby considered themselves inappropriately placed within their group. These individuals were more apt to manifest behaviors which would be disruptive to their group. Again, the implication is that congruence is the desired, pleasant, nondisruptive state, both for the individual and for the group of which he is a member.

Exline and Ziller experimentally varied the status congruence of the individuals in small discussion groups on the dimensions of voting power and task ability. Their findings indicated that congruent groups were more congenial and showed greater discussion agreement than incongruent groups. The authors further suggested that if their situation had permitted it, there was an indication that the incongruent groups would have changed towards a congruent status structure. Thus, once again, we have the implication that incongruence is undesirable and that there are tendencies towards the development of congruent status structures within groups.

Although it was not presented in this context, the findings and interpretation of a study by Kleiner, Parker, and Taylor[16] are also relevant.

[7] Warner and Lunt, *op. cit.*

[8] Centers, *op. cit.*

[9] Lenski, *op. cit.*

[10] Stuart Adams, "Status Congruency as a Variable in Small Group Performance," *Social Forces*, **32** (October, 1953), pp. 16–22.

[11] Ralph V. Exline and Robert C. Ziller, "Status Congruency and Interpersonal Conflict in Decision-making Groups," *Human Relations*, **12** (April, 1959), pp. 147–162.

[12] It is to be noted that the variable of status crystallization or congruence may be considered a characteristic of the social structure and a characteristic of a particular unit of that structure, e.g. an individual. That is, one may meaningfully speak of the extent to which a given social organization—e.g. a small group, an organization, or a society—has evolved a crystallized or congruent status structure; and one may also speak of the extent to which a given person's status positions are crytallized or congruent.

[13] Emile Benoit-Smullyan, "Status, Status Types, and Status Interrelations," *American Sociological Review*, **9** (April, 1944), pp. 151–161.

[14] George C. Homans, *Social Behavior: Its Elementary Forms*, New York: Harcourt, Brace & World, Inc., 1961.

[15] Leon Festinger, *A Theory of Cognitive Dissonance*, Evanston: Row, Peterson, 1957.

[16] As reported in an unpublished dittoed note seen by the

They hypothesized a relationship between the level of aspiration-level of achievement discrepancy and the incidence of mental illness. Their rationale suggested that this discrepancy produced frustration and stress for the individual, who responded by a flight into illness. They used educational rank as a measure of the individual's level of aspiration, and occupational rank as a measure of achievement. The discrepancy of which they speak, therefore, is an index of status congruence as employed, for example, by Lenski. Furthermore, the postulation of frustration as a reaction to this discrepancy directly parallels Lenski's interpretation and is consistent with the findings and interpretation of the small group studies of Adams and of Exline and Ziller. It is interesting to note, however, that whereas Lenski suggests and empirically finds that this state of frustration leads to active attempts to change the system (e.g. liberal political attitudes and behavior), Kleiner suggests and generally finds that it leads to a higher incidence of mental illness. Both approaches, however, suggest that incongruence is an undesirable state and that individuals will attempt to cope with it in some manner. Different coping techniques therefore become another issue of relevance in the further examination of this variable. Some persons may be expected to reduce status incongruence by means of flight into fantasy and illness (Kleiner); whereas others may attempt to reduce it by means of active efforts to change the social system or their relation to it (Lenski).[17]

Continuing our examination of relevant literature, it is valuable to take note of a distinction which Bales has made in his theory and supported by his research findings.[18] Although Bales pre-

---

author while at the Research Center for Group Dynamics of the University of Michigan in 1960.

[17] Is this not also a point which is implied by Merton? Cf. Robert Merton, *Social Theory and Social Structure*, Glencoe, Ill.: Free Press, 1957. His formulation of five different types of responses to the discrepancy between societal goals and sanctioned means to attain these goals may be considered as expressing the manner by which persons located in different segments of the social system are expected to react to status incongruence. "Conformity" is a response of those persons who presently occupy congruent status positions, while "innovation," "ritualism," "retreatism," and "rebellion" represent responses of persons in incongruent positions. Retreatism or withdrawal, including a psychotic reaction, thus becomes comparable to the response suggested by Kleiner, while rebellion, or actively seeking to change the system, becomes comparable to the response suggested by Lenski.

[18] Robert F. Bales, "Adaptive and Integrative Changes as Sources of Strain in Social Systems," in A. Paul Hare, Edgar F. Borgatta, and Robert F. Bales, editors, *Small Groups*, New York: Knopf, 1955, pp. 127–131; and "Task Roles and Social

sented his material in a somewhat different context, as with the work of Kleiner, there is a similarity to the variable of status congruence that demands further exploration. In general, Bales has distinguished between task leaders and socioemotional leaders within small discussion groups. He suggests that it is difficult for the same person to fulfill both functions, each of which is necessary for the group to continue operating effectively. Bales' method for identifying the task specialist and the socioemotional specialist involves ranking group members according to various categories of participation or interaction. Thus the most active individual (i.e. the most highly ranking) on giving suggestions and orientation may be identified as the task specialist, while the highest ranking individual on giving positive emotion or support may be identified as the socioemotional leader.

At first glance, it appears that the Bales' finding that it is *unusual* for the same person to head both ranks (i.e. fulfill both types of functions) is opposed to the previous findings which indicated the existence of a tendency toward status congruence. This is an instance of a person who ranks high on one dimension and low on another: obviously, therefore, it is an instance of status incongruence. However, as treated by Bales, this is not an undesirable state, but rather appears to be the more typical, felicitous condition of small group functioning. This finding may mean simply that one cannot rank *high* on both dimensions, but implies nothing about an incongruity for other ranks; or it may mean that differential ranking is *not necessarily* incongruent and undesirable. Assuming this latter point is correct, there is a particularly significant conclusion to be drawn: differential ranking does not *by itself* produce status incongruence and tendencies towards congruence. Although the preceding authors (e.g., Lenski, Adams, Exline and Ziller, and Benoit-Smullyan) have implied that differential ranking defines status incongruence and produces desires or pressures towards change, we would like to anticipate our later theoretical development at this point by briefly suggesting an alternate proposal.

It appears that the meaningful sense in which rank positions may be said to be incongruent and that tendencies towards status equilibration exist does not occur with *any* discrepancy between the positions, but rather, with any discrepancy that implies inconsistent expectations for the behavior of the occupants of the positions. This consideration suggests that it is not the mere location on a status hierarchy that is important, but rather, the expectations connected with that location. It further implies that a given individual may occupy a low rank in one hierarchy and a high rank in

---

Roles in Problem-solving Groups," in Eleanor E. Maccoby, Theodore M. Newcomb, and Eugene L. Hartley, editors, *Readings in Social Psychology*, New York: Henry Holt, 1958, pp. 437–447.

another and *not* be under pressure to change, if there is a consistency between the expectations coincident with those two positions. And finally, it implies that the dimensions which have been selected for research by Lenski, by Adams, by Exline and Ziller, and by Kleiner, are dimensions in which there is a high correspondence between positional discrepancy and expectational inconsistency, even though this apparently is not the case for the two major dimensions of which Bales speaks. And, in fact, Bales' theory points out that the inconsistency exists among the expectations connected with similar ranking on both dimensions rather than with differential ranking on each.

All of the preceding, much of which we shall develop further in the following sections, suggests the importance of empirical research directed towards identifying the nature of the expectations which correspond to the different ranking systems of a society, organization, or group, and towards identifying the mechanisms by which these expectations are shaped and altered to be congruent with the changing needs of the society, organization, or group.

THEORIES OF COGNITIVE CONSISTENCY

There has been a growing interest in psychology in the cognitive factors involved in behavior. The focus of the attitude change theories of Katz and Stotland,[19] Osgood, Suci, and Tannenbaum,[20] and Rosenberg, Hovland, McGuire, Abelson, and Brehm,[21] has involved a principle of cognitive consistency. In general terms, the individual is seen as motivated to maintain consistency among his cognitions or aspects of his cognitions, and attitude change may be brought about by introducing an inconsistency among certain of these elements.

The approach to interpersonal behavior suggested by Heider[22] and formalized by Cartwright and Harary,[23] as well as the approaches of Newcomb[24] and of Festinger,[25] are also similar in their emphasis on individual tendencies towards maintaining cognitive balance, symmetry, or consonance. Zajonc[26] summarizes many of these similarities in his recent review.

Each of the approaches has supported its theoretical orientation with empirical evidence suggesting that people apparently do establish relationships between themselves and others that could be characterized as balanced or symmetric or that persons do act in a manner designed to reduce dissonance.

The cognitive units tending towards consistency which these theories typically discuss include sets of attitudes towards persons and objects, two sets of attitudes or beliefs, and expectations and behavior. It is this final cognitive unit of expectation, and specifically Festinger's theory with which we shall deal further.

Festinger[27] has suggested that one form of cognitive dissonance involves a discrepancy between expectation and occurrence. Thus persons who expect that the world will end on a particular day experience dissonance when that day comes and passes and the world continues to exist.[28] Similarly, one can interpret the findings of Aronson and Mills,[29] showing greater attraction to a group with a severe initiation ceremony as compared with one less severe, in terms of the discrepancy between expectation or belief and occurrence. It would be dissonant to maintain the belief that one endured so severe an initiation for so unimportant a group; therefore, the group must be highly attractive and important. We would add that this must be so, of course, because one has the *underlying expectation* that high effort, high embarrassment, high severity of initiation, etc. goes with high reward. In order to maintain this underlying expectation, one alters his valuation of the group. That is to say, the person maintains that the expected relationship between hard work (severity of initiation, etc.) and reward is positive. Thus, when given a situation involving hard work, he completes this relation according to expectation by positing high reward value to the object, group,

[19] Daniel Katz and Ezra Stotland, "A Preliminary Statement to a Theory of Attitude Structure and Change," in Sigmund Koch, editor, *Psychology: A Study of a Science, V. 3*, New York: McGraw-Hill, 1959.

[20] Charles E. Osgood, George J. Suci, and Percy H. Tannenbaum, *The Measurement of Meaning*, Urbana, Ill.: University of Illinois Press, 1957.

[21] Milton J. Rosenberg, Carl I. Hovland, William J. McGuire, Robert P. Abelson, and Jack W. Brehm, *Attitude Organization and Change: An Analysis of Consistency Among Attitude Components*, New Haven: Yale University Press, 1960.

[22] Fritz Heider, "Attitudes and Cognitive Organization," *Journal of Psychology*, 21 (January, 1946), pp. 107–112; and *The Psychology of Interpersonal Relations*, New York: Wiley, 1958.

[23] Dorwin Cartwright and Frank Harary, "Structural Balance: A Generalization of Heider's Theory," *Psychological Review*, 63 (September, 1956), pp. 277–293.

[24] Theodore M. Newcomb, "An Approach to the Study of Communicative Acts," *Psychological Review*, 60 (November, 1953), pp. 393–404; and "Individual Systems of Orientation," in Sigmund Koch, editor. *Psychology: A Study of a Science, V. 3*, New York: McGraw-Hill, 1959.

[25] Festinger, *op. cit.*

[26] Robert B. Zajonc, "The Concepts of Balance, Congruity, and Dissonance," *Public Opinion Quarterly*, 24 (Summer, 1960), pp. 280–296.

[27] Festinger, *op. cit.*

[28] Leon Festinger, Henry W. Riecken, and Stanley Schachter, "When Prophecy Fails," in Eleanor E. Maccoby, Theodore M. Newcomb, and Eugene L. Hartley, editors, *Readings in Social Psychology*, New York: Henry Holt, 1958, pp. 156–163.

[29] Elliot Aronson and Judson Mills, "The Effect of Severity of Initiation on Liking for a Group," *Journal of Abnormal and Social Psychology*, 59 (July, 1959), pp. 177–181.

person, etc. This is referred to by Festinger as an example of maintaining consonance.

We shall now expand this idea by assuming that it is useful to deal with the psychological tendencies towards cognitive consistency in terms of expectancy units. Persons can then be characterized by their tendencies to maintain a consistency among expectations. That is, they function cognitively so as to maintain a consistency among the various expectations which they hold and between expectation and occurrence.

STATUS INCONGRUENCE, EXPECTANCY IN-CONGRUENCE, AND COGNITIVE DISSONANCE

We are now in a position to deal with the sociological variable of status congruence in the same terms we have selected for discussing the psychological tendencies towards cognitive consistency. To complete this step, we must first deal with the relationship between rank position and expectation. Let us make the assumption that one aspect of each position—or set of positions—along a given status dimension consists of certain expectations for the behavior of the occupant of that position. Thus, for example, a person ranking high in education may meaningfully be said to have certain expectations held by others and by himself for his behavior. A similar parallel between rank position and expectation can be drawn for other dimensions along which persons can be ranked. It is to be noted that this assumption is analogous to that made in role theory in speaking of positions in the structure of society and expectations connected to these positions.[30]

By the preceding assumption, we have now drawn a complete parallel between a condition of status incongruence and a condition of expectancy incongruence, or cognitive dissonance in Festinger's terminology.

Let us be a bit more specific on this point by examining two status dimensions, A and B, and the *underlying expectation* specifying the nature of the relationship to be expected between A and B. It is possible to speak of various positions or ranks along dimension A (R_{1A}, R_{2A}, ... R_{nA}), and various positions or ranks along dimension B (R_{1B}, R_{2B}, ... R_{nB}). Corresponding to each position along A are certain expectations pertaining to the behavior of the occupant of that position (e_{R1A}, e_{R2A}, ... e_{RnA}). A similar situation exists for each position along B. The underlying expectation is seen as linking the rank positions of A and B including their corresponding expectations.

Let us next define inconsistency or incongruity between A and B in a manner parallel to Festinger's definition of dissonance:[31] That is, A implies not B. We then conclude that when the underlying expectation maintains that A and B are positively related such that if R_{1A} then R_{1B}, an instance in which we find R_{1A} and R_{5B} is an instance of status incongruence (as typically used to refer to differential rank positions) *and* an instance of expectancy incongruence or dissonance. However, when the underlying expectation maintains that A and B are negatively related such that if R_{1A} then R_{5B}, an instance in which we find R_{1A} and R_{5B} is an instance of status incongruence (as defined by differential ranking), but is *not* an instance of expectancy incongruence or dissonance. Assuming a tendency towards congruence, we expect change in the former case but not in the latter. Thus we arrive at the point suggested earlier in our consideration of Bales; mere difference in rank position does not necessarily function as Lenski and the others have posited.

To summarize, we have suggested that one can treat the sociological variable of status congruence in the same terms useful in treating psychological theories of cognitive consistency, specifically, in terms of a more general theory of expectancy congruence.

TOWARDS AN EXPECTANCY CONGRUENCE MODEL OF INTERPERSONAL BEHAVIOR

We shall continue our examination of the general principle of expectancy congruence by presenting and discussing some of the assumptions underlying the model. In developing the model itself, we employ assumptions that are similar to those employed by G. H. Mead[32] and to those suggested as the basis for the *A-B-X* model of Newcomb[33] and the communication and social motivation models of Festinger.[34] We begin with a set of assumptions within a functionalist framework. From these assumptions, we derive certain implications for the functioning of individuals and of collectivities. Basically, we attempt to derive conclusions which pertain to intraindividual and inter-individual pressures towards cognitive consistency (expectancy congruence). Thus, this model is seen as relevant to psychological theories of individual cognitive behavior as well as to social psychological theories of group and collective behavior. As previously, our aim is to deal with the variable of status congruence as an example of the operation

---

[30] See Theodore R. Sarbin, "Role Theory," in Gardner Lindzey, editor, *Handbook of Social Psychology, V. 1*, Cambridge: Addison-Wesley, 1954.

[31] Festinger, *op. cit.*

[32] George H. Mead, *Mind, Self, and Society,* Chicago: University of Chicago Press, 1934.

[33] Newcomb, *op. cit.*

[34] Leon Festinger, "Informal Social Communication," *Psychological Review,* **57** (September, 1950), pp. 271–282; and "Motivation Leading to Social Behavior," in Marshall R. Jones, editor, *Nebraska Symposium on Motivation,* Lincoln, Neb.: University of Nebraska Press, 1954.

of this model. To this end we conclude this article with a brief consideration of the findings of the initial studies cited by Lenski, Adams, and Exline and Ziller in the context of the expectancy congruence model.

We should warn the reader at this point that we are not presenting the following as a formally derived theory with primitives, postulates, theorems, etc. But rather, we shall endeavor to discuss our propositions in a logical manner without presenting the more elegant outlines of a formal theory. We shall number our major paragraphs in order to provide easier reference and to emphasize the logical order of the propositions.

1. Let us begin with the central assumption that one of the basic requirements of individual and collective survival—in other words, a requirement basic to the continued existence of a social order—is a degree of coordination among the actions of two or more persons involved in any particular interaction situation. This assumption implies each individual's necessary dependence on other individuals for his own survival.

2. Let us next assume that among other factors, this coordination itself requires a degree of anticipatory knowledge about the behavior which may be expected of the other participants in the particular interaction situation. This knowledge permits the regulation of one's own behavior vis-à-vis the others with whom one is interacting. We shall further assume that this anticipatory knowledge exists within the person (P) in the form of expectations about his and the other's (O's) behavior.[35] These assumptions are similar to those advanced many years ago by G. H. Mead[36] and presently supported by those working in role theory.[37]

3. Over time, and we assume, through a series of child and adult experiences including intentional instruction, incidental learning, and learning of a trial-and-error sort, individuals (and larger units, including groups, organizations, and societies) develop a model of their physical and their social world. This model is assumed to contain the expectations, hypotheses, or hunches the individual maintains about his own behavior, the behavior of other persons, and about the physical environment. For purposes of this paper, we shall not deal with the expectations involving the physical environment, but rather shall concentrate solely upon

those involving one's self and other persons—i.e., the social environment.

This "world view" is similar to what those in the area of person perception have discussed in terms of the individual's cognitive system or theory of personality.[38] It is also similar to what has been referred to as the individual's "cognitive map" of his world.[39] In many respects, it is also comparable to what Bruner has referred to in his discussion of the individual's development of models and strategies for dealing effectively with his environment.[40]

When the unit we deal with is not the individual, but the group, organization, or society, we may speak of the norms, the values, and the ideology of the collectivity as being parallel to the individual's world view, model, or strategy. In point of fact, much of the individual's own model is a socially shared model of expectations, commonly treated under the rubric of "norms."

4. We next assume that an internally consistent or reliable model is more useful in the coordination of interactions than an unreliable model. That is, a set of expectations which is internally consistent provides the individual and the collectivity with potentially nonconflicting organizations of the social environment and thus provides relatively nonconflicting guidelines for action and interaction.

It also seems plausible to maintain that not only is an internally consistent set of expectations useful, but also, a valid set is more useful to the individual and the collectivity than an invalid set. By validity, we refer to the match or fit between expectation and input. A model or set of expectations which fits or matches the input from the environment within a tolerated range of error permits better coping

[35] It is important to note that we are not implying that this anticipatory knowledge is necessary for a cooperative as contrasted with a competitive interaction situation. An expectation about the other's behavior must be maintained, whether this other be friend or foe.

[36] Mead, *op. cit.*

[37] See for example, Merton, *op. cit.*; Sarbin, *op. cit.*; and Tamotsu Shibutani, *Society and Personality*, Englewood Cliffs, N.J.: Prentice-Hall, Inc., 1961.

[38] Leonard Berkowitz, "The Judgmental Process in Personality Functioning," *Psychological Review*, **67** (March, 1960), pp. 130–142; Jerome Bruner, David Shapiro and Renato Tagiuri, "The Meaning of Traits in Isolation and in Combination," in Renato Tagiuri and Luigi Petrullo, editors, *Person Perception and Interpersonal Behavior*, Stanford, Calif.: Stanford University Press, 1958; and Edward E. Jones and John W. Thibaut, "Interaction Goals as Bases of Inference in Interpersonal Perception," in Renato Tagiuri and Luigi Petrullo, editors, *Person Perception and Interpersonal Behavior*, Stanford, Calif.: Stanford University Press, 1958.

[39] Edward C. Tolman, "Cognitive Maps in Rats and Men," from, *Collected Papers in Psychology*, Berkeley: University of California Press, 1951.

[40] Jerome S. Bruner, "The Cognitive Consequences of Early Sensory Deprivation," in Philip Solomon, Philip E. Kubzansky, P. Herbert Leiderman, Jack H. Mendelson, Richard Trumbull, and Donald Wexler, editors, *Sensory Deprivation*, Cambridge: Harvard University Press, 1961.

with the environment, and thus, better coordination of action and interaction.[41] (See Festinger's treatment of a similar point in the 1954 Nebraska Symposium on Motivation.)

Based on the assumed necessity for a reliable and a valid model of the environment for the coordination of interaction, we postulate the existence of tendencies towards the achievement and maintenance of both an internally consistent and an externally valid set of expectations. We refer to the preceding as the *principle of expectancy congruence*. Because we are speaking of a consistency among expectations as well as between expectation and environmental input, this principle refers to these two distinguishable types of congruence.

SOME IMPORTANT ASPECTS OF THE PRINCIPLE OF EXPECTANCY CONGRUENCE

1. One aspect of this principle is comparable to the concern of the various psychological theories of cognitive consistency which we previously discussed.

2. Another aspect, and one which is of greater immediate concern in this article, suggests that individual tendencies towards expectancy congruence give rise to socially communicated, interpersonal pressures for one's self and others to present pictures of themselves which are

congruent with what is expected. When others behave in a manner which is congruent with our expectations for them, we are better able to coordinate our actions and interactions with them, i.e., our model provides an accurate picture of the social environment.

Furthermore, *O*'s deviation from expectation is a condition which is particularly painful to *P*, as he can no longer so easily coordinate his and *O*'s actions. Deviation of any kind (e.g., disagreement in opinion, belief, or attitude) does not necessarily give rise to these pressures, but rather, only *unexpected* deviation has this effect. Therefore, the fact that two friends disagree in opinion would not in and of itself produce pressures towards agreement as some theories would suggest.[42] In fact, there may be no pressures towards agreement, but instead pressures towards maintaining disagreement if this state is congruent with what each expects, e.g., with the underlying expectation. That one may empirically find pressures towards opinion agreement between two friends suggests that this is the expected state. Where agreement is not found, however, this may be as balanced, symmetric, and felicitous a state as a state of agreement, if it conforms to expectation. What has been referred to as "an agreement to disagree" basically reflects this underlying expectation to which we are referring.

3. In an analogous manner, deviation of a group member from the group's opinion on an issue will produce pressures towards uniformity of opinion,[43] only when this deviation is also a deviation from expectation for that particular group member. Implied in this model therefore is the possibility of certain group members' holding opinions discrepant from other group members but under no pressure to change, because this state is congruent with expectations for those members. Note the difference between this derivation and that of the Festinger-Schachter model,[44] which suggests that pressures operate towards uniformity of opinion as a function of the increasing discrepancy of a member's opinion from the group's opinion. We are suggesting that it is *not necessarily* a uniformity of opinion that is sought and towards which pressures are directed, but rather, a conformity to expectation. Therefore, homogeneity of opinion is not necessarily the desired end state; congruence with expectation is. Where the underlying expectation or group norm maintains that all group members with-

---

[41] We further suggest that there are individual differences not only with respect to expectations, but also with respect to tolerance of error or mismatch. To use the language of statistics, persons may be seen to vary in their tolerance of the discrepancy between the expected and the observed occurrence of an event. Some persons may find satisfaction with a *p*-value (probability that one would be incorrect in stating that there is no difference between what was expected and what was observed) of .50 or higher, while others may demand *p*-values approaching the .05 level. Additionally, it seems plausible to maintain that these *p*-values not only differ across persons, but within a given person across situations. For example, in a situation in which knowledge about the other's behavior is particularly important (such as for one's own survival), a *p*-value of .001 or less may be seen as necessary; whereas, in other, less important situations, the same individual may demand a less stringent level of significance.

The material in psychology which deals with tolerance of ambiguity and which relates this tolerance to certain personality traits or cognitive styles is of obvious relevance in this context. Cf. for example, Jack Block and Jeanne Block, "An Interpersonal Experiment on Reactions to Authority," *Human Relations,* 5 (January, 1952), pp. 91–98; Else Frenkel-Brunswik, "A Study of Prejudice in Children," *Human Relations,* 1 (July, 1948), pp. 295–306; and Abraham H. Maslow, "The Authoritarian Character Structure," *Journal of Social Psychology,* 18 (November, 1943), pp. 401–411.

[42] Cartwright and Harary, *op. cit.*; Heider, *op. cit.*; and Newcomb, *op. cit.*

[43] Stanley Schachter, "Deviation, Rejection, and Communication," *Journal of Abnormal and Social Psychology,* 46 (September, 1951), pp. 190–207.

[44] Festinger, *op. cit.*, 1950, 1954; and Schachter, *op. cit.*

out exception should have the same opinion, then opinion deviation is an instance of deviation from expectation, and pressures towards expectancy congruence are brought to bear on group members.

4. There is one further aspect of this model which must be discussed before examining the relationship between it and the earlier research and theory on the variable of status congruence. Assuming that each individual potentially is the locus of a multiplicity of expectations for his behavior, some of which may be incongruent with one another, we can examine the consequences of this condition within the context of the principle of expectancy congruence. One of the first and most obvious consequences involves the individual's own efforts to achieve and maintain a congruence among these various expectations for his behavior. These efforts would direct our attention to the aspect of role theory which is discussed under the title of role conflict. This presents an instance of an individual under conflicting expectations. We shall not deal with this consequence, but rather shall examine the consequences of this state for others with whom P interacts.

According to the expectancy congruence principle, P will be the recipient of socially communicated pressures from various O's to achieve and maintain a congruence among the expectations for his behavior. To the extent that P presents multiple faces to these others (because he is subject to multiple expectations), they too will be in an undesirable situation and will seek to change it towards a picture of P which is congruent, e.g. which is uni-faced rather than multi-faced. Therefore, P will be under pressures from others to present a picture of himself which is consistent.[45] He finds himself in a situation which is *doubly* unpleasant. In the first place, multiple, incongruent expectations may make it difficult for him to maintain a consistent picture of himself; and in the second place, multiple, incongruent expectations may make it difficult for others to interact with him and to coordinate their behavior with his.

An example presented to the author by a student in an interviewing course may make the above problem clearer. This student was a nurse who had two major aspects to her role.

One aspect dictated that she be a strict supervisor of a group of nursing trainees. The second aspect, on the other hand, dictated that she be a warm, compassionate counsellor, helping the trainees handle any particularly difficult interpersonal problems they faced. She recognized a problem in relating to the trainees, as she could not easily coordinate the different, incongruent expectations demanded as aspects of this nurse-role. We would further suggest that this situation of multiple, disparate expectations is *equally* a problem for all those trainees interacting with her. Each time they confront her they must ask themselves, "Which hat is she wearing?" "Is she the strict supervisor with punitive powers; or is she the warm, compassionate, understanding counsellor?" Until this question is answered by them, they are unable to relate to her and to coordinate their actions with hers. Thus the multiple, incongruent expectations are a problem for all participants in the interaction situation, and, as we have suggested, lead to pressures on the part of both interactants to achieve and maintain a state in which the expectations centering about P are congruent with one another: a state of expectancy congruence.

Let us simplify the preceding and continue to refer to a person in a situation of multiple, incongruent expectations as a multi-faced person (note the colloquial use of "two-faced" in this context) and then examine this approach a bit further. Assuming, as we have done, that a multi-faced person is undesirable to himself personally and to those with whom he interacts, what happens in those groups and organizations in which a certain degree of "multi-facedness" is required? In other words, some key persons in a group or organization may have as part of their roles the necessary characteristic of being multi-faced. Thus, for example, the bureaucrat may be forced to show one face to his fellow workers and another face to his clients or to his family. The question then becomes one of investigating the means whereby such key personnel are given supports by their group or organization that enable them and others to continue functioning in this manner. An organization may have formal and informal rules that serve to insulate the key man from encountering those persons who may see his many faces; and similarly, there may be rules that serve to limit the nature of the contact between those various persons. Thus, formal lines of communication and stresses towards impersonal relationships within some groups and organizations may be most helpful in this respect.

---

[45] We do not intend to ignore the possibility that O may achieve congruence by changing his own set of expectations rather than by applying pressures to P. We recognize this as a distinct possibility, but wish to pursue the consequences of the interpersonal approach in this article. We would suggest that the pressures of which we speak are nearly always communicated in varying degrees of obviousness in all interpersonal situations, e.g., from a lifted eyebrow, to a subtle glance, to a spoken word. And, we would add, this occurs most often prior to P's changing his own expectations about O.

INTERPERSONAL PRESSURES TOWARDS STATUS CONGRUENCE

We are now in a position to conclude our presentation by reexamining the research and theory on the variable of status congruence using the model just discussed.

The major findings involving the variable of status congruence suggest that incongruence in status ranks is an undesirable state as it leads to frustration and a desire for change. It was left relatively unexplained as to why this should be and why tendencies toward status equilibration, crystallization, or congruence should exist. According to the expectancy congruence model, however, an explanation is readily available. Both P and O find incongruence undesirable and frustrating in that it hinders their necessary coordination of interaction. With incongruence, the world is unorganized and difficult to cope with; thus both P and O seek to achieve and maintain a congruence of status positions, i.e., a congruence of expectations. Placing one's self and others into status positions is one means of ordering the social environment to facilitate coordinated interaction. Therefore, both intrapersonal and interpersonal effort is directed towards a congruence of expectations, a condition which is found with a congruent status structure.

Another aspect of the status congruence research and theory suggests that groups having a high degree of status incongruence are characterized by lack of mutual trust, reduced friendliness, and at times, by reduced productivity. From the model which we have suggested, each of these findings can be easily explained.

As we have seen, both P and O find congruence of expectation a desirable state and are subject to pressures to attain this state. To the extent that change towards congruence is impaired or impossible—that is, to the extent that an individual cannot change his positions within a given ranking system towards congruence with his other rank positions, or, to the extent that the group cannot develop a congruent status structure for its members—there will be dissatisfaction and continued frustration. The Adams finding reporting that groups high in status congruence showed a greater degree of mutual trust, greater friendship, and greater intimacy than groups low in status congruence is a reflection of this state of affairs. The multi-faced individual (the status or

expectancy incongruent individual) quite obviously is the kind of person that one would find difficult to trust, be friendly, and intimate with. And, by extension, it is not surprising that a group having a large number of such persons (a group low in status congruence) should be characterized as Adams has done.

It is now only one step further to explain the reduction in productivity that occurs within low congruent groups. Given the inconsistency in expectations for the other's behavior, this reduction may stem very simply from each individual's inability easily to coordinate his behavior with the behavior of others of his group. Or, this reduction may stem from the group's lack of cohesiveness, increase in tension, and increased concern with group maintenance rather than task problems. Such a group may expend much of its effort on achieving a congruence or a consistency of expectations, or working to defend against the apparent inconsistencies which exist, and thus have little energy remaining to devote to the task. Their "hidden agenda" of congruence-seeking and incongruence-defending, therefore, may readily serve to reduce their productive efficiency.

To summarize, we have suggested that the conditions necessary for the continuation of the social order, which are also the conditions necessary for the continuation of the individual who is at all points dependent on that social order, include at minimum an anticipatory knowledge of the behavior which may be expected of the other participants in a given interaction situation. The organization of this anticipatory knowledge into a model of expectations about the social and physical environment, and the demands for an internally consistent and an externally valid model provide the basic framework for deriving predictions about individual and group behavior, and for explaining the already existing theory and research on the variable of status congruence.

Coordinating status position with expectation and status congruence with expectancy congruence permits one to discuss status equilibration or status congruence tendencies within individuals and within social structures in terms of the more general principle of expectancy congruence. The effects of low status congruence for the individual as well as for the group—e.g., dissatisfaction, lowered productivity, lowered cohesiveness—become a function of the problems involved in coordinating one's behavior with the behavior of others in a situation which is characterized by multiple and conflicting expectations for one's and the other's behavior.

A CONCEPTUAL FRAMEWORK AND SOME EMPIRICAL DATA REGARDING COMPARISONS OF SOCIAL REWARDS *

In recent years a number of theorists[a] have developed concepts to deal with the fact that a person's reaction to rewards and costs is not always in proportion to their magnitude. Satisfaction or dissatisfaction with reward-cost outcomes appears to be affected by expectations as to the appropriateness or fairness of the outcomes. In determining what is appropriate, individuals compare their outcomes with those of other persons.

In the following selection Patchen offers a theory that explains an individual's satisfaction with rewards or costs in terms of their perceived dissonance or consonance with rewards received by other persons. Where an individual is similar to the comparison person on variables related to outcomes, such as education, seniority, or experience, he will be satisfied if he has a similar outcome (such as salary). Homans[b] has referred to these variables related to outcomes as *investments*. Unlike most theories postulating a tendency to avoid imbalance or dissonance, Patchen suggests a condition where balance or consonance is not sought. When the individual does not perceive himself as personally responsible for his outcome, he may be motivated to make dissonant comparisons. He may compare himself with others who are similar to him but who received higher wages. Since he perceives this situation as not his own fault, he can react with righteous indignation. In a sense, however, this is not a departure from balance theory. Such a comparison provides cognitive elements consistent with his feelings of indignation and his demands for higher status.

28.

A Conceptual Framework and Some Empirical Data Regarding Comparisons of Social Rewards[1]

MARTIN PATCHEN
UNIVERSITY OF MICHIGAN

A number of investigations, including the wartime researches reported in the *American Soldier* volumes, have made it clear that people's aspirations, satisfactions, and self-evaluations are determined not so much by their objective position as by their standing relative to specific persons with whom they compare (1, 5, 6, 8, 9). These findings raise general questions about what determines how an individual will react to a given comparison—e.g., whether with satisfaction or with dissatisfaction. They also raise general questions about what determines the *choice* of specific comparisons from among a number of possible alternatives.

Festinger (3) and Davis (2) have presented formal theoretical analyses of the comparison process. Davis states that he has not attempted to derive the formal relations between his theory and that of Festinger, though he suggests that his theory treats comparisons "where perceptions and evaluations are unambiguous" while Festinger's theory treats comparisons "where perceptions and evaluations are ambiguous" (2, p. 282).

The present paper points out what appear to be serious weaknesses in Davis's formulation of comparison phenomena. A conceptual approach to the comparison process will be outlined which is intended to be more general than either the Davis or Festinger formulation. This conceptual approach will treat comparisons in terms closely related to the theory of dissonance proposed by Festinger (4). Our consideration of what deter-

* The selection following the editorial introduction is reprinted from "A conceptual framework and some empirical data regarding comparisons of social rewards," *Sociometry*, 1961, **24**, 136–156, by permission of the author and the American Sociological Association.

[a] R. K. Merton & Alice S. Kitt. Contributions to the theory of reference group behavior. In R. K. Merton & P. F. Lazars-

feld (eds.), *Continuities in social research: Studies in the scope and method of "The American soldier."* New York: The Free Press of Glencoe, 1950. Pp. 40–105. J. W. Thibaut & H. H. Kelley. *The social psychology of groups.* New York: John Wiley & Sons, Inc., 1959. G. C. Homans. *Social behavior: Its elementary forms.* New York: Harcourt, Brace & World, Inc., 1961.

[b] Homans. *Ibid.*

[1] The research reported here is part of a larger study conducted by the Organizational Behavior and Change Programs for the Survey Research Center. The author is indebted to Dr. Carol Slater for many useful comments and suggestions during the formulation of the research theory and operations and for a critical reading of an earlier draft of this paper. This paper has also benefited from critical readings of the earlier draft by Dr. Arnold S. Tannenbaum and Dr. Donald C. Pelz. The study was under the general supervision of Dr. Floyd C. Mann who played an important part in making the research possible. Most of the data and ideas presented here are part of a doctoral dissertation (7) submitted to the University of Michigan in August 1959. The members of the doctoral committee, especially Dr. Theodore M. Newcomb, chairman, contributed useful criticisms of and suggestions for the research.

mines the choice of comparisons will, in turn, suggest some implications for dissonance theory. Data relevant to these theoretical ideas, from a study of wage comparisons made by workers in an oil refinery, will be presented.

SOME THEORETICAL IDEAS

The subjective meaning of given comparisons

Davis divides comparisons into those made with members of an "in-group" (same marital status, same education, etc.) and those made with members of an "out-group" (2, p. 283ff.). The meaning of comparisons to those in an in-group is clear. For example, as Davis points out, those who are deprived with respect to some social reward, and who compare to someone in the same in-group who is not deprived, will experience feelings of relative deprivation and, presumably, dissatisfaction. However, the meaning of comparisons with those in an out-group are not as clear. Those who are deprived and who compare to an out-group person will, Davis says, experience an "attitude" of "relative subordination." Those who are not deprived and compare to an out-group person who is deprived, will experience an "attitude" of "relative superiority" (2, p. 283). But how will the comparer *react* to his position of, say, relative subordination compared to the out-group person? Will he be satisfied? Will he maintain a feeling of high self-esteem? Or will he be dissatisfied, angry, or ashamed?

We obviously cannot answer these questions until we know what the "out-group" is, what characteristics it has, and what relevance these characteristics are seen by the comparers as having for deprivation with regard to some social reward. Without knowing these things, we cannot predict the subjective meaning of the comparisons made with this "out-group."

This point is of very general significance. It applies not only to comparisons to true out-groups —in the sense of persons who are widely and generally different from the comparer. It applies also to the large number of comparisons to persons who are similar to the comparer in some ways but different in others. Take the case of wage comparisons. A man may compare to someone who has generally equal education, but the comparison person may have three years of college instead of four, or a year of post-graduate work, or have gone to an Ivy League College instead of a state university, or majored in a different subject. Or, given complete identity of education, the comparison person may differ in any one of a number of other characteristics—age, family background, seniority, etc.—which are rel-

evant to the wage comparison. Indeed, when we consider specific comparisons, the lines between in-groups and out-groups blur. The question of how the individual will react to various comparisons where the comparison person differs from himself in ways *other* than on the dimension being judged becomes, therefore, very important.

Festinger shows an awareness of the importance of the relative position of comparer and comparison person on a *variety* of dimensions when he states the hypothesis, "If persons who are very divergent from one's own opinion or ability are perceived as different from oneself on *attributes consistent with the divergence,* the tendency to narrow the range of comparability becomes stronger" (3, p. 180). But, rather than considering additional attributes only in their possible role of limiting the range of comparisons, we may consider comparison on such secondary attributes as a fundamental part of the comparison process.

It is possible to think of any given social comparison as not one, but two or more, simultaneous comparisons. On the one hand individuals compare themselves on a primary dimension being judged (e.g., earnings). But comparisons on this primary dimension cannot be made in a cognitive vacuum. Such comparisons become meaningful to the individual only when he also compares himself to others on secondary dimensions which are believed to be bases of standing on the primary dimension (e.g., skill, seniority, education—where pay is the primary dimension) or which are otherwise relevant to standing on the primary dimension (e.g., for pay, how interesting various jobs are).

Continuing in our use of the example of wage comparisons,[2] the individual, in effect, makes a cognitive relation of the following sort:

$$\frac{\text{my earnings}}{\text{his (their) earnings}} \quad \frac{\text{compared}}{\text{to}} \quad \frac{\text{my position on dimensions related to earnings}}{\text{his (their) position on dimensions related to earnings}}$$

We may define a *perceived consonant comparison* as one in which the comparer perceives one side of this relation (i.e., the ratio of one's own earnings to another's earnings) as congruent with, or appropriate to, the other side of the relation (i.e., the ratio of one's own position on related dimensions to another's position on re-

---

[2] The present discussion is phrased in terms of wage comparisons in order to give substantive flavor to abstract ideas and because the research to be described has been concerned with wage comparisons. However, the general conception is thought to hold true for other types of social comparisons as well, especially those of other social rewards—e.g., prestige, popularity, rank, affection, and material goods.

lated dimensions). Similarly, a *perceived dissonant comparison* is defined as one in which the comparer perceives the ratio on one side of the relation as incongruent with, or inappropriate to, the ratio on the other side of the relation.[3]

It is also possible to distinguish among comparisons according to the degree of *objective* dissonance present. Some comparisons—e.g., to men of the same education and age as the comparer who are earning more than he—provide more objective bases for the comparer to perceive dissonance in than do other comparisons—e.g., to older men with more schooling who are earning more than he. We define *objectively consonant comparisons* as those in which the ratio of the comparer's position on dimensions relevant to pay to another's position on these relevant dimensions is culturally considered congruent with, or appropriate to, the ratio of their earnings. *Objectively dissonant comparisons* are, similarly, defined as those in which the ratio of the two persons' positions on dimensions relevant to pay is culturally considered incongruent with, or inappropriate to, the ratio of their earnings.[4]

From the preceding general description of the

comparison process, it is apparent that the following kinds of pay comparisons (as shown in Figure 1) are likely to be perceived as *dissonant in favor of the comparison person:*

1. Comparison to someone earning *more*—who is generally *similar* to the comparer on attributes related to earnings (cell *F*).
2. Comparison to someone earning *more*—who is generally *inferior* to the comparer on attributes related to pay (cell *I*).
3. Comparison to someone earning the *same*—who is generally *inferior* on attributes related to pay (cell *H*).

The following types of comparisons (again shown in Figure 1) are likely to be perceived as *dissonant in favor of the comparer:*

1. Comparisons to those earning *less*—who are generally *superior* to the comparer on attributes related to earnings (cell *A*).
2. Comparisons to those earning *less*—who are generally *similar* to the comparer on attributes related to earnings (cell *D*).
3. Comparisons to those earning the *same*—who are generally *superior* to the comparer on attributes related to earnings (cell *B*).

Cell *E* of Figure 1 shows the type of comparison which is most likely to be perceived as consonant—i.e., comparisons to those who earn the *same* as oneself and who are also closely *similar* on attributes relevant to earnings. It would be

[3] This definition appears closely similar to Festinger's definition of dissonance, although the present formulation was conceived without intentional linkage to Festinger's work. Festinger states, "Two cognitive elements are in a dissonant relation if, considering these two alone, the obverse of one follows from the other" (4, pp. 260–261).

[4] It is sometimes useful to separate presently consonant comparisons into those which will remain consonant over time and those which are *potentially* dissonant. This subject is discussed in detail elsewhere (7).

FIGURE 1. Types of wage comparisons.

OVERALL POSITION OF COMPARISON PERSON ON ATTRIBUTES RELEVANT TO EARNINGS	COMPARISON PERSON		
	EARNS LESS	EARNS SAME	EARNS MORE
SUPERIOR	DISSONANT—IN FAVOR OF COMPARER *A*	DISSONANT—IN FAVOR OF COMPARER *B*	1. CONSONANT 2. DISSONANT—IN FAVOR OF COMPARISON PERSON 3. DISSONANT—IN FAVOR OF COMPARER *C*
SIMILAR	DISSONANT—IN FAVOR OF COMPARER *D*	CONSONANT *E*	DISSONANT—IN FAVOR OF COMPARISON PERSON *F*
INFERIOR	1. CONSONANT 2. DISSONANT—IN FAVOR OF COMPARISON PERSON 3. DISSONANT—IN FAVOR OF COMPARER *G*	DISSONANT—IN FAVOR OF COMPARISON PERSON *H*	DISSONANT—IN FAVOR OF COMPARISON PERSON *I*

expected that perfect consonance in comparisons —either as objectively determined by the observer or as perceived by the comparer—is rare. However, it is probable that many comparisons which are close to perfect consonance may—for all practical purposes—be treated as consonant.

Perhaps the most interesting cells in Figure 1 are cells *C* and *G*. Cell *C,* for example, shows the possible types of comparisons which may occur when the comparison person earns more than the comparer and is also generally superior to the comparer on attributes relevant to earnings. Such comparisons may be consonant, dissonant in favor of the comparison person, or dissonant in favor of the comparer. Which it is depends on *how much more* the comparison person earns in relation to *how much superior* he is considered.

Some concrete comparisons which fit in cell *C,* drawn from interviews with oil workers, should make this point clearer.

Comparison type *C*1 (consonant) is illustrated by the remarks of a plant protection worker who compared his earnings to that of a certified accountant who earns more than himself. The comparer said he was "satisfied" with the way their earnings compared, explaining, "He has more education; he is a college graduate; he should be earning more."

Comparison type *C*2 (dissonant in favor of comparison person) is illustrated by the case of an assistant mechanic who chose "the fellow I work with"—a full mechanic—with whom to compare his earnings. The assistant said he was "not too satisfied" with the way their earnings compared, explaining, "We do the same work and there's three pay rates difference; I didn't have my papers when he did; he's quite a bit older than I am. He had 'em for quite a few years." While this man is willing to acknowledge the other to be superior to him in some ways, he evidently doesn't think the amount of difference justifies three rates of difference in pay.

Comparison type *C*3 (dissonant in favor of comparer) is illustrated by the case of a welder who chooses for comparison his brother-in-law who is a chemist and who earns more than he. The welder checks the most extreme category of satisfaction with the comparison ("very satisfied") and comments, "Well, he has gone to the University for five years and the difference in our wages is very small." In a similar case, a production worker who compared to a teacher who earned more than he, commented, "Considering the difference in our educations, I figure I'm doing better than he is."

These cases illustrate vividly why it is necessary to go beyond a mere identification of the reference groups or persons who are pertinent to given individuals. Such an approach tends to assume that once the comparison persons are identified, it is immediately obvious whether the comparison is favorable to the comparer (e.g., by whether he earns more or less). The present analysis indicates that identifying relevant comparison persons is only one part of the job of understanding the comparisons involved.

If the picture of the comparison process outlined above is adequate, then we should be able to predict individuals' satisfaction with specific wage comparisons when we have sufficient objective information about how the comparer and comparison person stand on dimensions culturally considered relevant to pay, as well as about the difference in their earnings.

Specifically, we would expect the following hypothesis to be supported:

Hypothesis 1. Satisfaction with wage comparisons will be a function not of objective difference in earnings, in itself, but of the objective dissonance of the comparison as a whole.

We would expect also, if our picture of the comparison process is meaningful, that individuals will consciously base their feelings of satisfaction or dissatisfaction with wage comparisons not on the actual money difference, nor on their need for money, nor on why they would like to have the money, but on the appropriateness of the wage difference in view of other relevant differences between themselves and the comparison persons.

We may state this expectation more formally, as follows:

Hypothesis 2. Men who are satisfied with specific wage comparisons will explain their satisfaction in terms of a consonance between relative wage standing and relative standing on attributes related to pay; men who are dissatisfied with specific wage comparisons will explain their dissatisfaction in terms of a dissonance between relative wage standing and standing on attributes relevant to pay.

The choice of comparisons

What determines which specific comparisons, from among many possible alternatives, will be chosen? Davis's crucial assumption, in this regard, is that "Within the population comparisons are random" (2, p. 282). Though he admits that this assumption may appear dubious, he sees "no reason to introduce a more complicated one." The rest of Davis's further theoretical derivations rest on this fundamental assumption.

It seems likely that some of the variance in the choice of comparisons can be accounted for on the basis of Davis's assumption of randomness. However, the present theoretical approach to comparisons would emphasize also that some individuals have stronger *motivation* than do others to choose dissonant rather than consonant comparisons.

One determinant of the individual's motivation

to choose dissonant or consonant comparisons was expected to be whether or not he accepts *personal responsibility* for his present position. If the individual sees himself as responsible for his present job position, a dissonant wage comparison will make him feel ashamed. Compared to the other person, he is a failure. For men who accept personal responsibility for their fate, there should, therefore, be strong pressures to avoid such dissonant comparisons.

This picture of motivations which impel the individual to choose consonant comparisons has parallels to Festinger's discussion of the forces which determine the choice of comparisons. Festinger sees the motivational push behind comparisons as the drive to evaluate oneself (one's opinions or abilities). However, the individual wants this evaluation to be favorable, to show him as being as good as or a little better than others like himself. Festinger states:

> The action to reduce the discrepancy which exists is, in the case of opinions, a relatively uncomplicated pressure towards uniformity. When and if uniformity of opinion is achieved there is a state of social quiescence. In the case of abilities, however, the action to reduce discrepancies interacts with the unidirectional push to do better and better. The resolution of these two pressures, which act simultaneously, is a state of affairs where all the members are relatively close together with respect to some specific ability, but not completely uniform. The pressures cease acting on a person if he is just slightly better than the others (3, p. 172).

In the terminology used in this paper, the individual is described as motivated to choose comparisons which are at least consonant.

However, according to the present theory, the comparer may, in some cases, be motivated to make comparisons which are dissonant in favor of the other person. For the man who rejects personal responsibility—who blames his boss, the union, society, etc.—for the existence of the dissonance, dissonant comparisons will usually evoke righteous indignation, instead of feelings of shame. Such a comparer can also use dissonant comparisons to justify protests over his present status and to legitimate (to himself as well as to others) a claim that he deserves a higher status.

For the case of wage comparisons, the following hypothesis concerning personal responsibility is advanced:

Hypothesis 3. Men who see the responsibility for their occupational and wage position as not being their own will be more likely than others to choose dissonant wage comparisons.

If hypothesis 3 is correct, we would expect

as a corollary that "non-responsible" men will, more often than "responsible" men, be dissatisfied with wage comparisons.

It may be noted that the question of the acceptance or non-acceptance of personal responsibility, which is so relevant to wage comparisons, probably has little relevance for the types of comparisons—opinions and abilities—discussed by Festinger. In most instances the individual would be hard put to blame his opinions or his abilities on someone else. But comparisons such as those concerning prestige, material goods and affection relate to things which are determined to some extent by other people. If we imagine a continuum which shows the relevance of personal responsibility to comparisons, then the types of comparisons which Festinger discusses would cover only one part of the continuum.

Another difference between Festinger's theory of comparison processes and the present theoretical approach may be noted. Festinger stresses the importance to the comparer of narrowing the range of comparisons to those like himself. Where the comparer's main motivation is evaluation of the self *per se* (as perhaps in comparisons of some opinions and abilities), such pressures to narrow the range of comparisons may be very strong. It may also be that, where it is difficult to compare some attribute with accuracy (e.g., again, in the case of some opinions and abilities), then a narrowing of the range of comparisons will be encouraged. However, in the case of other comparisons, such as wage comparisons, we would not expect such pressures to narrow the range of comparability to be strong. For if the comparer is actually motivated to create dissonance, such dissonance can sometimes best be established in comparisons to those who are unlike the comparer on the attribute being judged. For example, the most common and direct way to make a dissonant wage comparison is to compare to someone whose earnings are *much higher* than one's own but, who is, nevertheless, similar to oneself in some relevant ways.

Finally, the present theoretical approach has some interesting implications for the general theory of dissonance which Festinger has proposed (4). Festinger postulates that when dissonance occurs, forces to reduce this dissonance will arise. Festinger also discusses factors which create resistance to the reduction of dissonance. However, he seems to hold that, whatever the resistance to its reduction, the dissonance itself is anxiety producing. The present conception of dissonance with regard to comparisons of social rewards assumes, however, that under certain conditions even great dissonance may produce little anxiety and that the dissonance itself may serve the purpose of the comparer.

RESEARCH SETTING AND OPERATIONS

Having outlined a conceptual framework for understanding comparisons and having stated three hypotheses, we turn now to the presentation of some empirical data which bear on these ideas.

The site

The research reported here was conducted at an oil refinery located in a small Canadian city of approximately 40,000 population. Several other oil and chemical plants are located in this area. There are about 1500 non-supervisory employees working at the refinery. All employees, except a few office workers, are male and only men were interviewed. Almost all of the men are married and the great majority have children.

The largest group (34 per cent) work at traditional trades—such as pipe-fitter, mason, machinist—in the task of maintaining refinery equipment. Another large group of men (31 per cent) control and regulate the actual production of oil, jobs which require the watching and adjusting of control dials, as well as related tasks. Smaller groups of men work at assembly-line jobs, mainly at packaging and manufacturing oil drums (15 per cent), at the testing laboratory (6 per cent), at common labor and janitorial work (8 per cent), and at other miscellaneous jobs, such as driving trucks (6 per cent).

TABLE 1 *Satisfaction with Wage Comparisons to Those Earning More, in Relation to Occupational Level of Comparison Person**

OCCUPATIONAL LEVEL OF UPWARD COMPARISON PERSON	MEAN SATIS-FACTION WITH COMPARISON†	NUMBER OF COMPARERS‡
Professional	2.23	66
Clerical or sales	2.33	24
Proprietor of own business; manager	2.42	64
Blue-collar: foreman	2.59	76
Blue-collar: skilled or semi-skilled	2.63	252
All other (including farm and no mention)	2.43	37
Total	2.52	519

* Low scores indicate greater satisfaction with comparisons.
† Solid line joining two mean scores indicates that the difference is significant at the .01 level (1-tailed *t* test). Broken line joining two mean scores indicates that the difference is significant at the .10 level (1-tailed *t* test). ‡ For each comparer, a maximum of one comparison in a single row is included in the table, to avoid giving any comparer greater weight than any other. Where a comparer chose two upward comparison persons of the same occupational level, the first comparison was taken.

Sample

A one-third sample of male non-supervisory employees was interviewed. This sample was stratified by occupational groups and by pay level. Excluding those who could not be reached for interviewing, the number of men included in the final sample was 489, or 90.5 per cent of the original sample drawn.

Measures

During the interview, the respondent was told: "Now I'd like to ask you a few questions about how your earnings compare with the wages of other people you know about. Who would be someone either here at 'Atlas' or outside the refinery whose yearly earnings are *different* from yours?"[5] After one comparison person was named and identified as to kind of work, the respondent was asked: "Who would be someone else whose yearly earnings are different from yours?" For each of the two comparison persons, the following information is available:

Direction of comparison. The respondent was asked: "Is he earning more or less than you are right now?"

Occupational level of comparison person. Responses concerning the type of work done by the comparison persons, as described by the respondent, were coded into these ten occupational categories: (*a*) Professionals; (*b*) Proprietors and Managers; (*c*) Clerical or Sales; (*d*) Blue-collar, foreman; (*e*) Blue-collar, skilled and semi-skilled, non-supervisory; (*f*) Blue-collar, unskilled; (*g*) Blue-collar, unspecified; (*h*) Farm Owners and Farm Workers; (*i*) Unemployed; (*j*) Other.

It seems reasonable to assume that those who are on a different occupational level from our respondents will differ from the respondents in a number of ways which are culturally considered relevant to pay. These differences include educational level, social class, style of life, and the kinds of skills involved in work. Comparison persons who are professional men are most likely to be superior to our blue-collar respondents in all of these ways. Men in white-collar occupations (clerical and sales) and men who are proprietors or managers of businesses are also likely to have backgrounds different from those of our respondents, though not so much superior as that of professional persons.

Respondent's satisfaction with the way earnings now compare. After a respondent had indicated

[5] This rather indirect way of obtaining wage comparisons was adopted after more direct questions caused resentment and defensiveness among some respondents during exploratory interviews. Since time pressure permitted only two comparisons to be obtained and probed, comparisons only to those with *different* earnings were asked for. This restriction was intended to maximize the chances for dissonant comparisons to be chosen.

whether he or the comparison person was earning more, he was asked, "Which of these statements best shows how you feel about the way your earnings now compare to his earnings?" He was then handed a card which listed five alternatives, ranging from "very satisfied" to "not at all satisfied."

Reasons for satisfaction or dissatisfaction with comparison. After the respondent indicated his degree of satisfaction with the way earnings compare, he was asked, "Could you tell me why you feel this way?" The great majority of responses to this question were in terms of comparison on dimensions other than pay. These responses were coded in terms of the type of dimension compared on and the placement the respondent gave himself in relation to the comparison person on this non-pay dimension (see Table 2).

Other data available on each respondent include:

Absolute pay rate. These were available from company records.

Relative pay position. Respondents reported their age, education, length of service at the refinery, and the occupations of their brothers and brothers-in-law. On each of these criteria, every respondent was coded as below the median, at the median, or above the median on pay for men like himself. For example, the distribution on pay for men in each age category was calculated so that every man in the category was assigned a score showing his relative position on pay for men of his age. In

the same manner, each man was given a score showing his pay position relative to men of his educational category, relative to men of his seniority category, and relative to men of his family. In addition to the scores showing each man's relative pay position on each of these four dimensions, an overall index of relative pay position was constructed by adding each man's score (corresponding to below, at, or above the median) on all four dimensions.

Perception of personal responsibility for wage position. This is indicated by answers to two questions asked in the interview. (*a*) "For men who grew up when you did, how much would you say a man's chances for getting ahead in life depended on himself and how much on things beyond his control?" (Five alternatives were given on a printed card, ranging from "Almost entirely on the man himself" to "Not at all on the man himself.") (*b*) "Thinking about Atlas, how much would you say advancement usually depends on how well a man can do a job and how much on other things?" (Five alternatives were given on a printed card, ranging from "Almost entirely on how well a man can do a job" to "Not at all on how well a man can do a job.") These questions were intended to tap two separate, though related, components of personal responsibility in the life history of the individual. When numbers from one

SOCIAL REWARDS

233

TABLE 2 *Reasons Given by Respondents for Feeling Satisfied or Dissatisfied with Specific Comparisons to Persons Who Earn More** (Read table vertically)

REASONS GIVEN FOR FEELING OF SATISFACTION OR DISSATISFACTION	DEGREE OF SATISFACTION WITH COMPARISON		
	Satisfied %	Neither Satisfied nor Dissatisfied %	Dissatisfied %
Respondent has compensating advantages	44.6	19.5	0.0
Financial	16.1	5.4	0.0
Non-financial	28.5	14.1	0.0
Comparison person is superior	55.8	34.8	17.8
In what his job requires (education, skill, etc.)	44.6	22.8	13.7
In seniority, experience, age	6.8	8.7	1.4
In personal qualities	4.4	3.3	2.7
Comparison person's job is different unspecified	8.0	16.3	2.7
Respondent is equal or superior	1.2	9.8	75.4
In what his job requires (education, skill, etc.)	0.8	8.7	64.4
In seniority, experience, age	0.4	1.1	11.0
Respondent is not interested in comparing earnings	5.6	18.5	0.0
Respondent earns enough for his needs	2.8	4.4	0.0
Respondent wants more money, higher living standard	0.0	0.0	8.2
Other, or vague	3.6	10.9	16.4
Number of comparers	(249)	(92)	(73)

* The percentage of reasons in each column add up to more than 100, since a maximum of two reasons was coded for each respondent. The reasons given by each man for his feelings about a maximum of one comparison are included in any single column.

to five are assigned to alternative answers to each of these questions, there is a moderate positive correlation between acceptance of responsibility as measured by one question and as measured by the other ($r = +.29$). Moreover, each question, taken separately, was found to have a similar relation to the direction of comparisons chosen and to satisfaction with such comparisons. An index of acceptance of personal responsibility was constructed simply by adding each respondent's scores on the two questions.

Consonance and dissonance

With the present data we can distinguish well only a limited number of concrete types of consonance and dissonance from among the many possible types shown in Figure 1. Comparisons to those earning the same as the comparer (cells B, E, and H of Figure 1) are not available, since we asked men to choose persons whose earnings are different from their own.

The data available also make it difficult to classify various comparisons to those earning less than the comparer (cells A, D, and G) as more or less dissonant. This is because comparison persons who earn less than our respondents are almost all on the same general occupational level (blue-collar, non-supervisory) and it is not possible to tell whether these comparison persons are objectively superior, similar, or inferior on attributes relevant to earnings.

However, when we examine comparisons to those who earn *more* than the comparer, it is possible to make some rough distinctions between those comparisons which are objectively consonant and those which are objectively dissonant in favor of the comparison person. Comparisons to those who earn more but are on a higher occupational level fall in cell C and may, in general, be considered as more objectively consonant than comparisons to those on the same occupational level who earn more (cell F).[6] This is because higher earnings for persons on a higher occupational level (with accompanying higher social status, higher education, etc.) are, in general, culturally defined as appropriate, while differences in earnings for men on the same occupational level are not as often culturally defined as appropriate.

RESULTS

Objective dissonance and satisfaction

Our first hypothesis is that satisfaction with earnings will be a function not of the difference in

[6] The number of comparisons to persons who earn more but who are on a lower occupational level is too small to be included in the analysis.

earnings, as such, but of the difference in earnings in relation to the objective status differences between comparer and comparison person—i.e., of the objective dissonance of the comparison. A specific prediction based on this hypothesis was that men who choose "upward" wage comparison persons on the same occupational level as themselves (Cell F of Figure 1) will more often be dissatisfied with such comparisons than will men who choose upward comparison persons of a higher occupational level (Cell C of Figure 1). This prediction ignores the absolute amount of difference in earnings among men on various occupational levels. However, since the gap in earnings is likely to be larger between occupational levels than within them, this factor should work against our hypothesis, rather than for it.

Table 1 presents the data on satisfaction with upward comparisons,[7] separately for different occupational levels of the person with whom comparison is made. Those who choose comparison persons who earn more but who are on a higher occupational level are more satisfied with the comparisons than are men who choose comparison persons who earn more but are on their own occupational level. This difference is most marked when we compare satisfaction with comparison persons who are professionals to satisfaction with comparison persons who are blue-collar non-supervisory personnel like our respondents (difference between means significant at beyond .01 level; one-tailed t test). However, men are also more satisfied with comparisons to "clerical-sales" or "proprietory-managerial" persons who earn more than themselves than they are with comparisons to blue-collar workers who earn more than they do (difference between means significant at .10 level in both cases). These data consistently support hypothesis 1.

Perceived consonance and dissonance

We have predicted not only that *objective* dissonance will lead to feelings of dissatisfaction with comparisons, but that feelings of satisfaction or dissatisfaction will be *subjectively* based on perceptions of consonance or dissonance (hypothesis 2). Table 2 shows the reasons given by respondents for feelings of satisfaction or dissatisfaction with comparisons to those who earn more than themselves.

[7] The greater the satisfaction a man expressed with the specific comparisons he chose, the more content he was with his wages. A questionnaire item asked respondents, in a context other than that of comparisons, "How well do you feel you've done up to now as far as earnings go?" At one extreme, among those who said they were "very satisfied" with both wage comparisons chosen, 90.2 per cent said they felt they had, in general, done "very well" or "quite well" with respect to their earnings. At the other extreme, among men who said they were "not too satisfied" or "not at all satisfied" with both specific wage comparisons, only 16.0 per cent said they had, in general, done "very well" or "quite well."

Reasons for feeling satisfied

Of those who said they are satisfied with comparisons to men who earn more, over half (56 per cent) mentioned ways in which comparison persons are superior to themselves, thus justifying the difference in wages. More education, more seniority, being older, having more skills, having more responsibility, and having worked harder for advancement are among the superior attributes of the comparison person named.

A large proportion (about 45 per cent) of those who expressed satisfaction with upward comparisons explained their feelings by pointing to compensating advantages which they enjoy. Such items as having a better benefit program at Atlas, working more steadily, liking their own work better, and having a cleaner job are typical of the compensating advantages mentioned.

About 8 per cent of those satisfied emphasized the difference in jobs per se, without specifying which man deserves more pay. These men mentioned the fact of working for different companies, different departments, or different industries, implying that these essential differences explain the difference in wages. About 6 per cent of those satisfied said they were not interested in comparing wages; about 1 per cent mentioned ways in which they are equal or superior to the men who earn more; and about 4 per cent gave other reasons.

These data show that an overwhelming majority of men explain their satisfaction with upward comparisons in terms of differences beween themselves and the comparison person on dimensions related directly or indirectly to pay. These differences are usually either some superiority of the comparison person or some compensating advantage enjoyed by the respondent. In either case, what these men seem to be saying, in effect, is: "I am satisfied to be earning less, because there is some other difference between us which makes the wage difference okay." Or, in our theoretical terms, "I am satisfied because the difference in wages is consonant with other differences between us."

It is noteworthy that so few respondents (about 3 per cent) answered merely in terms of the wage difference—saying they earned enough for their needs—without relating the wage difference to some other relevant differences between the individuals.

Reason for dissatisfaction

Among those who are dissatisfied with earning less than comparison persons, a large majority (about 75 per cent) justify their feeling in terms of their own equality or superiority in ways directly relevant to pay. Mention of one's own high level of education, skill, responsibility, seniority, and experience and/or the comparison person's low standing in these respects are typical of the kinds of reasons included in this category.

Again, very few men explained their dissatis-faction merely in terms of the money difference or in the closely related terms of their wish for more material things. Only 8 per cent mentioned these reasons and, among these men, many gave additional answers in terms of the relative standing of comparer and comparison person on attributes other than earnings.

About 18 per cent of those dissatisfied also mention some *superiority* of the comparison person—most often in an attempt to give both sides of the issue. Three per cent mention the differences in occupation, industry, etc.

There are also a relatively large number of answers (about 16 per cent) by dissatisfied men which do not fit in the categories mentioned. Detailed examination of these uncategorized answers reveals that many are vague and non-specific, sometimes a mere restatement of dissatisfaction.

The data for dissatisfied men thus also support hypothesis 2. The great majority of men explain their feeling of dissatisfaction in terms of dissonance between differences in pay and differences on attributes related to pay.

In general, Table 2 provides striking empirical confirmation of a basic tenet of the conceptual scheme presented—that comparisons on some primary dimension (e.g., pay) are almost always made in the context of simultaneous comparisons on other culturally relevant dimensions.

Reasons for feeling "neutral" about comparison

The reasons given by those who say they are "neither satisfied nor dissatisfied" with upward comparisons indicate that their "neutrality" of feeling is based on cross-pressures exerted by perceptions of consonance and perceptions of dissonance. About one-third of these men mention some way in which the *comparison person* is superior, but about 10 per cent mention some way in which they themselves are equal or superior.

The most striking difference shown by this group is the relatively large proportion (about 19 per cent) who say they are not interested in comparing earnings. There appears to be a tendency in this group to avoid thinking about comparisons and to shut off their feelings about comparisons ("neither satisfied nor dissatisfied") when they are forced to compare.

Responsibility and dissonance

Our third hypothesis is that men who accept personal responsibility for their occupational fate will be more likely than others to choose consonant comparisons. One specific expectation derived from this hypothesis was that, among men who choose comparison persons who earn more than themselves, those who accept personal responsibility will be more likely than others to choose persons on a higher occupational level (Cell *C*).

In general, the data tend to support this prediction. But the differences among those who accept varying degrees of responsibility are small and statistically non-significant. However, when we consider separately those men who differ in their position on the Relative Pay Index, a more complete picture emerges. Men who stand medium or high on the Relative Pay Index tend to choose a high proportion of consonant comparisons regardless of whether or not they accept responsibility for their present position. But among men whose pay is low compared to others like themselves (low on Relative Pay Index), acceptance or rejection of personal responsibility for this poor position makes a difference in the choice of consonant comparisons. Table 3 shows this result. Especially noteworthy in this table is the fact that, among those who are relatively low on pay and accept responsibility, 19.2 per cent choose

TABLE 3   Occupational Level of "Upward" Comparison Persons Chosen by Men in Low Relative Pay Position, in Relation to Whether Comparer Accepts Personal Responsibility for His Position,†*

OCCUPATIONAL LEVEL OF UPWARD COMPARISON PERSON	RESPONSIBILITY ACCEPTED BY COMPARER		
	Little %	Moderate %	Great %
Professional	4.8	8.8	19.2
Clerical-sales	1.6	2.9	0.0
Manager-proprietor	16.1	4.4	11.5
Blue-collar, foreman	9.7	16.2	13.5
Blue-collar, skilled, semi-skilled	67.7	57.4	40.4
Other‡	0.0	10.3	15.4
Total	100.0	100.0	100.0
N of comparers	62	68	52

* For each respondent, only the first upward comparison chosen is included in this table. † Solid line joining two percentages indicates difference is significant at the .01 level (1-tailed tests except "Other" category, where 2-tailed test was used, since difference was not specifically predicted). Dashed line indicates difference is significant at .05 level (1-tailed test). ‡ Includes primarily comparison persons in farm occupations and in occupations which could not be sufficiently identified. Also included in "Other" are unskilled or unemployed.

TABLE 4   Mean Scores of Present Satisfaction* with Upward Comparisons, in Relation to Comparer's Relative Pay Position and Acceptance of Responsibility†,‡ (Number of comparers in parentheses)

RELATIVE PAY POSITION	ACCEPTANCE OF RESPONSIBILITY			
	Little	Moderate	Great	Total
Low	3.02 (64)	2.60 (68)	2.38 (52)	2.68 (184)
Medium	2.43 (41)	2.20 (27)	2.21 (17)	2.31 (85)
High	2.28 (44)	2.12 (33)	2.22 (37)	2.21 (114)
Total	2.64 (149)	2.39 (128)	2.30 (106)	2.46 (383)

* Lower score indicates greater satisfaction.   † Three men who did not answer both questions comprising the acceptance of responsibility index are not included in this table.   ‡ Solid line joining two mean scores indicates that the difference is significant at the .01 level or beyond (1-tailed *t* test). Dashed line joining two mean scores indicates significant difference at the .05 level or beyond (1-tailed *t* test).

upward comparison persons who are professionals (consonant comparisons) while among those who stand relatively low but reject responsibility, only 4.8 per cent choose professionals (*p* of difference < .01; one-tailed test). And while those who accept great personal responsibility choose only 40.4 per cent of upward comparisons on their own occupational level, those who accept little personal responsibility choose 67.7 per cent upward comparisons on their own occupational level (*p* of difference < .01; two-tailed test).

These data, while presenting some evidence that "non-responsible" men more often choose consonant comparisons, undoubtedly underestimate the percentage of consonant comparisons chosen by all groups, since only one specific type of consonance is distinguished. It seems probable that the differences between the comparisons chosen by the "responsible" and "non-responsible" groups would be greater if our measures of consonance and dissonance were more refined.

The data concerning the choice of consonant and dissonant comparisons are exactly paralleled by the results concerning satisfaction with comparisons. Table 4 shows that the combination of low relative pay position and rejection of personal responsibility brings a sharp decrease in satisfaction with upward comparisons. Among those whose relative pay position is low, men who reject personal responsibility are significantly more likely than those who accept moderate or great responsibility to be dissatisfied with comparisons

($p < .01$ for each difference; one-tailed t tests). Similarly, among those who reject responsibility, men who stand relatively low on pay are significantly more likely than those whose position is medium or high to be dissatisfied ($p < .01$ for each difference; one-tailed t tests). In other words, the same persons who were most likely to choose objectively dissonant comparisons were also most likely to be subjectively dissatisfied with comparisons. This parallel, while not surprising, gives a reassuring consistency to the data.

These results concerning the effect of feelings about personal responsibility on the choice of and satisfaction with comparisons generally support hypothesis 3. However, the data qualify and broaden the hypothesis. They indicate that the *combination* of an unfavorable position with regard to some social reward and rejection of personal responsibility for one's fate with regard to this reward will lead to the choice of dissonant comparisons. These data are also consistent with our assumption that an important motivation behind the choice of dissonant comparisons is the wish to protest one's present status and to help legitimate a claim for higher status. Men whose present objective wage position is low but who reject responsibility for this low position would be especially likely to have these motives.

The general conclusion that comparisons are often motivated is supported by other data from the present study concerning the effect of mobility chances on the choice of comparisons. These data, presented elsewhere (7), show that men whose upward mobility chances are relatively poor and uncertain are more likely to choose dissonant comparisons than are men whose upward mobility chances are assured. Again, however, the factor of personal responsibility is important, since men with uncertain mobility chances were most likely to choose dissonant comparisons when they reject responsibility for their occupational position.

SUMMARY

This paper has presented a conceptual framework for categorizing comparisons in terms of consonance and dissonance. A number of specific empirical types of consonant and dissonant wage comparisons were indicated. One advantage of this conceptual approach over previous formulations, it was argued, is to enable us better to predict the affective reaction (satisfaction-dissatisfaction) to specific kinds of comparisons.

It was hypothesized that individuals' satisfaction with wage comparisons will be a function of the objective and perceived dissonance of the comparisons, as defined, rather than of the difference in earnings alone. Data relevant to these predictions from a study of wage comparisons among workers at an oil refinery were presented. These data generally support the hypothesis that satisfaction with wage comparisons is based on the consonance or dissonance of the total comparison rather than on the wage difference alone.

Concerning the choice of comparisons, it was postulated that such choices are not, as Davis has assumed, wholly random, but are often motivated. One possible motive is the wish to protest one's present status and to claim a higher status. It was hypothesized that those who reject personal responsibility for their job position will be more likely to have such a motive and would be more likely, therefore, to choose dissonant wage comparisons. The data support this prediction for men whose wage position, relative to those like themselves, is low. These data also give support to the general proposition that the individual may tolerate and even seek dissonance in his situation if he rejects personal responsibility for the dissonance.

REFERENCES

1. CHAPMAN, D. W., and J. VOLKMANN, "A Social Determinant of the Level of Aspiration," *Journal of Abnormal and Social Psychology,* 1939, **34,** 225–238.

2. DAVIS, J. A., "A Formal Interpretation of the Theory of Relative Deprivation," *Sociometry,* 1959, **22,** 280–296.

3. FESTINGER, L., "A Theory of Social Comparison Processes," *Human Relations,* 1954, **7,** 117–140.

4. FESTINGER, L., *A Theory of Cognitive Dissonance,* Evanston, Illinois: Row, Peterson and Co., 1957.

5. HYMAN, H., "The Psychology of Status," *Archives of Psychology,* 1942, **38,** 15.

6. McINTOSH, A., "Differential Effect of the Status of the Competing Group on Levels of Aspiration," *American Journal of Psychology,* 1942, **55,** 546–554.

7. PATCHEN, M., "The Choice of Wage Comparisons," Ph.D. dissertation, University of Michigan, 1959.

8. PATCHEN, M., "The Effect of Reference Group Standards on Job Satisfactions," *Human Relations,* 1958, **11,** 303–314.

9. STOUFFER, S. A., and others, *The American Soldier,* Vols. I and II of *Studies in Social Psychology in World War II,* Princeton, New Jersey: Princeton University Press, 1949–50.

SOCIAL INFLUENCES ON INDIVIDUAL JUDGMENT✻

In the selection below Deutsch and Gerard offer a two-process theory of social influence and provide some evidence in its support. They note that earlier studies failed to distinguish between two kinds of social influence. The first, *informational* social influence, occurs when a subject is led to accept information obtained from another person as evidence about reality. The second, *normative* social influence, occurs when a subject accepts influence from another person because of his motivation to conform to that person's expectations.

Their experiment is designed to allow these two types of influence to operate separately. Of particular interest is the finding that normative social influences can operate to *increase* the independence of individual judgment. Earlier work had cast the social influence variable largely in the role of destroying personal integrity. This selection is an excellent example of how refinement of a particular concept can lead to new and crucial observations which result in a considerable advance in the understanding of a phenomenon.

29.

A Study of Normative and Informational Social Influences upon Individual Judgment

MORTON DEUTSCH
COLUMBIA UNIVERSITY

HAROLD B. GERARD[1]
UNIVERSITY OF CALIFORNIA, RIVERSIDE

By now, many experimental studies (e.g., 1, 3, 6) have demonstrated that individual psychological processes are subject to social influences. Most investigators, however, have not distinguished among different kinds of social influences; rather, they have carelessly used the term "group" influence to characterize the impact of many different kinds of social factors. In fact, a review of the major experiments in this area—e.g., those by Sherif (6), Asch (1), Bovard (3)—would indicate that the subjects (Ss) in these experiments as they made their judgments were *not* functioning as *members* of a group in any simple or obvious manner. The S, in the usual experiment in this area, made perceptual judgments in the physical presence of others after hearing their judgments. Typically, the S was *not* given experimental instructions which made him feel that he was a member of a group faced with a common task requiring cooperative effort for its most effective solution. If "group" influences were at work in the foregoing experiments, they were subtly and indirectly created rather than purposefully created by the experimenter.

HYPOTHESES

The purpose of this paper is to consider two types of social influence, "normative" and "informational," which we believe were operative in the experiments mentioned above, and to report the results of an experiment bearing upon hypotheses that are particularly relevant to the former influence. We shall define a *normative social influence* as an influence to conform with the positive expectations[2] of another.[3] An *informational social influence* may be defined as an influence to accept information obtained from another as *evidence* about reality. Commonly these two types of influence are found together. However, it is possible to conform behaviorally with the expectations of others and say things which one disbelieves but which agree with the beliefs of others. Also, it is possible that one will accept an opponent's beliefs as evidence about reality even though one has no motivation to agree with him, per se.

Our hypotheses are particularly relevant to normative social influence upon individual judgment. We shall not elaborate the theoretical rationales for the hypotheses, since they are for the most part obvious and they follow from other theoretical writings (e.g., 4, 5).

Hypothesis I. Normative social influence upon individual judgments will be greater among individuals forming a group than among an ag-

✻ The selection following the editorial introduction is reprinted from "A study of normative and informational social influences upon individual judgment," *Journal of Abnormal and Social Psychology*, 1955, 51, 629–636, by permission of the authors and the American Psychological Association.

[1] This research was conducted under a grant from the Office of Naval Research, Contract No. NONR 285(10).

[2] By positive expectations we mean to refer to those expectations whose fulfillment by another leads to or reinforces positive rather than negative feelings, and whose nonfulfillment leads to the opposite, to alienation rather than solidarity; conformity to negative expectations, on the other hand, leads to or reinforces negative rather than positive feelings.

[3] The term *another* is being used inclusively to refer to "another person," to a "group," or to one's "self." Thus, a normative social influence can result from the expectations of oneself, or of a group, or of another person.

gregation of individuals who do not compose a group.[4]

That is, even when susceptibility to informational social influence is equated, we would predict that the greater susceptibility to normative social influence among group members would be reflected in the greater group influence upon individual judgment. This is not to say that individuals, even when they are not group members, may not have some motivation to conform to the expectations of others—e.g., so as to ingratiate themselves or so as to avoid ridicule.

Hypothesis II. Normative social influence upon individual judgment will be reduced when the individual perceives that his judgment cannot be identified or, more generally, when the individual perceives no pressure to conform directed at him from others.

Hypothesis III. Normative social influence to conform to one's own judgment will reduce the impact of the normative social influence to conform to the judgment of others.

Hypothesis IV. Normative social influence to conform to one's own judgment from another as well as from oneself will be stronger than normative social influence from oneself.

Normative social influence from oneself to conform to one's own judgment may be thought of as an internalized social process in which the individual holds expectations with regard to his own behavior; conforming to positive self-expectations leads to feelings of self-esteem or self-approval while nonconformity leads to feelings of anxiety or guilt. In general, one would expect that the strength of these internalized self-expectations would reflect the individual's prior experiences with them as sources of need satisfaction—e.g., by conforming to his own judgments or by self-reliance he has won approval from such significant others as his parents. As Hypothesis IV indicates, we believe that contemporaneous social pressure to conform to one's own judgment may supplement, and perhaps be even stronger than, the individual's internalized pressure to conform to his own judgment.

[4] Generally one would also expect that group members would be more likely to take the judgments of other group members as trustworthy evidence for forming judgments about reality and, hence, they would be more susceptible to informational social influence than would nongroup members. The greater trustworthiness usually reflects more experience of the reliability of the judgments of other members and more confidence in the benevolence of their motivations. However, when group members have had no prior experience together and when it is apparent in both the group and nongroup situations that the others are motivated and in a position to report correct judgments, there is no reason to expect differential susceptibility to informational social influence among group and nongroup members.

Two additional hypotheses, dealing with the effect of difficulty of judgment, are relevant to one of the experimental variations. They follow:

Hypothesis V. The more uncertain the individual is about the correctness of his judgment, the more likely he is to be susceptible to both normative and informational social influences in making his judgment.

Hypothesis VI. The more uncertain the individual is about the correctness of the judgment of others, the less likely he is to be susceptible to informational social influence in making his judgment.[5]

METHOD

Subjects. One hundred and one college students from psychology courses at New York University were employed as Ss. The study was defined for the Ss as an experimental study of perception.

Procedure. We employed the experimental situation developed by Asch (1) with certain modifications and variations which are specified below. For detailed description of the procedures utilized by Asch and replicated in this experiment, Asch's publication should be consulted. The basic features of the Asch situation are: (a) the Ss are instructed that they are participating in a perceptual experiment, wherein they have to match accurately the length of a given line with one of three lines; (b) correct judgments are easy to

[5] Although we have no data relevant to this hypothesis, we present it to qualify Hypothesis V and to counteract an assumption in some of the current social psychological literature. Thus, Festinger (5) has written that where no physical reality basis exists for the establishment of the validity of one's belief, one is dependent upon social reality (i.e., upon the beliefs of others). Similarly, Asch (2) has indicated that group influence grows stronger as the judgmental situation diminishes in clarity. The implication of Hypothesis VI is that if an individual perceives that a situation is objectively difficult to judge—that others as well as he experience the situation in the same way (i.e., as being difficult and as having uncertainty about their judgments)—he will not trust their judgments any more than he trusts his own. It is only as his confidence in their judgments increases (e.g., because he deems that agreement among three uncertain judges provides more reliable evidence than one uncertain judge) that the judgments of others will have informational social influence. However (at any particular level of confidence in the judgment of others), one can predict that as his confidence in his own judgment decreases he will be more susceptible to normative social influence. With decreasing self-confidence there is likely to be less of a commitment to one's own judgment and, hence, less influence not to conform to the judgments of others.

make; (c) in each experimental session there is only one *naive S*, the other participants, while ostensibly *S*s, are in fact "stooges" who carry out the experimenter's instructions; (d) each participant (i.e., the naive *S* and the stooges) has to indicate his judgments publicly; (e) on 12 of the 18 perceptual judgments the stooges announce wrong and unanimous judgments, the errors of the stooges are large and clearly in error; (f) the naive *S* and the stooges are in a face-to-face relationship and have been previously acquainted with one another.[6]

To test the hypotheses set forth in the foregoing section, the following experimental variations upon Asch's situation were employed.

1. The face-to-face situation. This was an exact replication of Asch's situation except for the following minor modifications: (a) Only three stooges, rather than eight, were employed;[7] (b) the *S* and the stooges were unacquainted prior to the experiment; and (c) two series of 18 judgments were employed. In one series (the visual series), the lines were physically present when the *S* and the stooges announced their

judgments; in the other series (the memory series), the lines were removed before any one announced his judgment. In the memory series, approximately three seconds after the lines were removed the first stooge was asked to announce his judgment. The sequences of visual and memory series were alternated so that approximately half the *S*s had the memory series first and half had the visual series first.

2. The anonymous situation. This situation was identical with the face-to-face situation except for the following differences: (a) Instead of sitting in the visual presence of each other, the *S*s were separated by partitions which prevented them from talking to each other or seeing one another; (b) Instead of announcing their judgments by voice, the *S*s indicated their judgments by pressing a button; (c) No stooges were employed. Each *S* was led to believe he was Subject No. 3, and the others were No. 1, No. 2, and No. 4. He was told that when the experimenter called out "Subject No. 3" he was to indicate his judgment by pressing one of three buttons (*A, B,* or *C*) which corresponded to what he thought the correct line was. When an *S* pressed a given button, a corresponding bulb lit on his own panel and on a hidden master panel. Presumably the appropriate bulb also lit on the panels of each of the other *S*s, but, in fact, the bulbs on any *S*'s panel were not connected to the buttons of the other *S*s. When the experimenter called for the judgments of Subject No. 1, of Subject No. 2, and of Subject No. 4, a concealed accomplice manipulated master switches which lit bulbs on each of the *S*'s panels that corresponded to judgments presumably being made by these respective *S*s. Subjects No. 1, No. 2, and No. 4 were, in effect, "electrical stooges" whose judgments were indicated on the panels of the four naive *S*s (all of whom were Subject No. 3) by an accomplice of the experimenter who manipulated master switches controlling the lights on the panels of the naive *S*s. The pattern of judgments followed by the "electrical stooges" was the same as that followed by the "live stooges" in the face-to-face situation. (d) In providing a rationale for being labeled Subject No. 3 for each of the naive *S*s, we explained that due to the complicated wiring setup, the *S*'s number had no relation to his seating position. Implicitly, we assumed that each *S* would realize that it would be impossible for the others to identify that a judgment was being made by him rather than by any of two others. However, it is apparent from postexperiment questionnaires that many of the *S*s did not realize this. It seems likely that if we had made the anonymous character of the judgments clear and explicit to the *S*s, the effects of this experimental variation would have been even more marked.

3. The group situation. This situation was identical to the anonymous situation except that the subjects were instructed as follows:

> **This group is one of twenty similar groups who are participating in this experiment. We want to see how accurately you can make judgments. We**

---

[6] Inspection of the Asch situation would suggest that informational social influence would be strongly operative. As Asch has put it (2, p. 461):

> The subject knows (a) that the issue is one of fact; (b) that a correct result is possible; (c) that only one result is correct; (d) that the others and he are oriented to and reporting about the same objectively given relations; (e) that the group is in unanimous opposition at certain points with him.

He further perceives that the others are motivated to report a correct judgment. In such a situation, the subject's accumulated past experience would lead him to expect that he could rely on the judgments of others, especially if they all agreed. That is, even if his eyes were closed he might feel that he could safely risk his life on the assumption that the unanimous judgments of the others were correct. This is a strong informational social influence and one would expect it to be overriding except for the fact that the subject has his eyes open and receives information from a source which he also feels to be completely trustworthy—i.e., from his own perceptual apparatus. The subject is placed in strong conflict because the evidences from two sources of trustworthy information are in opposition.

In the Asch situation, it is apparent that, in addition to informational social influence, normative social influence is likely to be operating. The naive *S* is in a face-to-face situation with acquaintances and he may be motivated to conform to their judgments in order to avoid being ridiculed, or being negatively evaluated, or even possibly out of a sense of obligation. While it may be impossible to remove completely the impact of normative social influence upon any socialized being, it is evident that the Asch situation allows much opportunity for this type of influence to operate.

[7] Asch found that three stooges were about as effective in influencing the *S*s as eight.

TABLE 1 *Mean Number of Socially Influenced Errors in Individual Judgment Among Group Members and Among Non-members*

EXPERIMENTAL TREATMENT	N	MEMORY SERIES	VISUAL SERIES	TOTAL
Group, anonymous, no commitment	15	6.87	5.60	12.47
Nongroup, anonymous, no commitment	13	3.15	2.77	5.92
		p VALUES*		
		.01	.05	.001

* Based on a *t* test, using one tail of the distribution.

are going to give a reward to the five best groups—the five groups that make the fewest errors on the series of judgments that you are given. The reward will be a pair of tickets to a Broadway play of your own choosing for each member of the winning group. An error will be counted any time one of you makes an incorrect judgment. That is, on any given card the group can make as many as four errors if you each judge incorrectly or you can make no errors if you each judge correctly. The five groups that make the best scores will be rewarded.

4. The self-commitment variation. This variation was employed in both the face-to-face and anonymous situations. In it, each S was given a sheet of paper on which to write down his judgment before he was exposed to the judgments of the others. He was told not to sign the sheet of paper and that it would not be collected at the end of the experiment. After the first series of 18 judgments, the Ss threw away their sheets. The Ss did not erase their recorded judgments after each trial as they did in the Magic Pad self-commitment variation.

4A. The Magic Pad self-commitment variation. This variation was employed in the anonymous situation. In it, each S was given a Magic Writing Pad on which to write down his judgment before he was exposed to

the judgments of the others. After each S had been exposed to the judgment of the others and had indicated his own judgment, he erased his judgment on the Magic Writing Pad by lifting up the plastic covering. It was made convincingly clear to the S that only he would ever know what he had written down on the pad.

5. The public commitment variation. This variation was employed in both the face-to-face situation and in the anonymous situation. In it, the Ss followed the same procedure as in the self-commitment variation except that they wrote down their initial judgments on sheets of paper which they signed and which they knew were to be handed to the experimenter after each series of 18 judgments.

RESULTS

The primary data used in the analysis of the results are the errors made by the Ss which were in the direction of the errors made by the stooges. We shall present first the data which are relevant to our hypotheses; later we shall present other information.

Hypothesis I. The data relevant to the first hypothesis are presented in Table 1. The table presents a comparison of the anonymous situation in which the individuals were motivated to act as a group with the anonymous situation in which there was no direct attempt to induce membership motivation; in both situations, no self or public commitment was made. The data provide strong support for the prediction that the normative social influence upon individual judgments will be greater among individuals forming a group than among individuals who do not compose a group. The average member of the group made more than twice as many errors as the comparable individual who did not participate in the task as a member of a group.

Qualitative data from a postexperimental questionnaire, in which we asked the S to describe any feelings he had about himself or about the others during the experiment, also support Hypothesis I. Seven out of the fifteen Ss in the "group" condition spontaneously mentioned a felt

TABLE 2 *Mean Number of Socially Influenced Errors in Individual Judgment in the Anonymous and in the Face-to-face Situations*

SITUATION	NO COMMITMENT				SELF-COMMITMENT				PUBLIC COMMITMENT			
	Visual	Memory	Total	N	Visual	Memory	Total	N	Visual	Memory	Total	N
Face-to-face	3.00	4.08	7.08	13	.92	.75	1.67	12	1.13	1.39	2.52	13
Anonymous	2.77	3.15	5.92	13	.64	.73	1.37	11	.92	.46	1.38	13

obligation to the other group members; none of the individuals in the non-group condition mentioned any feeling of obligation to go along with the others.

Hypothesis II. To test the second hypothesis, it is necessary to compare the data from the face-to-face and anonymous situations among the

TABLE 3   *p Values* for Various Comparisons of Socially Influenced Errors in the Anonymous and Face-to-face Situations*

COMPARISON	TOTAL ERRORS
A vs. *F*	.001
A vs. *F*, no commitment	.001
A vs. *F*, self-commitment	.10
A vs. *F*, public commitment	.001
Interaction of commitment with *A-F*	.01

* *p* values are based on *t* tests, using one tail of distribution, derived from analyses of variation.

TABLE 4   *p Values* for Various Comparisons of Socially Influenced Errors in the Different Commitment Treatments*

COMPARISON	TOTAL ERRORS	ERRORS ON VISUAL SERIES	ERRORS ON MEMORY SERIES
No commitment vs. public commitment, *F*	.001	.01	.001
No commitment vs. self-commitment, *F*	.001	.01	.001
Self-commitment vs. public commitment, *F*	.01	NS	NS
No commitment vs. self-commitment, *A*	.001	.01	.01
No commitment vs. public commitment, *A*	.001	.01	.002
Self-commitment vs. public commitment, *A*	NS	NS	NS

* *p* values are based on *t* tests, using one tail of the distribution, and derived from the analyses of variation.

individuals who were otherwise exposed to similar experimental treatments. Tables 2 and 3 present the relevant data. It is apparent that there was less social influence upon individual judgment in the anonymous as compared with the face-to-face situation. This lessening of social influence is at the .001 level of statistical confidence even when the comparisons include the "commitment variations" as well as both the visual and the memory series of judgments. The interaction between the commitment variations and the anonymous, face-to-face variations, which is statistically significant, is such as to reduce the over-all differences between the anonymous and face-to-face situation; the differences between the face-to-face and the anonymous situations are most strongly brought out when there is no commitment. Similarly, if we compare the anonymous and face-to-face situations, employing the memory rather than the visual series, the effect of the normative influence upon judgments in the face-to-face situation is increased somewhat, but not significantly. That is, as we eliminate counter-normative influences (i.e., the "commitment") and as we weaken reality restraints (i.e., employ the "memory" rather than "visual" series), the normative influences in the face-to-face situation operate more freely.

The support for Hypothesis II is particularly striking in light of the fact that, due to faulty experimental procedure, the "anonymous" character of the anonymous situation was not sufficiently impressed on some of the *S*s. For these *S*s, the anonymous situation merely protected them from the immediate, visually accessible pressure to conform arising from the lifted eyebrows and expressions of amazement by the stooges in the face-to-face situation. Complete feeling of anonymity would probably have strengthened the results.

Hypothesis III and IV. Tables 4, 5, and 6 present results showing the influence of the different commitment variations. The public and the self-commitment variations markedly reduce the socially influenced errors in both the face-to-face and anonymous situations. In other words, the data provide strong support for Hypothesis III which asserts that normative social influence to conform to one's own judgment will reduce the impact of the normative influence to conform to the judgment of others.

TABLE 5   *Mean Number of Socially Influenced Errors in Judgments in the Anonymous Situation as Affected by the Commitment Variations*

NO COMMITMENT				MAGIC PAD SELF-COMMITMENT				SELF-COMMITMENT				PUBLIC COMMITMENT			
Visual	Memory	Total	*N*	Visual	Memory	Total	*N*	Visual	Memory	Total	*N*	Visual	Memory	Total	*N*
2.77	3.15	5.92	13	1.63	2.27	3.90	11	.64	.73	1.37	11	.92	.46	1.38	13

The data with regard to the influence of self-commitment are ambiguous in implication since the results of the two self-commitment variations —i.e., the "Magic Pad self-commitment" and the "self-commitment"—are not the same. The first self-commitment variation produced results which are essentially the same as the public commitment variation, markedly reducing socially influenced errors. The Magic Pad self-commitment variation produced results which were different from the no commitment variation, reducing the errors to an extent which is statistically significant; however, unlike the first self-commitment variation, the Magic Pad self-commitment was significantly less effective than the public commitment in reducing socially influenced errors.

Our hunch is that the *S*s in the first self-commitment variation perceived the commitment situation as though it were a public commitment and that this is the explanation of the lack of differences between these two variations. That is, writing their judgments indelibly supported the belief that "others can see what I have written." The *S*s in the Magic Pad self-commitment variation, on the other hand, were literally wiping their initial judgments away in such a manner that they would be inaccessible to anyone. Hence, in the Magic Pad variation, the normative influences to conform to one's own judgment had to be sustained by the *S* himself. Normative influences from the *S*'s self (to be, in a sense, true to himself) were undoubtedly also operating in the non-commitment variation. What the Magic Pad did was to prevent the *S* from distorting his recollection of his independent judgment after being exposed to the judgments of the others. Further, there is a theoretical basis for assuming that the commitment to a judgment or decision is increased following the occurrence of behavior based upon it. Hence, the behavior of writing one's judgment down on the Magic Pad makes the original decision less tentative and less subject to change. However, it is apparent that this internally sustained influence to conform with one's own judgment was not as strong as the combination of external and self-motivated influences. These results support our fourth hypothesis.

Hypothesis V. Table 7 presents a comparison of the errors made on the visual and on the memory series of judgments. It is apparent that the *S*s were less influenced by the judgments of others when the judgments were made on a visual rather than on a memory basis. It is also evident from the data of Table 2 that the differences between the visual and memory series were reduced or disappeared when the *S*s wrote down their initial, independent judgments. These results support our fifth hypothesis which asserts that the more uncertain the individual is about the correctness of his judgment, the more likely he is to be susceptible to social influences in making his judgment. Further support comes from the questionnaire

data. Out of the 90 *S*s who filled out questionnaires, 51 indicated that they were more certain of their judgment when the lines were visually present, 2 were more certain when they were absent, and 39 were equally certain in both instances.

Being exposed first to the memory series rather than the visual series had the effect of making the *S*s more susceptible to social influence upon their judgments throughout both series of judgments. In other words, an *S* was more likely to make socially influenced errors on the memory series and, having allowed himself to be influenced by the others on this first series of judgments, he was more likely to be influenced on the visual series than if he had not previously participated in the memory series. It is as though once having given in to the social influence (and it is easier to give in when one is less certain about one's

TABLE 6   *p Values* for Various Comparisons of Socially Influenced Errors in the Different Commitment Variations*

COMPARISON	TOTAL ERRORS	ERRORS ON VISUAL SERIES	ERRORS ON MEMORY SERIES
No commitment vs. Magic Pad self-commitment	.05	NS	NS
Magic Pad self-commitment vs. self-commitment	.005	NS	.05
Magic Pad self-commitment vs. public commitment	.001	NS	.01

* *p* values are based on *t* tests using one tail of the distribution.

TABLE 7   *Socially Influenced Errors in Individual Judgments as Affected by the Stimulus to Be Judged (Visual or Memory)*

	N	MEAN NUMBER OF ERRORS	p VALUE
Errors on visual series	99	2.20	.005*
Errors on memory series	99	2.60	
Total errors when visual series was first	51	4.12	.005
Total errors when memory series was first	48	5.71	

* Based on a *t* test of differences between visual and memory series for each subject.

judgment), the *S* is more susceptible to further social influences.

DISCUSSION

A central thesis of this experiment has been that prior experiments which have been concerned with "group" influence upon individual judgment have, in fact, only incidentally been concerned with the type of social influence most specifically associated with groups, namely "normative social influence." Our results indicate that, even when normative social influence in the direction of an incorrect judgment is largely removed (as in the anonymous situation), more errors are made by our *S*s than by a control group of *S*s making their judgments when alone.[8] It seems reasonable to conclude that the *S*, even if not normatively influenced, may be influenced by the others in the sense that the judgments of others are taken to be a more or less trustworthy source of information about the objective reality with which he and the others are confronted.

It is not surprising that the judgments of others (particularly when they are perceived to be motivated and competent to judge accurately) should be taken as evidence to be weighed in coming to one's own judgment. From birth on, we learn that the perceptions and judgments of others are frequently reliable sources of evidence about reality. Hence, it is to be expected that if the perceptions by two or more people of the same objective situation are discrepant, each will tend to re-examine his own view and that of the others to see if they can be reconciled. This process of mutual influence does not necessarily indicate the operation of normative social influence as distinct from informational social influence. Essentially the same process (except that the influence is likely to be unilateral) can go on in interaction with a measuring or computing machine. For example, suppose one were to judge which of two lines is longer (as in the Müller-Lyer illusion) and then were given information that a measuring instrument (which past experience had led one to believe was infallible) came up with a different answer; certainly one might be influenced by this information. This influence could hardly be called a normative influence except in the most indirect sense.

While the results of prior experiments of "group" influence upon perception can be largely explained in terms of non-normative social influence, there is little doubt that normative influences were incidentally operative. However, these were the casual normative influences which

can not be completely eliminated from any human situation, rather than normative influences deriving from specific group membership. Our experimental results indicate that when a group situation is created, even when the group situation is as trivial and artificial as it was in our groups, the normative social influences are grossly increased, producing considerably more errors in individual judgment.

The implications of the foregoing result are not particularly optimistic for those who place a high value on the ability of an individual to resist group pressures which run counter to his individual judgment. In the experimental situation we employed, the *S*, by allowing himself to be influenced by the others, in effect acquiesced in the distortion of his judgment and denied the authenticity of his own immediate experience. The strength of the normative social influences that were generated in the course of our experiment was small; had it been stronger, one would have expected even more distortion and submission.

Our findings, with regard to the commitment variations, do, however, suggest that normative social influences can be utilized to buttress as well as to undermine individual integrity. In other words, normative social influence can be exerted to help make an individual be an individual and not merely a mirror or puppet of the group. Groups can demand of their members that they have self-respect, that they value their own experience, that they be capable of acting without slavish regard for popularity. Unless groups encourage their members to express their own, independent judgments, group consensus is likely to be an empty achievement. Group process which rests on the distortion of individual experience undermines its own potential for creativity and productiveness.

SUMMARY AND CONCLUSIONS

Employing modifications of the Asch situation, an experiment was carried out to test hypotheses concerning the effects of normative and informational social influences upon individual judgment. The hypotheses received strong support from the experimental data.

In discussion of our results, the thesis was advanced that prior studies of "group" influence upon individual judgment were only incidentally studies of the type of social influence most specifically associated with groups—i.e., of normative social influence. The role of normative social influence in buttressing as well as undermining individual experience was considered.

REFERENCES

1. Asch, S. E. Effects of group pressure upon the modification and distortion of judgments. In H. Guetzkow (Ed.), *Groups, leader-*

[8] Asch (2) reports that his control group of *S*s made an average of considerably less than one error per *S*.

ship and men. Pittsburgh: Carnegie Press, 1951. Pp. 177–190.
2. Asch, S. E. *Social psychology.* New York: Prentice-Hall, 1952.
3. Bovard, E. W. Group structure and perception. *J. abnorm. soc. Psychol.,* 1951, **46,** 398–405.
4. Deutsch, M. A theory of cooperation and competition. *Hum. Relat.,* 1949, **2,** 129–152.

5. Festinger, L. Informal social communication. *Psychol. Rev.* 1950, **57,** 271–282.
6. Sherif, M. A study of some social factors in perception. *Arch. Psychol.,* 1935, **27,** No. 187.

CONFORMITY AND COMMITMENT TO THE GROUP *

In a further analysis of certain puzzling results in the study reported in the previous selection, Gerard advances the understanding of the social influence process. In a face-to-face condition, yielding or refusing to yield when confronted with unanimity of judgments contrary to one's own persisted on subsequent trials. In an anonymous condition, where other persons were unaware of one's response, this was not the case. Gerard suggests that public confrontation of one's actions establishes a commitment to a public image which acts as a barrier against change. This holds whether the action is in line with the group or against the group. In terms of rewards and costs exchanged in the influence process, the costs of changing one's position increase once a person's position becomes publicly established. As Gerard notes, the costs take the form of dissonance which is maximized under conditions of commitment. This selection is another illustration of how unanticipated findings often lead the way to a theoretical advance.

30.

Conformity and Commitment to the Group

HAROLD B. GERARD
UNIVERSITY OF CALIFORNIA, RIVERSIDE

As reported by Asch (1956), an individual who asserts his independence at the outset, in the face of successive disagreement with others, tends, over time, to remain independent. This tendency, it was hypothesized here, is due to the commitment to one's stand when confronting the others publicly. Data were examined from an experiment in which the individual experienced the same sequence of discrepant judgments used by Asch either with or without public confrontation. These data indicate that continued adamance

* The selection following the editorial introduction is reprinted from "Conformity and commitment to the group," *Journal of Abnormal and Social Psychology,* 1964, **68,** 209–211, by permission of the author and the American Psychological Association.

occurs only with public confrontation. Also, with confrontation, the individual who tends to yield to the others does so with greater frequency as compared with the no confrontation situation. This bimodal reaction occurring with confrontation, it was suggested, offers evidence for the effects of a stronger commitment to behavior in a public situation.

Processes involving an individual's tendency to yield or maintain his independence when confronted with disagreement from others have been the subject of some intensive investigation. One of the workers in the field, Asch (1956), devised a situation, the features of which are as follows. The subjects, who are seated side by side, are instructed that they are participating in a perception experiment in which they have to match, by inspection at a distance, the length of a given line with one of three comparison lines. In each experimental session there is only one naive subject. The other participants, while ostensibly subjects, are in fact paid participants who carry out the experimenter's instructions. Each participant (that is, the naive subject and each paid participant) has to announce his judgments publicly and in full view of the others. On 12 of the 18 judgmental trials the paid participants, who always agree with one another, announce judgments which are clearly wrong. The task itself is perceptually unambiguous, that is, in the absence of the false consensus subjects make no errors.

Asch found that if a subject was independent of the others at the outset, that is, did not yield his judgment in favor of theirs, he tended to remain independent to the end of the series of judgments. Since the amount of evidence disconfirming the subject's own judgments increases with successive disagreement we would expect his confidence in his ability to decrease and his tendency to yield, therefore, to increase over time. Thus, a subject who was adamant at the outset would tend to relent with continued confrontation of discrepant judgments. The fact that this did not occur in Asch's work is puzzling.

We propose that the key to understanding this apparent lack of an increase in the tendency to yield to the group consensus over time lies in the nature of a face-to-face confrontation. Where the individual can be personally identified with his judgments he is responding not only to the apparent discrepancy in information about the stimulus but also to what he believes are the expectations of the others as to what his response should be. In a face-to-face situation an avowal of a discrepant stand is a public commitment to the group of one's stalwartness. Any change in this behavior in the direction of yielding would violate this image not only to oneself but to the group. We would therefore expect that an individual who started out deviating publicly in Asch's experiment would, as Asch discovered, continue to do so in the face of continued disagreement. If, however, we assume that the individual's confidence decreases with successive disagreement we would expect that where the individual *has not* been identified publicly with a deviant stand he would tend, with successive disagreement, to yield his own judgments and adopt those of the others.

In a previous experiment by Deutsch and Gerard (1955), which was stimulated by Asch's work, a situation was created in which to test the above derivation by comparing the effects of discrepant information with and without a public commitment to the group.[1] We therefore decided to take a new look at these old data.

Four subjects at a time (a naive one and three paid participants) were run in the standard face-to-face situation utilized by Asch. The subjects responded serially on each trial with the naive subject always in the third position. Other subjects responded anonymously. This latter condition, which has been used in a great deal of research since, was identical with the face-to-face situation except for the following differences. The four subjects sat in adjoining cubicles and were not able to see or talk to each other. They pressed a button to indicate their choice. No paid participants were employed since each subject was led to believe that he was Subject "3," and that the others were "1," "2," and "4." Each subject was told that when the experimenter called for the choice of Subject 3 he was to indicate his judgment by pressing one of three buttons (labeled *A, B,* or *C*) depending upon which of the three lines (also labeled *A, B,* and *C*) he believed to be correct. Judgments were called for in numerical sequence and the choices were displayed on a panel of lights. The pre-programed choices for the bogus Subjects 1, 2, and 4 were displayed to the subject at the appropriate time. The subject's own choices registered only on his panel and

were recorded in the control room. In both the anonymous and face-to-face conditions 36 trials were administered as two identical series of the 18 used by Asch.

There is some evidence in the postexperimental questionnaire, not reported in the original article, which indicates that compared with the anonymous condition, the face-to-face condition was both more stressful and produced greater ego involvement. One question asked the subjects to estimate the number of times he disagreed with the others. An average of 19.8 disagreements were perceived in the face-to-face treatment as compared with 15.8 in the anonymous treatment ($p < .02$ by t). Since under both treatments the others deviated from the correct answer on the same number of trials, the perception of a greater number of disagreements may be taken as evidence of a more pronounced effect of the disagreement. The difference cannot be explained away on the basis of the number of disagreements existing taking into account the number of yielding responses since, as reported in the original paper, there was more yielding in the face-to-face treatment.

Another question asked the subject to indicate if at any time he had ever answered as the others did against his own first choice even though he thought the others wrong. In the anonymous treatment approximately one in four of the subjects indicated that they did so whereas not a single subject in the face-to-face situation said that he did. This is so again despite the greater number of yielding responses produced in the face-to-face treatment. This tendency for the subjects in the face-to-face treatment to deny that he yielded to the others suggests either a greater tendency to maintain "face" or an actual change in his perceptions due to public pressure.

During the first series of 18 trials, 25 of the 75 subjects[2] turned in an errorless performance; 13 in the anonymous and 12 in the face-to-face treatment. During the second series only 4 of these remained adamant in the anonymous treatment as compared with 9 in the face-to-face treatment ($p < .05$ by chi square). Thus, confidence in one's initial choice does appear to decrease with continued disagreement. In corroboration of Asch's results, this manifests to a lesser extent in the face-to-face treatment. The

TABLE 1   *Total Number of Errors for Both Series*

	0 ERRORS	1–4 ERRORS	5 OR MORE ERRORS
Anonymous	4	25	8
Face-to-face	9	11	18

---

[1] Self-commitment and commitment to the experimenter were varied in the original experiment. Here we are considering commitment to the discrepant majority.

[2] There were 101 subjects in the original experiment, however, 26 of these were in treatments which were not counterbalanced for the present purposes.

questionnaire data suggest that this is not due to any decrease in the perceived discrepancy (more likely an increase) but rather to the effects of public commitment.

How does this greater adamance in the face-to-face treatment square with the fact that, on the average, there was also more yielding there than in the anonymous treatment? Table 1 reveals the answer. Indicated are the number of completely adamant subjects (those making no errors), those who yielded a few times (1–4 errors), and those yielding a relatively large number of times (5 or more errors). The break between 4 and 5 errors produced the best median split for the 62 subjects making at least 1 error. There is a preponderance of subjects in both the "0" and "5 or more" categories in the face-to-face as compared with the anonymous condition ($p <$ .01 by chi square). Thus, there is both greater adamance and greater yielding with public confrontation. In line with our hypothesis, there is greater commitment to the behavior in a public situation be it yielding or independence. This commitment presumably involves the individual's concern with the estimate of himself he sees reflected in the attitudes of the others toward him. The individual assumes that the others prefer that he agree with them and is, therefore, concerned with possible censure. The yielder in the face-to-face situation is presumably motivated by these considerations. This was discussed fully in the original article.

In their recent review and critique of work on dissonance theory, Brehm and Cohen (1962) stress the importance of commitment for the arousal of dissonance. When two sets of cogni-tions held by the individual are not consistent with one another dissonance will arise to the extent that one of these sets is resistant to change. Commitment to a behavior serves to fix the cognitions associated with it. Subsequent dissonance reduction results in a weakening of the cognitions for which there was no strong commitment. This further affirms and supports the behavior to which the individual had initially committed himself. In our situation publicity produces a commitment. A person who tended to be independent would be more so in public. Similarly, a person who tends to conform would conform more in public. In terms of our interpretation above, taking either an independent or a conforming stand in public tends to fix the stand due to the negative consequences attendant on changing it.

REFERENCES

ASCH, S. E. Studies of independence and conformity: I. A minority of one against a unanimous majority. *Psychol. Monogr.*, 1956, **70** (9, Whole No. 416).

BREHM, J. W., & COHEN, A. R. *Explorations of cognitive dissonance.* New York: Wiley, 1962.

DEUTSCH, M., & GERARD, H. B. A study of normative and informational social influences upon individual judgment. *J. abnorm. soc. Psychol.*, 1955, **51,** 629–636.

LEADERSHIP AND INTERPERSONAL POWER *

Early studies of leadership, like those of interpersonal attraction and social power, focused on individual characteristics. Leaders were compared with followers on a wide variety of physical, personality, and social dimensions in an attempt to identify the determinants of leadership. While this approach was consistent with a conception of leadership held by men of practical affairs, it proved surprisingly fruitless. Next, research interest shifted to identifying actions of group members that could be considered leadership behavior. This approach made clear that such behavior was rarely, if ever, the monopoly of one person in a group, but instead was variously distributed among them. The new insight gradually led to a reformulation of the problem in terms of the question: What determines the distribution of leadership acts in a group? The general answer to his question was that the distribution was a function of the demands of the situation and the relevant characteristics of *all* group members.

The emphasis on all members, followers as well as leaders, led to a third stage of conceptualization which viewed leadership in terms of the twin processes of role differentiation and role allocation. In response to situational demands, a differentiation in function among group members emerges, with certain persons engaging in leadership behavior more frequently than others. The role of leader is allocated to these individuals. Basic to these processes is a pattern of exchange in which the followers acquiesce to the guidance of the leaders in exchange for the satisfaction of achieving group goals and of meeting their own social emotional needs. This development of a working relation between leaders and followers is illustrated in the following selection. The frequency of attempts to lead and the success of such attempts are shown to depend on the acquiescence of the followers.

* The selection following the editorial introduction is reprinted from "Leadership and interpersonal power," in D. Cartwright (Ed.), *Studies in Social Power*, Ann Arbor, Michigan: Institute for Social Research, 1959, pp. 118–149, by permission of the authors, the editor, and publisher.

31.

Leadership and Interpersonal Power[1]

JOHN R. P. FRENCH, JR.
INSTITUTE FOR SOCIAL RESEARCH, OSLO, NORWAY

RICHARD SNYDER
UNIVERSITY OF CALIFORNIA, SANTA CRUZ

Leadership is the subject of much recent research because of its practical importance rather than its conceptual clarity. Though useful as a popular term denoting a broad area of phenomena, "leadership" requires a more limited definition in order to become a useful scientific concept.

We propose a restricted definition of leadership in terms of power: Leadership is the *potential social influence of one part of the group over another*. If one member has power over another, then he has some degree of leadership. Usually every member has some degree of influence over others in an informal group; in other words the leadership is widely distributed throughout the group. Those who are popularly called "followers" are members with less leadership, either because of their personal qualities or because of their subordinate role.

In a formal organization, the influence of the followers and of the leaders is partly determined by the legitimate authority of the positions they occupy. Thus the part of a group which has leadership may be a superordinate position or role regardless of the person who occupies it. In this case the study of leadership involves the study of role relationships as well as interpersonal relations.

This conception implies that leadership is a property of the group rather than a characteristic of an individual—though personality traits may, of course, be determinants of influence. It is the *relationship* which is important, and we must look at both sides of it. We are immediately led to ask, What determines the amount and kind of influence which the leader will attempt to exert? And what determines the extent to which the followers will accept these influence attempts? In answering these questions we will pay particular attention to the more or less enduring interpersonal and interrole relations existing between the inducer who attempts influence and the recipient toward whom it is directed.

THE HYPOTHESES

Two experiments were designed to test three hypotheses about the determinants of attempted influence and four hypotheses about the effectiveness of these attempts.

The determinants of attempted influence. The basic assumption underlying these hypotheses is that attempts to influence others are instrumental acts whose occurrence is determined by the perceived probability of success in achieving some goal. Therefore influence attempts will occur if the inducer perceives a readiness of the recipient to accept his influence[2] and if he believes that the induced behavior will, in fact, lead him to his goal. Three hypotheses were derived from these assumptions.[3]

Hypothesis I-1. The amount of influence attempted by a leader (or member) over a given recipient increases with increasing acceptance of him by that recipient.

This hypothesis assumes that the amount of influence attempted will be proportional to the perceived probability of success. Presumably the leader will assume that an influence attempt will more probably succeed where the recipient likes him (see Hypothesis II-1 below). At the low end of the scale, where there is dislike between leader and follower, this hypothesis is in line with Newcomb's principles of autistic hostility (11).

Hypothesis I-2. The amount of influence attempted by a leader (or member) increases with increasing certainty in his own opinion.

The measure of the leader's certainty is presumably a measure of his subjective probability that events will prove him correct. Accordingly, the more certain he is, the more strongly he will try to influence others in order to attain either his own goal or a group goal.

Hypothesis I-3. The amount of influence attempted by a lead (or member) increases with decreasing certainty of opposing opinion in the recipient.

Again this hypothesis stems directly from the assumption that the attempt to exert influence is

[1] This work was supported under contract with Detachment No. 3 of the Human Resources Research Center, a part of the Technical Training Command of the United States Air Force. The authors wish to acknowledge the help of many members of this unit in collecting and analyzing the data. Particular thanks go to Mr. John V. Moore, for whom the project represented a major responsibility over a period of many months, and to Dr. Arthur Hoehn who did many analyses of the data.

[2] This assumption is directly in line with Festinger's hypothesis that the strength of the force to communicate to a group member increases with perception that the recipient will change his opinion in the desired direction (4).

[3] These assumptions permit the derivation of several additional hypotheses. In general we would expect that any determinant of the effectiveness of influence attempts will also be a determinant of the amount of influence attempted provided the leader understands this factor and can perceive its operation in his followers. Thus, for example, the preliminary field study found that noncommissioned officers will attempt more influence in areas where it is clear that they have the backing of their superiors.

guided by the perceived probability of success. Where the recipient shows great certainty in his opposing opinions, he will be perceived as strongly resistant to influence, but where he is uncertain he will seem more inducible.

The determinants of the effectiveness of influence attempted. The behavior of the recipient in response to an influence attempt will be determined, among other things, by the nature of his social relations with the inducer. Our problem here is to try to isolate the relevant dimensions of this relationship. Obviously many can be described which seem reasonably likely determinants of influence. Considering both the findings of previous research and the requirements of conceptual clarity, we have chosen three dimensions which promise to be conceptually independent and empirically uncorrelated: (*a*) the recipient likes the inducer, (*b*) the recipient accepts the authority of the inducer's role, (*c*) the recipient accepts the inducer as an expert **(9)**.

Hypothesis II-1. The effectiveness of an attempt by a leader (or member) to influence another member of the group increases with increasing acceptance of the leader by the recipient.

This hypothesis was earlier confirmed by Back **(1)**. Parallel findings show that the influence of the group over the member is determined by the attractiveness of the group for the member **(6, 12, 13)**. Thus both these hypotheses may be subsumed under the more general hypothesis that the influence of an inducing agent (either group or individual), over a person is a function of the attractiveness of the inducing agent for the person.

Hypothesis II-2. The effectiveness of an influence attempt by the leader increases with increasing readiness of the follower to accept the authority conferred by the leader's role.

What is ordinarily called authority in a military organization combines two factors which should be distinguished. (*a*) The authority of an officer over his men includes *coercive power*, i.e., the ability to punish his subordinates for noncompliance with his orders. (*b*) It also includes a predisposition on the part of the subordinate willingly to accept the influence of the officer because he perceives it as *legitimate*. Presumably coercive power will lead to overt conformity without covert change of attitude on the part of the subordinate **(5)**. The acceptance of authority as legitimate, on the other hand, should produce covert changes in attitudes and behavior as well as overt conformity. Hypothesis II-2, since it deals only with the acceptance of authority as legitimate, predicts changes in the private opinions and covert behavior of the men.

Hypothesis II-3. The effectiveness of an influence attempt by the leader (or member) increases with increasing perception that he is an expert in the area of the influence attempt.

This common sense hypothesis also has a long research history, whether as the effect of "expert opinion" **(10)** or "source credibility" **(8)**. Eventually this hypothesis should be refined with respect to the areas of expertness, the interrelations among them, and the relation of this dimension to other dimensions of interpersonal perception. However, our data do not permit such refined analyses.

Hypothesis II-4. The total amount of influence effected by a leader (or member) over a member increases with increases in the amount of influence attempted.

At the low extreme, it seems obvious that one can expect no influence if there is no communication and no attempt at influence. However, the relation between these two variables is not obviously a linear one: it might well be that attempts to influence beyond a certain level, especially if these attempts are not seen as legitimate, might well result in reduced effectiveness. However, within the more usual range of behavior exhibited by a leader, we would expect a monotonically increasing relationship.

The preliminary field study. Before describing the methods used in these two experiments, it will be worth reporting some of the relevant findings from a preliminary field study **(2)**. This study was conducted on the line maintenance personnel of two aircraft maintenance squadrons located at a training base. The relevant data were collected largely through the use of written questionnaires dealing with a number of attitudes toward matters of concern to the men and of importance to the performance of their daily work. The same questionnaire was used to measure the attitudes of the noncommissioned officers who supervised the men. For each attitude, the noncommissioned officer was asked how strongly he attempted to influence his men to believe as he did. Measures of the acceptance of supervisors were supplied largely by ranked sociometric choices made from lists of the personnel in the entire squadron. Our major measures of the influence of the noncommissioned officer over his airmen consisted of measures showing how closely the airman's attitude was related to the attitude of his noncommissioned officer and to the official beliefs and attitudes which the noncommissioned officer is supposed to support.

In analyzing the amount of influence attempted by noncommissioned officers, we found: (*a*) the closer the noncommissioned officer's own attitude to the officially approved attitudes of the Air Force, the stronger his influence attempts; (*b*) the noncommissioned officer attempts much stronger influence on attitudes relevant to the work of the group than on attitudes and opinions unrelated to the work; (*c*) but there is no relation between the acceptance of the leader and the strength of influence he attempts. The surprising lack of clear positive findings on (*c*) suggested the need for more carefully controlled research, employing less subjective measures of influence attempted.

The effectiveness of the leader tended to be related to his acceptance both as a spare-time companion and as a crew chief. Finally there was some support for the hypothesis that the stronger the influence attempted by the leader, the greater the amount of change he produced in the attitudes of his subordinates. Both of these determinants of effectiveness seemed to require further checking with better measures of effectiveness. The present experiments check these findings (see Hypotheses I-1, II-1, and II-4).

METHODS

Design of the experiments

The main reason for employing the experimental method in this phase of research was to test more unequivocally our major hypotheses about the influence of the leader as related to interpersonal relations, and in particular, to determine the direction of causation in these relationships. The experimental design involved two parts sufficiently independent to be considered as two separate experiments. The first —the group judgment test—was designed to study the influence of the leader on the opinions and judgments of his followers, while the second—a card-sorting task —was intended to measure his influence on productivity. The first experiment tested the influence of the leader in a free discussion situation where he was permitted to attempt as much influence as he liked using any method he could devise. In the second, both the methods of influence employed and the amount of influence attempted were held constant in order to discover whether there was a *direct* relationship between the effectiveness of attempted influence and the interpersonal relations between leader and follower.

Both experiments employed much more carefully controlled measurement of the effectiveness of influence than was possible in the field study. Instead of inferring the existence of an influence process from the relationship of the airman's opinion to the opinion of his noncommissioned officer, we brought the influence process into the laboratory and measured the actual changes induced by the leader. In the group judgment test this was accomplished by having the airmen record private judgments before discussion with the noncommissioned officer and after the discussion. In the card-sorting experiment the influence of inductions from the leader was measured by the actual change in the quantity and quality of work performed by the group of airmen.

The major independent variables of interpersonal relationship between leader and followers were not manipulated directly because we could find no method

for producing sufficiently large changes in these already established relationships. Instead we selected as subjects all noncommissioned officers of a given classification and hoped that the actual interpersonal relationships with the airmen would show enough variation to permit testing of our hypotheses.

The procedure may be summarized briefly:

1. From existing small work groups in the Air Force we selected the supervisor and three members chosen as far as practicable at random. When they arrived at the experimental room, they were told that their cooperation was needed in several research projects, that they were not being tested in any way, and that they would not be identified.

2. Each subject answered privately a written questionnaire measuring the major independent variables of interpersonal relationships.

3. Next, each group participated in the group judgment test. In this experiment each of the members in the group made a number of individual judgments from a set of stimulus figures. Unknown to the subjects these figures were not all the same. Slightly different forms of each figure were distributed in a way designed to produce planned patterns of disagreement within the group. After the members had completed their preliminary judgment, they held a discussion under instructions to try to reach agreement. After the discussion the group members again recorded their private judgments. Observational data provided the measures of attempted influence, and the changes from the preliminary to the final judgment provided a measure of the effectiveness of influence attempted.

4. Finally, the subjects were presented with the card-sorting task as an investigation of different ways of organizing a group. Three airmen were assigned a task of hand-sorting punched cards according to the number of holes in each card. A scoring system, depending upon the total number of cards sorted, the number correctly sorted, and the number of errors, was described and was stated to be the basis for comparing groups of different organization. The noncommissioned officer in charge of the group was assigned the task of checking the work of his three airmen, of comparing their results with those of other groups, and giving the group members instructions which would enable them to improve their performance. He was located in an adjoining room and was required to send all communications to his group by written notes. Actually he was asked to copy four standard notes, the first two instructing the group to slow down in order to make fewer errors, the last two instructing them to speed up. This aspect of the design was similar to the experiment of Schachter, Ellertson, McBride, and Gregory (**13**).

Subjects. Each group consisted of the supervisor and three of his subordinates taken from groups of instructors in the technical training schools at Chanute Air Force Base, Illinois. In our study, we used only noncommissioned officer supervisors and enlisted men serving under them.

We did not request subjects by name, because we hoped to give them as good an assurance of anonymity as possible, in order to increase the validity of their ratings of each other on the "Group Questionnaire," which provided our data on interpersonal relations. In arranging for subjects, we asked the organizations concerned to select men alphabetically by last name to accompany the supervisors. Probably this procedure was followed in most cases, but we know there were some deviations. To the extent that there was any systematic selection of subjects it may have had the effect of reducing the range in our interpersonal variables; but it is hard to see how it could have introduced any bias into the results obtained.

Thirty-six experimental groups were studied during the spring of 1952. From all of these we obtained usable data for the group judgment test. However, in the card-sorting experiment, mainly because of scheduling difficulties, only 26 groups yielded data which could be used in the final analysis.

The measures of interpersonal relations

Personal acceptance. By acceptance we mean essentially personal attractiveness to, or popularity with, another person. We recognize that there may be several different reasons why one person likes another, and also that one person may like another in certain situations more than in others. However, the variable of personal attractiveness or acceptance has considerable generality and can be treated as though it were approximately unidimensional.

The group questionnaire included four items designed as measures of acceptance. The blunt question "How well do you like him?" was from the beginning regarded as the major measure of this variable, with the other three items included as possible refinements. Since this major measure gave a better distribution of responses and apparently higher validity, it was the only measure used in the analysis. This measure of personal acceptance was:

How well do you like him?

A. He's my best friend in the Air Force.
B. He's one of my best friends.
C. He's a good friend of mine.
D. I like him a lot and would like to know him better.
E. I like him fairly well.
F. I don't have much feeling about him one way or the other.
G. I don't like him very much.
H. I dislike him.

Perceived authority. By perceived authority we mean the disposition of a person to perceive as appropriate and to accept the amount of authority possessed by a person who is in a superior role. We are explicitly interested in the authority inherent in the formal roles of an authority structure.

The questionnaire item for measuring the per-

ceived authority of the noncommissioned officer was as follows:

If he wants to use it, how much authority does the typical NCOIC[4] have over the men he supervises?

—— very little authority
—— some authority: but not much
—— a fair amount of authority
—— quite a lot of authority
—— a great deal of authority

Originally this item was intended to be part of a composite measure which also included an item on the airman's attitudes towards whether the noncommissioned officer had too much or too little authority. However, since less than 2 per cent of the subjects reported that he had too much authority, the analysis was performed with only this one item.

Perceived expertness. It is believed that this factor is particularly important in areas where expertness is perceived as necessary, as for example in the technical aspects of aircraft maintenance. In the card-sorting experiment we did not expect expertness to be at all relevant because we had selected activities where practically no skill or ability or intelligence was required. The group judgment test was obviously a task requiring expertness although it was not easy to specify the type of ability required. Accordingly our operational measure was the question:

Would you say he was very intelligent, about average, or what?

A. One of the brighest men I know.
B. Very bright—well above average.
C. A little above average.
D. About average.
E. A little below average.
F. A lot below average.

The group judgment test

The central idea of the group judgment test was to create a controlled discussion in which to measure the influence of the leader. We wanted an even division of opinion in the group in order to balance the pressures to change opinions. In addition we wanted the leader to be opposed equally often to each of his three men. In order to control the patterns of disagreement among members in the group, we adopted the techniques used by Back (1). Two subjects were presented with one form and the other two subjects with slightly different versions of geometric figures requiring judgments of the relative length of lines or the relative areas of plane figures (see Figure 1). In Form I, line *B* is slightly shorter than

---

4 Noncommissioned officer in charge.

line *A,* but in Form II the difference is reversed. Thus there should be a 2–2 division of opinion in the group.

Twelve such items were constructed so that it would be possible to pair each individual with every other individual four times in even opinion splits. Thus, in each group the members received forms as follows:

NO. OF ITEMS	RECEIVED FORM I	RECEIVED FORM II
4	Leader & Member 1	Member 2 & Member 3
4	Leader & Member 2	Member 1 & Member 3
4	Leader & Member 3	Member 1 & Member 2

Considerable work was required for the development of the items used. The problem was to get two forms of each item in which the differences between the figures to be compared were sufficiently great to produce the desired judgment fairly consistently, yet not so great that these judgments would be made with a great deal of confidence. We assumed that too high certainty of judgments was undesirable because it would reduce the probability of change of opinion, in line with Hypothesis I-3. In order to get the optimum amount of difference between the two figures of an item, four or five forms of each item were submitted to a group of 61 naive subjects as a "visual comparison test." On the basis of these pre-test data, twelve

FIGURE 1. The two forms of item 7 from the group judgment test.

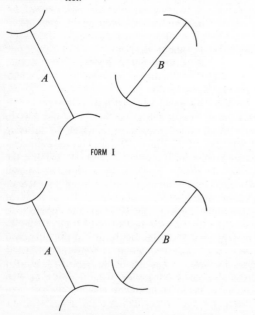

FORM I

FORM II

items were selected designed to produce 2–2 splits in opinion. In the actual experiment 63 per cent of them did in fact produce such splits. In order to reduce suspicion about the amount of disagreement in the group, two additional items were included on which all four subjects received the same form. The test items and the answer booklet containing 5-point rating scales for certainty of judgment are reported in full by Snyder (**14**).

Administration of the group judgment test

After the subjects had completed the written questionnaires, the experimenter told them that the Air Force was concerned with discrepancies in intelligence reports from agents assigned to the same geographical area, and that it was felt that "discussion between the agents might eliminate these discrepancies." The experiment was justified as an investigation of the accuracy of a group report compared to initial individual reports and post-discussion individual reports.

Seven of the visual comparison items were then presented to the subjects with instructions to make private judgments on the relative magnitude of the two figures in each item, without making any measurements, and to indicate their certainty of each judgment. Subjects were told that they would then discuss their judgments together, and finally would rejudge privately. It was suggested that they might want to jot down a few notes on their answer sheets since they would not have the geometric figures before them during the discussion.

As each subject completed his preliminary judgments the experimenter picked up his test booklet but left the answer sheets for use in the discussion. Subjects then discussed each item in order, with instructions to reach a public group decision as to the "correct" answer. The regular supervisors were designated as group leaders in this decision-making process.

After reaching a group decision on an item, each subject returned to his answer sheet, made another private judgment, and again indicated his degree of certainty before discussing the next item.

After subjects judged, discussed, and rejudged each of the first seven items, the answer sheets were collected and the remaining seven items were administered using the same procedure.

Two attempts were made to increase the pressure toward a change of opinion on the part of the subjects. First, each group was required to reach a decision on a group answer. Second, in giving the instructions, the experimenter commented that "our experience so far has shown that most men are able to improve their answers a lot after the discussion."

On items where there were 2–2 splits the conflict between the two sides frequently was so difficult to resolve that the subjects would appeal to the experimenter for some solution to the dilemma. Evidently they were highly involved and task oriented. There seemed to be no suspicions concerning the validity of the differences in opinion.

Measurement of influence attempts. In order to test our major hypotheses we had to have data on how much—or how hard—each subject attempted to influence the opinions of the others in his group. These measures had to be specific to the content of the test items, since our measures of effectiveness consisted of changes in the test items. After some initial attempts to use more elaborate instruments, we divided all verbal interactions into three observational categories: (a) influence attempts, (b) opinion change, (c) other.

1. Influence attempts. In this category were recorded only communications about the content of the item upon which the group was attempting to reach agreement. The following types of attempted influence were included:

    a. an initial statement of the judgment made, *if it was elaborated, defended as correct, or stated with emphasis;*

    b. reiterations of an opinion previously stated;

    c. statements about the stimulus figures of which the intent, as judged by the observers, was to defend the opinion held by the speaker;

    d. communications apparently calculated to reduce the certainty of an opponent's opinion or to question the basis of his judgment;

    e. communications questioning the ability of an opponent to make the required judgments, including joking attacks, such as "I guess you need some glasses;"

    f. statements indicating rejection of influence attempted by others.

2. Opinion change. This category might equally well have been designated "acceptance of influence" because it was defined as including all communications indicating overt compliance with an influence attempt. The category "opinion change" was designed quite specifically to provide evidence of overt acceptance of influence, regardless of whether it appeared that the person had actually (covertly) changed his opinion or not. Scored in this category were:

    a. remarks indicating that the individual had actually changed his judgment;

    b. statements indicating reduced confidence in an initial judgment;

    c. statements conceding the validity of an opponent's reasoning or arguments, unless such statements were clearly "rhetorical" (for example, such responses as, "You may have a point there, but I'm still sure the triangle was bigger," would be scored simply as "influence attempt," but the response, "I'm not so sure you're not right, after all," would be scored as "opinion change");

    d. remarks conceding the group decision to the opposing side, even when qualified by a clear statement that the person had not changed his own opinion.

3. Other. The interaction scored under this heading included all communications not recorded in one of the other categories. Much of the interaction so scored could be very easily discriminated, because it consisted of all the communications which did not deal directly with the test material. Thus, it included all "procedural" interaction and all irrelevant or "out-of-field" remarks. It also included remarks aimed at establishing the characteristics of the item under discussion.

The unit in our measure of interaction was the single uninterrupted speech. The temporal sequence of these units within the observation of the single test item was not recorded but the distinction between items was maintained. The observers recorded the person initiating a communication but not the person to whom it was addressed because during the pre-test it became clear that practically all of the interaction categorized as attempted influence was directed toward persons who held the opposite opinion and that it was reaching the two opponents equally.

Computations of the reliability of observation were based upon data from two observers who were both present at 25 of the 29 experimental sessions from which usable observational records were obtained. We selected a sample of about 17 per cent of the data by picking ten groups at random and including, from half of these groups, scores on seven odd-numbered items and, from the remaining half, scores on the seven even-numbered items. An observation "score" was defined as the number of interactions recorded for a single subject in one category on one item. Since there were four subjects in each group, our estimates of reliability are based on 280 scores in each observation category.

We first calculated inter-observer reliability coefficients for "influence attempts" and for "total participation" (the sum of scores in all three categories). The product moment correlation in each case was .92, indicating only fairly good reliability considering the fact that we threw together data from groups and from items which varied greatly in the total volume of interaction recorded.

One further question of reliability was investigated. Could the observers discriminate "influence attempts" from other communications? To answer this question we correlated "influence scores" with the next largest category—"other." The resulting coefficient of .41, while highly significant statistically, is still low enough to prove in conjunction with the high reliability coefficients that the discrimination of influence attempts was meaningful.

Since one of the two regular observers was present

at all but one experimental session, his records were used exclusively where possible.

The card-sorting experiment

Experimental task. The card-sorting experiment has already been described as an experiment involving a production task. Several general considerations determined the nature of the task selected. First, the task should be simple and require a minimum of skill or ability so that individual differences would not be a major factor determining performance and so that we could ignore any effects of learning, at least after a very brief familiarization period. Second, the task should permit easy and reliable measurement of both the quantity and quality of performance. Third, the task should be as routine and uninteresting as possible so that the restraining forces of satiation would prevent maximum performance even during the short time of the experiment. If the subjects were already producing as much as possible, there could be no increase in production in response to the influence attempted by the supervisor.

The task selected involved a hand-sorting of machine tabulating cards of the familiar type used in IBM equipment. These cards were punched with holes and had to be classified according to the number of holes. The only way the subjects could sort the cards correctly was to count the holes. The measure of quantity was the number of cards sorted, and the measure of quality was the proportion of cards correctly sorted.

The number of holes in each card ranged from 21 to 25. This number was great enough so that the cards could not be sorted by direct inspection; instead the subjects had to go through the boring procedure of counting each hole. Yet the time required to classify each card was so short that no substantial variation in performance measure would be due to units of production partially completed at the time the cards were collected.

All three sorters in the experiment placed the cards into a single five-compartment tray. Thus from their point of view the task was a group task and the product could be measured only as a group product. We may assume that most of them perceived that the supervisor had no information about what they produced as individuals. Hence, they were to a degree "protected" from the supervisor and at the same time they were prevented from effectively competing with one another for the supervisor's approval. In short, we had created a cooperative group in which the actions of any member had equal consequences for all four.

Administration of the card-sorting experiment. This experiment was presented to the subjects as a study of the best way to *organize* a group to do a job—how the work should be divided up, how it should be supervised, and so on. The experimenter explained the standardized task and the scoring system for comparing different groups. He pointed out that the task, like many routine jobs in the Air Force, would be organized so that the supervisor could not work right with his men. Instead he would be working in another room. In order to prevent too close supervision, the experimenter explained, the man in charge would be required to communicate to his subordinates by written notes. He would be given certain information about the speed and accuracy achieved by other groups, and this information could be used as a basis for sending written instructions to his own group concerning the quantity and quality of their work.

After the leader had been taken from the room and the subjects had worked for several minutes, the experimenter came back, picked up the filled tray, replaced it with an empty one, and carried the sorted cards into the other room, ostensibly to be checked by the supervisor. For the purpose of recording performance, the total sorting time was divided into nine periods of four minutes each. The first three periods were used as a base line against which to measure changes in productivity and errors. For the next three periods the subjects were induced by the supervisor to work slowly; they received the first message at the beginning of Period 5. The last three periods were fast periods with the subjects receiving messages to speed up at the beginning of Period 7 and again at the beginning of Period 8.

Influence attempts by the supervisor. As soon as he had been separated from the other members of the group, each supervisor was given a brief explanation of the experiment and asked to copy off in his own handwriting each of the four messages on a separate slip of paper. The messages, in order of delivery to the sorters, were the following:

1. "Too many mistakes. Take it slower."
2. "Slow down a lot. It will give us a better score in the end."
3. "It's going fine. Forget about mistakes and try for speed."
4. "Sort as fast as you can. Never mind about mistakes. Let's try for a record."

It was hoped that the apparent inconsistency between the first two and the last two notes would appear plausible to the subjects because of the elaborate scoring system and the detailed description of the supervisor's job given by the experimenter. As it turned out, this effort at plausibility may not have been entirely successful, as indicated by the informal group interviews conducted with subjects at the end of each experimental session. Comments by some of these subjects did suggest that there was some suspicion about the content of the notes, but how frequently there was enough suspicion to have an important effect on the responses is impossible to judge accurately.

Nevertheless these highly controlled, experimental, influence attempts by the supervisor did have an effect on the performance of the sorters.

The regular trend in Table 1 indicates that the messages influenced the behavior of the sorters. Despite considerable variation in over-all performance, every group worked faster in the "fast periods" than in the "base periods." All but four of the groups worked more slowly in the "slow periods" than in the "base periods." We can conclude that the experimentally controlled influence was successful.

RESULTS OF THE GROUP JUDGMENT EXPERIMENT

Determinants of attempted influence

Acceptance. Hypothesis I-1 predicts that the amount of influence attempted by a leader (or member) will increase with increasing acceptance of him. Comparing leaders of different groups, we should find that the more accepted leaders attempt more influence. Within a group we should find that the leader (or member) directs more influence toward those who accept him.

The correlations for testing the predictions comparing different groups are presented in Table 2.

As predicted, those leaders who are more accepted by their subordinates tend to attempt more influence ($r=.28$, $p=.08$). Likewise, members attempt more influence when they are more accepted by the leader ($r=.54$, $p<.01$). These two confirmations of the hypothesis are not independent since the amount of influence attempted by the leader correlates .55 with the amount attempted by the members of the same group. However, if we partial out the amount of influence attempted by the leader, the correlation between influence attempted by members and acceptance of the members by the leader drops only to .50.

All the other correlations in Table 2 are not significant, so we can rule out the alternative hypothesis that the amount of influence attempted by an inducer is determined by how much he likes the inducee.

Considering all the correlations in Table 2, it is clear that the amount of influence attempted in the group is determined by a process of interaction in which the behavior of all persons is highly interdependent. Though it cannot be inferred with certainty, the results suggest that the leader is able to set the tone for his group to a high degree, even in a situation where his official position seems largely irrelevant. This interpretation is supported by a multiple correlation of .69 between the amount of influence attempted by members and the amount attempted by their leader together with the extent to which they are accepted by their leader. That is, the amount of influence attempted by a member is determined by the amount attempted by his leader and how much the leader likes him. This may be considered quite a high correlation since certainty of initial opinion (the other known determinant of attempted influence) is not taken into account here.

In order to test the prediction from Hypothesis

I-1 that a person *within* a group will direct more influence toward those who like him, two additional analyses were made—one for leaders and one for members. Within a group any inducer, for example the leader, will on various items attempt influence toward three *pairs* of opponents: members 1 and 2, members 1 and 3, and members 2 and 3. For each group, the mean number of influence attempts made to the pair of opponents with lowest acceptance of the leader was subtracted from the mean number made to the pair with highest acceptance of the leader. This turned out to be a relatively crude analysis because of the number of tied scores for acceptance and because of the overlapping membership in the high and low pairs. In both analyses, the differences were in the predicted direction but not significantly different from zero.

A third method of analyzing the data combines

TABLE 1 *Group Mean Production and Errors for Each Period of the Card Sorting Experiment**

	MEAN NUMBER OF CARDS SORTED	MEAN PERCENTAGE OF ERRORS
Base periods: 1	54.2	12.1%
2	54.3	8.1
3	56.3	8.4
Slow periods: 4	48.1	5.8
5	44.7	5.8
6	49.4	5.2
Fast periods: 7	60.4	6.2
8	64.8	9.7
9	69.5	7.9

* Based on 25 rather than 26 groups, since for one group an error in collecting the cards prevents separating periods 5 and 6.

TABLE 2 *Correlations Relevant to Acceptance and Attempted Influence*

	1	2	3	4
1. Acceptance of leader by members		.18	.28	.12
2. Acceptance of members by the leader			.20	.54
3. Influence attempted by the leader				.55
4. Influence attempted by members				

Notes: 1. *N* for all correlations is 29, the number of groups from which we have observation data. 2. The measure of acceptance of leader by members is the sum of all the ratings of the leader by the members. The measure of acceptance of members is the sum of the ratings of those members by the leader. 3. The measure of influence attempted is the mean frequency per item (and per person) for all items where an initial 2–2 split occurred.

the effects of variations within and among groups. Treating each item separately, we tabulated the acceptance scores for the particular opponents on that item and the amount of influence attempted by the leader on the same item. The mean influence score, when both opponents accepted the leader highly, was 5.12; when the acceptance by one was high but by the other was low, the mean influence score was 4.01; when acceptance by both opponents was low, the influence attempted was 2.67. In short, almost twice as much influence is attempted toward high- as toward low-accepting opponents.

Certainty. Our remaining hypotheses in Group I relate the strength of attempted influence to the degree of certainty characterizing the opinions of the participants in a discussion. The analysis has been restricted to the data relating to leaders, not only because we are mainly concerned with the influence attempts of leaders, but also because the interdependence of all the factors operating in the group leads to difficulties in interpreting findings from an analysis in which each of the several members is considered separately as providing an independent test.

Our measures of certainty were the certainty ratings which accompanied the judgments made by the subjects on each of the test figures. These ratings were assigned values from 1, "completely certain" to 5, "very uncertain." In this analysis, we shall be concerned only with the ratings accompanying the preliminary judgments. As a subject's certainty changed, it undoubtedly had an effect upon his readiness to attempt influence, but to take this into account would require not only the final certainty ratings but also a continuous record of changes during the discussion, which could not be obtained.

Hypothesis I-2 states: The amount of influence attempted by a leader (or member) increases with increasing certainty in his own opinion. The first two analyses made to test this hypothesis parallel the "among groups" and "within groups" analyses used in the study of the acceptance variable. First, for each leader the mean initial certainty rating and the mean number of influence attempts made by the leader on the 2-2 split items were calculated. A Pearson r was then computed between these 29 pairs of means. The obtained r was $-.31$ which is in the expected direction and is statistically significant at the .05 level. Thus, in accordance with the hypothesis, leaders with relatively high initial certainty tended to make more influence attempts than leaders with relatively low initial certainty.

Hypothesis I-2 also predicts that a leader will tend to make more influence attempts on those items on which he is relatively certain than on those on which he is relatively uncertain. The test of this prediction was done as follows: for each leader, items with certainty ratings of 1 ("completely certain") and 2 ("quite certain") were placed in one set and those with certainty ratings 3 ("fairly certain"), 4 ("rather uncertain"), and 5 ("very uncertain") were placed in another. Eight of the leaders made initial certainty ratings which were all in the "high-certainty" set, and two made all their ratings at the low-certainty level. An analysis for the remaining 19 leaders showed an average of 1.27 more influence attempts per item for the "high-" than for the "low-certainty" items. A t-test for correlated measures indicates this is statistically significant at the .08 level ($t=1.88$, $df=18$, two-tailed test).

The magnitude of the relationship stated in Hypothesis I-2 can be best demonstrated by an analysis which combines the two effects reported above. We categorized all of the items from all of the leaders according to the leader's initial certainty on the particular item. For each category, Table 3 shows the mean number of influence attempts per item made by the leader.

From the three analyses together, we may conclude that there is a substantial and significant relationship confirming Hypothesis I-2.

The final hypothesis in this group is Hypothesis I-3: The amount of influence attempted by a leader (or member) increases with decreasing certainty of opposing opinion in the recipient. Here, if data on recipiency of influence attempts were more complete, leader influence could be related to the certainty of each opponent separately. Since these data could not be obtained reliably, the certainty of both opponents must be considered jointly, and the test of this hypothesis is perhaps somewhat less powerful as a consequence.

The method of analysis used was similar to that for Hypothesis I-2. Both "among groups" and "within groups" analyses were accomplished. First, the opponents' mean certainty rating per item was determined for each group, and these mean certainty ratings were correlated with the mean numbers of influence attempts of the respective leaders. The obtained Pearson r was .07 ($N=29$). This is far from statistically significant.

TABLE 3   Leader's Certainty as a Determinant of His Influence Attempts

	LEADER'S INITIAL CERTAINTY	MEAN LEADER INFLUENCE ATTEMPTS	NUMBER OF ITEMS
High	1	4.60	62
	2	4.95	92
	3	3.14	49
Low	4 and 5*	2.06	16

* These categories were combined because category 5 was used only a few times on initial judgment.

In the "within groups" analysis, the mean certainty of the two opponents was computed for each item. Then for each leader the items were divided into those on which the opponents showed high certainty (all items for which the opponents' mean certainty rating was 2.00 or less) and those on which they showed low certainty (all items for which the opponents' mean rating was greater than 2.00). The mean number of leader influence attempts per item was computed separately for each of the two sets of items for each leader. Finally, the algebraic difference in number of influence attempts made on the two sets of items was calculated for each leader, and a *t*-test was performed on the distribution of differences. For the 24 groups in which there were one or more items in each of the two categories, the mean difference in average number of leader influence attempts was .61. Though in the predicted direction, this difference is significant at only the .15 level.

In order to examine the combined effects of variations within and among leaders, we made a cross-break (similar to Table 3) of the mean influence attempted for items categorized according to the certainty of the opponents. The results showed no relation except for a slight trend at the extremes.

Thus all three analyses are consistent in showing no significant confirmation of Hypothesis I-3. Since most groups started the discussion by sharing their judgments and certainty ratings, the negative results are probably not due to inadequate perception of the opponent's certainty. It seems more likely that a contrary process was operating simultaneously: when the opponent was less certain he changed more quickly and hence the leader could attempt less influence and still obtain his objective.

Determinants of the effectiveness of the leader

The remaining hypotheses concern effectiveness of attempted influence. According to these hypotheses, the noncommissioned officer will be more successful in influencing his subordinates to the extent that they like him, they accept the authority of his role, they perceive him as an expert,[5] and he attempts more influence.

The analyses for these hypotheses focus on the covert influence rather than the overt influence of the leader. Thus the opinion changes dealt with are changes from initial private opinion to final private opinion rather than changes from initial private opinion to the group answer. Likewise the changes in certainty of opinion reflect private, covert influence. However, a few comments about

the leaders' overt influence seem appropriate. Each test situation provided by the group judgment test was an equilibrium situation, i.e., the subjects found themselves in a decision situation in which—for the group to accomplish its task of submitting a group answer—it was necessary for one side or the other to give way. Usually as soon as any one person had indicated a change of opinion, the discussion moved rapidly to a close, either with or without the expressed agreement of the remaining member. Despite the fact that the experimental activity was far removed from the usual role of the noncommissioned officer, the final group answer more frequently agreed with the initial private opinion of the leader and his partner than with the initial opinions of the leader's opponents ($p=.02$ by chi^2). Also, there was a tendency (not statistically significant) for the noncommissioned officer's influence on the group answer to be related to his acceptance by his opponents.

As already indicated, our chief interest is in the covert opinion changes. In 161 (or 59 per cent) of the 273 2-2 split situations for which data were obtained, at least one group member made such a change. The leader showed less tendency to change opinion than did the leader's partner and the leader's partner less than the leader's opponents, but the differences were small.

Opinion changes in relation to acceptance. Hypothesis II-1 says the more the group leader is accepted by another member of the group, the more effective will be his attempts to influence this member. One can, on the basis of this hypothesis, predict that the leaders who are highly accepted by their subordinates will be more effective in producing opinion changes than will leaders who are not so highly accepted. This prediction has been tested by comparing leaders among groups.

For each group we computed two indices: the sum of the three members' acceptance of the leader, and an index of leader effectiveness. In this situation, the success of the leader in influencing his group includes inducing his opponents to change their opinions, preventing his partner from switching to the opposite side, and resisting a change of his own opinion. Accordingly, this index of leader effectiveness scored positively changes by opponents and negatively changes by the leader and by his partner. The analysis utilizing this index yielded a Pearson *r* of .38 (*p* is approximately .03), so Hypothesis II-1 is confirmed using this measure of leader effectiveness.[6]

The above test of Hypothesis II-1 is somewhat

---

[5] The three interpersonal variables were found to have little relationship to each other. The highest intercorrelation among them was .27 ($N = 36$) between members' acceptance of the leader and the degree of expertness they perceived the leader to have.

[6] An index consisting of only the changes of opinion by the opponents yielded an insignificant trend in the same direction.

crude because it neglects: (a) the fact that leaders tended to have most influence over the members who liked them most (as predicted by the hypothesis), and (b) the influence of the opponent on the leader (Hypothesis II-1 would predict that leaders will change most toward opponents whom they like most). Therefore an analysis which includes the two-way influence process should account for more of the variance in leader effectiveness than does the simple index summing acceptance of the leader by the three group members. Using the full scale of answers to the question "How well do you like him?" each leader-opponent pair was classified into one of three categories: (a) the leader is more highly accepted by the subordinate than the subordinate is by the leader, (b) they accept each other equally, and (c) the leader is less highly accepted. For each opponent a tabulation was made of the number of 2-2 split items on which he changed toward the leader and the number of items on which he did not change. Change in opponent opinion occurred in 29 per cent of the 235 cases where the leader was more highly accepted, 20 per cent of the 185 cases where the leader was equally accepted, and in only 15 per cent of the 127 cases where the leader was less highly accepted. Thus the leader accomplishes almost twice as much influence when he is better liked than when he is less liked by his opponent.

Changes in certainty in relation to acceptance. The certainty ratings which accompanied the subjects' judgments on each item were obtained to provide an indicator of the effectiveness of influence attempts which would be more sensitive than the all-or-none measures based on opinion change. Two predictions regarding the relation of opponents' certainty ratings and acceptance of the leader were made on the basis of Hypothesis II-1. First, for opponents who changed their opinions from disagreeing with the leader on initial private judgment to agreeing with him on final private judgment, we would predict that high acceptors of the leader would be more confident of their new judgment than low acceptors. In other words, one would anticipate a positive correlation between acceptance of the leader and the certainty which the opponents have in their new judgments. The reasoning is that those who accept the leader more highly will be more dependent upon him for feeling their judgments are correct; having changed from disagreement to agreement with the leader, they will have a relatively greater sense of support for their final judgments. Second, those opponents who do not change will have their opinions shaken somewhat and they will respond by decreasing their certainty ratings.

Analyses were made both among groups and within groups to test the first prediction among opponents who changed toward the leader. The among-groups analysis was based on only 19 groups, some groups being omitted because certainty ratings were not available and some because there was not more than one instance in which an opponent made a change in judgment toward the leader. This analysis yielded an r of .53 ($p < .01$), indicating that those groups in which the members were more accepting of the leader tended to be those whose members were more certain of their new opinions. On the other hand the within-groups analysis failed to confirm the hypothesis although it was in the predicted direction. This analysis involved comparison of the mean certainty scores of the high-accepting and the low-accepting opponent in 16 groups. Since most opponents made only one or two changes from disagreement to agreement with the leader, the mean certainty scores involved are not very reliable. The low reliability and the small number of groups could account for failure to achieve a statistically significant result.

The second prediction about the relation of the opponent's certainty ratings and his acceptance of the leader was tested using only an opponent who did not change his opinion to agree with the leader and who knew (on the basis of the group discussion and public group decision) that his final judgment was different from the leader's final judgment. The prediction was that such opponents who were high acceptors would show more decrease (or less increase) in certainty from initial to final private judgment than would low acceptors. This prediction is based on much the same rationale as the first prediction, namely, that high acceptors are more dependent upon the leader for support for their opinions and thus will be more influenced toward uncertainty by expressions of counter-opinion on the part of the leader.

Examination of the data shows that, under the conditions specified by the second prediction, opponents tended to feel increased confidence in their judgments regardless of the level of their acceptance of the leader. However, the degree of increased confidence in judgments counter to the leader's was less in the case of high than in the case of low acceptors. The correlation was $-.29$ ($N=25$, $p=.08$), meaning that there was a near-significant tendency for the groups with high leader acceptance to be those in which opponents registered relatively small increases in certainty of judgment.

The within-groups analysis for the second prediction involved computing separately for each nonchanging opponent in each group the mean change in certainty ratings on items which met the necessary specifications. Then, in each group, the mean certainty change for the opponent with lowest leader acceptance was subtracted from that for the opponent with highest leader acceptance. The mean of the differences so obtained was $-.82$, showing that, on the average, the high acceptor in a group registered a smaller degree of increase in certainty than did the low acceptor in the same group. The mean difference of $-.82$ on the certainty scale is significantly different from zero at the .03 level of confidence ($N=22$, $t=2.00$, $df=21$).

Summary of the evidence for Hypothesis II-1. All of the evidence supports the hypothesis that the effectiveness of an attempt by a leader (or member) to influence another member of the group increases with increasing acceptance of the leader by the recipient.

1. More accepted leaders have more influence ($r=.38$, $p=.03$).
2. The leader accomplishes more influence when he is better liked by his opponent than when his opponent is better liked by him.
3. Opponents who changed their opinions toward the leader who was better liked were more certain of their new opinions ($r=.53$, $p<.01$). Within groups there was a trend in the same direction.
4. Opponents who did not change their opinions were less certain when they liked the leader more ($r=-.29$, $p=.08$ among groups; and $p=.03$ within groups).

Perceived authority as a determinant of effectiveness. Hypothesis II-2 states: the effectiveness of an influence attempt by the leader increases with increasing readiness of the follower to accept the authority conferred by the leader's role.

The analyses of changes in opinion (using differences within groups and the Pearson correlation among groups) showed no relation to perceived authority. However, a cross-break of the data suggests a curvilinear relationship between perceived authority of the leader and his effectiveness in changing opponents' opinions. Subjects who said that the typical noncommissioned officer has "a good deal of authority" were influenced by their own supervisors almost twice as much as those who responded with "a great deal of authority" or only "a fair amount."

Perceived expertness as a determinant of effectiveness. Hypothesis II-3 states: the effectiveness of an influence attempt by the leader (or member) increases with increasing perception that he is an expert in the area of the influence attempt. Analyses were made both among groups and within groups to test this hypothesis.

For the among-groups analysis, a Pearson r was computed between group indices for perceived expertness and leader effectiveness (the same measure used in the analysis of acceptance).[7] The obtained correlation was $-.32$ ($N=36$). Since high scores on the perceived expertness measure represent low perceived expertness, this correla-

tion is in the expected direction and significant beyond the .05 level.

The procedure used for the within-groups analysis was the same as that used in connection with acceptance of the leader. A leader effectiveness index (based only on changes in opponent judgment to conform to leader judgment) was computed separately for each opponent in each group. Then, from each group, two opponents were selected: the one who perceived the most expertness in the leader and the one who perceived the least. The leader effectiveness score for the opponent who perceived the least expertness was, in each group, subtracted from the leader effectiveness score for the opponent who perceived the most expertness, and a t-test was made to determine whether the mean of the distribution of differences in leader effectiveness scores was significantly different from zero. The obtained mean of the differences in leader effectiveness was .10, significant between the .05 and .10 level ($t=1.59$, $df=29$).[8] As one would expect, this much cruder analysis yields a less significant relationship.[9]

Effectiveness and attempted influence. The final hypothesis predicts that the total amount of influence effected by a leader over a member will increase with increasing influence attempts by the leader.

Using both previous measures of effectiveness, two analyses of the relation within groups and two analyses among groups were made. None of these four analyses showed a significant relation.

On theoretical grounds, we would expect no relationship where the acceptance of the leader was zero; where the leader was disliked, an inverse relation. Accordingly it seemed wise to try an analysis which controlled on acceptance of the leader. We also know that the amount of influence attempted by the leader correlates .55 with the amount attempted by the members (cf. Table 2). In such an argument between opposing sides, it seems likely that absolute increases in the frequency of influence attempted by the leader were being offset by corresponding increases by his opponents. Thus the analysis should also examine the amount of influence attempted by the leader *relative to* the amount attempted by members.

In the last 29 groups, where observational data were available, there were 218 items on which two members opposed the leader and his partner. Thus there were 436 cases where the change of opinion

---

[7] An index consisting of only the changes of opinion by the opponents again yielded a lower correlation of $-.19$.

[8] In the within-group analysis, six cases were lost because all three members in these groups made the same response on the item used to measure perceived expertness of the leader.

[9] An analysis which drew on both the variance within groups and the variance among groups confirmed Hypothesis II-3 at the .01 level.

of one opponent could be related to the amount of influence directed by the leader toward the pair of opponents.

Table 4 shows the percentage of these cases where the opponent changed his final private opinion to agree with the leader. In the upper half of the table, opinion change is related to the absolute frequency of influence attempted by the leader; in the lower half, opinion change is related to the amount of influence attempted by the leader expressed as a percentage of the total amount of influence attempted by all four members of the group. In both halves, Table 4 gives the breakdown for high and low acceptance of the leader by the opponent.

For highly accepted leaders there appears to be a curvilinear relation between effectiveness and absolute frequency of influence attempted, but this curvilinearity disappears when using the relative measure of influence attempted. A weaker trend of the same kind occurs for leaders who are low on acceptance. Clearly, there is no substantial correspondence between the greatest absolute attempts and the greatest relative attempts, or we should obtain the same type of relationship for both measures. Instead the greatest absolute frequency is associated with the smallest change

TABLE 4 *Opinion Change in Relation to Attempted Influence*

ABSOLUTE FREQUENCY OF INFLUENCE ATTEMPTED BY THE LEADER	PERCENTAGE OPINION CHANGE BY OPPONENTS WHERE ACCEPTANCE OF THE LEADER WAS:	
	High	Low
0 to 2	21.1 (109)*	17.3 (75)
3 to 5	27.4 (91)	23.6 (55)
6 to 8	43.8 (32)	18.8 (16)
9 or more	13.0 (46)	16.7 (12)
	24.5 (278)	19.6 (158)
INFLUENCE ATTEMPTED BY LEADER AS A PERCENTAGE OF TOTAL		
0 to 9%	9.8 (41)	10.5 (19)
10 to 19%	23.8 (63)	15.8 (57)
20 to 29%	17.6 (74)	15.0 (40)
30 to 39%	24.6 (57)	33.3 (21)
40% or more	51.0 (43)	33.3 (21)
	24.5 (278)	19.6 (158)

* Figures in parentheses indicate the number of cases on which the percentage in each cell is based.

whereas the greatest relative frequency is associated with the greatest change. Thus it appears to have been the "last word" which was important in producing change—in our conceptualization, it was the extra increment in a balanced system of mounting forces which finally produced a resultant sufficient to overcome the restraining force against change of opinion by one of the members. The highly accepted leaders were prepared to make more frequent attempts (see Table 2) to test the limits of their effectiveness, but they also got the last word more frequently.

In summary, the predicted relation of effectiveness to absolute frequency of influence attempted was not supported, perhaps because of a trend toward a curvilinear relation. Effectiveness was related to the relative frequency of influence attempted, though the significance of this relationship was not tested.

RESULTS OF THE CARD-SORTING EXPERIMENT

The aims of the card-sorting experiment, in contrast to those of the group judgment test, were quite circumscribed: (a) to test Hypothesis II-1 which asserts that the more the leader (or member) is accepted by another member of the group, the more effective will be his attempts to influence this member; and (b) to determine the relation between leader effectiveness and members' acceptance of the authority of the noncommissioned officer role. In addition, the relation between leader effectiveness and group members' acceptance of one another was examined.

The measure of leader effectiveness used in the card-sorting experiment consisted of the ratio: number of cards correctly sorted during the last two speed-up periods, to total number of cards correctly sorted in all periods.

Some of the principal characteristics of this measure of leader effectiveness and the reasons why these characteristics appeared desirable may be listed.

1. The measure reflects the extent to which output during "fast" periods exceeded output during "slow" and "base" periods. Response to "fast" and "slow" instructions are both weighted to some degree in this single measure.
2. The measure involves comparison between output during the last two "fast" periods and total output rather than between all three "fast" periods and total output. In designing the experiment a satiating task was purposely chosen with the hope of maximizing the restraining forces on the sorters. Actually, production continued to mount throughout the last three periods; but observations indicated, and comments in post-experimental interviews confirmed, that the need to relax increased rapidly for the sorters as the experiment drew to a close. If our reasoning is valid, differences in effective-

ness should be most evident toward the end of a session. The decision was therefore made to base computations of increase in output upon performance in the last two rather than all three of the "fast" periods.

3. The measure, by counting only correct sorts, considers quality as well as quantity of output. The messages introducing the fast periods of the experiment had instructed the subjects to "forget about mistakes" in the interest of speed, but in the context of the task as it had been defined for the subjects, the instruction could be taken literally only by someone who wanted to defeat the purpose of the attempted influence. The correlation between change in speed and change in percentage error from the slow to the fast periods was found to be $-.31$ ($N = 78$, the number of card-sorters) showing that those who increased their output the most tended to be those who increased their errors the least. Apparently, the second set of messages, regardless of their precise wording, had the effect of establishing a generalized pressure toward improved performance; and, as suspected, subjects who responded least readily to the pressure for speed were most ready to take advantage of the permission to relax on accuracy. On this basis, the conclusion was drawn that quality as well as quantity of performance needed to be taken into account.

Acceptance and effectiveness of the leader

The analysis employed for studying the relationship between acceptance of the leader and effectiveness of the leader was an "among-groups" analysis. In other words, an index of effectiveness of the leaders and an index of acceptance of the leader (the sum of the ratings of the leader by the three members) were obtained for each of the 26 groups, and the correlation between the pairs of indices was computed. The correlation was .42, showing that the more effective leaders tended to be those who were most highly accepted by their men. Since the obtained r is in the direction predicted and significant at better than the .05 level, the results of the card-sorting experiment confirm Hypothesis II-1.

Perceived authority and effectiveness of the leader

The among-groups correlation of leader effectiveness and the amount of authority group members perceived as residing in the noncommissioned officer role was only .08. The tendency toward a curvilinear relationship which was found in analysis of the group judgment test failed to show up in the card-sorting experiment.

Cohesiveness and effectiveness of the leader

It seems reasonable to expect that a leader will be effective in influencing his men partly through his ability to influence group standards. If this be the case, the leader's effectiveness should be greater in cohesive groups where the members are attracted to one another, for we know that more cohesive groups have more influence over their members (1, 6, 12, 13). In the card-sorting experiment this prediction is supported by an obtained correlation of .31, significant at approximately the .06 level, between intermember acceptance and leader effectiveness.

Finally, a multiple correlation coefficient was computed between leader effectiveness on the one hand and the two variables of acceptance of the leader and intermember acceptance on the other. The multiple correlation coefficient and the correlations involved in its computation were as follows:

Effectiveness (1) vs Acceptance of Leader (2)	.42
Effectiveness (1) vs Intermember Acceptance (3)	.31
Acceptance of Leader (2) vs Intermember Acceptance (3)	.64
Multiple Correlation ($R_{1.23}$)	.54

These results suggest that a sizable portion of the group-to-group variance in leader effectiveness can be accounted for in terms of members' acceptance of the leader and of one another. Also of interest is the strong tendency ($r = .64$) for groups in which members accept one another highly to be groups in which the members express a high degree of acceptance of the leader.

SUMMARY AND CONCLUSIONS

Two experiments were conducted to test seven hypotheses about the exertion of influence on judgments and behavior in small groups.

Determinants of influence attempted

In the preliminary field study, the amount of attempted influence reported by the noncommissioned officer was strongly related to organizational factors (the extent to which his own attitudes were officially approved and the relevance of the attitudes to the job), but was not related to interpersonal acceptance. In the first experiment these organizational factors were minimized by using judgments or opinions unrelated to the jobs of the subjects; hence interpersonal factors should account for more of the variance.

Hypothesis I-1. The amount of influence attempted by a leader (or member) over a given recipient increases with increasing acceptance of him by the recipient. Taken together, the several analyses of this relation for leaders and for members both within and among groups gives strong confirmation of the hypothesis. Apparently it is a more important determinant for members ($r=.54$) than for formal leaders ($r=.28$).

Hypothesis I-2. The amount of influence attempted by a leader (or member) increases with increasing certainty in his own opinion. Taken together, the three analyses (for the leaders only) significantly confirm the hypothesis.

Hypothesis I-3. The amount of influence attempted by a leader (or member) increases with decreasing certainty of opposing opinion in the recipient. Three separate analyses are consistent in showing no significant confirmation of the hypothesis. Perhaps there was a contrary process operating simultaneously: when the opponent was less certain he changed more quickly, and hence the leader could attempt less influence and still reach his goal. Both of these opposing processes are consistent with the basic assumption that the occurrence of an influence attempt is determined by the perceived probability of success in achieving some goal.

Determinants of effectiveness

In the field study there was a tendency for influence on opinions to be correlated with interpersonal relations. The first experiment strongly confirms this finding and demonstrates that the interpersonal relation is the independent variable. The second experiment further confirms the finding and extends it to the ability of the leader to influence the productivity of the group.

Hypothesis II-1. The effectiveness of an attempt by a leader (or member) to influence another member of the group increases with increasing acceptance of the leader by the recipient. This hypothesis was significantly confirmed for leader influence on: opinion changes ($r=.38$), changes in the certainty of these opinions ($r=.53$ and $r=.29$), and the productivity of the group ($r=.42$). In this test, the quantity and quality of influence attempts were exactly controlled. The leader's effectiveness in changing opinion is even more strongly related to *reciprocal* acceptance (how much the leader is accepted *relative to* how much he accepts the recipient) when there is opposition between the two. In the production experiment, where there is no such opposition, the effectiveness of the leader is also related to how much the members accept one another ($r=.31$).

Hypothesis II-2. The effectiveness of an influence attempt by the leader increases with increasing readiness of the follower to accept the authority conferred by the leader's role. The data from both experiments failed to confirm this hypothesis. It is possible that the measure of authority was inadequate or that the

experimental situation excluded the operation of formal authority.[10]

Hypothesis II-3. The effectiveness of an influence attempt by the leader (or member) increases with increasing perception that he is an expert in the area of the influence attempt. In the experiment on opinions this hypothesis was supported by the variance among groups ($r=.32$) and by a similar trend within groups ($.05$ $p=.10$).

Hypothesis II-4. The total amount of influence effected by a leader over a member increases with increases in the amount of influence attempted. As in the field study, this hypothesis was not supported in the first experiment, perhaps because of a trend toward a curvilinear relation. However, effectiveness was related to the *relative* amount of influence attempted, though the significance of this relation could not be tested.

REFERENCES

1. BACK, K. W. Influence through social communication. *J. abnorm. soc. Psychol.,* 1951, **46,** 9–23.
2. BIDDLE, B. J., FRENCH, J. R. P., JR., & MOORE, J. W. Some aspects of leadership in the small work group. A report to the U. S. Air Force, 1953.
3. CARTWRIGHT, D., & ZANDER, A. *Group dynamics: research and theory.* Evanston: Row, Peterson, 1953.
4. FESTINGER, L. Informal social communication. *Psychol. Rev.,* 1950, **57,** 271–282.
5. FESTINGER, L. An analysis of compliant behavior. In M. Sherif & M. O. Wilson (Eds.). *Group relations at the crossroads.* New York: Harper, 1953.
6. FESTINGER, L., SCHACHTER, S., & BACK, K. *Social pressures in informal groups.* New York: Harper, 1950.
7. HAVRON, M. D., FAY, R. J., & GOODACRE, D. M. Research on the effectiveness of small military units, PRS Report No. 885, Washington: Personnel Research Section, Adjutant General's Office, U. S. Army, 1951.
8. HOVLAND, C. I., & WEISS, W. The influence of source credibility on communication effectiveness. *Publ. Opin. Quart.,* 1951, **15,** 635–650.
9. LIPPITT, R., POLANSKY, N., REDL, F., & ROSEN, S. The dynamics of power. *Hum. Relat.,* 1952, **5,** 37–64.
10. MOORE, H. T. The comparative influence of majority and expert opinion. *Amer. J. Psychol.,* 1921, **32,** 16–20.

---

[10] A subsequent experiment by John R. P. French, Jr., and Bertram Raven confirms the hypothesis.

11. NEWCOMB, T. Autistic hostility and social reality. *Hum. Relat.*, 1947, **1**, 69–87.

12. SCHACHTER, S. Deviation, rejection, and communication. *J. abnorm. soc. Psychol.*, 1951, **46**, 190–207.

13. SCHACHTER, S., ELLERTSON, N., McBRIDE, D., & GREGORY, D. An experimental study of cohesiveness and productivity. *Hum. Relat.*, 1951, **4**, 229–238.

14. SNYDER, R. An experimental study of the influence of leaders in small work groups. Unpublished doctor's dissertation, Massachusetts Institute of Technology, 1953.

COMPETENCE AND CONFORMITY IN THE ACCEPTANCE OF INFLUENCE*

The problem posed by Hollander in this selection, the relation between conformity and status, has been touched on before. While the evidence suggests that conformity to the norms of a group increases a group member's status, the study by Harvey and Consalvi[a] indicated that persons highest in status conform less than those intermediate in this respect. If low status is associated with low conformity, and intermediate status with high conformity, we might well expect high status to be associated with very high conformity. This is not the case; the high-status individuals exhibit only moderate conformity. A related problem emerges in connection with leadership structures.

Leaders are expected to display in their behavior the values of the group. Yet in their role as innovator they must on occasion deviate from these values. Hollander has provided a conceptual solution to these contradictions. He suggests that as a person emerges as a leader he gains status by virtue of his conformity to group values and his competence in contributing to group goal achievement. Such increments gained in the process of becoming a leader can be thought of as units of "idiosyncrasy credits" which he may later draw upon when he deviates from group norms in order to perform leadership actions at variance with group norms. Hollander then performs an ingenious experiment in which he successfully tests a number of predictions derived from this conceptualization.

32.

Competence and Conformity in the Acceptance of Influence[1]

E. P. HOLLANDER
UNIVERSITY OF BUFFALO

When one member influences others in his group it is often because he is competent in a focal group activity. A member may show such competence by individual actions that further the attainment of group goals (cf. Carter, 1954); more specific situational demands may variously favor the ascent of the expediter, advocate, or what Bales and Slater (1955) have termed the task specialist. An additional condition for the acceptance of influence involves the member's perceived adherence to the normative behaviors and attitudes of his group. His record of conformity to these expectancies serves to sustain eligibility of the sort Brown (1936) calls "membership character."

A person who exhibits both competence and conformity should eventually reach a threshold at which it becomes appropriate in the eyes of others for him to assert influence; and insofar as these assertions are accepted he emerges as a leader. But it is still necessary to account for the "nonconformity" that leaders display as they innovate and alter group norms. Certain shifts must therefore occur in the expectancies applicable to an individual as he proceeds from gaining status to maintaining it.

This process has been considered recently in a theoretical model of status emergence (Hollander, 1958). It features the prospect that behavior perceived to be nonconformity for one member may not be so perceived for another. Such differentiations are seen to be made as a function of status, conceived as an accumulation of positively disposed impressions termed "idiosyncrasy credits." A person gains credits, i.e., rises in status, by showing competence and by conforming to the expectancies applicable to him at the time. Eventually his credits allow him to nonconform with

* The selection following the editorial introduction is reprinted from "Competence and conformity in the acceptance of influence," *Journal of Abnormal and Social Psychology*, 1960, **61**, 365–369, by permission of the author and the American Psychological Association.

[a] Harvey, O. J., & Consalvi. Status and conformity to pressures in informal groups. *J. abnorm. soc. Psychol.*, 1960, **60**, 182–187.

[1] This paper is based upon a study completed under ONR Contract 1849(00), while the author was at the Carnegie Institute of Technology. The views expressed here are those of the author and do not necessarily reflect those of the Department of the Navy.

The considerable assistance of H. Edwin Titus in this study is gratefully acknowledged.

Parts of the paper were reported at the symposium on "Recent Conceptions in Influence and Authority Process," held under the auspices of Division 8 at the 1959 APA Convention.

greater impunity.[2] Moreover, he is then subject to a new set of expectancies which direct the assertion of influence. Thus, whether for lack of motivation or misperception, his failure to take innovative action may cause him to lose status.[3]

It is readily predictable that in task oriented groups a member giving evidence of competence on the group task should with time gain in influence. If he simply nonconforms to the procedures agreed upon, the opposite effect should be observed. But the sequential relationship of nonconformity to competence is especially critical.

From the model, it should follow that, with a relatively constant level of manifest competence, the influence of a person who nonconforms *early* in the course of group interaction should be more drastically curtailed than in the case of a person who nonconforms *later*. Indeed, a reversal of effect would be predicted in the latter instance. Once a member has accumulated credits, his nonconformity to general procedure should serve as a confirming or signalizing feature of his status, thereby enhancing his influence. Accordingly, it may be hypothesized that given equivalent degrees of task competence, a member should achieve greater acceptance of his influence when he has conformed in the past and is now nonconforming than he should when nonconformity precedes conformity.

METHOD

Design

Twelve groups, each composed of four male subjects, were engaged in a task involving a sequence of 15 trials. A group choice was required for each trial from among the row alternatives in a 7 × 7 payoff matrix (see Figure 1). In every group, a fifth member was a confederate whose prearranged response was contrived to be correct on all but four trials,

[2] This is a newer formulation of an observation long since made regarding the latitude provided leaders (e.g., Homans, 1950, p. 416). It is further elaborated in Hollander (1959).
[3] This proposition is consistent with various findings suggestive of the greater social perceptiveness of leaders (e.g., Chowdhry & Newcomb, 1952).

i.e., 2, 3, 6, and 12, thus reflecting considerable competence on the task. All interactions among participants took place through a system of microphones and headsets from partitioned booths. Subjects were assigned numbers from 1 to 5 for communicating with one another. The central manipulation was the confederate's nonconformity to procedures agreed upon by each group in a pretrial discussion. In terms of a division of the 15 trials into three zones—early, middle, and late—of 5 trials each, six treatments were applied: nonconformity throughout, nonconformity for the first two zones, for the first zone alone, for the last two zones, for the last zone alone, and a control with no nonconformity. In one set of treatments the confederate was designated number 5, and in the other number 4, to test possible position effects. Acceptance of the confederate's influence was measured by the number of trials by zone in which his recommended response was accepted as the group's. This was supplemented by post-interaction assessments.

Subjects

The 48 subjects were all juniors in the College of Engineering and Science at the Carnegie Institute of Technology. All had volunteered from introductory psychology sections after being told only that they would be taking part in a study of problem solving in groups. Care was taken in composing the 12 groups so as to avoid either placing acquaintances together or having membership known in advance. Thus, no two subjects from the same class section were used in the same group, and subjects reported at staggered times to different rooms. By the time a subject reached the laboratory room where the experiment was actually conducted, he had been kept apart from the others and was not aware of their identity. The subjects never saw one another during the entire procedure, nor were their names ever used among them.

Instructions and set

Once seated and assigned a number, every subject was given a sheet of instructions and the matrix used for the task. These instructions fell into two parts, both of which were reviewed aloud with each subject individually, and then with the entire group over the communication network. The first part cautioned the subjects to always identify themselves by number (e.g., "This is Station 3 . . .") before speaking and not to use names or other self-identifying references. The second part acquainted them with the procedures

FIGURE 1. Matrix used in group task.

	GREEN	RED	BLUE	YELLOW	BROWN	ORANGE	BLACK
ABLE	−1	−12	+5	−1	−2	+15	−4
BAKER	+10	−1	−2	−7	+4	−3	−1
CHARLIE	−5	+5	−3	+3	−11	−1	+12
DOG	+5	−7	+10	−2	−5	+1	−2
EASY	−4	−1	−1	+1	+13	−10	+2
FOX	−6	+15	−5	−1	−3	−1	+1
GEORGE	−1	−1	−2	+10	+4	−2	−8

to be used, emphasized the aspect of competition against a "system," and established the basis for evident procedural norms. It read as follows:

1. You will be working with others on a problem involving a matrix of plus and minus values. Everyone has the same matrix before him. The goal is to amass as many plus units as possible, and to avoid minus units. Units are worth 1 cent each to the group; the group begins with a credit of 200 units. You cannot lose your own money, therefore. There will be fifteen trials in all.

2. In any one trial, the task involved is for the group to agree on just *one* row—identified by Able, Baker, Charlie, etc.—which seems to have strategic value. Once the group has determined a row, the experimenter will announce the column color which comes up on that trial. The intersecting cells indicate the payoff. Following this announcement, there will be thirty seconds of silence during which group members can think individually about the best strategy for the next trial, in terms of their notion about the system; note please that there are several approximations to the system, although the equation underlying it is quite complex. But work at it.

3. At the beginning of each trial the group members must report, one at a time, in some order, as to what they think would be the best row choice on the upcoming trial. Members may "pass" until the third time around, but must announce a choice then. Following this, groups will have three minutes on each trial to discuss choices and reach some agreement; this can be a simple majority, or unanimous decision; it is up to the group to decide. If a decision is not reached in three minutes, the group loses 5 units.

4. Before beginning the trials, the group will have five minutes to discuss these points: (*a*) The order of reporting; (*b*) How to determine the group choice for a given trial; (*c*) How to divide up the money at the end. These decisions are always subject to change, if the group has time and can agree. After the 15th trial, group members may have as much as five minutes to settle any outstanding decisions. Then headsets

are to be removed, but group members remain seated for further instructions, and the individual payment of funds.

Instruments and procedure

The matrix was specially constructed for this study to present an ambiguous but plausible task in which alternatives were only marginally discrete from one another.[4] The number of columns and rows was selected to enlarge the range of possibilities beyond the number of group members, while still retaining comprehensibility. The fact that the rows are unequal in algebraic sum appears to be less important as a feature in choice than the number and magnitude of positive and negative values in each; there is moreover the complicating feature of processing the outcome of the last trials in evaluating the choice for the next. All considered, the matrix was admirably suited to the requirements for ambiguity, challenge, conflict, immediate reinforcement, and ready manipulation by the experimenter.

The confederate, operating as either 4 or 5 in the groups, suggested a choice that differed trial by trial from those offered by other members; this was prearranged but subject to modification as required. Since subjects rather typically perceived alternatives differently, his behavior was not unusual, especially during the early trials. For the 11 trials in which the confederate's row choice was "correct," the color that "came up" was contrived to yield a high plus value without at the same time providing a similar value for intersection with another person's row choice. Had his recommendation been followed by the group on these trials, high payoffs would have accrued.

The device of a 5-minute pretrial discussion had special utility for establishing common group expectancies, in the form of procedures, from which the confederate could deviate when called for in the design. Predictable decisions on these matters were reached unfailingly. But their importance lay in having a *public affirmation* of member intent. Thus, on order of reporting, it was quickly agreed to follow the order of the numbers assigned members. Each group, despite minor variants suggested, decided on simple majority rule. Regarding division of funds, equal sharing prevailed, sometimes with the proviso that the issue be taken up again at the end.

In the zones calling for nonconformity, the confederate violated these procedures by speaking out of prescribed turn, by questioning the utility of majority rule, and by unsupported—but not harsh—challenges to the recommendations made by others. He manifested such behaviors on an approximate frequency of at least one of these per trial with a mean of two

---

[4] The matrix is an adaptation, at least in spirit, of a smaller one used with success by Moore and Berkowitz (1956).

per trial considered optimum. Thus, he would break in with his choice immediately after an earlier respondent had spoken and before the next in sequence could do so; when there were periods of silence during a trial he would observe aloud that maybe majority rule did not work so well; and he would show a lack of enthusiasm for the choice offered by various others on the matter of basis. Lest he lose credibility and become a caricature, in all instances he chose his moments with care and retained an evident spontaneity of expression.[5]

RESULTS AND DISCUSSION

The task gave quite satisfactory signs of engrossing the subjects. There was much talk about the "system" and a good deal of delving into its basis, possibly made the more so by the subjects' academic background; the returned matrices were littered with diagrams, notations, and calculations. Though quite meaningless in fact, the confederate's tentative accounts of his "reasoning" were evidently treated with seriousness, perhaps as much because of the contrived time constraint,

[5] The same person, H. E. Titus, was the confederate throughout.

which prevented probing, as of his jargon regarding "rotations" and "block shifts." In any case, the confederate at no time claimed to have the system completely in hand. He delayed his response from the sixth trial onward to suggest calculation of an optimum choice in the face of conflicting alternatives; and the four trials on which he was "wrong" were spaced to signify progressive improvement, but not total perfection.

Most pertinent, however, is the fact that there were no manifestations of suspicion concerning the confederate's authenticity. The others seemed to believe that he was one of them and that he was "cracking" the system; the post-interaction data were in full agreement.

Since all of the interactions were available on tape, it was possible to derive a number of indices of acceptance of influence. The most broadly revealing of these appeared to be the frequency of trials on which the confederate's recommended solution was followed.

In Table 1 this index is employed to discern the effects of three major variables. The analysis is arranged by zones (Z) of trials, and in terms of the confederate's nonconformity (NC) in the *current* zone and immediate *past* zone.[6] The

[6] For Zone I, the "past zone" refers to the discussion period. If he was to nonconform there, the confederate would question majority rule and suggest that the division of funds be left until the end rather than agree then on equal shares.

TABLE 1 *Mean Number of Trials on Which a Group Accepts Confederate's Recommended Solution*

CONFEDERATE'S PREVIOUS CONFORMITY	ZONE I (TRIALS 1–5)		ZONE II (TRIALS 6–10)		ZONE III (TRIALS 11–15)	
	Nonconforming*	Conforming	Nonconforming	Conforming	Nonconforming	Conforming
With Procedural nonconformity in immediate *past* zone	1.67		3.25	3.00	4.00	5.00
	6†		4	2	4	2
Without Procedural nonconformity in immediate *past* zone		2.00	5.00	3.75	5.00	4.75
		6	2	4	2	4

Analysis of Variance

SOURCE	SS	df	MS	F
Current nonconformity	.20	1	.200	
Zones	47.05	2	23.525	35.01§
Past nonconformity	3.36	1	3.360	5.00‡
Int: Current $NC \times Z$	1.22	2	.610	
Int: Current $NC \times$ past NC	13.52	1	13.520	20.12§
Int: $Z \times$ past NC	.72	2	.360	
Int: Current $NC \times Z \times$ past NC	4.11	2	2.055	3.06
Residual	16.12	24	.672	
Total	86.30	35		

* Confederate showed procedural nonconformity on the trials in this zone.   † Indicates number of groups upon which cell is based.
‡ $p < .05$.   § $p < .001$.

means given in each cell indicate the number of trials, out of five per zone, on which the confederate's choice was also the group's. In a chi square test, the effect of position upon this measure was found to be nonsignificant, and is therefore omitted as a distinction in the analysis of variance.

The significant F secured from Zones is in accord with prediction. It reveals the ongoing effect of task competence in increasing the acceptance of the confederate's choice, to be seen in the rising means across zones. While current nonconformity does not yield a significant effect, past nonconformity does. Viewing the table horizontally, one finds that the means for "without" *past NC* exceed the means for "with" *past NC* in all instances but one. Regarding the significant interaction of *current* and *past NC*, the combination "without-without" has a sequence (2.00, 3.75, 4.75) of persistently higher value than has "with-with" (1.67, 3.25, 4.00); this, too, is in line with prediction. Finally, the maximum value of 5.00 in Zone II for the combination "without" *past NC* but "with" *current NC* confirms the key prediction from the model, at least within the context of the relative magnitudes there; the same value is also seen in Zone III for the identical combination; still another reading of 5.00 holds there, however, for the inverse combination, but in a tight range of values quite beyond separation of effects for interpretation.

Considerable consistency was found too in the post-interaction data. On the item "overall contribution to the group activity," 44 of the 48 subjects ranked the confederate first; on the item "influence over the group's decisions," 45 of the 48 ranked him first. Two things bear emphasis in this regard: subjects had to individually write in the numbers of group members next to rank, hence demanding recall; and their polarity of response cut across all six treatments, despite significant differences among these in the actual *acceptance of influence.* That the confederate therefore made an impact is clear; but that it had selective consequences depending upon the timing of his nonconformity is equally clear.

In detail, then, the findings are in keeping with the predictions made from the model. The operational variable for measuring acceptance of influence was confined to the task itself, but nontask elements are touched as well. In that respect, the findings corroborate the subtle development of differential impressions as a function of even limited interpersonal behavior.

Some unquantified but clearly suggestive data are worth mentioning in this regard. Where, for example, the confederate began nonconforming *after* the first zone, his behavior was accepted with minimal challenge; by the third zone, his suggestion that majority rule was faulty yielded a rubber stamping of his choice. Again, if he had already accrued credit, his pattern of interrupting

people out of turn not only went unhindered but was taken up by some others. Quite different effects were elicited if the confederate exhibited nonconformity from the *outset,* notably such comments of censure as "That's not the way we agreed to do it, five."

The findings are especially indicative of the stochastic element of social interaction and its consequence for changing perception. Especially interesting is the fact that these effects are produced even in a relatively brief span of time.

SUMMARY

A study was conducted to test the relationship between competence on a group task and conformity or nonconformity to procedural norms in determining a person's ability to influence other group members. Data were gathered from 12 groups engaged in a problem solving task under controlled conditions. Each was made up of five members one of whom was a confederate who evidenced a high degree of competence during the 15 trials. His nonconformity to the procedural norms agreed upon by the group was introduced at various times, early, middle, or late, in the sequence of trials. Influence was measured by the number of trials (per segment of the entire sequence) in which the confederate's recommended solution was accepted as the group's choice. As a broad effect, it was found that a significant increase in his influence occurred as the trials progressed, presumably as a function of the successive evidences of competence. Past conformity by the confederate was also found to be positively and significantly related to the acceptance of his influence; finally, there was a statistically significant interaction between past and current nonconformity reflected in high influence in the groups in which the confederate had conformed earlier in the sequence of trials but was presently nonconforming. These results were all thoroughly consistent with predictions made from the "idiosyncrasy credit" model of conformity and status.

REFERENCES

BALES, R. F., & SLATER, P. E. Role differentiation in small decision-making groups. In T. Parsons, R. F. Bales, et al. (Eds.), *Family, socialization, and interaction process.* Glencoe, Ill.: Free Press, 1955.

BROWN, J. F. *Psychology and the social order.* New York: McGraw-Hill, 1936.

CARTER, L. F. Recording and evaluating the performance of individuals as members of small groups. *Personnel Psychol.,* 1954, **7,** 477–484.

CHOWDHRY, KAMLA, & NEWCOMB, T. M. The relative abilities of leaders and non-leaders to estimate opinions of their own groups. *J. abnorm. soc. Psychol.*, 1952, **47**, 51–57.

HOLLANDER, E. P. Conformity, status, and idiosyncrasy credit. *Psychol. Rev.*, 1958, **65**, 117–127.

HOLLANDER, E. P. Some points of reinterpretation regarding social conformity. *Soc. Rev.*, 1959, **7**, 159–168.

HOMANS, G. C. *The human group.* New York: Harcourt, Brace, 1950.

MOORE, O. K., & BERKOWITZ, M. I. Problem solving and social interaction. *ONR tech. Rep.*, 1956, No. 1. (Contract Nonr-609(16), Yale University Department of Sociology)

LEADERSHIP: INSTRUMENTAL AND SOCIAL-EMOTIONAL FUNCTIONS*

In the following selection Verba has brought together in an instructive fashion the research relevant to a basic problem in leadership: the inherent antithesis between instrumental and social-emotional leadership, between directing others toward task accomplishment and meeting their emotional needs, between getting the job done and being liked. Verba emphasizes throughout the contemporary view of leadership in terms of processes, such as role differentiation, legitimization, etc., rather than in terms of the traits of leaders. A methodological lesson also emerges from his analysis. Phenomena observed in a laboratory inevitably reflect some of the unique characteristics of this setting and cannot be expected to take the same form in the everyday world. In this instance the special conditions of the laboratory heightened the conflict between the two leadership functions, favoring their allocation to two different individuals. The answer to why this conflict and this particular solution do not occur so frequently in everyday situations produced a considerable theoretical advance through specifying the conditions under which these two leadership functions will be exercised by different persons or by the same person.

33.

Leadership: Affective and Instrumental

SIDNEY VERBA
STANFORD UNIVERSITY

CONFLICTING EXPECTATIONS: THEIR RESOLUTION IN SMALL GROUPS

The two leaders. To shed some light upon the way in which the conflict between instrumental and affective leadership is resolved, we turn first to the small group experimental literature. The resolution of the conflict in these small groups will then be compared with the resolution in larger,

on-going social systems. In the small groups studied by Bales and his associates, the conflict between instrumental and affective leadership is resolved by a differentiation within the leadership role. In these groups different individuals tend to specialize in the instrumental leadership role and in the socio-emotional leadership role. The evidence for this role differentiation is found in the material cited above: those members highly selected by the group by an affective criterion were not likely to be selected by the group as having contributed to the instrumental task, nor were they likely to be active in giving the group direction toward the accomplishment of that task. On the other hand, the individual selected by the group as contributing the most to the external task (Best Ideas) was also highly selected as contributing most to the instrumental aspect of the internal group task (Best Guidance). High choice by one criterion was closely correlated with high choice by the other, and the individual rated lowest by one was likely to be lowest by the other. The findings by Bales and his associates that the leadership role tends to be split between a task-oriented instrumental leader and a "sociometric star" is supported by small group studies of other authors. Both Gibb and Olmstead found that affective choice did not correlate highly with choice by an instrumental criterion. And Cattell and Stice in a factor analysis of leader characteristics found that different characteristics are associated with leadership defined in "syntality" terms (i.e., in terms of contribution to changes in group productivity) and leadership defined by an affective sociometric criterion.[1]

* The selection following the editorial introduction is reprinted from "Leadership: Affective and instrumental," in *Small Groups and Political Behavior: A Study of Leadership*, Princeton, N.J.: Princeton University Press, 1961, pp. 161–184, by permission of the author and publisher.

[1] Bales, in Parsons, Bales, and Shils, *Working Papers . . . ,* p. 147; Michael S. Olmstead, "Orientation and Role in the Small Group," *Am. Soc. Rev.*, **19** (1959), pp. 741–51; and Cattell and Stice, *Hum. Rel.*, **7** (1954). It should be pointed out that role differentiation of this sort is a tendency in small groups, not something that happens in every small group—even in experimental situations. See Robert F. Bales and Philip E. Slater, "Notes on 'Role Differentiation in Small Experimental Groups': Reply to Dr. Wheeler," *Sociometry*, **20** (1957), pp. 152–55. However, Parsons and Bales (*Family, Socialization . . .* , chap. 7) suggest that this role differentiation has a high level of generality. Morris Zelditch (*ibid.*, chap.

Activities of the two leaders. The fact that group leadership tends to be split between two individuals is reflected not only in the fact that group members choose different individuals by socio-emotional and instrumental criteria, but also in the fact that the behavior patterns of the individuals thus selected differ. When one looks at the interaction rates of the group members most highly selected on the basis of the socio-emotional and the instrumental (Best Ideas) criteria, one finds significant differences. The socio-emotional leader tends to initiate and receive more interactions in the socio-emotional categories of interaction than does the task specialist. He gives and receives more solidarity and tension-release interactions. The task specialist, on the other hand, is more active in giving opinions and suggestions; and he receives larger amounts of agreement, questions, and negative reactions. The difference between the behavior of the two leaders is best described by Slater: "The most salient general difference between the rates of interaction of the two types of leaders is the tendency for the Idea man to initiate interactions more heavily in Area *B* (Problem Solving Attempts) and the Best-liked man in Area *A* (Positive reactions). . . . On the Receiving end, the situation is largely reversed, with the Idea man receiving more agreement, questions and negative reactions, while the Best-liked man receives more problem solving attempts, and more solidarity and tension release. The general picture is thus one of specialization and complementarity, with the Idea man concentrating on the task and playing a more aggressive role, while the Best-liked man concentrates more on social emotional problems, giving rewards, and playing a more passive role."[2] The qualitative ratings given the two leaders by the group members are thus reflected in their quantitative interaction rates.

The difference between the two specialists extends to the attitudes of these two group members. Not only do they specialize in certain areas of the group activity, but they receive their satisfactions from those areas. The instrumental leader, it has already been suggested, is relatively less motivated to receive positive affective responses from the group. His personal satisfactions derive not from the affective responses of the group

members, but from the instrumental task directly. For the "sociometric star," on the other hand, ". . . *primary* satisfaction derives from his success in his role as promoter of solidarity and provider of opportunities for tension release. . . ."[3] The socio-emotional leader also tends to be more accepting of the other group members, while the task specialist differentiates among the other members in the degree to which he accepts them. On the sociometric question in which the group members were asked to rate the other members on the degree to which they liked them, 42 per cent of the socio-emotional leaders did not differentiate among the members (they said, in effect, "I like everybody") while only 20 per cent of the task leaders did not so differentiate.[4]

Relations between the two leaders. The balance between affective tone and instrumental accomplishment is maintained in these groups, then, by the development of two leaders. The disturbance in the expressive area caused by the instrumental directives of the task leader is countered by positive affective reactions from the socio-emotional leader. In understanding this process, it is important to note the relations between the two leaders. Bales and Slater found that the two had close relations, one with the other. The task and socio-emotional leaders tended to interact more frequently with each other than did any other pair of members; and, what is equally significant, tended to agree more frequently with each other.[5] In this way, it may be suggested, the task leader receives indirectly through the socio-emotional leader the expressive support that he could not directly obtain because of his instrumental role. That such a coalition between the two group

---

6) presents evidence for such a role differentiation within the nuclear family between the father (the instrumental leader) and the mother (the affective leader). We shall, however, look at the development of leadership bifurcation as an hypothesis to be tested in different situations. As we shall see, in some social situations there are mechanisms that lower the level of functional necessity of this role differentiation.

[2] Slater, in Hare, Borgatta, and Bales, eds., *Small Groups*, p. 507. See Bales and Slater, in Parsons and Bales, *Family, Socialization* . . . , p. 279, table 6, for the rates of interaction of the two specialists; and *ibid.*, pp. 280–83, for the tests of significance that have been applied to the data.

[3] Bales, in Parsons, Bales, and Shils, *Working Papers* . . . , p. 250. The distinction between the two types of leaders based upon the source of their satisfaction from participation in the group is similar to the distinction between various organizational clientele made by Barnard and Simon.

It bears a close resemblance as well to the distinction drawn by Harold Lasswell (based on quite different psychological evidence) between the two political types—administrator and agitator. "The essential mark of the agitator is the high value he places upon the emotional response of the public" (*Psychopathology and Politics*, p. 78). Administrators, on the other hand, ". . . are distinguished by the values they place upon coordinated effort in continuing activity." Whereas agitators are emotionally involved with the people with whom they deal politically, the administrators ". . . display an impersonal interest in the task of the organization itself. . . ." (*ibid.*, p. 263).

[4] Bales and Slater, *op. cit.*, p. 294. The difference is significant at the .06 level using a Chi square test.

[5] *Ibid.*, pp. 282–84.

leaders is important for the effective functioning of the group is suggested by a comparison made by Bales and Slater between High Status Consensus groups and Low Status Consensus groups.[6] In the former type of group—in which, as was pointed out earlier, task accomplishment and member satisfaction are both higher—the relationships between the two leaders are statistically significant. In the Low Consensus groups, though there is a tendency for the two leaders to interact with each other, the pattern is neither as consistent nor as strong.[7]

CONFLICTING EXPECTATIONS: THEIR RESOLUTION IN ON-GOING SYSTEMS

The conflict in expectations placed upon leaders has now been spelled out. In small experimental groups we have found that this conflict is resolved by the development of two leaders—an affective and a task leader—accompanied by an implicit coalition between the two men. On-going social systems, including political systems, must also deal with instrumental and affective relationships. Political systems, as well as small groups, depend upon inputs from their members of both instrumental activities (contributions of resources, services, etc.) and affect (loyalty, respect, etc.). And these systems maintain the adherence of their members by outputs in both these areas: specific services as well as affective rewards for participation in the system.[8] The model suggested by the

---

[6] For a definition of these two types of groups, see *ibid.*, pp. 274–77.

[7] *Ibid.*, pp. 283–84. The discovery of the dual functions of leaders and the fact that these functions tend to be split between two different group members suggest one reason why low correlations have been found between various measures of influence. We may define influence, as does March, in terms of its effect on the recipient of the influence attempt—i.e., ". . . if the individual deviates from the predicted path of behavior, influence has occurred. . . ." (J. G. March, "An Introduction to the Theory and Measurement of Influence," *Am. Pol. Sci. Rev.*, **49** [1955], p. 435.) Under this definition, influence may have a single result: changing the behavior of the recipient of the influence attempt. But several behaviors may be required of the influential to accomplish this. An influence act may, for instance, have an instrumental and affective component. And, as the studies cited in the text indicate, the two components of such an act may be divided between two individuals. Studies that find a low correlation among measures of influence may not be demonstrating the weakness of these measures, but may reflect the complexity of the influence act and the fact that a single influence act may be performed by several influentials at once.

[8] This analysis of political systems is suggested by David Easton, "An Approach to the Analysis of Political Systems," *World Politics*, **9** (1957), pp. 383–400.

---

studies of experimental groups suggests that the conflict between the affective and the instrumental aspects might best be resolved by a bifurcation of the leadership function. Faced with this conflict, does the on-going social system develop such a differentiated leadership structure, or are other mechanisms available to it to resolve this conflict? Clearly we can give no final answer to such a broad question. But a preliminary attempt to explore the resolution of this conflict in on-going social systems will be rewarding both in heightening our understanding of these systems and, what is more important in terms of this present study, in helping us to specify some of the differences between processes in experimental and non-experimental systems. An understanding of these differences is essential if we are to attempt to apply the results of experimental studies to non-experimental systems.

Special characteristics of small group leadership. When one attempts to compare the way in which the conflict between the two group tasks is handled in experimental and non-experimental systems, one is struck by certain special characteristics of the culture of the experimental laboratory—characteristics that tend systematically to affect the nature of the relations between the two tasks. The situation in the experimental groups is such as to raise the level of conflict between instrumental control and affective acceptance above that which one would expect in non-experimental situations. This heightened conflict derives from the external culture of these groups as well as from the internal structure.

The experimental groups discussed by Bales and his associates and by Gibb commence their interaction with a leaderless internal structure. No leader has been appointed or sanctioned by the experimenter. The object of these experiments is to see the way in which leadership structures develop in response to the group task. But the behavior of the leader with no external support who must emerge from a group differs significantly from the behavior of a leader who has some external sanction for his leadership position. In a series of experiments, Launor Carter found that group leaders who had been appointed by the experimenter were less active in expressing opinions, in arguing, and in defending their positions from attack than were group leaders who emerged on their own. "It appears that in the appointed situation, the leader may conceive of his role as that of a coordinator of activity or as an agent through which the group can accomplish its goal. In the emergent group, on the other hand, the person who becomes the leader may take over the leadership by energetic action and by trying to get the other members to accept his leadership."[9] The emergent leader, it would seem, is engaged in a

---

[9] Carter, *et al.*, in Cartwright and Zander, eds., *Group Dynamics*, p. 557.

struggle for power in the group. His directive acts are not supported by the sanction of the experimenter's appointment and are not expected by the group members. If his directives are to be accepted he must exert his direction more vigorously than must an appointed leader. And increased vigor leads to increased resistance.

This position is supported by studies of leaders who have developed high status in a group over time. As their status becomes more secure, they can afford to "let up" and lower their amount of directive acts without risking their position. Thus Heinicke and Bales found that in later meetings of a group in which a high-status individual had emerged, the high-status person performed fewer directive acts than he had performed in the group meetings that preceded his achievement of high status.[10] March suggests a similar tendency for leaders, selected as such on a post-session sociometric test, to reduce their overt attempts to influence other group members in those cases where such overt behavior does not seem to be necessary.[11] Moreover, leaders in on-going groups with diffuse and long-term relations are able to delegate their leadership in particular instrumental areas without risking their overall position. Whyte's description of the street corner gang leader is instructive in this connection: "It is my observation that interaction can be patterned and still have no resemblance to the stereotype of autocratic leadership. Take for example, Doc in the Nortons gang as described in my *Street Corner Society*. Doc gave the impression of being very unaggressive in that he did not often come out with ideas for action for the group. On the contrary there were many occasions when members of the group would suggest actions that the group subsequently carried out. But note this important point. The suggestions were always made to Doc and were not acted upon positively unless Doc gave at least his acquiescence. I observed that activity involving the whole group would be initiated either through the acceptance by Doc of suggestions presented by others or by proposals directed from Doc to the group."[12]

[10] Heinicke and Bales, *Sociometry*, 16 (1953), pp. 35–37.
[11] March, *Sociometry*, 19 (1956).
[12] W. F. Whyte, unpublished paper, quoted in Heinicke and Bales, *op. cit.*, p. 36.

That longer-lived groups are not beset by such a sharp split between instrumental and affective aspects of leadership suggests that, as experimental groups continue their interaction over time, the division between the two leaders should diminish. One would expect that the split between the two forms of leadership would be quite sharp during the first few group sessions before any leadership structure had been developed, but that as a consistent leader emerged whose control attempts came to be expected by the members, the negative affect in response to his control attempts would diminish. The experimental evidence on this point is mixed. Slater found that as the meetings of his experimental groups progressed, the percentage of times in which the same member held the

This description of leadership in an on-going group with a history of interactions suggests that experimental groups with no previous experience together differ in a systematic way from such systems. Insofar as members are similar in age, insofar as they are similar in status in the external culture of the group, and insofar as the experimenter supplies no sanction for any particular leadership structure, any directive attempt by a group member will be looked upon as a challenge to the other members. With no status consensus among the group members at the beginning of interaction and no status guides, would-be leaders in the new experimental groups are placed in a clear power struggle. The increased vigor necessary to control the group increases the negative reaction to the leader and heightens the conflict between acceptance and instrumental control.

The nature of the task in the small experimental groups also tends to heighten the conflict between the affective and instrumental aspects of the leadership function. Insofar as the accomplishment of the group task is important to the group members, those leaders who contribute to the accomplishment of that task will be rewarded with positive affect from the group members. But in the experimental groups considered above, the group task is assigned to the group by the experimenter and is not one toward which the members are highly motivated. The members may recognize that a particular individual contributed more to the accomplishment of the task, but they will not like that group member any more because of this.[13] Furthermore the use of college students

highest position on Best Ideas and Best-liked fell considerably —from 56.6 per cent of the time in the first meeting to 8.8 per cent of the time in the fourth. (Significant by Chi square at the .01 level. See Slater in Hare, Borgatta, and Bales, eds., *Small Groups*, p. 504, table 4.) Gibb, on the other hand, reports a tendency for the split between affective choice and instrumental leadership to diminish over time (*ibid.*, p. 536, table 3). It is in any case doubtful whether the groups used by Slater or by Gibb had sufficient time together to test the hypothesis that the leadership split will diminish over time. (There were four sessions in the Slater experiment, and three in the experiment by Gibb.)

Furthermore, our hypothesis states that as the group progresses over time, instrumental controls will receive less negative affect. This does not mean they will necessarily receive positive affect. As a stable group structure develops, group members may begin to differentiate themselves more from the group leader and direct their positive affect toward peers in the group rather than toward the higher-status leader.

[13] In a replication of the Bales experiment, Philp and Dunphy increased the motivation of the experimental subjects to accomplish the task set for them. The subjects were told that group performance would be taken into consideration in deciding upon class grades. Under this situation of heightened

of similar age may well create groups that negatively value the exertion of direct interpersonal
influence. The evidence from the experiment by
Hemphill cited above suggests a reluctance to use
interpersonal influence in these groups. Similarly,
Beatrice Shriver found that there were definite
cultural limits beyond which group members selected as leaders by the experimenter would not
go in exerting influence in the group. Thus the
group leaders balked at selecting certain group
members to receive higher rewards for their participation in the group. When it was suggested
that they give bonuses to the most effective group
members, the leaders either refused to make such
a selection or did so by some random means
(flipping coins, throwing darts).[14]

In the experiments, therefore, individuals who
do not value highly interpersonal control by
others are brought together in groups where the
exercise of such control has no external backing
from some extra-group hierarchy. The members
are unknown to each other and have no apparent
status differences such that one member would
be expected to exert more influence in the group
than another. Under these circumstances it is no
wonder that the most active group member, even
if he contributes the most to group performance,
will tend to be rejected by the group on socio-
emotional criteria. His control attempts are viewed
as arbitrary and as direct personal challenges. And
such directives are likely to arouse negative reactions. As Frank has put it, "Resistance to an
activity is readily aroused if it involves submitting to an arbitrary personal demand of someone else, and it is thereby equivalent to a personal
defeat."[15]

Legitimate leadership. Such arbitrary interpersonal
influence exists when the recipient of the influence
attempt does not consider that attempt legitimate
—i.e., when the recipient does not feel that the
leader *should* perform the acts he does perform.
In cases where there is a non-legitimate use of
interpersonal influence, followers may accept the
directives of leaders because the leader controls
certain sanctions or because of a desire to see
the group task accomplished, but such influence

relationships are likely to cause resistance and to
be unstable. On the other hand, if the recipient
of the directive believes that directive to be right
and proper, resistance will not develop. Where,
as in the experimental work by Carter described
above, the appointed leader had his position legitimized by the experimenter, he was not rejected
by the group nor did he have to engage in as
much overt influence. A more striking example
of the difference between legitimate leadership
that is expected and non-legitimate leadership is
found in the contrasting reaction to the directives
of the emergent leader and the directives of the
experimenter himself. One often forgets that there
is an authority figure in the leaderless experimental groups—the experimenter. He is usually older
and of higher status. Above all, by entering the
experimental situation the group members expect
his directives and accept them as legitimate. Consequently, unlike their rejection of the emergent
leader, experimental subjects follow the directives
of the experimenter without complaint or resistance. In fact, Frank reports the failure of an
experiment to measure resistance to unpleasant
tasks because subjects could not be induced to
resist any task assigned them by the experimenter.[16]

In on-going groups and organizations, it is the
development of a *legitimate* leadership structure
rather than the development of a dual leadership
structure that constitutes the major way in which
the conflict between affective and instrumental
leadership is resolved. In a study of 72 on-going
chaired committees in business and government,
Berkowitz found that when the chairman who was
expected to control the group did so, the satisfaction of the group members increased. Negative
reactions developed only when he failed to perform as expected. Furthermore, and this is significant, when the chairman performed as expected
and controlled the group, control attempts initiated by other group members led to the rejection of those members by the group—just as the
control attempts of the non-legitimized leaders in
the experimental groups led to negative reactions.
But where the chairman did not perform as expected, the group member who attempted to fill
the gap was not rejected by the group.[17] In groups

---

motivation to accomplish the task, affective-instrumental conflict was not as strong as in the work of Bales. See Hugh
Philp and Dexter Dunphy, "Development Trends in Small
Groups," *Sociometry,* 22 (1959), pp. 162–74. A similar finding
is reported by March, *ibid.,* 19 (1956), pp. 260–61.

[14] B. Shriver, unpublished Ph.D. dissertation, cited in Launor
Carter, *Annual Status Report,* Office of Naval Research, Contract Nbonr-241, Task Order V, Feb. 1, 1952.

[15] J. D. Frank, "Experimental Studies of Personal Pressure and
Resistance," *J. General Psychology,* 30 (1944), pp. 23–56.

[16] *Ibid.*

[17] Berkowitz, *J. Abnorm. Soc. Psych.* (1953). Several other
studies support this point. Heyns compared two sets of experimental groups. In one set a high-status leader performed
the leadership acts expected of him. In the other set of groups,
the leader did not so perform. In the first case, where the control
of the leader was expected and the leader did in fact exercise such
control, attempts to lead the group by other members resulted
in their rejection on a sociometric test after the group session.
In the groups where the leader did not perform as expected,
control attempts by other members resulted in their receiving
higher rankings on a post-session sociometric test. (R. W.
Heyns, "Effects of Variations in Leadership on Participant

in which there is an expected leadership pattern, negative affect will be engendered not by the control attempts of the legitimate leader, but by a failure of that leader to perform as expected; or if he performs as expected, by individuals who challenge his leadership.

The negative reactions to leader non-performance suggest that the model developed by Bales and his associates must be modified when the instrumental control attempts come from a legitimate leader. When control attempts are initiated by someone who is expected to initiate them, the disequilibrating force is not the control attempt, but any opposition that may develop to that control. Violation of the directive, not the directive itself, disturbs the smooth functioning of the group. In this case, the equilibrating mechanism is the sanction that the leader or the other group members employ to enforce acceptance of the directive.

Role of norms in follower compliance. One of the most effective ways in which the instrumental directives of a group leader acquire legitimacy and avoid being received as personal, arbitrary challenges to the group members is for the leader to be perceived as acting not as an individual but as the agent of some impersonal force, such as the "demands of the situation" or the group traditions and norms. The invocation of some external authority by the group leader relieves the follower of the burden of accepting the control of another individual. Thibaut and Kelley, in a study of power relations in the dyad, conclude that group norms have the effect of reducing the tension between the more powerful and the less powerful

member of the group. The impersonalization of expectations of behavior through the adoption of norms makes the influence relationship between the more and the less powerful group member more stable and palatable for both of them. For the less powerful member, the use of controls without a normative base would make those controls arbitrary and unpredictable, and lead to resistance on his part. For the more powerful member of a dyad, the use of purely personal power would also be unpleasant. He must either reduce his attempted control (and thereby perhaps endanger the accomplishment of the group goal) or risk the negative reactions of the other member. Thus the exercise of control in the name of a set of norms that legitimizes the control is to the advantage of both leader and follower. Alvin Gouldner makes a similar point in relation to bureaucratic organizations. The advantage of impersonal rules in a bureaucratic situation is not that these rules completely replace interpersonal influence, but that they make that influence less visible. In a society that stresses equalitarian norms, this reduction in the visibility of control increases legitimacy and reduces tensions.[18]

Impersonalization of control has been noted to be an effective means of social control in a number of contexts. Mannheim maintains that a key transition point in the development of human societies occurs when regulation of conduct ceases to be carried on in the name of an individual and begins to be exercised in the name of the needs of the group. Primitive groups, he points out, develop social functions that must be performed if the group is to survive. "Provision for such necessary functions is the external source and motivation of regulation in contrast to mere person-to-person relationships. The collective responsibility calls for recurrent and lasting functions, including that of leadership. The leader may give orders to the subordinate members of his team and on occasion use physical or psychological pressures. In so doing, he links his personal, physical and mental strength to an objective function. . . . In this situation a strange metamorphosis occurs: the 'archaic' experience of purely personal power is linked to and, so to speak, transfused into the social function. . . . The metamorphosis is also significant because it demarcates the beginning of the process that substitutes the control of man by institutions and organizations for that of man by man. . . ."[19]

Behavior in Discussion Groups," unpublished Ph.D. dissertation, University of Michigan, 1948.) Similar findings are reported by Crockett, *J. Abnorm. Soc. Psych.* (1955).

That the group member from whom the other group members expect control attempts will be rejected not for these attempts but for violating the group's expectation that he will exercise such control is supported by a finding in the classic Lippitt and White experiments. They found that of the three leader styles they used—the democratic, the authoritarian, and the laissez-faire—the style least liked by the children in the groups was the laissez-faire. Since the group leaders were adults appointed as leaders of the children's clubs, it is likely that the rejection of the laissez-faire leader, whose instructions were to keep his activity down to a minimum, resulted from his violations of the children's expectations that he would lead. See White and Lippitt, in Cartwright and Zander, eds. *Group Dynamics.*

Informal leadership, it would seem, arises in general as a gap-filler when formal leadership does not perform as expected. Kahn and Katz, for instance, point out that in production groups led by supervisors who did not perform differentiated leadership functions, an informal leader who spoke for the group was more likely to arise than in those groups where the supervisor performed the differentiated leadership functions expected of him. Kahn and Katz, in *ibid.*

[18] Thibaut and Kelley, *The Social Psychology of Groups,* chap. 8; and A. W. Gouldner, *Patterns of Industrial Bureaucracy* (Glencoe, Ill.: Free Press, 1954). See also March and Simon, *Organizations,* p. 44.

[19] Mannheim, *Freedom, Power* . . . , pp. 51–52.

Mary Parker Follett has emphasized the greater effectiveness of impersonal control in industrial situations. If industrial managers are to receive acceptance for their directives, she suggests, they must phrase those directives as coming from the "demands of the situation."[20] Blau gives an example of the way in which the introduction of statistical records of performance in a bureaucratic situation reduced negative reactions to criticism by supervisors. Rather than the subordinate receiving criticism from the superior as an individual, the subordinate perceived the criticism as engendered by the objective records, which were allowed to "speak for themselves."[21] The impersonalization of control is an especially useful technique in situations where individual autonomy is highly valued and in which challenges to that autonomy are likely to lead to strong negative reactions. Micaud and Crozier, writing of controls in French administration, suggest that it is the depersonalization of the control of subordinates by superiors in the name of traditional rules of conduct that allows the inferior personnel to accept the directives and maintain their dignity.[22] And impersonalization has been found to be an effective technique in that bastion of individuality, the French Chamber of Deputies. Melnick and Leites discuss the tendency of members of the Chamber jealously to guard their independence when it is challenged by personal persuasion. On the other hand, they will bow to constraint when it comes in the guise of the "force of events." "Before the first ballot [for President of the Republic] no power of human persuasion could convince an important majority of the URAS to support an outside candidate. But . . . face to face with the figures they . . . readily accept this policy. Submission to the dictates of the event is not regarded as incompatible with freedom of movement. On the contrary, the individual seems to feel that in heeding the lesson derived from the facts he is making full use of his freedom, while he would feel very differently about accepting the opinion of a colleague or leader. . . . He does not chafe at the constraint [the events] impose on him, for it is impersonal. . . ."[23]

Role of norms in leader motivation. The introduction of norms in on-going situations is a technique for mitigating the negative affect of the followers and for increasing the probability that they will comply with the directives of the leadership structure. Norms also operate upon the group leader. By insulating him from the negative affective reactions of followers, they make it easier for him to engage in task-oriented activities. The particular norm that operates to insulate the leader from the affective response of his followers is the norm of social distance. Studies cited above have shown that instrumental leaders tend to cut themselves off from satisfactory affective relationships with other group members and that leaders must to some extent be willing to accept this lack of affective support. The isolation of group leaders has been noted in many contexts. In a review of group studies, Chapin notes that individuals highly chosen by the group on various sociometric criteria rarely reciprocate choices they receive. Their highly chosen position sets them apart from the other group members.[24] Rieken and Homans emphasize the tendency of the group leader—especially in highly structured groups—to be cut off from his followers. "A ship captain at sea is socially the most isolated man in the world. Ashore, he drinks—with other captains."[25] The distance between the leader and his followers, enforced in on-going structured groups and organizations by social distance norms, allows the leader to perform more adequately as an instrumental leader by lowering his susceptibility to the affective reactions of the group. This hypothesis is supported by Fiedler in a study of on-going groups in military and business organizations. Those groups were more effective whose leaders were avoidant and distant from the followers.[26] Similar findings are reported in studies of air crews.[27] And Blau, in his study of a bureaucratic organization, suggests that bureaucratic authority cannot be as effectively exercised by supervisors having close informal ties with their subordinates as it can by more distant supervisors.[28]

---

[20] Mary Parker Follett, *Freedom and Coordination* (London: Management Publications Trust, 1949), p. 22.

[21] Blau, *Dynamics of Bureaucracy*, p. 40.

[22] Micaud, manuscript, chap. 2, p. 7; Crozier, *Esprit* (1957); and Crozier, *Rev. Française de Sci. Pol.* (1956).

[23] Constantin Melnick and Nathan Leites, *House Without Windows: France Selects a President* (Evanston, Ill.: Row, Peterson, 1958), p. 34.

[24] Chapin, *Am. Soc. Rev.* (1950).

[25] Riecken and Homans, in Lindzey, ed., *Handbook . . .* , p. 825. Harry Truman has written that "To be President of the United States is to be lonely, very lonely at times of great decisions." *Year of Decisions: The Truman Memoirs*, Vol. 1 (New York: Doubleday, 1956), p. ix.

[26] See Fred L. Fiedler, "A Note on Leadership Theory: The Effect of Social Barriers on Leaders and Followers," *Sociometry*, **20** (1957), pp. 87–94.

[27] Halpin found a negative relationship between a crew's rating of the "consideration" of the aircraft commander and that commander's effectiveness as rated by his superiors. *J. Abnorm. Soc. Psych.* (1954). Fruchter, Blake, and Mouton report that ". . . the crews that rated aircraft commanders highest for making crew membership more enjoyable, accepting responsibility, etc., were least effective in terms of the performance criterion." Benjamin Fruchter, Robert R. Blake, and Jane S. Mouton, "Some Dimensions of Interpersonal Relations in Three-Man Crews," *Psychological Monographs*, **71** (1957), no. 448.

[28] Blau, *op.cit.*, pp. 162 and 167–71.

When the leader does not have close personal ties with his followers, he can make decisions on instrumental grounds, rather than on particularistic personal grounds. Just as the development of norms in the group allows the leader to carry on instrumental activities without the negative affective reactions that might lower his instrumental effectiveness, so the development of norms leading to social distance enables him to function effectively in the instrumental area without being dependent upon the affective responses of his followers.

The process of legitimation. The development of the type of leadership found in experimental groups (leadership perceived by followers to be arbitrary and personal) into the type found in most on-going systems (leadership perceived to be impersonal and proper)—i.e., the process of legitimation of leadership—is probably one of the most important processes in political affairs. How does leadership that is seized by an individual with no sanction from the group become leadership that is accepted and expected by the group? Laboratory studies of groups with no expectations of leadership might be an excellent place to study this question. Do the laboratory studies thus far shed light upon this process of the legitimization of leadership? Unfortunately, at this time the answer is probably no.

The development of a legitimate leadership structure out of the leaderless group structure found at the beginning of the experimental studies would have to move through three stages. In the first place, certain members of the group must, in response to the group task, begin to differentiate their activities from those of the other group members. Secondly, the other group members must perceive the difference in the behavior of the group member or members who devote themselves more directly to the group task. And, lastly, the group members must come to regard this differentiated activity as right and proper. The first stage is reached in almost all experimental groups studied. Behavior counts show that significant differences in the behavior of the various members can be found in the first meetings of the new groups. The second stage, the recognition of the differing activity patterns, is also reached in many small group studies. But it is difficult to say if the third and crucial stage is reached—the stage at which the group members come to consider the differentiated activity of the group leader or leaders right and proper. The problem is that the small groups cited above do not deal with expectations of leadership. This can be seen in the conception of role used in these studies. Role as defined by Slater is ". . . a more or less coherent and unified system of items of interpersonal behavior."[29] A group role is thus defined by the

particular behaviors (as measured by interaction counts) in which a member engages. This definition does not take into account the expectations others may hold about the role performer.[30] The existence of expectations as to the leader's behavior is not observed directly in these studies, but is ". . . inferred from consistencies in overt behavior, consensus on ratings, and congruence between behavior and received ratings."[31] This inference is not necessarily valid. That a group member behaves in a certain consistent way and that the other group members agree that he is so behaving do not necessarily imply that the other group members sanction this behavior. The assumption that they do not sanction the leader's behavior is supported by the evidence that he receives negative affect for his instrumental control. In view of the absence of direct measures of expectation, we must agree with the cautious comment of Bales and Slater that "The degree to which differentiated roles in the fully structural sense appear in these small decision-making groups is perhaps a moot point."[32]

Since expectations of behavior are so significant for ongoing groups, it is to be hoped that small group researchers will begin to deal with them directly. One problem is that even those studies that do deal with legitimacy deal with it as an independent variable—i.e., legitimacy is introduced by the experimenter to see how it affects some dependent variable such as productivity or acceptance.[33] But if we wish to study the develop-

---

[29] Slater, in Hare, Borgatta, and Bales, eds., *Small Groups,* p. 498.

[30] A more usual definition of role would be in terms of the expected proper behavior for the occupant of a particular status. Thus Hartley and Hartley define social role as ". . . an organized pattern of expectancies that relate to the tasks, demeanors, attitudes, values, and reciprocal relationships to be maintained by persons occupying specific membership positions and fulfilling definable functions in any group. The emphasis here is on expectancies rather than on behavior because the role is defined by what others expect of the person filling it." (Eugene L. Hartley and Ruth E. Hartley, *Fundamentals of Social Psychology* [New York: Knopf, 1952], p. 486.) This is not to argue that the definition of role in the work of Bales, Slater, and their associates is a "wrong" definition. Role has been defined in many ways; at times, as a set of behaviors. (See Gross, *et al., Explorations in Role Analysis,* p. 14.) The definition of role used in these studies has been emphasized because it sheds light upon the types of relationships studied in these experiments.

[31] Bales and Slater, in Parsons and Bales, eds., *Family, Socialization . . . ,* p. 260.

[32] *Ibid.*

[33] See Bertram H. Raven and J. R. P. French, "Legitimate Power, Coercive Power and Observability in Social Influence," *Sociometry,* **21** (1958), pp. 83–97; and J. R. P. French, H. William Morrison, and George Levinger, "Coercive Power and Forces Affecting Conformity" (forthcoming).

ment of legitimate leadership, we must hope for studies of legitimacy as a dependent variable. What group structures, for instance, are conducive to the development of leadership that is accepted by the group? What sort of behavior on the part of an emergent leader indicates to group members that they ought to accord legitimacy to this individual? What type of task encourages the growth of legitimate leadership? These are some of the questions the answers to which would greatly increase our knowledge of political behavior. The small leaderless experimental groups may differ from on-going groups in that they have no pattern of expectations of differentiated leadership behavior. In some ways this limits the usefulness of these small groups for analysis of on-going social systems. But it also presents the possibility of studying in these small groups the process by which such expectations develop.

EXPERIMENTAL GROUPS AND ON-GOING SOCIAL SYSTEMS COMPARED

Experimental groups and on-going systems resolve the problem of conflict within the leadership role in different ways. The existence of these differences, however, does not imply that experimental studies are useless in understanding behavior in on-going social systems. It is to be hoped in fact that the very process of specifying some of the differences between experimental groups and on-going groups has added somewhat to our understanding of the processes in the latter. In any case, such specification of the differences between the two systems is necessary if studies relating the two levels are to be attempted.

Some similarities between the two systems. It should be pointed out that the differences between the two systems may not be as great as would first seem. The balance between instrumental control and affect is achieved in experimental groups by role differentiation within the leadership role. In on-going groups the balance may be achieved by the development of a leadership structure in which the instrumental control attempts are not identified with the personal arbitrary will of the leader. In both cases, the effects of negative affect in response to instrumental control attempts are mitigated by separating the responsibility for the instrumental directive. In the experimental group, this is accomplished by the development of two leaders. In the on-going situation, the responsibility for instrumental acts is projected on to the demands of the situation or the group norms.

Leadership role differentiation in on-going systems. Furthermore, the need for instrumental achieve-

ment as well as for affective satisfactions may, even in on-going groups, best be met by the development of a dual leadership structure. We have emphasized above that instrumental leadership in on-going groups may be insulated from negative reactions by a normative pattern that legitimizes the instrumental control. But this does not mean that instrumental leadership in an on-going social system is the best source of positive affective outputs to the groups members. It may well be that under certain circumstances the need for positive affective outputs is best satisfied by the development of a dual leadership structure.[34]

There are certainly situations in which a separation of the instrumental and affective aspects of group leadership plays an important part in the functioning of the system. Argyris, for instance, points out some of the difficulties that prevent formal organizations from satisfying the affective need of participants. In response to these needs a separate informal organization and leadership structure develops, better able to deal with the expressive aspects of the participation in the organization.[35] Similarly, Barnard points out that the informal organization is largely concerned with "feeling in the ranks."[36] And it is useful in this connection to remember Bagehot's classic distinction between the efficient and the dignified parts of the British Constitution—a distinction similar to that between instrumental and affective leadership. The two parts of the British Constitution perform different functions: ". . . first, those which excite and preserve the reverence of the population—the *dignified* parts . . .; and, next, the *efficient* parts—those by which it, in fact, works and rules." The important point is that though the efficient parts perform the actual instrumental functions, the dignified parts motivate individuals to participate in the system. "The dignified parts of the government are those which bring it force—which attract its motive power. The efficient parts only employ that power."[37]

There are probably many other situations in on-going groups where a division of the leadership function operates to increase the group effectiveness. But if we wish to test the proposition that it is the absence of normative expectations in experimental groups that leads to the tension between affective and instrumental leadership, it may be better to look at the structure of leadership in on-going social systems where the actions of the leader are not sanctioned by his followers. One situation in which leaders are forced to en-

---

[34] Parsons maintains that the role differentiation observed in the small experimental group is a general pattern of group structuring to deal with the affective and instrumental aspects of group interaction. He bases this largely on certain similarities between patterns in the experimental groups and in the nuclear family. See Parsons and Bales, *op. cit.*, p. 381.

[35] Chris Argyris, *Personality and Organization,* chap. 4.

[36] Barnard, *Functions . . .* , p. 169.

[37] Walter Bagehot, *The English Constitution* (London: D. Appleton, 1920), pp. 72–76.

gage in such unsanctioned activities arises when a group is faced with a new challenge and demand for change from the external environment. If, because of training or values, the traditional group leader is unable to deal with the new group problems, he may be replaced by a new leadership structure that does not have the fund of acceptance of the traditional leader. In situations of this nature, if the system is to remain stable, a bifurcation of leadership would be a way of balancing the new instrumental demands and the affective needs of the members. Eisenstadt points out that such a division of labor into an instrumental and a socio-emotional leadership is one of the most effective means by which immigrant groups in Israel can adjust to their new environment. "If the principal economic and political positions which are directly related to the institutional framework of the absorbing society are successfully performed by the new elite, and if the old elite is satisfied with performing more 'private' expressive functions (religious, ritual, etc.) there exists at least the possibility of a positive group transformation."[38]

Functional differentiation is, therefore, a means of solving the conflict caused by new demands upon group leaders. In a book on the problems facing professional "change agents" in group and community work, Lippitt, Watson, and Westley suggest that this division of labor can be consciously used in attempts to change communities and groups. They discuss the negative affective reactions that can arise in response to attempts to change a community. The "change agent," while avoiding too close a relationship with the client, must keep this negative affect to a minimum and must try if possible to develop positive affect with the group he is trying to change. One technique that has been tried by community workers is the use of teams of workers, some of whom are oriented solely toward the task at hand and some of whom are oriented toward a sympathetic emotional relationship with the client.[39]

A division of the leadership function may also be a useful technique when an instrumental act is likely to result in a sharp negative reaction. It is a common political practice for leaders to delegate control functions to a "scapegoat" leader when those controls are ones of which the followers are not likely to approve. Thus informal leaders—a Colonel House or a Harry Hopkins —may be used by the President to expedite unpopular changes. Or unpopular policies may be associated with a subordinate leader rather than with the President himself. The delegation of unpopular control acts to a "scapegoat" leader as a means of protecting the group leader from negative affect may be especially useful when the leader leads several groups at once. In these cases an act satisfying one group may not satisfy another. Machiavelli writes of the technique employed by the kings of France when faced with conflicting demands from the nobles and the masses. The king wished to relieve himself ". . . of the dissatisfaction that he might incur among the nobles by favoring the people, and among the people by favoring the nobles. He therefore established a third judge that, without direct charge of the king, kept in check the great and favored the lesser people. . . . From which another notable rule can be drawn, that princes should let the carrying out of unpopular duties devolve on others, and bestow favors themselves."[40]

CONCLUSION

This chapter has explored an aspect of the leader-follower relationship found to be significant in both small experimental groups and in on-going social systems. The use of a leadership problem common to both levels has given us a frame of reference within which the two systems can be compared. Though there are significant similarities between the ways in which this problem is resolved in the two systems, there are also significant differences. The latter have been traced largely to the special culture of the experimental situation.

The differences between the two levels do not destroy the usefulness of studies on one level for understanding relations on the other. Rather, *if these differences are known*, the small experimental group can be used as a model of relations in on-going situations. Both the ways in which the on-going system accords with and the ways in which it differs from the experimental model will increase our knowledge of on-going social systems. Further, it has been suggested that certain significant social processes in on-going situations —in particular, normative expectations of the followers—might fruitfully be built into the experimental studies. That connections between the experimental and the on-going situations cannot be made on a one-to-one basis does not imply that all such connections are useless. Cautious and continuing attempts to relate the two systems show promise of increasing our fund of knowledge of social and political processes.

The relationship between instrumental and affective aspects of social systems is highy significant for the understanding of political behavior. Political systems must provide their members with both types of outputs—the instrumental and the affective. In what ways can actual political systems provide both at once? Is it possible for an elite group of a society to perform both instrumental and affective leadership functions? Or

[38] Eisenstadt, *Int. Soc. Sci. Bull.* (1956).

[39] Ronald Lippitt, Jeanne Watson and Bruce Westley, *The Dynamics of Planned Change* (New York: Harcourt, Brace, 1958).

[40] Niccolo Machiavelli, *The Prince* (New York: Modern Library, 1940), pp. 69–70.

do most systems have separate elites for this? Can the individual member of a political system receive affective outputs from non-political relationships—the family, for instance—that lower the pressure on the political system to provide them?

These questions and many others are suggested by the analysis of leadership problems in this chapter. The student of political systems and organizations would do well to consider the often neglected relationship between affective and instrumental outputs of these systems and organiza-

tions. In particular, the attachment to political symbols and the effect of this attachment on instrumental effectiveness deserve study. Is low or negative affect always associated with low instrumental output? Was pre-Gaullist France such a system? Or can low affect be combined with high instrumental output? Are the USSR and China systems of this nature? If low affect can be combined with high instrumental output, what special mechanisms are required? Will such systems tend to be coercive?

It is hoped that the attempt to relate small group studies of a significant leadership problem with that problem as it exists in on-going systems has suggested an important political relationship that deserves further study.

THE CONTINGENCY MODEL: A THEORY OF LEADERSHIP EFFECTIVENESS[*]

Since the early work of Lewin, Lippitt, and White,[a] the consequences of leadership style have been the focus of numerous studies. While a variety of terms have been applied to what the initial investigators called democratic and authoritarian leadership climates, these two polar types are reflected in the distinction drawn by Fiedler between the leader who is accepting, permissive, considerate, and person-oriented and one who is directive, controlling, and task-oriented. Conclusions drawn from most studies favored the former type of leader as the most desirable. In part, as Gibb[b] has noted, this may well have reflected a cultural bias in favor of democratic leadership, a bias against which even the scientific investigator was not immune. The fact that in the initial investigation the quantity of production was greater under authoritarian leadership seemed to have had relatively little effect on later discussions of the problem.

Other investigations, such as that of Shaw,[c] showing greater quality and quantity of production under authoritarian leadership, and those of Morse[d] and Berkowitz,[e] showing lower levels of satisfaction

under democratic conditions, suggested that the earlier position that gave almost unqualified scientific approval to the accepting, permissive, person-oriented style of leadership should be modified. As Gibb[f] has suggested, under certain circumstances authoritarian leadership might be expected to have more favorable consequences. Only recently, however, has there been a systematic attempt to delineate these circumstances. In the selection below, Fiedler presents a theoretical model that attempts to specify the condition under which each type of leadership is more effective. This model, suggested by previously gathered data, is then tested by a reanalysis of this data in terms of the model. Finally, he submits his theoretical model to new data gathered explicitly to test it. This last step is necessary since up to this point the model, while consistent with the data which originally suggested it, might have fit only these data and not a new sample. By applying it to data based on a new sample, Fiedler has added considerably to the external validity of the study.

* The selection following the editorial introduction is reprinted from "The contingency model: A theory of leadership effectiveness," a paper based on research conducted under Office of Naval Research Contracts 170–106, N6–ori–07135, and RN 177–472, Nonr 1834(36), by permission of the author.

[a] K. Lewin, R. Lippitt, & R. K. White. Patterns of aggressive behavior in experimentally created social climates. *J. soc. Psychol.*, 1939, **10**, 271–299.

[b] C. A. Gibb. Leadership. In G. Lindzey (ed.), *Handbook of social psychology.* Vol. 2. Reading, Mass.: Addison-Wesley Publishing Co., Inc., 1954. Pp. 877–920.

[c] M. E. Shaw. A comparison of two types of leadership in various communication nets. *J. abnorm. soc. Psychol.*, 1955, **50**, 127–134.

[d] Nancy Morse. *Satisfactions in the white-collar-job.* Ann Arbor, Mich.: University of Michigan, Survey Research Center, 1953.

[e] L. Berkowitz. Sharing leadership in small, decision-making groups. *J. abnorm. soc. Psychol.*, 1953, **48**, 231–238.

34.

The Contingency Model: A Theory of Leadership Effectiveness[1]

FRED E. FIEDLER
UNIVERSITY OF ILLINOIS

ABSTRACT

A "contingency model" is proposed for predicting leadership effectiveness of small task groups. The model induced

[f] Gibb. *Op. cit.*

[1] The present paper is mainly based on research conducted under Office of Naval Research Contracts 170–106, N6–ori–07135 (Fred E. Fiedler, Principal Investigator) and RN 177–472, Nonr 1834(36), (Fred E. Fiedler, C. E. Osgood, L. M. Stolurow, and H. C. Triandis, Principal Investigators). The writer is especially indebted to his colleagues, A. R. Bass, L. J. Cronbach, M. Fish-

from previously obtained data on over 800 groups postulates that the prediction of leader performance, based on the leader's attitude and behavior measures, is contingent upon adequate classification of group situations and group tasks within which the leader must operate. The model predicts that directive, managerial, active leaders perform best under conditions which provide them with either considerable, or with relatively little effective power. Permissive, considerate, non-directive leaders perform best in group situations intermediate in the degree of effective power which the leader has at his disposal. The model was tested and extended by reanalyses of available data as well as a major experiment which is briefly described. The findings suggest a resolution of the theoretical controversy on the desirability of authoritarian, decisive, controlling leadership and supervision versus non-directive, permissive, and democratic leadership.

Leadership, as a problem in social psychology, has dealt primarily with two questions, namely, how one becomes a leader, and how one can become a *good* leader, that is, how one develops effective group performance. Since a number of excellent reviews (e.g., Stogdill, 1948; Gibb, 1954; Mann, 1959; Bass, 1960), have already dealt with the first question we shall not be concerned with it in the present paper.

The second question, whether a given leader will be more or less effective than others in similar situations, has been a more difficult problem of research and has received correspondingly less attention in the psychological literature. The theoretical status of the problem is well reflected by Browne and Cohn's (1958) statement that ". . . leadership literature is a mass of content without coagulating substances to bring it together or to produce coordination . . ." McGrath (1962), in making a similar point, ascribed this situation to the tendency of investigators to select different variables and to work with idiosyncratic measures and definitions of leadership. He also pointed out, however, that most researchers in this area have gravitated toward two presumably crucial clusters of leadership attitudes and behaviors. These are the critical, directive, autocratic, task-oriented versus the democratic, permissive, considerate, person-oriented type of leadership. While this categorization is admittedly oversimplified, the major controversy in this area has been between the more orthodox viewpoint, reflected in traditional supervisory training and military doctrine that

the leader should be decisive and forceful, that he should do the planning and thinking for the groups, and that he should coordinate, direct and evaluate his men's actions. The other viewpoint, reflected in the newer human relations oriented training and in the philosophy behind non-directive and brain-storming technique stresses the need for democratic, permissive, group-oriented leadership techniques. Both schools of thought have strong adherents and there is evidence supporting both points of view (Gibb, 1954; Hare, 1962).

While one can always rationalize that contradictory findings by other investigators are due to poor research design, or different tests and criteria, such problems present difficulties if they appear in one's own research. We have, during the past thirteen years, conducted a large number of studies on leadership and group performance, using the same operational definitions and essentially similar leader attitude measures. The inconsistencies which we obtained in our own research program demanded an integrative theoretical formulation which would adequately account for the seemingly confusing results.

The studies which we conducted used as the major predictor of group performance an interpersonal perception or attitude score which is derived from the leader's description of his most and of his least preferred co-workers. He is asked to think of all others with whom he has ever worked, and then to describe first the person with whom he worked best (his most preferred co-worker) and then the person with whom he could work least well (his least preferred co-worker, or *LPC*). These descriptions are obtained, wherever possible, before the leader is assigned to his team. However, even when we deal with already existing groups, these descriptions tend to be of individuals whom the subject has known in the past rather than of persons with whom he works at the time of testing.

The descriptions are typically made on 20 eight-point bi-polar adjective scales, similar to Osgood's Semantic Differential (Osgood, et al., 1957), e.g.,

Pleasant__:__:__:__:__:__:__:__Unpleasant

Friendly __:__:__:__:__:__:__:__Unfriendly

These items are scaled on an evaluative dimension, giving a score of 8 to the most favorable pole (i.e., Friendly, Pleasant) and a score of 1 to the least favorable pole. Two main scores have been derived from these descriptions. The first one, which was used in our earlier studies, is based on the profile similarity measure *D* (Cronbach and Gleser, 1953) between the descriptions of the most and of the least preferred co-worker. This core, called the Assumed Similarity between

bein, J. E. McGrath, W. A. T. Meuwese, C. E. Osgood, H. C. Triandis, and L. R. Tucker, who offered invaluable suggestions and criticisms at various stages of the work.

Opposites, or *ASo*, indicates the degree to which the individual perceives the two opposites on his co-worker continuum as similar or different. The second score is simply based on the individual's description of his least preferred co-worker, *LPC*, and indicates the degree to which the subject evaluates his *LPC* in a relatively favorable or unfavorable manner. The two measures are highly correlated (.80 to .95) and will here be treated as interchangeable.

We have had considerable difficulty in interpreting these scores since they appear to be uncorrelated with the usual personality and attitude measures. They are, however, related to the Ohio State University studies' "Initiation of structure" and "Consideration" dimensions (Stogdill and Coons, 1957). Extensive content analysis (Meuwese and Oonk, 1960; Julian and McGrath, 1963; Morris and Fiedler, 1964) and a series of studies by Hawkins (1962) as well as research by Bass, Fiedler, and Krueger (1964) have given consistent results. These indicate that the person with high *LPC* or *ASo*, who perceives his least preferred co-worker in a relatively favorable, accepting manner, tends to be more accepting, permissive, considerate, and person-oriented in his relations with group members. The person who perceives his most and least preferred co-workers as quite different, and who sees his least preferred co-worker in a very unfavorable, rejecting manner tends to be directive, task-oriented and controlling on task relevant group behaviors in his interactions.

ASo and *LPC* scores correlated highly with group performance in a wide variety of studies, although, as mentioned above, not consistently in the same direction. For example, in two samples of high school basketball teams the sociometrically chosen leader's *ASo* score correlated −.69 and −.58 with the percent of games won by teams and −.51 with the accuracy of surveying of civil engineer teams (Fiedler, 1954), and the melter foreman's *ASo* score correlated −.52 with tonnage output of open-hearth shops (Cleven and Fiedler, 1956). These negative correlations indicate that *low ASo* or *LPC* scores were associated with good group performance, i.e., that these groups performed better under managing, directive leaders than under more permissive, accepting leaders. However, while the *ASo* score of the sociometrically accepted company manager correlated also negatively (−.70) with the net income of consumer cooperatives, the board chairman's *ASo* score under the same circumstances correlated +.62 (Godfrey, Fiedler, and Hall, 1959). Thus, groups with different tasks seemed to require different leader attitudes. In a more recent study of group creativity in Holland, the leader's *LPC* score correlated with perform-

ance +.75 in religiously homogeneous groups with formally appointed leaders, but −.72 in religiously heterogeneous groups; and while the correlation was +.75 in homogeneous groups with appointed leaders it was −.64 in homogeneous groups having emergent (sociometrically nominated leaders). (Fiedler, Meuwese and Oonk, 1961.)

The results of these investigations clearly showed that the direction and magnitude of the correlations were contingent upon the nature of the group-task situation with which the leader had to deal. Our problem resolved itself then into (*a*) developing a meaningful system for categorizing group-task situations; (*b*) inducing the underlying theoretical model which would integrate the seemingly inconsistent results obtained in our studies, and (*c*) testing the validity of the model by adequate research.

DEVELOPMENT OF THE MODEL

Key definitions. We shall here be concerned solely with "interacting" rather than "co-acting" task groups. By an interacting task group we mean a face-to-face team situation (such as a basketball team) in which the members work *interdependently* on a common goal. In groups of this type, the individual's contributions cannot readily be separated from total group performance. In a co-acting group, however, such as a bowling or a rifle team, the group performance is generally determined by summing the members' individual performance scores.

We shall define the leader as the group member who is officially appointed or elected to direct and coordinate group action. In groups in which no one has been so designated, we have identified the informal leader by means of sociometric preference questions such as asking group members to name the person who was most influential in the group, or whom they would most prefer to have as a leader in a similar task.

The leader's effectiveness is here defined in terms of the group's performance on the assigned primary task. Thus, although a company manager may have, as one of his tasks, the job of maintaining good relations with his customers, his main job, and the one on which he is in the final analysis evaluated, consists of the long range profitability of the company. Good relations with customers, or high morale and low labor turnover may well contribute to success, but they would not be the basic criteria by this definition.

The categorization of group-task situations. Leadership is essentially a problem of wielding influence and power. When we say that different types of groups require different types of leadership we imply that they require a different relationship by which the leader wields power and influence. Since it is easier to wield power in some groups than in others, an attempt to categorize groups might well begin by asking what conditions in the group-task situation will facilitate or inhibit the leader's exercise of power. On the basis of our previous work we postulated three important aspects in the total situation which influence the leader's role.

1. Leader-member relations. The leader who is personally attractive to his group members, and who is respected by his group, enjoys considerable power (French, 1956). In fact, if he has the confidence and loyalty of his men he has less need of official rank. This dimension can generally be measured by means of sociometric indices or by group atmosphere scales (Cf. Fiedler, 1962) which indicate the degree to which the leader experiences the groups as pleasant and well disposed toward him.

2. Task structure. The task generally implies an order "from above" which incorporates the authority of the superior organization. The group member who refuses to comply must be prepared to face disciplinary action by the higher authority. For example, a squad member who fails to perform a lawful command of his sergeant may have to answer to his regimental commander. However, compliance with a task order can be enforced only if the task is relatively well structured, i.e., if it is capable of being programmed, or spelled out step by step. One cannot effectively force a group to perform well on an unstructured task such as developing a new product or writing a good play.

Thus, the leader who has a structured task can depend on the backing of his superior organizations, but if he has an unstructured task the leader must rely on his own resources to inspire and motivate his men. The unstructured task thus provides the leader with much less effective power than does the highly structured task.

We operationalized this dimension by utilizing four of the aspects which Shaw (1962) recently proposed for the classification of group task. These are, (*a*) decision *verifiability*, the degree to which the correctness of the solution can be demonstrated objectively; (*b*) *goal clarity,* the degree to which the task requirements are clearly stated or known to the group; (*c*) *goal path multiplicity*, the degree to which there are many or few procedures available for performing the task (reverse scoring); and (*d*) *solution specificity*, the degree to which there is one rather than an infinite number of correct solutions (e.g., writing a story vs. solving an equation). Ratings based on these four dimensions have yielded interrater reliabilities of .80 to .90.

Position power. The third dimension is defined by the power inherent in the position of leadership irrespective of the occupant's personal relations with his members. This includes the rewards and punishments which are officially or traditionally at the leader's disposal, his authority as defined by the group's rules and by-laws, and the

organizational support given to him in dealing with his men. This dimension can be operationally defined by means of a check list (Fiedler, 1964) containing items such as "Leader can effect promotion or demotion," "Leader enjoys special rank and status in real life which sets him apart from, and above his group members." The medium interrater agreement of four independent judges rating 35 group situations was .95.

A three dimensional group classification. Group-task situations can now be rated on the basis of the three dimensions of leader-member relations, task structure, and position power. This locates each group in a three dimensional space. A rough categorization can be accomplished by halving each of the dimensions so that we obtain an eight celled cube (Fig. 1). We can now determine whether the correlations between leader attitudes and group performance within each of these eight cells, or octants, are relatively similar in magnitude and direction. If they are, we can infer that the group classification has been successfully accomplished since it shows that groups falling within the same octant require similar leader attitudes.

An earlier paper has summarized 52 group-task situations which are based on our previous studies (Fiedler, 1964). These 52 group-task situations have been ordered into the eight octants. As can be seen from Table 1, groups falling within the same octant show correlations between the leader's *ASo* or *LPC* score and the group performance criterion which are relatively similar in magnitude and direction. We can thus infer that the group classification has been accomplished with at least reasonable success.

Consideration of Figure 1 suggests a further classification of the cells in term of the effective

FIGURE 1. A model for the classification of group-task situations.

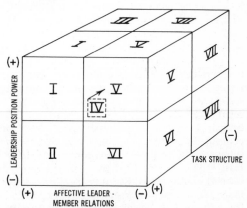

power which the group-task situation places at the leader's disposal, or more precisely, the favorableness of the situation for the leader's exercise of his power and influence.

Such an ordering can be accomplished without difficulty at the extreme poles of the continuum. A liked and trusted leader with high rank and a structured task is in a more favorable position than is a disliked and powerless leader with an ambiguous task. The intermediate steps pose certain theoretical and methodological problems. To collapse a three-dimensional system into a unidimensional one implies in Coombs' terms a partial order or a lexicographic system for which there is no unique solution. Such an ordering must, therefore, be done either intuitively or in accordance with some reasonable assumptions. In the present instance we have postulated that the most important dimension in the system is the leader-member relationship since the highly liked and respected leader is less in need of position power or the power of the higher authority incorporated in the task structure. The second-most important dimension in most group-task situations is the task structure since a leader with a highly structured task does not require a powerful leader position. (For example, privates or non-commissioned officers in the army are at times called upon to lead or instruct officers in certain highly structured tasks such as demonstrating a new weapon, or, for example, teaching medical officers close order drill—though not in unstructured tasks such as planning new policies on strategy.) This leads us here to order the group-task situations first on leader-member relations, then on task structure, and finally on position power. While admittedly not a unique solution, the resulting ordering constitutes a reasonable continuum which indicates the degree of the leader's effective power in the group.[2]

[2] Another cell should be added which contains real-life groups which reject their leader. Exercise of power would be very dif-

As was already apparent from Table 1, the relationship between leader attitudes and group performance is contingent upon the accurate classification of the group-task situation. A more meaningful model of this contingency relationship emerges when we now plot the correlation between *LPC* or *ASo* and group performance on the one hand, against the octants ordered on the effective power, or favorableness-for-the-leader dimension on the other. This is shown on Figure 2. Note that each point in the plot is a *correlation* predicting leadership performance or group effectiveness. The plot therefore represents 53 *sets of groups* totalling over 800 separate groups.

As Figure 2 shows, managing, controlling, directive (low *LPC*) leaders perform most effectively either under very favorable or under very unfavorable situations. Hence we obtain negative correlations between *LPC* and group performance scores. Considerate, permissive, accepting leaders obtain optimal group performance under situations intermediate in favorableness. These are situations in which (*a*) the task is structured, but the leader is disliked and must, therefore, be diplomatic; (*b*) the liked leader has an ambiguous, unstructured task and must, therefore, draw upon the creativity and cooperation of his members. Here we obtain positive correlations between *LPC* and group performance scores. Where the task is highly structured and the leader is well-liked, non-directive behavior or permissive attitudes (such as asking how the group ought to proceed with a missile count-down) is neither appropriate nor beneficial. Where the situation is quite unfavorable, e.g., where the disliked chairman of a volunteer group faces an ambiguous task, the leader might as well be autocratic and directive since a positive, non-directive leadership style under these conditions might result in complete inactivity on the part of the group. This model,

ficult in this situation and such a cell should be placed at the extreme negative end of the continuum. Such cases are treated in the section on validation.

TABLE 1   Median Correlation between Leader LPC and Group Performance in Various Octants

	LEADER-MEMBER RELATIONS	TASK STRUCTURE	POSITION POWER	MEDIAN CORRELATION	NUMBER OF RELATIONS INCLUDED IN MEDIAN
Octant I	Good	Structured	Strong	−.52	8
Octant II	Good	Structured	Weak	−.58	3
Octant III	Good	Unstructured	Strong	−.41	4
Octant IV	Good	Unstructured	Weak	.47	10
Octant V	Mod. poor	Structured	Strong	.42	6
Octant VI	Mod. poor	Structured	Weak		0
Octant VII	Mod. poor	Unstructured	Strong	.05	10
Octant VIII	Mod. poor	Unstructured	Weak	−.43	12

thus, tends to shed some light on the apparent inconsistencies in our own data as well as in data obtained by other investigators.

EMPIRICAL TESTS EXTENSION OF THE MODEL

The basic hypothesis of the model suggests that the directive, controlling, task oriented (low *LPC*) leader will be most successful in group-task situations which are either very favorable or else very unfavorable for the leader. The permissive, considerate, human relations oriented (high *LPC*) leader will perform best under conditions which are intermediate in favorableness. This hypothesis was tested by re-analyzing data from previous studies as well as by a major experiment specifically designed to test the model. Both are briefly described below.

Re-analyses of previous studies

As we indicated before, there is reason to believe that the relationship between the leader and his members is the most important of the three dimensions for classifying group-task situations. The problem of exercising leadership will be a relatively easy one in group-task situations in which the leader is not only liked by his crew and gets along well with his group, but in which the task is structured and the leader has a relatively powerful position. The situation will be somewhat more difficult if the leader under these circumstances has an only moderately good relationship

with his group members, and it will be quite difficult if the leader-member relations are very poor, if the group members reject or actively dislike the leader. Ordinarily this does not occur in laboratory studies. It does happen, however, that real-life groups strongly reject leaders—sometimes to the point of sabotaging the task. Since such a situation would present a very difficult problem in leadership, we would expect better performance from the task-oriented, controlling leader, and hence a negative correlation between the leader's *ASo* or *LPC* score and his group's performance. This result appeared in one study of bomber crews for which we already had the appropriate data, and it was tested by new analyses in two other studies.

Bomber crew study. A study was conducted on B-29 bomber crews (Fiedler, 1955) where the criterion of performance consisted of radar bomb scores. This is the average circular error, or accuracy of hitting the target by means of radar procedures. The crews were classified on the basis of their relationship between the aircraft commander and his crew. The crews were ordered on whether or not (*a*) the aircraft commander was the most chosen member of the crew, and (*b*) the aircraft commander sociometrically en-

FIGURE 2. Correlations of leader *LPC* and group performance plotted against octants, i.e., favorableness of group-task situation for leader.

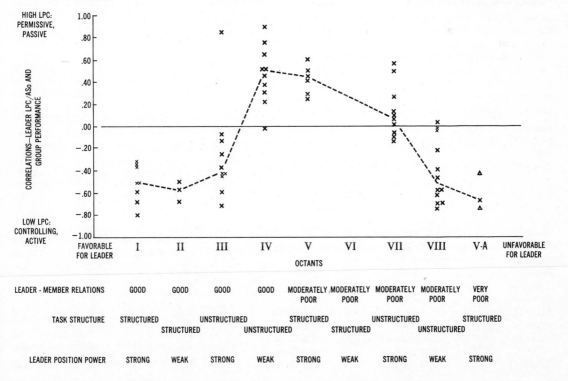

dorsed his keymen on his radar bombing team (the radar observer and navigator).

The results of this analysis are presented in Table 2. As can be seen, the correlations between *ASo* and crew performance are highly negative in crews having very good and very poor leader-group relations, but they tend to be positive in the intermediate range.

TABLE 2 *Correlations between Aircraft Commander's (AC's) ASo Score and Radar Bomb Scores Under Different Patterns of Sociometric Choices in B-29 Bomber Crews**

	RHO	N
AC is most preferred crew member and chooses keymen (K)	−.81	10
AC is most preferred crew member and is neutral to K	−.14	6
AC is most preferred crew member and does not choose K	.43	6
AC is not most preferred crew member but chooses K	−.03	18
AC is not most preferred crew member and is neutral to K	−.80	5
AC is not most preferred crew member and does not choose K	−.67	7

* Table adapted from Fiedler (1955).

TABLE 3 *Correlations between Leader LPC Scores and Anti-aircraft Artillery Crew Performance*

	RHO	N
Most highly chosen crew commanders	−.34	10
Middle range in sociometric choices	.49	10
Lowest chosen crew commanders	−.42	10

TABLE 4 *Correlations between General Manager's ASo Score and Company Net Income*

	RHO	N
Gen. mgr. is most chosen by board and staff (ASo perf.)	−.67	10
Gen. mgr. is chosen by board, but rejected by staff	.20	6
Gen. mgr. is rejected by board, but chosen by staff	.26	6
Gen. mgr. is rejected by board and staff	−.75	7

Anti-aircraft artillery crews. A second set of data came from a study of anti-aircraft artillery crews (Hutchins and Fiedler, 1960). Here the criterion of crew performance consisted of scores indicating the "location and acquisition" of unidentified aircraft. These crews were subdivided on the basis of leader-crew relations by separately correlating the leader's *LPC* score with group performance (*a*) for the ten crews which most highly chose their crew commander, (*b*) the ten which were in the intermediate range, and (*c*) the ten crews which gave the least favorable sociometric choices to their leader. These data are presented in Table 3.

Consumer cooperative companies. Finally we reanalyzed data from a study of 31 consumer cooperatives (Godfrey, Fiedler and Hall, 1959) in which the criterion of performance consisted of the per cent of company net income over a three year period. The companies were subdivided into those in which the general manager was sociometrically chosen (*a*) by his board of directors as well as by his staff of assistant managers, (*b*) those in which the general manager was chosen by his board but not his staff, or (*c*) by his staff but not his board, and (*d*) the companies in which the general manager was rejected, or not chosen, by both board of directors and staff. (Table 4.)

As these tables, and Figure 3 show, the task-oriented, managing, low *LPC* leaders performed best under very favorable and under very unfavorable situations, while the permissive, considerate leaders performed best under conditions intermediate in favorableness. These data, therefore, clearly support the hypothesis derived from the model.

Experimental test of the contingency model

In cooperation with the Belgian Naval Forces we recently conducted a major study which served in part as a specific test of the model. Only aspects immediately relevant to the test are here described. The investigation was conducted in Belgium where the French and Dutch speaking (or Flemish) sectors of the country have been involved in a long standing and frequently acrimonious dispute. This conflict centers about the use of language, but it also involves a host of other cultural factors which differentiate the 60 per cent Flemish and 40 per cent French speaking population groups in Wallonie and Brussels. This "linguistic problem" which is rooted in the beginning of Belgium's national history, has in recent years been the cause of continuous public controversy, frequent protest meetings, and occasional riots.

The linguistic problem is of particular interest here since a group, consisting of members whose mother tongue, culture, and attitudes differ, will clearly present a more difficult problem in leadership than a group whose members share the same language and culture. We were thus able to test the major hypothesis of the model as well as to extend the research by investigating the type of leadership which linguistically and culturally heterogeneous groups require.

Design. The experiment was conducted at the naval training center at Ste. Croix-Bruges.[3] It utilized 48 career petty officers and 240 recruits who had been selected from a pool of 546 men on the basis of a pre-test in which we obtained *LPC*, intelligence, attitude, and language comprehension scores.

The experiment was specifically designed to incorporate the three major group classification dimensions shown on Figure 1, namely, leader-member relations, position power, and task structure. It also added the additional dimension of group homogeneity vs. heterogeneity. Specifically,

[3] This investigation was conducted in collaboration with Dr. J. M. Nuttin (Jr.) and his students while the author was Ford Faculty Research Fellow at the University of Louvain, 1963–1964. The experiment, undertaken with permission of Commodore L. Petit-jean, then Chief of Staff of the Belgian Naval Forces, was carried out at the Centre de Formation Navale, Ste. Croix-Bruges. The writer wishes to express his especial gratitude and appreciation to the commandant of the center, Captain V. Van Laethem, who not only made the personnel and the facilities of the center available to us, but whose active participation in the planning and the execution of the project made this study possible. We are also most grateful to Dr. U. Bouvier, Director of the Center for Social Studies, Ministry of Defense, to Capt. W. Cafferata, USN, the senior U. S. Naval representative of the Military Assistance and Advisory Group, Brussels, and to Cmdr. J. Robison, U. S. Naval Attache in Brussels, who provided liaison and guidance.

48 groups had leaders with high position power (petty officers) while 48 had leaders with low position power (recruits); 48 groups began with the unstructured task, while the other 48 groups began with two structured tasks; 48 groups were homogeneous, consisting of three French or three Dutch speaking men, while the other 48 groups were heterogeneous, consisting of a French speaking leader and two Flemish members, or a Dutch speaking, Flemish leader and two French speaking members. The quality of the leader-member relations was measured as in our previous studies by means of a group atmosphere scale which the leader completed after each task session.

Group performance criteria. Two essentially identical structured tasks were administered. Each lasted 25 minutes and required the groups to find the shortest route for a ship which, given certain fuel capacity and required ports of call, had to make a round trip calling at respectively ten or twelve ports. The tasks were objectively scored on the basis of sea miles required for the trip. Appropriate corrections and penalties were assigned for errors.

The unstructured task required the groups to compose a letter to young men of 16 and 17 years, urging them to choose the Belgian Navy as a career. The letter was to be approximately 200 words in length and had to be completed in 35 minutes. Each of the letters, depending upon the language in which it was written, was then rated

FIGURE 3. Correlations between leader *LPC* or *ASo* scores and group performance under three conditions of leader acceptance by the group in studies of bomber crews, anti-aircraft artillery crews and consumer cooperatives.

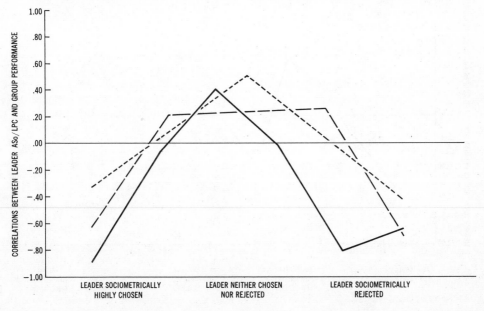

by Dutch or by French speaking judges on style and use of language, as well as interest value, originality, and persuasiveness. Estimated reliability was .92 and .86 for Dutch and French speaking judges, respectively.

It should be noted in this connection that the task of writing a letter is not as unstructured as might have been desirable for this experiment. The form of any letter of this type is fairly standardized, and its content was, of course, suggested by the instructions. The navy officers with whom we consulted throughout the study considered it unwise, however, to give a highly unstructured task, such as writing a fable or proposing a new policy, since tasks of this nature were likely to threaten the men and to cause resentment and poor cooperation. High and low task-structure is, therefore, less well differentiated in this study than it has been in previous investigations.

Results. The contingency model specifies that the controlling, managing, low *LPC* leaders will be most effective either in very favorable or else in relatively unfavorable group-task situations, while the permissive, considerate, high *LPC* leaders will be more effective in situations intermediate in difficulty.

The basic test of the hypothesis requires, therefore, that we order the group-task situations, represented in this experiment, in terms of the difficulty which they are likely to present for the leader. Since there are 16 cells in the design, the size of the sample within each cell (namely 6 groups) is, of course, extremely small. However, where the conditions are reasonably replicated by other cells, the relationship can be estimated from the median rank-order correlations.

The hypothesis can be tested most readily with correlations of leader *LPC* and group performance in homogeneous groups on the more reliably scorable second structured task. These conditions approximate most closely those represented on Figure 3, on bomber and anti-aircraft crews and consumer cooperatives. We have here made the

FIGURE 4. Median correlations between leader *LCP* and group performance scores plotted against favorableness-for-leader scale in the Belgian Navy study.

CODE FOR TWO DIGIT NUMBERS FIGURE INDICATING THE TYPE OF GROUP INVOLVED:

Composition	Position Power	High Group Atmos.	Low Group Atmos.	Task	1st Pres.	2nd Pres.
Homogeneous	High	1	5	Structured I	1	2
Homogeneous	Low	2	6	Structured II	3	4
Heterogeneous	High	3	7	Unstructured	5	6
Heterogeneous	Low	4	8			

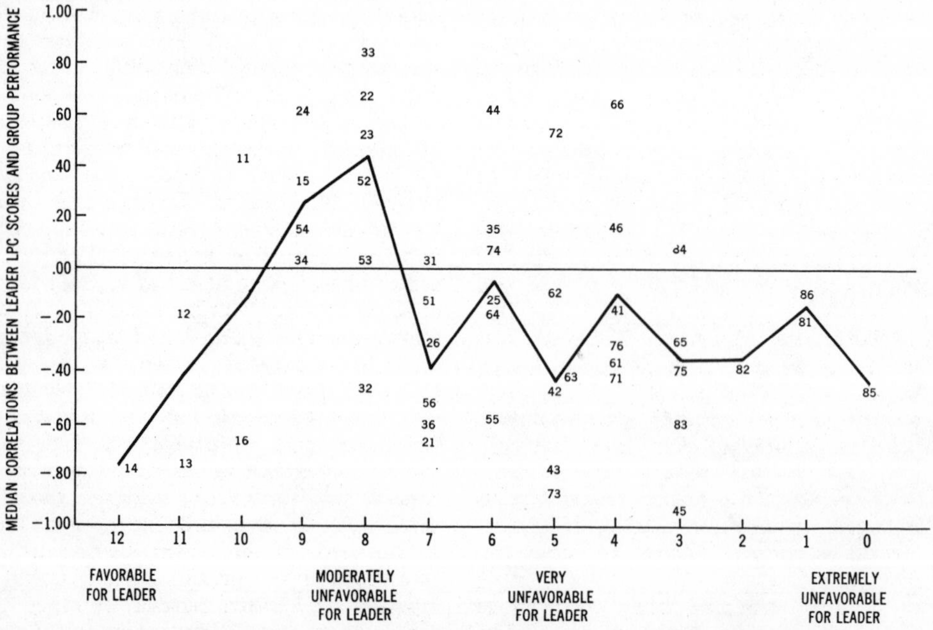

fairly obvious assumption that the powerful leader or the leader who feels liked and accepted faces an easier group-task situation than low ranking leaders and those who see the groups as unpleasant and tense. Each situation is represented by two cells of six groups, each. Since there were two orders of presentation—half the groups worked first on the structured task, the other half on the unstructured task, arranging the group-task situations in order of favorableness for the leader then gives us the following results:

	ORDER 1	ORDER 2
High group atmosphere and high position power	−.77	−.77
High group atmosphere and low position power	+.60	+.50
Low group atmosphere and high position power	+.16	+.01
Low group atmosphere and low position power	−.16	−.43

These are, of course, the trends in size and magnitude of correlations which the model predicts. Low *LPC* leaders are again most effective in favorable and unfavorable group-task situations; the more permissive, considerate high *LPC* leaders were more effective in the intermediate situations.

Extending the model to include heterogeneous groups requires that we make a number of additional assumptions for weighting each of the group-task dimensions so that all 48 cells (i.e., 16 cells × 3 tasks) can be reasonably ordered on the same scale. We have here assigned equal weights of 3 to the favorable poles of the major dimensions, i.e., to homogeneity, high group atmosphere, and high position power. A weight of one was assigned to the first structured task, and a weight of two to the second structured task on the assumption that the structured task makes the group-task situation somewhat more favorable than the unstructured task, and that the practice and learning effect inherent in performing a second, practically identical task, will make the group-task situation still more favorable for the leader. Finally, a weight of one was given to the "second presentation," that is, the group task which occurred toward the end of the session, on the assumption that the leader by that time had gotten to know his group members and had learned to work with them more effectively, thus again increasing the favorableness of his group-task situation to a certain extent.

The resulting weighting system leads to a scale from 12 to 0 points, with 12 as the most favorable pole. If we now plot the median correlation coefficients of the 48 group-task situations against the scale indicating the favorableness of the situation for the leader, we obtain the curve presented on Figure 4.

As can be seen, we again obtain a curvilinear relationship which resembles that shown on Fig-

ure 2. Heterogeneous groups with low position power and/or poor leader-member relations fall below point 6 on the scale, and thus tend to perform better with controlling, directive, low *LPC* leaders. Only under otherwise very favorable conditions do heterogeneous groups perform better with permissive, considerate high *LPC* leaders, that is, in group-task situations characterized by high group atmosphere as well as high position power, four of the six correlations (66%) are positive, while only five of eighteen (28%) are positive in the less favorable group-task situations.

It is interesting to note that the curve is rather flat and characterized by relatively low negative correlations as we go toward the very unfavorable end of the scale. This result supports Meuwese's (1964) recent study which showed that correlations between leader *LPC* as well as between leader intelligence and group performance tend to become attenuated under conditions of relative stress. These findings suggest that the leader's ability to influence and control the group decreases beyond a certain point of stress and difficulty in the group-task situation.

DISCUSSION

The contingency model seeks to reconcile results which up to now had to be considered inconsistent and difficult to understand. We have here attempted to develop a theoretical framework which can provide guidance for further research. While the model will undoubtedly undergo modifications and elaboration as data become available, it provides an additional step toward a better understanding of leadership processes required in different situations. We have here tried to specify exactly the type of leadership which different group task-situations require.

The model has a number of important implications for selection and training, as well as for the placement of leaders and organizational strategy. Our research suggests, first of all, that we can utilize a very broad spectrum of individuals for positions of leadership. The problem becomes one of placement and training rather than of selection since both the permissive, democratic, human-relations oriented, and the managing, autocratic, task-oriented leader can be effectively utilized. Leaders can be trained to recognize their own style of leadership as well as the conditions which are most compatible with their style.

The model also points to a variety of administrative and supervisory strategies which the organization can adopt to fit the group-task situation to the needs of the leader. Tasks can, after all, be structured to a greater or lesser extent by giving very specific and detailed, or vague and general instructions; the position power of the group leader can be increased or decreased and even the congeniality of a group, and its acceptance of the leader can be affected by appropriate adminstration action, such as for instance increasing or decreasing the group's homogeneity.

The model also throws new light on phenomena which were rather difficult to fit into our usual ideas about measurement in social psychology. Why, for example, should groups differ so markedly in their performance on nearly parallel tasks? The model—and our data—show that the situation becomes easier for the leader as the group moves from the novel to the already known group-task situations. The leaders who excel under relatively novel and therefore more difficult conditions are not necessarily those who excel under those which are more routine, or better known and therefore more favorable. Likewise, we find that different types of task structure require different types of leader behavior. Thus, in a research project's early phases the project director tends to be democratic and permissive; everyone is urged to contribute to the plan and to criticize all aspects of the design. This situation changes radically in the more structured phase when the research design is frozen and the experiment is underway. Here the research director tends to become managing, controlling, and highly autocratic and woe betide the assistant who attempts to be creative in giving instructions to subjects, or in his timing of tests. A similar situation is often found in business organizations where the routine operation tends to be well structured and calls for a managing, directive leadership. The situation becomes suddenly unstructured when a crisis occurs. Under these conditions the number of discussions, meetings, and conferences increases sharply so as to give everyone an opportunity to express his views.

At best, this model is of course only a partial theory of leadership. The leader's intellectual and task-relevant abilities, and the members' skills and motivation, all play a role in affecting the group's performance. It is to be hoped that these other important aspects of group interaction can be incorporated into the model in the not too distant future.

REFERENCES

BASS, A. R., FIEDLER, F. E. and KRUEGER, S. Personality correlates of assumed similarity (ASo) and related scores. Urbana, Ill.: Group Effectiveness Research Laboratory, University of Illinois, 1964.

BASS, B. M. *Leadership, psychology and organizational behavior.* New York: Harper Brothers, 1960.

BROWNE, C. G. and COHN, T. S. (Eds.) *The study of leadership.* Danville, Illinois. The Interstate Printers and Publishers, 1958.

CLEVEN, W. A. and FIEDLER, F. E. Interpersonal perceptions of open hearth foremen and steel production. *J. appl. Psychol.* 1956, **40**, 312–314.

CRONBACH, J. J. and GLESER, GOLDENE C. Assessing similarity between profiles. *Psychol. Bull.,* 1953, **50**, 456–473.

FIEDLER, F. E. Assumed similarity measures as predictors of team effectiveness. *J. abnorm. soc. Psychol.,* 1954, **49**, 381–388.

FIEDLER, F. E. Leader attitudes, group climate, and group creativity. *J. abnorm. soc. Psychol.,* 1962, **64**, 308–318.

FIEDLER, F. E. A contingency model of leadership effectiveness. In L. Berkowitz (Ed.) *Advances in experimental social psychology,* New York: Academic Press, 1964, Vol. I.

FIEDLER, F. E. and MEUWESE, W. A. T. The leader's contribution to performance in cohesive and uncohesive groups. *J. abnorm. soc. Psychol.,* 1963, **67**, 83–87.

FIEDLER, F. E., MEUWESE, W. A. T. and OONK, SOPHIE. Performance of laboratory tasks requiring group creativity. *Acta Psychologica,* 1961, **18**, 100–119.

FRENCH, J. R. P., JR. A formal theory of social power. *Psychol. Rev.,* 1956, **63**, 181–194.

GIBB, C. A. "Leadership" in G. Lindzey (Ed.) *Handbook of social psychology,* Vol. II, Cambridge, Mass.: Addison-Wesley, 1954.

GODFREY, ELEANOR P., FIEDLER, F. E. and HALL, D. M. *Boards, management, and company success.* Danville, Illinois: Interstate Printers and Publishers, 1959.

HARE, A. P. *Handbook of small group research.* New York: Free Press, 1962.

HAWKINS, C. A study of factors mediating a relationship between leader rating behavior and group productivity. Unpublished Ph.D. dissertation, University of Minnesota, 1962.

HUTCHINS, E. B. and FIEDLER, F. E. Task-oriented and quasi-therapeutic role functions of the leader in small military groups. *Sociometry,* 1960, **23**, 293–406.

JULIAN, J. W. and McGRATH, J. E. The influence of leader and member behavior on the adjustment and task effectiveness of negotiation groups. Urbana, Ill.: Group Effectiveness Research Laboratory, University of Illinois, 1963.

McGRATH, J. E. A summary of small group research studies. Arlington, Va.: Human Sciences Research Inc., 1962 (Litho.).

MANN, R. D. A review of the relationship between personality and performance in small groups. *Psychol. Bull.,* 1959, **56**, 241–270.

MEUWESE, W. A. T. The effect of the leader's ability and interpersonal attitudes on group creativity under varying conditions of stress. Unpublished doctoral dissertation, University of Amsterdam, 1964.

MORRIS, C. G., and FIEDLER, F. E. Application of a new system of interaction analysis to the relationships between leader attitudes and behavior in problem solving groups. Urbana, Ill.: Group Effectiveness Research Laboratory, University of Illinois, 1964.

OSGOOD, C. A., SUCI, G. A. and TANNENBAUM, P. H. *The measurement of meaning.* Urbana, Ill.: University of Illinois Press, 1957.

SHAW, M. E. Annual Technical Report, 1962. Gaines-

ville, Florida: University of Florida, 1962 (Mimeo.).

STOGDILL, R. Personal factors associated with leadership: a survey of the literature. *J. of Psychol.*, 1948, **25**, 35–71.

STOGDILL, R. M. and COONS, A. E. Leader behavior: its description and measurement. Columbus, Ohio: Ohio State University, *Research Monograph*, No. 88, 1957.

DIMENSIONS OF MEMBER SATISFACTION IN SMALL GROUPS *

One important process in science is the comparison of data from various investigations on a general topic in order to discover what generalizations can be drawn and to spell out the conditions under which they hold. Through this process, results that at first appear contradictory are reconciled. A comparison of the conditions of different experiments often leads to the discovery of new variables that account for differences in findings. In the following selection, in the attempt to discover its determinants, Heslin and Dunphy review studies in which member satisfaction was a dependent variable. Because the analysis covers three different types of specialized groups—the family, the therapy group, and the formal organization—the conclusions drawn are apt to have high external validity.

35.

Three Dimensions of Member Satisfaction in Small Groups

RICHARD HESLIN
DEXTER DUNPHY
HARVARD UNIVERSITY

INTRODUCTION

In social psychology and in enterprises such as business and industry, continuing interest has centered on the factors contributing to group member satisfaction or dissatisfaction. Usually member satisfaction has been referred to as 'morale', but since the term morale has not always been used consistently, this paper reviews small group studies which present findings that are relevant to 'member satisfaction with the group.' The use of the phrase 'member satisfaction with the group' clearly limits the sources of satisfaction

* The selection following the editorial introduction is reprinted from "Three dimensions of member satisfaction in small groups," *Human Relations*, 1964, **17**, 99–112, by permission of the authors and Tavistock Publications.

to the membership group itself and also allows for application of the concept to all kinds of groups. In this paper, therefore, we have examined member satisfaction in all studies in our sample whether it was referred to as morale or cohesion, or by any other term.

METHOD OF INVESTIGATION

Search of the literature was facilitated by the use of a collection of detailed abstracts of 450 small group studies, the abstracts being mounted on edge punch cards. The abstracts were made by the authors from published collections of small group annotations (Hare, 1962; Altman, Pendleton & Terauds, 1960), from published collections of small group studies (e.g. Cartwright & Zander, 1953, 1960; Hare Borgatta & Bales, 1955), and from a systematic search of the major journals publishing small group studies from 1955 to 1962. After being entered on an edge punch card, each study was coded according to a systematic scheme of content categories. Four main content divisions were made: (*i*) social system—structural state; (*ii*) social system—process and change; (*iii*) individual—structural state; (*iv*) individual—action. Within each of these divisons were listed appropriate variables considered in small group studies. For instance, under 'social system—structural state' the following variables appeared: subgroups and cliques; leader; other roles; power and influence; size and spatial relationships. In all, thirty variables were distinguished, and to each a particular hole on the punch card was allocated. Any study dealing with one of these variables had the portion of the card between the appropriate hole and the edge of the card clipped open with an adaptation of a ticket punch, changing the hole to a slot. A sorting needle inserted into a given hole in a group of cards and then lifted causes the cards on which that hole has been clipped to drop out, while the others stay on the needle. Reports of studies which contained results relevant to 'member satisfaction' were located by this method, this final procedure taking only a few seconds. All thirty-seven cards gathered in this manner have been considered in this study. The present article therefore attempts not only to make a significant contribution to the existing state of knowledge on an important aspect of small group theory, but also to demonstrate the usefulness of a coding scheme such as the one described above. For, though the initial process of reading and abstracting journal articles is time-consuming and laborious, once it is done, the researcher can conduct a search of the literature on any one of a large number of variables, and combinations of these variables, in a few minutes. The method has the added advantage of forcing the theorist to consider the results of studies which may not support his theory and which in other circumstances might slip his memory.

After culling the thirty-seven abstracts from the general collection of studies, the authors attempted to sort them by inspection on the basis of similarities or consistencies in research findings. This sorting process resulted in the hypothesis of the present article, namely: that three variables may account for a major proportion of variance associated with small group member satisfaction, and that these three variables may be readily defined in operational terms.

ANALYSIS

Dimension 1—Status consensus

Of the thirty-seven studies reviewed here, thirteen have findings which support the notion that status consensus is an important dimension underlying variations in member satisfaction. A number of studies by Bales and his associates at the Harvard Laboratory of Social Relations emphasized the initial importance of the problem of establishing status consensus and the effect of the resolution, or non-resolution, of this problem for group morale. In 1953, Bales noted the existence of different interaction patterns for groups with high and low member satisfaction. Taking the most satisfied group and the least satisfied group of sixteen laboratory groups, Bales found that the most satisfied attained a higher rate of suggestions, more often followed by positive reactions and less often by negative reactions and questions, than did the most dissatisfied group. Suggesting that a preponderance of positive reactions over negative reactions represents a state of equilibrium, Bales in this and subsequent studies (quoted below) attempted to specify the conditions under which such a state is most likely to develop. Such a state appears to be brought about most readily by the group's reaching status consensus, defined as consensus about the relative status of all group members. Bales found that the major point of disequilibrium (preponderance of negative over positive reactions) occurs in the second session

of laboratory-type problem-solving groups. It is at this point that the greatest conflict occurs and member satisfaction with the group is lowest. Groups with high status consensus were found to pass out of this state of disequilibrium soonest, with an accompanying rise in member satisfaction. Heinicke & Bales (1953) reported that groups classified as High and Low on status consensus both experienced a status conflict in the early sessions. But this status conflict was resolved earlier for the High groups, whose members were also in general more satisfied both with the group and with the group's solution of the problems than were the members of the Low groups. This pressure toward a congruent status structure can also be seen in the study by Exline & Ziller (1959).

More recently Shelley (1960a; 1960b) has reported similar findings for non-laboratory groups (girls' clubs) and suggested two modified definitions of status consensus. Both of these correlated more highly with member satisfaction than did Bales's measure, which relied on the ranking of all members by all members. The recommended measures stress consensus about the highest-ranking group member rather than consensus about the relative status of all group members. Shelley showed that these two measures of status consensus were both correlated 0.50 with satisfaction with the group.

Consistent with the idea that the degree of status consensus strongly influences member satisfaction is Hare's finding (1952) that where there was greater 'factionalism' in groups there was less satisfaction. Factionalism indicates lack of agreement about an appropriate leader, i.e. lack of status consensus. A parallel finding is that of Carlson (1960), who found the extent of 'clique structure' (i.e. perceived cliqueiness) identified by group leaders and by observers to be related negatively to four measures of member satisfaction. Although the equation of perceived clique structure with lack of status consensus may not be immediately apparent, it appears to us that 'cliqueishness' is virtually synonymous with factionalism. Certainly, leaders would be more likely to perceive cliqueishness where it implied some threat to their status.

The four studies dealt with above may be summarized as follows: the degree of status consensus, particularly consensus about the status of the task leader, exercises a significant influence on member satisfaction with the group. Where status consensus is high, member satisfaction tends to be high; where status consensus is low, member satisfaction tends to be low.

There is evidence that alternative sets of role structures can produce high status consensus, and that the particular structure which is developed depends on the human resources available to the group. The most satisfactory solution, in the sense that status consensus is more readily achieved, is the emergence of a leader who is a 'great man,' i.e. who can play a particular type of multifunctional leadership role. This has been brought out most clearly in a study by Borgatta, Couch & Bales (1954), in which 'great men' were identified in laboratory groups. On the basis of the results of a factor analysis of interpersonal behavior, great men were defined as persons scoring high on the factors of group goal facilitation, individual prominence, and group sociability. It was found that great men tended to remain great men over a series of sessions and that the groups in which they participated were higher on member satisfaction (as measured by higher rates of agreement, indicative of solidarity and tension release, and by lower rates of showing tension) than the groups in which great men did not participate.

A study which yielded similar results in an organizational setting was conducted by Kahn & Katz (1960). These authors attempted to identify the characteristics of supervisors in industry who led productive, in contrast to less productive, crews. They concluded that the supervisors of high-producing groups, which were also those highest on member satisfaction, possessed both the technological skills needed to support group tasks and the ability to help members to satisfy their important needs. The supervisor of a group with high member satisfaction characteristically played a differentiated role, delegated authority, and was high on 'supportiveness' or 'employee orientation.'

Both of these studies indicate that where the leader plays a role that is high both on task and on social-emotional (instrumental and affective) type acts, satisfaction will be higher than in groups where the leader is more specialized in his action.

Obviously not every group will have a potential great man available to fill the leadership role. However it appears possible in such circumstances to achieve a high level of satisfaction by the establishment of an alternative set of complementary roles which together perform the same group functions as the great man role. These functions are divided between two specialists instead of being performed by one. This form of role differentiation has been described by Bales (1953), Bales & Slater (1955), and Slater (1955). These studies point to the emergence in many groups of a task leader who symbolizes the demands of task accomplishment and of a social-emotional leader who symbolizes the demands of individual member needs. The task leader is invariably the highest participator, is ranked highest by group members on ideas and guidance, but is comparatively low on liking in comparison with the majority of the other group members. By contrast, the social-emotional leader is usually the second highest participator, is ranked particularly high on liking by his fellow group members, but is remarkably low on ideas and guidance. Bales has established that, where there is a coalition

between these specialists so that the roles are mutually supportive, member satisfaction rises and conflict is low. However, where there is a competitive relationship between the specialists, member satisfaction remains low and conflict remains high.

Summarizing these studies, we may conclude: status consensus is most readily achieved where a great man emerges—a great man being regarded as a high participator whose behaviour reveals high counts on acts devoted to both group task and group maintenance functions. Failing the emergence of a great man as leader, status consensus may also be achieved through the development of two differentiated but complementary and mutually supportive leadership roles, specialized alternatively about group task and group maintenance functions.

It is appropriate to consider how the existence of a formal structure and, in particular, of formal or 'imposed' leadership, affects satisfaction through status consensus. Two studies throw some light on this question. Cohen, Bennis & Wolkon (1962) compared elected and appointed leaders in 'wheel' and 'circle' communication nets. It was found that elected leaders retained their positions when groups moved from a wheel to a circle net, whereas appointed leaders were replaced when the group shifted. This result indicates that, where the leader was appointed, there was an incongruence between the formal and the informal group structures, an incongruence which was resolved in the circle formation. Since this incongruence centered on the appointed leader's position only, it seems clear that the existence of the appointed leader created a lack of status consensus which was resolved in favor of the informal leader in the changeover to a new group formation. Significantly, member satisfaction was highest in circle nets, but higher still for those groups who replaced their appointed leader with a leader of their own selection. Similarly, Goldman, Bolen & Martin (1961) studied laboratory groups with and without imposed leaders, finding that groups without imposed leaders expressed significantly greater enjoyment than did those with imposed leaders. We suggest that these findings indicate an explanation for the fact that the 'problem of low morale' is endemic in organizations. In organizational settings the achievement of a high level of status consensus is made difficult by the clash of 'headship' (Gibb, 1947) with leadership, the incongruency of formal and informal structures. It is significant that organizations have evolved characteristic ways of handling this incongruency by the selective recruitment of individuals possessing high status characteristics and by heaping symbols of authority upon them.

The achievement of status consensus also appears to be facilitated where group members clearly perceive the leader's competence in relation to the group task. Hamblin, Miller & Wiggins (1961) tested three competing theories involving independent derivations of the hypothesis that organization morale varies directly with the competence of the leader. It was found that only perceived competence independently controlled a significant amount of the variance of morale.

In summary, an important dimension of member satisfaction in small groups is the degree of status consensus among group members. Where status consensus is high, member satisfaction tends to be high; where status consensus is low, member satisfaction tends to be low. Status consensus is more readily achieved in groups where: (i) a leader emerges who plays a role high on both group task and group maintenance functions (great man); or alternatively (ii) two complementary and mutually supportive leader roles emerge, one specialized in the group task achievement, the other in group maintenance; and (iii) the great man or task specialist is perceived to be competent by the group members. Conversely, status consensus, and hence member satisfaction, will tend to be low where there is competition for leadership status, especially where competition leads to factionalism or cliqueishness. The likelihood of this happening would appear to be increased by: (i) the absence of a potential great man; (ii) the imposition of an incongruent formal leader upon a group; (iii) the perception by group members of the leader's incompetence.

Two appropriate operational definitions of status consensus are: (i) the degree of agreement shown in the rankings given to the highest-ranked individual, as used by Shelley; (ii) if the group has a formal or imposed leader, consensus is the degree to which the group rates the leader highly on adequacy as a choice for the position.

Dimension 2—Perception of progress toward group goals

A number of studies suggest that progress toward the group goals is also a crucial factor in member satisfaction. Significantly, it is the members' perception of this progress, rather than the actual progress, which is important, as was shown in a study by Shaw (1954). Shaw varied the complexity of problems which small groups had to solve, using communication networks. The groups working on simple problems both reached a solution more quickly and were more satisfied than the groups working on complex problems. The simple frustration involved in solving difficult problems without the knowledge that they are more difficult than usual appears to result in lowered member satisfaction.

Let us look at a study which investigated directly the frustrating quality of 'non' goal attainment. French (1941) used failure in goal achievement to frustrate two kinds of groups (eight previously organized groups, e.g. basketball teams, and eight newly formed groups) by presenting them with insoluble problems to solve. Two kinds of reaction to the frustration were observed: in the unorganized groups a division among the members (faction) occurred; within the organized groups there was no actual division of the group, but both inter-member aggression and signs of disorganization increased. Although French did not make any direct measure of satisfaction, we can probably regard the schisms and aggression as indicators of heightened dissatisfaction with the perceived stagnation in goal attainment progress.

Deprivation of goal attainment was also used in the more recent experiment by Hamblin (1958), where groups were placed in a crisis situation (failure at a modification of a shuffleboard game). When the group goal was not being attained, a reduction in member satisfaction was observed and a search for more successful means to achieve the goal was initiated.

When the needs of individual members are strong and are in conflict with the goal-directed activity of the group, both member satisfaction and goal attainment tend to be reduced. In a study by Fouriezos, Hutt & Guetzkow (1950) members' attempts to satisfy these needs were called 'self-oriented need' behavior. This kind of behavior was coded into the following five categories: dependency, status, dominance, aggression, and catharsis. The highest incidence of self-oriented need behavior was found in groups where members rated themselves lowest on satisfaction in general and on satisfaction with the group processes in particular. When an individual is expressing sentiments categorizable in one of the five categories, it is clear that he is not wholly involved in striving for the group, and some of the effort in the group is being used in other interests besides the attainment of group goals. This situation appears to be akin to the basis of Cattell's synergy, i.e. the total energy going into the group from the individuals (1948). This question of conflict between the group's task-directed activity and personal goals is related to the manner of structuring the means of obtaining rewards (Deutsch, 1949). Deutsch found that cooperatively organized groups were more successful than competitively organized groups in speed and quality of group productivity, and also that their members were more friendly toward one another. The competitive group members performed the same task (group solutions of Human Relation problems and puzzles) as the cooperative groups, but the former were informed that the best person in the group was to be rewarded whereas the latter were told that the best group would be rewarded. Under the competitive system member satisfaction was not contingent on group goal attainment but on individual member goal attainment. In fact, goal attainment by a fellow member would result in dissatisfaction for the others in the group. Deutsch interprets the differences between the two kinds of group as due to the close identity between member personal goals and group goals in the cooperative group; in the competitive group, on the other hand, group goals are only adopted in so far as they do not conflict with personal goals.

In contrast to this concern with own needs regardless of group needs, high involvement was experienced by the subjects in Shaw's (1958) 'com con' net (all members communicate to all members). They were more successful (completing their problems in less time) than hierarchically organized 'star' net subjects, and were more satisfied with their group. Raven & Rietsema (1957) obtained results which are also germane to the area of member involvement in goal attainment. In their study, a group atmosphere was simulated for a subject by means of recordings of three individuals working on a building task. The clarity of the 'group's' goals and activities was varied by varying the recording used. Each subject was given the task of cutting out cardboard for his group. The subjects who heard the unambiguous recording of their group working on the task felt warmer and more secure, and liked the group more, than the subjects who heard the vague, uninformative recording. They also adapted to the group's rather than their own goals when placed in a goal conflict situation. The differences in attitude may be attributed to the fact that it was virtually impossible for the subject in the 'unclear' situation to be involved with what his group was doing, owing to his inability to know with any degree of certainty what was going on. As far as involvement in group goal-directed effort was concerned, the feeling of these subjects approached that of a nonmember. An experiment by Rosenthal & Cofer (1948) also demonstrates a relationship between goal attainment and satisfaction. The experimenters 'planted' in the experimental groups an individual who behaved in an indifferent, neglectful manner toward the dart-throwing task. As the experiment continued, the attitude of the experimental group members toward the experiment, goal attainment, and the group itself became less favorable, while the attitude of the control group members became more favorable. Those in the experimental groups felt that their group was less effective than an average group, and consequently experienced less satisfaction.

Not only does goal attainment influence member satisfaction, but apparently satisfaction with a group can cause the type of behavior conducive to goal attainment. In many natural groups these two variables can best be viewed in an interactional, mutually supportive relationship. For example, the quality of a plan to improve cooperative housing was positively related to the

satisfaction with project life of the members in the contributing houses (Darley, Gross & Martin, 1952). We can assume that it was not the success that came from a high achievement on this particular goal (the report)—nor probably on any other single goal—that caused the high morale in the group, but rather that it was a variety of factors conducive to high involvement, which in turn contributed to both high satisfaction and success. In the various endeavors undertaken, some similar type of interactional relation was also probably at work in the offices studied by Katz, Maccoby & Morse (1950). They found that the members of high-producing offices had more pride in the group than had the members of low-producing offices.

Good progress toward group goals is associated with high member satisfaction, and, conversely, failure to maintain achievement in relation to group goals tends to reduce satisfaction.

This variable could be operationally defined by having members rate the group on the extent to which they feel it is moving toward its goals and then computing the average of these ratings for a group score.

Dimension 3—Perceived freedom to participate

'If I don't play on the first team, you can't use my ball.' These words can immobilize the sandlot preparations for a baseball game. The desire of the team member to put competent players in the important positions is in conflict with the desire of this player to participate in the game. To him, and to many others like him, a satisfying group experience involves reaching a desired level of personal participation. In order to understand the effects of differential participation, the subject has been brought into the experimental laboratory. The most rigorous attempts in this area have been communication network studies, where the extremes of communicability can be created and compared. From the viewpoint of any one position in a communication network these extremes are: (*i*) a subject may communicate to and receive messages from all of the other subjects (high centrality); or (*ii*) a subject may communicate to no one and receive information from only one person (low centrality). What does centrality mean in the experimental situation? The centrality of a subject's position influences: (*i*) the amount of information he will have; (*ii*) his importance in moving the group toward its goals; and (*iii*) his sense of being a part of the group. In communication net research these are aspects of member participation.

Bavelas (1950) describes research performed by Leavitt (1951) and others, in which four basic network 'designs' were analyzed: the wheel,

Y, line, and circle. Satisfaction was found to be higher for members of the circle net group (where everyone communicated to two other persons) than for those in a wheel net (four members communicate with one member who communicates with all). The positions in the net were each analyzed for relative centrality. It was found that the average 'morale' of those subjects in the more central positions was 7.8, while the average was 4.6 for subjects in less central or peripheral positions. This high participation is positively related to satisfaction since members in central positions have higher satisfaction than those in less central positions. Similar results were obtained by Berkowitz (1956) using a star design, by Shaw (1954) using wheel and circle nets, and by Cohen, Bennis & Wolkon (1962), described above, when they analyzed the effect of change on satisfaction by position. As well as analyzing the individual positions, averages of group satisfaction in differing communication net patterns can be compared.

Shaw (1958) found that members of 'com con' nets (everyone communicates to everyone) had a significantly greater average satisfaction than members of star nets (four-man wheel). Cohen *et al.* (1962), in analyzing the effect of change from one communication net type to another, found that the average satisfaction decreased significantly in groups going from the circle to the wheel and increased significantly in groups going from the wheel to the circle.

From communication net studies, it therefore appears that: groups with more equally distributed participation have a higher average member satisfaction than groups with unequal participation among members.

However, this finding seems to be contradicted by a study by Berkowitz (1953), where low participation by members was *positively* related to member satisfaction. How, if at all, can these apparently contradictory results be reconciled? The simple statement of findings given above masks the important aspect of situational differences. Communication net studies usually employ *peers*, often students, none of whom has had any previous experience of the task and who would therefore expect to participate to about the same extent. By contrast, Berkowitz studied executives in business and government conferences. In the conferences, outside skill and knowledge differentials would be important factors. Therefore, junior or less knowledgeable members would expect to participate to a smaller degree than others, and there would be a general expectation that the formal organization conference procedure would be followed.

The clue to the divergent results thus appears to lie in the differing expectations of members about the extent to which they can and should legitimately participate. If they feel free to fulfill their expectation about participation, satisfaction will be high. Since their expectation of participation is low, relative to the leader, they are satisfied when this relationship is realized. In groups of this type, the high value placed on goal attainment and status consensus, our two other variables, also partly explains the relatively low value placed on participation.

Bavelas (1942) has described a field experiment in which one member of each of three matched pairs of playground leaders was given instruction in group-centered and democratic techniques of leadership (which allowed the children more autonomy). The training had a marked effect on the behavior of the trained leaders when compared with that of their matched partners. The group-centered leader had groups which were higher in enthusiasm and which persisted longer than those of the more authoritarian classroom-style leader. Children in a play situation, in contrast to executives in a decision-making conference situation, do not have to restrain their participation rates to attain their goals.

Work with adults has also given support for the importance of participation-with-guidance as against direction. Another situation significantly different from the decision-making conference was studied by Coch & French (1948). In a field experiment, they varied the amount of participation allowed to factory workers in implementing a change in work procedure. Workers who were simply informed of a change in production methods, given the reasons for the change, and given an opportunity to ask questions (the usual procedure), were highly resistant to the innovation, were antagonistic toward their superiors, and had a high rate of discontinuing working for the company. The group of workers who were allowed to send representatives to work out the change-over procedure had no one quitting the job, a cooperative atmosphere among themselves, and a good relearning rate. In the group in which all the members participated in the transition, resistance and aggression were notably absent and satisfaction appeared to be high. It seems that, in the changeover situation, the worker's need to participate rises, since his welfare is directly affected. Allowing for increased participation to meet his increased expectations thus results in high member satisfaction.

In groups in which the main task is mediated through verbal means, i.e. discussion groups, decision-making groups, therapy groups, etc., freedom to participate can be looked upon as the opportunity to speak when a relevant idea comes to one's mind. Hare (1952) found that in a boy-scout discussion group, member satisfaction with the discussion went down as group size increased from five to twelve. Because only so many can speak in a given period of time, increasing group size is tantamount to placing restriction on the speaking time of all but the most assertive members. Singer & Goldman (1954) provide further support for the satisfaction-lowering effect of restricting the opportunities for members to express themselves. Their subjects were chronic schizophrenics in two psychotherapy groups, with ten patients in each. They manipulated the atmosphere of the groups by conducting one of them in a classroom style, using lectures, and the other in a democratic or group-centered manner. The latter group was rated higher in morale in both actions and verbalization. Preston & Heintz (1949), in analyzing the influence of participatory versus supervisory leadership on group judgement, found that participatory subjects were more satisfied with the group decision more often than supervisory subjects. Analogous effects of participation were found by Flanders (1951). Learner-centered groups were lower in interpersonal anxiety, hostility, apathy, and emotional disintegration, and were higher on learning, than teacher-centered groups. Finally, Hare (1953) found a trend (non-significant) indicating that groups under participatory leadership were more satisfied than groups under supervisory leadership.

In summary, all persons in a group do not have an equal need to participate (Borgatta & Bales, 1953), nor is freedom to participate the only desire that members have, as we have seen in the earlier sections. However, it is one important aspect of group behavior which is associated with member satisfaction, and appears to be particularly relevant to the satisfaction of basic member needs. It may be operationally defined by having the members rate the degree to which they have each felt free to participate in the group and then averaging these ratings for the group.

DISCUSSION

A survey of thirty-seven studies has shown member satisfaction to be related to three variables: (i) status consensus; (ii) perceived goal attainment; and (iii) perceived freedom to participate. Two studies in our sample are of particular interest because they have measurements related to all three of these variables and to member satisfaction. In the first, an observational study, it was found that members of high-performing rifle squads (high perceived goal attainment) reported fewer disagreements on how the leader ran the squad (high status consensus) and took more unauthorized initiative (perceived freedom to participate) than members of low-performing rifle squads. These high-performing squads had higher member satisfaction as indicated by: more pride in their squad, more socialization together after hours, and more satisfaction with their status (Goodacre, 1953). High measures on all three variables were thus correlated with high member satisfaction. Similar results were found in a study (mentioned earlier) which used laboratory groups of students (Goldman, Bolen & Martin, 1961).

For different groups there was imposed or non-imposed leadership, and equal or unequal reward structure. Groups with an equal reward structure and non-imposed leadership had the highest performance on the problem-solving task and the highest member satisfaction. These groups had been able: (i) to select their own most appropriate leadership approach (high status consensus); (ii) to be structured such that the members felt fewer constraints against participation (high perceived freedom to participate); and (iii) to succeed in achieving the goal (high perceived goal attainment).

We can therefore conclude that variations in the three variables we have isolated operate to influence member satisfaction in all fully fledged group situations. However, we feel that a scheme such as this should not only draw together the results of existing experimental and observational studies, but should also contribute to our understanding by generating means of improving member satisfaction in more permanent groups. Accordingly, three groups of major significance in social life today—the nuclear family, the therapy group, and the formal organization group—will be examined to indicate the usefulness of this scheme.

Parsons & Bales (1955) have stressed that the basic functions of the nuclear family are two: 'First, the primary socialization of children . . .; second, the stabilization of the adult personalities of the population of the society' (p. 16). The family may be characterized therefore as a small group whose major goals are providing for many of the important generalized social-emotional needs of the members and the socialization of the children. Accordingly, in relation to *participation* we may postulate that the satisfaction of family members will be reduced when: (i) the family fails to meet the level of member expectations, socially or emotionally (e.g. respect, humor, intimacy); (ii) family members perceive that they have little freedom to participate in deciding on or implementing important family concerns. In relation to *goal attainment* we may postulate that member satisfaction will tend to be reduced when: (iii) the family fails to maintain the expected rate of progress in socializing a child or children (e.g. low school grades, delinquency) and/or does not maintain its expected position among the other families which it uses as a larger reference group. Similarly, in relation to *status consensus* we may postulate that the satisfaction of family members will be reduced when: (iv) there is lack of consensus about the relative status of family members and particularly about the relative status of the parents (high-status persons).

With regard to points (i) and (iii) above, we feel that supportive evidence is unnecessary since a few moments' reflection will bring to mind many experiences which confirm them. In regard to (*ii*) and (*iv*), it is interesting that these points are paralleled by two schools of child-rearing theory: one which advocates permissive child-rearing practices emphasizing the children's participation in decisions concerning the family group as a whole (the child should be both seen and heard); and the other recommending the importance of a clear authority differential with the father as unquestionable head of the family. It appears to us that from the point of view of the satisfaction of family members both approaches have values —one stressing member participation and the other status consensus. It seems likely that the tendency for popular support to swing, pendulum fashion, from one position to the other indicates the necessity of recognizing both variables. In addition, the widespread feeling that one parent is never an adequate substitute for two indicates that the 'great parent' is even more rare than the 'great man' leader, and that the more usual way of achieving status consensus in the family, as elsewhere, is by establishing two differentiated and mutually supportive roles. The same principles which create a high level of satisfaction in other types of group appear also to operate in the family.

In efforts to change families in order to increase member satisfaction, such as occur in marriage guidance or counseling, we suggest the usefulness of examining members' expectations on the three variables and of taking steps either to change the expectations or to change the external or internal structure of the family until the situation approximates the expectations.

The therapy or training group represents an interesting example of our thesis, since in this case particular variables are manipulated by the trainer (or therapist) to produce certain desired effects. Here the members are faced from the first session with a leader who will not assume the usual authority role. Those who normally establish a dependent or counter-dependent relationship with a group leader find it impossible to create such a relationship. Doubts occur as to the leader's capability as a trainer and the resulting frustration reactions are used by the trainer to understand member motivations and to force the members to recognize these motivations. Member satisfaction in the early stages in such groups is notoriously low (e.g. see Bion, 1961) and we suggest that the reasons for this are as follows: although member *participation* is high in these groups, *status consensus* is made impossible, since any ascendant leader cannot function effectively in competition with the trainer. Similarly, perceived *goal achievement* is low in early sessions,

since members perceive an exacerbation of group problems rather than an alleviation of them. It is only after defense mechanisms have been recognized and attitudes have changed that the trainer plays a more positive role and in so doing re-creates status consensus, raises perceived goal attainment with positive statements, and so increases member satisfaction. We suggest, therefore, that the trainer, by manipulating two important variables, reduces member satisfaction in the early stages of the group process. This satisfaction-reduction is used to motivate the search for a more meaningful means of construing the members' relationships with each other and with the trainer than those learned in childhood situations.

The third type of group is one of the most discussed groups in a natural setting, the formal organizational work group such as exists in many businesses. We have already discussed such groups, suggesting reasons why difficulties concerning *status consensus* are likely to affect member satisfaction adversely. We noted that for a considerable time this recurring problem has been coped with by such measures as: (*i*) legitimizing occupancy of the high position by the recruitment to it of persons with unmistakable marks of success, such as degrees or former occupancy of other high-status positions; (*ii*) choosing individuals with high status in other spheres such as fame, social prestige, wealth, age; (*iii*) granting symbols of status such as titles, a superior office, a high salary, rituals of authority; and (*iv*) placing the occupant in a position where crucial information is available to him and not to others.

Member *participation* in formal organization groups is usually concerned with implementing decisions rather than making them, and is best understood in terms of the member's expectations of the amount and type of participation he ought to have. In regard to our third variable, we suggest an important factor which has been generally neglected. For whereas high *goal attainment* has always been sought and emphasized in formal organizations, frequently the importance of providing feedback to members has been ignored. Our review of the literature has suggested that it is not goal attainment *per se* which leads to increased member satisfaction but rather perception by members of the group's progress towards its goals. Where an organization is aiming to increase the satisfaction of its members, particular attention should be paid to the setting of realistically attainable short-term goals, and to the prompt non-perfunctory communication to members of progress toward and attainment of these goals.

SUMMARY

Detailed abstracts were made by the authors of 450 small group studies, selected mainly on the basis of recency of publication and/or inclusion in published collections of such studies. By use of a manual retrieval system, all studies dealing with 'member satisfaction' were extracted from the collection. These studies were then carefully perused for consistencies in their findings. On the basis of this review of the literature, it is proposed that a substantial amount of the variance in the satisfaction of members in small groups can be accounted for by variation along three other major dimensions. They are: (*i*) status consensus, i.e. the degree of consensus in the group concerning leadership; (*ii*) perceived progress toward group goals; and (*iii*) perceived freedom to participate. All relevant research findings of the thirty-seven studies appear to be interpretable and understandable in terms of these three dimensions. The three variables are shown to provide insight into the dynamics of member satisfaction in three specialized types of small group: the family, the therapy group, and the formal organizational work group.

REFERENCES

ALTMAN, I., PENDLETON, CATHERINE A. & TERAUDS, ANITA (1960). Annotations of small group research studies. Arlington, Va.: Human Sciences Research, Inc., October.

BALES, R. F. (1953). The equilibrium problem in small groups. In T. Parsons, R. F. Bales & E. A. Shils (Eds.), *Working papers in the theory of action.* Glencoe, Ill.: Free Press. Pp. 11–161.

BALES, R. F. & SLATER, P. E. (1955). Role differentiation in small decision-making groups. In T. Parsons & R. F. Bales (Eds.), *Family, socialization and interaction process.* Glencoe, Ill.: Free Press.

BAVELAS, A. (1942). Morale and the training of leaders. In G. Watson (Ed.), *Civilian morale.* New York: Reynal & Hitchcock. Pp. 143–65.

BAVELAS, A. (1950). Communication patterns in task groups. *J. acoustical Soc. Amer.* **22,** 725–30.

BERKOWITZ, L. (1953). Sharing leadership in small, decision-making groups. *J. abnorm. soc. Psychol.* **48,** 231–38.

BERKOWITZ, L. (1956). Personality and group position. *Sociometry* **19,** 210–22.

BION, W. R. (1961). *Experiences in groups.* London: Tavistock Publications; New York: Basic Books.

BORGATTA, E. F. & BALES, R. F. (1953). Interaction of individuals in reconstituted groups. *Sociometry* **16,** 302–20.

BORGATTA, E. F., COUCH, A. S. & BALES, R. F. (1954). Some findings relevant to the great man theory of leadership. *Amer. sociol. Rev.* **19,** 755–59.

CARLSON, E. R. (1960). Clique structure and member satisfaction in groups. *Sociometry* **23,** 327–37.

CARTWRIGHT, D. & ZANDER, A. (Eds.) (1953). *Group dynamics: research and theory.* Evanston, Ill.: Row, Peterson; London: Tavistock Publications, 1954. Second edition, 1960.

CATTELL, R. B. (1948). Concepts and methods in the measurement of group syntality. *Psychol. Rev.* **55,** 48–63.

COCH, L. & FRENCH, J. R. P., JR. (1948). Overcoming resistance to change. *Hum. Relat.* **1,** 512–32.

COHEN, A. M., BENNIS, W. G. & WOLKON, G. H. (1962). The effect of changes in communication networks on the behavior of problem-solving groups. *Sociometry* **25,** 177–96.

DARLEY, J. G., GROSS, N. & MARTIN, W. E. (1952). Studies in group behavior: factors associated with the productivity of groups. *J. appl. Psychol.* **36,** 396–403.

DEUTSCH, M. (1949). An experimental study of the effects of cooperation and competition upon group process. *Hum. Relat.* **2,** 199–231.

EXLINE, R. V. & ZILLER, R. C. (1959). Status congruency and interpersonal conflict in decision-making groups. *Hum. Relat.* **12,** 147–61.

FLANDERS, N. A. (1951). Personal-social anxiety as a factor in experimental learning situations. *J. educ. Res.* **45,** 100–10.

FOURIEZOS, N. T., HUTT, M. L. & GUETZKOW, H. (1950). Measurement of self-oriented needs in discussion groups. *J. abnorm. soc. Psychol.* **45,** 682–90.

FRENCH, J. R. P., JR. (1941). The disruption and cohesion of groups. *J. abnorm. soc. Psychol.* **36,** 361–77.

GIBB, C. A. (1947). The principles and traits of leadership. *J. abnorm. soc. Psychol.* **42,** 267–84.

GOLDMAN, M., BOLEN, M. & MARTIN, R. (1961). Some conditions under which groups operate and how this affects their performance. *J. soc. Psychol.* **54,** 47–56.

GOODACRE, D. M. (1953). Group characteristics of good and poor performing combat units. *Sociometry* **16,** 168–78.

HAMBLIN, R. L. (1958). Leadership and crisis. *Sociometry* **21,** 322–35.

HAMBLIN, R. L., MILLER, K. & WIGGINS, J. A. (1961). Group morale and competence of the leader. *Sociometry* **24,** 295–311.

HARE, A. P. (1952). A study of interaction and consensus in different sized groups. *Amer. sociol. Rev.* **17,** 261–67.

HARE, A. P. (1953). Small group discussions with participatory and supervisory leadership.

J. abnorm. soc. Psychol. **48**, 273–75.

HARE, A. P. (1962). *Handbook of small group research.* New York: Free Press.

HARE, A. P., BORGATTA, E. F. & BALES, R. F. (Eds.) (1955). *Small groups: studies in social interaction.* New York: Knopf.

HEINICKE, C. & BALES, R. F. (1953). Development trends in the structure of small groups. *Sociometry* **16**, 7–38.

KAHN, R. L. & KATZ, D. (1960). Leadership practices in relation to productivity and morale. In D. Cartwright & A. Zander (Eds.). *Group dynamics.* New York: Harper & Row; London: Tavistock Publications. Pp. 554–70.

KATZ, D., MACCOBY, N. & MORSE, NANCY C. (1950). Productivity, supervision and morale in an office situation. Ann Arbor, Mich.: Univ. of Michigan.

LEAVITT, H. J. (1951). Some effects of certain communication patterns on group performance. *J. abnorm. soc. Psychol.* **46**, 38–50.

PARSONS, T. & BALES, R. F. (Eds.) (1955). *Family, socialization and interaction process.* Glencoe, Ill.: Free Press.

PRESTON, M. G. & HEINTZ, R. K. (1949). Effects of participatory versus supervisory leadership on group judgment. *J. abnorm. soc. Psychol.* **44**, 345–55.

RAVEN, B. H. & RIETSEMA, JAN (1957). The effects of varied clarity of group goal and group path upon the individual and his relation to his group. *Hum. Relat.* **10**, 29–45.

ROSENTHAL, D. & COFER, C. N. (1948). The effect on group performance of an indifferent and neglectful attitude shown by one group member. *J. exp. Psychol.* **38**, 568–77.

SHAW, M. E. (1954). Some effects of problem complexity upon problem solution efficiency in different communication nets. *J. exp. Psychol.* **48**, 211–17.

SHAW, M. E. (1958). Some effects of irrelevant information upon problem-solving by small groups. *J. soc. Psychol.* **47**, 33–7.

SHELLEY, H. P. (1960a). Status consensus, leadership, and satisfaction with the group. *J. soc. Psychol.* **51**, 157–64.

SHELLEY, H. P. (1960b). Focussed leadership and cohesiveness in small groups. *Sociometry* **23**, 209–16.

SINGER, J. L. & GOLDMAN, G. D. (1954). Experimentally contrasted social atmospheres in group psychotherapy with chronic schizophrenics. *J. soc. Psychol.* **40**, 23–37.

SLATER, P. E. (1955). Role differentiation in small groups. *Amer. sociol. Rev.* **20**, 300–10.

BRAINSTORMING IN GROUPS AND CREATIVE THINKING *

Occasionally a psychological technique seizes the imagination of the public and receives widespread acceptance. For example, during the Korean War, news media gave much attention to the Communist efforts to "brainwash" American prisoners of war, and many people became convinced that the Communists had invented a diabolical new psychological weapon. Another example is the interest in "subliminal advertising" that was initiated by reports of experiments in movie theaters whereby flashing the phrases "Eat Popcorn" and "Drink Coca-Cola" on the screen at an exposure below the recognition threshold supposedly led the audiences to eat and drink voraciously. Such reports even led to a congressional investigation of these subliminal techniques.

There is a methodological lesson in such reactions. They are usually based upon inadequate experiments, distorted reports, or misinterpretations of the results obtained. Typically, the reports are not available for firsthand observation or else they cannot be checked after the fact. When such fads are followed up by carefully designed studies, the original interpretations usually have to be radically altered.

In the present selection, the investigators present an experiment carefully designed to determine the effects on creativity of group participation when using the popular brainstorming technique. Brainstorming activity is established by a set of rules that are supposed to free the individual's thought processes from his usual inhibitions, enabling him to have a larger number of more creative ideas. Usually these rules are applied in a group situation, because it is thought that interaction among the members facilitates the flow of ideas. The investigators do *not* test the efficacy of brainstorming rules, but they do determine whether group interaction is essential to their application. To accomplish this, group performance must be compared with individual performance in some appropriate fashion. This comparison is carried out by use of the *nominal* group, composed of individuals who have actually worked alone but whose performances are combined to provide a control comparison for the performances of actual groups. Methodological innovations of this sort are often a prerequisite to the solution of a theoretical question.

* The selection following the editorial introduction is reprinted from "Does group participation when using branstorming facilitate or inhibit creative thinking?" *Administrative Science Quarterly*, 1958, 3, 23–47, by permission of the authors and publisher.

Does Group Participation When Using Brainstorming Facilitate or Inhibit Creative Thinking?

DONALD W. TAYLOR
YALE UNIVERSITY

PAUL C. BERRY
UNIVERSITY OF MINNESOTA

CLIFFORD H. BLOCK
WASHINGTON, D. C.

In an experiment designed to answer the title question, twelve groups of four men each and forty-eight individuals followed the four basic rules of brainstorming in attacking the same three problems in the same order. Upon completion of the experiment, a table of random numbers was used to divide the forty-eight individual subjects into twelve nominal groups of four men each. The performance of each nominal group was then scored as though its members had actually worked together. The achievement of these nominal groups thus provided a measure of the performance to be expected if group participation neither facilitates nor inhibits creative thinking. When compared with that of the twelve nominal groups, the performance of the twelve real groups was found to be markedly inferior with respect to: (*a*) mean total number of ideas produced; (*b*) mean number of unique ideas produced; · (*c*) three different measures which weighted the ideas produced differentially with respect to quality. To the extent that the results of the present experiment can be generalized, it must be concluded that group participation when using brainstorming inhibits creative thinking.[1]

Brainstorming was originated and first used by Alex F. Osborn in 1939 in the advertising agency Batten, Barton, Durstine & Osborn, which he then headed.[2] Within recent years its use has grown rapidly. A large number of major companies, units of the Army, Navy, and Air Force, and various federal, state, and local civilian agencies have employed the technique, and instruction has been given in a number of colleges and universities in its use.[3] Although an occasional critical voice has been raised,[4] brainstorming may be said to have achieved wide acceptance as a means of facilitating creative thinking.

The purpose of brainstorming is to free individuals from inhibition, self-criticism, and criticism by others in order that in response to a specific problem they may produce as many different ideas as possible. The assumption is that the larger the number of ideas produced, the greater the probability of achieving an effective solution. Brainstorming is characterized by four basic rules:

(*1*) *Criticism is ruled out.* Adverse judgment of ideas must be withheld until later.

(*2*) *"Free-wheeling" is welcomed.* The wilder the idea, the better; it is easier to tame down than to think up.

(*3*) *Quantity is wanted.* The greater the number of ideas, the more the likelihood of winners.

(*4*) *Combination and improvement are sought.* In addition to contributing ideas of their own, participants should suggest how ideas of others can be turned into *better* ideas; or how two or more ideas can be joined into still another idea.[5]

Brainstorming ordinarily involves not only following the four basic rules but also group collaboration in attacking the problem. Osborn emphasizes the value of group interaction in facilitating the flow of ideas.[6] It was this characteristic of brainstorming which was of primary interest in the present study.

Certain rather informal experiments very briefly described by Osborn appear to support the view that group collaboration in brainstorming does increase production of ideas.[7] Moreover, many practical experiences described by Osborn also seem to provide support persuasive of this view. An adequate answer to the question, however, demands adequately controlled experiments

---

[1] The experiment reported here is one in a series of psychological studies of problem solving being carried out under Project NR 150–166 and supported by Contract Nonr 609(20) between Yale University and the Office of Naval Research. The present article presents essentially the same information, omitting only certain details of experimental procedure and statistical analysis, as the following technical report previously issued under the contract: Donald W. Taylor, Paul C. Berry, and Clifford H. Block, *Does Group Participation When Using Brainstorming Facilitate or Inhibit Creative Thinking?* (New Haven: Departments of Industrial Administration and Psychology, Yale University, 1957). Copies of this technical report are available in major university libraries. Permission is granted for reproduction, translation, publication, use, and disposal of the present article in whole or in part by or for the United States Government.

[2] Alex F. Osborn, *Applied Imagination*, rev. ed. (New York, 1957).

[3] *Ibid.* See also Brainstorming—New Ways to Find New Ideas, *Time*, **69** (Feb. 18, 1957) 90.

[4] Bernard S. Benson, Let's Toss This Idea Up . . . *Fortune*, **56** (Oct. 1957), 145–146.

[5] Osborn, *Applied Imagination*, p. 84.

[6] *Ibid.*, pp. 82–83.

[7] *Ibid.*, pp. 82, 228.

appropriately designed and with results subjected to thorough statistical analysis. No such experiment was known to the authors of the present report—certainly none has been published in sufficient detail to permit evaluation of the design, the analysis, and the conclusions reached.

The present experiment employed a design previously developed by Taylor for use in studies of group problem solving where the problems involved have logically correct solutions.[8] Earlier studies of such group problem solving were concerned with a comparison of the achievement of groups of various sizes with that of individuals. However, the performance of a group should be superior to that of an individual, simply because in the group more individuals are working on the problem. On the assumption of the appropriate null hypothesis, namely, that working in a group has no effect either positive or negative upon individual performance, Taylor[9] and Lorge and Solomon[10] independently have presented a simple mathematical model for predicting the performance of a group of a given size from a knowledge of individual performance. By comparing actual group achievement with that predicted from the model, one can determine whether group participation facilitates or inhibits problem solving.

Taylor has also developed an experimental design which provides an alternative method of testing the same null hypothesis as that represented by the model.[11] Individuals are randomly assigned to work either alone or in groups of a given size on a series of problems. The number of individuals working alone should be about equal to that working in groups. After the experiment is completed, those who actually worked alone are divided at random into nominal groups of the same size as the real groups. The performance of the nominal groups is then scored as though the members of the group had worked together. The achievement of the nominal groups thus provides a measure of the performance to be expected under the null hypothesis. If the performance of the real groups is superior to that of the nominal groups, group participation facilitates performance; if it is inferior, group participation inhibits it.

---

[8] Donald W. Taylor, "Problem Solving by Groups," in *Proceedings of the Fourteenth International Congress of Psychology, Montreal, June 1954* (Amsterdam, 1955), pp. 218–219. See also Donald W. Taylor and Olga W. McNemar, "Problem Solving and Thinking," in Calvin P. Stone, ed., *Annual Review of Psychology* (Stanford, Calif., 1955), VI, 455–482.

[9] Taylor, *op. cit.*

[10] Irving Lorge and Herbert Solomon, Two Models of Group Behavior in the Solution of Eureka-Type Problems, *Psychometrika*, **20** (1955), 139–148.

[11] Taylor, *op. cit.*

This design, with appropriate modification in the scoring of responses for nominal groups, was employed in the present experiment to provide an answer to the question: Does group participation when using brainstorming facilitate or inhibit creative thinking?

THE EXPERIMENT

Subjects

The ninety-six Yale juniors and seniors who served as subjects in this experiment were all at the time enrolled in a course in Psychology of Personnel Administration taught by the first author. Each week, in addition to two lectures to the entire class, the course included an analysis of a case carried out in small discussion groups;[12] each group had its own student leader, this task being rotated among the members of the group. As a result of such case discussion and of the way in which subjects were assigned, each real group in the present experiment was not, as often must be the case in studies of group problem solving, an *ad hoc* group of individuals meeting for the first time; instead, each real group included men who not only knew each other but who also had worked together effectively in small-group discussion over a considerable period of time. At the same time, the procedure used in assigning subjects was such that those assigned to work in groups and those assigned to work alone could legitimately be regarded as random samples from the same population.

For the case discussions, the class was divided into five sections of about equal size which met at different times during the week. These five sections were in turn divided into two discussion groups of about nine to eleven men each which met simultaneously in separate rooms; the instructor divided his time between the two groups meeting simultaneously. The following procedure was used to assign half of the ninety-six men to work in real groups of four and the other half to work alone. From each of the ten discussion groups in the class, four men were picked at random to form an experimental group, thus providing ten experimental groups; and from two of the ten discussion groups, an additional four men were picked at random to provide two more groups, for a total of twelve experimental groups. The remaining men in the ten discussion groups, forty-eight in all, served as individual subjects. Two points perhaps should be added here. The original registration of members of the class in the five sections was dependent primarily upon class schedules and had no known relation to ability. The division of these sections into two discussion groups was also unrelated to ability.

---

[12] Each period was devoted to discussion of a case selected from John D. Glover and Ralph M. Hower, *The Administrator* (Homewood, Ill., 1957). By the beginning of the present experiment, each group had completed a total of six cases.

Problems

Considerable pretesting was carried out in an effort to ensure that the problems selected for use in the present experiment would be as suitable as possible for attack by the brainstorming procedure and also for use with Yale students. Initially, several problems were selected from those suggested by Osborn as appropriate for use with brainstorming;[13] others were originated by the present writers, and some were obtained from other sources. With Yale students both individually and in small groups used as subjects, a total of about twenty problems was tried out; none of those, of course, who participated in these pretests served as subjects in the main experiment. On the basis of this pretesting, three problems were selected which seemed to be of interest to Yale students, productive of many and varied responses, and appropriate for use with brainstorming. The three problems were as follows:

1. Each year a great many American tourists go to visit Europe. But now suppose that our country wished to get many more European tourists to come to visit America during their vacations. What steps can you suggest that would get more European tourists to come to this country?
2. We don't think this is very likely to happen, but imagine for a moment what would happen if everyone born after 1960 had an extra thumb on each hand. This extra thumb will be built just as the present one is, but located on the other side of the hand. It faces inward, so that it can press against the fingers, just as the regular thumb does now. Here is a picture to help you see how it will be. (A line drawing of a hand with two thumbs was shown by the experimenter at this point in the reading of the problem and then left in full view on the table during the entire period of work on the problem.[14]) Now the question is: What practical benefits or difficulties will arise when people start having this extra thumb?
3. Because of the rapidly increasing birth rate beginning in the 1940s, it is now clear that by 1970 public school enrollment will be very much greater than it is today. In fact, it has been estimated that if the student-teacher ratio were to be maintained at what it is today, 50 per cent of all individuals graduating from college would have to be induced to enter teaching. What different steps might be taken to insure that schools will continue to provide instruction at least equal in effectiveness to that now provided?

For brevity's sake, the three problems were re-

ferred to as the "Tourists Problem," the "Thumbs Problem," and the "Teachers Problem."[15]

Procedure

In a single experimental session lasting about one hour, the three problems were presented in the order in which they are listed above to each of the twelve groups and to each of the forty-eight individuals. The second and third authors of the present report conducted the sessions, each one conducting six group and twenty-four individual sessions. The assignment of groups and individuals to experimenters was largely a matter of chance. Group and individual sessions were alternated in such a way that on any given date about the same proportion of group and individual sessions had been completed.

Both experimenters were advanced graduate students in psychology. Both were familiar with Osborn's writing concerning brainstorming. Both had participated in the pretesting described above and thereby gained experience with the procedures of brainstorming. Both personally believed that group brainstorming was an effective procedure for facilitating the production of ideas.

Very shortly before the present experiment began, one lecture to the class as a whole was devoted to creative thinking, with particular attention to brainstorming. The origin, nature, and widespread use of brainstorming was described, the purpose being to create interest in the procedure and as favorable as possible an attitude toward it. The shortage of controlled experimental studies of this and similar procedures was described. Finally, the students were asked to participate as subjects in the experiment and were promised a report of the results when it was available.

During the pretesting, both with individuals and with small groups, attention was devoted to the question of what length of time should be allowed for work on each of the problems selected for use. What was wanted was a span of time long enough so that members of groups of four would have adequate opportunity to express all the ideas which occurred to them within the working period and at the same time short enough so that individuals would not become bored by being forced to continue work on a problem long after they had essentially exhausted their ideas. Pretesting showed that the rate at which ideas were produced on the problems decreased with time. A time limit of twelve minutes was finally selected as one which would permit group members to express all ideas occurring to them within

[13] Alex F. Osborn, *A Manual of Instruction for Teachers Using the Textbook "Applied Imagination"* (New York, 1953).

[14] For a copy of the line drawing, see Taylor, Berry, and Block, *op. cit.,* p. 6.

[15] Although the third problem would be more accurately described as the education problem, it was called the "Teachers Problem" for the sake of symmetry.

the work period (though not to exhaust all possible ideas) and yet which would not result in excessive periods of silence for individual subjects. Actually, for both individuals and groups, appreciable periods of silence appeared between responses near the end of the twelve minutes.

Instructions

The experimenter began each group or individual session by reading aloud instructions,[16] the first part of which was designed to ensure a high degree of subject motivation. First, it was explained that the experiment was part of a program of research on problem solving and creative thinking being carried on under a contract with the Office of Naval Research. Secondly, each subject was asked to read the first three paragraphs (about 60 per cent) of a one-page feature article on brainstorming which, by coincidence, had appeared a few weeks earlier in *Time*.[17] These three paragraphs were quite favorable to brainstorming, describing its use in major U.S. companies. Finally, subjects were specifically asked to do as well as they could, and it was impressed upon them that the success of the experiment was contingent upon such effort.

The second part of the instructions was designed to make certain that subjects fully understood the nature of brainstorming. The four basic rules, as already described, were explained.

The instructions included a brief explanation that, because writing was slow and inaccurate, the discussion of each problem would be recorded (using an Edison *Voicewriter* and conference microphone). Subjects were also requested to avoid discussing any of the problems with anyone at Yale until the experiment was completed; evidence available indicates that this request was generally honored.

Opportunity was provided for questions and, finally, the four basic rules were reiterated. The experimenter presented each problem by reading it aloud to the individual or group. If any question was raised, it was answered by rereading part or all of the original statement. The actual copy of the problem was never given to the individual or group. On those few occasions when a critical comment was made during work on a problem, the experimenter called attention again to the basic rule against criticism. Comments volunteered by many of the students during the experiment support the belief that with a few possible exceptions they were motivated to do as well as they could. Those who participated as members

---

[16] For a copy of the instructions, see Taylor, Berry, and Block, *op. cit.*, pp. 37–39.

[17] Brainstorming—New Ways to Find New Ideas, *Time*, **69** (Feb. 18, 1957), 90.

of groups seemed particularly enthusiastic about their experience.

RESULTS

The first step following the completion of the experimental sessions was the division of the forty-eight individual subjects into twelve nominal groups of four each. This was done in order to permit comparison of real group performance not only with that of individuals but also with that to be expected on the basis of the hypothesis that working in the group has no effect either positive or negative upon the performance of its members. A table of random numbers was employed to divide the twenty-four individual subjects who had worked with the first experimenter into six nominal groups of four; the same procedure was used to divide the twenty-four who had worked with the second experimenter into an additional six nominal groups. This particular procedure was necessary if a test were to be made of any possible difference between the two sets of six nominal groups resulting from differences between the experimenters. Inspection of the data later obtained, however, revealed no possible significant difference between experimenters in the results.

Next, an essentially complete typewritten transcript was made of the recording of the responses of each real group and of each individual subject to each of the three problems. An analysis of all the transcripts for the Tourists Problem resulted in the preparation of a master list of all the different steps suggested to "get more European tourists to come to this country." Similar analyses yielded for the Thumbs Problem a master list of all the different suggestions of "what practical benefits or difficulties will arise when people start having this extra thumb," and for the Teachers Problem a master list of all the different steps that "might be taken to insure that schools will continue to provide instruction at least equal in effectiveness to that now provided." The three master lists were, of course, organized in terms of appropriate categories and subcategories. After preparation, each list was carefully reexamined to make certain that no essentially similar item appeared twice. What constituted a discriminable difference between two suggestions depended, of course, upon the judgment of the individual preparing the list, but in general it may be said that whenever the second suggestion appeared clearly to add something to the first, it was regarded as a different suggestion. The master list for the Tourists Problem included a total of 483 different steps, for the Thumbs Problem a total of 791 different consequences, and for the Teachers Problem a total of 513 different steps. The magnitude of such lists may be visualized from the fact that, when typed on sheets measuring 8½ by 11 inches, the Tourists list covered 14 pages, the Thumbs list 32 pages, and the Teachers list 17 pages.

For each master list, sets of data sheets were

prepared matching the list in such a way that the analysis of the protocol for any individual or real group could be recorded simply by placing a check in the row and column corresponding respectively to the particular idea and the particular group or individual. Four adjoining columns were used to record the analyses of the protocols for the individuals included in each nominal group of four. In a single adjacent column, a check mark was placed whenever a check had been made in that row for any one or more of the four individuals. Thus this column provided a record of nominal-group performance, consistent with the requirement of the experimental design that the nominal group be scored as though the members had worked together.[18] If any member of the nominal group presented an idea, the group was regarded as having presented it. If two or more members of the nominal group presented the same idea, it was still recorded as only one idea. The total number of different ideas presented by each real group, individual, or nominal group was obtained simply by taking the total number of check marks in the appropriate column.

Table 1 presents the mean number of responses by individuals and real groups to each of the three problems. On each of the three problems, the mean number of ideas presented by real groups is much larger than that presented by individuals. The appropriate analysis of variance[19] briefly summarized in Table 1 shows that this difference between real groups and individuals with an F of 71.2 is significant at well beyond the .0001 level.[20] The analysis also shows that the differ-

[18] The procedure described had not only the advantage of clerical and computational convenience but also the more important advantage of avoiding any possible effect of bias upon the scoring of nominal-group performance. Judgments of whether two similar ideas are the same or different are necessarily somewhat subjective. Had nominal-group scores been obtained by working directly with the original protocols, such judgments would have been made with knowledge of whether the two similar ideas had been produced by two members of the same nominal group. Such knowledge might conceivably have biased the judgments. In the procedure employed here, such judgments were made in the course of the construction of the master lists and without such knowledge.

[19] The analyses of variance reported in Tables 1, 2, 3, 5, 6, and 7 all involve what is described as a "Type I Mixed Design" by E. F. Lindquist, *Design and Analysis of Experiments in Psychology and Education* (Boston, 1953), pp. 266–273. To save space, only the most essential information resulting from the several analyses is presented in the tables just cited. For summaries of the same analyses in more conventional form, including both sums of squares and mean squares, see Taylor, Berry, and Block, *op. cit.*, pp. 13, 15, 17, 24–26.

[20] In other words, the probability is less than 1 in 10,000 of obtaining by chance a difference as large or larger than that between real groups and individuals reported in Table 1. Those unfamiliar with analysis of variance many wish to consult Quinn McNemar, *Psychological Statistics* (New York, 1955), pp. 243 ff.

ences among the three problems in mean number of responses is significant at the .001 level and that the interaction between the two primary variables is also significant.[21]

Table 2 shows that the mean number of responses produced by nominal groups was considerably larger than that produced by real groups on each of the three problems. The analysis of variance indicates that this superiority of nominal to real groups is significant at far beyond the .0001 level. The difference among the three problems in number of responses is again significant, but in this case the interaction does not even approach significance.

It seemed important to compare the performance of real and nominal groups not only in terms of the number of ideas produced but also in terms

TABLE 1 *Mean Total Number of Responses to Each Problem by Individuals and Real Groups*

	TOURISTS	THUMBS	TEACHERS	MEAN OF MEANS
Individuals	20.7	19.9	18.2	19.6
Real groups	38.4	41.3	32.6	37.5
Mean of means	29.6	30.6	25.4	
Analysis of variance	d.f.	F	p	
Individuals *vs.* real groups	1, 58	71.2	.0001	
Among problems	2, 116	8.5	.001	
Interaction	2, 116	4.96	.01	

TABLE 2 *Mean Total Number of Responses to Each Problem by Real Groups and Nominal Groups*

	TOURISTS	THUMBS	TEACHERS	MEAN OF MEANS
Real groups	38.4	41.3	32.6	37.5
Nominal groups	68.3	72.6	63.5	68.1
Mean of means	53.4	57.0	48.0	
Analysis of variance	d.f.	F	p	
Real *vs.* nominal groups	1, 22	96.3	.0001	
Among problems	2, 44	7.8	.005	
Interaction	2, 44	.09		

[21] Interaction refers to the variation in the effect of one independent variable upon the dependent variable as a function of a second independent variable (see McNemar, *op. cit.*, pp. 283, 301–303).

of the originality and quality of these ideas. For this purpose, additional analyses were undertaken.

A large proportion of the responses to any one of the problems was, of course, produced by more than one of the nominal or real groups, a small number of the ideas on each of the problems being suggested by nearly all of the twenty-four groups. On each problem, however, an appreciable number of suggestions was made by only one of the twenty-four groups; these may be described as unique responses. The number of such unique ideas provides one satisfactory measure of the originality of the performance of a particular group.

In Table 3 are given the mean number of unique responses produced by real and nominal groups on each of the three problems. The superiority of the nominal to the real groups on this measure is significant at the .005 level. The difference among the three problems in mean number of unique responses is also significant, but the interaction is not.

Comparison of Table 3 with Table 2 suggests that the difference between nominal and real groups in number of unique responses might result simply from the difference between the two in total number of responses, in other words, that nominal groups might produce more unique responses just because they produce more responses. To test this hypothesis, the method of analysis of covariance was employed, with the number of responses to each problem as the control variable.[22] For each of the three problems a separate

analysis of variance was carried out and then extended to include an analysis of covariance.[23]

The separate analyses of variance for the three problems yielded results consistent with those of the over-all analysis of variance reported in Table 3. The superiority of nominal to real groups in number of unique responses is significant at the .02 level for the Thumbs Problem and at the .001 level for the Teachers Problem, although it just reaches the .06 level for the Tourists Problem. The analyses of covariance show that after adjustment for differences in total number of responses, there is no significant difference between real and nominal groups in number of unique responses on either the Tourists Problem or the Teachers Problem.[24] On the Thumbs Problem, however, the difference after adjustment is significant at the .02 level. Moreover, computation of the adjusted means shows that this difference actually favors the real groups. In other words, when allowance is made for difference in total number of responses produced, the real groups produced more unique responses than the nominal groups, but only on the Thumbs Problem.

Detailed examination of the 483 different suggestions for solution of the Tourists Problem and of the 513 different suggestions for solution of the Teachers Problem indicated that these suggestions differed in quality with respect to at least three dimensions: feasibility, effectiveness, and generality. Accordingly, five-step rating scales were constructed for use in measuring these three. The intention was to construct scales such that the successive steps on each scale would be subjectively equal, each step would be relatively unambiguous, and all five steps would actually be used in rating. After some pretesting and revision, three scales were obtained which were considered acceptable for use.

The 791 different responses made to the Thumbs Problem differed from those made to the other two problems in that they represented anticipated consequences instead of suggested steps for solution. For this reason only one of the three rating scales constructed for rating responses to the other two problems, namely, generality, ap-

TABLE 3 Mean Numbers of Unique Responses to Each Problem

	TOURISTS	THUMBS	TEACHERS	MEAN OF MEANS
Real groups	7.5	17.7	7.3	10.8
Nominal groups	13.7	28.1	17.5	19.8
Mean of means	10.6	22.9	12.4	

Analysis of variance	d.f.	F	p
Real *vs.* nominal groups	1, 22	11.4	.005
Among problems	2, 44	42.1	.0001
Interaction	2, 44	1.29	

[22] The analysis of covariance provides a method for determining whether there is any significant difference between nominal and real groups in number of unique ideas produced after allowance is made for the difference in total number of ideas produced, the number of unique ideas being correlated with the total number of ideas. For an introduction to analysis of covariance, see McNemar, *op. cit.*, pp. 343 ff.

[23] Initially it appeared appropriate to extend the analysis of variance reported in Table 3 to include an analysis of covariance by using the general procedure described by Lindquist, *op. cit.*, pp. 332–333. One of the assumptions, however, which would be involved in such an analysis for all three problems simultaneously would be that the regressions within the six subgroups are both linear and homogeneous (*ibid.*, p. 323). Inspection of the appropriate scatter diagrams suggested that the slope coefficients for the real and nominal groups were homogeneous on each of the three problems but that those for the Thumbs Problem differed considerably from those for the other two problems. Accordingly, it was decided to carry out separate analyses of covariance for the three problems.

[24] For the conventional tables summarizing these three analyses of variance and of covariance, see Taylor, Berry, and Block, *op. cit.*, pp. 18–19.

peared equally applicable in the case of the Thumbs Problem. For this problem, however, analogous to feasibility and effectiveness on the other problems were the dimensions of probability and significance, respectively. Accordingly, two additional rating scales were constructed by the same method to measure these latter variables.[25]

All three authors of the present report participated in the rating of the responses to the three problems. The first author rated the responses to the Tourists, Thumbs, and Teachers Problems on effectiveness, probability, and generality, respectively; the second author on generality, significance, and feasibility, respectively; and the third author on feasibility, generality, and effectiveness, respectively. Thus the responses to each problem were rated on three different scales by three different raters, presumably increasing the independence of the ratings of the three characteristics. Each rater employed a different scale for each of the three problems, thus presumably minimizing the possibility that a single idiosyncratic interpretation of any of the scales would occur for all three problems. Since the use of a single scale for a single problem required the making of 483 to 791 judgments, and hence a great deal of time, it was not considered worth while to have the ratings replicated. The mean rating for all responses to the Tourists Problem was 3.27 on feasibility, 1.97 on effectiveness, and 2.20 on generality; for all responses to the Thumbs Problem, 2.04 on probability, 1.88 on significance, and 2.21 on generality; for all responses to the Teachers Problem, 2.83 on feasibility, 2.69 on effectiveness, and 2.39 on generality.

The intercorrelations among the dimensions rated are given in Table 4 for each of the three problems. Although all the correlations except one are significantly different from zero at the .01 level, the fact that all are relatively small suggests that the dimensions chosen for rating may be reasonably independent. It should be added, of course, that since the ratings being correlated were made by different raters, the obtained coefficients are probably somewhat lower than they would otherwise be because of the limited reliability of the ratings.

One additional point concerning the procedure used in rating deserves emphasis. All ratings were made of the responses as they appeared on the master list for the given problem and without any knowledge of whether the response had been made by real or nominal groups. This was done, of course, to eliminate any possible tendency of any rater to bias his ratings to favor either real or nominal groups.

After the ratings were all recorded on the master lists, these lists were then used in conjunction with the matched data sheets to obtain scores

[25] For a copy of each of the five rating scales, see Taylor, Berry, and Block, op. cit., pp. 40–42. Inspection of these scales provides the best available definition of each of the variables.

on each of the three rated dimensions on each problem for each of the real and nominal groups. The score for each group for a given problem and a given dimension was simply the sum of the ratings on that dimension of the responses given by the group to that problem.

TABLE 4 Intercorrelations among Ratings of Responses to Each of Three Problems

	FEASIBILITY vs. EFFECTIVENESS	FEASIBILITY vs. GENERALITY	EFFECTIVENESS vs. GENERALITY
Tourists	.25*	−.01	.27*
Teachers	.15*	.16*	.35*
	PROBABILITY vs. SIGNIFICANCE	PROBABILITY vs. GENERALITY	SIGNIFICANCE vs. GENERALITY
Thumbs	35*	.10*	.38*

* Significant at or beyond the .01 level.

TABLE 5 Feasibility, Effectiveness, and Generality of Responses to Tourists Problem

	FEASIBILITY	EFFEC-TIVENESS	GENER-ALITY	MEAN OF MEANS
Real groups	129.1	75.3	82.4	95.6
Nominal groups	215.1	133.0	141.1	163.1
Mean of means	172.1	104.1	111.8	

Analysis of variance	d.f.	F	p
Real vs. nominal groups	1, 22	43.5	.0001
Among measures	2, 44	199.2	.0001
Interaction	2, 44	9.3	.001

TABLE 6 Probability, Significance, and Generality of Responses to Thumbs Problem

	PROBABILITY	SIGNIFI-CANCE	GENER-ALITY	MEAN OF MEANS
Real groups	80.3	78.7	92.1	83.7
Nominal groups	157.3	133.2	155.8	148.8
Mean of means	118.8	106.0	124.0	

Analysis of variance	d.f.	F	p
Real vs. nominal groups	1, 22	114.6	.0001
Among measures	2, 44	4.60	.05
Interaction	2, 44	1.49	

A comparison of the mean scores of real and nominal groups on each of the three rated dimensions is presented in Tables 5, 6, and 7 for the Tourists, Thumbs, and Teachers Problems, respectively. On each of the three dimensions for each of the three problems, the mean for the nominal groups is much larger than that for the real groups. The analyses of variance summarized in Tables 5, 6, and 7 show that this superiority of the nominal to the real groups is significant well beyond the .0001 level for each of the three problems. The differences among the three measures are also significant for all three problems, and the interaction is significant for only the Tourists and Teachers Problems; these latter findings, however, are of limited interest because of the nature of the measures involved.

Comparison of Tables 5, 6, and 7 with Table 2 suggests that, as was true of unique responses for two of the problems, the differences between nominal and real groups on each of the rated dimensions for each of the three problems might have resulted simply from the difference between such groups in total number of responses. The score of a nominal or real group on any given quality dimension depends both on the rating of each idea given and on the total number of ideas produced. If the average rating on such a dimension is the same for the nominal as for the real groups, then the difference in score on that dimension would reflect only the difference in total number of responses. To determine whether there was any significant difference between nominal and real groups on these measures weighted for quality after allowance is made for difference in total number of responses, an analysis of covariance was carried out for each of the three problems.[26]

TABLE 7 *Feasibility, Effectiveness, and Generality of Responses to Teachers Problem*

	FEASIBILITY	EFFEC-TIVENESS	GENER-ALITY	MEAN OF MEANS
Real groups	92.6	90.4	78.5	87.2
Nominal groups	179.6	163.3	148.5	163.8
Mean of means	136.0	126.9	113.5	
Analysis of variance	*d.f.*		*F*	*p*
Real *vs.* nominal groups	1, 22		55.5	.0001
Among measures	2, 44		38.7	.0001
Interaction	2, 44		6.21	.005

[26] Inspection of the appropriate scatter diagrams indicated that the regressions of each of the three rated variables upon total responses not only were linear for both real and nominal

After adjustment for differences in total number of responses, no significant differences remain between real and nominal groups on the three measures for either the Tourists or the Teachers Problem. After adjustment, however, the difference on the Thumbs Problem remains significant at the .03 level.[27] Computation of the adjusted means shows that this remaining difference still favors the nominal groups. Thus for the Thumbs, but not for the Tourists and Teachers Problems, there is a superiority of the nominal over the real groups on the three quality measures over and above that accounted for by a superiority in total number of responses.

DISCUSSION

The comparisons of primary interest in the several analyses are, of course, those between the performance of real groups and that of individuals or of nominal groups. The analyses, however, also involved other comparisons to which attention may best be given first.

Three different problems were employed in the experiment, the purpose being to give greater generality to the results; if only a single problem had been employed the question might well have been raised whether the results could be generalized beyond that problem. Significant differences were found among the three problems in mean total number of responses (Tables 1 and 2) and also in mean number of unique responses (Table 3). But these findings are of little interest because different problems would obviously be expected to produce different numbers of ideas and also different numbers of unique ideas.

On both the Tourists Problem (Table 5) and the Teachers Problem (Table 7), significant differences were obtained among the mean scores based upon differential weighting of the ideas produced with respect to feasibility, effectiveness, and generality, respectively. Similarly, significant differences were obtained for the Thumbs Problem (Table 6) among the mean scores on the three measures involving differential weighting with respect to probability, significance, and generality, respectively.[28] These findings, however, are also of little interest, since the differences between means on these measures depend directly upon

groups but had essentially the same slope in all six subgroups. Accordingly, since the other assumptions involved in such a procedure (Lindquist, *op. cit.*, p. 323) appeared to be satisfied, the analyses of variance reported in Tables 5, 6, and 7 were extended to include the corresponding analyses of covariance (*ibid.*, pp. 332–333).

[27] For more complete information concerning the results of the analyses of covariance, see Taylor, Berry, and Block, *op. cit.*, pp. 24–26.

[28] These analyses were carried out for a problem at a time rather than a measure at a time because the Thumbs Problem involved different measures from the other two.

the particular scales employed to rate the ideas. Changes in the rating scales would change the magnitude and even the direction of the differences between such means.

The first important finding was that on each of the three problems the mean total number of ideas produced by the twelve groups was considerably larger than the mean number produced by the forty-eight individuals, the difference being highly significant (Table 1). It is true that the interaction is significant, indicating that the difference between real group and individual performance does vary among the three problems. But on all three problems group performance is clearly superior to individual performance. Such group superiority may very well account for the widespread impression that group participation does facilitate production of ideas. The individual who compares his own performance working alone with that of a group in which he participates at another time may understandably conclude that group interaction stimulates creative thinking, whether or not this is in fact the case. Many of those participating in the groups in the present experiment made comments indicating that they believed such participation had been stimulating.

The comparison of group performance with individual performance does not, however, provide an adequate answer to the question: Does group participation when using brainstorming facilitate or inhibit creative thinking? To answer this question, the performance of the twelve real groups was compared with that of the twelve nominal groups on each of the three problems with respect to (a) mean total number of ideas produced, (b) mean number of unique ideas produced, and (c) the three measures which involved the weighting of the ideas with respect to quality. The results of these several analyses were both clear-cut and consistent.

The performance of the twelve real groups is markedly inferior to that of the twelve nominal groups both in terms of number of ideas produced (Table 2) and in terms of number of unique ideas produced (Table 3). Since in neither case was the interaction significant, these findings apply equally to all three problems. The mean scores of the real groups on the three weighted measures were also markedly inferior to those of the nominal groups for the Tourists (Table 5), Thumbs (Table 6), and Teachers Problem (Table 7). In the case of the Thumbs Problem, the fact that the interaction is not significant indicates that the same result was obtained with all three measures. In the case of both the Tourists and Teachers Problems, this interaction is significant. On both problems, however, although the magnitude of the difference varies, the real group mean scores on all three measures are quite inferior to those of nominal groups (Tables 5 and 7). In brief, the performance of the real groups is inferior to that of the nominal groups on all three

problems with respect to each and all of the measures of performance employed.

To the extent that the results of the present experiment can be generalized, it must be concluded that group participation when using brainstorming *inhibits* creative thinking. What accounts for such inhibition? Although data are not available to provide an adequate answer, two suggestions may be made. In brainstorming strong emphasis is placed upon avoiding criticism both of one's own ideas and of the ideas of others. Nevertheless, it appears probable that the individual working in a group feels less free of possible criticism by others even when such criticism is not expressed at the time than does the individual working alone. To the extent that this is true, group participation is inhibiting. A second reason is that group participation may reduce the number of different ideas produced. A given number of individuals working in a group appear more likely to pursue the same train of thought—to have the same set or the same approach to the problem—than do the same number of individuals working alone. The greater the variety of set, train of thought, or approach, the greater would be the expected number of different ideas produced. To the extent that group participation reduces such variety, it inhibits production of ideas.

Certain supplementary analyses were carried out to aid in the interpretation of the major comparisons. To determine whether any significant differences between nominal and real groups would remain in number of unique responses after allowance had been made for difference in total number of responses, analyses of covariance were carried out for each of the three problems. These analyses showed that after adjustment with total number of responses as the control variable, the difference in number of unique responses is no longer significant for either the Tourists or the Teachers Problem. This finding may be interpreted to indicate that on these two problems the superiority of nominal over real groups is largely a matter of difference in number of responses and not, in addition, of any difference in the uniqueness or originality of the responses produced. In contrast, the analysis of covariance for the Thumbs Problem showed that, after adjustment for differences in total number of responses, the difference in number of unique responses not only is significant but actually favors the real groups. In other words, the degree of uniqueness of whatever responses were produced was somewhat greater for real than for nominal groups, but only on this one problem. To avoid any possible confusion at this point, it may be worth stating again the more important finding reported above that with respect to *number* of unique responses the nominal groups were superior to the real groups on all three of the problems.

A similar analysis of covariance was carried out for each of the three problems to determine whether differences between the nominal and real groups on the three quality measures also resulted simply from the difference in total number of responses. The results of such analyses showed that, after adjustment for differences in total number of responses, no significant differences between nominal and real groups remained on the three measures involving weighting for feasibility, effectiveness, and generality, respectively, for either the Tourists or the Teachers Problem. In contrast, after such adjustment for differences in total number of responses, significant differences favoring the nominal groups remain for the Thumbs Problem on the measures weighted for probability, significance, and generality of ideas, respectively. Taken together, these findings may be interpreted to mean that the superiority of nominal over real groups on the three quality measures is largely a matter of difference in number of responses and only to a limited degree, if any, a matter of difference in the quality of the ideas produced. But it must be kept in mind that because the nominal groups produce more ideas they also produce more ideas which equal or exceed any given level of quality.

To what extent can the conclusion be generalized that group participation when using brainstorming inhibits creative thinking? Would different results be obtained if some other kind of problems were employed, if the subjects were highly trained in brainstorming, if more time were allowed for work on each problem, or if the size of group were increased? To answer these questions fully would require, of course, additional careful experimentation. That any or all such possible changes in conditions would be expected to alter essentially the conclusion reached is by no means clear.

Would the inferiority of real to nominal group performance disappear with some other kind of problem? Even more important, would real-group performance actually be superior to that of nominal groups? An affirmative answer to the first question appears doubtful and to the second even more improbable. On the basis of rather extensive pretesting, the three problems employed were selected from about twenty to be as appropriate as possible for use with brainstorming and also for use with Yale students. These problems appear to be generally similar to those which brainstorming is ordinarily accustomed to attack. Moreover, the question is not whether following the basic rules of brainstorming would be more effective with some other kind of problems; in such a case, the performance of nominal as well as real groups would be improved. Rather, the question is whether with some other kind of problem group participation when using brainstorming will facilitate, and not inhibit, performance. If such facilitation should be obtained in a carefully controlled experiment, a new question would arise as to the kinds of problems with which group participation is facilitating .and with which it is inhibiting. Finally, it should be pointed out that the three problems were rather heterogeneous in character, thus increasing the generality of the results. The Thumbs Problem is clearly of a different type from the other two; the Teachers Problem appears to depend more heavily upon previously acquired, directly relevant knowledge than does the Tourists Problem.

More training and experience in following the basic rules of brainstorming than that received by the present subjects might well be expected to facilitate production of ideas. But such training and experience would be expected to improve the performance of nominal as well as of real groups. Indeed, it appears probable that with more highly trained subjects essentially the same conclusion would be reached as in the present study.

The time limit of twelve minutes for each problem was chosen, on the basis of considerable pretesting, as one which would permit group members to express all ideas occurring to them within the work period and at the same time not result in excessive periods of silence for individual subjects.[29] In the actual experimental sessions, appreciable periods of science appeared between responses near the end of the twelve minutes. Doubling or tripling the time allowed would, of course, increase the number of ideas produced by real groups, but it would also increase the number produced by nominal groups. It is possible that allowing more time would reduce the degree of superiority of nominal over real groups. It appears improbable, however, that such superiority would be eliminated and even more improbable that with any reasonable increase in time real group production of ideas would actually become superior to that of nominal groups. It is worth noting that the number of ideas per problem produced by real groups within twelve minutes compares favorably with the number reported for groups working considerably longer on other problems.[30] The mean number per problem varied

---

[29] Question has been raised concerning the fact that the four individuals in a nominal group were each allotted twelve minutes per problem for a total of forty-eight minutes, whereas the real group was only allotted twelve minutes. This statement, of course, misses the point. What is relevant is the fact that the number of man-minutes devoted to a problem by the four members of a real group was forty-eight, precisely the same as for the four members of a nominal group.

[30] Osborn, *Applied Imagination.*

from 32.6 for the Teachers to 41.3 for the Thumbs Problem (Table 2). Some individual groups, of course, produced a considerably larger number of ideas on each of these problems.

Osborn suggests that the optimum size for a brainstorming group is between five and ten.[31] The choice of four as the group size in the present experiment was based upon the fact that only about ninety-six men with appropriate experience in small discussion groups were available, together with the fact that N in the statistical analysis of this type of experiment is not the number of individual subjects but the number of groups. Increasing the size of the real groups to five or larger would probably increase the number of ideas produced, but it is also probable that an equal, if indeed not greater, increase would occur in the number of ideas produced by nominal groups of equal size. Hence increasing the size of the group would not be expected to alter the conclusion reached here.

The burden of proof would appear to be upon those who believe that with some change or changes in conditions group participation when using brainstorming will be found not to inhibit creative thinking, but instead to facilitate it.

It may be appropriate to emphasize in closing that the present experiment includes no evaluation of the basic rules of brainstorming—only an examination of the effects of group participation when using brainstorming. Such an evaluation would require experiments designed to compare the creativity of individuals or groups following the four basic rules with creativity of individuals or groups following some other procedure.

POSTSCRIPT

The brainstorming study just reported produces the conviction that, instead of facilitating creativity, group participation inhibits it. Scientific conclusions are always tentative, however; experiments are continually being revived with some new variable introduced. Often such further work requires that the original conclusions be considerably modified. This may be illustrated with a later investigation which introduced two variables not previously included: group cohesiveness and ego-involving problems.[a] In order that cohesive two-man groups might be created, individuals were permitted to choose a partner preferred for brainstorming activities. The problems used in the previous study were considered non-ego-involving; these were compared with a problem closely related to the individual's occupational activities. The result was that, on the ego-involving problem, cohesive groups were superior to nominal groups in the number of unique solutions produced. There were no differences among groups on the non-ego-involving problems.

CONFORMITY TO THE NORM OF PREJUDICE *

A treatment of group behavior would be incomplete without some attention to relations between groups. The most intensively researched facet of such relations is attitudes toward minority groups. The predominance of this *social problem* perspective is somewhat unfortunate, for, as a result, the field of intergroup relations lacks adequate theoretical development and a broad empirical base. Some progress may be made, however, by using concepts developed in other phases of social psychology and applying them to intergroup relations.

From our previous discussion of conformity to norms, we would expect that, once prejudice and discrimination against an outgroup are well established, the accompanying cognitions and feelings concerning the outgroup acquire a normative quality. Members of the ingroup share these attitudes and expect each other to conform to them. The selection below demonstrates in a convincing fashion that social norms are an important factor in maintaining prejudices. It has the merit of testing the hypothesis in two quite different societies where prejudice toward the Negro is strong: the United States and South Africa.

In applying the survey method to this problem, the investigator has wisely compared various subgroups to specify more clearly relations between variables. For example, he asks whether individuals identified as conforming more strongly to social norms in general are also more prejudiced. A positive answer strengthens the argument that prejudice represents at least in part conformity to a norm of prejudice. He attempts to rule out the possibility that conformers are more prejudiced because they have more authoritarian personalities. He compares conformers with nonconformers on a measure of authoritarian personality traits to eliminate this alternative explanation.

---

[31] *Ibid.*, p. 87.

* The selection following the editorial introduction is reprinted from "Personality and sociocultural factors in intergroup attitudes: A cross-national comparison," *Journal of Conflict Resolution*, 1958, **2**, 29–42, by permission of the author and publisher.

[a] D. Cohen, J. W. Whitmyre, & W. H. Funk. Effect of group cohesiveness and training upon creative thinking. *J. Applied Psychol.*, 1960, **44**, 319–322.

37.

Personality and Sociocultural Factors in Intergroup Attitudes: A Cross-national Comparison[1]

THOMAS F. PETTIGREW
HARVARD UNIVERSITY

I. INTRODUCTION

Along the continuum of prejudice theories, two extreme positions have been popular. One strongly emphasizes the personality of the bigot and neglects his cultural milieu; the other views intolerance as a mere reflection of cultural norms and neglects individual differences. Recent evidence lends little support to either pole. As further data are gathered with more refined research tools, it becomes increasingly apparent that the psychological and sociological correlates of prejudice are elaborately intertwined and that both are essential to provide an adequate theoretical framework for this complex phenomenon.

Carrying this viewpoint further, Smith, Bruner, and White (38, pp. 41–44) have delineated three functions that attitudes may serve for an individual. First, there is the *object-appraisal* function; attitudes aid in the process of understanding "reality" as it is defined by the culture. Second, attitudes can play a *social-adjustment* role by contributing to the individual's identification with, or differentiation from, various reference groups. It should be noted that both these functions—object appraisal and social adjustment—are important reflections on the personality level of sociocultural conditions. But the most studied function of attitudes, *externalization,* is somewhat unique. "Externalization occurs when an individual, often responding unconsciously, senses an analogy between a perceived environmental event and some unresolved inner problem . . . [and] adopts an attitude . . . which is a transformed version of his way of dealing with his inner difficulty." Such a process may serve to reduce anxiety. The principal psychological theories of prejudice—frustration-aggression (9), psychoanalytic (20), and authoritarianism (1)—all deal chiefly with this third process.

External expression of inner conflict is relatively more independent of sociocultural factors than are the other functions of attitudes. Indeed, a heuristic distinction between externalized personality variables and sociological variables contributes to our understanding of much that is known about intergroup conflict.

Minard's observations of race relations in the coal-mining county of McDowell, West Virginia, serve as a direct illustration of the point (26). The general pattern in this region consists of white and Negro miners being integrated below the ground and almost completely segregated above the ground. Minard estimates that roughly 60 per cent of the white miners manage to reverse roles almost completely; they can accept Negroes as equals in the mines but cannot accept them as equals elsewhere. Furthermore, he feels that, at one extreme, about 20 per cent accept the black miners as equals in both situations, while, at the other extreme, about 20 per cent never accept them in either situation. In our terms, the behavior of the majority of these whites studied by Minard can be predicted largely by sociocultural expectations, and the behavior of the consistent minorities can be accounted for largely by externalized personality variables.

The research literature abounds with further examples in which a separation of psychological and sociological factors is helpful. The many papers on interracial contact in housing (7, 40), at work (11), and in the army (39) show the marked effects that can brought about by certain changes in the social situation between races. But personality factors are still operating. Usually these studies report that some individuals hold favorable attitudes toward minorities even before the contact and that other individuals still hold unfavorable attitudes after the contact. Many of these studies also find that the changes brought about by the contact are quite specific and delimited in nature. That is, the intergroup changes occur only under a narrow range of conditions, since the basic personality orientations of the participants have not changed fundamentally. Thus white department-store employees become more accepting of Negroes in the work situation after equal status contact but not in other situations (11). And the attitudes of white army personnel toward the Negro as a fighting man improve after equal status contact in combat, but their attitudes toward the Negro as a social companion do not change (39).

Desegregation findings furnish further illustrations where the distinction is useful. Social demands for racial desegregation and the irresistible trend of the times are counteracting personality predispositions in many communities. Thus a 1954 public opinion survey in Oklahoma found an overwhelming majority of the residents sternly against desegregation, and yet today mixed schools have become accepted throughout most of the state without incident (17). And in Wilmington, Delaware, two years after successful school integration without apparent public opposition, a

[1] This article is a revision of a paper delivered in September, 1957, at the New York meetings of the American Psychological Association. The author wishes to express his deep appreciation to Professor Gordon W. Allport for his advice and encouragement and to Dr. Herbert Kelman, this issue's special editor, for his theoretical and editorial suggestions.

poll indicated that only a minority approved of the school desegregation decision of the Supreme Court (17). Indeed, this discrepancy between opinions and demands is a general phenomenon throughout the borders states. Hyman and Sheatsley (16) report that only 31 per cent of the white population in those border areas that have already integrated their school systems indorse desegregation.

This conflict between authority-supported cultural changes and personal preferences is underscored by another finding that public opinion polls have uncovered in the South. Several investigators have independently shown that respondents themselves make a distinction between what they individually favor and what they expect to happen in their community. Thus the huge majority of southern whites favor racial segregation, but most of them also feel that desegregation is inevitable (16, 28).

Finally, the work originally done by La Piere (19) in 1934 and more recently replicated in different contexts by Saenger and Gilbert (34) and by Kutner, Wilkins, and Yarrow (18) furnishes further justification for a theoretical separation of social and externalization aspects of intergroup conflict. These investigations illustrate the results of conflicting personality predispositions and actual social situations with minority-group members; frequently the face-to-face conditions override previous practices.

Such work has led several authorities in the field to make the sociocultural and personality differentiation. Psychologist G. W. Allport discusses the two classes of factors separately in his definitive volume, *The Nature of Prejudice* (2), and sociologist Arnold Rose makes a similar distinction in a recent theoretical article on intergroup relations (33).

The present paper is a summary report on research conducted chiefly to gain cross-national perspective on these two sets of prejudice factors. The studies were made in two parts of the world where racial conflict today is highlighted and cultural sanctions of intolerance are intense and explicit: the Union of South Africa and the southern United States. First, a more detailed report of previously unpublished data will be presented on the South African study. Following this, a comparison will be made with the southern United States based on a summary of data presented in detail elsewhere (29).

II. RACIAL PREJUDICE IN THE UNION OF SOUTH AFRICA[2]

The limited evidence available supports the general belief that white South Africans are unusually

prejudiced against Africans (14, 21, 24). This raises the intriguing question as to whether this increased hostility represents (*a*) more externalizing personality potential for prejudice among South Africans, (*b*) the effects of different cultural norms and pressures, or (*c*) both of these.

To provide a tentative answer, a questionnaire study was undertaken of the racial attitudes of students at the English-speaking University of Natal in the Union of South Africa. A non-random sample of 627 undergraduates—approximately one-third of the entire university—completed an anonymous instrument containing three scales and a number of background items.[3] The three scales are a thirteen-item measure of authoritarianism (*F* scale) whose statements are shown in Table 2, a sixteen-item measure of social conformity (*C* scale) whose statements are shown in Table 3, and an eighteen-item measure of anti-African attitudes (*A* scale) whose statements are shown in Table 8.[4] Background in-

TABLE 1 *Correlations between Anti-African Scale (A) and Authoritarianism (F) and Conformity (C) Scales**

VARIABLES	ETHNIC GROUP†	
	Afrikaners	English
N	50	513
A and *F*	+0.56	+0.46
A and *C*	+0.42	+0.46

* All four of these product-moment correlations are significantly different from zero at better than the 1 per cent level of confidence. The scale scores that were correlated vary between 0 and 10. They were calculated on the basis of +4 for agree strongly, +3 for agree, +2 for omitted response, +1 for disagree and 0 for disagree strongly for each item, and then the total scores were collapsed into the 0–10 categories for machine analysis.   † Separate analyses by ethnic group are made necessary by the sharply divergent *A*-scale means of the two groups (see Table 7).

particularly Professor Arnold Lloyd (now of the University of Witwatersrand), Dr. Hamisch Dickie-Clark, Miss Len Kuyper, Dr. Jack Mann, and Professor Max Marwick (now of the University of Witwatersrand).

[3] Comparisons between this one-third sample and the total student body of the University of Natal reveal that, in terms of sex, age, and field of concentration, the sample's distributions are quite similar to the student body at large.

[4] All thirteen of the F-scale items are from the original California study on authoritarianism (1, pp. 255–57); the C scale is a new scale composed of both new items and adaptations from the conformity measures of Hoffman (15) and MacCrone (22); and fourteen of the A-scale items are new, while four are adaptations from the E scale (1, items 8, 31, and 34 on p. 105 and item 29 on p. 117).

[2] This investigation was conducted during 1956 when the author was an honorary research associate of the University of Natal's Institute for Social Research. The study would not have been possible without the aid of the institute's co-operative staff,

formation includes place of birth, political party preference, father's occupation, and ethnic-group membership.

Taken as a group, these students evidence considerable hostility toward Africans, accepting in large degree the white-supremacy ideology so adamantly propounded by the present government of their country. Thus 72 per cent of the sample agree that "there is something inherently primitive and uncivilized in the native, as shown in his music and extreme aggressiveness"; and 69 per cent agree that "manual labor seems to fit the native mentality better than more skilled and responsible work." And yet their F-scale responses are roughly comparable to those of American student populations.[5] Thus these South

[5] Comparisons across diverse groups with varying forms of the F scale are difficult and tenuous at best. American college sam-

Africans are sharply prejudiced against blacks without possessing any greater externalizing personality potential for intolerance than peoples in more tolerant areas.

In addition, authoritarianism correlates with anti-African attitudes at a level comparable to relationships between authoritarianism and prejudice in other parts of the world. Table 1 shows that the A and F scales correlate $+0.56$ among the Afrikaans-speaking members of the sample and $+0.46$ among the English-speaking members. Similar scales typically correlate in the fifties in

ples generally average slightly below the neutral point on F-scale statements, while the present South African sample averages slightly above the neutral point. This small difference can probably be accounted for by (*a*) the use of a disproportionate number of high-agreement items in the thirteen-item F scale employed with the South African sample and (*b*) the inclusion in the South African group of fields of concentration not usually included in tested American college groups (e.g., agriculture) whose members tend to score high on the F scale (due probably to social class factors).

TABLE 2 *Anti-African Prejudice and F-Scale Items*

F-SCALE ITEM	PERCENTAGE AGREEMENT*		$2\times2\ \chi^2$	p
	Less Prejudiced Half	More Prejudiced Half		
a. Nowadays when so many different kinds of people move around and mix together so much, a person has to be especially careful not to catch an infection or disease from them	13.6	33.2	33.5	0.001
b. There is hardly anything lower than a person who does not feel a great love and respect for his parents	52.6	70.5	21.2	.001
c. People can be put into two distinct classes: the weak and the strong	23.5	37.8	15.1	.001
d. Most of our social problems would be solved if we could somehow get rid of the immoral, crooked, and feebleminded people	45.4	60.6	14.8	.001
e. The most important thing a child should learn is obedience to his parents	79.8	90.2	13.2	.001
f. Every person should have faith in some supernatural power whose decisions he obeys without question	46.7	60.9	13.0	.001
g. When a person has a problem or worry, it is best for him not to think about it, but to keep busy with more cheerful things	39.4	53.2	11.8	.001
h. Nowadays more and more people are prying into matters that should remain private and personal	63.5	74.5	8.6	.01
i. If people would talk less and work more, everybody would be better off	67.8	78.2	8.3	.01
j. An insult to our honor should always be punished	31.8	40.3	4.7	.05
k. No sane, normal person would ever think of hurting a close friend or relative	67.9	76.6	4.3	.05
l. Science has its place, but there are many important things that can never possibly be understood by the human mind	80.7	85.8	2.9	0.10
m. Some day it will probably be shown that astrology can explain a lot of things	44.4	48.0	0.9	n.s.

* The respondent was given four categories: agree strongly, agree, disagree, and disagree strongly. Percentage agreement is calculated by combining the first two of these replies. This footnote applies to Table 3 also.

American college samples.[6] The *C*-scale measure of social conformity—employed for the first time in this investigation—relates to the *A*-scale scores significantly, too, in both ethnic groups (Table 1).

More detailed analyses of the *F* and *C* scales' relationships with anti-African attitudes are provided in Tables 2 and 3. Each of the thirteen authoritarian statements separates the less and more prejudiced halves of the sample in the predicted direction, seven of the differences proving to be significant at better than the 0.001 level of confidence. The sixteen *C*-scale items predict almost as well; the more anti-African students in every case agree more often than the less prejudiced. Perhaps the conforming attitude of the

[6] Again, comparisons are difficult. Correlations between long-form F scales and ethnocentrism scales (measuring prejudice against a variety of out-groups) have sometimes reached the sixties and even occasionally the seventies in American college samples (1, 2, 5). But correlations of the magnitude found in this study have been consistently reported when—as in this study—a short-form F scale and a prejudice scale against a single out-group are related.

bigots is capsuled in the first item of Table 3. While only a third of the tolerant members of the group agree with the statement, over half the prejudiced students feel that "it's better to go along with the crowd than to be a martyr."

These personality relationships suggest (*a*) that personality factors are as important correlates of prejudice in this sample as they are in other, non-South African samples; (*b*) that social conformity (as measured by the *C* scale) is a particularly crucial personality variable in this sample's attitudes toward Africans; and (*c*) that personality components do not in themselves account for the heightened intolerance of this sample.

We must turn to sociocultural factors to explain the extreme prejudice of these respondents, and the unusual importance of these variables is made clear by the data. For instance, the 560 students who were born on the African continent are significantly more intolerant of Africans than the remaining 65, but they are *not* more authori-

TABLE 3   *Anti-African Prejudice and C-Scale Items*

C-SCALE ITEM	PERCENTAGE AGREEMENT*			
	Less Prejudiced Half	More Prejudiced Half	2×2 χ^2	*p*
a. It's better to go along with the crowd than to be a martyr	34.8	53.2	21.8	0.001
b. When almost everyone agrees on something, there is little reason to oppose it	16.6	31.1	18.5	.001
c. Adherence to convention produces the best kind of citizen	31.8	46.8	14.9	.001
d. To be successful, a group's members must act and think alike	45.7	60.0	12.5	.001
e. It is important for friends to have similar opinions	28.5	42.2	12.1	.001
f. It is more important to be loyal and conform to our own group than to try to co-operate with other groups	25.6	38.5	11.7	.001
g. We should alter our needs to fit society's demands rather than change society to fit our needs	42.4	55.1	11.4	.001
h. A good group member should agree with the other members	21.2	33.2	11.1	.001
i. It is best not to express your views when in the company of friends who disagree with you	23.8	32.9	6.1	.02
j. Before a person does something, he should try to consider how his friends will react to it	54.6	63.1	4.4	.05
k. To become a success these days, a person has to act in the way that others expect him to act	33.2	41.5	4.2	.05
l. A group cannot expect to maintain its identity unless its members all think and feel in very much the same way	59.3	66.8	3.9	.05
m. It is one's duty to conform to the passing demands of the world and to suppress those personal desires that do not fit these demands	43.7	51.1	3.4	.10
n. A person should adapt his ideas and his behavior to the group that happens to be with him at the time	45.7	52.6	3.1	.10
o. It is extremely uncomfortable to go accidentally to a formal party in street clothes	78.5	83.1	2.0	.20
p. To get along well in a group, you have to follow the lead of others	27.2	31.1	1.1	0.30

tarian. Table 4 shows that those not born in Africa are much less likely to fall into the most prejudiced third of the distribution than other sample members. And yet the two groups do not differ significantly in their F-scale scores. More thoroughly influenced throughout their lives by the culture's definition of the white man's situation in Africa, students born on the Dark Continent are more anti-African without the usual personality concomitants of ethnocentrism.

Another such relationship involves students who support the Nationalist party—the pro-*Apartheid* political faction that is presently in power. Table 5 indicates that these respondents score significantly higher on the A scale than their fellow undergraduates, but these two groups do not differ on the F scale. Again a prejudice difference is not accompanied by a personality potential difference. These relationships with political party preference and prejudice hold for

TABLE 4 *Place of Birth and Anti-African Prejudice**

ANTI-AFRICAN ATTITUDES†		PLACE OF BIRTH	
	N	On African Continent 560	Not on African Continent 65
Least prejudiced	176	28%	29%
Medium prejudiced	246	38%	54%
Most prejudiced	203	34%	17%

* 2×3 chi-square $= 9.33$; $p < 0.01$. † The least prejudiced are the students who rated A-scale scores from 0 through 4 by disagreeing with a heavy majority of the items; the medium prejudiced received scores of either 5 or 6 by agreeing with roughly half of the 18 A-scale items; and the most prejudiced obtained scores of 7 through 10 by agreeing with a majority of the statements.

TABLE 5 *Political Party Preference and Anti-African Prejudice**.

ANTI-AFRICAN ATTITUDES		POLITICAL PARTY PREFERENCE†	
	N	Nationalist Party 72	Other Parties 483
Least prejudiced	157	8%	35%
Medium prejudiced	210	26%	36%
Most prejudiced	188	66%	29%

* 2×3 chi-square $= 38.60$; $p < 0.001$. † Seventy-two of the 627 students did not indicate any political preference.

TABLE 6 *Father's Occupational Status and Anti-African Prejudice**

ANTI-AFRICAN ATTITUDES		FATHER'S OCCUPATIONAL STATUS†	
	N	Manual 146	Non-manual 417
Less prejudiced half	280	34%	55%
More prejudiced half	283	66%	45%

* 2×2 chi-square $= 18.90$; $p < 0.001$. † Sixty-four of the 627 students did not indicate their fathers' occupations.

each of the major ethnic groups—Afrikaners and English—considered separately.

Two other comparisons yield statistically significant differences in both authoritarianism and anti-African prejudice. Table 6 indicates that those sample members whose fathers are manually employed are significantly more intolerant of the African than those whose fathers are non-manually employed. The two groups differ in the same manner in their F-scale scores. But when authoritarianism is controlled for, the groups still differ significantly in their attitudes toward blacks.[7] In other words, the children of manual fathers are more prejudiced and more authoritarian than other students, and they remain more prejudiced even after the difference in authoritarianism is partialed out of the relationship. These upwardly mobile students must be carefully in step with the mores to establish firmly their rise in the social structure, and the mores of South Africa lead to intolerance.

Table 7 shows the sharp difference between the Afrikaner and English subjects in the sample. Afrikaners are both more anti-African and more authoritarian, and, when the F-scale differences are corrected for, they remain significantly more hostile to the African.[8] These 50 students are directly subject to the national ethos and have no

[7] Authoritarianism can be controlled out in two ways. First, separate chi-square analyses of father's employment and anti-African attitudes were made for low and high F-scale halves. Second, the A- and F-scale scores were employed in an analysis of covariance that partialed out F scores. Both analyses indicate that father's employment is a significant correlate of anti-African attitudes even after authoritarianism is controlled out of the relationship.

[8] Authoritarianism was controlled out by both of the analyses described in the previous footnote. With their F-scale differences corrected for, Afrikaners in the sample are still significantly more hostile to the African than the English students. The cultural determination of this ethnic-group difference is made apparent when we survey the attitudes of the English students toward the Indians of South Africa. In sharp contrast to their African attitudes, the English members of the sample are considerably more anti-Indian—one-fifth of them "wish someone would kill all of them."

TABLE 7 *Ethnic Group and Anti-African Prejudice**

ANTI-AFRICAN ATTITUDES		ETHNIC GROUP†	
	N	Afrikaners 50	English 513
Less prejudiced half	264	14%	50%
More prejudiced half	299	86%	50%

* 2×2 chi-square = 23.7; $p < 0.001$. † Ethnic group is determined by both the student's own ethnic identification and the principal language spoken in his home. Sixty-four of the students identified with other groups (e.g., Jewish, French, German) and are not included in this analysis.

conflicting national reference, as many English-speaking South Africans have in Great Britain. Like the upwardly mobile, they are in roles that demand unusual conformity.

Table 8 clarifies further the ethnic differences in attitudes toward the Africans. Sixteen of the A scale's eighteen statements significantly separate the Afrikaners from the English, the former scoring higher in all cases. And, moreover, there is a definite trend in these differences. The five items which discriminate poorest between the ethnic groups (items n through r) are all stereotyped-belief statements; they refer to the standard traits frequently associated with Africans—lazy, primitive, happy-go-lucky, and bad-smelling. Conversely, five of the six best discriminators (items b through f) are all exclusion-discrimination statements; they deny equal rights to Africans in employment, housing, and voting. Afrikaans-speaking and English-speaking students, then, do not differ sharply in the degree to which they harbor the

TABLE 8 *Ethnic-group Differences on A-Scale Items*

A-SCALE ITEMS	PERCENTAGE AGREEMENT*		$2 \times 2 \; \chi^2$	p
	Afrikaners	English		
a. Because of their primitive background, natives will always have a greater tendency toward crimes of violence than Europeans	70.0	34.9	33.6	0.001
b. Native musicians are sometimes as good as Europeans at swing music and jazz, but it is a mistake to have mixed native-European bands	86.0	54.2	18.8	.001
c. Most of the natives would become officious, overbearing, and disagreeable if not kept in their place	80.0	48.3	18.2	.001
d. Laws which would force equal employment opportunities for both the natives and Europeans would not be fair to European employers	74.0	44.2	16.2	.001
e. The natives have their rights, but it is best to keep them in their own districts and schools and to prevent too much contact with Europeans	86.0	63.7	9.9	.01
f. The natives do not deserve the right to vote	64.0	41.3	9.5	.01
g. The natives will never have the intelligence and organizing ability to run a modern industrial society	42.0	23.2	8.7	.01
h. As the native will never properly absorb our civilization, the only solution is to let him develop along his own lines	68.0	46.3	8.6	.01
i. Manual labor seems to fit the native mentality better than more skilled and responsible work	88.0	68.9	8.0	.01
j. Seldom, if ever, is a native superior to most Europeans intellectually	72.0	52.2	7.1	.01
k. The natives tend to be overly emotional	66.0	46.5	7.1	.01
l. Because of his immaturity, the South African native is likely to be led into all sorts of mischief and should therefore be strictly controlled in his own best interests	92.0	75.6	6.9	.01
m. The granting of wide educational opportunities to natives is a dangerous thing	36.0	19.9	6.9	.01
n. Most natives are lazy and lack ambition	60.0	44.1	4.6	.05
o. There is something inherently primitive and uncivilized in the native, as shown in his music and extreme aggressiveness	86.0	72.1	4.4	.05
p. Due to the differences in innate endowment, the Bantu race will always be inferior to the white race	54.0	39.6	4.0	.05
q. Most of the natives are happy-go-lucky and irresponsible	70.0	60.0	1.9	0.20
r. In spite of what some claim, the natives do have a different and more pronounced body odor than Europeans	84.0	81.5	0.2	n.s.

* Percentage agreement calculated as in Table 2.

traditional stereotype of the African, but they do possess markedly divergent views on discrimination against the African. A key to these differences may be provided in the lone exception to this trend, item *a*. Seven out of every ten Afrikaners, as compared with only a third of the English, believe that the "natives will always have a greater tendency toward crimes of violence than Europeans." Strong projection may be operating for those agreeing with this statement, but, in any event, it suggests that physical fear of the black man is especially prevalent among our Afrikaans-speaking respondents and that this may be the fundamental motivation for their emphasis on excluding and discriminating against the African.

All these findings point to the crucial role of the cultural milieu in shaping the attitudes of the white South African toward the blacks in his midst. While externalizing personality factors do not account for the students' unusually prejudiced attitudes concerning Africans, variables which reflect the dominant norms of the white society prove to be important. Students who are especially responsive to these norms—those who were born in Africa, those who identify with the Nationalist party, those who are upwardly mobile, and those who have been molded by the conservative traditions of the Afrikaans-speaking people—tend to be intolerant of Africans to some degree, regardless of their basic personality structure.

III. RACIAL PREJUDICE IN THE SOUTHERN UNITED STATES

Similar considerations led to an earlier comparative study of anti-Negro prejudice in the southern and northern United States. While considerable evidence indicates that white southerners are typically more intolerant of the Negro than white northerners (16, 27, 30, 35, 36, 39), little work has been focused on the factors underlying this difference. But, like the South African data, the scant data available suggest that sociocultural and not externalization factors may be the crucial determinants of the contrasting regional attitudes toward the Negro.

Thus, if the South did have more externalizing personality potential for prejudice than other American areas, it should also be more anti-Semitic.[9] But Roper (31, 32) has twice found in his national polls that the South is one of the most tolerant regions toward Jews, and Prothro (30) has noted that 40 per cent of his adult white

[9] This is true because the prejudiced personality is predisposed to disliking all socially recognized out-groups—Negroes, Jews, Catholics, etc.—and not just one. Being functionally necessary, prejudice generalizes to out-groups of all varieties (1, 2, 13).

Louisiana sample is at the same time favorable in its attitudes toward Jews and highly anti-Negro. Furthermore, there is no evidence that the stern family pattern associated with "prejudiced personalities" (1, 12) is more prevalent in the South than in the North (6, 8). And, finally, the few white southern populations that have been given the *F* scale have obtained means that fall easily within the range of means reported for non-southern populations (1, 25, 37).

Rose categorically concludes: "There is no evidence that 'authoritarian personality' or frustration-aggression or scapegoating, or any known source of 'prejudice' in the psychological sense, is any more prevalent in the South than in the North" (33). And Prothro adds: "Situational, historical and cultural factors appear to be of considerable, perhaps major, import in addition to personality dynamics" in determining anti-Negro attitudes in the South (30).

In testing these ideas in the two regions, different methods were employed than those used in South Africa. Public opinion polling techniques were utilized with 366 randomly selected white adults in eight roughly matched communities in the North and South. The four small southern towns, located in Georgia and North Carolina, were chosen to have Negro population percentages ranging from 10 to 45 per cent, while the small northern towns, all located in New England, have less than 1 per cent Negroes each.

The interview schedule contained a ten-item measure of authoritarianism (*F* scale), an eight-item measure of anti-Semitism (*A-S* scale), and a twelve-item measure of anti-Negro prejudice (*N* scale), together with numerous background questions.[10] The poll purported to be concerned with the effects of the mass media upon public opinion, and it seems largely due to this guise that the blatantly phrased prejudice statements caused no interview breakoffs.

Of greatest immediate interest is the striking similarity in these results with those of the South African investigation. First, the southern sample is considerably more anti-Negro than the northern sample but is *not* more authoritarian. Similar to

[10] There is considerable overlap in items used in the two investigations. Again, all ten of the *F* items are taken from the work of Adorno *et al.* (1); seven were used in South Africa (Table 2, items *a, b, c, f, h, i,* and *k*); and the others are items 1, 13, and 21 of p. 255 in *The Authoritarian Personality* (1). The *A-S* items are all from the California investigations, too (1, items 3, 4, 13, 15, 22, and 24 on pp. 68–69 and items 4 and 15 on p. 70). Save for the word substitutions of "white" for "European" and "Negro" for "native," all twelve *N*-scale items were used in the South African *A* scale (Table 8, items *b, c, d, e, f, j, k, m, n, o, q,* and *r*). That virtually the same prejudice and authoritarian statements can be successfully used in the Union of South Africa and in the northern and southern United States suggests that racial prejudice and its personality concomitants take extremely similar forms in many parts of the Western world.

the Afrikaner-English differences (Table 8), the southerners respond in the more prejudiced direction on each of the *N*-scale statements but are most unique in their extreme attitudes concerning excluding and discriminating against the Negro. That is, southerners and northerners in the samples both share in large degree the lazy, primitive, happy-go-lucky, and bad-smelling stereotype of the Negro, but southerners far more than northerners wish to deny equal rights to the Negro in employment, housing, and voting. And yet there is no difference in the externalization potential for intolerance; the *F*-scale means of the two samples are almost identical.

Further similarities to the South African data support the contention that personality dynamics, such as authoritarianism, are not responsible for the sharp North-South divergence in attitudes toward the Negro. When age and education are partialed out,[11] the *N* and *F* scales correlate to a comparable degree in the two populations. Moreover, with age and education partialed out again, the *N* and *A-S* scales relate at equivalent levels in the two regional samples. In other words, the externalizing prejudiced personality as tapped by the *F* and *A-S* scales does not account for any more of the anti-Negro variance in the southern sample than it does in the northern sample. This finding, combined with the previously mentioned fact that the two groups do not differ in their *F*-scale responses, indicates that externalization factors do not explain the heightened bigotry of the southerners. As with the South African results, we must turn to social variables in an effort to account for the regional discrepancy in attitudes toward the Negro.

All six of the sociocultural dimensions tested yield meaningful relationships with Negro prejudice in the southern sample: sex, church attendance, social mobility, political party identification, armed service, and education. These variables reflect southern culture in a manner similar to the social variables tested in the South African study. And as in South Africa, those southerners, who by their roles in the social structure can be anticipated to be conforming to the dictates of the culture, prove to be more prejudiced against Negroes than their counterparts. For example, females, the "carriers of culture," are significantly more anti-Negro than men in the southern sample but *not* in the northern sample.

Two other groups of southerners who manifest conforming behavior in other areas are also more intolerant of Negroes.[12] Respondents who have

been to church within the week are significantly more anti-Negro than those who have not been within the month, and there is a tendency (though not statistically significant) for the upwardly mobile to be more anti-Negro than others in the non-manual occupational class. The latter result recalls the finding in the South African study that students whose fathers are manual workers tend to be more anti-African (Table 6). In the northern sample, no such trends appear. Protestant churchgoers in the North tend to be more tolerant of the Negro than Protestant non-attenders, and no relationship between upward mobility and attitudes toward Negroes is discernible. Conformity to northern norms—unlike conformity to southern or South African norms—is not associated with hostility for the black man.

In contrast to the conformers, southerners who evidence deviance from the mores in some area of social life tend to be *less* anti-Negro. Non-attenders of church furnish one example. Another example are respondents who explicitly identify themselves as political independents, which also represents a degree of deviance: they tend to be considerably more tolerant of the Negro than are southerners who consider themselves either Democrats or Republicans.[13] Again, no such discrepancy occurs in the northern population.

Downward mobility has been noted by other investigators to be positively related to intolerance in the North (3, 10), and this finding is replicated in the present northern data. But in the southern data a striking reversal occurs. The downwardly mobile in the South are much less anti-Negro than other manually employed respondents, though the two groups do not differ in authoritarianism. Perhaps in a culture that emphasizes status and family background, that makes a sharp distinction between "poor whites" and "respectable whites," and that cherishes its aristocratic traditions (4, 6, 8), the downwardly mobile southerner learns to reject much of his culture. And rejecting the culture's stress on tradition and status makes it easier to reject also the culture's dicta concerning the Negro.

Two groups of southerners—armed service veterans and the highly educated—are potential deviants from southern culture simply because their special experience and study have brought them into contact with other ways of life. And, as we

---

[11] This was not necessary in the South African data because the college sample is relatively homogeneous in terms of age and education. In heterogeneous, randomly drawn adult samples, however, age and education must be controlled, since both authoritarianism and prejudice are positively related to age and negatively related to education (2, 5, 16, 23).

[12] The church attendance, social mobility, political party identification, and armed service findings reported here were all

established with matched-pair analyses. This design made it possible to control the age, education, and sex variables out of these relationships. The detailed results are published elsewhere (29).

[13] It might be thought that Republican party membership in the South constitutes deviance, too. Actually, the "solid South" is not that politically solid; three of the four southern communities polled have favored some Republican candidates in recent elections.

might expect, we find that both veterans and college-educated southerners are considerably more tolerant of the Negro than non-veterans and the poorly educated. Veterans in both regions prove to be more authoritarian than non-veterans,[14] and, consistent with this, northern veterans are less tolerant of Negroes than northerners who had not served. Education is negatively related to *N*-scales scores in the northern sample, too, but significantly less than in the southern sample. Exposure to non-southern culture leads to deviance from the strict southern norms concerning the Negro; little wonder that southerners who have been out of the region for any considerable length of time are generally viewed as suspect by their neighbors upon return.

These consistent relationships with social factors in the southern data have been interpreted in terms of conformity and deviance from the narrowly prescribed mores of small-town southern life. Evidence for such an analysis comes from a final intra-southern difference. Southern communities with high Negro population ratios (38 and 45 per cent) have significantly higher *N*-scale means than the other communities sampled in the South with low Negro ratios (10 and 18 per cent), though they are *not* different in authoritarianism or anti-Semitism. In southern areas with the most intensely anti-Negro norms, prejudice against the black southerner is greater, even though there is not a greater amount of externalizing personality potential for prejudice.

Though limited by the restricted samples employed, this evidence indicates that sociocultural factors—as in the South African sample—are indeed the key to the regional difference in attitudes toward the Negro. In spite of the marked contrast in samples and method between the two investigations, both the South African and the southern results underline the unique importance of social variables in prejudice that is sanctioned by the cultural norms.

IV. SUMMARY AND CONCLUSIONS

Finely interwoven personality and sociocultural variables together form the foundation upon which a broad and satisfactory theory of racial prejudice must be built. Neither set of factors can be neglected, but a heuristic separation between the relatively culture-free externalization factors and social factors aids analysis. The present paper uses this distinction to interpret prejudice data from two parts of the world with tense racial conflict—the Union of South Africa and the southern United States.

Externalization factors such as authoritarianism are associated with prejudice in both the South African and the southern samples at levels roughly comparable with other areas. Data from the South African students hint, however, that susceptibility to conform may be an unusually important psychological component of prejudice in regions where the cultural norms positively sanction intolerance. In addition, there is no indication in either of these samples that there is any more externalizing personality potential for prejudice in these areas than in more tolerant parts of the globe.

The extensive racial prejudice of the South African and southern groups seems directly linked with the antiblack dictates of the two cultures. Sociocultural factors which reflect the mores consistently relate to prejudice—place of birth, political party preference, upward mobility, and ethnic-group membership in the South African data and sex, church attendance, social mobility, political party identification, armed service, and education in the southern data. The pattern is clear: conformity to South African or southern mores is associated with racial intolerance, while deviance from these mores is associated with racial tolerance.

Taken together with other published work, these limited results suggest a broad, cross-national hypothesis:

In areas with historically imbedded traditions of racial intolerance, externalizing personality factors underlying prejudice remain important, but sociocultural factors are unusually crucial and account for the heightened racial hostility.

Should future, more extensive, research support such a hypothesis, its implications for prejudice theory would be considerable. Regions or peoples with heightened prejudice against a particular outgroup would not necessarily be thought of as harboring more authoritarianism; the special conflict may reflect the operation of particular historical, cultural, and social factors. Such a prospect may be encouraging to many action programs—efforts which typically are more successful at changing a person's relation to his culture than they are at changing basic personality structure. Desegregation is a case in point. The success of the movement in the South does not depend—this hypothesis would contend—on changing the deeply ingrained orientations of prejudice-prone personalities; rather, it rests on the effectiveness with which racial integration now going on in the South can restructure the mores to which so many culturally intolerant southerners conform.

A second implication of the hypothesis is that personality factors such as authoritarianism and susceptibility to conform cannot be overlooked in understanding bigotry even in parts of the world like the Union of South Africa and the southern United States. Most psychological approaches to prejudice, it has been noted, are concerned chiefly with the externalization function of attitudes. Perhaps, as the object-appraisal and social-adjustment functions of attitudes are studied in more detail, the direct personality concomitants of cultural pressures will be isolated and better understood.

[14] Presumably this increased authoritarianism of veterans is related to their service experience in authoritarian environments, though Christie (5) failed to note an increase in *F* scores of army recruits after six weeks of infantry basic training.

REFERENCES

1. ADORNO, T. W., FRENKEL-BRUNSWIK, ELSE, LEVINSON, D. J., and SANFORD, R. N. *The Authoritarian Personality.* New York: Harper & Bros., 1950.
2. ALLPORT, G. W. *The Nature of Prejudice.* Cambridge, Mass.: Addison-Wesley Press, 1954.
3. BETTELHEIM, B., and JANOWITZ, M. *Dynamics of Prejudice.* New York: Harper & Bros., 1950.
4. CASH, W. *The Mind of the South.* New York: Knopf, 1941.
5. CHRISTIE, R. "Authoritarianism Re-examined." In R. CHRISTIE and M. JAHODA (eds.), *Studies in the Scope and Method of "The Authoritarian Personality,"* pp. 123–96. Glencoe, Ill.: Free Press, 1954.
6. DAVIS, A., GARDNER, B., and GARDNER, MARY. *Deep South.* Chicago: University of Chicago Press, 1941.
7. DEUTSCH, M., and COLLINS, M. *Interracial Housing.* Minneapolis: University of Minnesota Press, 1951.
8. DOLLARD, J. *Caste and Class in a Southern Town.* New Haven, Conn.: Yale University Press, 1937.
9. DOLLARD, J., DOOB, L., MILLER, N., MOWRER, O., and SEARS, R. *Frustration and Aggression.* New Haven, Conn.: Yale University Press, 1939.
10. GREENBLUM, J., and PEARLIN, L. "Vertical Mobility and Prejudice: A Socio-psychological Analysis." In R. BENDIX and S. LIPSET (eds.), *Class, Status, and Power,* pp. 480–91. Glencoe, Ill.: Free Press, 1953.
11. HARDING, J., and HOGREFE, R. "Attitudes of White Department Store Employees toward Negro Co-workers," *Journal of Social Issues,* VIII, No. 1 (1952), 18–28.
12. HARRIS, D. B., GOUGH, H. G., and MARTIN, W. E. "Children's Ethnic Attitudes. II. Relationship to Parental Beliefs concerning Child Training," *Child Development,* XXI (1950), 169–81.
13. HARTLEY, E. L. *Problems in Prejudice.* New York: Kings Crown Press, 1946.
14. HELLMANN, ELLEN (ed.). *Handbook on Race Relations in South Africa.* Cape Town, South Africa: Oxford University Press, 1949.
15. HOFFMAN, M. L. "Some Psychodynamic Factors in Compulsive Conformity," *Journal of Abnormal and Social Psychology,* XLVIII (1953), 383–93.
16. HYMAN, H. H., and SHEATSLEY, P. B. "Attitudes toward Desegregation," *Scientific American,* CXCV (1956), 35–39.
17. JONES, E. "City Limits." In D. SHOEMAKER (ed.), *With All Deliberate Speed,* pp. 71–87. New York: Harper & Bros., 1957.
18. KUTNER, B., WILKINS, CAROL, and YARROW, PENNY. "Verbal Attitudes and Overt Behavior Involving Racial Prejudice," *Journal of Abnormal and Social Psychology,* XLVII (1952), 649–52.
19. LA PIERE, R. T. "Attitudes versus Actions," *Social Forces,* XIII (1934), 230–37.
20. MCLEAN, HELEN V. "Psychodynamic Factors in Racial Relations," *Annals of the American Academy of Political and Social Science,* CCXLIV (1946), 159–66.
21. MACCRONE, I. D. *Race Attitudes in South Africa.* London: Oxford University Press, 1937.
22. ———. "Ethnocentric Ideology and Ethnocentrism," *Proceedings of the South African Psychological Association,* IV (1953), 21–24.
23. MACKINNON, W. J., and CENTERS, R. "Authoritarianism and Urban Stratification," *American Journal of Sociology,* XLI (1956), 610–20.
24. MALHERBE, E. G. *Race Attitudes and Education.* Johannesburg, South Africa: Institute of Race Relations, 1946.
25. MILTON, O. "Presidential Choice and Performance on a Scale of Authoritarianism," *American Psychologist,* VII (1952), 597–98.
26. MINARD, R. D. "Race Relations in the Pocahontas Coal Field," *Journal of Social Issues,* VIII, No. 1 (1952), 29–44.
27. MYRDAL, G. *An American Dilemma.* New York: Harper & Bros., 1944.
28. PETTIGREW, T. F. "Desegregation and Its Chances for Success: Northern and Southern Views," *Social Forces,* XXXV (1957), 339–44.
29. ———. "Regional Differences in Anti-Negro Prejudice" (manuscript presently submitted for publication).
30. PROTHRO, E. T. "Ethnocentrism and Anti-Negro Attitudes in the Deep South," *Journal of Abnormal and Social Psychology,* XLVII (1952), 105–8.
31. ROPER, E. "United States Anti-Semites," *Fortune,* XXXIII (1946), 257–60.
32. ———. "United States Anti-Semites," *Fortune,* XXXVI (1947), 5–10.
33. ROSE, A. M. "Intergroup Relations vs. Prejudice: Pertinent Theory for the Study of Social Change," *Social Problems,* IV (1956), 173–76.
34. SAENGER, G., and GILBERT, EMILY. "Customer Reactions to the Integration of Negro Sales Personnel," *International Journal of Opinion and Attitude Research,* IV (1950), 57–76.
35. SAMELSON, BABETTE. "The Patterning of Attitudes and Beliefs Regarding the American Negro: An Analysis of Public Opinion." Unpublished doctoral dissertation, Radcliffe College, 1945.
36. SIMS, V. M., and PATRICK, J. R. "Attitude to-

wards the Negro of Northern and Southern College Students," *Journal of Social
Psychology,* VII (1936), 192–204.
37. SMITH, C. U., and PROTHRO, J. W. "Ethnic Differences in Authoritarian Personality,"
Social Forces, XXXV (1957), 334–38.
38. SMITH, M. B., BRUNER, J. S., and WHITE, R. W.
Opinions and Personality. New York:
John Wiley & Sons, 1956.

39. STOUFFER, S. A., SUCHMAN, E. A., DEVINNEY,
L. C., STAR, SHIRLEY A., and WILLIAMS,
R. M., JR. *The American Soldier: Adjust-
ment during Army Life.* ("Studies in
Social Psychology in World War II,"
Vol. I.) Princeton: Princeton University
Press, 1949.
40. WILNER, D. M., WALKLEY, R. P., and COOK,
S. W. "Residential Proximity and Inter-
group Relations in Public Housing Proj-
ects," *Journal of Social Issues,* VIII, No.
1 (1952), 45–69.

SHARED THREAT AND REDUCTION OF PREJUDICE *

The present selection is a good illustration of the
superiority of the laboratory study for precisely
testing an hypothesis. The experiment reported
tests a well-known hypothesis: that a situation
will produce more favorable attitudes of group
members toward each other if the participants
experience a common fate and shared goals. This
hypothesis also applies to relations between
groups. Two groups working together against a
common enemy might be expected to be drawn
toward a closer friendship. In the present selection,
Burnstein and McRae call attention to an earlier
study that attempted to test this hypothesis by
provoking in individuals some anxiety concerning
disasters that confront communities as a whole.
This type of shared threat has the advantage of
being analogous to a real field situation; however,
the investigators noted that in this hypothetical
situation the feeling that one shared these threats
equally with all others in the community, including
minority groups, may have been rather weak. Thus,
they designed and executed an experiment testing
the hypothesis in small, five-man groups. While it
is more difficult to generalize from this small-group
situation to one involving entire communities, regions, or nations, the principle can be more clearly
tested in the small-group setting.

38.

Some Effects of Shared Threat and Prejudice in Racially Mixed Groups[1]

EUGENE BURNSTEIN
ADIE V. McRAE
UNIVERSITY OF TEXAS

When members of a social system are threatened,
marked changes seem to occur in social relation-

ships (Jacobson & Schachter, 1954; Schachter,
Nuttin, de Monchaux, Maucorps, Osmer, Duijker,
Rommetveit, & Israel, 1954). Where the consequences of the threat and the responsibilities for
coping with it are shared, an increase in group
cohesion and a reduction in disruptive antago-
nisms may occur (French, 1941; Leighton, 1945;
Pepitone & Kleiner, 1957; Sherif & Sherif, 1953;
Wright, 1943).[2] The application of this general
finding to the study of particular social problems
can have important consequences. If the social
system in question is a society, community, or
group containing distinct religious or racial subgroups, concern about a shared threat may lead
to a decrease in the amount of hostility expressed
toward these minorities.

In the first explicit attempt to test the hypothesis that shared threat reduced social prejudice,
Feshbach and Singer (1957) presented a set of
questions to individuals designed to provoke concern about dangers which confront the community
as a whole, e.g., floods, hurricanes, atomic attack.
Immediately afterward a social prejudice questionnaire was administered. Responses on the final

* The selection following the editorial introduction is reprinted
from "Some effects of shared threat and prejudice in racially
mixed groups," *Journal of Abnormal and Social Psychology,*
1962, **64**, 257–263, by permission of the senior author and the
American Psychological Association.
[1] This research was supported in part by the United States Air

Force under Contract No. AF 49(638)–460 monitored by the
Air Force Office of Scientific Research of the Air Research and
Development Command and the University of Texas Research
Institute.
[2] A shared threat has also been observed to increase hostility
among group members. In Nazi concentration camps, inmates
went so far as to identify themselves with the source of the
threat (Bettelheim, 1943; Cohen, 1953). At present it is not
completely clear what are the necessary and sufficient conditions for a shared threat to reduce intermember hostility.
However, a review of the literature suggests the important
determinants are (*a*) the overwhelming nature of the threat,
(*b*) the degree to which group action can ameliorate the threat,
and (*c*) the degree to which members equally share the consequences of the threat and the responsibilities for coping
with it. In the concentration camp the threat was quite overwhelming. Group action provided little amelioration; in fact,
for many inmates a reduction in threat was only possible by
dissociating themselves from the group. Treatment varied with
the category of the inmate, and little role differentiation occurred other than imposed by the camp administration.

questionnaire were compared to those the person made a month earlier. The authors reasoned as follows:

> Under the impact of a common threat . . . one's reference group may become the population that is subjected to the danger. If this reference group now includes both Negro and white, whereas under ordinary stimulus conditions the reference group has been primarily the white population, then the social distance between white and Negro should decrease, with a corresponding decrement in social prejudice (p. 412).

The results gave only weak support to the hypothesis. However, there are considerations which suggest the shared threat induced by this method may have been relatively weak.

Requiring people to think about a community-wide disaster does not insure that they view it as one in which the suffering and responsibilities are equally distributed among all community members. In a pilot study conducted by the senior author, 47 male students in the elementary psychology course at the University of Texas were administered the first four of the five "Flood and Hurricane Threat questions" from Feshbach and Singer (1957). In addition they were asked if such a disaster struck Austin, Texas, would all or nearly all socioeconomic levels, ethnic groups, or neighborhoods be equally affected. Only 27% thought this to be likely. Over 30% thought that there would be large differences among various groups in the degree to which they suffered from such disasters. Similar differences occurred in regard to the distribution of the burden for coping with the disaster. Therefore, given this method of induction, the extent to which the subjects perceived the threat to be shared is ambiguous.

Furthermore, in a highly complex social system such as a community, multiple group membership is the rule. During a disaster, the person may experience severe role conflicts. In spite of the perception that the threat is shared equally by all community members, the role of a father, neighbor, or plant manager may be more salient than that of community citizen. This phenomenon is vividly documented by Killian (1952) in his study of the Texas City explosion and of three tornado-torn towns in Oklahoma. Thus, even when a shared threat is perceived to exist in a community setting, it is uncertain whether the community as a whole or some subsystem will become the salient reference group. In the latter case, minorities within the community remain outgroups in terms of the social relations which are salient for the person at that time. Under such conditions, social prejudice may be unaffected.

In order to test the hypotheses that shared threat reduces the expression of hostility toward minorities either one of two general procedures

can be used to minimize these processes which vitiate the threat induction: some method may be introduced to assure that the person faced by a community-wide threat takes the community as the salient reference group, or the threat may be induced in a simpler social system in which the number of group memberships available to the person is sharply reduced. Both procedures attempt to decrease the likelihood that roles or reference groups external to the threatened social system become salient. The present experiment utilizes the second method. Members of racially mixed groups cooperate to solve a logical problem. In these groups, failure is clearly shared by all members. At the same time all members have a role in coping with the status loss that results from failure (Deutsch, 1953). The social system, furthermore, is simple enough so that under the threat of status loss few, if any, alternative roles are likely to become salient other than membership in the particular problem solving group.

Another source of variation in the expression of hostility toward an individual Negro that should be controlled is the attitude of the other members toward this racial group as a whole. The stronger the person's anti-Negro attitudes, the more likely is he to be hostile toward a Negro member of his problem solving group. Thus, in the present study anti-Negro attitudes as well as shared threat will be examined.

If the expression of hostility toward a Negro group member varies directly with the strength of anti-Negro attitudes and inversely with the degree of shared threat, then the following predictions can be made: (*a*) high prejudiced individuals under nonthreatening conditions will express the greatest amount of hostility toward the Negro member; (*b*) low prejudiced individuals under shared threat will express the least amount of hostility toward the Negro member; (*c*) high prejudiced individuals under shared threat and low prejudiced individuals under nonthreatening conditions will display an intermediate amount of hostility toward the minority group member. In the situation under study hostility may be manifested in direct evaluations made of the Negro, in the frequency with which the Negro is rejected from the group, and in the avoidance of communication with him during the problem solving interaction.

METHOD

Subjects and confederate. Forty-eight male students in the elementary psychology course at the University of Texas were used as subjects. Participation fulfilled a course requirement. Several weeks before the experiment they were assessed as to their level of anti-Negro prejudice by means of Holtzman's D scale

(Kelly, Ferson, & Holtzman, 1958), in the form of a "Student Attitude and Opinion Questionnaire." This was administered by the instructors in a number of the sections of the course. The distribution of prejudice scores was split at the median; subjects falling above the median were considered high in prejudice, those below the median, low in prejudice. In order to minimize the possibility of prior acquaintanceship, the four subjects used in each experimental group were drawn from separate sections.

A Negro confederate was paid to serve as a member in all experimental groups. The four other members were, in one half of the groups, all high prejudiced subjects, in the other half, all low prejudiced subjects. The confederate participated in several pilot groups to attain maximum familiarity and skill with the type of problem to be used in the experiment. It was necessary to tell him about all phases of the experiment and its objectives. The only information that was withheld from him was the extent of prejudice of the subjects with whom he was to work.

Procedure. Six groups were run with low prejudiced subjects and six with high prejudiced subjects. Within each of these two conditions of prejudice, shared threat was induced in half of the group, while a nonthreatening or successful state of affairs was induced in the other half. The design, therefore, consisted of three groups of four subjects, plus the confederate, under each of the following conditions: High Prejudice, Nonthreat (*HPNT*); Low Prejudice, Nonthreat (*LPNT*); High Prejudice, Threat (*HPT*); and Low Prejudice, Threat (*LPT*).

Communication among the subjects occurred around a table similar to that used by Leavitt (1951). The subjects were seated so that each was separated from the next by a vertical partition extending from a post in the center of the table. The center post had slots allowing subjects to push written messages to other members. Direct communication was permitted among all members. Messages were written on colored cards corresponding to the color of the cubicle from which each subject operated.

As each subject arrived he was given a seat in front of his cubicle. When all subjects had taken their places, they were asked to stand and see who the other members were but not to engage in any conversation. A copy of the instructions was given to each member and they were asked to follow as the experimenter read them aloud. In summary form, the instructions were as follows:

> The purpose of this procedure is to evaluate how groups work together in solving problems when communication is limited to written messages. It has been found that a procedure such as this can be used to single out groups with different levels of skillfulness, ef-

ficiency, and creativity. The university recently has become quite interested in estimating how productively undergraduates can work together in groups. They have suggested that the Psychology Department initiate this program of evaluating groups of students with respect to these qualities. Thus, a record will be kept for the university administration of the performance of the group participating in this preliminary testing. Skillful, efficient, and creative group problem solving will be reflected in the time that it takes the group to solve the problem, i.e., how long after starting before every member has the correct answer. Each member will receive a grade that is based on how well his group performs in solving these problems. This means, of course, that everybody in the group gets the same grade. The grade a group receives will depend on how its performance compares to that of a large number of other groups of college students in Texas who have worked on the same type of problem in the same type of situation.

During the reading of the instructions the subjects were standing facing each other.

All groups were given four successive problems to solve—Leavitt's (1951) "common symbol" problem. They were instructed that each member had been given a different set of symbols and that their task, as a group, was to discover the symbol that was common to all members. When a member knew what this symbol was, he was to put it on a white slip and place it on top of his section of the center post. The group was considered to have completed the problem when all members had placed their white slip on the center post.

At the conclusion of Task 2, subjects were told to stand, stretch their legs, but not to converse. They were seated and given an evaluation of their performance. Half of the high prejudiced groups and half of the low prejudiced groups (*HPNT* and *LPNT*) were told that their performance was well above average. The remaining high prejudiced and low prejudiced groups (*HPT* and *LPT*) were informed that they had performed poorly compared to the average performance of similar groups. The experimenter reinforced these evaluations by making two or three positive or negative statements about the group's performance during or immediately after both Tasks 3 and 4. At the end of Task 4, the experimenter similarly evaluated the groups with respect to their overall performance. While the final evaluation was made subjects were standing in front of their cubicle facing each other.

Immediately following the final evaluation a postquestionnaire was administered. On six-point scales, subjects rated the experimenter in terms of his "competence as a psychologist" and in terms of their "liking" for him. Similarly, the test situation was rated for its "fairness," its "worthwhileness" and its "interest." To partially assess the success of the threat induction, subjects were asked to rate how "depressed" they felt at the results of the test. Three items allowed subjects to evaluate the other four members. Two of these items involved ranking members in terms of their contribution to the solutions and in terms of who the subjects liked best. The third item required subjects to rate other members for their estimated "communication and problem solving skill in everyday life." At the end of the questionnaire subjects were given a sheet which asked if they wished to replace one of the present members with a new one from the subject pool at the next testing session. If they did desire to do so, they were to indicate the rejected member by encircling one of the four listed colors which corresponded to the color of his cubicle.

After completing the questionnaires, subjects were given a full explanation of the nature of the experiments.

RESULTS

An analysis of variance of the mean times required for task completion by the four experimental groups indicates that completion time decreases significantly over trials ($F = 8.06$, $p < .001$). This is in accord with Leavitt's (1951) findings regarding improvement in performances over successive tasks.

To assess the success of the threat induction, two t tests were made, one on the self-ratings of depression as a result of the test, another on the subjects' ratings of themselves and other white members for their communication and problem solving skills in everyday life. The tests indicated that threatened subjects felt more depressed than nonthreatening subjects ($t = 2.82$, $p < .01$). Similarly, threatened subjects graded themselves and other white members significantly lower in everyday communication skills than nonthreatened subjects ($t = 3.67$, $p < .001$). There were no reliable differences as a function of threat in regard to the subjects' evaluations of the experimenter and of the test situation.

To determine differences in hostile expression resulting from shared threat and prejudiced attitude, t tests were run on the postquestionnaire items in which the subjects ranked the confederate in terms of contribution to task solutions, liking for him, and in which they estimated his everyday communication and problem solving skill. It was predicted that maximum hostility would be expressed in $HPNT$ conditions; the least in the LPT conditions; while HPT and $LPNT$ subjects would express an intermediate amount. In Table 1 the mean rank for contribution to the solutions given to the Negro confederate are presented. A rank of 1 indicates the greatest contribution, a rank of 5, the least contribution. The order of these mean ranks correspond exactly to the predicted order. However, only the differences between $HPNT$ and HPT and between $HPNT$ and LPT are statistically reliable. The difference between $HPNT$ and $LPNT$ approaches, but does not reach an acceptable level of significance ($p < .10$). For the mean rank given to the Negro confederate in regard to "liking," a

TABLE 1   Evaluation of Negro Confederate

	MEAN TASK CONTRIBUTION RANK		MEAN LIABILITY RANK		MEAN SKILL RATIO	
	Shared Treat		Shared Treat		Shared Treat	
	Present	Absent	Present	Absent	Present	Absent
Prejudice						
High	2.58	4.33	2.60	3.25	1.02	1.37
Low	2.42	3.25	2.58	2.83	.91	1.17
Difference tested	t		t			t
HPNT vs. HPT	3.12¶		2.57§			2.50§
HPNT vs. LPT	3.42¶		2.16‡			2.52§
HPNT vs. LPNT	1.85†		1.02*			
LPT vs. LPNT	1.28*					1.33*
LPT vs. HPT						

* Not significant.   † Significant at .10 level.   ‡ Significant at .05 level.   § Significant at .02 level.   ¶ Significant at .005 level.

score of 1 indicates the greatest relative liking for the confederate, 4 indicates the least liking. The Negro would be expected to be ranked lowest in the *HPNT* condition, highest in the *LPT* condition, and intermediate in the *LPNT* and *HPT* conditions. The results show the order of mean ranks once again conform to what was hypothesized. Only the differences between *HPNT* and *HPT* and between *HPNT* and *LPT* are significant. On the third item, subjects were required to estimate their fellow members' everyday communication and problem solving skill. In the context of this item, hostility may be expressed toward the Negro by rating him lower than the other group members. Ratings of group members, however, were shown to be biased by the presence or absence of threat. This is corrected by using a ratio of the rating given to the Negro by each subject over the mean rating given by the subject to all other members. A high degree of similarity between the Negro's rating and the mean rating is indicated as the ratio approaches 1. A ratio greater than 1 means that the confederate is considered less skillful than the average group member, less than 1 indicates he is considered more skillful than the average. Once again the obtained order fits the prediction exactly. However, only the differences between *HPNT* and *HPT* and between *HPNT* and *LPT* are significant.

With respect to the more general hypothesis that shared threat reduces the expression of hostility toward the confederate, responses to the above three items were analyzed by *t* tests for subjects exposed to shared threat and those not exposed, regardless of prejudice. The mean ranks given to the confederate on the first two items and the mean ratio given on the last item by threatened individuals were 2.50, 2.54, and 0.96, respectively. The same means for nonthreatened subjects were 3.70, 3.04, and 1.27, respectively. The difference between threatened and nonthreatened subjects on the first item was significant at the .005 level; the difference on the second item was significant at the .05 level; and the difference between the ratios was significant at the .01 level.

If they wished, subjects were given the opportunity to vote privately on rejecting a member from the group. In the *HPNT* condition 9 of the 12 subjects decided to reject a member. Of these 9 rejections, 6 were of the Negro confederate. With 9 subjects making use of their privilege to reject 1 of the 4 members in their group, it is highly improbable that as large or a larger number of these rejections would be directed toward one member by chance ($p < .01$). In the *LPNT* condition, 8 subjects wished to reject another member. The confederate received 3 of these rejections. Both in the *HPT* and *LPT* conditions 9 subjects decided to reject another member; and in each of these conditions 2 rejections were directed toward the confederate. In none of the latter three conditions did the frequency of rejecting the confederate depart significantly from what would be expected by chance alone. Thus, only under the *HPNT* condition, where the strongest expression of hostility toward the confederate was expected to occur, is the Negro rejected more frequently than chance.

Another significant source of information concerning the orientation of the members toward the Negro is the proportion of the task messages sent to him during the course of the problem solving interaction. Earlier studies have shown that interpersonal dislike can be coordinated to an increase in the barriers to communication (Festinger, Cartwright, Barber, Fleischl, Gottsdanker, Keysen, & Leavitt, 1948; Festinger, Schachter, & Back, 1950; Potashin, 1946). Thus, it is reasonable to expect that the amount of task communication with the Negro would vary inversely with the degree of hostility felt toward him. The total number of messages each subject sent to all other subjects was counted. The percentage of this total which the subject sent to the confederate was then computed. This was done only for those tasks following the initial induction of shared threat, i.e., Tasks 3 and 4. The analysis of variance of these percentages indicates that only the *F* ratio (4.64) for prejudice is significant ($p < .05$). The differences between threat conditions and between tasks did not approach significance. Figure 1 shows that the low prejudiced subjects, both threatened and nonthreatened, sent a greater proportion of their messages on Tasks 3 and 4 to the confederate than subjects in either high prejudiced condition.

FIGURE 1. Percentage of messages sent to Negro confederate by Low Prejudiced, Nonthreatened (*LPNT*) groups, High Prejudiced, Nonthreatened (*HPNT*) groups, Low Prejudiced, Threatened (*LPT*) groups, and High Prejudiced, Threatened (*HPT*) groups over the four tasks.

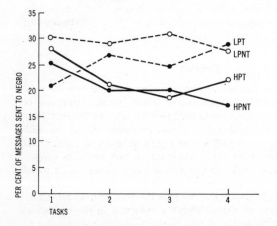

It appears that the expression of hostility toward a Negro group member varies directly with the strength of anti-Negro attitudes, and inversely with the degree of shared threat. Moreover, prejudice against Negroes as a group may be expressed through a reduction in communication to an individual Negro. This is similar to Schachter's (1960) observations regarding communication to a persistent deviant. Of course, since there could be no question of the Negro changing his "deviant" position, i.e., his status as a Negro, there was no initial rise in communication to the confederate as was found by Schachter during the early phases of interaction. Moreover, it is interesting to note that avoidance of communication with the Negro by high prejudiced subjects occurred in a situation where messages were of an impersonal, task oriented nature and where the Negro member possessed information of value to other members in solving the problem.

The prediction that shared threat would inhibit tendencies to avoid communication with the Negro was not confirmed. No difference in communication to the confederate appeared as a function of shared threat. There are a number of possible explanations as to why shared threat reduced the expression of hostility toward the Negro in terms of direct evaluation on the postquestionnaire, but had no effect on the tendency to avoid communication with him. The first bears on the procedure used to induce the threatening and nonthreatening conditions. It will be recalled that the evaluations of the group's performance by the experimenter, which was the means whereby threat was induced, was not made until after the second task. This was relatively late in the problem solving process. The reorganization of the person's initial attitude toward the Negro may take some time. Thus, attitude change may not have occurred in time to appreciably affect task communication. This explanation loses some of its force when one notes in Figure 1 that the differences in communication to the Negro as a function of prejudice occurs more markedly in the second two tasks than on the first two. An ongoing attitude change process should at least prevent such a difference from becoming more pronounced. Nevertheless, it might still be argued that with partitioned cubicles, a relatively long period of time is required before subjects become impressed with the fact that one member is a Negro; and still later, more time is needed for failure and status loss to sink in. Thus, the experiment may have obtained a sample of behavior when the subjects had fully noted the presence of the Negro but before the shared threat had an appreciable effect on communication. On this basis it would be predicted that if more than four tasks were given, subjects in the *HPT* condition would eventually begin to increase communication with the confederate.

A second line of reasoning assumes that avoidance of communication is a less direct form of hostile expression than rating the person as poor with respect to certain valued attributes. It also focuses on what is being affected by the induction of shared threat. Are prejudiced attitudes being remolded, or are the expressions of hostility stemming from such attitudes being inhibited without any underlying attitude change? If attitude change had occurred under shared threat, less overall hostility, direct and indirect, should be expressed toward the confederate. This did not occur. If, however, shared threat served to inhibit direct aggression without modifying prejudiced attitudes, our expectation would be quite different. In this case, it would be anticipated that high prejudiced individuals confronted by a common threat would express a smaller amount of direct hostility toward a minority group member than equally prejudiced but unthreatened individuals. Both groups, nevertheless, would be expected to express a similar amount of indirect hostility (avoidance of communication with the Negro) which would be greater than that manifested by less prejudiced individuals.

Finally, discriminatory behavior based on cultural norms and the affective orientation toward Negroes may under certain conditions be uncorrelated. One can follow the discriminatory practices of one's group without necessarily entertaining feelings of hostility. This suggests a third possible interpretation. Since about 75% of the items on the prejudice scale used in this study concern appropriate behavior toward Negroes, a high anti-Negro prejudice score may indicate that the person has strongly internalized the discriminatory behavior patterns of Texas culture. The strength of these norms regarding behavior may not be appreciably modified by a momentary event in a temporary group. Thus, the shared threat induced may have produced a positive change in the affective orientation toward the Negro group member while having no influence on conformity to cultural patterns which stress avoidance of equal status interaction.

SUMMARY

The purpose of this experiment was to test the relationship between shared threat and the expression of prejudice hypothesized by Feshbach and Singer (1957). Forty-eight subjects, varying with respect to anti-Negro prejudice, were placed under conditions of shared threat or nonthreat, in task oriented, cooperative work groups. A Negro confederate was a member in each group.

It was found, as hypothesized, that under conditions of shared threat a reduction in the expression of prejudice occurs in terms of direct evaluation of the Negro by other group members on a posttask questionnaire. No significant differences in the amount of communication to the confederate occurred as a result of the threat induction. However, significantly fewer messages were addressed to the Negro by the high prejudiced subjects, regardless of the presence or absence of shared threat.

REFERENCES

BETTELHEIM, B. Individual and mass behavior in extreme situations. *J. abnorm. soc. Psychol.,* 1943, **38,** 417–452.

COHEN, E. A. *Human behavior in the concentration camp.* New York: Norton, 1953.

DEUTSCH, M. The effects of cooperation and competition upon group processes. In D. Cartwright & A. Zander (Eds.), *Group dynamics research and theory.* Evanston, Ill.: Row, Peterson, 1953. Pp. 319–353.

FESHBACH, S., & SINGER, R. The effects of personal and shared threat upon social prejudice. *J. abnorm. soc. Psychol.,* 1957, **54,** 411–416.

FESTINGER, L., CARTWRIGHT, D., BARBER, KATHLEEN, FLEISCHL, JULIET, GOTTSDANKER, JOSEPHINE, KEYSEN, ANNETTE, & LEAVITT, GLORIA. A study of a rumor: Its origin and spread. *Hum. Relat.,* 1948, **1,** 464–486.

FESTINGER, L., SCHACHTER, S., & BACK, K. *Social pressures in informal groups: A study of a housing community.* New York: Harper, 1950.

FRENCH, J. R. P., JR. The disruption and cohesion of groups. *J. Psychol.,* 1941, **36,** 361–377.

JACOBSON, E., & SCHACHTER, S. (Eds.) Cross-national research: A case study. *J. soc. Issues,* 1954, **10**(4), 5–68.

KELLEY, J. G., FERSON, J. E., & HOLTZMAN, W. H. The measurement of attitudes toward the Negro in the South. *J. soc. Psychol.,* 1958, **48,** 305–317.

KILLIAN, L. M. The significance of multiple-group membership in disaster. *Amer. J. Sociol.,* 1952, **57,** 309–314.

LEAVITT, H. J. Some effects of certain communication patterns on group performance. *J. abnorm. soc. Psychol.,* 1951, **46,** 38–50.

LEIGHTON, A. *The governing of men.* Princeton: Princeton Univer. Press, 1945.

PEPITONE, A., & KLEINER, R. The effects of threat and frustration on group cohesiveness. *J. abnorm. soc. Psychol.,* 1957, **54,** 192–199.

POTASHIN, R. A sociometric study of children's friendships. *Sociometry,* 1946, **9,** 48–70.

SCHACHTER, S. Deviation, rejection, and communication. In D. Cartwright & A. Zander (Eds.), *Group dynamics research and theory.* Evanston, Ill.: Row, Peterson, 1960. Pp. 223–248.

SCHACHTER, S., NUTTIN, J., DEMONCHAUX, CECILY, MAUCORPS, P. H., OSMER, D., DUIJKER, H., ROMMETVEIT, R., & ISRAEL, J. Cross-cultural experiments on threat and rejection. *Hum. Relat.,* 1954, **7,** 403–440.

SHERIF, M., & SHERIF, C. *Groups in harmony and tension.* New York: Harpers, 1943.

WRIGHT, M. E. The influence of frustration on the social relations of children. *Charact. Pers.,* 1943, **12,** 111–122.

A **major** source of regularity in the interaction between individuals is the institutional structure. The latter consists of shared systems of normative expectations that constrain the behavior of group members. The terms "normative" and "constrain" refer to the obligatory character of these cognitive guides to interaction. In varying degrees, persons are supposed to behave in accordance with these expectations. Such systems are analyzed in terms of the concepts of status or position and role. The first two, frequently used interchangeably, refer most commonly to a location in a social relation. Persons categorized in a position or status are expected to behave in certain ways toward other persons located in related positions. These cognitions concerning appropriate feelings or behavior are referred to as role expectations.

In recent years, many social psychological studies have focused on the consequences of various characteristics of these systems for the individual and also the group. Basic to this research has been the idea of role strain. Individuals are seen as experiencing psychological discomfort in varying degrees when attempting to meet role expectations. In part, such strain may arise because of incompatibilities between such individual attributes as abilities or personality characteristics and the role expectations in question. In part, however, they arise out of the characteristics of the systems themselves. A system may be so organized that an individual finds himself subject to conflicting or competing expectations. Or he is required to shift from one position to another that demands opposite behaviors. Or he is inadequately rewarded for role performance. Such system variables are emphasized in the studies reproduced in this section. These investigations underscore the fact that difficulties in human relations are not necessarily due to deficiencies within the individual, but may arise because of historically developed defects within the system of relations that structures the interaction of group members.

The first selection, by Wardwell, and the second, by Kahn and his colleagues, illustrate a number of sources of role strain. The remaining selections deal with ways in which strain is prevented, or when it occurs, resolved. While discussion so far has emphasized social system features that create strain, other features and mechanisms have the effect of reducing strain. This is the subject of the third article by Toby. The last two selections focus on the individual and the ways in which he behaves under conditions of role strain. The first of these, by Gross, Mason, and McEachern, provides a basis for predicting which set of conflicting expectations a person in a role conflict situation is apt to honor. The second, by Goode, emphasizes resolution of strain by modification of the conflicting expectations through a process of bargaining between role partners.

PART FIVE

THE INDIVIDUAL AND THE SOCIAL SYSTEM

REDUCTION OF STRAIN IN A MARGINAL SOCIAL ROLE[*]

In one of the earliest studies of role strain, Wardwell, in his analysis of the role of the chiropractor, illustrates three sources. One source of strain lies in the lack of clarity and consensus concerning the expectations which make up the role. Chiropractors, their patients, and the general public are uncertain and disagree as to the nature of chiropractic practice. A second source of strain exists in certain incompatibilities in the role itself. A third source, which in part stems from the first, arises because the chiropractor defines the rights of his role to include rewards that others are not willing to accord him. The second part of this article analyzes the ways in which position occupants handle role strain. Of particular interest is the emergence of certain shared beliefs including the ideology of an oppressed minority and a treatment philosophy; these serve to reduce some of the strains inherent in the role. This kind of reaction to structurally induced strain may well be the origin of many ideological elements in a culture.

39.

The Reduction of Strain in a Marginal Social Role

WALTER I. WARDWELL
UNIVERSITY OF CONNECTICUT

The purpose of this paper is to contribute to the development of role theory through application of Leonard Cottrell's propositions concerning role adjustment to an empirical case—that of the chiropractor.[1] The following seem for Cottrell to be the most important factors contributing to role adjustment: (1) the degree of clarity with which the role is defined: specifically, the proportion of social situations for which there are explicit definitions of action agreed upon by all relevant parties; (2) the compatibility of alternate role behaviors required of a person in a given status position; and (3) satisfactory attainment of the goals highly valued in the subcultural group. He also states that "the amount of tension, anxiety, and frustration generated by the attempt to discover and play a given role is an index of the individual's adjustment to such a role." However, it is not enough

merely to isolate sources of strain. Other elements in the situation are patterns of strain reduction. Although Cottrell explicitly mentions that role adjustment varies with "the accessibility of substitute gratifications," he does not pursue this notion further or mention any other patterns of strain reduction. But analysis of them is as essential as analysis of the sources of strain.

Deficiency in any of the three aspects of role adjustment which Cottrell enumerates exemplifies what Talcott Parsons in his lectures has called "socially structured strain." "Social structure" consists of culturally defined behavior patterns appropriate to various status positions which may be viewed as its "parts."[2,3] When the definition of role behavior is vague or inconsistent (Cottrell's first and second points), the social structure is impaired and roles are subject to strain. Socially structured strain also appears in situations where the goals defined as appropriate for a role cannot be attained (Cottrell's third point). Although the reasons for nonattainment of goals may be idiosyncratic to the individual or otherwise "accidental," consistent nonattainment of goals by incumbents of a role probably results from ambiguity in the definition of the role. Since this is so, Cottrell's third factor in role adjustment, (3) above, may be regarded as a corollary or special case of the first (1).

Strain in a social role produces tension, anxiety, or frustration. The role concept is the link between the sciences of sociology and psychology, and the development of role theory is a necessary preliminary to their eventual integration into a unified body of theory. Not all strain-reduction patterns are "reactions" to frustration, but those that are should be explicable in psychodynamic terms. The following are the principal types of psychological reaction to tension and frustration: (1) aggression (the best known statement of this is Dollard's "frustration-aggression" hypothesis);[4] (2) regression to earlier, that is, infantile or more primitive, modes of behavior; (3) withdrawal, either physical or symbolic, from the frustrating situation (physical withdrawal is often, however,

* The selection following the editorial introduction is reprinted from "The reduction of strain in a marginal social role," American Journal of Sociology, 1955, 61, 16–24, by permission of the author and the University of Chicago Press.
1 "The Adjustment of the Individual to His Age and Sex Roles," American Sociological Review, VII (1942), 617–20.

2 The above represents the static view. From the point of view of dynamic process the terms corresponding to status and social structure are role and social system. The various roles and role complexes are interdependent "parts" of the social system which through their interaction maintain the system as a going concern.
3 Cf. Talcott Parsons, The Social System (Glencoe, Ill.: Free Press, 1951) pp. 70ff.
4 John Dollard, Frustration and Aggression (New Haven: Yale University Press, 1939).

no more feasible than is a forthright effort to remove the source of frustration); and (4) *accommodative behavior*, either overt or entirely mental: substitute goals may be adopted or the same goals may be sought by substitute means; cognitive reorganization may facilitate adjustment to the existing situation or may justify the adoption of other means to the original goals, a kind of rationalization.

There is a continuous feedback to the source of strain which is an important phase of the interactive process. A vicious circle often results in which cause and effect cannot be determined but which nevertheless exhibits a certain directionality —in which, as it were, the horse and his cart are running side by side.

STRAIN IN THE ROLE OF THE CHIROPRACTOR

To make these propositions more meaningful through empirical application, the role of the chiropractor in contemporary American society seems peculiarly well adapted. It is a social role that is marginal to the well-institutionalized role of the doctor. On the one hand, chiropractors practice their healing art as doctors, while, on the other, they are officially condemned by the American Medical Association as impostors in the doctor's role. The public is confused, although its evaluation of them is in general less harsh than that of organized medicine. The chiropractor's role is marginal to that of the physician in at least the following five respects: (1) amount of technical competence; (2) breadth of scope of practice; (3) legal status; (4) income; and (5) prestige.[5] The role's marginality derives from the fact that chiropractors claim to be doctors of a special kind and are so regarded by many people but that society at large does not accord them this status.

As Cottrell implies, lack of clarity in the definition of the role hampers adjustment, producing strain. In addition to ambiguity in the definition of the role of any doctor, the chiropractor's role is ambiguous for several other reasons. There is vast ignorance on the part of patients and potential patients as to what chiropractors do, and, more important, chiropractors themselves disagree on the question of what chiropractic treatment should be. The "straights" limit themselves to spinal manipulation alone, sometimes "adjusting" only upper cervical vertebrae, while the "mixers" also use heat, light, air, water, exercise, diet regulation, and electric modalities in their treatment. State

[5] For further discussion of the concept of marginality of a social role and a descriptive summary of the contemporary role of the chiropractor see the writer's "A Marginal Professional Role: The Chiropractor," *Social Forces*, XXX (1952), 339–48. For additional details consult the writer's doctoral dissertation, "Social Strain and Social Adjustment in the Marginal Role of the Chiropractor" (Department of Social Relations, Harvard University, 1951).

laws differ as widely in the scope of practice they permit. In most states chiropractors are limited to spinal manipulation and simple hygienic measures, while in others they may perform minor surgery, practice obstetrics, and sign death certificates. In four states, Massachusetts, New York, Mississippi, and Louisiana, they are not licensed at all but are prosecuted (they would say "persecuted") for practicing medicine without a license. The law is usually haphazardly enforced, however, with the result that the chiropractors in those states practice more or less openly. In certain other states many chiropractors depart from the exact provisions of the law. It is no wonder that, "the public, where it has any knowledge at all of it, has a confused opinion of chiropractic."

Interviews with chiropractors in a state where they are not licensed reveal this tension and frustration:

> We in_____are martyrs to chiropractic.
> . . . My brother left the state because he couldn't take it any longer—not knowing whether the next person who came into his office was going to be the one to testify against him in court. . . . The worst thing about being a chiropractor is that you have to practice behind locked doors.[6]
>
> I am thinking of giving up practice and getting an agency of some kind. It would be better than the uncertainty of practicing as it is now, which is like having an ax hanging over your head all the time.

Cottrell's second proposition focuses on the incompatibility of alternate role behaviors required of one in a given status. Lee, for example, has distinguished three aspects of the role of the physician: (1) the scientist-warrior on the frontiers of knowledge; (2) the gentle technician-savior of the sick; and (3) the retailer of medical knowledge, a scarce commodity which has been obtained by labor, sacrifice, and cash.[7] While these roles are often combined in specific persons, there are elements of incompatibility in them, particularly in the last two: between motivation in the humanitarian-altruistic and in the economic-egocentric roles ("collectivity-orientation" versus "self-orientation" in Parsons' terminology).[8]

Parsons has shown that there is no necessary conflict for physicians between long-range self-interest and short-run collectivity-orientation in

[6] All quotations, unless otherwise indicated, are from interviews with chiropractors in Massachusetts.
[7] Paraphrased from Alfred M. Lee, "The Social Dynamics of the Physician's Status," *Psychiatry*, VII (1944), 372.
[8] *Op. cit.*, pp. 60–61.

their dealing with individual patients in a well-integrated social situation.[9] However, since our society is not perfectly integrated, there may well exist conflict between the two. Oswald Hall has found that physicians excluded from the inner fraternity of the medical profession follow individualistic careers. These are set apart from other types "by the keen competition for patients and fees and by the conception of a medical practice as a commercial venture in which success is measured by income and number of patients."[10] The social situation of the chiropractor is certainly not well integrated. It is not surprising that, although most chiropractors appear to have well internalized the doctor's obligations pertaining to helping the sick, others follow the role of business entrepreneur in their day-today orientation toward patients. Hence we get such extreme statements as the following:

> I try to be a businessman as well as a professional man. I am interested in getting my fee. If a man gets a treatment and doesn't have the money to pay for it, I tell him I expect to be paid for my work. If he gets a second treatment and doesn't have the money to pay for it, I tell him in no uncertain terms that I don't do business that way. . . . I don't solicit or encourage charity cases.

On the third prerequisite of adjustment, the attainment of highly valued goals, chiropractors are disadvantaged in comparison with physicians. Their incomes are lower than those of physicians on the average, but that troubles them less than their failure to achieve recognition as competent doctors of a respected healing art. Patients come to them "when they have exhausted medical science and their money," one chiropractor lamented. Even in states where they are licensed, chiropractors normally do not share the use of tax-supported medical facilities such as hospitals and laboratories. Official AMA publications continue to call chiropractic "quackery," chiropractors "charlatans," and chiropractic patients "psychos," "hypochondriacs," or "dupes." (The chiropractic patient is thereby also cast in a marginal social role.) Chiropractic must therefore be "sold" to new patients, and this is a nuisance. Even convinced patients may have to be persuaded to try chiropractic for ailments other than those pertaining to muscles and joints or those for which

they have previously been helped by a chiropractor. All this lowers the chiropractor's estimation of himself.

In states without licensing legislation this lack of recognition is impressed on the chiropractor even more strongly. Especially, do chiropractors resent having their motives impugned:

> It's not right that we're treated as criminals. The legislators should take that into consideration no matter what they think about chiropractic. We're doing good work helping people who are sick. We are not hiding out. We go before the legislature each year to try to get a license. If we stayed in hiding, it would be different.

> It isn't fair for the government to provide a jury trial for Communists and not for me. I am an American if there ever was one. My ancestors helped settle the state of Iowa.

PATTERNS OF STRAIN REDUCTION

Strain-reducing patterns in chiropractors' behavior include several types of aggressive behavior, active efforts to remove the source of strain, physical withdrawal, and indications of what may be called "symbolic withdrawal." We find deviant patterns which enable chiropractors to attain money and power by means that are considered unethical or illegal, and we find rationalizations of this behavior. Cognitive accommodation takes the form of a well-developed ideology explaining the chiropractors' unfortunate social position and their unhappy relationship to the medical profession. This we call the "ideology of an oppressed minority."

And we find a chiropractic "philosophy" which defines the therapeutic situation in such a way as to reduce the amount of tension involved in it and to explain why failures occur as well as cures. Let us examine these strain-reducing patterns.

Realistic patterns. Realistic reactions to the strain of practicing in states without a licensing law include the following: (1) uniting for mutual aid, both informally and in associations which provide insurance protection and experienced defence counsel; (2) practicing under the guise of physiotherapists or masseurs; (3) restricting practice to "safe" illnesses and trusted patients; (4) participation in civic and fraternal activities in order to gain community acceptance, and (5) attempting to obtain a favorable licensing law by engaging in campaigns to educate the public, organizing patients into laymen's units for the purpose of exerting pressure on legislators, and forming friendships with politically important people.

Chiropractors attribute their failure to obtain favorable legislation almost completely to the opposition of medical interests. They believe that

[9] Talcott Parsons, "The Professions and Social Structure" and "The Motivation of Economic Activities," in *Essays in Sociological Theory* (Glencoe, Ill.: Free Press, 1949), chaps. viii and ix.
[10] "Types of Medical Careers," *American Journal of Sociology,* LV (1949), 249.

their lack of success is due principally to medicine's superior financial resources. Nevertheless, legislative campaigns are important episodes for them. Although the united front barely conceals the internal friction and contention that make of organized chiropractic a divided house, in general these campaigns are waged enthusiastically. There is always hope that "this time" the bill will pass. The money is contributed. Time and effort are devoted to attending meetings, contacting legislators, and encouraging patients to lend their support. The issue is talked up on all sides, debated publicly within legislative walls, and occasionally reported in the newspapers. Even if a law is not obtained, certain advantages have accrued; chiropractic has presented its case, obtained publicity, and perhaps won new friends. In any event, chiropractors have themselves been actively doing something to enhance their interests. Such behavior provides psychological satisfactions even if it does not succeed in accomplishing its stated purpose. Hence it performs the function of reducing strain in the chiropractic role.

Aggressive patterns. Aggression may be expressed in overt behavior or verbally. It may be directed at the source of frustration or at a substitute target. The substitute target may bear a symbolic relationship to the source of frustration, or it may simply serve as a convenient scapegoat on which to displace aggression. If no scapegoat is available aggression may be directed toward the members of one's own group (symbolically an intropunitive[11] response). We are concerned not with aggression directed toward the chiropractor but with how he handles his own aggression. Most of it is verbal and directed primarily against organized medicine, which is conceived to be the main source of frustration. Secondarily aggression is directed against legislators who enact and political authorities who enforce the laws unfavorable to chiropractic, both of which are viewed as tools of a powerful medical monopoly. For example:

> I want to talk to you on the American Mendicant's Association — otherwise known as the medical octopus, the medical trust, and this phraseology is not merely a convenient term used to express our disgust and contempt for a certain small body of political medical men who control a much larger body of sincere scientific medical men—it is in truth all that we call it, a trust using constrictive methods. First organized as an educational and protective association, it has spread its tentacles out over the entire country like a vampire. It controls the sur-

> roundings of your birth, milk supply, water supply, food supply, the sanitation in your house. . . . The A.M.A. controls the time you are born and the time you die. They help both. . . . There is no trust like it in existence. Of late years it has degenerated into a vast political machine, the biggest dam to medical progress the world has ever seen. It condems every method, every procedure, every theory, idea or help to humanity that does not originate within and financially help to fill the pockets of its own ranks.[12]

Mixers frequently show more hostility toward straights, whom they view as obstacles to scientific progress, than they do toward physicians. The straights often reciprocate, for they regard mixers as having deserted the straight-and-narrow path of chiropractic by going part way over to medicine. The straights tend to repress their feelings of inferiority to physicians and emphasize the differences between chiropractic and medicine. Since mixers represent the real continuity between the two therapies, they are a symbolically appropriate, as well as more convenient and vulnerable, target for aggression displaced from medicine.

A chiropractor can also express his aggressive urges against patients not only verbally but overtly, that is, through giving them vigorous "adjustments." We are not referring here to possible sadism but to the simple fact that patients are available and suitable objects for the displacement of hostility.

Withdrawal patterns. Professional mortality has always been a problem to the chiropractors. Many practitioners have abandoned their profession completely, while others have practiced only part time. A pattern of symbolic withdrawal would be to limit one's practice to a narrow ("safe") range of illnesses, not as a realistic adjustment to the hazards of practice, but as a defensive reaction to anxiety.

Patterns involving deviant means to cultural goals. We have already referred to the commercial aspect of the doctor's role as an alternative in a badly integrated social situation. It can serve to reduce strain only if it leads to attainment of some of the goals highly valued in the culture. Among the commercial alternatives of the chiropractor's role are such practices as secret remedies

[11] Saul Rosenzweig, "An Outline of Frustration Theory," in J. Hunt (ed.), *Personality and the Behavior Disorders* (New York: Ronald Press, 1944), chap. xi, p. 383.

[12] B. J. Palmer, *The Tyranny of Therapeutic Transgressions, or an Exposé of an Invisible Government* (Davenport, Iowa: Universal Chiropractors Association, 1916), pp. 42–43.

(selling new techniques for a fee), fee-splitting, soliciting patients, and advertising. Of course these are the very evils that beset the medical profession, but they are probably more frequent among chiropractors. It is reported:

> One enterprising Los Angeles chiropractor has the front of a large house covered with a series of neon legends in letters at least eighteen inches high. These signs flash on and off in sequence and read, "FEAR," "WORRY," "NERVOUSNESS," "NEUROSIS," — Dr._____.[13]

There is little doubt that some chiropractors take unfair advantage of their patients (as do some physicians) by means that are unethical or illegal, such as exaggerating illnesses, promising cures, giving excessive treatment, and overcharging. Such behavior is of course a cause as well as a result of the chiropractor's marginal role. As a matter of fact, these patterns are good examples of the interdependence between socially structured strain and patterns of reaction to it.

The following excerpts illustrate deviant behavior patterns:

> My brother never liked practicing in _____. He took over the practice of a man who was an alarmist. He (the alarmist) would tell people they had cancer when they didn't, just as with some M.D.'s every cold is pneumonia; then he would cure them of it.

> I once helped out_____while he went on vacation. When he got back, he told me that I would never get rich at chiropractic because I tend to minimize the patient's condition instead of playing it up. He said: "They come to you because they are sick or they think they are sick. Don't tell them they are not as bad as they thought. Tell them they're twice as bad as they thought." He said he would demonstrate on a patient who was waiting to see him. The patient was a new one whom I had gotten over a sacroiliac in four treatments. I had scheduled the fifth appointment after_____'s return so that the patient could meet his regular chiropractor. _____ examined him and said: "You're just beginning

to get well!" He sold him fifty dollars' worth of X-rays and talked him into taking some more treatments.

Rationalization of deviant patterns. It is not difficult for a chiropractor to justify practicing in spite of laws requiring possession of a medical or "limited medical" license. The arguments used are simple: chiropractors have a new type of healing art which the medical monopoly wants to keep from the public in order to prevent financial loss to themselves; until chiropractors obtain sufficient public support to get the laws changed, they are justified in technically violating them; they are bringing relief and health to the suffering sick, many of whom medicine has failed to help. The following statements clearly show these attitudes:

> I believe that if we keep our conscience clear then we can feel all right even if the legal authorities say we are not. Anything honest and legitimate is OK. What is a license anyway? It just lets you perform legally.

> Decency is an innate quality, while respectability is what is conferred upon us by society. . . . The A.M.A. made osteopathy respectable and osteopathy died. Beware of respectability! . . . If we are decent, society will eventually confer respectability.[14]

More interesting from our point of view are the rationalizations by which chiropractors justify unprofessional and unethical patterns of behavior. Voluminous advertising is regarded as essential to make the new healing art known and to answer the accusations of organized medicine. Solicitation is believed necessary in order to wean patients away from their childhood indoctrination, reinforced by constant "propaganda," that they should see a *medical* doctor when ill. If grandiose claims and impossible promises are made for chiropractic, these, they argue, are warranted by the "miraculous" cures that chiropractic sometimes achieves and the strong possibility that it might help almost any illness. It should be tried anyway. "It is not true to say 'We did everything possible' unless chiropractic was included" is a sentiment often met with in chiropractic literature. And if they sometimes exploit patients financially, this is considered no different from what medical doctors frequently do. To give adjustments to a hypochondriac is considered no more reprehensible than to prescribe pink pills and, they reason, is far better than unnecessary surgery. The greater the amount of mental conflict, the more necessary does rationalization become. The rationalizations here discussed are especially effective because they

---

[13] Malcolm H. Bissell, Jr., "A Preliminary Investigation of Chiropractic in California" (unpublished paper, Department of Sociology, University of Chicago, 1950). This is an extreme case, as are all those cited in this section, but such cases often best illustrate general trends.

[14] James G. Greggerson, *Seven Essays* (pamphlet) (n.p., n.d.) p. 21.

are patterned, that is, available and used by others subject to the same structured strain.

Accommodative patterns involving cognitive reorganization. Chiropractors have what we call an ideology of an oppressed minority. However, there are two other cognitive patterns which serve to reduce role tension.

First, there is chiropractic "philosophy"—principles of therapy together with the reasons therefor. Although these are regarded as having been scientifically verified, most chiropractors accept them on faith and use facts only to substantiate them as best they can.[15] These "first principles" structure the therapeutic situation for the chiropractor in an important way. The philosophy postulates a causal relationship between normal nerve functioning and health. Therapy is effected by locating interferences with nerve functioning, principally vertebral impingements, and correcting them, usually by manipulation. If tissue change has not gone too far, the patient will regain health; otherwise not. Surgical intervention is only necessary when tissue degeneration has taken place. The cause of sickness is thus given by the philosophy, and so is the technique for its removal. If the patient is not restored to health even when the chiropractor acts in accordance with the philosophy, this poses another problem to be "handled" cognitively. How is it accomplished? One explanation has just been noted—tissue degeneration may have progressed so far as to make a cure impossible. Another is that the spinal "subluxation" may have existed so long as to make correction well-nigh impossible. But even in other cases of failure chiropractic philosophy is not questioned:

> The principle of chiropractic is unlimited, but chiropractors cannot always apply it adequately.

> Chiropractic philosophy is perfect. It is beautiful, almost like a religion. The innate intelligence in each person is like a part of God. The only difficulty is that chiropractic philosophy is not always properly applied.

Thus in any given case human frailty rather than inadequacy of the principle itself accounts for failure to effect a cure.

If the chiropractic principle is so sacred that it can never be questioned, then this is cultism, not science. Yet it serves the function of decreasing role tension. It structures the therapeutic situation by eliminating doubt, for it supplies all the answers. It thus gives the practitioner confidence in situations whose outcome, in the nature of the

case, is uncertain. If a cure does not result, it is not the principle but the chiropractor who is at fault, and he should strive to apply the principle better next time. While this "philosophy" should not be considered primarily a reaction to a strain in the chiropractor's role, it performs the function of reducing strain. (It may be noted in passing that, from another point of view, the cultist aspects of chiropractic *produce* strain.)

The second cognitive pattern which reduces strain is related to the first: it is that chiropractic is separate and distinct from medicine. In fact, the two are sometimes thought of as complete opposites of each other. Chiropractic uses "natural healing methods" while medicine injects drugs, poisons, and foreign substances into the body and excises organs and tissues which should better be left in the body. "I believe medicine and chiropractic are incompatible—diametrically opposed to one another. One of them will kill the other off, but I don't know which one." If chiropractic is a science separate and distinct from medicine, a number of legal and psychological advantages result. First, there can then be no reason to expect chiropractors to study the same subjects as physicians or to be able to pass the same type of licensing examination; there should be a separate set of laws regulating the practice of chiropractic just as there are for dentistry and optometry. Second, chiropractors need not feel inferior to physicians if they are members of distinct healing arts. This attitude allows the chiropractor to express his feelings of personal inadequacy by way of condemnation of medical science and the medical profession for its inability to cure the sick. Instead of having to admit that he is inferior in training and social standing to the physician, he can define his situation as follows: "I am not an inferior kind of medical doctor. I am a practitioner as different from the physician as day is from night. My training is fully adequate for the type of healing I engage in. It is true that my legal and social standing is not so high as it should be, but that is something we chiropractors must strive to rectify. We need legislative and educational campaigns to bring about the recognition that chiropractic so richly deserves." In this structuring of attitudes the belief that chiropractic and medicine are opposite in nature plays a key part.

The chiropractic ideology of an oppressed minority may be stated as follows: Although this is nominally a free country, chiropractors do not have real freedom, inasmuch as their constitutional rights to life, liberty, and the pursuit of happiness are being thwarted by a powerful medical monopoly; The AMA and the "drug trusts" care only for their own financial well-being and not for the health of the citizenry; medical doctors

---

[15] But there is scientific support for much that chiropractors do, and some medical research supports chiropractic's principles. Cf. references in the writer's "A Marginal Professional Role: The Chiropractor," *op. cit.*, p. 341, and his doctoral dissertation, *op. cit.*, pp. 120–125.

prefer to treat symptoms with drugs and opiates or remove diseased tissue by surgery rather than allow chiropractors to remove the *cause* of disease; since the medical monopoly fears that its profits will be cut if chiropractic and natural healing methods become generally available, it raises every possible obstacle to the chiropractors' efforts; it does not hesitate to bribe legislators in order to gain its ends; it enforces a censorship on magazines, newspapers, and radio programs through its power to withhold pharmaceutical advertising; while it keeps people ignorant of chiropractic, it bombards them with free advertising in the form of news releases glorifying medical achievements and the latest wonder drug.

Chiropractors in general believe that the main reason they are persecuted is that their competition threatens the prestige and vested interests of the medical profession. The latter, they reason, is insincere in its protestation that it acts on behalf of the public welfare, since most chiropractic cures have been effected 'on previous medical failures. They accuse medical leaders of arguing in two directions at the same time: insisting that chiropractic has no scientific validity whatsoever, while at the same time protesting that they have no objection to anyone's practicing chiropractic providing he has first passed the regular medical examination. Thus, when the doctors say that chiropractors could practice under medical prescription, that shows that they either recognize some benefit to chiropractic therapy or that they are scheming hereby to prevent chiropractors from gaining access to patients. Individual physicians are said often to approve of chiropractors and to co-operate with them in aiding the sick, but to be impotent in the face of organized medicine and the drug trusts. Finally, at the same time that medicine pretends to regard chiropractic as pure quackery, it is incorporating into itself chiropractic principles and techniques, though under such new designations as "physical medicine" and "physiatry," and is "discovering" vertebral impingements and manipulative techniques that have been known to chiropractors for a long time.

This ideology enters into ·the definition of the chiropractor's situation in the following ways:

1. It accounts for the failure of chiropractic to gain scientific acceptance as a system of therapeutics. The blame is attributed to medically biased research workers. The fact that some physicians have adopted chiropractic and others expound theories nearly identical to it has convinced many chiropractors that it is only the influence of organized medicine and the drug interests that prevents the scientific truth of chiropractic from becoming more generally accepted. Consequently, the chiropractic prin-

ciple need not be called into question even though scientists in general have not accepted it.

2. It accounts for the present sociological status of chiropractors, that is, for the fact that they are not fully accepted as doctors under the law or by society at large. Again the "medical monopoly" is blamed for their plight. And there is just enough basis in fact for the belief that a medical monopoly exists and that organized medicine is principally responsible for the legal restrictions on chiropractors to permit the ideology to function in this way. In the first place, it is organized medicine that actively opposes chiropractic legislation and prods law-enforcement officials to see that the enacted statutes are obeyed. In the second place, organized medicine has accepted co-operative working agreements with related professions (e.g., dentistry, podiatry, optometry) only when these have accepted a limited status subordinate to medicine. Professions which refuse to accept the status of "limited medicine" (osteopathy, chiropractic, naturopathy) are still officially regarded as cults and are excluded from participation in medical activities and installations.[16] In the third place, the medical profession has been restrictive in accepting candidates for training and rather reactionary in its general social orientation:

> The medical profession has promoted or permitted itself to be a party to the promotion of intergroup, interracial, and interreligious tensions by setting up quota systems in medical schools, by barring certain races and religions from representation among the employees or even patients of many hospitals, and by being a party to that crowning and unscientific indignity to the American Negro, the Jim-Crowed blood bank and plasma supply.[17]

In the fourth place, drug and pharmaceutical concerns appear to have had some influence on AMA policy.[18] And, in the fifth place, a partial censorship of news unfavorable to medical and drug interests apparently exists.[19] But, true or not, chiropractors firmly believe in a "medical monopoly" and blame it for the present social and legal status of chiropractic.

3. It includes a moral justification of the chiropractors' cause. Chiropractors maintain that it

---

[16] Cf. "Associating with Osteopaths" (editorial), *Medical Economics,* February, 1941, p. 39.

[17] Lee, *op. cit.,* p. 376.

[18] Cf. James Rorty, *American Medicine Mobilizes* (New York: W. W. Norton & Co., 1939) *passim.*

[19] Cf. George Seldes, *Freedom of the Press* (Indianapolis: Bobbs-Merrill Co., 1935) chap. iii, "Bad Medicine"; and Annie Hale, *These Cults* (New York: National Health Foundation, 1926), pp. 193–99.

is right that they should continue to practice in spite of the legal and social restrictions simply because chiropractic is the "natural" way of gaining and retaining health and because it eliminates the "cause" of disease. It is also right because it has produced cures in cases where medicine has failed and because it helps suffering humanity without regard for the latter's ability to pay. In contrast, the medical profession's sins of omission and commission and its violations of professional ethics are magnified. This serves to excuse the chiropractors' own failings and to emphasize their moral righteousness.

> Medical men, despite their far-flung claims of interest in public health, actually are motivated by the fact that the chiropractic practitioner is taking away patients from them; and taking away patients *means taking away fees.* This economic factor is behind the desire to destroy the science.[20]

Sometimes the chiropractor's rationalization seems to be as simple as this: "I am making a living at chiropractic. That must mean that my patients are satisfied. Therefore I am doing some good for them and hence am morally justified in continuing to practice." There is nothing more reassuring to a doctor than to see his patients get well. Whether it was his doing or not, he ordinarily is given, and takes, credit for the cure. But, whatever their reasoning, most chiropractors, even in states where they are not licensed, feel that they are engaged in a perfectly legitimate undertaking.

4. It defines the situation for future action. It even becomes at times militant and has produced such slogans as "Go to jail for chiropractic!" It is significant that the ideology focuses the chiropractor's attention on the politicolegal sphere rather than on the theory and practice of chiropractic itself, thus projecting the source of difficulty outside the profession. Consequently, the primary effort need not be directed toward self-improvement. The main goal becomes the correction of legal iniquities either by a campaign of public education or by some other program to obtain favorable legislation.

---

[20] *ABC of Establishing Chiropractic* (pamphlet) (New York: American Bureau of Chiropractic, 1929), p. 9.

5. It justifies almost any means of combatting medicolegal "oppression." The reasoning is that, when one is being kicked, it is all right to kick back; dirty fighting invites reprisal, and since the medical monopoly resorts to censorship and political deals, chiropractic must do the same if it is to survive.

These, then, are the ways in which the conception of himself as a member of an oppressed minority structures the environment for the chiropractor. Holding this set of ideas about his situation greatly facilitates the chiropractor's adjustment to his role. It answers for him, on a small scale, of course, some of life's basic problems: What is my relationship to other people? What should be my relationship to the world? How can I account for the discrepancy between what *is* and what *ought* to be? (This is parallel to the problem of evil in theology, for the chiropractor the evil principle being monopolistic medicine.) What goals should a person in my position strive for? And what are the ways by which these goals can be achieved? Throughout, the question of the legitimacy of the chiropractor's role is at stake. Everyone needs a system of ideas that will provide answers to life's basic problems. The cognitive aspect of religion does this for the most important problems of meaning. Similarly, in a more limited way, an ideology does the same thing for participants in a "social movement." The chiropractic "cause" is in many respects a kind of social movement uniting chiropractors and patients working toward reform. American society has seen many social movements, though none just like chiropractic. Each typically has an ideology which performs functions similar to those of the chiropractic ideology—namely, structuring the environment as an action-determinant. This of course is what is meant by the phrase "defining the situation for action." The chiropractic ideology is an accommodative pattern, facilitating adaptation to the chiropractor's role. It is true that this part of the definition of the chiropractor's situation for action partly constitutes his role and may even exert some effect on the objective situation in which chiropractors act, but the ideology as a whole certainly also provides a pattern of adjustment for the chiropractor.

ROLE AND AMBIGUITY *

The selection below, taken from studies of organizational stress, focuses on strain arising from role ambiguity. Role ambiguity is conceived as a function of the discrepancy between the information available to a position occupant and that necessary for the adequate performance of his role. These studies were carried on in a parallel fashion in two research settings. One was an intensive study of 53 selected individuals occupying positions at various levels in a variety of industrial organizations. Each of these focal persons was interviewed at length. In addition, other persons designated as role senders—superiors, subordinates, and peers in the organization who hold expectations regarding his behavior—were similarly interviewed. This made it possible to obtain measures of role ambiguity and role conflict.

To assess the extent to which the findings of this intensive study could be generalized, a nationwide survey of role conflict and role ambiguity was conducted. In all, some 1,300 interviews were conducted with persons in a probability sample chosen from a population consisting of all adults over eighteen years of age living in private households in the nation. The replies of those 725 persons who were gainfully employed for at least twenty hours of work per week were the focus of analysis. This second investigation not only increased the external validity of the findings reported by these investigators, but served an additional epidemiological function. The findings of the national survey provided a description of the frequency and distribution of these sources of role strain throughout the working population.

40.

Role Ambiguity

ROBERT L. KAHN
UNIVERSITY OF MICHIGAN
DONALD M. WOLFE
CASE INSTITUTE OF TECHNOLOGY
ROBERT P. QUINN
UNIVERSITY OF MICHIGAN
J. DIEDRICK SNOEK
SMITH COLLEGE
ROBERT A. ROSENTHAL
JEWISH BOARD OF GUARDIANS, NEW YORK

Like role conflict, role ambiguity is costly for the person and for the organizational unit in which he works. Efficient goal-directed behavior is based on predictability of future events. A person generally has only limited control over future outcomes in which he may have a substantial interest. To the extent that he can realistically anticipate events beyond his control, he can direct his behavior toward producing more rather than fewer favorable outcomes.

Three conditions seem essential in determining such predictability: (1) The person must be able to anticipate with fair accuracy the consequences of his own actions. If he performs act A, how sure is he that event B (a desired effect) will follow? And how confident is he that X (an unwanted event) will not be produced? He needs to have usable knowledge about means-ends connections in situations where he can produce or withhold the means. (2) He needs to be aware of the determinants of relevant events which he does not produce, and of the likelihood of their occurrence. (3) He must be able to depend on the stability of a host of other surrounding conditions, that is, the "ground" that defines the "figure" of the changing events with which he deals directly. For example, everyone depends on the stability of stationary objects and on the reliability of the law of gravity. This chair will hold me just as it has in the past. The panic of an earthquake partially arises from the failure of the natural world, which is taken so for granted, to meet our expectations.

In complex social organizations the degree of predictability, though substantial, is significantly less than that accorded physical events. In addition to physical laws, a variety of social and cultural conditions must remain constant if people are to behave effectively. Words must maintain their meanings; the rules of the game must remain unchanged or at least intelligible. Changing them changes the world itself—to our delight when Lewis Carroll lets Alice slip through the looking glass, or to our terror when Kafka's metamorphosis confronts us.

The problem of predictability is further complicated for each person in an organization because he is surrounded by other actors who are trying to produce changes which will optimize their own rewards and satisfactions. Their actions represent sources of change over which the person may have little or no control, and which he can predict only in the grossest terms.

But the greatest difficulty may lie in the person's inability to anticipate clearly the consequences of his own acts. Often his goals in

* The selection following the editorial introduction is reprinted from "Role ambiguity," pp. 72–95 of *Organizational stress:*

Studies in role conflict and ambiguity. New York: John Wiley & Sons, 1964, by permission of the authors and the publisher.

organizational life are attainable only if ne can influence others to assist him, and interpersonal influence can seldom be accomplished with certainty. Moreover, efforts to produce desired changes in organizations, even when successful, often produce unanticipated secondary changes as well. One is seldom secure in the knowledge that his efforts will produce only those effects he desires and expects.

Clarity and predictability are thus required for effective movement toward goals, and in complex social systems, despite their characteristic emphasis on authority and rule, clarity and predictability are difficult to achieve. When the goals for the person are set by the objectives and requirements of the organization, ambiguity may limit his effectiveness and productivity on the job, as well as his ability to coordinate with others. To the extent that his goals stem from his own needs and values, ambiguity may be a major source of frustration and anxiety. Ambiguity thus poses a problem for both the individual and the system.

SCOPE OF THE PROBLEM

Role ambiguity is a direct function of the discrepancy between the information available to the person and that which is required for adequate performance of his role. Subjectively it is the difference between his actual state of knowledge and that which would provide adequate satisfaction of his personal needs and values. Virtually none of us knows *all* that we would like to know about the conditions surrounding our lives. We never predict with absolute certainty how things will turn out. To some degree, ambiguity is a fact of life for everyone, a condition with which we have become all too familiar. Most of us, however, are able to function reasonably well in our various roles in spite of the uncertainty.

To what extent, then, is ambiguity a problem for general concern? Data from the national survey of the labor force indicate that it is a source of stress for a substantial number of people.[1]

> 35 per cent are disturbed by lack of clarity about the scope and responsibilities of their jobs;
>
> 29 per cent are bothered by ambiguity about what their co-workers expect of them;
>
> 38 per cent are distressed because they cannot get information required to perform their jobs adequately.

While these people report some significant stress because ambiguity interferes with effective task performance, other responses emphasize the personal costs of ambiguity.

> 31 per cent are disturbed by lack of information about opportunities for advancement in the organization;

> 32 per cent are under tension because they are uncertain about their superiors' evaluations of them.

But these findings reflect only those cases in which ambiguity reaches admittedly stressful proportions. Other studies suggest that lack of desired information in organizations is even more widespread. A report of factory workers in a heavy industry is illustrative.

> Only 9 per cent reported that they were kept very well informed on what was happening in the company, yet 66 per cent said they wanted such information and 64 per cent said that other employees also wanted it.
>
> Only 10 per cent knew where they stood with their foremen, and 45 per cent said that *much* of the time they did *not* know. Yet 76 per cent wanted this information and 67 per cent said that others also wanted it.[2]

Other studies show comparable numbers who lack information about significant aspects of their work situation. Problems of ambiguity in the work situation are widespread and constitute important sources of stress for a great many people in the American labor force.

SOURCES OF ROLE AMBIGUITY

The major objective of this chapter is an increased understanding of the emotional and interpersonal consequences of ambiguity. That understanding will be enhanced by briefly considering some of the determinants of ambiguity. Three general conditions are significant: organizational complexity, rapid organizational change, and current managerial philosophies.

Complexity of modern organizations

Although the modern industrial organization is the creation of the minds of men, it has grown in size and complexity to the point that no single person can comprehend at a given moment more than a small bit of that which is to be known about it.

In very small operations a manager might well know all the employees personally, their peculiar strengths, habits, and limitations. He may understand the requirements of each task and function to be performed for organizational effectiveness. With effort and intelligence he may know fairly well "what's going on" in his organization, and other members can be equally well informed.

But in companies of even a few hundred members, such familiarity with the organization is virtually impossible. With increased size the structure of the organization becomes much more complex. The division of labor becomes more differentiated and specialized; more levels of supervision are introduced to maintain coordination and control; and more people become involved in organizational planning. In many industries advanced technology adds to the complexity; no single person can be adequately trained in all the relevant technical areas. The fact that size and complexity of organizations exceed the individual's span of comprehension probably accounts for much of the role ambiguity found today.

Rate of organizational change

If size and complexity even in the steady state pose major problems for comprehension, it is still more difficult to maintain an adequate understanding of the organization during peoiods of change. Yet rapid change is perhaps the dominant characteristic of our culture.

Changes of three kinds pervade American organizations and contribute to ambiguity. First, there is the fact of organizational growth. Many companies are increasing in size at a rapid rate, and an almost essential companion of growth is reorganization. Tendencies toward decentralization represent, in part, an effort to control the confusion produced by rapid growth and increased complexity.

Second, changes in technology require associated changes in the social structure of organizations. New techniques for performing work are introduced continually. They often impose rearrangements of and within work groups. New techniques virtually always require revisions in role expectations toward those employing them, revisions which often must be learned through a complicated process of testing and retesting. Certain technological innovations, for example, electronic data processing and operations research, are themselves intended to cope with problems of organizational complexity and ambiguity created by other new technologies.

Third, many organizations in American industry are characterized by frequent personnel changes. Not only is employee turnover a general problem, but frequent transfer and reassignments within organizations are common. The early weeks of a person's new assignment, during which he is learning his role, are fraught with ambiguity for him. Insofar as he performs the role differently from his predecessor and holds different expectations toward his associates, he also creates problems of ambiguity for them. Unfortunately for the solution of such problems, in some companies it is rare for a person and all his role senders to remain as an intact role set for more than a few weeks or months at a time. Changes in the personnel of nearly every set are sufficiently common to be the rule rather than the exception. Such changes constitute a major source of role ambiguity.

Because interdependence is such a dominant feature of organizations, the effects of change are difficult to contain. A change in any one part of the system creates changes in other parts as well. When changes are continually introduced in various parts of the organization, the total system may be in a state of constant flux.

Because organizations are open systems, changes in them may stem from changes in the environment. The problem of predictability of the environment is illustrated by the growing numbers of staff positions in large organizations charged with the responsibility of long-range forecasting, an uncertain art at best. Changes in markets, in sources of supply, and in financing must be met with appropriate intraorganizational changes. For many organizations internal interdependence, vulnerability to outside influence, and rapidly accelerating environmental change make a combined assault on the stability which is the strength of organizational process. Substantial degrees of ambiguity in many parts of the organization are almost inevitably the outcome.

Managerial philosophy and ambiguity

Role ambiguity is often the unintended consequence of factors that are largely beyond the control of any organizational member. It may also result from practices and procedures that members develop and persist in quite intentionally. Ambiguity has been described as growing out of problems in generating adequate and dependable information about issues which concern people in organizations. In complex situations undergoing rapid change, such information is difficult to obtain. But even when a relatively clear perspective can be generated—when the required information has been developed—it is seldom dispersed to all those who feel a need for it. Most organizations have rather restricted channels of communication.

The restricted flow of information is in part unintended. An individual in a key organizational position is often insensitive to the extent to which others would like to share information he possesses. He may be unbelieving or merely unaware that sharing information with others would be helpful to them and perhaps to the whole organization. Through inertia, through lack of consideration, and through lack of awareness the organizational word often does not "get around." This is too often true, but it is only part of the truth. The blockage of communication is often overdetermined. The attitudes and working assumptions of executives and supervisors as well as rank and file contribute to failure of information spread in several ways.

In *The Caine Mutiny* Herman Wouk described one organization in terms which have been echoed by members of many: "The navy was designed by geniuses to be run by idiots." A more flattering statement of this theoretical position would assert that although the organization as a whole must be coordinated within the framework of a rational over-all design, each member need not understand that design. As long as each man performs his own role and abides by the regulations, the system will run itself. All that is required of individual members (save, perhaps, for top managers) is that they know the general rules and their own responsibilities. If they have the information required for performing their own jobs, the rest is none of their business. In deciding whether or not to pass on certain information, the question, according to this set of assumptions, is not whether the other person would *like* to know, but whether he *needs* to know in order to get his job done. Logical requirements are acknowledged; psychological requirements are denied.

Generally, this is not an impossible set of assumptions. Many a system comes near to running itself on this basis. Members do muddle through without knowing "where they fit in the infinite scheme of things." At times of crucial decision every organization has its well-guarded secrets. Crucial decisions in hierarchical organizations are almost always made behind closed doors, supposedly to control the spread of rumors (which spread fastest when important doors are closed) and to increase the likelihood of successful implementation once the decision is made. There are many arguments for the restriction and control of information, including the time and effort required to keep everyone well informed. Consistent research findings that link completeness of communication to organizational effectiveness have yet to overcome them.

Let us consider just one other set of factors which limits free and open shaping of information in organizations. Control over the behavior of members is the essence of social organizations. Each member is charged with certain responsibilities and is subject to sanctions if he fails to carry them out properly. Each member is vulnerable. He must use sound judgment, make wise decisions, and act with skill and dispatch—or at least appear to. Therefore, each member is motivated to have at hand all the information relevant to his decisions and actions, including their evaluation by others. But he is less vulnerable if others do *not* also have that information. His decisions cannot be challenged if no one else has an adequate basis for judging them. Each person, therefore, has substantial reason for wanting to be better informed than anyone else on matters affecting his work. If one wants to control the behavior of others but be master of his own organizational fate, he is tempted to arrange for complete and undistorted information flowing to himself, but to filter and control the information flowing to others.

Such manipulation of information flow threatens the basis for sound decisions and cannot be

used on a wide scale without dire consequences. In the extreme it is bound to be self-defeating. Although it has few public defenders, many people at all organizational levels practice it regularly and enthusiastically

Restriction of information is one of the few techniques available to subordinates for influencing superiors, and they so use it.

THE AMBIGUITY EXPERIENCE AND ITS EMOTIONAL CONSEQUENCES

There are many factors producing ambiguity in organizations, many reasons why more than a third of the American labor force is disturbed by the lack of information required either for the performance of their jobs or for the attainment of their personal goals. Ambiguity, for many of them, is determined by several factors in combination and its costs paid in many places. Let us consider first the costs of ambiguity in the work role as they appear in the case of Nighter, a general foreman on the evening shift in an assembly plant. In addition to a rather difficult conflict stemming from the opposing demands of his superior and his counterpart on the day shift, Nighter is at times virutally overcome with ambiguity. Some sources of his ambiguity are identified in the following exchange:

> Q: How long have you been General Foreman?
> A: Well, I was a foreman for a year-and-a-half and then I was general foreman for a year-and-a-half, two years, I guess; then I was superintendent for about five years, and now I'm general foreman again for about two years.
> Q: You came down to this plant as general foreman?
> A: No. I was superintendent here when we first opened up, see? Then they wanted to shift everybody around because they were not satisfied with the way things were running, so . . .
> Q: How do you feel about all this shifting up and down?
> A: Well, there's a lot of confusion. You get used to the policies of one man and how he operates and before you know it he's gone and you get somebody else and there is all this shifting around. It finally gets to the point where production loses complete control of the area and it's all run from the front end up here and some of them don't

even know what a block is. I'm serious about it. Maybe somebody thinks it's a good policy, I don't know, but nothing has been solved. The conditions that existed out there, I think they're worse today than they were before, when there was a stable supervisory force out there. I don't know. They seem to want to keep the supervisors in a turmoil all the time.

And turmoil pretty well characterizes his experience. He goes on, describing a combination of conflictful and ambiguous circumstances:

. . . Well, what was happening there was that you'd come in in the morning and you'd start going through your division out there. You probably would get in here about 6:30 and about a quarter to eight or eight fifteen we'd have a meeting up front which would last about two hours. You'd go back to the department and start to go to another department and before you knew it you got another call because you had another meeting to go to some place. You might be three hours there and then you got another start and something else would take you away from the job—somebody from Planning would come in, or somebody from Budget — then at night about five o'clock we'd have another meeting until about 7:30 and they would want to know what the hell happened in the department. Why, hell, you haven't spent enough time out there to know exactly what the hell has taken place. You might be in the plant 12 hours a day, but you might be in the department about 2½ hours because of all the meetings they had around here. So when you couldn't spend any time going out and talking with your supervisors and getting your general foreman around to find out just what the problems were, well, you didn't know your job. So you can't go to meetings for six to eight hours a day and expect to know what the hell is going on out on the floor, and be able to run it.

Under such pressures Nighter's tension and anxiety finally gave way to resignation, with substantial loss of self-esteem:

Q: Are things worse in this plant than in any of the other plants?

A: Things are worse in this plant than in any other place I've ever known.

Q: How so?

A: Well, the constant shake-ups around here.

Q: Do they ever give you any explanation of why they do that?

A: Well, I didn't need an explanation for that. When they made a switch in personnel around here, well, the first thing they told me was that they would like me to give up—it was brought about in a roundabout way—to give up the superintendent's job. So I figured, well, hell I wasn't going to do it just because somebody was telling me to without my actually recognizing why. You know, they actually didn't have the power or anything. It finally got so bad that I figured it wasn't worth it—health and everything else—I was getting nervous. Normally I'm relaxed in the things I do. I try to think things out. I figured the job wasn't worth the money so I told them they could have the superintendent's job and if they wanted me as a general foreman around here I'd be glad to serve in that capacity and if I could help them—I knew that they were short on the afternoon shift—I told them I'd be glad to go on afternoons to help them out and I told them I would do whatever they wanted me to do.

Q: Did they ever explain what they thought it was that you were doing wrong?

A: No. They just said that I didn't know how to handle the job which I had handled for five years.

Apathy and feelings of futility accompany his resignation:

Q: It must be pretty damn hard on a guy though to get promoted and demoted—back and forth all the time? Is it kind of hard on you?

A: Well, it doesn't do you any good. I know I used to spend a lot of time on things like quality control, labor relations, and read books on how contracts should be written out, interpret contracts and stuff like that. Well, on top of that you'd be in and out of here and you were spending something like twelve hours a day in the plant. Coming in on Saturdays on your own time checking up and stuff like that.

Well, they change things and they assume a lot of things, so we try it their way. It's been hard. Like I say while I was keeping myself primed on items like that, I don't any more. I'm being fair about it. I don't bother any more.

Q: How clear are you about what the people around you expect of you?

A: Well, as far as what they expect from me, there's never been an actual discussion of it. No one has ever actually told me what they expect of me. I go out and do the best that I can the best way I know how.

Q: But you don't always know what they . . .

A: I don't always know what they think of it.

Q: Is there any particular part of your job where you are not clear about what people expect?

A: Well, a guy likes to know where he stands in a group, what his future might hold for him, somebody to have a heart to heart talk to say what's wrong and not wait until the last minute and then keep harping about something that you have no control over. I say I like to know where I stand. I would like to have somebody tell me which way I'm headed and if I'm going about it the wrong way, I would like for them to tell me. I'd like to please somebody rather than displease and be kept in the dark. That's the way everybody is around here. Nobody knows where the hell they stand.

The pathos in Nighter's words reflects the strain of a person bound into a situation he can neither control nor understand. Much as he would like to "do right" by the organization, he does not know what doing right means. Moreover, he learns only indirectly that he has failed; his job is taken away without explanation, or at least without one that he can understand and accept. It is perhaps understandable that his feelings of helplessness and futility are expressed with a touch of bitterness.

Another supervisor in a manufacturing plant is even more bitter about the ambiguity in his role. Maintainer (a general foreman in the maintenance department) was transferred to the evening shift without warning or explanation. This is how he describes that episode:

A: They don't tell you when they move you. Are you doing a bum job, or a good job? They don't ask you; they don't tell you nothing. You are in the dark. Now, what did I do wrong, that is all you think of.

Well, if they came around and said, "I got a job here I want to put you on for a while. We're having a lot of trouble." Well, I will go in and dig in. They don't do that. They say, "You start over here." That's it.

Am I doing a good job? What's the matter with the other guy, why did they take him out? They don't tell you nothing. They don't ask any questions. They don't tell you what the hell is up.

The way that I was told about going on the second shift was a guy that I don't work for, a guy I don't know at all, some stranger, he came over and says, "Hey, I hear you got to go on second shift." Well, Mr. X. just made out a chart and put me on second shift. I guess someone seen the chart and my name was on the chart.

Q: Who came down and told you officially that you were on second shift?

A: Well, the manager's assistant came over and says, "Hey, didn't anyone ever talk to you about the second shift?" I says, "Hell no, I hope I don't have to go on second shift." "Well," he says, "I guess you have to. They got you on the list, on that sheet up there." He showed me the sheet. So there I was.

Q: Well, do you think you will ever find out why all this happened?

A: I probably won't.

Q: Do you think if you went up to the front office they would tell you?

A: They would probably give me a silly answer. That's the way this damn place operates.

In frustration and bitterness, Maintainer's voice cracked several times during the above exchange. Although he is generally clear about his responsibilities and feels technically qualified to carry them out, he is understaffed and under a great deal of pressure. Moreover, he feels that his superiors do not appreciate the difficulty of maintaining a complex semiautomated assembly line.

Q: What parts of your work do you find most stressful?

A: Well, like I say, it is people giving orders and nobody knows what the hell they want you to do. Like when I was on days, when a machine would break down, there would be about fifteen white collars there and they all stand there popping questions. "How long before it will be done? How long will it take you?" You didn't know what the hell was the matter with the machine because you couldn't get near the goddamn thing.

And in another part of the interview:

Q: How often are you bothered by feeling you won't be able to satisfy the conflicting demands of your superiors?

A: Well, when you don't get no support from different people, well, sometimes you say, "What the hell is the use." I do the best I can and that's that.

Q: I suppose that bothers you quite a bit?

A: Yeh, it bothers you all the time. When you are trying to do a job, and you've been doing it right and doing a good job all along and somebody comes along and says you ain't doing a good job and won't give you an answer why or what for, then you begin to wonder. Nobody tells you. You go and ask and they shrug their shoulders. They give you a cold shoulder.

As disgruntled as Maintainer is, one wonders why he does not leave the organization. He feels that past pay increases and the pension plan have bound him into the system. A move would be too costly for him at this stage in his career. He also has a strong personal investment in the organization, which remains in spite of recent reverses:

Q: What about your present plans? Are you thinking of making a change in jobs in the future?

A: Oh, the way it is going now, anything is welcome.

Q: Are you thinking about looking for another job?

A: No, I got so much time in here, and I think that I've done my duty. As far as I'm concerned, I'm still trying to do my duty. I'm satisfied with working for the corporation and I've got a little investment of myself in here. I'd like to follow it through. I wouldn't like to switch jobs now.

Perseverance and stiff upper lip notwithstanding, Maintainer is suffering substantial strain. The ambiguity and apparent capriciousness of his work environment almost have him down:

If you know the reason for it, it would be all right. If they would give you some actual facts, it wouldn't hurt a guy so much. If your supervisors would come over and talk with you, there is usually a solution no matter how big the problem or how small. But these guys don't even talk it over with you.

Q: It seems that all you have been trying to do is find out what the story is?

A: That's right. I don't think anyone should have to work in the dark. Would you like to? I just want a square deal. Why, if I can get a square deal and some decent answers, I'll be satisfied. But you don't get that here.

Now, I'm not trying to get revenge or nothing like that. I just want working conditions. I want something to be happy about. I come to that door and say, "Goddamn, I got to come into this damn place again." That is the way you feel. (His voice breaks.) No kidding. And I'm not the only one. This is throughout. Everyone feels the same.

SOME CONCLUSIONS ON THE NATURE OF ROLE AMBIGUITY

These cases give some illustration of the variety of forms role ambiguity takes. Various aspects of the role and of the situation surrounding it may be ambiguous. The person may be uncertain about the scope of his responsibilities, about what is expected of him by others, about what behaviors will be effective in meeting these expectations. The organizational structure may be ambiguous; he may be unclear about who has a legitimate right to influence him or about the limits of his authority over others. Confusion may center around organizational rules and regulations, around conditions under which various sanctions might be applied, or around what the sanctions might be. Ambiguity about how one is evaluated by his associates, about how satisfied they are with his behavior, seems to be a common problem. There may be uncertainty about job security or opportunities for advancement.

Both Nighter and Maintainer suffer ambiguities in several different areas. Some of these are relevant to their personal satisfaction and to the gratification of personal needs (the socioemotional aspects of the role), while others are more relevant to task performance. Lack of structure in these two areas can be expected to have some similar consequences but some differential effects as well.

There are almost as many kinds of emotional reaction to ambiguity as there are foci of ambiguity. Tension, anxiety, and fear are common concomitants of uncertainty; anger and hostility also can be aroused. Nighter and Maintainer both expressed feelings of futility and apathy; they do not feel that they can do much about their situations and are no longer sufficiently motivated to try.

There is another point to be taken from these cases. Although ambiguity is stressful in its own right, the strain is even greater when the capriciousness of the environment has been demonstrated in past experience. Both Nighter and Maintainer are bitter about abrupt transfers, and for them ambiguity has taken on a new meaning as the prelude to unwanted change. When one has been burned in the past, he has additional reason to fear a fire behind the smoke of ambiguity. The world becomes not merely unknown, but hostile and dangerous.

The case material, although providing a dramatic portrayal of the problem of ambiguity, should be regarded as a source of hypotheses rather than a test of them. Quantitative statistical evidence for some of the conclusions drawn above is available from the intensive study. The analysis which follows is based on this evidence and deals with the consequences of the ambiguity experience. In neither of the current studies was a comprehensive effort made to measure the degree of objective role ambiguity.

Table 1 presents the correlations between three measures of experienced ambiguity and four measures of emotional reaction. Column 1, the general index of experienced ambiguity, indicates that the emotional consequences of role ambiguity are very much like those of role conflict. Ambiguity leads to increased emotional tension and to decreased satisfaction with one's job. It also contributes significantly to a sense of futility and to a loss of self-confidence. Conclusions about the personal costs of ambiguity are well supported statistically. Columns 2 and 3 represent the experience of ambiguity in the task and socioemotional areas, respectively. Correlations between emotional reactions of the focal person and lack of clarity on his part regarding role expectations others hold for him are presented in column 2; column 3 presents comparable correlations with uncertainty about how he is evaluated by his associates. Tension is associated with ambiguity in both areas, but some interesting differences are found in other emotional responses.

Ambiguity about role expectations tends to lead to dissatisfaction with the job in general and to feelings of futility. If a worker does not know what he is expected to do in his job, he cannot act appropriately; his sense of effectiveness as an active agent is seriously curtailed. Paraphrasing

Nighter's reaction (quoted above): "What's the use of going to a lot of extra work trying to keep up to date in various fields which might be relevant to the job; it won't get you anywhere if you don't know what they want of you." A feeling of effectiveness depends first of all on knowing what the job is, what it requires. On the other hand, ambiguity regarding role expectations is not so detrimental to self-confidence; the problem is in the environment, not in the self.

In contrast, uncertainty about how satisfied others are with one's behavior does not contribute significantly to job dissatisfaction or to feelings of futility. The intrinsic value of the job is not seriously challenged by ambiguity in evaluations, and the person is generally able to go on working. For the most part, his sense of effectiveness in the job is only moderately curtailed when others fail to provide adequate evaluative feedback. However, absence of information about how one is esteemed by his associates is a major source of tension and a serious detriment to self-confidence. Self-confidence is generally rooted in a process of reflected appraisals from others. When the "looking-glass self" is seen dimly, confidence is undermined almost as much as when it is seen negatively. Absence of evaluate feedback (or the presence of garbled feedback) may be almost as ego threatening as deprecating feedback.

MEDIATING EFFECTS OF NEED FOR COGNITION

Although the data just given have supported the general hypothesis that the greater the ambiguity

TABLE 1 *Correlations between Measures of Experienced Ambiguity and Various Emotional Reactions (from the intensive study, $N = 53$)*

EMOTIONAL REACTION	EXPERIENCED AMBIGUITY MEASURES		
	Ambiguity Index	Role Expectations	Evaluations
a. Tension	.51†	.44†	.40†
b. Job satisfaction	−.32*	−.33*	−.17
c. Futility‡	.41†	.34*	.20
d. Self-confidence‡	−.27*	−.20	−.44†

* $p < 0.05$. † $p < 0.01$. ‡ Futility and self-confidence are codes based on materials from the second focal interview. Both variables are intended to represent dimensions of a sense of effectiveness in dealing with one's environment. A person coded low in self-confidence is one who experiences a loss of effectiveness as a personal shortcoming. A person coded high in futility is one who regards his attempts at environmental mastery as being in vain either because of personal limitations or insurmountable environmental obstacles.

an individual experiences the greater will be his experience of tension, the role of individual personality differences in this affective response must also be considered.

A number of theorists[3] have postulated a need —variously called need for cognition, need for structure, or intolerance of ambiguity—which is a measurable characteristic of the organism and which may operate independently of other needs. Cohen, Stotland, and Wolfe define this need as follows:

> Need for cognition can be defined as a need to structure relevant situations in meaningful, integrated ways. It is a need to understand and make reasonable the experiential world. "Meaningfulness" and "integration" are individually defined in that they vary with the person's past experience and capacity for such integration. For any given individual different situations will be differentially important for the arousal and satisfaction of the need. In addition any given situation will have

differential importance for the arousal and satisfaction of the cognition need (p. 291).

On the basis of this definition Cohen, Stotland, and Wolfe tested the hypothesis that the association between ambiguity and frustration would be more pronounced among individuals characterized by a high need for cognition than among those with a low need for cognition. The measure of the need for cognition in this laboratory study consisted of a group of forced-choice reactions to a wide variety of hypothetical situations. Here is an example of such a situation, with "*b*" as the alternative keyed for need for cognition:

> Participation in a discussion group for solving a problem is most satisfying when:
> *a.* the problem is vital to you and to others in the group
> *b.* the problem is clear and the purpose of the group is evident
> *c.* the group is small and the discussion friendly

The data indicated that all of those individuals subjected to an ambiguous stimulus were more negatively affected than those who were given a structured stimulus, and that this negative reaction was the more pronounced for those scoring high on the need-for-cognition measure.

Our intensive study data permitted the testing of this same hypothesis. Table 1 (*a*) has already demonstrated a substantial association between experienced ambiguity and tension scores. Figure 1 adds an important qualification, dividing intensive study respondents into groups of high and low scorers on the Cohen, Stotland, and Wolfe measure of need for cognition. The figure indicates that the effects of experienced ambiguity on tension scores are considerably more pronounced for those scoring high in need for cognition. The emotional consequences of ambiguity cannot, therefore, be fully appreciated without a consideration of the motivational characteristics of the individual experiencing the ambiguity.

RELATION BETWEEN AMBIGUITY AND CONFLICT

Since the consequences of conflict and ambiguity are similar, the question of their relationship with each other arises. There are several reasons for expecting them to be associated. (*1*) The presence of conflicting role pressures may create uncertainty for the focal person. If various people press him to do different or even inconsistent things, he may not know what to do. Although each expectation may be clear, in combination they may add up to confusion rather than clarity. (*2*) If the role is ambiguous for the focal person, it probably is so for many of his role senders as well. Conflicting pressures might be more likely

[3] Cohen, A. R., Stotland, E., & Wolfe, D. An experimental investigation of need for cognition. *J. abnorm. soc. Psychol.*, 1955, **51**, 291–294; Katz, D., & Sarnoff, I. Motivational bases of attitude change. *J. abnorm. soc. Psychol.*, 1954, **49**, 115–124; Maslow, A. A theory of human motivation. *Psychol. Rev.*, 1943, **50**, 370–396; Murphy, G., Personality. New York: Harper, 1947.

FIGURE 1. Tension in relation to experienced ambiguity and need for cognition (from the intensive study).

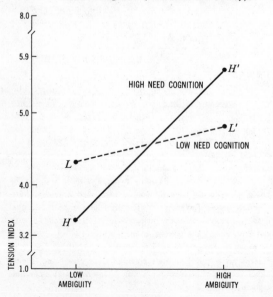

under such circumstances, because the senders are unaware of the inconsistency in their demands. (3) Some of the conditions cited as sources of ambiguity—organizational size and complexity, rapid change, differential objectives of subparts of the organization—are also sources of conflict. Role conflict and role ambiguity share to some degree the same spawning ground.

But only modest, generally insignificant correlations are found between measures of *objective* conflict and of experienced ambiguity. It appears that conflict and ambiguity are independent sources of stress; either or both of them may be present in any given role. Table 2 presents a fourfold comparison of the effects of conflict and ambiguity on tension. It is apparent that the presence of either one is tension producing, and in about the same degree. The highest level of tension occurs under the combined conditions of high conflict and high ambiguity, although the combination is not significantly more stressful than either one alone.

INTERPERSONAL CONSEQUENCES OF AMBIGUITY

Role conflicts are generally stressful, producing tension and dissatisfaction. Commonly this leads to such coping behaviors as rejection of or withdrawal from those role senders who are producing the stress, thereby weakening further such affective interpersonal bonds as trust, respect, and liking. Ambiguity in various aspects of occupational role is similarly distressing—the emotional costs of role ambiguity are much like those of role conflict. The question now becomes: Are the techniques used for coping with ambiguity the same as those used for conflict, and are they equally detrimental to interpersonal relationships?

Evidence relevant to this question is found in Table 3. Three general implications are particularly worth noting. First, it is difficult to maintain close bonds with associates when confronted with an ambiguous environment. This is especially true for feelings of trust in others. Just as one loses confidence in self with increasing uncertainty (see Table 1d), he loses confidence in the cooperativeness and good intentions of others as well (Table 3a). Ambiguity has a somewhat less pronounced influence on respect and apparently none on liking for others in the work situation.

Second, not all areas of ambiguity are equally relevant to interpersonal relations. Ambiguity about role expectations held by others and directed toward the self is stressful and tends to undermine trust, but is not related to interpersonal attraction. However, uncertainty about the way one is evaluated by his associates—how satisfied they are with his behavior—is significantly related to trust, respect, and liking. The socioemotional flavor of ambiguity about interpersonal evaluations makes it a source of emotional strain and a deterrent to close, supportive social relations.

Third, a severe reduction in communication is more evident when the stress stems from conflicting role pressures than when it involves ambiguity; the correlations in Table 3d are modest compared to the strong findings on the effects of conflict on communication. This difference is of considerable theoretical significance. Reduction in the frequency of communication is interpreted as a defensive withdrawal from a stressful situation. If the stress is created by role conflict—by attempts of others to change one's behavior—a withdrawal from those others may be an effective way of reducing the stress at least temporarily. Evasive tactics may help us temporarily to avoid the pains induced by others. Social withdrawal may not be desirable coping procedure from the organizational view, but it is nevertheless reinforced in conflict situations.

In ambiguous situations, which also produce emotional strain, there is no doubt a similar tendency to withdraw. In this case, however, withdrawal is self-defeating immediately as well as in the long run. Ambiguity is after all lack of in-

TABLE 2 *The Effects of Conflict and Ambiguity on Tension* (from the intensive study)*

DEGREE OF EXPERIENCED AMBIGUITY	DEGREE OF ROLE CONFLICT		
	High	Low	p
High	5.3	5.0	n.s.
	(15)	(9)	
Low	4.9	3.4	<0.05
	(12)	(16)	
p	n.s.	<0.05	

* *p*-values based on *t*-tests between means. Figure in parentheses below each mean is the *N* upon which the mean is based.

TABLE 3 *Correlations between Measures of Experienced Ambiguity and Various Dimensions of Interpersonal Relations (from the intensive study, N = 53)*

INTERPERSONAL VARIABLE	EXPERIENCED AMBIGUITY MEASURES		
	Ambiguity Index	Role Expectations	Evaluations
a. Trust in senders	−.38†	−.32*	−.42†
b. Respect for senders	−.24	−.17	−.29*
c. Liking for senders	.02	.23	−.30*
d. Communication frequency	−.10	−.14	−.26

* *p* < 0.05.   † *p* < 0.01.

formation, and withdrawal reduces still further the opportunity to acquire information. A far more effective technique for coping with ambiguity would be to increase the frequency of communication with others in the situation, to engage them as information gatherers and providers. Many people in organizations use just this method. If they are unclear about what they can do at some time or about what others expect of them, they go and ask; they seek clarity by means of increased communications. Unfortunately, many others do just the reverse, and it is the rare person indeed who continues to seek out information from others if his early efforts have been discouraged. If ambiguity persists in spite of efforts at communication, most people reach a point at which they quit trying, and communication rates deteriorate. At this point the direction of causality may be reversed, with reduced communication generating still greater ambiguity.

Thus the modest correlations in Table 3*d* probably reflect opposing tendencies: the attempt to bring clarity out of ambiguity by means of increased communication, and the attempt to avoid tension by withdrawing from a stressful situation. The second of these responses seems to be more typical when the ambiguity centers around evaluations by others. Under this condition there is

FIGURE 2. The receipt of negative evaluation as a problem in cognitive balance.

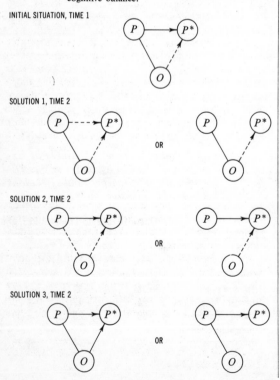

INITIAL SITUATION, TIME 1

SOLUTION 1, TIME 2

OR

SOLUTION 2, TIME 2

OR

SOLUTION 3, TIME 2

OR

more evidence of withdrawal than of active seeking for information about how satisfied others are with one's behavior. This may be true because it is often both embarrassing and dangerous to inquire about how well one is doing—embarrassing because in our culture at least it is "unmanly" to appear too concerned about how well liked and esteemed one is, and dangerous because of the consequent loss in self-esteem upon learning that in fact others think very little of you. For some people it is easier to fear the worst than to know the worst about oneself.

The question then becomes: Does ambiguity about others' satisfaction with oneself really imply some state of dissatisfaction on their part? Do those who withhold evaluative information in fact perceive the focal person negatively? There are good reasons for thinking that they might. Perceptions of one's associates are not easily communicated nor are such communications easily received, especially if they contain unfavorable elements. For reasons of etiquette, if nothing else, the more negative people's attitudes toward each other, the less evaluative feedback takes place.

Even if unfavorable evaluations are expressed, they may not be "heard." The experienced ambiguity may reflect a defensive distortion of signals which are clearly sent. Such distortions are prevalent partially because of their effectiveness in maintaining self-esteem. We have already seen that ambiguity constitutes a threat to self-esteem, undermining self-confidence (Table 1*d*). But direct reports from others about disliked aspects of the self are even more threatening. Thus a confusion of such messages—a retreat into uncertainty—may be an important defensive maneuver in the service of self-esteem.

There is yet another reason for failing to receive negative evaluations from others. A common response to derogatory comments from others is a hostile counterattack. But aggression, no matter how well founded in righteous indignation, is so destructive to fruitful collaborative relations that it must often be suppressed in situations of continued interdependence. When people must work closely together, as is typical in industrial organizations, there is good reason to expect derogatory feedback to be suppressed both at the source (by those holding the unfavorable evaluations) and at the point of reception (by those who would be offended by them).

The problem becomes clear when the situation is expressed in terms of the theory of cognitive balance.[4] Figure 2 represents a person, *P*, another person, *O*, and *P*'s self-image, *P**. At the outset, we assume *P* would like to see himself in a favorable light, indicated by the solid line from *P* to *P**. Given that *P* and *O* must maintain a positive work relationship (the *P-O* line), if *O* does not share this favorable view (dotted line from *O* to *P**),

[4] Cartwright, D., & Harary, F. Structural balance: a generalization of Heider's theory. *Psychol. Rev.*, 1956, **63**, 277–293.

the situation is potentially unbalanced. The balance can be restored in any of three ways: (*1*) the *P-P** connection can be changed to negative (*P* loses self-esteem) or eliminated (as in isolation or projection defenses); (*2*) the *P-O* bond can be changed to negative (*P* becomes hostile toward *O*) or eliminated (*P* avoids working with *O*); and (*3*) the *O-P** line can be changed to positive (*O* appears to like, respect, approve of *P**) or eliminated (*O*'s evaluation of *P** becomes ambiguous).

The first balancing mechanism—changing attitudes toward the self in a negative way—is very costly to *P*, too costly to use other than as a last resort, and may be pathological in the extreme. The second—deterioration of *P-O* relations—is probably quite common but costly for collaboration. Few organizations can long tolerate overt hostility between persons who are highly interdependent. The third alternative—distortion of *O*'s evaluation of *P**—is perhaps the most economical for all the participants. From the viewpoint of the total system, it may even be functional in maintaining necessary working relations for *O* to withhold unfavorable comment toward *P*, and for *P* to fail to read negative connotations into any comments *O* does make. In some organizations efforts are being directed toward finding constructive ways of giving and receiving critical feedback. The work of the National Training Laboratories provides the outstanding example.

This discussion suggests that unfavorable and often uncommunicated evaluations by associates are experienced by the focal person as ambiguity about how he is evaluated. There is indeed quantitative evidence in support of this conclusion. Role senders' perceptions of the focal person are summarized in five Public Image factor scores, based on their ratings of him on a series of 22 trait-descriptive adjectives. Four of the five Public Image factors are significantly correlated with ambiguity about others' evaluations. The more the associates of the focal person see him as emotionally unstable, as lacking assertive self-confidence, as being unbusinesslike or unsociable, the

more uncertain he is about how satisfied they are with him.

SUMMARY

Like role conflict, then, role ambiguity emerges as a prevalent condition in organizational life. Among its probable sources are the growing complexity of organizations, the rapid pace of technological change in our society, and the pervasiveness of certain managerial practices that deliberately foster ambiguity.

In an absolute sense role ambiguity exists when the information available to a person is less than is required for adequate performance of his role. Two types of ambiguity may be distinguished in terms of the focus of the individual's feelings of uncertainty. The first results from lack of information concerning the proper definition of the job, its goals and the permissible means for implementing them. This type of ambiguity concerns the *tasks* the individual is expected to perform, in contrast to a second set of concerns relating to the *socioemotional* aspects of his role performance. This second kind of ambiguity manifests itself in a person's concern about his standing in the eyes of others and about the consequences of his actions for the attainment of his personal goals.

Both kinds of ambiguity are associated with increased tension and reduced trust in associates. But whereas task ambiguity tends to create dissatisfaction with the job and feelings of futility, ambiguity about one's evaluation by others appears to undermine both the individual's relations with them and his self-confidence.

On the whole the effects of ambiguity resemble those of role conflict. These two conditions nevertheless occur independently of each other. Thus it is largely by chance that a person may find himself in a work environment that is both ambiguous and conflictful. When this occurs, however, he tends to suffer strains not significantly more severe than those evoked by either conflict or ambiguity alone.

SOME VARIABLES IN ROLE CONFLICT ANALYSIS *

The welter of expectations associated with the many positions a person occupies in his relations with others inevitably include conflicting demands. Yet he experiences much less strain than might be expected from an examination of such inconsistencies in the social structure. In the theoretical essay which follows Toby suggests a number of mechanisms that operate in social situations to provide smooth and socially accepted solutions to dilemmas posed by role conflict. Where these do not operate, he describes a variety of ways in which the individual may react under the pressure of the strain induced by being subject to conflicting expectations.

The reader should also bear in mind the point made by Toby in the beginning of his essay that over a period of time role strain generates change in role expectations so that inconsistencies are eradicated. As such, role strain becomes a source of social change.

---

* The selection following the editorial introduction is reprinted from "Some variables in role conflict analysis," *Social Forces,* 1952, **30**, 323–327, by permission of the author and University of North Carolina Press.

41.

Some Variables in Role Conflict Analysis[1]

JACKSON TOBY
RUTGERS UNIVERSITY

Social roles are the institutionally proper ways for an individual to participate in his society and thus satisfy his needs and wants. But roles are also *demands* upon the individual, norms which prescribe certain acts and forbid others. These demands come from the various groups in which the individual holds membership: his family, peer group, social class, occupational group, and so on. Usually the individual's role in one group is quite distinct from his role in another group. A man can be both a *father* and a *factory worker* at the same time. But sometimes role obligations are difficult to reconcile. Thus, the non-com is subject to one set of pressures from commissioned officers in authority over him and to another from his fellow enlisted men. Such competing obligations have been labeled "role conflicts," and several studies exist of verbal responses to hypothetical role conflict situations.[2]

It is obvious that an individual in a role conflict situation is uncomfortable. For him, the crossfire of competing claims is an obnoxious problem to be solved as quickly as possible. From society's point of view, however, role conflicts may be useful; they often give a social system flexibility by providing an entering wedge for social change. For example, Gunnar Myrdal points out that white Americans face a role conflict over the status of Negroes.[3] The subordinate status of Negroes has a certain traditional legitimacy. But this inferiority of status, ascribed on a racial basis, is not compatible with the American creed, with the norms by which we define the role of a human being in a democratic state. Hence white Americans are inhibited in their tendency to "keep the Negro in his place" because of their conflicting role of

democrat.[4] Therefore, Myrdal predicts the gradual deinstitutionalization of the ascribed inferior status for Negroes.

Valuable as role conflict may be as an initiator of necessary change, it is not entirely desirable from the viewpoint of the social system either. For, after all, a social system must make provisions for stability as well as for progress. Some control over incompatible claims must exist in every society—lest available motivation be channeled into internal tensions instead of into the maintenance of the social structure. If a social system is too flexible, stable expectations cannot exist, and anomie results. Hence, even in a society as dynamic as ours, mechanisms must exist to provide minimum control over role conflicts. These mechanisms are institutionalized. They serve to prevent inevitable strains from developing into disruptive intra-society conflicts. The following are a few of the more obvious integrative mechanisms of American society:

HIERARCHIES OF ROLE OBLIGATIONS

Role conflicts resemble a jurisdictional dispute between two unions in that both the groups defining the roles of the individual insist that their claim is the legitimate one. Further, just as jurisdictional disputes are exceptional enough in union activity to be newsworthy, so role conflicts are unusual in that they represent situations where the institutionalized system of priorities have proved insufficient to avert friction. To illustrate the ordinary operation of this system of priorities, consider the following question we posed to Harvard undergraduates:

> Imagine that your mother is en route to Cambridge and has sent a wire asking you to meet her train at South Station at 9 p.m. Suppose you have a seminar meeting from 8 to 10 that evening, and you have been scheduled to deliver a paper. You have no way of leaving a message for your mother at the station and no friend who can meet her for you. What would you probably do?

The students questioned were unanimous in saying that they would attend the seminar and explain to their mother later why they were unable to meet her. When pressed further, they usually added that they were sure that their mother would consider the presentation of a seminar paper more important than meeting her train. One respondent went so far as to say that his mother

[1] In the course of empirical studies of role conflict directed by Professor Samuel A. Stouffer and financed by an Air Force contract, the theoretical formulations embodied in this paper were developed. Since the basic concepts were arrived at in conversations with Professor Stouffer, it is difficult to say where his thoughts leave off and those of the writer begin.

[2] Samuel A. Stouffer, "An Analysis of Conflicting Social Norms," *American Sociological Review*, 14 (1949), pp. 707–717.

Samuel A. Stouffer and Jackson Toby, "Role Conflicts and Personality," *American Journal of Sociology*, 16 (1951), pp. 395–406.

[3] Gunnar Myrdal, *An American Dilemma* (New York: Harper & Brothers, 1944).

[4] Myrdal also considers a role conflict of Negro Americans: Shall they accept a subservient position in the hopes of largesse from the dominant majority? Or should they protest the denial of their democratic rights at the risk of greater hostility and further deprivations?

would have expected him to attend the seminar and would have been angry if he had cut the seminar to meet her train.

Similarly, a death in the immediate family is recognized as compelling reason for not appearing at one's place of business; kinship obligations have so clear a priority under such circumstances that a person who fulfilled his occupational obligations instead of staying home with his family would probably be regarded as peculiar by his fellow workers. In other words, institutionalization is more specific than the mere cataloguing of an individual's rights and obligations vis-a-vis other individuals and groups. Rights and obligations are defined *relative* to one another. The applicability of a claim depends in part upon the absence of other legitimate claims. Thus, the "excuse" is a highly important sociological category. *It is an approved technique for avoiding sanctions by asserting that an equally high or higher claim prevented the individual from fulfilling his obligations.* Excuses are most prevalent in informal interpersonal relations, but even the law recognizes their validity. For example, the obligation to respect human life is violated whenever one person kills another. But, under circumstances where the "excuse" of self-defense can be established, penalties are waived.

THE ACCIDENT

Another kind of legitimate non-compliance, a cousin of the "excuse," is the claim of the actor that his failure to fulfill his obligations is involuntary. No higher claims are invoked, but the actor escapes sanctions by demonstrating that circumstances beyond his control prevented him from carrying out his good intentions. For example, a bomber crew may not complete its combat mission because of engine trouble. Of course, only if the individual's failure to fulfill his obligations is regarded as involuntary will he remain in good standing with the group. Quite obviously, some claims of "accident" are fabricated for the purpose of avoiding penalties. Hence group skepticism is necessary to check abuses. (In the case of motorcycle policemen, skepticism verges on utter disbelief.) Even though the group is not in a position to investigate whether the accident really happened, a rough calculation of probabilities can usually be made. An individual can blame his tardiness on the public transportation system occasionally, but not daily.

RITUALS FOR REDUCING SOCIAL FRICTION: ETIQUETTE

Emily Post is sometimes ridiculed by people who pride themselves on being rational. They naively suppose that etiquette consists of meaningless ceremonials, for they do not realize the importance of prescribed rituals in solving the dilemmas of

daily life. Consider the chaos of competing demands for social recognition which would ensue if etiquette did not exist. Etiquette formalizes the rank order of claims for deference, thus avoiding in most cases the problem of deciding between one individual's right to attention and another's. The very arbitrariness of the ritual takes the problem out of the realm of idiosyncratic judgment; precedence is automatically evaluated according to the institutionalized criteria. Less specific than etiquette but analogous in function are rules of social intercourse like "first come, first served."

In the play of small children we see what happens before etiquette is institutionalized. Tom steps on Dick's foot. Dick pushes him off with a vigorous shove. "You don't need to push that hard," says Tom, pushing him back. And the fight is on. After they have beaten one another up and gone home in tears, a parent may feel called upon to heal the breach. Observe what he does. Instead of insisting that Tom was wrong and should be ashamed of himself (or that Dick should not have started the pushing), the peace-maker ignores the question of fault and seeks to induce the boys to apologize *mutually and to shake hands.*

With adults there is less likelihood for essentially trivial issues to produce conflict. The automatic apology of two strangers who accidentally collide on a busy street illustrates the integrative function of etiquette. In effect, each of the parties to the collision says, "I don't know whether I am responsible for this situation, but *if* I am, you have a right to be angry with me, a right that I pray you will not exercise." By defining the situation as one in which both parties must abase themselves, society enables each to keep his self-respect. Each may feel in his heart of hearts, "Why can't that stupid ass watch where he's going?" But overtly each *plays the role of the guilty party* whether he feels he has been miscast or not.

LEGITIMATE DECEPTION: TACT

Lies are generally regarded as reprehensible, and truth is held to be a virtue. But there are certain circumstances—held to be exceptional—where it is considered "tactless" to tell the truth, where the "white lie" is regarded as the proper response. Consider an example of such circumstances: Tom invites Mary to go to dinner with him on a certain evening. Mary does not like Tom, so she refuses the invitation, fabricating a previous appointment as the reason for not accepting his invitation. She may or may not deceive him. If she has on another occasion rejected a proposed "date," he may recognize that the "previous appointment" may have been her way of indicating that she does not care for his company. But Tom has no right to become indignant, for Mary has been *tactful*. True, she refused the invitation, which was an injury, especially if he suspects the motive for her refusal. But she does not add insult to injury by explaining it.

This solicitude for the feelings of others is the circumstance that makes the white lie socially "right." The ordinary lie is unreservedly disapproved because it lacks precisely this quality. It is a selfish attempt to manipulate other people by controlling their access to information. Tact, on the other hand, is institutionalized deception for the primary purpose of sparing the feelings of others. Mary did not lie to Tom because she feared losing a friend if she did not consider his feelings. Tactful behavior is a social obligation of adults. We are trained to avoid hurting one another because otherwise it would be too difficult to control the aggressions and hostilities at large in the system.[5]

SEGREGATION OF ROLES

Another important device for preventing role conflicts is the definition of roles so that attendant circumstances have to be appropriate in order to activate the role behavior in question. For example, the personnel director of a corporation has a role obligation to hire the best qualified people; he also has obligations to his family. But if his daughter were looking for a job and did not have the qualifications for any that were open, no one would accuse him of failing in his father role because he did not hire her. In our society the occupational and the familial roles are *defined* as segregated. Nepotism, though it occurs, is regarded as a fault rather than a virtue.

The fact that the same person is properly treated differently when he occupies different roles is of incalculable importance in clarifying the limits of obligations. An Air Force major who is in command of a fighter squadron is entitled to one kind of treatment from a pilot in his squadron because he is a major and quite different treatment because he is the Commanding Officer. And it may be important to understand when the major is occupying one role, when the other, and when he occupies neither. At the Officers Club, for instance, it may be appropriate to regard him in the role of friend. Interestingly enough, officers frequently dress in civilian clothes at their clubs, perhaps because this has functional significance

for the segregation of military roles from the roles appropriate to convivial interaction.

In spite of these various mechanisms to prevent incipient conflicts from developing, individuals do find themselves in situations where two or more groups make incompatible demands upon them. This is due in part to the imperfect integration of all social systems; if the integrative mechanism functioned perfectly, *true* role conflicts would be impossible. By true role conflicts, we refer to situations where the claims of the two groups are institutionally defined as legitimate, but where there exists no institutionalized formula for making the demands compatible. However, pseudo-role conflicts arise even where true role conflicts are impossible, and these appear very much like the genuine article to the individuals involved. By pseudo-role conflicts, we refer to situations where the claims of the two groups are institutionally defined as legitimate but where a skillful individual might have prevented the conflict from arising.[6] For example, the anguish resulting from appointments at two widely removed places at the same time is potentially avoidable. Nevertheless, whether an individual is caught in a true or a pseudo-role conflict, there are only a limited number of alternatives open to him:

Repudiation of his role in one group. The individual gets out of the dilemma but in a manner analogous to Alexander's cutting of the Gordian knot. Complete repudiation of role obligations is a drastic solution, inviting sanctions from the group which is defied. Depending on the group's importance to him—his identification with it and the severity of the sanctions it is likely to impose—he may be unable to face the consequences of defiance. A sergeant whose commanding officer instructs him to enforce an unpopular regulation may not be willing either to disobey his superior or to outrage the sentiments of his men. Other sergeants might be willing to enforce the regulation, no matter how their men griped. Still others might refuse to carry out the order.

Playing off one group against the other. The individual achieves a precarious equilibrium by indicating to each group the incompatible demands simultaneously being made upon him by the other. In this way he induces each group to mitigate its demands sufficiently so that his role obligations are compatible. A union official might be under pressure from union members to press for a substantial wage increase and under pressure from the Federal Government to hold the line against inflation. If he could convince the rank and file that the national welfare permitted only a small wage increase and the appropriate federal agency that a token wage boost was necessary to avert a wildcat strike, the problem would be solved. There

---

[5] Children seem to have much more overt conflict than adults, i.e., arguments as well as physical aggressions. Perhaps this difference can be explained as due in part to a difference in the employment of tact. It would be interesting to experiment with children and see whether lessons in tact could diminish intragroup friction.

[6] This notion of variability in skill at avoiding pseudo-role conflicts was suggested by Professor Talcott Parsons.

is a certain similarity between this technique of re-solving a role conflict and the invoking of institutionalized priorities to prevent the conflict from arising. But an important difference should be noted. The individual who plays off one group against another does not have institutionalized backing for his compromise. It is by dint of his personal skill in negotiation and his ability to communicate his plight and invoke sympathy that he solves the problem.

Stalling until the pressures subside. If the cross-pressures are of a *temporary* nature, it may be possible for the individual to postpone making a decision until one or both of the groups relax their demands. Stalling is, however, not passive waiting; it is an art. It involves placating and promising while the competing obligations are not being fulfilled. A role conflict amenable to such a tactic occurs when a woman comes to visit her son and daughter-in-law, and the two women resent one another. The son might stall until his mother's visit is over, thus avoiding a fight with either his wife or his mother.

Redefinition of the role (or roles). The individual reacts upon the situation and changes it so that the role expectations are no longer incompatible. For example, the daughter of immigrant parents may be able to redefine her role in the family according to American patterns, thus resolving the conflicting claims of her parents and her girl friends. Of course the opportunities for reeducating a group are comparatively infrequent. More often, a different type of redefinition of role is possible. The individual does not change the role requirements of the group, but he finds a formula whereby his behavior can, by Procrustean efforts, be defined as fulfilling the requirements. For example, suppose that the parents of an adolescent boy forbid him to drink intoxicating beverages, whereas his friends drink a good deal and bring pressure upon him to join them. He might solve this role conflict by drinking beer—if he could convince his parents that "beer isn't liquor" and his friends that beer is a manly and highly satisfactory "drink."

The double life. The individual takes advantage of the fact that he is not simultaneously in contact with both groups. He plays the approved role in each group, ignoring its expectations when in contact with the other. Deception is a vital element in this solution, and thus it is limited to circumstances where deception is possible. Moreover, this sort of deception, unlike the white lie, is entirely self-oriented and would be recognized as such by others—if they found out about it. It is not always necessary to practice *double* deception. That is to say, one of the groups might have no objection to the individual's playing a different role when not in contact with it. A nudist colony would, for example, probably approve of its members wearing clothes "on the outside." But nudists might still have to keep their membership in the colony secret.

Escape from the field. The individual may find his position in the cross-fire so unpleasant that he moves to a different social system. Of course this does not necessarily imply geographic mobility, although that is the most common device. A foreman under pressure both from his superiors in the company and from the shop steward of the union may resign his job. Escape from the field, through similar to role repudiation, involves retirement from *both* groups and withdrawal from the effective range of their sanctions. Suicide would be the limiting case.

Illness. If the pressures become unbearable and the individual does not perceive as appropriate to his problem any of the above mentioned devices, he may become prey to mental or physical illness. Illness is an excuse for failing to conform to role expectations, an excuse which has general acceptability. Thus, we might call this a solution to the conflict. On the other hand, it may simply signify the breakdown of the coping mechanisms of the organism under the pressure of the problem.

To sum up: Institutionalized techniques exist for preventing role conflicts from arising. These are not perfect, however, and role conflicts arise. But there are only a limited number of possible solutions to these dilemmas. The problem for research is the conditions under which one solution is chosen over another.

EXPLORATIONS IN ROLE ANALYSIS *

The following selection is drawn from a work which has had a crucial part in the development of re-search in this area. In their longer work, the authors, Gross, Mason, and McEachern, reviewed the empirical and theoretical research on role strain and drew together a set of conceptual tools for role analysis that is widely employed today. Focusing on the role of the school superintendent and his relation to school boards, they carried out a

* The selection following the editorial introduction is excerpted from *Explorations in Role Analysis*, New York: John Wiley & Sons, 1958, pp. 281–318, by permission of the authors and the publisher.

series of analyses designed to assess the nature of role consensus and to reveal some of its determinants, to study the extent of conformity to role expectations, and to develop and test a theory of role conflict resolution. The latter is the subject of the portion of the study reproduced here.

Their account of the development of their role conflict theory illustrates the cumulative character of scientific inquiry. A number of elements were suggested by previous lines of research. The variable of legitimacy or illegitimacy of role expectations was emphasized in a study by Getzels and Guba[a] of conflict between the role of teacher and military officer in a military staff school. They pointed out that the teacher role is subordinate to that of military officer. The first obligation of the instructors was to those legitimate expectations that stemmed from the fact that they were officers in a military organization. The importance of individual predispositions was highlighted by a series of studies beginning with the work of Stouffer and Toby.[b] These two investigators found that individuals confronted with a series of situations involving conflict between a particularistic obligation—an obligation to a friend—and a universalistic obligation—toward society—tended to favor either one type or the other.

Gross, Mason, and McEachern develop their theory in terms of the legitimacy or illegitimacy of an expectation, and the extent to which sanctions—a form of punishment—are apt to be applied for not conforming to the expectation. By assuming that an individual has a certain orientation toward legitimacy and toward sanctions, they are able to predict how he might react in a role situation involving conflicting expectations that are classifiable in terms of legitimacy and sanctions. For example, an individual clearly oriented toward legitimacy who is less concerned about sanctions would easily resolve a conflict between two expectations that both involve sanctions but which differ in legitimacy—he would choose the more legitimate one. By combining in a single theory these several variables from earlier studies, Gross, Mason, and McEachern show how the successive addition of variables increases the predictive power of a theory.

Subsequent applications of this theory[c] suggest that these theoretical variables may not account for as much of the variance in conflict resolution

[a] J. W. Getzels & E. G. Guba. Role, role conflict, and effectiveness. *Amer. sociol. Rev.*, 1954, **19**, 164–175.

[b] S. A. Stouffer & J. Toby. Role conflict and personality. *Amer. J. Sociol.*, 1951, **56**, 395–406.

[c] F. A. Shull, Jr., & D. C. Miller. Role-conflict behavior in administration: A study in the validation of a theory of role-conflict resolution. Paper read at Amer. Sociol. Ass., New York, August, 1960. J. Ehrlich, J. W. Rinehart, & C. Howell. The study of role conflict: Explorations in methodology. *Sociometry*, 1962, **25**, 85–97.

in role groups other than school superintendents and boards. Nevertheless, Gross and his colleagues appear to have isolated important variables in the process of role conflict resolution.

42.

A Theory of Role Conflict Resolution

NEAL GROSS
HARVARD UNIVERSITY

WARD S. MASON
U.S. AGENCY FOR INTERNATIONAL DEVELOPMENT, SAN SALVADOR

ALEXANDER W. McEACHERN
UNIVERSITY OF SOUTHERN CALIFORNIA

We have shown that when confronted with role conflict position incumbents adopt different resolution techniques. The question for which the theory to be presented and tested in this chapter attempts to provide an answer is why people adopt different resolutions. A number of suggestive explanations of these differences may be taken from the literature.

Parsons, for example, in his brief treatment of the resolution of role conflict, says that:

> . . . differences have to be adjusted by an ordering or allocation of the claims of the different role expectations to which the actor is subject. This ordering occurs by priority scales, by occasion, e.g., time and place, and by distribution among alters. . . .[1]

Toby has suggested, "Institutionalized techniques exist for preventing role conflicts from arising."[2] These include role obligation hierarchies (excuses), an actor's claim that his lack of fulfillment of an obligation is involuntary (unavoidable "accidents"), etiquette rituals, and "legitimate" deception like the white lie. When these techniques cannot be used Toby suggests that an actor has only a limited number of alternatives available to him. These include repudiation of his role in one group, playing off one group against the other, stalling, redefinition of the role (or roles), the "double life," escape from the field, and illness. He concludes his paper with the observation that "The problem for research is the conditions under which one solution is chosen over another."[3]

Getzels and Guba have suggested that the analysis "of the effective handling of role conflict might well be pushed forward within the three concepts involved in these conditions: the choice of major role, the congruence of needs and expectations, and the legitimacy of expectations

[1] Talcott Parsons, *The Social System* (Glencoe: The Free Press, 1951), p. 280.

[2] Jackson Toby, "Some Variables in Role Conflict Analysis," *Social Forces*, XXX (1952), p. 327.

[3] *Ibid.*, p. 327.

within the situation."[4] A major role is the one to which the actor commits himself at the point of decision-making in a role conflict. They view the decision as a function of (1) the role "that is most compatible with his needs" (congruence of needs and expectations), and (2) the legitimacy of the expectations: "If the individual chooses as his major role the one that is also the legitimate role in the situation he is less likely to be affected by conflicts or the threat of sanctions than when he chooses some alternate role."[5]

Stouffer and Toby investigated the relationship between a personality dimension and the resolution of "role conflict." They asked college students to say what their behavior would be when exposed to a series of hypothetical situations in which they had to select between two conflicting obligations. The choice in each case was between an obligation to a friend and one to society. Their study showed that the students could be classified on a unidimensional scale according to their tendencies to resolve dilemmas in a universalistic or particularistic way, and they say, ". . . (that) the results encourage one to believe that we can develop good measures of individual predisposition to a bias in a universalistic or particularistic direction."[6]

The preceding study stimulated Mishler to investigate the hypothesis that a particularistic role orientation is positively related to the characteristics of the authoritarian personality. Whereas Stouffer and Toby viewed one's role orientation as a personality bias, Mishler viewed it as a kind of behavior to which he related personality measures. He concluded that,

> The present study has shown that tendencies towards engaging in the same social behavior may be found within a number of different personality structures. . . . Two types of particularistic persons were found. One is oriented towards satisfaction and security in *internal* goals and is *cynical* about other persons. The second is oriented toward satisfaction and security in *external* goals and is *rebellious* against authority and social rules. Correspondingly two types of universalistic persons were found. One is *internally* oriented and has a *benign* attitude toward others. The other is *externally* oriented and *conforms* to authority and social rules.[7]

These previous formulations suggest certain strategic variables that deserve consideration in an attempt to formulate a theory of role conflict resolution. Getzels and Guba stress that the legitimacy of expectations and the congruency between personalistic needs and expectations may be the crucial dimensions affecting the resolution of the dilemma, that is, which role is selected as the major one. The empirical findings of Stouffer and Toby suggest the advisability of focusing attention on the actor's *predisposition* to behave in certain ways when faced with a role conflict. In the role conflict situations studied some actors tended to have a particularistic while others had a universalistic orientation to the situation. It is of further interest that Mishler's findings indicated that individuals with different types of personality structures tended to resolve the role conflicts in similar ways. This, of course, still leaves open the question of the conditions under which actors with different personality structures act in similar and in different ways.

It is worthy of comment that these prior formulations have directed little explicit consideration to the dimension of sanctions as a factor that may have an important bearing on the resolution of role conflict. Although the dimension of sanctions is central to Stouffer's basic formulation of role conflict,[8] it does not enter into the Stouffer-Toby analyses of the resolution of role conflict. In the Getzels-Guba approach to the problem it does not enter as a central variable. We shall try to give it a more strategic position in our theoretical approach to the resolution of role conflict.

Although each of these students of role conflict analysis is aware that in addition to conforming to one role or another, there are other possibilities of resolving the role conflict, their theoretical approaches to the problem are based on an actor's conforming to one or the other of the incompatible expectations or choosing one or the other of the roles. Little or no theoretical consideration is given in these formulations to the conditions under which an actor will engage in a compromise or avoidance behavior. For example, Getzels and Guba say:

> Theoretically, an individual in a role conflict situation may resolve the conflict—always omitting the possibility of changing the situation or withdrawing from it entirely—either by compromise or exclusion. He may attempt to stand midway between the conflicting roles, giving equal due to both roles, shifting from one to another as

[4] J. W. Getzels and E. G. Guba, "Role, Role Conflict and Effectiveness," *American Sociological Review*, XIX (1954), p. 175.

[5] *Ibid.*, p. 174.

[6] Samuel A. Stouffer and Jackson Toby, "Role Conflict and Personality," *American Journal of Sociology*, LVI (1951), p. 400.

[7] Elliot G. Mishler, "Personality Characteristics and the Resolution of Role Conflicts," *Public Opinion Quarterly*, XVII (1953), pp. 134–135.

[8] Samuel A. Stouffer, "An Analysis of Conflicting Social Norms," *American Sociological Review*, XIV (1949), pp. 707–717.

he believes the occasion demands, or he may choose one role as his significant frame of reference and assimilate all other roles in the situation to it. In actual practice it would seem that the situation at Air University—and one may well wonder whether this is not general to most situations—establishes the latter alternative as the one more likely to find acceptance. There seems to be a *major role* to which one must commit himself in order to determine his action at choice points, despite contrary expectations attaching to other roles he may simultaneously occupy.[9]

A major limitation of this *conclusion* is that it discards too easily other alternatives available to an actor in a role conflict situation. It precludes consideration of compromise and avoidance behaviors. Another characteristic of this formulation deserves emphasis. The Getzels-Guba approach assumes that role conflicts occur only when an actor simultaneously occupies multiple positions to which are attached conflicting expectations. It is not surprising then that the theory focuses on the factors involved in an actor's selecting one position as the major position.

For our purposes such a formulation is distinctly limited. This is the case because it will be recalled that we have recognized that an actor may be exposed to role conflict as a consequence of his occupancy of a single position (intrarole conflict). For example, teachers and school board members may be perceived as holding conflicting expectations for their superintendent, *as a superintendent*. A theory which requires that an actor choose a major position (or role) is of no utility for understanding intrarole conflict resolution.

In addition, the theoretical scheme we require must yield predictions from among four alternatives an actor may choose in resolving a role conflict. When an actor perceives his exposure to a role conflict situation in which there are two incompatible expectations, A and B, there are four alternative behaviors available by means of which he can resolve the conflict, in the sense of making a decision. The actor may: (*1*) conform to expectation A, (*2*) conform to expectation B, (*3*) perform some *compromise* behavior which represents an attempt to conform in part to both expectations, or (*4*) attempt to *avoid* conforming to either of the expectations.

For example, a superintendent could conform to the expectation held by his teachers that as their superintendent he should attempt to secure the highest possible increases in salary for them. On the other hand he could conform to the expectation held by his school board that he should try to minimize the salary increases for teachers. Or alternatively, he could compromise by attempting to negotiate a salary increase that would represent less than the teachers demanded and more than his school board originally wanted to give Or finally, he could remove himself from the situation by taking the position that the school board should negotiate with the teachers directly, removing himself from his intermediate position between them in the social hierarchy of the school system. A theory of role conflict resolution must therefore provide a basis on which to make predictions concerning which of these four alternative resolutions an actor will adopt.

The starting point for this exploratory effort to develop such a theory is the actor's definition of the role conflict situation according to two elements, legitimacy and sanctions. The first is his feeling about the legitimacy or illegitimacy of each of the incompatible expectations that he perceives is held for him in the situation. The second is his perception of the sanctions to which he will be exposed for nonconformity to each of the incompatible expectations. A third element of the theory, his orientation to legitimacy and sanctions, will be introduced later. For the moment our concern will be with how the legitimacy and sanctions dimensions can affect decision-making. First, we shall examine the possible influence of each of these elements singly, and then how they operate in combination.

The legitimacy dimension. We shall assume that actors are predisposed to conform to expectations they perceive as legitimate, perceived obligations, and are predisposed to avoid conforming to expectations which they perceive as illegitimate, perceived pressures. That is, if an actor feels that an individual or group has a right to expect him to behave in conformity with a given expectation he will be predisposed to conform to it. An individual who defines an expectation held by others for his behavior as illegitimate will be predisposed not to conform to it since failure to grant the other individual a right to expect a particular behavior implies the actor's rejection of his re-

FIGURE 1. Behavior predicted for four types of role conflicts on the basis of the "legitimacy assumption." * Legitimacy abbreviations: L = expectation perceived as legitimate; I = expectation perceived as illegitimate. † Behavior abbreviations: a = conformity to expectation A; b = conformity to expectation B; c = compromise; d = avoidance.

TYPE	1		2		3		4	
EXPECTATION	A	B	A	B	A	B	A	B
LEGITIMACY *	L	L	L	I	I	L	I	I
BEHAVIOR †	c		a		b		d	

[9] Getzels and Guba, *op. cit.*, pp. 173–174.

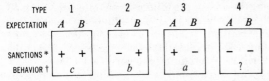

FIGURE 2. Behavior predicted for four types of role conflicts on the basis of the "sanctions assumption." * Sanctions abbreviations: + = strong negative sanctions applied for nonconformity to the expectation; − = strong negative sanctions not applied for nonconformity to the expectation. † Behavior abbreviations: a = conformity to expectation A; b = conformity to expectation B; c = compromise; d = avoidance; ? = no prediction possible.

sponsibility to conform to it. The assumption we have made with respect to the response of position incumbents to "legitimate" expectations is based on the reasoning that failure to conform to an expectation which is perceived as legitimate will result in negative internal sanctions.

If an actor perceives his exposure to two incompatible expectations, A and B, then, using only the criterion of legitimacy there are four possible types into which the situation the actor perceives as confronting him may fall. These are: (1) A and B are both perceived as legitimate; (2) A is perceived as legitimate, and B is perceived as illegitimate; (3) B is perceived as legitimate, and A is perceived as illegitimate; (4) A and B are both perceived as illegitimate.

On the assumption that an actor is predisposed to conform only to legitimate expectations we would make the predictions presented in Figure 1.

In the second and third situations the prediction would be that the actor would conform to the legitimate expectation and reject or ignore the illegitimate one. In the first situation, since the actor desires to conform to both expectations even though they are incompatible, he would try to conform in part to both of them by adopting some form of compromise behavior. In the fourth case, since he considers both expectations illegitimate, he would be predisposed to conform to neither of them and therefore would engage in some type of avoidance behavior.

Given information only about an actor's perceptions of the legitimacy of the incompatible expectations we would emerge with this set of predictions. What would be predicted if we based our reasoning *only* on the sanctions dimension?

The sanctions dimension. We will assume that if an actor perceives that failure to conform to an expectation will result in the application of strong negative sanctions the actor will be predisposed to conform to it. This assumption is based on what Parsons has termed the "gratificational aspect of the need disposition" of the actor.[10] If an actor

---

[10] Parsons, *op. cit.*

wants to maximize gratification from his interactions, he will be predisposed to behave in a manner that will minimize the negative sanctions (or maximize the positive ones) to which he perceives he might be exposed in his interactions. If he feels that nonconformity to an expectation will result in slight or no negative (or positive) sanctions, this element in his perception of the situation will have little or no effect on his behavior.

If an actor is exposed to two incompatible expectations, A and B, and we consider only his perception of the negative sanctions that will be applied by those who hold the A and B expectations for nonconformity to their expectations, and if we catgorize the negative sanctions into strong and weak, we secure the types of situations and predictions about behavior which are presented in Figure 2.

FIGURE 3. Behavior predicted for sixteen types of role conflicts on the basis of the "sanctions" and "legitimacy" assumptions. (The abbreviations used in this figure are as follows: legitimacy abbreviations: L = expectation perceived as legitimate, I = expectation perceived as illegitimate; sanctions abbreviations: + = strong negative sanctions applied for nonconformity to the expectation, − = strong negative sanctions not applied for nonconformity to the expectation; behavior abbreviations: a = conformity expectation A, b = conformity to expectation B, c = compromise, d = avoidance, and ? = no prediction possible.)

TYPE	1		2		3		4	
EXPECTATION	A	B	A	B	A	B	A	B
LEGITIMACY	L	L	L	L	L	L	L	L
SANCTIONS	+	+	−	+	+	−	−	−
BEHAVIOR	c		?		?		c	

TYPE	5		6		7		8	
EXPECTATION	A	B	A	B	A	B	A	B
LEGITIMACY	L	I	L	I	L	I	L	I
SANCTIONS	+	+	−	+	+	−	−	−
BEHAVIOR	?		?		a		a	

TYPE	9		10		11		12	
EXPECTATION	A	B	A	B	A	B	A	B
LEGITIMACY	I	L	I	L	I	L	I	L
SANCTIONS	+	+	−	+	+	−	−	−
BEHAVIOR	?		b		?		b	

TYPE	13		14		15		16	
EXPECTATION	A	B	A	B	A	B	A	B
LEGITIMACY	I	I	I	I	I	I	I	I
SANCTIONS	+	+	−	+	+	−	−	−
BEHAVIOR	?		?		?		d	

In the second and third situations he would conform to the expectation for nonconformity to which he perceived the greater negative sanctions. In the first, since nonconformity to either *A* or *B* would result in heavy negative sanctions he would try to compromise in order to minimize sanctions. Such a decision would, we assume, maximize his gratification from the situation. In the fourth case, we have no basis for prediction because he would not be predisposed to conform to either *A* or *B*.

Although for theoretical purposes we have examined each of the dimensions of legitimacy and sanctions separately, we assume that for any role conflict situation the actor perceives both of these dimensions and takes them into account in his decision-making. What predictions could be made when both the legitimacy and sanctions dimensions are taken into account? The sixteen combinations of the four types of legitimacy and four types of sanctions situations are presented in Figure 3.

On the basis of the assumptions made for the separate effects of the legitimacy and sanctions dimensions we could make predictions for behavior for these cells in Figure 3:

Cell *1*. Compromise behavior, because both dimensions predispose compromise behavior.

Cell *4*. Compromise behavior, because the legitimacy dimension predisposes to a compromise and the sanctions dimension has no effect.

Cell *7*. Conformity to *A*, because both dimensions predispose conformity to *A*.

Cell *8*. Conformity to *A*, because the legitimacy dimension predisposes conformity to *A* and the sanctions dimension has no effect.

Cell *10*. Conformity to *B*, because both dimensions predispose conformity to *B*.

Cell *12*. Conformity to *B* because the legitimacy dimension predisposes conformity to *B* and the sanctions dimension has no effect.

Cell *16*. Avoidance behavior, because the legitimacy dimension predisposes avoidance of both *A* and *B* and the sanctions dimension has no effect.

However, for the other nine cells it is not possible with only these two assumptions to make predictions about behavior. This is the case because (*1*) the legitimacy and sanctions dimensions predispose to conformity to opposite expectations (Cells 6 and 11), (*2*) one dimension predisposes a compromise behavior and the other conformity to one of the expectations (Cells 2, 3, 5, 9), (*3*)

one dimension predisposes avoidance behavior and the other predisposes conformity to one of the expectations (Cells 14 and 15), and (*4*) one dimension predisposes avoidance behavior and the other a compromise behavior (Cell 13).

The two assumptions regarding the impact of legitimacy and sanctions on the resolution of role conflicts are inadequate in combination to provide a basis for predicting how an actor will behave in the majority of the logically possible situations in which they could occur. What is needed is a third element in the theory that will allow us to make predictions concerning how an actor will behave when he is confronted with all possible types of situations, rather than only a part of them.

Two factors were inadequate because assumptions about them provided no basis for predictions when an actor was exposed to a role conflict in which the legitimacy and sanctions elements predisposed him to undertake different behaviors. They provided no logical basis for predicting which of the behaviors he would select. This inadequacy suggests that a theory of role conflict resolution must make use not only of an actor's perceptions of the elements in the situation, but of his predisposition to give primacy to one or the other of them in his decision-making.

The starting point for such a theory is still an actor's definition of a role conflict situation. We assume that actors will have perceptions of the legitimacy or illegitimacy of the expectations of the sanctions to which they will be exposed as a consequence of their nonconformity to each of them. We now introduce the additional assumption that individuals may be differentiated according to their primacy of orientation to the legitimacy or to the sanctions dimensions of the expectations in the situation. We shall posit three types of orientations to expectations, and for each of them we shall present a different set of predictions.

The first type characterizes the person who, when faced with a role conflict, gives primacy to the legitimacy dimension. His definition of the situations places stress on *the right* of others to hold the expectations he perceives they hold for him and de-emphasizes the sanctions he thinks will be applied to him for nonconformity to them. We shall characterize such a person as having a *moral* orientation to expectations. Since his concern is primarily with the legitimacy of the expectations he will be predisposed to behave in a role conflict situation in such a manner that will allow him to fulfill legitimate expectations and to reject illegitimate ones. He will behave according to the predictions presented earlier when we examined the logical consequences of taking only the legitimacy dimension into account in role conflict situations. If one of the incompatible expectations is viewed as legitimate and the other is not, he will be predisposed to conform to the

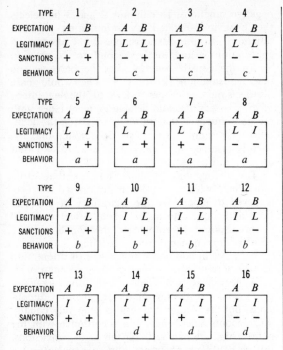

FIGURE 4. Behavior predicted for sixteen types of role conflicts for individuals with a "moral orientation." (The abbreviations used in this figure are as follows: legitimacy abbreviations: L = expectation perceived as legitimate, I = expectation perceived as illegitimate; sanctions abbreviations: + = strong negative sanctions applied for nonconformity to the expectation, − = strong negative sanctions not applied for nonconformity to the expectation; behavior abbreviations: a = conformity to expectation A, b = conformity to expectation B, c = compromise, and d = avoidance.)

legitimate expectation. If both are legitimate he will adopt a compromise behavior in order to conform, at least in part, to both of them. If both are perceived as illegitimate he will be predisposed to conform to neither of them and will adopt in consequence some type of avoidance behavior. In short, for an individual with such an orientation to expectations we can ignore his perceptions of the sanctions dimension in making predictions about his behavior. From his definition of the legitimacy of the expectations we can make predictions about his behavior. Thus, for the sixteen possible situations when the legitimacy and sanctions dimensions are combined we would make the predictions given in Figure 4.

The second type of primacy of orientation to expectations may be described as *expedient*. An individual who has this orientation is one who gives priority to the sanctions over the legitimacy dimension of the expectations perceived as held by others. Such a person is primarily concerned with minimizing the negative sanctions involved in

the role conflict situation. His orientation is based on a desire to be self-protective, to provide the best defense for himself in view of the relative severity of the negative sanctions he feels others will apply to him for nonconformity to their expectations. Whether others have a right to hold certain expectations is irrelevant or of secondary importance to him. Such an individual will be predisposed to behave, when exposed to different types of sanctions situations, in the manner indicated in our earlier consideration of the logical behavioral consequences of taking into account only the sanctions dimension in resolving role conflicts.

When he perceives strong negative sanctions for nonconformity to one expectation and weaker negative sanctions for nonconformity to the other, he will conform to the expectation which would

FIGURE 5. Behavior predicted for sixteen types of role conflicts for individuals with an "expedient orientation." (The abbreviations used in this figure are as follows: legitimacy abbreviations: L = expectation perceived as legitimate, I = expectation perceived as illegitimate; sanctions abbreviations: + = strong negative sanctions applied for nonconformity to the expectation, − = strong negative sanctions not applied for nonconformity to the expectation; behavior abbreviations: a = conformity to expectation A, b = conformity to expectation B, c = compromise, and d = avoidance.)

TYPE	1	2	3	4
EXPECTATION	A B	A B	A B	A B
LEGITIMACY	L L	L L	L L	L L
SANCTIONS	+ +	− +	+ −	− −
BEHAVIOR	c	b	a	c

TYPE	5	6	7	8
EXPECTATION	A B	A B	A B	A B
LEGITIMACY	L I	L I	L I	L I
SANCTIONS	+ +	− +	+ −	− −
BEHAVIOR	c	b	a	a

TYPE	9	10	11	12
EXPECTATION	A B	A B	A B	A B
LEGITIMACY	I L	I L	I L	I L
SANCTIONS	+ +	− +	+ −	− −
BEHAVIOR	c	b	a	b

TYPE	13	14	15	16
EXPECTATION	A B	A B	A B	A B
LEGITIMACY	I I	I I	I I	I I
SANCTIONS	+ +	− +	+ −	− −
BEHAVIOR	c	b	a	d

result in the stronger negative sanctions for non-conformity. If he perceives that equally strong negative sanctions result from both, he will compromise in order to minimize negative sanctions. If he perceives no negative sanctions for nonconformity to either of the expectations, the sanctions dimension will be of no value as a predictor of his behavior. In this instance the other factor in the model, the legitimacy dimension, would remain as the only basis for predicting his behavior. From the sixteen possible situations when the logical possibilities of the legitimacy and sanctions dimensions are combined, for expedients, we would make the predictions presented in Figure 5.

Since all the situations in the first column result in strong negative sanctions for nonconformity to expectations A and B, the actor will compromise in order to minimize both sets of

FIGURE 6. Behavior predicted for sixteen types of role conflicts for individuals with a "moral-expedient" orientation. (The abbreviations used in this figure are as follows: legitimacy abbreviations: L = expectation perceived as legitimate, I = expectation perceived as illegitimate; sanction abbreviations: $+$ = strong negative sanctions applied for nonconformity to the expectation, $-$ = strong negative sanctions not applied for nonconformity to the expectation; behavior abbreviations: a = conformity to expectation A, b = conformity to expectation B, c = compromise, and d = avoidance.)

TYPE	1		2		3		4	
EXPECTATION	A	B	A	B	A	B	A	B
LEGITIMACY	L	L	L	L	L	L	L	L
SANCTIONS	$+$	$+$	$-$	$+$	$+$	$-$	$-$	$-$
BEHAVIOR	c		b		a		c	

TYPE	5		6		7		8	
EXPECTATION	A	B	A	B	A	B	A	B
LEGITIMACY	L	I	L	I	L	I	L	I
SANCTIONS	$+$	$+$	$-$	$+$	$+$	$-$	$-$	$-$
BEHAVIOR	a		c		a		a	

TYPE	9		10		11		12	
EXPECTATION	A	B	A	B	A	B	A	B
LEGITIMACY	I	L	I	L	I	L	I	L
SANCTIONS	$+$	$+$	$-$	$+$	$+$	$-$	$-$	$-$
BEHAVIOR	b		b		c		b	

TYPE	13		14		15		16	
EXPECTATION	A	B	A	B	A	B	A	B
LEGITIMACY	I	I	I	I	I	I	I	I
SANCTIONS	$+$	$+$	$-$	$+$	$+$	$-$	$-$	$-$
BEHAVIOR	c		b		a		d	

negative sanctions. In columns 2 and 3 he selects the behavior dictated by minimizing negative sanctions. In the first instance he conforms to expectation B and in the second to expectation A. In the fourth column since he perceives no negative sanctions as operative he would base his decision on his perception of the legitimacy of the expectations and behave in accordance with the consequences that result from using the legitimacy criterion as the basis of decision-making. In this instance his behavior is exactly like that of a moralist.

The theory has posited thus far that those individuals with a moral orientation will be predisposed to emphasize the legitimacy of expectations and those with an expedient orientation will be predisposed to emphasize the sanctions they perceive for nonconformity to them.

We posit in addition a third type of orientation to expectations, the *moral-expedient* orientation.

A person who has this orientation does not give primacy to the legitimacy or sanctions dimensions, but takes both dimensions relatively equally into account and behaves in accordance with the perceived "net balance" of the two dimensions. Let us call such an orientation to expectations a moral-expedient or *M-E* orientation.

For some role conflict situations the decisions of an individual with an *M-E* orientation are relatively simple since both the legitimacy and sanctions elements lead him to the same behavior. If, for example, expectation A is perceived as legitimate and expectation B is viewed as illegitimate and if he perceives greater negative sanctions for nonconformity to expectation A than for nonconformity to B, he will conform to expectation A. In general, if using only the legitimacy dimension leads him to the same behavior as if he were using only the sanctions dimension, then there is no problem for him. Either criterion for behavior leads him to the same behavior.

By examining Figures 4 and 5 and observing which cell combinations of the legitimacy and sanctions dimensions lead to the same behavior we can easily isolate all the nonproblematic situations for him.

What is required is a basis for predicting his behavior in the other 9 cells.

A person with a *M-E* orientation is one who takes both the legitimacy and sanctions dimensions into account and is predisposed to adopt a behavior that emerges from a balancing of these two dimensions. Thus, if expectations A and B are both viewed as legitimate but he perceives greater negative sanctions for nonconformity to A than to B, then he will conform to expectation A. Weighing the two dimensions would result in clear cut resolutions of the role conflict in cells 2, 3, 5, 9, 14, and 15. In each of these instances on the basis of the sanctions and legitimacy dimensions there are two predispositions to one of the behaviors and only one to the other. For example, in cell 3 of Figure 6 both expectations are viewed as legitimate but there are heavier negative sanctions for nonconformity to the *A* than to the *B* expectation. Therefore, the *M-E* will conform to the *A* expectation. In cell 9 the sanctions dimension for both expectations is equivalent so the actor will base his decision on the legitimacy criterion and therefore conform to the perceived legitimate expectation, in this case *B*.

How would a *M-E* behave when the two dimensions would lead him to conform to opposite expectations, as in cells 6 and 11? In cell 6, the legitimacy dimension would require conformity to expectation *A,* but the sanctions dimension would lead to conformity to expectation *B*. Since the actor is a *M-E* he will engage in a compromise behavior because this seems to be the best balancing of the two dimensions when they lead to opposite behaviors; he is predisposed to do *A* on the basis of legitimacy, and *B* on the basis of sanctions, and therefore predisposed to both *A* and *B,* or to compromise.

We are left with one additional cell in Figure 6, cell 13. In this instance neither of the expectations are viewed as legitimate but nonconformity to both is perceived as leading to strong negative sanctions. The moralistic dimension of his orientation leads him to an avoidance behavior and the sanctions dimension suggests a compromise. In this instance it is clear that he will not conform to expectation *A* or *B*. To minimize sanctions he would compromise or try to conform to both *A* and *B,* and to emphasize legitimacy he would avoid or fail to conform to both *A* and *B*. It is clear that an avoidance reaction does not conform at all to either *A* or *B*; but it is equally clear that a compromise fails to conform in part to both *A* and *B,* and therefore is in part, an avoidance. Consequently, the most probable resolution of situations of this kind by moral-expedients would be a compromise, which in part avoids and in part conforms to both expectations.

Figure 6 summarizes the predictions made on the basis of the three dimensions of legitimacy, sanctions and orientation for moral expedients, and Figures 4 and 5 together with 6 comprise the predictions made on the basis of the theory. The assumptions with respect to the legitimacy, sanctions, and orientation dimensions provide bases for the prediction of behavior under all forty-eight of the possible conditions under which position incumbents may be faced with role conflict. Given these conditions, it is possible to predict the behavior by means of which individuals will resolve the role conflicts with which they perceive they are faced.

Methodology. To isolate the role conflicts to which the superintendent was exposed, the basic procedure was to present the respondent with four structured potential role conflict situations. For each situation three alternatives were given re-

garding the expectations that eighteen potentially relevant groups or individuals might hold. The superintendent was then asked to indicate which of the three statements most nearly represented the expectation he perceived each alter held for his behavior in the situation. If his responses revealed that contradictory expectations were held for his behavior and he validated our interpretation of them, we designated the situation as a role conflict.

After the respondent had indicated what expectations, if any, he perceived each of the eighteen listed groups and individuals held for him, the interviewer attempted to determine his feelings about the legitimacy of these expectations. The definition of legitimacy employed was the actor's perception of the right the others had to hold the expectation. If he perceived that the others had a right to hold the expectation, we will call it a perceived obligation or a *legitimate expectation*. If he perceived that the others did not have a right to hold it, we will call it a perceived pressure or an *illegitimate expectation*.

The respondent was asked to indicate for each group or individual whom he had said held a definite expectation for his behavior (responses in the *A* or *B* columns) whether "you think the individual or group named *has a right to expect you to do this*." He was asked to place a circle around the expectation of each individual or group which he believed to be a legitimate expectation. The superintendent's perception of the legitimacy of the expectations obtained through this procedure then allowed us to classify each role conflict situation into one of the four following types: expectations *A* and *B* both perceived as legitimate (*LL*); expectation *A* perceived as legitimate and *B* as illegitimate (*LI*); expectation *A* perceived as illegitimate and *B* as legitimate (*IL*); and expectations *A* and *B* both perceived as illegitimate (*II*).

After the legitimacy operation had been performed by the superintendent the interviewer began questioning the superintendent about his perception of the sanctions involved in the situation and about the way he resolved the role conflict. He also asked the superintendent to indicate the extent to which the situation "worried him" and why he undertook the particular course of action he reported to resolve the role conflict. He was asked to indicate how those who expected him to conform to expectation *A,* and then those who expected him to conform to expectation *B,* would react if he did not do what they expected of him. For 94 percent of the situations there was no disagreement between two coders on the classification of these sanctions. For those situations in which disagreement occurred the coders discussed in detail the reasons for the disagreement and finally developed a single judgment about a categorization of the role conflict on the basis of the sanctions.

The coding of the superintendent's resolution of the role conflict was derived from his response to the question, "What do you do in this situation?" There was 98 percent agreement between the coders on this operation and the disagreements were resolved in the same way as were those for the sanctions dimension.

The remaining element of the theory that requires consideration is the superintendent's orientation to expectations. That is, it was necessary to classify him as a moralist, expedient, or moral-expedient. The superintendent's responses to the Superintendent Performances Instrument provided the data used for this categorization. Each item in this instrument refers to expectations that could be applied to a superintendent. He was asked for the thirty-seven expectation items in this instrument, "As a school superintendent, what obligation do you feel that you have to do or not to do the following things." The response categories were: absolutely must, preferably should, may or may not, preferably should not, absolutely must not.

We reasoned that a person who would typically react to expectations that may be applied to him

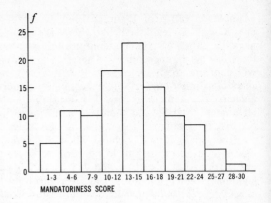

FIGURE 7. Frequency distribution of superintendents' mandatoriness scores on the superintendent performances instrument.

in terms of "it depends" is one who possesses an expedient orientation to expectations. He would be an individual who would tend to give heavy weight to sanctions in his interactions and slight weight to the legitimacy of expectations held for him. In operational terms he would respond to the expectation items with the preferably should, preferably should not, or may or may not response categories.

On the other hand a person whose typical response is not a contingent one, but is in terms of "I absolutely must" or "absolutely must not" carry out expectations, is one whose primacy of

---

TABLE 1 *Theoretical Predictions and Proportion Correct in a Test of a Theory of Role Conflict Resolution*

a. THE THEORETICAL PREDICTIONS OF BEHAVIOR FOR MORALISTS, MORAL-EXPEDIENTS, AND EXPEDIENTS IN SIXTEEN TYPES OF ROLE CONFLICTS*

	MORALISTS				MORAL-EXPEDIENTS				EXPEDIENTS			
TYPE	1	2	3	4	1	2	3	4	1	2	3	4
EXPECTATION	A B	A B	A B	A B	A B	A B	A B	A B	A B	A B	A B	A B
LEGITIMACY	L L	L L	L L	L L	L L	L L	L L	L L	L L	L L	L L	L L
SANCTIONS	+ +	− +	+ −	− −	+ +	− +	+ −	− −	+ +	− +	+ −	− −
BEHAVIOR	c	c	c	c	c	b	a	c	c	b	a	c
TYPE	5	6	7	8	5	6	7	8	5	6	7	8
EXPECTATION	A B	A B	A B	A B	A B	A B	A B	A B	A B	A B	A B	A B
LEGITIMACY	L I	L I	L I	L I	L I	L I	L I	L I	L I	L I	L I	L I
SANCTIONS	+ +	− +	+ −	− −	+ +	− +	+ −	− −	+ +	− +	+ −	− −
BEHAVIOR	a	a	a	a	a	c	a	a	c	b	a	a
TYPE	9	10	11	12	9	10	11	12	9	10	11	12
EXPECTATION	A B	A B	A B	A B	A B	A B	A B	A B	A B	A B	A B	A B
LEGITIMACY	I L	I L	I L	I L	I L	I L	I L	I L	I L	I L	I L	I L
SANCTIONS	+ +	− +	+ −	− −	+ +	− +	+ −	− −	+ +	− +	+ −	− −
BEHAVIOR	b	b	b	b	b	b	c	b	c	b	a	b
TYPE	13	14	15	16	13	14	15	16	13	14	15	16
EXPECTATION	A B	A B	A B	A B	A B	A B	A B	A B	A B	A B	A B	A B
LEGITIMACY	I I	I I	I I	I I	I I	I I	I I	I I	I I	I I	I I	I I
SANCTIONS	+ +	− +	+ −	− −	+ +	− +	+ −	− −	+ +	− +	+ −	− −
BEHAVIOR	d	d	d	d	c	b	a	d	c	b	a	d

* The abbreviations used in the table of theoretical predictions are as follows: legitimacy abbreviations: L = expectation perceived as legitimate, I = expectation perceived as illegitimate; sanctions abbreviations: + = strong negative sanctions applied for nonconformity to the expectation, − = strong negative sanctions not applied for nonconformity to the expectation; behavior abbreviations: a = conformity to expectation A, b = conformity to expectation B, c = compromise, and d = avoidance.

TABLE 1 (continued)

b. PROPORTION OF CORRECT PREDICTIONS FOR SIXTEEN TYPES OF ROLE CONFLICTS FOR MORALISTS (*M*), MORAL-EXPEDIENTS (*M-E*), AND EXPEDIENTS (*E*) IN FOUR SITUATIONS †

PERSONNEL HIRING AND PROMOTION

M ($N = 15$, $p_{correct} = .87$)

0	0	0	0
4/5	0/1	9/9	0
0	0	0	0
0	0	0	0

M-E ($N = 36$, $p_{correct} = .97$)

0	0	0	0
0/1	3/3	31/31	1/1
0	0	0	0
0	0	0	0

E ($N = 17$, $p_{correct} = 1.00$)

0	0	0	0
0	5/5	12/12	0
0	0	0	0
0	0	0	0

TOTAL OF M, M-E AND E ($N = 68$, $p_{correct} = .96$)

0	0	0	0
4/6	8/9	52/52	1/1
0	0	0	0
0	0	0	0

TIME ALLOCATION

M ($N = 10$, $p_{correct} = .50$)

0	0/1	2/4	0
0	0	3/3	0
0	0	0/1	0
0	0	0/1	0

M-E ($N = 28$, $p_{correct} = .82$)

2/2	0	13/13	1/2
0	0	1/1	0/1
0/3	1/1	2/2	2/2
1/1	0	0	0

E ($N = 10$, $p_{correct} = 1.00$)

0	0	6/6	0
0	0	0	1/1
0	0	2/2	0
0	0	1/1	0

TOTAL OF M, M-E AND E ($N = 48$, $p_{correct} = .79$)

2/2	0/1	21/23	1/2
0	0	4/4	1/2
0/3	1/1	4/5	2/2
1/1	0	1/2	0

TEACHER SALARY RECOMMENDATIONS

M ($N = 19$, $p_{correct} = .95$)

2/2	1/1	0	0
3/4	4/4	7/7	1/1
0	0	0	0
0	0	0	0

M-E ($N = 43$, $p_{correct} = .88$)

5/6	2/2	6/6	0/1
3/4	2/3	19/20	1/1
0	0	0	0
0	0	0	0

E ($N = 23$, $p_{correct} = .91$)

1/3	2/2	2/2	0
3/3	4/4	7/7	0
0	0	0	0
1/1	0	1/1	0

TOTAL OF M, M-E AND E ($N = 85$, $p_{correct} = .91$)

8/11	5/5	8/8	0/1
9/11	10/11	33/34	2/2
0	0	0	0
1/1	0	1/1	0

BUDGET RECOMMENDATIONS

M ($N = 18$, $p_{correct} = .83$)

0	0	1/2	0
1/1	1/2	12/12	0/1
0	0	0	0
0	0	0	0

M-E ($N = 50$, $p_{correct} = .96$)

10/10	1/1	14/15	0
2/3	1/1	19/19	1/1
0	0	0	0
0	0	0	0

E ($N = 22$, $p_{correct} = .96$)

4/5	0	4/4	1/1
4/4	2/2	6/6	0
0	0	0	0
0	0	0	0

TOTAL OF M, M-E AND E ($N = 90$, $p_{correct} = .93$)

14/15	1/1	19/21	1/1
7/8	4/5	37/37	1/2
0	0	0	0
0	0	0	0

TOTAL OF FOUR SITUATIONS

M ($N = 62$, $p_{correct} = .82$)

2/2	1/2	3/6	0
8/10	5/7	31/31	1/2
0	0	0/1	0
0	0	0/1	0

M-E ($N = 157$, $p_{correct} = .92$)

17/18	3/3	33/34	1/3
5/8	6/7	70/71	3/4
0/3	1/1	2/2	2/2
1/1	0	0	0

E ($N = 72$, $p_{correct} = .96$)

5/8	2/2	12/12	1/1
7/7	11/11	25/25	1/1
0	0	2/2	0
1/1	0	2/2	0

TOTAL OF M, M-E AND E

24/28	6/7	48/52	2/4
20/25	22/25	126/127	5/7
0/3	1/1	4/5	2/2
2/2	0	2/3	0

GRAND TOTAL $N = 291$
GRAND TOTAL $p_{correct} = .91$

---

† The cells of each of the sixteen-fold tables correspond to the numbered "legitimacy-sanctions" types (1–16) of the table of theoretical predictions.

orientation is to their rectitude. He does not think in terms of factors in the situation that would lessen his obligations. Such a person would be predisposed "to honor" legitimate expectations regardless of the sanctions involved in the situation. Such a person would be a moralist.

One who shows neither of these patterns of responses to expectations, but falls between the conditional and mandatory categories, would possess the characteristic required for the moral-expedient orientation. This orientation to expectations suggests that he is the type of person who would tend to take *both* the sanctions and legitimacy dimensions into account in reacting to perceived expectations.

This line of reasoning led to the following procedure. Each superintendent was given a score of 1 for each item in the Superintendent Performances Instrument for which he gave a mandatory response (absolutely must or absolutely must not). This provided a range of scores from 1 through 30 for the 37 items in the instrument. The distribution of mandatoriness scores can be seen in Figure 7. The estimated reliability of the scores is .884.[11] These scores were then split into the following three categories: 1–9, 10–18 and 19–30. On the reasoning outlined above those superintendents who fell into the low mandatoriness group (1–9) were defined as the expedients; those who fell into the high mandatoriness group (19–30) were considered moralists; and those who fell in the middle category (10–18) were categorized as moral-expedients.

A test of the theory. If we accept each of these operational indexes as adequately representing the variables and conditions described by the theory of role conflict resolution we can use them to perform an exploratory test. Superintendents who perceived their exposure to incompatible expectations in each of the four role conflict situations were categorized according to the perceived legitimacy of the expectations, the perceived sanctions to which they would be exposed for failure to conform to the expectations, and according to whether they were "moralists," "moral-expedi-

ents," or "expedients." The theory allows predictions of the behavior of superintendents of sixteen "legitimacy-sanctions" types for each of the orientation types. By comparing the behavior predicted on the basis of the theory for each of these forty-eight types with the actual behavior of superintendents who fell within these categories for each role conflict situation, we may say whether or not the theory has led in each case to the correct prediction.

In Table 1 are presented the proportion of correct predictions for each of the forty-eight types for each role conflict situation. Although it would be possible to interpret the prediction for each of the forty-eight types separately as a testable hypothesis, this seemed indefensible on two counts. The first is that it seemed unlikely that there would be enough cases in many of the cells to allow for tests of the significance of the proportion correctly predicted. The second is that the theory can be considered implicative of only one general hypothesis, that the perceived legitimacy, perceived sanctions, and orientation are related to behavior in a particular though complex way, and that given particular conditions for each of these three phenomena a particular *prediction* can be made for behavior. It was felt that the theory as stated could be compared directly to a hypothesis describing how one or more predictor variables determines a criterion variable. For example, if it is hypothesized that height and weight are positively related to strength, then, if the hypothesis is quantitatively precise, given particular values of height and weight, *predictions* can be made of the particular value of strength. To interpret predictions for particular values of the predictor variables as hypotheses, and test them as such, suggests both a lack of confidence in the general theoretical description of the relationships among the variables of concern, and as well, a probably unjustified confidence in the extensity of the data available with which to make the tests.

On the basis of this reasoning it was decided to perform a single test of the theory of role conflict resolution for each situation, interpreting this theory as providing one general hypothesis about the ways in which the three predictors, legitimacy, sanctions, and orientation, are related among themselves, and how these in turn are related to the criterion, behavior. It is nevertheless important to present and to some extent discuss whatever differences may be apparent in the degrees of success with which the behavior of superintendents in different categories can be predicted.

As can be seen in Table 1, for 264 of the 291 role conflict cases (91 percent) the theory led to the correct prediction. Since, however, the four role conflict situations are not independent, in order to test the theory it is necessary to ask whether the proportion of correct predictions obtained for each situation could have occurred by chance. To answer this question, the number of

---

[11] In computing the reliability of these scores the total instrument was divided into separate halves. An attempt was made to insure parallel halves by matching on both proportion giving a mandatory response p and correlation with total scores r. Each item was represented by a point on a scatter diagram, the abscissa of which represented r and the ordinate p. A circle was drawn around the matched pairs and one member of each pair was randomly assigned to each half. The scores on the two halves were then correlated ($r_{AB} = .792$), and finally the reliability estimated by the Spearman-Brown formula for doble lengths ($r_{TT} = .884$).

correct and of incorrect predictions were compared with the number expected on the basis of two hypothetical "chance" models, the first we shall call the "chance expectancy" model, and the second and more stringent of the two, the "proportionate expectancy" model. The "chance expectancy" model assumes that each of the four alternative behaviors will occur by chance with equal frequency. With this assumption, the expected proportion of correct predictions is .25, and of incorrect, .75. Comparing the expected frequencies computed on the basis of this model with the frequencies obtained on the basis of the theory, results in the case of each situation in differences which are significant at the .01 level.

This "chance expectancy" model is perhaps not realistic considering the actual frequencies of the four alternative behaviors, and is certainly not the most stringent model with which the theory might be compared. Since it is known that the four alternative behaviors do not occur with equal frequency, a more stringent model would attempt to take these disparities into account and would require that each of the behaviors be selected "by chance" with the frequency with which it is known to occur. In two of the situations, "Hiring" and "Time Allocation," the fourth alternative, "avoidance," does not occur at all, in the

TABLE 2   A Comparison of the Proportion of Correct Predictions Obtained on the Basis of a "Theory of Role Conflict Resolution" with the Proportion Expected on the Basis of a "Chance Expectancy Model"

SITUATION	NUMBER OF CASES	PROPORTION OF CORRECT PREDICTIONS BY THE "THEORY"	PROPORTION OF CORRECT PREDICTIONS EXPECTED BY "CHANCE"	t	PROBABILITY LESS THAN
Personnel hiring and promotion	68	.96	.25	8.41	.01
Time allocation	48	.79	.25	5.32	.01
Teacher salary recommendations	85	.91	.25	8.70	.01
Budget recommendations	90	.93	.25	9.26	.01

TABLE 3   A Comparison of the Proportion of Correct Predictions Obtained on the Basis of a "Theory of Role Conflict Resolution" with the Proportion Expected on the Basis of a "Proportionate-expectancy Model"

SITUATION	NUMBER OF CASES	PROPORTION OF CORRECT PREDICTIONS BY THE "THEORY"	PROPORTION OF CORRECT PREDICTIONS EXPECTED BY THE "MODEL"*	t	PROBABILITY LESS THAN
Personnel hiring and promotion	68	.96	.72	3.73	.01
Time allocation	48	.79	.51	2.80	.01
Teacher salary recommendations	85	.91	.46	6.26	.01
Budget recommendations	90	.93	.55	5.94	.01

* The definition of the proportion of correct predictions expected in each situation if the four alternative behaviors occur by chance with the frequency with which they actually occur is based on the information in the following table:

SITUATION	NUMBER OF CASES	PROPORTIONS OF ROLE CONFLICTS RESOLVED WITH BEHAVIORS $a, b, c,$ AND d				PROPORTION EXPECTED $(p_a{}^2 + p_b{}^2 + p_c{}^2 + p_d{}^2)$
		p_a	p_b	p_c	p_d	
Personnel hiring and promotion	68	.838	.103	.059	.000	.72
Time allocation	48	.667	.083	.250	.000	.51
Teacher salary recommendations	85	.635	.094	.212	.059	.46
Budget recommendations	90	.689	.033	.267	.011	.55

"Budget" situation it occurs only once, and in the "Salary" only five times. A more extreme example will perhaps clarify our reason for also using the "proportionate expectancy" model with which to compare the theory. Suppose that it had been possible to specify twenty alternative behaviors that could be selected in each situation. Even though sixteen of them never occurred at all, the proportion of correct predictions which would be expected on the basis of "chance" would be 1/20, or .05. A comparison of the theory with such a chance model, based on twenty alternative possible behaviors, would appear to be, if not a capitalization on chance, at least a misrepresentation of realistic possibilities. With the assumption that each of the behaviors is selected "by chance" with the frequency with which it is known to occur, the expected proportion of correct predictions for each of the four situations has been computed on the basis of the data presented in Table 3. The difference between the proportions expected in each situation according to the "proportionate expectancy" model and the proportions obtained on the basis of the theory is in each case significant at the .01 level.

We are consequently led to the conclusion on the basis of the comparisons between the "chance" model and theory, as well as between the "proportionate" model and the theory, that the findings provide significant support for the theory in four role conflict situations.

Although evidence has been obtained which can be interpreted as supporting the general hypothesis based on the theory, there are several observations which can be made about Table 1 suggesting limitations to the acceptability of this conclusion. The first is of the number of cells in which there are either very few or no cases. While it is true that an absence of cases in any cell is an interesting finding, it does not allow conclusions with respect to the validity of the theory for the whole range of types of role conflict situations for which predictions can be made. There are two cells in the "Grand Total" matrix which yield no cases, and nine others which yield seven or less. When these are broken down by situation and by orientation, there are many more cells which are inadequately or not at all represented. The most extreme case is found for "expedients" in the "Hiring" situation, where there are fourteen of the sixteen cells in which no cases occur.

Another possible limiting circumstance is the fact that there are interesting differences among the proportions of correct predictions for different categorizations of the data. For all four situations combined, for example, the proportion of correct predictions is highest for the "expedients" (.96), next highest for the "moral-expedients" (.92) and lowest for the "moralists" (.82). Differenti-

ating the role conflicts by situation and combining superintendents of all three orientations, as we did in testing the theory, we find that the highest proportion of correct predictions is obtained in the "Hiring" situation (.96), the next highest in the "Budget" (.93), the next in the "Salary" (.91), and the lowest in the "Time Allocation" situation (.79). This last finding is perhaps interesting in that the "Time Allocation" situation is the only one of the four which involves expectations arising because of the superintendents' incumbency of two positions, or inter-role conflicts. The point of these observations is that there are differences within the data for which the theory can in no way account.

The general tests by means of which this theory of role conflict resolution has been empirically examined provide significant support for it. Nevertheless, since both the theory and the operations by means of which it has been tested are exploratory, it is important to ask, and as far as possible try to answer, first, whether there are significant factors in the determination of behavior in the face of incompatible expectation situations which this theory ignores, and second, whether or not the complexities involved in the theory are necessary to a successful prediction of behavior in these situations. The first of these questions is of the completeness of the theory; does it fail to take account of significant and relevant variables which could influence behavior in situations of this kind? The second question is of the parsimony of the theory; does it include factors which are unnecessary for an adequate understanding and prediction of behavior? Neither of these questions can be given a definitive answer, but both can and will be explored within the limitations of the data available.

In considering the first of these questions, of the completeness of the theory of role conflict resolution, it would seem appropriate to examine the cases for which the theory failed to provide a basis for a correct prediction. If some factor or factors have been left out of the theory which should be included, suggestions as to their nature are likely to be found in the responses of superintendents whose behavior was not correctly predicted on the basis of the theory. Since the prediction was incorrect, the behavior could not have been determined in the way the theory posits, and some other factors are likely to be relevant. This reasoning assumes, however, that the operations by means of which the theory has been tested are entirely adequate, which, when considering the exploratory nature of our analysis, is an assumption we do not feel justified in accepting. We feel that it is necessary to admit two possible sources of error in the tests which have been made: The first is the possible inadequacy of the theory, and the second the possible inadequacy of the operations by means of which it has been tested.

Of the 291 situations in which superintendents

were exposed to incompatible expectations, the theory led to correct predictions in 264 cases. The remaining 27 were errors, and these 27 are the basis for this re-examination. Eight of these 27 errors arose in the "Salary" dilemma. The behavior of 5 of these 8 superintendents was coded as "avoidance" when, according to the theory, a "compromise" behavior was predicted. One of these superintendents said, "When the teachers make their demands I put it in the hands of the school committee. I just don't recommend. (Why do you do this?) The school committee has the authority and the responsibility. It's too hot for me; I let the school committee handle it." It might be suggested on the basis of this response that the theory as it was presented fails to recognize the possibility that negative sanctions may be minimized as much by avoidance as by compromise. Furthermore, if the formal definition of a position does not require incumbents to make certain decisions, as for example, decisions with respect to salary schedules, even though such incumbents recognize legitimate expectations with respect to these decisions, they may in the face of a dilemma resort to the formal definition as a justification for "avoiding" the obligations they recognize. It is interesting that all five of these superintendents have either an "expedient" or a "moral-expedient" orientation.

The six errors which were made in the "Budget" situation have nothing in common with one another, and although an interpretation could be offered of each one, the most likely explanation of their occurrence would appear to be the inadequacy of the operations.

Two of the three errors which were made in the "Hiring" situation suggest that there are limits to the strength of sanctions under which individuals with a "moral" orientation will continue to behave as moralists. In both of these cases, the superintendents perceived the "merit" expectation as legitimate, and the alternative as illegitimate. Since these superintendents were "moralists," the prediction was that they would conform to the "merit" alternative. This was incorrect; they conformed to the expectation they perceived as "illegitimate" and in both cases explained their behavior by reference to the strong negative sanctions which would result if they did not. In reviewing the interview protocols it became apparent that both of these superintendents were confronted with extreme sanctions and felt that it would serve no purpose for them to lose their jobs and be replaced by a superintendent who might not even recognize the legitimate expectation, let alone conform to it. Two suggestions might be made on the basis of these errors. The first is that there are limits to the strength of sanctions which individuals with a "moral" orientation can ignore. The second is more general. It might be suggested that the theory should be revised to allow for degrees of both "legitimacy" and "sanctions" and should make use of both of these factors as variables,

rather than as dichotomies, in a prediction formula. That the theory does not do this must be recognized as an inadequacy, although it is one with which it would have been impossible to deal in this exploratory study. It would have been possible, of course, to develop the theory so as to take sanctions and legitimacy into account as variables, but with our data and operational procedures it would have been impossible to test it. In this sense it is recognized that not only the test, but the theory itself is exploratory.

The third error made for the "Hiring" situation can be accounted for by the inadequate operational procedures. This superintendent made a clear distinction between "professional" and "nonprofessional" staff. For the first group he said only the "merit" expectation was legitimate, and that strong negative sanctions would be applied only for failure to conform to this expectation, and he said he did conform to the "merit" expectation. For the "nonprofessionals" this superintendent recognized no legitimate expectations, perceived sanctions only for the "nonmerit" alternative, and he conformed to this "nonmerit" alternative. In order to include this superintendent in the analysis it was necessary to combine his separate responses for the two groups of employees he distinguished. The result was that his behavior was coded as "compromise" since he conformed to both expectations in part. This was incorrect since only one expectation, "merit," was perceived as legitimate, strongly negative sanctions were perceived as resulting from failure to conform to both, and his orientation was "moral-expedient." More rigid operational definitions would have resulted in the exclusion of this superintendent from the analysis, but considering the latitude for interpretation which it was necessary to allow the coders, it did not seem justifiable to make this exclusion in the course of testing the theory.

The "Time Allocation" situation was the one on which the largest proportion of errors was made, 10 of the 48 cases being predicted incorrectly. Since this is the only situation in which the superintendent was exposed to inter-role conflict we may ask whether there is some other factor operating in this situation which did not enter in the other three situations and which the theory does not take into account. Two conclusions, which can perhaps be subsumed under one, are suggested by the responses of a number of these superintendents for whom the theory led to the incorrect prediction. Given incompatible expectations stemming from an individual's incumbency of two positions, some of our respondents invoked a "priority among positions" explanation of their behavior. Although according to their perceptions of the legitimacy and the sanctions and their orientation, the theory would lead to the prediction of a compromise, a number of superintendents said they "spent most evenings on school business," because, "It's my job." Other

TABLE 4 *Theoretical Predictions and Proportion of Correct Predictions Based on a Prediction Model Using the "Legitimacy Assumption"*

1. THE THEORETICAL PREDICTIONS OF BEHAVIOR IN FOUR TYPES OF ROLE CONFLICTS*

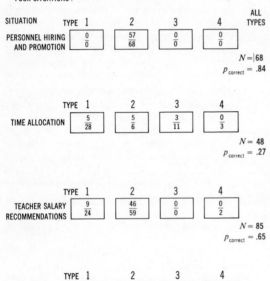

TYPE	1		2		3		4	
EXPECTATION	A	B	A	B	A	B	A	B
LEGITIMACY	L	L	L	I	I	L	I	I
BEHAVIOR	c		a		b		d	

2. PROPORTION OF CORRECT PREDICTIONS FOR FOUR TYPES OF ROLE CONFLICT IN FOUR SITUATIONS†

SITUATION	TYPE 1	2	3	4	ALL TYPES
PERSONNEL HIRING AND PROMOTION	0/0	57/68	0/0	0/0	$N = 68$ $p_{correct} = .84$
TIME ALLOCATION	5/28	5/6	3/11	0/3	$N = 48$ $p_{correct} = .27$
TEACHER SALARY RECOMMENDATIONS	9/24	46/59	0/0	0/2	$N = 85$ $p_{correct} = .65$
BUDGET RECOMMENDATIONS	17/38	42/52	0/0	0/0	$N = 90$ $p_{correct} = .66$
TOTAL OF FOUR SITUATIONS	31/90	150/185	3/11	0/5	$N = 291$ $p_{correct} = .63$

* The abbreviations used in the table of theoretical predictions are as follows: legitimacy abbreviations L = expectation perceived as legitimate, I = expectation perceived as illegitimate; behavior abbreviations: a = conformity to expectation A, b = conformity to expectation B, c = compromise d = avoidance.
† The four types of these tables correspond to the four "legitimacy" types of the table of theoretical predictions.

superintendents said "I feel I *should* be there," which suggests that they held an expectation for themselves to which they conformed irrespective of the other conditions in the situation. The theory takes into account neither the "priority among positions" nor the position incumbent's "own expectations." If an expectation for one position takes priority over an expectation for another position, it might be inferred that the incumbent perceives one as "more" legitimate than the other. Similarly, if a position incumbent does something because as he says in effect, "I expect this of myself," here too this might be inferred to be the "more" legitimate of the expectations to which he perceives he is exposed. These inferences return us to the suggestion that if the theory could have taken "legitimacy" and "sanctions" into account as variables rather than as dichotomies, it would have been a more precise theory in the sense of resulting in a larger proportion of correct predictions.

The conclusions which are suggested by this examination of the errors made in testing this theory of role conflict resolution may be summarized. First, it was suggested that the formal definition of a position with respect to a particular decision may influence the alternative behavior selected by a position incumbent. Second, the theory failed to recognize the possibility that negative sanctions *may* be minimized as much by avoidance as by compromise, depending on the particular situation, the nature of the sanctions, and the possibilities for "formal avoidance." Third, if it is operationally feasible to test such a revised theory, it can be suggested that the inclusion of perceived legitimacy and sanctions as variables rather than as dichotomies in a theory of role conflict resolution would be more accurately descriptive of the effects of these factors in determining behavior. Fourth, the expectations of an individual holds for himself may not be congruent with the expectations he perceives and may influence his behavior independently of the perceived expectations and their legitimacy. And finally, in inter-role conflict situations, the expectations for one position may take priority over the expectations for the other, irrespective of the perceived legitimacy of either.

From an examination of the 27 instances in which the theory of role conflict resolution led to incorrect predictions, we were led to posit certain possible additional variables which might be relevant under certain circumstances. It remains true however, that in 264, or 91 percent, of the cases the theory led to the correct prediction, which suggests that the theory, as far as prediction is concerned, is reasonably adequate as it was presented. But on this criterion, of degree of successful prediction, it is possible that a model using only some of the factors involved in the theory would prove as adequate. This is the second question we shall ask about this theory of role conflict resolution: Is it a parsimonious theory, or does it include factors and assumptions which are unnecessary for the successful prediction of behavior?

In an attempt to answer this question three prediction models were developed each of which is based on some of the assumptions involved in the theory. Each of these prediction models will be presented and compared with the theory. Whether or not the theory allows us to make significantly more correct predictions in each of the four situations than each of the models will be considered the tests of whether or not the theory is more or less adequate on the criterion of successful prediction, which is, however, only one criterion against which the success of a theory can be evaluated. While we would be willing to defend the theory of role conflict resolution on logical grounds, we do not construe the findings to be presented as in any way supporting this defense. The theory is open to argument independently of the data and the findings, but the data and the findings can provide suggestions for its acceptance, revision, or rejection.

The first prediction model is based on the assumptions with respect to the perceived legitimacy of incompatible expectations. If position incumbents are predisposed to conform to legitimate expectations and predisposed not to conform to illegitimate expectations, it is possible to make predictions about a position incumbent's behavior in the face of two incompatible expectations of four types. The four types and the predicted behavior were presented on page 354 and are summarized again in Table 4. Basing our predictions solely on this model, the results are presented in the second part of Table 4. Overall, this model provides 63 percent correct predictions.

The second model is based on the assumptions with respect to the perceived sanctions resulting from nonconformity to the incompatible expectations. If a position incumbent perceives that nonconformity to an expectation will result in strong negative sanctions, he will be predisposed to conform to it. If he perceives weak negative sanctions for nonconformity to a given expectation, he will not be predisposed either to conform or not to conform to it. On the basis of these assumptions it is possible to make predictions for three of the four possible types of situations in which there are two incompatible expectations to each of which an actor may perceive strong or weak negative sanctions for nonconformity. These types and the predictions based on these assumptions were presented on page 355 and summarized again in Table 5. Since for the fourth type in which no sanctions are perceived, no prediction can be made, we must accept any cases falling in this category as errors as far as predicting behavior is concerned. The results of using this second prediction model are presented in the second part of Table 5. Overall, this second model provides 82 percent correct predictions.

A third model may be based on both these

sets of assumptions with respect to legitimacy and sanctions, and as well, on the assumption that the predispositions derived from legitimacy and

TABLE 5   *Theoretical Predictions and Proportion of Correct Predictions Based on a Prediction Model Using the "Sanctions Assumption"*

1. THE THEORETICAL PREDICTIONS OF BEHAVIOR IN FOUR TYPES OF ROLE CONFLICTS*

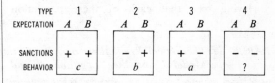

2. PROPORTION OF CORRECT PREDICTIONS FOR FOUR TYPES OF ROLE CONFLICT IN FOUR SITUATIONS †

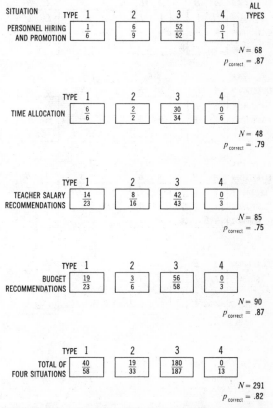

SITUATION	TYPE 1	2	3	4	ALL TYPES
PERSONNEL HIRING AND PROMOTION	$\frac{1}{6}$	$\frac{6}{9}$	$\frac{52}{52}$	$\frac{0}{1}$	$N = 68$ $p_{correct} = .87$
TIME ALLOCATION	$\frac{6}{6}$	$\frac{2}{2}$	$\frac{30}{34}$	$\frac{0}{6}$	$N = 48$ $p_{correct} = .79$
TEACHER SALARY RECOMMENDATIONS	$\frac{14}{23}$	$\frac{8}{16}$	$\frac{42}{43}$	$\frac{0}{3}$	$N = 85$ $p_{correct} = .75$
BUDGET RECOMMENDATIONS	$\frac{19}{23}$	$\frac{3}{6}$	$\frac{56}{58}$	$\frac{0}{3}$	$N = 90$ $p_{correct} = .87$
TOTAL OF FOUR SITUATIONS	$\frac{40}{58}$	$\frac{19}{33}$	$\frac{180}{187}$	$\frac{0}{13}$	$N = 291$ $p_{correct} = .82$

* The abbreviations used in the table of theoretical predictions are as follows: sanctions abbreviations: + = strong negative sanctions applied for nonconformity to the expectation, − = strong negative sanctions not applied for nonconformity to the expectation; behavior abbreviations: a = conformity to expectation A, b = conformity to expectation B, c = compromise, d = avoidance, and ? = no prediction possible.   † The four types of these tables correspond to the four "sanctions" types of the table of theoretical predictions.

from sanctions combine equally in predisposing behavior. This model is equivalent to that part of the theory which defined the predictions for position incumbents with a "moral-expedient" orientation, which is presented on page 355 and is summarized again in Table 6. Basing our predictions solely on this model, the results are as presented in the second part of Table 6. Overall, this third model provides 83 percent correct predictions.

Having seen that each of these prediction models provides a sizable proportion of correct predictions, it is necessary to ask whether or not the theory is significantly better according to this prediction criterion. The comparisons between the number of correct predictions obtained on the basis of the "theory" and the number obtained on the basis of each of the "prediction models" for each of the four situations are presented in Table 7. We may conclude that the "theory" provides significantly more correct predictions than the "legitimacy model" in all four situations, but that only in the "Salary" situation does it provide significantly more correct predictions than do the "sanctions" and the "legitimacy-sanctions" models. Does this finding imply that the "sanctions" and

---

TABLE 6 *Theoretical Predictions and Proportion of Correct Predictions Based on a Prediction Model Using the "Legitimacy" and "Sanctions" Assumptions*

1. THE THEORETICAL PREDICTIONS OF BEHAVIOR IN SIXTEEN TYPES OF ROLE CONFLICTS*

TYPE	1		2		3		4	
EXPECTATION	A	B	A	B	A	B	A	B
LEGITIMACY	L	L	L	L	L	L	L	L
SANCTIONS	+	+	−	+	+	−	−	−
BEHAVIOR	c		b		a		c	

TYPE	5		6		7		8	
EXPECTATION	A	B	A	B	A	B	A	B
LEGITIMACY	L	I	L	I	L	I	L	I
SANCTIONS	+	+	−	+	+	−	−	−
BEHAVIOR	a		c		a		a	

TYPE	9		10		11		12	
EXPECTATION	A	B	A	B	A	B	A	B
LEGITIMACY	I	L	I	L	I	L	I	L
SANCTIONS	+	+	−	+	+	−	−	−
BEHAVIOR	b		b		c		b	

TYPE	13		14		15		16	
EXPECTATION	A	B	A	B	A	B	A	B
LEGITIMACY	I	I	I	I	I	I	I	I
SANCTIONS	+	+	−	+	+	−	−	−
BEHAVIOR	c		b		a		d	

2. PROPORTION OF CORRECT PREDICTIONS FOR SIXTEEN TYPES OF ROLE CONFLICTS IN FOUR SITUATIONS †

PERSONNEL HIRING AND PROMOTION

0	0	0	0
$\frac{4}{6}$	$\frac{3}{9}$	$\frac{52}{52}$	$\frac{1}{1}$
0	0	0	0
0	0	0	0

$N = 68$
$p_{correct} = .88$

TIME ALLOCATION

$\frac{2}{2}$	$\frac{1}{1}$	$\frac{21}{23}$	$\frac{1}{2}$
0	0	$\frac{4}{4}$	$\frac{1}{2}$
$\frac{0}{3}$	$\frac{1}{1}$	$\frac{2}{5}$	$\frac{2}{2}$
$\frac{1}{1}$	0	$\frac{2}{2}$	0

$N = 48$
$p_{correct} = .79$

TEACHER SALARY RECOMMENDATIONS

$\frac{8}{11}$	$\frac{4}{5}$	$\frac{8}{8}$	$\frac{0}{1}$
$\frac{6}{11}$	$\frac{2}{11}$	$\frac{33}{34}$	$\frac{2}{2}$
0	0	0	0
$\frac{1}{1}$	0	$\frac{1}{1}$	0

$N = 85$
$p_{correct} = .77$

BUDGET RECOMMENDATIONS

$\frac{14}{15}$	$\frac{1}{1}$	$\frac{19}{21}$	$\frac{1}{1}$
$\frac{3}{8}$	$\frac{2}{5}$	$\frac{37}{37}$	$\frac{1}{2}$
0	0	0	0
0	0	0	0

$N = 90$
$p_{correct} = .87$

TOTAL OF FOUR SITUATIONS

$\frac{24}{28}$	$\frac{6}{7}$	$\frac{48}{52}$	$\frac{2}{4}$
$\frac{13}{25}$	$\frac{7}{25}$	$\frac{126}{127}$	$\frac{5}{7}$
$\frac{0}{3}$	$\frac{1}{1}$	$\frac{2}{5}$	$\frac{2}{2}$
$\frac{2}{2}$	0	$\frac{3}{3}$	0

TOTAL $N = 291$
$p_{correct} = .83$

---

* The abbreviations used in the table of theoretical predictions are as follows: legitimacy abbreviations: L = expectation perceived as illegitimate, I = expectation perceived as illegitimate; sanctions abbreviations: + = strong negative sanctions applied for nonconformity to the the expectation, − = strong negative sanctions not applied for nonconformity to the expectation; behavior abbreviations: a = conformity to expectation A, b = conformity to expectation B, c = compromise, and d = avoidance. † The cells of each of the sixteen-fold tables correspond to the numbered "legitimacy-sanctions" types (1–16) of the table of theoretical predictions.

TABLE 7 *Comparisons of the Proportion of Correct Predictions Obtained Using a "Theory of Role Conflict Resolution" and the Proportion Obtained Using Three "Prediction Models" in Four Situations*

SITUATION	NUMBER OF CASES	PROPORTION OF CORRECT PREDICTIONS BY THE "THEORY"	PROPORTION OF CORRECT PREDICTIONS BY THE "MODEL"	x^{2*}	PROBABILITY LESS THAN
1. Comparison of the "theory" and the "legitimacy model"					
Personnel hiring and promotion	68	.96	.84	6.12	.05
Time allocation	48	.79	.27	23.04	.01
Teacher salary recommendations	85	.91	.65	18.38	.01
Budget recommendations	90	.93	.66	21.33	.01
2. Comparison of the "theory" and the "sanctions model"					
Personnel hiring and promotion	68	.96	.87	2.50	not sig.
Time allocation	48	.79	.79	0.00	not sig.
Teacher salary recommendations	85	.91	.75	8.47	.01
Budget recommendations	90	.93	.87	2.50	not sig.
3. Comparison of the "theory" and the "legitimacy-sanctions model"					
Personnel hiring and promotion	68	.96	.88	3.20	not sig.
Time allocation	48	.79	.79	0.00	not sig.
Teacher salary recommendations	85	.91	.76	10.08	.01
Budget recommendations	90	.93	.87	2.50	not sig.

* For comparing proportions obtained on the same individuals a chi-square different from that ordinarily used is required. For an appropriate treatment of this problem, see, for example, Helen M. Walker and Joseph Lev, *Statistical Inference* (New York: Henry Holt and Company, 1953), pp. 102–103.

TABLE 8 *A Comparison of the Number of Correct Predictions Obtained Using a "Theory of Role Conflict Resolution" and the Number Obtained Using Each of Three "Prediction Models" for Cases of Role Conflict in Which the "Theory" and the "Model" Led to Different Predictions*

SITUATION	NUMBER OF CASES FOR WHICH THE PREDICTIONS OF THE "MODEL" AND THE "THEORY" DIFFERED	NUMBER OF CORRECT PREDICTIONS BY THE "THEORY"	NUMBER OF CORRECT PREDICTIONS BY THE "MODEL"	NUMBER OF CASES FOR WHICH NEITHER THE "THEORY" NOR THE "MODEL" WAS CORRECT
1. Comparison of the "theory" and the "legitimacy model"				
Personnel hiring and promotion	8	8	0	0
Time allocation	25	25	0	0
Teacher salary recommendations	24	23	1	0
Budget recommendations	27	26	1	0
All four situations	84	82	2	0
2. Comparison of the "theory" and the "sanctions model"				
Personnel hiring and promotion	11	8	2	1
Time allocation	19	8	8	3
Teacher salary recommendations	19	15	2	2
Budget recommendations	12	8	2	2
All four situations	61	39	14	8
3. Comparison of the "theory" and the "legitimacy-sanctions model"				
Personnel hiring and promotion	6	5	0	1
Time allocation	10	4	4	2
Teacher salary recommendations	12	12	0	0
Budget recommendations	10	8	2	0
All four situations	38	29	6	3

"legitimacy-sanctions" models are as useful as the theory for predicting role conflict resolution? For the purpose of predicting the resolution of all role conflicts in three of the four situations, we would conclude that it does.

Another consideration, however, suggests a modification of this conclusion. The theory leads to exactly the same predictions as each of the models for a large proportion of the cases. Whether or not the theory is significantly better than each of the models consequently depends only on those cases for which the theory leads to a prediction different from that made on the basis of the models. When there are only a few such cases for any one comparison, it becomes much more difficult if not impossible for the theory to provide significantly more correct predictions. Although it would be inappropriate to apply a significance test to the difference between the number of correct predictions made on the basis of the theory and a model only in the cases for which the theory makes a *different* prediction from that made by a model, it is clearly relevant to compare them on this criterion using only these cases.

Table 8 presents the number of correct and incorrect predictions made by the theory and by each of the three prediction models for each situation for *only those cases* in which the theory led to a prediction which differed from the one made on the basis of each of the models. For example, there were 8 cases in the "Hiring" situation for which the theory led to a prediction which differed from that made on the basis of the "legitimacy" model. In all 8 cases the theory led to the correct prediction and the model to the incorrect prediction. Comparing the theory with the "legitimacy" model for all four situations we may conclude that the theory is almost without exception more accurate. For 82 of the 84 role conflicts on which the theory and the "legitimacy" model led to different predictions in the four situations the theory was correct; in only 2 of the 84 cases did the "legitimacy" model lead to the correct prediction.

The comparisons between the theory and the other two models cannot be given quite so clear an interpretation, although it is only the "Time Allocation" situation in which the theory does not clearly lead to more correct predictions than does either the "sanctions" or the "legitimacy-sanctions" model. In the "Time Allocation" situation both prediction models lead to as many correct predictions as the theory (8 out of 19 in the case of the "sanctions" model and 4 out of 10 in the case of the "legitimacy-sanctions" model). In the remaining three situations, however, the theory consistently leads to more correct predictions than

either model. Overall, in the 61 cases for which the theory led to a prediction different from that to which the "sanctions" model led, the theory led to the correct one in 39 cases and the model in only 14. In 8 cases neither of them led to the correct prediction. Of the 38 cases for which the theory and the "legitimacy-sanctions" model differed, the theory led to the correct prediction in 29 and the model in 6. In 3 cases neither led to the correct prediction. These findings lead us to the conclusion that for those cases in which the theory led to a different prediction than we made on the basis of the models, the theory of role conflict resolution which we have examined leads to more correct predictions, in all but the single inter-role conflict situation ("Time Allocation"), than does any one of the three alternative "prediction models" with which it has been compared. To this extent, we may conclude that the theory satisfies the requirement of parsimony.

SUMMARY

A theory of role conflict resolution has been presented which allows for the prediction of behavior, according to four alternative courses of action, when an individual is confronted with two incompatible expectations. The theory describes relationships among the perceived legitimacy of the expectations, the perceived sanctions resulting from nonconformity to them, the orientation of the individual to these legitimacy and sanctions dimensions, and his behavior. The accuracy of the predictions to which this theory led for school superintendents in four "incompatible expectation situations" was tested, and the evidence was interpreted as supporting the theory. In addition, an examination was made of the cases in which the theory led to an incorrect prediction, and suggestions made on the basis of this re-examination as to factors which were operative in these cases which the theory failed to take into account. Finally, the theory was compared with three prediction models, each of which was based on only some of the assumptions necessary for the theory. The conclusion was drawn that the theory was satisfactorily parsimonious relative to the success with which it allowed predictions of behavior.

Two relatively clear advantages may be claimed for this theory. The first is that it is concerned with and takes account of incompatible expectations stemming from an individual's incumbency of one or more positions. The basic phenomena with which the theory is concerned are incompatible expectation situations, and consequently both inter- and intrarole conflicts may be subsumed under it. The second advantage we would claim derives from the theory's concern with "expectations," whether legitimate or illegitimate, rather than "obligations" which may be considered to be legitimate expectations. Although illegitimate expectations are not obligations, their existence poses a dilemma for position incumbents for whom they are held. This theory of role conflict resolution takes account of and allows predictions about dilemmas of both kinds.

Although it is recognized that there are two limitations to this theory, both of these may, with appropriate modifications, be taken care of without changing the basic assumptions about relationships which the theory makes. The first, which has already been mentioned, is that both the legitimacy and the sanctions dimensions are dealt with as dichotomies, whereas a more precise theory would be based on their treatment as continuous variables. By elaborating the theory to take this into account and developing operational procedures by means of which to test the elaborated theory, it is felt that this limitation could be removed. Neither of these was practicable in the present study, since without the empirical test, it would be impossible to evaluate the necessity for or success of the theoretical elaboration. The second limitation which is recognized is that the theory as it has been presented can deal with incompatible expectation situations in which there are only two incongruent expectations. If there are three incompatible expectations for a position incumbent in one situation, the present theory would not serve as a basis for predicting his behavior. However, by simply extending the number of alternative behaviors (for example, to 8 in the case of 3 incompatible expectations) the theory would allow for the prediction of which of the 8 alternative courses of action an individual would take under different conditions of perceived legitimacy and sanctions (there would be 64 different conditions for which it would be necessary to make predictions for each of the 3 differently oriented types of individuals). The same assumptions would serve, and except in numerical detail, the theory would be unchanged.

More severe, perhaps, are the limitations we feel constrained to place on the test which has been presented of the theory. Aside from the possible inadequacy of the operational procedures we employed to define "perceived legitimacy," "perceived sanctions," "behavior," and "orientation," it must be pointed out that both the situations for which tests could be made

and the position incumbents who were the respondents are quite restricted. For example, only one of the four situations was concerned with incompatible expectations stemming from superintendents' occupancy of two positions, or "inter-role conflict" situations, and in this case the theory provided the smallest proportion of correct predictions: only 79 percent as compared with 91 percent of all situations combined (see Table 1). The suggestion, based on an examination of those cases in which errors were made, that there may be in some cases a "priority among positions" points up the inadequacy of our test. It was impossible to examine this possibility in detail with our data, although it would seem necessary to do so before giving credence to the implication of the theory that it would apply to all incompatible expectation situations. Furthermore, the fact that superintendents are members of a "profession" would suggest that the "moral-expediency" dimension may be more cogent for their decisions than for the decisions of delinquents, for example.

Despite these possible inadequacies we would like to emphasize that a special point was made of using concepts in this theory which are widely applicable. The perceptions of incumbents of any position with respect to the expectations to which they are exposed, the legitimacy of the expectations, and the probable sanctions resulting from failure to conform to them are all concepts which are capable of operational definition under almost any conceivable condition. Furthermore, whether or not position incumbents are primarily oriented to the legitimacy or to the sanctions dimensions should be capable of operational specification no matter what the "absolute meaning" of legitimacy and sanctions may be for different incumbents of different positions. The isolation of these relatively serviceable conceptual elements of a theory of role conflict resolution may prove suggestive for further empirical explorations.

A THEORY OF ROLE STRAIN *

The conception of the institutional structure implicit in the work reviewed so far is analogous to the script of a play. The role expectations attached to each position are like the lines in the script for each of the parts. Strain is experienced by the actors when the play is poorly written: the lines are not clear, they require an actor to say or do incompatible things, etc. In the theoretical essay which follows, Goode abandons this static con-

ception of the social structure, and presents a conceptualization in which the actors contribute actively to the form that this structure takes. Moreover, this active process occurs over a period of time and involves a series of adjustments calculated to minimize, but not eliminate, strain. A central idea in his formulation is that role strain is inevitable. It results not just from poorly developed systems of relations, but is inevitable in any system because persons are not adequately motivated to carry out all their role obligations. In fact, the sheer volume and complexity of such demands make it inevitable that actors will experience strain.

Starting from the standpoint that strain is in-

* The selection following the editorial introduction is reprinted from "A theory of role strain," *American Sociological Review*, 1960, **25**, 483–496, by permission of the author and the American Sociological Association.

evitable, Goode suggests that the crucial problem facing an individual is one of allocating his role performances in a manner which minimizes strain. Each actor does this through a series of bargains with his various role partners. These bargains reflect in part the actor's relative power in the role market and, in part, limits imposed by third parties who enforce the going price for a given role performance. In this analysis the resolution of role strain becomes a basic societal process. Goode's approach provides a much more dynamic model of the social structure, and should this conceptual alternative prove useful in the development and testing of new empirical relations, it may well succeed the conceptual formulations that have guided most of the research on role strain.

43.

A Theory of Role Strain[1]

WILLIAM J. GOODE
COLUMBIA UNIVERSITY

When social structures are viewed as made up of roles, social stability is not explicable as a function of (a) the normative consensual commitment of individuals or (b) normative integration. Instead, dissensus and role strain —the difficulty of fulfilling role demands—are normal. In a sequence of role bargains, the individual's choices are shaped by mechanisms, outlined here, through which he organizes his total role system and performs well or ill in any role relationship. Reduction of role strain is allocated or economic in form, but the economic model is different. "Third parties" interact with an individual and his alter, to keep their bargain within institutionalized limits. The larger social structure is held in place by role strains. The cumulative pattern of all such role bargains determines the flow of performances to all institutions. The research utility of this conception is explained.

The present paper is based on the general view that institutions are made up of role relationships, and approaches both social action and social

structure through the notion of "role strain," the felt difficulty in fulfilling role obligations. Role relations are seen as a sequence of "role bargains," and as a continuing process of selection among alternative role behaviors, in which each individual seeks to reduce his role strain. These choices determine the allocations of role performances to all institutions of the society. Within the limited compass of this paper, only a few of the possible implications of role strain as a theoretical approach can be explored.

The widespread notion that institutions are made up of roles is fruitful because it links a somewhat more easily observable phenomenon, social behavior, to an important but less easily observable abstraction, social structure. In functionalist terms, this notion also links the observed acts and inferred values of the individual with the institutional imperatives or requisites of the society. At the same time, by focusing on the elements in the individual's action decision, it avoids the pitfall of supposing that people carry out their obligations because these are "functional" for the society.

Approaching role interaction in terms of role strain offers the possibility of buttressing more adequately the empirical weaknesses of the most widely accepted theoretical view of society,[2] according to which the continuity of social roles, and thus the maintenance of the society, is mainly a function of two major variables: the normative, consensual commitment of the individuals of the society; and the integration among the norms held by those individuals. Although this view is superior to earlier ones,[3] it fails to explain how a complex urban society keeps going[4] because it does not account for the following awkward empirical facts:[5]

1. Some individuals do not accept even supposedly central values of the society.

[1] Completed under National Institute of Mental Health Grant No. 2526-S.

I am indebted to several of my colleagues for criticism of this and related papers, and especially to Amitai Etzioni, Johan Galtung, Robert K. Merton, Charles H. Page, Morris Zelditch, and Hans L. Zetterberg.

[2] I prefer to call this the "Lintonian model" (Ralph Linton, *The Study of Man*, New York: Appleton-Century, 1936), although Linton is not, of course, the creator of this model. Rather, he summed up a generation of thought about social structure in a clear and illuminating fashion, so that for many years the definitions and statements in this book were widely cited by both anthropologists and sociologists. Of course, "everyone knows" these weaknesses, but our basic model is not thereby changed to account for them.

[3] For a systematic statement of several earlier models, see Talcott Parsons, *The Structure of Social Action*, New York: McGraw-Hill, 1937, Chapter 2.

[4] For an earlier discussion relevant to this paper, see William J. Goode, "Contemporary Thinking about Primitive Religion," *Soziologus*, 5 (1955), pp. 122–131; also in Morton Fried (editor), *Readings in Anthropology*, New York: Crowell, 1959, Vol. II, pp. 450–460.

[5] For a good exposition of certain aspects of dissensus as they apply to American society, see Robin W. Williams, *American Society*, New York: Knopf, 1956, esp. pp. 352 ff.

2. Individuals vary in their emotional commitment to both important and less important values.
3. This value commitment varies by class strata, and by other characteristics of social position, for example, age, sex, occupation, geographic region, and religion.
4. Even when individuals accept a given value, some of them also have a strong or weak "latent commitment" to very different or contradictory values.[6]
5. Conformity with normative prescriptions is not a simple function of value commitment; there may be value commitment without conformity or conformity without commitment.
6. When individuals' social positions change, they may change both their behavior and their value orientations.
7. The values, ideals, and role obligations of every individual are at times in conflict.

Under the current conception of roles as units of social structures, presumably we should observe the role decisions of individuals in order to see how the society continues. On first view, as can be seen from the above list of points, the basis of social stability or integration seems precarious, and the decisions of the individual puzzling. For even when "the norms of the society" are fully accepted by the individual, they are not adequate guides for individual action. Order cannot be imposed by any *general* solution for all role decisions, since the total set of role obligations is probably unique for every individual. On the other hand, the individual may face different types of role demands and conflicts, which he feels as "role strains" when he wishes to carry out specific obligations.

In the immediately following sections, the major sources and types of role strain are specified, and thereafter the two main sets of mechanisms which the individual may use to reduce role strain are analyzed.

TYPES OF ROLE STRAIN

It is an axiom, rarely expressed, of social theory that the individuals who face common role obligations *can* generally fulfill them. Indeed, most theories of stratification and criminality require such an assumption, and common opinion uses it as a basis for its moral demands on the individual. We may suppose, as a corollary, that there are theoretical limits to the specific demands which societies may make of men. In addition,

the "theorem of institutional integration"[7] is roughly correct as an orienting idea: people generally *want* to do what they are supposed to do, and this is what the society needs to have done in order to continue.

Yet, with respect to any given norm or role obligation, there are always some persons who cannot conform, by reason of individuality or situation: they do not have sufficient resources, energy, and so on. A wider view of all such obligations discloses the following types or sources of role strain:

First, even when role demands are not onerous, difficult, or displeasing, they are required at particular times and places. Consequently, virtually no role demand is such a spontaneous pleasure that conformity with it is always automatic.

Second, all individuals take part in many *different* role relationships, for each of which there will be somewhat different obligations.[8] Among these, there may be either contradictory performances required (the bigamous husband; the infantry lieutenant who must order his close friend to risk his life in battle) or conflicts of time, place, or resources. These are conflicts of allocation (civic as against home obligations).

Third, each role relationship typically demands *several* activities or responses. Again, there may be inconsistencies (what the husband does to balance his family budget may impair his emotional relations with the members of his household). There may be different but not quite contradictory norms which may be applied to the various behavioral demands of the same role (the clergyman as the emotionally neutral counselor, but as a praising or condemnatory spiritual guide). Perhaps most jobs fall into this category, in that their various demands create some strain as between the norms of quantity and quality, technical excellence and human relations skills, and universalism and particularism.

Finally, many role relationships are "role sets," that is, the individual engages, by virtue of *one* of his positions, in several role relationships with different individuals.[9]

---

[6] Charles H. Page has reminded me that role diversity is not confined to modern societies, as the work of functionalist anthropologists (e.g., Malinowski's *Crime and Custom* and Benedict's *Patterns of Culture*) has shown. This empirical fact is of considerable theoretical consequence, especially for the relations between adjacent social strata or castes, or between conquerors and the conquered.

[7] This is the label which Talcott Parsons has suggested for the view, generally accepted since Durkheim's *Division of Labor*, that the maintenance of the society rests on desires of individuals to do things which must be done if the society is to survive. *The Social System*, Glencoe, Ill.: Free Press, 1949, pp. 36–43.

[8] In this paper, I distinguish role and status on the basis of only "degree of institutionalization": all role relations are somewhat institutionalized, but statuses are more fully institutionalized.

[9] Cf. Robert K. Merton, *Social Theory and Social Structure*, Glencoe, Ill.: Free Press, 1957, pp. 369ff. For its use in an

The individual is thus likely to face a wide, distracting, and sometimes conflicting array of role obligations. If he conforms fully or adequately in one direction, fulfillment will be difficult in another. Even if he feels lonely, and would like to engage in additional role relationships, it is likely that he cannot fully discharge all the obligations he already faces. He cannot meet all these demands to the satisfaction of all the persons who are part of his total role network. Role strain—difficulty in meeting given role demands—is therefore normal. In general, *the individual's total role obligations are overdemanding.*

Consequently, although the theorem of institutional integration, or the assumption of norm commitment, offers an explanation for the fulfillment of the duties imposed by a single norm, it does not account for the integration of an individual's total role system, or the integration among the role systems of various individuals, which presumably make up the social structure. The individual's problem is how to make his whole role system manageable, that is, how to allocate his energies and skills so as to reduce role strain to some bearable proportions. For the larger social structure, the problem is one of integrating such role systems—by allocating the flow of role performances so that various institutional activities are accomplished.

THE REDUCTION OF ROLE STRAIN: EGO'S CHOICE

A sensitizing or orienting notion in functionalist as well as system theory—perhaps more properly called one element in the definition of a "system" —is that a strain is likely to be associated with some mechanisms for reducing it.[10] The individ-

ual can utilize two main sets of techniques for reducing his role strain: those which determine whether or when he will enter or leave a role relationship; and those which have to do with the actual role bargain which the individual makes or carries out with another.

Ego's manipulation of his role structure. Ego has at his disposal several ways of determining whether or when he will accept a role relationship:

1. Compartmentalization. This may be defined on the psychological level as the ability to ignore the problem of consistency. Socially, role relations tend toward compartmentalization because the individual makes his demands on another and feels them to be legitimate, in specific situations where he can avoid taking much account of the claims on that person. There seems to be no overall set of societal values which explicitly requires consistency or integration from the individual. The process of compartmentalization works mainly by (*a*) location and context and (*b*) situational urgency or crisis. The latter process permits the individual to meet the crisis on its own terms, setting aside for the moment the role demands which he was meeting prior to the crisis.

2. Delegation. This may be seen, at least in part, as one way of achieving compartmentalization. If, for example, secular counseling is inconsistent with the clergyman's moral leadership role, he may be able to delegate it. If secular manipulation by a church is inconsistent with its sacredness, it may delegate some secular acts to lay leaders or to specialized religious orders. A wife may delegate housekeeping, and some of the socialization and nursing of the child. Note, however, that the societal hierarchy of values is indicated by what may *not* be delegated: for example, the professor may not hire a ghost writer to produce his monographs, and the student may not delegate examinations.

3. Elimination of role relationships.[11] Curtailment may be difficult, since many of our role obligations flow from our status positions, such as those in the job or family, which are not easily eliminated. Of course, we can stop associating with a kinsman because of the demands he makes on us, and if our work-group sets norms which are too high for us to meet we can seek another job. Aside from social and even legal limits on role curtailment, however, some continuing role interaction is necessary to maintain the individual's self-image and possibly his personality structure: for example, many people feel "lost" upon retirement—their social existence is no longer validated.

4. Extension. The individual may expand his

---

empirical study, see Mary Jean Huntington, "The Development of a Professional Self Image," in R. K. Merton *et al.,* editors, *The Student-Physician,* Cambridge: Harvard University Press, 1957, pp. 180ff.

[10] Merton's "mechanisms" operate to *articulate* role sets; see Robert K. Merton, "The Role Set: Problems in Sociological Theory," *British Journal of Sociology,* 8 (June, 1957), pp. 113ff. Here, we are concerned with a more general problem, which includes role sets as a special source of role strain. Moreover, Merton is concerned with only one of our problems, integrating the total role systems of all individuals in a demarcated social system; while we are, in addition, concerned with the problem of the individual in integrating his own role system. Several of our mechanisms, then, are paralleled by Merton's. Compartmentalization partly corresponds, for example, to two of his—observability of the individual's role activities and observability of conflicting demands by members of the role set. Our mechanism of hierarchy or stratification, assigning higher or lower values to particular role demands, corresponds

to two of Merton's—the relative importance of statuses and differences of power among members of the role set.

[11] This, again, is a general case of which Merton's "abridging the role-set" is a special example (*ibid.,* p. 117).

role relations in order to plead these commitments as an excuse for not fulfilling certain obligations. A departmental chairman, for example, may become active in university affairs so that he can meet his colleagues' demands for time with the plea that other duties (known to his colleagues) are pressing. In addition, the individual may expand his role system so as to *facilitate* other role demands, for instance, joining an exclusive club so as to meet people to whom he can sell stocks and bonds.

5. Obstacles against the indefinite expansion of ego's role system. Although the individual may reduce his felt strain by expanding his role system and thereby diminishing the level of required performance for any one of his obligations, this process is also limited: After a possible initial reduction, *Role strain begins to increase more rapidly with a larger number of roles than do the corresponding role rewards or counterpayments from alter.* This differential is based on the limited role resources at individual's commands. The rewards cannot increase at the same rate as the expansion even if at first he increases his skill in role manipulation, because eventually he must begin to fail in some of his obligations, as he adds more relationships; consequently, his alters will not carry out the counter-performances which are expected for that role relationship. Consequently, he cannot indefinitely expand his role system.

6. Barriers against intrusion. The individual may use several techniques for preventing others from initiating, or even continuing, role relationships—the executive hires a secretary through whom appointments must be made, the professor goes on a sabbatical leave. The administrator uses such devices consciously, and one of the most common complaints of high level professionals and executives is that they have no time. This feeling is closely connected with the fact that they *do* have time, that is, they may dispose of their time as they see fit. Precisely because such men face and accept a wider array of role opportunities, demands, and even temptations than do others, they must make more choices and feel greater role strain. At the same time, being in demand offers some satisfaction, as does the freedom to choose. At lower occupational ranks, as well as in less open social systems where duties are more narrowly prescribed, fewer choices can or need be made.

Settling or carrying out the terms of the role relationship. The total role structure functions so as to reduce role strain. The techniques outlined above determine whether an individual will have a role relationship with another, but they do not specify what performances the individual will carry out for another. A common decision process underlies the individual's sequence of role performance as well as their total pattern.

1. The role relationship viewed as a transaction or "bargain." In his personal role system, the individual faces the same problem he faces in his economic life: he has limited resources to be allocated among alternative ends. The larger social system, too, is like the economic system, for the problem in both is one of integration, of motivating people to stop doing X and start doing Y, whether this is economic production or religious behavior.

Because economic structures are also social structures, and economic decisions are also role decisions, it might be argued that economic propositions are simply "special cases" of sociological propositions.[12] In a more rigorous methodological sense, however, this claim may be viewed skeptically, since at present the former body of propositions cannot be deduced from the latter.[13] Rather, economic theory may be a fruitful source of sociological ideas, because its theoretical structure is more advanced than that of sociology. Since the precise relation between economic and sociological propositions is not yet fully ascertained, economic vocabulary and ideas are mainly used in the succeeding analysis for clarity of presentation, and the correctness of propositions which are developed here is independent of their possible homologs in economics.[14] In this view, economic performance is one type of role per-

---

[12] Some structural differences between the two cases, however, should be noted: (*1*) There are specialized economic *producers*, for example, wheat farmers who offer only one product on the market, but no corresponding sociological positions in which the individual offers only one type of role performance. Some political, religious, military, or occupational leaders do "produce" their services for a large number of people, but they must all carry out many other roles as well in the "role market." Every adult must take part as producer in a minimum number of such role markets. (*2*) Correspondingly, in the economic sphere all participate in several markets as *buyers;* in the role sphere they act in several markets as *both* sellers and buyers. (*3*) Correlatively, our entrance into the economic *producer* or *seller* activities may be long delayed, and we may retire from them early if we have enough money, but as long as we live we must remain in the role market: we need other people, and they demand us. (*4*) We may accumulate enough money so as to be able to purchase more than we can use, or produce more than we can sell, in the economic sphere; but in the role system we probably always ask more on the whole than our alters can give, and are unable to give as much as they demand.

[13] The most elaborate recent attempt to state the relations between the two is Talcott Parsons and Neil J. Smelser, *Economy and Society,* Glencoe, Ill.: Free Press, 1956.

[14] Again, however, correctness is independent of their origin. It is equally clear that they parallel certain conceptions of psychodynamics, but again their sociological value is independent of their usefulness in that field.

formance, a restricted case in which economists attempt to express role performance, reward, and punishment in monetary terms.[15] In both, the individual must respond to legitimate demands made on him (role expectations, services, goods, or demands for money) by carrying out his role obligations (performances, goods or money payments). Through the perception of alternative role strains or goods-services-money costs, the individual adjusts the various demands made upon him, by moving from one role action to another. Both types of transactions, of course, express *evaluations* of goods, performances, and money.

In his role decisions, as in his economic decisions, the individual seeks to keep his felt strain, role cost, or monetary and performance cost at a minimum, and may even apply some rationality to the problem. At the same time, a variety of pressures will force him to accept some solutions which are not pleasant. His decisions are also frequently habitual rather than calculated, and even when calculated may not achieve his goal. Rather, they are the most promising, or the best choice he sees. Since the analysis of such behavior would focus on the act and its accompanying or preceding decision, the research approach of "decision analysis" seems appropriate to ascertain the course of events which led to the act.[16]

In role behavior, we begin to experience strain, worry, anxiety, or the pressures of others if we devote more time and attention to one role obligation than we feel we should, or than others feel we should. This strain may be felt because, given a finite sum of role resources, too much has already been expended; or because the individual feels that relative to a given value the cost is too high. The relative strength of such pressures from different obligations determines, then, the individual's role allocation pattern within his total role system. This system is the resultant of all

[15] Anthropologists have noted for over a generation that economic theory needs a more general framework to take account of the non-monetary aspects of economic action in non-Western societies. Cf. Bronislaw Malinowski, "Primitive Economics of the Trobriand Islanders," *Economic Journal* 31 (March, 1921), pp. 1–16. See also Malinowski's earlier article, "The Economic Aspects of the Intichiuma Ceremonies," *Festskrift Tillagnad Edward Westermarck*, Helsingfors: 1912; and *Argonauts of the Western Pacific*, London: Routledge, 1922. Also Raymond Firth, *Primitive Economics of the New Zealand Maori*, New York: Dutton, 1929. For a discussion of the interaction of economic roles and religious roles, see William J. Goode, *Religion Among the Primitives*, Glencoe, Ill.: Free Press, 1951, Chapters 5, 6.

[16] See the several discussions in Paul F. Lazarsfeld and Morris Rosenberg, editors, *The Language of Social Research*, Glencoe, Ill.: Free Press, 1955, pp. 387–448.

such strains. Analysis of role allocation requires, of course, that we know the individual's *internal* demands, that is, the demands which he makes on himself, and which thus contribute to his willingness to perform well or not.[17]

The process of strain allocation is facilitated somewhat, as noted above, by ego's ability to manipulate his role structure. On the other hand, the structure is kept in existence by, and is based on, the process of allocation. For example, with reference to the norms of adequate role performance, to be considered later, the white child in the South may gradually learn that his parents will disapprove a close friendship with a Negro boy, but (especially in rural regions) may not disapprove a casual friendship. The "caste" role definitions state that in the former relationship he is over-performing, that is, "paying too much." Such social pressures, expressed in both individual and social mechanisms, are homologous to those in the economic market, where commodities also have a "going price," based on accepted relative evaluations. Correspondingly, the individual expresses moral disapproval when his role partner performs much less well than usual, or demands far more than usual.

In all societies, the child is taught the "value of things," whether they are material objects or role performances, by impressing upon him *that* he must allocate his role performances, and *how* he should allocate them.[18] These structural elements are considered in a later section.

2. Setting the role price in the role bargain. The level of role performance which the individual finally decides upon, the "role price," is the resultant of the interaction between three supply-demand factors: (*a*) his pre-existing or autonomous norm commitment—his desire to carry out the performance; (*b*) his judgment as to how much his role partner will punish or reward him for his performance; and (*c*) the esteem or disesteem with which the peripheral social networks or important reference groups ("third parties") will respond to *both* ego's performance and to alter's attempts to make ego perform adequately.

The individual will perform well ("pay high") if he *wants* very much to carry out this role obligation as against others. He will devote much more time and energy to his job if he really enjoys his work, or is deeply committed normatively to its aims. The individual's willingness to carry out

[17] Price in an elementary economics textbook, determined by the intersection of supply and demand, requires no such datum (i.e., why or whence the demand is not relevant), and thus the model is simpler than the role model. However, more sophisticated economics, as well as the economic practitioner, must distinguish various components or sources of demand.

[18] Doubtless, however, the lessons can be made more explicit and conclusive when the "value" can be expressed in dollars rather than in the equally intangible (but more difficult to measure) moral or esthetic considerations.

the role performance varies, being a function of the intrinsic gratifications in the activity, the prospective gain from having carried out the activity, and the internal self-reward or self-punishment from conscience pangs or shame or a sense of virtue, or the like.

With reference to what ego expects alter to do in turn, he is more likely to over-perform, or perform well if alter can and will (relative to others) reward ego well or pay him well for a good or poor execution of his role obligations. Thus, my predictions as to what will make my beloved smile or frown will affect my performance greatly; but if she loves me while I love her only little, then the same smiles or frowns will have less effect on my role performances for her.[19] Similarly, as will be noted below in more detail, alter's power, esteem, and resources affect ego's performance because they allow alter to punish or reward ego more fully. The individual perceives these consequences cognitively and responds to them emotionally. If, then, the individual aspires to be accepted by a higher ranking individual or group, he may have to perform more adequately than for one of his own rank. This last proposition requires a further distinction. Alter may be able, because of his position, to reward ego more than alter rewards others in a similar status, but this additional reward may be no more than a socially accepted premium for extra performance. On the other hand, the additional reward may sometimes be viewed by those others as beyond the appropriate amount. Or the individual may over-perform in one activity of his role relationship to compensate for a poor performance in another—say, the poor breadwinner who tries to be a good companion to his children. Such further consequences of higher performance and higher reward may at times be taken into account by both role partners in making their role bargain.

If alter asks that ego perform consistently better than he is able or willing to do, then he may ease his allocation strain by severing his relationship with that individual or group and by seeking new role relationships in which the allocation strain is less.[20]

3. *Limitations on a "free role bargain."* The third component in ego's decision to perform his role bargain is the network of role relationship—"the third party" or parties—with which ego and alter are in interaction. If either individual is able to exploit the other by driving an especially hard

role bargain, such third parties may try to influence either or both to change the relationship back toward the "going role price." Not only do they feel this to be their duty, but they have an interest in the matter as well, since (*a*) the exploiting individual may begin to demand that much, or pay that little, in his role relations with them; and (*b*) because the exploited individual may thereby perform less well in his role relations with them. These pressures from third parties include the demand that either ego or alter punish or reward the other for his performances or failures.[21]

It is not theoretically or empirically clear whether such third parties must always be a limited reference group, or can at times be the entire society. Many of the norms of reference groups appear to be special definitions or applications of similar norms of the larger society. Certain groups, such as criminal gangs or power cliques in a revolutionary political party, may give radical twists of meaning to the norms of the larger society. Under such circumstances, the interaction of pressures on ego and alter from various third parties can be complex. We suppose that *which* third party is most important in a given role transaction between ego and alter is a function of the degree of concern felt by various third parties and of the amount of pressures that any of them can bring to bear on either ego or alter.

STRUCTURAL LIMITS AND DETERMINANTS

Strain-reducing mechanisms. The individual can thus reduce his role strain somewhat: first, by selecting a set of roles which are singly less onerous, as mutually supportive as he can manage, and minimally conflicting; and, second, by obtaining as gratifying or value-productive a bargain as he can with each alter in his total role pattern.

As the existence of third parties attests, however, both sets of ego's techniques are limited and determined by a larger structural context within which such decisions are made. Not all such structural elements reduce ego's role strain; indeed, they may increase it, since they may enforce actions which are required for the society rather than the individual. Essentially, whether they increase or reduce the individual's role strain, they determine which of the first set of mechanisms ego may use, and on what terms. Similarly, they determine whether ego and alter may or must bargain freely, to either's disadvantage, or

[19] Cf. Willard Waller's "Principle of Least Interest" in Willard Waller and Reuben Hill, *The Family*, New York: Dryden, 1952, pp. 191–192.

[20] Cf. Leon Festinger's Derivation C, in "A Theory of Social Comparison Processes," *Reprint Services No. 22*, Laboratory for Research in Social Relations, University of Minnesota, 1955, p. 123. Also see No. 24, "Self-Evaluation as a Function of Attraction to the Group," by Leon Festinger, Jane Torrey, and Ben Willerman.

[21] Note, for example, the potential "seduction" of the mother by the child; the mother wishes to please the child to make him happy, and may have to be reminded by others that she is "spoiling" him.

to what extent either can or must remain in an advantageous or costly bargaining position. The most important of such elements are perhaps the following:

1. Hierarchy of evaluations. Social evaluations are the source of the individual's evaluations, but even if only the frequently occurring types of choices are considered, such evaluations reveal complex patterns.[22] Some sort of overall value hierarchy seems to be accepted in every society, but aside from individual idiosyncrasies, both situational and role characteristics may change the evaluation of given acts. Indeed, all individuals may accept contradictory values in some areas of action, which are expressed under different circumstances. Here, the most important of these qualifying factors are: (*a*) the social position of ego (one should pay some respect to elders, but if one is, say, 30 years of age, one may pay less); (*b*) the social position of alter (the power, prestige, or resources of alter may affect ego's decision); (*c*) the content of the performance by ego or alter (mother-nurse obligations are more important than housekeeper-laundress duties); and (*d*) situational urgency or crisis. When ego gives the excuse of an urgent situation, alter usually retaliates less severely. However, when several crises occur simultaneously, the allocation of role performances is likely to be decided instead by reference to more general rankings of value.[23]

These illustrations suggest how structural factors help to determine ego's willingness to perform or his performance, in an existing role relationship (Type 1*b*), and though they reduce his uncertainty as to what he should or must do, they also may increase his obligations. At the same time, these same factors also determine in part whether or when ego will include the relationship at all (Type 1*a*) in his total role system (for example, a noted physicist should engage in a technical correspondence with a fellow physicist, but may refuse to appear on a popular television show; even a passing stranger is expected to give needed aid in a rescue operation).

This set of interacting factors is complex, but gives some guidance in role interaction. Since

there is a loose, society-wide hierarchy of evaluations, and both individuals and their reference groups or "third parties" may be committed to a somewhat different hierarchy of values, at least the following combinations of evaluations may occur:

EVALUATIONS BY:	EVALUATIONS OF:		
	Task Content	Rank of Alter	Situational Urgency
Society			
Reference groups or third parties			
Alter			
Ego			

2. Third parties. Though third parties figure most prominently in the bargaining within an existing role relationship, especially those which are more fully institutionalized (statuses), they also take part in ego's manipulation of his role structure, since they may be concerned with his total social position. For example, families are criticized by kinsmen, neighbors, and friends if they do not press their children in the direction of assuming a wider range of roles and more demanding roles as they grow older.

3. Norms of adequacy. These define what is an acceptable role performance.[24] Norms of adequacy are observable even in jobs which set nearly limitless ideals of performance, such as the higher levels of art and science, for they are gauged to the experience, age, rank, and esteem of the individual. For example, a young instructor need not perform as well as a full professor; but to achieve that rank he must perform as well as his seniors believe they performed at his rank. Such norms also apply to the total system of roles assumed by the individual. The individual may criticize another not only when the latter's specific performance fails to meet such criteria, but also when the latter's range of roles is too narrow (the wife complains, "We never go out and meet people") or too wide (the husband complains, "You take care of everything in the community except me").

The individual must assume more roles in an urban society than in primitive or peasant society, and the norm of functional specificity applies to a higher proportion of them. This norm permits individuals to bargain within a narrower range, but also, by limiting the mutual obligations of individuals (and thus tending to reduce role strain), it permits them to assume a larger number of roles than would otherwise be possible.

---

[22] Norman Miller has used data from the Cornell Values Study to show how various combinations of social positions affect expression of value in *Social Class Differences among American College Students*, Ph.D. thesis, Columbia University, 1958.

[23] In an unpublished paper on "doubling" (the living together of relatives who are not members of the same nuclear family), Morris Zelditch has used approximately these categories to analyze the conditions under which the claim to such a right is likely to be respected.

[24] This mechanism is akin to, though not identical with, Merton's "mutual social support among status occupants." Merton, "The Role Set . . . ," *op. cit.*, p. 116.

This, then, is a role system basis for the generally observed phenomenon of *Gesellschaft* or secondary relations in urban society.

4. Linkage or dissociation of role obligations in different institutional orders. The fulfillment of role obligations in one institutional order either rests on or requires a performance in another.[25] Thus, to carry out the obligations of father requires the fulfillment of job obligations. Such doubled obligations are among the strongest in the society, in the sense that ego may insist on rather advantageous terms if he is asked to neglect them in favor of some other obligation. Linking two institutional orders in this fashion limits ego's freedom to manipulate his role system.

At the same time, there are barriers against combining various roles, even when the individual might find such a linkage congenial. (For example: a military rule against officers fraternizing intimately with enlisted men; a regulation forbidding one to be both a lawyer and a partner of a certified public accountant.) In an open society, some role combinations are permitted which would be viewed as incongruous or prohibited in a feudal or caste society.

Such pressures are expressed in part by the punishments which the individual may have to face if he insists on entering disapproved combinations of roles. The barriers against some combinations also apply to a special case of role expansion: entrance into certain very demanding statuses, those which require nearly continuous performance, are subject to frequent crises or urgencies, and are highly evaluated.[26] Even in our own society there are not many such statuses. The combination of two or more sets of potential crises and responsibilities would make for considerable role strain, so that few individuals would care to enter them; but in addition organizational rules sometimes, and common social attitudes usually, oppose such combinations.—The priest may not be a mother; the head of a hospital may not be a high political leader.

5. Ascriptive statuses. All statuses, but especially ascriptive statuses, limit somewhat ego's ability to bargain, since social pressures to conform to their norms are stronger than for less institutionalized roles. Some of these require exchanges of performances between specific individuals (I cannot search for the mother who will serve my needs best, as she cannot look for a more filial child) while others (female, Negro, "native American") embody expectations between status segments of the population. The former are more restrictive than the latter, but both types narrow considerably the area in which individuals can work out a set of performances based on their own desires and bargaining power. Because individuals do not usually leave most ascriptive statuses, some may have to pay a higher role price than they would in an entirely free role market, or may be able (if their ascription status is high in prestige and power) to exact from others a higher role performance.[27] The psychological dimensions of these limitations are not relevant for our discussion. It should be noted, however, that at least one important element in the persistence of personality patterns is to be found in these limitations: the role structure remains fairly stable because the individual cannot make many free role bargains and thus change his role system or the demands made on him, and consequently the individual personality structure is also maintained by the same structural elements.[28]

6. Lack of profit in mutual role deviation. Since two role partners depend in part on each other's mutual performance for their own continuing interaction with other persons, mutual role deviation will only rarely reduce their role strain. It might be advantageous to me if my superior permits me to loaf on the job, but only infrequently can he also profit from my loafing. Consequently, both ego and alter have a smaller range of choices, and the demands of the institutional order or organization are more likely to be met. When, moreover, in spite of these interlocking controls, ego and alter do find a mode of deviation which is mutually profitable—the bribed policeman and the professional criminal, the smothering mother and the son who wants to be dependent—concerned outsiders, third parties, or even a larger segment of the society are likely to disapprove and retaliate more strongly than when either ego or alter deviates one-sidedly.

On the other hand, there is the special case in which ego and alter share the same status—as colleagues or adolescent peers, for example. They are then under similar pressures from others, and may seek similar deviant solutions; they may gang together and profit collectively in certain ways from their deviation.[29]

---

[25] I have described this mechanism of institutional integration in some detail in *Religion Among the Primitives, op. cit.,* Chapters 5–10.

[26] Perhaps the third characteristic is merely a corollary of the first two.

[27] Although the matter cannot be pursued here, it seems likely that in economic terms we are dealing here with the phenomena of the "differentiated product"—ego cannot accept a given role performance from just anyone, but from the specific people with whom he is in interaction—and of oligopoly—ego can patronize only a limited number of suppliers or sellers. Moreover, with respect to certain roles, both supply and demand are relatively inelastic.

[28] Cf. C. Addison Hickman and Manford H. Kuhn, *Individuals, Groups, and Economic Behavior,* New York: Dryden, 1956, p. 38.

[29] Albert K. Cohen has discussed one example of this special

*Less desirable statuses: Efforts to change the role
barbain.* The preceding analysis of how ego and
alter decide whether, when, or how well they will
carry out their role obligations permits the deduction of the proposition that when an individual's
norm commitment or desire to perform is *low*
with respect to a given status—in our society,
many women, Negroes, and adolescents reject
one or more of the obligations imposed on them;
perhaps slaves in all societies do—then alter must
bring greater pressure to bear on him in order
to ensure what alter judges to be an adequate
performance. If the individual does under-per-
form, he is less likely to have strong feelings of
self-failure or disesteem; he may feel no more
than some recognition of, and perhaps anxiety
about, possible sanctions from alter.

Individuals are especially conscious that they
are "training" others in both child and adult
socialization, if those others are suspected of being
weakly committed to their role obligations. Thus,
most Whites in the South have for generations
held that all Whites have an obligation to remind
the Negro by punishment and reward that he
"should keep in his place," and that punishment
of the Negro is especially called for when he
shows evidence that he does not accept that place.
It is the heretic, not the sinner, who is the more
dangerous. It is particularly when the members
of a subordinate status begin to deny normatively
their usual obligations that third parties become
aroused and more sensitive to evidence of deviation in either performance or norm commitment.
On the other hand, individuals in a formerly subordinate status may, over time, acquire further
bargaining power, while those in a superior status
may gradually come to feel less committed to the
maintenance of the former role pattern.

THE FAMILY AS A ROLE BUDGET CENTER

For adult or child, the family is the main center
of role allocation, and thus assumes a key position in solutions of role strain. Most individuals
must account to their families for what they spend
in time, energy, and money outside the family.
And ascriptive status obligations of high evaluation or primacy are found in the family. More
important, however, is the fact that family members are often the only persons who are likely
to know how an individual is allocating his *total*
role energies, managing his whole role system;
or that he is spending "too much" time in one role

obligation and retiring from others. Consequently,
family relations form the most immediate and
persistent set of interactions which are of importance in social control. Formal withdrawal
from these relationships is difficult, and informal
withdrawal arouses both individual guilt feelings
and pressures from others.

Moreover, since the family is a role allocation
center, where one's alters know about one's total
role obligations and fulfillments, it also becomes
a vantage point from which to view one's total
role system in perspective. Because it is a set of
status obligations which change little from day
to day and from which escape is difficult, role
alternatives can be evaluated against a fairly
stable background. Consequently, other family
members can and do give advice as to how to
allocate energies from a "secure center." Thus it
is from this center that one learns the basic procedures of balancing role strains.

Finally, family roles are "old shoe" roles in
which expectations and performances have become
well meshed so that individuals can relax in them.
In Western society, it is mainly the occupational
statuses which are graded by fine levels of prestige,
just as achievement within occupations is rewarded
by fine degrees of esteem. It is not that within
jobs one is held to standards, while within families
one is not.[30] It is rather that, first, socialization
on the basis of status ascription within the family
fits individual expectations to habitual performances and, second, rankings of family performances are made in only very rough categories of
esteem. The intense sentiments within the family
cushion individual strain by inducing each person
to make concessions, to give sympathy, to the
others. Of course, greater strain is experienced
when they do not. These status rights and obligations become, then, "role retreats" or "role
escapes," with demands which are felt to be less
stringent, or in which somewhat more acceptable
private bargains have been made among the various members of the group. One's performance is
not graded by the whole society, and one's family
compares one's family performance to only a
limited extent with that of other people in other
families.

The existence of unranked or grossly ranked
performance statuses or roles may permit the
individual to give a higher proportion of his energy
to the ranked performance statuses. The institutions which contain such statuses vary. For example, in contemporary Western society, the
layman's religious performances, like his familial
performances, are ranked only roughly, but at
one time evaluation of the former was more differentiated. However, familial performance apparently is never ranked in fine gradation in any

---

case at length in *Delinquent Boys*, Glencoe, Ill.: Free Press, 1955.
It requires, among other factors, special ecological conditions
and the possibility of communication among those in the
same situation.

[30] See Melvin Tumin's discussion of incentives in various non-
occupational statuses in "Rewards and Task Orientations,"
American Sociological Review, 20 (August, 1955), pp. 419–422.

society.[31] Here, an implicit structural proposition may be made explicit: the greater the degree of achievement orientation in a system of roles, the finer the gradation of prestige rankings within that system or organization.[32]

ROLE STRAIN AND THE LARGER SOCIAL STRUCTURE

Social structures are made up of role relationships, which in turn are made up of role transactions. Ego's efforts to reduce his role strain determine the allocation of his energies to various role obligations, and thus determine the flow of performances to the institutions of the society. Consequently, the sum of role decisions determines what *degree* of integration exists among various elements of the social structure. While these role performances accomplish whatever is done to meet the needs of the society, nevertheless the latter may not be adequately served. It is quite possible that what gets done is not enough, or that it will be ineffectively done. As already noted, the role demands made by one institutional order often conflict with those made by another—at a minimum, because the "ideal" fulfillment in each is not qualified by other institutional demands and would require much of any person's available resources. Many such conflicting strains frequently result in changes in the social structure. Within smaller sub-systems, such as churches, corporations, schools, and political parties, the total flow of available personal resources may be so disintegrative or ineffective that the system fails to survive. In addition, the total role performances in some societies have failed to maintain the social structure as a whole.

Thus, though the sum of role performances ordinarily maintains a society, it may also change the society or fail to keep it going. There is no necessary harmony among all role performances, even though these are based ultimately on the values of the society which are at least to some extent harmonious with one another. Role theory does not, even in the general form propounded

here, explain why some activities are ranked higher than others, why some activities which help to maintain the society are ranked higher, or why there is some "fit" between the role decisions of individuals and what a society needs for survival.

The total efforts of individuals to reduce their role strain within structural limitations directly determines the profile, structure, or pattern of the social system. But whether the resulting societal pattern is "harmonious" or integrated, or whether it is even effective in maintaining that society, are separate empirical questions.

SUMMARY AND CONCLUSIONS

The present paper attempts to develop role theory by exploiting the well-known notion that societal structures are made up of roles. The analysis takes as its point of departure the manifest empirical inadequacies, noted in the first section, of a widely current view of social stability, namely, that the continuity of a social system is mainly a function of two major variables: (*a*) the normative, consensual commitment of the individuals of the society; and (*b*) the integration among the norms held by those individuals. Accepting dissensus, nonconformity, and conflicts among norms and roles as the usual state of affairs, the paper develops the idea that the total role system of the individual is unique and over-demanding. The individual cannot satisfy fully all demands, and must move through a continuous sequence of role decisions and bargains, by which he attempts to adjust these demands. These choices and the execution of the decisions are made somewhat easier by the existence of mechanisms which the individual may use to organize his role system, or to obtain a better bargain in a given role. In addition, the social structure determines how much freedom in manipulation he possesses.

The individual utilizes such mechanisms and carries out his sequences of role behaviors through an underlying decision process, in which he seeks to reduce his role strain, his felt difficulty in carrying out his obligations. The form or pattern of his process may be compared to that of the economic decision: the allocation of scarce resources—role energies, time, emotions, goods—among alternative ends, which are the role obligations owed by the individual. The role performances which the individual can exact from others are what he gets in exchange.

It is to the individual's interest in attempting to reduce his role strain to demand as much as he can and perform as little, but since this is also true for others, there are limits on how advantageous a role bargain he can make. He requires some role performance from particular people. His own social rank or the importance of the task he is to perform may put him in a disadvantageous position from which to

---

[31] Partly because of the difficulty of outsiders observing crucial performances within it; partly, also, because of the difficulty of measuring relative achievement except in universalistic terms, as against the particularistic-ascriptive character of familial roles. Note, however, the creation by both Nazi Germany and Soviet Russia of a family title for very fertile mothers (an observable behavior).

[32] Note in this connection the case of China, the most family-oriented civilization. In comparison with other major civilizations, the Chinese developed a more complex ranking of kinship positions—and a more explicit ranking of familial performances. (See Marion J. Levy, Jr., *The Family Revolution in Modern China*, Cambridge: Harvard University Press, 1949, esp. Chapter 3). Various individuals have figured in Chinese history as "family heroes," that is, those who performed their family duties exceedingly well.

make a bargain. Beyond the immediate role relationship of two role partners stands a network of roles with which one or both are in interaction, and these third parties have both a direct and an indirect interest in their role transactions. The more institutionalized roles are statuses, which are backed more strongly by third parties. The latter sanction ego and alter when these two have made a free role bargain which is far from the going role price. The demands of the third parties may include the requirement that ego or alter punish the other for his failure to perform adequately.

Under this conception of role interaction, the bargains which some individuals make will be consistently disadvantageous to them: the best role price which they can make will be a poor one, even by their own standards. However, no one can ever escape the role market. The continuity of the individual's total role pattern, then, may be great even when he does not have a strong normative commitment to some of his less desirable roles. Like any structure or organized pattern, the role pattern is held in place by both internal and external forces—in this case, the role pressures from other individuals. Therefore, not only is role strain a normal experience for the individual, but since the individual processes of reducing role strain determine the total allocation of role performances to the social institutions, the total balances and imbalances of role strains create whatever stability the social structure possesses. On the other hand, precisely because each individual is under some strain and would prefer to be under less, and in particular would prefer to get more for his role performances than he now receives, various changes external to his own role system may alter the kind of role bargains

he can and will make. Each individual system is partly held in place by the systems of other people, their demands, and their counter-performances—which ego needs as a basis for his own activities. Consequently, in a society such as ours, where each individual has a very complex role system and in which numerous individuals have a relatively low intensity of norm commitment to many of their role obligations, changes in these external demands and performances may permit considerable change in the individual's system.

The cumulative pattern of all such role bargains determines the flow of performances to all social institutions and thus to the needs of the society for survival. Nevertheless, the factors here considered may not in fact insure the survival of a society, or of an organization within it. The quantity or quality of individual performances may undermine or fail to maintain the system. These larger consequences of individual role bargains can be traced out, but they figure only rarely in the individual role decision.

With respect to its utility in empirical research, this conception permits a more adequate delineation of social structures by focussing on their more observable elements, the role transactions. This permits such questions as: Would you increase the time and energy you now give to role relationship *X*? Or, granted that these are the ideal obligations of this relationship, how little can you get away with performing? Or, by probing the decision, it is possible to ascertain why the individual has moved from one role transaction to another, or from one role organization to another. Finally, this conception is especially useful in tracing out the articulation between one institution or organization and another, by following the sequence of an individual's role performance and their effects on the role performances of other individuals with relation to different institutional orders.

A **common** focus of Parts Four and Five was the more or less endur-ing structural properties of interaction. In Part Four, emphasis was placed on subinstitutional structures, most notably in the small-group setting; in Part Five, emphasis was mainly on institutional structures as conceptualized by role theory. The selections in Part Six also deal with interaction, but concentrate upon moment-to-moment exchange, on the sequential, give-and-take properties of interaction. Interest lies in discovering the order and regularity that underly this fluid process and in identifying the functional signifi-cance of the regularities. Special attention is given to the individual's definition of the situation and its consequences for his behavior toward the other person.

Although sociologists trained in the tradition called **symbolic interactionism** have long had a central interest in interaction proc-esses, recently other social psychologists have turned their attention in this direction. This trend is illustrated by the current interest in exchange theory, game theory, and the various empirical studies of bargaining and other topics that have grown out of these theories. Moreover, experimental methods have now developed to the point where they are capable of coping with the complexities of such inter-action, and they promise to provide the necessary data to test and further revise theoretical conceptualizations that until now have had very little empirical support of an experimental nature.

PART SIX

ONGOING INTERACTION PROCESSES

EMBARRASSMENT AND THE ANALYSIS OF ROLE REQUIREMENTS *

The following analysis by Gross and Stone re-sembles the previous one in focusing primarily on a conceptual analysis of interaction. Instances of embarrassment are considered disruptive of on-going interaction; they make it difficult or im-possible to perform one's role. Thus, an analysis of such instances is very useful for identifying the necessary requirements for adequate performance of one's role in everyday interaction. One thousand recalled instances of embarrassment were collected from college students, evening division students, and friends. These were classified and their major characteristics identified.

The three major requirements for role per-formance are identity, poise, and confidence in established identity and poise. By identity is meant the establishment of an individual in a defined position in a social situation; both he and the other person share a common definition of his identity. Any actions, events, or properties of the situation that contradict his identity are apt to give rise to embarrassment and to disrupt the interaction. Poise refers to the individual's control over self and situation; loss of poise provokes em-barrassment. Confidence enables both parties to ignore potentially disruptive events.

The present selection, like the previous one, furthers our understanding of ongoing interaction, in this case by emphasizing the underlying require-ments for role performance. The next step in the further development of this work would require a closer articulation between the concepts presented here and empirical data. In particular, experimental work is required to raise the level of certainty concerning these ideas.

44.

Embarrassment and the Analysis of Role Requirements[1]

EDWARD GROSS
GREGORY P. STONE
UNIVERSITY OF MINNESOTA

ABSTRACT

Since embarrassment incapacitates per-sons for continued role performance, it can provide an indicator of basic re-quirements of role performance. Study of one thousand instances of recalled embarrassment revealed three major requirements: identity, poise, and con-

* The selection following the editorial introduction is reprinted from "Embarrassment and the analysis of role requirements," *American Journal of Sociology*, 1964, **70**, 1–15, by permission of the authors and the University of Chicago Press.

[1] Revision of a paper read at the annual meeting of the Mid-west Sociological Society, April, 1963.

fidence in established identity and poise. The analysis of identity reveals the significance of adjunct roles and reserve and relict identities. Disturbances of poise revolve about the handling of spaces, props, equipment, clothing, and the body. Violations of confidence are prevented by performance norms. Finally, deliberate embarrassment is shown to have major social functions.

Attitudes, in the view of George Herbert Mead, are incipient acts. Meaningful discourse requires that discussants take one another's attitudes—incorporate one another's incipient activities—in their conversation. Since all social transactions are marked by meaningful communication, discursive or not, whenever people come together, they bring futures into one another's presence. They are ready, balanced, *poised* for the upcoming discussion. The discussion, of course, remands futures to a momentary present, where they are always somewhat inexactly realized, and relegates them in their altered form to the collective past we call memory. New futures are constantly built up in discussions. Indeed, they must be, else the discussion is over and the transaction is ended. Without a future, there is nothing else to be done, nothing left to say. Every social transaction, therefore, requires that the participants be poised at the outset and that poise be maintained as the transaction unfolds, until there is an accord that each can turn to other things and carry other futures away to other circles.

Poise is not enough. The futures that are presented, imperfectly realized, and re-established must be relevant. Relevance is achieved by establishing the *identities* of those who are caught up in the transaction. Futures or attitudes are anchored in identities. We speak of *role* as consensual attitudes mobilized by an announced and ratified identity. In social transactions, then, persons must announce who they are to enable each one to ready himself with reference to appropriate futures, providing attitudes which others may take or assume. Often announced identities are complementary, establishing the transaction as a social relationship, for many identities presuppose counteridentities. Whether or not this is the case, the maintenance of one's identity assists the maintenance of the other.[2]

Furthermore, all transactions are transactions through time. It is not enough that identity and poise be established. They must be continuously reaffirmed, maintained, and provisions made for their repair in case of breakdown. Role performers count on this. We attempt here to limn the structure of transactions by examining instances where identities have been misplaced or forgotten, where poise has been lost or destroyed, or where, for any reason, confidence that identities and poise will be maintained has been undermined. We have in mind instances of embarrassment, whether or not deliberately perpetrated.

EMBARRASSMENT AND THE ANALYSIS OF ROLE REQUIREMENTS

Embarrassment exaggerates the core dimensions of social transactions, bringing them to the eye of the observer in an almost naked state. Embarrassment occurs whenever some *central* assumption in a transaction has been *unexpectedly* and unqualifiedly discredited for at least one participant. The result is that he is incapacitated for continued role performance.[3] Moreover, embarrassment is infectious. It may spread out, incapacitating others not previously incapacitated. It is destructive dis-ease. In the wreckage left by embarrassment lie the broken foundations of social transactions. By examining such ruins, the investigator can reconstruct the architecture they represent.

To explore this idea, recollections of embarrassment were expressly solicited from two groups of subjects: (*1*) approximately 800 students enrolled in introductory sociology courses; and (*2*) about 80 students enrolled in an evening extension class. Not solicited, but gratefully received, were many examples volunteered by colleagues and friends who had heard of our interest in the subject. Finally we drew upon many recollections of embarrassment we had experienced ourselves. Through these means at least one thousand specimens of embarrassment were secured.

We found that embarrassments frequently occurred in situations requiring continuous and coordinated role performance—speeches, ceremonies, processions, or working concerts. In such situations embarrassment is particularly noticeable because it is so devastating. Forgetting one's lines,

---

[2] Alfred R. Lindesmith and Anselm L. Strauss assert that *every* role presupposes a counter-role. There is a sense in which the assertion is correct, as in Kenneth Burke's "paradox of substance," but it may also be somewhat misleading in sociological analysis. Specifically, there is a role of cigarette smoker, but the role is not really dependent for its establish-

ment on the counter-role of non-smoker in the sense that the parental role is dependent upon child roles and vice versa. Thus, in some social transactions the establishment and maintenance of one identity may be very helpful for the establishment and maintenance of a counter-identity; in other transactions, this may not be the case at all (see Lindesmith and Strauss, *Social Psychology* [New York: Dryden Press, 1956], pp. 379–80; and Kenneth Burke, *A Grammar of Motives* [New York: Prentice-Hall, 1945], pp. 21–58).

[3] Not all incapacitated persons are always embarrassed or embarrassing, because others have come to expect their *incapacities* and are consequently prepared for them.

forgetting the wedding ring, stumbling in a cafeteria line, or handing a colleague the wrong tool, when these things occur without qualification, bring the performance to an obviously premature and unexpected halt. At the same time, manifestations of the embarrassment—blushing fumbling, stuttering, sweating[4]—coerce awareness of the social damage and the need for immediate repair. In some instances, the damage may be potentially so great that embarrassment cannot be allowed to spread among the role performers. The incapacity may be qualified, totally ignored, or pretended out of existence.[5] For example, a minister, noting the best man's frantic search for an absent wedding ring, whispers to him to ignore it, and all conspire to continue the drama with an imaginary ring. Such rescues are not always possible. Hence we suggest that every enduring social relation will provide means of preventing embarrassment, so that the entire transaction will not collapse when embarrassment occurs. A second general observation would take into account that some stages in the life cycle, for example, adolescence in our society, generate more frequent embarrassments than others. These are points to which we shall return.

To get at the content of embarrassment, we classified the instances in categories that remained as close to the specimens as possible. A total of seventy-four such categories were developed, some of which were forced choices between friends, public mistakes, exposure of false front, being caught in a cover story, misnaming, forgetting names, slips of the tongue, body exposure, invasions of others' back regions, uncontrollable laughter, drunkenness in the presence of sobriety (or vice versa), loss of visceral control, and the sudden recognition of wounds or other stigmata. Further inspection of these categories disclosed that most could be included in three general areas: (1) inappropriate identity; (2) loss of poise; (3) disturbance of the assumptions persons make about one another in social transactions.

Since embarrassment always incapacitates persons for role performance (to embarrass is, literally, to bar or stop), a close analysis of the conditions under which it occurs is especially fruitful in the revelation of the requirements *necessary* for role-playing, role-taking, role-making, and role performance in general. These role requirements are thus seen to include the establishment of identity, poise, and valid assumptions about one another among all the parties of a social transaction. We turn now to the analysis of those role requirements.

IDENTITY AND POISE

In every social transaction, selves must be established, defined, and accepted by the parties. Every person in the company of others is, in a sense, obligated to bring his best self forward to meet the selves of others also presumably best fitted to the occasion. When one is "not himself" in the presence of others who expect him to be just that, as in cases where his mood carries him away either by spontaneous seizure (uncontrollable laughter or tears) or by induced seizure (drunkenness), embarrassment ensues. Similarly, when one is "shown up" to other parties to the transaction by the exposure of unacceptable moral qualifications or inappropriate motives, embarrassment sets in all around. However, the concept, self, is a rather gross concept, and we wish to single out two phases that frequently provided focal points for embarrassment—identity and poise.[6]

Identity. Identity is the substantive dimension of the self.

> Almost all writers using the term imply that identity establishes what and where the person is in social terms. It is not a substitute word for "self." Instead, when one has identity, he is *situated*—that is, cast in the shape of a social object by the acknowledgement of his participation or membership in social relations. One's identity is established when others *place* him as a social object by assigning the same words of identity that he appropriates for himself or *announces*. It is in the coincidence of placements and announcements that identity becomes a meaning of the self.[7]

Moreover, as we have already pointed out, identity stands at the base of role. When inappropriate identities are established or appropriate identities are lost, role performance is impossible.

If identity *locates* the person in social terms, it follows that locations or spaces emerge as symbols of identity, since social relations are spatially distributed. Moreover, as Goffman has remarked,[8] there must be a certain coherence between one's personal appearance and the setting in which he

[4] Erving Goffman, in "Embarrassment and Social Organization," *American Journal of Sociology*, LXII (November, 1956), 264–71, describes these manifestations vividly.

[5] A more general discussion of this phenomenon, under the rubric civil inattention is provided in Erving Goffman, *Behavior in Public Places* (New York: Free Press of Glencoe, 1963), pp. 83–88 and *passim*.

[6] Other dimensions of the self—value and mood—will be taken up in subsequent publications.

[7] Gregory P. Stone, "Appearance and the Self," in Arnold Rose (ed.), *Human Behavior and Social Processes* (Boston: Houghton Mifflin, 1962), p. 93.

[8] Erving Goffman, *The Presentation of Self in Everyday Life* (New York: Doubleday Anchor Books, 1959), p. 25.

appears. Otherwise embarrassment may ensue with the resulting incapacitation for role performance. Sexual identity is pervasively established by personal appearance, and a frequent source of embarrassment among our subjects was the presence of one sex in a setting reserved for the other. Both men and women reported inadvertent invasions of spaces set aside for the other sex with consequent embarrassment and humiliation. The implication of such inadvertent invasions is, of course, that one literally does not know where one is, that one literally has no identity in the situation, or that the identity one is putting forward is so absurd as to render the proposed role performance totally irrelevant. Everyone is embarrassed, and such manifestations as, for example, cries and screams, heighten the dis-ease. In such situations, laughter cannot be enjoined to reduce the seriousness of the unexpected collapse of the encounter, and only flight can insure that one will not be buried in the wreckage.

To establish *what* he is in social terms, each person assembles a set of apparent[9] symbols which he carries about as he moves from transaction to transaction. Such symbols include the shaping of the hair, painting of the face, clothing, cards of identity, other contents of wallets and purses, and sundry additional marks and ornaments. The items in the set must cohere, and the set must be complete. Taken together, these apparent symbols have been called *identity documents,*[10] in that they enable others to validate announced identities. Embarrassment often resulted when our subjects made personal appearances with either invalid or incomplete identity documents. It was embarrassing for many, for example, to announce their identities as customers at restaurants or stores, perform the customer role and then, when the crucial validation of this identity was requested— the payoff—to discover that the wallet had been left at home.

Because the social participation of men in American society is relatively more frequently caught up in the central structures, for example, the structure of work, than is the social participation of women who are relatively more immersed in interpersonal relations, the identities put for-

ward by men are often *titles;* by women, often *names.* Except for very unusual titles,[11] such identities are shared, and their presentation has the consequence of bringing people together. Names, on the other hand, mark people off from one another. So it is that a frequent source of embarrassment for women in our society occurs when they appear together in precisely the same dress. Their identity documents are invalidated. The embarrassment may be minimized, however, if the space in which they make their personal appearance is large enough. In one instance, both women met the situation by spending an entire evening on different sides of the ballroom in which their embarrassing confrontation occurred, attempting to secure validation from social circles with minimal intersection, or, at least, where intersection was temporally attenuated. Men, on the other hand, will be embarrassed if their clothing does not resemble the dress of the other men present in public and official encounters. Except for "the old school tie," their neckties seem to serve as numbers on a uniform, marking each man off from every other. Out of uniform, their structural membership cannot be visibly established, and role performance is rendered extremely difficult, if not impossible.[12]

Not only are identities undocumented, they are also misplaced, as in misnaming or forgetting, or other incomplete placements. One relatively frequent source of embarrassment we categorized as "damaging someone's personal representation." This included cases of ethnically colored sneers in the presence of one who, in fact, belonged to the deprecated ethnic group but did not put that identity forward, or behind-the-back slurs about a woman who turned out to be the listener's wife. The victim of such misplacement, however inadvertent, will find it difficult to continue the transaction or to present the relevant identity to the perpetrators of the embarrassment in the future. The awkwardness is reflexive. Those who are responsible for the misplacement will experience the same difficulties and dis-ease.

Other sources of embarrassment anchored in identity suggest a basic characteristic of all human transactions, which, as Strauss puts it, are "carried on in thickly peopled and complexly imaged con-

---

[9] We use the term "appearance" to designate that dimension of a social transaction given over to identifications of the participants. Apparent symbols are those symbols used to communicate such identifications. They are often non-verbal. Appearance seems, to us, a more useful term than Goffman's "front" (*ibid.*), which in everyday speech connotes misrepresentation.

[10] Erving Goffman, *Stigma* (Englewood Cliffs, N.J.: Prentice-Hall, 1963), pp. 59–62. Goffman confines the concept to personal identity, but his own discussion extends it to include matters of social identity.

[11] For example, the title, "honorary citizen of the United States," which was conferred on Winston Churchill, serves the function of a name, since this title has only been conferred a few times. Compare the titles, "professor," "manager," "punch-press operator," and the like.

[12] The implication of the discussion is that structured activities are uniformed, while interpersonal activities emphasize individuation in dress. Erving Goffman suggests, in correspondence, that what may be reflected here is the company people keep in their transactions. The work of men in our society is ordinarily teamwork, and teams are uniformed, but housework performed by a wife is solitary work and does not require a uniformed appearance, though the "housedress" might be so regarded.

texts."[13] One always brings to transactions more identities than are necessary for his role performance. As a consequence, two or more roles are usually performed at once by each participant.[14]

If we designate the relevant roles in transactions as *dominant roles*[15] then we may note that *adjunct roles*—a type of side involvement, as Goffman would have it,[16] or better, a type of side *activity*—are usually performed in parallel with dominant role performance. Specifically, a lecturer may smoke cigarettes or a pipe while carrying out the dominant performance, or one may carry on a heated conversation with a passenger while operating a motor vehicle. Moreover, symbols of *reserve identities* are often carried into social transactions. Ordinarily, they are concealed, as when a court judge wears his golfing clothes beneath his robes. Finally, symbols of abandoned or *relict identities* may persist in settings where they have no relevance for dominant role performances.[17] For example, photographs of the performer as an infant may be thrust into a transaction

by a doting mother or wife, or one's newly constituted household may still contain the symbols of a previous marriage.

In these respects, the probability of avoiding embarrassment is a function of at least two factors: (*1*) the extent to which adjunct roles, reserve identities and relict identities are not incongruent with the dominant role performance;[18] and (*2*) the allocation of prime attention to the dominant role performance so that less attention is directed toward adjunct role performance, reserve identities, and relict identities. Thus the professor risks embarrassment should the performance of his sex role appear to be the main activity in transactions with female students where the professorial role is dominant—for example, if the student pulls her skirt over her knees with clearly more force than necessary. The judge may not enter the courtroom in a golf cap, nor may the husband dwell on the symbols of a past marriage in the presence of a new wife while entertaining guests in his home. Similarly, should adjunct role performance prove inept, as when the smoking lecturer ignites the contents of a wastebasket or the argumentative driver fails to observe the car in front in time to avert a collision, attention is diverted from the dominant role performance. Even without the golf cap, should the judge's robe be caught so that his golfing attire is suddenly revealed in the courtroom, the transactions of the court will be disturbed. Fetishistic devotion to the symbols of relict identities by bereaved persons is embarrassing even to well-meaning visitors.

However, the matter of avoiding incongruence and allocating attention appropriately among the several identities a performer brings to a transaction verges very closely on matters of poise, as we shall see. Matters of poise converge on the necessity of controlling representations of the self, and identity-symbols are important self-representations.

Personal poise. Presentation of the self in social transactions extends considerably beyond making the appropriate personal appearance. It includes the presentation of an entire situation. Components of situations, however, are often representations of self, and in this sense self and situation are two sides of the same coin. Personal poise refers to the performer's control over self and situation, and whatever disturbs that control, depriving the transaction, as we have said before, of any relevant future, is incapacitating and consequently embarrassing.

[13] Anselm L. Strauss, *Mirrors and Masks* (Glencoe, Ill.: Free Press, 1959), p. 57.

[14] This observation and the ensuing discussion constitute a contribution to and extension of present perspectives on role conflict. Most discussions conceive of such conflict as internalized contradictory obligations. They do not consider simultaneous multiple-role performances. An exception is Everett C. Hughes' discussion of the Negro physician innocently summoned to attend a prejudiced emergency case in "Dilemmas and Contradictions in Status," *American Journal of Sociology*, L (March, 1945), 353–59.

[15] We have rewritten this discussion to relate to Goffman's classification which came to our attention after we had prepared an earlier version of this article. Goffman distinguishes between what people do in transactions and what the situation calls for. He recognizes that people do many things at once in their encounters and distinguishes those activities that command most of their attention and energies from those which are less demanding of energy and time. Here, the distinction is made between *main* and *size involvements*. On the other hand, situations often call for multiple activities. Those which are central to the situation, Goffman speaks of as *dominant involvements*; others are called *subordinate involvements*. Dominant roles, therefore, are those that are central to the transactional situation—what the participants have come together to do (see Goffman, *Behavior in Public Places*, pp. 43–59).

[16] Adjunct roles are one type of side involvement or activity. We focus on them because we are concerned here with identity difficulties. There are other side *activities* which are *not* necessarily adjunct *roles*, namely, sporadic nosepicking, scratching, coughing, sneezing, or stomach growling, which are relevant to matters of embarrassment, but not to the conceptualization of the problem in these terms. Of course, such activities, insofar as they are consistently proposed and anticipated, may become incorporated in the *personal role* (always an adjunct role in official transactions), as in the case of Billy Gilbert, the fabulous sneezer.

[17] This phenomenon provides the main theme and source of horror and mystery in Daphne du Maurier's now classic *Rebecca*.

[18] Adjunct roles, reserve identities, and relict identities need not cohere with the dominant role; they simply must not clash so that the attention of participants in a transaction is not completely diverted from the dominant role performance.

Loss of poise was a major dimension in our scrutiny of embarrassment, and its analysis can do much to shed light on the components of social situations—a necessary task, because the concept, "situation," is quite difficult to specify and operationalize. Working from the outside in, so to speak, we wish to single out five[19] elements of self and situation with reference to which loss of control gave rise to considerable embarrassment.

First, *spaces* must be so arranged and maintained that they are role-enabling. This is sometimes difficult to control, since people appear in spaces that belong to others, over which they exercise no authority and for which they are not responsible. Students, invited to faculty parties where faculty members behave like faculty members, will "tighten up" to the extent that the students' role performance is seriously impeded. To avoid embarrassment, people will go to great lengths to insure their appearance in appropriate places, and to some to be deprived of access to a particular setting is to limit performance drastically.

Spaces are often fixed in location and have boundaries. As such they may partake of the character of territories or domains: a particular person (or persons) is "in command" (it is "his" domain) and most familiar with it, and the territory is in continual danger of being invaded (deliberately or inadvertently). Embarrassments were reported for both of these features of space. Being "in command" and familiar with an area means knowing where the back regions are and having the right of access to them. The host at a party in his own home, however much he may be vanishing,[20] is at least the person in whose territory the gathering takes place. Should a guest spill food on his clothes, he has no choice but to suffer embarrassment for the remainder of the party. The host, by contrast, can retire to his bedroom and change his clothes quickly, often before the momentary loss of poise becomes known. A striking case of the man "in command" of a territory is the person delivering a speech to a fixed audience in a closed room. In being presented to the audience, he may even be told, "The floor is yours." To underline his exclusive domain, the speaker may wait until waiters clear the last table of cups and saucers and the doors are closed. In such a setting, where the audience is not free to leave, the speaker is now in great danger of embarrassing his audience unless his speech is such that the audience is not let down. Should he show lack of poise, the audience will feel embarrassed for him, yet be unable to escape, for that would further embarrass him. Hence they will suffer silently, hoping for a short speech.

In a situation reported to us, the discussant at a professional meeting was able to save the situation. The speaker was a man of national reputation—one of the pillars of his discipline. To everyone's dismay and embarrassment, he proceeded to give a pedestrian address of the caliber of an undergraduate term essay. Everyone hoped the discussant would save them, and he did. His tactic was to make clear to the audience that the identity presented by the speaker was not his real identity. This result he accomplished by reminding the audience of the major contributions of the speaker, by claiming the paper presented must be interpreted as evidence that the speaker was still productive, and that all could expect even more important contributions in the future. When the audience thundered applause, they were not simply expressing their agreement with the discussant's appraisal of the speaker: they were also thanking him for saving them all from embarrassment by putting the speaker back in command of the territory.

We have already touched upon problems presented by invasions of spaces, and little more need be said. Persons lose poise when they discover they are in places forbidden to them, for the proscription itself means they have no identity there and hence cannot act. They can do little except withdraw quickly. It is interesting that children are continually invading the territories of others—who can control the course of a sharply hit baseball?—and part of the process of socialization consists of indications of the importance of boundaries. Whether territories are crescive or contrived affects the possibility of invasion. When they are contrived and boundaries are marked, the invader knows he has crossed the boundary and is embarrassed if caught. With crescive territories inadvertent invasions occur, as when a tourist reports discovery of a "quaint" area of the city only to be met with the sly smiles of those who know that the area is the local prostitution region.

Such considerations raise questions concerning both how boundaries are defined and how boundary violations may be prevented. Walls provide physical limits, but do not necessarily prevent communications from passing through.[21] Hence walls work best when there is also tacit agreement to ignore audible communication on the other side of the wall. Embarrassment frequently occurs when persons on one side of the wall learn that intimate matters have been communicated to persons on the other side. A common protective device is for the captive listeners to become very quiet so that their receipt of the communication

---

[19] The five components to be discussed—spaces, props, equipment, clothing, and the body—are not offered as an exhaustive list. We have been able to distinguish close to forty such elements.

[20] David Riesman, Robert J. Potter, and Jeanne Watson, "The Vanishing Host," *Human Organization*, XIX (Spring, 1960), 17–21.

[21] See Erving Goffman, *Behavior in Public Places*, pp. 151–52.

will not be discovered by the unsuspecting intimates. When no physical boundaries are present, a group gathered in one section of a room may have developed a common mood which is bounded by a certain space that defines the limits of their engagement to one another. The entry of someone new may be followed by an embarrassed hush. It is not necessary that the group should have been talking about that person. Rather, since moods take time to build up, it will take time for the newcomer to "get with it" and it may not be worth the group's trouble to "fill him in." However unintentionally, he has destroyed a mood that took some effort to build up and he will suffer for it, if only by being stared at or by an obvious change of subject. In some cases, when the mood is partially sustained by alcohol, one can prepare the newcomer immediately for the mood by loud shouts that the group is "three drinks ahead" of him and by thrusting a drink into his hand without delay. So, too, a function of foyers, halls, anterooms, and other buffer zones or decompression chambers around settings is to prepare such newcomers and hence reduce the likelihood of their embarrassing both themselves and those inside.

Spaces, then, include bounded areas within which transactions go on. The boundaries may be more or less sharply defined, that is, walled in or marked off by the distances that separate one encounter from another. Overstepping the bounds is a source of embarrassment, signaling a loss of poise. Consequently, the boundaries are usually controlled and patrolled and come to represent the selves of those who are authorized to cross them.

A second component of self and situation that must be controlled to maintain poise is here designated *props*. Props are arranged around settings in an orderly manner commonly called décor. Ordinarily they are not moved about during a transaction, except as emergencies arise, to facilitate the movement of people about the setting and to protect the props from damage. In some cases, their adherence to settings is guaranteed by law. Wall-to-wall carpeting, mirrors attached to walls, and curtain fixtures, for example, may not be removed from houses, even though ownership of such domestic settings may change hands. The arrangement of less adhesive props within a setting may mark off or suggest (as in the case of "room dividers") smaller subsettings facilitating the division of large assemblies into more intimate circles. Moreover, although props are ordinarily not moved about *during* transactions, they are typically rearranged or replaced between major changes of scene, marking off changes in life situations.[22]

Perhaps just because of their intimate connection with the life situations of those who control them,[23] loss of control over props is a more frequent (though usually milder) source of embarrassment than the violation of boundaries. When one stumbles over his own furniture or slips on his own throw rug, doubt may be cast on the extent to which such props represent, in fact, the self and situation of the person or team members who have arranged them. Gifts of props are frequently embarrassing to the recipients. Thus an artist (or would-be artist) may foist a painting on a friend without recognizing that the painting is contrary to the recipient's aesthetic taste. Moreover, the artist may expect that his work will be given a prominent display commensurate with his investment. A conflict is immediately established between loyalty to the artist-friend and loyalty to the recipient's self. A way out is to include the prop in question only in those situations where the donor is present, but this may become tedious, depending on the frequency and scheduling of visiting. A classic case is the wealthy relative's gift of a self-photograph, which must be dragged out of the closet for display when the relative visits.

Clashing differences in domestic décor will usually terminate or restrict house-to-house visiting. Because of this, many wartime friendships have been abruptly ended shortly after the cessation of hostilities and demobilization. In a common military setting, servicemen would meet and become close friends, sometimes building up life-and-death obligations to one another. They would eagerly anticipate extending their hard-won intimacy into the workaday world of peacetime. Then, when they met in one or the other's home, the glaring incompatibility in décor would silently signal an incompatibility in life situation. Such embarrassing confrontations would be covered over with empty promises and futile vows to meet again, and the former friends would part as embarrassed strangers. If incompatibilities in décor can bring about the estrangement of friends who owe their lives to one another, we can see how

---

[22] David Riesman and Howard Roseborough, in a discussion of family careers, indicate the linkage between the rearrangement of props and the rearrangement of life situations: "One of our Kansas City respondents, whose existence had been wrapped up in her daughters' social life, when asked what she did when the daughters married and moved away, said that she slept more—and redecorated the living room. Still another became more active in church work—and redecorated the vestry" ("Careers and Consumer Behavior," in Lincoln Clark [ed.], *Consumer Behavior*, Vol. II: *The Life Cycle and Consumer Behavior* [New York: New York University Press, 1955], p. 14).

[23] Striking examples are provided by Harvey W. Zorbaugh in Ernest W. Burgess (ed.), *The Urban Community* (Chicago: University of Chicago Press, 1926), pp. 103–4; and in Anonymous, *Street-Walker* (New York: Gramercy Publishing Co., 1962), pp. 46–48.

props and their arrangement become powerful guaranties of the exclusiveness of social circles and status strata.

Much of our earlier discussion of adjunct roles, reserve identities, and relict identities applies to props. The porcelain dinnerware may always be kept visibly in reserve for special guests, and this very fact may be embarrassing to some dinner guests who are reminded that they are not so special after all, while, for other guests, anything but the everyday props would be embarrassing. Relict props also present a potential for embarrassment, persisting as they do when one's new life-situation has made them obsolete. The table at which a woman used to sit while dining with a former husband is obviously still quite serviceable, but it is probably best to buy another.

Third, every social transaction requires the manipulation of *equipment*. If props are ordinarily stationary during encounters, equipment is typically moved about, handled, or touched.[24] Equipment can range from words to physical objects, and a loss of control over such equipment is a frequent source of embarrassment. Here are included slips of the tongue, sudden dumbness when speech is called for, stalling cars in traffic, dropping bowling balls, spilling food, and tool failures. Equipment appearances that cast doubt on the adequacy of control are illustrated by the clanking motor, the match burning down to the fingers, tarnished silverware, or rusty work tools. Equipment sometimes extends beyond what is actually handled in the transaction to include the stage props. Indeed, items of equipment in disuse, reserve equipment, often become props—the Cadillac in the driveway or the silver service on the shelf—and there is a point at which the objects used or scheduled for use in a situation are both equipment and props. At one instant, the items of

a table setting lie immobile as props; at the next, they are taken up and transformed into equipment. The close linkage of equipment and props may be responsible for the fact that *embarrassment* at times not only *infects* the participants in the transaction but the *objects* as well. For example, at a formal dinner, a speaker was discovered with his fly zipper undone. On being informed of this embarrassing oversight after he was reseated, he proceeded to make the requisite adjustments, unknowingly catching the table cloth in his trousers. When obliged to rise again at the close of the proceedings, he took the stage props with him and of course scattered the dinner tools about the setting in such a way that others were forced to doubt his control. His poise was lost in the situation.

Just as props may be adjunct to the dominant role performance, held in reserve, or relict, so may equipment. Indeed, as we have said, reserve equipment is often an important part of décor.

Fourth, *clothing* must be maintained, controlled, and coherently arranged. Its very appearance must communicate this. Torn clothing, frayed cuffs, stained neckties, and unpolished shoes are felt as embarrassing in situations where they are expected to be untorn, neat, clean, and polished. Clothing is of special importance since, as William James observed,[25] it is as much a part of the self as the body—a part of what he called the "material me." Moreover, since it is so close to the body, it conveys the impression of body maintenance, paradoxically, by concealing body-maintenance activities.[26] Hence, the double wrap—outer clothes and underclothes. Underclothes bear the marks of body maintenance and tonic state, and their unexpected exposure is a frequent source of embarrassment. The broken brassière strap sometimes produces a shift in appearance that few women (or men, for that matter) will fail to perceive as embarrassing.

Fifth, the *body* must always be in a state of readiness to act, and its appearance must make this clear. Hence any evidence of unreadiness or clumsiness is embarrassing. Examples include loss of whole body control (stumbling, trembling, or fainting), loss of visceral control (flatulence, involuntary urination, or drooling), and the communication of other "signs of the animal." The actress who is photographed from her "bad side" loses poise, for it shakes the foundation on which her fame rests. So does the person who is embarrassed about pimples, warts, or missing limbs, as well as those embarrassed in his presence.

Ordinarily, persons will avoid recognizing such stigmata, turn their eyes away, and pretend them out of existence, but on occasion stigmata will

---

[24] Whether objects in a situation are meant to be moved, manipulated, or taken up provides an important differentiating dimension between equipment on the one hand and props (as well as clothing, to be discussed shortly) on the other. Equipment is meant to be moved, manipulated, or taken up *during* a social transaction whereas clothing and props are expected to remain unchanged during a social transaction but will be moved, manipulated, or taken up *between* social transactions. To change props, as in burning the portrait of an old girl friend (or to change clothes, as in taking off a necktie), signals a change in the situation. The special case of the strip-tease dancer is no exception, for her act transforms clothes into equipment. The reference above to the "stickiness" of props may now be seen as another way of describing the fact that they are not moved, manipulated, or taken up during transactions, but remain unchanged for the course of the transaction. Clothing is equally sticky but the object to which it sticks differs. Clothing sticks to the body; props stick to the settings.

[25] William James, *Psychology* (New York: Henry Holt & Co., 1892), pp. 177–78.
[26] A complete exposition of the body-maintenance function of clothing is set forth in an advertisement for Jockey briefs, entitled: "A Frank Discussion: What Wives Should Know about Male Support," *Good Housekeeping*, May 1963, p. 237.

obtrude upon the situation causing embarrassment all around. A case in point was a minor flirtation reported by one of our students. Seated in a library a short distance from a beautiful girl, the student began the requisite gestural invitation to a more intimate conversation. The girl turned, smiling, to acknowledge the bid, revealing an amputated left arm. Our student's gestural line was brought to a crashing halt. Embarrassed, he abandoned the role he was building even before the foundation was laid, pretending that his inviting gestures were directed toward some imaginary audience suggested by his reading. Such stigmata publicize body-maintenance activities, and, when they are established in social transactions, interfere with role performances. The pimples on the face of the job applicant cast doubt on his maturity, and, consequently, on his qualifications for any job requiring such maturity.

All this is to say that self and situation must be in a perpetual condition of poise or readiness, adequately maintained, and in good repair. Such maintenance and the keeping of self in a state of good repair obviously require energy and time. While engaged in maintenance or repair, the person is, for that time, unable to play the role. Hence we may expect that persons will, in order to avoid casting doubt on their ability to play a role, deliberately play down or conceal maintenance and repair activity. Speakers know that spontaneity cannot be left to chance but must be prepared for, even rehearsed. Yet, obviously information on the amount of preparation it took to be spontaneous would destroy the audience's belief in the spontaneity. Outer clothes require underclothes, as social life requires an underlife (which is, of course, also social).[27]

MAINTENANCE OF CONFIDENCE

When identities have been validated and persons poised, interaction may begin. Its continuation, however, requires that a scaffolding be erected and that attention be given to preventing this scaffolding from collapsing. The scaffold develops as the relationship becomes stabilized. In time persons come to expect that the way they place the other is the way the other announces himself, and that poise will continue to be maintained. Persons

[27] Consider the fact that the physician often needs time and opportunity to consult medical books and colleagues before he can render an authoritative medical diagnosis. A structural assurance is provided by his having been taught to make diagnoses slowly. Through time thus gained, he takes advantage of informal encounters with colleagues and spare moments between patients when he can consult medical books. A direct revelation of his need for such aids and his rather unsystematic way of getting them would be embarrassing. Yet it is in the patient's best interest that they be kept secret from him, otherwise the patient would be in the position of having to pass judgment on a professional practice when he is, in fact, too involved to render an objective judgment.

now begin to count on these expectations and to have confidence in them. But at any time they may be violated. It was such violations of confidence that made up the greatest single source of embarrassment in our examples. Perhaps this is only an acknowledgment that the parties to every transaction must always maintain themselves *in role* to permit the requisite role-taking, or that identity-switching ought not to be accomplished so abruptly that others are left floundering in the encounter as they grope for the new futures that the new identity implies.

This is all the more important in situations where roles are tightly linked together as in situations involving a division of labor. In one instance, a group of social scientists was presenting a progress report of research to a representative of the client subsidizing the research. The principal investigator's presentation was filled out by comments from the other researchers, his professional peers. Negatively critical comments were held to a bare minimum. Suddenly the principal investigator overstepped the bounds. He made a claim that they were well on the road to confirming a hypothesis which, if confirmed, would represent a major contribution. Actually, his colleagues (our informant was one of them) knew that they were very far indeed from confirming the hypothesis. They first sought to catch the leader's eye to look for a hidden message. Receiving none, they lowered their eyes to the table, bit their lips, and fell silent. In the presence of the client's representative, they felt they could not "call" their leader for that would be embarrassing, but they did seek him out immediately afterward for an explanation. The leader agreed that they were right, but said his claim was politic, that new data might well turn up, and that it was clearly too late to remedy the situation.

Careful examination of this case reveals a more basic reason for the researchers' hesitance to embarrass the leader before the client's representative. If their leader were revealed to be the kind of person who goes beyond the data (or to be a plain liar), serious question could have been raised about the kind of men who willingly work with such a person. Thus they found themselves coerced into unwilling collusion. It was not simply that their jobs depended on continued satisfaction of the client. Rather, they were unwilling to say to themselves and to the client's representative that they were the kind of researchers who would be party to a fraud. To embarrass the leader, then, would have meant embarrassing themselves by casting serious question upon their identities as researchers. Indeed, it was their desire to cling to their identities that led, not long afterward (and after several other similar experiences), to the breakup of the research team.

Just as, in time, an identity may be discredited, so too may poise be upset. Should this occur, each must be able to assume that the other will render assistance if he gets into such control trouble, and each must be secure in the knowledge that the assumption is tenable. Persons will be alert for incipient signs of such trouble—irrelevant attitudes—and attempt to avert the consequences. Goffman has provided many examples in his discussion of dramaturgical loyalty, discipline, and circumspection in the presentation of the self, pointing out protective practices that are employed, such as clearing one's throat before interrupting a conversation, knocking on doors before entering an occupied room, or begging the other's pardon before an intrusion.[28]

The danger that one's confidence in the other's continued identity or his ability to maintain his poise may be destroyed leads to the generation of a set of *performance norms.* These are social protections against embarrassment.[29] If persons adhere to them, the probability of embarrassment is reduced. We discovered two major performance norms.

First, *the standards of role performance almost always allow for flexibility and tolerance.* One is rarely, if ever, totally in role (an exception might be highly ritualized performances, where to acknowledge breaches of expectation is devastatingly embarrassing).[30] To illustrate, we expect one another to give attention to what is going on in our transactions, but the attention we anticipate is always *optimal,* never total. To lock the other person completely in one's glance and refuse to let go is very embarrassing. A rigid attention is coerced eventuating in a loss of poise. One is rapt in the other's future and deprived of control almost like the hypotist's subject. Similarly, never to give one's attention to the other is role-incapacitating. If one focuses his gaze not on the other's eyes, but on his forehead, let us say, the encounter is visibly disturbed.[31] Norms allowing for flexibility and tolerance permit the parties to social transactions ordinarily to assume that they will not be held to rigid standards of conduct and that temporary lapses will be overlooked. The norm is respected

by drinking companions who both understand how it is to have had a drop too much and who can also be counted on not to hold another to everything he says, does, or suggests. So, too, colleagues are persons who know enough to embarrass one another but can ordinarily be trusted not to do so. The exclusiveness of colleague groups can be seen, therefore, as a collective defense against embarrassment.

The second performance norm was that of *giving the other fellow the benefit of the doubt.* For the transaction to go on at all, one has at least to give the other fellow a *chance* to play the role he seeks to play. Clearly, if everyone went around watching for chances to embarrass others, so many would be incapacitated for role performance that society would collapse. Such considerate behavior is probably characteristic of all human society, because of the dependence of social relations on role performance. A part of socialization, therefore, must deal with the prevention of embarrassment by the teaching of tact. People must learn not only not to embarrass others, but to ignore the lapses that can be embarrassing whenever they occur. In addition, people must learn to *cope* with embarrassment. Consequently, embarrassment will occasionally be deliberately perpetrated to ready people for role incapacitation when it occurs.

DELIBERATE EMBARRASSMENT

Although we have emphasized up to this point instances of embarrassment which arise from wholly unexpected acts and revelations, the unexpected is often deliberately perpetrated. Examples are practical jokes, teasing, initiation into secret societies, puncturing false fronts, and public degradation. Since embarrassment appears to represent social damage that is not at all easily repaired, we might well ask why the condition may be deliberately established. The embarrassed person stands exposed as incapable of continued role performance—a person who cannot be depended upon. In his presence, all must pause and review their assessments and expectations. Whatever they decide, the transaction is halted, and those dependent upon it are deprived of the realization of the futures that they have entrusted to others.

Embarrassments, therefore, always have careers. One person embarrasses others whose hurried attempts to salvage the situation merely call further attention to the embarrassment. A point may be reached where no repair is possible—the embarrassed person breaks into tears, flees, or, in the classic case, commits suicide—not to save face, but because face has been destroyed beyond repair.[32] Other terminations are possible, as we have shown. The embarrassing situation may be transformed by humor—laughed off—to define it as

[28] Goffman, *The Presentation of Self in Everyday Life,* pp. 212–33.

[29] Implicit in Georg Simmel, *The Sociology of Georg Simmel,* trans. Kurt H. Wolff (Glencoe, Ill.: Free Press, 1950), p. 308.

[30] See the discussion of "role distance" in Erving Goffman, *Encounters* (Indianapolis, Ind.: Bobbs-Merrill Co., 1961), pp. 105–52.

[31] Here we are speaking of what Edward T. Hall calls the "gaze line." He points out there are cultural variations in this phenomenon. See his "A System for the Notation of Proxemic Behavior," *American Anthropologist,* LXV (October, 1963), 1012–14.

[32] Goffman, "On Face-Works," *Psychiatry,* XVIII (August, 1955), 213–31.

unserious and to invite others to symbolize their solidarity with the embarrassed person by joining in the laughter.[33] Blame may be diverted away from the transaction and placed on others on the outside. The embarrassed one may fall sick. There are numerous outcomes, and, while some are less drastic than others, none is completely devoid of risk. Why is it, then, that embarrassment may be deliberately perpetrated? There are at least three reasons or social functions that may be attributed to deliberate embarrassment.

First, since embarrassing situations are inevitable in social life, persons must be schooled to maintain poise when poise is threatened, to maintain the identities they have established in social situations in the face of discreditation, and to sustain the confidence others have built up about matters. Deliberate embarrassment acts to socialize young people with these skills. Consequently, all young children trip one another, push, disarrange one another's clothing and other items of personal appearance. Besides being fun, such play[34] socializes the child in the maintenance of poise despite direct physical attacks on his "balance." Indeed, young children will spin about, inducing dizziness as they unknowingly test their ability to handle the imbalance in the play that Roger Caillois speaks of as *ilinx* or vertigo.[35] But socialization continues throughout life, and adult men, for example, test who can maintain poise in the face of the other's loss by playing at "drinking the other under the table." The roller coaster and tilt-a-whirl, and less upsetting machines like the merry-go-round and ferris wheel can be interpreted as a technology available to test poise.[36] Almost by definition, every game is a test of poise, but some sports place particular emphasis upon such tests—ski-jumping and gymnastics.[37] Announced identities are also challenged and impugned in play, as in "name-calling," and such teasing often reaches out to call into question everything one seeks to establish about himself in social encounters:

Shame! Shame! Double shame!
Everybody knows your name!

[33] See Ruth Laub Coser, "Some Social Functions of Laughter: A Study of Humor in a Hospital Setting," *Human Relations,* XII (May, 1959), 171–82.

[34] Careful attention must be given to all phases of children's play, which includes very much more than the anticipatory and fantastic dramas emphasized by George H. Mead.

[35] "The Structure and Classification of Games," *Diogenes,* No. 12 (Winter, 1955), pp. 62–75.

[36] A definite age-grading of the technology may be noticed in our society. The mildest test of poise is provided for the very young—the merry-go-round—and the devilish devices seem to be reserved for the middle and late teen-agers.

[37] Poise is an essential part of the commercialized tumbling exhibitions we call wrestling. Interviews with professional wrestlers by one of the writers establish that the most feared "opponent" is not at all the most fierce, but the neophyte, upon whose poise the established professional cannot rely.

The child, of course, learns the institutionalized replies to such tests of identity and self-confidence which throw the challenge back:

My name, my name is Puddin' Tame.
Ask me again and I'll tell you the same!

As others have noted, the challenges and responses inherent in such tests of poise, identity, and self-confidence often assume a pattern of interactive insult. The classic case is "playing the dozens."[38]

If one function of deliberate embarrassment is socialization, we would guess that such tests would be concentrated in the formative years and in other periods of major status passage. Our survey of adults in the evening extension class showed this to be true. When we asked them to recall the time of their lives when they were frequently embarrassed, the adolescent years were most commonly mentioned. Instances of deliberate embarrassment also included hazings and the humiliation which accompanied socialization into the armed forces. It may well be that every move into an established social world—every major *rite de passage*—is facilitated by the deliberate perpetration of embarrassing tests of poise, identity, and self-knowledge.[39]

Second, embarrassment is deliberately perpetrated as a negative sanction as in "calling" the one who is giving an undesirable performance. Since embarrassment does incapacitate the person from performing his role, it can clearly be used to stop someone from playing a role that might discredit a collectivity. Empirical categories include public reprimands, exposure of false fronts,

[38] This game, found most commonly among American Negroes, is never carried on between two isolated antagonists, but requires the physical presence of peers who evaluate each insult and goad the players to heightened performances. The antagonists and their peers are usually members of the same in-group, again emphasizing the socializing function of the play. As the insults become more and more acrid, one antagonist may "break down" (lose poise) and suggest fighting. That person is perceived as having failed the test, and the group then moves to prevent a fight from actually occurring. For Negroes, the ability to take insults without breaking down is clearly functional for survival in Negro-white interaction (see John Dollard, "The Dozens: Dialectic of Insult," *The American Imago,* I [November, 1939], 3–25; Ralph E. Berdie, "'Playing the Dozens'" *Journal of Abnormal and Social Psychology,* XLII [January, 1947], 120–21; and Cornelius L. Golightly and Israel Scheffler, "'Playing the Dozens': A Research Note," *Journal of Abnormal and Social Psychology,* XLIII [January, 1948], 104–5).

[39] An interesting comment on this point was made by Erving Goffman in a personal communication: "Since the theater is *the* place for the issue of poise, could our extensive high-school theatrical movement then be part of the socialization you speak of?"

open gossip and cattiness, or embarrassment perpetrated as a retaliation for an earlier embarrassment. In some of these cases, a person is exposed as having no right to play the role he has laid claim to, because the identity in which his role is anchored is invalid. In others, the person is punished by terminating his role performance so that he can no longer enjoy its perquisites.

A third function of deliberate embarrassment is the establishment and maintenance of power. The technique here is rather more subtle than those we have discussed. Specifically, the scene may be laid for embarrassment so that only by following the line established by the one who sets the scene may embarrassment be avoided. In this case, one assures himself that his decision will carry the day by guaranteeing that any alternative will result in irreparable damage to the whole collectivity. Organizational policy changes, for example, may be accomplished by cloaking them in a cover story impregnated with the organizational ideology. To resist the proposed changes, consequently, risks the discreditation of the entire organization. Another example is to be found in "kicking an official upstairs." The decision will be reached in a policy-making discussion where the official in question may be present. In the discussion, emphasis will be given to the official's qualifications for the new post so that the "stage

manager" leads a new self forward to replace the old self of the official in question. Discreditation of the new self, particularly in the official's presence, would wreak such damage on the transaction that it must be foregone and the "manager's" decision conceded.[40]

CONCLUSION

In this paper, we have inquired into the conditions necessary for role performance. Embarrassment has been employed as a sensitive indicator of those conditions, for that which embarrasses incapacitates role performance. Our data have led us to describe the conditions for role performance in terms of identity, poise, and sustained confidence in one another. When these become disturbed and discredited, role performance cannot continue. Consequently, provisions for the avoidance or prevention of embarrassment, or quick recovery from embarrassment when it does occur are of key importance to any society or social transaction, and devices to insure the avoidance and minimization of embarrassment will be part of every persisting social relationship. Specifically, tests of identity, poise, and self-knowledge will be institutionalized in every society. Such devices, like all mechanisms of social control, are capable of manipulation and may well be exploited to establish and maintain power in social transactions. Yet, deliberate or not, embarrassment is as general a sociological concept as is role.

TOWARD A THEORY OF INTERPERSONAL TACTICS *

In the present selection Weinstein elaborates the analyses of interaction contained in the previous two selections by emphasizing its purposive character. Focus is upon the means by which an individual goes about getting other persons to do his bidding. Thus, the purpose of the interaction and the techniques by which the individual elicits from the other person the desired responses are at the center of the present analysis.

As in the previous selections, a working consensus on the identities of the participants is essential for successful interaction. Many of the techniques for influencing the other person revolve around establishing consensus on a particular identity for oneself or the other person. Thus, a person may drop names to suggest he is a person of high status; or he may specifically designate the other person as a good friend of his, thereby reminding him that the obligation of friendship requires him to accede to the imposed request.

Various other techniques include revealing or disavowing motives, stating an alibi, and displaying involvement to enhance credibility.

Weinstein is currently pursuing a program of empirical research designed to test and further revise his conceptualizations.

45.

Toward a Theory of Interpersonal Tactics

EUGENE A. WEINSTEIN
VANDERBILT UNIVERSITY

The interplay of self and society is the core of sociological social psychology. Until the last decade, however, theoretical innovations in this area have been meager. Most sociologists have been content to stand pat with three of a kind, Cooley, Mead, and Thomas.

* The selection following the editorial introduction consists of a paper presented at a meeting of the American Sociological Association, Montreal, Canada, August, 1964, and is printed here by permission of the author.

[40] Erving Goffman describes a similar process by which persons are channeled through a "betrayal funnel" into a mental hospital (see "The Moral Career of the Mental Patient," *Psychiatry*, XXII [May, 1959], 123–42).

If there is a new look in our theory, it is the greater attention given to the idea that people bring personal purposes into all interaction. Foote and Cottrell link this up with self theory in relating identity and interpersonal competence, the ability to successfully achieve one's own purposes in relation to others.[1] Goode notes that personal goals are more important than the heavily structural Lintonian concept of role implies.[2] Homans and Thibaut and Kelley both emphasize the pursuit of individual goals as the foundation of interaction, making the problem of whether a relationship continues or not central to their analyses.[3] Yet few of these treatments are very clear about process. Just how personal goals are pursued, the *modus vivendi* of interaction, is left as a residual category. The most prominent treatment of this problem is found in Goffman's work and the intellectual debt this paper owes to Goffman is enormous.[4] In a very real sense, it is but a formalization and slight extension of his ideas.

The logic of Goffman's analysis of interaction is essentially functionalist. His focus of study, the encounter, is seen as a miniscule social system. Goffman outlines the requirements of the system for self-maintenance and effective functioning. He goes on to describe what happens when certain requirements are not met, the conditions which create a breakdown in the system, and various modes of adaptation of the encounter-as-system to disequilibrating events.[5]

What is shadowy in all his discussion are the personal purposes of the actors involved. It is here that we pick up the thread, attempting to tie together the goal oriented approaches of Goode, Homans and Thibaut and Kelley to Goffman. The chief concepts introduced are two: The interpersonal task, the response of the other(s) the actor attempts to elicit, and lines of action, behavior directed toward the task response. The central problem in the study of interaction becomes the relationship between these two. How are lines of action organized in pursuing interpersonal tasks? "How do people go about the business of getting others to do, think or feel what they want them to?"[6]

Interpersonal tasks are pursued (and sometimes even formulated) in encounters. Thus the functional requirements of encounters act as interactional constraints upon goal-oriented behavior and the nature of these constraints must be understood. Perhaps the most basic of these requirements is what Goffman calls the "working consensus." In Goffman's terms, the working consensus is a tacit agreement as to whose claims to what issues will be temporarily honored.[7] It is an agreement as to what the nature of reality is to be, the definition of the situation jointly subscribed to (although not necessarily believed in) by participants in the encounter.

The concept of working consensus has broader definitional implications. For our purposes, these implications may be extended to relate more explicitly to the personal goals of the actors involved. Encounters are embedded in situations, the symbolic content of which changes with each line of action. As situations change so may their definitions by the several participants. Yet situations tend not to be in complete flux. There appear to be boundaries to the moment-to-moment changes in definitions of the situation as well as boundaries to the kinds of tasks which are pursuable and the kinds of lines of action used to pursue them in any encounter. These boundaries are provided by the working consensus and give some stability and structure to the encounter. Four conditions, each dependent on the others preceding, must be satisfied for a working consensus to develop.

1. Each of the participants must indicate willingness to receive communication from the others.
2. At least some of the participants must communicate a claim to pursue certain types of interpersonal tasks and the right to employ particular lines of action.
3. The particular kind of communication within its situational context must imply that a delimited set of tasks will be pursued using a delimited set of lines of action.
4. These implications cannot be overtly denied. If a working consensus is to be established and maintained, no participant can deny another's right to pursue certain types of tasks or his right to employ particular lines of action in doing so.

Since these rights are normatively allocated to roles, or, more precisely, social identities, the working consensus necessarily involves agreement upon the social identities of the participants.[8] Not

[1] Nelson Foote and Leonard S. Cottrell, Jr., *Identity and Interpersonal Competence* (Chicago: University of Chicago Press, 1955).

[2] William J. Goode, "A Theory of Role Strain," *American Sociological Review*, 25 (August 1960) pp. 483–496; and "Norm Commitment and Conformity To Role-Status Obligations," *American Journal of Sociology*, 66, (November 1960) pp. 246–258.

[3] George C. Homans, *Social Behavior, Its Elementary Forms*, (New York: Harcourt, Brace and World, 1961); and John W. Thibaut and Harold H. Kelley, *The Social Psychology of Groups* (New York: John Wiley and Sons, 1959).

[4] Erving Goffman, *The Presentation of Self in Everyday Life* (Garden City, New Jersey: Anchor Books, Doubleday, 1959); and *Encounters* (Indianapolis: Bobbs-Merrill, 1961).

[5] Goffman, *op. cit.* Also "Embarrassment and Social Organization," *American Journal of Sociology*, 62 (November 1956) pp. 264–271.

[6] Eugene Weinstein and Paul Deutschberger, "Some Dimensions of Altercasting," *Sociometry*, 4 (December 1963), p. 455.

[7] Goffman, *Presentation of Self*, pp. 9–10.

[8] *Ibid.*

only the identity claimed by the actor for himself, but those he may actively assign to others in the situation by what has been called "altercasting" must be mutually acceptable.[9] If not, the working consensus, and the interaction it serves to structure cannot be maintained. The alternatives are breakdown in the episode of interaction or renegotiation of the terms of the working consensus.

Any actor has a double problem in interaction. He has his interpersonal tasks. But he is involved with other actors, each with their own purposes and associated preference orderings which, in all likelihood, are somewhat different from his. As Goode emphasizes, the actor, in seeking to achieve his own goals in the encounter, must also keep the others bound in the relationship.[10] The working consensus must be maintained. Of particular importance in this, as Goffman notes, is maintaining the acceptability of the identities of the participants, his own included. Thus, we should expect to find that many lines of action are designed to serve this double function, pursuing goals and promoting or maintaining identities congruent with those goals. We turn now to examining some commonly used interpersonal tactics in the light of their double imperative. The neologisms coined in the process are not, as will become apparent, to be taken too seriously.

INSURING APPROPRIATE INTERPRETATION

One of the prime requisites of a successful line of action is that it have the meaning for the other intended by the actor. Goffman describes how important content is dramatized, unimportant or contradictory content is suppressed as a means of guiding inferences. We shall be concerned with further amplifying his analysis, focussing on lines of action which insure that inappropriate *evaluative* implications regarding one's own identity or the identity of the other are not made. Such lines of action form an important segment of that vast class of acts which might be called communication about communication.

When an act can have several meanings to another, which carry different evaluative implications regarding the actor, one way of trying to insure favorable evaluation is to offer an interpretation prior to action (pre-interpretation or printerp). "Now, be sure not to take this the wrong way. I don't want you to think. . . ." Printerps may also function to protect or enhance the identity of the other. Not uncommon is the printerp which, by

first asserting that nothing detrimental about the other is intended, allows us to insult them at will.

However, not all communication about communication takes place prior to action. The other's response may provide us with information that he has drawn inferences from our acts which are undesired. Posterps are used as corrective devices. "Oh no, that's not what I meant . . ." followed by some statement taking the apparent evaluative sting out of some prior acts is a ubiquitous post-interpretation.

Printerps and posterps can serve a number of functions in the attempt to direct the evaluative implications of lines of action. Sometimes, we find ourselves in circumstances in which we feel impelled to maintain interaction but in which we fear our acts or communications will not meet the evaluative standards appropriate for the situation. One common line of action is to apologize in advance for what is to come (pre-apology which is readily abbreviated to prepalog). "I'm not quite sure of this . . . but . . . ," or "Off the top of my head, I'd say . . ." are examples of prepalogs which request the others not to negatively evaluate the actor. Akin to these are prepalogs of the form, "I'm really not a very good . . . (tennis player, bridge player, cook, etc.)" which request others to apply less stringent evaluative criteria in judging the actor's performance in the encounter. Both forms serve a common function; they are attempts to divorce evaluation of the actor (and hence, the acceptability of his identity) from evaluation of his actions.

The prepalog may also be a useful tool in securing overt assurances concerning the acceptability of one's identity. Statements making overt negative references to self are so frequently met with responses of denial or assurance that they have acquired a label in the common parlance, "fishing."

An important type of communication about communication, subsumable under the more generic categories of pre- and post-interpretation, are statements about the causes of or which reveal the motives for one's actions (motive revelations or motrels). Motrels are invaluable tools for either associating or dissociating identities and actions. Personalized motrels are those in which the actor refers to causes of his behavior which are within his rational control implying that particularistic value choices are open to him. The actor thus assumes responsibility for the evaluative implications of his acts. In depersonalized motrels, the actor refers to causes of behavior beyond his control, his biology, random happenstance, universalistic normative prescriptions and the like—in short, alibis. The differences between them can be best seen in differential responses to requests.

When one makes a request, he implicitly indicates that both he and it are worthy of consideration. The rejection of a request entails risks for both parties. In consequence, there is an elaborate

---

[9] Weinstein and Deutschberger, *op. cit.*

[10] Goode, *op. cit.* Also cf. Eugene Weinstein and Paul Deutschberger, "Tasks, Bargains, and Identities in Social Interaction," *Social Forces*, 42 (May 1964), 451–456.

set of lines of action regarding the making, accepting, and denying of requests.

One defensive device for the minimization of risk by the actor (especially the risk of being seen as presuming beyond his rights) is to make the request without actually asking. This often takes the form of communicating a need without asking the other to fill it. Assent in such cases tends to take the form of a personalized motrel, e.g. "I'd be glad to. . . ." In extended sequences this can be countered with, "I really don't want to impose," a very useful gambit. It deserves as a prepalog and, at the same time, casts the other into the role of defending the reasonableness of the request.

Depersonalized motrels predominate when denying other's requests. They serve to deny not only the request, but, because one's response is beyond one's control, they also implicitly deny any negative implications concerning the requestor. Thus one divorces the *other's* identity from one's acts.

Another tactic which serves the same function is the altruistic motrel, a statement that one's acts are being made for the benefit of the other. Children rapidly become expert at discounting such claims when they preface parental action. Such statements attempt to establish a working consensus in which acts potentially threatening to certain aspects of the other's identity can be made. The motrel both assures the other of overall acceptance, and claims for the actor a relationship of intimacy with him.

In this latter respect, altruistic motrels are one (of a large number) of tactics used to enhance the credibility of what one says. Presumably, those who have our best interests at heart will provide us with valid information so we can maximize the effectiveness of our own actions. The altruistic motrel thus shifts the question of credibility of the act to its preface. It attaches the actor's identity to what follows, meaning that the other has a good deal more to disbelieve. Overt disbelief by the other runs the risk of being construed as a rejection of the actor.

A similar pattern is seen in another credibility enhancing tactic, the display of involvement. Involvement is indexed by the intensity of the action expressed in decibel level, qualifying adjectives, inflections, bodily gestures, etc. When great involvement in one's actions is displayed by such means, especially in communication about such intrapersonal "facts" as feelings, disbelief of the communication has greater implications for discrediting the actor's identity. Others may be hesitant to display doubt under such conditions because it runs a greater risk of disrupting the working consensus. That the display of involvement itself must be credible is well attested to in the Shakespearean admonition, "the lady doth protest too much, me thinks."

A final tactic in the same vein is the icon (short for identity confirmation). Here we are concerned with the actor's droppings—name dropping, place dropping, experience dropping, and the like. "After 25 years of experience in this business . . ." or, "Back at Harvard. . . ." One function of such acts is to legitimize information given. Again, the question of credibility shifts to the preface with the actor in essence saying believe what I say because of what I am. Icons may be directed at other types of tasks as well. They are handy tools for establishing relative evaluative superiority in an encounter, especially when the characteristics referred to are gratuitously offered, have high social evaluation, and are unequally distributed among the other participants, in essence, the ploy.[11]

In addition to their tongue-in-cheek terminology, the small sample of lines of action reviewed have a common theme. They illustrate ways the problem of managing evaluative implications is dealt with in everyday social intercourse. Many are techniques for either associating or dissociating one's face (or the face of the other) from one's acts. Facework would be an excellent name for the process had Goffman not preempted the term for a somewhat different idea.[12] Its ubiquity attests to the importance of maintaining the acceptability of the identities of the participants in an encounter. But why this importance? Or is it important? Perhaps what we have been describing are merely instances of middle-class politeness with its show of concern for the feelings of others.

An answer to this question may come from re-asking one raised earlier in this paper,—how are lines of action selected in relation to interpersonal tasks? We can offer the hypothesis that those lines of action will tend to be used which maximize the likelihood of task success (even allowing for wide individual differences in interpersonal competence). One might hold that maximization is due to conscious rationality in the selection of interpersonal tactics. And certainly we have introspective evidence in support of this. Who cannot recall thinking ahead to an upcoming encounter, focussing on just what might be the best impression to convey, the best tone to strike, the best tack to take to achieve our purposes? But a good deal of our tactics are not consciously selected. Many lines of action, well designed to elicit task responses from others are used, not because we are aware of their tactical advantages but because we have learned they are situationally appropriate. We may use prepalogs or motrels in order to satisfy, in our own eyes, standards of tactfulness we have internalized and not particu-

---

[11] Goffman makes a similar point in "On Facework," *Psychiatry,* **18** (August 1955) 213–255.

[12] *Ibid.*

larly because we recognize that they help to keep the other bound in the relationship so we can get him to do what we want.

Yet it is precisely this capacity to facilitate goal directed interaction that accounts for the importance of the rules of polite intercourse and their centrality in socialization. That they predominate in middle-class socialization is not surprising since middle-class goals are pursued more frequently in interpersonal relations; much more of lower-class life is concerned with action toward inanimate objects. Moreover, even among the middle class, the rules of polite intercourse are most likely to be violated in relationships to which commitment is the strongest. Contrast the treatment sometimes received by wives and children with that received by clients or by well dressed strangers for that matter.

A strong argument can be made for the functional necessity of tactics which serve to preserve the acceptability of the identities of participants in interaction. They do more than save feelings; they help to preserve the working consensus providing the structure within which encounters can be maintained and interpersonal tasks pursued. If the sociologist's principal abstraction, social structure, has any concrete expression it is to be found in countless myriad everyday social encounters. The operation of this larger structure is dependent upon the successful functioning of the microscopic and episodic action systems generated in these encounters. And these, in turn, are dependent upon conditions which will allow interpersonal tasks to be effectively pursued. If social structure is to be stable, in the long run individuals must be successful in achieving personal purposes.

STRESS AND CONTRACTUAL NORMS IN A BARGAINING SITUATION *

The selections covered so far in Part Six have been attempts to conceptualize interaction situations of relatively brief duration, situations that spring up according to the demands of the moment and are shortly succeeded by a new situation. Discussion has rested on direct observation in the field or on the use of survey procedures.

In the present selection Thibaut and Faucheux report a laboratory experiment on an interaction situation involving bargaining. A game-playing situation is established so that the two parties are mutually dependent upon each other's actions for gain. One member is also established as having more power than the other. The situation is arranged so that if the high-power member makes a large gain, the low-power member can only make a small one, and so that under certain circumstances the low-power individual can gain more by leaving the dyad. This motivates each member to arrive at an agreement with the other concerning his action; each is capable of depriving the other of gain, but with cooperation, each can achieve a moderate gain. Thus, the major purpose of the experiment is to test the conditions under which contractual agreements arise between mutually dependent parties.

Aside from its provision of experimental evidence, such experimentation contributes to theory in requiring the investigator to state in clearly specified terms the conditions under which a phenomenon will occur. He is required to formulate his hypotheses in precise language, and he must conceive of operations that represent the variables he wishes to study. The manipulation of theoretically relevant variables is more convincing than interpretations of data made subsequently to the collection of the material, as is often the case in field studies. Thus experiments of this type have considerably more internal validity than studies based on participant observation or the use of survey procedures.

46.

The Development of Contractual Norms in a Bargaining Situation under Two Types of Stress[1]

JOHN THIBAUT
UNIVERSITY OF NORTH CAROLINA
CLAUDE FAUCHEUX
CENTRE NATIONAL DE LA RECHERCHE
SCIENTIFIQUE, PARIS

The point of view that biological and social systems respond to stress with various adaptive mechanisms, the effects of which often protect the systems from collapse or disruption, has been stated and illustrated by Bertalanffy (1951), Selye

---

* The selection following the editorial introduction is reprinted from "The development of contractual norms in a bargaining situation under two types of stress," *Journal of Experimental Social Psychology*, 1965, 1, 89–102, by permission of the authors and the Academic Press.

[1] This research was done while Thibaut was a Special U.S. Public Health Service Fellow at the Sorbonne. Both authors were attached to the Laboratoire de Psychologie Sociale de la Faculté des Lettres et Sciences Humaines de l'Université de Paris. Facilities for the present research were provided by CREDS of Montrouge. The research is also part of the program of the Organization Research Group at the University of North Carolina. The ORG is supported by the Office of Naval Research under contract Nonr-855(04). The assistance of M. W. Doise in the conduct of this research is gratefully acknowledged.

(1950), and, with particular reference to psychological systems, by James Miller (1955). Although this conception seems to be an important one for the understanding of group phenomena, its usefulness in predicting social behavior is very limited, and its validity must remain unsupported unless a more detailed theoretical and experimental analysis is made of the processes by which groups respond to various types of stress.

It will be suggested in the following paragraphs that when power differentiation exists in a group whose members have a background of high interdependence and highly convergent interests, the introduction of both external and internal threats to the continued viability of the group creates the conditions for the emergence of norms which to a significant degree reduce the disruptive consequences of the threats.

To present the analysis as simply as possible, let us suppose the existence of a dyad in which the members' interests are highly interdependent and harmonious and in which one member is able potentially to exert more influence on the other than he receives. This situation is strongly favorable to the maintenance of membership. The high degree of interdependence of outcomes means that each member is heavily dependent on the other for positive outcomes and that alternative relationships outside the dyad are relatively unattractive. Motivations to disrupt the dyad by forming mutually exclusive relationships with external alternatives are likely to be minimal. Hence there is little or no need for policing the loyalty of the members or for developing norms that forbid disloyalty.

Furthermore, in this simplified situation the highly convergent interests of the members means that there is no real problem in the sharing of the outcomes produced by the group's efforts. Thibaut and Kelley (1959, Chapter II) show that when members' outcomes are perfectly correspondent (i.e., where there is a positive correlation of unity between member outcomes over the cells of the matrix describing their joint behaviors), the member holding the higher potential power is unable to use that power to advantage himself at the expense of the other. He cannot help himself without also helping the other, nor hurt the other without hurting himself. Hence, in this situation there is no need for the development of norms governing the sharing of outcomes or protecting the weak from exploitation.

The description of such harmony and mutual dependence suggests two types of stress that might threaten the maintenance of such a dyad:[2]

(1) Conflict of interest. This "internal" stress will develop when any factors so reduce the correspondence of member outcomes that they become

negatively correlated. As conflict of interest increases so does the degree of "usable" power of the member whose power is greater. The likelihood that this power will be used against his interests constitues a real threat to the low-power member. In order to protect himself against serious reductions in his share of the outcomes, he will be expected to appeal to norms of "equity" and "fair sharing."

(2) Improved alternatives outside the group. This "external" stress will appear whenever outcomes available outside the dyad become attractive enough to compete with those available inside. This stress threatens the interdependence of the group members. Good external alternatives may, of course, be attractive to both group members. However, if there exists in the dyad a degree of conflict of interest, this will create enough potential advantage to the high-power member so that in evaluating his probable share of the outcomes he is likely to remain loyal to the group. It is the low-power member, then, who will respond with greater alacrity to the increasingly attractive external alternative. The potential disloyalty of the low-power member thus constitutes a real threat to the high-power member. In order to preserve the integrity of the group within which he holds the advantage, he will be expected to appeal to norms of "loyalty" and "group spirit."

To make appeals for the invocation of norms is not, of course, a sufficient condition for their realization. The high-power member cannot realistically expect that the low-power one will respond favorably to a contractual restraint on his "disloyalty" unless the eschewing of the temptation to "disloyalty" can be compensated for in some fashion. Nor can the low-power member entertain realistic hopes of a normative approach to "fair sharing" unless he can in some way compensate the high-power member for inhibiting his use of power. How can this compensation be achieved? There is one striking solution which suggests itself.

When *both* external and internal stresses are high, each member is threatened by behaviors which the other is tempted to perform, and each member's appeal is to a rule of behavior, a norm, which will forbid such threatening behaviors. Thus a type of "interdependence" appears in which each member's acceptance of the other's appeal is compensated for by a reduction in threat. The low-power member's agreement to inhibit his "disloyalty" is compensated for by the high-power member's willingness to impose restraint on the use of his power. This argument can be put in another way. Only when both types of stress are high are both members motivated to invoke a norm; furthermore, it is only under these conditions that the low-power member is provided with

---

[2] Of course, it is possible for either of these stresses to be sufficiently high so that in fact the group does disrupt. It is assumed in the following that the level of stress, though high, is not overwhelmingly so.

sufficient "counter power," through the presence of an attractive external alternative, to bargain effectively with the high-power member. If this reasoning is correct, two mutually dependent threats may generate norms of behavior which embody the adaptive mechanisms that support the continued integrity of the group.

DESIGN OF THE EXPERIMENT

To explore the foregoing theoretical formulation, an experiment was designed in which two Ss were confronted with a bargaining task. The situation in which the Ss were placed was one which permitted the manipulation of the attractiveness of the external alternative and the degree of conflict of interest. At a standard point of time in the course of the experiment, an opportunity was introduced for the Ss to regulate their bargaining normatively by forming contracts. The frequency and characteristics of the contracts constituted the main dependent variables.

Preliminary procedure. At the beginning of each experimental session, one member of each dyad was randomly assigned to the high-power position (designated P) and the other to the low-power position (designated X). The Ss remained in the same power position throughout the experiment. The Ss in each dyad were seated at a table facing one another, with a cardboard screen rising to eye level placed between them. The Ss in each dyad were instructed not to compete with one another in the bargaining game that was to be played, but rather to compete with the other Ss who were in the same power position, i.e., all P's were in competition, and all X's were in competition. In order to facilitate the instruction of the Ss, to provide practice at the bargaining task, and to create the necessary background of uniformly high interdependence and harmony, all dyads were initially confronted with the same simple task. The task consisted of bargaining for points to be won by playing the game summarized in a matrix (Fig. 1) presented to each S. The procedure for playing the game was as follows. By open discussion, the two Ss arrived at a tentative agreement about their joint behavior. When this tentative agreement was reached, P re-

corded it on a printed form provided for this purpose. Each S then recorded privately his actual decision about what he would play. In this decision he was not obliged to honor the tentative agreement reached earlier; duplicity was thus possible. When the actual decisions were reached, they were announced publicly and recorded by P. The play was repeated with the same matrix for three trials.

In playing the game, each S had three options among which to decide. He could play either of the two columns (or rows) of the matrix or he could play the external alternative. If both Ss played the external alternative, each received one point. However, if one S played the external alternative, while the other played a column (or row) of the matrix, the first received one point while the latter received zero. The alternative was thus a dependable (though in this instance, a paltry) outcome that each S could attain quite independently of the other's behavior, and it also provided a method for threatening one's partner.

The outcomes to be received from playing the columns and rows of the matrix reflect the interdependence of the Ss. For both players to receive the maximum outcomes (30 points) available in the present matrix, P must play a while X plays y. If P played b while X played z, each would receive 25 points.

However, in the remaining two cells of the matrix, by and az, the outcomes accruing to each player depended on the degree to which P exercised his power. It will be recalled from the discussion in the preceding section that "usable" power depends directly on the degree of conflict of interest (noncorrespondence of outcomes) present in the interdependent situation of the group members. Hence, power can be used only when the outcomes to the members from a given joint action are different. This leads to the experimental definition and manipulation of power in this experiment; P was instructed that in any such cells in which the outcomes to the Ss differed, he was empowered to take for himself any number of points from the smaller of the two values up to the larger, leaving the remaining points to X. Thus, if either by or az were played, P was empowered to take any number of points from 3 to 10. If, for example, P took 8 points, X would receive 5. These rules governing the bargaining procedure, the consequences of playing the external alternative, and the use and meaning of power remained invariant throughout the experiment.

Note in this preliminary matrix that the harmonious solution (ay, leading to 30 points apiece) is the obviously dominant solution, that the conflictual solutions (in which power can be exercised) are relatively unattractive, and that the external alternative (1 point) is extremely low and hence mutual dependence on intradyadic cooperation is strongly reinforced.

Experimental treatments. After the three trials of the preliminary phase, the experiment proper began and the experimental manipulations were introduced. The treatments consisted of varying both the level of the external alternative and the degree of conflict of interest in the dyadic situation. The essential charac-

FIGURE 1. Matrix summarizing the game played during the preliminary phase of the experiment.

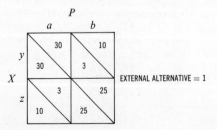

EXTERNAL ALTERNATIVE = 1

teristics of each of the four experimental conditions can be most succinctly described by the matrix governing the play in each of the conditions. Figure 2 shows the matrices representing high and low conflict of interest and the accompanying external alternatives. Pairing the values of the two variables results in the four conditions: high conflict-high alternative (*HH*), high conflict-low alternative (*HL*), low conflict-high alternative (*LH*), and low conflict-low alternative (*LL*). It should be observed that, in general, the points to be bargained for are higher in the experimental treatments than in the matrix of the preliminary phase, and that the cells containing the largest total number of points are no longer the harmonious solutions. Note too that the single difference between the matrices for high and low conflict consists in the size of discrepancy between the points contained in the cells of the main diagonal: in all other respects, including the total number of points available, the two matrices are identical. The level of the external alternative when high (35) begins to compete effectively with the matrix values; when low (10) this is not so.

It is perhaps apparent that the *HH* condition is designed to create high stress from both external and internal sources, the *HL* and *LH* conditions to produce mixed degrees of stress, and the *LL* condition little stress of either sort.

The dyads in each treatment used the same assigned matrix and alternative for the remainder of the experiment. The standard sequence which governed the remaining phases of the experiment was as follows: (*1*) three trials played with the new matrix and alternative followed by a brief questionnaire; (*2*) three additional trials with the same matrix and alternative; and finally (*3*) an opportunity to form contractual agreements which would govern the last three trials on the same matrix and alternative.[3]

Dependent measures. In addition to the tentative agreements, the actual choices in bargaining, and the outcomes received by *P* and by *X* on each trial, the dependent measures in the experiment included the interpolated questionnaire and the contractual decisions.

The *questionnaire* which was introduced after the first three trials on the experimental matrices asked each *S* to indicate on a 100-point scale the degree of his concern or anxiety about the fairness or equity of the division of points and about the likelihood that his partner would play the external alternatives. After each *S* had made his responses in private, the questionnaires were exchanged between partners. This device thus had two aims: to stimulate oral communication between partners about the variables being manipulated in the experiment and to gain data about the degree to which these variables were apprehended by and mattered to the *S*s.

After the sixth trial on the experimental matrices the procedure for forming *contracts* was introduced. The *E* emphasized that contracts were entirely volun-

tary and that they need not be formed unless the *S*s wanted them. On each of the three following trials each *S* recorded privately: (*1*) whether or not he wanted a contract to be formed, and (*2*) if in fact he wanted a contract to be formed, the single *rule* (among three presented to him) that he would most prefer to have incorporated in the contract and the type and amount of *sanction* that he would like to have applied to violations of any contractual rules.

The three rules among which each *S* wanting a contract had to choose were as follows:

EA-rule: it is prohibited to play the *external alternative* on this trial if a tentative agreement has been reached to play within the matrix.

D-rule: if on this trial a tentative agreement has been reached concerning the *division and distribution* of points between the partners, it is prohibited in the actual play to change the distribution agreed upon.

RC-rule: if on this trial a tentative agreement has been reached such that each partner is to play a specific *row or column* of the matrix, it is prohibited to shift in the actual play to the other row or column.

It will be apparent that the first two rules are designed to prohibit the kinds of behavior which on theoretical grounds may be expected to threaten differentially the two partners (whose anxiety about specifically these two sources of threat was earlier measured by the brief questionnaire). The third rule, which involves a type of behavior less central to the present research, was introduced primarily as a plausible third alternative which would permit the forma-

FIGURE 2. Matrices representing high and low conflict of interest and high and low levels of the external alternative.

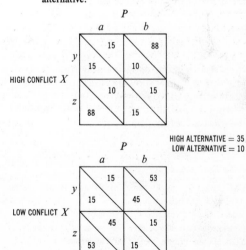

HIGH ALTERNATIVE = 35
LOW ALTERNATIVE = 10

---

[3] A final questionnaire, also administered, is discussed elsewhere (Faucheux and Thibaut, in press).

tion of types of contracts other than those envisaged by our theoretical formulation.

The two types of *sanction* afforded the Ss were indemnities and fines. Indemnities referred to payments (in points) the violator of a rule must make to the injured party. Fines referred to payments (in points) to be made by the violator to E. In the private recording of his preference for aspects of a contract, S could indicate any number of points between zero and 100 to be applied as an indemnity and/or as a fine.

After recording their individual preferences, the partners discussed the matter and decided whether to form a contract, and if a contract were to be formed, the rules and sanctions to be incorporated. The Ss were permitted to include in their contracts as many of the three rules as they liked and either or both types of sanctions. This procedure was repeated for three trials. Adherence to the various provisions of contracts was monitored and enforced by E.

Subjects and administration. Sixteen young adults of both sexes were formed into 8 dyads for the pretest. The experimental treatment was administered separately to each dyad, and the entire proceeding was tape-recorded. The Ss for the experiment proper were 100 14-year-old boys from two public schools in the suburbs of Paris: one at Chatenay and the other at Montrouge.[4] After the elimination from the sample of 2 dyads for failure to adhere to the instructions, there remained 24 dyads from each school. Six dyads at each school were assigned to each of the four treatments, making a total of 48 dyads, 12 for each treatment.

At each of the schools, the six dyads assigned to a given treatment were seated at widely separated tables in one large room, and the administration of the experiment thus proceeded simultaneously for all six dyads.[5]

RESULTS

In presenting the experimental findings, we shall proceed by first showing the objective situation confronting the Ss, then moving to the Ss' perception of this situation, and finally inquiring into the process of contract-formation and the characteristics of the contracts adopted.

The bargaining situation. There are two main aspects to the situation in which the Ss find them-

[4] We wish to thank Mademoiselle Hamel, Inspectrice de l'Enseignement Primaire; M. Forestier, Director of the School of Montrouge; M. Vlaeminkx, Director of the School of Chatenay; Madame Mongroville, directrice, and M. Pechberty (Centre d'Orientation Professionnelle de Montrouge).

[5] The assistance of Monique Fichelet, Marie Moscovici, Ferida Rasheed, and W. Doise in administering the experiment is gratefully acknowledged.

selves. These two aspects can be summarized by referring to the difference between the partners in the numbers of points won in the actual bargaining and to the frequencies with which the Ss chose to play the external alternative.

In presenting the data on points won in bargaining, let us consider the six trials that occurred before the opportunity to form contracts was introduced. (Data from the preliminary trials with the training matrix are, of course, omitted, since the experimental variations had not at that point been introduced.) Total points won in bargaining by dyads during these six trials show no mean differences among the four treatments. Dyads in the various treatments, therefore, were equally successful in their total productivity. On the other hand, the various treatments were not alike with respect to the share of the points won by P and X. Table 1 shows the mean differences between P and X in points received over the six trials before contracts were permitted. Although the variances from condition to condition are not homogeneous, it is plain that the sharing of points is much more nearly equal under low conflict of interest than under high. (High and low conflict of interest are different by analysis of variance: $F = 12.24$, $p < .001$.) A closely related finding is that under high conflict of interest there were 8 dyads in which on 19 occasions P failed to respect the agreement about sharing of points, but when conflict of interest was low, there were only 5 such instances in a total of 2 dyads. Hence, under conditions of high conflict of interest, X's share of the points is far exceeded by P's share, and the reduction of this disparity may pose a major problem for X.

The second aspect of the bargaining situation to be summarized here is the incidence of opting for the external alternative. It was frequently observed that an S would threaten to play the alternative without in fact doing so. Since these threats were not recorded (except in the pretests), the present data refer only to actual instances of playing the alternative. Table 2 shows, for all dyads in which either member at any time played the alternative, the number of dyads in which P was the first or only member to play the alternative, X was the first or only one to do so, or both members did so simultaneously. Note first that a total of 14 (58%) of the dyads in the High-Alternative conditions showed at least one instance of playing the alternative, as against only 4 (17%) of those in the Low-Alternative conditions. This difference yields a χ^2 of 7.20, which is significant at the .01 level. Note also that the initiative in playing the alternative rested mainly with X: in 11 dyads X was the first or only member to do so, but in only one dyad did P show this behavior. Hence, how to prevent X from playing the alternative may pose for P a major problem.

The partners' perception of the situation. Though it may seem clear that the partners theoretically should have and empirically do have the problems just outlined, it may be important to assess the degree to which these problems actually are perceived by the partners and matter to them.

It will be recalled that after the first block of three trials on the experimental matrices, a brief questionnaire was administered, partly to stimulate communication between the partners about "fair sharing" and "loyalty" to the dyad, and partly to gain information about the degree to which at that stage the partners were concerned about these two problems. Our theoretical formulation would lead us to expect that P would be more concerned in the High-Alternative than in the Low-Alternative conditions about his partner's playing the alternative, and that X would be more concerned about equitable sharing in the High-Conflict than in the Low-Conflict conditions.

As to the first of these predictions, although P does in fact have a greater degree of concern when the alternative is high than when it is low (the means are 37.30 and 26.58, respectively), this difference does not reach an acceptable level of statistical significance. The second prediction, however, is clearly confirmed. X's concern about fair sharing is greater when conflict of interest is high than when it is low. The means are 38.34 and 25.71, respectively, and the variance analysis yields an F of 4.42, which is significant at the .05 level.

An analysis rather similar to that just summarized can be made from the Ss' preference for various types of rules to be incorporated in contracts. It will be recalled that at the beginning of each of the three trials during which contracts were permitted, each S had the opportunity to record privately his preferences for various aspects of a contract which might be negotiated with his partner. From our formulation it might be expected that, in all conditions, P's preference would exceed that of X from a rule prohibiting the use of the external alternative, and that X's preference would exceed that of P for a rule prohibiting the violation of any agreement reached about the sharing of points between the partners. Both of these expectations are strongly confirmed. In every one of the four conditions P preferred prohibiting the alternative more frequently than did X, the combined probabilities reaching significance at the .01 level. (However, this difference in frequency of preference was not significantly greater under High-Alternative than under Low-Alternative conditions.) Similarly, in every condition X preferred more frequently than did P a rule protecting any agreements about sharing, again with combined probabilities reaching the .01 level. (But again, too, this difference in frequency of preference was not significantly greater when conflict of interest was high than when it was low.)

The contract. Throughout the following presentation of results, the term contract will be reserved for written agreements specifying at least one rule to be observed and including a sanction for viola-

tion in the form of an indemnity. (Fines were so infrequently attached to contracts that we will omit any consideration of them in this discussion.)

Let us now turn to the various measures which reflect the over-all frequency and intensity of contractual activity in the four conditions. Table 3 summarizes these data. The HH condition shows clear superiority on each of the five measures.

Dyads in the HH condition formed on the average 2.75 contracts (the absolute limit being 3.00), as compared with means of less than two contracts in the other three conditions. An analysis of variance yields an F for interaction of 5.51, which is significant at the .05 level.

Similarly, all 12 of the HH dyads formed at least one contract, while only 64% of the dyads in the remaining conditions did so. This difference between HH and the other conditions combined is significant by χ^2 (4.25) at the .05 level.

The same pattern is revealed by the frequency with which dyads included both rules prohibiting

TABLE 1 *Mean Differences between P and X in Points Received during the Six Trials Preceding the Contract Period*

CONFLICT OF INTEREST		LEVEL OF EXTERNAL ALTERNATIVE	
		High	Low
High	M^*	61.62	70.96
	SD	62.40	97.90
Low	M	2.79	3.25
	SD	16.71	48.73

* In all four conditions the mean difference signifies the preponderance of P's share over X's.

TABLE 2 *Total Numbers of Dyads in the Various Treatments in Which One or Both Members at Any Time Played the Alternative, with Specification of the Order of Doing So*

CONFLICT OF INTEREST		LEVEL OF EXTERNAL ALTERNATIVE	
		High	Low
High	P first	0	0
	X first	5	3
	Simultaneous	4	0
	Total	9	3
Low	P first	1	0
	X first	2	1
	Simultaneous	2	0
	Total	5	1

the playing of the external alternative and rules protecting agreements concerning the division of points. In all, 75% of the *HH* dyads formed such contracts, but only 19% of the remaining dyads did so. This difference yields a χ^2 of 10.13, which is significant at well beyond the .01 level.

The mean size of indemnity for violation of contractual provisions is also atypically high in the *HH* condition. The *F*-ratio for interaction resulting from the analysis of variance was 4.93, which is significant at the .05 level.

Finally, an index was constructed to estimate for each dyad the over-all quantity and intensity of its contractual activity by multiplying the number of rules adopted times the magnitude of indemnity to be paid for violations. The shapes of the resulting distributions are markedly different from condition to condition, and hence a variance analysis was not attempted. However, the Mann-Whitney test distinguishes the *HH* condition from the other conditions combined, yielding a *p* of exactly .02.

A word about the *effectiveness* of the contracts both from the point of view of the joint profit of the dyads and the division of points between the partners: To make the relevant comparisons, let us consider the joint profit of dyads for the six trials that preceded the contract period. The mean joint profit for these six trials was slightly higher for the 35 dyads that later formed contracts than for the 13 dyads that did not form

TABLE 3 *Frequency and Intensity of Contractual Activity in the Various Treatments*

CONFLICT OF INTEREST	LEVEL OF EXTERNAL ALTERNATIVE	
	High	Low
Mean number of contracts	2.75	1.33
Number of dyads forming one or more contracts	12	6
High Number of dyads adopting both *EA*- and *D*-rules*	9	2
Mean indemnity	65.56	26.39
Index of quantity and intensity	315.83	175.00
Mean number of contracts	1.67	1.92
Number of dyads forming one or more contracts	9	8
Low Number of dyads adopting both *EA*- and *D*-rules*	2	3
Mean indemnity	35.83	42.22
Index of quantity and intensity	194.17	184.17

* *EA*-rules are prohibitions against playing the alternative; *D*-rules protect agreements about the division of points.

contracts. Of the dyads forming contracts, 57% achieved the maximum possible joint profit (98 points) on each of the six trials, while only 31% of the "noncontractual" dyads achieved this level of joint profit. In spite of this initially higher level (though it is statistically nonsignificant), 86% of the dyads forming contracts maintained or increased their joint profit over the three trials of the contract period, while only 78% of the "noncontractual" dyads maintained or increased their initial levels of joint profit.

A more crucial test concerns the efficacy of contracts in reducing disparities in points received by the partners. If one compares the disparity in points received by the partners during the initial six trials with that of the three trials of the contract period, the efficacy of contracts becomes clear. In not a single one of the 13 dyads forming no contracts was there a reduction in this interpartner disparity from the initial trials to the contract trials. However 15 of the contractual dyads (including 8 from the *HH* treatment) showed reduced disparities during the contract phase. This difference yields a χ^2 of 6.23, which is significant at the .02 level.

DISCUSSION AND CONCLUSIONS

Although the task confronting the *S*s in the present research was to bargain for points in the context of a game defined by the given matrix, the focus of the study has been not so much on the microscopic analysis of game-playing behavior as on the game situation as a device for studying the development of contractual agreements. The aim of the study, to relate the genesis of contracts to the joint application of external and internal stresses on groups containing members of unequal power, appears to have been realized.

Nevertheless, there are two aspects of the process of game-playing in the present experiment that require comment. The first has to do with the exercise of power in the bargaining process. The reader will have observed that the matrices employed in this research created an interdependence between the players such that neither partner could attain large outcomes without the cooperation of the other. The manipulation of the external alternative set the limit of outcomes that each player could dependably attain by his own efforts alone. From this point of view, then, the partners were equally dependent on one another for any outcomes superior to those of the external alternative.

Hence it may be difficult to see wherein lies the superior power of *P*. The answer to this question appears to be that both partners accept the *E*'s definition of *P*'s power and find it plausible that the person endowed with superior power should aim for the larger share of the group's rewards. In any case, if *P* is to compete successfully with other *P*s he is forced to strain the upper limits of his possibilities. It is perhaps this aspiration for affluence, activated by *E*'s definition of the possible prerogatives of power, which holds P to the interdependent solution, while at the same time driving X to abandon it. Moreover, both partners apparently felt it in accord with their experience in other groups, that the powerful member will have greater "usable" power as the conflict of interest increases. The present manipulation of P's power, aimed at insuring this relationship of usable power to conflict of interest, was crystallized during the pretests on the basis of reassuring evidence from the comments of Ss.

The second comment on the game-playing process concerns the intensity of the bargaining activity and the involvement of the Ss. There is no doubt that these were maximal in the HH condition and (though this must be said less confidently) that they were minimal in the LL condition. Though precise timing of the bargaining sessions was not attempted, it is worth noting that, both at Chatenay and Montrouge, the order of time taken to complete the experiment was, from greatest to least: HH, HL, LH, and LL.

A word about the LL condition: From the point of view of global theories of cohesiveness, this is the condition which should produce dyads of the greatest cohesiveness. The minimal external stress on such dyads means that, with minimally attractive external alternatives, the resultant motivation to remain in the group should be high. And minimal internal stress should mean that the attractiveness of the group would not be unnecessarily reduced by intermember conflict. It is entirely possible that such dyads would be maximally effective in enforcing conformity to any norms that existed in the group. But from the present research it seems unlikely that such norms, at least of the sort discussed here (of equity and loyalty), will be generated from within the group in the absence of temptations to violate them.

REFERENCES

BERTALANFFY, L. VON. Theoretical models in biology and psychology. *J. Pers.*, 1951, **20**, 24–38.

FAUCHEUX, C., AND THIBAUT, J. L'approche clinique et experimentale de la genèse des normes contractuelles dans differentes conditions de conflit et de menace. *Bull. C.E.R.P., Paris,* in press.

MILLER, J. G. Toward a general theory for the behavioral sciences. *Amer. Psychol.*, 1955, **10**, 513–531.

SELYE, H. The physiology and pathology of exposure to stress: a treatise based on the concepts of the general-adaptation syndrome and the diseases of adaptation. Montreal: Acta, 1950.

THIBAUT, J., AND KELLEY, H. *The social psychology of groups.* New York: Wiley, 1959.

CONFORMITY AS AN INGRATIATION TACTIC*

A common theme throughout this section has been the presentation of self so as to further interaction goals. In the present selection Jones and Jones describe an experiment in which subjects present themselves as conforming to the opinions of another person in order to appear attractive to him. Their experiment is part of a program of research on *ingratiation*, which is defined as behavior directed toward increasing one's attractiveness to another person.[a] An ingratiation technique well known in everyday interaction is flattery; the conformity technique is perhaps less obvious.

That conformity to the opinions of another person should lead him to like the conformer is suggested by both theory and empirical evidence. Newcomb's theory of interpersonal attraction, discussed earlier, states that when A and B have similar feelings toward X, this symmetrical condition induces mutual liking. The experiment below, however, suggests that there is an optimum or normative degree of similarity that produces maximum attraction—a degree that is less than equality.

In this experiment subjects under two different conditions were faced with a dilemma. Subjects in one condition were given the impression that their opinions on thirty different items deviated markedly from those of the person they were to impress. If they appeared to agree with him to gain his approval they would not be true to themselves; if they expressed their true opinions, they might alienate him. Subjects in another condition were led to believe that the target person had opinions identical with their own on the thirty items. If they presented their true opinions they would violate the normative prescription against slavish conformity that appears to operate in most social situations and thus be disliked. But if they deviated from their opinions to avoid such an impression, they would not be true to themselves.

Two other conditions were also introduced, one where it was important for the subject to appear attractive to the other person, and another where it was not. The experimenter predicted that where the subjects were especially dependent on the other person's opinion, those subjects having identical opinions to the target person would ingratiate

---

* The selection following the editorial introduction is reprinted from "Optimum conformity as an ingratiation tactic," *Journal of Personality,* 1964, **32**, 436–458, by permission of the authors and Duke University Press.
[a] E. E. Jones, *Ingratuation: A social psychological analysis.* New York: Appleton-Century-Crofts, 1964.

themselves by appearing less conforming, and those having discrepant opinions would ingratiate themselves by appearing more conforming.

The investigation is especially instructive because it illustrates the complexities encountered in attempting to study experimentally aspects of ongoing interaction. As will be seen, the results were not quite as expected. From other information collected in the study, the investigators present a plausible interpretation of the findings, an interpretation consistent with theory, but highly tentative because it is a postexperimental analysis. Such analyses are desirable and useful primarily as a basis for further experimentation, where the validity of the new hypotheses is tested.

47.

Optimum Conformity as an Ingratiation Tactic[1]

ROBERT G. JONES
DAVIDSON COLLEGE

EDWARD E. JONES
DUKE UNIVERSITY

The present investigation concerns the manner in which a person resolves a particular dilemma in making himself attractive to another. It is one of a series of studies investigating the use of restricted communication opportunities for ingratiating self-presentations. If a person is concerned with presenting an attractive "face" to another and has been apprized of the other's opinions, a convenient and common way to accomplish this is to express opinions which are highly similar to those of the other, to agree with him or at least to minimize the degree of disagreement. A number of studies have shown that Ss do reduce the discrepancy between their private opinions and the stated opinions of another when motivated to be approved or accepted by him (Deutsch & Gerard, 1955; Thibaut & Strickland, 1956; Jones, Gergen, & Jones, 1963). But the resulting opinion conformity is rarely if ever complete, and even if the "conformer" is especially concerned with making himself attractive, he will most likely express a few minor disagreements in a setting of general agreement. This will be true for two reasons: (*a*) the potential ingratiator in our culture is unwilling to acknowledge to himself that he is willing to change his views markedly to gain attraction, and (*b*) for strategic reasons he will wish to avoid arousing suspicions in the target person that his agreement has been managed for

[1] This study is part of a research program supported by NSF G-21955. The authors wish to thank Kent Earnhardt for his invaluable help in preparing the messages for the experimental sessions.

its manipulative effects. He is most likely to arouse such suspicions if his opinions are monotonously close to the target person's in a setting where he is obviously dependent on the target person for favors, approval, or more generally, attraction.

A study by Jones, Jones, and Gergen (1963) showed that slavish agreement in such a setting does indeed give rise to the impression that the person agreeing is self-promoting, lacking in candor, and generally disliked. In that study, bystanders were exposed to a tape-recorded opinion exchange allegedly between two students like themselves. Following instructions given on the recording, one of these students always expressed his opinions after hearing the opinions of the other. It was so arranged that the degree of agreement was always very close in one treatment and moderately close or variable in another treatment. A cross-cutting variation presented the opinion interchange in two different contexts: approximately half the Ss heard the interchange described on the recording as a preliminary to a lucrative and attractive experiment—*if* the students ended up attracted to each other; the remaining Ss heard the interchange presented as a first impression session in which candor and accurate self-revelation were crucial. The major dependent variable was the rated impression of the student forced to go second in the recorded interchange. As predicted, Ss disliked and deprecated this student when the context raised the importance of attraction and he responded with slavish opinion agreement.

But, one might ask, what would the implications be if this high degree of agreement were genuine and coincidental? Would not the second speaker, then, be unfairly judged in the eyes of others if he spoke his true opinions? If the second speaker did hold the same opinions as the first, he would be victimized by the situation and forced into a dilemma of self-presentation: whether to be true to his opinions in the face of agreement with another, and quite possibly have his intention misunderstood, or whether to vary his opinions in an effort to avoid the imputation of manipulative intentions. The present investigation sought to determine whether such a combination of events would be perceived as a dilemma and whether the implied threat of being labeled a self-promoting conformist would lead Ss to adopt mild nonconformity as a tactic of ingratiation.

In spite of the many technical problems involved in proceeding to explore these questions, the possibility of demonstrating that we sometimes modify our opinions in order to make them seem autonomously determined, seemed worth the experimental effort. In the experiment to be described, each S was involved in an exchange of opinions with another person who always came first in expressing his views on each issue. For approximately half the Ss, it was arranged so that the initiator always expressed the opinions which had been endorsed in an earlier session by the S; i.e., the initiator pre-empted the S's opinions (Same condition). The remaining Ss were exposed to opinions from the initiator which varied systematically from their own earlier recorded ones (Discrepant condition). As in the "bystander" experiment, the interchange was set in one of two distinct contexts. Ss were either motivated to make themselves attractive (High-Dependence condition) or to be accurate (Low-Dependence condition). The major dependent variable was the extent to which the S agreed with the initiator in the experimental situation, though confidence and attraction ratings were also gathered to shed further light on the dilemma and its resolution.

The major hypothesis of the present study rests on two important conditions: (*1*) reasonable opinion stability over time; (*2*) realization by the S that a person dislikes someone who agrees with him only for ulterior reasons. Stability of the particular opinions involved is a precondition for subjective victimization, for if the S's opinions at the time of the experiment cannot be predicted from his opinions at an earlier date, there is no effective way to arrange for the initiator to pre-empt them. The hypothesis also assumes that the S has some appreciation for the cognitive dynamics of the initiator—the uses to which he is likely to put combined information about the setting and the S's behavior—or no true dilemma will exist for him. If these conditions hold, then the following prediction seems a straight-forward derivation from the theoretical argument developed above: When there is a high discrepancy between A's incoming opinions and B's previously recorded opinions, B will agree more closely with A in the High-Dependence than in the Low-Dependence condition. When A pre-empts B's previously recorded opinions on every issue, B will agree more closely with A in the Low-Dependence than in the High-Dependence condition. Statistically, the hypothesis predicts an interaction between opinion discrepancy and dependence in the production of initiator-subject agreement.

METHOD

Subjects

Sixty male volunteers from the Duke introductory psychology course participated in the experiment in groups of five. Eleven Ss, scattered across the various conditions, indicated suspicion of the experimental procedure. Data from these Ss were not included in the data analysis, though the results would not have been altered by their inclusion. The results were based on the remaining 49 Ss: 10 in the High-Same, 11 in the Low-Same, 15 in the High-Discrepant and 13 in the Low-Discrepant groups.[2] In addition, two control

[2] Since internal analysis of the Discrepant conditions was anticipated, slightly more Ss were run in these cells. Also, on occasions when only four Ss showed up, a paid assistant sat through the instructions as S.

groups were also run. In one (consisting of nine Ss) high dependence instructions were given but the Ss initiated rather than responded to each message. In the other, 20 randomly selected students from the same introductory class filled out the opinion-rating form at the beginning and end of the semester in a classroom setting. In neither control group could the S be directly affected by an incoming opinion message and any conceivable effects of the setting itself on the expression of opinions could be studied by comparing the two.

Experimental instructions:
High and low dependence

The crucial opinion exchange was set in one of two contexts which differed in the extent to which the S was dependent on the opinion initiator for the attainment of a desired goal. Dependence is herein used, then, in the sense specified by Thibaut and Kelley (1959), as the reciprocal of power rather than a regressive emotional condition. The supervisor has more power than the judge in the present experiment, because he can provide both more positive and more negative outcomes for the S. It may help the reader to consider that the normal or usual conditions of self-presentation, where dependence is neither high nor low, give rise to a joint concern with being attractive (congenial, acceptable, etc.) and with being faithful to one's private feelings. The High-Dependence condition was designed to make the former concern of greater importance than the latter, while the Low-Dependence condition was designed to reverse this differential concern. Neither, then, is necessarily more normal or neutral than the other.

High dependence. The experiment began with five Ss and the E seated around a large conference desk. Prominently displayed on the desk were five place cards reading "Supervisor," "Production Manager," "Copy Writer," "Copy Writer," and "Worker." On a nearby table was arrayed a stack of magazines, colored paper, scissors, a glue bottle, and similar art supplies. After introducing himself, the E informed the Ss he was studying productivity in groups with two different kinds of organizational structure. One arrangement had the person most attractive to the leader immediately under him in the chain of command, the other arrangement placed that person at the bottom of the chain of command. The E then said the present group would be organized along the former lines to produce advertising copy—as he nodded to the supply of materials on the table. Next he enumerated the jobs in the work group and deliberately moved the place cards around the desk indicating where the job holders would subsequently be located. The supervisor, he continued, would be selected at random by a roll of the die and the other positions would be determined by how attractive he judged each of the others to be on the basis of an exchange of opinions. The *E* then stated that for the present group the person judged most attractive by the supervisor would be the production manager and the one judged least attractive would be the worker; the other two would be the copy writers. After relative attraction to the supervisor had been determined on the basis of an opinion exchange in another room, he continued, the group would return to the office, each would assume his assigned position around the desk, and together they would work for 30 minutes on advertising copy. The clear implication was that everyone would know how everyone else had been rated by the supervisor and it was expected that *S*s would get emotionally involved in such a popularity contest.

Low-dependence variation. *S*s in the Low-Dependence conditions were instructed in the same setting except the place cards, magazines, etc., had been removed. The *E* explained that he was interested in what sorts of persons are "highly sensitive and accurate in their appraisals of other people." He indicated that earlier studies were open to question because they involved one person judging only one other and chance accuracy could never be ruled out. His innovation in this research was to have a judge who would make appraisals of four persons. In this way he could more carefully select accurate judges and compare their personalities with inaccurate judges. The test of a judge's accuracy, it was explained, was carefully controlled by only allowing him to have information about the others which he could gather from an opinion exchange. After stating that the judge for that session would be determined by a roll of a die, the *E* emphasized that the other *S*s had a delicate task too, because they would have to present themselves as honestly as possible in the opinion exchange if their judge was to have a fair chance of being accurate in his subsequent appraisals of them. Then the *E* asked each *S* to fill out a slip naming the two persons on campus who could give the best evaluations of him; these persons were to be contacted by the *E* within the week. Ratings made by the two friends would be pooled with the *S*'s own rating of himself to determine the standard by which to compare the judge's accuracy. The *E* concluded this part of the instructions by commenting that he hoped the judge from that group would prove to be highly accurate.

Cross-cutting variation:
Same and discrepant messages

When the *E* had concluded the instructions pertaining to the dependence variable, he went on to explain that attractiveness (in the High-Dependence condition) or accuracy (in the Low-Dependence condition) would be determined by a message exchange to be held in another room where there were a number of small booths. Each *S*, he continued, would enter a

separate booth after which the supervisor/judge would be randomly selected. The supervisor/judge (hereafter called Target Person or Target) would then begin sending messages to the others. They were to answer each as it was received and send it back—the *E* serving as messenger. The anonymity provided by the booths, it was suggested, would rule out the possibility of bias based on prior acquaintance (though *S*s were not allowed to participate in the experiment with friends), physical appearance, and the like. In the High-Dependence condition the *E* also commented that keeping the precise identity of each correspondent from the supervisor would put them all on an equal footing at the beginning. The *E* concluded by asking if there were any questions, briefly answered any which arose, and then led the *S*s to the other room where they were arbitrarily assigned to separate booths.

In planning the experimental design, it was assumed that a victimization effect would result from a combination of High Dependence and the receipt of opinions identical to the *S*'s. That is, the *S* would run the risk of appearing opportunistic if he expressed his true opinions. Opinions from the Target in this, the Same condition, and its counterpart, the Discrepancy condition, were prepared on the basis of each *S*'s responses to a "Campus Opinion Questionnaire." This questionnaire was administered to all male students in the introductory course early in the semester. It was composed of 50 opinion items, each accompanied by a 12-point scale running from "Agree Completely" to "Disagree Completely." *S*s were asked to check their agreement or disagreement with each statement.

The "Campus Opinion Questionnaire" also asked the *S*s to check those statements they found unusually important. It was suggested that this could be determined by "whether it would make any difference in how much you liked a new acquaintance if he held a very different opinion from yours on the item." Thirty items were selected for the opinion exchange portion of the experiment: the 10 checked important by all *S*s most frequently, the 10 checked least frequently, and the 10 in the middle range of frequency. While no specific hypotheses were formulated concerning this variation in item importance, it seemed quite possible that *S*s would respond differently to important and unimportant items in resolving the victimization dilemma.

Each *S* in the experiment received the messages in a different random order with the following restrictions: five middle important items began the exchange, and five concluded it. The high and low items were randomly presented between with five high and five low in messages 6-15 and 16-25.

The opinion items themselves ranged over a wide variety of topical issues and pertained to academic, social, political and personal matters. Two low important items were: (*a*) It will only be a matter of years before the horse becomes as extinct as the buffalo, and (*b*) Some way should be found to restrict any influence the alumni have over university policies and programs. Two middle important items were: (a) Television programs have become so bad that we should seriously consider federally sponsored programming during certain hours of the day, and (b) College student government associations are generally useless and don't deserve the support of the students. Two high important items were: (a) Negroes should be more severely punished for crimes against whites than for crimes against other Negroes, and (b) A belief in God is necessary in order to give a stable base to ethical standards in society.

Once in the booths, Ss in the Same condition were exposed to opinion ratings from the Target which were identical to their own pre-experimental ratings. Ss in the Discrepant condition received Target opinions which were four points removed from the S's pre-ratings either in the direction of greater agreement or disagreement. It was possible to maintain the deception that these opinions were actually coming from a naïve supervisor or judge because, of course, each S was isolated and prearranged messages tailored to the S's own opinions could be delivered by the E.

A number of steps were taken to facilitate the deception involved and to reinforce the experimental inductions. After the S had entered his booth, he was visited by the E who reiterated the significance of the messages. In the High-Dependence conditions, the E emphasized that the attractiveness rating would be based entirely on the S's replies to incoming messages. Low-Dependence Ss were reminded to express their true opinions and to avoid trying to impress the judge. The S was then given a copy of the rating form which would allegedly be used by the supervisor or judge in assessing the S. These rating forms had been carefully constructed to reflect the clearly evaluative emphasis of the assessment in the High-Dependence conditions and the clearly nonevaluative emphasis in the Low-Dependence conditions. Ss in the latter conditions, for example, saw that the judge always had to choose among positive or among negative attributes and never between the two types.

As the interchange began, the S received two introductory messages which were designed to convey the Target Person's clear understanding of the Dependence instructions (high or low). These were followed by a series of 30 messages, allegedly coming from, and after a few minutes picked up for delivery to, the Target Person. On each of these messages the opinion statement, worded identically to one on the earlier Campus Opinion Questionnaire, was printed twice with a 12-point scale of agree-disagree under each printing. The Target had presumably circled a number reflecting his opinion on the upper scale, and the S was to respond by circling a number on the lower scale. In addition, the S was asked to express, on a five-point scale, the degree of confidence he had in the correctness of his position on each issue.

The postexperimental questionnaire

When the message exchange was completed the E gave to each S a final questionnaire, commenting

that it would take the supervisor/judge a while to make his rating and indicating his interest in some additional information. The questionnaire included seven questions. The first asked the S to rate the supervisor/judge on four dimensions: attractiveness, soundness, intelligence, and candor. The second question asked separately how much of an effort the S had made to gain the (a) approval and (b) respect of the person sending the messages. The S was to check in each case one of five pertinent statements placed in descending order of concern with approval and respect. The intention here was to establish the effect of the dependence instructions. As a check on perceived influence, question three inquired whether or not the S had been influenced either to agree or disagree with the other person's opinions. The fourth question was directed toward the same interest and asked the Ss to indicate the number of items in which they had felt pressure to agree, disagree or had felt no pressure at all. The fifth question asked how similar the Ss' initial private opinions were to the other person's. The final two questions asked to what extent the Ss felt they were agreeing too much, or disagreeing too much.

When the questionnaires were completed, the Ss returned to the office where the experimenter declared the experiment was over, disclosed all deceptions and discussed with the Ss the scientific purpose of the study. They were then asked not to discuss the experiment with others.

RESULTS

Validation of experimental inductions

Before examining the data relevant to the major hypothesis, it is necessary to establish whether the specific objectives of the experimental inductions were achieved, and whether the opinion ratings had sufficient temporal stability to permit a true pre-empting of opinion in the Same conditions.

Dependence variation. Instructions in the High-Dependence condition made it clear to the S that he was in an attractiveness or popularity contest the results of which would be brought to the attention of his fellow Ss. The instructions themselves gave no hints concerning the components of attractiveness, but a copy of the supervisor's evaluation sheet was made available to the High-Dependence Ss and from this it was clear that they would be eventually judged on attributes relating both to affection and respect. If the dependence variation was effective, there should be evidence in the postexperimental questionnaire that High-Dependence Ss were more concerned with being liked and respected than Low-Dependence Ss. This was indeed the case; on separate questions the Highs expressed more concern with being liked ($F = 23.01$, $p < .001$) and with being respected ($F = 19.79$, $p < .001$) by the supervisor.

Discrepancy variation. Evidence concerning the differential perception of same and discrepant messages was also provided by the postexperimental questionnaire. Here Ss were asked to indicate the similarity between the supervisor's opinions and their own. As expected, Ss in the Same conditions perceived less discrepancy than did Ss in the Discrepant conditions ($F = 69.96$, $p < .001$). Ss in the Same conditions also found the Target more likeable ($F = 12.88$, $p < .001$), more sound ($F = 57.94$, $p < .001$), more brilliant ($F = 15.96$, $p < .001$), and more candid ($F = 13.43$, $p < .001$).

Opinion stability. Questions concerning the extent to which unreliability of opinion rating was a

TABLE 1 *Discrepancy from Target and from Before Scores (comparison of experimental and control Ss)*

EXPERIMENTAL Ss		Discrepancy from Target*		Discrepancy from Before Scores†	
		High Dep.	Low Dep.	High Dep.	Low Dep.
Same	$\overline{X}$	1.47	1.67	1.47	1.67
	SD	.67	.37	.67	.37
	N	10	11	10	11
Discrepant	$\overline{X}$	2.68	3.45	2.13	1.98
	SD	.46	.34	.38	.43
	N	15	13	15	13

CONTROL Ss	Laboratory (C_1)	Classroom (C_2)
$\overline{X}$	2.15	2.09
SD	.56	.55
N	9	20

* These values represent the average difference per item between the S's and the Target opinion ratings. Thus, the lower the discrepancy score, the greater the agreement with the Target. Comparisons: Same vs. Discrepant, $p < .001$; High vs. Low, $p < .01$; Interaction, $p < .05$.   † Since the Target's ratings are identical to the S's ratings in the Same condition, the means are the same in the first row of the table. In the third and fourth columns, the lower the score, the less the change (direction disregarded) from before to after rating. Comparisons between experimental and control Ss: Control (C_1+C_2) vs. High Same, $p < .02$; vs. Low Same, $p < .06$; vs. High Discrepant, n.s.; vs. Low Discrepant, n.s.

factor in the experiment are difficult to answer except by circumstantial evidence. Rating changes by the experimental subjects were presumably a mixture in unknown proportions of unsystematic pre-post variation and systematic changes effected by the experimental variables. Evidence from two control groups, however, suggests that the amount of unsystematic opinion change was considerable. A first control group (C_1 was exposed to the High-Dependence instructions in the experimental situation but in the opinion exchange these Ss always preceded rather than followed the prospective supervisor. A second control group (C_2) consisted of 20 randomly chosen students who twice filled out the opinion questionnaire—once toward the beginning and once at the end of the semester. The average scale change per opinion item (direction disregarded) was 2.13 for C_1 and 2.09 for C_2 respectively. Since we may assume that these values estimate the amount of unsystematic change occurring in the experimental conditions as well, pre-conditions for a true "victimization dilemma" were probably not achieved. Ss in the Same conditions viewed the opinions received as considerably closer to their own than those in the Discrepancy conditions, but there is serious doubt that the average S in the former conditions felt his precise opinions were pre-empted. As we shall see, therefore, the phenomenal situation of the Ss in the High-Dependence-Same conditions was rather different from that specified as a precondition for the main hypothesis.

Perception of influence and victimization. In spite of the undoubted pre-experimental changes in opinion characterizing all Ss, there still is some evidence from the final questionnaire that Ss in the Same conditions were more aware of influence pressures than those in the Discrepant conditions. (The dependence variation did not seem to affect this kind of awareness one way or the other.) Same condition Ss generally denied that they felt any influence to agree or disagree with the incoming statement, but they still acknowledged more influence than did Ss in the Discrepant conditions ($F = 6.02$, $p < .05$). Similarly, when asked if they felt they had "agreed too much," all Ss tended to deny this as a problem. Nevertheless, the Same condition Ss once again were less vigorous in their denial ($F = 9.90$, $p < .01$). It would seem, then, that being exposed to a sequence of opinions agreeing closely with one's own created at least some detectable conflict, regardless of the social context in which this exposure occurred. The probable nature of this conflict will be discussed below.

Opinion conformity: Accommodation to target's opinions

The main hypothesis of the present investigation predicted an interaction among the two independent variables in affecting the final discrepancy between the Target's and the S's opinions. A smaller discrepancy was predicted in the Low-Dependence-Same condition than in High Dependence Same; a larger discrepancy was predicted in Low Dependence Discrepant than in High Dependence Discrepant. As Table 1 shows, the predicted interaction was indeed significant (along with both main effects), but the reverse of differences specified in the prediction did not occur. When there is a fairly sizeable discrepancy between two persons' opinions and the importance of attraction is made salient, the individual responding second attempts to reduce this discrepancy beyond that expected in a comparison condition where the initial discrepancy is as great but attraction is minimized. This portion of the predicted interaction was confirmed to a highly significant extent ($t = 5.03$, $p < .001$). When the initial discrepancy is minimal, however, the results do not show a reversal of this effect: instead, there is no reliable difference in resulting discrepancy as a function of the salience of attraction (i.e., the dependence variable), and the mean difference is in the same direction as that in the Discrepant conditions. As the significant main effect for Dependence implies, pressures to be attractive produce change in the direction of conformity regardless of the degree of initial discrepancy, though the interaction tells us that this change is much greater when the discrepancy is substantial. Only in a relative sense, then, is the main hypothesis confirmed and the discrepancy results may be accounted for without reference to any effects of victimization. For one thing, Ss in the Discrepant conditions have more room for movement in the Target's direction than those in the Same conditions. It might also be noted that item importance did not greatly affect the observed variations in opinion discrepancy, though the High-Same Ss should show slightly more conformity on important than on unimportant items (cf. Jones, Gergen, Gumpert, & Thibaut, 1965). Finally, there were no systematic effects as a function of item sequence or position.

Signs of a self-presentation dilemma

The present study was mainly concerned with the potential dilemma facing Ss in the High-Dependence-Same condition, with the remaining conditions serving as points of comparison. As originally described, the dilemma was to emerge out of competing pressures to be true to one's own opinion's while avoiding the appearance of slavish and manipulative conformity. In view of the instability of Ss' opinion ratings, and the resulting fact that their opinion during the experimental session could not be accurately pre-empted by a repetition of their previously recorded ratings, there is serious question that such a dilemma was in fact created. The question remains serious in view of the failure of Ss in the Same conditions to confirm the hypothesis on the discrepancy or conformity data. But there are interesting data from other sources which argue that a kind of dilemma *was* created

in the High-Same Ss. For these Ss the problem was not, as initially proposed, one of remaining true to their own opinions while avoiding the appearance of conformity. Instead, however, the Ss faced a more benign dilemma: how to gain attraction and respect by conforming without appearing to conform and without having to acknowledge their conformity to themselves. The remainder of this section will concern itself with the evidence bearing on this dilemma and its resolution.

Perhaps the first thing to note is the fact of high variability in the High-Same cell. Ss in this cell vary from each other in discrepancy score more than Ss in the Low-Same cell ($F_{9, 10} = 3.28$; $p < .05$). A reasonable interpretation of this difference would suggest greater conformity conflict in the High-Same Ss. Relative to the Low-Same cell, some High-Same Ss showed more agreement with the Target and some showed less, suggesting that the position of the Target was more of a factor in determining their position. The Target's opinions were either more attractive or more repelling, but not apt to be ignored by the High-Same Ss. That the tendency to conform or to resist influence represented a general (if implicit) decision is suggested by the lack of any differences in variability across items. Thus, relative to Ss in other conditions there was no greater tendency for Ss in the High-Same condition to conform more on some items than others.

The conflict hypothesis becomes more plausible when some of the correlates of conformity in the High-Same cell are examined. As Table 2 shows, this is the only condition in which there is a significant positive correlation between attraction to the Target (as measured by a postexperimental questionnaire item) and conformity. In fact, in spite of the small samples involved, this correlation is significantly greater ($p < .01$) than the non-significant negative correlation in the Low-Same cell. Interpreting the psychological meaning of such a correlation involves the consideration of three major alternatives. It may be that Ss who happen to find themselves in closer agreement with the Target therefore like him better, or it may be that those who start out feeling positively toward the Target therefore agree with him more. While both of these alternatives are plausible, there does not seem to be any reason why either should characterize the High-Same group and not lead to similar correlations in the other cells. A third alternative is that those who tend to conform in a situation where too much agreement might be suspect, attempt to justify this conformity to themselves by increasing their liking for the Target. In other words, the high correlations in the High-Same cell may reflect the operation of dissonance reduction processes (cf. Festinger, 1957): dissonance is produced when the cognition that one is honest and consistent coexists with the cognition that one yields solely to win favor. By convincing himself that the Target person is likeable, the S thus reduces the dissonance created by conformity. Since the conditions for dissonance are not present to the same degree in the other cells, the correlations there are negligible.

Table 2 also presents evidence of a relationship between expressed desire to be respected on the one hand, and conformity in the High-Same and High-Discrepancy cells. In the High-Same cell, the relationship between these variables appeared to be curvilinear by inspection. Therefore, each discrepancy score was subtracted from the cell median (ignoring sign) to produce a derived "optimum conformity" score. Thus, the optimum conformity score is a measure of the degree to which the S in question overconformed or under-

TABLE 2 Relationships between: (a) Opinion Conformity and Liking the Target, (b) Opinion Conformity and Desire to Be Respected, and (c) Optimum Conformity Index and Desire to Be Respected (Product moment correlations)

a. OPINION CONFORMITY AND LIKING THE TARGET

	Dependence	
	High	Low
Same	.774†	−.321
Discrepant	.276	.102

b. OPINION CONFORMITY AND DESIRE TO BE RESPECTED

	Dependence	
	High	Low
Same	−.095	−.387
Discrepant	.563†	.189

c. OPTIMUM CONFORMITY INDEX* AND DESIRE TO BE RESPECTED

	Dependence	
	High	Low
Same	.461	−.051
Discrepant	.064	.163

* Derived by taking the absolute value of the discrepancy between the cell median score and the S's score. † p < .01.

conformed relative to the median S. The only correlation which approaches significance is that in the High-Same cell where the coefficient of .461 suggests that the desire to be respected relates to moderate conformity. It would be dangerous to make too much of this *ad hoc* result obtained with a derived score, but the fact that a curvilinear relationship exists does make good psychological sense. When a premium is placed on "being attractive to a Target and the Target is aware of this," those Ss most concerned with obtaining this goal adopt an optimum strategy of moderate conformity. A loss of respect is risked either if they conform too obviously or if they hold opinions too much at variance with those of the Target. When attraction is still salient but there is no danger of being judged a manipulative conformist, one would expect this curvilinear relationship to change into a linear one with desire for respect being related positively to degree of agreement with the target person. That this is indeed the case is clearly suggested by the significant correlation between raw discrepancy score and desire to be respected in the High-Discrepant cell. Ss in this cell had no need to fear being perceived as conforming for manipulative reasons. Their problem was rather to show enough agreement with the supervisor to avoid being judged ridiculous in his eyes and thus unworthy of his respect.

It is hardly surprising that the desire to be respected is positively correlated with the desire to be liked (coefficients ranging from .605 to .803). If in Table 2 ratings indicating the desire to be liked are substituted for ratings of desire to be respected, the correlations are similar but slightly lower in magnitude. But there is theoretically relevant evidence that Ss do make a distinction between being liked and respected in their efforts to be ingratiating, and that this distinction bears a logical relationship to conformity in their mind. The means in Table 3 strongly suggest that Ss respond to the dilemma created in receiving the Target's opinions by modifying their goals or aspirations in the situation. When "concern for being liked" and "concern for being respected" are scored separately and placed in a mixed factorial design, two significant results emerge from the resulting analysis of variance. As indicated previously, Ss in the High-Dependence condition are more concerned both with being liked and with being respected than Ss in the Low-Dependence condition. In addition, the significant interaction reflects the fact that Ss in the same conditions express more interest in being liked, while Ss in the Discrepant conditions express more interest in being respected. Putting together the relevant evidence, we may conclude that Ss are swept along by the discrepancy variation into a resulting position of rather close agreement (in the Same condition) or rather great disagreement (Discrepant condition). Their respective goals or "desires" are then, apparently, changed to accom-

TABLE 3 *Concern with Being Liked and with Being Respected*

A. MEAN AND STANDARD DEVIATION FOR EACH GROUP ON BOTH ITEMS*

		Concern for Being Liked†		Concern for Being Respected†	
		Dependence		Dependence	
		High	Low	High	Low
Same	$\bar{X}$	3.1	1.8	2.7	1.6
	SD	.57	.92	.95	.70
Discrepant	$\bar{X}$	2.6	1.4	3.3	1.7
	SD	.97	.70	.95	.95

B. SUMMARY OF ANALYSIS OF VARIANCE

Source	DF	MS	F
Between Ss	39	17.94	33.90§
B: Dependence (H-L)	1	33.80	
C: Discrepancy (S-D)	1	.05	
B × C	1	.20	
Error (b)	36	.997	
Within Ss	40	20.00	
A: Like-respect	1	.20	
A × B	1	.05	
A × C	1	3.20	7.16‡
A × B × C	1	.45	
Error (w)	36	.447	
Total	79		

* N for all groups is 10. Nine Ss were randomly discarded to equate cell frequencies for this analysis. † Higher scores signify greater concern with the given attribute. ‡ $p < .05$. § $p < .001$.

modate their perceived accomplishments: Ss who are swept into agreement tend to relinquish the goal of being respected; Ss who are in disagreement tend to relinquish the goal of being liked.

Confidence ratings and ingratiation

In addition to recording their opinions on each message form received, the Ss indicated their confidence on a scale from 1 (much confidence) to 5 (little confidence). These confidence scores may be examined in a number of different ways. The analyses attempted were those which seemed to give promise of relating the expression of confidence to ingratiation pressures. This becomes particularly pertinent following our realization that conformity itself (in the Same conditions at least) was not put to clear use as an instrument of ingratiation. Perhaps, then, variations in confidence might serve as a more subtle and less risky tactic in making oneself attractive.

By averaging each S's confidence scores across the 30 opinion items, it is possible to obtain an over-all confidence measure. As Table 4 shows, S's in the crucial High-Same cell are almost significantly more confident than Ss in the Low-Same cell ($p < .10$) and are significantly more confident than all other Ss combined ($p < .05$). It is tempting to conclude that Ss facing the dilemma of wanting to be attractive without running the risks of slavish conformity, attempt to further their aim by a combination of moderately high conformity and high self-confidence in their opinions. A breakdown of items into those of high, intermediate, and low importance (as in Table 4) shows that this difference in confidence scores appears only for items of intermediate and especially of high importance. It is relevant to point out that the High-Same Ss show greater conformity in the important than the unimportant items while the Low-Same Ss conform more on the unimportant items. However, since this "interaction" is far from significant, the confidence of High-Same Ss on important items cannot be completely accounted for by their increased agreement with the Target. The pattern of confidence ratings across levels of importance is at least consistent with the hypothesis that important issues are likely to be more salient in the process of

TABLE 4 *Confidence Ratings by Conditions as a Function of Item Importance*

CONDITION		IMPORTANCE*			
		High	Intermediate	Low	Total
High same	$\bar{X}$	1.65	1.89	2.20	1.91
	SD	.39	.40	.48	.39
Low same	$\bar{X}$	1.96	2.20	2.28	2.15
	SD	.27	.28	.21	.20
p diff		.05	.06	n.s.	.10
High discrepant	$\bar{X}$	1.95	2.13	2.35	2.15
	SD	.37	.47	.49	.39
Low discrepant	$\bar{X}$	1.97	2.32	2.35	2.21
	SD	.45	.36	.34	.29
p diff		n.s.	n.s.	n.s.	n.s.
Column totals		1.88	2.14	2.30	
p diff		$p < .01$		$p < .06$	

* Low scores = High confidence.

gaining and awarding approval, so it is with respect to such issues that the tactical use of confidence ratings is apparent.

Turning to individual differences in the tendency to express confidence in one's opinions, there is a strong relationship between confidence and conformity which appears only in the High-Same cell. As Table 5 shows, those Ss who show the most conformity in this cell also express the greatest confidence in their opinions. It should be noted that this is a correlation between conformity and confidence across all items, and does not necessarily imply that confidence is highest in the High-Same group on those items where the resulting discrepancy is lowest. In fact, correlations of confidence and conformity taking individual items into account (and thus computing a correlation for each S) are uniformly low and do not vary significantly by conditions. We are thus left with the more general conclusion that, only in the High-Same cell, Ss who present themselves as confident (on the average) also express opinions which are similar to the Target's. A reasonable interpretation of the high correlation is that those Ss who employ the risky tactic of conformity in the High-Same cell emphasize their confidence in the attempt to signify their autonomy and their resistance to social influence. This strategy would present the Target with a pattern of congenial opinions independently developed. Those Ss who do not tend to agree as much, on the other hand, reduce their "disagreeableness" by expressing less confidence in their opinions.

DISCUSSION

Stated in its most general form, the main hypothesis of the present investigation was that a person who is obviously motivated to win the approval of another must avoid the Scylla of overconformity and the Charybdis of errant disagreement. The avoidance of conformity should be demonstrable if the person finds that his own opinions have been pre-empted by the very person he wants to impress. Under the circumstances, he can only be true to himself at the expense of being judged a self-seeking conformist. Therefore, attraction pressures should induce mild disagree-

TABLE 5 Relations between Opinion Conformity and Confidence

	HIGH DEP.	LOW DEP.
Same	.671*	−.213
Discrepant	.076	−.149

* p < .05.

ment. Obversely, the avoidance of extreme disagreement should be demonstrable if the person finds that his own opinions differ markedly from those of the person he is trying to impress. He can only be true to himself at the expense of offering offense to the other. Attraction pressures should thus reduce the discrepancy between the opinion expressed first and the reply. The results of the experiment clearly confirmed the disagreement-avoidance part of the hypothesis, but the evidence with respect to conformity-avoidance turned out to be equivocal and complex.

The conformity-avoidance part of the hypothesis was tested by comparing two conditions in which the opinion initiator presented opinions identical to those previously endorsed by the S. In one condition, attraction was the induced goal of the interchange, so that the S was dependent on the other person for approval (presumably some combination of liking and respect). In the comparison condition, dependence was minimized by instructions emphasizing accuracy and valid self-disclosure. Contrary to the hypothesized conformity-avoidance effect, Ss in the High-Dependence-Same condition showed slightly more conformity than those in the Low-Same condition. In our judgment, the hypothesis was probably not confirmed because of the basic instability of the S's opinion ratings. Thus, Ss in both "pre-empt" conditions could show general agreement without slavish conformity and still be convinced that they were expressing their true opinions.

While there is no evidence of conformity-avoidance in the discrepancy data, the High-Same Ss showed in a number of ways an implicit awareness of the dilemma posed by a setting in which too much conformity would negate their attraction strivings. In each of the following respects, unique findings were obtained in the High-Same cell:

(1) While the cell mean showed slightly less opinion discrepancy than the Low-Same cell, High-Same Ss were significantly more variable than Low-Same Ss.
(2) Those Ss who conformed more also liked the Target more. This relationship between conformity and postexperimental ratings of liking appeared only in the High-Same cell.
(3) Conforming Ss tended to express greater confidence in their opinions throughout the message exchange. This relationship was again found only in the High-Same cell.
(4) Ss in the High-Same cell were more confident in general than the other Ss and this is especially true when only the most important issues are considered.
(5) The High-Dependence instructions are associated with a relationship between "desire for respect" and degree of conformity. However, this relationship was positive and linear for the Discrepant condition Ss and curvilinear for the Same condition Ss. In the latter group, desire for respect (and to a lesser degree

desire to be liked) was highest in those *S*s showing intermediate conformity.

Putting together these ways in which the High-Same *S*s differed from those in other cells makes it possible to salvage a complicated but still meaningful picture of the subtleties of self-presentation in the service of attractiveness. Faced with the dilemma of impressing someone who expresses opinions very close to their own, *S*s show evidence of conflict and search for ways to (*a*) convince the other person of their sincere similarity of views and (*b*) convince themselves that agreement with the other is not merely manipulative in intent. It may be plausibly argued that the former goal was mediated by expressing much confidence when agreement was high and little confidence when agreement was low. In the first case, the *S* attempts to convince the other that he happens to agree but is independent and autonomous. In the second case, the *S* softens the impact of his disagreement by his lack of self-confidence, implying that ultimately closer agreement could be reached. The goal of self-justification was mediated by a general denial of being influenced and a tendency to see the Target as more likeable when he had an influence on the *S*s' opinions. In addition, there was evidence that High-Dependence *S*s rationalized their interpretation of attraction to accord with their ultimate discrepancy from the Target, Same *S*s claiming a greater interest in being liked than respected and the reverse being claimed by Discrepant *S*s.

In view of the technical difficulties encountered in the present study, it is not clear whether an effective pre-empting of opinions could be arranged. Any attempt to increase the reliability of opinion statements by using only well-crystallized issues or reducing the number of scale points also increases the expectancy of close opinion agreement and thus takes the sting from the dilemma. In any event, while it cannot be said that the present High-Same *S*s were truly victimized by the experimental arrangements, they did use their limited communication resources to reach for approval in the subtle ways recounted above. We may conclude, then, that these *S*s showed some awareness of the likely cognitive dynamics of the Target and shaped their behavior to take account of these dynamics.

SUMMARY

The present study was primarily concerned with variations in opinion expression as a function of two cross-cutting experimental treatments. *S*s engaged in an exchange of opinions with a target person, and in all cases the target person expressed his opinions first. In one treatment variation the target person expressed opinions identical to those the *S* had expressed on a prior questionnaire, or he expressed quite different opinions (Same versus Discrepant variation). The exchange took place in one of two contexts: the *S* was either led to believe that he was dependent on the other for an evaluation of his attractiveness as a person, or that his task was to present himself as accurately as possible (High- versus Low-Dependence variation). Since it was expected that *S*s in the High-Dependence treatment would wish to avoid being perceived as agreeing for devious or manipulative reasons, the prediction was that *S*s in the High-Dependence-Same condition would show less resultant conformity than those in the Low-Same condition, whereas those in the High-Discrepant condition would show more conformity than those in the Low-Discrepant condition. Only the second part of this hypothesis was confirmed. While *S*s in the High-Same condition did not show less conformity than those in the Low-Same condition, those who were most concerned with attraction in this cell showed moderate ("optimum") conformity and avoided consistent agreement or disagreement. In addition, the greater the opinion agreement in the High-Same condition, the greater the expressed confidence, and the greater the rated attraction for the target person. The results were interpreted as reflecting the existence of a "self-presentation dilemma" in the High-Same *S*s and as showing how these *S*s employed alternative ways to deal with the dilemma by the use of subtle variations in the communication resources available.

REFERENCES

DEUTSCH, M., & GERARD, H. B. A study of normative and informational social influence upon individual judgment. *J. abnorm. soc. Psychol.*, 1955, **51**, 629–636.

FESTINGER, L. *A theory of cognitive dissonance.* Evanston, Ill.: Row, Peterson, 1957.

JONES, E. E., GERGEN, K. J., GUMPERT, P., & THIBAUT, J. W. Some conditions affecting the use of ingratiation to influence performance evaluation. *J. Pers. soc. Psychol.*, 1965, **1**, 613–625.

JONES, E. E., GERGEN, K. J., & JONES, R. G. Tactics of ingratiation among leaders and subordinates in a status hierarchy. *Psychol. Monogr.*, 1963, **77**, 3 (Whole No. 566).

JONES, E. E., JONES, R. G., & GERGEN, K. J. Some conditions affecting the evaluation of a conformist. *J. Pers.*, 1963, **31**, 270–288.

THIBAUT, J. W., & KELLEY, H. H. *The social psychology of groups.* New York: Wiley, 1959.

THIBAUT, J. W., & STRICKLAND, L. S. Psychological set and social conformity. *J. Pers.*, 1956, **25**, 115–129.

Socialization is an interactional process whereby an individual's behavior is modified to conform to expectations held by members of the group to which he belongs. Although the term was formerly thought of as applying only to the process by which the child gradually acquires the behavior patterns expected of him, it has recently been broadened to include the processes by which the adult takes on behaviors appropriate to the expectations associated with a new position in a group, an organization, or society at large. Thus socialization occurs throughout life and is especially active at each transition phase, such as entering school, taking a job, getting married, entering military service, becoming a parent or a grandparent, and retiring.

Compared with most other areas of social psychology, the methodological sophistication and theoretical development of research on socialization are at a relatively low level. Much of our knowledge on socialization comes from observations of neurotic or psychotic patients, participant observation of groups, and atheoretical studies that use crude techniques and inadequate experimental designs. Because of this reliance on observational data, the level of certainty of knowledge in this area is low, and the lack of formal theory as an underpinning for research operations makes it difficult to draw definitive conclusions from the sprawling mass of empirical data. The last decade, however, has seen a marked expansion of experimental child psychology along with the adoption of more sophisticated research designs conducted in a theoretical context.

Selections included here are of several kinds. Some represent recent experimental approaches that are a step in the direction of more adequate research on socialization: they have a definite theoretical orientation and test hypotheses derived from it, using adequate controls. They deal with theories of identification and with the stability of the self concept. One article deals with the choice of variables in the study of socialization. Two selections employ the method of participant observation; one deals with socialization of plebes at a military academy, and the other with mental patients entering the hospital. They are included because of the high quality of ideas presented; such studies provide many suggestions for developing more formal theory. A speculative analysis spelling out the implications of changing patterns of child rearing in the United States for the adult behavior of the new generation is the subject matter of another selection. Finally, another article shows how the adequate analysis of field data provides a precise test of a significant hypothesis on role learning.

PART SEVEN

SOCIALIZATION

THE CHOICE OF VARIABLES IN THE STUDY OF SOCIALIZATION*

This first selection discusses some of the major classes of variables that have been used in socialization studies and provides some of the reasons why they have been a special focus of interest. Many of the problems arising in attempts to conceptualize a variable are outlined and illustrated. In particular, the problems encountered when a variable from one research context is applied in another are highlighted.

* The selection following the editorial introduction is reprinted from "The choice of variables in the study of socialization," Sociometry, 1961, 24, 357–371, by permission of the author and the American Sociological Association.

Much of the discussion hinges around three processes: (*1*) interaction between variables, (*2*) confounding of variables, and (*3*) failure to specify the conditions under which a relation holds. When a variable is studied in a new context, it may be modified by the presence of another variable. For example, withdrawal of love as a form of discipline has different effects in combination with differing degrees of warmth of the parent-child relation. Confounding of variables occurs when two or more independent variables vary together, making it difficult to identify the causal one. If a study shows that parents who more frequently reward their children for dependent behavior strengthen such behavior, it is possible that this is a function of the sheer amount of interaction between parent and child rather than its reward quality unless, of course, the amount of interaction is controlled or equated. Finally, relations between variables are apt to hold only where the history of parent-child interaction takes certain forms.

48.

The Choice of Variables in the Study of Socialization[1]

ELEANOR E. MACCOBY
STANFORD UNIVERSITY

Perhaps the greatest change that has occurred in the field of child development in the past 15 years has been the increasing emphasis on socialization. The change may be traced by comparing the more traditional textbooks with recent ones. The scholarly child psychology text by Munn (**16**), for example, does not bring up the topic of parent-child interaction until the 16th chapter, and here devotes only eight pages to a topic called "environmental influences and personality," a heading under which he presents all that the book has to say on "mothering," on Freudian theory of developmental stages, on ordinal position—in fact, on socialization in general. Contrast this with a book such as Watson's (**23**), in which more than half the book is devoted to a discussion of socialization theory and a detailed consideration of the impressive amounts of research that have recently been done on the subject.

The same increasing emphasis on socialization may be seen in the child-development journals. And, of course, the widespread research interest

[1] This article is a composite of two papers, one delivered at the Berkeley Conference on Personality Development in Childhood in April, 1960, and the other delivered at the American Psychological Association Meeting in New York in August, 1961.

in this topic has led to the development of several research instruments for the measurement of parental attitudes and behavior. There are the Fels scales (**2**), developed during the 40's, for the rating of parent behavior; the parent interview schedule developed by Sears and his associates at Harvard and Stanford (**21**), the parent attitude scales developed by Shoben at U.S.C. (**22**), and the widely-used Parent Attitude Research Instrument scales developed at the National Institutes of Health by Schaeffer and Bell (**20**), to mention only a few. Each investigator, when he sat down to make a first draft of his rating scale or interview schedule or attitude scale items, had to ask himself the question: What shall I measure? What are the important variables in parental behavior that ought to make a difference in the development of the child? The process of selecting and defining variables is, of course, the very heart of theory-making. There are as many possible variables as there are ideas about what causes what in human development. I cannot attempt here to give any sort of roster of variables; the task would be too great and might not prove very useful. I simply want to point out some of the major classes of variables that have been used and give a little of the history of the reasons why we have chosen to measure these things and not others and perhaps point to a few ways in which we could clarify the meaning of the dimension we are using.

Let us start with the traditional child psychologist, with his interests in motor development, emotional development, intelligence, concept formation, and personality development, all grounded in traditional principles of learning and maturation. He may look upon the current work in socialization with a jaundiced eye and inquire what the excitement is all about. He may feel that he has actually been studying socialization for years without calling it by this name. He might put his question this way: If it is true that socialization is the process of transmitting culture from one generation to another, and that the child acquires the modes of behavior prescribed by his culture through the process of learning, then how is the study of socialization any different from the study of learning itself? One might reply that in socialization studies, we study not only the child as learner but the parent as teacher. But a skeptic might still wonder how much difference this actually makes. For example, laboratory studies of learning have demonstrated that behavior which is followed by rewards will be strengthened, and its probability of recurrence will be increased. Now, if a student of socialization does a study of dependency, and discovers that parents who reward their children for dependency have more dependent children, has he really found out anything that we didn't know already?

In my opinion, it *is* valuable to carry out at the human level studies which attempt to employ the standard variables that have grown out of laboratory study on learning, where most of the work has been done on sub-human species. But, in the process of applying such variables to socialization studies, the variables almost perforce undergo certain modifications and elaborations, with the result that translating traditional behavior theory variables into the socialization setting sometimes results in the addition of something new, and the possibility of getting new kinds of principles.

Let me give an example. Suppose we wanted to study the effects of a particular schedule of reward. What do we mean by reward? The traditional approach to reward has been to produce a physiological drive, such as hunger or thirst, through deprivation; and then to reinforce the desired behavior by presenting a drive-relevant reinforcing stimulus. But even in fairly young children, a rapid development of complex motivation occurs, and this changes the nature of the reinforcements to which children will be responsive. B. F. Skinner encountered this fact when he was developing his teaching machines. The early models were devised so as to emit little pieces of chocolate candy whenever a child made the correct response. But it was soon evident that a child progressed through a series of arithmetic or spelling problems just as readily without the candy; in fact, the giving of candy sometimes disrupted the learning process. Skinner, therefore, abandoned the candy rewards, and the current models of his machine rely upon no other reward than the child's interest in doing his work correctly—buttressed, no doubt, by a certain amount of pressure from the teacher and parents. This incident illustrates a major question about the definition of variables: what happens to the variable "amount of reward" when it is translated into situations of teacher-child, or parent-child, interaction? In modern societies, children's physiological drives are regularly and quite fully satisfied and are seldom used as a basis for training. That is, most parents do not let the child get hungry, thirsty, wet, or overtired, and then make the satisfaction of these needs conditional on good behavior. Rather, the rewards used are money, a trip to the zoo, being allowed to stay up for a special TV program, etc. A gift of candy for some children becomes symbolic of affection instead of vice versa. Very commonly, behavior is reinforced simply through the giving of approval, affection, of attention. So the concept "reward," when it refers to the rewards which parents use in socializing their children is not directly comparable to the concept as it was originally developed in studies of animal learning. Of course, it is not really a new idea to point out that different kinds of organisms are capable of being rewarded by different kinds of things. It is clear enough that there are as many kinds of rewards as there are distinguishable motives, and that both motives and rewards vary between species and within species. But the new idea that has been added in socialization studies is that there may be distinguishable *classes* of rewards which may have different effects. The

primary distinction made in studies so far has been between material reward and praise. Material reward covers all instances of giving the child some object or privilege that he wants, conditional upon good behavior. Praise depends to some degree upon the previous establishment of a relationship between the socializing agent and the child, such that the approval of this particular adult is something the child wants. That is, the effectiveness of praise ought to depend upon the identity of the person doing the praising and upon this person's being someone the child loves, fears, or must depend upon for the satisfaction of needs.

The same kind of differentiation of a variable has occurred with respect to punishment. Students of the socialization process have been working under the assumption that not all kinds of aversive events following a child's act will have the same effect. The distinction most commonly made is that between physical punishment and so-called love-oriented discipline, or withdrawal of love. There are other categories of punishment, too, such as withdrawal of privileges and ridicule, which are less interesting than the first two because there are fewer hypotheses about their probable effects. Let us concentrate for a moment on the distinction between physical punishment and withdrawal of love. Physical punishment is easy enough to define, although in rating its frequency and severity, the researcher is always troubled about the problem of how to weigh slaps and shakings in relation to formal spankings. More tricky by far is the matter of defining withdrawal of love. Sears and his associates (**21**) have defined it as any act or statement on the part of the parent that threatens the affectional bond between the parent and child. This would include the mother's turning her back on the child, refusing to speak to him or smile at him or be in the same room with him, saying she doesn't like him when he does disapproved things, etc. The system of classification of techniques of discipline presented by Beverly Allinsmith in her chapter in Miller and Swanson's book, *Inner Conflict and Defense* (**1**), similarly emphasizes the distinction between "psychological" and "corporal" punishment, but defines psychological discipline somewhat differently. This classification for Allinsmith includes manipulating the child by shaming the child, appealing to his pride or guilt, and expressing disappointment over his misdeeds. But there is another dimension considered in the rating: namely, the amount of emotional control the mother displays in administering her discipline. Thus, if a mother shouts angrily at the child, "I hate you for doing that," Allinsmith would *not* classify this as psychological discipline, while Sears *et al.* would. But the mother who says calmly and perhaps coldly, "Now, dear, you know I don't like little boys who do that," would be classified as using psychological discipline in both systems. The difference in these two classification systems stems in part from two different views of the nature of the process which gives psychological discipline its effect. Sears *et al.* view it as a technique which arouses the child's anxiety over whether he is loved and approved of, and thereby elicits efforts on the child's part to regain his parents' approval by conforming, apologizing, or making amends. Allinsmith, on the other hand, emphasizes two things: (*a*) the *modeling* function of discipline, pointing out that a mother who loses her temper at the same time she is trying to teach the child to control his, will have a child who will do as the mother *does* rather than as she *says*; and (*b*) the target the child chooses for the aggressive impulses aroused in him as a consequence of punishment. The reasoning here is that the openly angry mother becomes a more legitimate target for the child's counter-aggression. The distinction between the two definitions of the dimension is further brought out when we consider the kinds of findings reported in the studies using them: Sears *et al.* found that withdrawal of love was associated with high development of conscience, physical punishment with low; Allinsmith found that psychological discipline, as she defined it, was associated with *indirect* fantasy expressions of aggression in the children they studied, corporal punishment with *direct* expression of aggression. All this illustrates the fact that fairly subtle differences in the definition of a dimension can affect the nature of child behavior that can be predicted from it. But more importantly, both these studies illustrate the fact that when we attempted to take over the variable "punishment" from the learning laboratories, we found it necessary to subdivide and differentiate the variable and gained predictive power by doing so.

I have been attempting to cite ways in which I think that socialization studies have improved upon some of the standard variables employed in laboratory studies. There are instances, alas, in which we have not taken note of the differences which exist between the laboratory and the standard socialization settings, and thus have failed to identify and make use of some potentially promising variables. For example, in laboratory studies, we can take it for granted that the experimenter is there during training sessions, administering either reinforcements or aversive stimuli in some orderly relationship to the subject's responses. In the parent-child relationship, the parent is by no means always functioning as a trainer, and parents differ greatly in the degree to which they do so. Some parents keep track quite continuously of what the child is doing, and engage in a constant flow of interaction, both verbal and non-verbal,

with the child. Other parents, for a substantial portion of the time they are with their children, are bored, busy, withdrawn, intoxicated, watching television, or subject to some other state or activity which precludes their responding to the child unless he becomes very insistent. In such a household the children are, of course, in a very different learning situation than children growing up with more wholly attentive parents. I think the sheer amount of interaction may in some cases be a more important variable for predicting characteristics of the child than the nature of the interaction that does occur. Let me give an example. In a study Dr. Lucy Rau and I are now doing at Stanford, we have selected groups of children who show discrepancies in their intellectual abilities. That is, we have one group of children who are good at verbal tasks but poor at number, another group who are good at spatial tasks but poor at verbal, etc. One of our students, Mrs. Bing, has interviewed the mothers of the children, and has also conducted some observation sessions in which the mother presents achievement tasks to the child while the observer records the kind and amount of the mother's involvement with the child's work. Mrs. Bing has found that it is the *amount,* rather than the *kind,* of mother-child interaction that best predicts what the child's pattern of intellectual skills will be. That is, the mothers of the highly verbal children use more praise, but also more criticism, than do the mothers of equally bright children whose area of special skill is non-verbal. Their total level of interaction with the child is greater, and this interaction includes the administration of what we would regard as aversive stimuli as well as reinforcements. The variable "amount of interaction" emerged in our factor analysis of the scales in the *Patterns of Child Rearing* study (**21**)—we titled this variable "responsible child-rearing orientation" for lack of a better name, but we never made much use of the variable because it did not fit in with the theoretical formulation of our study. But I suspect that for any future work in which we are trying to predict such things as the child's cognitive maturity level or his achievement motivation, we may find that this variable is a better predictor than the less global variables (such as amount of praise) that we have been relying on up till now.

So far, I have been discussing the process of translating variables from laboratory studies of learning to the socialization setting, and have pointed out that we have been successful in employing such variables as reward and punishment, but that in the process of using these variables, we have found useful ways of subdividing them. Let us consider the theoretical meaning of the elaborations of these variables that have occurred.

When we make the distinction between material reward and praise, and the distinction between love-oriented punishment and punishment that depends for its effect upon producing direct physical pain, we are really taking note of the fact that the effect of discipline, and in fact the very nature of the discipline that is possible to use with a child, depends upon the history of the relationship that has been developed between the child and the person who is training him. And here is a new class of variables that socialization studies have added to the list of variables derived from classical studies of learning. In laboratory studies of learning, it has not been found necessary (at least until very recently) to ask whether the experimental subject loved or hated the machine that was emitting pellets of food and drops of water, or whether the characteristics of the machine or person presenting the rewards made any difference in the effectiveness of the reinforcement. Socialization studies, on the other hand, have found the identity of the socializing agent, and certain of his personality characteristics, to be important.

The emphasis on the importance of the relationship between trainer and learner came, of course, out of psychodynamic theories of personality development. Learning theory and psychoanalytic theory differ, I think, with respect to what they believe the basic nature of the socialization process is. This is an oversimplification, but I believe it would be reasonably accurate to say that a learning theorist would regard socialization as a learning process in which certain actions of the child's are selected out by virtue of reinforcement, others tried and dropped because they are in some way punished or non-reinforced. The parents have a primary role in administering the rewards and punishments for the child's actions, although they do not necessarily do this deliberately and consciously as a teaching effort. And, of course, there are other sources of reward and punishment than the parents' reactions which will help to determine what behavior the child retains.

The psychoanalytic approach, on the other hand, would emphasize not the detailed learning of specific actions on the basis of their outcome, but the providing of conditions which will motivate the child to take on spontaneously the socialized behavior the parent wants him to have. The terms introjection, internalization, learning through role-playing, and identification have been used in this connection; they all refer to the child's tendency to copy, to take on as his own, the behavior, attitudes, and values of the significant people in his life, even when the socializing agents have not said "that's a good boy" or given him a piece of candy for performing these acts or holding these values. I will not go into the controversy concerning which so much has been written as to whether the child is more likely to identify with the person who is powerful and feared or with the person who is loved; nor will I discuss the several thoughtful efforts by personality theorists to reconcile the two points of view. The only im-

portant point for our consideration here is that the psychoanalytic view of socialization has led to an exploration of such variables as the warmth or hostility of the socializing agent toward the child.

There can be no doubt that measures of the warmth of the parent-child relationship have turned out to be enormously useful in socialization studies, in a number of ways. In some studies, warmth has been found to have a direct relationship to some dependent variable. For example, McCord and McCord (14) have found that warmth in fathers was associated with low crime rate in sons. In other studies, warmth has turned out to be a useful cross-cutting variable which interacts with other variables in such a way that other variables only begin to show their effects when the sample is first sub-divided into groups differing in parental warmth. For example, in the *Patterns of Child Rearing* study, Sears *et al.* (21) found that withdrawal of love is associated with rapid development of conscience, but only if this technique is employed by a warm mother; also that punishment for toilet accidents disrupts the toilet-training process, but that the greatest disruption occurs if punishment is administered by a cold mother.

Warmth also occupies a central role in socialization studies in its relationship to other measures of child-training variables. There have been, to my knowledge, three factor analyses carried out on sets of socialization variables. One of these was on the Fels parent behavior rating scales (18), one on the PARI (27), and one on the dimensions employed by Sears *et al.* in the *Patterns* study (21). In the latter two, warmth emerged as a fairly clear factor. In the first, there were two factors, one called "concern for the child" and the other called "parent-child harmony," which taken together are probably close to what is meant by warmth in the other two studies. It is clear, then, that both in terms of its predictive value for the child's behavior and its central place among the other interrelated child-training variables, warmth is a variable to be taken seriously. Why is it so important? I have already pointed out why the psychodynamic theorists believe it to be so—because of its role in producing identification. But the laboratory learning theorists can acknowledge its importance for another very simple reason. Before a parent can socialize a child, he must have established a relationship with the child such that the child will stay in the vicinity of the parent and orient himself toward the parent. A warm parent keeps the child responsive to his directions by providing an atmosphere in which the child has continuous expectations that good things will happen to him if he stays near his parent and responds to his parent's wishes. Fear of punishment can also make the child attentive to the parent, of course, but it establishes as well the conflicting motivation to escape out of reach of the punisher.

I'm sure I needn't belabor any further the notion that warmth is an important variable. But to say this is not enough. We still are faced with considerable difficulty in definition. It has been the experience of a number of people working with child-training data that they find themselves able to make reliable distinctions between mothers they call warm and mothers they call cold, and they find it possible to train others to make similar distinctions, but find it difficult indeed to define exactly what cues they are using to make the rating.

I suspect one source of difficulty is that the behavior we look for as indicating warmth varies with the age of the child the mother is dealing with. When the child is an infant, we are likely to label a mother as warm if she gives a good deal of the contact comfort that Harlow (8) has described. As the child grows older, the part played by the giving of contact comfort in the total constellation of warmth undoubtedly declines. When a child is ten, a mother seldom expresses her warm feelings for him by holding him on her lap. Rather, they are more likely to be expressed by the mother showing interest in the child and what he is doing, by helping unconditionally when help is needed, by being cordial and relaxed. Now warmth as expressed this way is not the same thing as giving contact comfort, and it is not to be expected that the same individuals would necessarily be good at both. Those of you who have read Brody's fascinating, detailed descriptions of mothers' behavior toward their infants (4) will perhaps have noted that the mothers who gave effective contact comfort, in the sense of holding the child comfortably and close, stroking it occasionally, imparting some rocking motion, handling it skillfully and gently in the process of caring for the child—the women who could do all these things well were not necessarily the same women who expressed delight and pride in their children, who noticed their little accomplishments, or who looked upon their infants as individuals. We should therefore not be surprised if there are low correlations between a mother's warmth toward her infant and her warmth toward the same child when it is older. If a primary ingredient of warmth is being able to gratify the child's needs unconditionally, and if the child's needs change from the infantile needs for being fed and being given contact comfort to the more mature needs for various kinds of ego support, then it is necessary for a mother to change considerably as her child

changes, in order to be warm towards him at all ages. Some mothers make this change more easily than others. It is true that Schaeffer and Bayley (19), in their longitudinal study of a group of mothers, did find a substantial degree of continuity in the degree of warmth displayed by a given mother toward a given child as the child grew older. There were undoubtedly individual differences in the ways warmth was manifested, and in the appropriateness of a mother's particular style of warmth-giving to the needs of her child at each developmental stage.

From the standpoint of making use of the variable in research, it appears that we should recognize that measuring the mother's current warmth at the time the child is, say, in nursery school or in the primary grades may not be an especially good index of how warm she was to the child as an infant. Furthermore, her warmth in infancy might predict quite different characteristics of the child than her warmth in middle childhood. If there is any relation at all between nurturance to an infant and its later personality traits, infant nurturance ought to relate only to those aspects of personality that presumably have their foundation in infancy—such as Erikson's dimension of trust (6), or various aspects of orality. Achievement motivation, on the other hand, if it is related to the mother's warmth at all, ought to be related to measures of this variable taken when the child is older. A finding of Bronfenbrenner's (5) seems to support this point about the importance of warmth-giving being appropraite to the developmental level of the child. He was studying high-school-aged children and employed several variables relating to the kind and amount of affectionate interchange between these adolescents and their parents. He measured the parents' affection-giving (in the sense of direct demonstrativeness), use of affective rewards, nurturance, and affiliative companionship. Among these variables, it was only the last one, affiliative companionship, that correlated with the child's current level of responsibility taking. We can speculate that this particular aspect of warmth is the one that fits in much better with an adolescent's needs than either giving him kisses or peanut butter sandwiches. All this means that warmth has to be defined in terms of parental responsiveness to the changing needs of the child.

I have referred to socialization variables that came originally from laboratory studies of learning, and that have been adapted for use in studying the socialization process. I have also referred to variables that originated in psychodynamic thinking. There is a set of variables that is difficult to classify in terms of these two theoretical systems; I am referring to the dimension "permissiveness vs. restrictiveness," which emerged in our factor analysis of the *Patterns* variables, and to the related dimension of "control vs. laissez-faire" which has come out of the factor analysis of the

PARI scales. The theoretical status of these variables is confusing because they relate to both psychoanalytic and learning theory, but the predictions from the two theories as to the probable effects of "permissiveness" or "control" are sometimes quite different. To cite a familiar example, there is the issue of what ought to be the effects of permissive treatment of the infant's sucking responses. The question is complex, but a simplified version of the opposing positions would be this: the learning theorist would argue that if an infant is permitted extensive sucking, his sucking habit will be strengthened, and he will be more likely to suck his thumb, pencils, etc., at a later age. The psychodynamic theorist would argue that permitting extensive infantile sucking satisfies oral needs and reduces the likelihood of excessive oral behavior at a later age. The same kind of difference of opinion can be found concerning whether permissive treatment of a child's aggressive or dependent responses should increase or decrease those responses. Now, of course, the fact that different theories produce different predictions concerning the effects of a variable is no reason for abandoning the variable. On the contrary, it is cause for rejoicing, and we should by all means continue to use the variable so that we can get data which will bear upon the validity of the theories. The trouble is that when we arrive at the point of trying to get agreement on the interpretation of findings, it sometimes turns out that the two schools of thought did not mean the same thing by "permissiveness." If a study shows that the more permissive parents are toward their children's aggression the more aggressive the children become, the psychodynamic theorist may say, "Well, by permissiveness I didn't mean *license*; the child must have limits set for him but he must also be allowed to express his feelings." If, on the other hand, a study shows that children heavily punished for aggression are more aggressive on the playground, or prefer aggressive TV programs, the learning theorist may say, "Well, of course, if the parents' methods of stopping aggression are such as to provide additional instigation to aggression, then their non-permissiveness won't eliminate the behavior." We begin to see that there are some hidden meanings in such a term as "permissiveness" and that we are dealing with several dimensions. Continuing with the example of aggression, we can see that permissiveness for aggression could mean the following things:

1. The mother holds the attitude that aggression is an acceptable, even desirable, form of behavior.
2. The mother does not like aggressive behavior and expects to limit it in her children, but feels that it is natural and inevitable at certain ages and so does not react strongly when her young child displays anger. A related definition of permissiveness would be pacing the demands

for self-control placed upon the child to correspond with his developmental level.
3. The mother is not especially interested in the child or is otherwise occupied, and does not act to stop or prevent his aggression because she does not notice what he is doing.
4. The mother does not act early in a sequence of her child's aggressive behavior, but waits till the behavior has become fairly intense.

And at the other end of the scale, the effect of *non*-permissiveness ought to depend upon how the non-permitting is done—whether by punishment, by reinforcing alternative behavior, by environmental control that removes the instigations to undesired behavior, or some other means. The basic point I wish to emphasize is that I believe "permissiveness" is not a unitary variable, and that we need to work more directly with its components.

So far I have discussed several classes of variables: the ones translated as directly as possible from laboratory studies of learning (e.g., amount and kind of reward and punishment), and variables such as warmth and permissiveness of the socializing agent, which have their origins more in psychodynamic theories. There is another class of variables which has been emerging as more and more important, namely the "social structure" variables. These variables have their origin largely in sociological thinking. I do not have time to give them more than the most cursory attention, but I do not believe they can be omitted if we are to do any sort of justice to the scope of significant variables employed in current socialization studies. One has only to list a few findings which have come out of the investigation of social structure factors to see how essential it has become to take them into account. Here is a brief sampling of such findings:

1. With adolescents, parents are most strict with children who are of the same sex as the dominant parent (**17**).
2. A mother's use of strongly dominant child-rearing techniques (called "unqualified power assertion" in this study) is related to her husband's F score (authoritarian personality score), but not to her own (**11**).
3. A mother's behavior toward her children is more closely related to her husband's education than her own, and her behavior is more closely related to her husband's education than is *his* behavior to his own education. Thus it appears that it is the family's social status, as indicated by the husband's education, that influences the mother's socialization practices (**5**).
4. Sons are more intra-punitive if their mothers are primarily responsible for discipline than

they are if their fathers are the primary disciplinarians (10).

5. Aspects of social organization such as whether residence is patrilocal, matrilocal, or neolocal, and whether marriage is polygamous or monogamous, determine such aspects of culture as the length of the postpartum sex taboo, the duration of exclusive mother-child sleeping arrangements, and the amount of authority the father has over the child; these factors in turn influence such socialization practices as the age of weaning, the severity of the socialization pressures which are directed toward breaking up the child's dependency upon the mother, and the existence and nature of puberty rites at adolescence. These socialization practices then in their turn influence certain aspects of personality, including certain culturally established defense systems (24, 25, 26).

6. When offered a choice between a small piece of candy now vs. a large one later, children from father-present homes can postpone gratification more easily than children from father-absent homes (15).

These findings all represent efforts to put socialization practices into a cultural or social-structural context. In each case, socialization practices are regarded as a link in a several-step chain, and consideration is given to the factors which determine the socialization practices themselves, as well as to the effects these practices in their turn have upon the child. It is clear that the way parents treat their children will be a function of their relationship to each other (especially of the distribution of authority between them), of the place the family has in the status system of the society in which the family resides, of the society's kinship system, etc. Of course, not every student of socialization need concern himself with all the steps in the complex sequence; he may, and often does, select a set of socialization practices and relate them to the child's behavior without going back to the conditions which led to these practices. But he needs to be aware of the degree to which socialization practices are embedded in a cultural context, and even needs to be alert to the possibility that the "same" socialization practice may have different effects when it is part of different cultural settings. So far, few studies have been planned or analyzed with this possibility in mind, but it might be worth some empirical examination.

It is time to make explicit an assumption that has been implicit so far about the constancy of personality from one situation to another and from one time to another. When we select aspects of parental behavior to study, and try to relate these to measured characteristics of the child, we usually measure what we believe to be reasonably pervasive, reasonably enduring "traits" of the parent and child. Orville Brim (3) in a recent paper, has leveled a direct attack at the notion of trait constancy. He has asserted that there is no such thing as a "warm" person, nor an "aggressive" person, nor a "dependent" person, but that behavior is specific to roles. This would mean that the same individual may be aggressive with his subordinates and dependent toward his boss; that a child may be emotionally expressive with his same-sexed age mates, but not with his teachers or his parents. The question of exactly how general personality traits are, is, of course, a matter that personality theorists have struggled with for many years. But our view of this matter will have some bearing upon our selection and definition of socialization variables. For if a child's behavior is going to be entirely specific to roles, then there is no point in trying to predict any generalized traits in the child; rather, we should be looking for those aspects of the socialization situation that will determine what behavior will be adopted by the child in each different role relationship in which he will find himself. If we wanted to find what socialization practices were associated with the child's becoming dominant or submissive, for example, we would have to study how his dominant behavior had been reacted to when he was playing with same-sexed siblings, and study this separately from the socialization of the same behavior when he was playing with opposite-sexed siblings. Only thus could we predict, according to Brim, how dominant he would be with other boys in the classroom; and we would have to make a separate prediction of his dominance with girls in the classroom. We have already been following Brim's advice, in essence, when we do studies in which we test how the child's behavior varies with the role characteristics of the person with whom he is interacting. A good example is Gewirtz and Baer's study on the interaction between the sex of the experimenter and the effects of interrupted nurturance (7). But to follow Brim's point further, we would have to investigate the ways in which the child's behavior toward specific categories of "others" was conditioned by differential socialization in these role relationships.

I do not believe that either socialization or the child's reaction tendencies are as role-specific as Brim claims; but obviously role differentiation does occur, and he is quite right in calling our attention to the fact that, for some variables at least, we should be studying socialization separately within roles. Actually, role is only one aspect of situational variability; we have known ever since the days of Hartshorne and May (9) that trait behavior like "honesty" is situation-specific. They found, for example, that the child who will cheat on the playground is not necessarily the same child who will cheat in the classroom, and that cheating is a function of the specific task presented to the child. This means that, in studying the effects of socialization, we either have to abandon efforts to predict characteristics like "honesty" and attempt to study only those characteristics of the child that are at least somewhat constant across situations, or we have to choose socialization variables that are themselves much more situation-specific, and make much more detailed predictions. An example of the utility of making socialization variables more specific to the situations they are intended to predict is provided in a study by Levy (13), in which it was found that a child's adjustment to a hospital experience was *not* a function of the parents having trained the child generally to meet many different kinds of stress situations; rather, the child's response to hospitalization was predicted only from the amount of training the parent gave in advance for the meeting of this *particular* stress situation.

The same sort of situation prevails with respect to trait constancy over time. In their recent article on dependency, Kagan and Moss (12) were able to present repeated measurements of dependency in the same group of individuals—measurements which began at the age of three and continued into the late twenties. The most notable feature of their findings was the absence of continuity in this trait. The children who were dependent at age three and four were not the same individuals who emerged as dependent in adulthood. There was simply no continuity at all for boys, while there was some, but not a great deal, for girls. Let us consider Kagan's findings from the standpoint of efforts to study the socialization practices that are related to dependency. The first and obvious point is that we cannot expect to find any characteristic of the parent's behavior that will correlate with dependency in the young child and also correlate with dependency when the child is an adolescent or adult. This is not to say that the only correlations we can hope for are those between socialization practices and child characteristics measured at the same point in time. It is of course most likely that we shall be able to find aspects of a parent's current behavior that correlate with characteristics his child is displaying at the same time. But it is also possible that we could find aspects of the parent's current behavior whose effects will not show up until later. That is, perhaps there were things the parents of Kagan's sample of children were doing when these children were three and four that had some bearing upon how dependent the children became at the age of ten or eleven. But it is clear enough that whatever these delayed-action variables are, they could hardly be the same variables as the ones which determined how dependent the children were at age three, since it was not the same children who were displaying large amounts of dependency behavior at the two ages.

I have pointed to the way in which different theoretical systems, and different social-science disciplines, have converged to define and elaborate some of the variables which have been used in studies of socialization. In some cases this convergence has produced useful new knowledge; in others it has produced confusion over the meaning of variables. More importantly, it has produced a startling range of findings which have not yet been integrated into a theory of socialization. This is a major task that remains to be done.

REFERENCES

1. ALLINSMITH, B., "Directness with which Anger is Expressed," in D. R. Miller and G. E. Swanson, eds., *Inner Conflict and Defense,* New York: Holt-Dryden, 1960.
2. BALDWIN, A. L., J. KALHORN, and F. H. BREESE, "The Appraisal of Parent Behavior," *Psychological Monographs,* 1949, **63,** No. 4.
3. BRIM, O. G., "Personality Development as Role Learning," in I. Iscoe and H. Stevenson, eds., *Personality Development in Children,* Austin, Texas: University of Texas Press, 1960.
4. BRODY, S., *Patterns of Mothering,* New York: International Universities Press, 1957.
5. BRONFENBRENNER, U., "Some Familial Antecedents of Responsibility and Leadership in Adolescents," (dittoed paper) Cornell University, 1959.
6. ERIKSON, E. H., *Childhood and Society,* New York: Norton, 1950.
7. GEWIRTZ, J. L., and D. M. BAER, "Does Brief Social 'Deprivation' Enhance the Effectiveness of a Social Reinforcer ('Approval')?" *American Psychologist,* 1956, **11,** 428–429.
8. HARLOW, H. F., "On the Nature of Love," *American Psychologist,* 1958, **13,** 673–685.
9. HARTSHORNE, H., and M. A. MAY, *Studies in Deceit,* New York: Macmillan, 1928.
10. HENRY, A. F., "Family Role Structure and Self-Blame," *Social Forces,* 1956, **35,** 34–38.
11. HOFFMAN, M. L., "Power Assertion by Parents and Its Impact on the Child," *Child Development,* 1960, **31,** 129–144.
12. KAGAN, J., and H. A. MOSS, "The Stability of Passive and Dependent Behavior from Childhood through Adulthood," *Child Development,* 1960, **31,** 577–591.
13. LEVY, E., "Children's Behavior Under Stress and Its Relation to Training by Parents to Respond to Stress Situation," *Child Development,* 1959, **30,** 307–324.

14. McCord, W., and J. McCord, *The Origins of Crime,* New York: Columbia University Press, 1959.

15. Mischel, W., "Preference for Delayed Reinforcement: An Experimental Study of Cultural Observation," *Journal of Abnormal and Social Psychology,* 1958, **56,** 57–61.

16. Munn, N. L., *The Evolution and Growth of Human Behavior,* Boston: Houghton Mifflin, 1955.

17. Papanek, M. L., "Family Structure and Child-Training Practices," Ph.D. dissertation (unpublished), Radcliffe College, 1954.

18. Roff, M., "A Factorial Study of the Fels Parent Behavior Scales," *Child Development,* 1949, **20,** 29–45.

19. Schaeffer, E. S., and N. Bayley, "Consistency of Maternal Behavior from Infancy to Pre-Adolescence," *Journal of Abnormal and Social Psychology,* 1960, **61,** 1–6.

20. Schaeffer, E. S., and R. Q. Bell, "Development of a Parental Attitude Research Instrument," *Child Development,* 1958, **29,** 339–361.

21. Sears, R. R., E. E. Maccoby, and H. Levin, *Patterns of Child Rearing,* Evanston, Illinois: Row-Peterson, 1957.

22. Shoben, E. J., "The Assessment of Parental Attitudes in Relation to Child Adjustment," *Genetic Psychology Monographs,* 1949, **39.**

23. Watson, R. I., *Psychology of the Child,* New York: Wiley, 1959.

24. Whiting, J. W. M., "Sin, Sorcery and the Superego," in M. R. Jones, ed., *Nebraska Symposium on Motivation,* Lincoln, Nebraska: University of Nebraska Press, 1959.

25. Whiting, J. W. M., E. H. Chasdi, H. F. Antonovsky, and B. C. Ayres, "The Learning of Values," in F. Kluckhohn and E. Vogt, eds., *The Peoples of Rimrock: A Comparative Study of Values Systems* (in press).

26. Whiting, J. W. M., R. Kluckhohn, and A. Anthony, "The Function of Male Initiation Rites at Puberty," in E. E. Maccoby, T. M. Newcomb, and E. L. Hartley, eds., *Readings in Social Psychology,* New York: Holt, 1958.

27. Zuckerman, M., B. Barrett-Ribback, I. Monashkin, and J. Norton, "Normative Data and Factor Analysis on the Parental Attitude Research Instrument," *Journal of Consulting Psychology,* 1958, **22,** 165–171.

SOCIALIZATION INTO THE MILITARY ACADEMY*

The selection below is written from the recollections of a sociologist who had experienced ten months as a cadet at the United States Coast Guard Academy. Dornbusch focuses upon those aspects of academy life which hasten the transition from the role of civilian to that of cadet and which prepare him for the later role of Coast Guard officer. He is interested in identifying conditions that facilitate rapid and maximum socialization. Such socialization processes operate in most groups where the entering member must make marked changes in at least some aspects of his life.

The socialization agent initiates the control process by "desocializing" the newcomer: he is deprived of his previous statuses. His communication and contacts with persons outside the group are restricted. The group exercises extensive control over rewards and punishments that he can experience. Within the group, units are organized to support the member in his new role. All these procedures are vividly illustrated in the article.

* The selection following the editorial introduction is reprinted from "The military academy as an assimilating institution," *Social Forces,* 1955, **33,** 316–321, by permission of the author and the University of North Carolina Press.

49.

The Military Academy as an Assimilating Institution[1]

SANFORD M. DORNBUSCH
STANFORD UNIVERSITY

The function of a military academy is to make officers out of civilians or enlisted men. The objective is accomplished by a twofold process of transmitting technical knowledge and of instilling in the candidates an outlook considered appropriate for members of the profession. This paper is concerned with the latter of these processes, the assimilating function of the military academy. Assimilation is viewed as "a process of interpenetration and fusion in which persons and groups acquire the memories, sentiments, and attitudes of other persons and groups, and, by sharing their experience and history, are incorporated with them in a common cultural life. . . . The unity thus achieved is not necessarily or even normally like-mindedness; it is rather a unity of experience

[1] The writer is indebted to Harold McDowell, Frank Miyamoto, Charles Bowerman, and Howard S. Becker for their constructive criticism of this paper.

and of orientation, out of which may develop a community of purpose and action."[2]

Data for this study consist almost entirely of retrospective material, based on ten months spent as a cadet at the United States Coast Guard Academy. The selective nature of memory obviously may introduce serious deficiencies in the present formulation. Unfortunately, it is unlikely that more objective evidence on life within the Academy will be forthcoming. Cadets cannot keep diaries, are formally forbidden to utter a word of criticism of the Academy to an outsider, and are informally limited in the matters which are to be discussed in letters or conversations. The lack of objective data is regrettable, but the process of assimilation is present here in an extreme form. Insight into this process can better be developed by the study of such an explicit, overt case of assimilation.

The Coast Guard Academy, like West Point and Annapolis, provides four years of training for a career as a regular officer. Unlike the other service academies, however, its cadet corps is small, seldom exceeding 350 cadets. This disparity in size probably produces comparable differences in the methods of informal social control. Therefore, all the findings reported here may not be applicable to the other academies. It is believed, however, that many of the mechanisms through which this military academy fulfills its assimilating function will be found in a wide variety of social institutions.

THE SUPPRESSION OF PRE-EXISTING STATUSES

The new cadet, or "swab," is the lowest of the low. The assignment of low status is useful in producing a correspondingly high evaluation of successfully completing the steps in an Academy career and requires that there be a loss of identity in terms of pre-existing statuses. This clean break with the past must be achieved in a relatively short period. For two months, therefore, the swab is not allowed to leave the base or to engage in social intercourse with non-cadets. This complete isolation helps to produce a unified group of swabs, rather than a heterogeneous collection of persons of high and low status. Uniforms are issued on the first day, and discussions of wealth and family background are taboo. Although the pay of the cadet is very low, he is not permitted to receive money from home. The role of the cadet must supersede other roles the individual has been accustomed to play. There are few clues left which will reveal social status in the outside world.[3]

It is clear that the existence of minority-group status on the part of some cadets would tend to break down this desired equality. The sole minority group present was the Jews, who, with a few exceptions, had been informally excluded before 1944. At that time 18 Jews were admitted in a class of 162. Their status as Jews made them objects of scrutiny by the upper classmen, so that their violations of rules were more often noted. Except for this "spotlight," however, the Jews reported no discrimination against them—they, too, were treated as swabs.

LEARNING NEW RULES AND ADJUSTMENT TO CONFLICTS BETWEEN RULES

There are two organized structures of rules which regulate the cadet's behavior. The first of these is the body of regulations of the Academy, considered by the public to be the primary source of control. These regulations are similar to the code of ethics of any profession. They serve in part as propaganda to influence outsiders. An additional function is to provide negative sanctions which are applied to violations of the second set of expectations, the informal rules. Offenses against the informal rules are merely labeled as breaches of the formal code, and the appropriate punishment according to the regulations is then imposed. This punitive system conceals the existence of the informal set of controls.

The informal traditions of the Academy are more functionally related to the existing set of circumstances than are the regulations, for although these traditions are fairly rigid, they are more easily forgotten or changed than are the formal regulations. Unlike other informal codes, the Academy code of traditions is in part written, appearing in a manual for entering cadets.

In case of conflict between the regulations and tradition, the regulations are superseded. For example, it is against the regulations to have candy in one's room. A first classman orders a swab to bring him candy. Caught en route by an officer, the swab offers no excuse and is given 15 demerits. First classmen are then informally told by the classmate involved that they are to withhold demerits for this swab until he has been excused for offenses totaling 15 demerits. Experience at an Academy teaches future officers that regulations are not considered of paramount importance when they conflict with informal codes—a principle noted by other observers.[4]

[2] Robert E. Park and Ernest W. Burgess, *Introduction to the Science of Sociology* (Chicago: University of Chicago Press, 1921), pp. 735, 737.

[3] Cf. Arnold Van Gennep, *Les Rites de Passage* (Paris: Emile Nourry, 1909). Translated by Everett C. Hughes in *Anthro-*

pology-Sociology 240, Special Readings (Chicago: University of Chicago Bookstore, 1948), Pt. II, p. 9.

[4] Ralph H. Turner, "The Navy Disbursing Officer As a Bureaucrat," *American Sociological Review*, XII (June 1946), 344 and

Sometimes situations arise in which the application of either form of control is circumvented by the commanding officer. The following case is an example. Cadets cannot drink, cannot smoke in public, can never go above the first floor in a hotel. It would seem quite clear, therefore, that the possessor of a venereal disease would be summarily dismissed. Cadets at the Academy believed that two upper-class cadets had contracted a venereal disease, were cured, and given no punishment. One of the cadets was an outstanding athlete, brilliant student, and popular classmate. Cadets were told that a direct appeal by the commanding officer to the Commandant of the Coast Guard resulted in the decision to hush up the entire affair, with the second cadet getting the same treatment as his more popular colleague. The event indicated the possibility of individualization of treatment when rules are violated by officers.

THE DEVELOPMENT OF SOLIDARITY

The control system operated through the class hierarchy. The first class, consisting of cadets in their third or fourth year at the Academy, are only nominally under the control of the officers of the Academy. Only one or two officers attempt to check on the activities of the first classmen, who are able to break most of the minor regulations with impunity. The first class is given almost complete control over the rest of the cadet corps. Informally, certain leading cadets are even called in to advise the officers on important disciplinary matters. There are one or two classes between the first classmen and the swabs, depending on the existence of a three- or four-year course. These middle classes haze the swabs. Hazing is forbidden by the regulations, but the practice is a hallowed tradition of the Academy. The first class demands that this hazing take place, and, since they have the power to give demerits, all members of the middle classes are compelled to haze the new cadets.

As a consequence of undergoing this very unpleasant experience together, the swab class develops remarkable unity. For example, if a cadet cannot answer an oral question addressed to him by his teacher, no other member of his class will answer. All reply, "I can't say, sir," leaving the teacher without a clue to the state of knowledge of this student compared to the rest of the class. This group cohesion persists throughout the Academy period, with first classmen refusing to give demerits to their classmates unless an officer directly orders them to do so.

The honor system, demanding that offenses by

348; Arnold Rose, "The Social Structure of the Army," *American Journal of Sociology*, LI (March 1946), 361.

classmates be reported, is not part of the Coast Guard Academy tradition. It seems probable that the honor system, if enforced, would tend to break down the social solidarity which the hazing develops within each class.

The basis for interclass solidarity, the development of group feeling on the part of the entire cadet corps, is not so obvious. It occurs through informal contacts between the upper classmen and swabs, a type of fraternalization which occurs despite the fact it traditionally is discouraged. The men who haze the swab and order him hazed live in the same wing of the dormitory that he does. Coming from an outside world which disapproves of authoritarian punishment and aggressiveness, they are ashamed of their behavior. They are eager to convince the swab that they are good fellows. They visit his room to explain why they are being so harsh this week or to tell of a mistake he is making. Close friendships sometimes arise through such behavior. These friendships must be concealed. One first classman often ordered his room cleaned by the writer as a "punishment," then settled down for an uninterrupted chat. Such informal contacts serve to unite the classes and spread a "we-feeling" through the Academy.

In addition, the knowledge of common interests and a common destiny serves as a unifying force that binds together all Academy graduates. This is expressed in the identification of the interest of the individual with the interest of the Coast Guard. A large appropriation or an increase in the size of the Coast Guard will speed the rate of promotion for all, whether ensign or captain. A winning football team at the Academy may familiarize more civilians with the name of their common alma mater. Good publicity for the Coast Guard raises the status of the Coast Guard officer.

The Coast Guard regulars are united in their disdain for the reserves. There are few reserve officers during peacetime, but in wartime the reserve officers soon outnumber the regulars. The reserves do not achieve the higher ranks, but they are a threat to the cadets and recent graduates of the Academy. The reserves receive in a few months the rank that the regulars reach only after four grueling years. The Academy men therefore protectively stigmatize the reserves as incompetents. If a cadet falters on the parade ground, he is told, "You're marching like a reserve." Swabs are told to square their shoulders while on liberty, "or else how will people know you are not a reserve?" Myths spring up—stories of reserve commanders who must call on regular ensigns for advice. The net effect is reassurance that although the interlopers may have the same rank, they do not have equal status.

Another out-group is constituted by the enlisted men, who are considered to be of inferior ability and eager for leadership. Segregation of cadets and enlisted men enables this view to be propagated. Moreover, such segregation helps to keep associations within higher status social groups. There is only one leak in this insulating dike. The pharmacist mates at sick bay have direct contact with the cadets, and are the only enlisted personnel whom cadets meet on an equal basis. The pharmacist mates take pleasure in reviling the Academy, labeling it "the p---k factory." Some of the cadets without military experience are puzzled by such an attitude, which is inconsistent with their acquired respect for the Academy.

THE DEVELOPMENT OF A BUREAUCRATIC SPIRIT

The military services provide an excellent example of a bureaucratic structure. The emphasis is upon the office with its sets of rights and duties, rather than on the man. It is a system of rules with little regard for the individual case. The method of promotion within the Coast Guard perfectly illustrates this bureaucratic character. Unlike the Army or Navy, promotions in the Coast Guard up to the rank of lieutenant-commander do not even depend on the evaluation of superior officers. Promotion comes solely according to seniority, which is based on class standing at the Academy. The 50th man in the 1947 class will be lieutenant-commander before the 51st man, and the latter will be promoted before the 1st man in the 1948 class.

The hazing system contributes directly to acceptance of the bureaucratic structure of the Coast Guard, for the system is always viewed by its participants as not involving the personal character of the swab or upper classman. One is not being hazed because the upper classman is a sadist, but because one is at the time in a junior status. Those who haze do not pretend to be superior to those who are being hazed. Since some of those who haze you will also try to teach you how to stay out of trouble, it becomes impossible to attribute evil characteristics to those who injure you. The swab knows he will have his turn at hazing others. At most, individual idiosyncrasies will just affect the type of hazing done.[5]

This emphasis on the relativity of status is explicitly made on the traditional Gizmo Day, on which the swabs and their hazers reverse roles. The swabs-for-a-day take their licking without flinching and do not seek revenge later, for they are aware that they are under the surveillance of the first classmen. After the saturnalia, the swabs are increasingly conscious of their inability to blame particular persons for their troubles.

[5] Compare this viewpoint with that expressed in Hugh Mullan, "The Regular Service Myth," *American Journal of Sociology,* LIII (January 1948), 280, where hazing is viewed as the expression of "pent-up sadism." Such individualistic interpretations do not take into account the existence of an institutional structure, or else they give psychological interpretations to social processes.

Upper classmen show the same resentment against the stringent restrictions upon their lives, and the manner in which they express themselves indicates a feeling of being ruled by impersonal forces. They say, "You can't buck the System." As one writer puts it, "The best attitude the new cadet can have is one of unquestioning acceptance of tradition and custom."

There is a complete absence of charismatic veneration of the Coast Guard heroes of the past and present. Stirring events are recalled, not as examples of the genius of a particular leader, but as part of the history of the great organization which they will serve. A captain is a cadet thirty years older and wiser. Such views prepare these men for their roles in the bureaucracy.

NEW SATISFACTIONS IN INTERACTION

A bureaucratic structure requires a stable set of mutual expectations among the occupants of offices. The Academy develops this ability to view the behavior of others in terms of a pre-ordained set of standards. In addition to preparing the cadet for later service as an officer, the predictability of the behavior of his fellows enables the cadet to achieve a high degree of internal stability. Although he engages in a continual bustle of activity, he always knows his place in the system and the degree to which he is fulfilling the expectations of his role.

Sharing common symbols and objects, the cadets interact with an ease of communication seldom found in everyday life. The cadet is told what is right and wrong, and, if he disagrees, there are few opportunities to translate mental reservations into action. The "generalized other" speaks with a unitary voice which is uncommon in modern societies. To illustrate, an upper classman ordered a swab to pick up some pieces of paper on the floor of a washroom. The latter refused and walked away. There were no repercussions. The swab knew that, if he refused, the upper classman would be startled by the choice of such an unconventional way of getting expelled from the Academy. Wondering what was happening, the upper classman would redefine his own behavior, seeing it as an attack on the high status of the cadet. Picking up litter in a washroom is "dirty work," fit only for enlisted men. The swab was sure that the upper classman shared this common universe of discourse and never considered the possibility that he would not agree on the definition of the situation.

Interaction with classmates can proceed on a level of confidence that only intimate friends achieve in the outside world. These men are in a union of sympathy, sharing the same troubles, never confiding secrets to upper classmen, never criticizing one another to outsiders. Each is close to only a few but is friendly with most of the men in his class.

When interacting with an upper classman in private, a different orientation is useful. The swab does not guess the reason why he is being addressed, but instead assumes a formal air of deference. If the upper classman says, "Aw cut it out," the swab relaxes. In this manner the role of the upper classman is explicitly denoted in each situation.

In addition to providing predictability of the behavior of others, the Academy provides a second set of satisfactions in the self-process. An increase in the cadet's self-esteem develops in conjunction with identification in his new role. Told that they are members of an elite group respected by the community, most cadets begin to feel at ease in a superordinate role. One may be a low-ranking cadet, but cadets as a group have high status. When cadets visit home for the first time, there is a conflict between the lofty role that they wish to play and the role to which their parents are accustomed. Upon return to the Academy, much conversation is concerned with the way things at home have changed.

This feeling of superiority helps to develop self-confidence in those cadets who previously had a low evaluation of themselves. It directly enters into relationships with girls, with whom many boys lack self-confidence. It soon becomes apparent that any cadet can get a date whenever he wishes, and he even begins to feel that he is a good "catch." The cadet's conception of himself is directly influenced by this new way of viewing the behavior of himself and others. As one cadet put it, "I used to be shy. Now I'm reserved."

SOCIAL MOBILITY

A desire for vertical social mobility on the part of many cadets serves as one means of legitimizing the traditional practices of the Academy. The cadets are told that they will be members of the social elite during the later stages of their career. The obstacles that they meet at the Academy are then viewed as the usual barriers to social mobility in the United States, a challenge to be surmounted.

Various practices at the Academy reinforce the cadets' feeling that they are learning how to enter the upper classes. There is a strong emphasis on etiquette, from calling cards to table manners. The Tactics Officer has been known to give long lectures on such topics as the manner of drinking soup from an almost empty bowl. The cadet must submit for approval the name of the girl he intends to take to the monthly formal dance. Girls attending the upper-class college in the vicinity are automatically acceptable, but some cadets claim

that their dates have been rejected because they are in a low status occupation such as waitress.

Another Academy tradition actively, though informally, encourages contact with higher status girls. After the swabs have been completely isolated for two months, they are invited to a dance at which all the girls are relatives or friends of Coast Guard officers. A week later the girls at the nearby college have a dance for the swabs. The next week end finds the swab compelled to invite an acceptable girl to a formal reception. He must necessarily choose from the only girls in the area whom he knows, those that he met during the recent hours of social intercourse.

JUSTIFICATION OF INSTITUTIONAL PRACTICES

In addition to the social mobility theme which views the rigors of Academy life as obstacles to upward mobility, there is a more open method of justifying traditionally legitimated ways of doing things. The phrase, "separating the men from the boys" is used to meet objections to practices which seem inefficient or foolish. Traditional standards are thus redefined as further tests of ability to take punishment. Harsh practices are defended as methods by which the insincere, incompetent, or undisciplined cadets are weeded out. Cadets who rebel and resign are merely showing lack of character.[6]

Almost all cadets accept to some extent this traditional view of resignations as admissions of defeat. Of the 162 entering cadets in 1944, only 52 graduated in 1948. Most of the 110 resignations were entirely voluntary without pressure from the Academy authorities. Most of these resignations came at a time when the hazing was comparatively moderate. Cadets who wish to resign do not leave at a time when the hazing might be considered the cause of their departure. One cadet's history illustrates this desire to have the resignation appear completely voluntary. Asked to resign because of his lack of physical coordination, he spent an entire year building up his physique, returned to the Academy, finished his swab year, and then joyously quit. "It took me three years, but I showed them."

Every cadet who voluntarily resigns is a threat to the morale of the cadet corps, since he has rejected the values of the Academy. Although cadets have enlisted for seven years and could theoretically be forced to remain at the Academy, the usual procedure is to isolate them from the swabs and rush acceptance of their resignation. During the period before the acceptance is final, the cadets who have resigned are freed from the usual duties of their classmates, which action effectively isolates them from cadets who might be affected by their contagious disenchantment.

---

[6] "At each step of the ceremonies he feels that he is brought a little closer, until at last he can feel himself a man among men." A. R. Radcliffe-Brown, *The Andaman Islanders* (Glencoe, Illinois: The Free Press, 1948), p. 279.

REALITY SHOCK

Everett C. Hughes has developed the concept of "reality shock," the sudden realization of the disparity between the way a job is envisaged before beginning work and the actual work situation.[7] In the course of its 75-year history the Coast Guard Academy has wittingly or unwittingly developed certain measures to lessen reality shock in the new ensign. The first classmen, soon to be officers, are aided in lessening the conflict between the internalized rules of the Academy world and the standards for officer conduct.

On a formal level the first classmen are often reminded that they are about to experience a relative decline in status. On their first ship they will be given the most disagreeable duties. The first classmen accept this and joke about how their attitudes will change under a harsh captain. On a more concrete level, first classmen are given weekend leaves during the last six months of their stay at the Academy. These leaves allow them to escape from the restrictive atmosphere of the nearby area. It is believed wise to let them engage in orgiastic behavior while still cadets, rather than suddenly release all controls upon graduation.

Rumors at the Academy also help to prepare the cadets for their jobs as officers. Several of the instructors at the Academy were supposed to have been transferred from sea duty because of their incompetence. Such tales protect the cadets from developing a romantic conception of the qualities of Coast Guard officers, as well as providing a

graphic illustration of how securely the bureaucratic structure protects officers from their own derelictions. In addition, many stories were told about a junior officer whose career at the Academy had been singularly brilliant. He had completely failed in his handling of enlisted men because he had carried over the high standards of the Academy. The cadets were thus oriented to a different conception of discipline when dealing with enlisted personnel.

CONCLUSION

The United States Coast Guard Academy performs an assimilating function. It isolates cadets from the outside world, helps them to identify themselves with a new role, and thus changes their self-conception. The manner in which the institution inculcates a bureaucratic spirit and prevents reality shock is also considered in this analysis.

The present investigation is admittedly fragmentary. Much of the most relevant material is simply not available. It is also clear that one cannot assume that this analysis applies completely to any other military academy. However, as an extreme example of an assimilating institution, there is considerable material which can be related to other institutions in a comparative framework.

FAMILY STRUCTURE AND SEX ROLE LEARNING *

In interacting with another person, an individual learns not only his own role, but also elements of the role of the other person. Before she enters nursing school, a trainee may have learned some elements of the nursing role from her association with nurses on those occasions when she was a patient. Learning elements of a role prior to entry into the position helps to ease the later transition into it.

The prevalence of this type of learning suggests, however, that frequent interaction with another person occupying a specific role category is likely to lead to assimilation into one's own personality of some of his characteristics, even though later entry into his position is not anticipated. The following selection tests this hypothesis through a statistical analysis of differences between the personalities of boys and girls who have same sex siblings and those who have opposite sex siblings. Boys having

[7] Miriam Wagenschein, Reality Shock. Unpublished M.A. thesis, Department of Sociology, University of Chicago, 1950.

* The selection following the editorial introduction is reprinted from "Family structure and sex role learning by children: A further analysis of Helen Koch's data," *Sociometry*, 1958, 21, 1–16, by permission of the author and the American Sociological Association.

sisters were expected to be somewhat more feminine than those having brothers, and sisters having brothers, more masculine than sisters having only sisters. In addition, age was expected to play a part: an older sibling was considered more likely to serve as a model than a younger one.

50.

Family Structure and Sex Role Learning by Children: A Further Analysis of Helen Koch's Data[1]

ORVILLE G. BRIM, JR.
RUSSELL SAGE FOUNDATION

The structure of a social group, delineated by variables such as size, age, sex, power, and prestige differences, is held to be a primary influence upon the patterns of interaction within the group, determining in major part the degree to which any two group members interact. It is held, sec-

[1] The author wishes to express his appreciation of the valuable assistance of Miss Arla McMillan in preparation of Tables 2 and 3.

ond, that social roles are learned through interaction with others, such interaction providing one with the opportunity to practice his own role as well as to take the role of the other. On this basis one may hypothesize that group structure, by influencing the degree of interaction between group members, would be related to the types of roles learned in the group; one would learn most completely those roles which he himself plays, as well as the roles of the others with whom he most frequently interacts. This argument is applied in this paper specifically to the relation between family structure, described in terms of age, sex, and ordinality of children, and the sex role learning by the children.

The process of role learning through interaction, which has been described in detail by Mead (**15**), Cottrell (**2**), and others, can be sketched as follows. One learns the behavior appropriate to his position in a group through interaction with others who hold normative beliefs about what his role should be and who are able to reward and punish him for correct and incorrect actions. As part of the same learning process, one acquires expectations of how others in the group will behave. The latter knowledge is indispensable to the actor, in that he must be able to predict what others expect of him, and how they will react to him, in order to guide his own role performance successfully. Accurate or erroneous understanding and prediction are respectively rewarding and punishing to the actor, and learning proceeds systematically through the elimination of incorrect responses and the strengthening of correct ones.

It has been the distinctive contribution of sociology to demonstrate that learning the role of others occurs through the actor's taking the role of the other, i.e., trying to act as the other would act. While this role-taking of the other can be overt, as with children who actively and dramatically play the role of the parent, it is commonly covert in adults, as with the husband who anticipates what his wife will say when he returns home late, or the employee who tries to foresee his employer's reaction when he asks for a raise.

It follows that, whether taking the role of others is overt or covert, certain responses (belonging to the role of the other) are in fact made, run through, completed, and rewarded if successful, i.e., accurate, and that this process adds to the repertoire of possible actions of a person those actions taken by others in their own roles. Such actions, as part of one's repertoire or pool of learned responses, are available for performance by an actor, not now simply in taking the role of the other, but as resources which he can use as part of his *own* role performances.

The critical fact is that the actor not only can,

but does, make use of responses learned in role-taking in his own role performances. There are two senses in which this happens. The first, which does not concern us in this paper, involves the direct transfer of the role of the other to a new and parallel status of one's own, where there is a straightforward adoption of the other's role. Such transfer may be appropriate and rewarded, as where the oldest child performs the role of the parent to his sibs, or simply interesting and tolerated, as where the new assistant professor plays the department chairman to the graduate students.

The second sense, which is our major concern here, involves a more complex process of convergence between one's own role and that of the other which he takes, where there is a spill-over of elements belonging to another's role into one's own performance when it is not necessarily appropriate. Our basic hypothesis, set forth by Cottrell (**2**) and others, is that interaction between two persons leads to assimilation of roles, to the incorporation of elements of the role of the other into the actor's role. Thus, one says, husbands and wives grow more alike through time, and long-time collaborators in research begin to think alike.

While not pretending to a full analysis of the process underlying assimilation, several causes can be described. First, the actor may note that the other is successful to a high degree in some of his behavior and consciously transfer to his own role such behavioral elements for trial. To the extent that they prove successful for him, in his performance, and are not eliminated through punishment from others for being inappropriate, he will adopt them. Second, faced with novel situations where his "own" behavior fails, the elements of others' roles are already learned and available for trial and hence would tend to be tried prior to the development of totally new responses; again, if successful, they tend to be assimilated to the role. Third, the actions learned by taking the role of others are ordinarily performed implicitly and under limited conditions, e.g., in interaction with the other. However, the cues which guide and elicit one's own role performance may be difficult to differentiate from cues eliciting taking the role of the other. It would appear that for the young child this is especially difficult, and data indeed show that the child has difficulty discriminating between reality and fantasy, between what his role is or even what his self is, and what belongs in the category of the "other." In this way, behavior learned through role-taking and appropriate to the other is confused with and undifferentiated from behavior learned as part of one's own role. The latter becomes tinged or diluted with characteristics belonging to someone else's role.

Among the hypotheses which are derivative of the general hypothesis of assimilation through interaction, two are pertinent here. First, the process of discrimination between what belongs to oneself and what belongs to the other is aided by the guidance of other persons. Thus, the parent helps the son differentiate between what belongs to him and what belongs to his sister; the fledgling nurse is assisted in a proper demeanor and in separating her duties from those of the physician. Rewards and punishments administered by others govern the discrimination process. Where the process of assimilation comes primarily from inability to discriminate between roles, it follows that where greater attention is paid to helping the learner discriminate, the process of assimilation is to a greater degree arrested.

Second, given two other persons with whom one interacts and who differ in power over the actor, i.e., differ in the degree to which they control rewards and punishments for the actor, one would predict that the actor would adopt more of the characteristics of the powerful, as contrasted to the less powerful, other person. This follows from the fact that it is more important to the actor to predict the behavior of the powerful figure, that he is motivated more strongly to take his role, that the rewards and punishments are more impressive and the learning consequently better. Interaction between two figures of unequal power should give a parallel result, namely, there would be a greater assimilation of the role of the other into the actor's role for the less powerful figure, for the same reasons as above. Thus the employee gravitates toward the boss more than the reverse, and the child becomes more like the parent than the other way around. However, this is not to imply that the more powerful figure need not take the role of the other, nor that he does not assimilate (to a lesser degree) elements from the other's role. The weaker figure always has some control over rewards and punishments, requiring therefore that his reaction be considered. The displeased employee can wound his boss through expressions of dislike, and the angry child can hurt his parents in a variety of ways, from refusing to eat to threatening to leave home.

Turning now to a consideration of sex-role learning specifically, pertinent reviews (1, 17) of the data show that sex-role prescriptions and actual performance begin early. The accepted position is that children in a family learn their appropriate sex roles primarily from their parents. There is remarkably little data, other than clinical materials, on this topic, perhaps because of its obviousness. What systematic data there is, is not inconsistent with the role learning propositions set forth above. Sears, Pintler, and Sears (14) have shown that in families where the father is absent the male child is slower to develop male sex-role traits than in families where the father is present, a finding predictable from the fact that there is no father whose role the child needs to take. Both Sears (13) and Payne and Mussen (12) have shown that father role-playing, identification with the father, and masculinity of attitudes are positively related to the father's being warm, affectionate, and rewarding. This strikes

one as the same type of finding as the first, but at the other end of the interaction range; insofar as warm, affectionate, and rewarding fathers interact more with their sons, or are perceived as such because they interact more, it follows that the sons have more experience in taking their role.

In regard to the effects of sibling characteristics upon sex-role learning, there is again almost no information. Fauls and Smith (3) report that only children choose sex-appropriate activities more often than do children with older same-sex siblings, a finding which seems to fit none of our role-learning propositions. While one might hold that the only child has more interaction, because of sibling absence, with his same-sex parent, hence learns his sex role better, one might equally say, especially for the young boys, that it is the cross-sex parent with whom the child interacts and hence the only child should not learn his sex role well. In any case, the finding serves to stress the limitations of the data we are to report, namely, that they pertain to variations within two-child families, and that generalization to families of varying sizes is unwarranted. We return to this point later.

Even with respect to theory concerning the effects of siblings on sex-role learning, we have not noted any systematic predictions in the literature. It seems to us implicit in Parsons' recent analysis (11) of sex-role learning in the nuclear family that when the child begins his differentiation between the father and mother sex roles he would be helped in making the differentiation if he had a cross-sex sibling; this is not formally stated, however, and we may be guilty of misinterpretation.

It is against this background of comparative absence of research and theory on the effects of siblings on sex-role learning that our own report must be viewed. The very valuable data on personality traits of children presented in recent publications by Helen Koch (4, 5, 6, 7, 8, 9, 10) provide the opportunity to apply several of the general hypotheses set forth above to the substantive area of sibling effects on sex-role learning. The specific application of these hypotheses can be summarized as follows:

First, one would predict that cross-sex, as compared with same-sex, siblings would possess more traits appropriate to the cross-sex role. When taking the role of the other in interaction, cross-sex siblings must take the role of the opposite sex, and the assimilation of roles as delineated above should take place.

Second, one would predict that this effect would be more noticeable for the younger, as compared with the older, sibling in that the latter is more powerful and is more able to differentiate his own from his sibling's role.

Third, on the assumption that siblings close in age interact more than those not close in age, one would predict that this effect would be more noticeable for the siblings who are closest together in age. This is in essence an extension of the first hypothesis to deal with variations in interaction within the cross-sex sibling groups.

PROCEDURES

Our description of procedures must of necessity be broken into two parts. The first consists of a brief description of the procedures in Helen Koch's original study; complete details are available in the publications cited previously. The

TABLE 1 *Traits Assignable to Male (Instrumental) or Female (Expressive) Roles*

TRAIT NAME	PERTAINS PRIMARILY TO INSTRUMENTAL (*I*) OR EXPRESSIVE (*E*) ROLE	TRAIT IS CONGRUENT (+) OR INCONGRUENT (−) CHARACTERISTIC OF ROLE
1. Tenacity	I	+
2. Aggressiveness	I	+
3. Curiosity	I	+
4. Ambition	I	+
5. Planfulness	I	+
6. Dawdling and procrastinating	I	−
7. Responsibleness	I	+
8. Originality	I	+
9. Competitiveness	I	+
10. Wavering in decision	I	−
11. Self-confidence	I	+
12. Anger	E	−
13. Quarrelsomeness	E	−
14. Revengefulness	E	−
15. Teasing	E	−
16. Extrapunitiveness	E	−
17. Insistence on rights	E	−
18. Exhibitionism	E	−
19. Uncooperativeness with group	E	−
20. Affectionateness	E	+
21. Obedience	E	+
22. Upset by defeat	E	−
23. Responds to sympathy and approval from adults	E	+
24. Jealousy	E	−
25. Speedy recovery from emotional disturbance	E	+
26. Cheerfulness	E	+
27. Kindness	E	+
28. Friendliness to adults	E	+
29. Friendliness to children	E	+
30. Negativism	E	−
31. Tattling	E	−

second consists of our mode of further analysis of the reported data.

In her series of papers Helen Koch has reported results from a major research project concerned with the relation between structural characteristics of the family, namely, sex of child, sex of sibling, ordinal position of child, and age difference between siblings, and the child's ratings on more than fifty personality traits. In her study, all subjects were obtained from the Chicago public schools and one large private school. The characteristics of the children used as subjects can be summarized as follows. All children were from unbroken, native-born, white, urban, two-child families. The children were five- and six-year-olds, free of any gross physical or mental defect. In most cases only one sibling in a family was a subject in the study.

The subjects numbered 384. "The experimental design included three sib-spacing levels, two ordinal positions, subjects of two sexes and siblings of two sexes. There were 48 children in each of the following categories—male with a male sib older, male with a male sib younger, male with a female sib older, male with a female sib younger, female with a male sib older, female with a male sib younger, female with a female sib older, and female with a female sib younger. Each of these groups of 48 children was composed of three sub-groups of 16 children, representing the following three sibling-age-difference levels; siblings differed in age by under two years, by two to four years, and four to six years, respectively. Hence our basic subgroups of 16 numbered 24" (7, p. 289). The groups were matched, approximately, on an individual subject basis with respect to age of child and father's occupational status.

Teachers' ratings were made for each child on 58 traits. The teachers, all of whom were women, were trained in a conference or two to make the ratings. No teacher rated a child with whom contact had been less than three months, and in most cases the contact ranged from six to nine months. The 58 traits included 24 of the Fels Child Behavior Scales, and 34 items from the California Behavior Inventory for Nursery School Children. All ratings were made on line scales, converted later to 9-point scales. Ratings on each trait were subsequently normalized, prior to analysis of the data.

The relation between personality trait ratings and the structure of the family from which the children came was assessed by analysis of variance for each of the 58 traits. Helen Koch presents in her publications the findings from the variance analyses. It is this data on which we made our further study.

The procedures for the further analysis involved several steps. First, the writer, with the assistance of three professional persons as additional judges,[2] judged each of the 58 traits in terms

[2] Dr. John Mann, Mr. David Glass, and Mr. David Lavin.

of its pertinence to either a masculine or feminine role. Our conception of the characteristics of the two sex roles was based on recent empirical studies describing sex-role differences in small problem-solving groups (16) and in the nuclear family (18), and on the major theoretical treatment of such differences by Talcott Parsons (11). In these studies the now-familiar distinction between the instrumental or task role and the expressive or social-emotional role in a social group is shown to be related to sex-role differentiation, particularly in the family, with the male customarily taking the instrumental role and the female the expressive role. Hence in the judging process our decision as to whether a trait was masculine or feminine was essentially dependent on whether we believed the trait to belong to the instrumental or expressive role respectively.

Substantial descriptive data are available on sex-role differences in children for some of the traits which we judged. These findings, summarized by Terman and Tyler (17), were consulted after the judging was completed and strongly corroborate our assignment of traits: e.g., male children are judged higher on traits we believed instrumental, such as dominance and aggression, and lower on traits we judged to pertain to the expressive role, such as affection and absence of negativism.

In judging the traits it was recognized that many of them would be part of the role requirements for both roles. However, it was clear that there exists for each of the roles what is essentially a rank order of characteristics in terms of their importance for the role. Hence the basis for our judgments was whether the trait appeared to be higher in the rank order of requirements for the instrumental or the expressive role. Traits which seemed pertinent to neither, e.g., stammering, or for which no judgment of greater importance could be made, e.g., curiosity, were not ascribed to either role and were omitted from subsequent steps in the analysis. It was possible to assign 31 of the 58 traits to either the instrumental or expressive role. Twenty of the 31 traits pertain to the expressive role, the children evidently having been rated on a predominantly female cluster of traits.

Some of the traits were stated in a negative way which made them, while pertinent to the role, incongruent with the role conception. Thus, "uncooperativeness with group" seemed clearly to be relevant to the expressive role but as an incongruent trait. In like manner, both affectionateness and jealousy seemed most important as aspects of the expressive role, the former being congruent with the role conception, the latter incongruent. It therefore was necessary to make a second judgment regarding each trait, namely, whether it was a congruent or incongruent aspect of the role to which it pertained.

Table 1 lists the 31 traits, the role to which they seemed most pertinent, and the indication

of whether the trait was a congruent or incongruent characteristic of the role.

With the judging of the traits completed, the next step was a careful reading of Helen Koch's findings. A tabulation was made of all differences on the 31 traits between the 16 basic subgroups reported by her as significant (close to or at the .05 level, based on the separate analyses of variance). Such differences involved single structural characteristics, e.g., first-born versus second-born; single interactions of characteristics, e.g., girls with brothers versus girls with sisters; and multiple interactions, e.g., first-born boys with sisters versus first-born boys with brothers. These significant differences in traits were then entered in some preliminary forms of Tables 2 and 3. The procedure for entering differences was somewhat complicated and is described as follows:

First with respect to a trait judged pertinent to the male or instrumental role, and considered a congruent aspect of that role: when any subgroup or groups were rated significantly higher than others on that trait, the number of the trait was entered in the high masculinity column for such a group; the subgroup or groups they were higher than, i.e., the low groups, had the number of the trait entered in the low masculinity column. Second, with respect to a male trait considered an incongruent aspect of the role: when any subgroup was rated higher than another on such a trait, the trait number was entered in the low masculinity column for such a group; for the group it was higher than, i.e., the low group, the trait number was entered in the high masculinity column. The procedure for the female or expressive traits was identical, except the female columns were used.

This procedure means that for any subgroup, entries in the high masculinity column consist of congruent male traits on which the group is high, and incongruent male traits on which it is low; entries in the low masculinity column consist of incongruent male traits on which the group is high, and congruent male traits on which it is low. Female column entries are read the same way. An example may be helpful at this point. Consider in Table 3 the subgroup "Younger Boy with Older Brother" at the four- to six-year age difference. In the high masculinity column the entry of trait number 2 means that the group was rated significantly high on aggressiveness; the entry of trait number 10 means that the group was rated significantly low on wavering in decision. In the low masculinity column, trait number 6 indicates a high rating on dawdling and procrastinating, while trait number 7 indicates a low rating on responsibleness.

The preliminary forms of Tables 2 and 3 were complicated and two further steps toward simplification were taken before reaching the present form. The initial tables were marred by the occurrence of duplicate trait-number entries in the cells, arising primarily from the multiple reporting of the original data and the multiple differences emerging between the various subgroups. Hence, where duplicate trait-entries occurred, only one entry was kept. The result is to make each entry read that that subgroup is significantly higher (or lower) than some other group or groups on that particular trait. Second, the tables were complicated by the fact that for all subgroups there

were at least some trait numbers which appeared in both the high and low subdivisions of either the male or female column. This indicated, of course, that a subgroup was higher (or lower) than some other group on that trait, but also lower (or higher) than still another group; i.e., on the ranking of mean ratings on the trait, the subgroup would have differed significantly from both the top and bottom ranks. To clarify the tables, and also substantially to increase the reliability of the subgroup differences reported here, all traits on which a subgroup had both high and low entries were dropped for that subgroup. In summary, the result of this step, combined with the one above, is to make each entry in the final tables read that that subgroup is significantly

TABLE 2 *Instrumental and Expressive Traits for Five- and Six-year-old Girls*

SUBJECTS	SIB AGE DIFFERENCE	MALE (OR INSTRUMENTAL) TRAITS		FEMALE (OR EXPRESSIVE) TRAITS	
		High Masculinity Ratings	Low Masculinity Ratings	High Femininity Ratings	Low Femininity Ratings
Older girl with younger sister	0–2 years	2, 5, 7	4, 6, 9, 10	13, 14, 15, 16, 17, 18, 19, 20, 21, 24, 30	22, 23, 25, 26, 27
	2–4 years	7	2, 4, 9, 10, 11	13, 14, 15, 16, 17, 18, 19, 20, 21, 24, 30	22, 23, 26, 27, 28
	4–6 years	7	2, 4, 6, 9, 10, 11	13, 14, 15, 16, 17, 18, 19, 20, 21, 24, 30	22, 23, 25, 26, 27, 28
Older girl with younger brother	0–2 years	1, 2, 3, 4, 5, 9, 10	6	13, 14, 15, 16, 19, 20, 21, 25, 26, 27, 30	22, 24
	2–4 years	1, 2, 3, 4, 9, 10	6	13, 14, 15, 16, 19, 20, 25, 26, 27, 30, 31	22, 24
	4–6 years	1, 2, 3, 4, 5, 7, 9, 10	6	13, 14, 15, 19, 20, 21, 25, 26, 27, 28, 30	22, 24, 31
Younger girl with older sister	0–2 years	2, 5, 6, 7, 8	3, 4, 9, 10, 11	12, 13, 14, 15, 16, 18, 19, 20, 21, 22, 23, 30	17, 25, 26, 27
	2–4 years		3, 4, 5, 8, 9, 10, 11	12, 13, 14, 15, 16, 18, 19, 20, 21, 22, 23, 30	17, 25, 26, 27, 28
	4–6 years	6, 7	2, 3, 4, 9, 10, 11	12, 13, 14, 15, 16, 18, 19, 20, 21, 22, 23, 30	17, 25, 26, 27, 28
Younger girl with older brother	0–2 years	1, 2, 4, 6, 7, 8, 9, 10, 11		12, 13, 14, 15, 16, 18, 19, 20, 21, 22, 23, 25, 26, 27, 28, 30	
	2–4 years	1, 4, 6, 7, 10, 11		12, 13, 14, 15, 16, 18, 19, 20, 21, 22, 23, 25, 26, 27, 28, 30	
	4–6 years	2, 4, 5, 10, 11		12, 13, 14, 15, 16, 18, 19, 20, 21, 22, 23, 25, 26, 27, 28, 30	

Note: Trait numbers refer to listing in Table 1. Traits entered in high masculinity rating column are male-congruent traits with high ratings, male-incongruent traits with low ratings. The reverse is true for low masculinity rating column. Female trait entries are made in the same manner.

higher (or lower) than one or more groups on that trait, and is significantly lower (or higher) than none.

RESULTS AND DISCUSSION

The data presented in Tables 2 and 3 can be brought to bear upon our hypotheses by considering the distribution by subgroups of the traits indicating high or low masculinity or femininity. Our concern is with the frequency of trait entries of the four types, rather than with the descriptive content of any particular trait. Essentially we give each separate trait an equal weight, then summarize in terms of masculinity (many high rating, few low rating entries) and of femininity, associated with each subgroup.

With respect to our first hypothesis, that through interaction and taking the role of the other the cross-sex sibs would have more traits of the opposite sex than would same-sex sibs, an examination of the distribution in Table 2 shows that this is clearly the case. Controlling for ordinality, the older girl with a younger brother has more high masculinity traits and fewer low masculinity traits, than does her counterpart, the older girl with a younger sister. This distribution of traits is even more pronounced for the girls in the second ordinal position, the younger girl with older brother being substantially higher on

TABLE 3 Instrumental and Expressive Traits for Five- and Six-year-old Boys

SUBJECTS	SIB AGE DIFFERENCE	MALE (OR INSTRUMENTAL) TRAITS		FEMALE (OR EXPRESSIVE) TRAITS	
		High Masculinity Ratings	Low Masculinity Ratings	High Femininity Ratings	Low Femininity Ratings
Older boy with younger brother	0–2 years	9, 10	1, 2, 7, 11		12, 13, 14, 15, 16, 19, 22, 23, 25, 26, 27, 30
	2–4 years	4, 9, 10	1, 2, 5, 7, 11		12, 13, 14, 15, 16, 19, 20, 21, 22, 23, 25, 26, 27, 28, 30
	4–6 years	2, 4, 9, 10	1, 7, 11		12, 13, 14, 15, 16, 19, 20, 22, 23, 25, 26, 27, 30, 31
Older boy with younger sister	0–2 years	11	2, 4, 7, 9, 10	25, 26, 27, 31	12, 13, 14, 15, 16, 17, 18, 19, 20, 21, 22, 23, 24, 30
	2–4 years	2, 3, 5, 11	4, 7, 9, 10	25, 26, 27, 28	12, 13, 14, 15, 16, 17, 18, 19, 20, 21, 22, 23, 24, 30
	4–6 years	3	2, 4, 7, 9, 10	25, 26, 27, 28	12, 13, 14, 15, 16, 17, 18, 19, 20, 21, 22, 23, 24, 30
Younger boy with older brother	0–2 years	4, 9, 10	1, 2, 3, 5, 6, 7, 8	22, 23, 24	13, 16, 18, 19, 20, 21, 25, 26, 27, 28, 30
	2–4 years	4, 9, 10	1, 3, 6, 7	22, 23, 24	13, 16, 18, 19, 20, 21, 25, 26, 27, 28, 30
	4–6 years	2, 4, 5, 8, 9, 10	6, 7	22, 23, 24, 29	13, 16, 18, 19, 20, 21, 25, 26, 27, 28, 30
Younger boy with older sister	0–2 years		2, 4, 5, 6, 7, 8, 9, 10	17, 22, 23, 24, 25, 26, 27	13, 19, 30
	2–4 years		2, 4, 6, 9, 10	17, 22, 23, 24, 25, 26, 27, 28	13, 16, 19, 20, 21, 30
	4–6 years		2, 4, 6, 7, 9, 10	17, 22, 23, 24, 25, 26, 27, 28	13, 16, 19, 20, 21, 30

Note: See note to Table 2.

masculinity than her counterpart with an older sister. One will note that the acquisition of male traits does not seem to reduce the number of feminine traits of the girls with brothers. The more accurate interpretation is that acquisition of such traits adds to their behavioral repertoire, probably with a resultant dilution of their femininity in behavior, but not a displacement.

Examination of Table 3 with respect to this first hypothesis indicates that it holds for boys also. While not pronounced for the boys in the eldest child position, the boy with the sister is feminine to a greater degree than the boy with the brother. For the boys who are second-born, the difference is clear: the boy with the older sister is substantially more feminine than his counterpart with an older brother. For the boy with the older sister the acquisition of feminine traits would seem to have displaced, rather than simply diluted, his masculinity and he thus contrasts with the girls for whom this did not occur. We can offer no explanation for this, but it may provide a lead for further study in this area.

In connection with this result, the role of the parent requires attention. While all would agree that parents actively assist cross-sex sibs in separating their sex roles, the data show they are unsuccessful in completely arresting the process of assimilation. Perhaps in earlier times, when children's sex roles were stressed more strongly, and perhaps today for some parents making an extreme effort, the effects of interaction would be reduced. However, it certainly appears that the average parent today cannot completely avoid the effects of such sib interaction. Even were more attention given by parents to cross-sex as opposed to same-sex sibs in this matter, we believe that the tremendously greater cross-sex interaction of the former would leave its mark.

With respect to our second hypothesis, that because of differences in control of rewards and punishments and in ability to discriminate between self and other roles the effects of role-taking would be more pronounced for the younger child, an examination of Tables 2 and 3 again seems to support the hypothesis. While the younger, as contrasted with the older, girl with a brother manifests only a slightly greater degree of masculinity, this difference for boys is quite striking: the younger, as contrasted with the older, boy with a sister is substantially more feminine.

With respect to our third hypothesis, that on the assumption of interaction varying inversely with age-gap and greater interaction producing greater role-taking, the effects of role-taking would be largest for the sibs closest in age, the results in both tables are negligible. One might discern some such relationship for the boy with an older sister, and the girl with an older brother, but even here it is tenuous. Because the assumption that interaction varies with sib age differences may in fact be untenable, we cannot in this instance say we have made a direct test of the hypothesis that more frequent interaction produces more role assimilation. Since the first hypothesis, which in essence states the same point, was so strongly confirmed, our inclination is to reject our assumption that interaction varies with age difference, at least to a degree sufficient to produce differences in role-taking.

There are two further aspects of Tables 2 and 3 which are quite noticeable and which need comment. We refer first to the fact that girls with brothers appear to be masculine to a greater degree than do any of the males themselves. The simplest and most likely explanation, hence the one which we favor, is that this result occurs because of certain biases in the teachers' ratings. We submit that teachers implicitly rated boys and girls on different scales, i.e., girls were implicitly rated on a girls' scale, boys on a boys' scale. The girl with an extreme masculine trait—extreme, that is, for a girl—receives a very high rating; a boy with the same absolute degree of such a trait, or even more of it, would on the boys' scale not be extreme and his rating consequently would be reduced. In the subsequent analysis of variance, where the male and female ratings are treated as if on the same absolute scale, certain girls extremely high for girls would score significantly higher than even certain boys high on the trait. To some extent we see the same effect in reverse for the younger boys with an older sister; while not being more feminine than girls, they almost tie certain girls, e.g., older girls with younger sisters. The probable use of different implicit rating scales, the implausibility of any group of girls being more masculine than all boys, and the important fact that when girls and boys are assuredly rated on the same absolute scale (e.g., **3, 17**) boys regularly outscore girls on masculine traits, all tend to support this interpretation.

The second additional aspect of the tables which merits discussion is that all girls seem to be more feminine than the boys are masculine; indeed, the major characteristic of the boys is to be antifeminine, not masculine. In part this is explained by the assumed bias in the ratings mentioned above; boys are outscored on their own traits by some girls. In part also this is explained by the preponderance of feminine traits used in the ratings, so that boys could only express their masculinity, as it were, by being rated low on such traits. In part, and an intriguing part indeed, it may be explained by certain developmental processes commonly assumed in clinical theory and recently put in a role theory context by Parsons (**11**, pp. 95-101). Parsons points out that both boy and girl first identify with the mother and tend to play an expressive role. In development the boy must break away and establish a new identification with the father, which is difficult and involves much new learning, in the role-taking sense. At the same time, the boy must "push far and hard to renounce dependency." Girls, continuing identification with the mother and the expressive role, face neither of these problems. It may be, then, that the girls' femininity and the boys' antifemininity and yet lack of masculinity which shows itself in Tables 2 and 3 arises in part because the children have been caught by the raters at an age where the boy is trying to shift his identification from mother to father.

To conclude, our analysis of Helen Koch's data indicates that cross-sex siblings tend to assimilate traits of the opposite sex, and that this effect is most pronounced in the younger of the two siblings. These findings support the role-learning theory presented here, and also stand as a substantive contribution to the area of sex-role learning. We wish now to stress two points mentioned earlier.

First, these findings must be subject to strict limitations to two-child families. Not only does the Fauls and Smith study demonstrate this limitation with regard to only-child families, but observation suggests that in larger families other variables come into play; e.g., in the four-child family with a three and one sex split, parents may actively help the solitary child in differentiating sex roles; or in the four-child family with a two and two split, siblings may pair off by sex and the cross-sex role-taking effect is minimized.

Second, with respect to the substantive value of these results, we would point out that even though parents must remain as the major source of sex-role learning, almost every child has a mother and father to learn from. Hence, the variations in type and amount of sex-role learning occur on top of this base, so to speak, and in this variability the effect of a same or a cross-sex sib may play as large or larger a role than variations in parental behavior, mixed versus single-sexed schooling, sex of neighborhood playmates, and the like. Speculations on the durable and considerable effects of sex of sib on sex-role learning thus seem warranted and lead one to consider problems such as the effect of sex of sibling on one's later role in the marital relation, on career choices, and on other correlates of the adult sex role.

SUMMARY

This paper reports some relations between ordinal position, sex of sibling, and sex-role learning by children in two-child families. The findings are based on a further analysis of Helen Koch's data relating personality traits of children to their sex, sex of sibling, ordinal position, and age difference from sibling. In this analysis the personality traits were classified as pertaining either to the instrumental (masculine) role or the expressive (feminine) role. The distribution of such traits in children as a correlate of family structure was then assessed.

General propositions describing role learning in terms of interaction with others, including taking the role of the other, leads to hypotheses that cross-sex siblings will have more traits of the opposite sex than will same-sex siblings, and that this effect will be greater for the younger, as contrasted with the older, sibling. Both hypotheses are confirmed by the data presented.

REFERENCES

1. BRIM, O. G., JR., "The Parent-Child Relation as a Social System: I. Parent and Child Roles," *Child Development*, 1957, **28**, 344–364.
2. COTTRELL, L. S., JR., "The Analysis of Situational Fields in Social Psychology," *American Sociological Review*, 1942, **7**, 370–382.
3. FAULS, L. B., and W. D. SMITH, "Sex Role Learning of Five-Year-Olds," *Journal of Genetic Psychology*, 1956, **89**, 105–117.
4. KOCH, H. L., "The Relation of 'Primary Mental Abilities' in Five- and Six-Year-Olds to Sex of Child and Characteristics of His Sibling," *Child Development*, 1954, **25**, 210–223.
5. KOCH, H. L., "Some Personality Correlates of Sex, Sibling Position, and Sex of Sibling Among Five- and Six-Year-Old Children," *Genetic Psychology Monographs*, 1955, **52**, 3–50.
6. KOCH, H. L., "The Relation of Certain Family Constellation Characteristics and the Attitudes of Children Toward Adults," *Child Development*, 1955, **26**, 13–40.
7. KOCH, H. L., "Attitudes of Children Toward Their Peers as Related to Certain Characteristics of Their Sibling," *Psychological Monographs*, 1956, **70**, No. 19, (whole No. 426).
8. KOCH, H. L., "Children's Work Attitudes and Sibling Characteristics," *Child Development*, 1956, **27**, 289–310.
9. KOCH, H. L., "Sibling Influence on Children's Speech," *Journal of Speech and Hearing Disorders*, 1956, **21**, 322–328.
10. KOCH, H. L., "Sissiness and Tomboyishness in Relation to Sibling Characteristics," *Journal of Genetic Psychology*, 1956, **88**, 231–244.
11. PARSONS, T., "Family Structure and the Socialization of the Child," in T. Parsons and R. F. Bales, *Family, Socialization and Interaction Process*, Glencoe, Illinois: Free Press, 1955.
12. PAYNE, D. E., and P. H. MUSSEN, "Parent-

Child Relations and Father Identification Among Adolescent Boys," *Journal of Abnormal and Social Psychology*, 1956, **52**, 359–362.

13. SEARS, P. S., "Child-Rearing Factors Related to Playing of Sex-Typed Roles," *American Psychologist*, 1953, **8**, 431 (abstract).

14. SEARS, R. R., M. H. PINTLER, and P. S. SEARS, "Effect of Father Separation on Pre-school Children's Doll Play Aggression," *Child Development*, 1946, **17**, 219–243.

15. STRAUSS, A., *The Social Psychology of George Herbert Mead*, Chicago: Phoenix Books, University of Chicago Press, 1956.

16. STRODTBECK, F. L., and R. D. MANN, "Sex Role Differentiation in Jury Deliberations," *Sociometry*, 1956, **19**, 3–11.

17. TERMAN, L. M., and L. E. TYLER, "Psychological Sex Differences," in L. Carmichael (ed.), *Manual of Child Psychology* (2nd ed.), New York: Wiley, 1954.

18. ZELDITCH, M., JR., "Role Differentiation in the Nuclear Family: A Comparative Study," in T. Parsons and R. F. Bales, *Family, Socialization and Interaction Process*, Glencoe, Illinois: Free Press, 1955.

BASES FOR CHOICE OF A MODEL IN IDENTIFICATION*

The selection to follow presents several theoretical bases for choosing a model to identify with. An experiment designed to allow children in a nursery school setting to make a choice on these several bases is conducted to test the interpretations. The results favoring certain models over others are discussed in terms of their relevance to existing notions of identification.

While a single experiment does not permit us to make a final decision in favor of a particular theory of identification, this type of experiment conducted in different contexts and under different conditions will ultimately lead to the development of more precise conceptualizations of identification which can be buttressed by empirical data that systematically pertain to such conceptualizations.

51.

A Comparative Test of the Status Envy, Social Power, and Secondary Reinforcement Theories of Identificatory Learning[1]

ALBERT BANDURA
DOROTHEA ROSS[2]
SHEILA A. ROSS
STANFORD UNIVERSITY

Predictions derived from 3 prominent theories of identificatory learning were tested in 3-person groups representing prototypes of the nuclear family. In 1 condition an adult assumed the role of controller of positive reinforcers. Another adult was the consumer of these resources, while the child, a participant observer in the triad, was essentially ignored. In a 2nd treatment condition, one adult controlled the rewarding resources; the child, however, was the recipient of the positive reinforcers, while the other adult was assigned a subordinate and powerless role. Following the experimental social interactions the 2 adult models exhibited divergent patterns of behavior in the presence of the child, and a measure was obtained of the degree to which the child subsequently patterned his behavior after that of the models. Children imitated primarily the model who possessed rewarding power rather than the competitor for the rewards. Moreover, power inversions on the part of the male and female models produced cross-sex imitation, particularly in girls.

Although it is generally assumed that social behavior is learned and modified through direct reward and punishment of instrumental responses, informal observation and laboratory study of the social learning process reveal that new responses may be rapidly acquired and existing behavioral repertoires may be considerably changed as a function of observing the behavior and attitudes exhibited by models (Bandura, 1962).

The latter type of learning is generally labeled "imitation" in behavior theory, and "identification" in most theories of personality. These concepts, however, are treated in the present paper as synonymous since both encompass the same be-

* The selection following the editorial introduction is reprinted from "A comparative test of the status envy, social power, and secondary reinforcement theories of identificatory learning," *Journal of Abnormal and Social Psychology*, 1963, **67**, 527–534, by permission of the authors and the American Psychological Association.

[1] This investigation was supported by Research Grant M-5162 from the National Institutes of Health, United States Public Health Service.

The authors are indebted to Beverly Busching, Malka Yaari, Nancy Wiggins, and John Steinbruner, who assisted in collecting the data.

[2] This research was carried out while the junior author was the recipient of an American Association of University Women International Fellowship for postdoctoral research.

havioral phenomenon, i.e., the tendency for a person to match the behavior, attitudes, or emotional reactions as exhibited by actual or symbolized models. While the defining properties of identification are essentially the same in different personality theories, a host of divergent learning conditions have been proposed as the necessary antecedent variables for matching or identificatory behavior (Bronfenbrenner, 1960; Freud, 1946; Freud, 1924, 1948; Kagan, 1958; Klein, 1949; Maccoby, 1959; Mowrer, 1950; Parsons, 1955; Sears, 1957; Whiting, 1960).

In the experiment reported in this paper predictions were derived from three of the more prominent theories of learning by identification, and tested in three-person groups representing prototypes of the nuclear family. In one condition of the experiment an adult assumed the role of controller of resources and positive reinforcers. Another adult was the consumer or recipient of these resources, while the child, a participant observer in the triad, was essentially ignored. In a second treatment condition, one adult controlled the resources; the child, however, was the recipient of the positive reinforcers and the other adult was assigned a subordinate and powerless role. An adult male and female served as models in each of the triads. For half the boys and girls in each condition the male model controlled and dispensed the rewarding resources, simulating the husband dominant family; for the remaining children, the female model mediated the positive resources as in the wife dominant home. Following the experimental social interactions the two adult models exhibited divergent patterns of behavior in the presence of the child, and a measure was obtained of the degree to which the child subsequently patterned his behavior after that of the models.

According to the *status envy theory* of identification recently proposed by Whiting (1959, 1960), when a child competes unsuccessfully with an adult for affection, attention, food, and care, the child will envy the consumer adult and consequently identify with him. Whiting's theory represents an extension of the Freudian defensive identification hypothesis that identificatory behavior is the outcome of rivalrous interaction between the child and the parent who occupies an envied consumer status. While Freud presents the child as in competition with the father primarily for the mother's sexual and affectional attention, Whiting regards any forms of reward, material and social, as valued resources around which rivalry may develop. The status envy theory thus predicts that the highest degree of imitation by the child will occur in the experimental condition in which the rivalrous adult consumes the resources desired by the child, with the consumer adult serving as the primary object of imitation.

In contrast to the envy theory, other writers (Maccoby, 1959; Mussen & Distler, 1959; Parsons, 1955) assume that the controller, rather than the consumer, of resources is the main source of imitative behavior. The *power theory* of social influence has received considerable attention in experimental social psychology, though not generally in the context of identification theories.

Social power is typically defined as the ability of a person to influence the behavior of others by controlling or mediating their positive and negative reinforcements. French and Raven (1959) have distinguished five types of power based on expertness, attractiveness, legitimacy, coerciveness, and rewarding power, each of which is believed to have somewhat differential effects on the social influence process. For example, the use of threat or coercion, in which the controller derives power from his ability to administer punishments, not only develops avoidance behavior toward the controller but also decreases his attractiveness and hence his effectiveness in altering the behavior of others beyond the immediate social influence setting (French, Morrison, & Levinger, 1960; Zipf, 1960). The use of reward power, in contrast, both fosters approach responses toward the power figure and increases his attractiveness or secondary reward value through the repeated association of his attributes with positive reinforcement. Attractiveness is assumed to extend the controller's power over a wide range of behavior (French & Raven, 1959).

In the present investigation power based upon the ability to dispense rewards was manipulated experimentally. In accordance with the social power theory of identification, but contrasting with the status envy hypothesis, one would predict that children will reproduce more of the behavior of the adult who controls positive reinforcers, than that of the powerless adult model, and that power inversions on the part of the male and female models will produce cross-sex imitation.

The *secondary reinforcement theory* of identification, which has been alluded to in the discussion of social power through attractiveness, has been elaborated in greatest detail by Mowrer (1950, 1958). According to this view, as a model mediates the child's biological and social rewards, the behavioral attributes of the model are paired repeatedly with positive reinforcement and thus acquire secondary reward value. On the basis of stimulus generalization, responses which match those of the model attain reinforcing value for the child in proportion to their similarity to those made by the model. Consequently, the child can administer positively conditioned reinforcers to himself simply by reproducing as closely as possible the model's positively valenced behavior. This theory predicts that the experimental condition in which the child was the recipient of positive reinforcements will yield the highest imitation scores with the model who dispensed the rewards serving as the primary source of imitative behavior.

METHOD

Subjects

The subjects were of 36 boys and 36 girls enrolled in the Stanford University Nursery School. They ranged in age from 33 to 65 months, although the variability was relatively small with most of the ages falling around the mean of 51 months.

An adult male and female served as models in the triads so as to reproduce possible power structures encountered in different types of family constellations. A female experimenter conducted the study for all 72 children.

Design and procedure

The subjects were assigned randomly to two experimental groups and one control group of 24 subjects each. Half the subjects in each group were males, and half were females.

High rewarding power was induced experimentally through the manipulation of material and social reinforcements, and the use of verbal structuring techniques. While accompanying the child to the experimental room, for example, the experimenter informed the child that the adult who assumed the role of controller owned the nursery school "surprise room," as well as a fabulous collection of play materials. After introducing the child to the controller, the experimenter asked whether the child may play in the surprise room. The controller explained that he was on his way to his car to fetch some of his most attractive toys, but the experimenter and the child could proceed to the room where he would join them shortly. As the controller left, the experimenter commented on how lucky they were to have access to the controller's play materials.

On the way to the experimental room they met the other adult who insisted on joining them but the experimenter informed her that she would have to obtain permission from the controller since he owned the room, and it was doubtful whether sufficient play materials were available for both the adult and the child. This brief encounter with the other adult was designed primarily to create the set that rewards were available to one person only and thereby to induce rivalrous feelings over the controller's resources.

As soon as the experimenter and the child arrived in the experimental room, they sat down at a small table and played with the few Lincoln Logs and two small cars that were provided. A short time later the other adult appeared and announced that the controller also granted her permission to play in the room.

The controller then entered carrying two large toy boxes containing a variety of highly attractive masculine and feminine toys, a colorful juice dispensing fountain, and an ample supply of cookies. As soon as the controller appeared on the scene, the experimenter departed.

For children in the Adult Consumer condition, the adult who assumed the role of consumer requested permission to play with the articles and the controller replied that, since the child appeared to be occupied at his table, the consumer was free to use the play materials. This monopolistic move by the consumer adult left the child stranded at a table with two relatively uninteresting toys.

During the 20-minute play session, the controller offered the consumer, among other things, miniature pinball machines, mechanical sparkling toys, kaleidoscopes, dolls, and actively participated with the consumer in dart games and other activities. To add to the credibility of the situation, both the controller and consumer devoted most of their attention to articles, such as the pinball machine and dart game, which could be used in adult appropriate activities. Throughout the interaction the controller was most helpful, supportive, and generous in dispensing social reinforcers in the form of praise, approval, and positive attention. The consumer, in turn, commented frequently on the controller's highly attractive resources so as to further enhance the controller's rewarding status. The consumer also verbalized considerable positive affect characteristic of a person experiencing positive reinforcements.

Approximately half way through the session, the controller remarked, "Say, you look hungry. I have just the thing for you." He then brought forth the soda fountain dispenser, poured colorful fruit juices into paper cups and served them to the consumer along with a generous supply of cookies. While the consumer was enjoying his snack, the controller turned on a "TV-radio" that played a nursery melody while a revolving dial displayed a series of storybook scenes.

Toward the end of the session, the controller informed the consumer that he will be leaving on a shopping trip to San Francisco that afternoon, and asked the consumer if there was anything special she would like him to buy for her. The consumer requested a super two-wheel bicycle, a high status object among the nursery school children. The controller promised to purchase the bicycle along with any other items the consumer might think of before the controller departed for the city.

The procedure for the Child Consumer condition was identical with that described above except the child was the recipient of the material rewards and the social reinforcement. During the session the other adult sat at the opposite end of the room engrossed in a book, and was totally ignored by the controller. In discussing the prospective San Francisco shopping trip, the controller mentioned to the child that he was planning to visit some toy stores in the city that afternoon, and asked for suggestions of attractive toys he might purchase for future play sessions with children.

For half the boys and girls in each treatment condition the male model controlled and dispensed the resources, simulating the husband dominant family; for the remaining children the female model mediated the positive resources as in the wife dominant home.

At the completion of the social interaction session the controller announced that he had a surprise game in his car that the three of them could play together. The controller then asked the other adult to fetch the experimenter to assist them with the game, and as soon as the adult departed, the controller removed the toys and assembled the imitation task apparatus.

Imitation task

The imitation task was essentially the same two-choice discrimination problem utilized in an earlier experiment (Bandura & Huston, 1961), except the response repertoires exhibited by the models were considerably extended, and the procedure used in the acquisition trials was somewhat modified.

The apparatus consisted of two small boxes with hinged lids, identical in color and size. The boxes were placed on stools approximately 4 feet apart and 8 feet from the starting point. On the lid of each box was a rubber doll.

As soon as the other adult returned with the experimenter, the controller asked both the child and the experimenter to be seated in the chairs along the side of the room, and the other adult to stand at the starting point, while the controller described the game they were about to play. The controller then explained that the experimenter would hide a picture sticker in one of the two boxes and the object of the game was to guess which box contained the sticker. The adults would have the first set of turns, following which the child would play the guessing game.

The discrimination problem was employed simply as a cover task that occupied the children's attention while at the same time permitted observation of the models as they performed divergent patterns of behavior during the discrimination trials in the absence of any set to attend to or learn the responses exhibited by the models.

Before commencing the trials, the controller invited the other participants to join him in selecting a "thinking cap" from hat racks containing two identical sets of four sailor caps, each of which had a different colored feather. The controller selected the green feathered hat, remarked, "Feather in the front" and wore the hat with the feather facing forward. The other model selected the yellow feathered hat, commented, "Feather in the back," and placed the hat on her head with the feather facing backward. The child then made his choice from the four hats in the lower rack and it was noted whether he matched the color preference, hat placement, and the verbal responses of the one or the other model.

The models then went to the starting point, the child returned to his seat, and the experimenter loaded both boxes with sticker pictures for the models' trials.

During the execution of each trial, each model exhibited a different set of relatively novel verbal and motor responses that were totally irrelevant to the discrimination problem to which the child's attention was directed. At the starting point the controller stood with his arms crossed, but at the experimenter's warning not to look, the controller placed his hands over his eyes, faced sideways, and asked, "Ready?" The other model stood with his arms on his hips, then squatted with his back turned to the boxes, and asked, "Now?"

As soon as the experimenter gave the signal for the first trial, the controller remarked, "Forward march" and began marching slowly toward the designated box repeating, "March, march, march." When he reached the box he said, "Sock him," hit the doll aggressively off the box, opened the lid and yelled, "Bingo," as he reached down for the sticker. He then remarked, "Lickit-sticket," as he pressed on the picture sticker with his thumb in the upper-right quadrant of a 24 × 24 inch sheet of plain white paper that hung on the wall immediately behind the boxes. The controller terminated the trial by replacing the doll facing sideways on the container with the comment, "Look in the mirror," and made a final verbal response, "There."

The other model then took her turn and performed a different set of imitative acts but equated with the controller's responses in terms of number, types of response classes represented, structural properties, and interest value. At the starting point, for example, she remarked, "Get set, go" and walked stiffly toward the boxes repeating "Left, right, left, right." When she reached the container she said, "Down and up," as she lay the doll down on the lid and opened the box. She then exclaimed, "A stickeroo," repeated, "Weto-smacko," and slapped on the sticker with the open hand in the lower-left quadrant of the sheet of paper. In terminating the trial, the model lay the doll on the lid of the container with the remark, "Lie down," and returned with her hands behind her back, and emitted the closing remark, "That's it."

The two sets of responses were counterbalanced by having the models display each pattern with half the subjects in each of the three groups.

The models performed alternately for four trials. At the conclusion of the fourth trial the controller explained that he had to check some materials in his car and while he and the other model were away the child may take his turns. Before they departed, however, the experimenter administered a picture preference test in which the models were asked to select their preferred picture from six different stickers pasted on a 5 × 8 inch card, after which the child was presented a similar card containing an identical set of stickers and requested to indicate his preference.

In addition to the introductory block of four trials by the models, the child's 15 total test trials were interspersed with three two-trial blocks by the models. The models were always absent from the room during the child's test series. This procedure was adopted in order to remove any imagined situational restraints against, or coercion for, the child to reproduce the models' responses. Moreover, demonstrations of delayed imitation in the absence of the model provides more decisive evidence for learning by means of imitation.

The models always selected different boxes, the right-left position varying from trial to trial in a fixed irregular order, and the controller always took the first turn. Although the models received stickers on each trial, the child was nonrewarded on one third of the trials in order to maintain his interest in the cover task.

At the beginning of each of the blocks of subjects' trials, the experimenter administered the picture preference test and the selection of stickers that matched the models' choices was recorded. In addition, on the eighth trial the models removed their hats and hung them in different locations in the room. If the child removed his hat during the session and placed it along side one or the other of the model's hats, this imitative act was also scored.

At the completion of the imitation phase of the experiment, the children were interviewed by the experimenter in order to determine whom they considered to be the controller of resources, and to assess their model preferences. The latter data were used as an index of attraction to the models. In addition, for the children in the adult consumer condition, the session was concluded by providing them the same lavish treatment accorded their adult rival.

Children in the control group had no prior social interaction with the models but participated with them in the imitative learning phase of the study. The experimenter assumed complete charge of the procedures and treated the models as though they were naive subjects. This control group was included primarily to determine the models' relative effectiveness as modeling stimuli. In addition, the models alternated between subjects in the order in which they executed the trials so as to test for the possibility of a primacy or a recency of exposure effect on imitative behavior.

Imitation scores

The imitation scores were obtained by summing the frequency of occurrence of the postural, verbal, and motor responses described in the preceding section, and the hat, color, and picture preferences that matched the selections of each of the two models.

The children's performances were scored by three raters who observed the experimental sessions through a one-way mirror from an adjoining observation room. The raters were provided with a separate check list of responses exhibited by each of the two models, and the scoring procedure simply involved checking the imitative responses performed by the children on each trial. In order to provide an estimate of interscorer reliability, the performances of 30% of the children were recorded simultaneously but independently by two observers. The raters were in perfect agreement on 95% of the specific imitative responses that they scored.

RESULTS

The control group data revealed that the two models were equally effective in eliciting imitative responses, the mean values being 17.83 and 20.46 for the male and female model, respectively; nor did the children display differential imitation of same-sex ($M = 22.30$) and opposite-sex ($M = 18.50$) models. Although children in the control group tended to imitate the second model ($M = 22.21$) to a somewhat greater extent than the one who performed first ($M = 16.08$) on each trial, suggesting a recency of exposure effect, the difference was not of statistically significant magnitude ($t = 1.60$).

Table 1 presents the mean imitation scores for children in each of the two experimental triads. A $2 \times 2 \times 2 \times 2$ mixed factorial analysis of variance was computed on these data in which the four factors in the design were sex of child, sex of the model who controlled the resources, adult versus child consumer, and the controller versus the other model as the source of imitative behavior.[3] As shown in Table 2, the findings of this study clearly support the social power theory of imitation. In both experimental treatments, regardless of whether the rival adult or the children themselves were the recipients of the rewarding resources, the model who possessed rewarding power was imitated to a greater degree than was the rival or the ignored model ($F = 40.61$, $p < .001$). Nor did the condition combining resource ownership with direct reinforcement of the child yield the highest imitation of the model who controlled and dispensed the positive rewards. The latter finding is particularly surprising since an earlier experiment based on two-person groups (Bandura & Huston, 1961), demonstrated that pairing of model with positive reinforcement substantially enhanced the occurrence of imitative behavior. An examination of the remaining significant interaction effects together with the postexperimental interview data suggest a possible explanation for the discrepant results.

TABLE 1 Mean Number of Imitative Responses Performed by Subgroups of Children in the Experimental Triads

SUBJECTS	OBJECTS OF IMITATION			
	Male	Female	Female	Male
	Controller	Consumer	Controller	Consumer
Girls	29.00	9.67	26.00	10.00
Boys	30.17	18.67	22.33	16.17
Total	29.59	14.17	24.17	13.09
	Controller	Ignored	Controller	Ignored
Girls	22.00	16.17	31.84	22.17
Boys	29.17	16.67	26.83	34.50
Total	25.59	16.42	29.34	28.34

[3] The assistance of Eleanor Willemsen with the statistical computations is gratefully acknowledged.

The differential in the controller-other model imitation was most pronounced when the male model was the controller of resources ($F = 4.76$, $p < .05$), particularly for boys. In fact, boys who were the recipients of rewarding resources mediated by the female model tended to favor the ignored male as their object of imitation. In the postexperiment interview a number of boys in this condition spontaneously expressed sympathy for the ignored male and mild criticism of the controller for not being more charitable with her bountiful resources (for example, "She doesn't share much. John played bravely even though she didn't even share. . . . She's a bit greedy.").

As a partial check on whether this factor would tend to diminish the differential imitation of the two models, six children—three boys and three girls—participated in a modified Child Consumer treatment in which, halfway through the social interaction session, the ignored adult was informed that he too may have access to the playthings. He replied that he was quite content to read his book. This modified procedure, which removed the rivalry and the exclusion of the model, yielded four times as much imitation of the controller relative to the model who was ignored by choice.

The significant triple interaction effect indicates that the differential in the controller-other model imitation was greatest when the same-sex model mediated the positive reinforcers, and this effect was more pronounced for boys than for girls.

The data presented so far demonstrate that manipulation of rewarding power had produced differential imitation of the behavior exhibited by the two models. In order to assess whether the dispensing of positive reinforcers in the prior social interaction influenced the overall level of matching responses, the imitation scores in each of the three groups were summed across models and analyzed using a Sex × Treatment design.

The mean total imitative responses for children in the Child Consumer, Adult Consumer, and the Control group were 50.21, 40.58, and 37.88, respectively. Analysis of variance of these data reveals a significant treatment effect ($F = 3.37$, $.025 < p < .05$). Further comparisons of pairs of means by the t test, show that children in the child rewarded condition displayed significantly more imitative behavior than did children both in the Adult Consumer treatment ($t = 2.19$, $p < .05$), and those in the Control group ($t = 2.48$, $p < .02$). The Adult Consumer and Control groups, however, did not differ from each other in this respect ($t = .54$).

The model preference patterns were identical for children in the two experimental conditions and consequently, the data were combined for the statistical analysis. Of the 48 children, 32 selected the model who possessed rewarding power as the more attractive, while 16 preferred the noncontrolling adult. The greater attractiveness of the rewarding model was significant beyond the .05 level ($\chi^2 = 5.34$). The experimental triad in which

boys were the recipients of positive reinforcers while the male model was ignored, and the female consumer-girl ignored subgroup, contributed the highest preference for the noncontrolling adult.

In addition to the experimental groups discussed in the preceding section, data are available for 9 children in the Adult Consumer condition, and for 11 children in the Child Consumer treatment who revealed, in their postexperimental interviews, that they had actually attributed rewarding power to the ignored or the consumer adult despite the elaborate experimental manipulations designed to establish differential power status. A number of these children were firmly convinced that only a male can possess resources and, therefore, the female dispensing the rewards was only an intermediary for the male model (for example, "He's the man and it's all his because he's a daddy. Mommy never really has things belong to her. . . . He's the daddy so it's his but he shares nice with the mommy. . . . He's the man and the man always really has the money and he lets ladies play too. John's good and polite and he has very good manners.") This view of resource ownership within the family constellation was often directly reinforced by the mothers (for example, "My mommy told me and Joan that the daddy really buys all the things, but the mommy looks after things."). Children who attributed the resource ownership to the consumer or ignored

TABLE 2 *Summary of the Analysis of Variance of the Imitation Scores*

SOURCE	df	MS	F
Between subjects	47	310.17	
Sex of subjects (A)	1	283.59	<1
Sex of controller model (B)	1	128.34	<1
Adult versus child consumer (C)	1	518.01	1.61
$A \times B$	1	23.01	<1
$A \times C$	1	1.76	<1
$B \times C$	1	742.59	2.31
$A \times B \times C$	1	21.10	<1
Error (b)	40	321.49	
Within subjects	48	113.24	
Controller versus other model (D)	1	2,025.84	40.61‡
$A \times D$	1	297.51	5.96*
$B \times D$	1	237.51	4.76*
$C \times D$	1	396.09	7.94†
$A \times B \times D$	1	256.76	5.15*
$A \times C \times D$	1	19.52	<1
$B \times C \times D$	1	23.02	<1
$A \times B \times C \times D$	1	184.00	3.69
Error (w)	40	49.88	

* $p < .05$.   † $p < .01$.   ‡ $p < .001$.

female model had considerable difficulty in explaining their selection (for example, "I just knowed it does. . . . I could tell, that's how."), perhaps, because the power structure they depicted is at variance with the widely accepted cultural norm.

As shown in Table 3, models who were attributed rewarding power elicited approximately twice as many matching responses than models who were perceived by the children as possessing no control over the rewarding resources. Because of the small and unequal number of cases in each cell, these data were not evaluated statistically. The differences, however, are marked and quite in accord with those produced by the experimentally manipulated variations in power status.

DISCUSSION

To the extent that the imitative behavior elicited in the present experiment may be considered an elementary prototype of identification within a nuclear family group, the data fail to support the interpretation of identificatory learning as the outcome of a rivalrous interaction between the child and the adult who occupies an envied status in respect to the consumption of highly desired resources. Children clearly identified with the source of rewarding power rather than with the competitor for these rewards. Moreover, power inversions on the part of the male and female models produced cross-sex imitation, particularly in girls. The differential readiness of boys and girls to imitate behavior exhibited by an opposite-sex model are consistent with findings reported by Brown (1956, 1958) that boys show a decided preference for the masculine role, whereas, ambivalence and masculine role preference are widespread among girls. These findings probably reflect both the differential cultural tolerance for cross-sex behavior displayed by males and females, and the privileged status and relatively greater positive reinforcement of masculine role behavior in our society.

Failure to develop sex appropriate behavior

has received considerable attention in the clinical literature and has customarily been assumed to be established and maintained by psychosexual threat and anxiety reducing mechanisms. Our findings strongly suggest, however, that external social learning variables, such as the distribution of rewarding power within the family constellation, may be highly influential in the formation of inverted sex role behavior.

Theories of identificatory learning have generally assumed that within the family setting the child's initial identification is confined to his mother, and that during early childhood boys must turn from the mother as the primary model to the father as the main source of imitative behavior. However, throughout the course of development children are provided with ample opportunities to observe the behavior of both parents. The results of the present experiment reveal that when children are exposed to multiple models they may select one or more of them as the primary source of behavior, but rarely reproduce all the elements of a single model's repertoire or confine their imitation to that model. Although the children adopted many of the characteristics of the model who possessed rewarding power, they also reproduced some of the elements of behavior exhibited by the model who occupied the subordinate role. Consequently, the children were not simply junior-size replicas of one or the other model; rather, they exhibited a relatively novel pattern of behavior representing an amalgam of elements from both models. Moreover, the specific admixture of behavioral elements varied from child to child. These findings provide considerable evidence for the seemingly paradoxical conclusion that imitation can in fact produce innovation of social behavior, and that within the same family even same-sex siblings may exhibit quite different response patterns, owing to their having selected for imitation different elements of their parents' response repertoires.

The association of a model with noncontingent positive reinforcement tends to increase the incidence of imitative behavior in two person groups (Bandura & Huston, 1961), whereas the addition of a same-sex third person who is denied access to desired rewards may provoke in children negative evaluations of the rewarding model and thereby decreases his potency as a modeling stimulus. These two sets of data demonstrate how learning principles based on an individual behavior model may be subject to strict limitations, since the introduction of additional social variables into the stimulus complex can produce significant changes in the functional relationships between relevant variables.

REFERENCES

BANDURA, A. Social learning through imitation. In M. R. Jones (Ed.), *Nebraska symposium*

TABLE 3 Imitation as a Function of Attributed Rewarding Power to the Models

TREATMENT CONDITION	OBJECTS OF IMITATION			
	Female Controller	Male Non-controller	Male Controller	Female Noncontroller
Adult consumer	24.0	12.3	29.8	14.6
Child consumer	18.2	6.7	35.5	16.2

on motivation: 1962. Lincoln: Univer. Nebraska Press, 1962. Pp. 211–269.

BANDURA, A., & HUSTON, ALETHA C. Identification as a process of incidental learning. *J. abnorm. soc. Psychol.,* 1961, **63,** 311–318.

BRONFENBRENNER, U. Freudian theories of identification and their derivatives. *Child Develpm.,* 1960, **31,** 15–40.

BROWN, D. G. Sex-role preference in young children. *Psychol. Monogr.,* 1956, **70** (14, Whole No. 421).

BROWN, D. G. Sex-role development in a changing culture. *Psychol. Bull.,* 1958, **55,** 232–242.

FRENCH, J. R. P., JR., MORRISON, H. W., & LEVINGER, G. Coercive power and forces affecting conformity. *J. abnorm. soc. Psychol.,* 1960, **61,** 93–101.

FRENCH, J. R. P., JR., & RAVEN, B. The bases of social power. In D. Cartwright (Ed.), *Studies in social power.* Ann Arbor, Mich.: Institute for Social Research, 1959. Pp. 150–167.

FREUD, ANNA. *The ego and the mechanisms of defense.* New York: International Univer. Press, 1946.

FREUD, S. The passing of the Oedipus-complex. In, *Collected papers.* Vol. 2. London: Hogarth Press, 1924. Pp. 269–282.

FREUD, S. *Group psychology and the analysis of the ego.* London: Hogarth Press, 1948.

KAGAN, J. The concept of identification. *Psychol. Rev.,* 1958, **65,** 296–305.

KLEIN, MELANIE. *The psycho-analysis of children.* London: Hogarth Press, 1949.

MACCOBY, ELEANOR E. Role-taking in childhood and its consequences for social learning. *Child Develpm.,* 1959, **30,** 239–252.

MOWRER, O. H. Identification: A link between learning theory and psychotherapy. In, *Learning theory and personality dynamics.* New York: Ronald Press, 1950. Pp. 69–94.

MOWRER, O. H. Hearing and speaking: An analysis of language learning. *J. speech hear. Disord.,* 1958, **23,** 143–152.

MUSSEN, P., & DISTLER, L. Masculinity, identification, and father-son relationships. *J. abnorm. soc. Psychol.,* 1959, **59,** 350–356.

PARSONS, T. Family structure and the socialization of the child. In T. Parsons & R. F. Bales (Eds.), *Family, socialization, and interaction process.* Glencoe, Ill.: Free Press, 1955. Pp. 35–131.

SEARS, R. R. Identification as a form of behavioral development. In D. B. Harris (Ed.), *The concept of development.* Minneapolis: Univer. Minnesota Press, 1957. Pp. 149–161.

WHITING, J. W. M. Sorcery, sin, and the superego: A cross-cultural study of some mechanisms of social control. In M. R. Jones (Ed.), *Nebraska symposium on motivation: 1959.* Lincoln: Univer. Nebraska Press, 1959. Pp. 174–195.

WHITING, J. W. M. Resource mediation and learning by identification. In I. Iscoe & H. W. Stevenson (Eds.), *Personality development in children.* Austin: Univer. Texas Press, 1960. Pp. 112–126.

ZIPF, SHEILA G. Resistance and conformity under reward and punishment. *J. abnorm. soc. Psychol.,* 1960, **61,** 102–109.

SOCIAL CLASS, FAMILY STRUCTURE, AND THE AMERICAN CHILD *

The selection below considers the changes in patterns of child rearing over the past twenty-five years, identifying different practices with different socioeconomic class levels. The effects of parental behaviors on child behavior are described, with particular emphasis on different optimal child-rearing practices for boys and for girls. Another important variable is an aspect of family structure: the relative degree of dominance ascribed to the father's position. The marked changes in child-rearing practices over the past few decades are expected to produce certain modifications in the behavior of the current generation as compared with past generations.

52.

The Changing American Child—A Speculative Analysis[1]

URIE BRONFENBRENNER
CORNELL UNIVERSITY

A QUESTION OF MOMENT

It is now a matter of scientific record that patterns of child rearing in the United States have changed appreciably over the past twenty-five years (Bron-

* The selection following the editorial introduction is reprinted from "The changing American child: A speculative analysis," *Journal of Social Issues,* 1961, **17,** 6–18, by permission of the author and the publisher.

[1] This paper draws heavily on results from a program of research being conducted by the author in collaboration with Edward C. Devereux and George J. Suci. The contribution of these colleagues to facts and ideas presented in this paper is gratefully acknowledged. The research program is supported in

fenbrenner, 1958). Middle class parents especially have moved away from the more rigid and strict styles of care and discipline advocated in the early Twenties and Thirties toward modes of response involving greater tolerance of the child's impulses and desires, freer expression of affection, and increased reliance on "psychological" methods of discipline, such as reasoning and appeals to guilt, as distinguished from more direct techniques like physical punishment. At the same time, the gap between the social classes in their goals and methods of child rearing appears to be narrowing, with working class parents beginning to adopt both the values and techniques of the middle class. Finally, there is dramatic correspondence between these observed shifts in parental values and behavior and the changing character of the attitudes and practices advocated in successive editions of such widely read manuals as the Children's Bureau bulletin on *Infant Care* and Spock's *Baby and Child Care*. Such correspondence should not be taken to mean that the expert has now become the principal instigator and instrument of social change, since the ideas of scientists and professional workers themselves reflect in part the operation of deep-rooted cultural processes. Nevertheless, the fact remains that changes in values and practices advocated by prestigeful professional figures can be substantially accelerated by rapid and widespread dissemination through the press, mass media of communication, and public discussion.

Given these facts, it becomes especially important to gauge the effect of the changes that are advocated and adopted. Nowhere is this issue more significant, both scientifically and socially, than in the sphere of familial values and behavior. It is certainly no trivial matter to ask whether the changes that have occurred in the attitudes and actions of parents over the past twenty-five years have been such as to affect the personality development of their children, so that the boys and girls of today are somewhat different in character structure from those of a decade or more ago. Or, to put the question more succinctly: has the changing American parent produced a changing American child?

A STRATEGY OF INFERENCE

Do we have any basis for answering this intriguing question? To begin with, do we have any evidence of changes in the behavior of children in successive decades analogous to those we have already been able to find for parents? If so, we could take an important first step toward a solu-

part with grants from the National Science Foundation and the National Institutes of Health.

tion of the problem. Unfortunately, in contrast to his gratifying experience in seeking and finding appropriate data on parents, the present writer has, to date, been unable to locate enough instances in which comparable methods of behavioral assessment have been employed with different groups of children of similar ages over an extended period of time. Although the absence of such material precludes any direct and unequivocal approach to the question at hand, it is nevertheless possible, through a series of inferences from facts already known, to arrive at some estimate of what the answer might be. Specifically, although as yet we have no comparable data on the relation between parental and child behavior for different families at successive points in time, we do have facts on the influence of parental treatment on child behavior at a given point in time; that is, we know that certain variations in parental behavior tend to be accompanied by systematic differences in the personality characteristics of children. If we are willing to assume that these same relationships obtained not only at a given moment but across different points in time, we are in a position to infer the possible effects on children of changing patterns of child rearing over the years. It is this strategy that we propose to follow.

THE CHANGING AMERICAN PARENT

We have already noted the major changes in parental behavior discerned in a recent analysis of data reported over a twenty-five year period. These secular trends may be summarized as follows:

1. Greater permissiveness toward the child's spontaneous desires
2. Freer expression of affection
3. Increased reliance on indirect "psychological" techniques of discipline (such as reasoning or appeals to guilt) vs. direct methods (like physical punishment, scolding, or threats)
4. In consequence of the above shifts in the direction of what are predominantly middle class values and techniques, a narrowing of the gap between social classes in their patterns of child rearing.

Since the above analysis was published, a new study has documented an additional trend. Bronson, Katten, and Livson (1959) have compared patterns of paternal and maternal authority and affection in two generations of families from the California Guidance Study. Unfortunately, the time span surveyed overlaps only partially with the twenty-five year period covered in our own analysis, the first California generation having been raised in the early 1900's and the second in the late '20's and early '30's. Accordingly, if we are to consider the California results along with the others cited above, we must make the somewhat risky assumption that a trend discerned in the first three decades of the century has continued in the same direction through the early 1950's. With this important qualification, an examination of the data cited by Bronson et al. (1959) points to still another, secular trend—a shift over the years in the pattern of parental role differentiation within the family. Specifically:

5. In succeeding generations the relative position of the father vis-à-vis the mother is shifting with the former becoming increasingly more affectionate and less authoritarian, and the latter becoming relatively more important as the agent of discipline, especially for boys.

"PSYCHOLOGICAL" TECHNIQUES OF DISCIPLINE AND THEIR EFFECTS

In pursuing our analytic strategy, we next seek evidence of the effects on the behavior of children of variations in parental treatment of the type noted in our inventory. We may begin by noting that the variables involved in the first three secular trends constitute a complex that has received considerable attention in recent research in parent-child relationships. Within the last three years, two sets of investigators, working independently, have called attention to the greater efficacy of "love-oriented" or "psychological" techniques in bringing about desired behavior in the child (Sears, Maccoby, and Levin, 1957; Miller and Swanson, 1958; 1960). The present writer, noting that such methods are especially favored by middle class parents, offered the following analysis of the nature of these techniques and the reasons for their effectiveness.

Such parents are, in the first place, more likely to overlook offenses, and when they do punish, they are less likely to ridicule or inflict physical pain. Instead, they reason with the youngster, isolate him, appeal to guilt, show disappointment—in short, convey in a variety of ways, on the one hand, the kind of behavior that is expected of the child; on the other, the realization that transgression means the interruption of a mutually valued relationship. . . .

These findings [of greater efficacy] mean that middle class parents, though in one sense more lenient in their discipline techniques, are using methods that are actually more compelling. Moreover, the compelling power of these practices is probably enhanced by the more permissive treatment accorded to middle class children in the early years of life. The successful use of withdrawal of love as a discipline technique implies the prior existence of a gratifying relationship; the more love present in the first instance, the greater the threat implied in its withdrawal (Bronfenbrenner, 1958).

It is now a well established fact that children from middle class families tend to excel those from lower class in many characteristics ordinarily regarded as desirable, such as self-control,

achievement, responsibility, leadership, popularity, and adjustment in general.[2] If, as seems plausible, such differences in behavior are attributable at least in part to class-linked variations in parental treatment, the strategy of inference we have adopted would appear on first blush to lead to a rather optimistic conclusion. Since, over the years, increasing numbers of parents have been adopting the more effective socialization techniques typically employed by the middle class, does it not follow that successive generations of children should show gains in the development of effective behavior and desirable personality characteristics?

Unfortunately, this welcome conclusion, however logical, is premature, for it fails to take into account all of the available facts.

SEX, SOCIALIZATION, AND SOCIAL CLASS

To begin with, the parental behaviors we have been discussing are differentially distributed not only by socio-economic status but also by sex. As we have pointed out elsewhere (Bronfenbrenner, 1961), girls are exposed to more affection and less punishment than boys, but at the same time are more likely to be subjected to "love-oriented" discipline of the type which encourages the development of internalized controls. And, consistent with our line of reasoning, girls are found repeatedly to be "more obedient, cooperative, and in general better socialized than boys at comparable age levels." But this is not the whole story.

> . . . At the same time, the research results indicate that girls tend to be more anxious, timid, dependent, and sensitive to rejection. If these differences are a function of differential treatment by parents, then it would seem that the more "efficient" methods of child rearing employed with girls involve some risk of what might be called "oversocialization" (Bronfenbrenner, 1961).

One could argue, of course, that the contrasting behaviors of boys and girls have less to do with differential parental treatment than with genetically-based maturational influences. Nevertheless, two independent lines of evidence suggest that socialization techniques do contribute to individual differences, *within the same sex*, precisely in the types of personality characteristics noted above. In the first place, variations in child behavior and parental treatment strikingly similar

[2] For a summary of findings on social class differences in children's behavior and personality characteristics, see Mussen, P. H., and Conger, J. J., *Child Development and Personality*. New York: Harper, 1956.

to those we have cited for the two sexes are reported in a recent comprehensive study of differences between first and later born children (Schachter, 1959). Like girls, first children receive more attention, are more likely to be exposed to "psychological" discipline, and end up more anxious and dependent, whereas later children, like boys, are more aggressive and self-confident.

A second line of evidence comes from our own current research. We have been concerned with the role of parents in the development of such "constructive" personality characteristics as responsibility and leadership among adolescent boys and girls. Our findings reveal not only the usual differences in adolescents' and parents' behaviors associated with the sex of the child, but also a striking contrast in the relationship between parental and child behaviors for the two sexes. To start on firm and familiar ground, girls are rated by their teachers as more responsible than boys, whereas the latter obtain higher scores on leadership. Expected differences similarly appear in the realm of parental behavior: girls receive more affection, praise, and companionship; boys are subjected to more physical punishment and achievement demands. Quite unanticipated, however, at least by us, was the finding that both parental affection and discipline appeared to facilitate effective psychological functioning in boys, but to impede the development of such constructive behavior in girls. Closer examination of our data indicated that both extremes of either affection or discipline were deleterious for all children, but that the process of socialization entailed somewhat different risks for the two sexes. Girls were especially susceptible to the detrimental influence of overprotection; boys to the ill effects of insufficient parental discipline and support. Or, to put it in more colloquial terms: boys suffered more often from too little taming, girls from too much.

In an attempt to account for this contrasting pattern of relationships, we proposed the notion of differential optimal levels of affection and authority for the two sexes.

The qualities of independence, initiative, and self-sufficiency, which are especially valued for boys in our culture, apparently require for their development a somewhat different balance of authority and affection than is found in the "love-oriented" strategy characteristically applied with girls. While an affectional context is important for the socialization of boys, it must evidently be accompanied by and be compatible with a strong component of parental discipline. Otherwise, the boy finds himself in the same situation as the girl, who, having received greater affection,

is more sensitive to its withdrawal, with the result that a little discipline goes a long way and strong authority is constricting rather than constructive (Bronfenbrenner, 1960).

What is more, available data suggest that this very process may already be operating for boys from upper middle class homes. To begin with, differential treatment of the sexes is at a minimum for these families. Contrasting parental attitudes and behaviors toward boys and girls are pronounced only at lower class levels, and decrease as one moves up the socio-economic scale (Kohn, 1959; Bronfenbrenner, 1960). Thus our own results show that it is primarily at lower middle class levels that boys get more punishment than girls, and the latter receive greater warmth and attention. With an increase in the family's social position, direct discipline drops off, especially for boys, and indulgence and protectiveness decrease for girls. As a result, patterns of parental treatment for the two sexes begin to converge. In like manner, we find that the differential effects of parental behavior on the two sexes are marked only in the lower middle class. It is here that girls especially risk being over-protected and boys not receiving sufficient discipline and support. In upper middle class the picture changes. Girls are not as readily debilitated by parental affection and power; nor is parental discipline as effective in fostering the development of responsibility and leadership in boys.

All these trends point to the conclusion that the "risks" experienced by each sex during the process of socialization tend to be somewhat different at different social class levels. Thus the danger of overprotection for girls is especially great in lower class families, but lower in upper middle class because of the decreased likelihood of overprotection. Analogously, boys are in greater danger of suffering from inadequate discipline and support in lower middle than in upper middle class. But the upper middle class boy, unlike the girl, exchanges one hazard for another. Since at this upper level the more potent "psychological" techniques of discipline are likely to be employed with both sexes, the boy presumably now too runs the risk of being "oversocialized," of losing some of his capacity for independent aggressive accomplishment.

Accordingly, if our line of reasoning is correct, we should expect a changing pattern of sex differences at successive socio-economic levels. Specifically, aspects of effective psychological functioning favoring girls should be most pronounced in the upper middle class; those favoring boys in the lower middle. A recent analysis of some of our data bears out this expectation. Girls excel boys on such variables as *responsibility* and *social acceptance* primarily at the higher socio-economic levels. In contrast, boys surpass girls on such traits as *leadership, level of aspiration,* and *competitiveness* almost exclusively in lower middle class. Indeed, with a rise in a family's social position, the differences tend to reverse themselves with girls now excelling boys.[3]

TRENDS IN PERSONALITY DEVELOPMENT: A FIRST APPROXIMATION

The implications for our original line of inquiry are clear. We are suggesting that the "love-oriented" socialization techniques, which over the past twenty-five years have been employed in increasing degree by American middle class families, may have negative as well as constructive aspects. While fostering the internalization of adult standards and the development of socialized behavior, they may also have the effect of undermining capacities for initiative and independence, particularly in boys. Males exposed to this "modern" pattern of child rearing might be expected to differ from their counterparts of a quarter century ago in being somewhat more conforming and anxious, less enterprising and self-sufficient, and, in general, possessing more of the virtues and liabilities commonly associated with feminine character structure.[4]

At long last, then, our strategy of inference has led us to a first major conclusion. The term "major" is appropriate since the conclusion takes as its points of departure and return four of the secular trends which served as the impetus for our inquiry. Specifically, through a series of empirical links and theoretical extrapolations, we have arrived at an estimate of the effects on children of the tendency of successive generations of parents to become progressively more permissive, to express affection more freely, to utilize "psychological" techniques of discipline, and, by moving in these directions to narrow the gap between the social classes in their patterns of child rearing.

FAMILY STRUCTURE AND PERSONALITY DEVELOPMENT

But one other secular trend remains to be considered: what of the changing pattern of parental role differentiation during the first three decades of the century? If our extrapolation is correct, the balance of power within the family has continued to shift with fathers yielding parental authority to mothers and taking on some of the nurturant and affectional functions traditionally associated with the maternal role. Again we have

---

[3] These shifts in sex difference with a rise in class status are significant at the 5% level of confidence (one-tailed test).

[4] Strikingly similar conclusions were reached almost fifteen years ago in a provocative essay by Arnold Green ("The Middle Class Male Child and Neurosis," *American Sociological Review*, 1946, 11, 31–41). With little to go on beyond scattered clinical observations and impressions, Green was able to detect many of the same trends which we have begun to discern in more recent systematic empirical data.

no direct evidence of the effects of such secular changes on successive generations of children, and must look for leads to analogous data on contemporaneous relationships.

We may begin by considering the contribution of each parent to the socialization processes we have examined thus far. Our data indicate that it is primarily mothers who tend to employ "love-oriented" techniques of discipline and fathers who rely on more direct methods like physical punishment. The above statement must be qualified, however, by reference to the sex of the child, for it is only in relation to boys that fathers use direct punishment more than mothers. More generally, . . . the results reveal a tendency for each parent to be somewhat more active, firm, and demanding with a child of the same sex, more lenient and indulgent with a child of the opposite sex. . . . The reversal is most complete with respect to discipline, with fathers being stricter with boys, mothers with girls. In the spheres of affection and protectiveness, there is no actual shift in preference, but the tendency to be especially warm and solicitous with girls is much more pronounced among fathers than among mothers. In fact, generally speaking, it is the father who is more likely to treat children of the two sexes differently (Bronfenbrenner, 1960).

Consistent with this pattern of results, it is primarily the behavior of fathers that accounts for the differential effects of parental behavior on the two sexes and for the individual differences within each sex. In other words, it is paternal authority and affection that tend especially to be salutary for sons but detrimental for daughters. But as might be anticipated from what we already know, these trends are pronounced only in the lower middle class; with a rise in the family's social status, both parents tend to have similar effects on their children, both within and across sexes. Such a trend is entirely to be expected since parental role differentiation tends to decrease markedly as one ascends the socio-economic ladder. It is almost exclusively in lower middle class homes that fathers are more strict with boys and mothers with girls. To the extent that direct discipline is employed in upper middle class families, it tends to be exercised by both parents equally. Here again we see a parallelism between shifts in parental behavior across time and social class in the direction of forms (in this instance of family structure) favored by the upper middle class group.

What kinds of children, then, can we expect to develop in families in which the father plays a predominantly affectionate role, and a relatively low level of discipline is exercised equally by both parents? A tentative answer to this question is supplied by a preliminary analysis of our data in which the relation between parental role structure and adolescent behavior was examined with controls for the family's social class position. The results of this analysis are summarized as follows: . . . Both responsibility and leadership are fostered by the relatively greater salience of the parent of the same sex. . . . Boys tend to be more responsible when the father rather than the mother is the principal disciplinarian; girls are more dependable when the mother is the major authority figure. . . . In short, boys thrive in a patriarchal context, girls in a matriarchal. . . . The most dependent and least dependable adolescents describe family arrangements that are neither patriarchal nor matriarchal, but equalitarian. To state the issue in more provocative form, our data suggest that the democratic family, which for so many years has been held up and aspired to as a model by professionals and enlightened laymen, tends to produce young people who "do not take initiative," "look to others for direction and decision," and "cannot be counted on to fulfill obligations" (Bronfenbrenner, 1960).

In the wake of so sweeping a conclusion, it is important to call attention to the tentative, if not tenuous character of our findings. The results were based on a single study employing crude questionnaire methods and rating scales. Also, our interpretation is limited by the somewhat "attenuated" character of most of the families classified as patriarchal or matriarchal in our sample. Extreme concentrations of power in one or another parent were comparatively rare. Had they been more frequent, we suspect the data would have shown that such extreme asymmetrical patterns of authority were detrimental rather than salutary for effective psychological development, perhaps even more disorganizing than equalitarian forms.

Nevertheless, our findings do find some peripheral support in the work of others. A number of investigations, for example, point to the special importance of the father in the socialization of boys (Bandura and Walters, 1959; Mussen and Distler, 1959). Further corroborative evidence appears in the growing series of studies of effects of paternal absence (Bach, 1946; Sears, Pintler and Sears, 1946; Lynn and Sawrey, 1959; Tiller, 1958). The absence of the father apparently not only affects the behavior of the child directly but also influences the mother in the direction of greater over-protectiveness. The effect of both these tendencies is especially critical for male children; boys from father-absent homes tend to be markedly more submissive and dependent. Studies dealing explicitly with the influence of parental role structure in intact families are few

and far between. Papanek (1957), in an unpublished doctoral dissertation, reports greater sex-role differentiation among children from homes in which the parental roles were differentiated. And in a carefully controlled study, Kohn and Clausen (1956) find that "schizophrenic patients more frequently than normal persons report that their mothers played a very strong authority role and the father a very weak authority role." Finally, what might best be called complementary evidence for our inferences regarding trends in family structure and their effects comes from the work of Miller, Swanson, and their associates (1958; 1960) on the differing patterns of behavior exhibited by families from *bureaucratic* and *entrepreneurial* work settings. These investigators argue that the entrepreneurial-bureaucratic dichotomy represents a new cleavage in American social structure that cuts across and overrides social class influences and carries with it is own characteristic patterns of family structure and socialization. Thus one investigation (Gold and Slater, 1958) contrasts the exercise of power in families of husbands employed in two kinds of job situations: *a*) those working in large organizations with three or more levels of supervision; *b*) those self-employed or working in small organizations with few levels of supervision. With appropriate controls for social class, equalitarian families were found more frequently in the bureaucratic groups; patriarchal and, to a lesser extent, matriarchal in the entrepreneurial setting. Another study (Miller and Swanson, 1958) shows that, in line with Miller and Swanson's hypotheses, parents from these same two groups tend to favor rather different ends and means of socialization, with entrepreneurial families putting considerably more emphasis on the development of independence and mastery and on the use of "psychological" techniques of discipline. These differences appear at both upper and lower middle class levels but are less pronounced in higher socio-economic strata. It is Miller and Swanson's belief, however, that the trend is toward the bureaucratic way of life, with its less structured patterns of family organization and child rearing. The evidence we have cited on secular changes in family structure and the inferences we have drawn regarding their possible effects on personality development are on the whole consistent with their views.

LOOKING FORWARD

If Miller and Swanson are correct in the prediction that America is moving toward a bureaucratic society that emphasizes, to put it colloquially, "getting along" rather than "getting ahead," then presumably we can look forward to ever increasing numbers of equalitarian families who, in turn, will produce successive generations of ever more adaptable but unaggressive "organization men."

But recent signs do not all point in this direction. In our review of secular trends in child rearing practices we detected in the data from the more recent studies a slowing up in the headlong rush toward greater permissiveness and toward reliance on indirect methods of discipline. We pointed out also that if the most recent editions of well-thumbed guidebooks on child care are as reliable harbingers of the future as they have been in the past, we can anticipate something of a return to the more explicit discipline techniques of an earlier era. Perhaps the most important forces, however, acting to redirect both the aims and methods of child rearing in America emanate from behind the Iron Curtain. With the firing of the first Sputnik, Achievement began to replace Adjustment as the highest goal of the American way of life. We have become concerned—perhaps even obsessed—with "education for excellent" and the maximal utilization of our intellectual resources. Already, ability grouping, and the guidance counsellor who is its prophet, have moved down from the junior high to the elementary school, and parents can be counted on to do their part in preparing their youngsters for survival in the new competitive world of applications and achievement tests.

But if a new trend in parental behavior is to develop, it must do so in the context of changes already under way. And if the focus of parental authority is shifting from husband to wife, then perhaps we should anticipate that pressures for achievement will be imposed primarily by mothers rather than fathers. Moreover, the mother's continuing strong emotional investment in the child should provide her with a powerful lever for evoking desired performance. It is noteworthy in this connection that recent studies of the familial origins of need-achievement point to the matriarchy as the optimal context for development of the motive to excel (Strodtbeck, 1958; Rosen and D'Andrade, 1959).

The prospect of a society in which socialization techniques are directed toward maximizing achievement drive is not altogether a pleasant one. As a number of investigators have shown (Baldwin, Kalhorn and Breese, 1945; Baldwin, 1948; Haggard, 1957; Winterbottom, 1958; Rosen and D'Andrade, 1959), high achievement motivation appears to flourish in a family atmosphere of "cold democracy" in which initial high levels of maternal involvement are followed by pressures for independence and accomplishment.[5] Nor

---

[5] Cold democracy under female administration appears to foster the development of achievement not only in the home but in the classroom as well. In a review of research on teaching effectiveness, Ackerman reports that teachers most successful in bringing about gains in achievement score for their pupils were judged "least considerate," while those thought friendly and congenial were least effective. (Ackerman, W. I., "Teacher Competence and Pupil Change," *Harvard Educational Review*, 1954, **24**, 273–289.)

does the product of this process give ground for reassurance. True, children from achievement-oriented homes excel in planfulness and performance, but they are also more aggressive, tense, domineering, and cruel (Baldwin, Kalhorn and Breese, 1945; Baldwin, 1948; Haggard, 1957). It would appear that education for excellence if pursued single-mindedly may entail some sobering social costs.

But by now we are in danger of having stretched our chain of inference beyond the strength of its weakest link. Our speculative analysis has become far more speculative than analytic and to pursue it further would bring us past the bounds of science into the realms of science fiction. In concluding our discussion, we would re-emphasize that speculations should, by their very nature, be held suspect. It is for good reason that, like "damn Yankees" they too carry their almost inseparable sobriquets: speculations are either "idle" or "wild." Given the scientific and social importance of the issues we have raised, we would dismiss the first of these labels out of hand, but the second cannot be disposed of so easily. Like the impetuous child, the "wild" speculation responds best to the sobering influence of friendly but firm discipline, in this instance from the hand of the behavioral scientist. As we look ahead to the next twenty-five years of human socialization, let us hope that the "optimal levels" of involvement and discipline can be achieved not only by the parent who is unavoidably engaged in the process, but also by the scientist who attempts to understand its working, and who—also unavoidably—contributes to shaping its course.

REFERENCES

1. BACH, G. R., "Father-Fantasies and Father-Typing in Father-Separated Children," *Child Development*, 1946, **17**, 63–79.

2. BALDWIN, A. L., KALHORN, J., AND BREESE, F. H., "The Appraisal of Parent Behavior," *Psychological Monographs*, 1945, **58**, No. 3 (Whole No. 268).

3. BALDWIN, A. L., "Socialization and the Parent-Child Relationship," *Child Development*, 1948, **19**, 127–136.

4. BANDURA, A., AND WALTERS, R. H., *Adolescent Aggression*. New York: Ronald Press, 1959.

5. BRONFENBRENNER, U., "Socialization and Social Class Through Time and Space," in Maccoby, E., Newcomb, T. M., and Hartley, E. L., *Readings in Social Psychology*. New York: Holt, 1958, pp. 400–425.

6. BRONFENBRENNER, U., "Some Familial Antecedents of Responsibility and Leadership in

Adolescents," in Petrullo, L., and Bass, B. M., *Leadership and Interpersonal Behavior*, New York: Holt, Rinehart, and Winston, 1961.

7. BRONSON, W. C., KATTEN, E. S., AND LIVSON, N., "Patterns of Authority and Affection in Two Generations," *Journal of Abnormal and Social Psychology*, 1959, **58**, pp. 143–152.

8. GOLD, M., AND SLATER, C., "Office, Factory, Store—and Family: A Study of Integration Setting," *American Sociological Review*, 1959, **23**, 64–74.

9. HAGGARD, E. A., "Socialization, Personality, and Academic Achievement in Gifted Children," *The School Review*, 1957, **65**, 388–414.

10. KOHN, M. L., AND CLAUSEN, J. A., "Parental Authority Behavior and Schizophrenia," *American Journal of Orthopsychiatry*, 1956, **26**, 297–313.

11. KOHN, M. L., "Social Class and Parental Values," *American Journal of Sociology*, 1959, **44**, 337–351.

12. LYNN, D. B., AND SAWREY, W. L., "The Effects of Father-Absence on Norwegian Boys and Girls," *Journal of Abnormal and Social Psychology*, 1959, **59**, 258–262.

13. MILLER, D. R., AND SWANSON, G. E., *The Changing American Parent*. New York: John Wiley, 1958.

14. MILLER, D. R., AND SWANSON, G. E., *Inner Conflict and Defense*. New York: Holt, 1960.

15. MUSSEN, P., AND DISTLER, L., "Masculinity, Identification, and Father-Son Relationships," *Journal of Abnormal and Social Psychology*, 1959, **59**, 350–356.

16. PAPANEK, M., *Authority and Interpersonal Relations in the Family*. Unpublished doctoral dissertation on file at the Radcliffe College Library, 1957.

17. ROSEN, B. L., AND D'ANDRADE, R., "The Psychosocial Origins of Achievement Motivation," *Sociometry*, 1959, **22**, 185–217.

18. SCHACHTER, S., *The Psychology of Affiliation*. Stanford, California: Stanford University Press, 1959.

19. SEARS, R. R., PINTLER, M. H., AND SEARS, P. S., "Effects of Father-Separation on Preschool Children's Doll Play Aggression," *Child Development*, 1946, **17**, 219–243.

20. SEARS, R. R., MACCOBY, ELEANOR, AND LEVIN, M., *Patterns of Child Rearing*. Evanston, Illinois: Row, Peterson, 1957.

21. STRODTBECK, F. L., "Family Interaction, Values, and Achievement" in McClelland, D. C., Baldwin, A. L., Bronfenbrenner, U., and Strodtbeck, F. L., *Talent and Society*. Princeton, New Jersey: Van Nostrand, 1958, pp. 135–194.

22. TILLER, P. O., "Father-Absence and Personality Development of Children in Sailor Families," *Nordisk Psykologis Monograph Series*, 1958, **9**.

23. WINTERBOTTOM, M. R., "The Relation of Need Achievement to Learning Experiences in Independence and Mastery," in Atkinson, J. W., *Motives in Fantasy, Action, and Society*. Princeton, New Jersey: Van Nostrand, 1958, pp. 453–494.

TRANSITION TO THE ROLE OF THE MENTAL PATIENT *

The selection below is the first portion of an article that describes the process by which an individual is led to define himself as a mental patient. Goffman's observations are based primarily upon a year spent in a Federal mental hospital in Washington, D.C., supplemented by brief studies of ward behavior in the National Institutes of Mental Health Clinical Center. He passed the day with patients and avoided social contacts with the hospital staff, but did not sleep in the wards. He kept extensive field notes on his observations. Essentially this is the method of participant observation described in the methodology section of this book.

Goffman uses the term *moral career* to describe the series of progressions by which the free citizen gradually comes to see himself as a mental patient. Except for this notion of ongoing process, the term moral career is used in much the same sense as we have employed the term *role*. The excerpt chosen covers only the prepatient phase, dealing with the events leading up to the hospitalization.

The powerful impact on the individual of his relations with other persons and their definitions of him is vividly described. Step by step, he is led to redefine his ideas of self, until he is ready to enter formally the mental hospital. At the same time he does not fully recognize the magnitude of change in self that he must undergo to become a patient until he is actually hospitalized. Relatives, psychiatrist, and other agents conspire to maintain an illusion of minimal difference between the life of a free citizen and a hospital patient until he is safely hospitalized. This makes the prepatient phase run more smoothly for all concerned, including the patient.

* The selection following the editorial introduction is reprinted from "The moral career of the mental patient," *Psychiatry: Journal for the Study of Interpersonal Processes*, 1959, **22**, 123–131, by permission of the author and the William Alanson White Psychiatric Foundation.

The Moral Career of the Mental Patient

ERVING GOFFMAN
UNIVERSITY OF CALIFORNIA, BERKELEY

Traditionally the term *career* has been reserved for those who expect to enjoy the rises laid out within a respectable profession. The term is coming to be used, however, in a broadened sense to refer to any social strand of any person's course through life. The perspective of natural history is taken: unique outcomes are neglected in favor of such changes over time as are basic and common to the members of a social category, although occurring independently to each of them. Such a career is not a thing that can be brilliant or disappointing; it can no more be a success than a failure. In this light, I want to consider the mental patient, drawing mainly upon data collected during a year's participant observation of patient social life in a public mental hospital,[1] wherein an attempt was made to take the patient's point of view.

One value of the concept of career is its two-sidedness. One side is linked to internal matters held dearly and closely, such as image of self and felt identity; the other side concerns official position, jural relations, and style of life, and is part of a publicly accessible institutional complex. The concept of career, then, allows one to move back and forth between the personal and the public, between the self and its significant society, without having overly to rely for data upon what the person says he thinks he imagines himself to be.

This paper, then, is an exercise in the institutional approach to the study of self. The main concern will be with the *moral* aspects of career—that is, the regular sequence of changes that career entails in the person's self and in his framework of imagery for judging himself and others.[2]

The category "mental patient" itself will be understood in one strictly sociological sense. In this perspective, the psychiatric view of a person becomes significant only in so far as this view itself alters his social fate—an alteration which seems to become fundamental in our society when, and only when, the person is put through the process of hospitalization.[3] I therefore exclude certain neighboring categories: the undiscovered candidates who would be judged "sick" by psychiatric standards but who never come to be viewed as such by themselves or others, although they may cause everyone a great deal of trouble;[4] the office patient whom a psychiatrist feels he can handle with drugs or shock on the outside; the mental client who engages in psychotherapeutic relationships. And I include anyone, however robust in temperament, who somehow gets caught up in the heavy machinery of mental hospital servicing. In this way the effects of being treated as a mental patient can be kept quite distinct from the effects upon a person's life of traits a clinician would view as psychopathological.[5] Persons who become mental hospital patients vary widely in the kind and degree of illness that a psychiatrist would impute to them, and in the attributes by which laymen would describe him. But once started on the way, they are confronted by some

---

lem of "identity" and sociological studies of work careers and "adult socialization."

[3] This point has recently been made by Elaine and John Cumming, *Closed Ranks;* Cambridge, Commonwealth Fund, Harvard Univ. Press, 1957; pp. 101–102. "Clinical experience supports the impression that many people define mental illness as 'That condition for which a person is treated in a mental hospital.' . . . Mental illness, it seems, is a condition which afflicts people who must go to a mental institution, but until they do almost anything they do is normal." Leila Deasy has pointed out to me the correspondence here with the situation in white collar crime. Of those who are detected in this activity, only the ones who do not manage to avoid going to prison find themselves accorded the social role of the criminal.

[4] Case records in mental hospitals are just now coming to be exploited to show the incredible amount of trouble a person may cause for himself and others before anyone begins to think about him psychiatrically, let alone take psychiatric action against him. See John A. Clausen and Marian Radke Yarrow, "Paths to the Mental Hospital," *J. Social Issues* (1955) 11:25–32; August B. Hollingshead and Frederick C. Redlich, *Social Class and Mental Illness;* New York, Wiley, 1958; pp. 173–174.

[5] An illustration of how this perspective may be taken to all forms of deviancy may be found in Edwin Lemert, *Social Pathology;* New York, McGraw-Hill, 1951; see especially pp. 74–76. A specific application to mental defectives may be found in Stewart E. Perry, "Some Theoretic Problems of Mental Deficiency and Their Action Implications," PSYCHIATRY (1954) 17:45–73; see especially p. 68.

---

[1] The study was conducted during 1955–56 under the auspices of the Laboratory of Socio-environmental Studies of the National Institute of Mental Health. I am grateful to the Laboratory Chief, John A. Clausen, and to Dr. Winfred Overholser, Superintendent, and the late Dr. Jay Hoffman, then First Assistant Physician of Saint Elizabeths Hospital, Washington, D.C., for the ideal cooperation they freely provided. A preliminary report is contained in Goffman, "Interpersonal Persuasion," pp. 117–193; in *Group Processes: Transactions of the Third Conference,* edited by Bertram Schaffner; New York, Josiah Macy, Jr. Foundation, 1957. A shorter version of this paper was presented at the Annual Meeting of the American Sociological Society, Washington, D.C., August, 1957.

[2] Material on moral career can be found in early social anthropological work on ceremonies of status transition, and in classic social psychological descriptions of those spectacular changes in one's view of self that can accompany participation in social movements and sects. Recently, new kinds of relevant data have been suggested by psychiatric interest in the prob-

importantly similar circumstances and respond to these in some importantly similar ways. Since these similarities do not come from mental illness, they would seem to occur in spite of it. It is thus a tribute to the power of social forces that the uniform status of mental patient can not only assure an aggregate of persons of common fate and eventually, because of this, a common character, but that this social reworking can be done upon what is perhaps the most obstinate diversity of human materials that can be brought together by society. Here there lacks only the frequent forming of a protective group-life by ex-patients to illustrate in full the classic cycle of response by which deviant subgroupings are psychodynamically formed in society.

This general sociological perspective is heavily reinforced by one key finding of sociologically oriented students in mental hospital research. As has been repeatedly shown in the study of non-literate societies, the awesomeness, distastefulness, and barbarity of a foreign culture can decrease in the degree that the student becomes familiar with the point of view to life that is taken by his subjects. Similarly, the student of mental hospitals can discover that the craziness or "sick behavior" claimed for the mental patient is by and large a product of the claimant's social distance from the situation that the patient is in, and is not primarily a product of mental illness. Whatever the refinements of the various patients' psychiatric diagnoses, and whatever the special ways in which social life on the "inside" is unique, the researcher can find that he is participating in a community not significantly different from any other he has studied.[6] Of course, while restricting himself to the off-ward grounds community of paroled patients, he may feel, as some patients do, that life in the locked wards is bizarre; and while on a locked admissions or convalescent ward, he may feel that chronic "back" wards are socially crazy places. But he need only move his sphere of sympathetic participation to the "worst" ward in the hospital, and this too can come into social focus as a place with a livable and continuously meaningful social world. This in no way denies that he will find a minority in any ward or patient group that continues to seem quite beyond the capacity to follow rules of social organization, or that the orderly fulfilment of normative expectations in patient society is partly made possible by strategic measures that have somehow come to be institutionalized in mental hospitals.

The career of the mental patient falls popularly

and naturalistically into three main phases: the period prior to entering the hospital, which I shall call the *prepatient phase*; the period in the hospital, the *inpatient phase*; the period after discharge from the hospital, should this occur, namely, the *ex-patient phase*.[7] This paper will deal only with the first two phases.

THE PREPATIENT PHASE

A relatively small group of prepatients come into the mental hospital willingly, because of their own idea of what will be good for them, or because of wholehearted agreement with the relevant members of their family. Presumably these recruits have found themselves acting in a way which is evidence to them that they are losing their minds or losing control of themselves. This view of oneself would seem to be one of the most pervasively threatening things that can happen to the self in our society, especially since it is likely to occur at a time when the person is in any case sufficiently troubled to exhibit the kind of symptom which he himself can see. As Sullivan described it,

> What we discover in the self-system of a person undergoing schizophrenic changes or schizophrenic processes, is then, in its simplest form, an extremely fear-marked puzzlement, consisting of the use of rather generalized and anything but exquisitely refined referential processes in an attempt to cope with what is essentially a failure at being human—a failure at being anything that one could respect as worth being.[8]

Coupled with the person's disintegrative re-evaluation of himself will be the new, almost equally pervasive circumstance of attempting to conceal from others what he takes to be the new fundamental facts about himself, and attempting to discover whether others too have discovered them.[9] Here I want to stress that perception of losing one's mind is based on culturally derived and socially engrained stereotypes as to the significance of symptoms such as hearing voices, losing temporal and spatial orientation, and sensing that one is being followed, and that many

---

[6] Conscientious objectors who voluntarily went to jail sometimes arrived at the same conclusion regarding criminal inmates. See, for example, Alfred Hassler, *Diary of a Self-made Convict;* Chicago, Regnery, 1954; p. 74.

[7] This simple picture is complicated by the somewhat special experience of roughly a third of ex-patients—namely, readmission to the hospital, this being the recidivist or "repatient" phase.

[8] Harry Stack Sullivan, *Clinical Studies in Psychiatry;* edited by Helen Swick Perry, Mary Ladd Gawel, and Martha Gibbon; New York, Norton, 1956; pp. 184–185.

[9] This moral experience can be contrasted with that of a person learning to become a marihuana addict, whose discovery that he can be "high" and still "op" effectively without being detected apparently leads to a new level of use. See Howard S. Becker, "Marihuana Use and Social Control," *Social Problems* (1955) 3:35–44; see especially pp. 40–41.

of the most spectacular and convincing of these symptoms in some instances psychiatrically signify merely a temporary emotional upset in a stressful situation, however terrifying to the person at the time. Similarly, the anxiety consequent upon this perception of oneself, and the strategies devised to reduce this anxiety, are not a product of abnormal psychology, but would be exhibited by any person socialized into our culture who came to conceive of himself as someone losing his mind. Interestingly, subcultures in American society apparently differ in the amount of ready imagery and encouragement they supply for such self-views, leading to differential rates of *self*-referral; the capacity to take this disintegrative view of oneself without psychiatric prompting seems to be one of the questionable cultural privileges of the upper classes.[10]

For the person who has come to see himself—with whatever justification—as mentally unbalanced, entrance to the mental hospital can sometimes bring relief, perhaps in part because of the sudden transformation in the structure of his basic social situations; instead of being to himself a questionable person trying to maintain a role as a full one, he can become an officially questioned person known to himself to be not so questionable as that. In other cases, hospitalization can make matters worse for the willing patient, confirming by the objective situation what has theretofore been a matter of the private experience of self.

Once the willing prepatient enters the hospital, he may go through the same routine of experiences as do those who enter unwillingly. In any case, it is the latter that I mainly want to consider, since in America at present these are by far the more numerous kind.[11] Their approach to the institution takes one of three classic forms: they come because they have been implored by their family or threatened with the abrogation of family ties unless they go "willingly"; they come by force under police escort; they come under misapprehension purposely induced by others, this last restricted mainly to youthful prepatients.

The prepatient's career may be seen in terms of an extrusory model; he starts out with relationships and rights, and ends up, at the beginning of his hospital stay, with hardly any of either. The moral aspects of this career, then, typically begin with the experience of abandonment, disloyalty, and embitterment. This is the case even though to others it may be obvious that he was

in need of treatment, and even though in the hospital he may soon come to agree.

The case histories of most mental patients document offense against some arrangement for face-to-face living—a domestic establishment, a work place, a semipublic organization such as a church or store, a public region such as a street or park. Often there is also a record of some *complainant*, some figure who takes that action against the offender which eventually leads to his hospitalization. This may not be the person who makes the first move, but it is the person who makes what turns out to be the first effective move. Here is the *social* beginning of the patient's career, regardless of where one might locate the psychological beginning of his mental illness.

The kinds of offenses which lead to hospitalization are felt to differ in nature from those which lead to other extrusory consequences—to imprisonment, divorce, loss of job, disownment, regional exile, noninstitutional psychiatric treatment, and so forth. But little seems known about these differentiating factors; and when one studies actual commitments, alternate outcomes frequently appear to have been possible. It seems true, moreover, that for every offense that leads to an effective complaint, there are many psychiatrically similar ones that never do. No action is taken; or action is taken which leads to other extrusory outcomes; or ineffective action is taken, leading to the mere pacifying or putting off of the person who complains. Thus, as Clausen and Yarrow have nicely shown, even offenders who are eventually hospitalized are likely to have had a long series of ineffective actions taken against them.[12]

Separating those offenses which could have been used as grounds for hospitalizing the offender from those that are so used, one finds a vast number of what students of occupation call career contingencies.[13] Some of these contingencies in the mental patient's career have been suggested, if not explored, such as socio-economic status, visibility of the offense, proximity to a mental hospital, amount of treatment facilities available, community regard for the type of treatment given in available hospitals, and so on.[14] For information about other contingencies one must rely on atroc-

---

[10] See footnote 2; Hollingshead and Redlich, p. 187, Table 6, where relative frequency is given of self-referral by social class grouping.

[11] The distinction employed here between willing and unwilling patients cuts across the legal one, of voluntary and committed, since some persons who are glad to come to the mental hospital may be legally committed, and of those who come only because of strong familial pressure, some may sign themselves in as voluntary patients.

[12] Clausen and Yarrow; see footnote 4.

[13] An explicit application of this notion to the field of mental health may be found in Edwin M. Lemert, "Legal Commitment and Social Control," *Sociology and Social Research* (1946) 30:370–378.

[14] For example, Jerome K. Meyers and Leslie Schaffer, "Social Stratification and Psychiatric Practice: A Study of an Outpatient Clinic," *Amer. Sociological Rev.* (1954) 19:307–310. Lemert, see footnote 5; pp. 402–403. *Patients in Mental Institutions, 1941;* Washington, D.C., Department of Commerce, Bureau of the Census, 1941; p. 2.

ity tales: a psychotic man is tolerated by his wife
until she finds herself a boy friend, or by his
adult children until they move from a house to
an apartment; an alcoholic is sent to a mental
hospital because the jail is full, and a drug addict
because he declines to avail himself of psychiatric
treatment on the outside; a rebellious adolescent
daughter can no longer be managed at home because she now threatens to have an open affair
with an unsuitable companion; and so on. Correspondingly there is an equally important set of
contingencies causing the person to by-pass this
fate. And should the person enter the hospital,
still another set of contingencies will help determine when he is to obtain a discharge—such
as the desire of his family for his return, the
availability of a "manageable" job, and so on.
The society's official view is that inmates of mental
hospitals are there primarily because they are
suffering from mental illness. However, in the
degree that the "mentally ill" outside hospitals
numerically approach or surpass those inside hospitals, one could say that mental patients *distinctively* suffer not from mental illness, but from
contingencies.

Career contingencies occur in conjunction with
a second feature of the prepatient's career—the
circuit of agents—and agencies—that participate
fatefully in his passage from civilian to patient
status.[15] Here is an instance of that increasingly
important class of social system whose elements
are agents and agencies, which are brought into
systemic connection through having to take up
and send on the same persons. Some of these
agent-roles will be cited now, with the understanding that in any concrete circuit a role may
be filled more than once, and a single person may
fill more than one of them.

First is the *next-of-relation*—the person whom
the prepatient sees as the most available of those
upon whom he should be able to most depend in
times of trouble; in this instance the last to doubt
his sanity and the first to have done everything
to save him from the fate which, it transpires,
he has been approaching. The patient's next-of-
relation is usually his next of kin; the special
term is introduced because he need not be. Second is the *complainant*, the person who retrospectively appears to have started the person on his
way to the hospital. Third are the *mediators*—
the sequence of agents and agencies to which the
prepatient is referred and through which he is
relayed and processed on his way to the hospital.
Here are included police, clergy, general medical
practitioners, office psychiatrists, personnel in pub-

lic clinics, lawyers, social service workers, school
teachers, and so on. One of these agents will have
the legal mandate to sanction commitment and
will exercise it, and so those agents who precede
him in the process will be involved in something
whose outcome is not yet settled. When the
mediators retire from the scene, the prepatient
has become an inpatient, and the significant agent
has become the hospital administrator.

While the complainant usually takes action in
a lay capacity as a citizen, an employer, a neighbor, or a kinsman, mediators tend to be specialists
and differ from those they serve in significant
ways. They have experience in handling trouble,
and some professional distance from what they
handle. Except in the case of policemen, and
perhaps some clergy, they tend to be more psychiatrically oriented than the lay public, and will
see the need for treatment at times when the
public does not.[16]

An interesting feature of these roles is the
functional effects of their interdigitation. For example, the feelings of the patient will be influenced
by whether or not the person who fills the role
of complainant also has the role of next-of-relation—an embarrassing combination more prevalent, apparently, in the higher classes than in the
lower.[17] Some of these emergent effects will be
considered now.[18]

In the prepatient's progress from home to the
hospital he may participate as a third person in
what he may come to experience as a kind of
alienative coalition. His next-of-relation presses
him into coming to "talk things over" with a
medical practitioner, an office psychiatrist, or
some other counselor. Disinclination on his part
may be met by threatening him with desertion,
disownment, or other legal action, or by stressing
the joint and explorative nature of the interview.
But typically the next-of-relation will have set
the interview up, in the sense of selecting the
professional, arranging for time, telling the professional something about the case, and so on.
This move effectively tends to establish the next-
of-relation as the responsible person to whom
pertinent findings can be divulged, while effectively establishing the other as the patient. The
prepatient often goes to the interview with the
understanding that he is going as an equal of
someone who is so bound together with him that
a third person could not come between them in

[15] For one circuit of agents and its bearing on career contingencies, see Oswald Hall, "The Stages of a Medical Career,"
Amer. J. Sociology (1948) 53:227–336.

[16] See Cumming, footnote 3; p. 92.

[17] Hollingshead and Redlich, footnote 4; p. 187.

[18] For an analysis of some of these circuit implications for the
inpatient, see Leila C. Deasy and Olive W. Quinn, "The Wife
of the Mental Patient and the Hospital Psychiatrist," *J. Social
Issues* (1955) 11:49–60. An interesting illustration of this kind
of analysis may also be found in Alan G. Gowman, "Blindness
and the Role of Companion," *Social Problems* (1956) 4:68–75.
A general statement may be found in Robert Merton, "The
Role Set: Problems in Sociological Theory," *British J. Sociology* (1957) 8:106–120.

fundamental matters; this, after all, is one way in which close relationships are defined in our society. Upon arrival at the office the prepatient suddenly finds that he and his next-of-relation have not been accorded the same roles, and apparently that a prior understanding between the professional and the next-of-relation has been put in operation against him. In the extreme but common case the professional first sees the prepatient alone, in the role of examiner and diagnostician, and then sees the next-of-relation alone, in the role of advisor, while carefully avoiding talking things over seriously with them both together.[19] And even in those nonconsultative cases where public officials must forcibly extract a person from a family that wants to tolerate him, the next-of-relation is likely to be induced to "go along" with the official action, so that even here the prepatient may feel that an alienative coalition has been formed against him.

The moral experience of being third man in such a coalition is likely to embitter the prepatient, especially since his troubles have already probably led to some estrangement from his next-of-relation. After he enters the hospital, continued visits by his next-of-relation can give the patient the "insight" that his own best interests were being served. But the initial visits may temporarily strengthen his feeling of abandonment; he is likely to beg his visitor to get him out or at least to get him more privileges and to sympathize with the monstrousness of his plight—to which the visitor ordinarily can respond only by trying to maintain a hopeful note, by not "hearing" the requests, or by assuring the patient that the medical authorities know about these things and are doing what is medically best. The visitor then nonchalantly goes back into a world that the patient has learned is incredibly thick with freedom and privileges, causing the patient to feel that his next-of-relation is merely adding a pious gloss to a clear case of traitorous desertion.

The depth to which the patient may feel betrayed by his next-of-relation seems to be increased by the fact that another witnesses his betrayal—a factor which is apparently significant in many three-party situations. An offended person may well act forbearantly and accommodatively toward an offender when the two are alone, choosing peace ahead of justice. The presence of a witness, however, seems to add something to the implications of the offense. For then it is beyond the power of the offended and offender to forget about, erase, or suppress what has happened; the offense has become a public social fact.[20] When the witness is a mental health commission, as is sometimes the case, the witnessed

betrayal can verge on a "degradation ceremony."[21] In such circumstances, the offended patient may feel that some kind of extensive reparative action is required before witnesses, if his honor and social weight are to be restored.

Two other aspects of sensed betrayal should be mentioned. First, those who suggest the possibility of another's entering a mental hospital are not likely to provide a realistic picture of how in fact it may strike him when he arrives. Often he is told that he will get required medical treatment and a rest, and may well be out in a few months or so. In some cases they may thus be concealing what they know, but I think, in general, they will be telling what they see as the truth. For here there is a quite relevant difference between patients and mediating professionals; mediators, more so than the public at large, may conceive of mental hospitals as short-term medical establishments where required rest and attention can be voluntarily obtained, and not as places of coerced exile. When the prepatient finally arrives he is likely to learn quite quickly, quite differently. He then finds that the information given him about life in the hospital has had the effect of his having put up less resistance to entering than he now sees he would have put up had he known the facts. Whatever the intentions of those who participated in his transition from person to patient, he may sense they have in effect "conned" him into his present predicament.

I am suggesting that the prepatient starts out with at least a portion of the rights, liberties, and satisfactions of the civilian and ends up on a psychiatric ward stripped of almost everything. The question here is *how* this stripping is managed. This is the second aspect of betrayal I want to consider.

As the prepatient may see it, the circuit of significant figures can function as a kind of *betrayal funnel*. Passage from person to patient may be effected through a series of linked stages, each managed by a different agent. While each stage tends to bring a sharp decrease in adult free status, each agent may try to maintain the fiction that no further decrease will occur. He may even manage to turn the prepatient over to the next agent while sustaining this note. Further, through words, cues, and gestures, the prepatient is implicitly asked by the current agent to join with him in sustaining a running line of polite small talk that tactfully avoids the administrative facts of the situation, becoming, with each stage, progressively more at odds with these facts. The spouse would rather not have to cry to get the prepatient to visit a psychiatrist; psychiatrists

[19] I have one case record of a man who claims he thought *he* was taking his wife to see the psychiatrist, not realizing until too late that his wife had made the arrangements.

[20] A paraphrase from Kurt Riezler, "The Social Psychology of Shame," *Amer. J. Sociology* (1943) 48:458.

[21] See Harold Garfinkel, "Conditions of Successful Degradation Ceremonies," *Amer. J. Sociology* (1956) 61:420–424.

would rather not have a scene when the prepatient learns that he and his spouse are being seen separately and in different ways; the police infrequently bring a prepatient to the hospital in a strait jacket, finding it much easier all around to give him a cigarette, some kindly words, and freedom to relax in the back seat of the patrol car; and finally, the admitting psychiatrist finds he can do his work better in the relative quiet and luxury of the "admission suite" where, as an incidental consequence, the notion can survive that a mental hospital is indeed a comforting place. If the prepatient heeds all of these implied requests and is reasonably decent about the whole thing, he can travel the whole circuit from home to hospital without forcing anyone to look directly at what is happening or to deal with the raw emotion that his situation might well cause him to express. His showing consideration for those who are moving him toward the hospital allows them to show consideration for him, with the joint result that these interactions can be sustained with some of the protective harmony characteristic of ordinary face-to-face dealings. But should the new patient cast his mind back over the sequence of steps leading to hospitalization, he may feel that everyone's *current* comfort was being busily sustained while his long-range welfare was being undermined. This realization may constitute a moral experience that further separates him for the time from the people on the outside.[22]

I would now like to look at the circuit of career agents from the point of view of the agents themselves. Mediators in the person's transition from civil to patient status—as well as his keepers, once he is in the hospital—have an interest in establishing a responsible next-of-relation as the patient's deputy or *guardian;* should there be no obvious candidate for the role, someone may be sought out and pressed into it. Thus while a person is gradually being transformed into a patient, a next-of-relation is gradually being transformed

into a guardian. With a guardian on the scene, the whole transition process can be kept tidy. He is likely to be familiar with the prepatient's civil involvements and business, and can tie up loose ends that might otherwise be left to entangle the hospital. Some of the prepatient's abrogated civil rights can be transferred to him, thus helping to sustain the legal fiction that while the prepatient does not actually have his rights he somehow actually has not lost them.

Inpatients commonly sense, at least for a time, that hospitalization is a massive unjust deprivation, and sometimes succeed in convincing a few persons on the outside that this is the case. It often turns out to be useful, then, for those identified with inflicting these deprivations, however justifiably, to be able to point to the cooperation and agreement of someone whose relationship to the patient places him above suspicion, firmly defining him as the person most likely to have the patient's personal interest at heart. If the guardian is satisfied with what is happening to the new inpatient, the world ought to be.[23]

Now it would seem that the greater the legitimate personal stake one party has in another, the better he can take the role of guardian to the other. But the structural arrangements in society which lead to the acknowledged merging of two persons' interests lead to additional consequences. For the person to whom the patient turns for help—for protection against such threats as involuntary commitment—is just the person to whom the mediators and hospital administrators logically turn for authorization. It is understandable, then, that some patients will come to sense, at least for a time, that the closeness of a relationship tells nothing of its trustworthiness.

There are still other functional effects emerging from this complement of roles. If and when the next-of-relation appeals to mediators for help in the trouble he is having with the prepatient, hospitalization may not, in fact, be in his mind. He may not even perceive the prepatient as mentally sick, or, if he does, he may not consistently hold to this view.[24] It is the circuit of mediators, with their greater psychiatric sophistication and their belief in the medical character of mental hospitals, that will often define the situation for the next-of-relation, assuring him that hospitalization is a possible solution and a good one, that it in-

---

[22] Concentration camp practices provide a good example of the function of the betrayal funnel in inducing cooperation and reducing struggle and fuss, although here the mediators could not be said to be acting in the best interests of the inmates. Police picking up persons from their homes would sometimes joke good-naturedly and offer to wait while coffee was being served. Gas chambers were fitted out like delousing rooms, and vicitms taking off their clothes were told to note where they were leaving them. The sick, aged, weak, or insane who were selected for extermination were sometimes driven away in Red Cross ambulances to camps referred to by terms such as "observation hospital." See David Boder, *I Did Not Interview the Dead;* Urbana, Univ. of Illinois Press, 1949; p. 81; and Elie A. Cohen, *Human Behavior in the Concentration Camp;* London, Cape, 1954; pp. 32, 37, 107.

[23] Interviews collected by the Clausen group at NIMH suggest that when a wife comes to be a guardian, the responsibility may disrupt previous distance from in-laws, leading either to a new supportive coalition with them or to a marked withdrawal from them.

[24] For an analysis of these nonpsychiatric kinds of perception, see Marian Radke Yarrow, Charlotte Green Schwartz, Harriet S. Murphy, and Leila Calhoun Deasy, "The Psychological Meaning of Mental Illness in the Family," *J. Social Issues* (1955) 11:12–24; Charlotte Green Schwartz, "Perspectives on Deviance: Wives' Definitions of their Husbands' Mental Illness," PSYCHIATRY (1957) 20:275–291.

volves no betrayal, but is rather a medical action taken in the best interests of the prepatient. Here the next-of-relation may learn that doing his duty to the prepatient may cause the prepatient to distrust and even hate him for the time. But the fact that this course of action may have had to be pointed out and prescribed by professionals, and be defined by them as a moral duty, relieves the next-of-relation of some of the guilt he may feel.[25] It is a poignant fact that an adult son or daughter may be pressed into the role of mediator, so that the hostility that might otherwise be directed against the spouse is passed on to the child.[26]

Once the prepatient is in the hospital, the same guilt-carrying function may become a significant part of the staff's job in regard to the next-of-relation.[27] These reasons for feeling that he himself has not betrayed the patient, even though the patient may then think so, can later provide the next-of-relation with a defensible line to take when visiting the patient in the hospital and a basis for hoping that the relationship can be re-established after its hospital moratorium. And of course this position, when sensed by the patient, can provide him with excuses for the next-of-relation, when and if he comes to look for them.[28]

Thus while the next-of-relation can perform important functions for the mediators and hospital administrators, they in turn can perform important functions for him. One finds, then, an emergent unintended exchange or reciprocation of functions, these functions themselves being often unintended.

The final point I want to consider about the prepatient's moral career is its peculiarly *retroactive* character. Until a person actually arrives at the hospital there usually seems no way of knowing for sure that he is destined to do so, given the determinative role of career contingencies.

And until the point of hospitalization is reached, he or others may not conceive of him as a person who is becoming a mental patient. However, since he will be held against his will in the hospital, his next-of-relation and the hospital staff will be in great need of a rationale for the hardships they are sponsoring. The medical elements of the staff will also need evidence that they are still in the trade they were trained for. These problems are eased, no doubt unintentionally, by the case-history construction that is placed on the patient's past life, this having the effect of demonstrating that all along he had been becoming sick, that he finally became very sick, and that if he had not been hospitalized much worse things would have happened to him—all of which, of course, may be true. Incidentally, if the patient wants to make sense out of his stay in the hospital, and, as already suggested, keep alive the possibility of once again conceiving of his next-of-relation as a decent, well-meaning person, then he too will have reason to believe some of this psychiatric work-up of his past.

Here is a very ticklish point for the sociology of careers. An important aspect of every career is the view the person constructs when he looks backward over his progress; in a sense, however, the whole of the prepatient career derives from this reconstruction. The fact of having had a prepatient career, starting with an effective complaint, becomes an important part of the mental patient's orientation, but this part can begin to be played only after hospitalization proves that what he had been having, but no longer has, is a career as a prepatient.

SELF AND CONSENSUS AMONG SIGNIFICANT OTHERS[*]

Like the previous selection, the present one also deals with the self concept and with the impact of the definition of self by other persons with whom one interacts. Here the approach is experimental, testing the hypothesis that, if significant other persons are perceived to agree on how an individual is defined, his self concept is more likely to be resistant to change than if he perceives them as having divergent definitions of him. This idea is important, for it identifies an aspect of the

---

[25] This guilt-carrying function is found, of course, in other role-complexes. Thus, when a middle-class couple engages in the process of legal separation or divorce, each of their lawyers usually takes the position that his job is to acquaint his client with all of the potential claims and rights, pressing his client into demanding these, in spite of any nicety of feelings about the rights and honorableness of the ex-partner. The client, in all good faith, can then say to self and to the ex-partner that the demands are being made only because the lawyer insists it is best to do so.

[26] Recorded in the Clausen data.

[27] This point is made by Cumming, see footnote 3; p. 129.

[28] There is an interesting contrast here with the moral career of the tuberculosis patient. I am told by Julius Roth that tuberculosis patients are likely to come to the hospital willingly, agreeing with their next-of-relation about treatment. Later in their hospital career, when they learn how long they yet have to stay and how depriving and irrational some of the hospital rulings are, they may seek to leave, be advised against this by the staff and by relatives, and only then begin to feel betrayed.

[*] The selection following the editorial introduction is reprinted from "Resistance to change in the self concept as a function of perceived consensus among significant others," *Sociometry*, 1963, **26**, 102–111, by permission of the authors and the American Sociological Association.

social environment that has important consequences for maintenance or change of self and personality.

The hypothesis was tested by choosing, for each individual, a self-ascribed trait that he believed five significant other persons generally attributed to him and a self-ascribed trait that he believed they did not. Strong pressure by means of a highly credible but false personality assessment was exerted to test the relative resistance to change of these two traits.

54.

Resistance to Change in the Self-concept as a Function of Consensus Among Significant Others[1]

CARL W. BACKMAN
PAUL F. SECORD
JERRY R. PEIRCE
UNIVERSITY OF NEVADA

The recent development of several cognitive theories promises a greater articulation between research and theory on the self-concept than has hitherto been the case. Interpersonal congruency theory, in particular, is concerned with stability and change in self. It suggests that the greater the number of significant other persons who are perceived to define an aspect of self congruently, the greater the resistance to change. The hypothesis was tested by choosing, for each individual, a self-ascribed trait that he believed five significant other persons generally attributed to him and a self-ascribed trait that he believed they did not. Strong pressure exerted toward changing these traits by means of a false personality assessment resulted in a greater change in the low consensus trait.

The self-concept has been the focus of considerable research and theorizing since the early work of James,[2] Cooley,[3] and Mead.[4] All too often,

however, research has not been guided except in a loose fashion by theory. Consequently the total accumulation of substantive findings has been disappointing.[5] At the same time, self-theory has remained vague and rudimentary. More recently the development of a number of cognitive theories[6] closely integrated with programs of systematic research has given promise of a greater articulation between research and theory in this area. While these theories in general have been concerned with the broader problem of stability and change of attitudes, their work has implications for attitudes pertaining to the self. One of these approaches, in particular, interpersonal congruency theory, while not focusing exclusively on the self, affords it a central place, and outlines the conditions under which the self remains stable or changes.

Basic to interpersonal congruency theory is the assumption that there exists within the cognitive organization of the individual a tendency to achieve a state of congruency between three components of what has been termed the interpersonal matrix. These components include an aspect of self of an individual (S), S's interpretation of his behavior relevant to that aspect, and S's perception of the related aspects of the other person (O) with whom he is interacting. Thus an interpersonal matrix is a recurring functional relation among these three components. S strives to achieve congruency among the components of the matrix. Congruency is a cognitive phenomenon; i.e., each component enters into a state of congruency only as a perceptual-cognitive experience on the part of S. All three components of the matrix are in a *state of congruency when S perceives his behavior and that of O as implying definitions of self congruent with relevant aspects of his self-concept.*

Forces that stabilize or bring about changes in either of the other two components of the matrix will, by virtue of this principle, affect the stability of the self. Sources of stability in S's behavior as well as that of O include the residues of previous experience—learned responses—as well as constancies in the stimulus environment. These con-

[1] This investigation was supported in part by a grant (M-3620) from the National Institute of Mental Health, United States Public Health Service.

[2] William James, *Principles of Psychology*, New York: Holt, 1890. 2 volumes.

[3] Charles H. Cooley, *Human Nature and the Social Order*, New York: Charles Scribner's Sons, 1902.

[4] George H. Mead, *Mind, Self, and Society from the Stand-*

point of a Social Behaviorist, Chicago: University of Chicago Press, 1934.

[5] Ruth C. Wylie, *The Self Concept*, Lincoln, Nebraska: University of Nebraska Press, 1961.

[6] Charles E. Osgood and Percy H. Tannenbaum, "The Principle of Congruity in the Prediction of Attitude Change," *Psychological Review*, 62 (Jan., 1955), pp. 42–55; Dorwin Cartwright and Frank Harary, "Structural Balance: A Generalization of Heider's Theory," *Psychological Review*, 63 (Sept., 1956), pp. 277–293; Leon Festinger, *A Theory of Cognitive Dissonance*, Evanston, Illinois: Row, Peterson, 1957; Milton J. Rosenberg and Robert P. Abelson, "An Analysis of Cognitive Balancing," in Carl I. Hovland and Milton J. Rosenberg, editors, *Attitude Organization and Change*, New Haven: Yale University Press, 1960, pp. 112–163; Fritz Heider, *The Psychology of Interpersonal Relations*, New York: Wiley, 1958.

stancies in turn result not only from the expectations that constitute the social system and guide the behavior of S and O, but also from the operation of a number of interpersonal processes that stem ultimately from the tendency to achieve congruency. While the role of the social system is recognized by most theories that regard the self as a reflection of the views of other persons toward S, these interpersonal processes require further comment. Interpersonal congruency theory, while recognizing the importance of the social structure in fashioning the self, does not view S as passive in the process. Rather S is seen as actively structuring his relations with others so as to achieve and maintain congruency. He does this in the following ways.

In the first place, he selectively interacts with other persons, preferring those who treat him in a manner congruent with his self-concept, and avoiding those who do not. Similarly, he selectively evaluates others, depending upon their attitudes toward him. He does this by liking those who treat him in a congruent fashion, and disliking those who do not. Thus he maximizes the effect of congruent actions and minimizes the effect of incongruent actions on the self-concept. He may also misperceive the actions of others toward him in the belief that they see him as he sees himself, when in actuality, their views of him are somewhat discrepant with his own. Finally, he develops certain behavior patterns that elicit from others reactions that are congruent with his self-definitions. These include not only manipulative behaviors calculated to evoke certain congruent responses, but also less self-conscious, more enduring actions that lead others to treat S in a manner congruent with his self-concept.

A final source of stability and change stems from the manner in which matrices are related to each other. A given matrix may be considered *relevant* to those matrices that contain one or more of the same or similar components as the given matrix. For example, an S who considers himself intelligent may exhibit behaviors in a variety of situations that are interpreted by him as congruent or incongruent with his belief concerning his intelligence. Thus he may obtain high grades in school, play expert chess, but may be a poor bridge player. With respect to the matrix component involving other persons, people may ask him for help in solving problems, he may generally win debates, but his father may criticize his intellectual accomplishments. Matrices having no components in common are considered irrelevant, and as having no effect upon each other.

Matrices vary with respect to *centricality*. The centricality of a matrix is a function of the number of relevant other matrices that stand in a supportive relation to it, and the value of the *O-components* in these matrices. The term *centricality* is chosen in preference to salience or centrality, since the latter terms already have several other established meanings in this field. The greater

the centricality of a matrix, the more resistant it is to change, and should it change, the greater the resultant shifts in other matrices. The present study is concerned with one aspect of centricality, namely, the relative number of *O-components* having congruent relations with a given aspect of self. The contribution of S's *behavior-components* to centricality is ignored for the purposes of the present paper. Put simply, the thesis of the present paper is as follows: If a variety of significant other persons are perceived by S to agree in defining an aspect of S's self-concept congruently, their views support each other and his self-concept. If this condition were to prevail, the particular aspect of self involved would be expected to be more resistant to change than if S were to perceive less consensus among significant others. Thus, the main hypothesis of the present study may be stated as follows:

The greater the number of significant other persons who are perceived to define an aspect of an individual's self-concept congruently, the more resistant to change is that aspect of self.

The hypothesis was tested by choosing for comparison, for each S, a self-ascribed trait on which S perceived high consensus to exist among five significant other persons, and a self-ascribed trait on which perceived consensus was low. Individuals were then subjected to strong pressure to change their perception of these traits, created by means of a highly credible, but false personality assessment. The degree of change in the high consensus trait was compared with change in the low consensus trait.

METHOD

To create strong pressure toward changing certain self-cognitions, it was necessary to have an assessment of S's personality that would be highly credible. This was accomplished by using only subjects willing to volunteer two Saturday mornings for a project in personality assessment. Subjects were offered a personality assessment as a reward for serving in the experiment. In this manner, only those Ss likely to believe in the validity of personality tests would be included. In addition, high credibility was obtained by presenting a rationale emphasizing prestigious sources and serious purpose: the investigation was presented as part of a cooperative research project sponsored by the National Institute of Mental Health, of the U.S. Public Health Service, with the University of Nevada as a cooperating institution. Mention was made of the fact that several sociologists and psychologists from the University of Nevada were participating in the project. The purported purpose of the project was to discover how much insight individuals had into their own personalities.

Subjects were undergraduate students from introductory classes in several fields of study. A total of forty students attended two sessions held one week apart.

Assessment devices. The various ranking forms and checklists used were based upon the 15 needs measured by the Edwards Personal Preference Schedule (EPPS).[7] These forms contained 15 brief statements each describing one need, adapted from the need descriptions appearing in the EPPS manual. For example, the need for *nurturance* was represented by the statement, "This person enjoys helping others," and the need for *exhibition* by, "This person likes to receive a lot of attention from others; to be the center of attention."

In the first session, the following instruments were administered.

1. Reflected-self checklist. *S* was asked to write down the names of five close friends or relatives whose opinion he valued. He was given one checklist form for each of these five persons. For each person, he was asked to select the five need-statements that he believed would be most likely to be assigned to him by that person. A twenty-minute break followed the completion of these forms.

2. Self-ranking form. *S* ranked himself from 1 to 15 on the 15 abbreviated need statements, from those he believed to be most characteristic to those he considered least characteristic.

3. Edwards Personal Preference Schedule and Gordon Personality Profile.[8] These standard tests were administered to lend credence to the assessment process. In addition, the EPPS was scored and profiles were distributed after the experiment had been completed and its real purpose explained to *S*.

In the second session, *S* was given a profile sheet indicating the rank order of the 15 needs supposedly characterizing him. Although he was told that professional psychologists had prepared the profile from a careful analysis of the personality tests and the other forms he had taken, actually the order of the needs was the same as *S*'s initial self-ranking, except that two needs from among the highest-ranking five had been moved eight rank-steps downward. The needs on the profile were described in some detail by a psychologist while *S* was given time to study the profile. Finally, these profiles were placed under the chairs in which the *S*s were seated, and *S* was asked to rank himself again on the 15 needs.

The two needs were selected for each *S* for manipulation by the following means. For each of the

[7] Allen Edwards, *Edwards Personal Preference Schedule,* New York: Psychological Corporation, 1954.

[8] Leonard V. Gordon, *Gordon Personal Profile,* New York: World Book Company, 1953.

five need statements ranking highest on the initial self-ranking form, a measure of consensus was obtained from the reflected self checklist. This consensus score ranged from 0 to 5 depending upon the number of significant other persons that *S* perceived as likely to assign the need to him. The following criteria were used to determine what two needs should be manipulated: (*a*) they had to be included in the five highest-ranking statements on the initial self-form, (*b*) one had to have relatively high consensus and the other low consensus, (*c*) they had to have adjacent ranks on the self-form, and (*d*) the needs had to be balanced for *saliency.*

The higher the ranking of the need-statement on the self-form, the more *salient* it is, and thus probably more resistant to change. But needs that rank high are also likely to be high on consensus, compared with lower-ranking needs. To control for saliency, the subjects were divided into two groups, and the needs to be manipulated selected in a counterbalanced design, as follows:

TYPE OF NEED	GROUP I	GROUP II
High consensus need	High saliency	Low saliency
Low consensus need	Low saliency	High saliency

In addition, the magnitude of the difference in consensus for each need pair selected for persons in Group I was matched with the magnitude of the difference in consensus of the need pair selected for Group II. Thus any difference obtained between high and low consensus needs in susceptibility to manipulation can legitimately be attributed to the effects of consensus alone, and not saliency.

RESULTS

Several factors point to successful manipulation of the two chosen traits. The great majority of subjects (30 on the high consensus trait; 26 on the low consensus trait) ranked the two manipulated traits lower after receiving the false assessment. Moreover, on the post-experimental questionnaire most subjects indicated that they had been surprised upon reading the assessment profile, particularly stressing the point that the position of certain traits surprised them. On the other hand, only a few subjects stated that they believed any profile traits in the assessment were invalid: they found the assessment credible even though a few traits were unexpected. Somewhat inconsistently, however, subjects in general were not conscious of making deliberate changes in their self-rankings subsequent to the manipulation. The success of the experimental manipulation was also apparent from the loud sighs of relief that arose when the subjects learned that they had been deceived with respect to the assessment.

The main hypothesis of the study, as stated previously, is that an aspect of self will be more resistant to change when *S* believes that there is consensus among significant other persons concerning that aspect. A need high in consensus and one low in consensus for each individual were manipulated downward in an attempt to secure movement of these needs on a second self-ranking form. In general several forces could be expected to be generated by this manipulation. One is a tendency to lower one's self-ratings on these two traits. Another is the arousal of resistance to change, and some individuals in whom resistance is aroused might even rank themselves higher than they did initially on the need. Resistance of this sort would be expected because the acceptance of an incongruent self-definition not only requires a change in the matrix containing that aspect but in all related matrices in which that aspect is imbedded. Thus the threat of widespread incongruence could easily create resistance to acceptance. More frequently, of course, this resistance effect might be expected for the high consensus trait. While these two forces are represented by downward and upward movement in self-ranks, respectively, a certain amount of random movement in both directions due to error of measurement will be superimposed upon these other movements. In order to examine the movement due to acceptance or resistance to manipulation uncontaminated by random movement, the best test of the hypothesis is a comparison of the movement of the high consensus trait with the movement for the low consensus trait.

Table 1 lists in the first two columns the number of steps that the high and low consensus need was moved by each individual. Downward movements are positively labeled; upward movements are given a negative sign. Relative movement, shown in the last column of Table 1, was determined by subtracting the movement of the high consensus trait from the low. If the relative movement represented by the difference score is positive, the hypothesis is supported for that subject. This analysis allows for random effects operating to move a need upward and still permits a test of the relative effects of the degree of consensus. For example, as indicated in the first row of Table 1, deference was chosen as the low consensus need for subject 1 and autonomy as the high consensus need. From the initial self-ranking to the post-manipulation self-ranking he moved deference 8 rank steps downward and autonomy 2 rank steps upward. This yields a net change of 10 steps in the direction of the hypothesis. As may be seen by inspection of the difference column, 26 individuals produced a net difference in the direction of the hypothesis, 2 showed no change, and 12 changed in an opposite direction. Table 2 offers a more precise comparison taking into account the magnitude of the change. The low consensus need moved an average of 3.43 rank steps, and the high consensus need only 1.75 rank steps. The magnitude of the differences between the two needs is significant at the .008

level as tested by the Wilcoxon signed-ranks test[9] ($T = 229.0$, $N = 40$, $z = 2.43$). Thus it appears that the reaction to information incongruent with self-definition is a function of the perceived consensus of opinion among significant others.

As a final check on whether the movement of the manipulated traits was in fact due to the false personality appraisal, for each individual two non-manipulated traits, differing in consensus by the same amount as the previously chosen manipulated traits, were selected for analysis. These traits were compared to determine whether the low consensus trait moved to a greater extent than the high. The mean difference between them was only 0.21, and the differences were not significant ($T = 342.5$, $N = 37$, $z = .135$, $P = .44$).

DISCUSSION

The relatively greater movement in the manipulated direction of the low consensus trait supports the theoretical position that the degree of resistance to the acceptance of an incongruent self-definition is a function of the number of interpersonal matrices supporting that self-definition. In this instance, the element of each matrix supporting or weakening resistance was represented by the perceived attitude of a different significant other person toward a given aspect of an individual's self-concept. The possibility that the differing resistance of the high and low consensus needs resulted from a difference in salience (importance of the trait to S, as indicated by its self-rank position) was ruled out by equating on salience the two kinds of needs manipulated. Social desirability was presumed to be similarly controlled by the same matching process.

Encountering information contrary to self-definitions will result in a threat to congruency that must be resolved in some manner. In many instances, congruency is retained without a change in self or behavior. This is much more likely to occur when perceived consensus is high than when it is low. As described in more detail elsewhere,[10] in his attempts to restore congruency an individual may employ one or more of the following modes of resolution. He may reduce his interaction with those whose definitions of his behavior threaten congruence and increase interaction with

[9] James V. Bradley, *Distribution-free Statistical Tests.* Washington, D.C.: United States Department of Commerce, Office of Technical Services, August, 1960.

[10] Paul F. Secord and Carl W. Backman, "Personality Theory and the Problem of Stability and Change in Individual Behavior: An Interpersonal Approach," *Psychological Review*, 68 (Jan., 1961), pp. 21–32.

others whose definitions he perceives as congruent. A second mode involves evaluating selected other persons positively or negatively depending upon whether they are behaving congruently with certain aspects of self: he increases his liking for

TABLE 1   Changes in High and Low Consensus Manipulated Traits for Each Subject

SUBJECT	TRAITS MANIPU- LATED LOW, HIGH	MOVEMENT OF		
		Low Consensus Trait	High Consensus Trait	Difference
1	Def, Aut	8	−2	10
2	Aut, Aff	8	0	8
3	Def, Aba	8	1	7
4	Chg, Nur	7	0	7
5	Aba, Nur	7	0	7
6	Def, Nur	6	−1	7
7	Agg, End	8	1	7
8	Int, Nur	5	0	5
9	Suc, Aff	5	0	5
10	Exh, Chg	5	0	5
11	Def, Chg	4	−1	5
12	Def, Aba	9	5	4
13	Chg, Suc	4	1	3
14	Aff, Int	3	0	3
15	Ord, Ach	5	2	3
16	Chg, Ach	6	3	3
17	Aba, Int	2	−1	3
18	Het, Def	5	2	3
19	Int, Chg	3	1	2
20	Het, End	5	3	2
21	Chg, Aba	5	3	2
22	Het, Chg	4	2	2
23	Het, Int	−1	−3	2
24	Exh, Ach	3	1	2
25	Ord, Ach	5	4	1
26	Aba, Het	1	0	1
27	Chg, Int	0	0	0
28	Chg, Aut	3	3	0
29	Int, Aut	0	1	−1
30	Aff, End	1	2	−1
31	Ach, Nur	0	1	−1
32	Het, Chg	0	2	−2
33	Exh, Ach	7	9	−2
34	Ach, Aba	−2	0	−2
35	Suc, Ach	−2	1	−3
36	Aba, Suc	1	5	−4
37	Dom, Ord	4	8	−4
38	Het, Dom	−3	4	−7
39	End, Nur	0	7	−7
40	Int, Aff	−2	6	−8

TABLE 2   Net Mean Movement of Manipulated Trait

LOW CONSENSUS	HIGH CONSENSUS	DIFFERENCE	P
3.43	1.75	1.68	<.008*

* Wilcoxon signed-ranks test: T=229.0; N=40; z=2.43, one-tailed.

those who behave in a congruent fashion and decreases his liking for those behaving incongruently. A third means of resolution is the misperception of the other person's behavior in a manner allowing congruency to be achieved. Finally, he may employ techniques permitting him to elicit congruent responses from the other person that confirm aspects of self.

For the most part, the experimental situation was designed so as to minimize the occurrence of these various forms of resolving incongruency while maintaining self unchanged. Some of these modes require situations outside the laboratory where the individual has freedom of interaction. Nevertheless, the minority of subjects who failed to change appreciably either manipulated trait may have questioned the validity of the assessment devices, the intentions, or the competence of the experimenter in order to support non-change.

Research on attitudes toward non-self objects is consistent with the findings of the present study. The well-known experiments of Asch[11] and Sherif[12] on the formation of judgments as a function of social pressure illustrate the effectiveness of actual consensus in the initial formation of attitudes and in resistance to change. More recent work by Festinger, Riecken, and Schachter,[13] Festinger,[14] Brehm,[15] and Cohen[16] on dissonance theory further document the point that resistance to change of attitudes is strongly tied to social support—perceived or actual—and that the behavior of individuals is often concerned with securing consonance among cognitive elements ("congruence" in the interpersonal approach).

The present study has been concerned entirely

[11] Solomon E. Asch, *Social Psychology*, New York: Prentice-Hall, 1952.

[12] Muzafer Sherif, *The Psychology of Social Norms*, New York: Harper and Brothers, 1936.

[13] Leon Festinger, Henry W. Riecken, and Stanley S. Schachter, *When Prophecy Fails*, Minneapolis: University of Minnesota Press, 1956.

[14] Leon Festinger, *A Theory of Cognitive Dissonance*, Evanston, Illinois: Row, Peterson, 1957.

[15] Jack W. Brehm, "A Dissonance Analysis of Attitude-discrepant Behavior," in Carl I. Hovland and Milton J. Rosenberg, editors, *Attitude Organization and Change*, New Haven: Yale University Press, 1960, pp. 164–197.

[16] Arthur R. Cohen, "Attitudinal Consequences of Induced Discrepancies Between Cognitions and Behavior," *Public Opinion Quarterly*, 24 (Summer, 1960), pp. 297–318.

with *perceived* consensus. The assumption is made, however, that there is a high but imperfect association between actual consensus and perceived consensus. Some evidence[17] for this association has been presented in a study of a living group. The fact that the association is not perfect provides some opportunity for the individual to perceive consensus as greater than it actually is, and interpersonal congruency theory predicts that perceptual distortion will generally occur in the direction of consensus in order to maximize congruency. This prediction is also supported by data. One direction for further study, however, might be the replication of the present study, using in addition the variable of the actual consensus among significant other persons.

PERSONALITY FACTORS IN RESOLUTION OF CONCEPTUAL INCONGRUITIES *

Theories pertaining to balance or dissonance agree that imbalance is an important condition often leading to attitude change. Our focus here on the self concept, itself a constellation of attitudes with the person as an object, suggests that information at variance with the self creates an imbalanced situation of considerable interest and importance. The selection below describes an experiment in which individuals were confronted with such information and analyzes several aspects of their reaction to this imbalanced state in terms of their personality characteristics.

Worth noting is that the investigator has built into his design means of assessing a considerable variety of ways in which the individual might react to an imbalanced situation concerning his self concept. For example, to restore balance, an individual might change self or he might discredit the source of the incongruous information. In investigating situations of this kind, the experimenter must collect data that enable him to determine whether or not such alternative reactions have occurred. If he has failed to anticipate certain responses to imbalance, his experiment might well yield negative findings leading to the unwarranted discard of the hypothesis that imbalance creates pressures for change.

55.

Personality Factors in Resolution of Conceptual Incongruities[1]

O. J. HARVEY
UNIVERSITY OF COLORADO

One hundred and eighty-eight subjects, from whom were obtained measures of authoritarianism, extra-intrapunitiveness and self esteem, were exposed to one of five gradations of fictitiously negative information about themselves from either a friend or relative stranger. Following the treatment, subjects rerated self, rerated source, recalled the ratings received and completed a questionnaire aimed at measuring such side effects as distortion, source discrediting and dissociation. The results duplicated the earlier findings of Harvey, Kelley and Shapiro, and in addition demonstrated the effects of another person's complete agreement with an individual's self ratings as well as the effects of extreme disagreement. Authoritarianism related significantly to all responses; the other two personality measures related to none.

That an individual will evolve a definition of a personally relevant situation is simultaneously one of psychology's most basic and well documented assumptions. It seems also that once such a concept or way of ordering comes into being it becomes resistant to change, its holder being disposed toward construing the world in ways consonant with it. This tendency toward conceptual maintenance is inferable from a host of behaviors, including selective perception and retention, affective arousal, and difference in stimulus thresholds when the inputs are evaluated as being too much at variance with the existing ways of reading the situation. It is quite possible, if not probable, that this tendency toward self-maintenance is a general property of all systems, conceptual, social, biological or physical. Analogous to entropy and other laws of thermodynamics, the actual state of system maintenance at a given

[17] Paul F. Secord and Carl W. Backman, "Liking, Selective Interaction, and Misperception in Congruent Interpersonal Relations," *Sociometry*, 25 (Dec., 1962), pp. 321–335.

* The selection following the editorial introduction is reprinted from "Personality factors in resolution of conceptual incongruities," *Sociometry*, 1962, **25**, 336–352, by permission of the author and the American Sociological Association.

[1] This study was completed in 1958, under a contract between the Group Psychology Branch, Office of Naval Research and Vanderbilt University, with which the author was at that time affiliated. The results reported herein were presented at a symposium of the American Psychological Association, "Intra-organismic Norms and the Organization of Behavior," September, 1958. Thanks are extended to ONR for its support and to Walter Reed for his help in collecting and analyzing the data. Reproduction of this study in whole or part is permitted for any purpose of the United States Government.

time is a net result of the contemporaneously opposing forces toward change and toward stability.

It is with reactions to induced system-environment asynchrony that this study is concerned. The system in this case represents an individual's concatenation of concepts about himself and the incongruity is in the form of unfavorable evaluations from another person. Change in concepts toward both the self and the source of the evaluations are among the more probable responses to such a situation.[2] While such changes would have the effect of reducing the concept-event incongruity, it is likely that if an individual was highly committed to both sets of concepts, other or additional conflict resolving responses would occur. Failure to perceive the incongruity, distorting it to the point of absurdity or in some other way discrediting the source, dissociation of the negative evaluations from the source, and error in recall of the unfavorable inputs are among the many such effects that might result. Such responses might lessen the likelihood of concepts being changed in the direction of the communication. The occurrence of such techniques of psychological gerrymandering should, of course, vary with a multiplicity of factors. Of these, this experiment varied the source and magnitude of the discrepant inputs along with the personality make-up of the recipients of the incongruities. Individuals with differing personalities were exposed to information about themselves of varying degrees of unfavorableness which was made to appear as having come from either a friend or a relative stranger.

It might be expected that a typical response to an extreme concept-event discrepancy would be to dissociate the event from the concept or in some way render it irrelevant. Yet the results so far indicate that as long as the source of the deviant input maintains credibility in the eyes of the recipient even highly incongruous communications from him lead the recipient to change his concept in the direction of the deviant event.[3] In

an earlier study which employed the same general method as this investigation,[4] the group of subjects that received the most extreme of three gradations of derogation lowered their self-ratings more than did the others. This same group also decreased the favorableness of their concepts toward the source of the negative evaluations more than the other groups as well as showing greater error in recall of the evaluations received. The effects of negatively discrepant events were further investigated in this study by varying the unfavorableness of the evaluations the subject received about himself in graded amounts from zero to as much as the experimental setup allowed.

The personality factors investigated included intolerance of ambiguity, extra- and intra-punitiveness, and self-esteem as assessed by a level of aspiration technique. Intolerance of ambiguity was assumed to dispose toward greater resistance to change of concept and toward a greater manifestation of other effects. Greater extra-punitiveness was expected to dispose an individual to become more unfavorable toward the person derogating him, while greater intra-punitiveness was anticipated to result in increased unfavorableness toward the self following negative feedback from another person. Recall and other effects were expected to follow a related pattern.

Self-esteem has been found to relate negatively to change in target concept,[5] but its relationship to change toward the source is more conjectural. It is theoretically possible that while becoming more negative toward himself as a consequence of deprecation, the person of low self-esteem might at the same time become more positive toward the source of the derogation as a consequence of the latter's confirming or reinforcing the unfavorable opinions he already held of himself. For this latter effect to occur, however, it would be necessary for the recipient of the negative communication to have fully accepted his self as of low value and to wish to maintain it in its unfavorable state, probably something that rarely or never occurs in real life.

The authoritativeness of the source (friend vs. stranger) was expected to interact both with personality and with the magnitude of discrepant evaluations.

METHOD

Subjects. The 188 experimental subjects were undergraduate students enrolled in introductory psychology and sociology courses at Vanderbilt University and George Peabody College for Teachers in the spring and summer of 1958. The experiment was carried out

[2] O. J. Harvey, Harold H. Kelley, and Martin M. Shapiro, "Reactions to Unfavorable Evaluations of the Self Made by Other Persons," *Journal of Personality,* 25 (June, 1957), pp. 393–411.

[3] Harvey, Kelley, and Shapiro, *op. cit.*; Charles E. Osgood and Percy H. Tannenbaum, "The Principle of Congruity in the Prediction of Attitude Change," *Psychological Review,* 62 (Jan., 1955), pp. 42–55; Carl I. Hovland and Henry A. Pritzker, "Extent of Opinion Change as a Function of Amount of Change Advocated," *Journal of Abnormal and Social Psychology,* **54,** (March, 1957), pp. 257–261; Solomon C. Goldberg, "Three Situational Determinants of Conformity to Social Norms," *Journal of Abnormal and Social Psychology,* 49 (July, 1954), pp. 325–329; O. J. Harvey, David E. Hunt, and Harold

M. Schroder, *Conceptual Systems and Personality Organization,* New York: Wiley, 1961.

[4] Harvey, Kelley, and Shapiro, *op. cif.*

[5] Irving Janis, "Personality Correlates of Susceptibility to Influence," *Journal of Personality,* 22 (June, 1954), pp. 504–518.

during regular classroom meetings with classes each of approximately 40 students.

Instruments. Changes in concept of self, concept of the source of the negative evaluations and recall of source's ratings were measured by a scale of fifteen social characteristics of importance to college students. Included in the scale, which was devised and used by Harvey, Kelley and Shapiro in an earlier study,[6] were three items on each of five general characteristics of friendliness, sincerity, broadmindedness, sense of humor and considerateness, arranged in a randomized order. Each characteristic was presented in graphic form with only the most favorable and the most unfavorable points labeled at opposite ends of a 14 centimeter line. Subject responded by checking the position on the line which he considered to be most representative of his concept of the referent being rated.

Subjects' attributed reasons for receipt of the negative information was ascertained by an eight-item questionnaire administered at the end of the experimental sessions.

The personality measures consisted of the California F Scale,[7] the scale of Webster, Sanford and Freedman,[8] the Rosenzweig Picture-Frustration Test[9] and a modified level of aspiration test on a digit-substitution task aimed at self-esteem.

The use of the digit-substitution task as a measure of self-esteem was a direct attempt at operationalizing James' formula, Self Esteem = Success/Pretensions.[10] Accordingly, subject indicated, without prior practice or subsequent performance, the highest, the lowest and the most probable number of digit-symbol substitutions he expected to attain during a one minute period, given the information that 100 was the highest possible score. From these three pieces of information two scores were computed for each subject: the range of aspiration (the difference between the lowest and highest expected attainment); and a ratio of the most probable performance to this range.

Procedure. The procedure is identical to that employed earlier by Harvey, Kelley and Shapiro[11] with the exceptions that the present study included an investigation of personality correlates of reactions to self-derogation as well as more variations in the negative information presented to the individual about himself. This particular procedure was repeated and enlarged because of its demonstrated effectiveness in producing strong conflict and significant changes in both the target concept and concept toward the source as well as a number of additional effects.

Overview. The data were collected in three sessions. In the first session each subject rated himself on a scale of important social characteristics. In the second session, each subject rated one other person in the class on this scale, the same person who he believed was rating him. The other person rated by the subject was in one variation a person who, according to earlier information, knew him well and in the other variation one who knew him only poorly. Subject was then exposed to the ratings that presumably had just been made of him by the other person (*source*), but which were in fact fictitious ratings prepared earlier by the experimenters. These ratings were more unfavorable than subject's ratings of himself by one of five variations, from complete similarity to extremely high devaluation. Following exposure to the negative ratings, subject then rerated himself, rerated the source, recalled the ratings the source had presumably made of him, and, finally, completed a questionnaire concerning his evaluation of the experiment and his interpretations of the source's unfavorable ratings of him. In the third session, made to appear as unrelated to the others, each subject completed the four personality measures.

First session. The experiment was introduced as a study in social perceptiveness, an ability that was to be determined by having each member of the class rate one other person in the class on social characteristics. It was suggested that before the other person was rated each should rate himself in order to gain familiarity and skill in usage of the scale. Subjects were urged to exercise extreme care in these ratings of themselves even though they were for practice. These "practice" ratings in reality were to be used as the basis for the rigged unfavorable ratings subjects were to receive subsequently, and to provide a baseline against which to determine shift in ratings of the self as a result of the experimental treatments. In order to increase the likelihood that each one would use the rating scale in approximately the same way, subjects were advised of the meanings of different points on the scale.

After the initial self-ratings were made, each subject was asked to list the names of the persons in class who knew him best and those who barely knew him. After the names were listed, subject rated on a scale from 1 to 10 how well their owners knew him. In order to establish some degree of psychological equivalence for such ratings, subject was advised to let 10 stand for the *one* person, whoever it was—in class or out—who knew him best and then make his ratings in relation to that. These ratings provided the basis for assigning the source to either the friend or

[6] Harvey, Kelley, and Shapiro, *op. cit.*

[7] Theodore W. Adorno, Else Frenkel-Brunswik, Daniel J. Levinson, and R. Nevitt Sanford, *The Authoritarian Personality*, New York: Harper and Brothers, 1950.

[8] Harold Webster, R. Nevitt Sanford, and Mervin Freedman, "A New Instrument for Studying Authoritarianism," *Journal of Psychology*, 40 (July, 1955), pp. 73–84.

[9] Sanford Rosenzweig, *Rosenzweig P-F Study, Revised Form for Adults*, 1948.

[10] William James, *Principles of Psychology*, New York: Henry Holt, 1890 (Dover Publication edition).

[11] Harvey, Kelley, and Shapiro, *op. cit.*

the stranger condition. All sources in the friend condition had been rated by subject as knowing him above the level of 5, and all sources in the stranger condition had been rated as knowing him below the level of 5.

Preparation of fictitious ratings. During the time interval between the first and second experimental sessions (approximately one week), subjects were assigned to the friend or stranger source condition, and within each were randomly distributed among the five discrepancy conditions (I through V) which determined the degree to which the fictitious ratings, prepared by the experimenter, were made to deviate negatively from subject's initial self-ratings. In discrepancy condition I (Zero discrepancy) the fictitious ratings were made to coincide with subject's initial self-ratings on all 15 of the social characteristics. In discrepancy conditions II, III and IV, the fictitious ratings were made to be lower than subject's self-ratings on 9 (*treatment*) items by 1, 4.1, and 6.7 centimeters respectively, but to be practically the same (with slight variations to prevent suspicion) on the 6 remaining (*non-treatment*) items. In discrepancy V, the ratings received by subject were more unfavorable than his self-ratings by 6.7 centimeters on all 15 items of the scale.

The friend vs. stranger source variation and five degrees of negative discrepancy provided a 10-cell design, with personality variables cutting across all cells. The number of subjects in each of the five discrepancies in the friend condition was I=17; II=17; III=17; IV=17; and V=18. The number in each of the discrepancies in the stranger condition was: I=20; II=21; III=22; IV=21; and V=18.

Second session. Each subject was asked first to rate the other person (source) from whom subsequently he would receive the fictitiously negative ratings of himself. Subjects were again reminded in the use of the scale. The difficulty in rating a relative stranger was acknowledged, but they were urged to do their best. They were assured that the ratings would be kept confidential and would be seen only by the experimenters. Each subject rated his assigned person in two ways: he placed R's on the scales to show how he thought the other person "really" was and T's to indicate how the other person "thought" he was (or would rate himself).

The ratings of others were quickly collected and subjects were instructed: "Now we want your help in evaluating the ratings the other person has made of you so we can determine how good a judge of others each of you is. The way we will do this is by letting you see the T ratings made of you." At this point the experimenter feigned great embarrassment because of his "error" in having the R and T ratings on the same sheet where the T ratings could not be seen without the R ratings also being seen. In an apologetic tone,

the experimenter asked if anyone objected to seeing the R ratings made of him. Before subjects had a chance to object, the experimenter substituted the prearranged fictitious ratings for the genuine ones and distributed the former to them. The acceptance of the fictitious ratings by the subjects as genuine is demonstrated by the fact that out of a total of almost 350 subjects in the earlier[12] and present study, only seven had to be discarded because of the discovery that the ratings were rigged, and then for such a simple reason that the ratings were not in pencil or in the same color of ink as had been used earlier by the source.

In order to insure that the unfavorableness of the rigged ratings was recognized, subjects were asked to determine their accuracy. They were instructed to place a small check at the point where they would rate themselves (thus providing a rerating of themselves), count the number of dashes between their own ratings and the T ratings the source had made of them, and then record this difference on the margin. Thus every subject was led to note the position on the scale where the other person had rated him, thereby reducing the likelihood that differences among the experimental conditions can be attributed to differential exposure to the fictitious ratings.

Self reratings were collected and subjects were then asked to rate the other person again. Doubly assured that there would be no mistake this time in keeping the ratings confidential, subjects were instructed, "Because of time shortage, make only R ratings of the other person this time, that is, how you think the other person 'really' is." They were then asked to recall the R ratings the other person had made of them by reproducing the ratings on the 15-item scale as best they could. As the last step, subjects filled out the 8-item questionnaire which gave them a chance to deny, dissociate and in other ways minimize the seriousness of the ratings the other had made of them. This was reserved as the last step in the experiment to prevent suggesting the possibility to the subjects earlier that the fictitious ratings were not in fact genuine.

At the end of the experiment the fictitious nature of the received ratings and the purpose of the experiment were explained. The explanation seemed to relieve completely the high emotional arousal generated by the experiment. A polling of the subjects indicated that practically all of them enjoyed (retrospectively, it might be added) participating in the study.

Third session. The four personality instruments were administered approximately two weeks after the second session. In order that subjects would not associate these tests with the earlier experiment, they were administered by a person (usually the class instructor) other than the previous experimenters.

RESULTS

1. Changes in self-ratings. An analysis of variance yielded no significant differences between

---

[12] *Ibid.*

the friend and stranger sources in the changes produced in subjects' self-ratings, on the nine treatment items $(F = .157)$. Variation in the negativity of the ratings, however, did significantly influence self-change $(F = 10.715, P < .001)$, as did the interaction of source and discrepancy $(F = 3.388, P < .05)$. The nature of this interaction can be inferred from Table 1. It will be noted that the two smallest discrepancies of the friend source and the smallest (zero) discrepancy of the stranger source resulted in subjects becoming more favorable in their self-ratings. In the other seven cells negative evaluations by the source resulted in subjects changing their ratings of themselves in the unfavorable direction. The effectiveness of the friend source in the most discrepant condition diminished markedly from the next to largest discrepancy, suggesting perhaps that it had surpassed the optimal magnitude for maximum effectiveness. This same diminution in effect of the most unfavorable source evaluations did not occur for the stranger source, however. A logical reason could be that in relation to the ill-defined expectations held of a relative stranger such devaluation could not be so unexpected, while for a friend to be equally deprecating would appear intolerably incongruous.

2. Changes in source ratings. Unlike the influence on self-ratings, the source of the negative feedback made a significant difference in changes in the ratings of the source $(F = 3.948, P < .05)$. So did the variation in the negativity of the fictitious information $(F = 7.789, P < .001)$, although unlike self changes, source and discrepancy did not interact significantly $(F = 1.859, P > .10)$. As can be seen from Table 2, agreement or near agreement of the source's with subject's self-ratings resulted in subject becoming more positive toward the source, particularly the stranger source. This implies that one would be more disposed to change favorably toward a relative stranger following a perceived compliment from him than toward a friend who made the same positive evaluation. When the ratings from the source became too unfavorable, both friends and strangers changed their opinion of him in the negative direction, the friends, however, tolerating less deprecation by the source than the strangers before commencing to devalue him.

The differences between reactions to the ratings of a friend and a relative stranger, again, probably result from well defined expectancies in relation to a friend and only ambiguous ones in relation to strangers. Expecting friends to say only nice things about us, negative affect and tendencies toward reciprocal derogation result when they depart from this, while we interpret favorably the same objective reaction from one whom we expect little from in the way of his evaluations of us. This may account for the seeming paradox noted in everyday life: the person who characteristically performs good deeds and behaves considerately toward others is evaluated as a scoundrel when he departs even slightly from what is taken for granted about him, whereas a *bona fide* scoundrel achieves the reverse effect by no more than a periodic good deed.

In line with the possibility of more definite expectancies about a friend, it should be noted that the tendency to become more unfavorable toward the source as the unfavorableness of the ratings increased is less for the friend source in the most extreme discrepancy, suggesting, in line with the possibility noted from Table 1, that the deviation of the source at this point had become so extreme that the effects of his evaluations had begun to diminish.

The results in Tables 1 and 2 provide a rather striking experimental demonstration of an everyday occurrence in interpersonal relations. Being a recipient of positive evaluations enhances one's opinion of both oneself and the perceived source of the favorable tidings. Being negatively appraised, on the other hand, leads one to think less well of himself and of the source of the un-

TABLE 1 Mean Changes in Self Ratings on the Nine Treatment Items

SOURCE	DISCREPANCIES (IN CENTIMETERS)				
	0	1	4.1	6.7 Treatment	6.7 Total
Friend	.130	.410	−.671	−1.474	−.212
Stranger	.559	−.177	−.380	− .686	−.800

TABLE 2 Mean Change in Ratings of Source on the Nine Treatment Items

SOURCE	DISCREPANCIES (IN CENTIMETERS)				
	0	1	4.1	6.7 Treatment	6.7 Total
Friend	.206	.135	−.947	−.557	−.488
Stranger	.516	.610	.060	.444	−.840

TABLE 3 Mean Errors in Recall of Ratings on Nine Treatment Items

SOURCE	DISCREPANCIES (IN CENTIMETERS)				
	0	1	4.1	6.7 Treatment	6.7 Total
Friend	.042	.657	1.452	1.403	.600
Stranger	.501	.576	1.014	2.056	−.114

complimentary appraisal. Changes in ratings of
self correlated .408 with changes in ratings of
the other, in accord with what very well may be
a principle in human interaction: One thinks of
the other as the other leads one to think of oneself.

3. Error in recall of ratings received. This was
determined by subtracting each person's reproduction of the ratings he received on the nine treatment items from the value of the fictitious ratings
presented to him on the same nine items. While
differences in the unfavorableness of the ratings
received significantly affected subjects' recall of
them ($F = 8.998$, $P < .001$), the differences in
sources had no effect ($F = .017$), nor did source
and discrepancy interact significantly ($F = 1.751$,
$P > .10$). The results in Table 3 show that errors
in recall tended to be in the favorable direction,
increasingly so with the larger discrepancies up
to the most extreme discrepancy, which again

TABLE 4 *Mean Ratings of Source's Errors in
Scale Usage, Carelessness in Following
Instructions and Lack of Seriousness
in His Ratings*

SOURCE	DISCREPANCIES (IN CENTIMETERS)				
	0	1	4.1	6.7 Treatment	6.7 Total
Friend	9.350	8.782	12.100	12.241	19.183
Stranger	10.825	13.352	14.277	14.602	20.489

TABLE 5 *Mean Ratings of Source's General
Carelessness and Lack of Social Sensitivity*

SOURCE	DISCREPANCIES (IN CENTIMETERS)				
	0	1	4.1	6.7 Treatment	6.7 Total
Friend	7.600	9.106	12.600	11.718	14.706
Stranger	8.855	11.376	14.141	13.400	15.856

TABLE 6 *Mean Change in Subject's Ratings of
How Well Source Knew Him*

SOURCE	DISCREPANCIES (IN CENTIMETERS)				
	0	1	4.1	6.7 Treatment	6.7 Total
Friend	0	−.588	−1.813	−1.235	−2.056
Stranger	.850	.762	.727	.286	.278

lessened in effect. Perhaps the extreme discrepancy was so compelling in its negativity that the
individuals could only minimally distort its reality;
or possibly the greater extremity of the evaluations
in this condition simply reduced their effectiveness.

4. Dissociation and discrediting of source. This
was measured by an eight-item questionnaire administered at the end of the experiment. These
questions asked subject to indicate his opinions
on: the seriousness of the source in his ratings
of him; how well source knew him; how closely
source followed instructions in rating him; whether
source may have been angry at him; whether he
and source had used the rating scales in the same
way; the degree of usual carelessness of source;
the general sensitivity of the source to other people; and how sure he was source had actually
made the ratings of him which he had seen. Questions that were assumed to measure related interpretations of source's negative ratings were
combined in the analyses.

*A. Scale usage, seriousness of ratings and care
in following instructions.* Both the source and discrepancy differences had a significant effect (respectively, $F = 4.263$, $P < .01$; $F = 9.761$, $P <
.001$) on the extent to which subjects indicated
they believed the source used the scale differently
from them, was not serious in his ratings, and
did not follow instructions in making his evaluations. From Table 4 it can be seen that these
beliefs increased with increased unfavorableness
of the received ratings, and were greater when
the ratings were from strangers than from friends.

*B. Depreciation of source (carelessness and
lack of social sensitivity).* The pattern of these
results is similar to those in *A*, above. Significant
differences occurred from both source and discrepancy variations (respectively, $F = 4.487$, $P
< .01$; $F = 11.123$, $P < .001$), with the source
tending to be rated as careless and socially insensitive as his presumed ratings became more
unfavorable. Table 5 shows this tendency to have
been more pronounced toward the stranger than
toward the friend source.

C. How well source knew subject. The change
in how well subject thought the source knew him
was determined by subtracting the acquaintance
score on the initial sociometric rating (first session) from the similar score obtained from the
questionnaire administered after devaluation by
the source. Significant differences were affected
by both discrepancy and source variations in the
extent to which subjects changed their opinions
of how well the sources knew them (respectively,
$F = 65.443$, $P < .001$; $F = 4.773$, $P < .01$). Results in Table 6 indicate that subjects in the friend
condition interpreted the unfavorable ratings from
the source as indicating he did not know them as
well as they had originally thought, while those
in the stranger treatment felt that the source
knew them better than they had estimated orig-

inally, but less well as the ratings from the source became more negative.

D. Attribution of anger to source. The results in Table 7 show the extent to which subjects attributed the ratings they received to anger of the source toward them. Friends significantly more than strangers ($F = 2.736$, $P < .10$) felt the source was angry at them for some reason, but the increased discrepancies did not contribute significantly to this feeling.

E. Certainty source actually made ratings. The results from this question, administered separately and as the very last step to avoid providing clues to the fictitious nature of ratings, are presented in Table 8. Friends significantly more than strangers claimed to have disbelieved the derogatory ratings they saw had actually been made by the source ($F = 2.325$, $P < .10$), and this disbelief increased significantly with the increased discrepancies ($F = 23.696$, $P < .001$).

5. Relationship of change in self and source ratings to discrediting and dissociation of source. The product-moment correlations between each of the five dissociative and discrediting responses described above ($A-E$) and changes in the ratings of both self and source were computed. Of these 10 correlations, only three were significant: Change in rating of source correlated $-.241$ ($P < .01$) with deprecation of source and $-.323$ ($P < .01$) with attribution of anger to the source. Thus the more subjects changed in their evaluation of the source, the weaker was the tendency for them to rate him as careless and lacking in social sensitivity and to attribute anger to him as the cause of the negative ratings. Also, the more a person changed in his self ratings the less he felt the source had been angry at him.

The analyses described thus far parallel very closely those carried out in the earlier study by Harvey, Kelley and Shapiro.[13] The present results corroborate those of the earlier study. The remaining results to be presented will deal with personality correlates of the preceding behavioral effects, which were one of the main concerns of this study.

6. Intolerance of ambiguity (authoritarianism) and reactions to negative information. The following results are based upon the measure of authoritarianism developed by Webster, Sanford and Freedman. Responses to both this scale and the F Scale were correlated with the effects to be listed, but the consistently higher relationship of the scale by Webster *et al.* to the variables under consideration has led to the omission in this report of the correlations with the F Scale. The correlation of .721 obtained between these two measures of authoritarianism indicate they were measuring very much the same thing.

In Table 9 are presented the correlations between authoritarianism and change in self ratings, change in source ratings and recall of ratings received from the source, all based on the nine treatment items. Authoritarianism related significantly negatively both to changes in ratings of self and of source and correlated positively with the tendency to distort the unfavorable ratings in the more favorable direction when recalling them. Thus the more authoritarian individuals were more disposed to keeping intact their initial attitudes toward self and source than were those lower in authoritarianism. The tendency toward greater favorable distortion in recalling the received ratings apparently augmented this attempt of the more authoritarian to resist changing his concept of self or source.

It should be noted that the negative correlation between opinion change and authoritarianism found in this study is different from the findings of a positive correlation between these variables

TABLE 7 Mean Magnitude of Anger Attributed to Source

SOURCE	DISCREPANCIES (IN CENTIMETERS)				
	0	1	4.1	6.7 Treatment	6.7 Total
Friend	1.033	.553	1.556	2.747	1.700
Stranger	.435	1.224	1.305	.995	1.139

TABLE 8 Mean Degree of Disbelief of Source Derogation

SOURCE	DISCREPANCIES (IN CENTIMETERS)				
	0	1	4.1	6.7 Treatment	6.7 Total
Friend	5.406	5.082	9.213	10.312	12.728
Stranger	4.590	5.767	8.677	10.305	9.556

TABLE 9 Correlation of Authoritarianism to Changes in Ratings of Self and Source and to Errors in Recall of Rating Received

	SELF CHANGE	SOURCE CHANGE	RECALL
r	$-.240$	$-.223$	.225
p	$<.01$	$<.05$	$<.05$

$N = 119$.

[13] *Ibid.*

in several other studies.[14] One logical explanation of this lies in the difference in the ego-relevance of the issue in this and the other studies. While the more authoritarian individual may follow the route of least resistance and yield to the evaluation of another person when the issue is of low relevance, it appears that when the issue becomes central to his self (as in this study) he responds with a greater tendency to ward off the threatening information and to keep it out of his system of relationships.

That the more authoritarian individual was more disturbed by the negative evaluations of him can possibly be inferred from Table 10, which shows the extent to which subjects at three levels of authoritarianism failed to discriminate, or generalized between the treatment and the non-treatment items of the raing scale, i.e., between the nine items on which the subject was actually marked down in the ratings he received and the six which did not differ from his initial self ratings. Most striking is the greater tendency for the more authoritarian individuals to have generalized their self change on the treatment items to the non-treatment ones. At the lowest level of authoritarianism subjects discriminated highly between the items on which they had been devalued and those on which they had not ($r = .119$). At the highest level of authoritarianism, on the other hand, the discrimination made between these two sets of items was markedly reduced ($r = .818$). The same tendency, but to a less pronounced degree, existed in change toward the source. The higher the authoritarianism, the less the discrimination between the treatment and non-treatment items in re-rating the source. Recall of the ratings received were not differentially affected by the different levels of authoritarianism.

Thus while the more authoritarian individuals are more resistant to changing their concepts and try harder to ward off the incongruous evaluations (Table 9), they appear at the same time to be more threatened by the negative information that does find its way into their semi-closed systems. This seems to have resulted in an over-mobilization or in a more extreme reaction that prevented them from discriminating between the treatment and non-treatment items. Instead of their failure to discriminate, stemming from a kind of conceptual disorganization resulting from being harder hit by the negative ratings, the equally plausible possibility exists that the more authoritarian individuals were so motivated to ward off the unfavorable information by keeping their conceptual systems closed that they failed to note the difference between the items. But in either case, whether they were mobilized to exclude the unfavorable information from their conceptual systems or were over-reacting to the information that was unsuccessfully warded off, it would seem that the more authoritarian persons are more likely to react to threat by becoming even more constricted in their existing way of ordering and defining the situation.

The correlations between authoritarianism and each of the five techniques of source discrediting and dissociation discussed earlier (A–E), were also computed. Three of these five correlations were significant. Authoritarianism correlated .514 ($P < .01$) with the tendency to lower one's estimate of how well the source knew him; .654 ($P < .01$) with the tendency to disclaim the likelihood that the source was angry at him; and .331 ($P < .01$) with the tendency to deny that the source had actually made the negative ratings.

7. Extra- and intra-punitiveness and reaction to negative information. Responses to the Rosenzweig Picture-Frustration Test were scored three ways: in terms of intrapunitiveness, extrapunitiveness, and relative extrapunitiveness, i.e., one's intrapunitive score subtracted from his extrapunitive score. The correlations of these three measures with self change, source change, recall of ratings received (all based on the nine treatment items), and authoritarianism (as measured by the newer scale) were all practically nil, not one even approaching statistical significance. The failure of the scores on the P-F Test to relate significantly to the variables in this study could be due to shortcomings of the P-T Test itself. No special attention is given in this instrument to the social relationship between the source and recipient of the frustration. An instrument more directly perti-

TABLE 10 *Generalization of Effects from the Nine Treatment to the Six Non-treatment Items on Self Change, Source Change and Recall of Ratings Received at Three Levels of Authoritarianism*

	LOWER (N=39)		MIDDLE (N=41)		UPPER (N=39)	
	r	p	r	p	r	p
Self change	.119	>.10	.250	<.01	.818	<.01
Source change	.182	<.05	.270	<.01	.432	<.01
Recall	.012	>.10	−.161	>.10	−.056	>.10

[14] Leonard Berkowitz and Richard M. Lundy, "Personality Characteristics Related to Susceptibility by Peers or Authority Figures," *Journal of Personality*, 25 (March, 1957), pp. 306–316; Richard S. Crutchfield, "Conformity and Character," *American Psychologist*, 10 (May, 1955), pp. 191–198; O. J. Harvey and Donald F. Caldwell, "Assimilation and Contrast Phenomena in Response to Environmental Variation," *Journal of Personality*, 27 (June, 1959), pp. 125–135.

nent to the responses studied here probably could be provided by including sets of picture-stimuli involving, among other things, persons of higher and lower status, friends and strangers.

8. Self-esteem and reactions to negative information. The measure of self-esteem was represented by a modified level of aspiration technique. From the three pieces of information each subject provided in relation to the digit-symbol substitution task (the very highest, the very lowest, and the most probable score he felt he was likely to achieve during a one-minute performance), two scores were computed: the range of aspiration, representing the difference between the highest and lowest expected performance; and a ratio of the most probable performance to the highest and lowest probable scores. These scores, like the P-F scores, related almost not at all to change in self-esteem and reaction to treatments such as the one in this study, because the technique of measuring self-esteem in this case was completely lacking in previous validation.

Thus of the personality measures employed in this study, only authoritarianism was significantly related in a consistent way to the variables under investigation.

SUMMARY

The main purpose of this study was to investigate the relationship between personality factors and reactions to negative information on an issue highly relevant to the self. The method employed was similar to that used earlier by Harvey, Kelley and Shapiro. Individuals with differing personalities were exposed to information about themselves which was by one of five gradations more unfavorable than their initial self-ratings and which were made to appear as having been made either by a friend or relative stranger. The personality factors studies included authoritarianism, as measured by the scale of Webster, Sanford and Freedman; extra- and intrapunitiveness, measured by the Rosenzweig P-F Test; and self-esteem, measured by a modified level of aspiration technique.

In addition to corroborating the findings of our earlier study, the effects of complimenting a person by agreeing with his evaluations of himself and the results of extremely negative evaluations were also demonstrated. In the first instance, the individual became more positive toward himself and at the same time became more favorable toward the source of the congruent evaluations. And in the latter instance some suggestive evidence was obtained that the extremely negative evaluations lost in effectiveness because of their extremity.

Of the personality factors studied, only authoritarianism related significantly to the responses measured. It related negatively to change in attitude toward self and toward source, and positively to distortion in the favorable direction of the negative ratings received. These effects were interpreted as indicating the more authoritarian individual is more resistant to changing his concepts toward highly ego-involving objects (self and friend in this study), while he may resolve the incongruity by yielding to another's position when the issue does not involve threat to his self. Further evidence of this was provided by an increase in loss of discrimination between characteristics on which the individual had been derogated and those on which he had not as authoritarianism increased. This was especially true in the reratings of self following the negative information, although it was similarly reflected in reratings of the source of the negative information.

The more authoritarian individuals were also more likely to try to keep their attitudes intact by minimizing the authoritativeness of the source and by disbelieving the source had actually made the ratings of him. At the same time they were more likely to deny that one reason the source may have rated them low was because he was angry at them for some reason.

SUBJECT INDEX